ENCYCLOPEDIA OF RENAISSANCE LITERATURE

ENCYCLOPEDIA OF RENAISSANCE LITERATURE

James Wyatt Cook

Facts On File
An imprint of Infobase Publishing

Encyclopedia of Renaissance Literature

Facts On File, Inc.
An imprint of Infobase Publishing
132 West 31st Street
New York NY 10001

Library of Congress Cataloging-in-Publication Data
Cook, James Wyatt, 1932–
    Encyclopedia of Renaissance literature / James Cook.— 1st ed.
        p. cm.
    Includes bibliographical references and index.
    ISBN 0-8160-5624-2 (hardcover : alk. paper) 1. European literature—Renaissance, 1450–1600—Bio-bibliography—Dictionaries. I. Facts On File, Inc. II. Title.
    PN721.C66 2005
    809'.894'09024—dc22

                                                        2004029417

Facts On File books are available at special discounts when purchased in bulk quantities for businesses, associations, institutions, or sales promotions. Please call our Special Sales Department in New York at (212) 967-8800 or (800) 322-8755.

You can find Facts On File on the World Wide Web at http://www.factsonfile.com

Text design by Rachel L. Berlin
Cover design by Smart Graphics

Printed in the United States of America

VB FOF 10 9 8 7 6 5 4 3 2 1

This book is printed on acid-free paper.

CONTENTS

This book is for our children and their spouses
Allison Amy and David Geoffrey
Kathleen Marie and Dean David
Mary Sharon and Christopher Wyatt;
Their kids:
Josh, Leo, Riley, and Sam;
and
All my former students and their beloveds, especially
Jim and Debbie
Dawn and Roger
Kevin and Tabitha
Sandra and Andrew
Sandra and Martha
Angela and Greg
Carol and Misha
Susan and Alex
Irene and Tom
Jon and Leslie
Scott and Pam
Paula Jean
Meghan
Lynne
Casey
Erica
Brad
Dave and Aiko
Anna and Matteo
Gl'altri Veneziani, 1998 e 99
And the wonderful staff at the Stockwell-Mudd Libraries of Albion College: Cheers!

ACKNOWLEDGMENTS

Every substantial project requires the help of many hands, and this one is no exception. As always, my first debt of gratitude is owing to my spouse of a short 51 years, Barbara. My first-draft editor and an unfailing cheerleader, Barbara restrains my verbosity and insists on shorter sentences. I feel deeply grateful. I am also grateful to my agent, Jodie Rhodes, who suggested this project, and to my ever-responsive and supportive editor at Facts On File, Jeff Soloway, whose patience, instantaneous response to queries, and mastery of the techniques of positive reinforcement have become legendary in our household.

Mike Van Houten has supported this project at every step with his expertise as a reference librarian. So have his colleagues Alice Wiley Moore, Carolyn Gaswick, Michelle Gerry, Cheryl Blackwell, and their fearless leader, John Kondelik. My thanks, as well, to John and the administration of Albion College for finding me congenial workspace near the resources I required to do this job.

Professor Ananda Lal of St. Xavier University, Kolkatta, vetted the initial list of Indian literary figures to be included in this volume and helpfully called my attention to certain matters of controversy.

I am also indebted to the hundreds of editors whose contributions to specialized reference volumes helped to shape my understanding of literary developments around the world during the 16th and 17th centuries. Rather than name them individually, I gratefully acknowledge having consulted the following references:

Bright, William, ed. *International Encyclopedia of Linguistics.* New York and Oxford: Oxford University Press, 1992.

Brockhaus Enzyklopädie. Wiesbaden: F. A. Brockhaus, 1969.

Datta, Amaresh, ed. *Encyclopedia of Indian Literature.* New Delhi: Sahitya Akademi, 1989.

Encyclopaedia Judaica. Jerusalem: The Macmillan Company, 1971.

Encyclopaedia of Islam. Leiden: E. J. Brill and London: Luzac and Company, ca. 1963–ca. 1980.

Garland, Mary, and Henry Garland. *The Oxford Companion to German Literature.* Oxford: Oxford University Press, 1997.

Grendler, Paul F., ed. *Encyclopedia of the Renaissance.* New York: Scribners, ca. 1999.

Konzett, Matthias, ed. *Encyclopedia of German Literature.* Chicago and London: Fitzroy Dearborn Publishers, 2000.

Mair, Victor H., ed. *The Columbia History of Chinese Literature.* New York: Columbia University Press, 2001.

New Catholic Encyclopedia. New York: McGraw Hill, 1967.

Russel, Rinaldina, ed. *The Feminist Encyclopedia of Italian Literature.* Westport, Conn.: Greenwood Press, 1997.

Singer, Isidore, et al., eds. *The Jewish Encyclopedia.* New York and London: Funk and Wagnalls, 1924.

Finally, permission to quote from Edward Granville Browne's translations from the Persian of Ṣā'ib of Tabriz in volume 4 of *A Literary History of Persia,* 1997, has been granted courtesy of Ibex Books.

INTRODUCTION

OVERVIEW AND GUIDE TO USE

This reference volume looks at literature written during the Renaissance epoch from an atypical perspective—a global one. Renaissance volumes historically have dealt exclusively with European literary phenomena or, more recently, with culturally European literary works expatriate in the New World as well. This book attempts to look at typical and significant literary effort around the world. It tries to take into account authors, compositions, movements, and literary types and terminology not only in European culture and its extensions, but also in the native cultures of the New World, in Asia, on the Indian subcontinent, and in the Muslim world both in and outside India. The period under consideration focuses mainly on the years 1500–1700, but the encyclopedia also glances back at a few important ancient and medieval precursors.

Most of the entries included here have been suggested by popular anthologies of literature. I have included entries, writers, and texts that are often covered in introductory college or advanced high-school classes because the primary intended reading audience for this book consists of students in these kinds of classes as well as their instructors. Most entries are followed by a selected bibliography of texts, intended as a recommended reading list for those students who want to look further into the topic.

Many of the writers, works, and literary movements discussed in this book sought innovation by looking back to ancient roots for inspiration. For example, the writers of the Ming dynasty (1368–1644) and the Early Qing (Ch'ing) dynasty (1644–1911) in China looked back for inspiration to the literature, especially the poetry of the Tang dynasty (618–907)—a period during which the Chinese invented printing by word blocks, and literature flourished. Under the influence of the Chinese Ming literary efflorescence, Korean and Japanese literature, often written in Chinese as well as in the native tongues, also blossomed during the years of the European Renaissance. The mid–15th-century invention of an alphabet for the Korean language gave impetus to the growth of literature in that language.

In Hindu India, a spiritual movement called bhakti had been gaining momentum since the ninth century. As its adherents spread its tenets across the length and breadth of the subcontinent, the movement developed characteristics comparable to some displayed by the Protestant Reformation and the Roman Catholic Counter-Reformation in Europe.

There appeared, for instance, a reaction against clerical monopolization of ancient texts by virtue of priests' mastery of the Sanskrit language. A prime feature of bhakti was the insistence of its saints that the way to salvation lay in devotion to God, a good heart, and kindness to one's neighbor. The movement de-emphasized abstruse and difficult theological doctrine. So rough parallels can be drawn between the populism of both the bhakti movements of India and the Protestant movements of the European Renaissance. In many instances, ancient Hindu Sanskrit texts were translated into the many emergent vernaculars of India, and in those translations, the emphases shifted to stress social justice and the love of such gods as Vishnu and Krishna. The bhakti movement also contributed to the appearance of a humanistic religion of the book, Sikhism, with its holy scripture, the *Adigranth.*

The love poetry of medieval Sufi Muslims, with its conventions of spirituality derived from human love, had made its way from North Africa to Spain and radiated from there to southern France and Italy. As this poetry traveled, its writers adapted it to their own poetic conventions. In Provence in the Middle Ages, this imported verse transformed into the poetry of the troubadours and their female counterparts, the trobaritz. Moving south from Provence, in Italy it became the poetry of the sweet new style, the *dolce stil nuovo,* employed by Dante and others. A founding figure of the European Renaissance, Francesco Petrarca (1304–74), took that poetry, infused it with classical erudition, with a close examination of his own interior autobiography, and with a poetic sensibility that, rated by its influence on others, has not since been equaled in the Western world. His verses set the standard and the tone for lyric poets in Europe for the next 200 years, and the history of lyric poetry in the West could be characterized as a tug of war between poets who followed Petrarch and poets who reacted against him.

In the Muslim world, however, the same verses that had developed in Europe in the way broadly outlined above took a different course. Muslim lyric verse took as its models the poems of Persia,

and in the Arabic of Egyptian writers and the Turkish of the Ottomans and the Turki of the Mughals of North India, poetic forms like the *rubá'i* and the *qasída* became ubiquitous. Prose biographies of important poets and poetic romances based on biblical or historical themes became ubiquitous, and in Turkey a shadow-puppet theater called *karagoz* developed. Among the Persian contributions to the literature of the Muslim world was the expansion of the capacity for local vernacular languages and dialects to achieve the greater power of expression that Arabic displayed.

In all the cultures thus far discussed, translation played a major role. An entry on the subject of translation attempts a cross-cultural overview of the results of efforts at translation around the world. Similar entries for comedy and tragedy, for instance, try to look comparatively at global literatures—even at a few examples of the oral literatures of Africa and Pacific Oceania. A student or a general reader can find here, then, a reasonably comprehensive view of and introduction to important writers, works, literary terms, and literary trends around the world for a period of more than 200 years.

The principle for the exclusion of certain literatures, on the other hand, has been stasis. Where few or no new literary developments characterize a literature from 1500 to 1700, as was the case, say, in Russia and the Byzantine Greek world, no entries appear.

A reader may trace cross-references of interest by pursuing the SMALL-CAPITALIZED words in the text to other alphabetically listed entries where they occur and, by following the guide thus provided, may achieve a more comprehensive view of a subject of interest.

A CLOSER LOOK

Of course, the term *renaissance* occurred first in a European context. The Italian artist Giorgio Vasari (1511–74) seems to have first used the word to characterize the developments in Italian architecture, painting, and sculpture that he described in the biographical sketches he included in his *Lives of the Artists*. Later writers expanded the meaning of the word to describe a flowering of new knowledge, a vastly expanded European acquaintance with the writings of ancient Greek and Roman authors, and a sensibility that expressed itself in novel artistic and literary forms that were often based on the works of the ancients.

Any term one applies as a broad descriptor of historical developments, of course, is necessarily retrospective. The widely credited initiator of the European Renaissance, Francesco Petrarca, did not wake up one morning and decide it was time to get the Renaissance under way; rather, his interests in classical antiquity sparked similar interests in others. His introspective examination of his emotional life as a unique phenomenon and his treatment of his love for a woman as a literal and figurative poetic subject reformed both European tastes in poetry and concepts of amatory psychology. Petrarch's thought and work exercised an unprecedented influence on European literature. Thus, though European figures before Petrarch and their works receive some notice here, they do so because Renaissance literary figures made important use of their writings or ideas.

Over time, scholars and historians came to think of developments other than those mentioned above as falling under the umbrella of what they meant by *renaissance*. Humanism emphasized translating the Greek classics first into Latin and later translating both Greek and Roman works into the vernacular languages of Europe. Rejecting and improving on the educational models of the medieval scholastics, humanists also came into the Renaissance fold by proposing a student-centered program of education founded on the practice of the ancients. Humanists such as Lorenzo Valla (1407–57) also developed new standards for recovering ancient texts—including the text of the Bible. The resultant reworking of the Scriptures and other ancient books provided another avenue of intellectual and literary development that became associated with the idea of the Renaissance.

The technological advance and cost benefit associated with the late 15th-century invention of European printing opened the world of letters to new classes of readers and of writers. Over the strenuous objections of some men, for instance, women's voices increasingly strove to be heard—and *were* heard—via the new medium of printed books.

Printing and new standards of textual criticism conspired to turn up the volume of already audible demands for vernacular translations of the Bible and for better source texts than St. Jerome's fourth- and fifth-century Vulgate Latin Bible provided. Increasingly insistent voices, such as those of Martin Luther and John Calvin, challenged the authority of the Roman Catholic Church hierarchy and ultimately broke ranks with it. As the literary effects of the Renaissance spread northward to the Scandinavian peninsula and to Denmark's political dependent, Iceland, those effects arrived primarily, though not exclusively, in Lutheran form. In response to Protestant competition and to internal demands for reform, the Roman Catholic Counter-Reformation also resulted from the tides and eddies swirling in the European Renaissance.

The age of European world exploration began with the Columbian voyages, and aspects of European Renaissance literary culture moved overseas. In the Americas, beyond finding technologically primitive peoples with oral literatures, the Europeans also encountered high civilizations, like those of the Inca and the Maya, who themselves had developed extensive written literatures, and a certain degree of literary exchange took place between the cultures. Some Europeans, such as the missionary Fray Bernardino de Sahagún (1499–1590), recognized the value of New World texts and made efforts to preserve them. Because the Christian Europeans tended to undervalue the worth of non-Christian texts, however, many were consigned to the flames. At the same time, such early descendents of European immigrants as Sor Juana Iñéz de la Cruz (1651–95) mirrored in their writing elements both of European and indigenous Amerindian cultures. Scholars such as Germaine Warkentin, Carolyn Podruchny, and their collaborators have urged "decentring" the Renaissance and recognizing that its operations took place on the western as well as on the eastern side of the Atlantic and in North as well as in South and Central America.

In Pacific Oceania, European explorers encountered an oral literary culture that extended from Hawaii to New Zealand, and the explorers themselves had an impact on that culture as they and their ships and equipment became a part of the subject matter of the tradition.

Beyond its operations in the New World, however, aspects of European Renaissance literary and religious culture traveled with such missionaries as the Italian Jesuit Roberto de Nobili (1577–1656) to distant India and China. The Portuguese Inquisition even had a branch office in India at Goa. There and in China, however, the Renaissance European literary culture imported by such missionaries encountered well-established literatures that were in some instances much older than their own. A certain amount of marginal early mixing took place, as when Nobili adopted the dress and aspect of high caste Hindus and wrote in the Tamil tongue in south India to win Christian converts—a strategy of cultural blending developed by missionaries that also experienced a degree of success in China, Japan, and North America.

In the native literary cultures of China, India, and, to a degree, Korea in the 16th and 17th centuries, however, movements were afoot that paralleled some associated with the European Renaissance. The most striking parallel in China, perhaps, involved writers of the late Ming and the early Qing dynasties. As I earlier noted, just as their European counterparts looked to the writers of classical antiquity for models and inspiration, so the Chinese poets of the 16th and 17th centuries looked back to the golden-age poets of the Tang dynasty. Another unrelated but nonetheless striking parallel appears in the fact that the late Ming is the great age of the Chinese historical and social novel. Similar forms also began to emerge about the same time in Europe. Beyond that, the early Qing dynasty saw the flowering of the Chinese short story or novella—a form to which Boc-

caccio gave currency in Europe in the late 14th century. China also saw an upsurge in writing by female authors, particularly poetry, during the period. As in Europe, Chinese writing shifted some of its focus away from historical and religious matters in the direction of personal affection and emotionality.

As for Korea, one finds a parallel between the European spread of printing and the mid–15th-century invention of a true alphabet for representing the Korean language. Prior to that invention, Korean literature was almost exclusively oral and consisted principally of folk tales and ephemera. The invention of the Korean alphabet gave the same sort of impetus to Korean letters that the invention of moveable type gave to writing in Europe.

In India the bhakti devotional movement noted above had begun as early as the eighth century. In the 16th and 17th centuries, the bhakti movement gave impetus to the translation of Hindu scriptural epics such as the *Mahabharata*, the *Ramayana*, the legends surrounding the blue god Krishna, and other works from North Indian Sanskrit and South Indian Dravidian classical tongues. As did people in Europe, the Indian masses needed devotional texts in the emerging vernacular languages that they spoke. The effect of these translations roughly paralleled some of those observable in Europe during the same period. The religious authority of high-caste, priestly Brahmins was undermined by the new access of the masses to Hindu scripture. To a degree paralleling Reformation Protestantism, bhakti valued purity of heart in the faithful more than it did obedience to traditional authority. Purity of heart and repeating the name or names of God were enough, some taught, to assure salvation. Generally, bhakti also rejected the rigidity of the caste system and encouraged the kind of freethinking that used to prevail among the European and New World Anabaptist communities. In any case, bhakti spawned such novels of social protest as *Sundari Malua* (Beautiful Malua) and many, many poems that were sung to traditional tunes in praise of Hindu deities associated with Vishnu.

One observes other parallels between Indian and European religio-literary activity in the 16th and 17th centuries. Just as Lutheranism and Calvinism emerged from a substitution of biblical for papal authority, from Renaissance humanism, and from the literary activity that surrounded the preservation and transmission of the text of the Bible, so another religion of the book, Sikhism, grew up in India. A coalescing of Hindu, Muslim, Indian humanistic beliefs and the social and devotional programs of bhakti, Sikhism was founded by its first guru, Nanak. For the benefit of the faithful, Sikhism's fifth guru compiled the faith's holy book, the *Adigranth,* largely from the writings of bhakti poets, especially Kabir. The book itself is now considered the fountainhead and permanent guide of the Sikh faith.

The literatures of Hindu India and Muslim Mughal India in the 16th and 17th centuries tended to blur a bit at the edges. Islamic scholars at the court of Akbar sometimes became interested in Hindu letters. At the North Indian Court in Delhi, Persian prototypes were as popular as they were in Kabul to the north. The Emperor Akbar in Agra tried to merge Muslim and Hindu religious traditions into a state faith, but the effort did not survive him.

This intermingling of faiths and traditions in India, nonetheless, is reminiscent of similar attempts at syncretism in the European Renaissance, as when Giovanni Pico della Mirandola (1463–94) attempted to reconcile Plato and Aristotle within the framework of a Christianity, informed both by ideas drawn from the Muslim world and Jewish mystical Kabbalism.

Jewish culture in the diaspora also made its contribution to European Renaissance letters not only through the importation of mystical writings like those of Yohanan Ben Isaac Alemanno (ca. 1433–ca. 1504) but also through the Neoplatonist doctrine espoused by Jehudah ben Isaac Abravanel (Leone Hebreo, ca. 1460–ca. 1521). Beyond that we find writings both in Hebrew and in the vernacular languages of Europe by such figures as Glückel of Hameln (1646–1724), whose recollections of the activities of the Jewish community in Germany contributed much to Renaissance historiography in the region. Leone de Sommi, Ebreo,

wrote the first extant Hebrew drama, *A Comedy of Betrothal* (1550).

In Islamic society, literature was largely traditional, and translation from one linguistic group to another provided, though not the sole, the principal innovation. The Muslim world was not immune, however, from at least one of the products of European global exploration—New World tobacco, a product that stirred some literary controversy.

Undoubtedly one could find other parallels to underscore the reasons that it is not disingenuous to entitle a work that deals so broadly with the literatures of different cultures an *Encyclopedia of Renaissance Literature.* Yet many cultures are omitted or sparsely represented here. Sub-Saharan Africa and Pacific Oceania are thinly represented because, though oral literature flourished there, it is difficult to determine dates of origin for the stories one finds. Other cultures, such as those of 16th- and 17th-century Russia and of the Byzantine Greek world do not appear because, as I earlier remarked, they seem to have been undergoing a period of literary stasis. What one might consider a renaissance or a parallel to it did not arrive in those cultures, as far as I can tell, until the 19th century.

I do not intend this volume for specialists. It is addressed principally to another important audience—to high-school students and their teachers, to undergraduates and their professors, to librarians, and to curious general readers. I hope that what such readers find here will lead them to the texts themselves. Those whose interests in the European Renaissance lead them beyond the covers of reference volumes, while consulting some of the primary texts, might well also wish to examine the basic modern critical document, Jakob Christoph Burckhardt's (1818–97) *The Civilisation of the Renaissance in Italy.* Such persons will also want to explore the indispensable work of Paul Oskar Kristellar (1905–99). Beyond the bibliographies at the end of most entries, references to Burckhardt and Kristellar, to other useful commentary, and to still useful older editions appear in the section "Selected Bibliography."

J. W. C.

Writers Covered, by Language of Composition

꧁ꕥ꧂

ARABIC

Faydī
Fuzûlî
Hubbi Qadin
Ibn Iyās
Kemál-Pasha-záde
Maqqari of Tlemcen, Ahmed al-, b. Muhammad
Shirbīnī, Yūsuf Al-
Suyūtī, Jalāl al-dīn al-
Tashköprü-záde family

ASSAMESE

Sankaradeva

BENGALI

Caitanya Deva, Krishna
Chakravarti, Mukundaram
Chandrabati
Dās, Vrindavān
Krishnadāsa Kavirāja Gosvāmi

CHINESE

Chen Jiru
Dong Yue
Duan Shuquing
Feng Menglong
Huang Xiumei
Kim Man-jung
Kong Shangren
Li Dongyang
Li Mengyang
Li Panlong
Li Yu
Lo Guanzhong
Pu Songling
Shi Naian
Tang Xianzu
Wang Duanshu
Wang Jiaoluan
Wang Shizhen
Wang Shizhen II
Wu Cheng'en
Xu Wei
Yang Jisheng
Yang Shen
Yuan Hongdao
Yu Tong

CONGOLESE (MONGO PEOPLE)

Anon. Epic of *Lianja and Nsongo*

DANISH

Bording, Anders
Kingo, Thomas Hansen
Palladius, Peder
Pedersen, Christiern
Tausen, Hans

ENGLISH

Ascham, Roger
Ashley, Robert
Bacon, Francis
Barclay, Alexander
Beaumont, Francis
Best, George
Bourchier, John, Lord Berners
Bunyan, John
Burton, Robert
Campion, Thomas
Carew, Thomas
Cartwright, William
Cary, Elizabeth Tanfield, first viscountess
  Falkland
Cavendish, George
Cavendish, Margaret
Caxton, William
Chapman, George
Clarendon, Edward Hyde, earl of
Constable, Henry
Crashaw, Richard
Cromwell, Oliver
Daniel, Samuel
Davies, Sir John
Dekker, Thomas
Deloney, Thomas
Denham, Sir John
Donne, John
Dryden, John
Dyer, Sir Edward
Earle, John
Elizabeth I
Elyot, Sir Thomas
Fletcher, John
Fletcher, Phineas
Florio, John

Ford, John
Foxe, John
Gascoigne, George
Greene, Robert
Greville, Fulke, first baron Brooke
Grimald, Nicholas
Hakluyt, Richard
Hall, Joseph
Herbert, George
Heywood, Thomas
Hobbes, Thomas
Hoby, Sir Thomas
Holinshed, Raphael
Hooker, Richard
James I
Jones, Inigo
Jonson, Ben
Kyd, Thomas
Kynaston, Sir Francis
Leland, John
Lodge, Thomas
Lyly, John
Marlowe, Christopher
Marston, John
Marvell, Andrew
Massinger, Philip
Middleton, Thomas
Milton, John
More, Sir (St.) Thomas
Nashe, Thomas
Norton, Thomas
Pembroke, Mary Herbert, countess of
Philips, Katherine
Rowley, William
Sackville, Thomas
Shakespeare, William
Shirley, James
Sidney, Sir Philip
Spenser, Edmund
Suckling, Sir John
Surrey, Henry Howard, earl of
Tourneur, Cyril
Trahern, Thomas
Tyndale, William
Udall, Nicholas
Vaughan, Henry

Vaux, Thomas Lord
Waller, Edmund
Walton, Izaak
Webster, John
Wilson, Thomas
Wroth, Lady Mary
Wyatt, Sir Thomas

FINNISH

Agricola, Michael
Erici, Ericus

FRENCH

Aubigné, Théodore-Agrippa d'
Baïf, Jean-Antoine de
Balzac, Jean-Louis Guez de
Bartas, Guillaume de Salluste, seigneur du
Bellay, Joachim du
Budé, Guillaume
Cartier, Jacques
Commynes, Philippe de
Corneille, Pierre
Crenne, Hélisenne de
Cyrano de Bergerac, Savinien de
Descartes, René
Des Roches, Madeleine and Catherine
Du Fail, Noël (pen name, Léon Ladulfi)
Du Guillet, Pernette
Gournay, Marie Le Jars de
Hardy, Alexandre
Jodelle, Étienne
La Fayette, Marie-Madelaine Pioche de la Vergne,
    comtesse de (Madame de La Fayette)
La Fontaine, Jean de
L' Hermite, François
Mairet, Jean
Malherbe, François de
Marguerite de Navarre
Marot, Clément
Molière
Montaigne, Michel Eyquem de
Anne-Marie-Louise d'Orléans, duchesse de
    Montpensier (La Grande Mademoiselle)
Rabelais, François

Racine, Jean
Rambouillet, Catherine de Vivonne, marquise de
Régnier, Mathurin
Ronsard, Pierre de
Rotrou, Jean de
Scarron, Paul
Scève, Maurice
Scudéry, Georges de
Scudéry, Madeleine de
Sorel, Charles
Urfé, Honoré d'
Viau, Théophile de

GERMAN

Abraham a Sancta Clara
Böhme, Jakob
Brant, Sebastian
Busche, Hermann von dem
Camerarius, Joachim
Dach, Simon
Fleming, Paul
Gerhardt, Paul
Glückel von Hameln
Greiffenberg, Catharina Regina von
Grimmelshausen, Hans Jacob Christoph von
Gryphius, Andreas
Hofmannswaldau, Christian Hofmann von
Luther, Martin
Melancthon, Philip
Opitz, Martin
Reuter, Christian
Spee von Langenfeld, Friedrich
Wickram, Jörg
Zwingli, Huldrych

GREEK

Chrysoloras, Manuel
Epicurus
Plato

GUJERATI

Akhā
Mīrā Bāī

HEBREW

Alemanno, Yohanan Ben Isaac
Archevolti, Samuel
Delmedigo, Elijah
Karo, Joseph Ben Ephraim
Sommi, Judah Leone ben Isaac
Zacuto, Moses ben Mordecai
Zarfati, Joseph

HINDI (INCLUDING BRAJ AND AVADHI)

Akhā
Bihari Lal
Bittalnāth
Jayisi, Malik Mohammad
Kabir
Keshavdās
Mīrā Bāī
Nabhādās
Nānak
Nandadāsa
Sūrdās
Tulsīdās
Vallabha (Vallabhāchārya)
Vyas, Harriram

ICELANDIC

Arason, Jón
Icelandic poets (see entry)
Icelandic translators, balladeers, annalists, and
   biographers (see entry)
Magnússon, Jón

ITALIAN

Abravanel, Jehudah ben Isaac
Andreini, Isabella
Aragona, Tullia d'
Aretino, Pietro
Ariosto, Ludovico
Battiferi, Laura
Bembo, Pietro
Boccaccio, Giovanni
Boiardo, Matteo Maria
Botero, Giovanni
Bruni, Leonardo
Bruno, Giordano
Campanella, Tommaso
Casa, Giovanni della
Castelvetro, Lodovico
Castiglione, Baldassare
Catherine of Genoa, Saint (Caterina Fieschi
   Adorno)
Cecchi, Giovanni Maria
Cellini, Benvenuto
Cereta Laura
Chrysoloras, Manuel
Colonna, Vittoria
Dante Alighieri
Ficino, Marsilio
Firenzuola, Agnolo
Fonte, Moderata (Modesta Pozzo Zorzi)
Franco, Veronica
Galilei, Galileo
Gámbera, Veronica
Guarini, Giovanni Battista
Machiavelli, Niccolò
Marinella, Lucrezia
Medici, Lorenzo de'
Michelangelo Buonarrotti (Michelagniolo di
   Lodovico Buonarroti)
Petrarch, Francis (Francesco Petrarca)
Pico della Mirandola, Giovanni
Poliziano, Angelo
Pulci, Antonia Tannini
Pulci, Bernardo
Pulci, Luca
Pulci, Luigi
Stampa, Gaspara
Sullam, Sara Coppio
Tarabotti, Archangela
Tasso, Torquato
Valla, Lorenzo
Vasari, Giorgio

JAPANESE

Bashō (Matsuo Bashō)
Chikamatsu Monzaemon
Saikaku (Ihara Saikaku)

KANNADA

Honnamma, Sañhiya
Purandaradasa

KOREAN

Hŏ Kyŏngbŏn
Hŏ Kyun
Kim Man-jung

LATIN AND NEO-LATIN

Agricola, Rudolphus
Boethius
Calvin, John
Celtis, Conradus
Cicero
Copernicus, Nicolaus
Descartes, René
Erasmus, Desiderius
Fleming, Paul
Greif, Andreas (Gryphius)
Lucretius
Luther, Martin
Mithradates, Flavius
More, Sir (St.) Thomas
Ovid
Petrarch, Francis
Plautus
Seneca
Spee von Langenfeld, Friedrich
Terrence
Valla, Lorenzo
Virgil
Zwingli, Huldrych

MALAYAM

Erutacan

MARATHI

Akhā
Bahinabai
Eknath

Tukārāma
Vitthal

MARSHALLESE

Man This Reef

NAHUATL

Anon. *Annals of Cuauhtitlan* in *The Codex Chimalpopoca*
Anon. "Songs in the Nahuatl language of Mexico"
Sahagún, Bernardino de

NORWEGIAN

Arrebo, Anders Christensen
Beyer, Absalon Pedersson
Dass, Petter
Engelbretsdatter, Dorothea

ORIYA

Dāsa, Atibadi Jagannātha
Dāsa, Dānakrishna
Five Friends (Achyutananda, Ananta, Balarama, Jagannatha, and Yasovanta)

PERSIAN

Faydī (later Fayyādī), Abu 'L-Fayd
Fudúlí
Gul-Badan Begum
Hátifí
Kemalpasazâde
Ṣā'ib of Tabriz
'Urfí of Shiraz

PORTUGUESE

Camões, Luíz Vaz De
Ferreira, António

PUNJABI

Akhā
Guru Arjan Dev

QUECHUA (INCAN)

Anon. "Elegy of the Great Inca Atawallpa"
Anon. Huarochiri Manuscript
Anon. *Play of Ollantay*
Anon. "Zithua Hymns"

QUICHE (MAYAN)

Anon. *Popul Vuh*

RAJASTANI

Mīrā Bāī
Ratnākaravarni

SANSKRIT

Krishnadāsa Kavirāja Gosvāmi
Vallabha (Villabhāchārya)
Vyas, Harriram
Vyāsa

SPANISH

Acosta, José de
Boscán Almogaver, Juan
Calderón de la Barca, Pedro
Carvajal y Mendoza, Luisa de
Cervantes Saavedra, Miguel de
Columbus, Christopher
Columbus, Ferdinand
Cortés, Hernán
Cruz, Sor Juana Inés de la
Díaz del Castillo, Bernal
Encina, Juan del
Erauso, Catalina de
Ercilla y Zúñiga, Alonso de
Fernández de Oviedo y Valdés, Gonzalo
Garcilaso de la Vega
Garcilaso de la Vega, The Inca
Gómara, Francesco López de
Góngora y Argote, Luis de
Lope de Vega Carpio, Félix
Rodríguez de Montalvo, Garci
Téllez, Gabriel (Molina Tirso de)

SWEDISH

Messenius, Johannes
Rosenhane, Gustaf (Skogekär Bergbo)
Stiernhielm, Georg
Wivallius, Lars

TAMIL

Nobili, Roberto de

TELEGU

Chemakura, Venkata Kavi
Krishnadevaraya
Molla, Atukuri

TONGAN

Anon., *Historic Poems of Tonga*

TURKISH AND TURKĪ

'Atá'í Nev'ízáde
Bābur (Zahīr-ud-Dīn Muhammad)
Bâkî
Fuzûlî
Háletí
Hubbi Qadin
Kâtib Çelebî
Kháqání
Kemalpasazâde
Lámi'í of Brusa
Nábí
Ná'ilí
Nev'í
Omer (Nef'i of Erzerum)
Süleyman I
Tashköprü-záde Family
Yahyá Effendi

URDU

Walī

AUTHORS' TIME LINE

❧❧❧

ANCIENT INFLUENCES

Dates	Author	Dates	Author
ca. 1500 B.C.E.	Vyāsa (See also *MAHAB-HARATA*)	1370–1444	Bruni, Leonardo
		1407–1457	Valla, Lorenzo
ca. 428–ca. 348 B.C.E.	Plato	1420–1491	Caxton, William
b. 384–322 B.C.E.	Aristotle	1423–1591	Tashköprü-záde family
341–271 B.C.E.	Epicurus	1432–1484	Pulci, Luigi
ca. 250–184 B.C.E.	Plautus, Titus Maccius	1433–1499	Ficino, Marsilio
ca. 190–159 B.C.E.	Terence, Publius Teren- tius Afer	1434–1494	Boiardo, Matteo Maria
		1435–1504	Alemanno, Yohanan Ben Isaac
106–43 B.C.E.	Cicero, Marcus Tullius		
ca. 99–55 B.C.E.	Lucretius	1440–1518	Kabir
70–19 B.C.E.	Virgil	ca. 1443–1485	Agricola, Rudolfus (Huysman, Roelof)
43 B.C.E.–7 C.E.	Ovid		
ca. 4 B.C.E.–ca. 65 C.E.	Seneca, Lucius Annacus (the younger)	1445–1505	al-Suyūtī, Jalāl al-dīn
		1447–1510	Catherine of Genoa, St.
480–524 or 525 C.E.	Boethius	ca. 1447–1511	Commynes, Philippe de
		1447–1516	Li Dongyang
		1448–1524	Ibn Iyās

13TH-, 14TH-, AND 15TH-CENTURY PRECURSORS AND EARLY RENAISSANCE FIGURES

Dates	Author	Dates	Author
		1449–1492	Medici, Lorenzo de
		ca. 1450–1483	Mithradates, Flavius
		1450–1547	Mīrā Bāī
1265–1321	Dante Alighieri	1451–1506	Columbus, Christopher
1290–ca. 1365	Shi Naian	1452–1501	Pulci, Antonia Tannini
1304–1374	Petrarch, Francis	1454–1494	Poliziano, Angelo
1313–1375	Boccaccio, Giovanni	1458–1521	Brant, Sebastian
1330–1400	Lo Guanzhong	1459–1508	Celtis, Conradus
ca. 1349–1415	Chrysoloras, Manuel	ca. 1460–1497	Delmedigo, Elijah

ca. 1460–ca. 1521	Abravanel, Jehudah ben Isaac
1463–1494	Pico della Mirandola, Giovanni
1466–1536	Erasmus, Desiderius
1467–1533	Bourchier, John, Lord Berners
1467–1540	Budé, Guillaume
1468–1534	Busche, Hermann von dem
1469–1499	Cereta, Laura
d. 1474	Pulci, Luca

16TH- AND 17TH-CENTURY AUTHORS

Five Friends

1468–ca. 1530	Juan del Encina
1468–1534	Kemalpasazâde (Ibn Kemal)
1469–1527	Machiavelli, Niccolò
1469–ca. 1639	Nānak
d. 1470	Pulci, Luca
1470–1547	Bembo, Pietro
ca. 1472–ca. 1531	Lámi'í of Brusa
1473–1530	Li Mengyang
1473–1543	Copernicus, Nicolaus
1474–1533	Ariosto, Ludovico
1475–1522	Barclay, Alexander
1475–1564	Michelangelo Buonarotti
1477–1542	Jayisi, Malik Muhammad
1478–1529	Castiglione, Baldassare
1478–1535	More, Sir (Saint) Thomas
1478–1557	Fernández de Oviedo y Valdés, Gonzalo
1479–1531	Vallabha
1480–1554	Pedersen, Christiern
1483–1530	Bābur (Zahīr-ud-Dīn Muhammad)
1483–1546	Luther, Martin
1483–1553	Rabelais, François
1483–1563	Sūrdās
1484–1531	Zwingli, Huldrych
1484–1550	Arason, Jón
1485–1533	Caitanya Deva, Krishna
1485–1547	Cortés, Hernán

1485–1550	Gámbara, Veronica
1485–1553	Chaitanya Deva, Krishna
d. 1487	Pulci, Bernardo
1488–1539	Columbus, Ferdinand
1488–1559	Yang Shen
1488–1575	Karo, Joseph Ben Ephraim
1490–1542	Boscán Almogaver, Juan
1490–1546	Elyot, Sir Thomas
1490–1547	Dāsa, Atibadi Jagannātha
1491–1557	Cartier, Jacques
1492–1547	Colonna, Vittoria
1492–1549	Margeurite d'Angoulême
1492–1556	Aretino, Pietro
1492–1584	Díaz del Castillo, Bernal
1493–1543	Firenzuola, Agnolo
1494–1566	Süleyman I
1494–1536	Tyndale, (Hütchins) William
1494–1576	Sachs, Hans (See MEISTERSINGER)
1494–1561	Tausen, Hans
ca. 1495–1556	Fuzûlî (Fuḍūlī) of Baghdad, Mehmed ibn Suleyman
1496–1544	Marot, Clément
1498–1569	Huang Xiumei
1499–1590	Sahagún, Bernardino de, Fray
Early 16th c.	Sankaradeva
mid-16th c.	Battiferi, Laura
16th c.	Dâs, Vrindavân
16th c.	Erutacan
16th c.	Molla, Atukuri
16th c.	Wang Jiaoluan
fl. mid-16th c.	Ratnākaravarni
fl. 1500	Montalvo, Garci Rodríguez de
ca. 1500–ca. 1562	Cavendish, George
1500–1571	Cellini, Benvenuto
1500–1574	Camerarius, Joachim
1500–1582	Wu Cheng'en
1501–1560	Scève, Maurice
1503–1536	Garcilaso de la Vega
1503–1542	Wyatt, Sir Thomas
1503–1576	Casa, Giovanni della

1503–1560	Palladius, Peder
1504–1536	Boleyn, Anne
1505–1554	Wickram, Georg
1505–1536	Udall, Nicholas
1505–1571	Castelvetro, Lodovico
ca. 1506–1552	Leland, John
ruled 1509–1530	Krishnadevaraya
ca. 1509–1557	Agricola, Michael
1509–1564	Calvin, John
1510–1556	Vaux, Thomas, Lord
1510–1566	Aragona, Tullia d'
ca. 1510–1598	Vyas, Harriram
ca. 1510–ca. 1600	Duan Shuqing
1511–1564	Gómara, Francesco López de
1511–1574	Vasari, Giorgio
1514–1570	Li Panlong
1515–after 1552	Crenne, Hélisenne de (Marguerite De Briet)
1515–1568	Ascham, Roger
1515–1611	Archevolti, Samuel
ca. 1515–1589	Bittaināth
1516–1587	Foxe, John
1517–1547	Surrey, Henry Howard, earl of
1518–1587	Cecchi, Giovanni Maria
1519–1562	Grimald, Nicholas
1520–1587	Des Roches, Madelaine
ca. 1520–1545	Du Guillet, Pernette
ca. 1520–1591	Du Fail, Noël
d. 1521	Hátifí, 'Abudu'lláh
1521–1593	Xu Wei
ca. 1522–1560	Bellay, Joachim du
1523–1554	Stampa, Gaspara
1523–1603	Gul-Badan Begum
1524–1580	Camões, Luíz Vaz De
1524–1585	Ronsard, Pierre de
ca. 1525–1577	Gascoigne, George
1525–1581	Wilson, Thomas
1526–1590	Wang Shizhen, II
1526–1600	Bâkî (Mahmud Abdül bâkî)
1527–1592	Sommi, Judah Leone ben Isaac
1527–1607	Krishnadāsa Kavirāja Gosvāmi
1528–1569	Ferreira, António
1528–1575	Beyer, Absalon Pedersson
1530–1666	Hoby, Sir Thomas
1532–1573	Jodelle, Étienne
1532–1584	Norton, Thomas
1532–1589	Baïf, Jean-Antoine de
1533–1592	Montaigne, Michel Eyquem de
1533–1594	Ercilla y Zúñiga, Alonso de
1533–1599	Eknath
ca. 1533–1599	Nev'í
1533–1603	Elizabeth I of England
1536–1608	Sackville, Thomas
1538–1612	Guarini, Giovanni Battista
1539–1600	Acosta, José de
1534–1616	Garcilaso de la Vega, The Inca
1543–1607	Dyer, Sir Edward
1543–1623	Tulsīdās
1544–1590	Bartas, Guillaume de Salluste, seigneur du
1544–1617	Botero, Giovanni
1545–1587	Des Roches, Catherine
1545–1614	Fries, Peder Clausson
ca. 1545–1625	Erici, Ericus
1546–1591	Franco, Veronica
1547–1595	Faydī
1547–1616	Cervantes Saavedra, Miguel de
1548–1600	Bruno, Giordano
fl. ca. 1550	Battiferi, Laura
ca. 1550–ca. 1600	Chakravarti, Mukundaram
ca. 1550–1600	Chandrabati
1550–1617	Tang Xianzu
1552–1630	Aubigné, Théodore-Agrippa d'
ca. 1552–1599	Spenser, Edmund
1552–1616	Hakluyt, Richard
1553–1625	Florio, John
1553–1644	Yahyá Effendi
1554–1586	Sidney, Sir Philip
1554–1600	Hooker, Richard
ca. 1554–1606	Lyly, John

1554–1628	Greville, Fulke, first baron Brooke
1555–1592	Fonte, Moderata
1555–1628	Malherbe, François de
1556–1605	Keshavdās
1558–1592	Greene, Robert
1558–1594	Kyd, Thomas
1558–1625	Lodge, Thomas
1558–1639	Chen Jiri
1559–1663	Bihari Lal
ca. 1560–1634	Chapman, George
1561–1621	Pembroke, Mary Herbert, countess of
1561–1626	Bacon, Francis, Viscount St. Albans
1561–1627	Góngara y Argote, Luis de
1562–1604	Andreini, Isabella
1562–1613	Constable, Henry
ca. 1562–1619	Daniel, Samuel
1562–1635	Lope de Vega Carpio, Félix
1563–1589	Hŏ Kyŏngbŏn
ca. 1563–ca. 1600	Deloney, Thomas
d. 1564?	Purandaradasa
1564–1593	Marlowe, Christopher
1564–1616	Shakespeare, William
1564–1642	Galilei, Galileo
1565–1641	Ashley, Roger
1565–1645	Gournay, Marie Le Jars de
ca. 1567–1601	Nashe, Thomas
1567–1620	Campion, Thomas
1568–1610	Yuan Hongdo
1568–1614	Carvajal y Mendoza, Luisa de
1568–1625	Urfé, Honoré d'
1568–1639	Campanella, Tommaso
1569–1618	Hŏ Kyun
1569–1626	Davies, Sir John
1570–1627	Middleton, Thomas
1570–1631	Háletí
1570–ca. 1662	Nabhâdâs
1571–1653	Marinella, Lucrezia
1572–1631	Donne, John
ca. 1572–1632	Dekker, Thomas
ca. 1572–ca. 1632	Hardy, Alexandre
1572–ca. 1635	Omer (Nef'i of Erzurum)
1572–1637	Jonson, Ben
1573–1613	Régnier, Mathurin
1573–1652	Jones, Inigo
1574–1641	Heywood, Thomas
1574–1646	Feng Menglong
1574–1656	Hall, Joseph
1575–1624	Böhme, Jakob
ca. 1575–1626	Tourneur, Cyril
1576–1634	Marston, John
1577–1640	Burton, Robert
1577–1656	Nobili, Roberto de
1579–1625	Fletcher, John
1579–1636	Messenius, Johannes
d. ca. 1580	Holinshed, Raphael
ca. 1580–ca. 1625	Webster, John
ca. 1580–1648	Molina, Tirso de
1582–1650	Fletcher, Phineas
1583–1634/5	'Atá'í, Nev'í-záde
1583–1640	Massinger, Philip
d. 1584 (?)	Best, George
1584–1616	Beaumont, Francis
fl. ca. 1585	Nanandāsa
ca. 1585–ca. 1642	Rowley, William
ca. 1586–1639	Cary, Elizabeth Tanfield, viscountess Falkland
ca. 1586–ca. 1639	Ford, John
1587–1637	Arrebo, Anders Christensen
1587–1642	Kynaston, Sir Francis
ca. 1587–ca. 1651	Wroth, Lady Mary
1588–1665	Rambouillet, Catherine de Vivonne, marquise de
1588–1679	Hobbes, Thomas
d. 1590/91	'Urfí of Shiraz
1590–1626	Viau, Théophile de
1591–1632	Maqqari of Tlemcen, Ahmed al-
1591–1635	Spee von Langenfeld, Friedrich
1592–1641	Sullam, Sara Coppio
1592–ca. 1650	Erauso, Catalina de
1593–1663	Herbert, George
1593–1683	Walton, Izaak

1595?–1640	Carew, Thomas	1615–1669	Denham, Sir John
1596–1650	Descartes, René	1616–1655	Yang Jisheng
1596–1666	Shirley, James	1616–1664	Greif, Andreas
1597–1639	Opitz, Martin		(Gryphius)
1597–1654	Balzac, Jean-Louis Guez de	1617–1679	Hofmannswaldau, Christian Hofmann von
1598–1672	Stiernhielm, Georg	1618–1704	Yu Tong
1599–1658	Cromwell, Oliver	1619–1655	Cyrano de Bergerac, Savinien de
late 16th or early 17th c.	Yehudah ben David	1619–1677	Bording, Anders
17th c.	Chemakura Venkata Kavi	1619–1684	Rosenhane, Gustaf
ft. ca. 1600	Hubbi Qadin (Ayishe)	1620–1686	Dong Yue
1600–1655	Akhā	ca. 1620–1697	Zacuto, Moses ben Mordecai
ca. 1600–1674	Sorel, Charles	1621–1678	Marvell, Andrew
1600–1681	Calderón de la Barca, Pedro	1621–1695	La Fontaine, Jean de
1601–1655	L'Hermite, François (Tristan)	ca. 1621–1695	Vaughan, Henry
		1621–1706	Wang Duanshu
ca. 1601–1665	Earle, John	1622–1673	Molière
1601–1667	Scudéry, Georges de	ca. 1622–1676	Grimmelshausen, Hans Jacob Christoph von
1601–1670	Sá'íb of Tabriz or Ishfanan	1623–1673	Cavendish, Margaret (née Lucas), duchess of Newcastle
1604–1652	Tarabotti, Archangela		
1604–1686	Mairet, Jean	1627–1693	Anne-Marie-Louise d'Orléans, duchesse de Montpensier
1605–1659	Dach, Simon		
1605–1669	Wivallius, Lars		
1605–1682	Browne, Sir Thomas	1628–1688	Bunyan, John
d. ca. 1606–1607	Kháqání	1628–1690	Vitthal
1606–1684	Corneille, Pierre	1628–1700	Bahinabai
1607–1687	Waller, Edmund	1630–1712	Nábí
1607–1649	Tukārāma	1631–1664	Philips, Katherine
1607–1656	Gerhardt, Paul	1631–1700	Dryden, John
1607–1701	Scudéry, Madeleine de	1633–1694	Greiffenberg, Catharina Regina von
1608–1674	Milton, John		
1609–1640	Fleming, Paul	1634–1693	La Fayette, Marie-Madeleine Pioche de la Vergne, comtesse de (Madame de La Fayette)
1609?–1642	Suckling, Sir John		
1609–1650	Rotrou, Jean de		
1609–1656	Kâtib Çelebî, (Hajji Khalifah)		
1609–1674	Clarendon, Edward Hyde, earl of	1634–1703	Kingo, Thomas Hansen
		1634–1711	Wang Shizhen II
1610–1660	Scarron, Paul	1635–1716	Engelbretsdatter, Dorothea
ca. 1610–1696	Magnússon, Jón		
1611–1643	Cartwright, William	1637–1674	Trahern, Thomas
1611–1679	Li Yu	1637–1692	Kim Man-jung
ca. 1613–1649	Crashaw, Richard	1639–1699	Racine, Jean

1640–1715	Pu Songling	1651–1695	Cruz, Sor Juana Inés de la
1642–1693	Saikaku (Ihara Saikaku)	1653–1724	Chikamatsu Monzaemon
1644–1694	Bashō (Matsuo Bashō)	1659 d.	Al-Shirbīnī, Yūsef
1644–1709	Abraham a Sancta Clara	1665–ca. 1712	Reuter, Christian
1645–1724	Glückel von Hameln	d. ca. 1666	Ná'ilí
d. ca. 1647	Fehím	ca. 1668–ca. 1707	Walī (Valī; Walī Muham-
1647–1707	Dass, Petter		mad; Walī Dakhanī)
1648–1718	Kong Shangren	late 17th c.	Honnamma, Sanciya
1650–1710	Dāsa, Dānakrishna		

A

abhanga (a verse form of India)

A run-on couplet of three-and-one-half metrical feet, the *abhanga*'s first two feet rhyme, but its last foot-and-a-half does not rhyme with the other two. (See POETIC METER.) Difficult to illustrate in rhymed English (or to master in the languages of India), the *abhanga* became the especially favored verse form of the accomplished Maharastran poet and Hindu saint, TUKĀRĀMA (1607–49), who used the form so effectively that few after him attempted it. One who did, however, was the female poet and saint BAHINABAI (1628–1700). When the *abhanga* is handled skillfully, its brevity gives it the force of a pithy EPIGRAM or of a Japanese HAIKU (a poem that is usually 17 syllables long). One of Tukārām's *abhangas* can be rendered into English like this:

> *Not sold in the bazaar, sainthood*
> *Is purchased by paying one's life—*
> *All else is bluster.*
>
> (Paraphrase mine, J. W. C.)

Bibliography

India Yogi. "Tukaram—The Heart of Marathi Devotional Poetry." Available online. URL: http://www. indiayogi.com/content/indsaints/ tukaram.asp. Downloaded on June 14, 2003.

Abhanga gatha (Collection of *Abhangas*) Tukārāma (after 1640)

A collection of some 4,500 short, pithy, poems in the Marathi language of INDIA by the most popular of Indian poet–saints, TUKĀRĀMA, this gathering of his work has acquired the status of Scripture. While at least some of the poems have likely been included under false pretenses, the vast majority of them seem to be the poet's own. Quite apart from the devotional aspects of his work, it is Tukārāma's working through the various emotional, spiritual, familial, and material difficulties of his own life in memorable verse that draws a reader's interest. He tells about his parents and their line of work as low-caste moneylenders. He recalls his childhood, discusses his brother, and decries the evils of the caste system. He talks of his wife and their child and of the way in which they starved to death in the terrible famine of 1630. He recounts the depression into which he fell following their deaths and his eventual victory over despair through the mystical contemplation of Godhead. He talks of his penance for the sin of hoping too little and of the help he received from a mentor—his guru, CHAITANYA DEVA.

In Western literature of a comparable sort, perhaps, the *Confessions of Saint Augustine* comes closest to matching the self-critical introspection that Tukārāma achieves.

The *Abhanga gatha* also contains much wisdom about the fruitful conduct of life. Some aspects of it provide a sort of self-help advice that accounts for at least a portion of its continuing popularity. Tukārāma rejects the authority of the Brahmins who viewed religious teaching as a high-caste prerogative and prefers straightforward, simple, colloquial language to the scholarly Sanskrit of the Brahmin tradition.

According to an undoubtedly apocryphal story that nonetheless appears in the collection itself, to punish the poet for writing about religion in Marathi instead of Sanskrit, jealous Brahmins seized the manuscript of the *Abhanga gatha* and threw it into the River Indrayani at the town of Dehu. Two weeks later, however, the river—presumably having had a chance to read and approve the collection—returned it to the author undamaged.

English versions of selections of the *Abhanga gatha* are widely available, though those translations' titles bear little resemblance to their Marathi original.

Bibliography

Tukārāma. *An Indian Peasant Mystic: Translations from Tukaram.* Translated by John S. Hoyland. London: H. R. Allenson, Ltd., 1932.

———. *Eating Hunger: Selections from the poems of Tukarama.* Translated by J. Nelson Fraser and K. B. Marathe. Cambridge, Mass.: RhwymBooks, 1998.

———. *Meditations of St. Tukarama.* Jodhpur, India: Marudhar Publishers, 1976.

———. *Says Tuka: Selected Poetry of Tukaram.* Translated by Dilip Chitre. New York: Penguin Books, 1991.

———. *The Poems of Tukarāma.* Translated by J. Nelson Fraser and K. B. Marathe. Reprint. Delhi: Motilal Banadarsidass, 1981.

Abraham a Sancta Clara (Johann Ulrich Megerle) (1644–1709)

An Augustinian friar who took the religious name Abraham, Megerle had been trained by both the Jesuits in Ingolstadt and the Benedictines in Salzburg, Austria. Ordained a priest in 1668, he began a career as a preacher in 1672 in Vienna where the style and content of his preaching attracted the favorable attention not only of his ordinary congregation, but also of the emperor, who named Megerle as imperial preacher.

In the late 1670s Megerle applied the satirical and witty style of his sermons to writing moral SATIRES with the object of reaching a wider audience and improving, as he thought, the lax behavior of the Viennese. His first such work, *Mercks Wien* (Take heed, Vienna! 1680) suggests a connection between the citizens' sinfulness and lack of seriousness and the twin plagues that threatened them: the bubonic plague that was raging at the time and the Turkish assault on Vienna. In 1683 another work in the same satirical vein, *Auf, auf, ihr Christen* (Rise up, rise up, you Christians) encourages the citizens of Vienna to cooperate and to resist the Turks stoutly.

Megerle's next work was a long (four volume), largely legendary biography of Judas Iscariot, the betrayer of Christ. The work appeared in installments for more than a decade: *Judas der Ertzschelm* (Judas, the leading rogue, 1486–95). It is marked by a wandering style of narration that suggests that its author could not resist an illustrative story or a sidelight.

Some of his later works belong to the genre of fools' literature that SEBASTIAN BRANT's *The Ship of Fools* and DESIDERIUS ERASMUS's *PRAISE OF FOLLY* also illustrate. The first of these, Megerle's *Wunderlicher Traum von einem grossen Narren-Nest* (A wonderful dream from a great fool's nest) appeared in 1703. It was followed by *Karn voller Narrn* (Coachfuls of fools, 1703). He returned to the genre later in the decade by poking fun first at a hundred follies typical of men, in a Latin-titled work, *Centifolium stultorum* (A hundred leaves of fools, 1709). He then did women the same courtesy in *Mala galina* (1713). The punning Latin title of this last work provides a glimpse into the intricate workings of Megerle's not-always-priestly sense of humor. While the principal meaning of *mala galina* is "a wicked hen," the phrase also admits a secondary translation as "a bearded hen."

In the brief interval between these two sets of fools' literature, Megerle continued his series of moral satires: *Heilsames Gemischgemasch* (A wholesome mishmash, 1704), *Hey! und Pfuy! Der Welt* (Hey and phooey! The World! 1707), and *Wohl angefüllter Wein-Keller* (The well-stocked wine cellar, 1710).

Megerle's works have remained in print in German since their first publication and good modern editions are available in that language. As of this writing, however, his work has not appeared in English translation.

Bibliography

Vivian, Kim, Frank Tobin, and Richard H. Lawson, eds. *Vom frühen Mittelalter bis zum Sturm und Drang: An Anthology of German Literature.* Volume I. Prospect Heights, Ill.: Waveland Press, Inc., 1998.

Abravanel, Jehudah ben Isaac (Leone Hebreo) (ca. 1460–ca. 1521)

Descended from Spanish and Portuguese Jews, the physician and philosophical scholar Jehudah Abravanel was among those who fled Spain in 1492 rather than undergo forced conversion to Christianity. In an effort to make him convert, in 1490 Spanish authorities planned to kidnap his child. Learning of the plot, Abravanel sent his son into Portugal where his father, Isaac Abravanel, had been an important statesman. There, however, the child was first held hostage and then, in 1495, was obliged to convert.

Abravanel fled to Italy where in 1502 he penned a touching poem lamenting his loss of the child he had not seen in 12 years. In the same year he began what was to become his most celebrated work. Writing in Italian, he became the first person to consider purely philosophical problems in that tongue in his celebrated *Dialoghi di amore* (Dialogues or conversations about love, 1535). In this work Abravanel develops the platonic view that the true, the good, and the beautiful are the ground of being and that love, governed by reason, is the principle that makes these attributes perceptible to the human mind. But love is higher than reason, and, in the hierarchy of the real, beauty is the highest characteristic because it is the central quality of God from which all other qualities take their being.

God is simultaneously knowledge, the knower, and that which is known. He is the lover, the loved, and in His primordial divine beauty, that which is loveable. In the earthly realm people can only perceive reflections of this divine reality. Likewise, only people can perceive these reflections. Humankind, therefore, becomes the link between the physical world and the intellective world of abstract truth, goodness, and beauty that God contemplates in God's own being.

To this neoplatonic view, Abravanel joins elements of mysticism from the Jewish kaballah and certain aspects of magic and astrology as well. His *Dialoghi* became enormously influential—except, ironically, in the Jewish community. In Italy five editions appeared in 15 years. In 1551 a French edition was addressed to Queen Catherine de' Medici of France, and shortly thereafter an edition appeared in Spanish addressed to King Philip II and translated by GARCILASO DE LA VEGA, the INCA. Partly owing to Abravanel's influence, cults of platonic love sprang up throughout Europe, precipitating a flood of Renaissance platonic love poems in almost all the languages of Europe.

Bibliography

Abravanel, Jehudah [Leone Ebreo]. *The Philosophy of Love.* Translated by F. Friedeberg-Seely and Jean H. Barnes. London: The Soncino Press, 1937.
Zinberg, Israel. *A History of Jewish Literature.* Translated and edited by Bernard Martin. Cincinnati, Ohio, and New York: Hebrew Union College Press and KTAV Publishing House, 1974.

Academy of the Cross (Accademia della Crusca)

Replacing the earlier Florentine Academy (founded ca. 1540), the Academy of the Cross—established in 1582 with the financial support of the Tuscan grand dukes—proposed to purify the Italian language and provide for it a literary standard. Both Italy's location as a Mediterranean linguistic crossroads and its mountainous terrain had contributed to the development of many regional and even local dialects, some of which were and still are mutually unintelligible. Italy today recognizes nine major dialect areas.

Coming at a moment in history when Latin still served as an international lingua franca and was the language of choice for writers who wished to be read beyond their own national borders, the academy promoted the Tuscan dialect as the vernacular ideal toward which educated Italians should strive. This made sense as the three most influential literary figures of Italy, DANTE, PETRARCH, and BOCCACCIO had all written in Tuscan—the language of Florence and its surrounding region.

As an important step in its linguistic campaign, the academy published the first great Italian dictionary, its *Vocabolario degli Accademici della Crusca* (Wordlist of the members of the Academy of the Cross, 1611). In addition to a list of words with their definitions that was approved for literary use, the first edition of the *Vocabolario* contains three indexes to the words, sayings, and Latin and Greek phrases sprinkled throughout the dictionary. The academy continued its program of dictionary publication until late in the 19th century, regularly updating its standards of philology and lexicography. When the first version of the fifth edition failed to meet those standards, the academy suppressed the work and began again.

It has published and continues to publish many other works as well. During the Renaissance it sometimes took sides in literary quarrels. In 1584 it defended, for example, PIETRO ARIOSTO's *ORLANDO FURIOSO* against the attack of Cammillo Pellegrino, who thought Ariosto's work a poor representative of the EPIC genre. It has also published editions (1726–27) of the works of DANTE, collections, catalogues, bulletins, and philological studies. It continues its work to this day.

For Italy the efforts of the Academy of the Cross in achieving a national standard has proved a great success. In Italy today people generally agree that the best Italian spoken is *"la lingua Toscana in bocca Romana"*—the Tuscan dialect as spoken by Romans.

Acosta, José de (1539–1600)

A Jesuit missionary to the native peoples of Peru, Acosta served in the New World from 1571 to 1587. While there he wrote a catechism in the local languages that had the distinction of being the first book printed in Peru. On his return to Spain, he first wrote in Latin a careful study of the difficulties missionaries faced while working among the indigenous peoples of the Americas, *De procuranda indorum salute* (On securing health for the Indies). He next catered to the intense public interest in the New World's exotic peoples and its exploration by writing on the basis of firsthand information the first work to consider the New World in the context of its relation with Europe. His *Historia natural y moral de las Indias* (Natural and moral history of the Indies) appeared in Spanish in 1590. It was soon translated into six languages and ran through 22 editions. In this work Acosta tried to organize his astronomical, geographic, metallurgical, botanical, zoological, social, and anthropological observations in Peru and Mexico according to the scientific tenets of his epoch and the thinking of the Jesuit order.

His career was interrupted in 1592–93 by his imprisonment for a short-lived resistance to his Jesuit superiors. After he conformed to their views, the Jesuits appointed Acosta to high administrative and academic office in Jesuit institutions in Valladolid and in Salamanca. He served there until his death.

Bibliography

Acosta, José de. *Natural and Moral History of the Indies.* Edited by Jane E. Mangan; translated by Frances López-Morillas; introduction and commentary by Walter Mignolo. Durham, N.C.: Duke University Press, 2002.

Burgaleta, Claudio M. *José de Acosta, S. J., 1540–1600: His Life and Thought.* Chicago: Jesuit Way, ca. 1999.

Actes and Monuments . . . (*Foxe's Book of Martyrs*) John Foxe (1563)

In 1554 while living in exile during the reign of the Roman Catholic English Queen Mary I, John Foxe published at Strasbourg in Latin the first modest installment of what was to become, after the Bible itself, the English-speaking world's most influential book of Renaissance Protestantism. The little Strasbourg volume, whose Latin title, *Rerum in ecclesia gestarum . . . commentarii,* translates as *Commentaries on matters in Church Affairs,* focused mainly on the persecution of the 14th-century English religious reformer John Wycliffe (ca. 1330–84) and his followers. It also treated a few Continental martyrs such as the Florentine monk Girolamo Savonarola (1452–98) and the Bohemian Wycliffite Jan Hus (ca. 1372–1415), both burned at the stake for heresy. It may be helpful to recall that, technically, martyrs are persons who, when given the choice, prefer death above renouncing their religious convictions.

Mary I's repression and executions of English Protestants provided further grist for Foxe's mill, and his friend and associate Edmund Grindal (ca. 1519–83) helped Foxe collect the new martyrs' stories. A much-expanded, second Latin edition of his work appeared at Basel in 1559.

When Elizabeth I succeeded Mary on the English throne in 1558, Grindal became bishop of London. On Foxe's return to England, Grindal ordained him. Back on British soil, Foxe set about translating, revising, and again greatly expanding the Basel edition. The first English version of Foxe's book, though its abbreviated title is *Actes and Monuments,* early came to be popularly called Foxe's Book of Martyrs. It appeared in 1563. By this time Foxe had included sections on the apostolic martyrs, on the martyrs created during four subsequent repressions of Christians under Roman emperors, and on the latest persecutions of European Protestants. Foxe continued expanding and revising the work throughout his lifetime. New and ever-larger editions appeared in 1570, 1576, and 1583. Posthumous ones have continued coming out ever since. A recent one even modernizes Foxe's Renaissance English.

In 1571 the convocation of the Anglican Church ordered that a copy of Foxe's now huge book be made available in every English Cathedral. Moreover, it directed that every British clergyman from the rank of archbishop down to and including that of resident canon should have a copy in his home for his own benefit and that of his visitors and servants.

A certain amount of controversy has surrounded Foxe's historiography. His detractors—usually not his co-religionists—have found fault with the accuracy of his history. His supporters—usually but not always his co-religionists—while admitting that Foxe was a propagandist for his faith—also defend the historical accuracy of his writing. The truth probably lies somewhere in between. On the basis of Roman civic records, the eminent 18th-century historian Edward Gibbon thought the numbers reported in early Christian accounts of Christians martyred as a result of repressions by Roman Emperors considerably exaggerated.

At the end of Foxe's life, the title of the first volume of the three in the last edition he personally compiled (1583) appeared as: *Actes and Monuments of Matters most Special and Memorable Happening in the Church, with an universal History of the Same, wherein is set forth at large the whole race and course of the Church from the primitive Age to these latter tymes of ours, with the bloudy times, horrible troubles, and great persecutions agaynst the true martyrs of Christ, sought and wrought as well by Heathen Emperours, as nowe lately practised by Romish Prelates, especially in this Realme of England and Scotland, Newly revised and recognised, partly also augmented and now for the fourth tyme agayn published and recomended to the studious Reader by its author John Foxe. . . .* Volumes 2 and 3 each had separate titles. Essentially, volume 2 examined the period of the reigns of Henry VIII through Elizabeth I, and volume 3 continued into the time of King Charles I. Subsequent editions under a long series of editors have continued adding material of various sorts to Foxe's compilation while at the same time abridging some of his original selections.

American editions have appended histories of missionary efforts in the United States and persecutions of Protestants wherever they have occurred.

Though 20th- and 21st-century editions would appear very different from his own to Foxe, chances are he would applaud most of the work of his successors, for they continue his agenda in the context of changing times. His work will undoubtedly go on appearing as a living, changing document as long as new candidates for inclusion continue to suffer religious persecution.

Bibliography

Foxe, John. *Foxe's Christian Martyrs of the World.* Westwood, N.J.: Barbour Books, ca. 1989.

Adi Granth (Sri Guru Granth Sahib; The Holy Scripture of the Sikhs) Guru Arjan Dev (Punjabi language, 1601 or 1604)

Compiled with careful attention by the fifth guru of the Sikh religion and a devoted team of scholars, the Adi Granth is the most revered object of the faith. The Sikhs' holy book's full modern title, Adi Sri Guru Granth Sahib, can be translated: The Most Revered and the Original Spiritual Adviser: the Great Work. Originally it was simply called The Book or The Manuscript, but it has subsequently acquired more elements in its title and an increasingly venerated status within the religion.

In 1708 Gobind Singh, the 10th guru of Sikhism, supplemented the text of The Book by including the writings of his father, Tegh Bahadur, the 9th guru. That done, Gobind Singh declared the line of human Gurus at an end and named the book itself the eternal Guru of the religion, investing it with the new title Sri Guru Granth Sahib. The word *Adi* was then added to distinguish the work from Gobind Singh's *The Book of the Tenth Master.*

As a physical item, the Adi Granth is cared for and revered in the Golden Temple in the city of Amritsar in the Punjab. As a literary compilation it is composed of three basic parts. The first of these contains liturgical material—a basic statement of faith called the *mul mantra* and hymns and prayers to be used in daily private worship. The second section comprises the bulk of the text—1,340 of 1,430 pages. It contains many verses and hymns, each of which is supposed to be sung to the tune of one of 31 ragas (ancient traditional patterns or modes in Indian music). Each subsection is headed by the title of one of the ragas.

The miscellaneous section includes a variety of verses in various measures that are not associated with particular tunes. These are arranged principally by authorship. The last of the miscellaneous inclusions is a matter of controversy and may be an unauthorized addition. Although the authorship of the individual songs and poems throughout the miscellaneous section is well known, all of the contributors used the name of the first guru, NĀNAK, as pen names.

One commentator on the Adi Granth has characterized it as "a poetical and musical tribute to the creator by a community of devout poets." The lyrics of poems address questions of cosmology, theology, the place of human beings in creation, philosophy, and science. It agrees with the big-bang theory of creation and holds that the Creator has established scientific principles to run the universe. It rejects miracles, magic, rituals, and many of the other trappings of Christo-Judeo-Islamic religions. It does, however, hold that the Creator responds to prayer and that people have free will and are held accountable for immoral and antisocial decisions and actions. The text emphasizes human equality, social service, hard work, and sharing wealth. It encourages socially responsible behavior and provides an accidental if partial parallel to the rise of European HUMANISM.

The Adi Granth has exercised incalculable influence on literary matters in India. First of all, it has encouraged literacy. Thousands of manuscript copies circulated long before the printing press arrived in northern India. No Sikh household can function without a copy. Second, the book stemmed the encroaching tide of Arabic script as the writing medium for representing the languages of India and encouraged the preservation of the native Punjabi Gurmukhi script. Third, because of the inclusiveness of the Adi Granth, it brings together from all over India elements of 500 years of indigenous Indian thinking. Fourth, in its rich variety it has provided models for subsequent writers such as the 17th-century poet Haria or Hari Das or the 18th- and 19th-century poet Bhai Darbari.

Finally, the challenging process that resulted in the compilation of the Adi Granth necessitated bringing together experts in a wide variety of disciplines. These included, among others, calligraphy, comparative philosophy, devotional music, explanations of the metaphors, symbols, and allegories in the texts, lexicography, and poetics. Its production therefore sparked an intellectual tradition within Sikhism that continues to operate.

Bibliography

Songs of the Saints from the Adi Granth. Edited and translated by Nirmal Dass. Albany, N.Y.: State University of New York Press, ca. 2000.

Sri Guru Granth Sahib in English Verse. Transcreated by Swami Rama. Dehra Dun, India: Himalayan Hospital Trust, ca. 1998.

The Essence of Sri Guru Granth Sahib. Edited and translated by Gurbachan Singh Makin. Chandigarh, India: Guru Teg Bahadur Educational Center, 1998–2000.

Advancement of Learning, The Francis Bacon (1605)

The first step in an enormous project of human improvement that BACON called the great instauration, or Renaissance, *The Advancement of Learning* is a systematic account of the improvements learning had experienced during the European Renaissance and of what else needed doing. After a flattering prologue addressed to King James I, whom Bacon found to be endowed with "the power and fortune of a king, the knowledge and illumination of a priest, and the learning . . . of a philosopher," in the first book of this treatise, Bacon discusses the "diseases" afflicting learning. He talks about the faults of churchmen, politics, and the learned that contribute to the diseases. Among these the first is that people study words rather than substance. The second is the study and discussion of pointless and meaningless subjects—including the query of medieval SCHOLASTICISM: How many angels can dance on the head of a pin? The third arises from misrepresentation of truth and the willingness of learners to be misled.

To these afflictions Bacon adds the propensity of learners either to be overly interested in antiquity or in novelty, with the result that they either mistrust new knowledge or fail to perceive the relevance of old knowledge to their current situations. To these errors he adds a learner's unwillingness to suspend judgment pending new information or more careful consideration. The greatest error of learners, however, is the misapplication of what is learned. Such misapplications include simply satisfying curiosity, entertainment, achieving fame, earning money, and winning arguments. The proper ends of learning, Bacon insists, involve glorifying God and improving the human condition.

Having considered these and other problems and pitfalls learners may encounter, Bacon continues by setting out in the 6th section of the first book a general program of mastery for learners to undertake. Bacon begins with God and the creation of the world as told in Genesis. He then suggests learning about angels from the Athenian Dionysius. From "spirits and intellectual forms," Bacon advises descending to "sensible and material forms." Bacon implies that Adam in Paradise invented the experimental method when he viewed and named the creatures. By extension he thinks that the study of the natural world is humanity's proper sphere. He notes that knowledge of the natural world did not bring about the fall, but rather knowledge in the moral sphere.

Bacon's secondary agenda throughout this discussion implicitly calls into question those who would confine their study to the Bible and avoid exploring scientific knowledge. Nonetheless, Bacon's first 13 points involve biblical studies. In the 14th he cites the fathers of the church as authorities for the study of pagan literature to round out the philosophical and moral education of Christians. Whether or not Christians should read pagan writers was a hotly debated issue of the Renaissance. Bacon insists that the learner master faith and science and philosophy as well, citing both divine evidence and human proofs of the dignity of knowledge.

The second book addresses as a central concern what kings and others have done to advance learning. Bacon considers that their most useful contributions include building colleges and establishing foundations. They can endow colleges with funds and grant them freedoms and privileges. They can help establish the regulations by which such colleges and foundations run. Persons of wealth and power can also build libraries and staff them. They can collect books for them or help them improve their collections. They can also encourage new authors, support producing new and better editions of the works of old ones, and commission new and better translations. Finally, they can endow professorships so that the learned can gather to study and teach.

With the 9th section of the second book, Bacon begins discussion of defects in the foundation of colleges and universities. First he notes that small salaries attract people of lesser capacities. Pay better, and hire better people, he advises. He also recommends equipping laboratories with scientific apparatus. He further suggests bringing in independent governors and distinguished visitors to review the work of colleges. He encourages greater exchange and cooperation among universities and insists that the learned write books to disseminate the fruits of their study and research. To a very considerable degree, Bacon's recommendations have been implemented in the modern university.

The rest of the second book of *The Advancement of Learning* addresses curricular matters and courses of study and the benefits deriving from various disciplines. Again, Bacon's ideas about categories of knowledge, curriculum, and method have influenced the development of institutions of higher learning from his own lifetime until the present moment.

He subdivides history into natural, civil, ecclesiastical, and literary. Knowledge he separates into divine, natural, and human philosophy with numerous appropriate subcategories in each division. His remarkable grasp, particularly, of the future role of the natural sciences both in education and in the improvement of the human condition appears most clearly in this second book. So does the emphasis that he puts on the experimental demonstration of facts rather than on reasoning by syllogism and theory.

Bacon did not live to complete the grand design he began with *The Advancement of Learning*, but that work essentially suggests its outline.

Bibliography

Bacon, Francis. *The Advancement of Learning*. Edited by Michael Kiernan. New York: Oxford University Press, 2000.

Adventures of Master F. J., The George Gascoigne (1573)

An example of ELIZABETHAN FICTION sometimes described as the first novel in the English language, *The Adventures of Master F. J.* first appeared as the only prose piece in GASCOIGNE'S anonymously published collection *A Hundredth Sundrie Flowres*. It reported an affair between F. J. and Mistress Elinor that was alleged to have occurred somewhere in the north of England.

The tendency of readers to want to see fiction as authorial biography (which in this case it may have been) led to enough speculation about the identity of the principals that Gascoigne denied the guesswork and claimed that the tale was a translation from an Italian author named Bartollo. That work, Gascoigne alleged, recounted a "fable" of the relationship between Ferdinando Jeronimi and Leonora de Valasco (Elinor). Not very many people then or since have believed Gascoigne's allegation, and many continue to think the story was grounded in an affair of his own.

The presentation of the story is innovatively complex. A narrator's voice, one belonging to a certain G. T., sometimes presents information independently. Sometimes G. T. indirectly quotes what F. J. has told him, or G. T. reflects on the action that has passed. Beyond that F. J. and Elinor exchange letters and love poems to which the reader has access. As a result, the reader's viewpoint constantly shifts to accommodate the new information provided by the various points of view.

Readers learn in Greene's revision of the work that F. J. has been invited to woo the lady Frances. Regrettably F. J. is instead smitten with Frances's sister-in-law, Elinor, to whom he writes a PETRARCHAN love poem that he delivers by dropping it down the front of her low-cut gown. She reads it with approval. As the affair develops the reader learns that F. J. is not Elinor's first extramarital lover.

Frances, in the meantime, has fallen in love with F. J. and becomes jealous of Elinor. When the lovers finally consummate their passion, the vigilant Frances is aware of it and creeps into their bedchamber unobserved.

Whereas the lovers conduct their affair under the pretext of nobility provided by the traditions of courtly love and the fashionable tenets of the cult of PLATONIC LOVE, the earthier narrator G. T. takes a much less noble, more pragmatic view of the matter. His unsentimental stance underscores the tawdry nature of the affair and posits simple lust as its motivator.

Frances, however, wishes to prove her love for F. J. by becoming his ally in his pursuit of Elinor, who rapidly loses interest in her new conquest. The general effect of the story is to satirize the posing associated with the cult of Platonic love.

In attempting to distance the work from the supposition of autobiographical content, Gascoigne reworked the story as it had appeared in 1573, including the detail about F. J.'s having come in the first place to woo Frances. Gascoigne also heightened the Italianate elements of the work, setting the end of the story in Venice and having F. J. drown his sorrows in a life of excess and debauchery while Frances sickens and dies of a broken heart. The sentimental ending of the second version undercuts without altogether vitiating the harshness of the first version's SATIRE.

Bibliography

Gascoigne, George. *A Hundredth Sundrie Flowres.* Edited by G. W. Pigman III. Oxford, U.K.: Clarendon Press, 2000.

Salzman, Paul. *English Prose Fiction: 1558–1700: A Critical History.* Oxford, U.K.: Clarendon Press, 1985.

Adventurous Simplicissimus, The Hans Jacob Christoph von Grimmelshausen (1669)

On its publication the partly autobiographical German novel, *Der Abendteuerliche Simplicissimus Teutsch* (*The Adventurous Simplicissimus*), catapulted its author into instant fame. The book concerns the experiences of a peasant boy. Reared exclusively on his father's farm, the child reaches the age of reason without knowing that he has a name, other than *lad*. Likewise, he knows neither of his parents' given or surnames. He is unaware, as well, that other people beyond the peasants on his family farm inhabit the world. Simplicissimus lives, in other words, in a state of nature until the soldiers come.

The story is set during the Thirty Years' War (1618–48)—a long and grueling European conflict remembered particularly for the cruelty of its soldiery on all sides to peasants in the countryside. The soldiers capture Simplicissimus's father, slaughter the livestock, violate the women, and steal or destroy the family's few possessions. One of the dairymaids is able to warn the boy that the soldiers will take him with them unless he runs away.

Simplicissimus flees into the forest where he learns to sleep in hollow trees and hold starvation at bay with what he can find. There a religious hermit discovers him, takes him in, adopts him, and educates him in Christian lore and in reading and writing. The hermit also takes the youth to the local church before the local folk arrive early each Sunday morning. There its pastor meets the pair's spiritual needs. The boy lives happily with his adoptive father until one day when the hermit has Simplicissimus help dig a grave for the old man. He explains death to the lad and tells him what to do when he passes. As soon as Simplicissimus understands, the hermit lies down in the grave and dies. After unsuccessfully attempting to revive the hermit, Simplicissimus follows his instructions, buries him, grieves for a long time, but eventually wanders off in search of the pastor.

He finds him, but not in the way he expected. Soldiers have come to the village and taken prisoners—the pastor among them. There follows a description of the unspeakable cruelty of the soldiers to their captives—always described from the point of view of the naïve and minimally judgmental Simplicissimus. This naive authorial point of view became GRIMMELSHAUSEN'S hallmark under the name *the simplician style.*

Simplicissimus leaves the village and returns to the hermit's dwelling in the woods, planning to dwell there in isolation from the world, but the soldiers come there too, plunder or destroy his few belongings—except for the hermit's Bible and a few books for which the soldiers have no use. They abduct Simplicissimus and take him to their overlord to whom they give the youth's books. The hermit's name appears in the Bible, as does the fact that he considers Simplicissimus his adoptive son. The lord of the castle where Simplicissimus is held proves to be the hermit's brother-in-law, and he makes the lad a page in his service.

In that capacity, Simplicissimus learns—mostly by observation rather than participation—about all sorts of worldly behavior: drinking until one is too addled or sick to continue, dancing, swearing, and sex. He also learns about hypocritical behavior.

Grimmelshausen follows Simplicissimus's progress through the world in a series of episodic chapters that are generally quite brief and that have clever titles. The young man is present at a witches' dance. He is kidnapped and pressed into military service by the Croats. He is jailed as an enchanter. He travels through the world—eventually as far away as Moscow. He marries twice—though the first time without really intending to. He rotates through a number of careers: a nobleman, a vagabond, a quack doctor, an itinerant actor, more than once a soldier, and a student.

In the book's 22nd chapter Simplicissimus and his real father are reunited.

Events from the Thirty Year's War appear in the book at regular intervals. This recurrent theme gives the work a thematic backbone. Because that war was a war of attrition that regularly involved the suffering of civilian populations rather than a war of great battles that were fought and won or lost in a few days' time, it presaged many of the conditions of warfare in the 20th and 21st centuries. One cannot read this work and the 20th-century novelist Jerzy Kosinski's *The Painted Bird* (1965) without perceiving a resonance between them that suggests Grimmelshausen's book provided Kosinski with a model.

Among the many reasons for certainty concerning the autobiographical nature of several of the episodes in Grimmelshausen's book, we find the fact that in *Simplicissimus's* subtitle Grimmelshausen has given the lad a name: Melchoir Sternfels von Fuchshaim. That name is an anagram of the author's own.

Bibliography

Grimmelshausen, Hans Jacob Christoph von. *The Adventurous Simplicissimus: Being the Description of the Life of a Strange Vagabond Named Melchoir Sternfels von Fuchshaim.* Translated by A. T. S. Goodrick. Lincoln: University of Nebraska Press, 1962.

Against Marriage   Anne-Marie-Louise d'Orléans, duchesse de Montpensier (La Grande Mademoiselle) (1660–1661)

An exchange of eight letters between the duchesse de MONTPENSIER and her friend Madame de Motteville, *Against Marriage* explores what relations between the sexes might ideally be in the upper reaches of the French social hierarchy.

The duchesse, remembered ultimately as La Grande Mademoiselle, proposes a society without marriage, courtship, or the conventional trappings of romantic feeling and the stylized rituals that accompanied both lighthearted and serious flirtation. She envisions a society drawn in part from PASTORAL literature. In her imagined realm, women can move freely among country pleasures, retreats at religious cloisters, and attendance at the court. They would sometimes occupy their time with reading and writing. At other times they would pursue charitable projects among the less fortunate. In her own life, the duchesse had already undertaken the role of heroic military leader in the civil strife that had afflicted France. She had actually ordered the cannons of the Bastille fired against the king's troops during one of the uprisings of the nobility and the bourgeoisie against royal autocracy that the French call the two Frondes (Slings, 1648–49 and 1651–53). The literary historian Carolyn Lougee Chappell has suggested that the pastoral elements in the activities that Mademoiselle Montpensier proposes may amount to a strategically safe literary cover for the passionately involved, sometimes politically subversive actions of the life that she historically led.

In her answering letters, Madame de Motteville plays the foil to La Grande Mademoiselle's proposals. Though her own two-year marriage when she was 18 to a man who was 90 when they wed might have embittered her toward married life, de Motteville nonetheless argued against the duchess, defending marriage as a protection for women against rapacious men and defending the flirtations of the court as necessary adjuncts to the institution.

Bibliography

H-France Book Reviews. October 2003. Carolyn Lougee Chappell. Available online. URL: http://www.uakron.edu/hfrance/reviews/chappell.html. Downloaded May 5, 2004.

Montpensier, Anne-Marie-Louise d'Orléans, duchesse de. *Against Marriage: The Correspondence of La Grande Mademoiselle.* Translated and edited by Joan DeJean. Chicago: University of Chicago Press, 2002.

Agricola, Michael (ca. 1509–1557)

See FINNISH LANGUAGE AND LITERATURE.

Agricola, Rudolphus (Roelof Huysman) (ca. 1443–1485)

Posterity remembers Agricola by the name under which he published rather than by his given name of Huysman. One of the earliest and certainly the most important of the representatives of northern HUMANISM, the Frisian Agricola profoundly influenced the development of Renaissance education and thought. In addition to mastering Latin and Greek and beyond his contributions in the literary realm, he also found time in his relatively short lifetime to excel as a painter and as a musician.

As a Latinist, Agricola edited and commented upon the work of BOETHIUS. He also edited the writings of the Roman historian Tacitus and Pliny's *Natural history.* His principal contribution to the intellectual climate of the Renaissance, however, derived from the system of critical thinking that he proposed in his *Three books on dialectical invention.* Like other Humanist thinkers, Agricola considered the system of thought and discussion employed by medieval scholasticism intellectually bankrupt. In its place he proposed an all-inclusive, systematic approach to thinking and reasoning. In his first book he discusses 24 topics (loci or TOPOI) for consideration. He then considers, first, how to formulate a question for investigation. Next, he proposes a method for thinking about and discussing a question. Finally, in the first of his three books, he discusses ways to explain the outcome of the investigation of a question.

His second book begins by explaining ways to recognize loci or *topoi* in a text. This book deeply affected the way in which literary research was conducted and taught. It sets forth a method for organizing a systematic program of studies. It became the basis for new school and university curricula all over Europe and throughout the Renaissance.

The third book of this influential series discusses various oratorical techniques for moving an audience and for meeting with its approval. Among those whom Agricola influenced, perhaps the most notable was ERASMUS. Agricola spoke to the students at Erasmus's boyhood school, and Erasmus recalled feeling inspired by what the elder Dutch scholar had to say. Agricola felt that his principal mission in life involved rescuing Christianity from the hands of ill-educated and superstitious churchmen and reconciling it with the clearly superior intellectual systems and learning of the ancient Romans and Greeks. Erasmus too found this program congenial.

Beyond these literary accomplishments, Agricola also composed a series of eight orations, one of which is remembered for its early if somewhat romanticized biography of PETRARCH.

In his capacity as a professional musician, Agricola served in Italy for a period as the organist to the court of Duke Ercole I d'Este.

Bibliography

Agricola, Rudolph. *Letters.* Translated by Adrie van der Laan and Fokke Akkerman. Tempe, Ariz.: Arizona Center for Medieval and Renaissance Studies, 2002.

Rudolph Agricola, Gronings Humanist, 1485–1985; tentoonstellingscatalogus. Groningen: Unviversiteitsbibliotheek, 1985.

Akbar, the Great (Abū-ul-Fath Jalāl-ud-Din-Muhammad) (1542–1605)

Mughal emperor of India from the age of 13 until his death, Akbar early overcame rebellion and civil war and later extended his control of India throughout the northern part of the subcontinent. A wise and tolerant ruler of subjects both Muslim and Hindu, Akbar also displayed a taste for Persian poetry and scholarship. As part of a program designed to demonstrate the intellectual equality of the Mughal Empire with Persia, Akbar imported numerous scholars and poets from Iran to his court at Agra.

Under his encouragement, literature, science, commerce, and the arts flourished. Akbar established the post of Persian poet laureate of the Mughal Empire, naming FAYDĪ as the first to hold the position. In an effort to encourage the peaceful coexistence of his Hindu and Muslim subjects, Akbar commissioned a team of translators, including Faydī to render into Persian portions of the Hindu EPICS *The Mahabharata* and the *Ramayana*.

Reared as a Muslim, Akbar developed a personal religious viewpoint that tried to combine elements of several faiths into a state religion. Predictably, this effort offended the conservatives of all religious points of view.

Under Akbar's rule, literary activity flourished producing a golden age of Persian poetry in North India.

Akha (1600–1655)

Originally a goldsmith by profession, Akha became a religious philosopher and a devotional poet in the bhakti tradition of India. He wrote mainly in the Gujerati language but also in Punjabi, in Hindi, and in the closely related Braj tongue. (See INDIA, LANGUAGES OF.)

Like many poets in the bhakti tradition, Akha began as a devotee of the Hindu deity Vishnu, but he moved beyond the vision of that early devotion to a more philosophical and perhaps even a deistic—though still devotional—philosophical position. Deists believe in God on the basis of reason and nature only without appeal to revelation and scripture. The system of thought he developed appears in his greatest poetic work, the *AKHEGITA* (1649). In it, he discusses knowledge, bhakti (devotion), the nature of Maya (illusion), and the identifying characteristics of persons who achieve greatness in life and liberation from illusion by the conduct of their lives and through divine grace.

A social critic and satirist as well as a poet, Akha ridiculed the caste system, the notion of untouchability, and competition among religious sects. Another of his Gujerati works, a satirizing book of humorous sestets called *Chappa,* caught the popular imagination and became a classic of populist sentiment—forwarding the agendas of the common people at the expense of religious establishments and their elitism. For this reason he chose to write in the Gujerati vernacular instead of the liturgical Sanskrit.

A mystical strain in Akha's poetry has occasioned critical comparisons between some of his work and that of the roughly contemporaneous English METAPHYSICAL POETRY AND POETS. Akha's poetic output was substantial and included seven major poems beyond those mentioned, along with a number of minor ones.

Bibliography

Akhā. *Wings of the Soul: Poems of Akhā, the Spiritual Poet of India.* Berkeley, Calif.: Asian Humanities Press, 1993.

Yashaschandra, Sitamshu. "From Hemacandra to Hind Svarāj: Region and Power in Gujarati Literary Culture." In *Literary Cultures in History: Reconstructions from South Asia,* 567–611, edited by Sheldon Pollock. Berkeley: University of California Press, 2003.

Akhegita (Akhā's songbook) Akhā (1649)

A metaphysical poem in the Gujerati language of India and modeled on the ancient Sanskritic *Bhagavadgita*, Akhegita makes what some consider the most important statement in Gujerati about God and the self. Some manuscripts of the document, scholar Umashankar Joshi tells us, allude to the work as "the great soul-liberating knowledge of the supreme spirit."

AKHĀ himself claimed that the work contained the secret of merging the self into the Absolute. To accomplish that end, Akhā addresses the topics of knowledge—especially of the self, of the nature of bhakti (devotion), of the renunciation necessary to achieve true knowledge, of the recognition of the illusory world perceived by the senses, and of the characteristics of the great souls who arrive at true insight and knowledge through the way they live their lives and divine grace. The work explores the life of the individual human spirit.

Akhā famously develops metaphors involving fish to illustrate the conditions of people who live without the knowledge he offers and those who live with it. The first are like a fish out of water suffocating for want of the life-giving fluid and burning with the need for union with God and the underlying reality beyond the physical world. The second, instead, are like a great fish that lives freely in the ocean, occasionally appearing on the surface, but mostly submerged in the great sea with which it is inseparably linked.

The *Akhegita* teaches that gurus are useless and that one must look within for the truth where, however hidden, the reality resides that will call the human spirit to it and reveal itself when the human being renounces the pleasures and attractions of the world of illusion. That reality, says Akhā, is Godhead itself—Brahma. The devotee who practices renunciation and seeks that truth will be refashioned in the likeness of the ultimate reality. The illusory world, instead, is like the infinity of reflections in facing mirrors or a magnificent edifice constructed of transparent glass.

In form, Akhā divides the *Akhegita* into 40 verse chapters (*kadavas*). Following every fourth chapter there is a song (*pada*), the last of which sings an ecstatic spiritual hymn.

Bibliography

Akhā. *Wings of the Soul: Poems of Akhā, the Spiritual Poet of India*. Berkeley, Calif.: Asian Humanities Press, 1993.

Yashaschandra, Sitamshu. "From Hemacandra to Hind Svarāj: Region and Power in Gujarati Literary Culture." In *Literary Cultures in History: Reconstructions from South Asia*, 567–611, edited by Sheldon Pollock. Berkeley: University of California Press, 2003.

Alchemist, The   Ben Jonson (1610)

First acted in 1610 by the King's Majesty's Servants and dedicated to LADY MARY WROTH, BEN JONSON'S verse SATIRE rings changes on the familiar topic of the trickster tricked.

In the extended absence of Love-wit from his house in London, his butler Jeremy, who is in fact a confidence man named Face, installs Subtle and Doll Common in Love-wit's dwelling. There Subtle practices a number of confidence games on a series of dupes whose various follies and appetites make them all eager to be parted from their money and possessions. A clerk, Dapper, becomes convinced that he is the nephew of the Queen of Fairies and that she will give him a spirit that will make him win at all games. Drugger, a tobacconist, seeks advice on the arrangement of his new shop and buys magical spells to bring in customers. The memorable Sir Epicure Mammon wishes to become the master of the Philosopher's Stone (believed by many to turn base metal into gold) so that he may incessantly indulge his insatiable sensual appetites. The wonderfully funny Anabaptists, the Deacon Ananias and his Pastor, Tribulation, display respectively the belligerent demeanor of persons convinced of their own righteousness and their logic-chopping willingness to sacrifice devout principle to potential profit. Like Sir Epicure, they believe that the alchemist Subtle will convert their base metals into gold and silver.

The con artists also give lessons in quarrelling to a character named Kastrill, who follows the fashion of picking fights and seeks a charm that will help him select his enemies advantageously. Subtle, Doll, and Face promise as well to arrange a match between a person they think to be a Spanish grandee and the widow Dame Pliant, Kastrill's sister. The grandee is actually a friend of Sir Epicure's, Surly by name, who has recognized the crooks for what they are. When he exposes them, however, they convince their dupes that Surly is lying. All cooperate in driving him from the house.

Much of the fun of the play arises from the inventiveness of the con artists in managing their business with each of their foolish marks and in keeping them apart as the crooks play various roles. Jonson also sets the audience up for a series of disappointed expectations. The first such surprise is Surly's failure to expose the crooks. The next comes when the master of the house, Love-wit, unexpectedly returns and the neighbors tell him of the crowd of visitors that have been frequenting his house. Face reverts to his role of butler and so bemuses the neighbors that they begin to doubt their own eyes. Just then, however, the dupes begin to arrive, and Face is finally obliged to tell Love-wit the truth. Love-wit forgives him, and the games continue.

The play opened with a quarrel between Face and Subtle that Doll settled by threatening to cut their throats if they would not be friends. As the play's end approaches, Doll and Subtle agree to deceive Face and to make off with their ill-gotten gains without paying him his share. Face, however, has anticipated them: We discover that he sent for Love-wit and that the officers of the law are at the door; Face tells Doll and Subtle to flee over the back wall.

Finally aware they have been tricked, the dupes arrive at the door with the constables. Finding the tricksters fled, Sir Epicure Mammon and the Anabaptists quarrel over the ownership of goods left in the cellar. Love-wit, in the meantime, has struck a match with Dame Pliant, thereby disappointing Surly's hopes. Pliant's brother, Kastrill, threatens Love-wit, who calls his bluff. Kastrill reverses course, promises a generous wedding gift, and enters the house with his sister and Love-wit to enjoy a smoke together. One of Jonson's best-loved plays, *The Alchemist* continues to delight audiences in the 21st century as it did in the 17th.

Bibliography

Jonson, Ben. *The Alchemist* in *Ben Jonson*. Volume 5. Edited by C. H. Herford and Percy Simpson. 1937. Reprint, Oxford: The Clarendon Press, 1971.

Aldine Press (1495–1597)

An important publisher of books addressed, at first, to the new but growing Renaissance market for works in Greek and Latin, the Aldine Press was founded in Venice by scholar–printer Aldus Manutius (ca. 1449–1515) (neé Aldo Manucci) together with a group of wealthy and influential business partners. The press's early publications included a five-volume edition of the works of ARISTOTLE and grammars and dictionaries of the Greek language.

In its early days, the press enjoyed a niche market with no European competition. In the last four years of the 15th century and the first few of the 16th, Aldus began to expand his list by publishing the works of HUMANIST authors who wrote in classical Latin and Greek, such as St. Catherine of Siena, AGNOLO POLIZIANO, PIETRO BEMBO, and ERASMUS. A steady stream of editions of classical writers regularly appeared as well.

The press continued to publish through three generations of direct heirs and in-laws, who sometimes disputed the right to control the company's assets. While the press never wholly lost sight of its founder's interest in the classics, it did introduce and expand a list of Italian works as well. Some of these proved very influential, for example, BALDESSARE CASTIGLIONE's *BOOK OF THE COURTIER* and several works of TORQUATO TASSO.

Certainly the early publishing house whose reputation has proved the most enduring, the Aldine Press pioneered the pocket-sized volume in 1501 with an edition of Virgil. In that same edition, italic type appeared for the first time. The imaginative beauty of the typefaces that the press employed and the attractive arrangement of words and woodcuts on the pages of Aldine books contributed significantly to overcoming the preference of wealthy book collectors for manuscript volumes and to silencing their objections to the new medium of printing from movable type. Aldus the elder, as the founding Manutius came to be called, designed typefaces like italic that were reminiscent of handwriting. Doubtless, such innovation contributed significantly to the growing European appetite for printed books.

Bibliography

Barker, Nicholas. *Aldus Manutius and the Development of Greek Script and Type in the Fifteenth Century.* New York: Fordham University Press, 1992.

Fletcher, H. George. *New Aldine Studies.* San Francisco: B. M. Rosenthal, Inc., 1988.

Alemanno, Yohanan Ben Isaac (ca. 1435–1504)

Descended from a French Jewish family of central European (Ashkenazi) origin, Alemanno was born in Cittá di Castello, Italy, not far from the town of Perugia. He later moved to Florence where he attended a Jewish school (yeshiva), and later still he earned a doctorate in medicine and in the liberal arts in Padua.

A gifted linguist, Alemanno was the master of Italian, Hebrew, Arabic, Latin, and probably French. Back in Florence, for a time he worked as a tutor to the children of a wealthy Jewish banker and literary patron, Yechiel da Pisa. While employed there, he became acquainted with GIOVANNI PICO DELLA MIRANDOLA, the brilliant Florentine humanist. The intellectual companionship between the two flourished as a result of their mutual interests in several subjects.

Prominent among these interests were magic and mysticism, particularly that characterizing the Jewish kabbalah. This mystical movement had developed from the study of a Medieval Hebrew version of Moses Maimonides's work, *The Guide for the Perplexed* (*Moreh Nevukhim*). It combined Neoplatonic mysticism with ARISTOTLE's philosophy and with the theology of the rabbinical and biblical traditions. Orthodox kabbalists rejected the study of secular subjects. Pico was interested to learn that Alemanno had begun to work on several manuscripts before coming to Florence. Pico encouraged him to finish them.

In response, Alemanno completed his commentary on the Song of Solomon's Ascent (*Heshek Slomo*). This is the only one of Alemanno's works currently available in an English edition. In Florence he also completed a work entitled *Hai ha-'olamin* (The immortal)—an encyclopedia that summarized for a thinking but not necessarily scholarly audience the work of the most significant Arab and Hebrew scientists and philosophers, viewed through the lens of Neoplatonist humanism. The ultimate objective of Alemanno's program of humanistic kabbalism was achieving union with God. On the path to that objective, those who learned their lessons would also acquire a magical control over both the earthly sphere and the celestial one.

Among Alemanno's other works in progress was a commentary on the Pentateuch from a kabbalistic standpoint. This work shares certain characteristics with Pico's own *Heptaplus,* which discusses the six days of Genesis from seven interpretative points of view. Alemanno's expertise may well have proved crucial in helping Giovanni Pico achieve his objective of constructing a Christian kabbalah.

Pico died in 1494. Sometime thereafter, certainly by 1497 when the Jews were expelled from Florence as they earlier had been from England, from Spain, and from France, Alemanno left his adopted city. Like his forebears in the desert, he wandered for a while. Then he returned to Mantua where he died without finishing the other works he had started. These are still available only in manuscript.

Bibliography

Lelli, Fabrizio. "Alemanno, Yohanan Ben Isaac." In *Encyclopedia of the Renaissance.* Vol. 1, edited by Paul F. Grendler. New York: Scribner, 1999.

Lesley, Arthur Michael, Jr. *"The Song of Solomon's Ascents" by Yohanan Alamano: Love and Human Perfection according to a Jewish Associate of Giovanni Pico della Mirandola.* Ann Arbor, Mich.: The University of Michigan Press, 1976.

allegory

Like a METAPHOR (life is a fountain) or a simile ("my love is like a red, red rose"), an allegory is a comparison that applies the qualities of one thing to another. Whereas a metaphor is likely to be a brief comparison, however, an allegory is likely to be extended, sometimes over the entire course of a literary work. Moreover, sometimes only one term of the comparison will be stated, and the reader is left to infer the other. In the hands of a master, allegory can become multilayered and deeply laden with meaning, enabling an author to imply—or a reader to infer—several matters simultaneously. EDMUND SPENSER, for example, in his unfinished epic THE FAERIE QUEENE, develops, among others, extended comparisons between Faerie Land and the human mind and soul and between Faerie Land and Elizabethan England. The characters and their actions represent human virtues and vices— sometimes simplistically, and sometimes in very complex ways. King Arthur represents all the virtues rolled into one. Queen ELIZABETH I, who commanded Spenser's unflagging admiration, appears and reappears as Gloriana, the Faerie Queen herself, as Belphoebe, the virgin huntress, and perhaps as Medina, a female character who represents the middle way.

Episodes in the text suggest political events in England, love relationships between men and women, seduction, fear of intimacy, the warfare between good and evil influences, the dangers of self-delusion and mistaking appearances for reality, and many other matters. Spenser himself wrote a letter to Sir WALTER RALEIGH, explaining (and perhaps slightly exaggerating) his use of "allegories' dark conceits" in *The Fairie Queene.*

The early church fathers had designed a four-level system of allegorical interpretation of Scripture called "Patristic exegesis"—explanation according to the Fathers. The first of these levels is literal; it tells you what happened. The second is what the Fathers meant by allegorical; it clarifies proper faith. The third level is the moral level; it teaches you how to behave. The fourth level is anagogical; from it one learns what to expect beyond this world in the realm of future glory. Scholars of Islam assert that skilled interpreters can read the *Koran* on 77 or more allegorical levels.

In Italy, DANTE, PETRARCH, and many of their successors understood and employed the patristic system of allegorical interpretation. Dante was long thought to have written a letter explaining the patristic system to Can Grande della Scala, the ruler of Verona who offered the poet protection in that city. Though Dante's authorship is now sus-

pect, the letter is nonetheless contemporary with him, and he does indeed employ the system. So did many other European authors, and although Protestant reformers did and do think the system overrefined and often attend only to the literal level, many non-Roman Catholic English authors continued to find the patristic system of allegorical interpretation useful to their literary purposes throughout and beyond our period.

See also TYPOLOGY.

Bibliography

Brittain, Simon. *Poetry, Symbol, and Allegory: Interpreting Metaphorical Language from Plato to the Present.* Charlottesville: University of Virginia Press, 2003.

Maclean, Hugh. *Edmund Spenser's Poetry,* 2nd ed. New York: W. W. Norton & Company, 1982.

Roche, Thomas P., Jr. *The Kindly Flame: A Study of the Third and Fourth Books of Spenser's "Faerie Queene."* Princeton, N.J.: Princeton University Press, 1964.

alternative literacies

Literacy means having the ability to look on a page at a group of standardized symbols that stand for the sounds of a language and to understand the meaning of the symbols. Sometimes such reading occurs at a much faster rate than hearing the same thing spoken. Wherever alphabets are used, each symbol represents a *phoneme*—a minimal unit of sound.

All the languages of the industrialized West, of Eastern European countries, of the Jewish and Arabic communities, and of Korea use the alphabet to represent their languages. Other sorts of representations do, however, exist. For instance, some systems of writing use syllabaries in which, as the name suggests, the symbols stand for syllables rather than phonemes. Some systems use logograms, in which a symbol stands for entire words. The Mayan writing system that Europeans encountered on their arrival in the New World in the 16th century combined a syllabary with logograms.

The Chinese, who were the first to develop movable type, use a system of ideographs to represent their language. In this system, a symbol may be a logogram and represent a single word, or it may be a true ideograph and represent a complex idea. While such a system can represent more language with less text, it lacks the economy and efficiency of alphabetic systems. With comparatively few symbols, an alphabet can represent the entire word stock of a language. Ideographic systems require many more symbols to achieve the same end. Before the use of computers displaced typewriters, a Chinese typewriter might require as many as 5,000 keys. Japanese writing early emulated the Chinese system, adapting it to the Japanese language. Since the 19th century, however, an alphabetic system has grown up alongside the older ideographic system in Japan.

Pictographic writing is yet another way to represent language to the eye. This is really a mixed system. Sometimes a picture will represent the thing it stands for, such as a drawing of a god. Other drawings will be ideographs that represent both the idea of and the word for *water* or a *mountain*. Still other symbols will represent phonemes, and others might simply depict an event. The pre-European-contact Nahuatl writing system in Mexico was of this mixed pictographic variety.

The Inca recorded their texts via a series of knotted strings. These string writings, called *quipu*, represented at least aspects of the Quechua language. Different-colored strings indicated different-subjects, and knots stood for numbers and their multiples and possibly also for words. The Quechua language survived the European conquest of the Inca and is today still spoken by some 10 million people throughout the Andes. It is one of the official languages spoken in Peru and in Ecuador. The conquering Spaniards, however, confiscated from the libraries that housed them the ancient *quipu* texts and burned them. We know that a rich heritage of drama, song, and poetry existed because some of it still lingers today. (See APU INCA ATAWALLPAMAN [THE ELEGY OF THE GREAT INCA ATAWALLPA] and AFUOLLANTAY [THE PLAY OF OLLANTAY].)

Language itself, of course, is vastly more ancient than writing. While, as the distinctive hallmark of the human species, language must share the entire history of *homo sapiens,* writing began only five or six thousand years ago. Even into the 20th century and certainly in the two centuries on which this book focuses, many languages had yet to acquire a means of graphic representation. For persons speaking languages that have no written representation, what one might refer to as *the book of memory* serves some of the same function as keeping written records. Also, societies without writing often have storytellers or genealogists who specialize in learning and passing along traditional narratives and family histories.

As the European explorers of the Renaissance encountered the preliterate societies of the Pacific, they discovered that some Pacific islanders could recite their genealogies for hundreds of generations. They also discovered that some, like the people of Guam, memorized and recited ancient poems that guided their navigation over the vast reaches of the Pacific Ocean. On the Philippine island of Mindanao, a preliterate, headhunting people, the Ifugao, had trained their memories to keep track of intergenerational obligations. If person one's grandfather, say, had borrowed a pig from person two and failed to pay the debt, the descendants of person two would know a pig was due them. They would also know the number of chickens due in interest.

As a consequence of their reliance on the book of memory, preliterate societies often possess an oral tradition containing a vast body of embryonic literary material. Stories pass down from generation to generation, sometimes changing form to accommodate the realities of different times or because a powerful figure modifies the story for political purposes. The tellers of the stories often develop oral formulas as an aid to memory. We see such formulas in Homer in his repetition of the phrase "rosy-fingered dawn," or in the *Beowulf* poet's often repeated line: "Beowulf, the son of Egetheow, spoke." Sometimes these formulas also serve as line fillers to meet audience expectations for certain POETIC METER. When someone finally writes down the stories, such formulas often are preserved and testify to the oral tradition that preceded the written versions. African oral epic exemplifies a tradition in which stories, often of uncertain age, began to be written down during the 17th century. This process of recording the oral literature of preliterate peoples continues today.

Bibliography

African Folktales. Edited by Paul Radin. Princeton, N.J.: Princeton University Press, 1964.

Baugh, Albert C., and Thomas Cable. *A History of the English Language.* Englewood Cliffs, N.J.: Prentice Hall, 1963.

León Portilla, Miguel, and Earl Shorris. *In the Languages of Kings.* New York: W. W. Norton, 2001.

Lockhart, James. *The Nahuas After the Conquest.* Stanford, Calif.: Stanford University Press, 1992.

Amadis of Gaul Garci Rodríguez de Montalvo (before 1505)

Adapted from an uncertain source, possibly in the Portuguese language, *Amadis of Gaul* was the most widely known and popular of the Renaissance works that continued the tradition of CHIVALRIC ROMANCE.

Amadis differs from its predecessors of the Middle Ages. The romances in the tradition of Charlemagne focused on the military exploits of heroes like Roland, and those in the tradition of King Arthur and his Round Table managed at the same time to focus on religion and on the trouble that illicit sex can stir up. Both older traditions, then, have didactic purposes as they embellish history to make it more palatable and to teach religious lessons. Rodríguez tries in *Amadis* to present an ideal paladin—a perfect knight who at once exemplifies the benefits of courage and of chastity as the principal cornerstones of the chivalric hero's character.

Both of the older traditions also mythologized persons who either had been or were thought to have been historical. Amadis, by contrast, is an imagined knight. The son of the nonexistent king of Wales, or Gaula as it is called, Amadis is born the illegitimate son of an English princess, Elisena. His mother in her shame sets her baby adrift on the sea. A Scottish knight rescues the child and takes him to England and Scotland, where Amadis grows up. There he eventually falls in love with the fictive Lisuarte, the daughter of an equally fictive king of England.

Meanwhile back in Wales, Elisena has married the imaginary Perion, king of Gaula, who fathers Amadis's half brother, Galaor. The lengthy adventures of the half-siblings, their battles and (mostly Galaor's) loves, their virtually interminable encounters with enchanters and giants, their variable standing in their ladies' favor, and their travels across England, France, Germany, and Turkey, and the eventual union of Amadis and Oriana occupy the first four books of Montalvo's adapted work. Unlike other authors of many chivalric romances whose attention shifts kaleidoscopically from one hero to another, Rodríguez's gaze rests steadily on the two brothers.

The fifth book—entirely Rodríguez's original though less successful creation—pretends to have been translated from Greek and follows the adventures of the earlier born Esplandian, the son of Amadis and Oriana. Esplandian's story picks up where it left off in the fourth book. He has just been dubbed a knight and armed, and he travels about the world essentially repeating his father's successes, trying to outdo them but without the same credibility. Most of the action takes place in the East with Muslims as the chief enemies. Almost all the locations are entirely fictional. Eventually Esplandian ends up as the emperor of the Byzantines at Constantinople, and his by now very aged father, Amadis, succeeds to the throne of England.

The style and literary verve of the first four books disappears from the fifth. It as almost as if Rodríguez was trying too hard on a subject he had already milked for what it was worth. Nonetheless, Rodríguez's *Amadis* and *Esplandian* prompted a spate of Spanish imitations. The adventures of a nephew, Florisando, appeared. Then came a grandson of Amadis, Lisuarte of Greece, and so on. Amadis's descendents and relatives also starred in stories in French. Eventually 12 books about Amadis and his kin appeared in Spanish and 24 in French.

Bibliography

Garci, Rodríguez de Montalvo. *Amadis of Gaul: A Novel of Chivalry . . . Books I and II.* Translated by Edwin B. Place and Herbert C. Behm. Lexington: University of Kentucky Press, 2003.

———. *The Labors of the very Brave Knight Esplandián.* Translated by William Thomas Little.

Binghamton, N.Y.: Center for Medieval and Early Renaissance Studies, State University of New York at Binghamton, 1992.

Aminta Torquato Tasso (1573)

Inspired by a performance of the third PASTORAL DRAMA written in Italy, Agostino Argenti's *Lo Sfortunato* (The unfortunate one), the great Italian poet Torquato Tasso launched immediately into writing one of his own. Three months of fevered effort produced *Aminta*. Widely regarded as a virtually perfect example of a pastoral play, *Aminta* is also celebrated for the elegance of its poetry and its linguistic style. It was the play that began the popular vogue for pastoral plays that briefly swept the Continent and endured into the 17th century. Tasso delighted his audience at the play's first performance at the Belvedere Palace in Ferrara by setting his play not in the region of Arcadia in ancient Greece, but rather just outside Ferrara near the Po River.

The play concerns a nymph, Sylvia, who has dedicated herself to the chaste service of the goddess Diana. The play's title character Aminta is a shepherd who is utterly in love with Sylvia but who is also bashful. In the play's first act Sylvia's older friend, Daphne, tells Sylvia of Aminta's love. Sylvia, however, is much more interested in serving the goddess and hunting in the woods. In the second scene, Aminta recounts the history of his passion and complains about Sylvia's chilly reception of his ardor.

Aminta, however, is not Sylvia's only suitor. A woodland satyr has also pursued her, but she has rejected his advances. As we learn in the first scene of the second act, the satyr's love has turned to vengeful hatred. He decides to surprise Sylvia while she bathes in a fountain, rape her, and kill her. The second scene finds Daphne discussing Aminta's case with his friend Thyrsis. She suggests that she is going with Sylvia to the fountain and that Thyrsis should bring Aminta so that he can press his case with Sylvia. When in the third scene Thyrsis follows that advice, the timid Aminta at first refuses to go. He does not wish to be forward. Ultimately convinced, however, he goes.

A singularly nondramatic aspect of Tasso's play arises from the actors' often talking about offstage action rather than portraying that action onstage. This is the case with the satyr's attempted attack on Sylvia. In the third act, Thyrsis reports to the chorus that Aminta has arrived in time to thwart the satyr's plan and save Sylvia. The satyr flees, but so does Sylvia without even thanking her rescuer. Disconsolate, Aminta decides on suicide, but Daphne prevents him. While Aminta is telling Daphne that she should have let him die, another nymph, Nerina, appears with the news that Sylvia has been attacked and eaten by wolves. Aminta runs off, this time determined to die.

As Act IV begins, no sooner has the shepherd left than Sylvia turns up undevoured. On learning that Aminta is mad with grief and intends to destroy himself, Sylvia's heart softens and she decides she loves him after all. In the second scene, however, another character, Ergasto, appears with the news that Aminta has thrown himself from a cliff and is indeed dead. Grieving, Sylvia and Daphne go off in search of the body.

In the fifth act, however, still another shepherd messenger, Elpino, arrives to inform the characters on stage and the audience that Aminta has landed in a soft bush and, far from being dead, is reveling in the arms of his beloved Sylvia. As the pastoral drama developed, more and more of the action appeared onstage instead of being reported.

Bibliography

Tasso, Torquato. *Aminta: A Pastoral Play*. Edited and translated by Charles Jernigan and Irene Marchegiani Jones. New York: Italica Press, 2000.

Anatomy of Melancholy, The Robert Burton (1621, 1624, 1628, 1638, and 1651)

Modern psychology labels as *depression* what BURTON called *melancholy*. The medical literature of Burton's era and that of earlier centuries back to classical times recognized melancholy as a disease and listed for it specific sets of symptoms. Its causes were partly attributed to sufferers' astrological profiles. People born under the sign of Saturn, as Burton himself was, were thought to be particularly susceptible.

Physicians also thought melancholy resulted from an imbalance in the *humors.* These were bodily fluids: blood, phlegm, yellow bile, and black bile whose balance in an individual was established at moment of birth by the configuration of the stars. Illness, according to the medical theory of the time, resulted from alterations in that balance. Too much black bile or phlegm was associated with a person's becoming a melancholiac. Persons of artistic temperament were sometimes thought to be melancholy by nature.

Burton's interest in the subject of melancholy was principally in its psychological effects, although as a student of HUMORAL MEDICINE, he believed in the physical origins of the symptoms of the disease. Burton said that he studied and wrote about the subject, first, so that he himself could avoid the symptoms of the affliction. Second, he remarked that he could not imagine a better use for his time that to try to find a way to help those who suffered from so widespread and debilitating a disease. In any case, he devoted his life to learning and making public everything there was to know on the subject. The result was a vast tapestry of specialized knowledge organized and presented by an intellect that was at once genuinely scientific, funny, sometimes wildly imaginative, and frequently satiric. It was written, moreover, in an engaging and unmistakably individual, lively prose style that makes frequent and witty use of Latin quotations that the author often translates for the reader immediately so that his humor arises from the interactions of the two languages.

The preface to the first edition is addressed to the reader by Burton's persona, Democritus Junior. Burton selected that name because he says he felt a kinship with the original, melancholy Greek philosopher. This preface is reminiscent of ERASMUS's introduction in his *PRAISE OF FOLLY*—a document doubtless influential in forming Burton's satiric manner. In it Burton defends his authority as a clergyman writing on a medical subject and says that he doesn't know how "to do a more general service and spend my time better than to . . . [show] how to prevent and cure so universal a malady. . . ."

In calling his work an *anatomy,* Burton has in mind the dissecting table, for he lays bare the symptoms, the causes, the circumstances, and the potential cures for every known category and subcategory of the disease, drawing quotations from everywhere and touching on all sorts of tangential issues, such as religion and the occult, as he explores with great sensitivity the darker reaches of the human mind.

Bibliography

Burton, Robert. *The Anatomy of Melancholy.* Edited by Thomas C. Faulkner, Nicholas K. Kiessling, and Rhonda L. Blair. 3 vols. Oxford and New York: Oxford University Press, 1989–1994.

———. *The Anatomy of Melancholy.* Edited by Holbrook Jackson. New York: New York Review of Books, ca. 2001.

Andreini, Isabella (1562–1604)

Hardly out of her teens, Isabella Andreini became a European celebrity. She was a close acquaintance of Marie de' Medici, queen of France, and maintained a friendly correspondence not only with the nobility and royalty of Europe, but also with Cardinal Cinthio Aldobrandini, who was the Vatican's man in charge of the CATHOLIC COUNTER-REFORMATION. To him she dedicated the second of her two volumes of lyric poems, her *Rime* (Rhymes), published in 1601 and 1603.

In these collections, Andreini asserted her place in the canon of Italian letters by composing SONNETS and EPISTOLARY SONNETS in the manner of PETRARCH, TERZA RIMA in the manner of DANTE, madrigals, ODES (*CANZONI,* or songs), ECLOGUES in the form of DRAMATIC MONOLOGUES, and CENTOS (*centoni*). In these centos, she expressed her thoughts in the words of others, selecting and joining lines from others' works to reflect her own feelings. Sometimes this technique also helped her distance herself from the depth of her emotion, as in her first cento (*Centone I*), one of three poems mourning the death of her friend Laura Guidiccioni Lucchesini.

She also wrote a PASTORAL DRAMA, *MIRTILLA* (1588), thereby asserting her justifiable claim as a literary successor of the renowned TORQUATO TASSO. In 1607 Andreini's husband and Flaminio Scala published fragments of dialogues that Andreini had composed. Some of these later turned up in the work of other playwrights, perhaps most notably in SHAKESPEARE's *Much Ado About Nothing*. Only recently have English translations of the work of this remarkable Italian poet and dramatist begun to appear.

Andreini exchanged many learned letters with HUMANIST scholars of her day, at least one of whom counted her a man (which he meant as a compliment) by virtue of what he thought to be her masculine understanding and mastery of ancient and modern languages, and of NEO-LATIN and Italian literature. Her learning was so highly regarded by her contemporaries that she was elected a member of the prestigious Academy of the *Intenti* at Pavia and endowed with the academic name of *Accesa*—the flaming or brilliant one.

Principally famous as an actress and singer with the acting troupe *I GELOSI,* which she and her husband Francesco Andreini owned, she contributed her own name to the cast of STOCK CHARACTERS associated with the COMMEDIA DELL' ARTE. She was the prototype "Isabella." In that capacity, her roles involved not only reciting memorized lines, but also much onstage invention and ad-libbing. She played fortunate Isabella, Isabella the astrologer, and jealous Isabella in plays of the same names— plays that she had a major hand in writing. She also performed in *Isabella's Jokes* and in her most celebrated play, *The Madness of Isabella*. Beyond this, as she assures us in the first poem of her collection of lyrics, she played male roles too. Her acting career, begun when she was 16, lasted most of her life. Renowned for her personal virtue, she helped improve the public image of actresses. She died tragically while miscarrying her eighth child.

Bibliography

Andreini, Isabella. *La Mirtilla: A Pastoral.* Translated by Julie D. Campbell. Tempe, Ariz.: Arizona Center for Medieval and Renaissance Studies, 2002.

———. *Selected Poems of Isabella Andreini.* Edited by Anne MacNeil. Translated by James Wyatt Cook. Lanham, Md.: Scarecrow Press, 2005.

Andromaque (*Andromache*) Jean Racine (1667)

Following JOHN DRYDEN's English translation of a passage from the third book of VIRGIL's *Aeneid* together with the plot of Euripedes' Greek tragedy on the same subject, Racine sets his play in the aftermath of the Greeks' victory over the Trojans. Achilles's son, Pyrrhus, holds as prisoners the slain Trojan prince Hector's wife, Andromache, and their son Astyanax. Astyanax is the legendary founder of the ancient French royal line.

Pyrrhus, now the king of Epirus, is betrothed to Hermione, the daughter of Helen of Troy and the Spartan King Menelaus. Despite that engagement, Pyrrhus has fallen in love with his captive Andromache. To further complicate the twisted love plot, Orestes, the son of Agamemnon and Clytemnestra, arrives as a Grecian ambassador to Epirus. Orestes is in love with Hermione, who, despite Pyrrhus's betrayal, remains madly though ambivalently devoted to the man who jilted her. Andromache, however, despite Pyrrhus's ardent wooing, is devoted only to her husband's memory and to the well being of Astyanax.

The play opens with a discussion between the just-arrived Orestes and his friend Pylades. Their conversation sets the stage by conveying to the audience the information in the preceding paragraphs and revealing that, in addition to his diplomatic mission, which is to achieve the sacrifice of Astyanax, Orestes ardently hopes to win Hermione's love now that Pyrrhus has proved false to her.

The second scene of Act I portrays the diplomatic negotiation between Orestes and Pyrrhus. Pyrrhus refuses to accede to the Greeks' request and suggests that Orestes pay a social call on Hermione. Pyrrhus's tutor, Phoenix, reproves him since Orestes's passion for Hermione is known. Pyrrhus, however, is hopeful that in view of the circumstances Hermione will voluntarily depart with Orestes.

Scene iv presents an encounter between Andromache and Pyrrhus. Pyrrhus declares his ardor, but Andromache sensibly tries to dissuade him, pointing out that a match between them would stir up all sorts of enmity. She begs him to let her and her son go and that Pyrrhus return to Hermione.

Act II finds Hermione reluctantly agreeing to see Orestes but fearful that he will mock her for being treated as she treated him. Her maid, Cleone, assures her that nothing of the sort will happen and that Orestes still adores her. Then the two women discuss the conflicting emotions of love and hate that Hermione feels for her faithless fiancé.

Orestes is admitted in scene ii and declares his continuing passion, citing Pyrrhus's faithlessness as grounds for her leaving him. Hermione, however, says that, as a Spartan princess, she is not free to make that decision. Either her father or her betrothed must release her from her responsibilities. She sends Orestes for a definitive answer, promising to leave with him if Pyrrhus rejects her.

After soliloquizing in scene iii about his hopes, in scene iv Orestes discovers that Pyrrhus has come to his senses and decided to do his duty to Greece by marrying Hermione after all. The audience discovers in the next scene, however, that his change of heart arises not from a renewed sense of duty but rather from having observed Andromache together with her son. He saw how she sought out Hector's lineaments in the boy's face, and Pyrrhus realized that he could never hope to displace Hector's memory.

Learning of Pyrrhus's about-face, Orestes is torn between his duty as a diplomat and his love for Hermione. He and Pylades opt for love over duty and decide to abduct her. Pylades convinces Pyrrhus that he must dissemble and not let his continued affection for Hermione show.

Act III, scene iv depicts an encounter between Andromache and Hermione. Andromache pleads for exile for herself and her son, but Hermione responds that she has no influence. Her father Menelaus is hardening Pyrrhus's heart against Astyanax.

In the sixth scene, Pyrrhus and Andromache meet once more. Andromache pleads her son's case again, and Pyrrhus tells her that it is too late, though had she asked before he would have set Astyanax free. Just as Andromache despairs, however, Pyrrhus once more reverses his field and tells her that he can save Astyanax if she will marry him after all. After much soul searching, Andromache

decides to visit Hector's tomb to seek guidance from his spirit.

In Act IV, scene i, the audience learns of the advice she received. Having secured Pyrrhus's promise of safety for her son if she will marry, Andromache will go through the ceremony and then, before the consummation of the union, commit suicide, thereby preserving her matronly honor. She is certain that she can depend upon Pyrrhus to keep his part of the bargain despite his grief and disappointment.

Learning of Pyrrhus's latest betrayal, Hermione extracts a promise from Orestes that he will murder Pyrrhus at the marriage altar. Then, fearing that Orestes will not keep his word, Hermione resolves to do the deed herself. At that moment (Act IV, scene v), Pyrrhus appears to give Hermione an opportunity to upbraid him for his faithlessness. She argues that his appearance is merely to scorn her. When he responds that theirs was to have been an arranged marriage and that she never loved him, she declares her ardor for him with a clarity and intensity that goes far toward making her one of the most memorable jilted women in the annals of theater. She advises him, finally, to lay his base heart bear upon the altar but to fear finding her there as well.

Hermione opens Act V with a soliloquy that reveals her conflicted emotions, cycling rapidly between love and hatred, between forgiveness and revenge. Then, in the second scene, her maid Cleone reports the wedding procession and Pyrrhus's joyful appearance. She also reports that Orestes and the Greeks are in the temple and that Orestes too seems trapped between his love for Hermione and his duty as an ambassador. Hermione determines that she will seek her own revenge and then commit suicide, but as scene iii opens, Orestes appears announcing that Pyrrhus is dying at the altar, slain by the Greeks.

Hermione now blames Orestes for Pyrrhus's death, asking by what right and on whose orders he had the Greeks kill her beloved. When he replies that he obeyed her, she reproves him for believing a maddened lover and sends him away. Orestes is overwhelmed with shame at having failed in his duty in attempting to please a mad woman.

In the play's final scene, Pylades reports that Andromache is marshalling the Epirans to seek out and destroy the Greeks and counsels a hasty retreat. Orestes demurs, saying that he must find Hermione. Pylades then tells him that she has committed suicide on the body of Pyrrhus. Orestes is driven mad by grief, hallucinates, and falls into unconsciousness. Pylades takes advantage of his state to bear him away to the ships, and the final curtain falls.

Throughout the play, Racine carefully observes the classical UNITIES of time, place, and action as well as the Greeks' prohibition against having characters die on stage.

Bibliography

Racine, Jean. *The Complete Plays of Jean Racine.* Translated by Samuel Solomon. New York: Random House, 1967.

Annals of Cuauhtitlan in The Codex Chimalpopoca (1570)

Following the Spanish conquest of Mexico, a group of missionaries arrived in 1521. Bent on converting the Mexicans to Christianity, the priests were anxious to destroy preconquest native manuscripts that might remind the Indians of their former ways. The priests also established schools and educated the most promising children as trilingual chroniclers who could replace the old histories with new ones that partly assimilated the old stories to European and Christian models. These students learned mainly Latin and the Nahuatl language of Central America but also studied Spanish. As a result of their education and subsequent compositions, Nahuatl enjoyed a brief literary Golden Age. The missionary-trained, Nahuatl chroniclers provided revisionist histories that partly assimilated native history to the views of their Spanish conquerors. A similar destruction and rewriting of chronicles had taken place more than a century earlier when the Aztecs assumed power in the Valley of Mexico.

Among the products of the 16th century's outpouring of Mexican chronicles were the *Annals of Cuauhtitlán.* The anonymous author, a citizen of that community, traced the real and mythic history of his city from the year 635 C.E.—a time so early, Aztec myths held, that the sun had yet to be born and the Toltec dynasties had not begun. The work continues, recording the names of rulers and the durations of their reigns from before the founding of Cuauhtitlán up to the actual founding of the city in 1318. In the course of that discussion, the author considers the fall and dissolution of the Toltecs in 1064. Thereafter he addresses the treachery and eventual defeat of the Tepaneca people in 1430. Then the author begins his consideration of the rise of the Aztec—the Mexica of Tenochtitlán—and the focus shifts away from Cuauhtitlán to the succession of Aztec rulers that terminates with their conquest by the Spaniards.

The work's basic structure is chronological in the manner of the earlier Central American histories that were written in pictures as opposed to the new *Annals* that were written in Nahuatl words with European letters. From time to time, however, the author departs from strict chronology to tell a story or recount a myth. *The Annals*'s principal value, however, arises from the sometimes unique information the work provides about the peoples and historical events that it chronicles and from the ethnographic details it supplies about the status of women, the Aztec system of land tenure, government, tribute, warfare, and human sacrifice.

Bibliography

History and Mythology of the Aztecs: The Codex Chimalpopoca. Translated from the Nahuatl by John Bierhorst. Tuscon, Ariz. and London: The University of Arizona Press, 1992.

Aragona, Tullia d' (1510–1556)

Born in Rome and reared in Sienna, Tullia d' Aragona followed her mother's profession of courtesan. Like many of her calling, she had been schooled in literature and music to make her an agreeable companion for members of the upper classes. The CATHOLIC COUNTER-REFORMATION and the moral strictures that followed the COUNCIL OF TRENT imposed tighter controls on courtesans, and, perhaps in an effort to become more acceptable to the social circles in which she preferred to move, she married in 1543.

By 1546 she had moved to Florence where she enjoyed the friendship and support of the philosopher Benedetto Varchi and of Duke Cosimo I de' Medici. She had also begun her own literary work. Fifty-six of her poems appeared in 1547 in a volume dedicated to the duchess. Aragona's poems are in the manner of PETRARCH, joining his forms to her experience. The volume also includes EPISTOLARY SONNETS. This verse collection, *Rime della Signora Tullia d' Aragona; et di diversi a lui* (The poems of Madam Tullia d'Aragona; and of various persons to her) preceded a volume of prose in the form of a dialogue, her *Dialogo della infinitá d'amore,* 1547 (Dialogue about the infinity of love). In the dialogue two speakers named Tullia and Varchi debate such questions as whether or not it is possible to love within limits, the comparative depth of love achievable by men and women, the comparative value of logic and experience, and the differences between vulgar and virtuous love.

In 1548 Aragona returned to Rome where she remained until her death. It may be that while there she penned a chivalric romance. One entitled *Il Meschino altrimenti desto il Guerrino* (The wretched fellow or the little warrior aroused) has tentatively been attributed to her.

Bibliography

Aragona, Tullia d'. *Dialogue on the Infinity of Love.* Edited and translated by Rinaldina Russell and Bruce Merry. Chicago: University of Chicago Press, 1997.

Arason, Jón (1484–1550)

Arason was the last Roman Catholic bishop of Iceland before 1536 when the king of Denmark, Christian III, imposed Protestantism on the island—then a Danish dependency. Like many Icelandic priests of the time, Arason did not observe the discipline of celibacy—he married and fathered a family. As a literary figure, Arason had brought the first printing press to Iceland around 1530, and he himself became the country's first printer. All the books he printed have regrettably been lost. Not only did he print books, however, he also wrote for them. He composed both secular and religious poetry of notable merit. A collection of his religious poems was edited by Finnur Jónson and published in Copenhagen, Denmark, in 1918. Apparently the only modern edition of a sample of Arason's SATIRE also was printed in Copenhagen in an 1869 collection of poems in the old Nordic languages. No English translation of any of his writing seems to be available.

Fiercely committed to his religious faith, Arason resisted Iceland's forced conversion to Lutheranism as its state religion. When the crown indicted him as an outlaw, he raised an army and with it took control of the Skálholt region. The national authorities arranged an ambush in which he and two of his sons, Ara and Bjorn, were captured. Already condemned, without formalities all three were executed on the spot by beheading.

Arason's life, career, and execution mark the passage from the Middle Ages to the Renaissance in Iceland. There he is regarded as a national hero, and his story has been the subject of biography, fiction, and drama. Of these, the only work available in English is a translation of a play by the Scandinavian dramatist Tryggvi Sveininbjörnsson.

Bibliography

Bach, Giovanni, et al. *The History of the Scandinavian Literatures.* Edited by Frederika Blanker. New York: Dial Press Inc., 1938.
Strindberg, August, Tryggvi Sveininbjörnsson et al. "Bishop Jón Arason," *Modern Scandinavian Plays.* New York: Liveright Publishing Corporation, 1954.

Araucana, La Alonso de Ercilla y Zúñiga (Part I, 1569; Part II, 1578; Part III, 1590)

Ercilla's long, historical poem about the resistance and subjugation of the Chilean province of Arauco by the Spanish conquerors in the New World was supposed to be an EPIC. From a formal point of view, the author's flawed understanding of an epic poem's characteristics left his objective unfulfilled.

From every other point of view the poem is among the most fascinating documents to issue from the European conquest of the Western Hemisphere.

Ercilla had spent nine years of his youth as a soldier fighting the Araucan Indians. The fierce resistance to Spanish rule mounted by the Araucans was a matter of wonder to the Europeans. The historian of Spanish literature, George Ticknor, quotes the playwright Luis de Belmonte as saying that the soil of the small territory of Arauco "is nourished with the bones of Spaniards" and that Alexander the Great had conquered much of the Middle East and India "with fewer soldiers than Arauco . . . cost Spain."

The first part of the poem traces with great statistical and geographical accuracy the opening episodes of the conflict. Ercilla describes the country and its inhabitants. He next traces through 15 cantos of the poem the battles, the diplomacy, the plots, and the exploits of the war. Ercilla wrote this part of the poem in rhymed eight-line stanzas between 1555 and 1563 while he was actually engaged in battle. For writing materials he used whatever came to hand, often drafting his verse on scraps of leather.

A close reading of the epic suggests that Ercilla was more sympathetic to the cause of the Indians than to that of the Spaniards, though his loyalty to his own heritage prevents him from directly saying so. He admired the Araucan's courage and determination, and his descriptions of their unrestrained behavior offer fascinating pictures of a world long past. He gives some of his Indian characters, like Colocólo in the second canto, some of the poem's most moving speeches.

Apparently Ercilla was not altogether satisfied with the versified, factual narrative that characterized the poem's first section. Therefore, though he maintained the same historical accuracy in the second part of the poem, he interspersed in it some of the usual devices of classical epic, such as bits of visionary ALLEGORY. Bellona, the Roman goddess of war, appears. The poet imagines a Spanish victory in France and introduces a magic cave where, under the spell of the magician Fiton, the poet envisions from South America the Spanish victory at the naval battle of Lepanto in the Mediterranean Sea. He also adds love interest with the moving stories of the Indian women Tegualda and Glaura. Tegualda's story involves her successful search for the body of her slain husband across the battlefield at night. A reader, Ticknor observes, finds more poetry but less history in the second section of La Araucana.

The poem's third section returns to chronicling the war itself. Again, however, to remind his readers of his poem's epic associations, Ercilla intersperses material drawn from VIRGIL. With true Spanish gallantry Ercilla defends the reputation of the Carthaginian Queen Dido against the aspersions that Virgil had cast upon it in the Aeneid. As he approaches the end of his poem, Ercilla turns in the 36th and 37th cantos to providing his reader with some autobiographical information. As much of what we know of him comes from that source and from other brief passages in the 13th canto of Part I, we have reason to be grateful for this personal aside.

In the poem's 37th and final canto, Ercilla also introduces a theoretical discussion of public and private rights to make war and the issue of the claims of the Spanish king to the throne of Portugal. He ends the poem with complaints about his private disappointments, his pitiable condition, and his resolution to seek solace in a religious life.

Another author, Osorio of Léon, later continued the poem (1597). The most interesting portions of the continuation include further factual details about Ercilla's life among the Araucans during the campaign.

Bibliography

Ercilla y Zúñiga, Alonso de. La Araucana. Translated by L. Carrera. New York: The Author, 2000.

Archevolti, Samuel (1515–1611)

A member of the Jewish community of Renaissance Venice, Archevolti composed liturgical poems in Hebrew that were incorporated into the Festival Prayer Book of Jewish enclaves throughout Italy. He was apparently one of those Jewish mystics devoted to the power of the kabbalah. His most important contribution to the Hebrew literary endeavors of his time was a highly regarded grammatical treatise entitled: Arugat Ha-Bosem (The fragrant garden bed [of the Hebrew language], 1603). Both original and lucid, Archevolti's work points up the most notable qualities of the Hebrew language. Beyond grammar, the work also discusses styles of oratory and both traditional and new forms of Hebrew poetry and meters. A Christian scholar named Buxtorf the Younger translated the last chapter of the work into Latin in 1660.

An important issue for Hebrew scholars throughout the European Middle Ages and the Renaissance involved what was called pointing. The ancient Hebrew alphabet represented consonant sounds only and made no provision for representing vowel sounds. That system may have served well at the time of composition of the Scriptures. In the intervening centuries Hebrew had undergone, however, the same sorts of sound changes that affect all languages. As a result, many readers of Scripture felt unsure how words should be pronounced. Hebrew scholars called exegetes or pointers employed great effort and erudition to restore certainty about which vowels occurred at which points. Moreover, there was debate over the way the Scriptures had historically been sung. Archevolti argued on the basis of the *Zohar*—a mystical work that appeared first in Spain about the year 1300—that both the vowel points and the musical notation for chanting the text had been given to Moses with the Ten Commandments at Sinai.

Bibliography

Zinberg, Israel. *A History of Jewish Literature: Italian Jewry in the Renaissance Era.* Vol. 4. Edited and translated by Bernard Martin. Cincinnati, Oh.: Hebrew Union College Press and New York: KTAV Publishing House, Inc., 1974.

Aretino, Pietro (1492–1556)

The multitalented son of a cobbler of Arezzo, Pietro Aretino rose to fame in the fields of painting, sculpture, and literature. Long infamous as a member of the not altogether misnamed "trinity of vice" (Aretino, MACHIAVELLI, and RABELAIS), by the time he was 30 Aretino had established himself in Rome as a poet and a painter. He came to public

notice with the publication of his pasquinades (1521). These were a series of SATIRES named for an ancient Roman statue called the *pasquino*. The citizens of the city annually decorated it with satiric verse. Aretino's poems made fun of the political maneuvering associated with the papal elections of 1521.

The year 1524 saw the publication of a collection of sonnets inspired by a group of 16 erotic engravings by Giulio Romano. Pope Clement VII had forbidden the circulation of the images. Perhaps as a result of Aretino's having incurred papal displeasure, someone tried to murder Aretino in 1525. As a result he left Rome in search of a safer and more congenial home. He first moved to Mantua under the protection of the Gonzaga family but settled at last in the republic of Venice. In that congenially liberal setting, he established himself as a friend and literary peer of the master painter Titian, who several times painted Aretino's likeness, and of the sculptor and architect Jacopo Sansovino, who designed the columned library on St. Mark's square.

In Venice, with its flourishing publishing industry, Aretino continued writing steadily in a wide variety of genres. Innovation and imagination were his watchwords. "Copy nature," was his motto. He had no patience with PETRARCHISM. As a playwright, he rejected the models of the Roman comedy that BEMBO had prescribed and CASTELVETRO's Aristotelian notions of TRAGEDY. Instead of drawing his characters from ancient Rome and Athens, he drew them from contemporary Italian life.

Although the freshness of this approach, his witty dialogue, and his mastery of satire delighted audiences, his plays generally lacked coherence. In his bitter comedy *La Cortegiana* (The courtesan or harlot) he parodies CASTIGLIONE's *Book of the Courtier.* Whereas Castiglione wrote a book designed to produce the perfect gentleman, Aretino mercilessly exposed the viciousness at the core of aristocratic and papal courts of his day. In this play a Siennese named Goro comes to Rome hoping to learn the ways of the court and perhaps become a cardinal. His tutor in courtly behavior, Master Andrea, teaches him slang and swaggering and explains the expectations for conduct at court. "The main thing a courtier needs to know," he says, "is how to curse." He then names among other courtly accomplishments gambling, jealousy, whoring, heresy, and many others in that vein. The play gives a central impression of sordid realism. It is also notable for its prologue's satirical parade of Italy's leading literary figures.

Aretino's comedy *Il Marescalco* (The Blacksmith) is probably his best. He examines the same social conditions that he does in *The Courtesan,* but the satire is much better humored. Here the plot concerns a wealthy dolt whose patron, the duke of Mantua, advises him to marry. Wishing to avoid both the condition and the expense, the smithy tries not to comply, but through argument and bullying the duke's courtiers and lackies drive him to take a wife. When the wedding is over, the dupe is relieved to discover that the marriage was a sham and that he has married a male page dressed as a woman.

Talenta, the name both of a play and its major character, is a study of the life of a courtesan. It is most notable for the credible portrayal of the depravity and self-deception of its heroine. In addition to these and other comedies, which helped set the stage for the production of thousands of 16th-century Italian comedies, Aretino also wrote a tragedy *Orazio* (*Horace*).

Worthy of note despite their crudity are Aretino's *Dialoghi* (*Dialogues*), especially the dialogue concerning court life that chronicles the insufferable and demeaning living conditions of the servants upon whom the opulent lives of the aristocracy depended.

Beyond these works Aretino wrote sonnets and other forms of poetry such as an EPIC parody *Orlandino,* which mocked BOIARDO's *ORLANDO INNAMORATO.* On one hand Aretino produced grossly indecent pornographic works: his lewd *Sonnetti lussuriosa* (*Sonnets*), his indecent *Dialogues,* and his vulgar *Ragionamenti* (*Arguments*). On the other hand, he penned touching religious romances, saints' lives, a life of Christ, and paraphrases of the Bible. Ironically his reputation and popularity rested heavily on these religious writings. His prose style later proved influential in forming the flowery and alliterative *euphuistic* style of JOHN LYLY in England. His invective against his enemies reappeared in a minor literary movement known as the literature of abuse.

His principal contribution, however, to Renaissance literature came with the publication of his letters in six volumes between 1538 and 1557. PETRARCH had collected his own Latin letters for posthumous publication, but Aretino was the first person to publish his own correspondence in Italian. In his volumes appear letters to friends and patrons, critical commentary on art and literature, stories of ordinary events, and curses against his enemies. This was his most financially successful publishing venture, and his letters started a trend for publishing correspondence all over Europe. If they did not directly influence MONTAIGNE's decision to compose essays from personal experience, they at least point in that direction.

Though Aretino was not one of the best writers of Renaissance Italy, he was one of its most original and prolific, one of its most effective prose stylists, and one of its most colorful characters. A probably apocryphal account says he died from "an excess of laughter," when, on hearing a dirty joke from his sister who ran a bordello, he threw himself back in his chair, flipped over, and broke his neck. His epitaph, however, is certainly real: "Here lies the Tuscan poet Aretino, who spoke ill of everyone except Christ, excusing himself [for this exception] by saying: "I don't know him." [Translation mine. J. W. C.]

Bibliography

Aretino, Pietro. *Aretino's Dialogues.* Translated by Raymond Rosenthal. New York: Stein and Day, 1971.

———. *The Letters of Pietro Aretino.* Translated by Thomas Caldecot Chubb. Hamden, Conn.: Archon Books, 1967.

———. *The Marescalco.* Translated by Leonard G. Sbrocchi and J. Douglas Campbell. Ottawa, Canada: Carleton University Centre for Renaissance Studies and Research, Dovehouse Editions, 1986.

———. *I modi. The Sixteen Pleasures: An Erotic Album of the Italian Renaissance.* Edited and translated by Lynne Lawner. Evanston, Ill.: Northwestern University Press, 1988.

———. *The Ragionamenti: the lives of nuns, the lives of married women, the lives of courtesans.* London: Odyssey Press, 1970.

Cairns, Christopher. *Pietro Aretino and the Republic of Venice: 1527–1556.* Florence, Italy: L. S. Olschki Editore, 1985.

Ariosto, Ludovico (1474–1533)

The eldest of 10 children, Ariosto was the son of the noble but not wealthy Count Niccolò Ariosto and his wife, Daria Malaguzzi. The young Ludovico had been privately educated in grammar and rhetoric and wished to pursue humanistic studies and Latin literature at the University of Ferrara. His father, like the fathers of PETRARCH and BOCCACCIO before him, proved unsympathetic, however, to his son's literary aspirations. The elder Ariosto insisted that his eldest son study law. Unenthusiastically, Ludovico complied. From 1492 through 1497, however, he also received private instruction in the humanities from Gregorio da Spoleto.

In 1500 Niccolò Ariosto died, leaving Ludovico the de facto father of a large family. Showing a flair for financial administration and exercising both care and prudence, he managed the family's modest resources to provide dowries for his sisters and adequate livings for his brothers. From the time of his father's death until 1503, Ariosto received a small stipend as the captain of Canossa—a ruined castle that required little if any of his attention. During this period he wrote Latin poetry that celebrated some of his love affairs. In 1503 he entered the service of Cardinal Ippolito d' Este, for whom he worked until 1517. Ariosto's salary, though modest, would have been enough had it been regularly paid, but he often had difficulty collecting it. Eventually, Ariosto and the cardinal parted company. The cardinal recognized Ariosto's poetic talent, but he did not altogether understand his

retainer's capacities. He wanted Ariosto to suspend versifying, take holy orders, and accompany him to fight against the Turks in Hungary. Ariosto refused these requests. Not only did he feel no calling for the priesthood, but he was also busily engaged in writing the poem that would become his masterpiece and one of most notable works of the Italian Renaissance, his ORLANDO FURIOSO (Roland gone mad).

Despite their failure to agree in this instance and notwithstanding their very different temperaments, the poet and the warrior priest did not entirely disconnect. In part because Ariosto's poem celebrated the house of Este, the cardinal generously financed the publication of the poem's first edition (1516) and secured the rights to the income from its sales to Ariosto. Unable, however, to accommodate the cardinal's requests, in 1517, Ariosto sought and found a new patron.

Unlike Cardinal d'Este, his brother Duke Alfonso I d'Este of Ferrara recognized how extraordinary Ariosto's literary abilities actually were. In 1518, therefore, the duke became Ariosto's patron and thereafter paid the poet handsomely for usually very limited service, supported three servants and two horses, and made it possible for Ariosto to buy his own house. He also left Ariosto free to write—at least most of the time. In his new post he was required to superintend the ducal theater, a congenial task that involved writing plays, supervising their production, and reading their prologues at performances. He had been involved in similar activities since his boyhood. The year 1508 saw the production of his play *Cassaria.* In 1509, *I Suppositi* (*The Pretenders*) followed. This play, the ultimate source of the story for the Broadway musical *The Fantastics,* so pleased Pope Leo that he requested its performance at the Vatican. Ariosto composed other comedies: *Il Negromante* (*The Necromancer*) also performed in Rome in 1510); *Lena* (performed in Ferrara in 1528), and the unfinished *La Scolastica* (Scholasticism). On Ariosto's recommendation, the duke built the first permanent theater in Ferrara in 1532; unfortunately, it burned down that same year. During his employment in Ferrara, Ariosto also produced some tellingly effective SATIRES.

Ariosto's agreeable employment in Ferrara, however, did not continue without interruption. For more than three years beginning in 1522—the year following the appearance of the second edition of Ariosto's masterpiece, Alfonso required the poet to serve as governor of the Este's mountain province of Garfagnana—a district also claimed by Lucca and Florence. With his typical grace, Ariosto performed his duties as the governor of a fractious people with tact and competence while he continued to polish and revise his *Orlando Furioso* for its third and definitive edition (1526). In 1525 Duke Alfonso recalled Ariosto to Ferrara where he found himself the literary jewel in the ducal coronet. The Este connection and Ariosto's growing fame brought him tributes from and the friendship of both the Florentine and the Roman branches of the Medici family and of ducal families of Mantua and Urbino as well.

Happily reestablished in Ferrara, Ariosto resumed his loving relationship with Alessandra Benucci Strozzi. Before her husband Tito Strozzi's death she and Ariosto had become involved, and they remained so throughout the poet's lifetime, marrying secretly not long before he died. Both the secrecy and the delay were probably occasioned by the fact that Ariosto received the financial benefit of certain church positions that paid him without expecting any work in return. He could not have continued to occupy them if he were married—or at least if it had been known that he was.

Ariosto's prospects continued to improve. On a diplomatic mission in late 1531, he became a friend of the supreme commander of the forces of the Spanish Holy Roman emperor, Charles V. This powerful man, Alfonso d'Avalos, marquis of Vasto warmly admired the poet's work. This he demonstrated, first, by granting an annual pension of 100 ducats and some jewelry to Ariosto. Second, in 1532, while in the city of Mantua, the marquis introduced Ariosto to the emperor himself. This might have resulted in the poet's rapid advancement to the highest levels of European honor and reward, but Ariosto's health had been in decline for over a year, and he continued to fail rapidly, dying at home in Ferrara in July of 1533.

Universally regarded as the finest Italian poet of the 16th century, Ariosto inherited the subject that made him famous from a talented predecessor at the Este court, MATTEO MARIA BOIARDO. Among other literary works of great merit, Boiardo too had set to work upon a CHIVALRIC EPIC, his *ORLANDO INNAMORATO* (Roland in love). He completed two parts of it but had only begun the third part when he died in 1494. What he had finished was published posthumously in 1495. Ariosto took up where Boiardo had left off, beginning work on *Orlando Furioso* about 1506.

Whereas Boiardo had woven a charming fabric, however, Ariosto loomed an inexhaustibly rich tapestry. His dexterity as a narrator has few equals. He leads his reader eagerly on through episode after episode of an enormous work, and his story line never falters. His characters display clearly individual traits and are drawn in credible psychological dimensions so that readers can relate to them. The characters and their stories excite and involve the emotions of the readers. And yet, through all the intricacies of the tale, Ariosto's playful sense of humor continually shines through, deconstructing the seriousness of the tale or making a subtle joke at the expense either of his characters or his patrons.

Above all, for those fortunate enough to be able to read the work in Italian, there is the musicality of Ariosto's flawlessly polished verse. Like EDMUND SPENSER in English, Ariosto is a poet's poet. Anyone aspiring to greatness as an Italian poet in any age would do well to study diligently at the feet of this master.

Bibliography

Ariosto, Ludovico. *Orlando Furioso.* Translated by Guido Waldman. London: Oxford University Press, 1974.

Marinelli, Peter V. *Ariosto and Boiardo: The Origins of Orlando Furioso.* Columbia: University Missouri Press, 1987.

Aristotle's *Poetics*

Born in Greece in 384 B.C.E., Aristotle mastered the entire realm of human knowledge of his time and place. A student of PLATO (427–347 B.C.E.) at that philosopher's academy in Athens, Aristotle also served as a tutor to the future King Alexander the Great. At about age 50, Aristotle founded a Lyceum in Athens where he taught until his death in 367 B.C.E.

Apparently, Aristotle's lecture notes survived at the school for centuries because, 300 years after the philosopher's death, Andronicus of Rhodes, the last headmaster of the lyceum, edited those notes and Aristotle's other surviving writings. Andronicus gave Aristotle's works their current organization, sequence, and titles.

The transmission of Aristotle's work from ancient times through the Middle Ages to the Renaissance is too complex to trace here in detail. Suffice it to say that in Western Europe only Aristotle's logical texts and some partial Greek commentaries on them reached the hands of the sixth-century Roman scholar and statesman BOETHIUS. In the East, however, the older, Greek manuscripts were unearthed and reedited at Byzantium in the ninth century, and many texts were preserved, commented upon, and transmitted via Arabic, Jewish, and Syriac scholars.

By the 12th century, nonetheless, only two works of Aristotle were available in Latin in Western Europe. Commercial and cultural contacts in the 13th century between Europe and the East, however, resulted in a flurry of translation. The *Poetics* itself was first translated into Latin from Greek by the Fleming, William of Moerbeke (active, ca. 1255–78). Improved translations and better-edited texts continued appearing in the late 15th and early 16th centuries. Not until commentators began to compare Aristotle's work with the Roman writer Horace's *Art of Poetry* in the 1540s, '50s, and '60s, however, did Aristotle's work begin to influence critical thinking about poetry seriously. Even then, commentators tended to confuse the principles of Aristotle and Horace. However, 1570 saw the publication of LUDOVICO CASTELVETRO's Italian translation and exposition of *The Poetics*. In his explanation, Castelvetro put forward

his own ideas about the nature of tragedy, and many of his readers conflated the commentator's thinking with Aristotle's.

Aristotle himself opens his work with a discussion of imitation or mimesis, which he labels the common principle of poetry, dancing, painting, and sculpture. He then turns to the question of higher and lower sorts of imitative arts, assigning TRAGEDY to the higher and COMEDY to the lower. He next considers various forms of poetry. Nondramatic narrative and lyric poetry he treats together as a single form. Dramatic poetry may also be narrative, or it may be pure, acted drama. A DRAMATIC MONOLOGUE such as Isabella Andreini's *Eclogue 3, Sorcery* or a soliloquy within a play would exemplify narrative, while any of SHAKESPEARE's plays would typify pure drama.

Aristotle next speculates on the psychological origins and growth of poetry, concluding that people have an instinct for harmony and an instinct for rhythm that give rise to poetic expression. Based on his familiarity with the work of Greek poets, Aristotle traces a split in the development of poetry. He perceives the split in the works of Homer and in the distinction between comedy and tragedy. He then traces the development of tragedy. Chapter 6 of *The Poetics* attributes six elements to tragedy: spectacle, lyric song, and diction, which he calls external elements. The other three, internal elements, include action or plot—the most important—then character, then thought.

Aristotle's next several chapters detail many of the issues discussed in the entry on tragedy, among others: the magnitude, wholeness, and organic connections of the incidents of the plot; an emphasis on poetic rather than historical truth, a preference for combining the unexpected with the apparently inevitable, and a distinction between simple and complex plots. He goes on to consider the hero's reversal of fortune and the superiority of an unhappy ending over POETIC JUSTICE. He then describes and exemplifies the way that pity and fear should arise in the audience as the result of the plot. The importance of ethical representation receives his attention.

Aristotle then devotes two full chapters (17 and 18) to advice for tragic poets about how to go about writing a tragedy, what to include, and what to leave out. He next considers diction and language and looks at EPIC poetry, tragedy, and history, comparing and contrasting them. Finally, his last two chapters consider objections brought against poetry and the difference between poetic truth and common reality. After weighing the comparative merits of epic poetry and tragedy, Aristotle concludes that the moral superiority of tragedy qualifies it for a higher regard.

The response of Renaissance critics and playwrights to the availability of new translations of and commentaries on *The Poetics*—particularly that of Castelvetro—took two forms. In Italy the critics generally treated the work as a prescriptive set of rules for drama, or they objected to that view, saying that new times required new forms and that the ancients should be models for the moderns, not their masters.

In France, after the publication of JEAN VAUQUELIN DE LE FRESNAYE's *Art of Poetry* (1605), French poets and dramatists increasingly took Aristotle's advice to heart. In England, SIR PHILIP SIDNEY's *Defense of Poesie* contributed to the discussion, as did JOHN MILTON's preface to *Samson Agonistes*.

The widespread, intense interest in this text and other ancient Greek and Roman documents was the central, defining characteristic of Renaissance HUMANISM—a word whose meaning has shifted radically in 21st-century America. A current phrase like *secular humanism* has hardly anything to do with the Renaissance meaning.

Bibliography

Butcher, S. H., trans. *Aristotle's Poetics*. New York: Hill and Wang, 1961.

Cooper, Lane. *Aristotle on the Art of Poetry*. New York: Harcourt, Brace and Co., 1913.

Herrick, Marvin T. *The Poetics of Aristotle in England*. New Haven, Conn.: Yale University Press, 1930, Rpt. 1976.

Kallendorf, Craig. "Aristotle and Cinquecento Poetics." In *Encyclopedia of the Renaissance*. Vol. 1, edited by Paul F. Grendler. New York: Scribner's, 1999.

Weinberg, Bernard. *A History of Literary Criticism in the Italian Renaissance*. Vol. 2. Chicago: University of Chicago Press, 1961.

Arrebo, Anders Christensen
(1587–1637)

A Norwegian poet, Arrebo is remembered principally for his posthumously published, immense EPIC poem *Hexaëmeron* (The six days, 1661). Although the poem has a Greek title, it is written in the Norwegian language. In the epic, its poet elaborates upon the biblical story of the world's creation in alexandrine meter (See POETIC METER). In 1536 King Christian III had imposed Protestant Christianity upon Denmark and Norway, then a Danish province. One of Arrebo's objectives in his choice of subjects was the introduction of aspects of the new faith to the Norwegian people. Arrebo also enjoyed a reputation as a poetic translator. From similar religious motives he rendered the Psalms from Latin into Norwegian verse, publishing them in 1623. A Protestant clergyman, Arrebo rose to become the Lutheran bishop of Trondheim.

Bibliography

Bach, Giovanni, et al. *The History of the Scandinavian Literatures*. Edited by Frederika Blanker. New York: Dial Press Inc., 1938.

Ascham, Roger (1515–1568)

A member of the "second generation of English Humanists" (See HUMANISM), Ascham was educated at St. John's College, Cambridge, where he continued his career, first, as a fellow and a reader in Greek. Then, in 1541 he became a lecturer in mathematics and in 1547 was appointed a public orator for the university. The next year, he became tutor to the Princess Elizabeth, for whom he also served as Latin Secretary after her accession to the throne. He had also held this important diplomatic post and others under her predecessors, Edward VI and Queen Mary.

He composed his first work, *Toxophilus,* for King Henry VIII in 1545. A treatise on archery modeled on the dialogues of CICERO, this work presents a discussion between Toxophilus, whose name means "one who loves the bow," and Philologus, "one who loves the word."

After apologizing to King Henry for not having written the book in Latin or Greek, and after defending his use of English on the grounds of its potential benefit to English readers, Ascham advises the king to require all Englishmen to become proficient in the use of the English long bow. Not only would universal training in the use of this armor-piercing weapon be useful in time of war, practicing with the bow, Ascham maintains, is an "honest . . . pastime for the mind . . . wholesome for the body, not vile for great men . . . [nor] costly for poor men."

Toxophilus provides an early example of an effort to improve English prose style by being at the same time scholarly and popular. Though it follows a classical model, it avoids INKHORN TERMS (unfamiliar borrowings from ancient tongues) while at the same time employing words of Greek and Latin derivation as appropriate to enrich a discourse that reflects good, plain, conversational English. (See ENGLISH LANGUAGE.) Henry VIII rewarded Ascham for the book with a pension.

Ascham's other notable English prose work, *The Scholemaster,* appeared posthumously in 1570. Ascham divided it into two books. In the first he suggests a number of principles for teaching and illustrates them with examples. To learn Latin, he advises having a student translate a passage into English and then, after an interval, back into Latin. Then the teacher should gently review and, together with the student, correct the work. Ascham is among the earliest in England to advise against beating as a motivator to learning. He reports a story about Lady Jane Gray, who thought that having stern parents and a gentle teacher was a combination that had most greatly benefited her education. He saw as the aim of education the capacity to serve God and country well, and he considered studying Greek and Roman classics and avoiding both popular romances and the vices of his contemporary Italy the preferred method for achieving that objective. The second book of *The Scholemaster* considers imitation of style. Ascham recommends imitating the best models, paraphrasing, and turning verse into prose and vice versa as pathways to mastery for students.

Ascham's work is wise, humane, and attractive. Especially the first book of *The Scholemaster* is as congenial as the man himself apparently was.

See also EDUCATION IN EUROPE.

Bibliography

Ascham, Roger. *English Works.* Edited by William Aldis Wright. Cambridge. U.K.: Cambridge University Press, 1904.

Daiches, David. *A Critical History of English Literature.* Vol. 1. New York: The Ronald Press, 1960.

Ashley, Robert (1565–1641)

Carefully educated in languages both at home and in a notable Southampton grammar school, Ashley received his university training at a trio of Oxford colleges: Hart Hall, Merton, and Magdalen. At Magdalen, he earned his B.A. in 1582 and his M.A. five years later. In 1587, as well, he was named professor of geometry at his alma mater. After holding that post for only a year, he moved to London to study law at the New Inn of the Temple. The next year, however, he interrupted that effort to return to his first love, the study of languages. He traveled and mastered French. Then, from 1593 to 1595 he completed his legal studies, but failing to secure important posts through patronage, he devoted the rest of a long career to study, translation, and travel.

It is as a translator that Ashley enters the history of literature. His principle works include a translation of DU BARTAS's French work *L'Uranie* (Urania) into Latin hexameters (1589), the translation into English (1594) of Louis Le Roy's *De la vicissitude ou variété des choses en l'univers* (*Of The Interchangeable Course, or Variety of Things in the Whole World,* 1577). His last work appeared in 1627 when he presented King Charles I a translation from the Spanish: *Almansor the Learned and Victorious King.*

Ashley is also remembered for an English essay, *Of Honour,* and for initiating the imitation of the prose style employed by the Roman SENECA among English essayists including FRANCIS BACON and JOSEPH HALL.

Bibliography

Ashley, Robert. *Of Honour.* Edited by Virgil B. Heltzel. San Marino, Calif.: Huntington Library, 1947.

Hebel, J. William, and Hoyt H. Hudson. *Prose of the English Renaissance.* New York: Appleton, Century, Crofts, Inc. 1952.

Leroy, Louis. *Of The Interchangeable Course, or Variety of Things in the Whole World, and the Concurrance of Arme. . . .* Translated by Robert Ashley. London: C. Yetswiert, 1594.

L'Astrée (Astrea) Honoré d'Urfé (Part I, 1607; Part II, 1610; Part III, 1619, Part IV, 1627)

Modern English speaking readers may never get the chance to peruse a translation of all of HONORÉ D'URFÉ'S vast, brilliant, and perplexing novel, *Astrea.* At this writing only the first part of the enormous work is available in a contemporary translation. Few modern readers in any Western European language, moreover, would have either the leisure, the patience, or the habits of mind required to plough through the whole of D'Urfé's masterpiece.

Yet a masterpiece the novel is, for in exquisitely crafted prose and verse the book epitomizes everything the Renaissance thought about love and love theory. Its vast array of characters talks ceaselessly about love. They write about love, theorize about love and its complexities, fall into love, fall out of love, scorn love, fear love, and frequently suffer near suicidal depression for love.

Principally a PASTORAL novel, *Astrea* also draws inspiration from CHIVALRIC ROMANCE and from the novellas of Italy, France, and Spain—particularly from CERVANTES's *Galatea.* It relies as well on models drawn from ancient Greek action stories and on the emergent French literature of sentiment for some of its love interest. It also draws on d'Urfé's personal experience of a 25-year-long passion for his sister-in-law, Diane du Châteaumorand. Aspects of her personality are thought to appear in the title character Astrea and perhaps in other female characters as well. Despite such personal allusion, however, the book is not principally biographical. While the novel resists classification, in at least one of its aspects it nonjudgmentally sets the optimism of Renaissance Platonic love theory over against a darker, more ancient, pre-Freudian view of Love as a cruel and tyrannical deity who rejoices in enslaving his human adherents. It also sets the cult of ennobling love against the pessimistic views of Saint Augustine of Hippo about the appetitive nature of human beings and their capacity for self-delusion concerning their motives.

Set in the French region of Forez—the region where d'Urfé grew up—the novel mythologizes local geography. D'Urfé moves the landscape 11 centuries back through time to fifth-century Gaul. In that time and place, D'Urfé would have his reader think, the Druids held sway, not worshiping their historical polytheistic pantheon, but rather devoted to the fictive Tautates, a triune deity that d'Urfé assimilates to the God of his Roman Catholic contemporaries. Through the Edenic landscape of ancient Forez runs the Lignon River. On one bank a group of shepherds live in rustic simplicity. Their forebears were nobles who withdrew from the life of the court to enjoy the pastoral life. On the other bank live the Druid nobility and priesthood, including the chief priest Adamas, one of the principal spokesmen for neoplatonic love theory and for the subordination of sexual love to human reason.

Interwoven plots concern dozens of sets of characters—often with very similar names and with problems whose patterns involve only minor variations from one another. These people find their way to Forez to work out their romantic problems. Typical of pastoral plotting is the continual deferment of lovers' gratification, and often even of their mutual understanding, so that a reader begins to wonder if a conclusion will ever arrive, and suspense is spun out beyond the capacity of most modern readers to wait or even to remember.

Mixed in among characters whose verbal allegiance, regardless of their actions, is to a finally unsustainable ideal of love, one finds other characters whose motives differ markedly from those of the idealistic shepherds like Celedon, who disguises himself as a woman to be near his beloved Astrea. Hylas is a character that rejects rational spirituality as playing any role whatever in love relationships; for him love is all about the temporary possession of a woman's beauty. He rejects out of hand the PETRARCHAN depression of the yearning, idealistic lover. Once any given love relationship has fulfilled its sensual purpose, for Hylas it is over, and the women that he uses regularly find that they have not much suffered on his account once he has abandoned them. Galathée is a female character who moves from man to man, though her motives differ from those of Hylas since she must dominate in her relationships.

Beyond Hylas, who at least represents a kind of joyous sensuality, male characters appear who are lecherous, cruel, and sadistic in their use of women. Gondebaud is a lecher, Childéric a debauchee and rapist. Sex and violence, disguised identity, an ongoing search for a theoretically once enjoyed but now lost state of happiness, transvestism, love triangles, sexual sublimation, a religion of love—all play interlacing roles in a sprawling, four-part novel that set out on an exhaustive exploration of the twisting byways of human passion and that required more than a lifetime to write.

D'Urfé died before Part IV was written. He had left extensive notes toward its completion, however. His secretary, Balthazar Baro, therefore undertook on his deceased employer's behalf to supply an ending that approximated what his employer would have done. Whereas, however, d'Urfé managed to remain so utterly nonjudgmental that a reader seeking an authorial viewpoint beyond learned didacticism is doomed to frustration, Baro did not quite share d'Urfé's capacity for suspended judgments. Yet if a central message can be carried away from this long canticle of a book whose language, both verse and prose, sings throughout, that message might be that the business of human loving in all its permutations constitutes a foolish enterprise.

The novel provoked CHARLES SOREL to write his SATIRE of pastoral literature *Le Berger extravagant* (The extravagant shepherd, 1627), in which the main character is driven mad by reading too many pastorals.

Bibliography

Hembree, James M. *Subjectivity and the Signs of Love: Discourse, Desire, and the Emergence of Modernity in Honoré d'Urfé's L'Astree.* New York: Peter Lang, 1997.

Hinds, Leonard. *Narrative Transformations from L'Astree to Le berger extravagant.* West Lafayette, Ind.: Purdue University Press, ca. 2002.

Horowitz, Louise K. *Honoré d'Urfé.* Boston: Twayne Publishers, ca. 1984.

Urfé, Honoré d'. *Astrea, Part I.* Translated by Steven Randall. Binghamton, N.Y.: Medieval and Renaissance Text Society, 1995.

Astrophel and Stella   Sir Philip Sidney (1591)

SIDNEY met Penelope Devereaux, the daughter of Lord Essex, when she was 13 years old. The pair later became engaged to marry. The match, however, was broken off for unknown reasons, and Penelope instead married Lord Rich. Their marriage proved unhappy, and Penelope eventually became the mistress of the Earl of Devonshire, subsequently securing a divorce from Rich. She and Devonshire scandalized England by marrying after Rich died.

Sidney, who died of a war wound in 1586, did not live to see the later developments in Penelope's life. While some argue that she is not the Stella to whom Sidney addressed his work, internal evidence suggests otherwise. In part to vent the pain he felt at her marriage to another, and in part to celebrate the love he still felt for Penelope, Sidney wrote a SONNET sequence in the manner of PETRARCH. In its title, *Stella* means "star" in Latin, and *Astrophel* is Greek for "one who loves a star." Like Petrarch, Sidney varies the forms of his sonnets and—particularly in their last six lines—introduces rhyming variations of his own. Like Petrarch, too, Sidney introduces longer songs into his collection to add variety. Although the collection circulated in manuscript, the Sidney family did not authorize its publication. The edition of 1591 was pirated, as was another in 1592. Finally in 1598 the family authorized an edition.

In the famous opening sonnet, the lover/author states his purpose in addressing his poems to Stella: "That . . . she . . . might take some pleasure of my paine / . . . and . . . [that he might] grace obtaine." He describes his difficulties in starting the sequence, trying to wring inspiration from his "Sunne-burnt braine," until, in the sonnet's last line, his MUSE resolves his quandary: "Foole saide My muse to mee, looke in thy heart and write."

In some of the poems of complaint, like the 24th or the 37th that first appeared in the authorized edition of 1598, Sidney indirectly assigns blame with the frequent use of the word *Rich*—identifying both the cause of his sorrow and perhaps subtly suggesting that the match with Lord Rich proved to be financially more advantageous for the Essex family than a match with the Sidneys.

Bibliography

Sidney, Sir Philip. *Astrophel and Stella*. Menston, U.K.: Scolar Press, 1970.

'Atá'í, Nev'í-záde ('Atá-ulláh)
(1583–1634/5)

A Turkish poet and biographer and the son of the learned poet NEV'Í, the young 'Atá'í studied under notable Turkish scholars and became a member of an elite scholarly and judicial class called *the learned* (*'ulama'*). In this capacity he served as a judge in several of the Ottoman Empire's dependencies in Eastern Europe—now the Balkan countries—before returning to the place of his birth, Constantinople, where he died.

As a biographer, 'Atá'í enlarged a running account of eminent members of the scholarly class to which 'Atá'í himself belonged. Entitled *Shaqá'iq-un-Nu'mániyya* (Crimson peony), this work had been begun in Arabic by the eldest member of the TASHKÖPRÜ–ZÁDE FAMILY (1423–1529) and translated into Turkish by Mejdí. The importance of this work for scholars results from the information it contains about the lives and accomplishments of the persons it chronicles.

The body of 'Atá'í's poetry is preserved in five books. Composed of four longer poems called *MESNEVÍS* plus a compilation of shorter poems, the five books are known as 'Atá'í's *Quintet*. Two of the *mesnevís*, the first and the third, respectively bear the titles *The Converse of Virgins* and *The Breath of Flowers*. These are composed of series of chapters or *breaths*. Each breath addresses some ethical or mystical question illustrated by a brief story drawn from legend or history. The second book, *The Seven Courses*, involves conversations among and monologues by seven spiritual mystics who describe their mystical ecstasies and the joys of the spiritual life. The fourth book, titled both the *Cup-bearer-Book* and *The World-Displayer*, belongs to a category of poetic production popular among 'Atá'í's contemporaries. It begins with long prayers and praises, recounts the Ascension to Heaven of the Prophet Mohammad, and contains verses in praise of the Sultan. These are followed by a statement of purpose for writing the book and, finally, by a long series (1561) of couplets interrupted occasionally by 12 RUBÁ'IS.

The fifth book of 'Atá'í's *Quintet* departs from the expectations for similar collections of five works. Ordinarily, the fifth would be another *mesneví*. Instead it is a random collection of poems called QASÍDA that honor great men, 150 GHAZELS, and a number of other poems of miscellaneous varieties.

A subsequent writer, Nedím, praised 'Atá'í as the preeminent author of *mesnevís*. Nedím, however, stands alone in this flattering appraisal. Most later critics consider 'Atá'í's work quite ordinary.

Bibliography

Bearman, P. J. et al. *The Encyclopedia of Islam*. Vol. 10, fascicules 177–178. Leiden: Brill, 2000.

Gibb, E. J. W. *A History of Ottoman Poetry*. Vol. 3. Edited by Edward G. Browne. London: Luzac and Company, 2nd ed., 1965.

Atheist's Tragedy, The   Cyril Tourneur
(1611)

This SENECAN TRAGEDY focuses on a finally unsuccessful attempt by the atheist, D'amville, to establish a dynasty by forcing a marriage between Castabella (whose name means *chaste and lovely*) and his own sickly son, Roussard. Castabella already has an understanding with the play's other good character, D'amville's nephew, Charlemont, who is away at war. Nonetheless, with the connivance of a Puritan preacher called Langbeau Snuffe and Castabella's promiscuous mother, Levidulcia, the marriage takes place, but Roussard is in no condition to consummate it.

With this strand of the action firmly in progress, in Act 2 D'amville takes the next step in an ambitious plan to gain control of a fortune. He murders his own brother and arranges a false report of Charlemont's death. This makes D'amville his brother's heir. The ghost of the father, Baron Montferrer, however, appears to Charlemont on a battlefield on the Continent and urges his son to return home but not to attempt to avenge him.

The plot continues with bedroom scenes, graveyard scenes, murders and attempted murders, an attempt by the Rev. Mr. Snuffe to seduce a dead body, and the suicide of Levidulcia in a paroxysm of regret over her profligate life—which has been in evidence both on stage and by report throughout the play.

In the final act, after the death by natural causes of the sickly Roussard, D'amville succeeds in having Charlemont wrongfully convicted of the murder of D'amville's confederate in crime, Borachio. Venting his spleen, D'amville insists on playing headsman and personally carrying out Charlemont's death sentence. As D'amville raises the axe to strike, however, he accidentally brains *himself*. In view of the interposition of Providence, the sentence against Charlemont is vacated. He and the still virginal Castabella are reunited, and the two inherit their respective family titles and fortunes. The play's last line underscores its moral: "Patience is the honest man's revenge" (V. ii. 303).

Bibliography

Tourneur, Cyril. *The Plays of Cyril Tourneur.* Edited by George Parfitt. Cambridge, U.K., and New York: Cambridge University Press, 1978.

atmanivedana (The biography of a soul)

Atmanivedana is a term with two meanings. In its first meaning, the word describes the ninth and highest stage of a Hindu's devotional quest for spiritual illumination. At this stage, the devotee becomes one with the universal soul. In its literary sense, an *atmanivedana* is a biography or, more usually, autobiography that, in keeping with the Hindu belief in repeated incarnations, traces the journey and experiences of an individual soul (*atman*) through successive lives, including the present one, in its journey towards enlightenment. The female Marathi poet BAHINABAI (1628–1700) wrote a celebrated example of an *atmanivedana*.

Aubigné, Théodore-Agrippa d'
(1552–1630)

A Huguenot (French Protestant) engineer, student of magic, courtier, administrator, author, and soldier, Aubigné's valor and military success led to his appointment by King Henry IV as governor of Maillezais and vice-admiral of Guienne and Brittany. Henry had reason to be grateful to Aubigné. When Queen Catherine de' Medici (1519–89) ordered the St. Bartholemew's day massacre of Huguenots (August 24, 1579), she had imprisoned Henry, then the protestant duke of Navarre, in the royal palace of that epoch, the Louvre. Aubigné was among those who helped Henry escape and survive to become king. Henry reigned until his assassination in 1610.

Aubigné's literary efforts, as he tells his children in the autobiography he composed for them, began at age seven when he translated Plato's *Crito*. Early in his career as a courtier and poet, he followed the example of PIERRE DE RONSARD, composing a cycle of 100 SONNETS in honor of Cassandre Salviati's niece, Diane (*Hécatomb à Diane*). The year 1571 saw the composition of a verse TRAGEDY, *Circé,* that Queen Catherine's son, Charles IX, admired. To the same year belongs Aubigné's collection of love poems, *Le Printemps* (Spring).

Generally acknowledged as his poetic masterpiece, *Les Tragiques* (The tragic ones), though written earlier, appeared in 1616. This seven-canto EPIC poem combines history and SATIRE as it recounts the course of the French religious wars. Though sometimes careless and lacking the polish displayed in the major epics of Italy and England, *Les Tragiques* nevertheless contains passages that reveal great poetic power, and its satirical depiction of fawning courtiers is biting.

The years after 1616 saw the publication of several prose works. Among these, the most important is his *Histoire universelle, 1550–1601* (Universal history of the years 1550–1601). In it he tries very hard to give a balanced view of human affairs during that period. His effort seems not to have succeeded with his countrymen. Published serially between 1616 and 1620, the *History* so offended the French Catholic regime that the Paris city hangman burned it publicly at the Sorbonne.

In 1620, at age 70, Aubigné retired to Geneva, Switzerland, where he lived until his death. While there he published *Aventures du Baron de Fœneste* (*The Adventures of Baron de Fœneste*). An entertaining, PICARESQUE story, this work portrays a parasitic aristocrat involved in court politics and is undoubtedly a composite of traits drawn from persons the author had known at the French court. In a similarly satiric vein Aubigné tells the story of the *Confession catholique du Sieur de Sancy* (Catholic confession of the Lord of Sancy)—the mock confession of a convert. This work was translated into English late in the 17th century but apparently not since.

The degree to which both Aubigné's poetic and prose works draw upon his personal experience sets him apart from most of his contemporaries with direct connections to the royal court.

Bibliography

Aubigné, Theodore-Agrippa d'. *Les tragiques: a translation with introduction and notes of Books, I, II, and III.* Translated by Jesse Zeldin. Ann Arbor, Mich.: University Microfilms, 1954.

Randall Coats, Catharine. *Subverting the System: D'Aubigne and Calvinism.* Kirksville, Mo.: University of Missouri Press, 1990.

Regosin, Richard. *The Poetry of Inspiration: Agrippa d'Aubigne's Les Tragiques.* Chapel Hill, N.C.: Duke University Press, 1970.

Autobiography of Lorenzo de' Medici the Magnificent, The: A Commentary on My Sonnets Lorenzo de' Medici (after 1492)

Had the uncrowned prince of Florence, Italy, LORENZO DE' MEDICI, been nothing other than a poet, history would have remembered him for the collection of 39 ITALIAN SONNETS that he gave the world, together with his prose remarks on the poems.

By organizing his collection in this way Lorenzo asserted his claim to a very high place in the history of Italian letters. His poems are written in the manner of the instigator of the European Renaissance FRANCIS PETRARCH—perhaps the most influential European lyric poet in history. Lorenzo's remarks on the poems, on the other hand, emulate the practice of DANTE ALIGHIERI in his partly autobiographical *La vita nuova* (*The New Life*) and his *Il convivio* (*Banquet*). Recalling his devotion to Beatrice, Dante—like Lorenzo after him—interspersed a literary–critical commentary between the texts of his poems in *The New Life*. In the *Banquet* Dante anticipates many of the arguments that Lorenzo employs in defending his choice of Italian rather than Latin for his poem. By emulating his two great Italian vernacular predecessors Lorenzo first invokes their traditions. He also lays claim to a place in their company and concurs in their assessment of the Italian language as an appropriate medium for a serious artist.

More than anything that Lorenzo ever wrote, his *Commentary* lays claim to being an autobiographical work. It is not, however, a record of deeds done and accomplishments—though he sometimes refers in passing to veiled but specific occurrences such as the murder of his older brother Giuliano at the Cathedral of Florence and his own narrow escape from the church. Rather the *Commentary* is an interior autobiography that chronicles his feelings about a beloved woman, Lucrezia Donati, his thoughts about HUMORAL MEDICINE as it related to his own rather melancholy disposition, and his conclusions about many of the major intellectual issues of his time. Above all, the *Commentary* conducts an ongoing interpretation of a talented poet's own analysis of the meaning of the poems he has written.

As the ruler of the city and the head of a far-flung banking empire, Lorenzo was the subject of an ongoing campaign of rumor and vilification by his enemies. In view of the fact that Lorenzo's manuscript circulated widely as he worked on it over the years, the literary historian William Kennedy has pointed to another function of

Lorenzo's collection. That function was political. At some level, Kennedy suggests, Lorenzo, who often felt persecuted and misunderstood, was trying to convince the readers of Dante and Petrarch—the people who mattered, the people in the know—that he deserved their support and admiration as a man, a thinker, and an artist.

Bibliography

Medici, Lorenzo de'. *The Autobiography of Lorenzo de' Medici The Magnificent: A Commentary on My Sonnets.* Translated and edited by James Wyatt Cook. 1995. Tempe, Ariz.: Arizona Center for Medieval and Renaissance Studies, 2000.

autos sacramentales (Spanish religious drama)

As in England, France, and Italy, the Spanish religious drama of the Renaissance was rooted in medieval dramatizations of passages of Scripture or BIBLICAL TROPES. Deriving from the Latin word *actus,* Spanish *auto* was applied to any solemn act. So, on the one hand, it was used to describe the biblical plays traditionally performed on Corpus Christi day—the holiday celebrating the body of Christ that had been established by papal edict in the 13th century. On the other hand, the same word could be applied to the act of burning someone at the stake, an auto-da-fé.

The medieval *autos sacramentales* had been acted in churches—usually by clergy and nuns. While such productions continued, and although the Spanish church authorities were reluctant to surrender their self-appointed authority over the performances, with the advent of the Renaissance the plays described as *autos* increasingly became the brainchildren of professional or quasi-professional playwrights.

The earliest of these was JUAN DE LA ENCINA (ca. 1468–1530) who, in addition to writing secular plays for the entertainment of members of the Spanish nobility and in fact founding the public secular drama of Spain in 1492, also wrote a series of six simple dialogues (which he called *eclogues*) for presentation at Christmas, Easter, Carnival, and Lent. In addition to these, he also authored quasi-religious plays that flattered his patrons and combined secular and religious elements. Sometimes these concern biblical personages and scenes, and sometimes they are drawn from the lives of saints.

Encina's life spanned the transition of the literature of Spain from the Middle Ages to the early Renaissance. The next professional Spanish playwright, however, to employ the matter of religious drama in his work was LOPE DE VEGA (1562–1635). Unlike Encina, Lope de Vega bends biblical matter to the sometimes fantastic requisites of his theatrical imagination. In his play *Spotless Purity,* Lope—as he is regularly called—brings together with the University of Salamanca, first, John the Baptist, then Job, David, and Jeremiah. Both the creation of the world and the nativity appear together in *The Birth of Christ.* Clearly the chronology of ordinary life was of no concern.

In sum, the general direction of the Spanish religious theater during the Renaissance lay toward a higher degree of secularization. Entertainment was substituted for religious indoctrination. In this respect, at least in the hands of professional playwrights, religious theater's development in Spain paralleled that throughout Europe.

Aztec Priests' Speech, The (1524)

A poem in the Nahuatl language, *The Aztec Priests' Speech* was written in reply to the attempts by a delegation of 12 Franciscan missionaries from Rome to convert the Aztec priests to Roman Catholicism. Revised and polished in 1564, it stands as a dignified, if hopeless, response of the defeated to conquerors who would have them give up their traditional ways and values.

After declaring that what they are about to say will not be open to further discussion and that they understand that their own words will not be in their future best interests, the Aztec priests courteously welcome their guests from beyond the sea, acknowledge their preeminence as conquerors, and recognize in them the form of the "Alldeity" the Franciscans represent. They also acknowledge their amazement at having felt the breath of the deity who spoke the word as reported in the Bible the Franciscans have brought.

The Aztec continue, acknowledging their unworthiness and subjection, but they reject the sign of the cross. They agonize because their gods are dead, and they exclaim in amazement over the differences between the missionaries' message and their Aztec ancestors' teaching about the gods. Then the Aztec priests begin to enumerate the benefits their gods conferred on them, including manliness and valor, clothing, fashion, plants, food, health, power, and minerals including the "godshit" that Europeans call gold. Moreover, the priests continue, their old deities conferred cities, power, honor, law, life, worldview, the Aztec way of life, the rites they practice, and the way they pray.

They beg the Franciscans to do nothing, to be cautious, and not to ruin what little is left after the Aztec's defeat and humiliation.

After this dignified but hopeless response, the Aztec priests invite the Franciscans to do with them whatever they please. The poem forces its reader to feel the utter dejection of a proud but subjected people that has exhausted its last hope of reprieve.

Bibliography

Brotherston, Gordon, and Edward Dorn, translators. "The Aztec Priests' Speech." In *Literatures of Asia, Africa, and Latin America,* edited by Willis Barnestone and Tony Barnstone, 1579–83. Upper Saddle River, N.J.: Prentice Hall, 1999.

B

Babylonian Captivity of the Church of God, On the Martin Luther (1520)

One of three or four documents setting forth the essence of MARTIN LUTHER's doctrinal disagreements with the theory and practice of Roman Catholicism as he found it in his time, *On the Babylonian Captivity . . .* discusses Luther's views concerning the sacraments of the church. Essentially he argues that the sacramental theology of the Middle Ages errs in naming seven sacraments: baptism, confirmation, the Eucharist, marriage, penance, holy orders, and extreme unction. Instead, Luther argues that Christ himself is the sacrament, and so only baptism in which one is freed from original sin, the Eucharist (holy communion) in which one literally (which Luther believed) or figuratively (which most Protestants think) partakes of Christ's body and blood, and maybe penance deserve to be considered sacraments.

Bābur (Zahīr-ud-Dīn Muhammad) (1483–1530)

King of Kabul as a child, then deposed, and subsequently, as a result of five superlatively successful military campaigns, the first Mughal emperor of India, Bābur was also a charming memoirist. Writing in the Chagatay Turkish called *Turkī*, he composed an autobiography, The history of Bābur (*Bābur-nāmeh*), which reveals him as a straightforward, unpretentious person who loved his family and friends. Bābur's work is also an important historical document, chronicling as it does his successes in founding a great empire.

Among other matters, he treats the difficulties he experienced as a deposed monarch who was too poor to afford either a hat or shoes, let alone support the attendants who had been constrained to leave him out of sheer want. He also reports the kindness shown him by his more fortunate relatives, the khan and begum of Tashkent. Concerning his conquest of India, he gives graphic and matter-of-fact descriptions of his battle tactics, those of his opponents, and the outcomes of his campaigns.

Bibliography

Bābur. *The Bāburnama: Memoirs of Bābur, Prince and Emperor.* Translated and edited by Wheeler M. Thackston; introduction by Salman Rushdie. New York: Modern Library, 2002.

Bacon, Francis, Viscount St. Albans (1561–1626)

So early did Bacon begin to reveal signs of his extraordinary intellect and his passion for philosophy that one commentator on his work suggests that Bacon "was never a child." He enrolled at Cambridge's Trinity College when he was only 12. At 14, annoyed with the constraining curriculum and with university rules, he withdrew, enrolling instead at Gray's Inn, where he studied law for a year.

He was well connected. His father, Sir Nicholas Bacon, was Lord Keeper of the Seals. His mother, Ann Cook, was the sister-in-law of one of QUEEN ELIZABETH's principal ministers, Lord Burghley, and Elizabeth herself called the boy her "young Lord Keeper." Undoubtedly as a result of those connections, he was invited to accompany the party of the British ambassador to France in 1576. He interrupted his legal studies to do so, spending three years there and writing his first book, *On the State of Europe.* This volume he published after returning to England. He was 19 years old.

Strangely, his evident endowments and his connections in high places did not lead to early advancement. In 1596, however, he did secure the post of queen's council. In that office he incurred the criticism of some of his future biographers by prosecuting his friend and patron, the earl of Essex, for treason in 1601. In fairness, however, Bacon had little recourse since Essex had led an insurrection.

The year 1597 saw the publication of his *Essays or Counsels, Civil and Moral*—a work whose title and content had been inspired by the writings of MICHEL DE MONTAIGNE. With that Bacon's fortunes improved. He was knighted in 1603, possibly as the result of the efforts of his new patron, the duke of Buckingham. In his *Essays* Bacon shows himself to be not only Montaigne's successor, but also the precursor of Benjamin Franklin and H. L. Mencken. His pithy maxims are both quotable and memorable: From *Of Marriage and Single Life:* "He that hath wife and children hath given hostages to fortune;" (He had married Alice Barham in 1606.) From *Of Revenge:* "Revenge is a kind of wild justice, which the more a man's nature runs to, the more ought law to weed it out;" from *Of Youth and Age:* "A man that is young in years may be old in hours, if he have lost no time;" from *Of Studies:* "Reading maketh a full man; conference [discussion] a ready man; and writing an exact man." Like Montaigne, Bacon is a man of a world clearly in

the process of becoming. One could not imagine him a century earlier.

Queen Elizabeth died in 1603, and after the accession to the throne of JAMES I, Bacon's career advanced more rapidly. During the next 17 years, he successively became: solicitor-general, attorney– general, privy councilor, lord keeper of the seals, lord high chancellor, Baron Verulam, and, finally, Viscount St. Albans. One would think that the responsibilities of such offices would keep even the most able person fully occupied, but Bacon's many writings continued appearing throughout the period both in English and in Latin. The publication in 1620 of one of his most important Latin works, *Novum Organum* (New Organon, 1620), advocated a new method of inductive, empirical logic. Then his public career fell apart.

He was indicted for allowing the duke of Buckingham to sway his decisions and also accused of taking bribes. Tried by the House of Lords, he pleaded guilty to 23 charges. The House of Lords fined him 40,000 pounds—an astronomical sum, sentenced him to prison for as long as it pleased the king, and barred him from further public office. He was released after two days, the fine was forgiven, and the king granted him a generous pension, but his days as a public servant had ended. For the last six years of his life, however, he lived in retirement, conducting scientific experiments and publishing other writings.

Whatever his shortcomings as a public official may have been, Bacon possessed one of the keenest intellects of his era. As a writer of English prose, he had no peer during his lifetime, and he contributed to the corpus of NEO-LATIN composition as well. Bacon made a significant contribution to British political history with his *History of Henry VII* (1622). This work is especially interesting for its narrative style, its psychological insights into the players, and the way he characterizes historical figures by attributing to them imaginary speeches that reveal their motives and methods of operation.

He called the writing project that he set for himself The Great Instauration—the great renewal or Renaissance. Essentially, what he proposed is the experimental method on which rests all scientific and technological progress. He took, as he wrote to

Lord Burghley in 1592, all knowledge as his province and divided his project into six stages: first, he meant to classify existing knowledge with a view to identifying its failings and holes. THE AD-VANCEMENT OF LEARNING (1605) represents that stage of the project. The second part of this immense undertaking is addressed in *Novum Organum* itself, and with the 1620 edition he published his objectives and plans for his Great Instauration. The other four subprojects of his master plan are represented only by fragmentary materials that he was in process of assembling. Although Bacon finally was less influential than, say, RENE DESCARTES either as a scientist or as a philosopher, he nevertheless played an important role in proposing and popularizing the possibility of a new, empirical method that avoided a priori assumptions—the foundation stone of scientific and technological progress.

Although he was an empiricist to the core, Bacon was no religious scoffer; he perceived, however, that theology was the proper province of theologians, not scientists (and vice versa). In 1624, while ill, Bacon translated the penitential Psalms into English verse.

During Lent in 1626, he busied himself experimenting with using snow as a refrigerant for food to determine the preservative qualities of low temperature. Chilled, he caught a cold that progressed into pneumonia and killed him on Easter day.

Bibliography

Bacon, Francis. *The Works of Francis Bacon.* 15 volumes. Edited by James Spedding et al. Boston: Brown and Taggard, 1860–64. Reprint, St. Claire Shores, Mich.: Scholarly Press, ca. 1969.

Daiches, David. *A Critical History of English Literature.* Vol. 1. New York: The Ronald Press, 1960.

Bahinabai (1628–1700)

A female saint and a poet in the Marathi language of India, Bahinabai wrote a series of 473 AB-HANGAS—brief rhyming poems—in the manner of TUKĀRĀMA OF DEHU, a poet and philosopher. Of these verses, the first 78 constitute an AT-MANIVEDANA—an autobiography of the progress of her soul through 12 previous lives, although it begins by detailing the current one. In it we learn that a *sadhu* or wandering holy man had foretold her birth and how her father found a gold piece not long after she was born. These events resulted in her family's regarding her birth as auspicious, and as a child she was especially cherished. As a further mark of her unusual qualities, instead of joining the other village children at play, she spent her time reciting the names of God.

Her parents contracted a marriage for her when she was only three years old with the stipulation that she remain in her parental home until she reached puberty. Although her husband was a scholar and, as she reports, "an excellent jewel of a man," he was also a widower 27 years her senior, and a number of her poems detail the marital difficulties the couple experienced. Some of these were occasioned by the teen-aged Bahinabai's increasing sense of religious calling and the visions that she began to experience. One of these involved the poet–saint Tukārām, who fed her honey. When people began to be convinced of Bahinabai's sanctity, they began to pay her visits. This enraged her husband, who was both a high-caste Brahmin and a religious mendicant who begged for a living. Enraged by the unsolicited visits of lower-caste persons, on several occasions, the husband beat his child bride.

Other verses recount the poet's very unusual experiences with a calf that accompanied her everywhere, would eat only from her hand, and take milk from its mother only when Bahinabai was present. The calf even insisted on accompanying her to worship and seemed to bow when the people did. As a result, people concluded that the calf was a *yogabhrasta,* one who had worshipped the Hindu deity Hari in a former life. A visiting holy man, Jayaram Svami, confirmed this. He advised Bahinabai's husband that she was herself a *yogabhrasta* and that the calf and its mother were her companions and "one with her in her religious life." The holy man congratulated the husband on his good fortune in having married Bahinabai and advised him not to "distress her any more" as, in performing her wifely duties, she would become the means of his salvation.

Bahinabai's charming verses provide a privileged glimpse into a woman's often-difficult life and her religious devotion in 17th-century village India.

Bibliography

Bahinabai. *Bahinabai: A Translation of Her Autobiography and Verses.* Translated by Justin E. Abbott. Poona, India: Scottish Mission Industries, 1929. Reprinted with a foreword by Anne Feldhaus. Delhi: Motilal Banarsidass, 1985.

———. *Bahina Bai [sic] and her Abhangas.* Translated into English verse by Krishna P. Bahadur. New Delhi: Munshiram Manoharlal Publishers, 1998.

Women Writing in India, 600 B.C. to the Present. Vol. 1. Edited by Susie Tharu and K. Lalita. New York: The Feminist Press at the City University of New York, 1990.

Baïf, Jean-Antoine de (1532–1589)

A French poet who in 1553 was named by PIERRE DE RONSARD among the seven literary stars who should be included in the French PLÉIADE, Baïf is principally remembered for his SONNETs. The author of several collections of love lyrics, Baïf made his most enduring contribution to French poetry with his introduction of the 12-syllable Alexandrine as the standard POETIC METER for the line of a French sonnet. He introduced that measure in the second collection of his lyrics in 1555—a collection he addressed to a woman named Francine.

Together with Ronsard and with JOACHIM DU BELLAY, Baïf studied poetry at the *Collège de Coqueret,* and like them he sought to apply the models of Greek and Latin poetry to the composition of French verse. His attempts to reform French spelling and to introduce blank verse that depended, as Latin and Greek had done, on long and short syllables rather than on heavier and lighter emphasis, produced only slight impact on French Renaissance literature.

Bibliography

Baïf, Jean-Antoine de. *Poems.* Edited by Malcolm Quainton. Oxford: Blackwell, 1970.

Bâkî (Mahmud Abdül Bâkî) (1526–1600)

Revered as the Poet-King—the greatest of all Ottoman lyric poets—Bâkî was born to a humble family of Constantinople and was early apprenticed to a saddle maker. His superior intelligence, however, soon became apparent and he shifted to the study of the law. During his student years he also began to write poetry, and one of his youthful works, *Hyacinth,* a QASÍDA, continues to be regarded among his most celebrated poems.

Around 1555–56 Bâkî gave one of his poems to the Ottoman Sultan Süleyman. The sultan found it delightful and welcomed Bâkî as one of his closest private friends. Except for a brief period when his enemies successfully conspired against him, Bâkî continued to enjoy the imperial favor not only of Süleyman but of his three successors as well. As a result he rose to a succession of prestigious legal positions in the empire. As another mark of the emperor's regard, Süleyman conferred on Bâkî a female companion whose name, *Túti Qadin,* meant "lady parrot" —a woman who was also literary and witty.

Critics and commentators remember Bâkî as a poet who modernized Turkish poetry by avoiding many phrases that earlier poets had overused and who employed fresh and striking language. In their evaluations of his poetry, the same writers also remark upon the purity of his style and the clarity of his meaning. From the point of view of subject matter, however, Bâkî's verse remained in the main stream of the poets who preceded him— flowers, spring, love, and wine comprised his principal subjects. In these poems on traditional subjects we find a parallel with the British CARPE DIEM poets.

An exception to the conventionality of Bâkî's choice of subjects, however, appears in the noblest of Bâkî's compositions, his *Elegy on Sultan Süleyman.* In that work the affection and gratitude Bâkî felt for his friend and benefactor, together with the poet's grief at the emperor's passing, spurred Bâkî to heights of original lyricism that he never again equaled. Another exception occurs in his early *Hyacinth,* written to honor his teacher, Qaramání–záde Mehemmed Efendi. This poem provides the reader with a tour de force of technical ingenuity, using the word *sunbul* (hyacinth) to end each of the last 49 lines after using words rhyming with *sunbul* in the 49 lines preceding its first use.

In addition to the substantial body of his lyric poetry, Bâkî translated legal and theological documents from Arabic into Turkish prose. He also collected and made translations of quotations from the Prophet. Critics of Turkish letters value his prose style for its clarity, its freedom from pointless adornment, and its careful balance.

Balance of Truth, The   Kâtib Çelebî (Haci Halifa) (before 1657)

The final work of Kâtib Çelebî, *The Balance of Truth* offers a frank, sensible, liberal, and often humorous discussion of a number of issues of Islamic behavior, doctrine, and observance that have sometimes proved contentious. The book is generally considered to be a model of good sense and good humor. After Çelebî made a pilgrimage to Mecca, he called himself Haci Halifa.

Two matters that Haci Halifa addresses and that still provoke heated discussion in many circles, both Muslim and non-Muslim, involve the consumption of coffee and tobacco. The former topic gains further interest from the fact that the author died in 1657 while drinking a cup of coffee.

Çelebî's essay on the beverage begins with a discussion of its origins in Yemen and a description of the way the Yemeni hill people prepared it and its supposed medicinal benefits. He finds it "suited to the ascetic life," and "sedative of lust." He then follows coffee into Asia Minor, where he says it arrived by sea about 1543.

Coffee's arrival was met with immediate resistance by Muslim clerics, who objected, perhaps on spurious grounds, to its being roasted and, from a stronger position, to the practice of consuming it in large gatherings where it passed from hand to hand. This practice, the clerics suggested, smacked of loose living. Some who resisted the importation of coffee went so far as to bore holes in the hulls of vessels carrying it, sending both ships and cargos to the bottom. All such measures, however, failed. Coffeehouses opened one after another, and en-

thusiastic coffee drinkers gathered. Drug addicts, Çelebî says, found that coffee intensified their experience and eagerly sought the substance.

As the coffeehouses proliferated, entertainers began to perform in them, increasing their attraction to the point that people neglected their jobs to participate in the fad. Then, Çelebî mordantly reports, people of all classes began to amuse themselves by knifing each other in the coffeehouses. This of course provoked a reaction from the authorities. The sultan closed all the coffeehouses in Istanbul—though those outside the city remained open. Moreover, Çelebî sensibly remarked, "such things do not admit of a perpetual ban."

Haci Halifa closes his brief treatise with a consideration of the medical nature of coffee according to the theories of HUMORAL MEDICINE. He considers coffee a cold, dry substance and discounts its heat in an infusion. Because it is dry, he says, it interferes with sleep and is a diuretic in a degree that varies with the predominate humor of the drinker. Persons whose disposition is melancholic—that is, ruled by black bile—will find that coffee produces insomnia and a morbid anxiety. Such people should, by implication, avoid coffee or at least drink it only with sugar. Those, on the other hand, especially women, whose temperament is naturally moist and in whom phlegm is the predominant humor will benefit from drinking much strong coffee.

In a similar fashion, Çelebî examines the history and progress of tobacco smoking. A Spanish ship's doctor on a voyage to the New World, the essayist reports, was suffering from a lymphatic disorder produced by his own phlegmatic (cold and watery) disposition and his months at sea. Following the rule of treatment by opposites, he sought a hot, dry substance to relieve his condition, and observing the natives burning tobacco, he fashioned a pipe and tried it. It helped. His countrymen took up the practice, and soon all the seamen began to smoke. From them, the practice spread through England, France, and Europe and eventually into the Islamic world, reaching Turkey in around 1601.

There, Çelebî says, people did not know that its original purpose among Europeans had been medicinal. They quickly became addicted to its use. The clergy and the civil authorities objected to tobacco's use, though in varying degrees. Some forbade it; some only disapproved it. Those addicted to its use, of course, argued that it was (or should be) permissible. That discussion continues about tobacco and other substances. In Çelebî's time the sultan himself forbade the use of tobacco, sometimes even punishing those who disobeyed his antismoking edict with death, but to no avail. The more he punished, the more people smoked. He eventually gave up.

Having considered the history of smoking tobacco and attempts at its prohibition, Haci Halifa attempts a rational consideration of the whole issue, considering both sides of seven related health, moral, social, and canonical issues. After giving fair and due consideration to both sides, he concludes that it is best "not to interfere with anyone in this respect, and that is all there is to it."

Bibliography

Chelebî, Kâtib. *Mīzzān-ul-Haaq (Balance of Truth)*. Translated by C. G. Pfander, 1910. Edited by W. St. Clair Tisdall. Villach, Austria, 1986.

Balzac, Jean-Louis Guez de (1597–1654)

One of the founding members of the French Academy in 1634, Balzac followed the example of Machiavelli in Italy by writing a political discourse entitled *The Prince* (1631). Unlike Machiavelli's treatise that instructed princes in policy, Balzac's work surveyed princes and their favorite courtiers. He also interested himself in philosophy and religion, publishing a treatise that combined ancient Greek stoicism with Christian ethics, *The Christian Socrates* (1652). In 1654 he published a discussion of life at the court, *Aristippe* (*Aristippus*—the name of a fourth-century Greek philosopher). This work his English translator considered to be Balzac's masterpiece. His principle contributions to French literature, however, arose from the influence he exercised over the development of 17th-century French prose writing and from the letters that he published in ever revised and expanded editions from 1624 until the end of his life.

Influenced by the affected purism favored in French poetry by François de Malherbe, Balzac set out to establish similar norms for prose. Though he had little that was new to say, he said it very elegantly in a style that shares some elements with the flowery prose of the English writer John Lyly in his *Euphues*. One commentator remarks of Balzac, "He made French prose eloquent by giving it cadence." Together with his fellow late Renaissance academicians, Balzac strove to purify and dignify French prose style and to establish for it a national norm. He also attempted to inculcate in the manners of the time the manliness of the ancient Roman patriot and the domestic and civic morality of the virtuous Frenchman.

Although modern critics do not much praise the content of his writing, collections of Balzac's works continued to be published in France well into the late 20th century and English translations of them into the 18th. Though his letters may owe some of their inspiration to Montaigne, they are largely sterile, abstract, and devoid of the personal qualities that make Montaigne so attractive. For Montaigne, the interest lay in what he found when he tested matters against his experience. For Balzac, the interest lay in the polished, rhetorical expression of a generality.

Bibliography

Bearman, P. J., et al. *The Encyclopaedia of Islam*. Vol. 1. Leiden: Brill, 1960.

Gibb, E. J. W. *A History of Ottoman Poetry*, 2nd ed. Vols. 1 and 3. Edited by Edward G. Browne. London: Luzac and Company, 1965.

Barclay, Alexander (ca. 1475–1552)

An English translator and satirist, Barclay introduced a new satirical spirit into English letters with his 1509 translation of Sebastian Brant's *Das Narrenschiff* (Ship of Fools, 1494). Not a German linguist, Barclay translated from the Latin (*Stultifera Naves*) of the Swiss translator Jacob Locher. Barclay's English, however, did not just mirror Brant and Locher's work: In his rhyme royal version, Barclay put aboard Brant's ship a wide array of fools from the local British scene. Barclay's passenger list expanded many times over the length of Brant's original.

Whereas medieval SATIRE had tended to ridicule the folly of sinners who were ensnared in the toils of one or more of the SEVEN DEADLY SINS, Brant and especially Barclay shifted the focus to social satire: the affectations of courtiers, the folly of keeping up with popular shifts in interest, or the silly enthusiasms of the crowd. Barclay introduces this new, HUMANIST strain of satire into England.

Following the method he pioneered in *The Ship of Fools,* Barclay translated and expanded five Latin ECLOGUES, three of the scholarly Pope Pius II (Aeneus or Enca Sylvius Piccolomini, 1405–64), and two of the Italian poet Baptista Mantuanus. With these works Barclay introduces into English a mode of classical poetry—the PASTORAL. His translations of the eclogues also make the first use of that mode to satirize contemporary English life. Writers such as JOHN SKELTON and EDMUND SPENSER later followed Barclay's early example.

See also POETIC METER.

Bibliography

Barclay, Alexander. *The Eclogues of Alexander Barclay.* Edited by Beatrice White. London: Oxford University Press, 1928.

Brant, Sebastian. *The Shyp of Fooles.* Translated by Alexander Barclay, 1509. Edited by Phyllis C. Robinson. Seal Harbor, Maine: High Loft, 1983.

Bartas, Guillaume de Salluste, seigneur du (1544–1590)

A French Huguenot (Protestant) nobleman, diplomat, musician, artist, and poet, Bartas was one of the Protestant aristocracy targeted but missed in the St. Bartholemew's Day massacre (August 24, 1579). A poetic disciple of PIERRE DE RONSARD and JOACHIM DU BELLAY, Bartas took up the latter's challenge for a French poet to produce a classical EPIC poem in the manner of VIRGIL. When Bartas asked Jeanne d'Albret, the queen of Navarre to suggest a subject, she chose a topic both biblical and feminist: the Hebrew heroine Judith's liberation of Jerusalem from the tyranny of Holofernes. Although the re-

sultant epic *Judith* (1565) does not enjoy a premier place in the annals of French poetry, writing it did hone Bartas's poetic skills. He produced a successful play on the same subject in 1574.

His next literary effort, The week (*La Semaine,* 1578) recounted as an epic poem the events of the first week of the world's creation as detailed in Genesis. This poem was a popular success, going through 20 editions in five years. Doubtless encouraged by its reception, Bartas began to work on a sequel that was also his deceased wife's memorial, The second week (*La Seconde Semaine,* 1584). Bartas's use of the word *week* in the second epic was figurative. He intended that week to stretch throughout biblical history to the Last Judgment. The 1584 edition gave readers a first installment. The balance never followed—at least not from his pen.

Bartas was a serious and talented Christian poet, and the combination did not win only a French audience for his work: His epics were translated into all the major European languages and into Latin as well. While 19th- and early 20th-century French critics sometimes have retrospectively found fault with Bartas's work, his own and immediately following generations greatly admired him, and his work proved enormously influential.

In 1605, Joshua Sylvester translated *La semaine* into English. Together with the Bible itself, the English version of the work was a major source of JOHN MILTON's *Paradise Lost.* As a Protestant poet who was able to weave together the classical manner dear to the hearts of his fellow HUMANISTS with subjects of great religious seriousness and moral edification, Bartas provided a template for those subsequent writers who shared his religious views and for the few who also shared his comprehensive mastery of the art forms and the fields of knowledge of his day.

Another of his works, Urania (*La Uranie,* the heavenly MUSE) develops his view of the calling of the Christian poet and his convictions about God's expectations for the poet who is also a priest.

See also VATES.

Bibliography

Bartas, Guillaume Salluste du. *The divine weeks and works of Guillaume de Saluste, Sieur du Bartas.*

Edited by Susan Snyder and translated by Josuah Sylvester. Oxford: Clarendon Press; New York: Oxford University Press, 1979.

———. *The works of Guillaume de Salluste, sieur Du Bartas, a critical edition with introduction, commentary, and variants. . . . [sic] Edited by Urban Tigner Holmes, Jr. et al. Chapel Hill: The University of North Carolina Press, ca. 1935.*

Bartholomew Fair   Ben Jonson (1614)

First performed on October 31 by Lady Elizabeth's Men at London's Hope Theater, *Bartholomew* (pronounced *Bartelmee*) *Fair* had its second performance before King James I the following day. An immediate success, it was the last of JONSON'S truly great plays.

In some respects it is a MORALITY PLAY—one that represents a literary subcategory of the European Renaissance, the literature of fools. At the annual Smithfield Fair held on St. Bartholomew's Day (August 24), Jonson assembles a representative selection of the citizens of London. Each character, however, also typifies some form of human vice or folly, and their names provide the keys. The fair swirls with figures like the doting but foolish husband Littlewit, his initially honest but eventually corruptible wife, Win (short for Win-the-Fight, not Winifred), and Win's widowed mother Dame Purecraft. Purecraft and one of her fortune-hunting suitors, Zeal-of-the-Land Busy, represent and satirize ignorant, proselytizing, grasping Puritans who loudly proclaim virtue and denounce vice but who are themselves running confidence schemes to bilk their more simpleminded co-religionists of their money.

The cast also features an overzealous justice of the peace, Adam Overdo, who attends the fair in disguise to root out abuses but who regularly misidentifies them. We meet as well Overdo's brother-in-law, Bartholomew Cokes, a well-to-do and credulous young man who willingly contributes to his own robbing and victimizing at the hands of every crook and con artist at the fair. He has a paid companion, Humphrey Wasp, who buzzes with anger at any remark addressed to him. Cokes is betrothed to Grace Wellborn, who is anxious to be rid of her gullible husband-to-be.

Other figures attending the fair include Winwife, another suitor for the hand and fortune of Dame Purecraft, and the man after whom Purecraft lusts, Winwife's friend Quarlous. Also in attendance is a pathetically mad figure named Trouble-All.

The fair's personnel and hangers-on include sellers of goods such as Lantern Leatherhead, who trades in hobbyhorses; Joan Trash, who hawks gingerbread; and the mistress of the fair's misrule, Ursula the pig-woman whose roast pork is one of the fair's main attractions and her bartender, Mooncalf. Also selling his wares is a vendor of BROADSIDE BALLADS, Nightengale. Nightengale's performances give his pickpocket confederate Ezekiel Edgeworth opportunities to take purses from his rapt listeners.

Others who ply their dubious trades at the fair include Punk Alice, a prostitute described as "mistress o' the game," and pimps Captain Whit and Jordan Knockem, who convince Win that a prostitute's life is preferable to that of an honest wife.

The fair, in short, represents the vanities, vices, and follies of the world in a setting populated by Londoners typical both of its citizens and of people everywhere with similar follies and vices.

The play opens with a stage keeper appearing to apologize for the delay in beginning the performance. Taking the audience into his confidence, the stage keeper pokes fun at the play's author, at his assistant, and at the play itself. The prompter then appears and sends the stage keeper away. After this the prompter reads a long pseudocontract between the author and the audience. This contract requires each member of the audience to arrive at an independent judgment of the play and to promise not to try to find allusions to celebrated persons hidden among the characters.

After this, the play proper begins by establishing the initial characteristics of the Littlewits, Cokes, Wasp, Dame Purecraft, Quarlous, and Busy. It also develops the device by which the Little-wits manage to get the Puritans Purecraft and Busy to a fair at all. Win pleads pregnancy and an all-consuming desire to eat some of the wonderful roast pig at the fair. This overcomes the objections of Busy, who decides that by eating pork he can demonstrate his disdain of Jews.

The play's last act features a puppet show within a play and Little-wit's pathetic grief at his wife's fall, to which his own neglect and folly principally contributed. In the last act too, Justice Overdo actually learns that his overzealous pursuit of wrongdoing was foolish.

The large number of characters and the almost cinematic changes of scene at the fair may make the play initially confusing for a reader. The same attributes, however, delighted then (and now delight) most viewers of a good production. One segment of the Renaissance audience, however, remained unamused. The play's unflattering portrayal of Puritans added impetus to their demands for the CLOSING OF THE THEATERS in England.

Bibliography

Jonson, Ben. *Bartholomew Fair* in *Ben Jonson*. 4th ed. Vol. 6. Edited by C. H. Herford Percy and Evelyn Simpson. Oxford: The Clarendon Press, 1986.

Bashō (Matsuo Munefusa, Matsuo Bashō) (1644–1694)

Japan's most celebrated poet and the unchallenged master of the haiku form, Bashō was born Matsuo Munefusa in the town of Ueno in Iga province. There he remained in the service of a samurai overlord and studied verse until he was 22 years old. He then wandered for a few years, continuing to study and write verse in the style of the Teimon school of poetry. In 1672 he settled in the city of Edo and came under the influence of Nishiyama Soin, the founder of the comic and allusive Danrin school of *haikai* poetry.

Whereas the Teimon school emphasized verbal linkages between the stanzas of poems, Danrin preferred to make such links conceptually. In Bashō 's day, the 17-syllable, three-line haiku stanza did not usually stand alone as an individual poem. Rather, the haiku appeared as the first stanza (hokku) of a series of linked verses *(haikai)*, which were often the result of collaboration by several poets. For example, a *haikai* poem entitled *Throughout the Town* (1690), begins with a haiku in the traditional form—three lines with five,

seven, and five syllables, respectively—and written by a poet named Bonchō. That first haiku is the poem's hokku, or its foundational stanza. The second stanza repeats the hokku and adds to it two lines of seven syllables each. The two added lines are called a tanka. Bashō wrote the second stanza of *Throughout the Town*. A third poet, Kyorai, added the poem's third stanza. In varying order, the three kept adding stanzas according to a formula until, in this instance, they achieved a sequence of 36 stanzas called a *kazan*.

> Here is a brief example of such a poem's
> two opening stanzas:
>   (Haiku as hokku)
>   *Fragrant pine needles*
> *Waves roll sparkling in sunlight*
>   *Southwesterly breeze*
>   (Hokku plus tanka)
>   *Fragrant pine needles*
> *Waves roll sparkling in sunlight*
>   *Southwesterly breeze*
> *The harmless drudge at his desk*
> *Writes examples in bad verse.*
>
>   (J. W. C.)

Gaining an enviable reputation as a poet and still known as Munefusa, Bashō attracted students and disciples, one of whom, in around 1680, built a hut for him in the country near Edo. This hut was called the *Bashō-an* (Banana-tree retreat), and from it Bashō took his literary name. In addition to collaborating with his students in the production of haikai poems, Bashō frequently journeyed around Japan and composed wonderful travel journals while on the road. Comparing these with the matter-of-fact journals kept by a companion of his wanderings reveals that some of Bashō's episodes are fictive while others render actual experiences with consummate art. The journals intersperse prose narrative with verse commentary—a literary combination called haibun. Bashō's most famous travel journal is widely considered to be the finest of its kind, *Narrow Road to the Interior*. The "interior" that the work approaches is simultaneously that of his country and the interior of the human soul.

In his artistic development, Bashō moved always in the direction of greater and greater simplicity and toward what a pair of his editors and translators, Willis and Tony Barnestone, call "a mood of desolate and lonely beauty, the Japanese sublime." The influence of Daoist thought and of Zen Bhuddism also appears in Bashō's work.

Bibliography

Bashō, Matsuo. *Narrow Road to the Interior.* Translated by Sam Himill and illustrated by Stephen Addiss. Boston: Shambhala and Random House, 1991.

———. *A Haiku Journey, Bashō's Narrow Road to a Far Province.* Translated by Dorothy Britton. Tokyo and New York: Kodansha International, 1980.

Ueda, Makoto. *Bashō and His Interpreters: Selected Hokku, with commentary.* Stanford, Calif.: Stanford University Press, 1991.

Battiferi, Laura (mid–16th century)

An early Italian poet and sonneteer in the style of FRANCIS OF PETRARCH, Battiferi was among the pioneers of women writing erudite poetry in Italy. While her work has not appeared in modern editions, she is nonetheless well remembered as a friend and correspondent of the painter and poet Agnolo Bronzino (1519–74). Bronzino painted a famous portrait of Battiferi in which she appears dressed in black with an icily severe expression on a face whose most prominent feature is a noble Roman nose. In her lap, her hands rest upon a volume of PETRARCH'S SONGBOOK.

Battles of Coxinga, The Chikamatsu Monzaemon (1715)

The most notable of CHIKAMATSU's highly mythologized history plays, *The Battles of Coxinga* depicts in five acts events that had occurred in the 1640s. The play's remarkable popularity arose mainly from the high quality of Chikamatsu's writing, but also from its spectacular exploitation of the possibilities of the puppet theater for which it was originally written. Later it was revised for performance by live actors in the Kabuki theater. The scenes set in China also piqued public interest. During the Tokugawa period of Japanese history (1603–1868), people were forbidden to travel abroad, and visits by foreigners were strictly limited to Dutch and Chinese traders who could do business only in a defined area of the port city of Nagasaki. Thus this play's Chinese scenes provided the audience with a surrogate travel opportunity.

The play opens in Nanjing in the court of the Chinese Ming emperor Shisōretsu with a commentary by the ever-present narrator setting the stage for the action. From him we learn that the emperor keeps numerous wives and concubines and that his favorite of them all, the Lady Kasei, is pregnant and expected to bear the heir to the throne. An ambassador from Tartary (Mongolia) speaks and explains that his king has fallen in love with Lady Kasei on hearing her beauty praised. He offers gifts and asks that she be sent to his king. The Chinese all consider the request unreasonable until an official named Ri Tōten reveals a pact he made with Tartary some years before. In exchange for food to relieve a Chinese famine, he promised the Tartars the next thing they might request from China.

The Chinese haughtily reject the ambassador's requests, underlining their contempt by throwing away the presents he brought. Infuriated he promises an immediate attack by Tartar troops. To defuse the situation, Ri Tōten demonstrates his loyalty by gouging out his own left eye and presenting it to the ambassador on a ceremonial baton. This impresses both the emperor and the ambassador, and the door remains open for further negotiation.

To show his appreciation for Ri Tōten's gesture, the emperor appoints him governor of Beijing and promises him the hand of Princess Sendan, the emperor's younger sister, in marriage. He proposes a flower tournament, however, to let fate decide if Sendan should consent to a marriage that she finds displeasing. The princess and her retainers who are armed with plum blossoms, do mock battle against Ri Tōten and his supporters, who are armed with cherry blossoms. The blooms respectively symbolize chastity and fecundity. Since the emperor has fixed the tournament, Sendan's side loses easily.

A loyal subject, Go Sankei, reproves the emperor's bad judgment in trusting the treacherous Ri Tōten. The emperor kicks Go Sankei in the forehead for offering this unwelcome opinion, but immediately the Tartars mount a sneak attack. Bairoku, the Tartar ambassador, confesses that he lied about his emperor's desire for the Lady Kasei: He really wants to kidnap her so that the Chinese emperor will have no heir.

As the battle rages, Ri Tōten murders the emperor and tries to kidnap the pregnant Lady Kasei. Go Sankei foils this attempt and tries to lead the empress to safety. She, however, is killed by a bullet. He quickly rescues her child by Caesarean section, kills his own baby, and places it in the Lady Kasei's womb to avoid a search for the rescued prince. In the confusion of battle, Go Sankei's wife, Ryūkakun rescues Princess Sendan, kills a would-be assassin, steals his boat, and spirits the princess away.

The second act opens back in Japan where, after some stage business involving a clam, a predatory bird—a shrike—and a fisherman named Watōnai, Princess Sendan washes up on the Japanese shore and is led to a retired Chinese court retainer, Tei Shiryū—also known as Ikkan—who is married to a Japanese wife. On hearing of the princess's misfortunes, Watōnai is able to interpret the meaning of the meeting between the shrike and the clam and to predict his own future. He realizes that he will become the general who will defeat the Tartars and restore the Ming dynasty to China's throne.

Returning to China to fulfill that destiny, Watōnai and Ikkan interrupt a tiger hunt in a bamboo forest. Watōnai and the tiger fight. Displaying superhuman strength, Watōnai vanquishes the beast without killing it. Just then the Tartar An Taijin arrives. He has been hunting the tiger as a present for Ri Tōten, who is now a governor for the Tartar emperor. A battle ensues. Watōnai and his new ally, the tiger, together kill An Taijin and overcome his forces, recruiting the survivors to their cause. Watōnai thereafter rides the tiger into battle, and the two become famous throughout the land for their invincible prowess in warfare.

The opening of Act Three finds Watōnai and his allies outside the Castle of the Lions—the most impregnable fortress of China. Its warden is the husband of the daughter that Ikkan-Tei Shiryū left behind when he fled China years before. Convinced of this, the daughter, Kinshōjo, admits to the castle her bound stepmother who has accompanied her husband and who poses no threat to the defending troops. Thereafter, the warden of the castle, Kanki, returns. In a hardly credible mishmash of conflicting loyalties and codes of martial honor, Kinshōjo commits suicide so her husband, Kanki, can join her half brother, Watōnai, as an ally against the Tartars. Kanki has been serving them because there was no heir of the Ming dynasty. Once the alliance is formed, Kanki renames Watōnai, dubbing him *Coxinga*. Overcome with happiness at the alliance and grief at the death of her newfound stepdaughter, Coxinga-Watōnai's mother commits suicide—a favorite device of Chikamatsu for ridding the stage of characters that have served their purpose.

Act IV traces the path of Princess Sendan and compresses five years of action into an extended Buddhist vision of the engagements between Coxinga's forces and the Tartars. These are viewed by the loyal Ming courtier Go Sankei from the vantage point of the Mountain of the Nine Immortals. This is a mythical Chinese peak from whose summit, legend has it, one can see all of China.

Act V begins with a war council at which Go Sankei and Kanki offer strategic advice for tricks to quell the Tartar enemies. Go Sankei wants to imprison hornets in tubes that the Tartars will open; Kanki proposes leaving the Tartars poisoned fruit in an abandoned camp. Coxinga, however, prefers the direct method and battle. A further disappointment, however, awaits the great warrior. The Tartars capture and kill his father, adding further impetus to his desire to overcome them. This he does in the play's final scene where the three allies cooperate in dismembering the villainous traitor Ri Tōten. The victors then offer prayers for the new emperor—the very baby whose life Go Sankei had sacrificed his own child to save in Act I.

Bibliography

Chikamatsu, Monzaemon. *Four Major Plays of Chikamatsu.* Translated by Donald Keene. New York: Columbia University Press, ca. 1998.

Beaumont, Francis (1584–1616)

Francis Beaumont was a younger son of a judge, also named Francis, of the court of common pleas. The Beaumonts belonged to the British country gentry and owned an estate at Grace-Dieu, Leicester. In 1598, the younger Beaumont was enrolled in his second year at Oxford when his father died. He withdrew from university and two years later enrolled as a member of the Inner Temple, evidently with the purpose of studying law. The record, however, does not suggest that he actually did. Instead he joined the circle of literary revelers that made the Mermaid Tavern their headquarters and there became close friends with BEN JONSON and Michael Drayton. Perhaps encouraged by his literary associates, Beaumont began to try his hand at poetry. The year 1602 saw a brief verse introduction to *Metamorphosis of Tobacco*—a piece written by his uncle, Sir John Beaumont. In that year, inspired by the Roman poet Ovid's *Metamorphosis,* Francis Beaumont may have written a long, erotic elaboration of Ovid's poem he entitled *Salmacis and Hermaphroditus.* He was only 18 at the time, however, and his authorship is open to question. During the next several years, Beaumont certainly penned a series of poems that introduced and praised plays written by Ben Jonson: VOLPONE (1605), *EPICOENE, OR THE SILENT WOMAN* (1609), and *Cataline* (1611).

Sometime around 1605 Beaumont met JOHN FLETCHER. The two became good friends and began one of the most successful theatrical collaborations of the Jacobean period. Together they wrote and produced *The Woman's Prize, or The Tamer Tamed* (after 1604: a sequel to SHAKESPEARE's *Taming of the Shrew*). Perhaps the two friends composed *The Woman Hater* (published anonymously in *1607*). They probably collaborated on *The Captain* (ca. 1608), and on *Four Plays or Moral Representations in One* (ca. 1608). These four pieces borrow the ti-

tles of PETRARCH's *Triumphs:* the triumphs of *Honor, Love, Death,* and *Time.* The first two triumphs are thought to be Beaumont's and the others Fletcher's. The friends' fruitful collaboration also produced *The Faithful Shepherdess* (ca. 1609), *Philaster* (ca. 1610), THE MAID'S TRAGEDY (1611), and *A KING AND NO KING* (1611). Considerable scholarly debate centers on the degree of credit each author should receive in these plays and in several others where it looks as if one or the other of the authors had a minor hand in contributing to the work of the other.

THE KNIGHT OF THE BURNING PESTLE (ca. 1611) seems principally and perhaps wholly Beaumont's work, but recent scholarship suggests slight traces of Fletcher's hand as well. Both wrote plays outside of their famous collaboration, often working with other playwrights—as was the frequent practice of the epoch. In general, Beaumont seems to have had the better critical judgment and Fletcher the quicker wit. Scholarship also credits Beaumont with the lion's share of the overall work.

The last edition of all the works in which either Beaumont, Fletcher, or both had a hand—that of Alexander Dyce in 1877—lists 56 plays. More recent discussion enumerates 59. Suffice it to say that the matter is complex. Critical voices become virtually unanimous, however, in pointing to *The Knight of the Burning Pestle* as Beaumont's comic masterpiece.

Beaumont married in 1613, only three years before his death. His friends considered his death at a relatively early age attributable to a mind never at rest, to overwork, and to his carousing style of life.

Bibliography

Beaumont, Francis. *The Knight of the Burning Pestle.* Edited by Sheldon P. Zitner. Manchester, U.K.; Dover, N.H.: Manchester University Press, ca. 1984.

Beaumont, Francis, and John Fletcher. *The Dramatic Works in the Beaumont and Fletcher Canon.* Cambridge, U.K.: Cambridge University Press, 1966; reissued 1996.

———. *The Works of Beaumont and Fletcher.* Edited by Alexander Dyce. New York: D. Appleton and Company, 1877.

Oliphant, E. H. C. *The Plays of Beaumont and Fletcher: an Attempt to Determine their Respective Shares and the Shares of Others.* New Haven, Conn.: Yale University Press, 1927.

Bellay, Joachim du (ca. 1522–1560)

An early defender of the French language as a medium of artistic expression and an influential poet, the young du Bellay withdrew from legal studies at the University of Poitiers to pursue poetry along with PIERRE DE RONSARD at the Collège de Coqueret. Studying the classic authors of ancient Greece and Rome, du Bellay learned to model his French poetry on their example and on that of the poets of the Italian Renaissance. He also became convinced that the French language was as noble a medium of expression as the classical languages. He perceived ways that, as Italian already had, French could be further enriched by imitating the classics and by expanding its vocabulary through resurrecting old words, inventing new ones, and introducing into poetry words previously confined to the discussion of technical subjects.

He organized his thinking about these matters into a treatise that set forth his views, his Defense and illustration of the French language (*Défense et illustration de la langue française,* 1549). Moreover, he applied his theories to his own PETRARCHIST, amorous SONNET sequence Olive (*L'Olive,* 1549–50), the first such work in French.

After conducting a critique of the mistakes made by earlier French poets, such as trying to write literary Latin and not testing the literary resources of the French language, du Bellay's *Défense* gives very specific guidance to would-be poets. A poet should not rely merely on talent but on knowledge as well, so poets must store their minds, not with the low examples of the Middle Ages, but with the noble works of the ancients. He counsels using the forms of the ODE and the sonnet to express emotion, the EPIGRAM and the SATIRE for witty composition, and the application to French of the ancient COMEDY and TRAGEDY. His fifth chapter deals with the EPIC. There he advises poets to rework such native French materials as the stories of

Tristan and *Lancelot* on the models of HOMER and VIRGIL.

Du Bellay's work proved exceedingly influential. The group of poets who took his advice and whose nucleus included du Bellay himself, Pierre Ronsard, and JEAN-ANTOINE DE BAÏF, has since become known as the PLÉIADE—originally a group of seven literary stars named by Pierre Ronsard. In fact many other French writers also followed Bellay's precepts, du BARTAS among them. Du Bellay's influence extended beyond France. In England, EDMUND SPENSER found both his discussion and his example useful.

In 1553, du Bellay visited Rome where he joined the household of a relative—Cardinal du Bellay—as chief steward. His two-year stay there deeply influenced his life and his art. His enthusiasm and his feeling for the pathos of a city much declined from its ancient grandeur appears in his 32-sonnet sequence the Antiquities of Rome (*Antiquités de Rome*) and in its companion 15-sonnet sequence Dream (*Songe,* 1558). Increasingly personal sonnets followed with his sequence Regrets (*Les regrets,* 1559). These poems catalogue his life and disappointments in Rome. He also wrote a collection of Latin lyrics (*Poemata*) on the same subjects. Among them he chronicles a sad passion for a woman he calls Faustina.

Despite his low opinion of translators, du Bellay himself translated the fourth book of Virgil's *Aeneid* (1552). In 1553, his Collection of poetry (*Recueil de poésie*) poked fun at the same Petrarchist style he had himself employed only a few years before. Of a satiric turn of mind, he sometimes mocks court poets in his *Poète courtisan* (A court poet, 1559). The title puns: It also means, *A fawning poet.* A late collection also attests to his more playful spirit. Various rustic games (*Les divers jeux rustiques*) contains comic portraits and a satiric treatment of the total deafness he suffered before his own early death. His love of the countryside around his native Anjou appears in what is perhaps his most famous if not the most characteristic poem of his mature artistry, A wheat winnower (*Vanneur de Blé*).

Bibliography

Bellay, Joachim du. *The Regrets: a Bilingual Edition.* Translated from the French and Latin by David R. Slavitt. Evanston, Ill.: Northwestern University Press, 2003.

Coleman, Dorothy G. *The Chaste Muse: A Study of Du Bellay's Poetry.* Leiden, Netherlands: Brill, 1980.

Hartley, David Julian, ed. *A Critical Edition of the Circumstantial Verse of Joachim Du Bellay.* Lewiston, N.Y.: E. Mellen Press, ca. 2000.

Katz, Richard A. *The Ordered Text: The Sonnet Sequences of Du Bellay.* New York: Peter Lang, 1985.

Shapiro, Norman R., trans. *Lyrics of the French Renaissance: Marot, Du Bellay, Ronsard.* New Haven, Conn.: Yale University Press, ca. 2002.

Tucker, George Hugo. *The Poet's Odyssey: Joachim Du Bellay and the Antiquities de Rome.* New York: Oxford University Press, 1990.

Bembo, Pietro (1470–1547)

A native of Venice, Bembo became a notable scholar and churchman. In the latter capacity he rose to become the secretary to Pope Leo X (1513). Pope Paul III elevated Bembo to cardinal in 1539. On the literary front, Bembo became interested in what generations of Italians had called the QUESTION OF THE LANGUAGE. Some erudite Italians like Ercole Strozzi had objected to Bembo that only Latin deserved serious attention—especially as the Italian language itself, with all its regional dialects and variants, had not yet developed a widely accepted literary standard. Bembo, however, perceived that the ancient languages held no self-evident advantages over the modern, so he set himself up as the champion of Tuscan, the language of Florence, as the single literary standard toward which all Italian authors should strive. To that end, he himself diligently studied as models the vernacular writings of FRANCIS PETRARCH and DANTE in verse and BOCCACCIO in prose. Apparently he perceived no irony in using the writings of the 14th century to construct a literary standard for the 16th.

To achieve purity of style, he polished his own works with unflagging industry. He is said to have revised his writing as many as 40 times, keeping separate files for each version. However compulsive this may seem, Bembo's influence produced the effect he desired. A significant number of talented writers chose to compose in the Italian vernacular and to observe Bembo's advice concerning the use of pure Tuscan. Even the best of the poets of his generation, LUDOVICO ARIOSTO, praised Bembo in his ORLANDO FURIOSO, naming the cardinal as the man who "raised our pure and sweet idiom up from its dismal, vulgar manner," (*Orlando Furioso,* xlvi, 15: translation mine). At the same time, however, Ariosto largely ignored Bembo's precepts in his own verse.

Several of Bembo's works contributed to his growing influence on the writers of Renaissance Italy. One of these was a Platonic dialogue about love—one inspired by and begun in the midst of a love affair in 1500 with Maria Savorgnan. The finished product, however, Bembo dedicated in 1505 to his later friend, Lucrezia Borgia, duchess of Ferrara. This work, *Gli Asolani* (The dwellers at Asolan)—the location of the garden of the queen of Persia tried in the progress of verse and prose conversations to fuse Christian, Platonic, and Aristotelian notions of spirituality. It also encouraged respect for women. Its publication expanded Bembo's broad courtly audience of both sexes and increased his approval among the powerful noble women who were the social arbiters of his time.

An important part of Bembo's program for Italian literary discourse involved his publication of critical editions of the work of the earlier Florentine writers he so admired. While still in Venice and before embarking on an ecclesiastical career, he published a critical edition of Petrarch's rhymes (*Rime,* 1501) and Dante's *Commedia* (1502), or as Bembo titled the work *Terze Rime* (named for Dante's interlocking three-lined rhymes: aba, bcb, cdc, etc.).

Assimilating the models of such earlier defenders of the Italian vernacular as Dante, LORENZO DE' MEDICI, and Leo Battista Alberti to his own thinking, Bembo spent years writing and polishing his prose discussions of the vernacular language (*Prose della volgar lingua*). He also prepared a grammar of the Italian language, his Grammatical rules (*Regole Grammaticali*), which went through 14 editions.

From these two works sprang future discussions of Italian linguistic issues for years to come.

Bembo's prescriptions for Italian did not escape severe criticism. PIETRO ARETINO considered him an impossibly dogmatic pedant, utterly out of touch with the lively idiom of contemporary usage. The Florentine Academy criticized Bembo's attempt to reduce good Italian to a closed system, and other writers, including the Jewish scholar JOSEPH BEN EPHRAIM KARO, the Neapolitan poet JACOPO SANNAZARO, and the literary critic LUDOVICO CASTELVETRO concurred. Even some of Bembo's admirers, such as BALDASSARE CASTIGLIONE, took indirect issue with the excessive purism and the backward looking straitjacket in which Bembo's slavish admiration of Petrarch's verse and Boccaccio's Latinate prose threatened to imprison not only Italian but also the other emerging vernaculars of Renaissance Europe. Both on the continent and in England, Bembo's influence gave rise to the phenomenon of PETRARCHISM in the composition of lyric poetry and to arbitrary ideas about usage deemed acceptable or not.

Bibliography

Bembo, Pietro. *Gli Asolani* [The Asolanians]. Translated by Rudolf B. Gottfried. Freeport, N.Y.: Books for Libraries Press, 1971.

Borgia, Lucrezia, and Pietro Bembo. *The Prettiest Love Letters in the World: Letters between Lucrezia Borgia & Pietro Bembo, 1503 to 1519.* Translated by Hugh Shankland. Boston: David R. Godine, 2001.

Best, George (d. 1584?)

While in the service of English knight Sir Christopher Hatton, George Best was sent to accompany explorer Martin Frobisher on the three voyages he undertook in 1576, 1577, and 1578 in a vain attempt to discover a northwest passage around the top of North America from Europe to the Orient and India. Immediately on his return, Best, who had been working enthusiastically on a manuscript throughout the voyages, issued *A True Discourse of the Late Voyages of Discovery* (1578). This work in turn was abridged by RICHARD HAKLUYT for inclusion in his own compilation, *The Principal Navigations, Voyages, Traffiques and Discoveries of the English Nation* (1589, and 1598–1600).

Following an extensive celebration of the variety of human accomplishment and of scientific and technological progress, Best focuses on the advances in the art of navigation, "one of the excellentest arts that ever hath been devised." He praises the compass, the sextant, and other instruments of travel across the open sea. Straying often from the description of Frobisher's voyage to touch upon the entire realm of ancient and modern discovery, geography, and cosmology, Best writes with great enthusiasm and conviction but in such a wandering manner that a modern reader in search of Frobisher's story may well lose patience with Best's telling of it. Hakluyt apparently did, for he deleted much of Best's collateral material from his own abridgement of Best's account of the voyage.

Anyone, however, who is interested in the early European exploration of the far northern reaches of the American continent will find Best's firsthand account rewarding despite its author's fondness for erudite digression.

Bibliography

Best, George. *The Three Voyages of Martin Frobisher, in Search of a passage to Cathaia and India by the North-west.* New York: B. Franklin, 1963.

Beyer, Absalon Pedersson (1528–1575)

The adopted son of the first Lutheran bishop of Bergen, Norway, Beyer became the most prominent Norwegian HUMANIST of his era. A Norwegian patriot, Beyer promoted both nationalism and the independence of his country from Denmark. His most influential work was his history and description of his country, *Concerning the Kingdom of Norway* (1567). He is also credited with the creation of several dramas in the Norwegian tongue, and he is known to have promoted the production of drama in his native Bergen, but none of his plays seems to have survived.

Bhaktamala (verse lives of Hindu poet–saints) Nabhādās (late 16th–early 17th century)

The first of several verse collections of the biographies of poet–saints associated with the spiritual reawakening (BHAKTI) that occurred in India from about 1450 through the 16th and 17th centuries and beyond, the *Bhaktamala* is an essential source of information for anyone seeking to understand the diversity of religious points of view represented in this movement that was at once literary, musical, popular, philosophical and devotional.

Nabhādās, the author of the *Bhaktamala,* composed the work in the *Brajbhasha* language. This tongue is a close relative of modern Hindi, though *Brajbhasha* achieved full literary status almost three centuries earlier. Though Nabhādās was himself a particular devotee of the Hindu deity Rama, the poets whose lives Nabhādās chronicles often celebrated other members of the Hindu pantheon or other manifestations of Rama. KABIR, for instance, venerated Vishnu. TULSĪDĀS introduces Rama's brother Bharata. Others adore and compose verse about the blue deity, Krishna or the goddess Chandi.

The *Bhaktamala* inspired imitators and commentators in several of the LANGUAGES OF INDIA.

bhakti

The effect of bhakti—a kind of emotional fervor that infused the devotional literature of India for the better part of a millennium—began to make itself felt as early as the ninth or 10th centuries. Bhakti, however, achieved its most influential expression in the work of the probably illiterate Hindi poet KABIR (1440–1518). Kabir hoped to see Hinduism and Islam amalgamate into a single monotheistic faith. To that end he dictated a number of brief, inspirational maxims and verses to a disciple named Bhagoji. These maxims teach that God is available to everyone and that through faith everyone can reach salvation and direct union with the divine. Some of Kabir's inspirational verses found their way directly into the hymns of NĀNAK (1469–ca. 1539), the founder of the Sikh religion.

Nānak translated some verses of Kabir and imitated others in the Punjabi language. Nānak was the first guru of Sikhism. One of his successors, Arjun, the fifth guru, collected Nānak's verses along with others into the sacred book of that religion, the *Granth.* As a result, the fervor of bhakti, with its mixture of both Islamic and Hindu elements, infused the literary traditions of the Sikhs.

Bhakti is not merely a literary phenomenon. It is also thought to have the power to renew people—to refashion them into religious persons. This quality appears prominently in the work of TULSĪDĀS (1532–1623), who sometimes wrote in the Avadhi and Braj tongues and even occasionally in late Sanskrit. Tulsīdās is also credited, however, with the creation of modern literary Hindi and with founding the golden age, 1500–1700, of the literature in that language. In his adaptation of the ancient EPIC of the Hindu god Rama, Tulsīdās introduces Rama's brother, Bharata, as the prototype of the new man—the man of bhakti—devout, reformed, and on the road to salvation.

Similar qualities appear in the work of writers who employ the bhakti tradition in other Indian languages, like the female BAHINABAI and her poetic inspiration TUKĀRĀM OF DEHU. Both of these saintly poets followed the tradition while writing in the Marathi language. Among the North Indian languages beyond those mentioned above, Gujerati, Kanada, Oriya, Bengali, Urdu, and Assamese also produced poets in the bhakti tradition. Among the southern Dravidian tongues, the bhakti tradition inspired work in Tamil, Malayam, and Telegu. (See INDIA, LANGUAGES OF.)

Whatever their language of composition, bhakti poems fall roughly into two groups. The first of these is the *saguá* (verse celebrating gods with visible attributes). Poems of this sort feature the gods Krishna and Ram, who take the shapes of human beings and interact with people. Both deities are visible forms of the less approachable Vishnu. The second sort of bhakti poem, the *nirguá* (without attributes) celebrates precisely the opposite tendencies. It calls into question the propriety of using images, parables, and rituals in worship. It tends to be more satiric and anticlerical. Though on the surface this may seem contradictory, in the end both roads lead to the same elevating outcome for those who take them.

Bibliography

Miller, Barbara Stoler. *Masterworks of Asian Literature in Comparative Perspective: A Guide for Teaching.* Armonk, N.Y. and London: M.E. Sharpe, 1994.

Renou, Louis. *Indian Literature.* Translated by Patrick Evans. New York: Walker and Company, 1964.

Bible in English

Portions of the Bible had been translated from the Vulgate Latin version into Old English (the language of *Beowulf*) as early as the seventh century. In the late 14th century, under the auspices of the English religious reformer John Wycliffe (ca. 1330–89), two translations of the Bible appeared in late Middle English (the language of Geoffrey Chaucer). The political upheaval, however, that surrounded the reform movement associated with the Wycliffites resulted in an ecclesiastical ruling in 1408 that banned translating the Bible into English. Ignoring this ban would have been no small matter, for the harsh penalties for that infraction included excommunication, trial as a heretic, and, if found guilty, being burned at the stake.

By the beginning of the 16th century, however, the English public increasingly demanded a vernacular bible. An Oxford trained scholar, WILLIAM TYNDALE, who was competent in both the Greek and Latin languages sought to meet that demand and asked permission from the bishop of London to do so. The bishop proved unsympathetic, however, so Tyndale tried to secure permission in a continental venue. He failed again when he tried to publish in Cologne, Germany, but in 1526, his luck happily changed. That year in the city of Worms, Germany, he published between 3,000 and 6,000 copies of the English New Testament he had translated directly from the Greek. The tale of its arrival in England involves high drama. The copies of the book were hidden in bales of cloth and smuggled past customs both on the Rhine and in the ports of England. Once ashore, it was quickly distributed.

The ecclesiastical authorities, however, proved vigilant. They intercepted most of the copies and publicly burned them in a ritual at St. Paul's Cathedral in London. As a result, only two copies are known to survive today. Enough copies remained in the Renaissance, however, that Tyndale's version provided the underpinning for all subsequent English New Testaments. David Daniell tells us that the Christmas stories, the parables of Jesus, the reports of the crucifixion, and certain passages of Paul's writing, such as his Epistle to the Romans, have all come down to us mainly in Tyndale's words.

Doubtless disappointed at the fate of his translation but nonetheless undaunted, Tyndale, still in Germany, studied Hebrew and began to work on translating the Old Testament. He completed the first five books of the Old Testament, the Pentateuch, and those books of the Old Testament that detail the history of the Jewish people. Then he was tricked into going to Antwerp. There he was arrested, tried for heresy, convicted, and, as an object lesson to other would-be translators, both strangled and burned to death on October 6, 1536.

This excessive though by no means unusual cruelty on the part of the authorities failed in its objective. In 1537 all Tyndal's translations from the Old Testament as well as his revision of the New Testament were printed. Had they not been, Tyndal would still have prevailed. In 1535 another translator, Miles Coverdale (1488–1569), using Tyndal's work as his principal source document, published the first complete Bible in early modern English. In 1539 with the blessing of King Henry VIII, Coverdale, again using Tyndale's work as his principal source document assembled the only Bible to enjoy the official blessing of the infant Anglican Church. Known as the *Great Bible,* it was distributed to every church in the realm.

On the death of Henry VIII, the Kingdom of England was plunged into a period of political turmoil that saw the brief reign (1547–53) of Edward VI, Henry's 10-year-old son by his third wife, Jane Seymour. The reign of the boy king was followed by the briefer elevation to the throne (10 days) of the unhappy Lady Jane Grey (1537–54). On August 3, 1553, Grey was succeeded on the throne by

Henry's elder daughter Mary I (1516–68), the child of Henry's first wife, Catherine of Aragon. A devout Catholic, Mary gradually restored the Roman church to its preeminence in the realm of England, and her officials persecuted Anglicans. As a result, many biblical scholars fled to Geneva, Switzerland. There, amid the scholarly resources they needed, including better texts than had been accessible to their predecessors, the exiles, still relying heavily on Tyndale, produced a masterwork, the *Geneva Bible.* Complete with almost every imaginable aid to a reader, this was the Bible that served during the long reign of ELIZABETH I (ruled 1558–1603). It was the bible that SHAKESPEARE knew, and its influence on Elizabethan literature can hardly be exaggerated.

Few Englishmen, however, were more conservative than the bishops of the church establishment. Despite advances in textual criticism and biblical scholarship, many of them remained adherents of the authority of the Latin Vulgate and felt that it, rather than documents of greater antiquity in the original languages, should be the basis of an English Bible. Accordingly they organized a none-too-successful translation, which appeared in 1567 and of course was labeled the *Bishop's Bible.* It too was heavily indebted to Tyndale. So was a Roman Catholic English translation that appeared in Rheims in 1582.

A half-century after the appearance of the *Geneva Bible,* interested persons prevailed upon KING JAMES I to initiate another translation. He agreed, though he required that the Bishop's Bible be the foundation document. In 1611 the *King James Bible* appeared. "It was," says David Daniell, Tyndale's biographer, "Tyndale's translation with a Latinate coloring."

A single example from the beatitudes will suggest the debt that Renaissance English Bible translation owes its martyred initiator:

From Tyndale's New Testament, 1534: "Blessed are ye when men revile you, and persecute you, and shall falsely say all manner of evil sayings against you for my sake."

From the Great Bible, 1539: "Blessed are ye, when men revile you, and persecute you, and shall falsely say all manner of evil sayings against you, for my sake."

From the Geneva Bible, 1560: "Blessed *are* ye when men revile you, and persecute *you,* and say all manner of evil against you for my sake, falsely."

From the Bishop's Bible, 1572: "Blessed are ye, when (*men*) shall revile you, and persecute (*you*), and lying, shall say all manner of evil saying against you, for my sake."

From the Rheims New Testament, 1582: "Blessed are ye when they shall revile you, and persecute you, and speak all that naught is against you, untruly, for my sake. . . .'"

From the King James Bible, 1611: "Blessed *are* ye, when men shall revile you, and persecute you, and shall say all manner of evil against you falsely for my sake."

Bibliography

Bruce, Frederick F. *The English Bible: A History of Translations.* London: Lutterworth Press, 1964.

Daniell, David. *William Tyndale: A Biography.* New Haven, Conn., and London: Yale University Press, 1994.

The Geneva Bible: The Annotated New Testament. 1602 Edition. Edited by Gerald T. Sheppard. New York: The Pilgrim Press, 1989.

Tyndale's New Testament. Edited by David Daniell. New Haven, Conn., and London: Yale University Press, 1995.

Tyndale's Old Testament: Being the Pentateuch of 1530, Joshua to 2 Chronicles of 1537, and Jonah. Edited by David Daniell. New Haven, Conn., and London: Yale University Press, 1992.

Bible in Europe

Throughout the Middle Ages, a Latin translation of the Bible called *The Vulgate* provided the text of the Scriptures known to and used by Western European churchmen. It was this version of the Scriptures that JOHANN GUTENBERG published at his printing shop in Mainz during the years 1454 and 1455. The Gutenberg Bible, also called the Forty-Two-Line Bible because each page contained that much text, was an almost perfect example of the printer's art, but it made no effort to improve the quality of the vulgate Latin text itself.

See also BIBLE IN ENGLISH.

In the 14th an 15th centuries, however, biblical manuscripts written in Hebrew and Greek began to find their way to Europe. Accompanying the resurgence of Renaissance interest in learning those languages, such scholars as LORENZO VALLA and Gianozzo Manetti (1396–1459) in Italy, Jacques Lefèvre d'Etaples (ca. 1455–1536) in France, and ERASMUS in the Netherlands developed methods for comparing versions of texts. In doing so they intended to correct corruptions and mistranslations that had crept into the Scriptures over centuries of recopying and reediting. Each of the last three named also actually translated either the entire Bible or portions of it. Manetti learned Hebrew and translated the Psalms. He also translated the New Testament and produced his versions together with the Vulgate and its Old Latin predecessor.

Lefèvre d'Etaples also retranslated the Psalms into Latin as well as St. Paul's Letters (1512) and other portions of the New Testament. He was hampered in this effort, however, by his limited command both of Greek and of Hebrew. Convinced of the need of the people and of the clergy as well for a Bible in the French that they knew rather than one in the Latin that they did not, Lefèvre d'Etaples eventually translated the Vulgate Bible into French. His translation appeared serially between 1523 and 1530. It later served as the basis for retranslations and revisions by JOHN CALVIN. Pierre Robert Olivétan also used Lefèvre d'Etaples's French version as well as the versions in Hebrew and Greek to provide the first French Protestant translation of the Bible (1535)—one that eventually came to be called the French Geneva Bible.

Influenced by the methods of textual criticism developed by Lorenzo Valla, Erasmus, then living in Basel, Switzerland, undertook an ambitious program of textual editing and translation. His first step involved publishing the New Testament in Greek (1516). Then during the next 19 years he accompanied the Greek text with a Latin translation that he edited and improved with each subsequent edition in 1519, 1522, 1527, and 1535 as better manuscripts became available to him for comparison.

The importance of the biases of translators in the transmission of biblical texts appears clearly in the versions of Lefèvre d'Etaples and Erasmus. Whereas the former was more pious and concerned with the contemplative life of the Christian and the adoration of Christ, the latter was more action oriented and concerned with the moral development of the individual.

Biblical commentary also played an important role in the transmission and improvement of scriptural texts during this period. Christian translators consulted Jewish scholars for explanations of Hebrew discussion about the meanings of the Scriptures. What the Christians learned, they added to their own commentaries. MARTIN LUTHER and Philip Melancthon, for example, had access in Wittenberg to Hebrew scholars like Matthäus Aurogallus (ca. 1490–1543) and Caspar Cruciger (1504–48), who helped inform the Germans' understanding of the text and influenced Luther's own admirable and elegant German translation (New Testament, from Erasmus's Greek, 1522; complete Bible, 1534). The consultation of Jewish experts was by no means limited to Protestant translators and commentators. Cardinal Tommaso de Vio (1469–1534) also sought the advice of Hebraists in preparing his extensive biblical commentaries.

While the efforts described above went forward, elsewhere teams were assembled to compare various versions of biblical texts with a view to producing more authoritative Scriptures. At the University of Alcalá de Henares in Spain, for example, Cardinal Francisco Jiménez de Cisneros (also known as Cajetan, 1436–1517)—the same person who had instructed Luther to recant—brought together the manuscripts and the talent necessary to produce a Bible with texts displayed together on a page in several languages. In addition to the cardinal himself, the team included three Hebraists, two Greek scholars, expert Latinists, and a very capable printer. The outcome, delayed by the cardinal's death, was the magnificent COMPLUTENSIAN POLYGLOT BIBLE (1521). A similar team effort was undertaken in Antwerp and resulted in The Antwerp Polyglot, an eight-volume bible in Hebrew, Syriac, Greek, and Latin (1572).

The interest of HUMANISM in recovering older versions of biblical texts and in improving the available translations became politicized to a degree by the disputes resulting from the Protestant Reformation and by the reform movements within the Roman Catholic Church itself. The Council of Trent (1545–63), which had been convened to address the need for reform within the Roman church and the crisis posed by the Protestants, added the matter of biblical authority to its long agenda. It wisely concluded that, if imperfect, the Vulgate nonetheless provided an adequate and authoritative guide for the instruction of Christians. At the same time the council did not close the door on improving and correcting the text. Pope Sixtus V (served 1585–90) appointed a commission to revise the Vulgate, but the result proved unsatisfactory—partly because the pope himself insisted on serving as an unqualified editor. Pope Clement VIII (served 1592–1605) empowered a commission to re-revise, and the resultant version of the Bible, known as the *Sisto–Clementine* version (1592) served as the approved Catholic version until the 20th century.

Translation of the Bible into the vernacular languages of Europe was a major literary enterprise of the Renaissance. The effort did not, however, meet with universal applause. In Spain, especially, the SPANISH INQUISITION resisted new translations. It suppressed an early Bible (1478) translated into the Catalan language by Bonifacio Ferrer. Only a single page survives. Another translator, Francisco de Enzinas, was jailed by the Inquisition even though his Spanish New Testament (1543) was published in Antwerp. A Spanish Old Testament was printed in Ferrara, Italy in 1553 to address the needs of Spanish Jews who had settled there after being expelled from Spain in 1492. The first complete translation of the Bible in the Spanish tongue was one prepared for Protestants by Cassiodoro de Reina. That Bible appeared in Basel in 1569.

Throughout the Renaissance, Jews, driven from pillar to post throughout the Diaspora by Christian intolerance, did not only provide counsel for Christian scholars. Rather they continued to read and discuss Scripture through the various lenses provided by their own Talmudic tradition, by traditions of Jewish law and theology, by the philosophic positions that had developed from the writings of PLATO and ARISTOTLE, and by the mysticism of the kabbalah. For them the Bible was not, as for some Christians, the sole source of spiritual guidance, but rather a starting point for discussion and interpretation in all fields of human interest.

As Lutheran Protestantism spread North to the Scandinavian peninsula and into Iceland, the impulse for vernacular Bible translations accompanied it. Translated by CHRISTIEN PEDERSEN, the Bible appeared in Danish in 1543. Oddur Gottskálksson's New Testament came out in Icelandic in 1540 and was followed in 1584 by Gudbrandur Thorláksson's entire Bible. Michael Agricola's Finnish New Testament arrived on the scene in 1548 and the whole Bible in 1642. (See FINNISH LANGUAGE AND LITERATURE.) In Swedish OLAUS PETRI published the New Testament in 1526 and the Old in 1541. ANDERS ARREBO translated the Psalms into Norwegian (before 1637).

Bibliography

Bach, Giovanni et al. *The History of the Scandinavian Literatures.* Edited by Frederika Blanker. New York: Dial Press Inc., 1938.

The Cambridge History of the Bible: The West from the Fathers to the Reformation. Edited by G. W. H. Lampe. Cambridge, U.K.: Cambridge University Press, 1969.

Twersky, Isadore, and Bernard Septimus, eds. *Jewish Thought in the Seventeenth Century.* Cambridge, Mass.: Harvard University Press, 1987.

biblical tropes

At some early moment in Christian history, worshipers began to elaborate Scripture readings by acting out portions of biblical passages, especially on the high holy days of the liturgical year. These dramatic elaborations are called tropes. The earliest recorded trope in England is the *Quem quaeritis* trope.

Performed in Latin for an Easter service in 1042 C.E., this little play depicts the moment in the resurrection story when Mary the mother of Jesus and Mary Magdalene come to Jesus' tomb to find the stone closing the entrance rolled away and an angel stationed outside the now empty tomb.

> *"Whom do you seek (Quem quaeritis) in the sepulcher, Christians?"* the angel asks.
>
> *"Jesus crucified,"* the women answer.
> *"He is not here, he has risen as he said he would; go and announce that he has risen from the sepulchre,"* the angel instructs them.

With that brief interchange begins the record of British theater.

In England, such tropes developed into MORALITY PLAYS and cycles of plays on biblical themes performed in several English cities on Corpus Christi day. In Italy they became *sacre rappresentazioni* (holy performances), first a folk form and then, in the early Renaissance, an art form practiced by quasi-professional playwrights and such skilled poets as ANTONIA PULCI. In Spain similar plays were called *AUTOS SACRE-MENTALES*, and in France miracle plays developed.

Biblical tropes continued to be performed throughout the Renaissance and are still performed today.

Bibliography

Daiches, David. *A Critical History of English Literature.* Vol. 1. New York: The Ronald Press Company, 1960.

Bihari Lal (1559–1663)

A poet in the Hindi tongue of northern India, Bihari wrote a collection of 713 couplets (*dohas*) called *Satsai*. His reputation rests exclusively on that collection. Composed in about 1630, Bihari's work was patronized by the king of Jaipur, Jaya Singh. Unlike most literary production in India during his period, Bihari's jewellike couplets, though occasionally colored with mystical, spiritual, or philosophical elements, are generally secular in content. Many are explicitly erotic, but within a relatively simple palette of subject matter, his verses manage to achieve deep meaning and subtlety and a kaleidoscopic variation on such topics as heroines and their classification and the physical beauties of women. Aside from the poems dealing with amorous topics, others deal with peace of mind, emotional detachment, and tactful public conduct.

Along with TULSĪDĀS, Bihari Lal is one of the two most admired poets of his time period in India. His work draws upon Sanskrit, Prakrit, and Persian predecessors and has been translated into several other Indian tongues. It has also generated an ocean of literary criticism.

biographers of Turkish poets
(16th Century)

Five notable biographers of Turkish poets flourished in the 16th century. First, the poet Sehí Bey (d. 1548) recorded the lives of poets from the founding of the Ottoman Empire until his own lifetime. A civil servant by profession, Sehí Bey titled his work *The Eight Paradises.*

Latífi of Qastamuni (d. ca. 1586) wrote a work of greater importance that treated the same subject matter more fully: *Tezkira* (Memoirs or Dictionary of the poets, 1546). Latífi's work existed only in manuscript until the late 19th century when it was finally printed.

A third work that treats the same earlier poets but that extends the list of poets until later in the 16th century flowed from the pen of Ashiq Çelebî (Pír Muhammed, d. ca. 1568–69). Ashiq Çelebî's discussion of poets contemporary with him is especially useful because he was personally acquainted with many of them.

The fourth of the 16th century's quintette of chroniclers of Turkish poets, Ahdi of Baghdad, only discussed his contemporaries in his *Rosebed of Poets* (1563). When dealing with the lives of poets contemporary with the authors, all four works seem reliable. Though the stories that the first three biographers tell concerning their predecessors' lives may be true, all three of them rely exclusively on traditions that had been handed down through the generations. On the other hand, their discussions of the poems themselves are more reliable since these have survived remarkably intact.

The fifth and most authoritative of the compilers of poets' biographies was named Qinalí-záde Hasan Çelebî. His dictionary of poets contains more than 600 entries and is divided into three sections. The first records the lives and works of Sultans who were also poets. The second treats poets who, though never rulers, were members of the imperial family. The third treats all the other poets Hasan Çelebî had notice of from the earliest times to his own. Although the book is a treasure trove of information about the poets and, particularly, of examples of their works, the longest entry is one devoted to the author's father—a poet of no reputation. Some critics also fault the book for excessive wordiness.

All the biographies of these 16th-century chroniclers share in common the practice of recounting more or less extended anecdotes about the poets' lives. Their successors of the 17th century put less emphasis on biography and more on literary discussion and example.

Bibliography

Gibb, E. J. W. *A History of Ottoman Poetry.* Edited by Edward G. Browne. London: Luzac and Company, 1965.

Birth of Christ, The   Lope de Vega Carpio (1641)

One of LOPE DE VEGA's religious dramas, *The Birth of Christ* opens with Satan and some allegorical figures representing Beauty and two of the DEADLY SINS conferring about God's creation of the world. On the approach of Adam and Eve accompanied by the allegorical characters Grace and Innocence, Satan and his companions hide behind some bushes. Grace and Innocence admire Adam and Eve's happy relationship and discuss God's purposes for the creation.

Following his usual practice, Lope introduces comedy into his serious subject matter. In this case Innocence is the character who plays the comic role. Also following his usual practice, Lope remains totally unconcerned about chronological order. Following the medieval tradition of plays about the creation, immediately after the fall, Satan and his fol-

lowers are exiled to Hell. Lope improves on this story by having the Virgin Mary accomplish this task some four millennia before she is born. Adhering more closely to Scripture, Lope has an angel escort Adam and Eve from Eden. Then the Divine Prince (Christ) and the Celestial Emperor (God) take the stage and hold a conference filled with subtle points of theology. They develop a plan for the redemption of humankind and send the angel Gabriel to Galilee to announce the Messiah's coming.

Despite their confinement in Hell, as the second act opens, Satan, Sin, and Death rejoice that they have conquered the world. To their annoyance and frustration, the allegorical figure of Divine Grace frees World, another allegorical character, from their clutches. To World's delight, Divine Grace announces that the Holy Family has arrived in Bethlehem and salvation is imminent. The scene shifts to Bethlehem where the story of Mary and Joseph's difficulties finding lodging is recounted, and the shepherds are presented joking and singing rough songs about the discomforts of a frosty night. Their fun is interrupted by an angel announcing Jesus' birth, and the shepherds hurry off in search of the child.

In the third and last act, the shepherds report on their visit to the mother and child at the manger, and Gypsies and Africans perform a dance (another of Lope's fanciful embellishments). Following the dance, the wise men appear bearing gifts and adoring the baby Jesus, and the play ends.

Bittalnāth   (Vitthalnath) (ca. 1515–1588)

A poet and singer of Hindi songs dedicated to the Hindu deity Krishna, Bittalnāth wrote a body of work that became linked with the routines of tending Krishna's idol. His poems are also associated with the Hindi versions of the traditions of BHAKTI (devotional reform) and the temporary secularization of Indian religion in the 16th and 17th centuries. Although based in popular rather than in high culture, Bittalnāth 's assertion of the secular and the socially new in India resembled parallel though unrelated developments in European Renaissance culture at about the same time. Together with other contemporary poets, Bittalnāth contributed to creating one of the earliest identifiable genres of poetic and musical literature in the then developing Hindi language.

blank verse

A line of blank verse typically contains 10 syllables. The first syllable of each foot receives a light stress and the second a heavier one. (See POETIC METER.) Within that general framework, individual feet of the line may depart from the norm to achieve variety, and line length may also vary by a syllable or two. Blank verse does not rhyme.

HENRY HOWARD, EARL OF SURREY (1517–47) invented blank verse as an unrhymed English equivalent for the dactylic hexameter line of ancient Greek and Latin for his translations from VIRGIL's *Aeneid.* Howard essentially took Chaucer's iambic pentameter line and deleted the rhyme. In his continuing experimentation with the line, Howard revealed to his contemporaries the musical qualities of spoken, unrhymed, English verse. Blank verse became the vehicle for some of the most celebrated and enduring monuments of English letters, including the plays of SHAKESPEARE and JOHN MILTON's EPIC poem, *PARADISE LOST.*

Boccaccio, Giovanni (1313–1375)

A friend and contemporary of the Italian poet FRANCESCO PETRARCA (PETRARCH), Boccaccio is a transitional figure between the Middle Ages and the Renaissance. Whereas the courtly literature of the medieval period had been principally about and addressed to the aristocracy, Boccaccio's sometimes extremely innovative literature often focuses on the common people—the tradespeople and the peasantry. In this way and in others, his work anticipates the literature of the next several centuries.

The illegitimate son of a tradesman of Certaldo and a Parisian adventuress, Boccaccio for a time took his father's advice and studied canon law. But the young man had vowed at the tomb of VIRGIL to devote his life to literary pursuits. This promise, after a brief interlude in the banking business in Naples, he kept. He was among the very earliest to embrace the classical studies that we associate with HUMANISM, and he proved pivotal in their development. When he and Petrarch agreed to study Greek, Boccaccio in fact did so while Petrarch merely carried a Greek copy of Homer in his saddlebags, hoping that some day he would acquire the skill to read it. As an artist, nevertheless, and without rancor Boccaccio considered himself inferior to both DANTE and Petrarch. His self-described greatest accomplishment was securing a professorship of Greek for Leontius Pilatus—the man from whom Boccaccio had himself learned to read the language.

The work for which the literary world principally remembers Boccaccio is his *Decameron* (1348–51). A framework tale addressed to an audience of women, the story begins with a graphic description of the ravages in Florence of the bubonic plague of 1348. At the Florentine church of Santa Maria Novella, a group of seven well-to-do young women agree to leave the plague-stricken city in the company of a group of three equally wealthy young men—the as yet Platonic lovers of three of the women. Once arrived with a procession of servants at a country estate, they agree to pass the time by telling stories—a story each for each of 10 days. Every morning, a member of the group serves as the ruler. The ruler either allows free rein or picks the topic and chooses the first teller, and the stories begin. The eight assigned topics cover a wide range of possibilities: the influence of fortune, the force of will power, stories of love with happy or tragic outcomes, quick-witted responses that get the speaker out of trouble, women who trick men and men who trick men, and, on the last day, examples of magnanimity.

Whatever the topic, many of the tales are about passion and its consequences, and they are told in a manner that leaves no maiden's cheek unblushing nor any illusion dear to the Middle Ages unpunctured. The story of the canonization of the profligate Ser Ciappelletto makes a mockery of confession, the last rites, and sainthood itself. Priests, monks, and the veneration of relics fare no better. The thoughtlessness and cruelty of lovers, marriage, informal bigamy, the falsity of knightly ideals, and the gullibility of peasants—all are treated with scornful sarcasm as the young people amuse themselves with stories that in other circumstances would have been considered outrageous. Yet Boccaccio balances this satirical attack on the outmoded ideals of a passing age with the beauty of his brief introductions to each day's activities. Implicit in the pages of the *Decameron* one finds not only the opening chapter of Renaissance imaginative fiction, but one also finds the original of both the modern short story and the modern novel. The stories are not simply a laundry list of tales. They interact. They reveal the personalities of their narrators. Their tellers sometimes complement and sometimes parody each other. Overall, the point of view expressed is that of the rising merchant classes to which Boccaccio himself belonged.

Also presaging Renaissance interest in the classics was the Latin work that Boccaccio completed, the *Genealogy of the Gods of the Gentiles* (*Genealogia deorum gentilium*), an encyclopedic work about classical mythology that had been begun by Boccaccio's friend and mentor, Paolo da Perugia, the royal librarian at Naples. In his *Filostrato* (ca. 1335), Boccaccio tells the story of Troilus and Cressida that is later retold by both Chaucer and SHAKESPEARE in England. An Italian prose epic, the *Filocolo* (ca. 1336) continues to blend Boccaccio's interest in classical literature with themes from the Middle Ages. Four or five years later, his *Thesiad of the Wedding of Emilia* (*Teseida delle nozze d'Emelia*) appeared. Continuing a story told by the Roman poet Statius in his *Thebiad,* this work in Italian verse stanzas provided both rather pedantic explanations of classical material for Boccaccio's readers and, more important, the model that would be followed by many Renaissance writers of verse epic from LUIGI PULCI, ARETINO, ARIOSTO, and TASSO in Italy to EDMUND SPENSER in England. Chaucer again drew from this work for the story of *The Knight's Tale* and for episodes in other works.

Boccaccio's simultaneous classicizing and modernizing continued in his later works. His *Comedy of the Florentine Nymphs* (*Commedia delle ninfe fiorentine, 1341–42*) alludes to and borrows from Dante while resurrecting the classical pastoral and combining with it Christian motifs. Another pastoral work, *Ninfale Fiesoleano* (The nymphs of Fiesole, 1344–46) recounts in octave stanzas a tragic love story in a pre-Christian rural setting. It also presents Boccaccio's own mythic account of the founding of the town of Fiesole. In assimilating the classical pastoral ideal of innocent nymphs and shepherds living happily in a rural landscape to the idea of an urban civil society that depends for the quality of its life upon its cultured citizenry, it anticipates yet another favorite theme of the Renaissance. Likewise, his terza-rima *Amorous Vision* (*Amorosa Visione, 1342–43*) looks backward to the model of the medieval dream vision a la Dante and employs the popular notion begun by Petrarch of a series of *triumphs* or allegorical parades of figures like Love, Glory, Love, Wealth, and Fortune.

In his *Elegia di madonna Fiammetta* (Elegy of Lady Fiammetta, 1343–44), Boccaccio achieves perhaps the best of his shorter works. He has Fiammetta tell her own heartrending story, and the incidents of the tale trigger interior monologues that achieve the kind of psychological realism that many modern writers strive for. For some Renaissance women writers, this work provided a useful model. The French writer, HÉLISENNE DE CRENNE partly retells and adapts the story to her own purposes.

Generally, a defender of women, in his *Corbaccio* (*Ugly Crow,* or *Coarse person,* after 1354) Boccaccio seems to stray into misogyny as he bitterly rings changes on a tale from the *Decameron* to satirize a woman who rejects a man's advances. Some readers defend the author by suggesting the tale's misogyny ironically represents the lover's viewpoint rather than that of Boccaccio.

In addition to the *Genealogy of the Gods* . . . discussed above, Boccaccio wrote a number of other works in Latin that proved influential among Renaissance writers in a variety of ways. His Latin song celebrating life in the country (*Bucolicum Carmen,* ca. 1372) revived the classical genre of the ECLOGUE, thereafter used by many Renaissance writers including EDMUND SPENSER in his *Shepherd's Calendar* (1579). He wrote an influential history of the *Fates of Illustrious Men* (*De casibus virorum illustrium,* 1355–73) and another about *Famous Women: De mulieribus claris* (1361). The latter became a central document in and a model for other works that contributed to the ongoing debate about the education of women, the worth of women, and the dignity of women that continues into the present moment. Also in Latin he penned a biography of Petrarch and a commentary on Dante. Along with those two great Tuscan predecessors, after his death posterity elevated Boccaccio to a place among the *Three Crowns—Le tre corone*—of Italian letters.

Bibliography

Boccaccio, Giovanni. *The Decameron.* Translated by G. H. McWilliam. London and New York: Penguin, 2nd ed., 1995

———. *Giovanni Boccaccio, the Life of Dante.* Translated by Vincenzo Zin Bollettino. New York: Garland, 1990.

———. *The Elegy of Madonna Fiametta sent by her to Women in Love.* Translated by Roberta L. Payne and Alexandra Hennessey Olsen. New York: Peter Lang, ca. 1992.

———. *Famous Women: De mulieribus claris.* English and Latin. Translated by Virginia Brown. Cambridge, Mass.: Harvard University Press, 2003.

———. *Nymphs of Fiesole.* Translated by Joseph Tusiani. Rutherford, Md.: Fairleigh Dickensen University Press, 1971.

Boethius (Ancius Manlius Severinus Boethius) (480–524 or 525 C.E.)

Also known to the Roman Catholic hagiarchy as Saint Severinus Boethius, Boethius was a vastly influential Roman polymath and statesman of the early Middle Ages. Though he wrote on many subjects including music, mathematics, philosophy, and theology, his translations of and commentaries on the work of ancient Greek logicians, particularly, helped define medieval, scholastic thinking and underpinned a good deal of church doctrine during the Middle Ages.

With the rise of Renaissance HUMANISM, however, with its new capacity for textual criticism and for restoring ancient texts to a condition closer to their originals than the ones with which Boethius had apparently worked, some humanists began to call into question Boethius's interpretations of classical Greek thought. LORENZO VALLA even doubted Boethius's status as a Christian. Valla argued that Boethius had been a pagan.

After careful consideration of all the available evidence, however, the Roman Catholic Church has taken the official position that Boethius was indeed a practicing Christian and in 1823 officially confirmed the long-standing practice in the city of Pavia, in whose cathedral he is likely buried, of honoring Boethius as a saint on October 23.

Boethius's work, particularly his *Consolation of Philosophy,* written in prison while he awaited execution by clubbing on trumped-up charges of embezzlement, continued to exercise important literary influence throughout the Renaissance and beyond.

Bibliography

Boethius. *The Consolation of Philosophy.* Translated by P. G. Walsh. Oxford and New York: Oxford University Press, 1999.

———. *The Consolation of Philosophy.* Translated by Richard H. Green. Mineola, N.Y.: Dover, 2002.

Herberman, Charles G., et al. *The Catholic Encyclopedia.* Volume 2. New York: The Encyclopedia Press, 1913.

Böhme, Jakob (1575–1624)

A German shoemaker who also became a lay theologian, Böhme circulated his first literary effort, *Aurora,* in manuscript among his fellow townspeople of Görlitz and published it in 1612. His work, which fuses Scripture and the pseudoscience of alchemy, so offended both a Lutheran pastor and the Görlitz town council that the council members forbade his ever writing anything again.

For six years Böhme heeded their injunction, but he felt driven to resume writing. In 1618 there appeared from the press his treatise *Von den drei Prinzipipien des Gottlichen Wesens* (*On the three principles of God's being*). That work was followed by: *On the Signs of Things* (*De Signatura rerum,* 1622), *A Great Mystery* (*Mysterium Magnum,* 1622–23), *Der Weg zu Christo* (*The way to Christ,* 1624), and finally the work reappeared that in 1612 had so offended his neighbors, *Aurora* (1634). Ekhard Bernstein reports Böhme to have believed that studying nature leads to understanding both "God's greatness . . . [and] the secrets of the universe."

Böhme's theology was influential in his own time, particularly among mystics. His later influence was felt among the German Romantic poets such as Fichte and Schilling and such philosophers as Spinoza and Hegel. His works continued appearing in translation in France and in England, where Isaac Newton and others studied them. They were also translated in Russia and, eventually, in the United States, where Ralph Waldo Emerson became interested in his thinking. Böhme believed that humanity, considered as a unit, is an androgynous being whose union the Virgin Mary symbolizes. Quasi-religious sects such as the Philadelphians (those believing in brotherly love) were also based on Böhme's teachings.

Bibliography

Böhme, Jakob. *Jacob Boehme's The Way to Christ.* Translated by John Joseph Stoudt. Westport, Conn.: The Greenwood Press, 1979.

———. *The Divine Couple: selections from the Mystical–alchemical treatises of Jacob Boehme and Disciples.* St. Paul, Minn.: Grailstone Press, 2001.

Bernstein, Eckhard. "Böhme, Jakob." In *Encyclopedia of the Renaissance.* Vol. 1, edited by Paul F. Grendler, 245. New York: Scribners, 1999.

Boiardo, Matteo Maria (1434–1494)

The count of Scandiano, Boiardo received his education in Ferrara and entered the service of the dukes of the Este family in that city. With Dukes Borso and Ercole I, he was linked closely by ties of friendship as well as by feudal obligation. In 1479 he married Taddea dei Gonzaga, daughter of the count of Novellara. On the Estes' behalf, Boiardo served both as a diplomat and as the military governor, first, of Modena in 1481 and then, from 1487 until his death, of Reggio Emilia. As a warrior and regional administrator, Boiardo enjoyed a reputation as a model of chivalrous behavior and as a merciful judge. He opposed capital punishment and did his best to govern without resorting to it.

Boiardo's best-remembered work, ORLANDO INNAMORATO, continues threads of the medieval *Chanson de Roland* by recounting in rhymed, eight-line stanzas the adventures and death of Charlemagne's nephew Roland. Regrettably Boiardo died before completing the masterwork, whose composition paid a courtly compliment to his patrons of the Este family. The incomplete work invited continuations by later authors, and many versions—some serious, some comic, and some satirical parodies—appeared in Italy, Spain, and England during the next two centuries.

Boiardo also wrote a number of lesser works. These include translations of *The Lives of Illustrious Men* by the Roman Cornelius Nepos; of Xenophon's Greek work, *The Education of Cyrus;* and of Riccobaldo's Latin *History of the Roman Empire.* These translations are all dedicated to the Este family, and in them Boiardo, with the confidence in the power of education that typified the spirit of HUMANISM, asserts the ability of history to teach good behavior and model good government. In addition, Boiardo translated *The Golden Ass* of the Roman Lucius Apuleius, and, from the Greek, Herodotus's *History of the Peloponnesian Wars.*

Composing poetry first in Latin (1460s and '70s) and later in Italian, Boiardo began his career with Latin verses praising the Este family. In Latin he also wrote some pastorals and some epigrams. In 1477 his *Amorum libri tres* (Three books on love) appeared in Italian. Modeled on the work of PETRARCH, this autobiographical collection of 180 poems explores the snares and pitfalls of love. These were followed in 1482–83 by 10 Italian ECLOGUEs, his *Pastorale,* in which shepherds discuss politics and personal matters. Finally, for production at the Este court in 1491, Boiardo wrote an Italian version of a classical comedy, *Il Timone* (Timon).

Bibliography

Boiardo, Matteo Maria. *Amorum Libri: The Lyric Poems of Matteo Maria Boiardo.* Translated by Andrea di Tommaso. Binghamton, N.Y.: Medieval and Renaissance Texts and Studies, State University of New York at Binghamton, 1993.

———. *Orlando Innamorato.* Translated by Charles S. Ross. West Lafayette, Ind.: Parlor Press, 2004.

Cavallo, Jo Ann. *Boiardo's Orlando innamorato: An Ethics of Desire.* Rutherford, N.J.: Rutgers University Press, 1993.

Boleyn, Anne (1504–1536)

Daughter of Sir Thomas Boleyn and Elizabeth Howard, Anne Boleyn secretly married Henry VIII in January 1533 before his divorce from Catherine of Aragon had become official. In May of the same year, Archbishop Cranmer approved Anne as Henry's legal spouse, and she was crowned queen of England. In September she gave birth to England's future queen, ELIZABETH I. Boleyn's only male child was stillborn in January 1536. On May 2 of that year, Henry had her arrested on charges of incest with her brother, Lord Rochford, and adultery with four commoners. After a secret commission investigated the charges, she and all the men were tried and convicted of high treason and condemned to death. Anne Boleyn's uncle, the third duke of Norfolk, Thomas Howard, pronounced her verdict. She was beheaded in the Tower of London on May 19, 1536. On May 30 Henry took Jane Seymour as his third wife.

In addition to being considered by many the proximate cause of the establishment of the Anglican Church with England's ruler at its head rather than the pope, Anne Boleyn also inspired SIR THOMAS WYATT's famous ENGLISH SONNET "Whoso list [wishes] to hunt, I know where is an hind [a deer] . . ."—an imitation and partial translation of a sonnet by PETRARCH. In his version Wyatt, who was himself one of Anne Boleyn's admirers, complains that the deer (which stands for Anne) wears a necklace of diamonds that spells out, first, the Latin phrase, *"noli me tangere"* (let no one touch me), followed by "for Caesar's [Henry's] I am." Anne Boleyn's tragic story has many times been recounted in history, fiction, opera, and folk song. Her ghost is said to stalk the Tower of London at midnight "with her head tucked underneath her arm."

Bibliography

Warnicke, Retha M. *The Rise and Fall of Anne Boleyn: Family Politics at the Court of Henry VIII.* New York: Cambridge University Press, 1989.

Book of the Courtier, The Baldassare Castiglione (1528)

Translated from Italian into English by SIR THOMAS HOBY as *The Book of the Courtier,* CASTIGLIONE'S *Il cortegiano,* which had been in preparation for over a decade, appeared in Venice in 1528 and became one of the most influential books of the European Renaissance. It follows PLATO as a model for the structure of its dialogues and nods both to Plato and CICERO in its choice of contemporary persons who will present points of view identifiable in many cases with their own. Despite these parallels *The Book of the Courtier* is nonetheless a stunningly original work. It aims to establish an ideal standard of behavior in aristocratic society while at the same time examining many issues of contemporary interest—PLATONIC LOVE, whether republics or autocratic states are better, the arts of painting and sculpture, the ideal consort for the ideal courtier, and so on.

The fiction of the work brings together a distinguished company of notable Italians and many of Castiglione's friends (some of whom had since died) at the court of Guidobaldo da Montefeltro, the duke of Urbino, in the year 1506. Borrowing a device from Plato's *Symposium,* Castiglione pretends that the remarks he assigns to various speakers are being reported to him after his return to Urbino from England, where he in fact accepted the Order of the Garter on his duke's behalf and where he himself was knighted (1506).

Castiglione divides his work into four books prefaced by an introductory letter. In the first book, the members of the company address the attributes of the perfect courtier: Of noble rank, he must be dignified, a skilled warrior, knowledgeable and adept in the arts and humanities, temperate, physically fit, graceful, and capable of achieving all he does with apparent ease.

Among the issues also considered in the first book appears the ongoing debate concerning the question of the Italian language (see ITALIAN LANGUAGE, THE ISSUE OF). In his introductory letter Castiglione defends his decision to use the vernacular language instead of Latin, and in the text a discourse occurs that ponders which of many Italian dialects to employ. PIETRO BEMBO had in real life insisted on preserving 14th-century Tuscan as a literary standard for 16th-century writers. A corollary of Bembo's position implied the artificial preservation in writing of many usages no longer current in the spoken language. Tactfully demurring from Bembo's view—which nonetheless receives a lucid exposition by one of the speakers—Castiglione suggested in his introductory letter that good manners require freedom from all affectation. That freedom is an absolute requisite for whatever the perfect courtier might do. It thus seemed strange to Castiglione to employ words in writing that people would avoid in conversation. In the body of the text he has the Florentine exile Giuliano de' Medici, duke of Nemours, agree, remarking that he would never use words of Petrarch and Boccaccio that were not current in good society.

The second book considers the ways a courtier can gracefully exhibit his attributes. Among these, the company concurs in approving correct behavior and easy, amusing conversation, with many entertaining examples of the latter.

The third book conducts, in the context of love and of identifying the attributes of a proper consort for the ideal courtier, an examination of the virtues of women. Although women are present and participate as questioners or moderators, it is the men who argue the various points of view presented. Nonetheless, the discussion defends women against the false accusations of the antifeminist tradition.

The last book treats the qualities of the courtier as a counselor of his overlord. This section stresses the necessity for speaking the truth as opposed to flattering and for the demonstration of accomplishments that will win a prince's confidence. This discussion flows into one that considers the comparative advantages of monarchies and republics. Finally, the conversation turns once more to the subject of love and how an aging courtier should conduct himself in a love relationship. The answer proposed involves PLATONIC LOVE. In a courtly compliment perhaps barbed with a good-natured joke, Castiglione assigns the lion's share of this genuinely moving discourse to Cardinal Pietro Bembo. As the cardinal explains to the company the steps by which a lover rises from the admiration of a beloved's physical attributes to an appreciation of her mental and moral qualities and finally to the contemplation of heavenly beauties and ideality itself, he illustrates his own discussion by becoming spellbound with the contemplation of the heavenly ideal. One of the women present returns him to Earth by gently plucking at his garment.

The Book of the Courtier was widely translated and imitated throughout Europe and was for years consulted by many as a guide to conduct. It also spawned some uncomplimentary parodies. PIETRO ARETINO's experience of court life as a lackey in Rome had convinced him that courtiers were a pack of flattering scoundrels who contemptuously lived on the backs of their servants and regularly practiced every conceivable vice. He therefore responded to Castiglione with *La cortegiana* (The courtesan or harlot), a bitter SATIRE that remorselessly exposes the vice and corruption of his contemporary aristocratic and papal courts.

Bibliography

Castiglione, Baldassare. *The Book of the Courtier: The* [Charles] *Singleton Translation.* Edited by Daniel Javitch. New York: W. W. Norton, 2002.

Woodhouse, J. R. *Baldesar Castiglione: A Reassessment of the Courtier.* Edinburgh: Edinburgh University Press, 1978.

Bording, Anders (1619–1677)

Anders Bording was the first writer to publish a regular news magazine in Denmark. His monthly periodical, *The Danish Mercury,* provided its readers with reports about matters of current interest. Moreover, it reported the monthly news in verse. Until well into the 19th century, European readers generally preferred to read verse instead of prose. The 19th-century English poet, Lord Byron, repressed his personal preference for prose writing because he found a wider and more profitable audience for verse. Bording's 17th-century publication acknowledged his Danish Renaissance readership's preference for poetry while at the same time meeting their interest in the news of the moment.

Boscán Almogaver, Juan (1490–1542)

A founding figure of the literary Renaissance in Spain, Juan Boscán tells us that he had been devoted to poetry since he was very young. Though he was himself a Catalonian aristocrat of Barcelona, at first he preferred writing verse in Castilian Spanish. The surviving examples of his earliest poems reflect the style of the Spanish verse of the 15th century. In 1526, however, on a visit to Grenada he became acquainted with Andrea Navagiero, the Venetian ambassador to the court of Charles V, who also happened to be in Granada. Navagiero, Boscán reports, challenged him to try his hand at verse forms "used by good Italian authors."

Taking up the challenge, Boscán at first found adapting Italian meters to Spanish difficult, but feeling that his work improved with practice, he continued writing "with increasing zeal." He also challenged his good friend GARCILASO DE LA VEGA to try his hand as well. The results of their efforts forever altered the direction of Spanish literature.

Boscán followed PETRARCH by bringing the rhyme structure of the ITALIAN SONNET into Castilian Spanish, which already employed the 11-syllable (hendecasyllabic) line. He also adapted to Spanish the freer structure of Petrarch's odes (*canzoni*), introduced *terza rima* (DANTE's rhyme scheme in the *Divine Comedy*), the eight-line rhyming stanza of ARIOSTO, and blank verse. Unlike Petrarch, whose songbook documents the trials of unrequited love, Boscán celebrates the domestic joys of his happy married life. His blank verse *Leandro* (Leander)—based on Musæus's Greek *Hero and Leander*—is almost 3000 lines long.

An early Spanish devotee of HUMANISM, Boscán's mastery of Greek also enabled him to translate a tragedy of EURIPIDES. This work, though licensed for publication, never appeared in print and has not been found. Though he published some of his translations, none of Boscán's original work appeared during his lifetime. He wrote, as he reports in a celebrated letter to the duchess of Soma, "to solace such faculties as I have and to go less heavily through . . . life." His wife published her deceased husband's writings in 1543 together with some of Garcilaso de la Vegas's work in four books. The first contains Boscán's pre-Italianate works. The second and third include his adaptations of the Italian mode to Spanish, his *Leandro,* and an allegory describing the courts of Love and of Jealousy. The fourth includes Garcilaso de la Vegas's work.

One of Boscán's most important contributions to Spanish Renaissance letters was his translation of BALDASSARE CASTIGLIONE's THE BOOK OF THE COURTIER. Castiglione served as Pope Clement VII's ambassador to Spain from 1525 until his death in 1529. While there, Castiglione prepared his manuscript for its Venetian publication in 1528. Castiglione himself may have given Garcilaso de la Vega a copy soon after its appearance. Garcilaso, in turn, sent his copy to Boscán together with a request that he translate it. Boscán complied, publishing the work in 1534 despite his opinion that translation is "a low vanity, beseeming men of little knowledge."

Bibliography

Boscán, Juan, and Garcilaso de la Vega. *Obras completas.* Edited by Carlos Claveria Laguarda. Madrid: Turner, 1995.

Darst, David H. *Juan Boscán.* Boston: Twayne Publishers, 1978.

Ticknor, George. *History of Spanish Literature.* New York: Gordian Press, 1965.

Botero, Giovanni (1544–1617)

A writer on government and political theory, Botero, like all Renaissance writers about affairs of state, was influenced by the ideas of NICCOLÒ MACHIAVELLI. Botero, however, took issue with Machiavelli and had original advice for the rulers of absolute monarchies. Botero perceived that the world was changing. He saw that with the rise of the merchant classes and the emergence of military tactics based on a wide range of new and more destructive weaponry, princes who wished to preserve their domains needed new governmental structures. They required professional civil servants, an efficient system of direct taxation that bypassed popular legislative assemblies, and careful, long-range military planning. Botero also supported the power of the Roman Catholic Church and the suppression of all other sects and religions. He anticipated modern political science by considering factors that could be quantified and measured, like demographics. Botero explored these topics in two influential works: *Della Ragion di stato* (On the reason of state, 1589) and *Delle cause della grandezza e magnificenza delle città* (On the causes of the greatness and magnificence of cities, 1606).

He was also the first political theorist to look beyond local and regional governments to consider the then developing system of European nations with the new capacity to project their power around the globe. In this context, he prepared his Universal reports (*Relazioni universali*) that appeared in installments between 1591 and 1596. This was a reference guide to the politics, geography, and ethnography of the known world. It included Asia and the New World as well as Europe and the Old World, and European leaders used his work heavily throughout the following century.

Bibliography

Birely, Robert. "Giovanni Botero," *The Counter Reformation Prince: Anti-Machiavellianism; or Catholic Statecraft in Early Modern Europe*. Chapel Hill, N.C.: University of North Carolina Press, 1990.

Botero, Giovanni. *The Reason of State and The Greatness of Cities*. Respectively translated by P. J. Waley and D. P. Waley and by Robert Peterson. London and New Haven, Conn.: Yale University Press, 1956.

Bourchier, John, Lord Berners
(1467–1533)

A close friend of King Henry VIII of England, Bourchier had early been a partisan of that king's father, Henry, then duke of Richmond, who eventually became England's King Henry VII. Thus closely and amicably connected with the throne, Bourchier enjoyed a distinguished career as a diplomat, a tourist, a soldier, a sometime imperfect linguist, and a translator. In the last capacity he made his most memorable contributions to the literature of the British Renaissance.

Almost singlehandedly Bourchier made the reading of history and historical romance a popular enterprise in 16th-century England. In 1534 he translated and published in English a French version of a Spanish translation of the originally Latin work of the Roman Emperor Marcus Aurelius, *The Golden Book of Marcus Aurelius*. In the same year he published an English version of the historical romance *Huon of Bordeaux*. This work belonged to the same cycle of romances concerning the court of Charlemagne as did the medieval French CHIVALRIC EPIC *The Song of Roland*—a poem that inspired many verse continuations in several languages during the Renaissance.

Soon after in a similar vein, Bourchier translated from French *Arthur of Little Britain* and from Spanish a romance by Diego de San Pedro, *The Castle of Love*. Principally, however, literary history remembers Bourchier for his masterpiece, his translation of the *Chronicles* of the Medieval Flemish historian Jean Froissart (ca. 1333–ca. 1405). Froissart had been consumed by his interest in the story of the wars between England and France that had been fought from 1326 until 1400. He traveled throughout France and England collecting materials for his history of those wars.

Bourchier's translation of Froissart was likely a principal source for WILLIAM SHAKESPEARE's history play, *Richard II*.

Bibliography

Froissart, Jean. *The Chronicles of England, France, Spain, and Other Places Adjoining*. Translated by John Bourchier. Edited by G. C. Macaulay. New York: Limited Editions Club, 1959.

Brant, Sebastian   (1458–1521)

A German HUMANIST from Strasbourg, Brant lived and worked in Basel until 1501 when that city opted to withdraw from the German Empire and join the Swiss Confederation. Brant achieved lasting literary fame with his poem, *Das Narrenschiff* (*The ship of fools*, 1494). The governing idea of this work is that a kind of Noah's Ark filled with fools of every description sets out on a voyage to the land of Narragonia—Foolsland. Like all writers of SATIRE, Brant has as his objective the moral improvement of the vicious and foolish. He hopes that some of his readers will recognize themselves among the irate, the gluttonous, the adulterous, the covetous, the vain, and the blasphemous who populate the ship. Brant hopes that others will perceive themselves in the portraits that he paints of passengers guilty of lesser folly: of indulgent parents, for instance, or of obsessed collectors of such material goods as books and paintings, and of those who put off until tomorrow what needs doing today. If such persons do recognize themselves, they will be led by their embarrassed recognition of their particular brand of folly to reform their ways—or at least so the author hoped.

Beautifully printed with high quality woodcuts by talented artists, Brant's 112-chapter work became an instant best-seller. To make it more accessible to the educated elite of Europe, Jacob Locher translated it in 1497 from German into Latin with the title *Stultifera naves*. *The Ship of Fools* initiated a long tradition of fools' literature. This tradition included, for example, ERASMUS'S *PRAISE OF FOLLY*. Widely translated into European vernacular tongues, *The Ship of Fools* has never been out of print, and it continues to inspire imitations. Motion pictures have been based on it, and its title has been repeatedly borrowed.

The overwhelming success of *The Ship of Fools* has obscured the memory of Brant's other important contributions to European letters. He was a tireless editor who had a hand in an estimated third of the works that appeared from the presses of Basel in the last 25 years of the 15th century. In 1498 he also published a volume of his own Latin poems. After his return to his native Strasbourg in the first year of the 16th century, he continued his work as author and editor. He edited Virgil and Terrence in Latin and wrote histories in German. He was a distinguished jurist who occupied Strasbourg's highest administrative offices and who also served as an imperial councilor and diplomat.

Bibliography

Brant, Sebastian. *The Shyp of Fooles*. Translated by Alexander Barclay. Edited by Phyllis C. Robinson. 1509. Reprint, Seal Harbor, Me.: High Loft, 1983.

broadside ballads

From at least medieval times, folk poets had written ballads to be sung to familiar tunes and sold on the street corners of English towns. While the medieval variety had been hand lettered or printed by means of wood blocks, the advent of the printing press had somewhat eased the labors of the many "ballad mongers" who made or supplemented a living in this fashion.

In the 16th and 17th centuries, doggerel poems were written on many subjects of popular interest. These might include murders, complaints about marital woes, events regarded as supernatural, politics, the births of monstrously malformed infants, or news from the front lines of the war of the moment. They might equally well address falling in love or encourage godly living or make libelous remarks about notable persons. In their topicality, in short, the ballads and ballad makers filled the niches occupied by 21st-century television news broadcasters, disc jockeys, television evangelists, talk-show hosts, and the composers of rap and rock lyrics. In fact, as news books became popular during the reign of ELIZABETH I, several ballad writers became the first English journalists.

Then as now, the political establishment frequently coopted the balladeers to produce political and religious propaganda and sway public opinion. This proved especially true under the reigns of the pre-Elizabethan Tudor monarchs who used the balladeers to support either the Anglican or the Roman Catholic establishments. Henry VIII and Edward Seymour, the first duke of Somerset and Protector of England during the minority of Henry's heir, Edward VI, both employed a famous Protestant balladeer, Gray of Reading, to produce ballads supporting the Anglican establishment. Another, William Birch, produced *A song between the Queen's Majesty and England* that casts *Bessy* (Elizabeth I) and *England* as lovers. The ballad recounts the difficulties Elizabeth bore while a princess sometimes fearing for her life. Hearing about Elizabeth's imprisonment in the tower and her subsequent house arrest, England says: "Why, dear Lady, I trow [trust], / Those madmen did not know / That ye were daughter unto King Harry, / and a princess of birth, / One of the noblest on earth, / And sister unto Queen Mary." The message is that those responsible can plead ignorance.

Bessy responds: "Yes, yet I must forgive / All such as do live, / If they will hereafter amend. . . ." The message: The queen is willing to let bygones be bygones. A somewhat more chilling message is implicit in the next lines, however, in which the queen asks God to bless those no longer here. Bessy will not balk at the exercise of power.

The name *broadside* alludes to the large sheet of paper on which the ballads were printed in black-letter type. In addition to the words of the verse and the name of the tune to which the ballad should be sung, a rough woodcut drawing often headed the sheet to attract the eyes of potential customers. In his *Microcosmography*, JOHN EARLE characterizes the broadside balladeers as "pot-poets" inspired by "thin drink" to compose verses that "go out in single sheets, and are chanted from market to market to a vile tune and a worse throat, whilst the poor country wench melts like her butter to hear them." (See CHARACTER WRITING.)

Other portrayals of broadside balladeers made their way into literature. SHAKESPEARE's Autolycus from *The Winter's Tale* (IV, iii) both sings ballads and offers them for sale. In BEN JONSON's BART-HOLEMEW FAIR a balladeer distracts a crowd while his confederate picks their pockets.

Some balladeers rose above John Earle's expectations for them. One notable example is THOMAS DELONEY who can fairly lay claim to having been England's first professional man of letters and novelist. Some ballads, moreover, were genuinely charming and survive in the performance repertoire today. *Lady Greensleeves* is perhaps the most notable example.

Bibliography

Preston, Cathy Lynn, and Michael J. Preston, eds. *The Other Print Tradition: Essays on Chapbooks, Broadsides and Related Ephemera*. New York: Garland, 1995.

Broken Heart, The John Ford (1633)

The possibility exists that *The Broken Heart* drew some of its inspiration from the real and complex love lives of some famous persons. These included SIR PHILIP SIDNEY and Penelope Devereaux, Lady Rich, the woman he calls *Stella* in his SONNETS. The play may also allude to the husband of her unhappy marriage, Robert, Lord Rich, and to the man whose mistress Devereaux–Rich became and remained until she shocked England by marrying him after her divorce from Rich. Her lover was Charles Blount, Lord Mountjoy and earl of Devonshire. No very firm evidence supports the direct connection between the play and these people. Some critics point to rough parallels between the play and the lives. Also, FORD's early poem, *Fame's Memorial*, was an ELEGY on the death of Charles Blount. This poem revealed a great deal of sympathy for Blount and his wife. Ford seems to have considered them highly principled and moral if unconventional.

In *The Broken Heart*, a young Spartan, Orgilus, has been betrothed to his beloved Penthea. Her father's untimely death, however, has left her fate in the hands of her brother Ithocles. Ithocles forces Penthea to marry Bassanes, an older man who becomes insanely jealous of his young wife. He bricks up windows lest she be seen from the street and at the height of his distraction publicly accuses Penthea and her brother of incest. Penthea, for her part, carefully observes her unwilling marriage vows, preserving her and Bassanes's honor although she still loves Orgilus.

Ithocles comes to regret his hasty and ill-advised decision to break the match his father had arranged for Penthea, and he attempts to win Orgilus's friendship. Orgilus pretends that Ithocles has succeeded.

In the meantime, Ithocles falls in love with the Spartan princess, Calantha, and she with him, and late in the play, her father, Amyclas the king, agrees to her request that she and Ithocles be allowed to marry despite the fact that arrangements were going forward to have her wed Nearchus, prince of Argos.

Penthea, who has patiently and honorably borne all her adversity, is at last driven insane by Bassanes's groundless jealousy, by her own conviction that by marrying Bassanes when she was betrothed to another she has become an adulteress, and by her unrequited love for Orgilus. Finally she stops eating and sleeping and starves herself to death. Her shrouded body is carried onstage seated in a chair. Orgilus sets chairs to either side of her corpse and invites Ithocles to sit and grieve with him. When Ithocles does so, he discovers that his chair is a mechanical trap that holds him motionless. Orgilus tells Ithocles that he intends to kill him to avenge Penthea's death. Ithocles encourages Orgilus to do so, and Orgilus stabs him twice—the second time to shorten Ithocles's agony.

In the final act, the princess Calantha, dressed in bridal finery and dancing at her wedding party, is three times interrupted with bad news. Her father Amyclas has died. News comes of Penthea's death, and finally Orgilus himself informs Calantha of Ithocles's murder. In her distraction, Calantha continues dancing as she absorbs the horror. Now queen of Sparta, Calantha condemns Orgilus to death and allows him to choose the manner of execution and his executioner. He elects to die by bleeding, opens one of his own veins on stage, and has Bassanes open another.

In the last scene of the play, Calantha provides for the future of Sparta by naming Nearchus her successor, makes wise arrangements for the welfare of faithful retainers, kisses the cold lips of Ithocles's corpse, and dies of a broken heart. The events of the last act fulfill the prophecy of the Oracle at Delphi as interpreted by another character, the philosopher Tecnicus. Tecnicus predicted that revenge would "prove its own executioner" and that "a lifeless trunk" would "wed a broken heart."

In this play as in others, Ford explores the psychological consequences of several subcategories of lovers' melancholy, following the symptoms and causes explored by ROBERT BURTON in his ANATOMY OF MELANCHOLY (1621). The play memorably supports the position that marriage should be based on love.

Bibliography

Anderson, Donald K. *John Ford.* New York: Twayne Publishers, 1972.

Ford, John. *'Tis Pity She's a Whore and Other Plays.* Edited by Marion Lomax. Oxford and New York: Oxford University Press, 1995.

Brooke, Fulke Greville, first baron

See GREVILLE, FULKE, FIRST BARON BROOKE.

Browne, Sir Thomas (1605–1682)

A physician and writer of eloquent prose, Browne studied first at Winchester College and then at Oxford University. After taking an Oxford M.A., Browne began the practice of medicine. Perhaps feeling the need for better preparation than Oxford then afforded, he later continued his medical studies at the outstanding European institutions of his time: Montpellier in France, the Medical College at the University of Padua in Italy, and the University of Leyden in the Netherlands, where he received his degree. Originally a Londoner, Browne established his medical practice permanently in Norwich in 1637.

Browne interested himself in all sorts of science as well as in religion. He conducted experiments to test his ideas empirically—a habit that associated him with the new science of his time. His objectives in doing so, however, differed from those of his fellow scientists because Browne's motives were principally religious ones. Rather than hoping to exercise greater control over the natural world, Browne wished to improve his capacity to worship God by better understanding God's creation.

In 1635 he wrote what was perhaps his greatest work, RELIGIO MEDICI, a unique spiritual autobiography. Very unusual works continued to characterize Browne's literary production. In 1646 he published Epidemic falsehood (*Pseudoxia Epidemica*); *or Enquiries into Very many received Tenets, and commonly presumed Truths.* He proposed in *Vulgar Errors,* as the work came to be called, to free the world from superstition. Following the model provided by FRANCIS BACON's *Idols and False Notions,* Browne's very complex work reveals much about its author without making significant progress toward achieving its announced aim. On the contrary, we discover that Browne was himself superstitious, believing in magic, astrology, alchemy, and witchcraft. In 1664, in fact, he himself testified in a witchcraft trial.

Next appeared *Hydriotaphia, Urn Burial* (1658). Occasioned by the discovery near Norfolk of some ancient urns containing the bones of deceased persons, Browne's essay seizes the opportunity to reflect at length on the mystery of death, the necessary anonymity of the vast majority of persons who lived in earlier times, and the folly of attempting to preserve their memory by elaborate tombs and monuments that are themselves destined to crumble. Only "the sufficiency of Christian Immortality," he concludes, "frustrates all earthly glory." Otherwise whether one is buried in "St. Innocent's Churchyard" or "the sands of Ægypt" does not matter at all.

Published together with *Urn Burial* was *The Garden of Cyrus* (1658). This very peculiar effort, intended to pair with his reflection on death by discussing life and growth, devotes considerable attention to the frequency with which the number five appeared in the cultivation of ancient gardens and how it also occurs in the configuration of plants and animals. Other less notable works appeared posthumously including *Miscellany Tracts* (1683), *Letter to a Friend* (1690), and a sequel to *Religio Medici* called *Christian Morals* (1716).

Married in 1641 to Dorothy Mileham, who survived him, Browne fathered 12 children, five of whom perished in childhood. King Charles II knighted him in 1671. Browne's style, particularly, makes him one of the most attractive prose writers of the late English Renaissance.

Bibliography

Browne, Sir Thomas. *The Major Works.* Edited by Constantine A. Patrides. Harmondsworth, U.K.: Penguin, 1977.

———. *Religio medici: A Letter to a Friend and Christian Morals.* Edited by W. A. Greenhill. Peru, Ill.: Sugden, Sherwood and Co., 1990.

———. *The Works of Sir Thomas Browne.* Edited by Geoffrey Keynes. 2nd ed., 4 vols. Chicago and London: University of Chicago Press, 1964.

Post, Jonathan F. S. *Sir Thomas Browne.* Boston: Twayne, 1987.

Bruni, Leonardo (1370–1444)

A prolific writer and translator, an influential historian and political theorist, and the outstanding Italian HUMANIST of his generation, Bruni was the bestselling author of the 15th century. He also held important ecclesiastical and civic posts in Rome and in Florence.

He had learned Latin in his native Arezzo, and sometime after his 20th birthday, he enrolled in the University of Florence, where he planned to study law. There, he became associated with the brilliant humanist circle surrounding the chancellor of Florence, Coluccio Salutati. He continued his studies of Latin literature, perfecting his style in Latin composition, and he mastered Greek under the tutelage of MANUEL CHRYSOLORAS, an educator who served in Florence as an emissary of the Byzantine emperor. From 1405 until 1414–15, except for a three-month interval in 1411, Bruni served in Rome as apostolic secretary to several popes. Then he returned permanently to Florence and the pursuit of literary activity.

Bruni's most notable work was his History of the Florentine people (*Historiarum Florentini populi*, 1415–44). Appearing serially in 12 volumes, the Florentine history traces the real—as opposed to the mythic—beginnings of Florence, the development of its institutions, its military history in defending itself against the ambitions of foreign powers, and the expansion of Florentine control in Tuscany until the year 1402. Four years before his death Bruni published a partly autobiographical continuation that addressed the events of his lifetime, a Commentary on the events of his time (*Rerum suo tempore gestarum commentarius*, 1440).

Bruni not only interested himself in recent Italian history, but he also addressed ancient Greek and Roman matters. Both Bruni's methods and his choice of subjects have gained him a reputation as the first modern historian. Writing in elegant Ciceronian Latin and using as sources the generally unknown writings of Greek historians, he took pains to fill in gaps in the available Latin record of ancient history. His Commentary on the first Punic war (*De Primo bello punico commentarius*, 1418–22) does this by replacing lost works of the

Roman historian Livy. His Commentary on Greek matters (*Rerum graecarum commentarius,* 1439) paints for his readers an earlier unavailable picture of Greece in the first part of the fourth century. His Italian war against the Goths (*De bello italico adversus Gothos,* 1441) reminded the city fathers of Florence that the Greeks had helped Italians against the Teutonic hordes in the sixth century. Others translated Bruni's books into Italian, and his work enjoyed wide circulation in both languages.

By no means limited to writing history, Bruni's literary activity included memoirs, literary theory, moral philosophy, advice on education, political and funeral oratory, a commentary on knighthood, the publication of his letters, many literary translations—mainly from Greek into Latin, two biographies in Latin, and two in Italian. His *Dialogues Dedicated to Pier Paolo Vergerio* (1405–06) portray the discussions of literature that took place in the circle surrounding Salutati. His discourse, On correct translation (*De recta interpretatione,* ca. 1420) gave Europe its first discussion ever of translation theory. Bruni defended the method of conveying the proper sense of a document rather than plodding along word-for-word. He wrote On literary study (*De studiis et literis,* 1422–25) and early translated St. Basil's Letter to young men (*Epistula ad adolescentes,* 1400). The saint's letter advised students (in this case his nephews) to read the best of pagan literature, and he cites the Bible in support of the idea that Christians derive moral benefit from such knowledge. One of the principal educational debates of the Renaissance addressed precisely this issue. Religious conservatives feared that reading classical authors would undermine and corrupt Christian youth.

Often Bruni's translations advanced humanist philosophical, educational, and methodological agendas. His translations from Aristotle challenged the traditions of medieval SCHOLASTICISM. His discussion of knighthood attacks medieval, romanticized notions of chivalry and reinterprets it as a kind of public service. His historical translations offered political advice to governing authorities. Bruni also undertook to translate all of PLATO. Though in the event he was unable to carry that

project to completion, he did complete four dialogues and parts of others.

Among his many other writings, his four biographies deserve particular mention. All of them celebrate Bruni's special heroes. First came his biography of CICERO, the *Cicero Novus* or New Cicero (1412–13), the Roman on whose writing Bruni had modeled his Latin style. Next appeared his life of ARISTOTLE (1429–30), who was the philosopher Bruni most admired. In 1436, biographies appeared of DANTE and of PETRARCH. Bruni felt that BOCCACCIO, in his biography, had paid Dante scant tribute for his military, scholarly, civic, and diplomatic accomplishments. In discussing Petrarch, Bruni emphasized his role in giving impetus to the rise of humanism by reviving the literary Latin of the Roman golden age.

Bruni's literary efforts and the high regard of Florentine leaders made him one of the wealthiest citizens of his city. He held high public office in the Florentine Republic. On his death, his city honored him with the unusual tribute of a public funeral. His remains repose in an elegant tomb in the Florentine church of Santa Croce.

Bibliography

Griffiths, Gordon, James Hankins, and David Thompson. *The Humanism of Leonardo Bruni: Selected Texts.* Binghamton, N.Y.: State University of New York, Medieval Texts and Studies, 1987.

Hankins, James, ed. *Renaissance Civic Humanism: Reappraisals and Reflections.* Cambridge, U.K.: Cambridge University Press, 2000.

———. *Repertorium Brunianum: A Critical Guide to the Writings of Leonardo Bruni.* Rome: *Fonti per la storia dell'Italia medievale,* 1997–2004.

Bruno, Giordano (1548–1600)

Although Bruno authored a significant literary output, he is principally remembered for other distinctions. He was one of what must be a very small group of persons to have been excommunicated by the Catholics, by the Calvinists, and by the Lutherans. Found guilty of heresy by the Roman INQUISITION, he was burned at the stake in Rome on

January 8, 1600, after an imprisonment and trial that had begun eight years earlier in Venice.

Bruno entered the Dominican order in 1565 and rose by stages to be ordained a priest in 1572. In 1576, however, he fled the order's priory in Naples, where he stood accused of heresy for reading the forbidden works of ERASMUS. Dodging the church authorities, Bruno became an itinerant professor, moving north through Rome, Venice, and Savoy, arriving eventually at Geneva where he briefly served as a professor of theology. His free-thinking ways, however, soon landed him in trouble with the Calvinists, so he moved on to Lyon and Toulouse. In Toulouse, he earned an M.A. and discoursed about ARISTOTLE, mathematics, and the memory system of the Spanish thinker, Ramón Lull. Naturally gifted with an astounding memory himself, Bruno studied carefully the systems of memorization that Lull had developed. Bruno later devised his own, which he published as The art of memory (*Ars memoriae,* ca. 1581). At about the same time he also published a discussion of Lull's system together with his additions.

Perhaps owing to his being continually on the move during this period, a number of Bruno's works have regrettably been lost: On the signs of the Times (*De' segni de' tempi*) was apparently published at Venice then lost, and The great key (*Clavis magna*) is said to have appeared at Toulouse. Also missing is a later work, On God's predicaments, developed from 30 lectures Bruno gave at Paris about Thomas Acquinas.

After a brief and unpleasant stint at Oxford (1583), where he lectured in Latin on the theories of COPERNICUS, Bruno returned to Paris. There he published a series of significant works. The first of these was another treatise on memorizing: The art of remembering (*Ars reminiscendi,* 1583). The others reflected Bruno's dangerous interest in magic and his equally risky rejection of received Catholic opinion about a geocentric universe. The latter was the subject of his *La cena de le ceneri* (Ash Wednesday supper, 1584) in which he both supported Copernicus and developed his own view of the infinity of the universe. This view he refined in later Italian works in which he characterized traditional religion as largely superstitious nonsense. He proposed that the universe is both an image of God and that it emanates from Him. He also perceived PLATONIC LOVE among people as a means by which to rise by stages to the direct contemplation of God—a view reflected in much early Renaissance love theory.

Continuing his itinerant ways, Bruno taught where he could and continued publishing. Some of his work fell within the pale of what was tolerable by Renaissance authority, like poems in Latin that discussed the possibility of the infinitely small and infinitely large in the cosmos. In his Italian work, On the infinite universe and worlds (*Del infinito universo e mondi,* 1584), Bruno's discussions of micro- and macrocosmology and of his belief in the probability of an infinite number of universes eerily anticipate some of the more startling implications of 21st-century physics and string theory. Of course, Bruno's method of arriving at his conclusions was deductive rather than empirical. Writers of science fiction have also found similar speculation attractive. But publishers seemingly found untouchable some of Bruno's other works on the occult, and several of his books about magic did not appear in print until late in the 19th century.

In 1591, a Venetian grandee, Giovanni Mocenigo, hoping to improve his own memory, invited Bruno to Venice as his teacher. Bruno accepted and traveled to Venice in the late summer of that year. By the following spring, Mocenigo had decided that his teacher was a dangerous man. When Bruno tried to return to Germany, Mocenigo had him arrested and charged before the Venetian Inquisition with a number of heretical views. At first, the Venetian inquisitors were disposed to dismiss the charges. Venice had always been more easy going in such matters than Rome. The old charge of heresy, however, was still on the Roman books. Informed of his detention, the Roman Inquisition contrived Bruno's extradition, and, although it took the better part of a decade to be finally decided, the rationalist freethinker's fate was sealed.

Bibliography

Bruno, Giordano. *The Ash Wednesday Supper.* Translated by Edward A. Gosselin and Lawrence S. Lerner. Toronto: University of Toronto Press, 1995.

———. *The Infinite in Giordano Bruno, with a Translation of His Dialogue Concerning the Cause, Principle, and One.* Translated by Sidney T. Greenberg. New York: King's Crown Press, 1950.

Yates, Frances A. *Giordano Bruno and the Hermetic Tradition.* London: Routledge, 1999.

Budé, Guillaume (1467–1540)

A French humanist, linguist, philosopher, physician, theologian, and lawyer, Budé proved enormously influential in establishing classical studies in France. He thereby became an important figure in the French transition from medieval to Renaissance culture. He was the first to apply the methods of textual criticism developed by LORENZO VALLA to the body of law and legal precedent that had descended from the ancients. In doing so, he demonstrated the corruption of the texts that arose as they were transmitted through the centuries. Also a translator from Greek and Latin and a commentator on ancient texts, he was interested in the monetary value and the systems of measurement of classical Greece and Rome. FRANÇOIS RABELAIS and his brother studied Greek and became acquainted with HUMANISM under Budé's tutelage.

Appointed secretary to King Louis XII, Budé sometimes also served as an ambassador to the papal court in Rome, as he did in 1502 and again in 1515. On his return from the second mission, the new king, FRANCIS I, named him royal librarian. In that capacity Budé assembled the collection that became the core of the French national library, the great *Bibliothèque Nationale.* At Budé's suggestion, the king established a trilingual national academy for the study of Greek, Latin, and Hebrew. That academy eventually developed into the *Collège de France.*

Budé's literary output was as massive as his work was influential. He wrote a Greek–Latin dictionary and published letters in both languages. He edited Virgil, prepared tracts on the best ways to study classical languages, penned discussions of philology, collected examples of princely behavior from among the ancients for the edification of the rulers of France, and wrote a stoic tract about the contempt in which one should hold the operations of FORTUNE. This list is far from exhaustive.

Budé exemplifies the sort of person in the history of literature who exercised great influence without being widely remembered by posterity.

Bunyan, John (1628–1688)

Born the son of a tinker in the village of Elstow, not far from Bedford, England, John Bunyan learned and practiced his father's trade. During the British civil war between the supporters of Parliament and those of the king, Bunyan was forced into military service on the side of Parliament in 1644. He continued to serve until his regiment was decommissioned in 1647. In that year he returned home and married his first wife. Her name has not survived, but in 1650 the couple's first daughter, Mary, was born blind. Some think the child may have been named for her mother. A second child, Elizabeth, followed in 1654, and two more came along before their mother died in 1658.

In 1655, however, the Bunyans moved from Elstow to Bedford and there became associated with the Bedford Separatist Church. In that congregation Bunyan came under the powerful spiritual influence of its founder John Gifford, who died that same year. Feeling himself called to preach, Bunyan began to do so in 1656, the year that also saw his first literary effort, *Some Gospel-truths Opened.* This work provoked a response from the Quakers whom it had attacked. Bunyan answered that response with a defense of his earlier work. The year of his wife's death saw the publication of *A Few Sighs from Hell; or the Groans of a Damned Soul.* Written in a plain and humble manner, this work nonetheless attempts to instill the fear of eternal damnation into the souls of hardened sinners. A clever editor achieved a witty journalistic coup by advertising the piece immediately above the announcement of OLIVER CROMWELL's death so that it appeared that the sighs and groans issued forth from the suffering soul of the former Lord Protector of England.

Although Bunyan's formal education had never proceeded beyond grammar school, together with his religious zeal and private reading, that education proved to be an adequate foundation to make Bunyan both a formidable preacher and a towering literary figure. His private reading of course included the BIBLE itself in at least two English translations, the Authorized Version and the Geneva Bible. He had combed the pages of Scripture in search of messages that God had surreptitiously included there for him alone—a frequent practice among Puritan believers with a penchant for TYPOLOGY and for finding hidden messages in nature and in texts. In addition to reams of puritanical tracts and sermons, Bunyan also had read MARTIN LUTHER's *Commentary on Galatians,* JOHN FOXE's *Book of Martyrs,* and Samuel Clark's *A Mirrour and Looking-glass for both Saints and Sinners.* His works also contain evidence of his familiarity with such poets as GEORGE HERBERT and Francis Quarles, the latter of whom also wrote religious tracts. Bunyan knew some works of fiction and the religious books of Arthur Dent and Bishop Lewis Bayley as well.

Two periods of imprisonment, the first from 1660 to 1672 (for unlicensed preaching) and the second for about half the year 1677 (for failing to attend Anglican services at his local parish church), gave Bunyan ample time for reading, writing, and reflection. He also, remarkably, found opportunities to continue preaching while jailed. The year before the first imprisonment—a year that saw the publication of his *The Doctrine of the Law and Grace Unfolded*—Bunyan had married a second wife, Elizabeth. She doggedly pursued obtaining her husband's release, but his enemies repeatedly thwarted her on technicalities. Though Bunyan's freedom was curtailed, his works continued to appear: *Profitable Meditations* (1661), *I Will Pray with the Spirit* (ca. 1663), *Christian Behaviour* (1663), *A Mapp shewing . . . Salvation and Damnation* (?), *One Thing is Needful* (?), *The Holy City, Prison Meditations,* and *The Resurrection of the Dead* (all three, 1665).

The following year, 1666, saw the publication of Bunyan's spiritual autobiography, *Grace Abounding.* Although Bunyan suffered from the fallout of the rancorous religious disputes of his day, he rarely allowed himself to be drawn into them. Instead, he continually emphasized his central message: God's grace was sufficient. Those who believed and accepted it would be saved. Also in 1666 he began to work on *A Christian Dialogue*—a work he completed around 1672. It is likely, as well, that he started to work on THE PILGRIM'S PROGRESS during his first, long imprisonment.

Just as technicalities had kept Bunyan in jail, technicalities also got him out. In January 1672 he was officially named the pastor of the Bedford Separatist Church (later known as the *Bunyan meeting*), and on being officially licensed as a Congregational preacher the following May, he was released. The responsibilities of his official appointment, however, hardly stemmed the flow of works from his busy pen. Although an enormous number of early editions of Bunyan's works that had been brought together for auction met accidental destruction by fire, leaving us ignorant of their initial publication dates, the period subsequent to his first imprisonment saw a spate of his new books: *The Barren Fig-Tree; A Confession of My Faith; A Defence of the Doctrine of Justification, By Faith in Jesus Christ; Differences in Judgment about Water Baptism, No Bar to Communion; A New and Useful Concordance to the Holy Bible.* All of these seem to have appeared before 1674. These were followed by: *Peaceable Principles and True* (1674); *Reprobation Asserted* (?); *Light for Them That Sit in Darkness* and *Instruction for the Ignorant* (both 1675). *Saved by Grace* and *The Strait Gate* followed in 1675.

His six-month-long imprisonment in 1677 enforced on him the leisure to finish the first part of the work by which posterity best remembers him, *Pilgrim's Progress* (Part I, 1678). The same year also saw issued *Come and Welcome, to Jesus Christ.* A trio of works followed in 1679, 1680, and 1682, respectively: *A Treatise of the Fear of God, The Life and Death of Mr. Badman,* and *The Holy War.* Two more works followed in 1683: *The Greatness of the Soul* and *A Case of Conscience Resolved.*

The year 1684 saw not only the publication of the second part of *Pilgrim's Progress,* but three lesser-known inspirational works as well. Until almost the moment of Bunyan's untimely death, more works of the same sort continued appearing. Notable among them was his *A Book for Boys and Girls,* whose charming wit especially exemplifies

Bunyan's lighter side and joy in good fun. Still more spiritual tracts appeared in the year of Bunyan's death, and his final sermon saw print the year following. A five-year hiatus in posthumous publication followed. Perhaps Mrs. Bunyan felt it best to withhold her husband's last works from the press. In the year of her passing, 1692, however, a dozen new titles appeared, mostly of sermons. After another six years, the final new work published in the 17th century appeared: *The Heavenly Footman.*

More than a half-century later, there came to light among the Bunyan family papers a journal that Bunyan had kept during his long imprisonment. It was published in 1765 under the title: *A Relation of the Imprisonment of Mr. John Bunyan.*

Not a member of the literary or the intellectual establishment of university-trained writers, Bunyan reflects in his work the mentality, understanding, and faith of ordinary folks in the last years of the 17th century. Even three centuries later, his work remains accessible to the understanding of those who, for whatever reason, may decide to read it. Christian evangelicals, particularly, will recognize in Bunyan's writing a shared and congenial viewpoint.

Bibliography

Bunyan, John. *The Complete Works of John Bunyan.* Edited by Henry Stebbing. New York: Johnson Reprint Corp., 1970.

Hargreaves, Cyril, et al. *Valiant Pilgrim: The Story of John Bunyan and Puritan England.* New York: Macmillan, 1950.

Sadler, Lynn Veach. *John Bunyan.* Boston: Twayne Publishers, 1979.

Burton, Robert (1577–1640)

A clergyman and the author of the *Anatomy of Melancholy,* Burton was educated at Oxford where, after a time at Brasenose College, he was elected in 1593 as a student in Christ Church College. He spent the rest of his life there among books, sometimes serving as the college librarian (1626 and later) and sometimes working among the books of the newly established Bodleian Library (1602). He also received appointments to two church parishes. Possibly these were essentially sinecures.

Burton also frequently penned Latin occasional poems mainly about significant events in the royal household. He contributed a drama in Latin, *Philosophaster* (1617), to the university's tradition of performing plays in that language. This is a rather rigid comedy about the pseudoscience of alchemy and the gullibility of those duped by its practitioners. Broadly its outlines suggest those of BEN JONSON's play, *The Alchemist.*

Burton's reputation, however, rests principally upon the book that he spent most of his adult life writing and revising for new editions. This work, his ANATOMY OF MELANCHOLY, first appeared in 1621. For this edition Burton adopted the pen name *Democritus Junior.* Four subsequent editions with changes and additions appeared during the author's lifetime. A final revision was published posthumously in 1651.

Burton's fascination with this subject may have stemmed from his own belief in astrology and in the influence of the stars and planets upon the personalities of human beings. He was born under the influence of Saturn—a fact that predisposed him to melancholy (depression), as he thought, though modern medicine might judge that genetic factors played a more determining role. Michael O'Connell, one of Burton's biographers, notes that some of his relations in previous generations had suffered from the affliction. The epitaph that Burton wrote for himself a few days before his death is of particular interest in this respect: Referring to himself as Democritus Junior, he says in Latin that melancholy gave him both life and death. This has led some to speculate (long after his death) that he committed suicide by hanging himself. Nothing, however, contemporary with his passing suggests such an end for him. O'Connell rather calls attention to Burton's morbid fascination with astrology and, from its perspective, the suggestions of ill health that his horoscope predicted as Burton neared the end of his 63rd year. Rather than suicide, O'Connell prefers the theory of a psychosomatic influence occasioned by Burton's belief in astrology. His falling ill and dying may have amounted to a self-fulfilling prophecy.

Bibliography

Burton, Robert. *The Anatomy of Melancholy.* Edited by Thomas C. Faulkner, Nicholas K. Kiessling, and Rhonda L. Blair. 3 vols. Oxford and New York: Oxford University Press, 1989–1994.

O'Connell, Michael. *Robert Burton.* Boston, 1986.

Vicari, Eleanor. *The View from Minerva's Tower: Learning and Imagination in "The Anatomy of Melancholy."* Toronto: University of Toronto Press, 1989.

Busche, Hermann von dem (1468–1534)

Although none of his work is available in modern editions or in English translation, Busche remains a notable literary figure of the Northern Renaissance. A devotee of HUMANISM, he studied at Münster and Heidelberg in Germany. In the latter city his mentor was the most important of the early humanists of Northern Europe, RUDOLPH AGRICOLA. Busche next journeyed to Italy; he continued his studies at Rome and in Bologna before returning to Germany. There he moved from town to town and position to position. His writings, both poetry and prose, began to appear in the first decade of the 16th century. Meanwhile he was hired at the University of Wittenberg to teach humanism. His appointment there was brief, however. The next year (1503) finds him receiving a bachelor's degree in law in the city of Leipzig and securing a salaried appointment as its university's official poet.

Apparently Bushe's personality was thorny. Opinionated and rude as well as brilliant, he regularly offended his superiors and was obliged to move on. This pattern repeated itself at Erfurt, and eventually, in 1516, also in Wesel, where he served for a year as headmaster in a Latin school before being terminated. His intellectual arrogance, however, had at least one positive attribute: it made him a formidable controversialist. He took sides in literary quarrels. He wrote a major defense of humanism, the Fortress of Humanity (*Vallum humanitatis,* 1518). Apparently Busche feared nothing except his own conscience. After Emperor Charles V ordered MARTIN LUTHER's books burned, Busche ardently, though unsuccessfully, supported the Protestant reformer in 1521 at Worms, where Luther was placed under the ban of the empire.

Busche also joined protests against such Roman Catholic customs as fasting during Lent. Ever the wandering scholar, Busche spent the last decade of his life teaching history and the humanities, first at Heidelberg and finally at Marberg, where the new university was more congenial to his Lutheran viewpoint.

Bibliography

Liessem, Hermann J. *De Hermanni Buschii vita et scriptis* (Concerning the life and writings of Hermann Busche). Bonn, Germany: Caroli Georgii, 1866.

Bussy d' Ambois George Chapman (1607)

Loosely based on events at the French royal court, *Bussy d' Ambois* is a SENECAN TRAGEDY. Its protagonist, Bussy, is recruited by Monsieur, the French King Henry's brother, in the hope that the hot-blooded Bussy can forward Monsieur's royal ambition by killing the king. Filled with a sense of his native honor and nobility, Bussy is quick to take offense, enjoys a duel with wit or rapier, and brooks no insult from anyone regardless of station. Introduced at court, his utter frankness charms the king, who is accustomed to empty flattery. At the same time, Bussy makes an enemy of the duke of Guise by publicly paying court to the duchess.

Insulted by partisans of the duke, Bussy and two seconds duel offstage with three of the duke's retainers. Graphically reported onstage by Nuntius, a messenger, we learn that Bussy has killed his man, Barrisor, and two other courtiers, L'Anou and Pyrhot, who had slain Bussy's seconds. Called before the king for judgment, Bussy appears with Monsieur who pleads on his behalf. At first not disposed to be lenient, the king is convinced by Bussy's defense of the privilege of defending one's honor as being beyond the reach of the law. Henry pardons Bussy and promotes him to the first rank of his courtiers.

It is not only King Henry who finds Bussy charming. So does Tamyra, the countess of Montsurrey, who, although she rejects the unwelcome advances of Monsieur, is so hopelessly smitten by Bussy that she sends her confessor, a friar who can summon demons, to conduct Bussy to her chamber. Their tryst, unfortunately, is observed by Tamyra's maid, Pero.

Monsieur finds that Bussy's friendship with the king has thwarted his plans. Bussy has known from the outset that the king's brother wants to mount the throne. He tells Monsieur that he will do anything asked of him except kill the king. In a wonderful scene, Bussy and Monsieur agree to share their honest opinions of each other. This produces one of the richest exchanges of insults in the history of stagecraft.

Now both sworn enemies of Bussy, Monsieur and Guise easily pry from Pero her mistress's secret. Monsieur makes the sign of the cuckold's horns at Count Montsurrey. He in turn accuses his wife of infidelity. She denies it, but the convinced Montsurrey tortures her by stabbing her nonfatally but repeatedly, onstage, until she writes Bussy a letter of invitation in her own blood. The friar interrupts this scene and drops dead of shock, after which his ghost figures prominently in the action.

Earlier, however, the friar had called up the spirit Behemoth and his attendant demons to find out what Bussy's enemies are up to. A counterspell partly thwarts this attempt, but the spirit agrees to find out more and reappear at Bussy's call. When he does so he tells Bussy not to heed his mistress's next summons or he will be murdered.

Montsurrey appears disguised as the friar and brings Tamyra's letter. Bussy concludes that the spirit has lied and goes to meet Tamyra. There, murderers await him. All but one of them flees, however, at the appearance of the friar's ghost. That one, Bussy kills. Then Montsurrey enters at the head of the rest of the murderers and they wound Bussy fatally. The friar's ghost admonishes Bussy to forgive them, which he does. Tamyra repents, Montsurrey forgives her but sends her away, and the friar's ghost recites the play's last lines.

Bibliography

Chapman, George. *Bussy d'Ambois.* Edited by Maurice Evans. New York: Hill and Wang, 1966.

Calderón de la Barca, Pedro
(1600–1681)

A prolific Spanish dramatist, a poet, a priest, and a soldier, Calderón was born in Madrid where, at age nine, he began his studies with the Jesuits. At the University of Salmanca, he studied theology, philosophy, and civil and canon law, graduating at the age of 19. Apparently at that early age he had already acquired a reputation as a playwright, though the grounds for that reputation are uncertain. In 1620 and again in 1622 he entered civic poetry contests in honor of San Isidro (Saint Isadore), and Calderón's entries both times won the praise of the era's major playwright, LOPE DE VEGA. In the second contest, Calderón won a prize as well.

Calderón wrote plays in a number of genres. Devoutly religious, he penned several full-length religious dramas and plays about the lives of saints. He also composed numerous *AUTOS SACRAMENTALES* (sacramental acts). These one-act religious dramas in verse sometimes combined scriptural with nationalistic themes. Peopled by such allegorical characters as the Divine Orpheus, who figured forth Christ, the *autos* were designed for performance on Corpus Christi day. About a hundred of them survive. These were accompanied by introductory songs called lauds or praises (*loas*) and were often interrupted by INTERLUDES as well so

that their performance time was almost as long as the three-act dramas he wrote for the commercial theater. He also wrote spectacular COURT ENTERTAINMENTS, and he composed many short farces and more than a hundred comedies and tragedies.

In the 1620s Calderón's literary career seems to have been occasionally interrupted by periods of military service in Italy (1625) and afterward in Flanders. He continued to write plays, nevertheless, and by 1632, the playwright Juan Perez de Montalvan tells us, Calderón had already had many plays produced, had won a number of public prizes, and had written a good many lyric poems.

The year 1623 saw a production at court of his earliest surviving play, *Amor, honor y podor* (Love, honor, and power). This play pits the conflicting claims of personal wishes against civic responsibility and the requirements of the Spanish code of honor, themes to which he would return many times in his secular plays. His best remembered play, *La vida es sueño* (*Life Is a Dream*, ca. 1630, revised 1635), anticipates the Freudian notion of the subconscious while it explores questions of liberty, politics, religious faith, knowledge, and what constitutes objective reality.

Some of Calderón's plays incorporate historical events, but he is never constrained by the requirements of realism, chronology, or geography. In his

Amar despues de la muerte (Love survives life) he sets his story in Grenada during the Moorish rebellion of 1568. The play's hero, a Moor named Tuzani, defends the honor of his beloved Clara Malec's aged father against an insulting Spaniard. In the second act, Tuzani marries Clara but must immediately leave her at a fortress while he goes to fight. The fortress briefly falls into Spanish hands, and a Spanish soldier kills Clara to steal her jewels. Tuzani arrives in time to observe the murder but not soon enough to stop it or to positively identify the killer. Disguising himself as a Spanish knight, Tuzani enters the enemy camp, identifies his wife's murderer, leads him to confirm his guilt by bragging, dispatches him with a single blow, and, overcoming all opposition, fights his way out of the Spanish encampment and escapes to the mountains. The swashbuckling events of this episode came to characterize a group of Calderón's plays known as the cape-and-sword dramas.

As a priest, Calderón was a constant critic of the Spanish code of honor that demanded revenge for insults. It also punished adulterous women with banishment or death. The code of honor seemed more consistent with demanding an eye for an eye than with Christian forgiveness. Two of his plays explore this theme by exploring the dangers of murdering an erring—or apparently erring—wife. In one, *El médico de su honor* (The physician of his own honor, 1637), a husband, Don Gutierrez, is misled by equivocal evidence into believing that his innocent wife has deceived him. Torn between his love for her and his sense of injured honor, he forces a physician to open a vein and bleed her to death. The physician, who is led blindfolded to and from the house, on exiting presses his bloody hand on the door. He then reports the crime to the king, who rushes to the house and insists that Gutierrez marry Leonore, a woman he had earlier jilted. The other play in this mode, The painter of his own dishonor (*El pintor de su deshonra*, ca. 1648) a husband kills his faithless wife and her lover. The fathers of the two murdered persons approve the action and volunteer to defend the husband against any consequences of his action.

In The great monster jealousy (*El Mayor Monstruo los Zelos*), Calderón examines the motives of Herod, Tetrarch of Judea, who commanded that in the event of his death his wife Mariamne should be killed to prevent her marrying or taking another lover. In a stroke of allegorical irony, the still living Herod accidentally strikes down his wife with his dagger, thus becoming in his own person the monster of jealousy.

While these plays reveal the dark side of Calderón's imagination, many of his comedies reveal his wit, his gentle sense of humor, and his seemingly inexhaustible fund of sometimes self-mocking and uproarious invention. In an entertaining frolic, *La Dama Duende* (The phantom lady, ca. 1629), one that Calderón himself seems to have particularly liked, a young woman, Doña Angela, uses a secret door leading from her rooms to a guest apartment to mystify a handsome young houseguest whom she admires. She moves furniture, leaves notes, bumps into his visitors in the dark, and leads him and his manservant to believe themselves haunted. Eventually, of course, the mystery unravels and the two young people are married.

In addition to his stage career and his tasks as a sort of master of the revels at the royal court, Calderón also managed to perform important administrative tasks for the church. When he died, although his burial was private and without ceremony as he had requested, a few days later the king accorded Calderón a magnificent state funeral in keeping with his status as a national treasure. His passing was mourned all over Europe.

Bibliography

Calderón de la Barca, Pedro. *Calderón Plays.* Translated by Gwynne Edwards. London: 1981.
———. *Four Comedies.* Translated by Kenneth Muir and annotated by Ann L. Mackenzie. Lexington: University of Kentucky Press, 1980.
———. *Three Comedies.* Translated by Kenneth Muir and Ann L. Mackenzie. Lexington: University of Kentucky Press, 1985.
———. *Life Is a Dream.* Translated by Stanley Appelbaum. Mineola, N.Y.: Dover Publications, 2002.

———. *Six Plays by Calderón*. Translated and edited by Edwin Honig. New York: Hill and Wang, 1993.

———. *The Phantom Lady*. Translated by Donald Beecher. Ottawa: Dovehouse Editions, 2002.

Gerstinger, Heinz. *Pedro Calderón de la Barca*. Translated from the German by Diana Stone Peters. New York: Ungar, 1973.

Lund, Harry. *Pedro Calderón de la Barca, a Biography*. Edinburgh, Tex.: Andres Noriega Press, 1963.

Parker, Mary, ed. *Spanish Dramatists of the Golden Age: A Bio-Bibliographical Sourcebook*. Westport, Conn.: Greenwood Press, 1998.

Calvin, John (Jean Chauvin) (1509–1564)

A HUMANIST scholar, religious thinker, and the founding father of a major wing of the PROTESTANT REFORMATION, Calvin was born in France at Noyon in Picardy. He began his university career as a student of Latin in Paris in 1523. There he had intended to prepare for the priesthood, but he changed his mind. Instead, from 1528 to 1531, he studied law in Orléans and later in Bruges. While there, he was swept up in the widespread student interest in the new humanism. Calvin adopted as his own humanism's pre-Lutheran objective—one cherished by Catholic humanists like ERASMUS—of fusing classical learning and Christian truth. To accomplish this, humanist scholars had adopted a program both of recovering pagan texts and of restoring the Bible to its original languages. Doing so would, as they thought, remove textual errors that had crept in over centuries of translation and manuscript recopying.

Devoted to that effort, Calvin undertook the study of Greek and Hebrew as well as continuing to master Latin. In 1532 the first fruits of Calvin's work appeared in his Latin *Commentary on Seneca's De Clementia* (about clemency). He had also helped prepare a statement of the theological principles of the humanist movement. This statement was included in a speech delivered by Nicholas Copp, the rector of the University of Paris. The speech, smacking too much of Protestantism with its emphasis on salvation by grace,

offended the authorities, and some of those who had participated in its preparation, including Calvin, wisely left Paris in 1533. Calvin went to Basel, Switzerland.

The precise moment at which Calvin officially switched his allegiance from Roman Catholicism to Protestantism has not been recorded. His study of theology in Basel, however, either confirmed or precipitated his decision to abandon the Roman Catholic communion. He began a systematic reading of and commentary upon the Scriptures. These eventually grew to address every book of the Bible except Revelations. Over the years Calvin shared his findings in extemporaneous lectures given to Protestant ministers-in-training who came to Switzerland to learn from him. These commentaries on the Bible plus discussions of theology and essays arguing his positions make up the bulk of his literary output. This was, in fact, enormous. His method of production depended on a corps of secretaries who recorded his lectures, sermons, and debates, wrote them up, and presented them to Calvin for his approval. In 1536 the first version of Calvin's *Christianae religionis Institutio* (*Institutes of the Christian religion*) appeared in Latin. This work continued to be reissued and enlarged throughout his lifetime, eventually reaching, in the definitive modern Latin edition, some 59 volumes. Additional volumes of previously unpublished sermons have since appeared, as have a dozen volumes of his *Commentaries*.

Calvin worked for much of his life in the city of Geneva, Switzerland, where Protestantism had been imposed as a result of a military treaty. He was first invited there in 1536 to spread Protestant doctrine among an unenthusiastic populace. His insistence, however, on the authority of clerics over laymen (including town councilors) and on having the power to excommunicate soon produced conflict with the secular authorities. It also produced a backlash from that portion of the populace called libertines who bridled at the moral and behavioral restraints of Calvin's doctrines. In 1538 he was consequently expelled from Geneva for a time.

He moved to Strasbourg where he married Idelette de Bure, the widow of one of his converts.

All the children of Calvin's marriage sadly died in infancy. During three years in Strasbourg, Calvin published his commentary on St. Paul's Letter to the Romans, served a church as its pastor, met Protestant leaders at various international conferences, engaged Roman Catholic theologians in debate, and came to be viewed as a major Protestant spokesman.

In the fall of 1541, Geneva invited Calvin to return. The Protestant establishment seemed threatened, and the town fathers felt that they needed a strong leader. Calvin made conditions. The town council met these by enacting a series of *Ecclesiastical Ordinances* on which Calvin insisted. These required religious education for children and adults, abolished Roman Catholicism, and regulated every aspect of public and private behavior. It also set up an ecclesiastical hierarchy with powers to enforce Calvinist points of view. Following almost a decade and a half of resistance from the libertines, Calvin prevailed, and theocracy flourished in Geneva.

Calvin's influence spread widely through the Continent and the British Isles and into North America. As it spread, it changed to meet the needs and perceptions of the various Reform communions into which Calvinism splintered—generally in directions more conservative than Calvin's own. Calvin's points of view in their several developments continue to color the activities, thinking, and public pronouncements of private individuals, clerics, and governmental authorities. Central to Calvin's doctrines is the elevation of Scripture as the sole authority in all matters where human reason and Christian doctrine seem to conflict. This view is not the same as biblical literalism since Calvin tempered his view of Scripture with the humanist rhetorical doctrine that the Scripture needed to be applied and interpreted to meet the needs of the time, place, and circumstances of the faithful. Calvin's own views also asserted the equality of the sexes, not the submission of the wife to the husband.

An argument might successfully be made that John Calvin was the most influential of all European Protestant Reformers. Certainly, his *Institutes* both in Latin and in translations enjoyed a readership that far surpassed that of any other religious literary document of the Renaissance except the Bible itself.

Bibliography

Calvin, John. *The Institutes of the Christian Religion.* Edited and translated by Tony Lane and Hillary Osborne. 1987. Reprint, Grand Rapids, Mich.: Baker Book House, 1996.

———. *Commentaries.* 12 vol. Edited by David W. Torrance and Thomas F. Torrance. Grand Rapids, Mich.: Eerdmans, 1959–1972.

Parker, T. H. L. *John Calvin: a Biography.* 1975. Reprint, London: Dent, 1987.

Camerarius, Joachim (1500–1574)

A supporter of MARTIN LUTHER and especially of the religious reformer Philip Melancthon, Camerarius taught classical languages at a series of German schools and universities, including the Universities of Erfurt, Wittenberg, Tübingen, and finally Leipzig. He also served for a time as the founding rector of the Latin school at Nürnberg. A devoted stoic HUMANIST and an ardent defender of the PROTESTANT REFORMATION in public debate, Camerarius authored a substantial literary output. He translated, edited, and wrote textbooks and commentaries about such Greek literary authors as Aesop, Homer, Sophocles, and the Greek mathematician Euclid. He did the same for such Roman writers as CICERO and PLAUTUS, and about such subjects as grammar, handwriting, and rhetoric.

A 1531 visit to the solar system by Halley's Comet heightened Camerarius's interest in astrology, which historically viewed comets as portents of disaster. Thereafter, he wrote about comets and translated, among other ancient astrological texts, the Egyptian–Greek astronomer Ptolemy's Collection of four books (*Tetrabiblos Syntaxis*). For a time Camerarius also toyed with casting horoscopes and predicting the future. Astrology in the 16th century was closely linked to another of his interests, medicine. Physicians of the period often cast horoscopes to determine what treatment might be most effective for patients. (See HUMORAL

MEDICINE.) In this connection he wrote texts on medicine and pharmacy.

Camerarius was also an active biographer. Having previously edited and published the letters of his friend and mentor Philip Melancthon, Camerarius penned a widely read biography of Melancthon (1566). Other biographical portraits and full-length biographies continued flowing from Camerarius's pen. These included a sketch of the famous artist Albrecht Dürer and full discussions of the German poet Helius Eobanus Hesus, the Lutheran bishop Count Georg von Anhalt, and of the Greek fabulist Aesop.

Among his religious works, Camerarius produced a life of Christ (*Historia Jesu Christi,* 1566), catechisms and works of religious instruction, and histories of ecumenical councils and the Moravian church. He also composed a hexameter poem in Greek and a series of ECLOGUEs that appeared posthumously in 1568. A German biography of Camerarius appeared in 2000.

Camões, Luíz Vaz De (1524–1580)

A Portuguese soldier from a poor family of the minor nobility, Camões studied as a charity student at the University of Coimbra where he began his literary career by writing a play for university performance, Amphitriton (*Amphitriões*). He fell in love with the willing Donna Caterina Ataide, but her father withheld approval for the match. After writing poems of lost love in the Italian manner, Camões enlisted in the army. He served at Ceuta in North Africa in 1549. Blinded in his right eye by a splinter, he returned to Lisbon, was imprisoned for street fighting, gained his freedom by reenlisting, and then spent the best part of the next two decades (1553–70) in the Portuguese trading colonies of Goa in southern India and Macao off the coast of China. While engaged in that colonial military service he employed his leisure to write plays, poems, and the major work for which he is principally remembered, *The Lusiad* (or *Lusiads*)—from the ancient name for Portugal (*Os Lusíadas,* 1572). Returning to Goa from Macao, where he had enjoyed a lucrative post, Camões lost everything he had earned in a shipwreck off Cambodia, but

he was able to save the precious manuscript of his *Lusiad.*

An EPIC poem in 10 cantos, Camões' masterpiece focuses on the historical voyages of Portuguese explorer Vasco da Gama around the Horn of Africa. Da Gama's voyages succeeded in opening a new trade route to the east and establishing the colonies where Camões had served. With this historical strand Camões combines, as VIRGIL's *Aeniad* had done for Rome, the mythic origins of Portugal, its past history, and a hopeful future development in which the nation would achieve its divinely appointed destiny. With these narrative threads, always pointing toward Christian Portugal as the inheritor of Roman greatness, Camões interweaves Roman and Trojan history, gods and goddesses from the Roman pantheon, and mutually reflecting events on Earth and in the heavens.

On *The Lusiad*'s publication, Camões received a small royal pension, but it was not nearly enough to relieve his poverty. He died penniless in a public hospital. The Portuguese people warmly remember him, however, and regard his epic as their national poem. His lyrics and elegies were published posthumously in 1595. His reputation as a poet has grown through time. Elizabeth Barrett Browning's celebrated *Sonnets from the Portuguese* translate lyrics of Camões.

Bibliography

Camões, Luis de. *The Lusiad: or The Discovery of India: An Epic Poem . . . with a Life of the Poet.* Translated and edited by William Julius Mickle. Fifth edition revised and edited by E. Raymond Hodges. New York: Gordon Press, 1975.

Campanella, Tommaso (1568–1639)

A philosopher, theologian, and poet, Campanella spent almost 30 years of his life imprisoned for heresy (twice) and for having conspired to overthrow Spanish rule in the Kingdom of Naples. He was tortured, and had he not feigned madness, he would certainly have been executed. But canon law prohibited executing the insane. During his long confinement (1597–1626), Campanella wrote prodigiously.

Campanella's difficulties with the Roman IN-QUISITION began with the publication of his first book in Latin, Philosophy demonstrated by the senses (*Philosophia sensibus demonstrata*) (1591). This work defended the work of a fellow philosopher, Bernardino Telesio, who advocated adding the perceptions of the senses to the arid rationalism of Aristotelian SCHOLASTICISM. An early empiricist and in some ways a forerunner of modern scientific method, Campanella was also a utopian thinker. In organizing a revolution, his goal had been to set up in the place of the Spanish rulers of Naples a polity where citizens followed their consciences in religious matters, where all property was held in common, and where amassing knowledge was the prime occupation.

His Italian work *La Città del Sole* (*The City of the Sun,* written 1602, published 1623) envisions an ideal state. In it, church and state combine into a single entity led by a ruler at once prince and pope. Despite its autocracy, the city of Solaria would be a place of freedom where reason ruled and where the state's responsibilities mainly included improving the lives of its citizen through science, education, and technology.

Despite Campanella's extended difficulties with ecclesiastical and civic authority, the church regarded him highly as a thinker and as a theologian. When, in 1616, Galileo Galilei was about to be tried for espousing a heliocentric view of the solar system, one of his judges, Cardinal Boniface Caetani, asked Campanella, though in prison, to provide a theological brief concerning the issues of the trial. Campanella strongly supported Galileo, not because he agreed with him, but because he thought it in the church's best interest to support free inquiry into scientific matters. Published in 1622, this discussion, *Apologia pro Galileo* (A defense of Galileo), is regarded as a classic argument for free thought and speech.

To Pope Urban VII, Campanella owed his eventual release from prison. Still threatened, he moved to Rome where his views continued to anger the Jesuits. In 1634 he moved again, this time to Paris under the protection of Cardinal Richelieu and supported by an annual stipend from the king.

Posterity owes the preservation of Campanella's poetry to a German scholar, Tobia Adami. Adami had secretly spirited away several of Campanella's manuscripts during visits to him in prison. In 1622 Adami chose representative samples of Campanella's Italian poems and published a collection of his selections. The poems treat many of the same themes that Campanella addresses in his philosophical works—the primacy of Nature as a teacher, the combination of matter, thought, and spirit in the composition of the human being, and the majesty of the universe as contrasted with the insignificance of the human creature.

Bibliography

Bonansea, Bernardino. *Tommaso Campanella: Renaissance Pioneer of Modern Thought.* Washington, D.C.: Catholic University of America Press, 1969.

Campanella, Tommaso. *A Defense of Galileo, the Mathematician from Florence.* Translated by R. J. Blackwell. Notre Dame, Ind.: University of Notre Dame Press, 1994.

———. *La città del sole: Dialogo Poetica. The City of the Sun: A Poetical Dialogue.* Italian and English, translated by Daniel J. Donno. Berkeley, Calif.: University of California Press, 1981.

Headley, John M. *Tommaso Campanella and the Transformation of the World.* Princeton, N.J.: Princeton University Press, 1997.

Campion, Thomas (1567–1620)

A British musician and poet, Campion studied at Peterhouse in Cambridge from 1581 to 1584 but did not graduate. He enrolled at Gray's Inn in London to study law but apparently found that occupation uncongenial. Eventually he earned a degree in medicine abroad.

His literary career began during the period of his legal studies. Five of Campion's poems appeared anonymously in an unauthorized edition of SIR PHILIP SIDNEY's ASTROPHEL AND STELLA in 1591. At the same time, more of Campion's verses were circulating in manuscript. Writing both in Latin and English, Campion published a collection of Latin EPIGRAMS in 1595. Collaborating with musician Philip Rosseter, Campion wrote both the music and the lyrics for all the songs in the first half of their *A Book of Airs* (1601).

Campion next turned to prose composition, publishing a critical discussion about writing verse, *Observations in the Art of English Poesy* (1602). This discussion argues for employing his variation on the unrhymed quantitative and accentual POETIC METER of the classical languages in English composition rather than using the traditional English system of rhyme and stress. His argument seems odd as he himself usually employed the English system in his lyrics, though he does use his lovely song *Rose-cheeked Laura* to illustrate his application of quantitative principles to composition in English verse. In any case Campion's argument in the *Observations* makes clear his own occasional confusion of musical and verbal accentual systems. SAMUEL DANIEL wrote a response attacking Campion's position, and BEN JONSON then wrote one that corrected both Daniel and Campion (1603). That exchange put the matter permanently to rest.

In 1604 Campion turned to composing court masques (see COURT ENTERTAINMENT). He wrote one of these royal entertainments that year and three more in 1613. Throughout his career, Campion continued contributing songs to collections published by others. In 1613 he returned to publishing collections of *Airs*, four of which appeared between that year and 1617. Campion's special talent for flawlessly combining lyrics and their musical settings distinguishes him as one of the finest writers of English Renaissance songs.

Bibliography

Campion, Thomas. *Campion's Works*. Selections edited by Percival Vivian. London and New York: Clarendon Press, 1966.

Campion, Thomas, and Philip Rosseter. *A Book of Ayres: Set Forth to be Song to the Lute, Orpherian, and Base Violl*. New York: Performers' Facsimiles, ca. 1992.

Hawkins, H. W. *Modern Love Elegies*. Manquin, Va.: Uppingham House, 2002.

cape-and-sword drama

An innovation of the Spanish playwright, LOPE DE VEGA CARPIO, cape-and-sword dramas took their name from the preferred style of dress of Spanish gentry. The costume was associated with gentlemen of the second rank, that is, of aristocrats below the rank of royalty, dukes, or counts but still of sufficient status to style themselves *Dons*.

The plays themselves featured romantic involvements among young people, gallantry, and swordplay. Murder, assassination, and mayhem of various sorts also figured prominently. Lope's COURT ENTERTAINMENT, *SAINT JOHN'S EVE* (1631), is a prime example of a cape-and-sword drama. The genre survives into modern filmmaking with movies about Zorro being the prototype.

Carew, Thomas   (1595?–1640)

A courtier in the service of King Charles I, Carew (pronounced Cary) had come to court following an early diplomatic career that took him to Venice (1613), to the Hague (1616), and to Paris (1619). In 1628 he secured his appointment as a member of the royal household—a position that he held for the rest of his life. He earned the friendship of Queen Caroline as a result of his discretion and quick thinking. The story goes that among Carew's duties was bearing a candle or lantern to light the king's way to the queen's bedchamber. Performing this task on one occasion, Carew entered the queen's room ahead of the king to find her in compromising circumstances with the Lord St. Albans, Henry Jermyn. Carew stumbled tactfully, dousing the light so that the king saw nothing.

A friend, admirer, and disciple of both BEN JONSON and JOHN DONNE, Carew also managed to combine their literary styles in his own splendid poems. Particularly famous is his *Elegy on the Death of Dr. Donne* (1633). Conveying a sense both of Donne's poetic accomplishment and his religious commitment as well as of Carew's heartfelt sorrow at the loss of his friend, Carew ends the poem with a four-line epitaph. This moving tribute suggests that in Donne's tomb lie "the king of wit" and two priests: one, the poet, a priest of

Apollo; the other, the Anglican Dean of St. Paul's Cathedral, a priest of the true God.

Carew also authored one of the loveliest, most sensuously textured, and most tastefully erotic poems in the English language, *A Rapture* (1640). In addition to his lyric poems, Carew authored a COURT MASQUE, The British sky or heaven (*Coelum Britannicum*), which he staged together with the scenery designer and landscape architect, INIGO JONES.

Not only did Carew owe much to the verse of his friends and contemporaries, but he also used as a model the work of Italian poet Giambattista Marino. A member of the cult of PLATONIC LOVE, which flourished at the court, Carew led a colorful personal life. He repented of it, it is said, upon his deathbed.

Bibliography

Carew, Thomas. *Poems of Thomas Carew.* Edited by Arthur Vincent. Freeport, N.Y.: Books for Libraries Press, 1972.

Selig, Edward I. *The Flourishing Wreath: A Study of Thomas Carew's Poetry.* New Haven, Conn.: Yale University Press, 1958.

Carnal Prayer Mat, The   Li Yu (1657)

The period from 1500 to 1700 proved to be among the great ages in the history of the Chinese erotic novel. Among those, LI YU's *The Carnal Prayer Mat* is the most original, most ribald, the funniest, and at the same time, as the book's translator Patrick Hanan observes, the most "outrageous, vulgar, [and] shocking." Over against those aspects of the work, Li sets careful and extended attention to dialogues against libertinism and in favor of the Buddhist tradition's emphasis on repentance and salvation. Li represses salaciousness for its own sake while emphasizing the humorous aspects of his subject.

The originality of the work's content is balanced, with a single exception, by the traditionality of the book's form. Following the practice of most Chinese novels, Li begins each chapter with a verse epigram. Next comes a brief lyric, followed by the text of the chapter proper. At the end of each chapter, Li introduces a formal innovation. He comments briefly in

his own voice on what has gone before. In doing so he adopts a theatrical practice of having a narrator act as interlocutor. He also expands this practice into an occasional dialogue between a reader and the author that interrupts the text.

Li devotes his first chapter to a tongue-in-cheek defense of the eroticism of the novel he is about to present. He argues that sex, when treated like medicine, is not harmful to humankind. Rather, he says, sex only becomes harmful when treated like food; in that case it can be fatal. He assures his reader that his principal motive is to repress licentiousness.

The second chapter begins the story proper. In it a baby who babbled in Sanskrit scriptures becomes a Buddhist monk with the religious name *Correct and Single* and the monastic name of *Lone Peak*. In addition to abstaining from the temptations of the flesh, he also refused to beg for money, explain Scripture, or to dwell on one of the sacred mountains of China. These were perceived as marks of unusual piety, and young men flocked to his residence begging to become his disciples. He was very selective about choosing them. One day a remarkably handsome young man enters Lone Peak's dwelling while the priest is meditating. After meditation, they converse, and the priest is willing to recruit the young man, who introduces himself by the pen name, Scholar Vesperus. The conversation reveals that, though Vesperus feels a religious calling, it is as yet a weak one and he has two desires that he first wishes to fulfill. First he wants to achieve rewards through his own efforts. He is reluctant, though, to confide his second desire. The priest correctly guesses that it is to marry the most beautiful girl in the world. There follows a rather intellectual discussion of sex and Vesperus's obsession with it as sexual behavior relates to rewards and punishments in the afterlife. The two men part, and Li's authorial persona informs the reader that Vesperus will thereafter be the novel's focus until the last chapter. In the critique of the first chapter, the author explains that he had tricked the reader into thinking that he would develop a homoerotic relationship between the characters, that the reader can expect more surprises of that sort, and that only Li Yu has the skill to provide them.

In the third chapter we follow the story of Vesperus as he uses a matchmaker to win the hand of Jade Scent—a beautiful young maiden. She is everything he had hoped for in a woman except that she is reticent about sex. Vesperus uses a book depicting various possibilities to remedy her lack of experience in this department, and he is idyllically happy with his wife. His father-in-law, however, is another story. He does not much like Vesperus and nags and criticizes the young man incessantly. When this becomes unbearable, Vesperus resolves to set out in search of new adventure. He tells his father-in-law he wants to find a teacher, take the government examinations, and make a success of himself, but that he does not want Jade Scent to think him deficient in his love for her, so the father-in-law should suggest it. The father-in-law agrees. Vesperus tries to leave one of his homosexual servants to keep an eye on Jade Scent. Here the reader for the first time learns that Vesperus's erotic tastes run to both women and men. The father-in-law rejects this offer, and Vesperus goes in search of new fields to conquer.

Conquering new fields becomes the central theme of much of the rest of the novel. All sorts of surprising interludes and novel complications develop, including reconstructive surgery to enhance Vesperus's prowess among women and other marriages. Like Don Juan in Mozart's opera *Don Giovanni*, Vesperus keeps a record of his conquests, and Cloud, Lucky Pearl, and Lucky Jade (three sisters who have been entertaining Vesperus) discover this in Chapter 15. As Vesperus not only recorded names but also had devised a rating system with commentary, the sisters learn exactly what he thinks of each of them.

In Chapter 19 the reader learns Vesperus's first wife, Jade Scent, once he had introduced her to the joys she experienced with him, could not live without them. She has in the interim become a prostitute, and Li Yu credits Vesperus with her fall. Vesperus visits the brothel in which she is employed. Jade Scent sees him, and thinking that he has come to have her arrested, she hangs herself rather than bear the ignomiy. Not long afterward a letter comes informing Vesperus that his second wife has run off with a lover.

Realizing that the time has come to seek redemption for all his past sins, Vesperus returns to the temple of Lone Peak where he takes the monastic name Stubborn Stone. In an act of penance, he emasculates himself. This is not, however, the story's denouement. Another character, Honest Quan, who throughout the story has been Vesperus' enemy, arrives on the scene also seeking salvation. He takes the Knave as his monastic name. The former enemies exchange forgiveness, and eventually all three, Lone Peak, Stubborn Stone, and the Knave die at intervals all seated in the lotus position of the compassionate Buddha.

Li Yu's comment on the final chapter intentionally leaves a reader perplexed. "This," he says, "truly is a book that mocks everything." He then paraphrases a quotation from a commentator on the writings of the Chinese sage Confucius: "Those who understand me will do so through *The Carnal Prayer Mat;* those who condemn me will also do so because of *The Carnal Prayer Mat.*"

Bibliography
Li Yu. *The Carnal Prayer Mat.* Translated by Patrick Hanan. 1990. New York: Honolulu: University of Hawai'i Press, 1996.

Carnival Songs of Florence
Although their roots probably reach back into earlier folk traditions, the origin of the Florentine Carnival Song as a Renaissance phenomenon and literary subspecies has been attributed to LORENZO DE' MEDICI (1449–92). A notable poet himself, this uncrowned ruler of Florence was ever vigilant in seeking ways to gain the support of ordinary Florentines through public entertainments of various kinds. As Antonfrancesco Grazzini (pen named *Il Lasca*—the Roach) tells the story in his celebrated collection, *Canti carnascialeschi* (Carnival songs, 1559), the Florentines were in the habit of parading through the streets masked, in costume, and singing satiric songs during the period preceding Lent called Carnival. Some walked, some rode on horseback, and others rode in decorated carts or chariots in allegorical parades called triumphs.

Seeing in this custom an opportunity for increasing popular enthusiasm for his leadership, Lorenzo commissioned the construction of elaborately designed and decorated carts to carry persons dressed in allegorical costume and singing songs whose lyrics, which were both appropriate to the allegorical characters and full of bawdy double entendre, Lorenzo had himself written. Singing and dancing and accompanied by musical instruments, Lorenzo's revelers paraded through the city in their carts. The Florentines loved it and viewed Lorenzo's inventiveness as a challenge to their own. Both the best artists of the city and the common folk took up the challenge and prepared their own irreverent and invariably suggestive songs on every imaginable subject: Gypsies, frog catchers, nymphs in love, runaway nuns, damned souls, and tortoise-shell cats—this list faintly suggests the range.

Bibliography

Medici, Lorenzo de'. *Carnival Song.* Translated by Walter Piston. Performed by Robert Palmer and others. Analog, 12-inch sound disk, 33 1/3 rpm, mono. Fleetwood, 1964.

carpe diem

A Latin phrase meaning "seize the day," carpe diem literature, especially lyric verse, promotes the idea that life is short and youth shorter, so people should live each day to its fullest. Male poets such as Robert Herrick and ANDREW MARVELL composed poems on that theme. Herrick's *To Virgins to Make Much of Time* and Marvell's *To his Coy Mistress* encourage young women to seize the amorous opportunities that present themselves lest they grow old and die having missed their chances.

Cartier, Jacques (1491–1557)

A French navigator and explorer, Cartier sailed the coast of North America and explored the St. Lawrence River, returning on three occasions in 1534, 1535, and 1541–42 and twice enduring the trials of the Canadian winter. These explorations laid the groundwork for France's claims to ownership of her North American colonies.

Cartier established the first trading post with the Iroquois Indians at a spot today called Taddousac on the western bank of the St. Lawrence near its confluence with the Saguenay. His relations with the Indians were characterized by mutual treachery, and Cartier did not scruple, on his first journey, against kidnapping some of his trading partners and taking them home to France. That the same two Iroquois he kidnapped returned with him and served as his guides on his second journey suggests that, at least in retrospect, they were not altogether displeased with their involuntary travels.

Cartier reached the sites both of Quebec City and of Montreal. At the latter location, rapids barred him from further exploration of the St. Lawrence, though the problems the shallow, swift water posed for a few miles might easily have been surmounted.

Cartier's journals of his voyages, with their accounts of new lands, exotic peoples, and the deadly, almost insurmountable hardships of the Canadian winter, commanded enormous popular interest and made a significant contribution to the Renaissance literature of exploration despite the fact that Cartier's own investigations might have achieved much more. Rather than explore overland or by Indian canoe, Cartier felt content to rely on the testimony of others and to repeat in his reports to the French king what he heard about vast treasures and potential routes to Asia further inland. Cartier preferred sailing saltwater.

After first appearing in French in 1545, Cartier's journals were immediately translated into Italian (1556) and then into English. A notable early translation was JOHN FLORIO's—perhaps from the Italian—in 1580. Good modern editions are available in both French and English.

Bibliography

Cartier, Jacques. *The Voyages of Jacques Cartier.* Edited by Ramsay Cook. Translated by Henry Percival Biggar. Toronto: University of Toronto Press, ca. 1993.
———. *Voyages en Nouvelle-France.* Edited and modernized by Robert Lahaise and Marie Couturier. Quebec: Hurtubise, ca. 1977.

Cartwright, William (1611–1643)

A member of the group of literary figures surrounding BEN JONSON—the *sons of Ben*—Cartwright was at once an Anglican priest, a popular lecturer on Aristotle at Oxford, a poet, and a playwright. His comedies and tragicomedies, performed in the university, were popular with Oxonians. One of his plays, *The Royall Slave: A Tragi-Comedy*, performed before King Charles I, met with the royal approval.

Among his best-remembered works is his poem, *No Platonic Love*. In it he parodies JOHN DONNE's poem, *The Ecstasie*, and rejects the notion, popular among his contemporaries, that a lover rises by stages from the admiration of a beloved's physical being, to admiration of the beloved's mind and virtues, and finally to a contemplation of godhead itself. Adherents of the cult of PLATONIC LOVE boast, Cartwright says, that "They souls to souls convey." Not so, he argues, "The body is the way."

His masterful style and satiric wit led Ben Jonson to remark of him, "My son Cartwright writes . . . like a man." Cartwright spent his adult life in Christ Church College, Oxford.

Bibliography

Cartwright, William. *Plays and Poems*. Edited by G. Blakemore Evans. Madison: University of Wisconsin Press, 1951.

Carvajal y Mendoza, Luisa de (1566–1614)

Orphaned as a child, Carvajal was reared by her uncle, the marquis of Almazán, as a strict and fervent Roman Catholic. Her religious zeal prompted her to remain single, though her desire for freedom of action apparently prevented her entering the convent. She chose to live in poverty and eventually convinced the Jesuits to send her as a missionary to England in an effort to bring the English back into the Roman Catholic fold.

She was a notable religious poet, writing in the tradition of medieval Spanish religious mystics on subjects that reveal her obsession with Christ, her determination to mortify the flesh, and her desire to achieve martyrdom. She also authored letters and autobiographical sketches.

Bibliography

Carvajal y Mendoza, Luisa de. *Epistolario y poesias* (A collection of letters and poems). Edited by Jesús Gonzáles Marañon and Camilo Maria Abad. Madrid: Ediciones Atlas, 1965.

———. *This Tight Embrace*. [English and Spanish Selections: Poems and Letters.] Edited and translated by Elizabeth Rhodes. Milwaukee, Wisc.: Marquette University Press, 2000.

Cary, Elizabeth Tanfield, first viscountess Falkland (ca. 1586–1639)

The daughter of an able and wealthy British jurist and his wife Elizabeth Symonds Tanfield, as a youngster Elizabeth Tanfield Cary became deeply versed in the study of languages and of theology.

In 1602 she married Sir Henry Cary, whose distinguished service to the Crown and connections at court brought him increasingly responsible civil appointments, though not always the financial rewards that he expected to accompany them. The year 1618 saw his appointment as comptroller of the royal household. Two years later the king created him Viscount Falkland. In 1622 he became lord lieutenant of Ireland, where he served until 1629 despite irregular payment of his disappointing salary and financial straits that arose from disagreements with his wife because of her religious convictions. In 1629 he returned to London as privy councilor to the king—a responsibility he exercised until his injury in a fall resulted in the amputation of his leg and, on the following day, 24 September 1633, his death.

Before that unfortunate event, Elizabeth Cary had pursued her literary interests and given birth to eight children. Five years before her marriage, the dedication to her of one of the letters in Michael Drayton's *England's Heroicall Epistles* (1597) suggests her early connection with the British literary scene. In about 1605 Cary penned the work for which she is principally remembered and the one whose attribution to her evokes the least controversy, THE TRAGEDY OF MIRIAM. Based on the story of the marriage between King Herod and the Princess Miriam and its disastrous outcome, this rhymed verse drama is the first original tragedy by a woman printed in England.

As early as 1624, members of Cary's family began to find her religious sentiments disturbing. Her studies of comparative religion led her to lean more and more toward a Roman Catholic position. Her father found her views on that subject so distasteful that in about that same year he disinherited her. The same issue led to an estrangement from her husband, for in 1625 she packed up four of her children and returned with them to England, leaving Lord Falkland and her other children in Ireland.

In 1626 she apparently wrote a history of the reign of Edward II, and the following year she expanded it. This attribution, though increasingly secure, still remains somewhat controversial. The mixed prose and verse work is distinguished by its attention to characterization and motive.

On November 14, 1626, Cary created a public scandal by openly and formally converting to Roman Catholicism. Her husband was appalled at what he considered her "Romish hipocrasy," and sought every means he could to procure a legal separation. He could not afford to maintain two households, and her conversion flaunted the Anglican establishment. Fortunately for Cary, King Charles I also had a Roman Catholic wife and sympathized with the point of view that a woman could exercise her conscience in such matters provided that she granted only spiritual allegiance to the pope and no temporal allegiance. Consequently, the king ordered Cary to provide his wife with 1,000 pounds per annum for her maintenance. The politics surrounding her decision, however, led to her being banned from the court when Cary accompanied Queen Caroline to mass. Cary was a highly visible public figure and a noblewoman to boot. Despite his private sympathy for her decision, the king could not appear to condone it lest others follow her example.

In 1630 Cary published in France what she considered to be her most important work, a translation of a treatise addressed to the king of England by Cardinal Jacques Davy du Perron: *The reply of the most illustrious Cardinall of Perron, to the answeare of the Kinge of Great Britaine.* Perron's work presented the arguments supporting the Roman Catholic position in the face of the Anglican establishment. Cary's scholarship and translation gained favorable attention in Rome.

Cary worked to convince her children to follow her into the Roman church, and two of her boys, Henry and Patrick, and four of her daughters, Lucy, Mary, Elizabeth, and Anne, did so, though Patrick eventually reconverted to Anglicanism. All of the Roman Catholic daughters, however, became nuns in France, and Lucy, who took the religious name Dame Maria, in 1645 at Cambrai, penned a biography of her mother, *Lady Falkland, Her Life.* This work remained in manuscript until the mid 19th century when it was discovered and belatedly published. Dame Maria's biographical models were the lives of saints, and that emphasis appears in her depiction of her mother.

Bibliography

Ferguson, Margaret W., Patrick Cullen, and Betty S. Travitsky, eds. *Works by and Attributed to Elizabeth Cary.* Aldershot, U.K.: Scolar Press, 1996.

Wolfe, Heather, ed. *Elizabeth Cary, Lady Falkland: Life and Letters.* Tempe, Ariz.: Arizona Center for Medieval and Renaissance Studies, Arizona State University, 2001.

Casa, Giovanni della (1503–1566)

Born a member of the Florentine nobility, Giovanni della Casa entered the priesthood and rose through its ranks, eventually becoming the archbishop of Benevento, the papal nuncio in Venice, and under Pope Paul IV, the Vatican's secretary of state. It seems that Casa made an enemy of Pier Paulo Vergerio, a Roman Catholic bishop who converted to Protestantism. Casa had prosecuted him for heresy in Venice in 1546. In retaliation, the exiled Vergerio made Casa and his work a target of Protestant accusations concerning the corruption of the clergy. Casa had in fact written an obscene, burlesque poem, A chapter about the oven (*Capitolo del*

Forno), and a Venetian woman had borne him a son, Quirino, whom the archbishop acknowledged. Neither of these matters was unusual at the time, but the resultant scandal may have prevented Casa from rising even higher in the church hierarchy.

Casa wrote both Latin poems and admirable Italian verse in the manner of PETRARCH. The Italian poems are particularly notable for the autobiographical view they provide of Casa's innermost thoughts and feelings and of his private conviction that his life had been wasted as a result of his youthful follies.

Casa is principally remembered in literary circles for an influential book that he wrote on manners. Addressed to the person from whose name it takes its title, *Galateo,* the book is a sort of companion volume to CASTIGLIONE's THE BOOK OF THE COURTIER. It instructs Galateo in such matters as styling his hair, using his napkin, and how to imply his meaning when his topic might be considered indelicate. In short, *Galateo* instructs a young gentleman about his behavior in polite society. Its popularity for a very long time suggests that it both identified and addressed a perceived social need.

Bibliography

Casa, Giovanni Della. *Galateo.* Translated and edited by Konrad Eisenbichler and Kenneth R. Bartlett. Toronto: Centre for Reformation and Renaissance Studies, ca. 1986.

Castelvetro, Lodovico (1505–1571)

The child of a noble family, Castelvetro was born in the city of Modena, Italy, and educated in the law at the Italian universities of Padua, Bologna, and Ferrara. Also interested in literature and in HUMANIST studies, he continued his education in languages and literature in the Tuscan city of Sienna before returning to his native Modena to teach law. He was active in literary affairs and became embroiled in a quarrel stemming from his unflattering assessment of the verse of a minor poet, Annibale Caro. This literary trifle flared into a major feud involving a killing and, eventually, a charge of heresy leveled against Castelvetro.

Rather than take his chances with the officers of the INQUISITION in Rome, Castelvetro fled to Paris and, as a result, was excommunicated from the Catholic Church. In Paris, Castelvetro undertook partly to translate from the Greek and partly to summarize ARISTOTLE'S POETICS. The translation was not always faithful to the original, and in trying to convey Aristotle's ideas about the sorts of decorum that TRAGEDY ought to preserve, Castelvetro elaborated on his source and invented the UNITIES of time, place, and action. He also preferred dramatic realism and did not require that poetry fulfill an educative mission. Its more proper role, as he thought, was simply to entertain. He also took issue with the idea that the poet was divinely inspired when the creative mood came along. He did not think that poets occupied the priestly role of VATES.

Castelvetro's readers often thought that the notion of the unities belonged to Aristotle, and the reverence with which dramatists and critics regarded the Greek philosopher was so great that many European playwrights—especially among the French—regarded the unities as rules for composition. The upshot was that Castelvetro's popularization of Aristotelian doctrine became one of the most influential pieces of all Renaissance literary criticism.

Bibliography

Charlton, H. B. *Castelvetro's Theory of Poetry.* Manchester, U.K.: Manchester University Press, 1913.

Castiglione, Baldassare (1478–1529)

A student of HUMANISM, a soldier, a diplomat, and a writer, Castiglione produced among other works one of the most influential books of the European Renaissance, THE BOOK OF THE COURTIER (1528). This work's four sections aim to establish an ideal standard of behavior in aristocratic society. At the same time the work examines many topics of contemporary interest such as PLATONIC LOVE, whether republics or autocratic states are better, the arts of painting and sculpture, and the ideal consort for the ideal courtier.

Aside from his most famous work, Castiglione also produced a pastoral ECLOGUE, Thyrsis (*Tirsi* [a shepherd's name], 1508). He wrote Italian poetry in the PETRARCHIST manner and penned poems in Latin as well. Beyond this he wrote a prologue to Cardinal Bibbiena's comedy, *Calendra* (1513). Much of Castiglione's extensive correspondence also survives and is available in modern Italian and English editions.

Bibliography

Ady, Julia Mary. *Baldassare Castiglione, The Perfect Courtier, His Life and Letters: 1478–1529.* 1908. New York: AMS Press, 1973.

Castiglione, Baldassare. *The Book of the Courtier: The* [Charles] *Singleton Translation.* Edited by Daniel Javitch. New York: W. W. Norton & Co., 2002.

Woodhouse, J. R. *Baldesar Castiglione: A Reassessment of the Courtier.* Edinburgh: Edinburgh University Press, 1978.

Castle of Perseverance, The

Written in verse in the early 15th century and last performed in England in 1536, the allegorical play *The Castle of Perseverance* is an important precursor of much Renaissance British drama and provides a sense of the native English tradition from which both Renaissance theater and British allegorical epic emerged. Along with two other plays of its sort, *Wisdom* and *Mankind, The Castle* reveals much about the staging and subject matter of longer plays, or *Macro Plays,* at the dawn of the Tudor period. A PSYCHOMACHIA (a battle between good and evil for possession of a soul), the play was resurrected at the University of Toronto in 1982. Played outdoors in the round in both the 16th and the 20th centuries, the play follows the fortunes of a character, Mankind, from birth to death and beyond. Before his birth, three kings named the World, the Flesh, and the Devil declare their intention to destroy Mankind. As soon as he comes into the world, Mankind acquires a guardian angel who tries to steer him in the direction of salvation and a demon who works hard at snaring his soul for hell.

A series of sets, erected according to the conventional principles of MORALIZED GEOGRAPHY help keep the audience attuned to Mankind's progress through the afternoon-long performance. At the center of the arena stands the Castle of Perseverance itself. As long as Mankind remains there in moral balance, he is guarded by the vigilance of his angel and of several characters who represent his virtues. But Mankind is often foolish, and he deserts the safety of virtuous living for the opportunities of the World and its king—located in the west. To the distress of his good angel and the virtues, he becomes ensnared for a time by the attractions of the harlot Lust and those of Gluttony, both of whom reside in the south and in the House of Luxury.

In the northeast, halfway between Heaven and Hell, stands the abode of Greed. For the aging Mankind, Greed represents the most serious temptation, and he deserts the Castle of Perseverance to dwell there. His tempting demon is overjoyed while his angel and his virtues weep with sorrow.

In due course, Mankind dies. Characters named Justice and Truth, argue that God must judge Mankind according to what he deserves, and the devil emerges from hell's mouth to claim his soul. But before that can happen, another character called Mercy reminds God that if people were judged only according to what they merit, hardly any would be saved. God tempers justice with mercy, and, much to the chagrin of the devil and the demon, Mankind is snatched from the jaws of hell and conducted to Heaven.

The play, which in Canada began with a herald announcing the action, ended there with a procession all around the arena. Grimacing threateningly at the audience, the devil, Lucifer, brought up the rear. In an unplanned sequel to the Toronto revival and much to everyone's delight, a child stepped from the audience to stroke the devil's fine, long, furry tail.

Concerned that such allegorical plays might encourage popery and undermine the Anglican establishment, Henry VIII's government suppressed their performance along with those of morality-play cycles in several English cities.

Bibliography

Eccles, Mark. *The Macro Plays: The Castle of Perseverance, Wisdom, Mankind.* London, New York, Toronto: Oxford University Press, 1969.

Hopper, Vincent Foster, and Gerald B. Lahey. *Medieval Mystery Plays*. Great Neck, N.Y.: Barron's Educational Series, 1962.

catharsis

Anyone who has ever seen a good production of WILLIAM SHAKESPEARE'S *KING LEAR* and who has sat stunned and drained as the final death march empties the stage has experienced what ARISTOTLE meant by catharsis. Shakespeare achieves this emotionally cleansing experience for the audience without closely observing the Aristotelian unities as the Renaissance generally understood them. In his *Poetics*, Aristotle argued that a good TRAGEDY produces in the audience a sense of identification with the tragic hero or heroine. As a result of that identification, the play produces in its viewers the emotions of pity and fear. The members of the audience pities the protagonist's misery and fears that fate might lead them into similar circumstances. The end of the play, however, relieves the audience of these emotions and produces a cleansing or *catharsis* that somehow leaves the audience morally improved.

Catherine of Genoa, Saint (Caterina Fieschi Adorno) (1447–1510)

Forced into an unwanted marriage with the reprobate Giuliano Adorno, Caterina Fieschi, who would have preferred the convent, began in 1473 to experience religious visions that included the bloody Christ carrying his cross. She became a religious ascetic. She wore a hairshirt—a garment made of animal skin with the hair side toward a person's body. Because this garment was usually not removed for bathing, vermin made their homes next to and within the skin of the wearer, resulting in the continual mortification of the flesh. In addition, she adopted other ascetic measures.

When her husband's business failed, he reformed his life. Together they began a ministry for the dying, the orphaned, and the poor that centered on the charitable hospital of Pammatone where her service continued without interruption despite her husband's death in 1497. Catherine's devotion attracted supporters among whom were a lawyer, Ettore Vernazza, and a devoted disciple, Cattaneo Marabotto. These two compiled from Catherine's reports the work that constituted St. Catherine of Genoa's indirect and somewhat belated contribution to the literature of the Renaissance, the Italian *Life of the Seraphic St. Catherine of Genoa* (published in 1737) that detailed her not-altogether-original view of purgatory as a step toward unity with Godhead.

Eventually, she became the salaried administrator of the hospital at Pammatone. Her responsibilities included supervising other nuns, priests, and physicians. She also dealt innovatively with the overwhelming demands on the hospital's services during plague times by erecting outside its walls ranks of tents to shelter the afflicted.

She was canonized by the Roman Catholic Church in 1737.

Bibliography

Catherine of Genoa, Saint. *Fire of Love! Understanding Purgatory*. Manchester, N.H.: Sophia Institute Press, ca. 1996.

———. *Purgation and Purgatory: The Spiritual Dialogue*. Translated by Serge Hughes. New York: Paulist Press, 1979.

Nugent, Donald Christopher. "Saint Catherine of Genoa: Mystic of Pure Love." In *Women Writers of the Renaissance and Reformation*, edited by Katharina M. Wilson, 67–80. Athens, Ga. and London: University of Georgia Press, 1987.

Catholic Counter-Reformation

As a result both of reform movements within the Roman Catholic Church and of reactions to the threat posed by the Protestant rebellion against the authority of the Holy See, the Roman Catholic Church underwent a notable spiritual revival and organizational and disciplinary reform in the 16th and 17th centuries.

Within the Roman church the reform movement was grounded in the thinking and activities of Christian HUMANISTS, of priests and nuns who were appalled by certain abuses that had crept into the practices of the church hierarchy—such as the sale of indulgences and the absentee holders of religious office who drew their salaries but rarely appeared. Leaders such as the Carmelites St. Theresa of Avila and St. John of the Cross contributed to a renewal of spiritual zeal with their written reports of mystical experience, their personal sanctity, and their organizational capacities. They and members of new religious orders such as the Jesuits (formed 1534) were also struck by the abysmal ignorance of the lower clergy and the reprehensible behavior of cloistered members of both sexes. The Jesuits and the Franciscans counted among those who undertook a global program of education for both laymen and clergy. The Barnabites (formed 1530) and the Ursulines (formed 1535) respectively undertook missionary efforts and applied Jesuit educational principles to training young girls.

Popes such as Paul III (served 1534–49), Paul IV (served 1555–59), and Pius IV (served 1559–65) convened the COUNCIL OF TRENT, reformed the Roman Curia, prohibited the sale of church offices and indulgences, and demanded high standards of personal behavior from the clergy.

On the literary front, the devotional writings of the saints named above characterize one sort of literary activity associated with the Counter-Reformation. The renewed zeal of the Catholic Church and its adherents appeared as well in the reflections of personal religious devotion in the writings of such poets as ISABELLA ANDREINI, in the vast religious epics of TORQUATO TASSO in Italy, and in the religious drama of France and Spain. There playwrights such as PIERRE CORNEILLE and PEDRO CALDERÓN DE LA BARCA brought the spirit of religious reform to the stages of their countries.

Perhaps, however, the writings of the Christian humanists finally produced the greatest impact both on the Counter-Reformation and on the subsequent history of the Roman Catholic Church. As early as the 15th century LORENZO VALLA had proposed new standards for textual criticism that would improve the text and, therefore, the authority of the Bible. DESIDERIUS ERASMUS applied these standards not only to his own translations of the Bible, but to his enormous output of translations of the works of the early Church fathers as well. Al-

though Erasmus's writings for a while appeared on the INDEX OF FORBIDDEN BOOKS, eventually Roman Catholic authorities came to approve of his work. Less controversial was the work of Spanish Cardinal Francisco Jiménez de Cisneros, founder of the University of Alcalá and director of the project that resulted in the COMPLUTENSIAN POLYGLOT BIBLE, whose editorial principles generally, but not always, followed those proposed by Valla. The church credits the English humanist saint and martyr, SIR THOMAS MORE with contributing to the principles on which the Counter-Reformation was founded.

Bibliography

Birely, Robert. *The Refashioning of Catholicism, 1450–1700: A Reassessment of the Counter-Reformation*. Washington, D.C.: Catholic University of America Press, 1999.

Luebke, David M., ed. *The Counter-Reformation: The Essential Readings*. Malden, Mass.: Blackwell, 1999.

O'Malley, John W. *Trent and All That: Renaming Catholicism in the Early Modern Era*. Cambridge, Mass.: Harvard University Press, 2000.

Cavalier lyric

A name originally used as a scornful term by PURITANS, the phrase *Cavalier lyric* has come to describe poems on the subject of love and the pleasures of living the amorous life while one is young and can seize the day—CARPE DIEM. Cavalier poets typically were associated with the court of King Charles I of England and included such writers as THOMAS CAREW, HENRY VAUGHAN, SIR JOHN SUCKLING, and KATHERINE PHILIPS.

Cavendish, George (ca. 1500–ca. 1562)

A faithful member of the staff of Cardinal Thomas Wolsey (ca. 1475–1530), Cavendish retired to his country estate after the cardinal died on his way to London to face charges of high treason. Wolsey had successfully positioned himself as the power behind the throne in Henry VIII's reign. He displeased the king, however, by dragging his feet in the matter of the king's divorce from his first wife, Catherine of Aragon.

As a close associate of the cardinal, Cavendish had access to the information required to write a biography of Wolsey, and he did so during the reign of Queen Mary I (1553–58). Scrupulously fair to the man that Cavendish characterizes as his "Lord and master," and whose capacities as the chief administrator of a kingdom he openly admires without for a moment glossing over his faults, Cavendish did not publish the work during his lifetime since it contained several equally even-handed portraits of living persons.

In portraying Wolsey's rise to the pinnacle of power, his arrogance, and his subsequent pitiable fall, Cavendish as a biographer conforms both to the expectations of factual reporting and of medieval notions of tragedy—the fall of a powerful individual as a result of the fickle operation of FORTUNE. That handling does no violence, however, to the biographer's subject since the facts of Wolsey's life conformed closely to the pattern.

Cavendish's occasionally hostile attitude toward aspects of the Anglican establishment appeared in his manuscript. As a result, the work did not see print during Elizabeth's reign or indeed until 1641. Nonetheless, a great many manuscript copies of the work circulated. SHAKESPEARE had probably seen one before writing his *Henry VIII*. When the work did finally appear in print, its editor altered it mercilessly to turn it into Puritan propaganda against the Anglican Archbishop Laud. Wolsey was turned into a cautionary example for ambitious clerics, and Cavendish's reputation as a biographer suffered undeserved damage.

In the 18th century a reliable version at last appeared that rescued both text and author. Finally in 1825 S. W. Singer carefully edited the text from Cavendish's own holograph manuscript.

Bibliography

Cavendish, George. *Thomas Wolsey, late Cardinal, his Life and Death*. Edited by Roger Lockyer. London: Folio Press and J. M. Dent, 1973.

Cavendish, Margaret (*née* Lucas), Duchess of Newcastle (1623–1673)

One of the most unusual of the self-constructed literary figures of the Renaissance, Cavendish was born to a wealthy Essex family. Her father died when she was only two, so throughout her childhood she had before her the example of her capable and independent mother. The Lucas family was firmly royalist in its political sympathies: Therefore in 1642 when civil war erupted in Britain, Mrs. Lucas moved with her eight children to Oxford where young Margaret became a maid of honor to Queen Henrietta Maria. When the queen went into exile in Paris in 1644, Margaret went with her. There she met William Cavendish, a widower 30 years her senior and the marquis of Newcastle, who wooed and won her hand. During the interregnum, the English estates of the marquis were confiscated. The couple moved to Antwerp. The now Countess Margaret returned to England in 1651 in an unsuccessful effort to secure compensation for her husband's seized lands and possessions, and while she was there she began her career as a writer.

On her return to Antwerp in 1653, she published both her *Poems and Fancies* and *Philosophical Fancies*. *Nature's Pictures drawn by Fancy's Pencil to the Life* followed in 1656.

With the restoration of the monarchy in 1660, the Cavendish couple returned to England and took up residence in the most habitable of the marquis's recovered estates. Margaret Cavendish had discovered the pleasures of writing and of constructing worlds within the imagination. In doing so, she created within her mind a persona for herself, and both in her artistic and her ordinary life she strove to be the person she imagined. She valued originality, and she fashioned costumes for herself that were pieced together from both men's and women's clothing. Her appearance and public behavior made some of her friends consider her mad. But she was only original and different. Women who wrote were discouraged from publishing—at least under their real names. The notoriety was considered vulgar. Rejecting this notion as a form of patriarchal control, Cavendish actively sought an audience and wanted a readership that valued both her work and who she was.

As a thinker she was essentially interested in categories and types, and her interest was wide ranging. It included the sciences and philosophy, and though her scientific speculations were routinely dismissed by her contemporaries and by later thinkers, her materialism and her atomism were both worthy of being propounded given the state of the physical sciences in her time. She was a skeptic, a feminist with a unique point of view, a utopian visionary, and a crafter of fictions that self-evidently combined fantasy and autobiography. She also freely combined genres and mixed prose and poetry to produce a life work that is genuinely unique in the annals of literature.

In *Nature's Pictures*, for example, Cavendish tells us she includes "feigned stories of natural descriptions" that are alternatively comic, tragicomic, poetic, romantic, philosophical, and historical, some in verse, some in prose, and some mixed. It is her most sustained attempt at combining categories. She published *Orations of Divers Sorts and Plays* in 1662. The following year *Philosophical and Physical Opinions* appeared, in 1664 two collections of letters, *Sociable Letters* and *Philosophical Letters*, were published.

In 1665 William Cavendish became the Duke, and Margaret the Duchess, of Newcastle. That year also saw the publication of a work she had written in Antwerp: *The World's Olio*—a collection of essays in which she outlines her thinking on a number of aesthetic, political, philosophical, and scientific subjects. In 1666 the work appeared for which she is principally remembered today, THE DESCRIPTION OF A NEW WORLD CALLED THE BLAZING WORLD. With it was printed her *Observations on Experimental Philosophy*.

In 1667 Cavendish published her husband's biography, the *Life of William Cavendish*. From that time until the end of her life, many of her earlier works were reissued, but only in 1668 did something new appear: *Plays never Before Printed*.

The 20th and 21st centuries have seen a renewed interest in and revised readings of the works of this singular and memorable author.

Bibliography

Cavendish, Margaret, Duchess of Newcastle. *The Description of A New World Called The Blazing World and Other Writings.* Edited by Kate Lilley. London: William Pickering, 1992. Reissued, Penguin, 2002.

Grant, Douglas. *Margaret the First: A Biography of Margaret Cavendish, Duchess of Newcastle, 1623–1673.* Toronto: University of Toronto Press, 1957.

Caxton, William (1420–1491)

Born in Kent, Caxton, who eventually became the first printer in England, early served as a London apprentice, becoming a member of the Mercers' Company. Beginning in the 1440s, he moved to the Continent where he became a successful member and eventually a governor of the Merchant Adventurers of Bruges, Belgium. He dealt on this company's behalf with the Hanseatic League and with the Duchy of Burgundy. In Burgundy he made an important connection with the sister of King Edward IV, Margaret, Duchess of Burgundy. In 1470 Caxton moved to Cologne where he apparently learned the printing business from Johann Schilling, whose shop he took over. Back in Bruges in 1473, with the Fleming calligrapher Colard Mansion to design type, he established another shop. At it he printed the first work set in type in the English language, his own translation of a French historical romance, *Recuyell* (a literary collection) *of the Historyes of Troy*, a work dedicated to the Duchess Margaret.

The year 1476 saw Caxton set up his printing business near the royal court in Westminster—a move that made him the first printer in England. A gifted translator, he rendered many works into English. These included *The Golden Legend* from the Latin of Jacobus Voragine's collection of saint's lives, and parts of works by BOETHIUS, CICERO, OVID, and VIRGIL. His shop produced the first printed editions of *The Canterbury Tales* of Geoffrey Chaucer (1477), John Gower's *Confessio amantis* (Confession of lovers), and of Thomas Mallory's *Morte d'Arthur* (1485). As a translator, Caxton followed his originals very closely and occasionally got lost in the long sentences that characterized the Latin of many of his originals. Yet this work of translation focused his attention closely on matters of English style. He tried to produce, he said, "English not over rude, ne curious, but in such terms as shall be understanden by God's grace." When in doubt about the clarity of his word choice, he sometimes double translated, using both an English and a French word together and leaving to his reader to decide which might be clearer. Coming at the very beginning of the early modern period of the English language, Caxton's prose provided a useful model for some of his successors.

Both in number and quality, the works that proceeded from his print shop outpaced the production of the competitors who, beginning in 1478, followed his lead in London and elsewhere in England. Altogether his shop produced about a hundred works during his lifetime with Caxton himself not only translating many of them but often also adding helpful commentaries that preceded or followed the text.

Caxton's apprentice, Wynken de Worde, succeeded him in the printing business. In 1495 de Worde issued Caxton's last translation. From the Latin *Vitas Patrem*, it contained accounts of the lives of those early church fathers who, like St. Jerome, had mortified their flesh and sought solitary inspiration in the desert. De Worde reported that Caxton had literally finished the translation on the last day of his life.

Caxton's press specialized in serving and at the same time helping to create the home market for books in English—a market that expanded rapidly throughout the Renaissance. About 30 of Caxton's works survive either as fragments or in single copies. Facsimile editions are available of some of his more famous books, such as his 1483 second edition of Chaucer, which is illustrated with woodcuts.

Bibliography

Hellinga, Lotte. *Caxton in Focus.* London: British Library, 1982.

Painter, George D. *William Caxton: A Quincentenary Biography of England's First Printer.* London: Chatto and Windus, 1976.

Cecchi, Giovanni Maria (1518–1587)

Nicknamed *Il comico* (the comedian) by his contemporary Florentine citizens, Giovanni Maria Cecchi authored more than 60 plays. In the early part of his career, these ran mostly to COMEDY or to mixed forms; later (after 1560) he turned primarily to religious subjects. His many comedies influenced the development of later Italian theater. In them one recognizes stock characters, perhaps borrowed from the classical Roman comedies of Plautus and Terrence but brought into Cecchi's contemporary theatrical scene as the recognizable stereotypes of Renaissance Italians: the boaster, the senile lover, the penny pincher, the flatterer. Cecchi's character types laid the foundation for several of the traditional characters or—as they were called—*masks* that populated the partly improvisational COMMEDIA DELL' ARTE (comedy of the guild) that followed him.

Beyond writing for the theater, Cecchi's literary activity included collecting and commenting on Florentine proverbs that he published in an undated edition. He also published sketches and anecdotes about France, Germany, Spain, and other countries: A collection of more portraits (*Compendio di piú rittratti*, 1575). He parodied and satirized the pedantic proceedings at the learned academies of his city in his Master Bartolino's idle prattling (*Cicalalmento di Maestro Bartolino*, 1582). He also penned a popularization in Italian of gospel stories and religious lessons to make them accessible to his fellow citizens who read and spoke no Latin.

The religious plays of his last period run to two volumes, though they have not been reedited since the late 19th century.

Bibliography

Cecchi, Giovanni Maria. *The Horned Owl.* Translated by Konrad Eisenbichler. Waterloo, Canada: University of Waterloo Press, 1981.

Radcliffe–Umstead, Douglas. *Carnival Comedy and Sacred Play: The Renaissance Dramas of Giovan Maria Cecchi.* Columbia: University of Missouri Press, 1986.

Cellini, Benvenuto (1500–1571)

A multitalented figure of the Italian Renaissance, Cellini was a master goldsmith, a sculptor, a designer and producer of commemorative medals, a slapdash poet, the author of a pair of how-to books, and an autobiographer.

His most famous work, his autobiography, LIFE OF BENVENUTO CELLINI, remained unpublished for almost a century and a half following his death, finally appearing in 1728. Except to the degree that his book circulated in manuscript, it did not, therefore, furnish a model for other Renaissance figures to follow. That probably is just as well since the autobiography is among the most florid exercises in egocentrism imaginable. By his own account he saved Rome virtually singlehandedly during the siege of 1527, killing, he claimed, the leader of a mercenary army of Spaniards and Germans, Constable Charles de Bourbon, (who did, in fact, fall there) and shooting the prince of Orange from the walls of Castel St. Angelo. Not merely the most resourceful soldier of his epoch, he also portrays himself as the most important artist of his age and his detractors as dolts or worse. By his own admission, however, he was also a swaggering bully, expert and ready in the exercise of arms, fighting and murdering freely as he pleased, and getting away with it because of the protection of admiring popes and kings and the other powerful of the Earth. Despite, or perhaps because of, Cellini's self-serving exaggerations and partly because of his fast-paced, breathless style, his autobiography makes exciting reading. It also contains valuable biographical material about many of Cellini's contemporaries, especially artists. Cellini was a prototype of the romantic hero, an unapologetic individualist who insisted on his own way.

His how-to books included a volume on the art of the goldsmith and another on sculpture. From time to time, these volumes also contain autobiographical snippets that provided Cellini's readers in his own epoch a taste of what 18th-century readers would discover in the autobiography. His poems were very conventional affairs, written in the PETRARCHIST mode to flatter patrons or address friends.

His work as a sculptor and goldsmith, on the other hand, was really among the finest of his age. He is especially remembered for his bronze *Perseus* with the head of Medusa (1553), other statues on mythological themes, his bronze busts of his contemporaries including one of his Florentine patron Cosimo I de' Medici, and for his magnificent golden salt cellars.

Bibliography

Cellini, Benvenuto. *The Autobiography of Benvenuto Cellini.* Translated by George Anthony Bull. New York: Penguin Books, 1998.

———. *The Treatises of Benvenuto Cellini on Goldsmithing and Sculpture.* Translated by C. R. Ashbee. New York: Dover Publications, 1967.

Celtis, Conradus (b. Konrad Pickel) (1459–1508)

A member of the second generation of northern HUMANISTS, Celtis studied at Cologne (B.A., 1479) and under the celebrated RUDOLFUS AGRICOLA at the University of Heidelberg (M.A., 1485), where he learned basic Greek and some Hebrew. Spending the next two years teaching poetry at the universities in Erfurt, Leipzig, and Rostock, he published a textbook, *The Art of Writing Verse and Song* (in Latin, 1486).

After a period of traveling in Italy, where he had contacts with several notable Italian humanists, in 1489 he went to Cracow to study astronomy, mathematics, and science. Back in Germany by 1492, he taught poetry at the university of Ingelstadt until an outbreak of the plague closed that institution, and he moved to Heidelberg, tutoring the sons of Philip, elector of the Palatinate. He ultimately settled in Vienna and became that university's professor of poetry.

Celtis always wrote NEO-LATIN verse, and his work is among the most innovative of his German contemporaries. In 1502 he published in Latin *Four Books of Love Poetry.* In this volume he fuses descriptions of his four mostly imaginary love affairs with depictions of German geography. Each affair takes place in a different one of Germany's four regions. The poem reveals Celtis's fascination with numerology as he examines the significance of the numbers four and nine, interweaving the various meanings of these numbers—nine muses, four seasons, nine signs of the Zodiac, four directions, and so on—into each of the four books.

During his lifetime, Celtis also busied himself throughout Germany, forming associations of persons who, regardless of social origin, shared interests in humanistic studies and literature. Inspired by the intellectual academies Celtis had observed in Italy, these groups undertook publishing projects, worked at collecting manuscripts, and offered mutual moral and intellectual support to their members.

Celtis died before he could bring to completion the ambitious program of writing and publishing he had set for himself. He had been especially fond of the Roman poet Horace (Quintus Horatius Flaccus, 65–8 B.C.E.), who is possibly the most widely read author in the European literary tradition. Thinking of himself as the German Horace, Celtis modeled another collection of Latin poems on the work of his Roman precursor. Using the earlier device of linking a region of Germany to each of his new *Four Books of Odes* . . . (1513), Celtis includes poems about his friends and some love poems as well. He wrote another collection, this time of EPIGRAMs modeled on the verse of the Romans Juvenal, Martial, and Persius. This frequently humorous collection contained poems that satirize Celtis's enemies and opponents. Others flatter his colleagues and patrons, and others still address lovers and saints. Celtis's admiring students saw to the publication of this posthumous edition.

Always an ardent advocate of the intellectual and cultural traditions of Germany, Celtis had begun one other major project before he died. He was preparing a work, *Germany Illustrated*, which would describe in Latin the history, geography, and people of his country. Only one sample of that work went to press, *Nürnberg* (in Latin, 1502). It paints an admirably full picture of that city, its people, its institutions and their workings, and its architecture in the early part of the 16th century.

Bibliography

Celtis, Conrad. *Selections*. Edited and translated by Leonard Forster. Cambridge, U.K.: Cambridge University Press, 1948.

Spitz, Lewis W. *Conrad Celtis: The German Arch-Humanist*. Cambridge, Mass.: Harvard University Press, 1957.

cento

Cento—an English word—has two meanings. First, it can be a collection of translations by many hands of the works of an author. In the 19th century, for example, the *Bohn Cento* was the only complete translation available in English of the 366 poems comprising PETRARCH's *Canzoniere*.

The second meaning alludes to a poem or collection of poems that an author has constructed by borrowing lines from one or more other authors and ordering them to express the arranger's thoughts and emotions. ISABELLA ANDREINI sometimes constructed poems in this way, borrowing lines from Petrarch and DANTE. Her verses illustrate two advantages to this mode of composition: First, the technique distances an author from powerful feeling. Andreini uses the method in a poem mourning the death of her friend Laura Guidiccioni Lucchesini. The distance she achieves from her own feeling makes the poem very effective. Second, employing the technique asserts an author's familiarity with the work of others and invites comparison—an invitation that implies an author deserves to be considered in the same league as the poet who originally wrote the lines.

central African epic

Because the literary tradition of central Africa remained exclusively oral well into the modern era, no one can say with precision exactly what time period saw the beginnings of the stories that have come to be associated with one now extant epic cycle or another. One can say that probably some of the stories associated with particular epics predate, perhaps by centuries, the year 1500. One can also say, this time with some certainty, that others of the stories were added to the cycles that contain them in the 200-year span on which this work principally focuses. Neither does supposing that some of the stories postdate the period of the European Renaissance seem unreasonable.

By 1500 European epics like those of Homer and Virgil that had been committed to ink and paper in ancient times admitted no new material. CHIVALRIC EPIC, on the other hand, remained open. One can trace the rich invention of story and parody from legends surrounding the courts of Charlemagne and Arthur through numerous European Renaissance writers from MATTEO BOIARDO's ORLANDO INNAMORATO, through the works a number of Italian writers, French writers, Portuguese writers, Spanish writers and English writers until MIGUEL DE CERVANTES SAAVEDRA's DON QUIXOTE DE LA MANCHA effectively closed off the genre as a serious medium of literary invention.

While drawing parallels between Central African and European chivalric epics is not always easy to do, one may safely say that the two forms share in common at least a degree of openness to the admission of new material into the cycles of song (in the broad sense of verse as well as vocal performance) and story. In Africa epics were and are intended for public performance, and material could be added or deleted from performance to performance. In Europe, chivalric epic was written either to be read privately or heard by a few persons gathered to hear another read aloud, and while a reader might skip or edit, the addition of new material had to wait on the authorial and publication processes. By contrast, Central African epics involve recitation, singing, mime, dancing, instrumental accompaniment, and lively audience participation. Sometimes, too, the lead performers in Central African epics feel a religious calling to perform. When this is the case, a spiritual dimension is added to what is more usually felt to be a reenactment of history—even when that history is mythic.

Despite their variability, certain general similarities do occur among Central African epics. While being performed they restructure the ordinary environment inhabited both by performers and audience members, all of whom temporarily inhabit an alternative, mythic world in which reenactment of the pasts of their real or imagined ancestors becomes possible. Second, no single performance of one of the epics ever seems to include all the stories associated with it. Third, the stories that frequently are included vary from locale to locale within a culture.

Most of the epics of Central Africa, however, do contain creation stories that account for the appearance and naming of people, animals, plants, and insects, but not necessarily of the creation of the world itself. They often trace the journeys of characters, the life stories of heroes, conquests, and the establishment of dynasties. They sometimes report wondrous events. Almost universally they are concerned with the search for food and its consumption and with the competition for food among relatives, often of different generations. They sometimes account for social roles and for the emergence of technologies associated with hunting and farming.

Typical of the epics of Central Africa is an epic cycle surviving among the Mongo peoples of the northeastern region of the Congo—LIANJA AND NSONGO (*Nsong'a Lianja*). The Mongo survive by hunting and by raising bananas, and they share their territory with a group of pygmies called the *Twa*, with whom they are economically interdependent. Anthropologist Steven Belcher tells us that the Mongo arrived in the region where they now live at least 200 years ago—perhaps longer. It may be safe to think that some of the episodes concerning migration and conquest date from the period just before their arrival in their present location. The consensus of scholars, however, is that the stories of migration and conquest rarely if ever concern the entire Mongo people, but rather isolated groups of them.

An epic tradition with a slightly different focus from that of the Mongo peoples is to be found among the BaNyanga people who live eastward in the Congo's Kivu region. Though the themes addressed in their *Mwindo Epic* parallel in many respects those of the Mongo, the performance aspects differ signficantly. First BaNyanga performers tend to view themselves as shamans and have often been initiated into a spirit cult. Second, although performances for paying (often Euro-American) audiences can be commissioned, the BaNyanga's preferred venue for performance is the hunting camp, and soliloquy rather than group singing seems the preferred mode of presentation. The *Mwindo Epic* focuses on strife between a father and his extraordinary son, Mwindo, who has supernatural powers. The two are reconciled after Mwindo rescues his father from the underworld. Some of the feats Mwindo accomplishes remind one of the feats performed by Hercules in Greco-Roman myth.

On the eastern coast of the Cameroons, a popular epic cycle seems to be in process of disappearing—or rather of converting into an elite literary entertainment. This is the epic concerning the figure Jeki la Njambe of the Duala people. The Duala have in the past few centuries become more concerned with commerce and trading than with conquest and subsistence. Therefore the conditions no longer exist that gave rise to their folk epic, and the people do not necessarily see their lives reflected in the cycle. Jeki's story parallels in its general outline the story of Mwindo. The elements of the cycle have been collected in two printed editions. Both of these give many more episodes of the story than would ever have been performed at one sitting, and their audience tends to be composed of those interested in folk lore and literary history.

The Ijo people dwell along riverbanks in the Nigerian delta region. Their regional epic sequence, the *Ozidi Saga,* may have its roots in an ancient story, but much of the story suggests more recent European contact. Ozidi's father, a local chieftain, is murdered by assassins and replaced by Ozidi's paternal uncle. Ozidi's grandmother, a sorceress of great power, rears the lad and undertakes his training as a warrior. As soon as he can, Ozidi undertakes a campaign of vengeance in which his grandmother's powers materially assist him and he regains the leadership. Thus far, the story could belong to any time period, and suggestions of a matrilineal society appear. After Ozidi successfully regains power, however, he begins to face adversaries who represent diseases of various sorts. One of these is a king who represents the tropical ailment elephantiasis, but eventually Ozidi must confront the Smallpox King, and we have clearly entered the period of European colonization of coastal Africa.

Other epic cycles, none earlier than the 18th century, present the stories of known, historical kings. An interesting aspect of these—one that suggests a long history of the practice—is their frequent rewriting to conform to new political realities. The 20th-century West by no means invented the notion of revising history to suit the whims, agendas, and priorities of conquerors.

Bibliography

Belcher, Stephen. *Epic Traditions of Africa.* Bloomington: The Indiana University Press, 1999.

Johnson, John William, Thomas Hale, and Stephen Belcher, eds. *Oral Epics from Africa: Vibrant Voices from a Vast Continent.* Bloomington: Indiana University Press, 1997.

Cereta, Laura (1469–1499)

Laura Cereta was an Italian HUMANIST of Brescia who had been educated in a convent school and tutored by her father in Latin, Greek, and mathematics. Widowed in her teens, she conducted a wide correspondence with male and female humanists of her epoch. In some of her letters she maintains an appropriately assertive posture against patronizing male humanists, and she presents a feminist point of view on many matters. Had her letters been made public earlier, they would have had more impact beyond her own relatively narrow circle. As it is, an edition of her work appeared in 1640. Consequently, one can say with one of her current editors and translators, Diana Robin, that Cereta's discussions often "anticipate" issues raised by later self-consciously feminist Renaissance writers.

Cereta's letters are particularly interesting for the autobiographical glimpses they provide into her sometimes difficult life and for the issues they examine from a woman's perspective. She is severely critical, for example, of women who disparage other women who have superior educations. She discusses her feelings as a daughter, as a bride, as a widow, and as the citizen of a city invaded by foreign troops.

Cereta also composed works modeled on PETRARCH and on the Roman Apuleius. These also were published posthumously.

Bibliography

Cereta, Laura. *Collected Letters of a Renaissance Feminist.* Edited and Translated by Diana Robin. Chicago: University of Chicago Press, 1997.

Rabil, Albert Jr. *Laura Cereta. Quattrocento Humanist.* Binghamton, N.Y.: Medieval and Renaissance Texts and Studies, State University of New York, 1981.

Cervantes Saavedra, Miguel de

(1547–1616)

Most widely remembered for his authorship of the two parts of DON QUIXOTE DE LA MANCHA, Cervantes also wrote plays, other prose, and poetry. Before he embarked on his literary career, however, he acquired a wide and varied experience of the world and of its hardships.

Although evidence exists of his having studied under a teacher who praised some of his verses, he does not seem to have had much if any formal university education. Cervantes himself, however, reports that he read widely from childhood, even perusing scraps of paper that the wind blew in his direction. Threatened by the severity of the Spanish law with the loss of his right hand and imprisonment for a youthful indiscretion, the 22-year-old Cervantes left Spain and spent a portion of 1569–70 in Rome as a retainer of Cardinal Giulio Acquaviva, undoubtedly coming into contact, while there, with Italian Renaissance artists, writers, and thinkers. Then he seized an opportunity to wipe his legal slate clean in Spain by enlisting in the Spanish army. As a soldier assigned to fight aboard ship, he served heroically in the famous naval Battle of Lepanto (October 7, 1571) where the Spanish fleet decisively defeated the Turks, turning the tide against their European ambitions. In that battle, Cervantes was wounded several times and lost, as a result, the use of his left hand and arm.

Released from the hospital at Messina in April 1572, he accompanied Marco Antonio Colonna to the Middle East. In 1573 Cervantes served in Tunis with Don John of Austria under the command of an admirable captain, Lope de Figueroa, and traveled with his regiment to Sicily and Italy again, this time spending about a year in Naples. He was discharged in 1575. His notable service procured him letters of commendation addressed from the duke of Sesa and from Don John to the king of Spain, and Cervantes, together with his brother Roderigo, set sail for home hoping to find significant employment.

Unfortunately, they suffered an all too common fate of 16th-century Mediterranean voyagers. Their ship was attacked and captured by Algerian pirates and its occupants taken to Algiers to be held for ransom. The letters that Cervantes carried worked against him. His captors thought they had snared a valuable prize and set a price for his freedom far beyond the means of his family to afford. His father had been an itinerant surgeon–barber who had always supported his family hand-to-mouth. It took the family three years to raise the money to free Roderigo and two more to secure Cervantes's release, which they did by sacrificing their daughters' dowries to the cause, by borrowing, and by accepting the charity of pious persons. For those five Algerian years, Cervantes served as a slave, first to two Europeans who had converted to Islam, one a Greek and the other a Venetian. Later he became the personal slave of the *dey* or ruler of Algiers, Hassan Pasha.

During this period of captivity Cervantes made several unsuccessful escape attempts, endured harsh punishments when they failed, and apparently gained a reputation for heroism and fortitude among the Christians of Algiers. The wonder is that he was neither impaled nor burned to death. It seems, however, that his literary career began in Algiers with a prose work—*News from Algiers* (*Información de Argel*)—detailing his escape attempts, his fidelity to the Christian faith, and his valor. Portions of this work or segments inspired by the events reported in it would reappear in Cervantes's later writings.

Back in Spain, Cervantes no longer had his letters of commendation. Except for his family, he was without connections. It is also possible that his family were *conversos*—that is, they may have converted from Judaism to escape expulsion from Spain in the late 15th century. If this is true, both prejudice and the law put Cervantes at a competitive disadvantage in finding employment. With his brother Roderigo, therefore, Cervantes set out around 1580–81 for Portugal in the army of the marqués de Santa Cruz and in 1582 sailed to fight in the Azores against those who refused to acknowledge the rule of the conqueror of Portugal, Philip II of Austria. Cervantes's work suggests a significant knowledge of and affection for Portuguese literature that doubtless dates to this period, and it may be that he became acquainted in Portugal with the popular literary form, the prose pastoral.

In any case, back in Spain in 1584, his next literary production took that form. He dedicated the work, *La Galatea,* to Marco Antonio Colonna, under whose standard he had earlier served. In this work, shepherds and shepherdesses thinly disguise a highly literate cast of characters. Certain autobiographical elements appear, such as the character Timbrio's captivity among the Moors. Following European pastorals elsewhere, *Galatea* tries to link Christian story and pagan myth and to modernize the recovered classic genre by introducing European Renaissance issues. Although the work as it stands runs to two substantial volumes, Cervantes did not consider it finished. He often alluded to his determination to finish it, although he never did.

Cervantes next tried his pen at drama. The secular Spanish theater was just entering in its infancy, and had Cervantes shown more natural talent as a playwright, the task of shaping its development might have fallen to him instead of to his contemporary LOPE DE VEGA.

Certainly, the events of Cervantes's own life seem dramatic enough to serve as grist for a playwright's mill, but he seems never to have acquired the knack for turning his experience into profitable drama. This was not for lack of trying. He himself tells us that he wrote "twenty or thirty" plays that were staged. Of these, nine survive. The best remembered of them is a play based on his Algerian captivity, *El Trato de Argel* (*The Algerian Affair*) in which he includes incidents based on his experience there. Another surviving play attempts to fuse Celtic and Roman history in Spain, constructing a patriotic national mythology by describing in *El cerco de la Numancia* (*The Siege of Numantia*) the

Roman siege with 80,000 men of the Celtic city of Numantia. Its 4,000 heroic defenders in fact held out for 14 years (16 in the play) until the last of them, a young boy, leaps to his death from a tower with the keys to the city's gate in his hand. The play celebrates the resolution of the Spanish character.

Both these plays were written in a hodgepodge of varied POETIC METER. The second features allegorical characters like Spain herself, the resurrection of a fallen soldier through black magic, and genuinely touching scenes between Numantian family members and lovers as they fall victim to famine during the siege of the city.

In 1584 Cervantes wooed and won Catalina Salazar Palacios, a resident of Esquivias, a small community in La Mancha. Shortly thereafter, unable to earn an adequate living in the theater despite the apparent success of his plays, he found employment requisitioning supplies to equip the Spanish armada for its ill-fated attempt to invade England. He also served as a none-too-successful tax collector whose accounts sometimes failed the scrutiny of government auditors. His applications for appointments to several vacant administrative posts in the New World were rejected despite his meritorious record of government service.

Beset by debts, Cervantes was supporting an extended family that included not only his wife but also the two sisters whose chances at marriage had been sacrificed with the dowries that freed him. His household also included his two illegitimate daughters and a servant. In these circumstances he began work on *Don Quixote*. In 1605, in Cervantes 58th year, while he was living in Valladolid, publication of its first part at last brought him instant literary fame—though little money.

The year 1606 found him back in Madrid, where he lived for the rest of his life. In 1613 his *EXEMPLARY STORIES* (*Novelas ejemplares*) appeared. In these he undermines by the examples of the tales themselves many of the prevailing literary orthodoxies of his era: the insistence on maintaining a single point of view, for example; or the objectivity of what is real as opposed to reality's dependence on one's subjective experience of the world. The literary theorists of the late 20th and early 21st centuries have designated Cervantes not only the first real Spanish representative of the Renaissance, but also the first modern, and they have claimed him as one of their own. As grounds for these laurels they cite the utter novelty of Cervantes's literary achievement both in these 12 tales and in the two parts of *Don Quixote*. They also point to his successful demonstration of the falsity of the critical theory of his age and country and to his anticipation of the cultural leveling that results from the internationalization of trade, commerce, and economic activity. The critics especially call attention to his apparent discovery (or rediscovery since great writers seem always to have known it) of what contemporary critics label INTERTEXTUALITY—the way one literary text speaks to another.

In 1614, Cervantes published a verse SATIRE in terza rima: Journey to Parnassus (*Viaje del Parnaso*). In this brief work, the god of poets, Apollo, calls all good poets to Mount Parnassus to help him evict the bad ones. Apollo sends Mercury, the messenger of the gods, in a ship rigged with examples of verses to seek Cervantes's advice on contemporary Spanish poets. In addition to providing his views on others, Cervantes remarks on his own work, which, as he tells us, has been neglected and little rewarded.

Still striving to profit from his prodigious talent, Cervantes turned once again to writing plays and farces, but in the decades that had elapsed since his earlier theatrical ventures, the plays of Lope de Vega had so shaped the expectations of audiences and producers and Lope himself so dominated the theatrical scene that Cervantes could not find a theater to produce his work. This was so even though his plays were shaped to meet the requirements of drama as established by Lope. Finally he did manage at least to find a publisher for eight plays and eight farces, or *Entremeses* (*Interludes*) as he called them. None seems to have actually been produced in his lifetime. Some of the full-length plays rework material deriving from Cervantes's Algerian captivity. Another concerns the conversion and rehabilitation of a notorious womanizer. Still another, *The Labyrinth of Love*, invokes chivalry as a theme. The farces in the collection seem livelier than the longer plays. One, "The Watchful Guard," may be based on Cervantes's experience as a soldier. Cervantes's characteristic sense of humor enlivens "The Pretended Biscayan." Another, "The Jealous Old Man," rewrites one of the *Exemplary Stories*. Perhaps more interesting than the plays and farces themselves is the preface to the work that traces the development of the Spanish theater and details the part that Cervantes perceived he had played in it.

A bogus second installment of *Don Quixote* that abused and insulted Cervantes appeared in 1614. Infuriated, Cervantes redoubled his efforts to finish the genuine version, which appeared for an eagerly waiting readership in October of 1615. Although the profits almost all went to the publisher, the glory was Cervantes's own.

One last work remained in the pen of the aging writer. This was a serious effort at romantic fiction entitled The trials of Persiles and Sigismunda, a Northern story (*Los Trabajos de Persiles y Sigismunda, Historia Setentrional*), which appeared posthumously in 1617. Modeled on Greek romances, this work concerns a prince of Iceland and a princess of Friesland as they travel in disguise through Cervantes's fantastic notion of the northern seas, ice islands, and Norse pirates. Eventually they arrive at Rome where, having at last overcome all their difficulties and having resumed their own identities, they marry and presumably live happily ever after. The journey has an allegorical overlay as the pair moves from the barely civilized margins of European culture to its fountainhead at Rome. Cervantes himself had a high opinion of this work, though posterity has not always accorded it a central place in his canon.

Aging, ill, and aware that he was dying, Cervantes met his end with the same resolution and serenity with which he had borne affliction throughout his life, though even near the end he continued to think he might finish his "Galatea."

Bibliography

Cervantes Saavedra, Miguel de. *Don Quijote: A New Translation, Backgrounds and Contexts, Criticism.* Translated by Burton Raffel. Edited by Diana de Armas Wilson. New York: W. W. Norton, ca. 1999.

———. *Exemplary Stories.* Translated by Leslie Lipson. New York: Oxford University Press, 1998.

———. *The Interludes of Cervantes.* Translated by S. Griswold Morley. New York: Greenwood Press, 1969.

———. *Journey to Parnassus.* Edited by James Y. Gibson. London: 1883.

———. *The Trials of Persiles and Sigismunda: A Northern Story.* Edited by Celia R. Weller and Clark A. Colahan. Berkeley, Calif.: University of California Press, 1989.

McCrory, Donald. *No Ordinary Man: The Life and Times of Miguel de Cervantes.* London and Chester Springs: P. Owen, 2002.

Chaitanya Bhāgavata (Songbook [about] Chaitanya, *Chatanya Mangal*)
Vrindavān Dās (mid-1540s)

Also called the *Chaitanya Mangal,* Dās's verse biography is the earliest of several accounts of the life of the Hindu saint CHAITANYA (1486–1533). By the devotees of the Hindu deity Vishnu, Chaitanya was thought to be an incarnation of Lord Krishna—one of Vishnu's manifestations—and Dās follows this line in his account of Chaitanya's life. Later biographers considered that Chaitanya embodied in his own person both Krishna and his beloved Radha.

In its first 12 chapters, the work follows Chaitanya from shortly after his birth through his life as a householder and husband to his embarking on his mission. The next 26 chapters detail his planning for and developing an influential movement to encourage the veneration of Vishnu as well as his decision to become an ascetic, itinerant poet, and preacher. The final 11 chapters address his early work among the people as an ascetic, holy man.

As biography, the book displays several shortcomings. It leaves out what is known of Chaitanya's birth, and it neglects important discussion of his later life as a holy man when the saint was perhaps at his most influential. It also suffers from the author's inability to collect as source material earlier, authoritative writings about Chaitanya in Sanskrit, and some of the book's details do not jibe with the earlier authorities' accounts. Dās's version should not, however, suffer too harshly in the judgment of the critics. His book was a labor of love that required him to invent the genre he crafted. He had no models of biographical writing to follow. That he did the best he could with the material available to him appears in the subsequent success of the biography, which has been regularly reprinted in several of the languages of INDIA. Finally, *Chaitanya Bhāgavata* itself provided a model that later and more sophisticated biographers could incorporate in their works about this important 16th-century Indian religious reformer.

See also *CHAITANYACHARITAMRITA* and KRISHNADĀSA KAVIRAJĀ GOSVĀMI.

Bibliography
Majumdar, A. K. *Chaitanya, His Life and Doctrine: A Study in Vaisnavism.* Bombay: Bharatiya Vidya Bhavan, 1969.

Mukherjee, Prabhat. *History of the Chaitanya Faith in Orissa.* New Delhi: R. Chaterjee, 1940. Reprint, Calcutta: R. Chatterjee, 1979.

Chaitanyacharitamrita Krishnadāsa
Kavirāja Gosvāmi (ca. 1585)

The most important of four biographies—really saint's lives or hagiographies—of the poet and saint Chaitanya Deva (1486–1532), *Chaitanyacharitamrita* (The journeys and good works of Chaitanya) is reputed to be the only true epic in the Bengali language of the Indian medieval period. KRISHNADĀSA'S bilingual, verse work contains 10,503 couplets in Bengali and 1,012 couplets in Sanskrit. (See INDIA, LANGUAGES OF.) Of the Sanskrit verses, Krishnadāsa newly composed 97 and took the rest strategically from Sanskrit scriptures or classical Sanskrit poems. The poet then artfully deployed these borrowings to achieve the religious and philosophical purposes described below.

Krishnadāsa's predecessor biographer, VRINDAVĀN DĀS (fl. 16th century), with no biographical models to follow, had pieced together his life of Chaitanya exclusively in Bengali and, working from inadequate sources, had focused on first half of the saint's life, on his religious training, on his organizational work in spreading the doctrines associated with the veneration of the Hindu deity

Vishnu manifested as Krishna (part of the Vaishnava movement), and on Chaitanya's social gospel.

In contrast, Krishnadāsa undertook to complete the saint's life story and to assimilate it to the elevated status that Chaitanya had achieved in the minds and hearts of his followers. The poet begins by tracing in the first of the work's three sections the 24 years Chaitanya spent as a householder. The second section begins with the saint's initiation into monastacism and an account of his pilgrimage journeys to various holy sites as he pursues his goal of union with Godhead. Chaitanya's followers came to believe that he incarnated in his inward person the Hindu deity Krishna and, in his outward, the beauty of Krishna's beloved consort Radha. This ALLEGORY represents both the enjoyer of God's love and the love that is enjoyed. In the final section of Krishnadāsa's version, a reader follows the saint around the subcontinent during his last 18 years as he preaches and clarifies for his listeners his doctrine of love for one's fellow creatures.

Krishnadāsa's objectives, however, were far broader than merely recounting the incidents of the saint's life. Literary historian Sudipta Kaviraj views this biography as a way of "*doing* religion"— of bringing Krishnadāsa's readers into the circle of the spiritual reawakening associated with the BHAKTI movement to which Chaitanya's contribution had proved enormous. Among other benefits, that movement had served as a corrective to the elitist and inflexible Brahmin philosophy that had dominated Hinduism before the bhakti movement began flourishing in the 15th century.

In his linguistic and literary strategies, therefore, Krishnadāsa reflects the fact that by his time bhakti and Brahminism had reached an accommodation. The traditions had merged. Both of them viewed Chaitanya as himself divine and accepted his writings and sayings as scripture. The biographer emphasizes this merging partly by moving back and forth between Sanskrit—the liturgical language of Brahminism—and Bengali—the language of the common people of Krishnadāsa's region. The same tactic appears in the mixture of verse forms that the author employs.

An associated strategy becomes apparent in Krishnadāsa's choice of subject matter. Whereas Vrindavān Dās had focused on Chaitanya's work among the common people, Krishnadāsa details his sermons and follows closely his discussions and disagreements with religious scholars whose allegiances were pledged to subtypes of bhakti that differed from Chaitanya's. The 21st-century scholar Kaviraj finds it significant that, as Krishnadāsa portrays the historical and biographical detail surrounding Chaitanya, the saint mostly speaks popular Bengali despite his reputation as a master of the finer points of classical Sanskrit. Kaviraj seems to consider this Krishnadāsa's silent commentary on the pre-bhakti problems of Brahminism. When, however, Krishnadāsa reports matters of theological doctrine, he always shifts into the most eloquent level of classical Sanskrit, expressing his subject in the verse forms and complex meters identified with the Brahminical tradition.

Bibliography

Datta, Amaresh, ed. *Encyclopedia of Indian Literature.* New Delhi: Sahitya Akademi, 1989.

Kaviraj, Sudipta. "The Two Histories of Literary Culture in Bengal." *Literary Cultures in History: Reconstructions from South Asia.* Berkeley, Calif.: University of California Press, 2003.

Krishnadāsa, K. G. *Sri Chaitanya Charitamrita.* English translation by A. C. Bhaktivedanta Swami Prabhup. Los Angeles: Bhaktivedanta Book Trust, ca. 1996.

Chakravarti, Mukundaram (ca. 1550– ca. 1600)

This distinguished Indian poet whose medium of expression was the Bengali language is best remembered for his long verse narrative in praise of the Hindu goddess Chandi (*Kavikankan–Chandi*). The popularity of Chakravarti's verse was responsible for a flowering among Bengalis of the cult of Shakti, which celebrated the creative power of God that was responsible for the creation of the world. The poetic impulse that Chakravarti began survived among successor poets into the mid-18th century. Often called the jewel of poets, Chakravarti wrote verse that readers value as a prime example of devotional poetry. Critics and historians also prize it for the vigor of its language and for its graphic descriptions of daily life in the villages of 16th-century Bengal.

Chandrabati (ca. 1550–1600)

An Indian poet in the Bengali language, Chandrabati was the daughter of an impoverished poet and singer, Bansidas. She is remembered for a number of important works. First among these is her short version of the epic celebrating the Hindu god Rama—a *Ramayana*. She prefaced this work with a traditionally obligatory autobiography so that we know the moving details of her life.

Although virtually destitute, her father taught her to read and write. Throughout her childhood she was devoted to a playmate, Joychandra, with whom she eventually fell in love, rejecting many other suitors in the expectation that he would be her husband. He, however, married someone else.

Devastated, Chandrabati had her father build a temple for her, and she became its keeper, devoting her life exclusively to poetry and religion and rejecting the eventual advances of the regretful Joychandra. Disconsolate, he committed suicide.

Although she was initially a poet in the religious BHAKTI tradition, Chandrabati later turned her attention to more contemporary matters and to social criticism. One of her surviving poems, Kenaram the dacoit or bandit (*Dasyu Kenaram*) chronicles the exploits of an outlaw. Her most important work is a long narrative opera (a *pala gan*) in ballad meter. Entitled Beautiful Malua (*Sundari Malua*), the work is divided into 28 parts and has 1,247 verses. The attribution of this work to Chandrabati is controversial. Though Susie Tharu and K. Lalita argue strongly in its favor, many scholars in India doubt Chandrabati's authorship.

While classical examples of this form usually deal with mythological material, Chandrabati instead uses it to address the hardships that ill-conceived and unjust laws called the black laws impose on women. She sets her story during the reign of AKBAR the Great, Mughal emperor of India (1556–1606). Though the laws in question had been earlier enacted, they continued in effect. In essence, the laws gave local landowners and government functionaries the power to tax subsistence farmers and villagers at whatever rates they could extort. Those families who could not pay were subject to having their women sequestered or jailed until payment was forthcoming.

Vaguely autobiographical in its general outline, the story concerns Malua and her childhood sweetheart Binod who eventually marry. Malua's beauty attracts the unwelcome attention of officials who abuse the power of the laws they administer to force the family and their relatives into impossible debt. When the family cannot pay, the officials reason, they will gain control of Malua. When the family manages to sell all they own and pay, one official who wants Malua for a concubine threatens to bury her husband alive if she does not submit to his lust. To save her husband, Malua agrees. In custody in the local *hauli* (jail), however, Malua is able to put the official off until her brothers come to her rescue. The family flees to its ancestral village outside the control of the lecher.

Once there, however, because Malua has been in jail, the village elders unjustly shun her and require her to live outside the village. When a snake bites Binod, Malua nurses her husband back to health, and the other women argue that this proves her virtue and worthiness to live among them. The elders refuse to be moved, however, and rather than continue to be a burden on her family, Malua drowns herself as the historical Joychandra had done.

The story is often presented from a woman's viewpoint, focusing on matters like recipes and the household chores that fell exclusively to village women in Chandrabati's time. Translator Madhuchhandra Karlekar has rendered portions of Chandrabati's poem into English.

Bibliography

Women Writing in India, 600 B.C. to the Present. Volume I. Edited by Susie Tharu and K. Lalita. New

York: The Feminist Press at the City University of New York, 1990.

Chapman, George (ca. 1560–1634)

British poet, playwright, and translator, Chapman was born in Hertfordshire and probably benefited from a university education. His first collection of poetry, *The Shadow of the Night*, appeared in 1594.

Best remembered as an early translator of Homer into English, Chapman published partial translations from the *Iliad* in 1598 and again in 1610. The following year saw Chapman's magnificent translation in heptameter couplets of the entire *Iliad* under the title *The Iliads of Homer, Prince of Poets*. This translation he completed under the patronage of Prince Henry, heir presumptive to the British throne, whose death in 1612 ended Chapman's access to the royal purse and forced him to scrabble for a living with his pen. In 1616 Chapman's translation of Homer's *Odyssey* in pentameter couplets appeared. In 1618 came *The Georgicks of Hesiod*, and in 1624 Chapman rounded out his career as a translator from the Greek with Homer's lesser works. Much admired as a translator, Chapman inspired a later poet of the first rank, John Keats (1795–1821), to praise his rendition of Homer in a celebratory poem, "On first looking into Chapman's Homer." Chapman also produced a little-remembered philosophical epic, *Euthymiae & Raptus* (1609). A translation of PE-TRARCH's Latin *Seven Penitential Psalms* followed in 1612, and another work, *The Divine Poem of Musaeus*, appeared in 1616.

While Chapman's lasting literary reputation rests principally on his genuinely remarkable capacities as a translator, he was also a gifted poet and figured among the most talented playwrights of his epoch. Like many among his contemporary dramatists, Chapman frequently cooperated with his colleagues in bringing productions to the stage. In a famous collaboration with BEN JONSON and JOHN MARSTON, Chapman had a hand in writing *Eastward Hoe!* (1605)—a play which the Scottish entourage of King JAMES I found offensive and which landed its authors in jail for a brief period. Another collaboration involved the playwright JAMES SHIRLEY, with whom Chapman produced both a COMEDY, *The Ball*, and a TRAGEDY, *The Tragedie of Chabot* (both 1639).

Chapman's independent authorship of drama is also substantial. The Admiral's Men enacted his first extant comedy, *The Blind Beggar of Alexandria*, in 1596. The next year the same company performed *A Humorous Day's Mirth*. Probably in 1599 another comedy, *All Fools*, appeared, although it did not see print in a reader's edition until 1605. A staged sequel to CHRISTOPHER MARLOWE's play, *Hero and Leander*, in 1598 was followed in 1601–02 by the production of a sprightly comedy, *The Gentleman Usher*. Several more comedies ensued: *May Day* (1601–02), *Monsieur D'Olive* (1604–05), and his most notable comedic work *The Widow's Tears* (1612). In 1607 and 1613, a pair of connected tragedies appeared: first, perhaps his best work, BUSSY D'AMBOIS, and its sequel, *The Revenge of Bussy D'Ambois*. The last work certainly ascribable to his single hand is the historical tragedy, *Caesar and Pompey* (1631).

The Widow's Tears is a bitter comedy whose unremitting SATIRE makes one wonder whether its author, too, may not have become embittered by the perennial poverty he endured despite his remarkable gifts.

Bibliography

Chapman, George. *Chapman's Homer*. Edited by Allardyce Nicoll and Garry Wills. Princeton, N.J.: Princeton University Press, 1998–2000.

Dekker, Thomas, George Chapman, and Ben Jonson. *The Roaring Girl and Other City Comedies*. Edited by James Knowles. New York: Oxford University Press, 2001.

Fraser, Russell A., and Norman Rabkin. *Drama of the English Renaissance: The Stuart Period*. New York: Macmillan, 1976.

Jacob, Alexander, ed. *The Roman Civil War in English Renaissance Tragedy: An Edition of Catiline, Caesar and Pompey, and Julius Caesar. . . .* Lewiston, N.Y.: Edwin Mellen Press, 2002.

Jonson, Ben, John Marston, and George Chapman. *Eastward Ho!* London: Nick Hern, 2002.

character writing

A *character* is a usually short, moral essay whose main object is the improvement of the reader's virtue. Generally, character essays begin with a definition of a virtue or a vice. Next comes an often satirical and ironic description of the behavior of a person who regularly illustrates the characteristic under consideration. The English pioneer of this sort of essay was JOSEPH HALL, an Anglican Bishop who partly modeled his work on the example of the 30 surviving *Characters* of the ancient Greek writer, Theophrastus, whose surviving work, however, characterizes only vices. Other British writers who followed Hall's example include Sir Thomas Overby, JOHN EARLE, John Stevens, and JOHN DRYDEN.

Bibliography

Hebel, J. William, and Hoyt H. Hudson. *Prose of the English Renaissance.* New York: Appleton, Century, Crofts, 1952.

Chast Mayd in Cheapside, A   Thomas Middleton (1611, published 1630)

Drawn from standard comic fare, the plot lines of this bitter SATIRE intertwine to expose the darker currents of life among London's 17th-century middle classes. Two young lovers, Moll and Touchwood Junior, are desperate to marry, but Moll's parents, the goldsmith Yellowhammer and his wife Maudlin, have other plans. They try to force Moll to marry the all too aptly named Sir Walter Whorehound. That gentleman has fathered a number of children, first with a Welch Gentlewoman, who was formerly his concubine but who will finish the play married to the hapless young Tim Yellowhammer. The mother of Whorehound's other brood is Mistress Allwit, whose husband happily prostitutes his wife in exchange for large payments from Sir Walter. Through much of the play Tim, a Cambridge student, and his tutor dispute in Latin syllogisms such questions as whether or not a fool has a rational nature. After a series of failed attempts to flee together, Moll and Touchwood Junior feign death. They are carried to church in their coffins and there rise up and marry.

Meanwhile we discover that Touchwood Senior, described as "a decayed gentleman," proves himself a highly potent sexual athlete who has left many a young woman pregnant and himself vulnerable to blackmail by women who feign innocence while plying the trade of prostitute. His virility proves useful in resolving the difficulties of Sir Oliver and Lady Kix whose inability to produce an heir—and thereby claim an inheritance dependent on their doing so—provokes terrible rows between them. The useful intervention of Touchwood Senior, however, resolves that difficulty to everyone's satisfaction.

Wounded in an onstage duel with the also wounded Touchwood Junior, Sir Oliver undergoes an unlikely reformation in the face of the death he fears. He reviles and renounces both the Allwits and his own illegitimate children. The Allwits, in turn, refuse to shelter him, badly hurt as he is, except in a toilet.

This summary aims to convey a sense of the skill and complexity of MIDDLETON's comic plots and demonstrates the unrelenting zeal of his satirical scalpel. No pretense, folly, or vice escapes it. Only Moll and Touchwood Junior survive relatively unscathed, though in their Cheapside milieu one has little hope of their continued moral health.

Bibliography

Dutton, Richard, ed. *Thomas Middleton: A Chaste Maid in Cheapside; Women beware Women; The Changeling; A Game at Chess.* New York: Oxford University Press, 1999.

Chemakura, Venkata Kavi   (17th century)

Renowned for his ingenuity as a wordsmith in the Telegu language of southern India, Venkata Kavi Chemakura was a soldier and court poet serving King Raghunatha Nayaka of Tanjore. His reputation rests principally on his narrative poem *VIJAYAVILASAM.* Though the poem retells an earlier story, the way Venkata Kavi exploits the musical possibilities of spoken Telegu sets him apart from his predecessors.

Not troubled by unbecoming modesty, Venkata Kavi claimed to be the offspring of the Hindu deity Lakshmanamatya and credits the Sun God with being his poetic muse. Though his *Vijayavilasam* catapulted him to fame, his other surviving work *The deeds of Sarangadhara* (*Sarangadhara Charita*), though popular, did not receive the same degree of public acclaim. This less popular survivor retells an earlier story of King Rajaraja's courtesan's passion for the king's son, Prince Sarangadhara. The prince resists the courtesan Chitrangi's advances. Angry and disappointed, she accuses the prince of molesting her. The furious father orders the amputation of his son's hands and feet. A wise man of the court, Machindranath, however, magically reverses this procedure with the result that a grateful prince becomes an initiate of the wizard's cult and assumes the name *Chaurangi*.

Though modern editions of both works appear in Telegu, neither as yet has found its way into English.

Chen Jiri (Ch'en Chi-jih) (1558–1639)

A Chinese novelist, dramatist, and writer of EPIGRAMS, Chen Jiri also wrote a biography of a friend's father. Most Chinese writers before Chen had earned their livings as civil servants. Working in government positions that required literate persons offered the principal employment opportunity for scholars in China almost until the end of the Ming dynasty in 1644. Chen, by contrast, was among the first able to earn his living with his writing brush. Though his work seems to have been admired by his immediate successors, they have not been widely remarked on by English-speaking historians of Chinese letters.

Chikamatsu Monzaemon (1653–1724)

A Japanese dramatist of the Tokugawa period (1603–1868), Chikamatsu Monzaemon has been sometimes called the SHAKESPEARE of Japan. His most important American student and translator, Donald Keene, considers this an unhappy comparison because it misleads speakers of both Japanese and English.

Chikamatsu wrote plays for each of the two principal venues that characterized the Tokugawa period. The first sort was a puppet theater called *Jōruri*. The second, the Kabuki, was the popular theater. In both sorts of theater the dialogue was sung as well as spoken. In the puppet theater, of course, the singing accompanied the manipulation of the inanimate characters. Kabuki theater was performed by male actors exclusively.

Chikamatsu, like other writers of his period, looked away from the aristocratic, Buddhist-oriented subjects that had dominated the literary scene in Japan before the 17th century. Like many of his contemporary writers, too, he came from a military family—his father had been a samurai. Moreover, Chikamatsu was writing for an audience predominantly composed of merchants. They liked their theater to be at once more spectacular, more action oriented, sexier, and more sentimental than the classic Noh drama.

Chikamatsu's first play for the puppet theater *The Soga Successors* (1683) drew an enthusiastic audience though its models were traditional. His next puppet drama, *Kagekiyo Victorious,* appeared two years later. Though the playwright had not yet achieved his full powers, the play met with tremendous success. It features a love triangle, jealousy and betrayals, a hero who can fly, a *Medea*-like subplot, a miracle, and a happy ending for the protagonist. *The Soga Successors* marks the turning point between the traditional puppet theater and the new puppet theater that was to follow. Whereas the old theater had been hidebound and formulaic, the new featured new sorts of plots and dialogue. Chikamatsu introduced a new sort of domestic drama to the puppet stage as well.

His play, *The LOVE SUICIDES AT SONEZAKI* (*Sonezaki Shinjū*, 1703) was an instant and overwhelming success, and by 1705 he had been named the staff playwright to the Emperor. For the rest of his career as a playwright, Chikamatsu focused on two sorts of plays: history plays and domestic plays about contemporary, ordinary citizens. Their subject matter for the latter was drawn from life. The popularity of *Sonezaki* was such that Chikamatsu created a subgenre of love suicide dramas, both those he wrote and those of others. These plays also stimulated such a fad for love suicides in real life that in 1722 an edict forbade plays with *shinjū* (love suicide) in their titles. Before that edict took effect, however, Chikamatsu had written *Two picture-books of love suicides* (1706), *The Love Suicides at the Women's Temple* (1708), and *The Love Suicides at Amijima* (1721).

In the play that brought the playwright the most renown, his history, *The BATTLES OF COXINGA*, Chikamatsu wrote first for the puppet theatre and then revised for the Kabuki stage. The play is probably more effective in the puppet version. It portrays scenes that might sicken the audience if live actors performed them: eye gouging, an onstage Caesarean section to produce a live heir from a dead empress, a bloody battle between a tiger and a hero. It also features distant vistas of battle, and a magical cloud bridge that wind-shreds out of existence, dropping those crossing it into the gorge below.

The balance of his major work includes *The Drum of the Waves of Horikawa* (1706), *Yosaku from Tamba* (1708), *The Courier for Hell* (1711), *Gonza the Lancer* (1717), *The Uprooted Pine* (1718), *The Girl from Hakata*, or *Love at Sea* (1719) and *The Woman-Killer and the Hell of Oil* (1721).

The female characters of Chikamatsu's plays are frequently big-hearted prostitutes with the capacity for deep emotion and love strong enough to lead them to self-destruction with their lovers. The heroes of these domestic tragedies lack the grandeur of their roughly contemporary counterparts in the Western tradition. Sometimes they are ineffectual men whose principal accomplishment is being loved by a generous-natured woman—and sometimes by more than one. Usually the heroes are drawn from the merchant classes, and generally their fates arise from their own faults. One should always bear in mind the utter isolation of Japan in the 16th and 17th centuries from virtually all other contemporary theatrical traditions. There was no cross-fertilization with western theater and precious little contemporary contact with any other Asian tradition. For Westerners, this may make the apparent modernity of Chikamatsu's middle-class heroes and themes all the more striking.

Most of Chickamatsu's plays continue to be acted on the Japanese stage. They are all available in good English translations.

Bibliography

Chickamazu, Monzaemon. *Four Major Plays of Chikamatsu*. Translated by Donald Keene. New York: Columbia University Press, 1998.

——. *The Love Suicide at Amijima: A Study of a Japaneses Domestic Tragedy. . . .* Edited and translated by Donald H. Shively. 1953. Ann Arbor, Mich.: Center for Japanese Studies, University of Michigan, 1991.

——. *Major Plays of Chikamatsu*. 1961. New York: Columbia University Press, ca. 1990.

Chinese drama, 17th century, theories of

Two rival points of view underlay the composition of much Chinese drama in the 17th century. The first articulated new ideas about how plays should be written. The basic outline of this view appeared in a miscellanous anthology of the writings of LI YÜ (1611–79). His as yet untranslated *Xian quing ou ji* (Casual expressions of idle feelings) set forth a manifesto for writing and producing drama written for a popular, Chinese audience. Whereas older drama had often been privately performed before a highly literate audience who enjoyed obscure reference to earlier literature, Li argued that the language of poetry produced for the stage should be free of such mystification. It should use clear, plain speech so that a popular audience speaking colloquial Chinese and including both illiterate men and uneducated women and children could understand the verse in which all Chinese productions were sung to music.

Li developed his views as the result of long years of practical stage experience. He also advised aspiring playwrights to follow his example in writing about love in its various forms. Love relationships always commanded audience interest. So did plays based on notable recent occurrences.

Li also suggested that would-be playwrights imagine how their material would play before an audience as they were composing. Li might be sitting at his table with his writing-brush in hand when he composed, but his mind was on stage addressing an audience in whose response he was vitally interested.

Li's anthology helped start a fashion for writing handbooks on how to write plays that culminated in a tradition of including introductory interlinear explanatory notes and critical remarks in the published versions of Chinese plays.

A contrasting theoretical viewpoint appeared in the writings of those critics who scorned Li's theory and his practice. It also was evident in the many plays still written in traditional style. Among the playwrights who clung to the older manner and subjects of composition was YU TONG (1618–1704), who loved to show off his learning in a high-flown literary manner. Another writer who looked back to better days was Wu Weiye (1609–71). An officer in the Ming dynasty that fell in 1644, Wu wrote plays in the high style. His favorite topic was the regrettable fall of dynasties.

See also CHINESE THEATER.

Bibliography

Dolby, William. *A History of Chinese Drama.* New York: Barnes and Noble, 1976.

Mair, Victor H., ed. *The Columbia History of Chinese Literature.* New York: Columbia University Press, 2001.

Chinese novels

The long fiction of the Ming dynasty (1368–1644), like other Chinese literary genres, looks back over centuries of telling and retelling, combining, refining, and shaping the materials that emerged in the 15th, 16th, and 17th centuries as a high point of the Chinese novelistic enterprise. Chinese novels in the 16th century generally treated historical subjects with a good deal of mythologizing and literary shaping so that behind each novel of the period stood substantial historical, artistic, and thematic precedents. Two important ones illustrate a process of growing novels by accretion.

SANGUO ZHI YANYI (*ROMANCE OF THE THREE KINGDOMS,* 1522) provides a helpful case history. Perhaps beginning from an account of the historical records that detailed Chinese civil wars during the second and third centuries, the basic form of the novel as we have it is sometimes attributed to a 14th-century writer named LO GUANZHONG. There seems, however, to be no hard evidence for that attribution. In any case the text of the novel grew by the 16th century to include an enormous cast of characters and a vast series of situations set forth in 240 sections that, for the 1522 edition (the earliest one extant), were compressed into 120 chapters. That version was further edited and a substantial critical commentary appended in a 1680 version that has ever since been the standard one.

Similarly, *THE STORY OF THE WATER MARGIN* (*Shuihu zhuan,* ca. 1550) begins from historical events that occurred early in the 12th century when a band of Robin Hood-like robbers led by Son Jiang inhabited the marshes of the Liangshan district and plied their trade. To that basic story, scholars Wilt Idema and Lloyd Haft tell us, details of the careers of other 12th-, 13th-, and 14th-century heroines and heroes, some real and some fictive, became attached with the help of a 14th-century writer, Shi Naian (Shih Nai-an; 1290–ca. 1365). As the story is told in its definitive 16th-century form, it includes 36 principal heroes and heroines and 72 secondary ones, each with his or her own characteristics and stories and each with his or her retinue of supporting characters.

Adding to the complexities resulting from simple accretion, two different traditions for transmitting the novel had grown up in two geographic areas. One set of texts originating around Fujian summarized a greater number of incidents. The other set, coming from the Nanjing–Hangzhou (Nanking Hangchow) area, treated fewer incidents but in greater detail. A no-nonsense sort of editor named Jin Shengtan (1608–61) gave the novel what has since been its definitive form. He reduced the novel from the 100- and 120-chapter versions of the competing traditions to a volume of 72 chapters. Jin stops the story at a point when all 108 principal and secondary heroes and heroines are meeting together. Then he adds a dream-sequence finale in which a single leader envisions the execution of the other 107. Jin also added a critical commentary—some of it interlinear—that often praised his own editorial emendations.

Another subset of novels dating from the mid-16th century includes historical romances that focus on particular events in Chinese history without bringing in extra material. The author of at least four such novels, Xiong Damu, wrote one of the best remembered of them, *Bei Song Zhizhuan* (History of the Northern Song, ca. 1550). This work celebrates the accomplishment and military exploits of generals belonging to the Yang family.

The increasing audience for novels of both sorts described above led publishers to meet the demand by sometimes reprinting older novels and sometimes by publishing new ones. The new texts nevertheless often drew their inspiration from earlier works. Among these is one of the most influential of all Chinese novels, the 100-chapter THE JOURNEY TO THE WEST (ca. 1592). The authorship of this fantasy fiction ALLEGORY is traditionally ascribed to WU CHENG'EN—a minor official in the Chinese civil service. The work traces, among other matters, the career of a monkey named Sun Wukong and the pilgrimage to India of a seventh century Chinese Buddhist monk, Xuanzang. In that context the novel manages both to be funny and to conduct a multilevel SATIRE exposing social ills and human folly. A magnificent English translation of the entire work appeared in 1977. The popularity of *The Journey to the West* led to a number of sequels. Among these the most notable is DONG YUE'S (1620–86) much shorter (16 chapters) work bearing the straightforward title *Supplement to the Journey to the West* (1641). Frankly allegorical and satirical, Dong Yue's book examines the effects of passion (*qing*) on the monkey Sun Wukong, who is victimized by a character named Mackerel. The word for that fish in Chinese is also *qing*, presumably pronounced with a different tonal pattern from the homynym meaning *passion*. Sun Wukong in due course became a featured character in a series of Chinese puppet plays.

Other long novels of the period address the supernatural and magic. One of these tries to find places in the Chinese creation myth for the many gods worshiped by common people in China. There as elsewhere in the world various localities or stones or trees or bodies of water have spirits or minor gods associated with them, and local belief may treat those spirits as tutelary deities. The author, probably either Xu Zhonglin or Lu Xixing, tries to achieve this by describing through the last 70 of the book's 100 chapters a prolonged series of battles between rival kings. When one of them eventually wins, all the common soldiers of the victor's army who were killed in battle are posthumously ennobled and deified.

Another work is analogous to the Renaissance literature of exploration in the European West. *The Record of the Western Ocean* reports expeditions to Arabia, India, and Southeast Asia led by the emperor's grand eunuch Sanbao in the 15th century.

The 16th and 17th centuries in China also witnessed the rise of the social novel. CHIN P'ING MEI TZ'U-HUA (*The Golden Lotus*, written ca. 1580, first published ca. 1619) generally gets credit for being the prototype. The plot explores with considerable pornographic glee the colorful domestic arrangements of a provincial apothecary, Xing Ximen, who eventually acquires six wives and some concubines. The story also traces Qing's shady business transactions and his inevitable ruin by his vices. The anonymous author of the story underlines the operation of retribution for sin and reward for good as central operating principles of the universe.

Bibliography

Anon. *The Golden Lotus.* Translated by Clement Egerton. London: Routledge, 1939. Reprint, New York: Paragon Book Gallery, 1962.

Idema, Wilt, and Lloyd Haft. *A Guide to Chinese Literature.* Ann Arbor, Mich.: Center for Chinese Studies, The University of Michigan, 1997.

Lo Guanzhong [?]. *Three Kingdoms: A Historical Novel.* Translated by Moss Roberts. Berkeley, Calif.: University of California Press, ca. 1991.

Mair, Victor H., ed. *The Columbia History of Chinese Literature.* New York: Columbia University Press, 2001.

Shih Nai-an [?]. *Water Margin.* Translated by J. H. Jackson. Edited by Jin Shengtan. New York: Paragon Book Reprint Corp., 1968.

Wu Ch'eng-en. *The Journey to the West.* Translated and Edited by Anthony C. Yu. Chicago: The University of Chicago Press, 1977.

Yang Xianyi, Lo Guanzhong, and Wu Cheng'en. *Excerpts from Three Classical Chinese Novels* [*Three Kingdoms, Journey to the West, and Flowers in the Mirror*]. Translated by Gladys Yang. Beijing: Chinese Literature, 1981.

Chinese short story collections
(ca. 1450–ca. 1700)

The 250-year period that includes the 16th and 17th centuries stands among the great ages of Chinese collections of short stories. Like most other literatures with long histories of both written and oral expression, Chinese stories look back to the performances of storytellers, to drama, to earlier novels and stories, to newsworthy reports, to historical occurrences, to traditional forms of prose and poetry, and even to brief anecdotes for their inspiration. As a result the stories display a rich and continual IN-TERTEXTUALITY, often quoting passages from preceding authors in the dialogue. The forms of the stories also at first reflected the traditional, especially the oral, sources from which they were drawn.

A 13th-century author, Lo Yeh, grouped Chinese short stories into eight categories. One dealt with demons and spirits, another with marvels. A third told stories of love and a fourth of lawsuits and court cases. Accounts of fights with swords or staves comprised Lo's fifth and sixth categories, and the seventh and eighth focused on immortal beings and religion and on sorcery. By the 16th century, the subjects of stories had expanded to include and favor stories about foolish behavior and its consequences, stories of romantic love, and stories of crime, detection, and punishment.

As happened in Europe in a totally unrelated but parallel development, the 16th century in China saw an expanded exploitation of the commercial possibilities inherent in publishing. Because the readership that purchased the collections came mainly from the middle and lower classes, it was to that audience that authors and publishers principally addressed their writing. The pages of the stories were populated as well by characters drawn from the classes for whom the stories were intended.

Novelty as well as tradition was valued by Chinese readers. Early in the 17th century, authors such as LI YU (1611–79) and Shi Chengjin began to experiment with the voice of the narrator, shifting the stance to reveal the thoughts of different characters or using the author's personal voice to narrate the tale.

The publications of Hong Pien (ca. late 15th–early 16th century) and FENG MENGLONG (1574–1646) helped develop a public taste for anthologies containing stories written either by earlier writers or by the persons who compiled the books. Hung's collection, *Sixty Stories,* had been lost but was partly recovered in the early 20th century so that some 29 of the stories he collected are now known. His was a watershed collection, for it began an enterprise that many others continued. Feng's work, however, was more extensive, more influential, and eventually included some 120 stories. He composed some 35 of these himself and extensively adapted and edited many of the other tales he chose to include in the three volumes that have come to be known collectively as "the three words" since each book has *words* in its title. Feng's selections and contributions to the collections often reflect his own disappointing career as a scholar and public official.

Feng's collaborator in the *words* projects, Langxian, may have contributed as many as 22 of the stories in the third of Feng's collections, *Constant Words to Awaken the World.* As opposed to Feng's tales, Langxian's focus on different interests. His reflect his interest in the natural world and a greater concern with inner experience, Taoist and Buddhist doctrines, heroic women, and the soul's achieving immortality.

The trend begun by the above collections continued throughout the 17th and into the 18th centuries. In the 17th, more than 20 collections of short stories appeared. As they developed, their subject matter grew increasingly erotic on the one hand and increasingly religious on the other. The Chinese phrase *hua pen* labels the genre of the individual tales included in the collections discussed in this entry. The phrase means simply "vernacular stories."

Bibliography

Feng Meng-lung. *Stories from a Ming Collection: The Art of the Chinese Story-Teller.* Translated by Cyril Birch. New York, Grove Press, 1958.

———. *Stories Old and New: A Ming Dynasty Collection Compiled by Feng Menglong.* Translated by Shuhui Yang and Yunqin Yang. Seattle: University of Washington Press, ca. 2000.

Lai Ming. *A History of Chinese Literature.* New York: The John Day Company, 1964.

Mair, Victor H., ed. *The Columbia History of Chinese Literature.* New York: Columbia University Press, 2001.

Chinese theater

In China the roots of theater probe deep into very ancient times, and one can trace some of them to nontheatrical street entertainments such as juggling, acrobatics, and martial-arts contests. Professional storytellers sought to amuse their audiences in the streets and came to specialize in recounting tales drawn from Chinese history, from Buddhist or Taoist religious traditions, or from accounts of love affairs or crimes.

Improvisational poets also amused the crowds by versifying to order on the spot. Singers sang, instrumentalists performed, and dancers danced. Though all these entertainments were eventually destined to contribute to the development of Chinese theater, a more specifically theatrical precursor also had its beginnings in street performance—two-person farce. It was this last element that eventually became the structural center for the textual portion of performances in China. This fact doubtlessly also accounts for the fact that tragedy, as it is known both in the West and in Japanese Noh plays, never developed on the Chinese stage.

The fact that Chinese theatrical texts must be written for preexisting tunes is a defining difference between Chinese theater and any variety of dramatic musical performance in the West. Well before the 16th and 17th centuries, some theatrical performances came to be associated with tunes that had originated in the north and that typically accompanied relatively short plays in the farce genre (*ZAZU*, or *tsa-chü*). These farces could be and were written on almost any subject. Increasingly in the 16th and 17th centuries, however, a popular taste developed, at first for longer dramas whose texts were written to accompany tunes from southern China, especially the regions around Jiangxi and Suzhou. These plays that looked to the music and to the more romantic performance traditions of the south were called *ch'uan-ch'i* or *chuanqi* plays. Like the greatest among them, *The PEONY PAVILION* by TANG XIANZU (1550–1616), they had multiple, melodramatic plots and often made the heroine more complex and interesting than the hero. Such plays also sometimes addressed social issues, as did YANG JISHENG's (1616–55) *The CRYING PHOENIX* (ca. 1570). That play celebrates the protests of a 16th-century city official against two generations of corrupt dictators. The second of them had died only five years before the play was performed.

Somewhat paradoxically, though the preference for southern tunes and plays written for them eventually drove the traditional farces out for a while, at the same time audiences began to demand that the southern-tune plays be shorter or that performances of individual portions of them be staged. Toward the end of the 16th century, an imaginative poet named XU WEI (1521–93) reintroduced the farce genre with a new set of rules that allowed for using both northern and southern tunes and for a variable length of one to four acts.

As theater developed commercially in China, three principal performance venues emerged. One of course was a place like a theater in a sizable city to which an audience could come and pay to see a staged performance. These big-city theaters, however, fell prey for a while to difficult economic times. During that interval, the very wealthy commissioned private performances in their homes, sometimes maintaining resident troupes of (usually female) actors. Beyond this, itinerant acting companies often traveled from village to village, staging performances in local temples. As a result, elaborate scenery of the sort that required machinery or stalwart stagehands to manipulate did not develop in China. In its place, rather, a stylized set of nonverbal conventions came to be understood mutually by players and by members of the audience.

Literary historians Wilt Idema and Lloyd Haft suggest a pair of examples. If an actor climbed on a chair and peered around, the audience understood that he was standing on a mountaintop or other high place. If he carried a riding crop, the audience understood that he was supposed to be on horseback. Such conventions eventually became both very elaborate and very subtle, requiring a knowledgeable audience. As the theater developed, however, whatever it lacked in sumptuous scenery, it made up for in gorgeous costuming and, sometimes, facial makeup.

In a development that parallels to a degree the comedy of the guild (COMMEDIA DELL' ARTE) in Italy, Chinese actors and actresses were assigned character types in which they specialized and which both men and women could portray regardless of the character's supposed sex.

Though the general characteristics of Chinese theater were already well developed by the 16th and 17th centuries, that epoch nevertheless saw some shifting of emphasis in what playwrights chose to write about and in the preferences of audiences for certain sorts of plays. It also saw the publication of many of the surviving versions of plays written in those two centuries and in earlier epochs as well. In an important development, publishers compiled anthologies of plays, and the collections sold well to the reading public. Once such anthologies became available for study, literary criticism soon followed. One sort brought a high level of professionalism to handbooks for writing drama. The most notable of these was authored by a playwright and producer, LI YU (ca. 1610–80). In his work, whose title translates "Casual Expressions of Idle Feelings," he sets forth a comprehensive theory for writing and producing plays. Another sort of critical commentary appeared between the lines in editions of plays. An edition of the famous *Romance of the Western Chamber* introduced this practice.

Such close critical analysis provided standards for playwrights to try to achieve. The analytical discussion challenged writers to change drama from a fairly light form of entertainment to serious, high art. Several playwrights met this challenge, including KONG SHANGREN (1648–1718), with his *PEACH BLOSSOM FAN* (1699), and Hung Sheng (1605–1704) with his *Palace of Eternal Youth* (ca. 1690). Both plays addressed serious political issues connected with the dissolution of the Ming dynasty.

The 16th and 17th centuries witnessed major developments in the history of the Chinese theater and produced several plays, such as *The Peony Pavillion*, that have never been surpassed and that, at least in part, remain in the active repertoire of Chinese theater.

See also CHINESE DRAMA, 17TH CENTURY, THEORIES OF.

Bibliography

Hung Sheng. *The Palace of Eternal Youth*. Translated by Hsien-yi Yang and Gladys Yang. Beijing: Foreign Languages Press, 1955.

Idema, Wilt, and Lloyd Haft. *A Guide to Chinese Literature*. Ann Arbor, Mich.: Center for Chinese Studies, The University of Michigan, 1996.

Mair, Victor H., ed. *The Columbia History of Chinese Literature*. New York: Columbia University Press, 2001.

Chinese women writers, 1500–1700

In earlier times Chinese women had often enjoyed enviable reputations as writers of odes (*shi*) and lyric poems (*ci*). These forms, however, throughout the 144 last years of the Ming and the 66 first years of the Qing dynasties considered here, lost much of their appeal for a broad spectrum of the reading public. Many readers came to prefer drama and prose narrative to personal poems. Women, nevertheless, continued to write in the older forms in ever increasing numbers. Some critics have argued that by choosing to write in antiquated forms, most women writers of 16th and 17th centuries in China enjoyed at best a marginal readership with antiquarian tastes.

HUANG XIUMEI (1498–1569) presents a notable exception to this generalization. Many of the poems that she exchanged with the husband from whom she was long separated by his political exile were deeply and, in one instance, sensationally erotic. That autobiographical eroticism in the context of her remarkable skill as a poet and of the painful details of her husband's absence separated her from all her female contemporaries.

The decision of women to write personal lyrics in the older manner did not imply a lack either of skill or talent. Rather it appears that they found congenial the capacity of the older forms to externalize and objectify their complex thoughts and feelings. Such was surely the case with the courtesan poet Liu Shi (1618–64). Together with her lover, Chen Zilong, she helped spark a widespread revival of interest in *ci* poetry that calls into question the notion that 16th- and 17th-century Chinese women poets marginalized themselves by using outmoded forms. Indeed, one of the women drawn to those forms, Xu Can (ca. 1610–post-1677) attracted critical attention as the best female writer of the age—one perhaps better than even the most notable of her predecessors in former ages.

Literary historian Kang-i Sun Chang convincingly suggests that a sharp rise in women's literacy began in the 16th century and that the encouragement of male editors who actively promoted women's work had much to do with a spate of anthologies of women's writing of *ci* and *shi* poems in a period when they were ostensibly not valued. The editor of one of these, *Compendium of poetry by renowned ladies* (1600), proposed that the poetry of women in traditional modes provided an antidote for the confusions of late Ming dynasty literary disagreements. Later editors agreed, and many insisted on anthologizing examples of *ci* and *shi* poems by contemporary female poets—not by ancient ones. Moreover, in selecting titles for their anthologies the editors made conscious efforts to associate the poems' female authors with such earlier successful schools of male poets as the EARLIER SEVEN MASTERS and the LATER SEVEN MASTERS. Kang-i Sun Chang cites two anthologies of poems by women writers whose titles contain the phrase "seven female talents." Late in the Ming period, she continues, women like Liu Shi and Wang Zuanshu themselves became editors and critics, and their contributions to literary discourse proved welcome.

It seems then that, contrary to conventional wisdom, the misogynist tradition, which often constrained and discouraged the literary activity of women in the Western World between 1500 and 1700, did not find a counterpart in the late Ming and early Qing periods in China. It seems instead that women discovered modes of expression that suited their voices and that they enjoyed the active support of male editors and publishers in attracting a receptive audience.

Bibliography

Women Writers of Traditional China: An Anthology of Poetry and Critcism. Edited by Kang-i Sun Chang, Haun Saussy, et al. Stanford, Calif.: Stanford University Press, 1999.

Yu, Pauline, ed. *Voices of the Song Lyric in China.* Berkeley, Calif.: University of California Press, 1994.

chivalric epic

In Renaissance literature, the medieval cycles of stories surrounding the courts of King Arthur in Britain and Charlemagne in France provided the raw materials for a kind of EPIC poem that celebrated the knightly virtues of Christian chivalry. In Italy examples of the type included ORLANDO INNAMORATO (Roland in love, 1487) by MATTEO MARIA BOIARDO, ORLANDO FURIOSO (Roland gone mad, 1516) by LUDOVICO ARIOSTO, and JERUSALEM DELIVERED (*Gerusalemme liberata*, 1581) by TORQUATO TASSO. In England, EDMUND SPENSER drew inspiration from his Italian predecessors while at the same time attempting to create in his THE FAERIE QUEENE, a protestant, national epic that celebrated the TUDOR dynasty and particularly its last representative, ELIZABETH I, in a multi-layered ALLEGORY.

A bit earlier (1572), the Portuguese LUÍS DE CAMÕES in his LUSIAD (*Os Lusíadas*, 1572) applied the conventions of the genre to extol Vasco da Gama's success in sailing around the Horn of Africa and opening a new trade route to India. Aspects of the genre also appear in the New-World epic of the Spaniard ALONZO ERCILLA Y ZÚÑIGA, *La Araucana*. This poem recounts the Spanish efforts to subdue the Aracanian peoples of Chile.

The chivalric code of conduct, however, was increasingly outmoded in a world rapidly developing more and more efficient and destructive methods of warfare. Armored knights, equipped with swords and lances and fighting from the backs of also armored warhorses, were simply no match for artillery—nor for that matter for the English longbow that also fired an armor-piercing projectile. This material reality was soon reflected in literature with the publication of MIGUEL DE CERVANTES SAAVEDRA's picaresque novel, *DON QUIXOTE DE LA MANCHA* (1605), which exposed the hopeless folly of the chivalric code. After that tale of "the knight of the sorrowful countenance," the chivalric epic that had once enshrined the knightly ideal lapsed into silence.

Bibliography

Anglo, Sydney, ed. *Chivalry in the Renaissance.* Woodbridge, U.K., and Rochester, N.Y.: Boydell Press, 1990.

Leslie, Michael. *Spenser's "fierce warres and faithfull loves": Martial and Chivalric Symbolism in The Faerie Queene.* Totowa, N.J.: Barnes and Noble, 1983.

Vitullo, Juliann M. *The Chivalric Epic in Medieval Italy.* Gainesville: University of Florida Press, 2000.

Christian Nobility of the German Nation, To the Martin Luther (1520)

In this subsequently published address to the princes of Germany, LUTHER argues that every Christian believer is a priest. Each Christian acquires this status at baptism. Thus neither the hierarchy of the church nor the saints themselves can claim the power of intercession. Moreover, as Luther reminded the princes assembled, the pope has no special brief for authoritative interpretation of Scripture. Although a papal decree (*Decretum Gratiani*, 1145) laid claim to that authority, the decree has no Scriptural basis. No baptized human being, Luther argues, has more or less authority to interpret Scripture.

Chronicle History of Perkin Warbeck, The: A Strange Truth John Ford (ca. 1634)

JOHN FORD based his only history play on one of the most bizarre episodes in British history. Perkin Warbeck, a native of Flanders, presented himself in 1490 at the court of Katherine, duchess of Burgundy—sister of King Edward IV of England. Warbeck claimed to be Richard, duke of York, the younger of Edward IV's two sons. Their uncle, Richard III, had caused the boys to be murdered in the Tower of London. If his story had been true, Warbeck had a legitimate claim to the English throne.

A convincing and possibly self-deluded liar, Warbeck attracted a series of unlikely if self-interested supporters. These included numerous Irishmen, King Charles VIII of France, and King James IV of Scotland. James not only protected Warbeck, he also married him to a Scottish princess of the blood, Katherine Gordon, daughter of George Gordon, earl of Huntly. In both history and the play, Katherine stood by her husband until his eventual execution in the tower.

Ford's play closely follows the fortunes of the imposter prince from his welcome in Scotland through the Scots' military campaign in support of his claims, his entering sanctuary in Hampshire at Beaulieu, his offstage surrender, and his eventual execution. Of greater interest in the play than Perkin Warbeck himself are several other characters. King Henry VII of England is presented as tenderhearted, approachable, wise, and just. Henry is distressed and upset when he discovers that his chief minister, Sir William Stanley—the man who had crowned him king when Richard fell at the Battle of Bosworth Field—treasonously supports Warbeck's party. Both the earl of Huntley and Katherine's earlier suitor Daliell are distinguished by their unflagging care of Katherine and their devotion to her well-being. Katherine herself is a model of constancy and shares her husband's fortunes until his execution. She swears to live as his widow. The historical Katherine broke that vow three times.

Historically, there is not a shred of doubt that Warbeck was a total fraud. If no other evidence were available, the 20th-century discovery of the remains of both young princes in the tower would have laid to rest any doubts on the subject. But even at the end of the 15th century the evidence against Warbeck was incontrovertible. Ford, however, manages to introduce a dramatic glimmer of possible truth in Warbeck's claim. Ford achieves this by endowing Warbeck with a princely demeanor and an unfailing eloquence. Ford's Warbeck also makes evident that he believes his own fantasy. He is offended at his secretary's suggestion that he is a fraud even though the secretary, Frion, is likely among those who hatched the plot. Ford's interest in psychological quirks never deserted him.

Ford's drama closely follows the accounts of the Warbeck incident that appear in Thomas Gainsford's *True and Wonderful History of Perkin Warbeck* (1618) and in SIR FRANCIS BACON's *History of the Reign of King Henry VII* (1621).

Bibliography

Anderson, Donald K., Jr. *John Ford.* New York: Twayne Publishers, 1972.

Ford, John. *Perkin Warbeck.*" In *'Tis Pity She's a Whore and Other Plays,* edited by Marion Lomax, 241–363. Oxford and New York: Oxford University Press, 1995.

Chrysoloras, Manuel (ca. 1349–1415)

The father of Greek language studies in Renaissance Italy, Chrysoloras first came to Venice in 1390 as an envoy of the Byzantine Emperor Manuel II. Two young Florentines, Roberto de' Rossi and Jacopo Angeli, traveled to Venice to call on Chrysoloras and indicated their desire to learn Greek. Later, with the backing of the Florentine Chancellor Coluccio Salutati and the Florentine Republic, Angeli recruited Chrysoloras to teach Greek in Florence beginning in 1397.

His teaching opened the way for the HUMANIST recovery of Greek classical texts. He also influenced and improved the style of translation from Greek documents. Whereas medieval attempts at translating the language had plodded from word to word, Chrysoloras encouraged his students to translate for intention and meaning. That method became the humanist standard.

Chief among Chrysoloras' students at Florence was the enormously influential humanist LEONARDO BRUNI, the author of a definitive history of the city of Florence and a careful translator whose work with Greek historians filled in numerous gaps in Italian knowledge of Greek and Roman history.

Chysoloras authored a Greek grammar that made the language accessible to students for more than 100 years. Because he wrote it in the form of a series of questions and answers, its title was the Greek word for "questions:" *Erotemata.*

As a personal ambition, Chrysoloras hoped to reunite the Greek Orthodox and Roman Catholic churches, and to that unachieved end he converted to the Roman communion and was ordained a priest. His role in opening the treasure chest of classical Greek letters for the benefit of Renaissance Europeans of the West, however, remains his most notable accomplishment.

Cicero, Marcus Tullius (106–43 B.C.E.)

A Roman senator, statesman, orator, and author, Cicero contributed his name to the English adjective *Ciceronian.* The word is used to describe an elegant and polished prose style. For many early HUMANIST writers, the Latin prose of Cicero provided a standard upon which to model their own NEO-LATIN compositions.

Cid, Le Pierre Corneille (1637)

Described by the playwright himself first as a TRAGI-COMEDY and in subsequent revisions (1648 and 1660) as a TRAGEDY, CORNEILLE's most famous play continues after almost four centuries to attract a large and enthusiastic audience. In writing his verse drama, *Le Cid,* Corneille followed the Spanish version penned by Guillén de Castro in 1618. The play concerns the early life and career of the medieval Spanish hero Rodrigo Diaz de Vivar (ca. 1043–99) who spent his military career serving first the Spanish, then the Moors, and finally his own interests. He eventually became the ruler of Valencia by conquest.

Vivar's soubriquet, the Cid (the lord), became the name by which history generally remembers him and both his real and his legendary career.

Corneille's version of the story focuses on Don Rodrique's young manhood, on his ill-starred love relationship with the lady Chimène, daughter of a count, Don Gomès, the general of the Spanish armies, and on the conflicts that arise when honor, public reputation, and the revenge code come into conflict with the young people's mutual attraction.

As the curtain rises, we find Chimène cross-questioning her maid, Elvire, about a conversation the maid has overheard. In the contention between Don Rodrique and Don Sancho for the hand of Chimène, Don Rodrique's suit has prevailed with her father. Though she is thrilled that her father has confirmed her own secret choice, Chimène feels troubled by fears of unhappiness.

In the next scene, the audience learns that the Spanish princess, the Infanta, also loves Don Rodrique. The Infanta will nonetheless be glad to see him marry her friend Chimène so that she can put aside her hopes for herself. Those hopes are inappropriate because of the difference in their rank, for the princess must wed royally.

Act I, scene iii presents a dialogue between Don Rodrique's father, Don Diegue, and Chimène's, Don Gomès. Although Gomès has succeeded Diegue as the supreme general of the king's armies, the king has seen fit to appoint Diegue as his son's tutor. Jealous at the old man's elevation to an honor Gomès thinks should have been his, Chimène's father sneeringly rejects Diegue's proposal of an alliance of their houses through marriage, and as words grow increasingly heated, Gomès strikes the old man, who draws his sword to defend his honor despite his weakness. Gomès easily disarms him and further insults him.

Scene iv finds Don Diegue raging, and in scene v he appeals to his son for revenge. On learning that his father's enemy is Don Gomès, Rodrique's hope of marrying Chimène vanishes, and in a series of lyrical stanzas he decides to die on the certainly invincible sword of her father rather than live without her.

Act II opens with the count regretting his rashness and wishing that the blow could be recalled, on the one hand, but on the other, haughtily telling the courtier Arias that Gomès feels assured of the king's continued favor since the kingdom's safety rests upon his military prowess. In the second scene, Rodrique challenges Gomès. The experienced warrior tries to dissuade Rodrique but eventually is goaded into accepting, remarking that only "a base son" would outlive "a father's honor."

Hearing of the quarrel, the Infanta and Chimène discuss its outcomes. Chimène despairs, and the Infanta offers to imprison Rodrique to protect him, but when she sends after him, she discovers that he and Gomès have already left the palace together "muttering angrily." Scene v revisits the Infanta's passion for Rodrique, and in scene vi the king expresses his displeasure at Gomès's disrespect and effrontery. A report of an approaching naval squadron of Moors is discussed, and, following the king's order to mount a double guard, in scene vii we learn that Rodrique has unexpectedly killed Gomès in an offstage duel. In the next scene, Chimène demands Rodrique's death as punishment for her father's demise while Diegue pleads on his son's behalf on the grounds of honor. As the curtain falls on Act II, the king promises to do justice.

In clarifying the play's central conflict between love and honor, Act III is the play's crux. First, Rodrique comes to Chimène's house so that the hand he loves may exact vengeance by killing him. The maid, seeing her mistress coming, hides Rodrique to spare Chimène greater pain. Escorted by Don Sancho, Chimène arrives. Sancho begs her to name him her champion so that he may avenge her by killing Rodrique. She demurs, saying that the king has promised justice but, failing that, promises to call on Sancho later if she needs him. On Sancho's exit, Rodrique comes out of hiding and begs Chimène to act as her own executioner. She refuses, admitting that, though circumstance has made Rodrique her mortal foe, she still loves him. The loving enemies explore the finer points of the double bind in which they find themselves, and Rodrique at length departs.

Act III, scene v reunites father and son. Rodrique tells Diegue that he has sacrificed all for him, but Diegue remarks that, while mistresses are many, honor requires his service. The father tells the son to present himself at once to the king as a replacement for Gomès. The enemy is at the gate, and the army needs a general.

As Act IV begins, we learn from the conversation of Chimène and Elvire, that Rodrique has successfully led the army against the Moors, won the battle in three hours, and captured two kings. The Infanta presses Chimène to give up her private vendetta in deference to the public welfare and to forgive Rodrique. Chimène, however, cannot bring herself to do so.

In the third scene of Act IV, the king confers on Rodrique the title with which the moors have labeled him, the Cid. Rodrique seeks the king's pardon for having sprung to the kingdom's defense without permission, and the king freely grants it. In the following scene, Chimène comes once again to press her suit for vengeance, and the king decides to test her. He reports that though Rodrique's forces were victorious, he himself was slain. Chimène faints, convincing the king of her love. When the king confronts her with this view, she insists that Rodrique be executed as a prisoner. She next calls on the cavaliers present to avenge her. She promises to marry the one who brings her Rodrique's head.

The king intervenes, saying that the custom of settling private feuds by dueling has cost the kingdom too many able men. Diegue, however, upbraids the king for overturning ancient custom and undermining honor. Persuaded, the king relents, and Sancho presents himself as Chimène's champion. The king permits the duel, but insists over her objections that Chimène marry the victor.

As Act V opens, Rodrique once more presents himself to Chimène, telling her of his intention to die in the upcoming duel. When no other argument can prevail against his resolution, she begs him to defend himself, conquer, and save her from having to marry Don Sancho, whom she despises. Ecstatic at the prospect of winning Chimène despite all, Rodrique agrees.

The second scene opens with the Infanta's fantasizing once more about Rodrique. The practical minded Leonora interrupts her reverie, telling her that, whatever happens, she can stop worrying. Rodrique will either die or marry. The Infanta, however, insists that the stakes have changed since Rodrique has become the Cid and that his new rank qualifies him as a potential husband for a princess.

In the event, Rodrique wins the duel, but spares Sancho's life on the grounds that blood risked on Chimène's behalf should not be shed. Sancho then goes to present Rodrique's sword to the king. Thinking Rodrique slain, the distraught Chimène declares her love at last. Finally, the fact that Rodrique lives emerges, and it seems the lovers will be united. But, leaving the door ajar for an eventual change of mind, Chimène persuades the king not to enforce his decree and insist on a peremptory marriage. The play ends with the question of the lovers' eventual union still open.

Bibliography

Carlin, Claire L. *Pierre Corneille Revisited.* New York: Twayne Publishers, 1998.

Corneille, Pierre. *The Cid.* In *Six Plays by Corneille and Racine.* New York: The Modern Library, 1931.

———. *The Cid.* In *Five Classic French Play,* edited and translated by Wallace Fowlie. 1962. Reprint, Mineola, N.Y.: Dover Publications, 1997.

ci poetry of China (*tz'u* poetry of China)

Ci poems developed in China as early as the 10th century but enjoyed a significant revival in the 17th. This form of poetry arose in response to the introduction into China of new sorts of musical instruments and unfamiliar tunes from central Asia. It differed from the older classical *shi* poems in several ways. *Ci* at first involved writing new words to be sung, often by women, to old tunes. It also employed many more elements of vernacular as opposed to courtly language. Almost all Chinese male poets were also civil servants. Only a tiny percentage of the population was literate, and those who could read and write almost always entered government service. As a result the language of the *ci* poets was not nearly as divorced from the classical Chinese idiom as are the lyrics of 21st-century popular music from formal prose in the Western world.

At first *ci* poems were expected to mirror the subject, length, line characteristics, and rhyming patterns of the songs whose tune they borrowed. Later, some flexibility was introduced in that a new tune could be composed for a new subject, but later poems using that tune were expected to follow its conventions. A principal difference between Chinese and European verse arises from the two facts that Chinese is a tonal language and that it tends to be monosyllabic. Single-syllable words using exactly the same vowels and consonants differentiate their meaning by the pitch at which they are spoken or by the tonal pattern within them. This means that many more rhymes are possible than in English, but because written Chinese characters convey tonality as well as pronunciation of consonants and vowels, rhyming words with identical consonant–vowel sequences can have very different meanings depending on tone.

Whereas European languages use either stress or syllable length to determine POETIC METER, Chinese substitutes tone levels for meter. This makes *ci* poems particularly difficult to compose since, in addition to its other requirements, a new poem's tonal patterns must conform exactly to those of the original.

Two principal sorts of *ci* developed. The first, *xiaoling*, short poems, were written in two stanzas, and were limited to no more than 58 Chinese characters. *Xiaoling* treated such topics as living life freely, the suffering resulting from a lover's absence, and the brevity of human life. The second sort of *ci*, called *manci*, was longer with two or three stanzas that employed from 60 to 240 characters. Its subjects included the lives of courtesans and their patrons, loneliness, and, as the form developed, the interior life of the author.

The major poets of the 17th-century revival of *ci* poetry were Chen Zilong (1608–47) and Nalan Xingde (1655–85). Chen's poems frequently were addressed to a courtesan with whom he fell in love. He became involved in politics and rebellion against the Manchu dynasty. Eventually he committed suicide. Probably the most outstanding poet of the *ci* revival, Nalan Xingde was himself a high official of the Manchu. His *ci* fell into the briefer category, the *xiaoling*, and are principally remembered for the clarity of their diction and the sincere quality of their sentiments. A number of *ci* poems also appear among the works of the female poet HUANG XIUMEI (1498–1569).

Attesting to the influence of the 17th-century *ci* revival among Chinese intellectuals are numerous commentaries written to explain the ALLEGORY implicit in *ci* poems. The explanations suggest that *ci* writers used the form to comment on and sometimes to criticize politics and politicians. The year 1687, moreover, saw the publication of the *Ci lü*, a compilation by Wan Shu of 875 patterns of *ci* tunes together with 1,496 variants. Another list compiled in 1715 listed 826 tunes and 2,306 variations.

Bibliography

Chang, Kang-i Sun. *The Late Ming Poet Ch'en Tzu-lung [Zilong]: Crisis of Love and Loyalism.* New Haven, Conn.: Yale University Press, 1991.

Women Writers of Traditional China: An Anthology of Poetry and Criticism. Edited by Kang-i Sun Chang, Haun Saussy, et al. Stanford, Calif.: Stanford University Press, 1999.

Clarendon, Edward Hyde, earl of
(1609–1674)

An ardent royalist, a historian of his times, and a counselor to both King Charles I and Charles II of England, Clarendon was twice forced to endure exile. First, as a result of the upheavals resulting from the English Civil War, in 1646 he fled with the king to the Scilly Isles off Land's End. While there, he began work on his *History of the Rebellion* (1702–04). Much later in his life, vilified by his enemies at the court of Charles II, Clarendon was once more obliged to go into exile, this time in France. There he spent his remaining days, completing the work he had begun earlier. His chronicle of the most significant political events in England during his time finally appeared posthumously almost a quarter-century after his death.

The balanced discussions in the text reflect the character of the man. He was a keen observer of people. He thought that even the king should operate within the constraints of the law—something that Stuart monarchs, believing as they did in the divine right of kings, always found difficult. Although Clarendon recognized the political faults of his monarch, Charles I, he judged him nonetheless to be "the best master . . . friend . . . husband . . . father . . . and Christian." that his age had produced. Clarendon's assessment of OLIVER CROMWELL was not nearly so complimentary: "He will be looked upon by posterity," says Hyde, after a long catalogue of Cromwell's virtues and vices, "as a brave, bad man."

His discussions of the English Civil War and its causes and outcomes have particular value coming, as they do, from a highly placed eyewitness and a fair-minded participant.

closet drama

One sort of closet drama includes plays written for private performance outside a theater with only a small audience or with none. Another use of the term involves the performance in private, perhaps by a group of readers, of plays originally written for performance in a theater. MARY HERBERT's rhymed verse tragedy *Antonius* (1592) exemplifies a play written for private performance only.

closing of the English theaters (1642)

Theater in 17th-century England had two traditional enemies. First, Puritan preachers railed against the ruinous effects that the graphic display of vice on stage produced on the characters of the audience, especially that segment of it that was young and impressionable. Second, government censors at the Stationers' Register, the agency responsible for licensing the publication of books and plays, looked with a jaundiced eye upon any dramatic situation that seemed to offer a comment on or criticism of contemporary politics.

Playwrights were sometimes jailed and fined when the censors or their political masters found their works objectionable. This had happened for instance to GEORGE CHAPMAN and his collaborators BEN JONSON and JOHN MARSTON whose *Eastward Hoe* had offended the Scottish supporters of KING JAMES I. THOMAS MIDDLETON and everyone connected with his *A Game at Chess* were summoned before a magistrate when the Spanish ambassador complained about the political commentary in that play.

Beyond the clerical opposition to the influence of the theater on social morality and the suspicions of the censors about its capacity for political meddling, the economics of theatrical production and class distinctions also played roles in a crisis that overtook the British theater in 1642. The great public arena theaters like the GLOBE and the Swan had increasingly attracted an ill-behaved, lower-class audience. Private theaters with much smaller seating capacities skimmed off the more affluent playgoers, but often still had difficulty meeting production costs. Making a profit became increasingly difficult for all concerned.

When, therefore, the Puritans came to power in 1640, the theater was a weak and easy target for a parliament that considered it a public danger on many grounds. The performance of plays was banned in England, and the theaters remained closed from 1642 until the Restoration of the Stuart line in 1660. The closure effectively ended the great Renaissance flowering of English theater—a period whose equal has not been seen since.

Nonetheless, records in the Greater Metropolitan London Record Office suggest that the production of plays did not entirely disappear during those 18 years. Rather it may instead have gone underground. Several 17th-century warrants preserved in that city archive charge Anglican churches with staging plays in their social halls. These ancient documents did not come to light until the 1990s.

Bibliography
Bentley, G. E. *The Jacobean and Caroline Stage.* 7 vols. Oxford: Oxford University Press, 1941–1968.

Colonna, Vittoria (1492–1547)

Daughter of Fabrizio Colonna, the grand marshall of Naples, and Angesina di Montefeltro, Vittoria Colonna was to become a central figure among Renaissance artists and writers. When Vittoria was only four years old, her family contracted a marriage for her with Ferrante Francesco D'Avelos, also four, the heir to the marquisate of Pescara. They married at 19 and lived happily together until D'Avelos was called to war. He was wounded in 1512, returned briefly to live with his wife, was recalled to duty in 1515, and though he survived for another 10 years, he became so involved in politics and intrigue that his wife never saw him again. He died, some thought of poison, in 1525. She, now the dowager marchioness of Pescara, never ceased cherishing her husband's memory, which became one of the principal subjects of her substantial body of poetry.

Study and religious reflection, with which Colonna had passed her time during her husband's absence, became at some point her twin passions. An accomplished Latinist, she founded a salon where illustrious Italians—particularly literary ones—were proud to be seen and to be included in her circle of friends. One of her closest friends was the Florentine sculptor, painter, and poet, MICHELANGELO BUONAROTI (1475–1564).

Her own poems included mostly sonnets in the Petrarchan manner on the death of her husband or on religion and morality. In those addressed to her husband, she often employs PETRARCH's device of listening while the god of Love speaks and recording his words. She calls her deceased husband her "handsome sun" and her "eternal light." In her 22nd sonnet she regrets that she and her husband were childless and at the same time celebrates the fruitfulness of their souls.

On the religious front, Colonna was not unacquainted with Protestant doctrine. She was probably sympathetic with it, especially with its evangelical call for active faith and purity of life. She nevertheless adhered to her devout Roman Catholicism, particularly to the elements of its 16th-century spiritual reformation, and she continued to venerate both the Virgin Mary and the saints. As she grew older, her poetry turned mostly to religious subjects. Her talent, intellect, social standing, and virtuous life made her one of the most celebrated Italian literary women of the Renaissance.

Bibliography

Bassanese, Fiora. "Vittoria Colonna (1492–1547)." In *Italian Women Writers: A Bio-Bibliographical Sourcebook,* 85–94, edited by Rinaldina Russell. Westport, Conn.: The Greenwood Press, 1994.

Garibaldi, Joseph. "Vittoria Colonna: Child, Woman, and Poet." In *Women Writers of the Renaissance and Reformation,* edited by Katharina M. Wilson, 22–46. Athens, Ga.: University of Georgia Press, 1987.

Russell, Rinaldina, ed. *The Feminist Encyclopedia of Italian Literature.* Westport, Conn.: Greenwood Press, 1997.

Columbus, Christopher (1451–1506)

Though Columbus's birthplace is a matter of some controversy, Genoa, Italy, is traditionally mentioned. After numerous attempts to convince European monarchs to finance his search for a sea passage to the East Indies, he finally convinced King Ferdinand and Queen Isabella of Spain to do so. In exchange for his service he was to become the grand admiral of Spain's navy and the governor of all the lands he claimed for the Spanish crown. Eventually he commanded four voyages to what he termed the "New World."

Rarely are ships' logs characterized as literature. Exceptions are warranted, however, and among them surely must be counted numerous entries in the logs that Christopher Columbus kept during his voyages of discovery. The logs for the first voyage reveal his progress across the sea (whose width he had underestimated as he had the entire circumference of the Earth). They record the fears of his sailors on losing sight of land and his decision to announce less distance than he actually made so that the men would think themselves closer to home. The logs recount such unusual sights as a falling meteor and the discovery of the Sargasso Sea—a broad region of the North Atlantic Ocean where the surface is covered with floating weed. They reveal his own fear that the men would mutiny and throw him overboard. The entries for October 11, 1492—the day on which Roderigo de Triana aboard the *Pinta* first sighted land—and for October 12, the day

Columbus's mariners first set foot in the Western Hemisphere, command special interest.

Once arrived on the islands off the coast of the American mainland, the logs contain Columbus's descriptions and assessments of the people he meets, his insistent quest for gold, and his conviction that "with 50 men you could subject everyone [on San Salvador] and make them do what you wished." Profiteering from slavery was clearly on his mind. He also credulously repeats an account of a distant tribe of one-eyed men with dogs' heads who ate human flesh. Only the last detail, of course, had basis in fact.

Columbus discovered Cuba later in 1492. Again the logs recount that fact and report the contacts that the Europeans made. The logs reveal as well that Columbus thought—or wanted his sponsors to think—that he was indeed very near the East Indies. He showed the native people examples of the spices he sought, and they assured him, though they themselves did not have such goods, that peoples to the southwest of them did. The log for Friday, November 23, 1492, introduces the word *cannibal* (*canibales*) from the Taino Indian language into the European vocabulary. Columbus's feeling for natural beauty often shines through as he describes the landscapes and harbors that he observes.

Columbus's letters to the Spanish monarchs are also of literary interest. They reflect his sense of mission. He felt himself divinely appointed to the task of great discovery. He reported for instance in a 1503 letter from Jamaica that once at Veragua, in a moment of great danger when he feared that hostile natives would destroy his anchored ship, he climbed into his ship's rigging to pray, fell asleep, and had a dream that he took to be the answer to his prayer. In the dream a voice assured him that all would be well.

The logs and other documents related to Columbus's adventures in the New World are easily accessible in Spanish, in English translation, and in translation in many other languages as well. Columbus's discovery gave impetus to one of the major literary thrusts of the Renaissance. The New World became both the subject of many literary works and a METAPHOR for discoveries of all sorts. It also laid the groundwork—although at a distance of some centuries—for the cultural pluralism that characterizes much of the thinking of our own epoch. For the indigenous peoples of the Americas in the meantime, however, Columbus's discovery of their homeland was an unparalleled disaster. Murder, thievery, forced conversion, extortion of wealth and entire countries, disease, famine, and betrayal followed inexorably from contact with Europeans.

Even in cases where the military strength of the peoples contacted led to treaties rather than to immediate and direct exploitation, a pattern of deception, dependency, and subjugation followed. In the last decade of the 20th century, the D'Arcy McNickle Center for the Study of the American Indian at the Newberry Library in Chicago conducted a comprehensive survey of treaties that Europeans and Euro-Americans had made with the indigenous and initially sovereign peoples of the Americas. At the outset of the project researchers expected to find between 1,000 and 2,000 treaties. By the time they finished, they had identified more than 20,000. The European and Euro-American signatories had unilaterally broken every one of them.

Bibliography

Columbus, Christopher. *The Log of Christopher Columbus.* Translated by Robert H. Fuson. Camden, Maine: International Marine Publishing, a Division of the McGraw-Hill Companies, 1987.

———. *The Log of Christopher Columbus: the First Voyage, Spring, Summer, and Fall, 1492.* Edited by Steve Lowe. Illustrated by Robert Sabuda. New York: Philomel Books, 1992.

Columbus, Ferdinand (Colón, Fernando) (1488–1539)

Devoted to scholarly pursuits and collecting books, Ferdinand Columbus was the son of the 37-year-old widower Christopher and his mistress, Beatriz Enríquez de Arana. As a boy Ferdinand lived with his mother in the city of Córdoba in his earliest years, but after his father's stunning success in discovering the New World, the lad received an appointment as a page in the household of Crown

Prince Don Juan. While there he acquired his life-long literary interests.

Those scholarly pursuits were interrupted, however, when in 1502 his father invited his 13-year-old son to join him on his fourth voyage to the New World—a voyage that proved by far the most difficult of Christopher Colombus's expeditions. On it Ferdinand demonstrated that his devotion to books was matched by his courage and fortitude. He was to return once more to the Americas, this time with his brother Diego in 1509. As governor of the island of Española, Diego put Ferdinand in charge of building monasteries and churches, but Ferdinand did not like the work and asked to return to Spain.

There, because of his extensive firsthand knowledge of the New World and of seamanship, he served in a consulting capacity to the Spanish and Portuguese Crowns on related matters. His rewards for that work and the income from his slaves and property in the New World made him independently wealthy. Much of his money he spent assembling a private library of 15,370 rare books and manuscripts. On his death he attempted to provide for the preservation of these books and to assure their availability to scholars by leaving them to the cathedral of Seville. He also left a plan for their preservation and the terms of consultation. His confidence in the reliability of the chapter, however, proved to be utterly misplaced, and his library was shamefully neglected with the result that only about 2,000 of its works remain. Happily, though these works still remain in the cathedral's library, the Biblioteca Colombina, they are better cared for now. The collection provides the crucial core of extant primary documents concerning Christopher Columbus's discovery of the New World.

Toward the end of his life, encouraged by both his own firsthand knowledge and his possession of his father's papers, Ferdinand decided to write his own biography of the explorer. He completed THE LIFE OF THE ADMIRAL CHRISTOPHER COLUMBUS around 1537, and the work first saw print in an Italian translation in 1571. No work about the discovery of America offers scholars and general readers greater rewards.

Bibliography

Colón, Fernando. *The Life of the Admiral Christopher Columbus by His Son Ferdinand.* Translated by Benjamin Keen. New Brunswick, N.J.: Rutgers University Press, ca. 1992.

———. *Historia del Almirante Cristobál Colón.* Edited by Luis Arranz Márquez. Madrid: Dastin, 2000.

comedy

Exposing human vice, folly, self-importance, and pretension seems to be a universal characteristic of comedy, and comedy itself appears throughout the world. Everywhere comedy, which does not necessarily have to be funny, tests human behavior against a set of cultural norms. In China, in the Muslim world, in Japan, in India, in Europe and elsewhere, foolish, vicious, asocial, or overly self-important characters risk ridicule and social isolation when comedy unmasks their vice, schemes, and pretenses.

Like TRAGEDY, European dramatic comedy probably traces its origins to Grecian religious festivals—particularly to a kind of song that honored the god Dionysius. The name of the group that sang the song *Comus* seems the source of the word *comedy* itself. In the so-called *old comedy,* represented by a group of 11 surviving plays by Aristophanes (425–388 B.C.E.), one can trace the outlines of the older religious festivals from which the genre sprang. The early comedy of Aristophanes ridiculed individuals like Socrates and Euripedes. His later work, however, shifted to focus more broadly on human folly and vice.

In ancient Rome, two writers of comedy became particular models for their successors: PLAUTUS, whose work is represented by 20 surviving plays, and TERENCE, whose remaining corpus contains six. Both these writers rang changes on a standard plot: Young people in love must overcome obstacles to fulfill their dreams. This plot seems never to lose its appeal, for there are always young people in love and confronted by difficulties. In the plays of the two Romans, the obstacles usually took the form of a set of STOCK CHARACTERS.

A braggart, the *MILES GLORIOSUS* (self-glorifying soldier), might be presented as a wealthy rival. Another character that interfered with the course of true love was a slave trader. He sometimes owned the heroine and wished to sell her favors to someone other than her young lover. Also, elderly parents who valued considerations other than love sometimes tried to control the heroine's love life. The young lover often has an associate, sometimes a slave or a flatterer, that helps him overcome the obstacles. Eventually, of course, true love wins the day and the lovers achieve their objective as the villains get their comic comeuppance.

Roman comedy seems to have continued to be known throughout medieval Europe, even though an almost exclusively religious drama prevailed, and this seemingly universal comedic thread of holding vice and pretense up to ridicule continued into Renaissance theater as well. We see it in the comedy of ARETINO, ARIOSTO, BRUNO, and MACHIAVELLI and in the partly improvisational *COMMEDIA DELL'ARTE* (comedy of the guild) in Italy. Similar explicit or implicit community standards for morals and behavior appear in the comedic elements of the religious and humanist drama throughout Europe.

In England a trend toward the secularization of native English religious comedy had begun as early as the 13th century. This trend continued, first with Renaissance HUMANIST INTERLUDES and then with frankly bawdy ones. Interludes were short plays performed between the courses of Renaissance banquets. A group of young playwrights called the UNIVERSITY WITS, having become acquainted with the plays of Plautus, began to imitate them. BEN JONSON, JOHN LYLY, ROBERT GREENE, and of course SHAKESPEARE all borrowed elements from the Roman comedy. Shakespeare, particularly, enlarged the capacities discovered there. Just as the older English drama had mixed comic and tragic or potentially tragic elements, so did Shakespeare and others. The result was tragicomedy or DARK COMEDY like Shakespeare's *THE WINTER'S TALE*.

French native theater of the Middle Ages also continued to influence the comedy of the Renaissance. Particularly influential were verse farces, of which hundreds survive, and DRAMATIC MONOLOGUES. A student of French theater, Barbara Bowen, maintains convincingly that the critical views of JOACHIM DU BELLAY have historically been overemphasized in discussions of French theatrical history. For instance, ÉTIENNE JODELLE's *Eugéne* is a Renaissance play that is usually mentioned as a radical departure from its medieval predecessors. In *Eugéne,* though, Bowen points out strong influences of earlier theater both on *Eugéne*'s form and on its content. Nonetheless, HUMANIST discussion of genre categories and of definitions deriving from ARISTOTLE's POETICS probably exercised more influence among French writers of comedy than among their English counterparts until the appearance of Jean Baptiste Poquelin or MOLIÈRE at the beginning of the period following the Renaissance, *The Enlightenment.*

Spanish comedy followed a course paralleling the English one. PEDRO CALDERÓN DE LA BARCA and LOPE DE VEGA mixed the matter of ordinary life with chivalric visions of days gone by in the Spanish *comedia*. *Don Juan*, by TIRSO DE MOLINA gave Mozart the prototype for his tragicomic opera *Don Giovanni*. Don Juan suffers the ultimate Christian tragedy in the loss of his soul, and the play appeals to the comedic impulse through his continual flouting of the norms of respectable behavior. In Spain, as in England, dramatic art strove to portray together the emotional and physical realities of life and its idealities as well.

Both comedic and tragic elements also appear in Chinese Opera. One of the most important theatrical poets of our period in China was TANG XIANZU (1550–1617), whose *PEONY PAVILLION* presents a tragicomic love story in 55 scenes.

In the Middle East, Arabic comedy sometimes was presented via shadow-figure plays and puppet shows that expose the very worst foibles of people—particularly sexual ones. One sort of puppet show, *KARAGÖZ* (the name both of the genre and its main character), became a popular mode of social and political criticism.

Finally, although all forms of Indian theater are essentially comedic, one that arose in the 16th century, the Ankia Nat of SANKARADEVA (d. 1568) portrays the wonderfully amusing adventures of Lord Krishna, a Hindu deity, including his amorous ones among a group of milkmaids.

Bibliography

Allen, Roger. *The Arabic Literary Heritage: The Development of its Genres and Criticism*. Cambridge, U.K.: Cambridge University Press, 1998.

Bowen, Barbara C. "French Drama," in Grendler, Paul F. *Encyclopedia of the Renaissance*. Vol. 2. New York: Charles Scribner's Sons, 1999.

Cowan, Louise, ed. *The Terrain of Comedy*. Dallas: Dallas Institute of Humanities and Culture, ca. 1984.

Lai Ming. *A History of Chinese Literature*. New York: The John Day Company, 1964.

Shipley, Joseph T. *Dictionary of World Literary Terms*. Boston: The Writer, Inc., 1970.

Sword of Truth. "The Immortal Land of Krishna—Assam." Available online. URL: http://www.swordoftruth.com/swordoftruth/multimedia/krishnapresentation/html/assampage. Downloaded on June 5, 2003.

Comedy of Betrothal, A *(Tsahut Badi-hutha de-quiddushin)* Leone de' Sommi (1560)

The earliest surviving drama in the Hebrew language, SOMMI'S five-act prose drama draws its character types from the Italian COMMEDIA DELL' ARTE and its plot from a postbiblical, oral, rabbinical narrative from the Hebrew Torah, the *Midrash Tanhuma*. Sommi wrote the original in biblical Hebrew.

A father is on the point of death. His only son and heir is traveling abroad. To protect the young man's inheritance, the father wills all he owns to a trusted slave and leaves his son the privilege of choosing any one thing from his estate. The father feels confident that his intelligent son will understand the ploy and will choose the slave, thereby regaining control of his father's fortune. The father's confidence in his son is well placed. His prospective in-laws, however, miss the point of the father's ingenuity.

Thinking that the father has disinherited the son, the in-laws break off their daughter's engagement to the young man. On his return, the son schemes to defeat his prospective in-laws' interference by making love to their daughter, whom he adores, in a vineyard. Under Jewish law this consummation would constitute a legitimate marriage with or without the parents' consent. A narrator in the drama, the Rabbi Amittai, whose name translates as "one who speaks the truth," resolves all dilemmas without the necessity of resorting to trickery.

Sommi's play directs social criticism at the matchmaking and marriage practices of the Jewish community in 16th-century Mantua. The drama was apparently performed in Mantua during Sommi's lifetime. It survives in the National Archives in that city in four manuscript copies, which suggests that the copies were acting versions. The play was revived both in Haifa and in Venice in the 1960s. A good English translation is available.

Bibliography

Sommi, Leone de'. *A Comedy of Betrothal (Tsahoth B'dihutha D'Kiddushin)*. Translated by Alfred S. Golding. Ottawa, Canada: Dovehouse Editions Canada, 1988.

comic relief

A characteristic often attributed to the TRAGEDY of WILLIAM SHAKESPEARE to contrast his plays with those of the ancient Greek tragedians. Whereas ARISTOTLE thought that tragedies should sweep from beginning to end with an unremitting sense of inevitability like the plays of Euripides and Sophocles, Shakespeare sometimes interrupted that flow with scenes like Act II, scene iii of MACBETH—the "drunken porter" scene. Interspersing such scenes, some suggest, appealed to the "groundlings"—the members of Shakespeare's audience who occupied the standing room in THE GLOBE THEATER and whose taste was too unrefined for unrelieved tragedy. While this may be true, it also seems at least equally likely that native English theater had historically included both serious and comedic elements and that Shakespeare and others drew on that tradition. *THE SECOND SHEPHERD'S PLAY* of the Wakefield Cycle of MORALITY PLAYS, performed from the 13th through the first third of the 16th centuries to celebrate the holiday of Corpus Christi, provides a typical example. In it, a representation of the adoration of the Magi at Christ's birth alternates with a comic parody of that serious action as group of country bumpkins named Col,

Gibb, and Daw fawn over a lamb dressed as a baby and, when the fraud is discovered, toss its perpetrator, Mac, in a blanket.

commedia dell' arte

Variously translated as "the comedy of the guild" or "the comedy of skill," the phrase *commedia dell' arte* describes a category of popular, largely improvisational theater that originated in Italy around the middle of the 16th century. The genre featured an ever-growing body of STOCK CHARACTERS—some representing regional Italian stereotypes. Some of the characters wore masks and costumes that have continued from that day to this to be identified with the roles their wearers played. Harlequin is one of these so-called masks recognizable by his black-and-white clown suit and his black mask. A physician from the city of Bologna, Graziano, is another, wearing the mask of the medieval plague doctor. Sometimes, a famous player such as ISABELLA ANDREINI contributed her own name to a character, and the role of Isabella became a fixture of the genre. Always there was a collection of clowns called Zanni (from which comes the English adjective *zany*) who carried on stage business and buffoonery. The actors could assume several roles, even cross-dressing as members of the opposite sex as the occasion warranted.

In its performance, commedia dell' arte had a good deal in common with 20th-century jazz concerts. The characters had before them a kind of outline of the play they were to perform, and from it they ad-libbed in much the same way that jazz musicians improvise their solos while following a basic chart.

While many troupes traveled around the countryside performing when and where they could and living hand-to-mouth, others became very well off. One of the more successful companies was THE GELOSI, run by Isabella Andreini and her husband Francesco. They and others like them traveled throughout Europe, and the fashion of the commedia spread to France and Germany where local companies sprang up in imitation of the Italians.

Though it flourished mainly in the 16th and 17th centuries, the commedia dell'arte continues to be performed in Italy to this day. It has also inspired playwrights and comedians to apply aspects of it to their own work as recently as the 20th century. One could argue, for instance, that Charlie Chaplin's persona in early films owed much to the clowns of the commedia, and the Italian Nobel Prize winner Dario Fo makes use of its conventions as well.

Bibliography

Cairns, Christopher, ed. *The Commedia dell'Arte from the Renaissance to Dario Fo.* Lewiston, N.Y.: E. Mellen Press, ca. 1989.

Henke, Robert. *Performance and Literature in the Commedia dell' Arte.* Cambridge and New York: Cambridge University Press, 2002.

commonplace books

The Renaissance commonplace books, at first regularly compiled in manuscript by students, scholars, writers, and readers, were later printed for commercial distribution as well. Commonplace books assembled topics of interest to the person compiling the book. (See TOPOS, TOPOI.) Schoolchildren compiled commonplace books to organize quotations from the materials they read. These they collected either under headings assigned by their teachers or under those that especially engaged the student. Usually, the compilers of commonplace books cross-referenced their entries both to other entries and to the works from which they were drawn. Essentially, this encyclopedia is a descendant of the kind of commonplace book that people organized alphabetically within a particular sphere of interest.

There were other sorts of organization as well: among others, Aristotelian categories of thought, proverbs, witty sayings, quotations supporting particular positions, and reflections on various categories of experience. BEN JONSON's *Timber, or Discoveries Made Upon Men and Matter* (1641) illustrates the kind of book based on experience. Preachers often compiled such books to organize ideas and quotations for sermons. It is altogether likely that commonplace books underlay collections of essays like those of MONTAIGNE, BACON, and DESCARTES.

The widespread Renaissance employment of commonplace books sprang from the interest HUMANIST writers took in the uses that ARISTOTLE, CICERO, and Quintilian had found for similar collections during classical antiquity. The Humanists RUDOLFUS AGRICOLA (1443–85) and DESIDERIUS ERASMUS (1466–1536), together with the Lutheran theologian and humanist Philip Melancthon (1497–1560) all shared a concern for the improvement of education. Those three developed the method of compiling private commonplace books that became standard across Europe throughout the two centuries on which this volume principally focuses. Moreover, a broad market, structured on similar principles, eventually developed for printed commonplace books.

Ann Moss tells us that commonplace books affected European compositional and conversational styles, causing both to be liberally sprinkled with quotations, rhetoric, and verbal ornament. She also suggests that, because of the intimate connection between such books and Latin schools that principally trained boys, the use of commonplace books produced both a like-minded European male elite and an accompanying exclusion of women from it.

Commonplace books give us a useful insight into Renaissance ideas of the organization of the human mind. Their widespread use also influenced the way in which Renaissance minds in fact were organized.

Bibliography
Moss, Ann. *Printed Commonplace Books and the Structuring of Renaissance Thought*. Oxford, U.K.: Oxford University Press, 1996.

Commynes, Philippe de (ca. 1447–1511)
Sometimes styled the French MACHIAVELLI (whom he met in the 1490s), Commynes was a French aristocrat who played major roles in the diplomacy and administrations of three French rulers, Louis XI, Charles VIII, and Louis XII.

His principal contribution to Renaissance literature came with the publication of his *Memoires* of the reign of Louis XI (ruled 1461–83). These were written between 1489 and 1492, and published in two preliminary editions in 1524 and 1528. The definitive edition appeared posthumously in 1552. Lucid, energetic and written from the perspective of an insider, Commynes's book examines not only the events of the reign of an astute ruler known as the spider king, but also the psychology, the motives, and the processes of decision making and action that produce social evolution. Using Louis XI's reign as his test case, Commynes tried to draw general conclusions about the way in which capable rulers and governments should conduct themselves.

The work is also interesting for its autobiographical glimpses into the life of a man who, as long as Louis XI lived, was FORTUNE's darling, but who fell from both her favor and his king's during the reign of Louis XII. He advises rulers to trust only themselves, to be suspicious of their advisors, and to leave nothing to the fickle operation of fortune.

His work proved highly influential in the Renaissance and beyond. It was widely translated and continues to reappear periodically in various languages.

Bibliography
Commynes, Philippe de. *Memoires: The Reign of Louis XI*. Translated by Michael Jones. Harmondsworth, U.K.: Penguin, 1972.

Compleat Angler, The   Izaak Walton (1653)
Subtitled *The Contemplative Man's Recreation*, IZAAK WALTON's charming book on fishing has the distinction of being, after the Bible, the bestselling book in the English language. In Walton's own lifetime it went through five editions—each one revised and enlarged by his hand. Many persons in every generation succeeding Walton's own have found his volume as congenial a companion as Walton himself must have been. Among them, not a few have been lured by the book to try their hands at the recreation its author so loved. Among those, some have found a lifelong passion in the art

of catching fish. Others, like the American author Nathaniel Hawthorne (1804–64), after the book had enticed them to try fishing, discovered they preferred reading about catching fish in Walton's work to the actual sport itself.

More than just a how-to book, Walton's work celebrates the joys of rural landscapes, innocent and comradely companionship, good food and drink, and the happiness that arises from the combination. The book also delights a reader with its colloquial, straightforward prose style. Walton almost makes a reader feel part of the company enjoying the charms of the English countryside. Most readers also find pleasing the poems and songs interspersed throughout the volume's pages.

The book, however, opens not along the banks of some stream but rather in London with the chance meeting of three men walking up Tottenham Hill. The three, whose Latinate names reflect their preferred sports, are a fisherman, Piscator, a hunter, Venator, and a devotee of falconry, Auceps. As they walk along together, the men agree to discuss the charms and advantages of their respective sports, not to scoff at each other, and to listen willingly to what the other two have to offer.

Auceps begins and discourses on the benefits of the element air. He sets a defense of the superiority of one of the Greek elements as a feature of the discourse. Piscator argues for the superiority of water and Venator of earth. Fire, of course, is not represented. Auceps supports his preference with quotations about birds from Scripture and provides a list of the species of fowl that a falconer may choose to train for the hunt.

Venator follows the model, praising both the sorts of game he hunts and the dogs he uses to track them. Piscator takes his turn, and as he finishes his initial praise of fishing, Auceps reaches his destination and leaves the other two, assuring them of the pleasure he has taken in their discourses and the personal regard he feels for his companions.

As Piscator and Venator stroll along together, Venator asks for more detail, and Piscator obliges, describing rivers, species of fish, and the psychological and emotional benefits of fishing. As the first chapter ends, the two have become such good friends that they agree that Piscator will join Venator the following day on an otter hunt. For the next two days after that, Venator will fish with Piscator.

The otter hunt proves successful, and there is time enough left for Piscator to catch a chubb for dinner at an Inn, where the hostess prepares the fish according to Piscator's instructions. Venator is so impressed that he makes Piscator his fishing teacher and extends their planned outing to five days.

The next two chapters, III and IV are devoted to discussing how to catch and prepare chubb and trout, respectively. In chapter IV, a charming digression takes place. Having caught both a trout and a chubb, the friends agree to share the trout for their supper. They give the chubb to a grateful pair of milkmaids, a mother and a daughter, who thank them for their gift by singing. The daughter sings CHRISTOPHER MARLOWE's "The Passionate Shepherd to his Love," (ca. 1599), and the mother replies by singing Sir Walter Raleigh's "The Nymph's Reply to the Shepherd" (1600).

Returning to the inn where they are lodging, the pair meet Piscator's brother and a friend of his. The obliging hostess prepares their dinner, and the men while away the evening by singing. The rest of the fifth chapter, which recounts the third and part of the fourth days of the outing, is devoted to instructions concerning trout fishing, fly tying, the various sorts of bait one should select under various circumstances. The friends enliven the day by singing and by telling amusing stories. The activities of the fourth day consume several chapters as different species of fish are described and the manner of trying to catch each one. The final chapter devoted to the activities of the fourth day bears the title, "Chapter XVI—Is of nothing or that which is nothing worth." In it the four men return from their day's fishing, dine, and again engage in conversation and the recitation of poems and singing. The bucolic absence of our contemporary electronic din is enough to inspire nostalgia for a world long passed.

Chapters XVII through XXI recount the fifth day. On it the men—now firm friends—walk back to London. As they go they describe the beauties of the scenes they pass. Piscator rounds out Venator's education with discussions of other fish and the various baits one needs for them. Piscator describes several rivers, instructs Venator in the construction and maintenance of fishponds, and gives him directions in the 21st chapter for making a rod and reel and choosing the colors for the rod and the line. As the book ends, there is much quoting of pastoral poetry, appropriate Scripture, Greek philosophers, and St. Augustine's *Confessions* on the subjects of friendship, virtuous living, contentment, enjoyment of the natural world, the goodness of God and nature, and the contribution that angling makes to all the above.

Walton's work closes with a verse of Scripture, 1 Thess. 4.2: "Study to be quiet."

Bibliography

Walton, Izaak. *The Compleat Angler, or, the Contemplative Man's Recreation.* Edited by Andrew Lang. New York: Dover Publications, 2003.

Complutensian Polyglot Bible

A triumph of the printer's art, the Complutensian Polyglot Bible was prepared at the new University of Alcalá (*Compluta* in Latin) de Henares in Spain by a team led by the founder of the university, the conservative Cardinal Francisco Jiménez de Cisneros (also known as Cajetan, 1436–1517)—the same person who had instructed MARTIN LUTHER to recant. Jiménez de Cisneros brought together the manuscripts and the talent necessary to produce a Bible with texts in several languages (including Latin, Greek, and Hebrew) displayed together on a page. In addition to the cardinal himself, the team included three Hebraists who were Jewish converts to Christianity, two Greek scholars, a Spanish HUMANIST Antonio de Nebrija, and, of course, a very capable printer. Securing the necessary papal permissions and the cardinal's death delayed publication until 1521.

This multilingual presentation of the Scripture had been partly inspired by the humanist goal of correcting biblical text through comparative examination of early originals. Jiménez de Cisneros's religious conservatism prompted him to insist on preserving as much of the officially approved Medieval Latin Bible (the Vulgate) as the ancient manuscripts allowed rather than achieving an entirely fresh edition of the Latin text. The team also made editorial choices that supported prevailing Roman Catholic viewpoints and at least once actually altered a passage from an ancient Greek manuscript to make it conform. Objecting to this approach, Nebrija withdrew from the project.

The finished work consisted of five volumes. Though the editorial decisions diminished the value of the work from the perspective of textual criticism, displaying alternate versions of Scripture together in original languages nonetheless provided a valuable service to biblical scholarship.

Bibliography

Bentley, Jerry H. *Humanism and Holy Writ: New Testament Scholarship in the Renaissance.* Princeton, N.J.: Princeton University Press, 1983.

composition

Renaissance ideas about imaginative composition—at least before MICHEL DE MONTAIGNE—did not often encourage authors simply to look in their hearts and write. Rather, writers in the Renaissance, especially poets, imagined that in the course of literary history most subjects had already been considered. The writer's job, then, rather than creating from scratch, involved learning a great deal about the way earlier authors and poets had treated their subjects and recombining the elements of those writings in ways that achieved depth or novel insight. Making the topics of earlier writers (see TOPOS) accessible to one's imagination involved a great deal of study and memorization. PETRARCH memorized 20,000 lines of VIRGIL, and JOHN MILTON literally studied himself blind preparing for their high calling as poets.

The motivation for such heroic effort arose in part from the conviction that the poet, when composing, performed a priestly function (see VATES). This view of the role of the poet as a sort of priest was, until quite recently, held all over the world. Except in western industrial society, it still is.

conceit

A *conceit* is a kind of METAPHOR that achieves its effect by making comparison between very unlike objects or ideas in the hope of achieving a fresh or novel insight. Among poets throughout Europe who imitated PETRARCH, "eyes like stars," "pearly teeth," "lips like cherries" and other such comparisons, which had perhaps once seemed fresh, became laughable through too frequent use. One artist even drew a picture of a "conceited lady" whose features were composed of the objects to which they had been compared. She was singularly unattractive. Reacting against this PETRARCHIST tradition, a school of poets in England developed the METAPHYSICAL CONCEIT. This school attempted to employ fresh and often far-fetched comparisons to enliven their verse.

See also JOHN DONNE, ANDREW MARVELL, and RICHARD CRASHAW.

concrete poems

The text of a concrete poem is arranged to represent the physical form of the subject of a poem. Two examples include "The Altar," and "Easter Wings" by GEORGE HERBERT. Here is the first of "Easter Wings'" two stanzas:

> Lord, who createdst man in wealth and store,
> Though foolishly he lost the same,
> Decaying more and more,
> Till he became
> Most poor:
> With thee
> O let me rise
> As larks, harmoniously,
> And sing this day thy victories:
> Then shall the fall further the flight in me.
> (1633)

The Renaissance interest in concrete poems, also called pattern poems, sprang from and revived an ancient Alexandrian Greek tradition of shaping poems like objects ranging from Pan's musical pipes to eggs.

Constable, Henry (1562–1613)

Educated at Cambridge and the son of a notable Warwickshire family, Henry Constable became a Roman Catholic convert while at university. As a result he lived much of his life abroad in France, though he traveled to and from the Continent. A composer of ENGLISH SONNETS, he published a brief sonnet sequence, *Diana*, in 1594. Though this contained only 23 poems, an expansion in 1595 included both Constable's own poems and those of others, including eight by SIR PHILIP SIDNEY. Other poems by Constable in praise of Sidney appeared in Sidney's own *Apologie for Poetrie* (1595). Four more of Constable's pastoral poems were included in *England's Helicon* (1600).

King JAMES I admired Constable's work sufficiently to include one of his sonnets in the king's own *Poetical Exercises* (1591). Perhaps on the strength of that admiration, Constable tried to influence James to permit Catholics greater religious freedom in England without penalty, but that effort proved unsuccessful. Because of their Catholic bias, Constable's religious sonnets did not see print until the 19th century.

His work was popular enough in his own era that at least one of his pastoral poems, "Damelus' Song to his Diaphenia," was set to music by Francis Pilkington and published in that musician's *First Book of Songs or Airs* in 1605.

Bibliography

Fleissner, Robert E. *Resolved to Love: The 1592 Edition of Henry Constable's Diana*. Salzburg: Institut für Anglistik und Amerikanistik, Universität Salzburg, 1980.

Copernicus, Nicolaus (1473–1543)

A Polish astronomer, a canon lawyer, a physician, an economic theorist, a regional administrator, and a translator, Copernicus stands in the first rank of the founders of modern science. Orphaned in about 1485, Copernicus became the ward of his uncle, Lucas Watzelrode. A priest, Watzelrode became the bishop of Varmia in 1489. As bishop, Watzelrode was in a position to smooth the young

Copernicus's way and did so, seeing to his education first at the cathedral school and later at the University of Cracow. Although Copernicus never became a priest, his uncle helped him secure a lifetime appointment to the chapter of canons at the cathedral of Frauenburg. He also held a concurrent appointment as *scholasticus* (scholar) at Breslau until 1538.

Sent by his colleagues to study canon law at the University of Bologna in 1496, Copernicus also pursued his interest in astronomy, making his first recorded observation there the following year. So successful was Copernicus's work that his professor, Domenicos Maria Novara, arranged for him to lecture on astronomy and mathematics in Rome, where he observed an eclipse of the moon in November 1500.

The year 1501 found him back in Frauenburg for his installation as a canon of the cathedral. Immediately thereafter he returned to Italy, where he received the doctorate in medicine from the University of Padua; then he moved on to Ferrara, whose university granted him a doctorate in canon law in 1503. He remained in Italy until 1505 when he returned to Prussia where, from 1507 until 1512, he served his uncle as secretary and personal physician. During this period he translated into Latin 85 Greek Letters of Theophylactus Simocatta. These dealt with ethical matters, love, and rural subjects. The translation appeared in 1509. Not only was Copernicus interested in making these letters available in a language read by most educated readers, but he also wished to improve his own Greek so that he could study the as yet untranslated *Almagest* of the ancient Egyptian Greek astronomer Ptolemy. Ptolemy's geocentric scheme for the universe had dominated astronomy since ancient times, and his ideas meshed with the Christian view that human beings were central to God's plan. (See COSMOLOGY.)

In 1513, the year following his uncle's death, Copernicus built an astronomical observatory and equipped it with the available instruments for celestial observation. These did not yet, of course, include a telescope. Based on his observations and the complex mathematical computations he made as a result of them, Copernicus concluded that Ptolemy had been wrong. Not the sphere of the Earth, but the sphere of the Sun was the center of the solar system. He accordingly drafted his most influential work, which both reconfigured astronomy and shook the foundations of theological thinking, his Little commentary (*Commentariolus*, written 1513–14). He understood its implications and was reluctant to publish it, though he did allow manuscript copies to circulate among a narrow circle of trusted friends. Only after 26 years did he allow friends who were also important members of the ecclesiastical hierarchy to convince him that he owed it to science to publish. His expanded and definitive discussion finally appeared in the last year of his life as: On the revolution of the heavenly spheres (*De revolutionibus orbium coelestium*, 1543).

A highly technical work, the book suffered from the decision of its editor to replace Copernicus's own introduction with an unsigned one by a Lutheran theologian, Andreas Oslander. This falsely denied that Copernicus intended to describe the real state of the solar system. Rather, Oslander claimed, it was a mathematical means for predicting the positions of heavenly bodies. That disclaimer, then generally attributed to Copernicus, plus the fact that he had dedicated the work to Pope Paul III, probably saved the work from early controversy. In 1616, however, after GALILEO GALILEI was forced to renounce his confirmation of Copernicus by telescopic observation, the book became prohibited reading for Roman Catholics until 1758.

As for Copernicus himself, during his lifetime he was far too busy to be burdened with worry about his posthumous reputation among theologians. At Frauenberg he served at various times as vicar general of his order, judge, tax collector, military governor, physician, and treasurer. These offices he apparently discharged with great competence and political astuteness. In the course of his duties he wrote a treatise on coinage that, by showing how debased coinage drives out more valuable money, anticipated Gresham's law. He also was responsible for revising the system of weights and measures of his region.

Bibliography

Copernicus, Nicolaus. *Three Copernican Treatises.* Translated and edited by Edward Rosen. New York: Octagon Books, 1971.

———. *Nicholas Copernicus on the Revolutions.* Edited and translated by Edward Rosen. Baltimore and London: Johns Hopkins University Press, 1978.

———. *Nicholas Copernicus Minor Works.* Translated and edited by Edward Rosen and Erna Hilfstein. Baltimore and London: Johns Hopkins University Press, 1985.

Mekarski, Stefan. *Nicholas Copernicus (Mikolaj Kopernik), 1473–1543.* Translated from the Polish by B. W. A. Massey. London: Polish Cultural Foundation, 1973.

Corneille, Pierre (1606–1684)

A French lawyer and devout church–warden in his hometown of Rouen in Normandy while at the same time an illustrious verse playwright in Paris, Corneille apparently moved easily between the two poles of his professional existence and between the two cities in which he worked.

His first play, *Mélite* (1629) is a COMEDY—a story of young love. An immediate success on the Paris stage, it established an eager audience for his work. He met his public's demand with a series of works over the next several years: *Clitandre,* a tragicomedy, *Médeé* (Medea), a TRAGEDY, and four other comedies. In these comedies he departs from the French Renaissance obsession with Roman subjects, drawing his material instead from the life around him as he does in his *Place Royale* (The Royal Plaza) or his *Galérie du Palais* (The gallery of the palace). The best of these early sentimental comedies, perhaps, is *La Veuve* (The widow) in which a confidence man is trapped in his own snares. For the fourth of these early comedies, he looked to Spain for inspiration, producing his uproarious *L'Illusion Comique* (The comic illusion).

At least once he collaborated with four other playwrights, bringing to the stage Cardinal Richelieu's *Comédie des Tuileries* (Comedy of the Tuileries, 1635.) This was a shrewd political move.

Richelieu was the power behind the throne, and he also harbored literary aspirations. By assisting him in realizing them, Corneille gained a powerful advocate.

His next major success and the triumph that brought him true fame was his tragicomedy, LE CID (1636). Corneille based his play on the story of the medieval Spanish national hero whose triumph over the Islamic invaders had made his life the stuff of legend. He took his material directly from a Spanish drama, *The Youthful Adventures of the Cid,* by the playwright, Guillen de Castro. Corneille reshaped the play by shifting its focus from incident to psychology. Although Corneille was always more interested in imitating life than in following critical dictates, he nevertheless tried to make his *Cid* conform more closely to the unities of time, place, and action proposed by the Italian LUDOVICO CASTELVETRO in the latter's commentary on ARISTOTLE's *POETICS*. The broad scope of the source play's action, however, doomed that attempt to partial failure, and the critical community accused Corneille both of breaking the rules of good dramaturgy and of stealing his material from the Spanish.

Surely offended, for the next three years Corneille attended to his legal affairs in Rouen before returning to the Paris stage with a new play. This tragedy, *Horace* (1639), conformed closely to the French Academy's preference for the unities, treated a subject from Roman history, and celebrated the virtue of patriotism. That formula established a pattern of moral tragedy approved by French critics and audiences alike—and by Cardinal Richelieu as well: Public duty always takes precedence over personal interest. Both Corneille and the playwrights succeeding him thereafter adhered closely to the model. *Cinna,* another verse tragedy on a Roman subject appeared in 1640. In 1643, with the appearance of *Polyeucte*—a play about a Christian martyr with that name—Corneille moves his theme of the subordination of personal interest to stoic heroism into the religious sphere. He then returns to the political arena with *La mort de Pompée* (The death of Pompey) later that same year.

Corneille's most celebrated comedy, *Le Menteur* (The liar), also appeared in 1643. Looking to Spain once more for his inspiration, he adapted Alarcón's *La Verdad Sospechosa* (The doubtful truth) for the French stage. The hero of the French version, Dorante, lies extravagantly and entertainingly throughout the play. His untruths do not arise from malice, however. Rather they arise from egocentrism and a romanticized view of himself. The play's success led Corneille to pen a sequel that failed to live up to the original. His tragedy *Rodogune* (1645)—named for a female character, a rival of the play's heroine, Cleopatra—was his personal favorite. Against the terror of the play's tragic ending, Corneille contrasts the fraternal affection of Cleopatra's two sons—an affection that persists despite their rivalry for the love of Rodogune.

Succeeding these dramas came a series of others that demonstrate Corneille's theatrical versatility. Named for one of the characters, the tragicomedy *Nicoméde* was followed by a musical play *Androméde* that depended mainly on spectacular effects for its interest. Then came another play with a Spanish theme, *Don Sanche d'Aragon*.

In the year 1647, Corneille achieved one of his personal goals. After being passed over twice, he finally was elected to the French Academy—the highest literary honor his countrymen could bestow. The period of his greatest theatrical achievement, however, had passed. In 1652 a tragedy, *Pertharite*, failed with the Parisian audiences, and Corneille entered a period of retirement from the stage. He returned to Rouen where his literary efforts were mainly directed to a verse translation of the *Imitation of Christ* and to preparing a printed edition of his plays together with explanatory prefaces and three essays on the art of the theater. This three-volume edition appeared in 1660.

He tried a comeback, and his tragedy, *Oedipe* (Oedipus), proved a success, but his play *Attila*, based on the career of Attila the Hun, failed. So did a play he wrote in 1670 in competition with RACINE, *Tite et Bérénice* (Titus and Berenice, respectively the son of the Roman Emperor Vespasian and the daughter of the Jewish king, Herod Agrippa I). Appearing eight days earlier, Racine's play on the same subject was a great success.

Living now in Paris with his younger brother Thomas, who also wrote plays, Pierre Corneille kept trying, and his later plays are obsessed with political subjects. The audiences, however, had lost interest in him. His last attempt to produce a new play came in 1674 with *Suréna*. Its failure ended his active theatrical career. He revised his works for publication—a task he completed in 1682—and died in 1684. His brother Thomas was elected to his place in the academy. On its behalf, his fellow academician and an even more able playwright, JEAN RACINE, wrote and delivered at Corneille's funeral a magnificent and heartfelt eulogy.

Bibliography

Abraham, Claude Kurt. *Pierre Corneille.* New York: Twayne Publishers, 1972.

Corneille, Pierre. *Horace.* Translated by Alan Brownjohn. Edited by David Clarke. London: Angel Books, ca. 1996.

———. *Seven Plays.* [*The Cid, Cinna, Horatius, Polyeucte, Rodognune, The Liar, Surenas*] Translated by Samuel Solomon. New York: Random House, 1969.

———. *Théâtre complet.* Edited by Alain Niderst. Paris: Presses universitaires de France, ca. 1984–ca. 1986.

Margitíc, Milorad R. *Corneille comique: Nine Studies of Pierre Corneille's Comedy with an Introduction and a Bibliography.* Seattle, Wash.: Papers on French Century Literature, 1982.

Cortés, Hernán (1485–1547)

The Spanish conquistador who subdued Mexico, Cortés was the son of a noble family of Medellín in the Estremedura region. In 1504 he sailed to San Domingo with Diégo Velásquez de Cuéllar. In 1511, he fought beside Velásquez in Cuba. In 1518 Velásquez appointed Cortés the leader of an expedition whose objective was the conquest of Mexico. The expedition seemed hardly sufficient to the task, being composed of 550 men with 10 cannon and 17 horses. Nonetheless, after landing on the Yucatán Peninsula, the small force overcame Tabasco and pressed on toward the Aztec capitol, Tenochtitlán, arriving at San Juan de Ulúa. There, messengers from Montezuma II, the Aztec ruler met Cortés and presented him with gifts from their king.

Cortés built a fortress and founded Veracruz, and to bolster the courage and resolution of his men he burned his ships. The party then resumed their march toward Tenochtitlán but confronted determined resistance at Tlaxcala. The Spaniards won the day and the allegiance of the Tlaxcalans. Evading an ambush at Cholula, Cortés and his party, whose numbers were now increased by Tlaxcalan allies, arrived at the Aztec capital on November 8, 1519. Received with honor by Montezuma and his court, Cortés repaid the Aztecs' courtesy by seizing the king and holding him captive until he swore to become the feudal vassal of the king of Spain.

This story and the rest of the history of his conquest of Mexico Cortés tells in his own words in a series of five reports he made to Holy Roman Emperor Charles V (King Charles I of Spain), who was also emperor of Mexico as a result of Cortés's efforts. The five reports, *cartas de relación,* went to Spain in 1519, 1520, 1522, 1524, and 1526. Written in straightforward prose, these eyewitness accounts vividly portray both the events and the people involved. The events in the conquest of Mexico synopsized above are taken from the reports of 1519 and 1520. Cortés' history benefits both from its author's being the protagonist and from the clarity of his style.

After serving as both captain general and governor of Mexico, Cortés returned famous, ennobled to the rank of marquis, and wealthy to Spain. He died near Seville and was survived by his second wife and their four children and also by five other children borne by Indian women, including one by the sister of Montezuma. He acknowledged these offspring and provided for them in his will. His body was later returned to the New World and rests in Mexico City, which Cortés built on the ruins of Tenochtitlán after he razed it in 1521.

Bibliography

Cortés, Hernán. *Letters from Mexico.* Edited and translated by Anthony Pagden. New Haven, Conn.: Yale University Press, 1986.

Thomas, Hugh. *Conquest: Montezuma, Cortés, and the Fall of Old Mexico.* New York: Simon and Schuster, 1993.

cosmology

Throughout much of the Renaissance the predominant view of the universe was the one proposed by the ancient Greek astronomer Ptolemy. The Earth stood immobile at the center of a vast series of nine spheres. These were made of a crystalline substance, and embedded in each sphere were the moon, the sun, each of the six planets then known, and the fixed stars. Beyond the ninth sphere was the *primum mobile*—the prime mover. This gave the spheres their initial motion, and, as the ninth sphere turned, it moved the eighth, which impelled the seventh, and so on. Beyond the prime mover was chaos, and, in the Christian view of things, also Heaven from which the Earth hung suspended by a golden chain known as the Great Chain of Being. This chain's links were composed of all sentient creatures from archangels at the top of chain to the least of God's living creation. As the spheres turned, their crystalline substance rubbed together and created a harmonious sound, "the music of the spheres," whose pleasing melody angels could hear.

Other ancient astronomers had proposed a heliocentric universe with a mobile Earth. The geocentric view, however, fit well with Christian notions of a providential creation that put Earth and, on it, humankind at the center of God's attention, concern, and care. Thus it was Ptolemaic cosmology that historically enjoyed the church's official stamp of approval and that gave DANTE and JOHN MILTON the model for their great allegorical epics.

Bibliography

Milton, John. *Paradise Lost and Selected Poetry and Prose.* Edited by Northrup Frye. New York: Rinehart, 1951.

Council of Trent   (1545–1563)

Convened in the northern Italian city of Trento as the 19th ecumenical council of the Roman Catholic Church, the Council of Trent's decisions affirmed the official stance of the church on many of the contentious issues that separated Roman Catholic from Protestant thinking. From a literary perspective, among other decisions made by the council during its long and twice interrupted deliberations, the council affirmed the Nicene Creed as the basis of Christian belief. It responded to the HUMANIST criticism of the textual corruption of the Latin Vulgate BIBLE by, first, definitively establishing the books to be included in the New and Old Testaments, and, second, by ruling that the Vulgate, whatever its textual inadequacies, was a sufficient authority for resolving questions of doctrine. This decision left open the door for improving the Bible's text by the new methods that humanism had developed while at the same time preserving the influence of the Vulgate. Another literary outcome of this debate appeared in the postcouncil revision of missals and breviaries—that is, of the instructional materials from which lay Catholics learned the tenets of their faith.

The Council of Trent after long debate narrowly rejected the Lutheran principle of justification by faith alone. It also affirmed the real as opposed to the symbolic presence of the body and blood of Christ in the Eucharist. These decisions troubled many reformers. So did the council's affirmation of the veneration of the Virgin Mary and of saints and their images. While those three rulings were not palatable to many in the reform movement, a decision that better pleased them required bishops to reside in their dioceses, thereby ending the possibility of the plurality bishoprics and limiting the temptation of accruing temporal power by that means. The council also addressed issues concerning the education and behavior of clergy whose ignorance and profligacy had become a matter of public and literary scorn and satirical comment.

Another matter of vast literary importance was implicit in the decisions of the Council of Trent. Those decisions provided the grounds on which a book would receive the approval—the *imprimatur* (let it be printed)—of the church authorities or whether a work would be listed on the church's INDEX OF FORBIDDEN BOOKS.

Bibliography

Chemnitz, Martin (1522–86). *Examination of the Council of Trent.* Translated from Latin by Fred Kramer. St. Louis, Mo.: Concordia Publishing House, 1971–ca. 1986.

Countesse of Montgomeries Urania, The   Lady Mary Wroth (1621)

Published together with her SONNET sequence *Pamphilia to Amphilanthus*, LADY MARY WROTH'S 1621 edition of what proved to be only the first part of her sprawling ROMANCE, *The Countesse of Montgomeries Urania*, provoked a bitter and sexist literary quarrel in London. Her book, the first long narrative fiction ever certainly published by an English woman, broke more than one of her era's taboos.

In the first place women—especially noble women—were tacitly expected to circulate their writings only in manuscript. Print publication was decidedly beneath them. Publishing for money was the province of the common scribbling classes and the prerogative of men only. In the second place, though much of *Urania* was indebted to works of CHIVALRIC and PASTORAL romance like GARCI RODRÍGUEZ DE MONTALVO'S *AMADIS OF GAUL*, LUDOVICO ARIOSTO'S *ORLANDO FURIOSO*, and EDMUND SPENSER'S *FAERIE QUEENE*, to MIGUEL DE CERVANTES SAAVEDRA'S *DON QUIXOTE DE LA MANCHA*, and especially to Wroth's uncle SIR PHILIP SIDNEY'S *ARCADIA*, lengthy portions of the work described thinly veiled goings on at the feverishly amorous court of James I. So when Wroth's book hit the streets in December 1621, the king found himself inundated with letters of complaint from influential noblemen who objected that Wroth had portrayed their private lives under the pretext of fiction.

Responding to the complaints, as Wroth's most notable 20th-century editor, Josephine A. Roberts, reports, Wroth wrote to George Villiers, the duke of Buckingham, asserting that the work had been pirated and that she had not intended to make *Urania* public. She told Villiers that she had demanded a halt to distribution and that she had applied for the king's permission to recover the copies that had already been sold. While that may be so, no record of the work's recall has been found, and Wroth was perennially in need of money to discharge the burdensome debts that she had inherited from her deceased husband.

Principally in prose but sprinkled through with SONNETS and occasionally with longer poems, the work has as its principal character the shepherdess Urania. The opening passages find her wandering about the countryside in a state of depression arising from love sickness. She strays into a cavern that shows signs of habitation, and there she finds a man stretched out on a flat stone, dressed like a religious hermit, and lying as still as the funeral statue he resembles. He begins, however, to speak, and readers discover that he too is pining away. His name is Perissus, and his affliction is a lost love, Limena, whose husband Philargus, as we also learn, was her murderer. Before her death Limena charged Perissus not to try to avenge her. Obeying her entreaties, Perissus went off to war and vented his sorrow by killing numerous enemy troops. This episode may fictionally displace some of the actual events surrounding the forced marriage of Sir Philip Sidney's beloved Penelope Devereaux to the wealthy Lord Rich. No actual murder was involved, but the hopes of the young people were shattered.

After the initial episode of Perissus, a reader discovers that the cause of Urania's depression is her feeling for Amphilanthus, heir to the kingdom of Naples. Amphilanthus is seeking his sister, kidnapped at birth, as Urania discovers when she runs into his kinsman, Parselius, the prince of Morea. The pastoral novel continues in this vein with a huge cast of characters many of whom are royalty or members of the nobility in the character of shepherds. They populate an Arcadian landscape that exists, not on the face of the planet in Italy, Albania, Romania, Greece, Hungary, or the other locales in which *Urania*'s action ostensibly occurs, but in the minds of those who subscribe to the views about love and its capacity for ennobling lovers that were popularized by PETRARCH and those subscribing to NEOPLATONISM and the associated cult of PLATONIC LOVE that heavily influenced the royal court under James I.

Distinguishing Wroth's work from the bulk of the European pastoral tradition in which she lo-

cates it, however, the reader finds at its narrative center a coterie of sensible and passionate women: Urania herself, her cousin, Philistella, the ladies Veralinda and Pamphilia, and others. These women in the guise of royal and noble shepherdesses and their involvement in, discussion of, and responses to the complex military action, sea voyages, allegorical episodes, and love relationships that swirl around them give the work a weight and balance that places it squarely at the cornerstone of women's writing in Britain.

The first part of *Urania* in the 1621 edition breaks off sharply without closure. There then follows a sonnet sequence of poems from Pamphilia to Amphilanthus. Some have suggested that Wroth intended this break to emulate the ending of her uncle Sir Philip Sidney's *Arcadia*, a work that Sidney left unfinished owing to his death as a result of an infected battle wound. No one seems to have known that there was much more of Wroth's already vast work until Josephine A. Roberts excavated it from the manuscripts held by Chicago's Newberry Library. Published for the first time in 1999 by Roberts's successor editors, the second part continues exactly from the place that the first part breaks off and continues the kaleidoscopic, episodic story through almost as many pages again as are included in the first part.

Bibliography

Wroth, Lady Mary. *The First Part of the Countess of Montgomery's Urania.* Edited by Josephine A. Roberts. Binghamton, N.Y.: Renaissance English Text Society . . . [and] Medieval and Renaissance Texts and Studies, 1995.

———. *The Second Part of the Countess of Montgomery's Urania.* Edited by Josephine A. Roberts and completed by Suzanne Gossett and Janel Mueller. Tempe, Ariz.: Renaissance English text Society . . . [and] Arizona Center for Medieval and Renaissance Studies, 1999.

Countess of Pembroke's Arcadia, The

(Old Arcadia) Sir Philip Sidney (1593)
Drawing on a growing interest in finding freshness in mixed modes, Sir PHILIP SIDNEY brought together

in his *Arcadia* the emergent Italian PASTORAL and the no longer so popular CHIVALRIC ROMANCE in his pastoral romance, *Arcadia*. Intended originally for private reading and dedicated to Sidney's sister Mary Herbert, The countess of Pembroke, the *Arcadia* circulated quite widely in manuscript from before 1590 before being brought to the press in a partial revision in 1593. For at least a century *Arcadia* remained the most cherished work mostly written in prose in the English language. It also contains verse. SONNETS and ECLOGUES also appear sprinkled throughout the text, and until late in the 19th century, English readers preferred verse to prose.

From the perspective of style, the *ARCADIA* offered a clear (and for most a preferable) stylistic alternative to what Sidney called "Eloquence . . . disguised . . . in a courtesan-like painted affectation . . ."—a style he obviously associated with JOHN LYLY's *EUPHUES*. Sidney's literary purposes derived from the classical objectives of literature, which had always been to please and to instruct. The latter of these ends Sidney had elaborated in his *THE DEFENCE OF POESIE*. Specifically the *Arcadia* was directed toward educating in proper behavior the members of the class to which Sidney himself belonged, the aristocrat—the courtier.

In form, the work is divided into five books—a feature that some regard as linking the book to the five acts of a theatrical performance. The first book begins, as does an EPIC, in the midst of matters with two Greek shepherds, Strephon and Claius, seated at the seaside and tearfully discussing their feelings of love. They interrupt their conversation when they see a small chest floating in the water and a half-drowned young man clinging to it. This proves to be the prince Musidorus. He is grief-stricken over the death at sea of his friend and fellow prince, Pyrocles, and asks that the shepherds help him go back to sea to recover the body. The sympathetic shepherds engage a fisherman to take them out. In due course they discover Pyrocles alive and clinging to the mast of a wrecked ship. Before they can rescue him, however, a pirate ship bears down on them, and the fisherman is compelled to flee or risk having the entire party pressed into slavery. They reluctantly leave Pyrocles to be captured.

Once more ashore the shepherds escort Musidorus from the land of Laconia, where they rescued him, to the house of Kalander in the happy land of Arcadia. The shepherds ask Musidorus to tell them about himself and his friend, but Musidorus gives false names and nothing more. He calls himself Palladius and his friend Daiphantus. Once arrived at Kalander's place Musidorus attempts to reward the shepherds, but they refuse. Then Musidorus falls ill. Kalendar sees to all his guest's needs and sets out to find his friend and to rescue him if possible.

The third chapter describes Kalander's lovely home and its sensuous statuary. Musidorus also learns about Arcadia, which proves to be an Edenic place ruled by a kind ruler, Basileus, and his much younger wife, Gynecia. He also hears of their beautiful daughters Pamela and Philoclea, and he learns in the fourth chapter of the strange decision their father has made to turn all his affairs and the education of his daughters over to a shepherd, Dametas, his ill-favored wife, Miso, and their daughter, Mopsa.

In the fifth chapter of Book I, matters grow more complex. The central issue of the chapter, however, concerns the fact that Kalander's son, Clitophon, has been captured and carried off by a people called the Helots. In chapter 6, Kalander mounts a military expedition against the Helots to recover his son, and Musidorus/Palladius joins it. In the heat of battle, Musidorus/Palladius fights against the captain of the Helots. The captain knocks off his enemy's helmet and instantly drops to one knee to yield up his sword. The captain proves to be Pyrocles/Daiphantus. Nightfall ends the general fighting, and the reunited friends negotiate a peace between the warring parties that recognizes the victory of the Arcadians. Back in Arcadia, Pyrocles recounts his adventures from the time of his being captured until his reunion with Musidorus.

The richly varied plot continually introduces new characters and episodes with a kaleidoscopic complexity impossible to trace here in any detailed way. The second book flashes back in the seventh chapter to the beginning of Pyrocles' and Musidorus's friendship and details their educations. The situations always present readers with examples of behavior on which the text passes judgment while inviting the reader to do likewise.

The *Arcadia*'s five books weave a rich tapestry of pastoral gardens, seafaring and warfare, noblemen and noblewomen, heroes and villains, shepherds and Amazons, kindness and unkindness, marriage feasts and spectacles. Its deliberate pace appealed to a leisured class of reader whose challenge was to fill—in a creatively or morally or intellectually rewarding way—the time that their wealth and servants freed for literary pursuits.

At the center of the swirl of character and incident, the two young princes emerge as courtiers whose capacities for unflinching martial heroism and gallant and correct participation in courteous society are constantly being improved or challenged by the situations they encounter and the people they meet. The work is informed by the philosophy of Aristotle, HUMANIST Christian stoicism, and a belief in the rationality of nature. It incorporates material from Italian, French, ancient Greek, and Dutch sources. Literary historians generally credit *The Old Arcadia* with being the first English prose work to elevate female characters to the status of heroines and to make their love interests a central feature of the plot.

Sidney himself had partly revised his work, but his untimely death left his revisions unfinished. His sister added material. Some of his editors made decisions about what should go where. The incompletion of certain episodes together with Sidney's own invitation to other authors to supply more led later writers to sign on. Just as the chivalric romances of BOIARDO and of ARIOSTO had invited imitators and writers of sequels, so Sidney's pastoral romance drew successor authors into the fold with emendations and additions well into the following century. It also contributed material to the work of Sidney's successors. BEAUMONT and FLETCHER used a female character, Zelmane, as the model for their Bellaria in their drama *Philaster* (1620). SHAKESPEARE's *KING LEAR* draws the subplot of Gloucester, Edgar, and Edmund from the second book of the *Arcadia*, and the 18th-century novelist Samuel Richardson was inspired by one of Sidney's female characters and named his first novel, *Pamela* (1749), for her.

Bibliography

Duncan-Jones, Katherine. *Sir Philip Sidney, Courtier Poet.* New Haven, Conn.: Yale University Press, 1991.

Salzman, Paul. *English Prose Fiction, 1558–1700: A Critical History.* Oxford, U.K.: Clarendon Press, 1985.

Sidney, Sir Philip. *The Countess of Pembroke's Arcadia (The Old Arcadia).* Edited by Katherine Duncan-Jones. Oxford, U.K.: Oxford University Press, 1999.

court entertainment: masque and spectacle

Throughout the Renaissance, dramatic entertainments for royalty or for the courts of the nobility were to be found everywhere throughout Europe. LUDOVICO ARIOSTO had prepared entertainments for the court of the dukes of the Este family at Ferarra in Italy, and magnificent spectacles were staged for the court of Louis XIV of France. The form of the court masque, however, achieved perhaps its most complex expression at the court of James I of England in the hands of the master playwright, BEN JONSON and the landscape architect and designer of stage effects, scenery, and machinery, Inigo Jones.

In Ferrara and in Rome a tradition of reading Latin plays at the ducal and papal courts sprang up as early as the 1480s. Italian versions of these plays followed soon after, and when Lucrezia Borgia married Alfonso d' Este in 1502, his father, Duke Ercole d' Este of Ferarra, pulled out all the stops. He converted the building now called the Palazzo della Ragione into a makeshift theater and assembled from all over Italy 110 actors and actresses together with dancers, scene painters, instrumentalists, and singers. The spectacular entertainments on that occasion included country dancers and ballets and actors portraying allegorical figures, satyrs, gladiators, turbaned Saracens, and other exotic roles. Each of the five nights during which this entertainment continued also saw produced a different comedy of the Roman playwright PLAUTUS. This extravagant court entertainment set the fashion for subsequent

Italian comedy by establishing the expectation that a play would be modeled on the five acts of the Roman comedy and would include dancing, music, allegorical representations, and elaborate scenery.

Court masques in England were usually written for a one-time performance at a state occasion or to celebrate a holiday. They made use of masked aristocrats, members of the court, to speak the dialogue, and the masques incorporated music and dancing and elaborate visual effects. They had as their objective the praise or sometimes the carefully couched instruction of the monarch and were also designed to impress visitors with the grandeur of the state and its governors. The performance of a masque was usually preliminary to a ball to which the members of the court, acting as masqueraders, led the audience at the masque's end.

Widely remarked on is Jonson's *The Masque of Blackness* in which the playwright appeared as an African at the queen's request. Queen Anne and her female companions also sometimes participated as actors as they did in *The Masque of Queens* (1609). In that masque as well, the queen suggested the introduction of an antimasque against which she and her companions could be set off to advantage. In this case, the antimasque featured allegorical representations of bad reputations while the queen and her company represented the good. This moral opposition in which good always prevailed over evil proved popular with masqueraders and spectators alike and thereafter was incorporated in many royal entertainments. As aristocrats could hardly be expected to play the parts of evildoers, professional actors came to be employed as the antimasqueraders.

Sometimes the subjects of masques became less abstract and more topical. Thomas Campion's *Lord Hay's Masque* (1607) voiced careful reservations about the union of the kingdoms of England and Scotland that King James was urging. Similarly, George Chapman's *Memorable Masque* (1613) slipped an advisory comment on colonial policy into a paean of praise for other royal diplomacy.

Outside the venue of the court, masques also saw service as plays within plays. One thinks of the masque of Cupid, god of love, which ironically turns into a multiple act of vengeance at the end of Thomas Middleton's *Women Beware Women.* Then too one recalls the *Masque of Ceres* in Shakespeare's *The Tempest* with which Prospero entertains the newly betrothed Miranda and Ferdinand.

Similar entertainments occurred elsewhere in Europe. A notable one in France took place at Versailles in the reign of Louis XIV where the young king staged a nine-day-long production celebrating his liaison with his mistress Louise Françoise de Labaume Leblanc, the duchess of La Vallière. This splendid fête, Pleasures of the enchanted island (*Plaisirs de l'Ile enchantée*, 1661) featured the famous French playwright Molière as the principal actor. Riding in a chariot and costumed as the Greek satyr–god Pan, Molière celebrated the king's ardor for the duchess in high-flown verse.

In the case of Louis XIV at Versailles, almost every detail of the king's daily routine from his rising to his retiring was a carefully staged public event. Formal entertainments then, even though they were ephemeral and rarely recurred, needed to inspire even more awe than the normal routine at Versailles. As a result, the shows involved enormous expense in their production and were breathtakingly spectacular.

In Spain, the poet Juan de Encina became the master of the revels for the court of the duke of Alva in 1492, and the religious and secular dramatic, verse eclogues that he wrote and produced both for those aristocrats and for King Ferdinand and Queen Isabella also enjoyed public performance and became the first nonreligious plays enacted in Spain. As a result, Encina is credited with founding the Spanish secular theater. The great Spanish playwrights of the Renaissance such as Pedro Calderón de la Barca and Lope de Vega were among Encina's successors in providing spectacular entertainments for the royalty and nobility of Spain.

The literary and social value of court masque and spectacle was a matter of disagreement among authors and spectators alike. Some, including Ben Jonson, thought of the court entertainment as a way for intellectual commoners, like himself, to exert influence on public policy. Others thought them frivolous and a needless drain on the public purse.

Bibliography

Béhar, Pierre, and Helen Watanabe O'Kelly. *Spectaculum Europaeum: Theatre and Spectacle in Europe (1580–1750)*. Wiesbaden: Harrassowitz, 1999.

Ben Jonson. Edited by C. H. Herford Percy and Evelyn Simpson. Oxford: The Clarendon Press, reissued 1988.

Holme, Bryan. *Princely Feasts and Festivals: Five Centuries of Pagentry and Spectacle*. New York: Thames and Hudson, 1988.

Strong, Roy C. *Splendor at Court: Renaissance Spectacle and the Theater of Power*. Boston: Houghton Mifflin, 1973.

courtly makers

A phrase employed by Richard Tottel (d. 1594), *courtly makers* labels the members of the first generation of Renaissance English poets to write in imitation of the Italian poet PETRARCH and his followers. This group most famously included SIR THOMAS WYATT, HENRY HOWARD, EARL OF SURREY, and NICHOLAS GRIMALD. Tottle used the phrase in an anthology, *Song and Sonnets* (1557), which came to be known as *Tottle's Miscellany*. Wyatt contributed 91 poems to the collection, Surrey 36, and Grimald 40. Tottle also included poems by poets of whose names he was uncertain. Later scholarship has identified some of these including THOMAS LORD VAUX, Sir John Cheke, William Gray, JOHN HEYWOOD, and THOMAS NORTON. The broad selection of subjects like love, grief, moral instruction, compliments, and philosophy, and the wide variety of forms and meters make the *Miscellany* a virtual manifesto of and showcase for the new poetry of Elizabethan England. The work's popularity attests to the intense public interest in the poems of this premier group of poets. The *Miscellany* saw nine editions in the 30 years following its first appearance. It also spawned a rash of imitators that proved equally popular.

Crashaw, Richard   (ca. 1613–1649)

Son of the Puritan preacher and poet William Crashaw (1572–1626), Richard Crashaw attended Cambridge University and in 1634 published a collection of religious poems in Latin, his *Book of Sacred Epigrams*. Although he had become a fellow of Peterborough College at Cambridge in 1635, his Catholic convictions prevented his Anglican ordination, and the fellowship was terminated in 1643. His devotion to Roman Catholicism seems to have been reinforced by reading a biography of the Spanish mystic St. Teresa of Avila that was translated into English in 1642. Following the loss of his fellowship, he immigrated to Paris, formally converted to Catholicism, and published a book of religious verse, *Steps to the Temple* (1646).

Both in his religious conviction and his poetry, Crashaw was an enthusiast. His poetry bubbles with energy and devotional fervor. His imagination sometimes overwhelms a reader with the irrepressible richness of his METAPHOR. He occasionally pushes the METAPHYSICAL CONCEIT beyond its effective limits into the realm of the almost ludicrous as when, in "Saint Mary Magdalene, or the weeper," he characterizes the weeping eyes of Magdalene as "two walking baths, two weeping motions, / Portable and compendious oceans."

Yet despite such lapses, even the most secular of modern readers can hardly fail to be moved by the sincerity and conviction of Crashaw's devotional poetry.

Bibliography

Crashaw, Richard. *The Complete Works of Richard Crashaw*. New York: AMS Press, 1983.

Crenne, Hélisenne de   (Marguerite de Briet) (ca. 1515–after 1552)

A French prose writer and epistolary novelist who took *Hélisenne* as her pen name, Marguerite de Briet was a native of the village of Abbeville in the French district of Picardy. There she somehow acquired an enviable HUMANIST and religious education—perhaps by being privately tutored. In about 1530 she married a country gentleman, Philippe

Fournel de Crasne, whence Crenne. This marriage apparently did not turn out happily since local records demonstrate that by 1539 the couple was legally separated.

The year 1538 saw the beginning of a successful writing career that established de Crenne as one of the major feminist controversialists of her time. Her first work, *Les Angoysses douloureuses qui procedent d'amours* (*The torments of love*), which may well reflect elements of her own life, interweaves in its three parts aspects of the chivalric and psychological novels and De Crenne's own self-consciousness as a creator of fiction.

In the first part of the book, its heroine, a lovely young woman whose name is also Hélisenne, recounts her marriage at age 11 to an older husband. She goes on to report how she subsequently fell in love with a younger man. The second and third parts of the book explore the painful outcomes of this difficult but not unusual situation.

Stylistically, some critics maintain, the first part of the book is superior to the second two parts, which seem to those critics to rely too heavily on chivalric romance. Both Constance Jordan and Lisa Neal, however, convincingly argue that the complex, derivative nature of parts two and three parallels the usual practice of Renaissance authors. Their borrowings indicate their erudition and their capacity to adopt and rework the production of their literary predecessors. Instead of signaling a failure of the writer's powers of invention, de Crenne's borrowings assert her claim to a place in the creative company of her literary forebears.

Neal, moreover, calls attention to the way that de Crenne continually readjusts the narrative framework of the second two parts, forcing a reader to rethink earlier assumptions about the meaning and significance of facts and episodes. This readjustment of the narrator's viewpoint occurs in all de Crenne's work, marking her as an important innovator in the French letters of her day.

De Crenne's first foray into book publishing drew an appreciative audience. A pair of her modern translators, Marianna M. Mustacchi and Paul J. Archambault, report that by 1560 *The Torments of Love* had gone through eight editions.

Surely encouraged by the success of her first work and perhaps enticed by a commission from her publisher, De Crenne immediately tried her hand at an epistolary novel, THE FAMILIAR AND INVECTIVE LETTERS (*Les Epistres familières et invectives*, 1539). She was apparently the first author in the French language to attempt to tell a story through a series of letters ostensibly written by several people. This work, which also appeared in eight editions by 1560, is composed of 13 personal letters and five invective ones. All 13 of the personal letters ostensibly come from the pen of the fictive Hélisenne. So do four of the five invectives, but the second of the series is ostensibly written by her husband who accuses her of intolerable infidelities and many of the faults that men have alleged against women in person and in print from time immemorial.

The final works in de Crenne's brief but successful literary career included a work on the model of the medieval dream vision, *Le Songe de Madame Hélisenne . . .* (The dream of Madame Hélisenne, 1540), and the first known complete translation into French of the first four books of VIRGIL's *Aeneid* (1541). De Crenne proved to be both a good translator and a useful annotator. The dream vision is an ALLEGORY that pits the characters Reason, Charity, and Chastity, on the one hand, against Shame and Sensuality on the other. These figures debate the comparative moral constitutions of men and women, concluding that far from being man's downfall, woman is man's glory.

After almost 500 years of virtual obscurity, de Crenne's work has undergone a reassessment long overdue. She is at last taking her rightful place among French literary innovators and fiction writers.

Bibliography

Crenne, Hélisenne de. *A Renaissance Woman: Hélisenne's Personal and Invective Letters.* Translated and Edited by Marianna M. Mustacchi and Paul J. Archambault. Syracuse, N.Y.: Syracuse University Press, 1986.

———. *Oeuvres.* 1560. Geneva. Slatkine Reprints, 1977.

———. *The Torments of Love: Hélisenne de Crenne.* Translated by Lisa Neal and Steven Randall. Minneapolis: University of Minnesota Press, 1996.

Jordan, Constance. *Renaissance Feminism: Literary Texts and Political Models.* Ithaca, N.Y.: Cornell University Press, 1990.

Cromwell, Oliver (1599–1658)

A farmer, a seemingly invincible soldier, and a parliamentarian, Cromwell became Lord Protector of England in 1653. In that role, he ruled England largely by decree, repeatedly dissolving Parliament when it questioned his edicts. Enormously important in the annals of British history and the 17th century Civil War (1642–51) that effectively ended the Renaissance in England, Cromwell was among those who supported and was responsible for the execution of King Charles I and the exile of his family in 1642. Beyond this, Cromwell's impact on literature stemmed mainly from his unwavering support for the Puritan cause and point of view. In the judgment of English Puritans, the theater was the workshop of the devil, luring apprentices away from work and sewing the seeds of vice in the minds of the populace. Governing authority had likewise always suspected the theater as a hotbed of sedition. These convergent viewpoints together with the rowdy behavior of audiences led to the CLOSING OF THE ENGLISH THEATERS in 1642.

Although Cromwell refused Parliament's offer of the British crown (1657), he accepted the opportunity to name his own successor. He selected his own son, Richard Cromwell (1626–1712). Though the younger Cromwell did succeed his father in September 1658, he proved ineffectual as a ruler. Parliament forced his abdication the following May and, in 1660, recalled Prince Charles Stuart from his French exile to the throne as Charles II of England.

Oliver Cromwell was buried in Westminster Abbey's tomb of kings. After the restoration, however, Charles II's courts of law tried Cromwell posthumously, found him guilty of high treason, exhumed his corpse, hanged it at the Tower of London, and reburied it there.

Bibliography

Coward, Barry. *The Cromwellian Protectorate.* New York: Manchester University Press, 2002.

Smith, David L., ed. *Cromwell and the Interregnum: The Essential Readings.* Malden, Mass.: Blackwell Publishing Company, 2003.

Cruz, Sor Juana Inés de la (Juana Ramírez de Asbaje y Santillana) (1651–1695)

A largely self-taught child prodigy, Juana Ramírez de Asbaje was born in the Mexican village of San Miguel de Nepantla between the volcanoes Ixtacihuatl and Popocatépetl. Intensely interested in everything around her, particularly physical phenomena, she anticipated on the basis of her observations modern theories about energy and gravity and Sir Isaac Newton's laws of inertia as well.

She learned to read at three and read omnivorously from books borrowed from the fine library of a well-to-do uncle. She also contrived to study and master Latin, setting goals for herself and cutting off her prized hair a few inches if she failed to reach the goal by the time her hair had grown a certain length. When she was only 12 she came to the attention of the faculty of the University of Mexico City. They arranged to have 40 professors from a variety of disciplines examine her, and, as Diego Callejas—her biographer who was apparently present—reports, none of them proved a match for her erudition.

Her reputation for learning resulted in her being invited while in her teens to become a lady-in-waiting to the countess of Paredes, wife of the Spanish viceroy in Mexico City. Ramírez de Asbaje remained in the countess's service, cutting a brilliant figure in the society of the vice-regal court for some five years. Though there were suitors aplenty, and although her uncle had provided her with a dowry, despite her extraordinary accomplishments and her beauty she chose not to marry. She determined instead to enter the church, becoming in 1669 a nun in the order of St. Jerome in the Convent of Santa Paula. Taking the religious name of Sor (Sister) Juana Inés de la Cruz, she amassed perhaps the finest library in the Americas, equipped her study with the scientific apparatus of her day such as the recently invented telescope and an astrolabe, and pursued from within the cloister a career in study, philosophical speculation, and writing. Friends also arranged to have some of her works published.

As the scholar Emilie L. Bergman convincingly argues, the decisions to enter the convent and to study was fraught with peril for a mind as unfettered as Sor Juana's. Though the order she joined valued her extraordinary capacities and at first encouraged her literary activities, her interest in philosophy, religion, and natural science inevitably put her on a collision course with the CATHOLIC COUNTER-REFORMATION and church authorities.

Before that confrontation occurred, however, she produced a substantial body of work, much of it commissioned by noble patrons. She was unquestionably the finest Spanish colonial poet of either sex. Despite the complexity of her poetry's allusiveness, she surpassed in skill and clarity the occasionally obscure verse of another notable colonial poet, LUIS DE GÓNGORA (1561–1627), whose verse she sometimes emulated. Convincing grounds for that assessment appear, first, in her 975-verse poem *The First Dream*. This work, de la Cruz observed, was the only one she remembered writing for her own pleasure. Taking its starting point from the medieval genre of the dream vision, the work imagines that the poet falls asleep and that her disembodied soul rises to a mountaintop. From that lofty vantage point, though the soul can see and understand many things, it cannot fathom all existence nor match the knowledge of the angels. In an intellectual tour-de-force of allusiveness that reveals de la Cruz's familiarity with ancient, medieval, and recent scientific and literary work, the poem conducts in 11- and seventh-syllable lines a philosophical analysis of the nature and potentiality of human knowledge that combines the perspectives of St. Thomas Aquinas and ARISTOTLE.

Her other verse included poems commemorating special occasions and epistolary poems addressed to members of the vice-regal court, love poems, autobiographical poems that tried to explain her special circumstances and atypical viewpoints, and religious poems. Her peasant songs (*villancicos*), the Nobel laureate Octavio Paz suggests, were written for religious observances and are especially notable because they reflect the language of the common people including elements from the various cultures that made up the Mexican population of her day—Mexican Indians, Congolese laborers, Spaniards, and Basques.

At the request of her patrons, Sor Juana also penned both secular and religious drama. If along with her plays one counts all the works, long and short, that she intended for performance, and if one considers those she collaborated in writing as well as those she penned alone, some 52 dramatic pieces survive. In the secular category we find two verse comedies whose form was partly inspired by the theater of LOPE DE VEGA: *The Trials of a Noble House* (*Los empeños de una casa*) and *Love is the Greater Labyrinth* (*Amor es más laberinto*). The second resulted from a collaboration between Sor Juana and Juan de Guevara.

A play in three acts, *The Trials of a Noble House* focuses on a love entanglement. A brother and sister, Don Pedro and Doña Anna, are in love with Doña Leonor and Don Carlos, respectively. But Leonor and Carlos are in love with each other. *Love Is the Greater Labyrinth* contains similar elements of plot joined with the story of Theseus and the Minotaur. Set in Minoan times on the Island of Crete the play makes erudite use of classical allusion.

Among Sor Juana's religious dramas, her allegorical sacramental drama EL DIVINO NARCISO (*THE DIVINE NARCISSUS*) combines the classical story of Echo and Narcissus with biblical elements and with the benefits God's grace confers on human nature. This work is generally considered her masterpiece.

Altogether, Sor Juana penned more than 50,000 lines of verse—about half of it designed for public performance and the other half for private reading. A considerable portion of this work appeared in print during her lifetime. In the 20th and 21st centuries, however, critical interest has focused principally on a prose work that Sor Juana wrote that defended her right as a woman to pursue a literary career and to engage in philosophical and religious debate. The confrontation between church authority and a too-thoughtful nun finally resulted from the unauthorized publication of Sor Juana's critique of a Portuguese theologian's work.

Apparently making Sor Juana a puppet in pursuing a complicated vendetta, her friend the bishop of Puebla, who had encouraged her to pen the work, first published it against her will and then wrote a fork-tongued condemnation of her pursuits and her opinions. Pretending to be a nun named Sor Philotea (Sister Love–God), the bishop sent his criticisms to Juana in a letter. In response, Sor Juana wrote a brilliant, courteous, tactful, and impassioned defense of her activities and intellectual pursuits. Her REPLY TO SOR PHILOTEA (1691) has become a fundamental document of modern feminism.

Notwithstanding her convictions about her rights as a woman and a nun to learn, to think, to write, to publish, and even to disagree with the positions of the masculine church hierarchy, Sor Juana had taken vows of poverty, chastity, and especially obedience. Powerless to resist her superiors' pressure, but also sincerely devoted to her religious calling, Sor Juana at last fell silent. She sold her library and scientific apparatus for the benefit of the poor and ceased her studies and her writing.

She died of pestilence contracted while caring for infected sisters of her convent.

Bibliography

Bergmann, Emilie L. "Sor Juana Inés de la Cruz: Dreaming in a Double Voice." *Women, Culture and Politics in Latin America.* Berkeley, Calif.: University of California Press, 1990.

Cruz, Sor Juana Inés de la. *The Divine Narcissus: El Divino Narciso.* Translated by Patricia A. Peters and Renée Domeier. Albuquerque: University of New Mexico Press, 1998.

Flynn, Gerard. *Sor Juana Inés de la Cruz.* New York: Twayne Publishers, Inc., 1971.

Mirrim, Stephanie. *Early Modern Women's Writing and Sor Juana Inés de la Cruz.* Nashville: Vanderbilt University Press, 1999.

Paz, Octavio. *Sor Juana or, The Traps of the Faith.* Translated by Margaret Sayers Peden. Cambridge, Mass.: The Belknap Press of Harvard University Press, 1988.

Schmidhuber, Guillermo, and Olga Martha Peña Doria. *The Three Secular Plays of Sor Juana Inés de la Cruz: A Critical Study.* Translated by Shelby Thacker. Lexington: The University Press of Kentucky, 2000.

Trueblood, Alan S., editor and translator. *A Sor Juana Anthology.* Cambridge, Mass.: Harvard University Press, 1988.

cupbearer poems   (*Sáqí Namá*)

A species of poem widespread throughout the Islamic world, cupbearer poems celebrated drinking wine and revelry. The activities described in the poem, however, were supposed to be understood as ALLEGORY. The drinking of wine represented the joys of life—often of the religious or spiritual life. Almost every significant poet in the Islamic world in the 16th and 17th centuries felt obliged to try to compose one.

Subject, not form, defines a cupbearer poem. Nonetheless, the poems generally appeared as a relatively lengthy composition in the MESNEVÍ form—a narrative constructed of a series of rhyming couplets. Poets might describe the cup; praise the person who carried it; describe the quality, taste, and color of the wine, the tavern where it was served, the entertainers in the tavern, the beauties of the women present, and so forth. Almost every cupbearer poem also contained a section instructing the reader on the correct interpretation of its allegory lest the poet be misunderstood to be praising the consumption of prohibited alcohol.

Among Turkish poets, OMER (NEF'I OF ERZURUM, 1572–ca. 1635) wrote a cupbearer poem that differed from most. It is celebrated for the jewellike quality of its five stanzas in praise of the crystal cup bearing the wine. More typical and among the longer representatives of the class is an example by the Turkish poet HÁLETÍ (1570–1631).

The opening and closing sections of his 15-section *Cupbearer Book* address the poet's praises to God. Some of the other 13 sections of the work's 515 narrative couplets contain the author's complaints about the sad conditions of his life. In addition to all the details characteristic of the cupbearer genre, Háletí's verses also contain descriptions of the seasons of the year and instructions for enjoying each season to the fullest. To this he adds criticism of conventional persons who do not make the most of life's party, and he invites them to join the revelry. FORTUNE is fickle; life is short; situations change by the minute. Take advantage of life's pleasures, the poet advises, when they present themselves. In Háletí's case as in others, a reader sometimes wonders about the exclusively allegorical intentions of the work.

The message of cupbearer books had much in common with Renaissance Europe's mistaken notions about the practices of the Greek philosopher EPICURUS, who, though in reality he preached moderation in all things, was popularly thought to have advised that we ought to "eat, drink, and be merry, for tomorrow we die."

Bibliography

Gibb, E. J. W. *A History of Ottoman Poetry.* Edited by Edward G. Browne. London: Luzac, 1965.

Cyrano de Bergerac, Savinien de
(1619–1655)

Remembered best for his enormous nose, Cyrano was a French soldier who reputedly fought more than a thousand duels to redress insults directed at his unusual appearance. He was also a poet and became a playwright when disabilities resulting from his wounds terminated his military career. Though his theatrical works sometimes lack polish and professionalism, they are nonetheless amusing and often highly original.

His first comedy, *Le Pedant Joué* (The amused pedant), appeared in 1654. This was followed by a tragedy, *La Mort d'Agrippina* (The death of Agrippina). It tells the story of the Roman Emperor Nero's mother Agrippina, who was murdered and butchered by her insane son.

Also an early writer of scientific fantasy fiction, Cyrano wittily imagines the political and social states of affairs on the surface of the Moon and of the Sun in his two compositions, *Histoire comique des éstats et Empires de la Lune* (The comical tale of the states and empires of the Moon, 1656) and *Histoire comique des éstats et Empires du Soleil* (The comical tale of the states and empires of the Sun, 1662).

Not among the brighter lights of Renaissance French theater, Cyrano has nevertheless remained in the public's memory owing to a 19th-century play by Edmond Rostand. This romantic comedy, entitled *Cyrano de Bergerac*, bears a very distant relationship to Cyrano's actual life. Rostand's play became the basis for a Hollywood film produced by RKO studios in 1950.

Bibliography

Rostand, Edmond. *Cyrano de Bergerac: A Heroic Comedy in Five Acts.* Translated by Christopher Fry. London and New York: Oxford University Press, 1975.

Dach, Simon (1605–1659)

As a professor of poetry at the University of Königsberg and musically gifted as well, Dach principally wrote poems commissioned for performance, sometimes to his own tunes, at weddings, christenings, funerals and other important occasions. He was a member of the Königsberg circle of poets and literary figures. With the exception of the poems included in a German and English score of a funeral cantata whose music was written by the composer Max Reger (1873–1916), none of Dach's verse has been translated into English. A modern German reprint of a 17th-century edition of his poetic works is available as is a German biography describing his position in the Königsberg literary group.

Bibliography

Reger, Max, et al. *Choralkantaten zu den Hauptfesten des evangelischen Kirchenjahres . . .* [Choral cantatas for the chief festivals of the evangelical liturgical year]. Stuttgart: Carus-Verlag, ca. 1990.

Daniel, Samuel (ca. 1562–1619)

A skillful English poet; a writer of court masques, (see COURT ENTERTAINMENT) plays, and prose criticism, and a translator, Daniel studied for three years at Magdalen Hall in Oxford but did not finish a degree. In 1585 he published a translation from the Italian, *The Worthy Tract of Paulus Jovius,* which was admired for the clarity of its English prose style. After traveling for a time on the Continent and making friends with literary figures in Italy, Daniel returned to England and became tutor to William Herbert (1580–1630), who would become the third earl of Pembroke. This position brought Daniel into contact with the literary circle of Mary Sidney Herbert, the countess of PEMBROKE. That association Daniel considered to be the best literary schooling he ever received. Under the influence of the members of that group, he began to write SONNETS. Twenty-eight of these appeared in an unauthorized edition of SIR PHILIP SIDNEY's *Astrophel and Stella* (1591). The following year, Daniel first published an authorized version of his own sonnet cycle *Delia,* and also his verse *Complaint of Rosamond.*

In 1595 the work appeared for which he is best remembered, his verse history of the Wars of the Roses: *A History of the Civil Wars between York and Lancaster.* In his opinion, history rather than fiction provided the proper subject matter of verse. He shifted to prose, however, for his last historical work, his *History of England* (1612). Another prose work important in the history of English literary criticism was his *Defense of Rhyme* (1602). Daniel wrote that work in response to THOMAS CAMPION's

Observations in the art of English Poesy (1602), in which Campion had mounted an attack on rhyme and on accentual verse.

Until JAMES I succeeded ELIZABETH I in 1603, Daniel's circumstances required him to continue as tutor to a succession of noble families—a vocation he found not altogether congenial. With the new court in power, however, the countess of Bedford recommended Daniel to Queen Anne, and Daniel received a royal commission to write the very first COURT ENTERTAINMENT of the reign, a masque called *The Vision of the Twelve Goddesses* (1604). Although BEN JONSON, who had a low opinion of Daniel's verse, soon took over writing masques, Queen Anne nevertheless conferred on Daniel a series of appointments in the royal household, and he directed a company of child actors at Bristol. One of Daniel's plays for this company, *Pilotas,* caused him some trouble as the censors thought it commented too directly on the earl of Essex's uprising against Queen Elizabeth.

In the 19th century, British poets Wordsworth and Coleridge both admired Daniel's work, particularly his verse history. Both his contemporaries and posterity have given Daniel's verse mixed reviews. Although his diction is universally admired, some of his work, especially his Lover of the muse (*Musophilus*, subtitled: *Containing a general defence of all learning*) and his verse letters offering unsolicited advice to members of the aristocracy, seem too schoolmasterly to please many tastes. Nonetheless, SHAKESPEARE seems to have been influenced by Daniel's choice of three quatrains and a couplet for the form of the ENGLISH SONNET and perhaps also by his verse rhetoric and diction.

Bibliography

Daniel, Samuel. *The Complete Works.* Edited by A. B. Grosart. Five volumes. London: 1899. Reissued, New York: Russell & Russell, 1963.

Danish drama

Discussions of Danish drama during the Renaissance mention the names of three playwrights worthy of note. Two of these wrote religious drama. Peder Jensen Hegelund (1542–1614), who was the bishop of Ripon, wrote a play based on the biblical story of Susanna and the elders and an allegorical drama entitled *Calunia* (Calumny). He also penned an almanac in both Danish and Latin, and he excerpted and synopsized the writings of the Protestant cleric Philip Melancthon.

The second writer of Danish religious plays, Hieronymus Justesen Ranch (1539–1607) staged: *King Solomon's Acclaim, Samson's Songs in Prison,* and *The Miserly Knave.*

A third playwright whose more secular work continues to attract the attention of historians of drama was Mogens Skeel (1650–94). Skeel authored popular comedy and dramatic SATIRE addressed to aristocratic and middle class audiences. Although modern Danish editions of the works of all three authors are available, no English translations exist.

Dante Alighieri (1265–1321)

One of the so-called three crowns (Tre corone) of Italian literature, Dante was the major Italian poet of the Middle Ages. His influence on subsequent literary history can hardly be exaggerated. One of his important contributions to a literary discussion that continued through and beyond the Renaissance resulted from his Latin treatise, On the eloquence of the vernacular tongue (*De vulgare eloquentia*). In it, Dante asserts the capacity of the Italian language of his day to handle lofty themes and subjects with grace and to express complex thoughts and distinctions both accurately and beautifully.

Among the later contributors to that discussion, LORENZO DE MEDICI wrote a defense of the vernacular tongue in which he repeats many of Dante's arguments and adds others of his own. Cardinal PIETRO BEMBO contributed to the debate, as did the ACADEMY OF THE CROSS (Accademia Della Crusca). This academy had as its objective the establishment of a norm for cultured spoken and for literary Italian. (See ITALIAN LANGUAGE.)

Bembo was almost singlehandedly responsible for a temporary decline in Dante's standing among Renaissance Italian readers. The cardinal thought Dante's language rough and "shaggy" and preferred the more lyrical smoothness of PETRARCH as the model for Italian letters.

Dante's major work, his COMMEDIA, now translated into English more than 60 times, provided a late medieval example of a long ALLEGORY. Renaissance poets who succeeded him and who, in part based on his example, used allegory in their EPIC work include TASSO, BOIARDO, and ARIOSTO in Italy, and EDMUND SPENSER and JOHN MILTON in England.

A member of the school of Medieval Italian poets who wrote in the "sweet new style," (*dolce stil novo*), Dante also provided the poets of the Renaissance with examples of an ITALIAN SONNET sequence, *La Vita Nuova* (The new life). That work became a model for commenting in prose on one's own sonnets—a practice followed by Lorenzo de' Medici and others. This practice helped point the way for Renaissance literary criticism.

Bibliography

Bloom, Harold, ed. *Dante Alighieri, 1265–1321.* Philadelphia, Pa.: Chelsea House Publishers, ca. 2003.

Dās, Vrindavān (16th century)

A verse biographer in the Bengali language of northern India, Dās wrote the first life of the Hindu saint Chaitanya Dev (1486–1533). Composed around 1650, it is Dās's only surviving work and perhaps his only one. Based both on the oral testimony of persons who had known the saint personally and on written sources, The songbook about Chaitanya (*Chaitanya Bhagāvata*) recounts the saint's life in three sections. The first one, composed of 12 chapters, details his life from birth to a visit he made to Gaya. The second section, 26 chapters long, depicts Chaitanya's preparations to undertake a religious revival of the worship of the Hindu deity Vishnu. It begins with his return from Gaya to Navadvipa—a famed center of Sanskritic learning—and it concludes with Chaitanya's renunciation of the world for the life of an ascetic. The final section of the book is 11 chapters long and follows the saint's career as a preacher, teacher, and religious mendicant from his departure from Navadvipa to the end of his life in Puri.

According to the beliefs of his contemporary and present followers, Chaitanya was the Hindu deity Lord Krishna incarnate, who assumed flesh in the person of the saint so that he could personally preach the religion of devotion (the *Bhakti Dharma*) and could ease the sufferings of people by leading them to the Lord. Chaitanya's central contribution to Indian religious thinking held that, after many rebirths, a faithful soul will at last be released from the cycle of being (*Sansara*) but neither into a void nor as a anonymous droplet in the ocean of ultimate being. Rather, Chaitanya held, individuals will retain their identities and enjoy their blissful participation in godhead.

Aside from the view it offers of the life of its primary subject, Dās's biography is also notable on other grounds. It pictures the economic, social, and political life of an important center of learning and Sanskritic culture during the reign of Hussein Shah (late 15th—early 16th century). It is also an original of its kind, for Dās had no models of previous biographical writing. He had to invent his genre. His book provided a model for subsequent biographers of the saint, most notably, perhaps, that of the Bengali EPIC poet, KRISHNADĀSA KAVIRĀJA GOSVĀMI (1527–1607). Dās's book remains in print in the Bengali tongue.

Bibliography

Majumdar, A. K. *Chaitanya, His Life and Doctrine: A Study in Vaisnavism.* Bombay: Bharatiya Vidya Bhavan, 1969.

Mukherjee, Prabhat. *History of the Chaitanya Faith in Orissa.* New Delhi: R. Chaterjee, 1940; Reprinted, Calcutta: R Chatterjee, 1979.

Dāsa, Atibadi Jagannātha (1490–1547)

A devotional poet in the Oriya language of INDIA, Dāsa not only penned numerous books on religious subjects associated with the veneration of the Hindu deity Vishnu but also first translated the ancient Sanskrit religious work, the *Bhagāvata*, into Oriya. This had the effect of making that fundamental document of the Hindu religion accessible to the common people in Orissa. Influenced by the Brahmins, the rulers of Orissa historically had mainly patronized writers in the Sanskrit tongue to the neglect of Oriya.

Encouraged by his mother, however, Dāsa began his translation of the *Bhagavata* in his 18th year. As it happened, sometime during 1509–10 the Hindu saint CHAITANYA DEVA KRISHNA, who was thought to be a living incarnation of the deity Krishna, visited Puri where Dāsa was working. Dāsa read a portion of his translation to the saint, who wholeheartedly approved the work. Then Dāsa requested that Chaitanya himself initiate him as a devotee of Vishnu. Perhaps sensitive to the political implications of doing so, Chaitanya suggested that the most notable devotional poet then composing in Oriya, Balarama Dasa, perform that task. Rather than disappoint the young translator altogether, however, Chaitanya rewarded him with the title *Atibadi* (greatly great). By that designation Dāsa was thereafter addressed—just as the 20th-century Indian leader, Mohandas K. Gandhi was often addressed by his honorific title *mahatma* (great soul).

Dāsa's finished translation of the *Bhāgavata* enjoyed instant and enormous popularity in Orissa. That renown, in turn, provoked the jealousy of the Sanskritic scholars who unsuccessfully attempted to discredit him.

His verse remains popular in India. More than a dozen modern editions of several of his works have appeared in Oriya since 1950. In his own lifetime, his work was written in manuscript on palm leaves, and a modern facsimile with English explanatory text exists. So does a short collection of bilingual selections from his works edited by Sitakant Mahapatra.

Bibliography

Dāsa, Jagannātha. *The Bhāghavata Purāna, An Illustrated Oriya Palmleaf Manuscript.* Edited by P. K. Mishra. New Delhi: Abhinav Publications, 1987.

Mahapatra, Sitakant, ed. *Jagannātha Dāsa: Bhāgavata.* New Delhi: Sahitya Akademi, 1989.

Dāsa, Dānakrishna (1650–1710)

Recognized as one of the great devotional poets in the Oriya language, Dāsa like most of his contemporaries wrote in the poetic tradition devoted to the celebration of the Hindu deity Vishnu—the Vaishnavite movement. Hindu deities often manifested themselves, or aspects of themselves, in more than one form. Aspects of Vishnu appeared in the deity Krishna and his lover Radha. Krishna, in turn, manifested himself sometimes as the deity Jagannath, also called Purushottam (the best of men). It was this manifestation to which Dāsa felt particularly devoted.

Dāsa's most celebrated work is the *RASAKALLOLA* (Waves of delight). After describing in the first of its 34 cantos the significance of Jagannath, it goes on to trace the birth of Lord Krishna and to recount that deity's traditional adventures including his childhood, his liking for butter, an attempt to assassinate him, and his amorous adventures among love-smitten milkmaids called *gopis*. Dāsa displayed his technical mastery of his language's verse forms by composing each of the 34 cantos of the poem in a different meter. The poem mainly focuses on the love of Krishna and Radha and on the intimate details of their erotic encounters, often so graphic that some critics find them offensive. It treats the same sort of material in detailing Krishna's adventures among the *gopis*.

The scholar Gopalchandra Mishra suggests that controversy surrounds the exact list of Dānakrishna Dāsa's writings. The problem stems from the fact that Dās or Dāsa is a very common surname and can also be traced to the existence of more than one Dānakrishna Dāsa who wrote devotional verse in Oriya at about the same time. Another work, however, that Mishra comfortably attributes to the author of *Rasakallola* is *Artatran Chautisa* (Ode of an afflicted soul). The title accurately represents the sorrow of the content.

Later poets imitated Dāsa's technical mastery with the result that history regards him as the founder of a school of poetry in the Oriya language. At this writing his work does not seem to have appeared in English translation.

Bibliography

Datta, Amaresh, ed. *Encyclopedia of Indian Literature.* New Delhi: Sakitya Akademi, 1987.

Dass, Petter (1647–1707)

A Norwegian preacher and poet whose reputation and influence stretched beyond his northern parish in Helgeland to the furthest reaches of his country, Dass is best remembered for his long topographical poem, The trumpet of the north country (*Norlands trompet,* 1678–92). In it he represents the manners and way of life of the Norwegian people and the rugged beauty of the Norwegian landscape with its forests, mountains, fiords, and coastline.

In addition to this longer work, Dass penned numerous shorter poems that circulated in manuscript and, among the illiterate, by word of mouth long before they were collected in a single printed volume. Prominent among Dass's shorter work is a poem, *The Song of the Dalesman* (1683), which enjoys continuing popularity.

Among the Norwegian people Dass's reputation as a minister passed into folklore. There he is represented as having such recourse to the forces of good that he could command the obedience of the devil himself.

Bibliography

Johnston, Andrew, trans. "Three poems by Petter Dass" in *Translations from the Norse.* Gloucester, U.K.: J. Bellows, Steam Press, ca. 1879.

Davies, Sir John (1569–1626)

An English jurist, parliamentarian, and public servant, Davies was also a poet of great wit and originality. Educated at Queen's College, Oxford, he joined the Middle Temple to practice law in London in 1588 and became acquainted with a number of London authors. His first work, *Orchestra,* was licensed for publication in 1594 and appeared partly finished two years later. A poem without parallel in English, *Orchestra* takes the art of dancing as its subject. Davies imagines that while the Greek poet Homer's hero Ulysses was off wandering, his chaste wife Penelope's suitor, Antinous, woos her with praise of dancing. The suitor catches her interest, and Penelope asks him to continue his discourse about the origins and universality of dancing. Antinous, in a long series of rhyme royal stanzas (seven-line, iambic pentameter stanzas, rhyming ababbcc), charmingly explains how everything in nature dances (the Earth excepted since *Orchestra*'s COSMOLOGY puts an immobile

Earth at the solar system's center) and how dancing characterizes both the gods and civilized persons. Though Antinous does not win Penelope's love, he does captivate her imagination. After that, Davies dismisses Terpsichore, the MUSE of the dance, and calls on the heavenly muse, Urania, to inspire a series of compliments for the work of great poets past and present.

The year 1599 saw the publication of *Hymns of Astræa,* a series of acrostic poems addressed to ELIZABETH I. In an acrostic, the first letters of each line, when read down the page, spell something. In this case, they spell ELISA BETHA REGINA— "Queen Elizabeth" in Latin. These were written during a period when Davies had been disbarred from the practice of law as a result of an assault he committed on a former friend, Richard Martin. This interval in Davies's legal career lasted until 1601, and he occupied the time in writing. In the same year as the *Hymns,* a long poem, *Nosce te ipsum* (Know thyself) appeared. This work proposed a series of philosophical arguments for the immortality of the human soul.

Davies also authored a number of witty epigrams and sonnets. He was not fond of the sugared, PETRARCHIST sonnets of the English poets of the 1590s. He therefore parodied them in a short (nine-poem) sonnet cycle called *Gulling Sonnets. Gull,* as Davies uses the term, alludes to simpletons who follow the latest fashion in dress and behavior but who are otherwise without admirable qualities. These sonnets reveal Davies's satirical wit and intellectuality—qualities that he shares with such contemporaries as GEORGE CHAPMAN and Sir WALTER RALEIGH and that anticipate similar ones in the poems of JOHN DONNE.

Davies's legal and political career followed a distinguished and sometimes colorful course. King James appointed him solicitor general of Ireland, and in 1613 he, as a Protestant, was elected speaker of the Irish Parliament. The Catholic members rioted, and Davies had to be lifted into the lap of his Catholic predecessor to assume his office. In the last year of Davies's life King James I appointed him lord chief justice of England, but Davies died of a stroke at a dinner party before he could assume that office.

Bibliography

Davies, John. *The Complete Works.* Edited by Alexander B. Grosart, 1878. Hildesheim: Olms, 1968.

Defence of Poesie, The *(An Apologie for Poetrie)* Sir Philip Sidney (1595)

In 1579 a failed playwright, Stephen Gosson (1554–1624) suddenly changed sides in the ongoing controversy about the theater and its effect on public morals. Perhaps Gosson, as he claimed, experienced a sudden moral conversion, or perhaps, as seems more likely, the faction of London puritans and preachers who considered the theater the devil's workshop hired him to pen an attack. In either case, Gosson published a tract, *The School of Abuse, Containing a Pleasant Invective against Poets, Pipers, Players, Jesters, and Such Like Caterpillers of a Commonwealth.* He dedicated the work to one of the most renowned noblemen and literary figures of the era, Sir PHILIP SIDNEY.

Several authors answered the attack, including THOMAS LODGE, whose *Reply to Gosson* also appeared in 1579. The best remembered among the several responses to Gosson, however, was that of the person to whom *The School of Abuse* was dedicated—the same Sir Philip Sidney. Sidney composed his answer in about 1580–82. It did not, however, appear in print until 1595 when two editions bearing the titles in this entry's headline appeared. Though Sidney never names Gosson, his response treats many of the same issues, and it has become a foundation stone of English literary criticism and theory.

In an easy, kindly, and witty discussion, Sidney sets straight those who undervalue poets and poetry. Poets, Sidney argues, are the first who illuminate the ignorant. They prepare the way for the acquisition of more difficult knowledge by making the exercise of the mind delightful to the mind. He observes further that the ancient historiographers and philosophers often wrote their works in verse.

Sidney goes on to underscore the role of the poet as priest, as (see *VATES*). Poets emulate creation by showing fallen humanity the perfection toward which imperfect human nature can strive.

By a *poet*, Sidney does not mean exclusively persons who write in verse. He uses the term, rather, to mean people who write imaginative literature of all sorts. He credits these creative writers with producing numerous benefits for their readers. Reading their works purify one's wit, enriches one's memory, hones one's judgment, and adds to one's store of knowledge—including self-knowledge and virtuous action, which are the highest of all accomplishments.

He defends the poet as producing greater benefit than philosophers and historians. Philosophers work by precept, says Sidney, and historians by example. The poet, however, combines their functions, instructing in both ways, making people enamored of virtue, and pleasing readers and listeners at the same time by appealing to their emotions as well as to their intellects. Virtue, Sidney concludes in his general discussion, is the object of all worldly learning, and poetry—which by Sidney's definition would include Scripture—is virtue's best teacher.

Sidney then turns his attention to the various subcategories of poems—comic, lyric, tragic, tragicomic, EPIC, and so forth, defending each subcategory by illustrating the manner in which it promotes virtue.

He then focuses specifically on verse, pointing out its affinity with music and its ease of memorization. As for poets themselves, Sidney addresses the age-old canard that, because poets speak of matters in the realm of the imagination they must necessarily be liars. Not so, Sidney insists. Because poets affirm nothing, they tell no lies. Instead they provide ALLEGORY and figurative language that assert within their metaphors complex truths that are difficult to state directly.

Having answered the objections of naive critics, Sidney acknowledges that it is possible to abuse poetry and use it to serve ends, like the promotion of vice, not natural to it. But, he asks, "shall the abuse of a thing make its right use odious?" He admits that there are "poetasters"—those who pretend to the reputation of poet when they are really no-talent frauds—like certain of our contemporary singers and musicians who are commercially packaged to appeal to or to create specific market tastes. Discerning readers and listeners, however, will soon find them out.

With a taste formed by classical and humanist learning and by a breadth of reading and a discerning intellect, Sidney praises the poetry of Chaucer, Spenser, and the EARL OF SURREY, while he condemns the widespread practice among his contemporary playwrights of mixing together comedy and tragedy. His objection to this practice stems from the psychology of laughter, which he thinks ought not to arise from wickedness but from a sense of disproportion or from delight. He also states a preference for the Aristotelian unities of time, place, and action, as these had been interpreted and popularized by the Italian LUDOVICO CASTELVETRO.

After further discussion of specific aspects of writing verse, Sidney concludes that the proper practice of poetry, far from being damnable or irrelevant, is one of the great glories of the human enterprise.

Bibliography

Sidney, Sir Philip. *Sir Philip Sidney's An Apology for Poetry, and Astrophil and Stella: Texts and Contexts.* Edited by Peter C. Herman. Glen Allen, Va.: College Publications, 2001.

Dekker, Thomas (ca. 1572–1632)

One of the breed of Renaissance London writers who managed to eke out a living by penning plays and pamphlets, Dekker seems to have been self-educated. Like other London playwrights whose livelihoods depended on rapidly serving the appetites of an audience demanding variety and a rapid turnover of stage productions, Dekker collaborated extensively. Though many of his plays have been lost, enough survive to permit a sound evaluation of his talent.

He had a special knack for portraying London life. An early play that he wrote alone, *The Shoemaker's Holiday* (1599), borrows the plot of a novel, *The Gentle Craft,* by THOMAS DELONEY. Portraying the life of Simon Eyre, a shoemaker in London who rose to become lord mayor, the play combines a detailed knowledge of life in the city with a gift for writing verse and a benign view of human nature. In the same year Dekker wrote *Old Fortunatus.* This play, taken from German folklore, tells the tale of the title character, Fortunatus, who is offered a choice among gifts by the goddess FORTUNE. He

foolishly picks great wealth and in doing so also unknowingly elects a sequence of events that leads to his own death and those of his two sons.

The HONEST WHORE, Dekker's most celebrated achievement, is a play in two parts. Part I (1604) resulted from Dekker's collaboration with Thomas Middleton, but part II (c. 1605) is considered the better play, and Dekker wrote it alone. While the setting of *The Honest Whore* is Italian, the language of the common characters is strictly lower-class London—a dialect of which Dekker was a master.

As a poet, Dekker ranks with the best of the English Renaissance stage. Exercising his remarkable gifts, however, did not bring him riches or even a comfortable living. To keep body and soul together, he was constrained to accept whatever literary hackwork came his way, and he spent almost three years of his life in debtors' prison (1613–16). And yet, he generally turned such hackwork into something worthy and notable as he does in his 1603 pamphlet *The Wonderful Year.* In it he gives one of his several descriptions of the horrors of the bubonic plague in London. Dekker achieves an effect comparable to BOCCACCIO's similar, though less emotional, account of the Florentine plague in the introduction to his *Decameron.* The same year, 1603, also saw the publication of another pamphlet, *The Bachelor's Banquet,* which spiritedly discusses the sufferings of wife-dominated husbands. Two other pamphlets of 1608, *Bellman of London* and *Lanthorn and Candlelight,* graphically depict the lives of vagabonds in London. His 1609 work, *The Gull's Hornbook* turns Renaissance books on etiquette and appropriate social behavior, like GIOVANNI DELLA CASA's *Galateo,* upside down. In this ironic elementary text for young men aspiring to be fashionable, Dekker satirically gives the rules by which a mindless fop in London should behave himself. His *Seven Deadly Sins of London* explores the city's seamier side. Indicative of his range, however, his 1609 pamphlet, *Fowre Birds of Noahs Ark,* is in its essence a work of religious devotion. It contains a series of heartfelt, moving prayers including one for a child, another for an apprentice, and others for prisoners, for men who work at dangerous jobs, "A Prayer to Stay the Pestilence," and another for the two universities. Dekker was also a master of CHARACTER WRITING and had a hand in creating masques and COURT ENTERTAINMENTS.

His collaborations with other playwrights produced numerous works for the stage. Particularly notable among these we find *Satiromastix* (1602). This collaboration with JOHN MARSTON poked not-very-good-natured fun at BEN JONSON, with whom Dekker had an ongoing feud. Dekker collaborated with JOHN WEBSTER on three plays published in 1608: *Westward Ho!* and *Northward Ho!* (two plays whose titles Ben Jonson parodied in *Eastward Ho!*). The other fruit of that year's collaboration was *The Famous History of Sir Thomas Wyat*. With PHILIP MASSINGER Dekker wrote another devotional work, *The Virgin Martyr* (1622). He also collaborated with JOHN FORD on *The Sun's Darling* (1624).

Plays about witches proved to be a popular subgenre on the Renaissance London stage. Some of these had their origin in actual witch trials and others were simply responses to audience fascination with the subject. Dekker, in collaboration with John Ford and WILLIAM ROWLEY, also made a powerful contribution to that literary type with the tragedy, *The Witch of Edmonton* (1623).

Bibliography

Dekker, Thomas. *The Honest Whore.* London: Globe Education: New York: Theatre Arts Books and Routledge, 1999.

———. *The Plague Pamphlets of Thomas Dekker.* Edited by F. P. Wilson. Norwood, Pa.: Norwood Editions, 1977.

———. *The Shoemaker's Holiday.* Adapted by Bernard Sahlins. Chicago: Ivan R. Dee, 2003.

———. *The Witch of Edmonton: a Critical Edition.* Edited by Etta Soiref Onat. New York: Garland Publishers, 1980.

———. *Thomas Dekker's The Pleasant Comedy of Old Fortunatus.* Edited by Suzanne Blow. Music composed by Riva Kuhl. Bessemer, Ala.: Colonial Press, ca. 1988.

Delmedigo, Elijah (ca. 1460–1497)

A Jewish rabbinical scholar, physician, and student of classical philosophy, Delmedigo had mastered the philosophical lore of the ancient Greeks as it was preserved in the Arabic tradition—especially in the writings of Ibn Rushd, better known to Medieval and Renaissance scholars as Averroës.

Early celebrated for his prodigious learning, at age 20 Delmedigo was invited by a Talmudic school in Padua to become its head. Delmedigo accepted and spent 1480–90 in Italy. His reputation spread, and the University of Padua asked him to arbitrate a philosophical disagreement that was raging in that institution. He was so successful that the university appointed him to occupy its chair of philosophy when he was only 23 years old.

Delmedigo found the HUMANISTS of Florence, Padua, Bassano, and Venice eager to learn from him and to commission both Delmedigo's own new texts and his translations of philosophic works from Hebrew into Latin as well. Among the works commissioned were Rushd's synopses of PLATO's *Republic* and ARISTOTLE's *Metaphysics*. He also summarized the Islamic philosopher's commentaries on Aristotle's About the soul (*De anima*). His writings contributed importantly to the dissemination of ancient knowledge among the humanist scholars of the Italian Renaissance.

Among Delmedigo's patrons, the Florentine humanist sage GIOVANNI PICO DELLA MIRANDOLA commissioned him to write in Latin commentaries and texts about the intellective soul and whether or not the soul could be immortal. When he had finished these for Pico, Delmedigo translated them into Hebrew for an audience of his own people. He did the same thing with a work about the substance of the celestial sphere that he translated into Latin for Pico from Ibn Rushd's Arabic. A part of his motivation for his translations into Hebrew arose from his desire to make secular knowledge more accessible to the Jewish community.

Scholars today are principally interested in a work Delmedigo wrote in Hebrew about religious issues, *Behinat ha-dat* (The examination of religion)—written after his return to his native Crete in 1490. In it Delmedigo argues for the compatibility of rabbinic faith with the revelations of the Hebrew prophets and also with the rationalism of the Greek and Arabic philosophers. He dismissed the Jewish Kabbalah with its magic and mysticism.

He also rejected Christian claims for the Incarnation of God as a human being, for salvation and the personal survival of the individual soul, teachings concerning the Trinity, and the transubstantiation of bread and wine into the actual body and blood of Christ in the Eucharist. He rejected as well the mystical claims of Giovanni Pico and those among his Florentine associates who sought to reconcile the idealism of Neoplatonic thinkers with both Christian and kabbalistic mysticism.

From a philosophical perspective, Delmedigo was personally committed to Aristotelian realism as interpreted and synthesized with the Arabic tradition by Ibn Rushd. Delmedigo considered the natural world to be intelligible and predictable without recourse to magic and mysticism. He thought of God as an eternal and self-contained creative mind whose creation was directly intelligible to his intellective creatures by means of philosophy. Nonetheless, he ardently maintained a fundamental distinction between religion and philosophy, and argued that if the two disciplines proved to be at odds one should rely on the truth of prophecy and tradition founded in the Torah. At the same time Delmedigo was himself a most tolerant man, and he recommended open-mindedness about and toleration for all religious points of view rather than making them the causes of strife, oppression, political control, and warfare.

His principle contributions to Renaissance literature resulted from his role as a popularizer of philosophical and rabbinical knowledge rather than as an innovative thinker. Modern editions are available in Hebrew.

Bibliography

Zinberg, Israel. *A History of Jewish Literature.* Translated and edited by Bernard Martin. Cincinnati, Ohio, and New York: Hebrew Union College Press and KTAV Publishing House, 1974.

Deloney, Thomas (ca. 1563–ca. 1600)

A British journalist and an early writer of prose fiction during the reign of ELIZABETH I, Deloney both celebrates the middle-class craftsworkers of London and addresses them as the principal audience for his stories. Deloney himself was a silk weaver and a member of the clothier's guild. His story JACK OF NEWBERRY (1597) traces the career of a fellow weaver whose success leads him to wealth and fame as an entrepreneur who employs many other weavers in the manufacture of clothing. Similarly, in *The Gentle Craft* (1597), Deloney follows the history of a real Londoner, Thomas Eyre. Eyre was a shoemaker who rose to become lord mayor of London. The playwright Thomas Dekker borrowed the plot of this novel for his play, *The Shoemaker's Holiday.*

In a third novel, *Thomas of Reading* (ca. 1599), Deloney once again celebrates a member of his own guild who travels to London in the company of other weavers to sell their wares after meeting together in an inn at Reading. Deloney's style of writing dialogue is interesting. Both in that dialogue and in his reporting of incident, as long as members of the middle class are speaking, the style is straightforward and utterly unaffected. But as soon as a member of the aristocracy speaks, the style becomes artificial in the manner of GEORGE LYLY's EUPHUES. In the third chapter of *Thomas of Reading,* for example, the runaway daughter of the earl of Shrewsbury is bewailing her misery: "What is become," she says, "of my rare jewels, my sumptuous fare, my waiting servants . . . and all my vain pleasures?" And she answers herself: "My pleasure is banished by displeasure, my friends fled like foes . . . my feasting turned to fasting, my rich array consumed to rags. . . ."

One suspects Deloney of having linguistic fun at the expense of the nobility, gently mocking the pretensions of the aristocratic classes by putting in their mouths the affected speech of Lyly's artificial prose style.

Bibliography

Deloney, Thomas: *The Novels of Thomas Deloney.* Edited by Merritt E. Lawlis. Westport, Conn.: Greenwood Press, 1978.

———. *The Works of Thomas Deloney.* Edited by Francis Oscar Mann. Oxford: The Clarendon Press, 1912.

Denham, Sir John (1615–1669)

Born in Dublin, Ireland, Denham earned a bachelor's degree at Trinity College, Oxford, and afterward studied law at Lincoln's Inn in London where he was admitted to the bar in 1639. Firmly royalist in his politics, he occupied high office under the Stuart monarchs. When civil war broke out in 1640, Denham was serving as the high sheriff of the county of Surrey. Fighting under the royalist standard, he was taken a prisoner but not held long, and he returned to Oxford. There he turned to writing a play. A tragedy based on actual events at the court of the sultan of Turkey, his *Sophy* (1641), which appealed to a popular interest in orientalism, was successfully staged at Blackfriar's Theater in London.

The work that earned him the greatest praise among his contemporaries and from the writers of the 17th and 18th centuries was a poem, *Cooper's Hill* (1642). It described and celebrated the beauty of the countryside and the economically beneficial agrarian and topographical features around Egham near London. An often-quoted passage praises the River Thames and its benefits to trade and agriculture. Restoration poet and dramatist John Dryden considered *Cooper's Hill* "the exact standard of good writing." The lexicographer Dr. Samuel Johnson awarded Denham the palm among poets of his generation for the strength of his verse, and Alexander Pope paid *Cooper's Hill* the ultimate compliment by imitating it in his poem, *Windsor Forest.*

During the INTERREGNUM, Denham served as a secret agent of the royalist cause, and when he was found out he fled for his life to the Continent where he continued his royalist work in various capacities. When the Stuart line was restored to the English throne in 1660, the king appointed Denham surveyor–general of the royal works and the following year knighted him. His remains rest at Westminster Abbey in the Poets' Corner.

Denham exemplifies a poet whose work earned him high praise from the critical community in his own era but whose stock subsequently fell. Later critics have not esteemed his work as highly as did his immediate successors.

Bibliography

Denham, John, Sir. *The Poetical Works.* Edited by Theodore Howard Banks. Hamden, Conn.: Archon Books, 1969.

——— and others. *Some Political Satires of the Seventeenth Century.* Edited by Edmund Goldsmid. Wilmington, Del.: Scholarly Resources, 1973.

O Hehir, Brendan. *Expans'd Hieroglyphicks; A Critical Edition of Sir John Denham's Coopers Hill.* Berkeley, Calif.: University of California Press, 1969.

Descartes, René (1596–1650)

A French philosopher, mathematician, and writer, the founder of modern philosophy, Descartes was born in the province of Touraine at La Haye, a town since renamed La Haye–Descartes in his honor. After studying 10 years with the Jesuits at La Flàche (1604–14), he attended university in Poitiers where he studied law, finishing his degree in 1616.

Descartes enjoyed an independent fortune. He therefore decided that volunteering for military service at his own expense would allow him opportunities for travel and reflection. He put that plan into practice and served first with the army of Maurice of Nassau in Holland. During that campaign he reflected about the relationship between geometry and music and wrote a treatise on that subject. While serving with the duke of Bavaria in Germany in the winter of 1619, Descartes experienced a sudden inspiration for a way to reconstruct philosophy on the model of mathematics. He would begin with the most basic of verifiable certainties and systematically develop a meticulously rational philosophy from that base. The undeniable certainty on which he based his system was his awareness of his own mental processes. "I think," he wrote in Latin, "therefore, I am (*Cogito, ergo sum*)."

Descartes continued traveling, thinking, making scientific observations, and pursuing his interests in the work of Tycho Brahe, Johannes Kepler, and GALILEO GALILEI, with whose view of a heliocentric solar system he agreed. He also worked at developing his philosophic system. He spent time in Germany, France, Italy, and in Holland, where in 1628 he settled down. In Holland, he reasoned, he would be able to follow his thought where it led him more freely than would be the case in France.

When he learned that the church had condemned Galileo's work, Descartes, who remained a Catholic throughout his life, was severely shaken. In fact, he destroyed the manuscript of a major scientific work, his *Traité du monde* (Treatise about the world), and resolved never to publish anything. Fortunately he changed his mind, but the work he destroyed never appeared in its original form. He decided at least to publish in French a popular summary of his thought. Accordingly, the year 1637 saw the anonymous publication of his *Discourse de la Méthode* (DISCOURSE ON THE METHOD). Later, his more technical works began to appear in Latin under his name. In 1641 his *Meditationes de Prima Philosophia* (Meditations about the first philosophy) appeared. This was followed in 1644 by the volume that rounded out his fundamental philosophical positions, his *Principia Philosophiae* (Principles of philosophy). He saw the division between mind and matter as the basic duality of creation. Absolute perfection was God's characteristic. Systematic doubt, empirical evidence, or, failing that, indubitable, mathematical deduction underpinned his methodology. He had long since proved that reasoning by syllogism produced error.

Descartes's work produced the sort of controversy he had hoped to avoid. Happily, it also attracted powerful supporters. One of these was the Princess Elizabeth, daughter of the elector of the Palatine, Frederick V. For her in 1649 he completed his *Traité des passions d' l'âme* (Treatise about the passions of the soul). Although the physiology that Descartes describes in this document reflects the medieval state of that science in his time, the document is thoroughly modern in seeing the causes of the passions as rooted in the body itself as opposed to arising from the struggle of good and evil for control of the soul. The passions themselves are neither good nor evil. Rather, their moral value depends on reason, will, and the consequences of the actions that arise from the passions.

Descartes's uncompromising rationalism attracted both criticism and the dangerous enmity of those who considered his views a threat to their religious convictions. He decided that Holland might no longer be a safe haven for him. Princess Elizabeth accordingly helped procure for him an invitation from Queen Catherine of Sweden to move to Stockholm and become the queen's tutor. He accepted her invitation and moved in 1649, but the Swedish winter and the queen's rigorous schedule of meeting Descartes for their discussions at 5 A.M. proved too much for him. Not long after arriving in Sweden he contracted pneumonia and died.

In addition to the works named above, Descartes wrote lesser philosophic works and made notable contributions to mathematics, especially in the fields of algebraic notation and coordinate geometry. He also provided astronomy with his useful theory of vortices.

One of the most private of men, Descartes did his best to stay out of the public view. He fathered one daughter, Francine, out of wedlock (1635). He adored her, and he never recovered from her death in 1640. It was probably just as well that he did not live to see his worst fears about the reception of his ideas realized. In 1663 the Congregation of the Index forbade circulating his work among Roman Catholic readers. Despite that ban, which came too late to have much impact, Descartes became and remains one of the most influential thinkers of the Renaissance.

Bibliography

Contingham, John, Robert Stoothoff, and Dugald Murdoch. *The Philosophical Writings of Descartes.* Cambridge, U.K.: Cambridge University Press, 1985, reprinted 1997.

Description of a New World, Called The Blazing World, The   Margaret Cavendish (1666)

In *The Blazing World,* a utopian romance unparalleled among women writers of the 17th century, CAVENDISH imagines that a nameless young woman is kidnapped and carried off on a merchant ship that passes from this world to a neighboring planet by sailing from the pole of this one directly to the pole of the next. The kidnapper and his crew all freeze to death during this crossing, but the young woman is saved from this fate by the heat of her own blazing virtue. Her survival provides evidence of her matchless worthiness, and the emperor of the Blazing World marries her and confers on her unlimited power to rule and govern as she pleased. These tasks she performs with skill and enthusiasm, putting down rebellion and governing equitably.

There is surely a metamorphosed autobiographical reference here as this essentially is how Margaret managed in her own household. In the preface to this work, Cavendish names herself "Margaret the First" of the imaginary world she has created. In the text itself, however, she assigns herself a cameo role in which Margaret Cavendish appears as the empress's scribe and court writer—a role that permits the author an opportunity to justify to the world what others considered her eccentric behavior. She explains that her "singularity" marks her right to define herself as she chooses rather than to accept the roles that a male-dominated society would prescribe for her.

The work achieves many of its effects by mixing together in the matrix of Cavendish's fantasy fiction many elements. These include philosophical matters, richly elaborated description, a kaleidoscopic consideration—often implicit—of the costs to women of male chauvinism, and a technique familiar to readers of French letters of the period, the construction of catalogues of lists or catalogues called *blazons*. These lists often feature sumptuously luxurious objects.

Cavendish considered that creating new worlds in fiction would provide women with opportunities to fulfill themselves in ways the real world denied them—opportunities to exercise in fictive realms some of the capacities men typically reserved to themselves.

Cavendish published *The Blazing World* together with a nonfiction discussion of natural philosophy, *Observations Upon Experimental Philosophy* (1666). This pairing created a kind of hybrid that greatly interested Cavendish. She felt sure that such pairing of kinds both created refreshing novelty and paralleled the mixing of traditionally male and female attributes that she tried to model for others in her own life and work. She

considered the two worlds represented in the jointly published works joined at the poles just like the two worlds in *The Blazing World*.

Bibliography

Cavendish, Margaret, Duchess of Newcastle. *The Description of a New World Called The Blazing World and other Writings*. Edited by Kate Lilley. London: William Pickering, 1992. Reissued, Penguin, 2002.

Des Roches, Madeleine (1520–1587) and Catherine (1545–1587)

The founders of a literary salon in the French city of Poitiers, Madeleine and her daughter Catherine Des Roches began publishing their works together in 1578 and continued to do so in collections of 1579, 1583, and 1586. The following year they both died in an outbreak of the bubonic plague.

Educated in the HUMANIST tradition, the Dames des Roches, as they were known, enjoyed a wide popular audience for their translations from the Latin, their letters, their dialogues in prose, and their plays. These last included both a PASTORAL play and a TRAGICOMEDY. They also wrote a sort of literary criticism and social commentary called salon responses. Notable among their collected writings is Catherine's SONNET sequence, though their poetic production was by no means limited to that single genre.

Their growing literary fame attracted numerous clever persons from as far away as Paris to their Poitiers salon to converse about literary subjects. An incident in which a flea was observed on the person of Catherine led to the publication of The flea of Madame Des Roches (*La puce de Madame des Roches*, 1582 and 1583) a collection of commentaries about the salon by those who regularly attended it.

American scholar Anne R. Larsen has recently edited and reissued in French the work of the Dames Des Roches, but only a few samples of their writings have as yet appeared in English.

Bibliography

Anne R. Larsen, ed. *Les Ouevres: Madelaine Des Roches, Catherine Des Roches; édition critique.* Geneva, Switzerland: Droz, 1993.

Díaz del Castillo, Bernal (1492–1584)

A Spanish soldier who accompanied HERNÁN CORTÉS on his expedition of Mexican conquest in 1519, Díaz retired to his estate in Central America (now in Guatemala) and in his old age recorded his earlier experiences. He was motivated to become a chronicler of the events of his youth by the errors he observed in the court chronicler LÓPEZ DE GÓMARA's official history of the Conquest. Díaz's True history of the discovery of New Spain (*Verdadera Historia de la conquista de la Nueva España,* 1632) captures the wonder of the experience of discovering an entirely new world. Díaz describes, for example, the entry of Cortés's small party of 400 into the Aztec capital Tenochtitlán on November 8, 1519. He records the meeting between the Aztec emperor Montezuma and Cortés and summarizes their conversation and behavior in fascinating detail, focusing on cultural differences and revealing the Aztec's dignified and diplomatic responses to Cortés's almost immediate suggestion that the Aztecs give up their traditional religion and convert to Christianity.

With a keen sense of what will interest readers and for what future generations will want to know, Díaz focuses on issues such as how Cortés was able to speak with the Aztecs, telling the stories of a shipwrecked Spaniard, Jerónimo de Aguilar, who had learned Mayan, and a Christian Indian girl, Doña Marina, whose joint efforts made possible Cortés's relatively easy communication with the indigenous peoples of the New World.

The *True History* is a treasure store of sociological and anthropological information about Aztec habits, manners, and mode of life that without Díaz' account might well have been irretrievably lost. Longer than Cortés' own reports of the same events, it also records more detail, treats the perspective of the Aztecs with greater objectivity, and reports events more impartially. Throughout the work, Díaz takes a keen delight in pointing out mistakes made by López de Gómara.

Bibliography

Díaz del Castillo, Bernal. *The Discovery and Conquest of Mexico 1517–1521* [selections]. Edited by Genaro García and Hugh Thomas. Translated by A. P. Maudslay. New York: Da Capo Press, 1996.

———. *The Conquest of New Spain.* Translated by J. M. Cohen. Baltimore, Md.: Penguin Books, 1963.

Discourse on the Method René Descartes (1637)

Included among DESCARTES's earliest published writings, his *Discourse on the Method of Rightly Conducting One's Reason and Seeking the Truth in the Sciences* begins with a brief autobiographical sketch of its author's intellectual development. He says that "good sense or reason" is the most widely distributed quality in the world and that he does not therefore presume to teach a method that everyone must learn to guide his or her reason correctly. As he considers that his own intellect is not significantly different from that of others, he will merely describe the method he has developed to guide his own reasoning in the hope that his readers will adopt those portions of it that seem congenial.

He goes on to describe his studies and the conclusions that he drew from them. It is well, he thought, to study other people and their ways to give us comparative grounds for evaluating our own presuppositions and practices and not to think that all customs but our own are ridiculous and irrational. At the same time, he cautions, too much traveling eventually makes a person a stranger to his own country. Similarly, too much time spent studying the history of past ages leaves one ignorant of one's own. Accordingly, after he had "escaped" the control of his tutors, he spent a good deal of time traveling and studying philosophy and mathematics—a discipline he especially cherished. Finally, he tells us, he resolved to look within himself and to study carefully what he discovered there as well.

Using his own experience as a touchstone, as had MONTAIGNE before him, Descartes resolved to proceed slowly, to reject the opinions of others, and to follow four cardinal rules. First, he decided to "avoid precipitate conclusions and preconceptions" and exclude anything doubtful from consideration. Second, he determined to examine problems in an orderly fashion and piecemeal rather than all at once. Third, he resolved to proceed from the simple to the complex. Fourth, he intended to be exhaustive in listing all relevant issues and subcategories so that nothing would be left out. He also meant to consider the problems he examined in a symbolic fashion, derived from the practices of algebra and geometry and to attempt to establish some philosophical first principles so that he could rebuild the edifice of his intellect, so to speak, from the ground up.

Having set forth these principles, Descartes next addressed the context within which he would put them in operation. He decided to obey the laws and customs of his country and to hold tentatively the most moderate among conflicting opinions until his method revealed another opinion to be correct. Then he would hew to that correct opinion even though others found it doubtful. He next decided he would try to master himself rather than FORTUNE. Finally he concluded that, among all others possible, the enterprise he had undertaken was the one most suitable for his capacities and interests.

Descartes spent, he tells us, the next nine years pursuing this program, all the while suspending judgments on many matters. He moved to Holland for eight of those years, living a solitary and reclusive life while following his plan. While there he began by rejecting every opinion and thought as illusory except the one that seemed to him undeniable: "I am thinking; therefore I exist." That phrase, often translated as, "I think; therefore I am," became the foundation stone of Descartes's philosophy. The *I* of the phrase, however, Descartes conceived of as an intellective entity independent of the body—an entity he called soul. Recognizing his own imperfections, Descartes thought that his imperfect soul must take its origins from a more perfect being and that being must be God, the "foundation of truth," as Descartes understood it.

Descartes continues by describing at length his conclusions about the human heart and the circulation of the blood that had recently been demonstrated by Gabriel Harvey. He also addresses other physiological questions. On these he brings to bear the medical theories of the ancients who attributed bodily movement to "animal spirits" that the heart distributed to the various parts of the body as required. He distinguishes between human beings and beasts based on the human capacity for speech, which he found provided evidence of a uniquely human rational soul—a soul he conceived of as having been specially created.

In the sixth part of the *Treatise on Method* Descartes tells us that he suppressed another document (one we now know to have been his *Treatise on Man*) when he learned of the Congregation of the Holy Office's—that is, the INQUISITION's—suppression and condemnation of Galileo Galilei's *Dialogue Concerning the Two Chief World Systems* in 1633. Descartes had read Galileo's work and had found nothing objectionable in it. Given the inquisitors' objections to Galileo, Descartes tactfully suggested that his own opinions might be wrong. Between the lines a reader finds Descartes's disinclination to meet a fate like Galileo's at the hands of the inquisitors.

Equally clearly implied and often directly expressed is Descartes's private conviction of the sufficiency of essentially scientific method to explain natural phenomena without recourse to scriptural revelation. Yet his fear of the Inquisition was sufficient to make him decide to suppress many of his writings during his lifetime. He compares the search for truth to battles. "We lose a battle," he says, "whenever we accept a false opinion concerning an important question of general significance." One might apply Descartes's dictum to the continuing rear-guard actions that certain groups continue to conduct against the thoroughly established truth of evolutionary theory.

To avoid just such controversy, Descartes says, he suppressed much of his thinking, and in the final section of his *Discourse on the Method* he defends his decision to defer allowing the publication of his work until after his death.

Bibliography

Descartes, René. *The Philosophical Writings of Descartes.* Volume I. Translated by John Cottingham, Robert Stoothoff, and Dugald Murdoch. 1985. Cambridge, U.K.: Cambridge University Press, 1997.

Discovery of the New World by Christopher Columbus, The Lope de Vega Carpio (1614)

One of LOPE DE VEGA'S most ambitious history plays, the action of the *Discovery of the New World* attempts to compress into an evening's entertainment 14 years of Christopher Columbus's activity beginning with his failed efforts to interest Don John of Portugal in his project and ending with the explorer's presentation of artifacts from the New World to Ferdinand and Isabella of Spain. In the interim, the audience is required to imagine itself present at the fall of the city of Granada, on the deck of Columbus's ship *Santa Maria* when his men mutiny, and with the discoverer in America.

The play is peopled not only with sailors, Spanish and Portuguese nobles, Moors from Granada, and American Indians, but allegorical figures also appear. These include representations of Christianity, a Demon, Idolatry, and Providence.

The central idea on which the play rests involves the benefits that will accrue to the peoples of the New World from their Christianization. Lope, however, who was himself a priest, seems to have little grasp of the nature of Native American religions. The scene that represents the indigenous Americans at worship before Europeans arrive pictures the Indians singing about such classical deities of Rome and Greece as Phoebus Apollo and Diana.

From the perspective of verisimilitude, the play does better in handling the character of Columbus. It catches the discoverer's sense of predestined mission and pictures him as kind and dignified. It also has the allegorical figure Idolatry argue strongly before the tribunal of Providence against the Spanish occupation of the New World on the grounds that the Spaniards are not truly motivated by religion but rather by a desire to profit.

In this play Lope extravagantly combines theatrical traditions of many sorts to stage a spectacular show. Historical accuracy, though occasionally achieved, is not a principal objective of the piece. Entertaining his audience, rather, is the goal at which Lope aims.

Bibliography

Vega Carpio, Lope de. *Translations of the American Plays of Lope de Vega: The Discovery of the New World, The Conquest of Araucania, Brazil Restored.* Edited and translated by Kenneth Stackhouse. Lewiston, N.Y.: E. Mellen Press, 2003.

Divine Narcissus, The Sor Juana Inés de la Cruz (ca. 1688)

A one-act, sacramental drama that was written in honor of the Holy Eucharist and intended for performance on the holiday of Corpus Christi, *The Divine Narcissus* presents an ALLEGORY. It brings together in a Christian PASTORAL the classical story of Narcissus, who stands for Christ, and Echo, who represents Satan. The names of the other characters suggest their functions in the play: Synagogue (divine revelation in the Old Testament), Gentile (pagan antiquity), Human Nature (a woman in search of her beloved Narcissus), Grace (the means to salvation through Christ), Pride, and Self-Love.

The play is prefaced by an introductory, five-scene playlet called a *loa.* This introductory piece features the characters Occident and America dressed in Aztec costume. Other characters include Religion, Zeal, Soldiers, and Musician. Essentially the introduction acquaints the audience with the benefits accruing to Occident and America from contact with European Religion, a character who restrains the severities of Zeal and Soldiers in dealing with indigenous peoples and institutions. The *loa* also realistically depicts the suspicion and resistance with which Occident and America greet that point of view.

The play proper begins with the characters Synagogue and Gentile calling on the people to praise Divine Narcissus/Christ. From the allegorical speeches, Human Nature perceives that divine mysteries are figured forth in their content, and scene 2 instructs the audience in the play's allegorical method. In the third scene, the villains appear in earnest: Echo confers with Pride and Self-Love about ways to subvert Narcissus. The third scene features a series of tableaux from the Old Testament—Cain and Abel, Enoch, Abraham and Isaac, and Noah. These suggest the dangers of self-love and pride, and point out the means the faithful may take to avoid their pitfalls. In the fourth scene, the interaction between Narcissus (Christ) and Echo (Satan) recalls the scriptural account of Christ's temptation in the desert. In the Bible Satan shows Christ the kingdoms of the world and offers them to him in exchange for his allegiance. In the play, Echo entices Narcissus with her wealth and, presenting an idol, tries to get the world and Narcissus to bow down before it.

In the meantime, Human Nature like a forlorn lover seeks her beloved Narcissus. Finally, Narcissus looks into the waters of a pool that has never known poison, observes his own likeness—which is also the likeness of Human Nature, and falls in love with it. This interesting artifice turns on its head the biblical notion, sometimes presented graphically in art and literature, that Eve beholds and loves her own countenance on the face of the serpent in the Garden of Eden.

While Narcissus remains entranced with the reflection of his countenance—at once God's and, in God's image, Human Nature's, Echo arrives. In a wonderful scene that assimilates the classical themes of the play to the Christian context, Echo is struck dumb with rage that Narcissus has perceived and loved in his own image both God and human beings. Struck dumb, Echo can only repeat the last words that Narcissus speaks—words that describe the final truth of the Satanic state: "I have pain, rage."

In the balance of the play, Narcissus recapitulates Christ's sacrifice for Human Nature, his spiritual bride, and Grace explains that he has chosen to remain on Earth in the form of a white flower, a METAPHOR for the Eucharist, the either literal or figurative sustaining body and blood of Christ for the Christian faithful.

This summary does not do justice either to the beauty of the language or the simple dignity of Sor Juana's lovely allegorical drama, but perhaps it will convey a sense of the outline of her religious masterwork, which in moving verse sets forth some of the central precepts of her faith as she attempts to dramatize the operation of Divine Grace in human life and the role of the Eucharist in that operation.

Bibliography

Cruz, Sor Juana Inés de la. The *Divine Narcissus: El Divino Narciso*. Translated by Patricia A. Peters and Renée Domeier. Albuquerque: University of New Mexico Press, 1988.

Doctor Faustus, The Tragical History of
Christopher Marlowe (ca. 1604)

A tragedy based on a then unpublished, loose English translation (ca. 1588) of a German prose original (anonymous, 1587), MARLOWE's powerful, iambic-pentameter verse play was likely written around 1589 but surely by 1592. The 15 years of repeated stage production that passed before the play's publication probably means that passages by other hands found their way into the 1604 text. In fact, a collaborator probably originally wrote the play's humorous scenes since Marlowe's genius did not tend in the comic direction.

From a formal perspective, Marlowe's work presents an interesting combination of a classical TRAGEDY and a medieval MORALITY PLAY. From the ancients Marlowe borrows a chorus to introduce and comment on the action and represent the judgments of public opinion. From the morality plays he introduces the SEVEN DEADLY SINS personified, evil and good angels, devils, and the general framework of a PSYCHOMACHIA—a conflict between the forces of good and evil for the salvation or destruction of a human soul.

The play's opening finds Dr. Faustus, a professor of theology at Wittenberg University, about to abandon his studies of theology and medicine to pursue the study of magic and alchemy. He is compelled by his desire to master all knowledge and the secrets of the universe. His good and evil angels, respectively, discourage him from and encourage him in this decision. He is, however, confirmed in his determination to pursue magic in conference with two magicians, Valdes and Cornelius.

In Act I, scene iii, Faustus summons up a devil, Mephistophilis, who appears in the garb of a Franciscan friar. A servant of Satan, Mephistophilis describes his own hellish torment as a fallen angel, but intent on his desire for knowledge, Faustus offers to exchange his soul if Satan will permit Mephistophilis to serve him. A comic scene follows, ending Act I. In the first scene of Act II, Faustus reflects on his decision to sell his soul. His good and bad angels discourage him and encourage him, but Faustus is firm in his decision. Mephistophilis returns to say that Satan has accepted. Faustus draws up an agreement that allows him to assume any form or to be an invisible spirit when he wishes. The agreement also gives him control of Mephistophilis for a period of 24 years. After that Faustus agrees that the devil may claim his soul. After having a discussion with Mephistophilis about hell—in which Faustus does not believe despite his new servant's assurances to the contrary—Faustus demands the fairest maid in Germany for a wife.

Mephistophilis balks at this request since marriage is a divinely instituted condition and a sacrament from which particular instances of God's grace follow. Mephistophilis instead offers Faustus a devil dressed like a woman. When Faustus refuses her, the devil promises to bring him the fairest courtesans. Already the devil is cheating on his bargain, but Faustus does not notice. Mephistophilis distracts him by giving Faustus a book that reveals the answers to all his questions about natural science and that gives him control of riches and power over warriors.

From time to time, Faustus vacillates about the decision he has made, but he always ends up reaffirming it. In Act III, Mephistophilis takes Faustus on a whirlwind tour of Europe, including Vatican City. Invisible, Faustus amuses himself by annoying the pope at dinner, snatching away his food and wine, and boxing the Pontiff on the ear.

Throughout the play, Faustus performs several magical acts—changing into a dog and a monkey a pair of apprentices who stole one of his books and tried to do magic themselves. He makes horns grow on the forehead of a knight and brings grapes in January from the other side of the world to please a duchess. With ever-greater frequency, however, as the end of his 24 years draws nearer, he reflects with regret on his coming damnation. In Act V, scene i, an old man tries to lead him to repentance, and Faustus says: "I do repent, and yet I do despair/ . . . What shall I do to shun the snares of death?"

Mephistophilis appears, calls Faustus a traitor, and threatens him. Faustus reaffirms his former oath to Lucifer and asks for Helen of Troy as his lover. She enters—though she is Helen in appearance only. She is in reality a female demon—a succubus. Faustus can no longer tell the difference: "Is this the face," he asks, "that launch'd a thousand ships, / And burnt the topless towers of Ilium [Troy]?"

He kisses her and finds that her kiss sucks his soul from his body. The old man pronounces his case hopeless, and the devils enter who will carry Faustus's body and soul to hell. In the play's final scene, the clock strikes 11. Faustus, knowing he has only an hour left to live makes a final effort at salvation. "O," he exclaims, "I'll leap up to my God! . . . / See, see where Christ's blood streams in the firmament! / One drop would save my soul—half a drop!" As the hour approaches, Faustus calls on God, hoping to remit some of his sentence in hell. He begs Lucifer to spare his soul. But it is too late. As the clock strikes midnight, the devils snatch Faustus away to hell, and the chorus supplies the moral of the story.

Conceivably there could be an ironic relationship between Faustus's story and Marlowe's biography. Marlowe was dismissed from university for atheism and was knifed to death in a tavern brawl.

Bibliography

Marlowe, Christopher. *Doctor Faustus.* Edited by Sylvan Barnet. New York: Signet Classics, ca. 2001.

Dom Japhet of Armenia Paul Scarron
(performed 1647, published 1653)

Possibly the most successful COMEDY by Paul Scarron, *Don Japhet* closely follows the action of a Spanish model, *El marqués de Cigarrel* (The marquis of Cigarrel) by Alonso de Castillo Solórzano. Scarron changes the organization by extending the play to five acts so that it meets the expectation for plays on the classical model.

The play intertwines two plot lines. In the first the title character, a foolish bumpkin named Dom Japhet, discovers that his folly and antics entertain King Charles V, who was called Charles the Wise. The king's favorable attention overwhelms Japhet's meager judgment, and he grows ridiculously self-important.

Set against that foolery Scarron develops the growing love of a pair of admirable young people, a peasant girl Léonore and Dom Alphonse, the disguised son of the Spanish ambassador to Rome, Pedro de Toledo. Alphonse finds employment as a servant to Dom Japhet so that he can woo Léonore anonymously. The audience discovers in the second scene, however, that Léonore has already discovered the true identity of her admirer in a letter he dropped. She has learned, moreover, that he is betrothed to a Spanish lady.

Léonore has fallen in love with Dom Alphonse, so when he urgently woos her, she puts him off, saying that her feelings toward him might change with time. This gives Alphonse the opportunity to break off his Spanish match and remain with her.

The plot grows more complex late in the first act when Dom Japhet also falls in love with Léonore at first sight. Shortly thereafter a letter arrives revealing that Léonore is also of noble birth, was left to be reared in simplicity, but now must assume her proper role in society. Dom Japhet employs his servant as an intermediary with Léonore, but when he arrives Alphonse speaks for himself (though feigning to speak for Japhet). Léonore understands the ruse and answers in the same spirit.

In the second act, Japhet reveals his literary kinship with the hero of DON QUIXOTE DE LA MANCHA, imagining himself comparable to a figure from CHIVALRIC ROMANCE like AMADIS OF GAUL.

Dom Japhet presses his suit; Léonore refuses him. He cannot imagine why. Like Don Quixote, Japhet becomes a laughing stock, finally suffering being stripped naked and having the contents of a chamber pot emptied on his head.

Scarron also introduces a secondary love interest with another young couple, Elvire and Dom Alvare. The townspeople arrange a mock marriage for Dom Japhet, ostensibly with a South American princess, Ahihua. Totally taken in by this foolery, Dom Japhet willingly participates in the false nuptials. They in turn provide an entertaining counterpoint when set against the real marriages of Elvire and Dom Alvare and Léonore and Dom Alphonse. A serious undercurrent in the play rewards the self-knowledgable young people while punishing Dom Japhet, an antihero who is self-deceiving to the point of madness.

Bibliography

Scarron, Paul. *The Whole Comical Works of Monsieur Scarron.* 2 vols. New York: Garland Publishers, 1973.

Dom Juan (*Don Juan*) Molière (1665)

MOLIÈRE was not the first to bring the story of what the poet and translator Richard Wilbur has called a "serial lover" to the European stage. TIRSO DE MOLINA had anticipated him on the Spanish stage with THE TRICKSTER OF SEVILLE (*El Burlador de Sevilla*, 1630), and a pair of Italian versions had been revised and translated for French performance before Molière brought his *Dom Juan,* a TRAGICOMEDY atypically written in prose rather than verse, to the French stage. There the playwright hoped the story's familiarity and its themes of sexual predation and heavenly retribution would play well with Parisian audiences.

The play opens with Dom Juan's valet, Sganarelle, praising the qualities of snuff to Elvire's squire, Gusman. Elvire, Dom Juan's wife, has sent Gusman to inquire why her husband suddenly departed without notice or leave-taking.

Sganarelle frankly tells Gusman that Dom Juan is a champion scoundrel who believes neither in Heaven or Hell—nor even in werewolves. Rather the Dom's entire existence is devoted to gratifying his unnatural sexual appetites. To accomplish that objective, Sganarelle says, Dom Juan will marry anyone or anything, any time—just as he has taken Elvire from the convent and married her. Sganarelle cautions Gusman, however, that if he repeats these confidences, Sganarelle will swear Gusman is a liar.

In the second scene, Dom Juan explains to Sganarelle that every new potential conquest is like a military campaign that he *must* win. He cannot, moreover, abide the notion of monogamous fidelity.

Sganarelle reproves Dom Juan for trifling with the sacrament of marriage. Heaven, Sganarelle feels certain, will punish the Dom. The audience next learns that the pair has returned to the town where, six months earlier, Dom Juan had killed the Commander. The valet opines that coming there was a bad idea, but Dom Juan confides that he envies the happiness of a pair of betrothed lovers he has observed and wishes to seduce the bride-to-be. He explains that he plans to abduct her during an outing on the sea. We also learn that Sganarelle disapproves of his master's behavior and apostasy.

In the third scene of Act I, Elvire herself arrives. She asks why Dom Juan has deserted her. He mockingly explains that his conscience has troubled him because he seduced her from a convent and that he fears heavenly retribution.

The next scene shifts the scene to the countryside where a peasant, Pierrot, is telling his beloved Charlotte that he rescued two men (Dom Juan and Sganarelle) from the sea and that when he left them to dry out, one of them was making eyes at Mathurin, a country girl. He then pokes fun at the excesses of the courtier's clothing.

Having failed in his abduction attempt when his boat overturned, Dom Juan picks Charlotte as his next victim. At first, Charlotte sensibly resists the Dom's blandishments, but when he swears he will marry her and Sganarelle confirms it, Charlotte agrees to marry the nobleman. Pierrot intervenes, and Dom Juan slaps him and a good deal of slapstick business follows. In scene iv, Mathurin enters and reveals that she too is engaged to Dom Juan. The girls argue over him, and in a series of asides the Dom deceives them both and convinces each of his intention to marry her.

Dom Juan finally exits, and Sganarelle warns both of the country maidens to stay in their village and be safe. When Dom Juan returns and overhears a portion of Sganarelle's warning, the quick-witted valet says he was merely giving examples of what the girls ought not to believe. Learning now, however, that a posse of 10 men is in pursuit of them, the two agree to disguise themselves and flee. Sganarelle resists the dom's suggestion that they exchange attire.

Act III's curtain rises on the two in disguise. Dom Juan appears in peasant garb, and Sganarelle is wearing a doctor's gown. He reports that people have been stopping him and asking for advice. Out of respect for his attire, he explains, he has prescribed for those who asked. Dom Juan suggests that Sganarelle's advice has as much chance of curing the ill as the advice of doctors. Sganarelle adds medicine to the list of things his master has no

faith in. This leads to a discussion on the subject of belief, and Sganarelle discovers that his master believes only in arithmetic.

Confirming this, in the next scene the pair encounters a poor man who spends his time in praying and begging alms. Dom Juan offers the man a gold coin if he will blaspheme. The poor man refuses.

As they pass through a forest, Dom Juan rescues a man from bandits. That man proves to be Dom Carlos, a member of the posse of Elvire's relatives seeking vengeance from Dom Juan. When Dom Carlos explains his mission, Dom Juan explains that he is a friend of the man they seek. He assures them that Dom Juan will be pleased to meet them on a field of honor at any time. In the next scene, Carlos's brother Alonso arrives, recognizes Dom Juan, and demands vengeance, but because Juan has saved his life, Carlos requests a delay.

Left alone, Dom Juan and Sganarelle happen upon the tomb, mausoleum, and statue of the slain Commander (La Statue du Commandeur). Dom Juan jokingly directs Sganarelle to asks the statue to dinner the following evening. When Sganarelle reluctantly does so, the statue nods its acceptance. Dom Juan disbelieves Sganarelle's report, but when the Dom himself repeats the invitation the statue nods again.

"So much for your free thinkers," says Sganarelle.

In the opening scene of the fourth act, Dom Juan tries to brush aside the statue's responses as an optical illusion. The next scene shifts to an attempt by Ragoutin, Dom Juan's tailor, to collect his bill. Ragoutin is put off with empty compliments and false expressions of interest in his family members—including the family pet. He leaves without a penny of what is due him.

Dom Juan's father, Dom Luis, visits next and blames his son because his life is a reproach both to his ancestry and to his title. Luis promises to exercise his patenal authority to put a stop to Dom Juan's depravity. Dom Juan responds by wishing for his father's death.

In Act IV, scene vi, Elvire reappears, this time veiled and in a religious habit. She has reformed her life, she reports, and entered a religious order. She warns Dom Juan that his dissolute life has brought him to the end of Heaven's patience and that he has but a day's time to reform. He was dear to her, she tells him, and she counsels immediate repentance and reform. In response Dom Juan unsuccessfully attempts to convince her to spend the night.

The Dom will reform, he tells Sganarelle in the next scene after 20 or 30 more years of the life he presently leads. The two begin their dinner, and as they eat, a knock comes at the door. The statue has kept his appointment. It joins the others at table and then invites Dom Juan to dinner the following night.

Act V opens with Dom Juan pretending to his father to renounce his evil ways. His father is overjoyed. After the old man's departure Sganarelle too expresses his joy at his master's conversion. Dom Juan assures his valet, however, that he is unchanged. Sganarelle is flabbergasted that the Statue's visit has not inspired either belief or fear. Dom Juan explains his imposture with a specch that could be a fable of our times: "The true believers," he says, "are easily hoodwinked by the false and blindly follow those who ape their piety." This serious moment is followed by comic business in which Sganarelle reproves his master with a self-evidently illogical argument.

Dom Carlos arrives to try to settle the matter of Donne Elvire's honor without bloodshed. But Dom Juan plays the hyprocite and claims that Heaven's will forbids that he live with her despite his earnest desire to do so.

In the play's penultimate scene, a specter appears with a final warning of Heaven's approaching judgement. Dom Juan rejects both the warning and repentance.

As life often does, so the play ends suddenly. In Act V, scene v, the statue reappears to remind Dom Juan of their appointment. Dom Juan willingly takes the Statue's extended hand, and amidst thunder and lightning, the statue leads him off to Hell. Left alone on stage, Sganarelle complains that no one is left to pay him his back wages.

Bibliography

Molière. *Dom Juan.* Translated by Richard Wilbur. San Diego, New York, and London: A Harvest Book, 2001.

Dong Yue (Tung Yüeh) (1620–1686)

The author of THE TOWER OF MYRIAD MIRRORS (HSI YU PU), likely the best of many sequels to the monumental Chinese novel THE JOURNEY TO THE WEST (ASI YU CHI), Dong early showed signs of extraordinary capacities. At the age of seven he studied the classical LANGUAGE OF INDIA, Sanskrit. By the age of nine he had learned to write essays in classical Chinese calligraphy. In his 19th year, however, he met with a stunning disappointment when he failed the imperial examination that qualified one for a job in the Chinese civil service. As he was married with a son to support, he cast about for other ways to earn a living.

The following year (1640) he wrote his masterpiece. It appeared in 1641. Dong may have written much else as well, but because he periodically burned the books that he wrote, much of his work went unpublished. He destroyed his books in 1643, 1646, and 1656. Though this may seem strange, Dong's religious convictions likely classed his own writings among the illusory trappings of a world in which attachment to things, even one's own brain-children, is both illusory and foolish.

In 1652 Dong fathered another son, and the following year he changed his name to Lin. His life-long interest in religious matters, however, continued to assert itself. After the third book burning, Dong/Lin vowed never to write again and entered the Lingyen Buddhist monastery under the religious name Nanqian (Nan–chien).

He reconsidered the vow he had taken against writing. Perhaps thinking that recounting his own spiritual adventures would be of more benefit to the world than the work he had destroyed, he wrote a retrospective diary in 1676.

His mother preceded him in death by only two years, and Dong died in a monastery whose Chinese name means *Evening Fragrance*.

Bibliography

Brandauer, Frederick P. *Tung Yüeh.* Boston, Mass.: Twayne Publishers, 1978.

Dong Yue. *The Tower of Myriad Mirrors: A Supplement to Journey to the West by Tung Yüeh.* Translated by Shuen-fu Lin and Larry J. Schulz. Ann

Arbor, Mich.: Center for Chinese Studies, the University of Michigan, 2000.

Donne, John (1572–1631)

An English poet and prose, John Donne was endowed with the kind of brilliance and personal charm that early promised a distinguished public career. Donne studied first, when only 12, at Oxford and then at Cambridge. While there Donne became a friend of the influential Sir Henry Wotten. Like many contemporaries who aspired to public office, beginning in 1592 Donne continued his education in the law at Lincoln's Inn in London.

Richard Baker in his *Chronicle of the Kings of England* (1643) tells us that throughout the 1580s and 1590s, Donne gained a reputation as "a great visitor of ladies, a great frequenter of plays, [and] a great writer of conceited verses." By *conceited*, Baker did not mean that Donne regarded himself too highly. Rather Baker meant that the poems Donne wrote contained the sort of sometimes far-fetched comparisons called METAPHYSICAL CONCEITS. Donne's wit, superb intelligence, and ironic turn of mind led him to reject the prevailing and well-worn PETRARCHIST mode of conventional lyric poetry in English and instead to write lines whose length and meters varied, to find fresh and sometimes startling images and metaphors, and to rely on intellect and wit rather than exclusively on feelings whose expression had become conventionalized. Other poets followed Donne's lead, and he became the founder of the metaphysical school of poetry.

Although always a prolific poet, throughout his life Donne resisted allowing his verse to be printed. He did make two exceptions to this policy, for in 1611 his two *Anniversaries* appeared. The first was a commemorative poem following the death of Elizabeth Drury, the daughter of a patron and benefactor, Sir Robert Drury. The second was a general meditation about death. Donne later said that he wished he had not allowed even these verses to see print during his lifetime.

His other poems did, however, circulate widely in manuscript, as was the fashion among upperclass Elizabethan writers who did not depend on their pens for their livelihoods. During the early (pre-1601) period of his production, his verse tended to be erotic, celebrating the joys of real or imagined love affairs, or to be cynical in tone, joking about lovers' fickleness. Poems like his *Song, Go and catch a falling star,* or *Woman's Constancy,* or *The Flea,* or *The sun rising* illustrate the tone of his earlier poems on the subject of love.

In 1597–98, Donne saw military service as a volunteer member of the earl of Essex's expeditions to Cadiz in Spain and to the Azores islands; such poems as *The Storm* and *The Calm* can be attributed to his experiences while serving. On his return, he became the secretary of Sir Thomas Egerton, the keeper of the Great Seal. Like FRANCIS BACON before him, Donne might himself have risen to that exalted office. In 1600 he fell in love, however, with his employer's niece, Anne More, and she with him.

Anne More had not yet quite reached the age of majority, and the difference in their social status made the couple despair of securing the necessary permission for their union, so in 1601 they married secretly and illegally. When this became public, the couple was forced to separate, Donne lost his position, and he was jailed for a time. Anne was spirited away to France where her father, Sir George More, hoped her ardor for Donne might cool and she would consent to an annulment. She disappointed her parent. When she reached the age of majority, she returned to Donne, and the couple parented a family of 12 children, of whom seven survived. Large as it was, the size of the family was not unusual for an era when high infant mortality was a fact of life. It was remarkable, however, that after Anne's death in 1617, Donne never remarried—the typical pattern of widowers—despite the large brood he had to rear alone.

Surely we owe several of Donne's most moving and best-remembered poems to his responses to his relationship with his spouse. *A Valediction* (farewell), *forbidding mourning* must describe the quality of the Donnes' mutual devotion. In that poem appear exquisitely original images of the unbreakable connections "like gold to airy thinness beat" that bind true lovers. Donne also develops the image of the legs of a compass ("stiff twin compasses") with one at the center that turns and leans in response to the one that "roams" as Anne was forced to do. *The Ecstasy* explores the relationship between spiritual and physical love in an effort to define the quality of the couple's shared feelings.

Other poems express both his sorrow at losing his wife, his hope for their eventual reunion in heaven, and his belief that love survives mortality. *Twicknam Garden* expresses the contrast between the exterior beauty of a springtime garden and the interior winter of the sorrowing poet. *The Relic* suggests that the speaker when deceased will continue to wear around his wrist "a bracelet of bright hair about the bone"—a bracelet made from the hair of his beloved and carried with him to the grave in hopes that an ancient legend might be true. Some believers in physical resurrection thought that, before ascending to heaven, the resurrected person would need to collect any body parts missing as a result of accident, amputation, or even, in the most extreme form, hair cuttings and nail parings. The hair bracelet with its sexual implication was a means for assuring a brief reunion of a loving couple before ascending to heaven where there would be no giving or taking in marriage.

The year 1601 marked a major turning point in Donne's life in ways beyond his marriage. In that year, after studying the subject exhaustively and concluding that he could in good conscience convert to the Anglican Church, he did so. This was a major step for the nephew of an eventual Roman Catholic saint, for Donne's maternal uncle was the martyred Sir Thomas More. Once Donne had converted, though, he allowed himself to be persuaded by an Anglican priest, Thomas Morton, to write some anti-Catholic tracts. He nevertheless resisted from at least 1607 until 1615 mounting pressure from his friends and even from King JAMES I to pursue a career in the church. Perhaps he still hoped to be appointed to public office, or perhaps he felt unsure of a clerical calling. In any case, Donne finally saw that the king was only willing to advance him in a career as an Anglican priest, and at age 41 he finally became convinced of his own suitability for that role and took priestly orders. Pleased, the king promoted him to the post of dean of St. Paul's Cathedral in 1621.

Religion had always been among the subjects for Donne's verse, but after he became a priest and after he channeled his authorial powers into writing his eloquent and powerful sermons, his poetic production also focused on spiritual matters. His *Holy Sonnets* and his *The Progresse of the Soule* represent the spiritual side of his body of verse. Frequently in them one gains a sense of Donne's own feelings of spiritual inadequacy. In the three verses of his *A Hymne to God the Father,* which repeatedly puns on Donne's own name, the poet acknowledges his own unworthiness, begs for forgiveness, and asserts his belief in divine mercy. In *Batter my heart three-personed God,* the first line of the 10th poem among the *Holy sonnets,* Donne uses images of warfare and pillage, blacksmithery, and forcible divorce while imploring God to mount an all-out attack on his reluctant soul so that it may be rescued from God's enemy and be saved. Number six of the same collection, the celebrated *Death Be Not Proud,* asserts Donne's conviction in the triumph of life eternal.

Donne also wrote verses in Latin. A famous example is one addressed to playwright BEN JONSON on the subject of his play *Volpone.* His prose production includes a set of *Paradoxes and Problems,* whose individual titles provide a good index to their content, for instance, "That a Wise Man is Known by Much Laughing." Another title asks, "Why Puritans make Long Sermons?" The text answers, "It is their duty to preach on till their Auditory [audience] wake." Donne also composed essays and CHARACTERS, devotions, SATIRES, verse letters, elegies, epigrams, and translations.

Donne's poetic reputation has waxed and waned as his readers and critics have valued or disvalued wit and ingenuity in matter and manner. The young poets of his own century strove to imitate him, but such 18th-century critics as Samuel Johnson, partly owing to the excesses of Donne's imitators, found his meters "rough," and others found his ingenuity perplexing. In the early 20th century, when intellectual poetry was in and *pretty* poetry out, Donne's star rose once more. His reputation parallels the history of publication of his work. His poems were first collected and posthumously published in 1633, and a succession of seven editions, also including his prose works, rapidly followed. Then, except for excerpts and textbook inclusions, his work lay relatively fallow until Sir Henry Grierson's careful edition of most of his poems in 1912. This collection was supplemented by at least 12 others of portions of Donne's production throughout the 20th century. At this writing, a new, monumental, and definitive variorum edition of his poetic work has begun to issue from the press. If the pattern holds, the 21st century will properly continue to value Donne as a talent of the highest rank.

When the great fire of London destroyed St. Paul's Cathedral in 1666, Donne's funerary effigy was among the few surviving monuments. That statue bearing Donne's likeness occupies a prominent place in Sir Christopher Wren's present cathedral (built 1675–1710).

Bibliography

Bald, R. C. *John Donne: A Life*. 1970. Reprint, Oxford: Clarendon Press, 1986.

Donne, John. *The Complete Poetry and Selected Prose of John Donne*. Edited by Charles M. Coffin, Denis Donoghue, and W. T. Chmielewski. New York: Modern Library, 2001.

———. *John Donne's Sermons on the Psalms and Gospels: with a Selection of Prayers and Meditations*. Edited by Evelyn M. Simpson. Berkeley, Calif.; University of California Press, 1963. Reprinted, 2003.

———. *Paradoxes and Problems*. Edited by Helen Peters. Oxford: Oxford University Press, 1980.

———. The *Divine Poems*. Edited by Helen Gardner. Oxford and New York: Oxford University Press, 2000.

———. *The Sermons of John Donne*. 10 volumes. Edited by George R. Potter and Evelyn M. Simpson. Berkeley and Los Angeles: The University of California Press, 1953–1962.

———. *The Variorum Edition of the Poetry of John Donne*. Edited by Gary A. Stringer. Bloomington, Ind.: University of Indiana Press, 1995–ca. 2003.

Don Quixote de la Mancha Miguel de Cervantes Saavedra (Part I, 1605; Part II, 1615)

Impoverished and nearing the end of the sixth decade of a hard and often disappointing life and of a sporadic and usually disappointing literary career, MIGUEL DE CERVANTES scored a minor victory. He managed to persuade a printer, Juan de la Cuesta and a bookseller publisher, Francisco de Robles, to offer for sale a shoddily printed volume, *The Ingenious Gentleman Don Quixote de la Mancha*. Certainly one of the most original novels ever written, *Don Quixote* has also proved to be the most enduring. Of all the books ever published in any Western European language, it has been more often translated and has appeared in more editions than any work other than the Bible.

The novel concerns a Spanish country gentleman named Quejana who owns a library filled with CHIVALRIC ROMANCES and volumes of poetry. The romances, with their stories of knights and battles and their conventions of questing, of defending the innocent, and of rescuing and wooing distressed maidens have so addled Signor Quejana's brain that he convinces himself he too has a chivalric mission. Like Roland, Lancelot, Amadis de Gaul, and numerous other heroes of a fiction Quejana takes for history, he will himself ride forth as Don Quixote to right wrongs, honor his lady, and—his central mission—restore the entire world to the Golden Age.

In the process of Don Quixote's effort to accomplish this impossible feat, Cervantes definitively exposes the nonsensical dimensions of the chivalric tradition and its codes. The book's introduction and its other apparatus parodies that which usually accompanied newly published work: It includes mock poems of praise and dedications. Cervantes also punctuates the text of Book I with literary digressions of several sorts, including interspersed novellas and pastorals.

In his role as author, Cervantes pretends that in a market he has discovered his history of Don Quixote written in Arabic by Cid Hamete Benengeli in some notebooks and on some scraps of paper. Cervantes pretends that he hires a Moorish Castillian to translate the work, and Cervantes's retelling is based faithfully on that translation.

Don Quixote is the first novel of the Western prose tradition to reflect in fiction the psychological growth and change that persons experience in real life. Before Cervantes, prose writers had offered their readers stereotyped characters. Even GIOVANNI BOCCACCIO in his *Decameron* presents recognizable types—the profligate priest, the gullible villager, the generous lover. Cervantes's major characters, however, Don Quixote and the shrewd peasant turned squire, Sancho Panza, develop and change as they live and confront their inward and outward experiences.

On Don Quixote's first adventure, he rides forth in a suit of old armor with a homemade, partly pasteboard helmet and visor on an old, withered, bag-of-bones horse he named Rocinante. Arriving at an inn, he has himself dubbed a knight. In the same inn several adventures occur at various times. Don Quixote fights with mule drivers, and he slashes a number of wine bags while dreaming he fights a giant. On the road as a knight errant, he frees a number of felons on their way to becoming galley slaves, and he parodies Christ's temptation in the desert.

Don Quixote's fantasy becomes his reality. If the evidence of his own senses or of Sancho Panza's advice tells him his fantasies are untrue, the Knight of the Mournful Countenance, as the Don calls himself, attributes the differences between objective reality and his perceptions to the work of magicians. He fights with windmills thinking they are giants. He commandeers a barber's basin, convinced it is the upper portion of an enchanted helmet. Yet all the while, though sometimes impatient with his squire's chattiness, he is considerate of Sancho Panza, and the reader watches genuine affection grow between the two main characters. Sancho sometimes displays shrewd judgment and insight. On other occasions he participates in Don Quixote's delusions—especially when he thinks about the island Don Quixote has promised to give him when the Don becomes a king or an emperor.

In La Mancha the local curate and the village barber together with Signor Quejana's relations and servants despair over the elderly gentleman's madness and conceive elaborate but unsuccessful ruses to distract him from his pursuit of knight errantry. Hoping to keep him at home and to cure him, they destroy the books that obsess him. As they select books for destruction, they conduct a literary–critical review of chivalric letters and pastoral poetry. Among the few works they spare from the flames are ALONSO DE ERCILLA Y ZÚÑIGA's *Araucana,* Juan Gutierrez Rufo's *Austriada,* and Cristóbal de Virues's *Montserrate*—two historical epics and a didactic poem.

A similar critical discussion takes place in chapter 68 near the end of Book I. There the curate and a canon of the church discuss the Spanish theater. They regret the decline of poetic tragedy from a standard set by several good examples. These include Cervantes's own *Numantia.* The conversation then turns to comedy and religious drama, which the clergymen agree have also fallen from their former glory. Playwrights, they conclude, pander to the tastes of the actors who pay them, and actors' tastes are flawed. To remedy the situation, they propose enlightened state censorship to protect the public interest and the quality of Spanish theater. These views may be those of Cervantes, though some have thought he merely imitated PLATO's *Republic.* After Sancho Panza attempts to explain to his wife what he has been doing, Part I ends with a series of epitaphs and sonnets that parody serious ones and were meant to amuse Cervantes's readers.

In the years that intervened between Cervantes's own Parts I and II of *Don Quixote,* someone writing under the pseudonym Alonzo Fernandez de Avellaneda penned a spurious second part that stole some of Cervantes's planned material. This work appeared in 1614. In it the writer heaped personal insults upon Cervantes. When the real Part II appeared in 1615, a furious Cervantes replied in kind in his introduction. The fake is also exposed in Part II's text in chapters 57 and following. Cervantes discovered the fraud after writing the first 56 and before he wrote the introduction.

Although in the English-speaking world Part I is better known, Part II is generally acknowledged to be the better book. More tightly plotted without the asides of Book I, more philosophical in the way it addresses questions about the subjective nature of reality, and more successful in the development of character, Part II of *Don Quixote* reveals a Cervantes who has at last fully developed his creative powers. In Part II, Don Quixote and Sancho become aware that a book has been written about them (and eventually that a literary fraud has been perpetrated upon them). Knight and squire discover that Part I is wildly popular and also that their fame precedes them. The discussion that follows gives Cervantes an opportunity to conduct a critical evaluation of Part I.

In Part II, as a result of Sancho Panza's clever trickery, Don Quixote finally comes face to face with a woman he believes to be the lady he serves, Doña Dulcinea del Toboso. In fact he finds himself in the presence of a peasant girl who thinks he is making fun of her, but Sancho convinces him that she is indeed his lady, changed by an enchanter into the shape that Don Quixote sees. In the second book as well, as a result of a series of accidents, Don Quixote actually wins a fight with the Knight of the Wood, who is really his friend Sansón Carrasco in disguise. Certain that he will be able to best Don Quixote in a joust, Carrasco is part of a plot by Signor Quejana's friends to make the madman stay at home for two years in hope of curing him.

By including the fame of Part I in Part II, Cervantes makes Sancho and Don Quixote welcome to a duke and his duchess. She has read Part I, recognizes the don and his squire, and she and her husband conspire with their servants to make Sancho and Don Quixote think Sancho really is the governor of the island of Barataria. Don Quixote gives Sancho a great deal of good advice, but Sancho's own peasant shrewdness and common sense provide the grounds upon which he is able to settle suits wisely and equitably.

After a number of other adventures, Don Quixote at last returns home and regains his sanity. In his right mind now and calling himself Alonso Quijano the Good (a change from Part I), he makes his will and dies. Having killed off one of the most memorable and fully realized characters in the history of fiction, Cervantes in the guise of Cid Hamete Benengeli ended the book with an ostensible address to the Cid's pen. In it he chastises the pretender who wrote the spurious continuation of his novel. He also warns other pretenders against resurrecting Don Quixote. "For me alone Don Quixote was born," he says, "and I for him." The world continues to delight in the outcome of both births.

Bibliography

Cervantes Saavedra, Miguel de. *Don Quijote de la Mancha*. Edited in Spanish by Francisco Rico et al. Barcelona: Critica, ca. 2001.

———. *Don Quixote*. Translated by Walter Starkie. New York: Signet Classic, 2001.

———. *Don Quixote de la Mancha*. Translated by Charles Jarvis. Oxford and New York: Oxford University Press, 1999.

drama

Drama can describe virtually any kind of performance—acted or not. Ordinarily, though, the term applies to a play written for performance by actors who impersonate the play's characters before an audience. The Renaissance was a particularly fruitful period for European drama. First, the period saw the survival and continued development of religious dramatic forms that had been introduced during the Middle Ages:—MIRACLE AND MORALITY PLAYS in England and France, *SACRE RAPPRESENTAZIONI* (sacred plays) in Italy, and *AUTOS SACRAMENTALES* (sacramental shows) in Spain. Second, the period witnessed the introduction of humanist elements into such older forms as INTERLUDES—brief plays written for performance between the courses of banquets—and the rapid development of a more secular theater.

In Italy PASTORAL DRAMA and the COMMEDIA DELL'ARTE (the comedy of the guild) developed. These latter dramas, in part written down but mostly improvised by the professionals of the theatrical guild, employed STOCK CHARACTERS represented by players in masks and costumes traditionally associated with the actors' roles. Whereas in Italy and elsewhere, pastoral plays—peopled by nymphs, shepherds, nature spirits, and demigods of the ancient Greek countryside—enjoyed public performance, in England they were sometimes written for private performance as CLOSET DRAMA.

Italian opera also originated during the 16th century and early on represented such classical and pastoral history and myths as the coronation of the Roman Empress, Poppaea, the wife of Nero, or like the story of Daphne (which was the subject of the very first Italian opera by Ottavio Rinuccini in 1594).

The principal driving force behind the flowering of European Renaissance drama was surely the continued survival of a few and the rediscovery of many of the classical dramas of ancient Greece and Rome. These provided models both for COMEDY and TRAGEDY that European playwrights in various countries and languages emulated closely. Also, in many cases, the writers combined with the newly rediscovered classical models elements of their earlier national drama to produce flourishing theater all over Europe. England, France, and Spain all produced especially rich theatrical traditions by combining the elements mentioned above with stunning innovations in stagecraft. The rise of commercial theater for the masses and the popularity of spectacular COURT ENTERTAINMENTS for the aristocracy added impetus to this remarkable spurt of theatrical development.

Elsewhere the era from 1500 to 1700 also saw dramatic innovation. In India the tradition of dramatic performance is also ancient, deep, and rich. It does not, however, include tragedy. Otherwise it parallels to a considerable degree the drama of Europe. Indian drama is religious in origin and maintains that connection throughout its long history. As a result, the characters of Indian drama tended to be drawn from gods whose stories the ancient great epics recounted or from a somewhat later tradition involving human stock characters—like a rascal, or like a stage manager. In the Assamese language in the 16th century however, the playwright, poet, painter, and musician SANKARADEVA (d. 1568) pioneered the still enthusiastically performed *Ankia Nat* drama. This involves a series of one-act musical plays in which actors in enormous masks represent gods, goddesses and animals as they depict the legend of the god Krishna.

In Middle Eastern languages, the Arabic and Turkish shadow puppet comedy called *KARAGÖZ* also appeared and flourished at this time, and in 1550 the Jewish poet LEONI DE SOMMI; wrote the first extant Hebrew drama: A comedy of betrothal (*Is zahut bedi-huta de-kiddushin*).

In sub-Saharan Africa, records of literary documents do not begin until the 18th century. In tribal areas village storytellers still sing creation myths of indeterminate age. Their performances hint at the existence of similar ones during the 16th and 17th centuries. Given the rich oral culture of Africa, once records do begin to appear, we can confidently suppose that the roots of the dramatic performances the records describe penetrate into our period and before. Nowadays professional storytellers called griots still perform in the English language an EPIC of old Mali: *Sundiata*.

In the New World, the zeal of missionary priests consigned to the flames as diabolical writings many Central American hieroglyphic manuscripts that might have told us something about dramatic performance among the indigenous peoples before European contact. We do, nevertheless, have hints that suggest the performance by shamans of poems and dances in which many persons participated. One such fragmentary remnant, *The Deadly Dance*, recounts the mass suicide of the Toltecs led by a shaman who danced, sang, and recited verse.

Among the Inca of Peru, a rich tradition of dramatic performance centered on a long cycle of Quechua-language kingship dramas based on the reigns of Inca monarchs. Some information about them was recorded in a unique system of knotted string writing called *quipu*. A few of their texts were recorded after European contact, like THE PLAY OF OLLANTAY, and others survived in the memories of their actors. On the murder by the Spanish of the Incan ruler Atawallpa in the 16th century, a new tragedy was added to the cycle that continues to be performed in the Andean highlands to this day.

In the Far East, dramatic performance enjoys a tradition thousands of years old. By the time of the European Renaissance, Chinese operatic drama had developed many expectations that governed both its composition and performance. In the 16th century, however, an extremely creative innovator broke free from the earlier rules. TANG XIANZU (1550–1617) charmed the most conservative critics and enchanted audiences with the novelty of his panoramic comedy, *The PEONY PAVILLION*—a tour de force of 56 scenes that forever changed the face of subsequent dramatic and operatic writing in China.

Human beings, it seems, feel a universal impulse to represent someone else either for the entertainment or for the religious instruction of an audience, or to characterize, invoke, or invite their gods.

Bibliography

Allied Arts in India. "Theatre Form Using Masks." Available online. URL: http://www.puppetindia. com/misc.htm. Downloaded on June 5, 2003.

Barnstone, Willis, and Tony Barnstone. *Literatures of Asia, Africa, and Latin America.* Upper Saddle River, N.J.: Prentice Hall, 1999.

Boone, Elizabeth Hill. *Stories in Red and Black: Pictorial Histories of the Aztecs and Mixtecs.* Austin, Tex.: University of Texas Press, 2000.

Boone, Elizabeth Hill, and Walter D. Mingolo. *Writing without Words: Alternative Literacies in Mesoamrica and the Andes.* Durham, N.C.: Duke University Press, 1994.

Chai, Ch'u, and Winberg Chai. *A Treasury of Chinese Literature.* New York: Appleton-Century, 1965.

Sword of Truth. "The Immortal Land of Krishna—Assam." Available online. URL: http://www.sword-oftruth.com/swordoftruth/multimedia/krishnapr esentation/html/assampage. Downloaded on June 5, 2003.

dramatic monologue

This poetic form, which can also be presented as prose, seems to have had its origins in the Middle Ages but was developed by several Renaissance practitioners. As the name suggests, a single speaker addresses a hearer who is not present. The content of the monologue reveals to the audience something important—even unintended—about the psychological or emotional state of the person speaking. Though it may be performed on stage, a dramatic monologue typically relies on word pictures instead of scenery to paint the situation in the minds of the audience.

Stand-alone examples of the genre exist during the Renaissance, including *Sorcery, Eclogue 3* by the Italian poet ISABELLA ANDREINI, in which a jilted lover attempts witchcraft to regain the affections of the shepherd who abandoned her. More commonly the dramatic monologue appears as a soliloquy embedded in a play, like that of Hamlet when he considers whether or not the ghost he has seen can be trusted.

Dream of Nine Clouds, A

See KIM MAN-JUNG.

Dryden, John (1631–1700)

A towering literary figure of the 17th century, John Dryden is typically counted among British Restoration rather than among Renaissance writers. His prolific and influential work, however, continued to develop literary currents begun in the Renaissance proper. For example, he contributed both to the practice and the theory of neoclassical drama, and he translated both Roman and Greek writers into English.

The first of 14 children born to Erasmus Dryden and his wife Mary, John Dryden may have received his earliest schooling in the village of Tichmarsh. Later, as a king's scholar, he attended London's Westminster school, and from its master, Dr. Richard Busby, Dryden acquired an enviable mastery of both Latin and Greek.

Even before he entered King's College, Cambridge, at the age of 19, Dryden began his literary career with the publication of an ELEGY in a collection of verse commemorating the death of Henry, Lord Hastings (1649). After Dryden took his Cambridge B.A. in 1654, little is known of him until 1659. In that year, however, he contributed a slight collection of verses to a cooperative venture with EDMUND WALLER and Thomas Spratt. Dryden's verses, "Heroique Stanzas to the Glorious Memory of Cromwell," appeared with his colleagues' eulogies in *Three Poems upon the Death of his late Highness Oliver Lord Protector of England.* Though this work may well have been an opportunistic venture by three young poets trying to make their way, Dryden's contribution would become for him a continuing embarrassment. When he became the British poet laureate under King Charles II, his detractors never failed to point to his praise of the king's most hated enemy.

Fortunately, he also published a work in celebration of Charles II's return to England in 1660, *Astrea Redux* (Astrea returned). Astrea was the Roman goddess of justice who had lived on Earth during the golden age. Thus the work's title contained a high compliment to the restored monarch.

The year 1663 saw both the production in London's reopened theater of the first of Dryden's many successful plays, *The Wild Gallant,* and his marriage to Lady Elizabeth Howard. His next play dealt with the conquest of Mexico by Cortés and the conqueror's love for an Aztec princess. The play, *The Indian Emperor,* had its initial run cut short, however, by an outbreak in London of the bubonic plague. The Drydens packed up and moved to Wiltshire until the danger had passed. There Dryden made good use of his time by writing the work that firmly established his reputation, *Annus Mirabilis, The Year of Wonders* (1667). The year alluded to in the title was 1666—both the plague year and the year of the great fire of London. Whereas antiroyalist sympathizers viewed the plague and the fire as God's punishment for allowing the king to return, Dryden treated the disasters as the last ditch effort by the ghosts of the usurpers and their living allies to destabilize the monarchy. The wonders to which he alludes are the Londoners' "true loyalty, invincible Courage, and unshaken Constancy"—the qualities with which the citizenry confronted the disasters. More than any other work, *The Year of Wonders* led to Dryden's appointment as poet laureate. He was invested in that office in 1668 on the death of his predecessor, Sir William Davenant. At the same time Dryden was appointed to write plays exclusively for the Theatre Royal.

His plays appeared with punctual regularity. Among the 28 plays that he would eventually pen for the British stage, those written for the Theatre Royal included, *Secret Love* (1667); *Tyrannic Love* (1669); and *The Conquest of Grenada, Parts I and II,* which is the prime example of the new English "heroic play," and *Marriage à la mode* (1670–71). The destruction of the Theatre Royal by fire, however, interrupted Dryden's string of stage successes. It was not resumed until a new theater was constructed in Drury Lane. Then Dryden first capitalized on the public taste for Oriental subjects with the production of *Aureng–Zebe* (1675), a play about an East Indian potentate. Dryden wrote one more major play, *All for Love* (1677), before terminating his association with the Theatre Royal.

Beyond writing *Annus Mirabilis* during his plague-enforced exile from London, Dryden had also composed an *Essay on Dramatic Poesy.* In it he developed his theoretical views about drama and discussed in that context the thinking of other European theorists about drama and its relation to nature. The work takes the form of a discussion whose participants represent various viewpoints on such subjects as the relative merit of the ancient and the modern or of the English and the French theater. Dryden himself participates in the guise of Neander. While respecting the work of the ancients, Dryden champions the work of moderns as superior and thinks that, as compared with freer-wheeling British dramatists, the French mistake observing the neo-Aristotelian rules—such as the UNITIES of time, place, and action—as the end rather than the means of dramatic performance. In that context, Dryden defends the cause of TRAGICOMEDY and finds in the English theater the fullest development of the neo-classical theatrical tradition. Dryden later penned a similar discourse on heroic poetry.

The great English lexicographer Dr. Samuel Johnson considered Dryden among the world's greatest writers, one to whom English letters owed the perfecting of its poetic meter, the "refinement" of the English language, and the "correction" of the nation's "sentiments." With respect to English poetry, Johnson said that Dryden "found it brick and left it marble."

Dryden's skeptical and satirical frame of mind regularly appears in his prose writings and in his poetry. Dryden sharpened his satirical pen in his poem *MacFlecknoe,* a work in which he excoriates the vapid critic and dull comic playwright, Thomas Shadwell. Nowhere, however, does Dryden exercise his talent for SATIRE to greater effect that in his political poem *Absalom and Achitophel.* The earl of Shaftesbury, Anthony Ashley Cooper, had put political pressure on King Charles II to name his illegitimate, Protestant son, the duke of Monmouth, heir to the throne. Perceiving a parallel between that circumstance and the biblical situation between King David and his rebellious son Absalom, who yielded to Achitophel's encouragement to rebel against his father, Dryden exploits that likeness to wonderful satiric effect.

Dryden was also an uncommonly gifted and industrious translator. From Latin he translated into English verse all the writings of VIRGIL, all of Persius, and selections from OVID, LUCRETIUS, Juvenal, and Horace. From the Greek he translated a portion of Homer's *Iliad,* Plutarch's biography of Alexander the Great, and selections from Theocritus. From Italian and from Middle English he respectively translated and then included in his own *Fables* (1700) works from Boccaccio and Chaucer. Beyond this he did numerous prose translations as well.

Notable among Dryden's many other literary accomplishments we find two significant religious poems. The first is *Religio Laici* (The religion of laymen, 1682). Essentially an Anglican document, the poem defends Scripture as the sufficient source of religious authority. The second, *The Hind and the Panther,* Dryden wrote after his conversion to Roman Catholicism in 1687. In this poetic allegory, the Roman Catholic Church is presented as the peaceful Hind (a deer) and the Anglican Church as the bloodthirsty Panther. Yet the poem's message is more balanced and thoughtful than this brief characterization implies, and it recognizes the political excesses and failures of both congregations.

Shortly after the publication of his *Fables,* Dryden died on Mayday, 1700. Both his influence and his legacy are enormous. The body of his works in their standard edition runs to 20 substantial volumes.

Bibliography

Hooker, E. N., and H. T. Swedenberg, Jr., et al., eds. *The Works of John Dryden.* 20 volumes. Los Angeles, Calif.: The University of California Press, 1956–89.

Plutarch, *The Life of Alexander the Great.* Translated by John Dryden. Edited by Arthur Hugh Clough. New York: Modern Library, 2004.

Walker, Keith, ed. *John Dryden, The Major Works.* New York: Oxford University Press, 2003.

Wasserman, George R. *John Dryden.* New York: Twayne Publishers, 1964.

Duan Shuquing (ca. 1510–ca. 1600)

A Chinese writer of both CI and SHI poems, Duan Shuquing was the daughter of a Confucian scholar, teacher, and civil servant Duan Tingbi, who taught his child to read and write. She married another Confucian scholar, Rui Ru, and lived into her 90s.

While many of Duan Shuquing's poems have been lost, some that survive have been translated into English by Charles H. Egan from a collection called *Lü chuang shi gao* (Drafts of poetry from the green gauze window). These examples are brief poems inspired by the observation of natural events—rain on autumn leaves, the call of geese, moon rise, a cuckoo's song. They reflect the elegiac sadness such observations evoke in the poet.

Bibliography

Kang-i Sun Chang et al., eds. *Women Writers of Traditional China.* Stanford, Calif.: Stanford University Press, 1999, pp. 202–07.

Duchess of Malfi, The   John Webster   (1614)

Especially dark and brooding examples of TRAGEDY, *The Duchess of Malfi* and *THE WHITE DEVIL* justify WEBSTER's reputation as the inheritor of WILLIAM SHAKESPEARE's mantle as the premier Renaissance British tragedian.

Performed by the theatrical company, The King's Men, both at the Blackfriars' and GLOBE THEATERS, the action of the play is based on an episode of early 16th-century Italian history involving Giovanna Piccolomini, the dowager duchess of Amalfi, who secretly married her major domo and bore him three children. Eventually discovering their sister's secret, her brothers plotted revenge for her having married without their permission, without the political advantage that an arranged marriage would have assured, and at the cost of their potentially inheriting her fortune.

To avoid the brothers' vengeance, the duchess's husband Antonio was forced to flee with their eldest child. Hired assassins, however, eventually killed him. Giovanna was also captured with her two youngest children and disappeared. The Italian writers, Matheo Bandello and Giraldi Cinthio, and the Frenchman, François de Belleforest, retold the story with embellishments. The English translators William Painter and George Whetstone translated Belleforest and Cinthio, respectively, and Webster used Painter's version as his primary source, though he consulted some of the others as well. Whereas Bandello and others had construed the story as principally the tragedy of the husband, Webster instead perceives it as the tragedy of a nobly independent woman.

The Duchess of Malfi opens at the duchess's court with an exchange between Delio and his friend, Antonio of Bologna, the duchess's steward, who has recently returned from France. Also present on stage at various times during the first scene we find the duchess's brothers, one being Ferdinand, duke of Calabria, and the other being an unnamed cardinal of the Roman Catholic Church. Beyond them we meet Daniel de Bosola, whom the brothers recruit as a spy in their sister's household; Cariola, the duchess's maid and confidante; and others. The brothers wring a promise from their sister that she will never marry. She, however, has already resolved on marrying Antonio. She also intends to keep the marriage secret. Although Antonio loves the duchess, he does not aspire to marry her. Thus she is forced to do the wooing. After first taking Cariola into her confidence, she asks Antonio to marry her toward the end of the play's first scene. Although he feels unworthy, he accepts. Then the maid Cariola appears, and in her presence the pair exchange their wedding vows according to a valid procedure called *per verba presenti*. By this means couples without recourse to priests can conduct their own weddings in the presence of a witness.

Though the pair is able for a time to keep their union secret, the duchess's pregnancies eventually give them away. Initially, Antonio is not suspected as the father of the duchess's children. Accused of debauchery by her brother, however, the duchess reveals that she is married, and Bosola is able to ferret out the identity of her husband. Maddened by his sister's actions, Ferdinand first presents her with a dead man's hand and tells her that her husband and two of her children are dead. Then he has Bosola bring in assassins who strangle her, the two children who are with her, and the maid Cariola. Overcome with grief and guilt at having arranged the murder of his twin sister, Ferdinand goes mad and thinks he is a wolf. He also refuses to pay Bosola the promised reward for his services.

Bosola's character is both the most fully developed and the most perplexing in the play. He is a brave and honest man who is at first blinded by his allegiance to the twisted Duke Ferdinand. In a debased parody of the duchess's proposal in the first act, in the fourth the cardinal's mistress, Julia, declares her love for Bosola. The cardinal interrupts them, confesses his complicity in the duchess's murder, and poisons Julia by having her kiss an envenomed book.

Eventually Bosola's pity for the murdered duchess leads him to swear to protect Antonio and the surviving eldest son from the plots of Duke Ferdinand and the cardinal. Ironically, Bosola accidentally kills Antonio. He then murders the cardinal. The crazed Ferdinand gives Bosola his death wound, but before he dies, Bosola kills Ferdinand as well. The only survivor of the tragic affair is the eldest child of the duchess and Antonio. At the play's end Delio sets about securing the dukedom of Amalfi for the duchess's only surviving child.

Bibliography

Webster, John. *The Duchess of Malfi: John Webster.* Edited by Dympna Callaghan. New York: St. Martin's Press, 2000.

Du Fail, Noël (Leon Ladulfi)
(ca. 1520–1591)

Under his pen name—an anagram of his own—Du Fail contributed a number of short stories, essays, and memoirs to a body of narrative prose considered among the best France had to offer during the Renaissance. Both a lawyer and a member of the French landed aristocracy, Du Fail preferred to conceal his identity when he published. His first and most notable literary work, Country conversations (*Propos Rustiques*), appeared in 1547. It presents ironically humorous social criticism in the guise of a series of dialogues conducted by rural villagers. The influence of the work of both GIOVANNI BOCCACCIO and of FRANÇOIS RABELAIS appears in Du Fail's deft and original handling of his material. Similar purposes and methods appear in his Idle stories (*Baliverneries,* 1548).

Though he continues as a social critic, his objectives become more directly historical, autobiographical, and didactic in his Memoirs . . . of the judgments of the Parliament of Brittany (*Memoires . . . des arrests du Parlement de Bretagne*, 1579) where the stylistic influence of MICHEL DE MONTAIGNE becomes more observable.

In his final work, Stories and conversations of Eutrapel (*Contes et discours d'Eutrapel*, 1585), Du Fail achieves a synthesis of his earlier episodic style, his mastery of anecdote and dialogue, and the personal essay to offer a commentary on his society, give advice, and assign responsibility for failures.

Du Guillet, Pernette (ca. 1520–1545)

A disciple of the French poet MAURICE SCÈVE (1501–1562), Pernette Du Guillet, a native of Lyon, was among the earliest Frenchwomen to write lyric verses in the PETRARCHIST tradition. Her contemporaries admired Du Guillet's poems, composed while she was very young, and although they have not yet been translated into English, they remain available in French in modern editions.

Du Guillet met Maurice Scève when she was only 16 years old. From that time they maintained an intensely affectionate relationship. Their mutual affection—whose sometimes passionate expression may have been confined exclusively to the literary realm—appears in both their works. Indeed, Du Guillet is the model for the fictive Délie—the lady of Scève's huge sequence of 10-line poems by the same name. Whereas Scève's treatment of his love for Du Guillet is characterized at times by sexual fantasy and jealousy of her husband, her love for him is an unwaveringly pure PLATONIC LOVE that has led her to spiritual and intellectual heights.

After Du Guillet's untimely death in a plague year, her husband Antoine Du Moulin arranged for the publication of her works: *Rymes de gentile et vertueuse Dame, D. Pernette du Guillet, Lyonnoise* (Rhymes of a gentle and virtuous lady, madam Pernette du Guillet of Lyon). The work appeared before the end of the year she died. It contains five ELEGIES, 60 EPIGRAMS, 10 ODES, and two letters.

The little we know about her life comes from her husband's preface to the 1545 edition of her work. She was competent in several Romance languages, including the Italian of Tuscany, the Spanish of Castile, and classical Latin. She also had mastered music and played, among other instruments, the lute and the harpsichord, and some of her lyrics were set to music in her own time.

Bibliography

Du Guillet, Pernette. *Poésies* [Poems]. Geneva: Slatkine Reprint, 1970.

———. *Rymes*. Geneva: Droz, 1968.

Hollier, Denis, ed. *A New History of French Literature.* Cambridge, Mass.: Harvard University Press, 1989.

Dyer, Sir Edward (1543–1607)

Although Dyer's reputation as a poet was widespread in his own time, not much of his work has survived. He was a member of the celebrated literary circle surrounding MARY SIDNEY HERBERT, COUNTESS OF PEMBROKE and was a friend both of her brother, SIR PHILIP SIDNEY and of poet FULK GREVILLE.

His best known surviving poem, *My Mind to me a Kingdom is,* gained popularity as a song performed in BEN JONSON's play *Every Man Out of His Humor* (Act I, Scene ii, ll. 11–14). It was also widely circulated as a BROADSIDE BALLAD—perhaps with an otherwise unknown stanza, and a version of it appeared in William Byrd's collection, *Psalms, Sonnets, and Songs* (1588). Another longer version appears in the Bodleian Library's manuscript of *The Countess of Pembroke's Arcadia* (Rawlinson Poetry MS. 85, 1598). It is this latter version that has usually been reprinted.

The poem reflects a contented man who seeks neither wealth nor fame, who enjoys a perfectly clear conscience, and who avoids worldly care as much as possible. Perhaps the disappearance of Dyer's other verse results from his satisfaction with a quiet life away from the public eye.

Bibliography

Clark, Andrew, ed. *The Shirburn Ballads, 1585–1616.* Oxford: Clarendon Press, 1907.

Dyer, Edward, Sir. *My Mind to Me a Kingdom Is.* Berkeley Heights, N.J.: Oriole Press, 1960.

Earle, John (ca. 1601–1665)

Educated in theology at Oxford, John Earle became the tutor to Charles, prince of Wales, before the exile of the royal family during the INTERREGNUM (1642–60). In 1642 Earle accompanied the royal family to France as chaplain to the prince, who in 1660 became King Charles II. Late in life, Earle rose through the Anglican hierarchy, becoming bishop of Worcester in 1662 and Salisbury in 1663.

He made an originally anonymous contribution to the English prose genre of CHARACTER WRITING with a collection of essays, *Microcosmography* (1628–29). The work found a ready audience and went through several editions with additional essays appearing in the later ones. Earle's witty SATIRE appears in his epigrammatic characterizations of the sorts of persons he especially disapproves. He defines a "Discontented Man" for instance, as "one that is fallen out with the world, and will be revenged upon himself . . . at last [falling] into that deadly melancholy to be a bitter hater of men." For characters whose foibles are often the object of demeaning humor but whose graces redeem them, however, Earle has a gentler touch. We see this illustrated in his character of "A Downright Scholar." The scholar's only fault, says Earle, "is that his mind is too much taken up with his mind." In explaining why the scholar is the butt of the fashionable world's sarcasm, Earle smiles at the scholar's peculiarities while turning the edge of his satire against the fashionable world itself.

Among the several essayists who contributed to writing characters, Earle's prose is the most nuanced and sophisticated.

Bibliography

Earle, John. *Microcosmography: A Piece of the World Discovered in Essays and Characters.* Edited by Harrold Osborne. St. Clair Shores, Mich.: Scholarly Press, 1978.

Earlier Seven Masters (*Quian Quizi*)

A group of Chinese writers of the early 16th century, the earlier seven masters (also called the seven scholars of an earlier period) united in their criticism of the work of a predecessor, LI DONGYANG (1447–1516). Their objection to Li Dongyang's writing and to the practices it represented rested upon their demand for important content as well as for beautiful language. Though Li Dongyang's writing looked to the same models the seven favored—the poets of the Tang dynasty (700–1000 C.E.)—the seven earlier masters thought the theories Li drew from the Tang poets emphasized style with little substantial content. They called for a return to the meatier example of the great authors of the Tang dynasty (700–1000), especially Du Fu (712–770). Du Fu had expressed in memorable language his deep concern with the sociopolitical problems of his time and had become revered by the Chinese as the saint of poetry (*shi sheng*).

The leaders of the earlier seven masters were Li Mengyang (1472–1530) and Ho Chingming (1483–1521). Other members included Kang Hai (1475–1540), and Wang Jiusi (1468–1551), who were notable authors of zazu—a sort of comedy. The last two authors named were responsible for spreading the notion of a group of masters. It appears that, though the members of the group did share common ideas, they had not ever been active together as a coterie. The poetry by the group's members was itself later criticized in turn for returning to language so archaic that people had trouble understanding it.

Bibliography

Idema, Wilt, and Lloyd Haft. *A Guide to Chinese Literature.* Ann Arbor, Mich.: Center for Chinese Studies, The University of Michigan, 1997.

Mair, Victor H., ed. *The Columbia History of Chinese Literature.* New York: Columbia University Press, 2001.

eclogue

The Renaissance eclogue reintroduced into European languages an ancient, classical genre of poem written by such poets as Virgil in 37 B.C.E., and by Theocritus (third century B.C.E.). Usually dramatic in content, the eclogue often contained a verse dialogue that concerned itself with rural matters. The 16th century in Italy saw the eclogue handled by such poets as Matteo Maria Boiardo and Isabella Andreini. In England, Edmund Spenser's *Shepherd's Calendar* is an example of the genre.

As the pastoral mode developed to include full-length drama and as pastoral romance became popular, the term *eclogue* came to allude principally to the verse form in which a work was cast. The term became separated from its originally rural subject matter.

Throughout the latter part of the Renaissance the name *eclogue* applied mainly to poems containing persons speaking a soliloquy or a dialogue that provided the main interest in the poem. Action rarely figured to any important degree. Rather, the sentiments expressed in the monologue or dialogue gave the eclogue its focus. Eventually, the form departed from its rustic roots and was set in urban landscapes.

education in Europe

In Renaissance Europe, new theories and methods of education began to emerge as a salient feature of the renewed interest in classical literature. In 1350 in Italy Petrarch had discovered a portion of Quintilian's *Oratorical Institute* (*Institutio oratoria*), and humanist Poggio Bracciolini found the rest in 1416. The *Institute* contained a program of education focused on turning male children into morally admirable adults who, because they were excellent orators, could fulfill their civic responsibilities. Quintilian proposed home schooling at the elementary level and counseled methods of instruction that capitalized on the natural interests of children, recognized their individual differences both in ability and in predisposition for certain subjects, and also considered children's psychological makeup. He also proposed what contemporary educational theorists, who regularly update him by renaming his concepts, would call "successive approximations to mastery"—a step-by-step approach. He also proposed rewarding the children as they succeeded in mastering new material—positive reinforcement. As compared with the practices of priests and monks in the earlier cathedral schools, Quintilian also proposed a wider-ranging curriculum. In contrast to them, he recommended against corporal and psychological punishment.

Spurred by the discovery of Quintilian's work and that of other classical educators, humanist writers began to suggest modern versions of portions of the liberal arts curriculum. Pier Paolo Vergerio (1370–1444), Leonardo Bruni (1370–1444) and others contributed to the discussion. Vittorino da Feltre (1378–1446) founded a celebrated boarding school at Mantua. There he combined a firm grounding in Greek, Latin, and the humanities with physical education and Christian religious instruction. He intended to achieve a sound mind and a stalwart Christian character in a strong and healthy body. (He did not emphasize such practical matters as mathematics and the sciences, perhaps because gentlemen left such matters to the hired help.) The boys who studied such a curriculum in Italy were destined to occupy important positions in their societies, and the ability to talk cogently and argue persuasively was an important object of their education. The study of literary and historical texts in their native (classical Latin and Greek) languages with generous portions of memorization thrown in and the construction of COMMONPLACE BOOKS as an aid to learning all received heavy stress.

Along with the humanist impulse itself, the interest in new methods of education and new curricula fanned out across continental Europe and the British Isles. In England, humanist education began at Christ Church in Canterbury and soon spread to London where John Colet instituted a school at St. Paul's Cathedral around 1505. Colet's friendship with ERASMUS of Rotterdam influenced both the curriculum and the texts used in that school and in the household of Sir THOMAS MORE. A humanist school was also established at the royal court where Henry VII and Henry VIII's children and those of noble families received their early training. Both ROGER ASCHAM and THOMAS ELYOT taught the humanist curriculum and wrote important treatises on the subject of education.

Late in the 15th century Queen Isabella of Castile patronized two humanist schools at the royal court, and humanists began to tutor aristocratic children. Within a century in Spain, by Richard Kagan's estimate, almost every community of more than 500 residents had a humanist Latin school. As Spain went, so went Portugal.

Early in the 16th century, the French began to adopt—and to adapt—the humanist curriculum. As in Spain, the incentive to do so came from the top. King FRANCIS I (1494–1547) encouraged civic leaders in their efforts to establish classical grammar schools in their towns and cities. The French combined the humanist models of Italy with ear-

lier Christian and scholastic models. The latter drew bitter satire from FRANÇOIS RABELAIS. The French university version of the Latin curriculum notably included the NEO-LATIN works of Italian humanist LORENZO VALLA among the examples of the middle echelons of good Latin compositional style that students mastered.

Similar schools and curricula developed in Germany, mainly in monasteries at first. In Germany and the Netherlands, the curriculum was carefully organized by grade and by subject. The fact that the printing press had made its first appearance in Germany and that its use there early became widespread increased the supply of affordable texts to German schools.

Jesuit schools became a pan-European phenomenon. The Jesuits synthesized humanist education based on Quintilian with the dialectic method of the University of Paris and with their own experience as educators. In addition to adding practical sciences to their curriculum, they also stressed the spiritual development of their charges and tempered those elements of humanist education that some viewed as counter to the church's teaching. By the year 1600, Jo Ann Hoeppner and Moran Cruz tell us, 236 Jesuit colleges operated around the world—including the New World and Japan. One of the most attractive features of Jesuit education arose from there being no tuition. The Jesuits taught as a part of their charitable mission.

The saturation of Europe with new schools created a Latin culture in which almost all educated European men above the artisan class participated. It created a common Continental, masculine culture. A number of women, particularly upper-class women, also gained access to the new curricula. Sometimes they were privately tutored or homeschooled. Several treatises encouraged the education of women. Among these was one by Erasmus, *The Abbot and the Learned Lady,* 1524. In Italy, such women as Cassandra Fedele (1465–1558) and Is-ABELLA ANDREINI (1562–1604) participated in humanist discourse. Those who, like the Venetian MODERATA FONTE (1555–1592), had been forced to scrabble an education together argued convincingly for expanded educational opportunities for women.

A similar pattern developed throughout the other countries of Europe. Education for women beyond primary school, where they could and did become literate, however, was the exception rather than the rule throughout the European Renaissance.

In addition to being the subject of formal treatises, education also received treatment in the imaginative literature of the period. A notable example occurs in FRANÇOIS RABELAIS's discussion in his *Gargantua* of the Abbey of Thélème, in which men and women study a humanist curriculum together and where the motto is "do what you please."

See also AGRICOLA, RUDOLPHUS; ERASMUS, DESIDERIUS.

Bibliography

Moran Cruz, Jo Ann Hoeppner. "Education." Vol. 2, *Encyclopedia of the Renaissance.* Edited by Paul F. Grendler. New York: Scribners, 1998.

Rabil, Albert, ed. *Renaissance Humanism: Foundations, Forms, and Legacy.* Volume 3. Philadelphia: University of Pennsylvania Press, 1988.

Simon, Joan. *Education and Society in Tudor England.* Cambridge, U.K.: Cambridge University Press, 1979.

Warnicke, Retha M. *Women of the English Renaissance and Reformation.* Westport, Conn.: Greenwood Press, 1983.

Woodward, William Harrison. *Studies in Education During the Age of the Renaissance, 1400–1600.* 1906. Cambridge, U.K.: Cambridge University Press, 1967.

Eknath (1533–1599)

Born in the town of Paithan in the state of Maharashtra, India, Eknath was a poet saint who composed in the Marathi language. Orphaned as an infant, he was brought up by his grandparents. Deeply religious from an early age, Eknath became a disciple of Janardan Swami with whom he studied for a number of years before going on pilgrimage and returning to his native village.

There he lived as a social reformer, rejecting all caste distinctions. For Eknath poetry was a means to bring the masses to a religious revival. He succeeded in doing this, revivifying the Maharastran Bhagawat cult. Contributing to this success was his collection of poetic aphorisms, the *Eknathi Bhagavata* (Songbook of Eknath). In this work he develops new interpretations of the relationships among people, the universe, and deity. He sought out literary forms to influence the masses, retelling the old epics and stories of India in modern forms that addressed the social and religious issues of his day. Each word in a poem, he thought, should be a stepping-stone on the path to spiritual development. He was a master of the ABHANGA, composing more than 3,000 of these brief, religious verses. He also composed in a form called the *gowlan* (milkmaids' songs). This sort of poem was associated with the famous stories of the milkmaids, or *gopis,* who fell in love with the Hindu deity Krishna.

He composed epics like the *Bhavarta RAMAYANA,* which retold with contemporary emphasis the stories surrounding the deity Rama. Similarly, in 1571 he composed the inspirational story of the marriage of Rukmini to Krishna—an ALLEGORY for the union of religious fervor with God. He adapted folk dramas called *bharudas* to inspire good attitudes and behavior in people and to achieve social reforms. These were and continue to be great artistic and social successes and are still performed in both the Marathi and Hindi languages.

Many of Eknath's minor works develop from older Sanskritic texts. As in his major works, however, he always reshapes that material with profound, new insights of his own. His greatest work, the *Eknathi Bagavatha,* has achieved the status of scripture among the devout Hindu population of India.

Bibliography

Macnicol, Nicol, trans. *The Psalms of the Maratha Saints: One Hundred and Eight Hymns Translated from the Marathi.* Calcutta: Association Press; London and New York: Oxford University Press, 1920.

elegy

An elegy is a poem that mourns a dead person or that expresses sorrow for the loss of happiness or for unreturned love. Originally a classical form defined by the Roman poet Propertius, the elegy was rediscovered by Renaissance poets. EDMUND

SPENSER's *Daphnaida* (1591) and JOHN MILTON's *LYCIDAS* (1637), which mourns the drowning of his promising young friend, Edward King, both provide examples of the form in English. In Italy, IS-ABELLA ANDREINI's lament for the death of her friend Laura Guidiccioni Lucchesini also illustrates the genre. Andreini's friend Gabriel Chiabrera practiced the form as well. Elsewhere LUÍS VAZ DE CAMÕENS wrote elegies in Portuguese. Recently discovered by Donald W. Foster is an elegy probably written by WILLIAM SHAKESPEARE in 1611 on the death of Master William Peter.

"Elegy of the Great Inca Atawallpa, The" (*Apu Inca Atawallpaman*)

Spoken by more than 10 million persons in the Andes region today, the Quechua language was spoken in several dialects by the Incan people at the moment of contact with the European invaders. (See also ALTERNATE LITERACIES.) The Incan emperor, Atawallpa, received the Spanish courteously. They, however, kidnapped and imprisoned him and extorted enormous sums of gold and other valuables, ostensibly as ransom. The Incas met the invaders' demands, but the Spanish nonetheless executed Atawallpa with a garrote.

Incan literature already had a rich tradition of drama and poetry and a unique system of writing, at least to keep records, with knotted string (*quipu*). That literary tradition included a cycle of dramas—still performed today—that were based on the reigns of Incan rulers. To that cycle was added the tragedy of Atawallpa. Among the literary productions in the wake of Atawallpa's murder, someone wrote an elegy that told his story and mourned his loss. Two notable American poets have undertaken to provide English readers with a taste of the Incan poetic tradition. M. S. Merwin has translated this elegy into English verse, and Mark Strand has provided other examples of poems written in the Quechua language.

Bibliography

18 Poems from the Quechua. Translated by Mark Strand. Cambridge, Mass.: H. Ferguson, 1971.

Merwin, W. S. *Selected Translations: 1948–1968*. New York: Atheneum, 1968.

Elizabeth I of England (1533–1603)

Conceived out of wedlock by and born to Henry VIII and his second wife ANNE BOLEYN, Elizabeth received a careful, HUMANIST education with a Protestant emphasis. As a child and young woman, she mastered both ancient and modern languages, acquiring fluency in Latin, Greek, Italian, and French.

The volatile religious situation in England that her father's rejection of papal authority had initiated grew even more precarious with the 1553 accession to the throne of Elizabeth's elder half sister, the Roman Catholic Queen Mary, and with her reversal of Henry's religious policy. The queen's suspicions also required the Princess Elizabeth to pick her way carefully through a perilous young womanhood. After the younger Sir Thomas Wyatt and Henry Gray, the marquis of Dorset, rebelled in 1554, Mary and her advisers actively considered executing Elizabeth.

On Elizabeth's accession to the throne, she restored the English monarch to the role of head of the English church. Her attitude toward the peaceful practice of the religion of one's conscience, however, was generally tolerant until a group of her Roman Catholic nobles rebelled in 1569 and Pope Pius V excommunicated her. Thereafter her policies became more actively Protestant.

On the literary front Elizabeth I herself made some notable contributions to English letters. First, she displayed her mastery of languages by translating several works into English. Among these from the French she translated Marguerite de Navarre's *Mirror of the Sinful Soul*. She also translated DESIDERIUS ERASMUS's Latin work *Dialogue of Faith*. She has also been doubtfully credited with penning some skillful English poems. George Puttenham, the author of the 1589 work *The Art of English Poesy* assigned her the first place among the poets of her reign for "sense, sweetness, and subtility [sic]" in every category of lyric and heroic poetry. Although the work that he ascribes to her authorship has not otherwise been authenticated, if it is hers, flattery discounted, she really was a skillful poet. One poem that begins "When I was young and fair . . ." chronicles its speaker's regret at having rejected all suitors. Another, "The doubt of future foes" tells of the speaker's current political fears and predicts policies to be implemented when the political situation changes.

Some of Elizabeth's speeches and many of her letters deserve mention as examples of effective public rhetoric and the theater of politics. One example of each must suffice here. Her reproof written December 6, 1559, to five Roman Catholic bishops who complained that she was embracing "schisms and heresies" is a classic. She tells the prelates that "Romish pastors" led her realm and people astray. She retorts that the bishops "hit us and our subjects in the teeth" with the assertion that Rome first planted the Catholic faith in England, and she cites the legend that the pre-Roman Catholic Joseph of Arimathea first brought Christianity to Britain after he had donated his tomb to Christ. She concludes by reminding them of her clemency in not invoking the punishments she might—strongly hinting that she will punish if they continue to resist her will. In this brilliant letter, she mimics the hortatory style of the bishops themselves.

Equally effective was a speech she gave to hearten her troops at Tilbury before the expected invasion of the Spanish Armada. She appeared before them wearing armor, assuring them that, despite her womanhood she had "the heart and stomach of a king."

Elizabeth's principal contribution to literature during and after her reign, however, came not as a result of her writing but rather as a result of the veneration accorded her by the chief poets of her realm. EDMUND SPENSER adored her, addressing his national EPIC The Faerie Queene to her, and representing her in its pages in numerous allegorical guises. (See ALLEGORY.) She appears as Gloriana, the fairy queen herself, as Belphoebe, the virgin huntress, and in other representations as well. The publisher of the first printed version of SIR PHILIP SIDNEY's posthumously published Arcadia (1590) added material depicting Elizabeth as the queen of Corinth, Helen, for whose hand the knights of Iberia (Spain) and Corinth (England) contended by jousting.

The queen's public image was carefully cultivated. Elizabeth was England. Both she and England were great. The poets knew it, applauded it, and were inspired by it. So did the lesser writers of the time including those who penned COURT ENTERTAINMENTS the emerging journalists, and the sometimes-paid propagandists who scribbled BROADSIDE BALLADS. All contributed to the elevation and maintenance of Elizabeth's public image as the Virgin Queen whose consort was her realm.

Bibliography

Elizabeth I. Elizabeth I: Collected Works. Edited by Leah S. Marcus, Janel Mueller, and Mary Beth Rose. Chicago and London: The University of Chicago Press, 2000.

Levin, Carole. "The Heart and Stomach of a King." Elizabeth I and the Politics of Sex and Power. Philadelphia: University of Pennsylvania Press, 1994.

MacCaffrey, Wallace. Elizabeth I. New York: E. Arnold, 1993.

Elizabethan chronicles

Writers of English prose in the 16th and 17th centuries worked at crafting an idiom of expression that would make English prose as flexible an instrument as they thought classical Latin and Greek to have been. A part of this effort addressed the composition of history, or chronicles. While such chronicles often focused on historical events, like their medieval predecessors Renaissance chronicles had as their principal object the illustration of the workings of Divine Providence in history. Among the earliest of the 16th-century English chroniclers, Edward Hall (ca. 1499–1547) examined with a friendly eye the rise and triumph of the Tudor dynasty in his Union of the two Noble and Illustre Families of Lancaster and York (1542). His perception of history as unfolding God's purposes for the ruling house of England may have helped establish the point of view that WILLIAM SHAKESPEARE adopted in his history plays that treat the same subject.

In composing and editing his famous *Chronicles* (1577), RAPHAEL HOLINSHED (d. ca. 1580) made use of Hall's work and of SIR THOMAS MORE's (1478–1535) earlier written (1513–14) but later published (1577) *History of Richard III,* which More had written in Latin. The original design for Holinshed's *Chronicles* projected a "universal cosmography," but the scope of the actual publication narrowed appreciably to focus on the British Isles. Treating geographical as well as historical subjects, Holinshed's work included sections written by other hands. William Harrison provided the *Description of England.* He also translated from the Scottish dialect of John Bellenden a *Description of Scotland.* This geographical treatise Bellenden had in turn translated from Hector Boece's (ca. 1465–1536) Latin *History of Scotland* (1527). The second edition of Holinshed's *Chronicles* included Irish as well as English and Scottish history and is the version that Shakespeare read and used in connection with his history plays.

The courtier and voyager, Sir WALTER RALEIGH (1552–1618) set out to chronicle the entire history of the world. In 1614 he published what he had so far accomplished. He had reached the year 186 B.C.E. He left it at that.

Though the chroniclers were often motivated by patriotism and by a desire to discover the moral lessons that history could teach the rulers of a state, not all of them addressed such broad questions. Many focused on narrower but nonetheless important antiquarian issues. Archbishop Matthew Parker (1504–75) and his associate John Joscelyn founded the study of the Anglo-Saxon (Old English) language. They were motivated by a desire to prove the continuity of a native English church from pre-Roman Catholic times, and Parker's Latin work *Concerning the Antiquities of the British Church* may well have been the first privately printed book in England.

JOHN LELAND (ca. 1506–1552) understood that the Anglican closing of Roman Catholic monasteries would result in scattering the contents of their libraries and the likely loss of much material that existed only in manuscript. He accordingly began a difficult and arduous search for manuscripts composed by early British authors. This

search culminated in a Latin work whose title translates *Commentaries on British Writers.* To Leland, to his contemporary John Bale (1495–1563), and to his successor John Pits (1560–1616)—scholars who sought out and chronicled the unprinted work of early English writers—belongs the credit for the foundation of English literary scholarship.

John Stow (1525–1605), with the help of Archbishop Parker, edited several medieval English chronicles that had previously existed only in manuscript. In 1565 he published his *Summary of English Chronicles,* and in 1580 produced *The Chronicles of England.* His most important contribution to chronicling English history came in 1598 with his *A Survey of London and Westminster,* which detailed their history, their government, and their antiquities from the time of the Norman Conquest (1066) until his own day.

First a master and then headmaster of Westminster School, William Camden (1551–1623) published the most significant antiquarian chronicle of the English Renaissance. This work, *Britannia,* appeared first in Latin in 1586 and in English in 1610. It conducted a comprehensive topographical survey of the British Isles. Camden also contributed a collection of Old English historians (1603), and chronicled *The Annals of the Reign of Elizabeth to 1588.*

Bibliography

Camden, William. *Remains Concerning Britain.* Edited by R. D. Dunn. Toronto: The University of Toronto Press, ca. 1984.

Dillon, Janette, ed. *Performance and Spectacle in Hall's Chronicle.* London: The Society for Theatre Research, 2002.

Hall, Edward. *The Union of the two Noble and Illustre Families of Lancastre and Yorke.* London: Richard Grafton, 1550.

Holinshed, Raphael. *Holinshed's Chronicles—England, Scotland, and Ireland.* Edited by Vernon F. Snow. New York: AMS Press, ca. 1976.

More, Thomas. *The History of King Richard III and Selections from the English and Latin Poems.* Edited by Richard S. Sylvester. New Haven. Conn.: Yale University Press, 1976.

Raleigh, Walter. *Sir Walter Raleigh: Selections from his History of the World. . . .* Edited by G. E. Hadow. St. Claire Shores, Mich.: Scholarly Press, 1978.

Stow, John. *A Survey of London.* Edited by Henry Morley and Antonia Fraser. Phoenix Mill, U.K., and Dover, N.H.: A. Sutton, 1994.

Elizabethan fiction

English prose style developed in the 16th century in a number of subgenres that included religious tracts, pamphlets, essays, translations, and letters. All of these made their own eventual contributions to the soon-to-emerge English novel, but the most important legacies of all the prose contributors to the style of imaginative fiction was undoubtedly, first, a spirited and colloquial use of the spoken language. Second, by contrast, was the influence of some of the musical effects that JOHN LYLY achieved with the highly artificial style of his two-part work EUPHUES.

From the perspective of plot, some early 16th-century English fiction drew its inspiration from classical sources and from an Italian genre—the *novella,* or brief tale. These provided grist for the mills of such translators as William Painter who in 1566–67 published two volumes of stories gleaned not only from classical sources and directly from the Italians but also from their French translators. Painter's two volume *Palace of Pleasure* contributed to the development of Elizabethan short fiction by elaborating on the plots of his sources and by explicitly drawing forth the morals of the stories he told. Following suit, George Pettie borrowed Painter's title and seems to have noticed and liked the alliterative possibilities it contained since he entitled his collection of stories *A Petite Pallace of Pettie His Pleasure* (1576).

Between the two *Palaces,* however, came GEORGE GASCOIGNE's work, *THE ADVENTURES OF MASTER F. J.* (1573)—a work sometimes awarded the accolade of being the first real English novel despite its brevity and its inclusion as the only prose piece in a collection of poems. Ostensibly a rendition of an Italian romance about Ferdinando Jeronimi and Leonora de Valasco, the work may instead have autobiographical overtones that Gascoigne has transferred into an Italianate setting. It is a story of F. J.'s misplaced love for Leonora, the sister-in-law of Frances, a girl F. J. is supposed to be wooing. Leonora is a faithless wife who takes and discards lovers easily. F. J. becomes one of these discarded lovers. Too late he discovers that Frances has loved him. She dies of a broken heart. F. J. launches into a dissolute life in an effort to forget his troubles, and the fickle Leonora continues her games of love without suffering or disaster. The work is surprisingly amoral in an age that wished to see POETIC JUSTICE done.

Certainly the most self-conscious attempt to develop an artificial, literary language for the production of English prose fiction was that of John Lyly in his romance *Euphues.* The first part of the work, *Euphues, The Anatomie of Wit,* appeared in 1579. It was followed in 1580 by *Euphues and his England.* Despite the overwrought quality of Lyly's prose to modern taste, its novelty brought it a brief period of widespread popularity and several imitators. The style relies heavily on the repetition of consonant sounds, as in the phrase Painter's *Palace of Pleasure,* on farfetched comparisons, and on frequent contrasts between direct opposites. Despite its artificiality, its influence on the musical qualities of subsequent English prose style proved both deep and lasting.

SIR PHILIP SIDNEY's less elaborately wrought *THE COUNTESS OF PEMBROKE'S ARCADIA,* a PASTORAL romance originally written for private reading aloud to a circle of family and friends, circulated first in manuscript about 1580 and in a revised printed edition in 1584. Both versions provided models of polished prose less artificial than Lyly's.

THOMAS LODGE imitated Lyly's style in a more palatable manner but with less success in romances whose plots derived from such Grecian stories as his *Rosalind* (1590). Another who rode the crest of the brief popularity of the Euphuistic style was ROBERT GREENE, perhaps England's first writer to make a living with his pen. Both his *Mamillia* (1580) and his *Gwydonius, The Carde of Fancie*

(1584) emulated Lyly's prose style. When the style went out of fashion, however, Greene quickly moderated his use of it, modeling his style on Sidney's more straightforward prose, as one sees in Greene's *Pandosto* (1588) and his *Menaphon* (1589).

In 1594 a stylistically unstable, novelistic work of fiction appeared from the pen of THOMAS NASH (ca. 1567–1601). This work, *THE UNFORTUNATE TRAVELLER*, seems above all to be a dazzling display of a degree of mastery so sure of itself that it disdains a predictable form. In its pages, Nash allows the book's hero, Jack Wilton, to become its narrative voice. Jack's point of view continually shifts—he is not an all-together reliable narrator. At one moment he is satiric, at another witty. Almost always he is an intellectual exhibitionist. His philosophical point of view seems usually nihilistic, though he may occasionally vary it with a moral observation. The novel bristles with violence and unapologetic savagery at one moment, but at another it can shift to lighthearted mockery of the PETRARCHIST tradition in European poetry. It may be a novel so far ahead of its time in terms of its readers' expectations that few if any of Nash's contemporaries were theoretically equipped to deal with its accomplishment. In part because it resists being fit into categories, *The Unfortunate Traveller* has become a darling of 20th- and 21st-century criticism.

Another early novelist in Elizabethan England, THOMAS DELONEY (ca. 1563–ca. 1600), composed three popular novels with plots drawn from the lives of Londoners of the merchant class. A silk weaver himself, Deloney grew interested in the careers and successes of other members of London's middle classes. The first of his three novels, *JACK OF NEWBERRY* (1597) traces the career of a fellow weaver whose success leads him to wealth and fame as an entrepreneur who employs many other weavers in the manufacture of clothing. His second, *The Gentle Craft* (1597), follows the history of a real Londoner, Thomas Eyre, a shoemaker who became Lord Mayor of London. That novel became the basis for the playwright THOMAS DEKKER's drama, *The Shoemaker's Holiday*. Deloney's last novel, *Thomas of Reading* (ca. 1599), recounts the adventures of several weavers who meet

at an inn in Reading and travel together to London on a sales trip. Deloney's style of writing dialogue reveals his sensitivity to the class distinctions that characterized the speech of Englishmen. The honest tradesmen speak clearly and straightforwardly while members of the upper classes speak in the self-consciously artificial manner that John Lyly had sought to popularize.

One sort of Elizabethan prose writing fell halfway between journalism and fiction. Perhaps the best example is Thomas Dekker's account of the London plague year of 1603—also the final year of the reign of Queen Elizabeth I. Dekker's grafting of fictive detail on a basic framework of fact in *THE WONDERFUL YEAR* (1603) makes for very effective prose indeed. It was a technique he continued to perfect through most of the first decade of the reign of Elizabeth's successor, King JAMES I.

Bibliography

Klein, Holger, David Margolies, and Janet Todd, eds. *Early English Prose Fiction*. Cambridge, U.K.: Cambridge University Press, 1997. CD-Rom.

Salzman, Paul. *An Anthology of Elizabethan Prose Fiction*. Oxford: Oxford University Press, 1985.

———. *English Prose Fiction, 1558–1700*. Oxford: The Clarendon Press, 1985.

Elyot, Sir Thomas (ca. 1490–1546)

An English scholar, diplomat, writer, student of medicine, lawyer, translator, and lexicographer, Elyot studied at Oxford University and at the Middle Temple in London. He was a friend of both SIR THOMAS MORE and of the HUMANIST scholar Thomas Linacre. Under Linacre's tutelage, Elyot studied both medicine and the Greek language.

As a public servant, he first was employed as an administrator under the powerful Cardinal Wolsey, but when Wolsey fell from power in 1529, Elyot withdrew to his country estate near Cambridge and wrote the work for which he is principally remembered, *The Book Named the Governour* (1531).

In this work he discusses the purposes and function of a state considered from a humanist and rationalist point of view. The state is to be both moderate and rational. It is to be headed by God's destined secular representative, the king, and managed by a group of "inferior governors"—the civil servants. This class of persons requires careful education from their earliest childhood, and the first section of Elyot's book prescribes the content, methods, and purposes of that education. The early curriculum emphasized the study of classical languages from the age of seven. The Greek and Roman authors whose works the youthful governors in training must study included Aristophanes, ARISTOTLE, Caesar, CICERO, Homer, Livy, Lucian, Ovid, PLATO, Quintilian, and Xenophon. A proper mastery of these authors, Elyot thought, would produce virtuous public servants with the managerial skills necessary to oversee both civil and military matters. For the creative use of the governors' recreational time, Elyot also prescribes instruction in music, sculpture, and painting and recommends exercise in the form of dancing, hunting, and archery. This discussion occupies about a third of the book. In the rest of *The Governour*, Elyot details the many virtues that should characterize a proper civil servant and gives examples of those virtues in operation.

As a result of *The Governour*'s success and perhaps through the influence of Henry VIII's advisor Thomas Cromwell, Elyot himself returned for a time to public service and was sent on an embassy to the Low Countries in an effort to arrange the arrest of the fugitive translator of the BIBLE into English, WILLIAM TYNDALE. Elyot also briefly served in 1532 as ambassador to Emperor Charles V. Since his mission was to secure the emperor's support for Henry VIII's divorce from his first wife, Catherine of Aragon, and since, as some political dialogues he later wrote reveal, Elyot was secretly her supporter, perhaps his heart was not in his duty. He definitively retired from the public arena that same year.

As a translator, Elyot rendered into English several Greek works including some from Isocrates, St. Cyprian, and Plutarch. He also translated some of GIOVANNI PICO DELLA MIRANDOLA's NEO-LATIN WRITINGS. The medical studies Elyot had pursued with Thomas Linacre resulted in a compendium of medical advice, *The Castle of Health* (ca. 1534), and

Elyot had the distinction of becoming the first English lexicographer, producing in 1538 an English–Latin dictionary. In this connection, as one with a humanist education in classical languages, Elyot shared the point of view that Greek and Latin were capable of more precise expression than was early 16th-century English. At the same time, he knew that the majority of his literate countrymen did not read those languages. He therefore felt duty-bound to extend the expressive capacities and the precision of the English language. To accomplish this, he provided his readers with an immediate explanation of words that he himself constructed on the basis of classical models or that he thought would be unfamiliar to his audience. He uses, for example, the word *tractability*, which he immediately follows with a parenthetical definition: "which is to be shortly persuaded and moved." In another instance, he uses the word *continence* and defines it, "which is a mean between chastity and inordinate lust."

Bibliography

Elyot, Thomas, Sir. *A Critical Edition of Sir Thomas Elyot's The Boke named the Governour*. Edited by Donald W. Rude. New York: Garland Publishers, 1992.

Lehmberg, Stanford. *Sir Thomas Elyot, Tudor Humanist*. New York: Greenwood Press, 1969.

Major, John. *Sir Thomas Elyot and Renaissance Humanism*. Lincoln, Neb.: University of Nebraska Press, 1964.

Encina, (Enzina), Juan del (ca. 1458– ca. 1530)

Credited with founding the secular theater in Spain, a courtier, a lawyer, a priest, a musician, and a poet, Encina was educated in the law at the University of Salamanca. Its rector recommended him to Fadrique I de Toledo, the duke of Alva (Alba), whose court Encina joined as master of the revels in 1492. To the duke and duchess of Alva, to their son Don Garcia de Toledo, and to the Spanish monarchs and their son he dedicated the four parts of the earliest edition of his collected poems, his Songbook (*Cansoniero*, 1496).

Encina's four-part collection found a receptive audience, and during the next two decades they went through six editions, some of them containing fresh material. The first three parts of the collection includes songs, lyric poems, and several representatives of medieval-style rustic songs (*villancicos*). They also contain quasi-historical poems with compliments for his royal patrons. In the fourth part of the collection, however, appear nine dramatic poems—a number that eventually grew to 14 plays of increasing length and complexity. These plays take the form of the classical ECLOGUE, but their spirit is Spanish. Their versification often follows older Spanish models. All of them include songs. One contains a dance, and one represents a brawl between students and townspeople in the marketplace of Salamanca. The dramatic poems were written as COURT ENTERTAINMENTS and had been at various times presented before the Spanish aristocrats who were named in their prefaces.

The public performance of Encina's plays, however, had begun in 1492 when he became master of the revels, and there is evidence that the author himself took part in their presentation. He began his career by paraphasing the *Eclogues* of VIRGIL, shaping them so they fit in with incidents that occurred during the reign of Ferdinand and Isabella. He also followed the models of the Spanish medieval religious drama, penning simple but imaginative dialogues for presentation at Christmas, Easter, Carnival, and Lent. His purely secular dramas include the *Auto del Repelon* (The enactment of the brawl, mentioned above), three romantic comedies, and the story of a suicidal, love-struck shepherd. Although none of Encina's plays can be considered great theater, they do seem to have been the first nonreligious drama performed publicly in Spain.

In about 1500, Encina moved to Rome and became a priest. His outstanding musical accomplishments led to his promotion to the post of musical master of the chapel of Pope Leo X—the highest post to which a 16th-century European musician could aspire. Encina broke up his extended career in Rome by making a pilgrimage to Jerusalem in 1518–20. The literary product of this extended journey was a not-much-read verse recitation of his religious experiences along the way.

Late in life, he enjoyed the income from a priory in Leon and retired to Spain. He was interred at the Cathedral in Salamanca.

Bibliography
Andrews, J. Richard. *Juan del Encina: Prometheus in Search of Prestige.* Berkeley: University of California Press, 1959.

Rio, Alberto del, and Miguel Angel Pérez Priego, eds. *Juan del Encina* [selections in Spanish]. Barcelona: Critica, ca. 2001.

Engelbretsdatter, Dorothea (1635–1716)
A Norwegian composer of hymn–tunes and lyrics, Engelbretsdatter is chiefly remembered as the first female poet of any significance in the canon of Scandinavian letters. Her reputation rests exclusively on the hymns she wrote.

English language in the Renaissance
In the century following the death of GEOFFREY CHAUCER in 1400 C.E., speakers of English, for reasons that are not altogether clear, began to pronounce certain vowel sounds further forward in their mouths. Some have proposed that widespread dental disease made the pronunciation of back vowels painful, but no one really knows. The result of this phenomenon is called the great vowel shift, which had mostly run its course by 1500.

Chaucer's East Midland dialect, which, as the speech of London, is the direct ancestor of modern English in all its worldwide manifestations, gave long vowels essentially the same values they had in continental European languages. *A* was pronounced as in *ta-ta. E* was pronounced to rhyme with the word *say* and was slower than the other vowels to shift, achieving its modern value in England between 1700 and 1800. Thus Shakespeare can pun, in *Henry IV*, Part I, on *reason*, and *raisin*, both of which sounded like the dried fruit. *I* was pronounced to rhyme with modern *be. O* and *u*, broke or diphthongized (two vowel sounds pronounced together) so that they came to rhyme with *slow* and *you*, respectively. The overall effect of these changes for Londoners in the reign of Queen Elizabeth made their English sound *then* very much the way that Modern Irish English sounds *now* in Dublin. Both 21st-century Irish and American English are more conservative in their pronunciation than is modern British English whose pronunciation has changed more radically in the last couple of centuries. While the foregoing discussion simplifies matters somewhat, it conveys the essential picture.

During the TUDOR and STUART periods, English, like the continental languages of the Renaissance, was busy establishing its credentials as a literary language on a par with classical Greek and Latin. Church or VULGATE LATIN had served as the common language of medieval Europe and had provided a diplomatic as well as a religious norm. JOHN MILTON, for instance, as late as the INTERREGNUM (1640–60 C.E.) performed the office of Latin secretary to the government of OLIVER CROMWELL—that is, Milton was the chief diplomat of England and conducted the nation's foreign affairs in Latin. Movements were afoot in the 16th century to "enrich" the English language with borrowings from scholarly Greek and Latin vocabulary. This sometimes resulted in the introduction of INKHORN TERMS—pedantic or clerical coinages that sometimes rendered the prose of their users virtually incomprehensible to ordinary Englishmen. Here is part of a letter that THOMAS WILSON scornfully attributed to a Lincolnshire clergyman seeking an appointment:

Pondering, *expending*, and *revoluting* within my selfe, your *ingent affability*, and *ingenious capacity* for *mundaine affairs*: I cannot but *celebrate*, & *extol* your *magnifical dexteritie* above all other. . . . But now I *relinquish* to *fatigate* your intelligence, with any more *frivolous verbositie*. . . .

The italicized words in this brief example struck Wilson as inkhorn terms—words essentially un-English. Some of them have nonetheless become standard. Many terms from classical Latin and Greek made their way into serviceable English as a result of conscious efforts by writers of the period to expand English vocabulary. Sir THOMAS ELYOT, in the first treatise on education printed in the English language, *The Governour* (1531), contributes several new words among which are *education* and *dedicate*—both from Latin roots and both first recorded in English in that work.

JOHN LYLY and others attempted as well to beautify writing by introducing a doggedly alliterative, flowery style that took its name from Lyly's work *EUPHUES*—the Euphuistic style: "O my Euphues, little dost thou know the sudden sorrow that I sustain for thy sweet sake, whose wit has bewitched me . . . whose comely feature without fault, whose filed speech without fraud hath wrapped me in this misfortune." Happily, Lyly's attempts did not long take serious hold on the imaginations of the more important Elizabethan writers—except perhaps as a matter of scorn.

The English language had from its origins been amenable to borrowings. Many terms from church Latin had entered the language during the Old English Period (440–1100 C.E.). So had numerous terms of Scandinavian origin including *she*, which displaced native Old English *heo*, and *they*, which replaced *hie* in the usually borrowing-proof pronoun paradigm. The Norman Conquest (1066 C.E.) and its aftermath had also expanded the English language with many thousand French words. The net result for Elizabethan and later English literature is a particularly rich kind of unusual, three-tiered language. Native Anglo-Saxon word stock provides a basic tier of discourse that includes among many other words most of those taboo in polite conversation, the names of live animals (*cow, swine, deer*), ancient farming tools (*plough, axe*), preconquest institutions (*church*), and a number of dialectical survivals not common in standard speech (*tote* for *carry*). (The italicized words in the following sentence are English borrowings from French, often with Latin sources further back.) The *French* and *Latin* word stock that the English *language acquired* so *abundantly* after the *Conquest provides* much of the *language* of *ordinary discourse*, of *fiction, poems, prose essays*, and plays. Another example of borrowing from French includes the names of animals cooked for the table (*beef, pork, venison*). Finally in this connection the terms introduced as a result of the operation of the interest of Renaissance HUMANISM in classical Latin and Greek serve as the medium for scientific and scholarly discussion. It was during the Renaissance that this three-legged paradigm largely took its present form.

At the same time, the English resisted repeated attempts to normalize their language officially. Whereas the French Academy and the Italian ACADEMY OF THE CROSS (*Accademia della crusca*) established recognized conventions for the literary languages of their countries, the only really effective norm for good English usage has until recently been social. Television and the recording industry have for the past several decades been changing that, but in England during the Renaissance, "good English" was the language as spoken by royalty and members of the upper classes in London—and as written for them and for a wealthy and highly literate middle class by sensible poets such as CHRISTOPHER MARLOWE and SIR THOMAS WYATT and by such thoughtful authors of prose as Thomas Hobbes.

English spelling in the Renaissance was pretty haphazard. Writers often spelled words the way they sounded, and their work was usually comprehensible. Some developed consistent practices within their own writing, but others' spelling, like that of ROBERT GREENE, even of the same words, varied greatly within single documents. "Correct" spelling, like correct punctuation, finally became a matter for printers' conventions and the makers of dictionaries.

Bibliography

Baugh, Albert C., and Thomas Cable. *A History of the English Language*. 1963. Reprint, Upper Saddle River, N.J.: Prentice-Hall, Inc., ca. 2002.

Blake, N. F. *A History of the English Language*. New York: New York University Press, 1996.

Bloomfield, Morton W., and Leonard Newmark. *A Linguistic Introduction to the History of English*. New York: Alfred A. Knopf, 1963.

Onions, C. T. *The Oxford Dictionary of English Etymology*. Oxford, U.K.: Oxford University Press, 1966.

English sonnet

The sonnet, which may have antecedents traceable to Arabic love poems, developed in Italy in the early 13th century. (See ITALIAN SONNET.) Largely in response to the work of FRANCESCO PETRARCA, the sonnet spread throughout Europe, and its form adapted to the metrical realities of the language in which it was written. Although its length can vary, the sonnet typically contains 14 lines with a variety of possible rhyme schemes. In England, SIR THOMAS WYATT brought the sonnet home from an Italian journey in 1527. Typically, the English sonnet has a line of 10 syllables, each syllable receiving alternating light and heavy stress to produce five metrical feet. Although English is in reality a language with four degrees of stress, the sonnet, particularly in the hands of apprentice poets, pretends that the language has two. This stress pattern is called iambic pentameter: ba DA, ba DA, ba DA, ba DA, ba DA. (See POETIC METER.) Good poets do not follow it slavishly, however. They vary the meter and also the number of syllables both for variety and effect. In the first line of one of his sonnets, "Whoso list to hunt, I know where is an hind," Sir Thomas Wyatt varies both meter and the numbers of syllables.

In addition to a fairly specific meter, the sonnet form also required the poet to rhyme—again, not slavishly—according to one of several possible formulas. The first eight lines might rhyme, abab abab, or abba abba. These eight lines made up the "octave." The next six, in the hands of the Italians, comprised the "sestet" and could rhyme, cd, cd, cd; cde cde; or cdc cdc. When they followed the latter two forms, the sestet was said to be composed of two tercets. Wyatt often constructed a sestet composed of two tercets that rhymed cdd cee—really a quatrain and a couplet. HENRY HOWARD, EARL OF SURREY, perceived Wyatt's innovation and improved on it, creating what was to become the typical Elizabethan rhyme scheme for the sonnet in English: abab cdcd efef gg, and abba cddc effe gg. JOHN MILTON reverted to the Petrarchan model.

Again following the example of Petrarch, writing sonnet cycles became popular throughout Europe. SHAKESPEARE, EDMUND SPENSER, and JOHN

Donne wrote famous ones. Spenser invented a new form of the sonnet for his cycle *The Amoretti:* abab cdcd efef gg—that is, three quatrains and a couplet. Donne employed a "crown of sonnets" to introduce his *Holy Sonnets.* A sonnet crown is a series of seven linked sonnets, the last line of the first also being the first line of the second, and so on.

Many sonnets treated love as their subject, and some of the comparison of the beauties of the beloved—eyes like stars, a walk like a goddess—got used so frequently that the better poets sometimes poked fun at them as in this illustrative first quatrain of Sonnet 130 of Shakespeare's cycle:

> My mistress' eyes are nothing like the sun;
> Coral is far more red than her lips' red;
> If snow be white, why then her breasts are
>   dun;
> If hairs be wires, black wires grow on her
>   head.

Though the poet finally turns the parody into a telling compliment in the final couplet:

> And yet, by heaven, I think my love as rare
> As any she belied with false compare.

Bibliography

Hebel, J William, and Hoyt H. Hudson. *Poetry of the English Renaissance, 1509–1660.* 1929. Reprinted, New York: F. S. Crofts & Co., 1936.

Shipley, Joseph T. *Dictionary of World Literary Terms.* Boston: The Writer, Inc. 1970.

epic

The epic mode of poetry has deep roots in the past of many cultures. Apparently epics arose in the ancient world from oral recitations of stories—many older than writing itself. These stories recount the deeds of heroes and gods, and they report facts and myths of central importance to the cultures that produced them. The Homeric epics, the *Iliad* and the *Odyssey* established the characteristics of the model for the ancient Mediterranean world, and Virgil imitated their form for his Roman national epic, the *Aeneid.*

The Middle-Eastern prototype is the *Gilgamesh* epic of ancient Sumeria—the oldest written epic known (before 3000 B.C.E.) and the source of some of the plot for the story of Noah in the Old Testament. The Hebrew Old Testament itself can be viewed as a literary epic or series of epics recounting the saga of Jewish culture. In ancient India the *Ramayana* and the *Mahabharata* arose, as did a series of lesser works the *Puranas.*

In the European Middle Ages, Germanic heroic cultures produced national epics: *Beowulf,* the *Niebelungenlied,* and the two Icelandic *Eddas.* Finland produced its *Kalevala.* The deeds of the warriors of the court of Charlemagne became material for a series of epics, beginning with the French epic, *The Song of Roland.* Though some of the writers of these medieval epics appear to have been familiar at least with Virgil, they were much freer than he in the forms they chose for expressing their material.

The Song of Roland together with Aristotle's discussion of epic poetry in his *Poetics* provided grist for the epic mills of several Renaissance poets in Italy and Spain. Earliest among them, Matteo Maria Boiardo wrote his *Orlando Innamorato* (Roland in love, 1483). Not long after, Ludovico Ariosto followed with his *Orlando Furioso* (Roland gone mad, 1532). Lesser but nonetheless worthy Italian poets contributed other epic poems. Their efforts were followed by that of the distinguished Torquato Tasso, whose Jerusalem delivered (*Gerusalemme Liberata*) appeared in the 1570s. In addition to being a major poet, Tasso wrote influential works on theory that combined Aristotle's ideas with Ariosto's practice. These treatises were carefully read both by such English literary theorists as Sir Philip Sidney and by the great epic poets of Renaissance England, Edmund Spenser and John Milton.

European Renaissance epics often follow certain formal conventions first observed by Homer. They often start, for example, as Homer's do by invoking a muse or an inspirational figure. (See Muses.) Once the muse begins singing through the poet, the action picks up in the middle of the matter and then flashes back as necessary to earlier events. All share a concern with matters of great magnitude played out against a national, or in the case of Milton, a universal background.

In at least three cases contemporary events provide the matter for Renaissance epic poets. The Portuguese poet LUÍS VAZ DE CAMÕES recounts Vasco da Gama's voyage to India around the Cape of Good Hope at the southern tip of Africa in *Os Lusíadas*—from the ancient name of the region of Portugal, Lusitania (THE LUSIAD). The French poet, AGRIPPA D'AUBIGNÉ treats the religious wars between his Protestant and Catholic countrymen in his epic *LES TRAGIQUES* (THE TRAGIC ONES). Finally, the Spaniard, ALONSO DE ERCILLA Y ZÚÑIGA treats the conquest of Chilean Indians by the Spanish in *LA ARAUCANA* (The Araucanian people).

In the New World, an epic work written in the mid-16th century is the *POPOL VUH* (Council Book). Composed in the Santa Cruz Quiche Mayan language in Latin script, the *Popol Vuh* seems drawn from one or more Mayan hieroglyphic manuscripts. This epic gives insight into the life, mythology, and thinking of pre-European contact Mayan civic and agricultural society. (See ALTERNATIVE LITERACIES.)

Renaissance era Europeans increasingly made contact with many preliterate cultures around the world. Explorers discovered that members of such cultures also communicate matters they deem crucial—like genealogies, creation myths, and stories about earlier rulers and gods—by means of oral epics. These were and often still are committed to memory by priests and storytellers and passed from one generation to the next in song or verse. Some episodes may be ancient and some fairly recent in origin. Typical of this oral tradition is the CENTRAL AFRICAN EPIC, LIANJA AND NSONGO (*Nsong'a Lianja*), the epic of the Mongo peoples of the central Congo region. In this story, which may well have originated during or about the time of the European Renaissance, a ruler named Lianja and his sister Nsongo travel among several different peoples, subduing each one.

Bibliography

Belcher, Stephen. *Epic Traditions of Africa.* Bloomington: Indiana University Press, 1999.

León-Portilla, Miguel, and Earl Shores. *In the Language of Kings: An Anthology of Mesoamerican Literature, Pre-Columbian to the Present.* New York: W. W. Norton and Company, 2001.

Epicoene, or *The Silent Woman* Ben Jonson (1609)

First acted by the Children of her Majesties Revels, one of England's several highly professional troops of child actors, BEN JONSON'S prose comedy, *The Silent Woman,* brilliantly interweaves themes from Roman comedy with the manners and morals of Elizabethan London and with a situation drawn from PIETRO ARETINO's Italian comedy, The blacksmith (*Il Marescalco*).

The central conflict of *The Silent Woman* arises from the desire of an aging bachelor, Morose, to deny a nephew, Dauphine Eugenie, his inheritance. To do this Morose contemplates wedlock and fathering an heir. But Morose suffers from a pathological sensitivity to any noise other than the sound of his own voice. He pads his door and his stairs to deaden the sounds of knocking and footfalls, and he insists that his servant, Mute, respond to his queries silently. Because of this affliction, Morose asks his barber, Cut-berd, to seek a mute woman. Cut-berd claims to have found a woman so quiet that Morose will be able to tolerate her company. Morose meets her, finds her quiet enough, and contracts a marriage with her.

Also populating the play we find a group of London women led by Lady Haughty and including Madam Centaur, Madame Mavis, and Mrs. Trusty. These women have organized themselves into a "college" whose purpose is to bring them together with the fashionable wits of the town and to increase the probability of their meeting suitable lovers. Regrettably, they are poor judges of character, and instead they attract the fops and fools, notably Sir Amorous La-Fool and John Daw.

Adding to the general hilarity we find Captain Thomas Otter—a *MILES GLORIOSUS* directly out of Roman comedy, and his wife. Otter calls his spouse "princess" to her face and defers to her in all things, but behind her back to his male acquaintance he disparages her unmercifully.

In his unraveling of all these situations, Jonson displays an unerring sense of comic stagecraft and singular ingenuity. Through the trickery of Dauphine and his friends Clerimont and True-wit, Morose contracts to marry the silent woman. Once the contract is signed, she becomes loud and demanding and reveals herself to be precisely the sort of woman he has feared throughout his life. La-Fool and Daw are each led to believe that the other wishes to murder him. The plotters contrive to kick La-Fool and to tweak Daw's nose painfully while each thinks the other has done it, and both have agreed not to discuss it further. This takes place in front of the college of women and clarifies for them the sort of men they have been entertaining. Both Centaur and Mavis become enamored of Dauphine, and each seeks to discredit the other.

Both La-Fool and Daw claim to have slept with the silent woman, and in an uproarious conclusion Clerimont and True-wit impersonate a canon lawyer and a cleric who advise Morose on the subject of how he might divorce Epicoene. Dauphine promises that he will free his uncle from the contract if Morose will release a portion of his income to him during his lifetime and consign the rest to him at his death. Morose willingly agrees, signs the necessary papers, and Dauphine reveals that Epicoene, the silent woman, is a boy. This is the device borrowed from *Il Marescalco*. Morose is free of his contract having been soundly punished with loud noise throughout the play for his recalcitrance. The fools and pretenders are all unmasked and all get their comeuppance.

The play makes extended use of Latin phrases in the mouths of the untutored to satirize types like canon lawyers and fops.

Bibliography

Jonson, Ben. *Ben Jonson*. Edited by C. H. Herford and Percy Simpson. Volume 5. Oxford: The Clarendon Press, 1937, 1954, and 1971.

Epicurus (341–270 B.C.E.)

A Greek philosopher and teacher, Epicurus founded a school and commune in an Athenian garden in about 306 B.C.E. There he taught the doctrine that temperance, moderation, and simplicity led to freedom from fear and to happiness. Those two qualities resulted from living a moral life, and that produced pleasure. Achieving moral pleasure was the central goal of life. Epicurus taught that the universe was materialistic, that the gods did not intervene in human affairs or concern themselves with the guilt or innocence of individuals, and that the human body and soul, like the rest of the universe, is composed of atoms. Death is not to be feared. It simply dissolves both body and soul together.

Though Epicurus is reputed to have written prolifically, only a few letters and fragments of his work have survived. We are—and the Renaissance was—acquainted with his work mainly through discussions of his teachings in the writings of the Romans CICERO, LUCRETIUS, and Plutarch. Because his materialist doctrines conflicted with the teachings of Christianity, Epicureanism was misrepresented to the medieval and Renaissance world. In the popular mind, the adjective *Epicurean* came to connote sensuality and libertinism. Thus we see on the Renaissance English stage a character like BEN JONSON's Sir Epicure Mammon in *THE ALCHEMIST*. Sir Epicure is devoted to every imaginable form of vice and excess.

In fact, Epicureanism and Stoicism were the two principal philosophies of ancient Greece, and the teachings of Epicurus attracted adherents for hundreds of years.

epigram

In contemporary usage *epigram* may refer to any brief, witty saying in verse or in prose. During the Renaissance, however, the label mainly applied to poems that imitated either those of the first-century C.E. Roman poet Martial (Marcus Valerius Martial) and the works of more than 300 writers collected in the sixth-century C.E. *Greek Anthology*. These included brief satirical poems particularly, but also epitaphs, compliments, amusing anecdotes, love poems, and verse for special occasions. In England, both BEN JONSON and ROBERT HERRICK wrote epigrams based on or borrowed from the *Greek Anthology*.

Bibliography

Shipley, Joseph T. *Dictionary of World Literary Terms.* Boston: The Writer, Inc., 1970.

epistolary sonnet

In Renaissance Italy a fashion developed for poets and even for people who did not regularly write poetry to exchange letters (*epistles*) written as sonnets. FRANCESCO PETRARCA, for example, once received a complimentary sonnet from a reader and admirer. The reader's sonnet, however, contained a formal error. Petrarch courteously replied with a sonnet that erred in exactly the same way at the same place.

ISABELLA ANDREINI often exchanged sonnets with friends and admirers and, on at least one occasion, with a harsh critic, Angelo Ingeniere. Ingeniere reproved Andreini for acting with too much art and too little matter. Andreini's response, dripping with sarcasm, put her correspondent firmly in his place.

The practice of exchanging epistolary sonnets became common throughout Renaissance Europe.

See also ENGLISH SONNET and ITALIAN SONNET.

Epithalamion (On the bed chamber)
Edmund Spenser (1595)

A 433-line marriage ODE written in 1594 as a wedding present for SPENSER'S second wife, Elizabeth Boyle, *Epithalamion* is a poem unprecedented and perhaps unparalleled in the English language.

Opening with an invocation addressed to all nine MUSES, Spenser implores their aid in praising his bride. The poem continues by imagining the day of the wedding from its dawn and the bride's awakening through her rising, bathing, dressing, and appearance. Though the poem is PASTORAL in its manner, its nymphs, shepherds, and allegorical rivers are Irish, and its setting is Ireland, where the wedding in fact occurred. The ode celebrates the groom's joy in the wedding day's arrival. It con-

jures up the music and minstrelsy of the local musicians, of the surrounding songbirds, and of a mighty church organ. It assimilates the Irish country wedding to the Roman wedding ritual employed by the poet Catullus (ca. 84–ca. 54 B.C.E.) in his *Ode 61*. Then it interweaves with those elements the amorous vernacular tradition of Renaissance Europe with a PETRARCHAN catalogue of the bride's beauties and a pair of compliments comparing the bride's appearance to that of Queen ELIZABETH I.

Once the poem has enumerated the bride's physical beauties, it continues to praise her moral excellences of "sweet love . . . constant chastity,/ Unspotted fayth . . . comely womanhood . . . honour . . . modesty . . . and virtue." So sanctified are the bride's attributes that the ordinarily awe-inspiring angels who fly about the altar seem to be only peeping cherubs fluttering about her face. Once the wedding has been solemnized, however, a celebratory party begins, and the IMAGES of the poem shift from Christian to pagan. As the wedding guests drink "by the belly full" the poet directs that the doorposts and walls be sprinkled with wine to invite the pagan deities Bacchus and Hymen—the god of wine who brings joy to a party and the god of marriage, respectively.

Eventually, the groom becomes impatient for the day to end, but at long last the bridesmaids put the bride to bed, and the groomsmen lead him to her. The poem now utters prayers to the deities and spirits of the classical, Christian, and Irish folkloristic traditions that nothing disturb the couple's first night together and that no evil omens or spirits intrude upon their peace.

After a joyous celebration of the couple's love-making, there follow prayers for the fruitfulness of their union. Again the deities addressed represent the classical pantheon as well as the Protestant traditions of the Christian faith, and the poem expresses the poet's hope for the couples' eternal participation in the heavenly joys of the saints.

As odes do, the poem ends with an address to the song itself that expresses in a compelling paradox the poet's hope that for "short time"—that is until the world ends—the poem will be an "end-lesse" monument to his beloved.

Epithalamion is one of the most exquisitely and elaborately wrought lyric creations of the English language, and the critical community has by no means as yet exhausted its analysis of Spenser's invention. As an instance of their discoveries, the literary critic Kent Hieatt observed that the movement of the Sun and the Moon through the lines of the poem on the wedding day corresponds with mathematical precision to the movement of the celestial orbs as they would have appeared in Ireland on the day of the wedding. If one were to establish a ratio between the minutes of the 24-hour wedding day and the lines of the poem less the introductory stanza and the address to the song, sunrise, sunset, and moonrise in the poem's development would take place exactly at the right times for the latitude and longitude of Spenser's wedding.

Bibliography

Hieatt, Kent A. *Short Time's Endless Monument: The Symbolism of the Numbers in Edmund Spenser's "Epithalamion."* New York: Columbia University Press, 1960.

Spenser, Edmund. *The Shorter Poems: Edmund Spenser.* Edited by Richard A. McCabe. London and New York: Penguin Books, 1999.

Erasmus, Desiderius (1466–1536)

A towering figure of Renaissance thought and letters, Erasmus and his elder brother Pieter were the illegitimate sons of a priest named Roger Girard and a widow whom we know only by her first name, Margaret. From 1475 until Girard's death in 1484 the boys were educated by the pious members of an evangelical order, the Brothers of the Common Life, at a school in Deventer, Holland. The boys' appointed guardians then enrolled them both as Augustinian canons, and Erasmus's guardian, who wished the lad to become a priest, sent him to study at s' Hertogenbosch. Although Erasmus resisted the priesthood, his choices were limited by his poverty, and in 1492 he was reluctantly ordained. In 1495–96 he attended the University of Paris as a student of theology, but the austere regimen enforced upon the students of the Collège de Montaigu where he resided severely undermined Erasmus's health. That plus the dim view that he took of the capacities of his professors and of their medieval methods of scholastic philosophy led him to withdraw from the university. The study of classical languages and literature and better methods of teaching became his overriding interests.

On withdrawing from the Sorbonne, Erasmus wrote a manual on the use of correspondence and the first of a series of *Colloquies,* both to be used in teaching conversational Latin. He also began to work as a private tutor, and in 1499 one of his pupils, the English nobleman William Blount, invited him to England for the first of three visits. While there, he became close friends with SIR THOMAS MORE and with the HUMANIST John Colet. Recognizing Erasmus's extraordinary gifts, these friends introduced him to people who could offer support for his work. After his return from this first English visit in 1500, Erasmus published a collection of *Adages* that he had gleaned from classical authors.

Between 1500 and 1504 Erasmus became one of a number of wandering scholars. Supporting himself by tutoring, he moved from one university to another while he mastered the Greek language and studied the writings of the early fathers of the Christian Church. In Antwerp in 1504 he published his Handbook for a Christian soldier (*Enchiridion militis Christiani*). This work urged a return to the piety and simplicity of early Christianity. Also in that year, Erasmus discovered the forgotten manuscript of LORENZO VALLA's annotations on the New Testament. In that document Valla had outlined his method for comparing ancient manuscripts to improve passages of Scripture that had been accidentally or intentionally changed over time. In 1505 Erasmus arranged for the publication of Valla's notes and began to apply their principles to his own study of the texts of Scripture. Later that year, he made his second trip to England.

Returning in 1506 he traveled to Italy where he was awarded the doctorate in theology from the University of Turin on the basis of his self-evident mastery of the discipline and without fulfilling the usual residency requirement. He continued to Venice where he edited for Aldo Manuzio and had access to Manuzio's fine library and the company of others interested in classical letters. Manuzio's ALDINE PRESS also issued a much-expanded revision of Erasmus's *Adages* in 1508. With that publication, Erasmus's renown soared.

The years 1509–14 saw Erasmus return for the final time to England. There he was able to teach Greek at Cambridge while translating the letters of St. Jerome and the writings of SENECA. Also, employing the textual methods of Lorenzo Valla, Erasmus worked on an improved translation of the New Testament. On his last English visit, Erasmus stayed with Sir Thomas More and dedicated to him what is likely Erasmus's most widely read book, THE PRAISE OF FOLLY. Its title puns on the accidental correspondence between the Greek word for fool and the name of Erasmus's host, *Encomium Moriae* (The praise of folly—and the praise of More).

This book imagines that the self-styled demigoddess Folly presents to an eager audience of students a lecture on folly's benefits. After introducing herself as the daughter of Plutus, the god of riches, and the nymph Neotes (youth), Folly claims credit for all sorts of human benefits, including procreation and happiness. She is forgetful, verbose, illogical, and disorganized. She produces irrelevant arguments and non sequitors. She is also exceedingly funny. Beneath Folly's discourse, the ironic and satiric pen of Erasmus deconstructs all she has to say in praise of herself until, in the final section of the book, he makes Folly change briefly into the Christian fool who, in believing the incredible, qualifies for life eternal. Here, more than in any other of Erasmus's works, the playful and attractive personality of the man shines through. Not everyone got his jokes, though, and at least one of Erasmus's contemporary readers reproved him for celebrating folly.

Erasmus's literary output was enormous, and he surely thought of *The Praise of Folly* as a playful exercise. His serious work involved, first, his translation and bilingual Greek and Latin edition of the New Testament. This appeared in Basel, Switzerland, in 1516, the year after Erasmus had moved there and established a working relationship with

the publisher John Froben. Erasmus's translation in four volumes of the work of St. Jerome appeared that same year, and many other translations of the work of the early church fathers followed: St. Cyprian (1520), Arnobius (1522), Hilarius (1523), Irenaeus (1526), Ambrose (1527), Augustine (1528), St. John Chrysostom (1530), Basil (1532), and Origen (1536). During this period in Basel, Erasmus's religious order, the Augustinians, made an effort to require him to rejoin the cloister, but Erasmus applied for and received a papal dispensation to live in the world and to wear the clothes of a layman rather than priestly garb.

His early interest in education continued unabated. Erasmus entertained high hopes for a program of education that fused evangelical Roman Catholicism with the learning of the ancient Greeks and Romans. He saw education as *the* essential humanizing factor in people's lives. Works on teaching and learning appeared from his pen at a steady pace: The method of study (*De ratione studii*, 1512), The education of a Christian Prince (*Institutio principis Christiani*, 1516), The method of true theology (*Ratio verae theologiae*, 1518), The antibarbarians (*Antibarbari*, 1520), The Ciceronian dialogue (*Dialogus Ciceronianus*, 1528), and On the education of children (*De pueris instituendis*, 1529). Among these works, the only one whose title is not self-explanatory, *The Antibarbarians*, defended teaching classical literature by pagan authors to Christian children. This was a hot-button issue of the day, and Erasmus argued against the proponents of a medieval scholastic education. Erasmus maintained that the ethical content and erudition of many Greek and Roman writers benefited children. To these pedagogical treatises, Erasmus added a number of texts for classroom use. To assist in teaching composition he penned On the foundations of an abundant style (*De copia*, 1512). He made the Greek grammar of Theodore Gaza accessible to Western European students by translating it into Latin in 1518. On writing letters (*De conscribendis epistolis*) followed in 1519.

Purely literary translation also attracted his interest. In addition to an innovative translation into

Latin verse of two Greek plays by Euripedes, he prepared critical Latin editions of the works of Roman authors. A representative though not exhaustive list of such editions includes the works of CICERO, PLAUTUS, Pliny, Seneca, Suetonius, and TERENCE.

A tireless correspondent, Erasmus sometimes penned as many as 40 letters a day. He wrote to almost everyone who was anyone in Europe. Some 3,000 of these have been published as part of a program for the posthumous publication of his works that he himself designed.

Erasmus's ambitious program for the improvement of society through a fusion of humanist and Christian education by means of liberal studies was undermined by the rise of Lutheranism, by the resultant split between Protestants and Catholics, and by the hardening of their respective positions. This new schism in the Christian community was not the kind of reformation for which Erasmus had hoped. He foresaw that the division between Protestant and Catholic would render unachievable the educational program in which he had reposed such faith and that factional strife would inevitably result. On principle, Erasmus opposed strife whether civil or religious, and he championed peace in such works as War is sweet to the inexperienced (*Bellam dulcis inexpertis,* 1515)—a treatise that should be required reading for all aspiring political leaders everywhere) and his Complaint of peace (*Querela pacis,* 1517). Not a pacifist and a firm supporter of just war, Erasmus nevertheless counseled negotiation in place of armed conflict.

Erasmus's later religious works led his critics to suspect him of secret Lutheran sympathies. His works became the targets of such conservative groups of censors as the theological faculty at the University of Paris and the Spanish INQUISITION. Certainly, by the end of his life, though he remained a priest, he felt estranged from Roman Catholicism, expressing in late works his reservations concerning the church's positions on eating meat and on the necessity for confession. When, in 1536, Pope Paul III made belated overtures, offering him a cardinal's hat with appropriate accompanying income, Erasmus declined and wrote one of his last treatises *On the Purity of the Church.* When death approached,

Erasmus met it without benefit of clergy and rejected the sacrament of extreme unction.

Erasmus's extraordinary contributions to Renaissance literature still command a fascinated audience, and his works continue to be translated and reissued.

Bibliography

Erasmus, Desiderius. *Collected Works.* Toronto: University of Toronto Press, 1974–present.

McConica, James. *Erasmus.* Oxford: Oxford University Press, 1991.

Tracey, James. *Erasmus of the Low Countries.* Berkeley: University of California Press, 1996.

Woodward, William Harrison. *Desiderius Erasmus: Concerning the Aim and Method of Education.* Cambridge, U.K.: Cambridge University Press, 1904. Reprint, New York: 1964.

Erauso, Catalina de   (1592–ca. 1650)

As a young woman of 15, the Basque Erauso fled from the convent where she was a novice, and she assumed the identity of a man. In that guise she enlisted as a Spanish soldier, serving first in Spain and then fighting in Peru and Chile until 1624 when her ruse was finally discovered. She was sent home in woman's clothing, but in 1629—after circulation of her story had earned her a military pension from King Philip IV of Spain and a papal dispensation from Urban VIII to continue dressing as a man—she returned to Mexico and resumed her masculine identity as a mule driver, Antonio de Erauso.

Erauso has been credited with writing an autobiography, though no manuscript of it is known to exist. Her story, which is verifiable in its essentials by reference to other documents, was the basis for a 1626 play by Pérez de Montalbán, The nun ensign (*La monja alférez*). In 1829 a book appeared that represented itself as a 1624 autobiography that she had either dictated or written during the time she spent in Spain before she returned to the New World: The story of the nun ensign, Madam Catalina de Erauso, written by herself (*Historia della monja alférez, Doña Catalina de Erauso, escrita por ella misma*). In the absence of a manuscript, scholars are uncertain if this really is an autobiography or a fictionalized account of Erauso's career. In either case the document is fascinating and available in modern editions in both Spanish and English. The Spanish critical edition also contains the known documents relating to Erauso's life and an earlier English translation as well.

Bibliography

Erauso, Catalina De. *Lieutenant Nun: Memoir of a Basque Transvestite in the New World.* Translated by Michele Stepto and Gabriel Stepto. Foreword by Marjorie Garber. Boston: Beacon Press, 1996.

———. *Vida i sucesos de la Monja Alférez. Autobiografia atribuida a Doña Catalina de Erauso.* Edited by Rima de Vallbona with an English translation by Fitzmaurice-Kelly. Tempe, Ariz.: University of Arizona Press, 1992.

Ercilla y Zúñiga, Alonso de (1533–1594)

A Spanish officer who volunteered and fought in Chile against the Araucanian Indians, Ercilla composed the first significant poem that was written in the New World in a European language. His LA ARAUCANA, (The Araucanians, published in three parts, 1569, 1578, and 1589) is an EPIC poem of more than 2,000 eight-line stanzas organized into 37 cantos. The poem celebrates the courage of the Spanish, of course, but to an even greater degree it praises the valor and heroism of the defending Indians.

All the events of the poem, as Ercilla tells King Phillip II in the epic's dedication to the ruler, are factual, and significant portions of the poem were actually written in the field (where its author spent nine years) on whatever came to hand—scraps of paper or even bits of leather. Not only did Ercilla have the advantage of being an eyewitness to the events his poem chronicles, but he is also a gifted poet with an eye for incident and an ear for the musicality of his language.

His poem, of course, reports the battles. We learn of the Indians' tactic of luring the Spaniards into their center by appearing to fall back and then surrounding and decimating them. Ercilla also takes us into the Araucanian councils, where we observe their disputes about who should lead

them. We see them accept an elder's advice to resolve the dispute by conferring the leadership on the man who can hold up a heavy log the longest. We see torture and execution. We learn of Ercilla's encounter with Tegualda, an Araucanian woman seeking her husband's body across the battlefield, and of her grief when she finds the corpse.

The success of Ercilla's epic poem about the Araucanian war inspired numerous imitations on the same subject and even a 33-canto extension of Ercilla's poem by a poet named Osorio, about whom little else is known. Neither the imitations nor the extension, however, matched the literary achievement of Ercilla's original. Behind that achievement, of course, stands Ercilla's recital of autobiographical and historical material fused with his mastery of and borrowings from epic models from VIRGIL to ARIOSTO. *La Araucana* pays tribute to those models in various ways. It adopts, for example, the stanzaic form of Ariosto's ORLANDO FURIOSO, and it digresses to rescue the Carthaginian Queen Dido's reputation from what Ercilla considers Virgil's misrepresentations about her in the *Aeneid*.

La Araucana continues to be eagerly read in the original and in translation.

Bibliography

Ercilla y Zúñiga, Alonso de. *La Auraucana.* Translated by L. Carrera. New York: The Author, ca. 2000.

Erici, Ericus (ca. 1545–1625)

See FINNISH LANGUAGE AND LITERATURE.

Erutacan (Ezhuthacan) (16th century)

Writing in the Malayalam language, the poet Erutacan composed that tongue's definitive version of the great EPIC poem of India, the MAHABHARATA. Spoken in southwestern India in Kerala, Malayam is one of the ancient Dravidian languages. These languages, indigenous to India, were once spoken throughout the continent before the expansion from the north of peoples speaking the Indo-European languages now prevalent throughout most of northern India. During the BHAKTI period of religious revival that includes the 16th and 17th centuries, the retelling and recasting of the legends of the *Mahabharata* and other stories of gods, heroes, and heroines for the various linguistic communities of India was among the chief characteristics of the continent's literature.

Euphues, The Anatomy of Wit   John Lyly (1578)

Euphues, a wealthy and witty but self-indulgent Athenian youth, moves to Naples, Italy, where he establishes himself and seeks out companions and friends. Observing his behavior, an elderly gentleman finds much to admire in Euphues's intelligence and his essential character, but he also finds much to criticize in his actions and conduct. The old fellow offers Euphues a great deal of unsolicited advice about conducting his life according to high standards. WILLIAM SHAKESPEARE parodies the advice in Polonius's foolish speech to his son Laertes in *Hamlet*. Euphues politely but firmly rejects the elder's advice, much preferring the company and counsel of companions his own age.

In Naples, Euphues acquires a best friend, Philautus. The Athenian youth also falls in love with a Neapolitan girl, Lucilla. She eventually proves fickle and throws Euphues over for a new love, Curio.

At last perceiving the error of his ways, Euphues returns to Athens where he seeks new friends, completes his education, and writes a long series of letters to his Neapolitan acquaintance. Much of the book's *very* slow action occurs in the context of a long sequence of dialogues that Euphues conducts with other characters. In its objectives, *Euphues* resembles other Renaissance volumes that concern themselves with the way in which a young gentleman can gain an education, amuse himself, conduct himself in his youth and in his old age, find friendship and love, behave honorably and appropriately in both sorts of relationships, improve his character, and in general live a satisfying and fulfilling life.

For literary historians, however, the principal interest of John Lyly's best-remembered work lies neither in its purposes nor in its plot. The work is remembered rather for its exaggeratedly artificial style. Although Lyly was not the first to use it, the flowery manner of the book's composition ever thereafter took its name, *euphuism* or the *euphuistic style*, from Lyly's 1578 volume and from its companion tome, Lyly's *Euphues and his England* (1580).

A brief analysis of the style reveals many of its features. First, Lyly constructs his sentences in clauses that balance and reflect each other both in grammatical structure and in word choice: "Fire cometh out of the hardest flint with the steel, oil out of the driest heat by the fire, love out of the stoniest heart by faith, by truth, by time." (I have slightly modernized Lyly's punctuation and spelling.) Second, he proliferates analogies from classical sources: ". . . in this manner did Pericles deal in civil affairs, after this did Architas the Tarentine, Dion the Syracusian, the Theban Epaminondas govern their cities." Third, he besieges the reader with assonance (the repetition of vowel sounds) and alliteration (the repetition of consonant sounds). Observe the repetition of *s* sounds in the following passage: "But yet I am not so senseless altogether to reject your service, which—if I were assured to proceed of a simple mind, it should not receive so simple a reward." Though one could point out a long list of other ingenuities, a final one involves his use of comparison and simile—a use that Shakespeare again directly parodies in a speech by Sir John Falstaff in HENRY IV, PART 1 when he says: "For as the camomile, the more it is trodden on, the faster it grows, [so] youth, the more it is wasted the sooner it wears." Shakespeare takes these words directly from the mouth of the old man who offers Euphues unwanted advice.

Read in the right frame of mind, *Euphues* can delight and amaze a modern reader—chiefly with the seemingly inexhaustible wellspring of Lyly's verbal acrobatics, apt if far-fetched comparisons, and ingenious structural inventions.

Bibliography
Lyly, John. *Euphues: The Anatomy of Wit; and Euphues and his England.* Edited by Leah Scragg. Manchester, U.K.: Manchester University Press, 2003.

Exemplary Stories (*Novelas ejemplates*)
Miguel de Cervantes Saavedra (1613)

In this collection of 12 brief tales, CERVANTES first tells "The Little Gypsy Girl," the story of Preciosa, the kidnapped child of a noble family, who, unaware of her origins, sings and dances for the entertainment of the wealthy and the sustenance of her captors. Next comes "The Generous Lover," a story grounded in Cervantes's experience in Algiers though set on Cyprus in 1572. There follows the tale of two young men, "Riconete and Cortadillo," which parodies the PICARESQUE mode of storytelling. So does its successor, "The Colloquy of the Dogs." Both the preceding tales are set in the underworld of Seville where Riconete and Cortadillo join the league of robbers and beggars. Their leader, Monopodio, is secretly in cahoots with the police authorities. The respectability of the charitable uses to which the grifters put their ill-gotten gains narrows the gap between the honest and the criminal classes. "The English–Spanish Woman" is the story that provides grounds for crediting Cervantes with anticipating the dilution of traditional culture that follows from the internationalization or globalization of trade. Other stories in the collection seem to have some basis in factual situations, including "The Fraudulent Marriage," "The Jealous Estremadurian" (a person from the Spanish region of Estremadura), and "The Pretended Aunt."

In these stories Cervantes undermines by the examples of the tales themselves many of the prevailing literary orthodoxies of his era, such as the insistence on maintaining a single point of view, for example, or the objectivity of what is real as opposed to reality's dependence on one's subjective experience of the world. The literary theorists of the late 20th and early 21st centuries have designated Cervantes not only the first real Spanish representative of the Renaissance, but also the first modern, and they have claimed him as one of their own. As grounds for these laurels they cite the utter novelty of Cervantes's literary achievement both in these 12 tales and in the two parts of *Don Quixote de la Mancha*.

Bibliography

Cervantes, Miguel de. *Exemplary Stories*. Edited by C. A. Jones. London: 1972.

———. *Exemplary Stories*. Translated by Lesley Lipson. New York: Oxford University Press, 1998.

F

Fables of La Fontaine, The   Jean de La Fontaine (1668 and 1678–1679)

Some think that LA FONTAINE undertook writing his fables, at least in part, to curry the royal favor of Louis XIV. To achieve this aim the poet's strategy seems to have been to create a children's book for the princes of the royal line. In so doing, La Fontaine hoped both to give the children pleasure and to instruct them by means of a series of didactic animal fables.

The long line of his predecessors in the fable genre stretched back through the Middle Ages to the Ancients, particularly to the Greek Fabulist Aesop (ca. 700 B.C.E.), to Hesiod two centuries before him, to ancient India before Hesiod, and finally into the mists of preliterate, oral storytelling. More recently, La Fontaine had before him the examples of several French antecedents who retold both Greek and Indian fables.

La Fontaine reworks many of the stories of his predecessors, but he tells them in charming and sophisticated verse and with a characteristic psychological and moral complexity that sets him apart from his literary forebears. Moreover, fine engravings added interest to his versions of the fables.

After opening the first book of the 1668 fables with a dedicatory stanza to the French crown prince, La Fontaine launches into recounting the tales themselves. He begins with "The Grasshopper and the Ant." Everyone who has read this tale in Aesop's version knows the moral: Work hard through the summer for winter will come. This the ant does while the grasshopper fiddles away the season. In the end the improvident grasshopper relies on the ant's drudgery and generosity to survive.

In La Fontaine's version, instead, the female grasshopper comes across as a Bohemian sort of artist who fiddles for the love of music even though her performance pays nothing (though La Fontaine seems to think it should). To survive, she must borrow from the ant. The ant in turn displays the characteristics of a self-satisfied, money-grubbing peasant. Although the ant grudgingly sustains the grasshopper, the ant meanly ridicules both her necessity and her love of her art. As a lesson for the crown prince, La Fontaine's version draws a more reflective and nuanced moral than the clear antithesis his sources offer.

Several fables scattered through the collection address a character flaw that persons in high places often find easy to acquire, a self-satisfaction that glosses over one's own deficiencies. "The Fox and the Crow," "The Beggar's Wallet," "The Two Mules," and "The Swallow and the Little Birds" variously approach this topic.

In "The Wolf and the Dog," the two main characters prove to be equally defensive about their styles of life. The wretched wolf barely keeps alive on what he is able to catch, but he thinks he nevertheless enjoys absolute freedom. The dog on the other hand tries to convince the wolf that domestication is a wonderful thing. It assures a full belly, and it gives one a sense of satisfaction at a job well done in guarding a human family. The observant wolf, however, notices the patch of skin on the dog's neck where his chain has worn off the hair. The dog has to admit that limited freedom is the price of his comfort and sense of worth and purpose. In most earlier versions, the wolf seems to get the best of the argument. Instead in La Fontaine the two seem like moral mirror images of each other. Each is certain of the superiority of his own point of view.

Sometimes it seems that La Fontaine's treatment of the material he borrows leaves the moral unchanged but heightens the fun. This happens in "The Town Rat and the Country Rat." The moral stays the same: Living in the country is better than living in a city. But in making this point, the poem is much funnier than its antecedents.

The poet never loses sight of his principal mission, the education of a prince. "The Wolf and the Lamb," presents a pair of lessons in power politics that are often repeated throughout the collection in different guises. First, the strong overcome the weak by reason of greed and power. Second, while they do so they argue for the necessity and virtue of their actions. Counterpoised against that lesson, however, is one to be drawn from the "Oak and the Reed" at the end of the first book. The Oak rules the wood and is its strongest inhabitant while the reed is among its weakest. Yet when the tempest comes, the Reed survives while the uprooted Oak comes crashing down.

La Fontaine's themes are many. Some of them seem autobiographical and concern the relation of artists and patrons like "Simonides and the Gods." Many assert the immutability of human nature, as does "The Cat Changed into a Woman." "The Lion in Love" seems to warn against loving outside one's station in a hierarchically organized society. When a lion and a shepherdess fall in love, dangers for both are implicit in the relationship.

The fables of 1668 both produced popular success and assured continued patronage. Moreover, in his poetic reworking of the fables of his sources, La Fontaine had found his own most characteristic and congenial mode of expression. Returning to the fable genre again a decade later, La Fontaine gave the world his most celebrated masterpiece, the *Fables* of 1678–79. In them the element of social SATIRE that had been perceptible in the first collection comes into sharper focus. A reader also perceives more subtle insights into the wellsprings of human motivation and the ironies implicit in the human condition.

In his dedication of the later collection to the marquise Françoise de Montespan, the mistress of King Louis XIV, La Fontaine lauds the merits of the fable as a literary genre. The fable, he suggests, has a way of winning both the affections of readers and their concurrence in its point of view. Then, with sudden contrast, a dark and brooding fable opens the second collection. The bubonic plague strikes the animal world. After much suffering and death the animals decide someone must be at fault. All agree that the Jonah among them must be put to death, and the donkey—the weakest among them— is the consensus choice. In an ironic ending, La Fontaine concludes that whatever courts decide must be right, even if they decide that black is white.

The recalcitrance of the clergy in refusing to pay an assessment in support of a war is lampooned in "The Rat who Retired from the World." La Fontaine's ever-present interest in diversity of literary form appears as he experiments with such double fables as "The Heron" and "The Maiden." The *Fables* provide an overwhelmingly rich source of pleasure and opportunities for analysis. They also clarify many of La Fontaine's own personal points of view, as in those that consider the artist and his art, or social issues, or, as in "An Animal on the Moon," the poet's interest in scientific matters of his time.

Bibliography

La Fontaine, Jean de. *The Complete Fables of Jean de la Fontaine.* Translated and edited by Norman B. Spector. Evanston, Ill.: Northwestern University Press, 1988.

Faerie Queene, The Edmund Spenser
(1596 and 1609)

Although never finished, EDMUND SPENSER's allegorical EPIC nonetheless remains the longest poem in the English language. Influenced by native English, by French, and by Italian CHIVALRIC ROMANCE, Spenser set out to write a national, Anglican epic that celebrated in a complex ALLEGORY the glories of Britain's actual and mythic history, of the Anglican Church establishment, and above all of the reigning monarch ELIZABETH I. To honor her, Spenser presented his ruler in various allegorical guises throughout his work. She appears as Gloriana, the Faerie Queene herself; as Belphoebe, the virgin huntress of the woods; as Medina, who represents the golden mean between excessive and faint commitment to virtue; and as Britomart, a female knight who rescues Amoretta from the enchanter Busirane.

As Spenser explained the plan of the poem's central allegory to Sir WALTER RALEIGH in a famous letter on the subject (1589), the poet proposed to present in each of 12 books a different knight-errant as the book's hero. Each of the 12 knights, said Spenser, would illustrate one of the 12 virtues ARISTOTLE had described in his *Nichomachean Ethics*. The overall hero of the Epic would be Prince Arthur, the destined consort for Gloriana. Arthur represented all the other knights' virtues rolled into one.

Spenser's letter has led later critics to try to identify each knight with one of Aristotle's virtues. While in some cases this seems easy, in others agreement has proved hard to reach. Perhaps poets should not be expected to follow too closely their original concepts, for as the work develops the allegories grow exceedingly complex. In addition to the four levels of allegory proposed by the church fathers for the interpretation of scripture called patristic exegesis, Spenser introduces political and historical allegory and several shades of moral and psychological allegory—making the poem a treasure trove for critics and scholars in search of subtle meaning.

Not all of Spenser's knights undertake their quests with the virtue they represent perfected in their own persons. This certainly proves to be the case with the Red Cross Knight, the hero of the epic's first book. Spencer's British readers recognized the red cross appearing on the knight's shield and tunic as the heraldic device of the patron saint of England, Saint George. The principal virtue of the Red Cross Knight is holiness, but, as a reader soon discovers, he needs help in perfecting it.

After calling on such classical deities as Mars, Venus and Cupid and on the chief classical muse of his inspiration—unnamed but most likely Clio, the muse of history, though also possibly Calliope, the muse of epic poetry—and after including among his muses his inspirational sovereign, Elizabeth I, Spenser opens the poem.

Book I begins with the action already well under way. A knight and a lady have already set out on the quest. He rides a warhorse, she a donkey. Behind them a dwarf, her servant, follows along. In a flashback well into Book I, the reader learns that the Red Cross knight and the lady have met at the court of Gloriana, the Faerie Queene herself.

The lady, Una, has come to Faerieland seeking help. A great dragon has enslaved her native city and its king and queen, her father and mother. She needs a champion, and Queen Gloriana appoints the as yet untried Red Cross Knight at his own request. It will be his first knightly quest. The three move forward into a pleasant wood, but the paths through it grow increasingly confusing. They choose the path most trodden, and it leads them to the mouth of a cave. The Red Cross Knight dismounts to confront whatever lurks within. The lady, Una, whose name means "the one" and who stands for truth, tries to restrain the knight. She tells him that the cave is the monster Error's den. The dwarf too advises instant flight.

Half woman, half serpent, Error daily gives birth to a thousand young who kennel in her mouth. She rushes from the cave, sees an armed knight, and tries to flee. Red Cross cuts off her retreat. She turns to fight and coils around him like a python. Una tells the knight to strangle Error before she crushes him. He tries, but Error vomits up on Red Cross her belly full of young monsters and prey. Dismayed at first, he summons his force and beheads Error. Her offspring instantly devour her body.

Pleased with the outcome of his first adventure, Red Cross, Una, and the dwarf continue on their way until they encounter an old man who invites them to spend the night in his hermitage. The hermit proves to be a Roman Catholic enchanter, Archimago, who after some talk of popes and saints calls up evil spirits to plague his guests' slumber. The Red Cross Knight, who by now has predictably fallen in love with Una, has his sleep disturbed by psychosexual dreams and a false show by Archimago that features Una's infidelity. In the layered allegory of the poem, Archimago at this stage chiefly represents hypocrisy.

Convinced by the dream that Una is not worth his trouble, the Red Cross Knight abandons her. When she wakes and finds him gone, she follows on her donkey with little hope of overtaking him. Archimago then employs his enchanter's skills to impersonate the Red Cross Knight.

The real knight, in the meantime, encounters a Saracen knight named Sansfoy (without faith) and a female companion dressed in scarlet and rich jewels. This lady is Duessa (falsehood) and is Una's opposite. The knights engage in combat. Red Cross slays Sansfoy, and Duessa claims that she was his unwilling prisoner and that her name is Fidessa— the faithful one.

Allegorically speaking, at this point in the narrative holiness in league with truth and commonsense (the dwarf) have overcome error but are not capable as yet of recognizing and overcoming ill will and guile. Manipulated by the arch magician, who for a militantly Protestant Spenser represents both the devil and the pope, holiness (Red Cross) is tricked into accepting duplicity or falsehood (Duessa posing as Fidessa) as the companion of his quest.

As they ride on together they encounter a bleeding tree that speaks to them. This enchanted being explains that he is Fradubbio, once misled by the witch Duessa, who seems beautiful to the waist but who is all deformed and serpentlike below. Duessa knows the truth of this, but she swoons and is then kissed from her faint by Red Cross.

Duessa guides the Red Cross Knight to the castle of the giant Orgoglio (pride), who imprisons him. In the meantime, Una wanders in the wood where she comes under the protection of a lion (symbol of Britain) that protects her until she encounters Prince Arthur. In due course, Arthur overcomes Orgoglio and frees a shamed and enfeebled Red Cross Knight. To recover and prepare to complete his quest, Red Cross goes to the House of Holiness where he learns repentance and how to achieve the bliss of heaven. Spiritually recovered, he resumes his mission and, after a three-day, touch-and-go battle with the dragon, Red Cross kills the beast and frees Una's city. In the course of the battle, the Dragon briefly entombs Red Cross in a well. Happily the well is the Well of Living Water, which restores the knight's strength. The episode allegorically reenacts the death and resurrection of Christ. In the last canto of Book I, the Red Cross Knight and Una—holiness and truth— are betrothed.

The second book recounts the adventures of Sir Guyon, the knight of temperance, who undertakes the destruction of the bower of bliss, home of the wanton witch Accrasia and a fountain whose waters poison those who drink from it with destructive sensuality, turning people into beasts. Unlike the Red Cross Knight, Guyon is already perfectly steadfast in his virtue. Accompanied by a religious mendicant, the Palmer, who represents right reason, Guyon is able to resist all sorts of temptations. After luring Guyon into the underworld, Mammon, the god of the world, tempts him with treasure and his daughter, Philotime (ambition). Guyon manfully resists. When he emerges from Mammon's home, however, he faints and has to be saved from assassins by Prince Arthur. Only when naked maidens bathing in the poisoned fountain attempt to entice him does Guyon briefly break into a lustful sweat, but the Palmer instantly notices and "reproves" his "wandering eyes."

In the course of Book II, Guyon visits the castle of Alma (the soul). This allegorical representation of the human body is under continual attack by twelve troops bent on its destruction. These represent the SEVEN DEADLY SINS and the five vices. Their commander, Maleger, represents both the attacks of physical disease and original sin.

Book III recounts the adventures of a female knight, Britomart, the mythic ancestress of the royal house of Britain and the allegorical representation of chastity. This book is full of magical encounters. Britomart falls in love with Artegall, whose image she sees in a magical mirror. Because she does not know if her love is real or illusory, Britomart falls into a depression. Her nurse and companion perceives the signs of love sickness and, after trying a number of home remedies, takes her ward to the cave of Merlin, the legendary magician of King Arthur. Merlin assures Britomart that Artegall is real and shows her a vision of the generations of British kings that will descend from their eventual union.

Among the wonderful characters appearing in Book III is Florimell. Her name means "honeyed flowers," and she represents female attractiveness. She is forever pursued by ill-intentioned would-be lovers and is always fleeing them. Among these Churl, the son of a witch who briefly shelters Florimell, is struck dumb by her beauty and dotes on her. Perceiving his feelings and rightly fearing lest his adoration turn to physical violence, Florimell escapes. Churl falls into such a life-threatening depression that his mother creates a False Florimell with eyes made from lamps, snow-white skin, golden wire for hair, and other attributes drawn from the hackneyed comparisons, called CONCEITS that were regularly employed by love poets in the PETRARCHIST tradition. False Florimell is the conceited lady of that tradition. Like most of the tradition's admiring readers, Spenser implies, Churl is too dumb to recognize the difference between true beauty and its shoddy representations in such poems.

In one of the most psychologically interesting episodes of *The Faerie Queene*, Florimell resists rape at the hands of an old fisherman and is rescued by Proteus, the sea god of Greek mythology who can shift his shape. Proteus then attempts to seduce Florimell by subtly perceiving the sort of man she wants and altering his behavior so that he seems to be that kind of person. Florimell intuits his intention, and continually changes her requirements until Proteus, having exhausted his repertoire, must let her go.

The varying forms of sexual passion and the capacity of chastity to control them constitute the central subject of Book III. Lust for lust's sake, as Spenser illustrates in the story of Hellenore and Paridell, leads to bestiality. At the same time, fear of sex in married love, one of the interpretations of the cause of Amoretta's sufferings in the castle of the evil enchanter Busirane, can be overcome by chastity. Britomart illustrates this by rescuing Amoretta, kidnapped from her wedding, after seeing her march in a parade of the slaves of the cruel tyrant Cupid. In this episode called the "Masque of Love," Cupid's victims appear in forms that represent their suffering at his hands. Amoretta marches holding her living heart in her hands before her, ripped from her breast and pierced through with Cupid's dart.

In Book III as well, Belphoebe (one of the representations of Queen Elizabeth I) rescues a wounded Prince Arthur and restores him to physical health, only to wound him worse when he falls in love with her. Also in this important section of the poem, the episode in the Garden of Adonis allegorically explores the role that sexuality plays in the continual renewal of the world.

The fourth book of *The Faerie Queene* explores friendship, and the fifth, which recounts the meeting between Britomart and Artegall, examines justice—the virtue that Artegall represents. Book VI presents Sir Calidore and examines the virtue of courtesy in terms of Calidore's quest to subdue the Blatant Beast—a monster with a thousand vicious tongues. The books touched on here plus two more cantos on the subject of mutability were all of the grand design for *The Faerie Queene* that Spenser completed before his death. The work substantiates the claim often made for Spenser that he is a poet's poet. Though our contemporary readers often find the poem's complex allegories, polished artifice, and intentionally archaic language difficult, those who persevere will be rewarded by one of the most musical poems in the language—one filled with incomparable depths of psychological and moral analysis.

Bibliography

King, Andrew. *The Faerie Queene and Middle English Romance: The Matter of Just Memory*. Oxford and New York: Clarendon Press, 2000.

Spenser, Edmund. *The Faerie Queene.* Edited by A. C. Hamilton, Hiroshi Yamashita, and Toshiyuki Suzuki. New York: Longmans, 2001.

Faithful Shepherd, The　(Il Pastor Fido)
Giovanni Battista Guarini　(1590)

Widely read in manuscript before its publication and subsequent first performance (1595), GUARINI's *The Faithful Shepherd* looks back to TORQUATO TASSO's much briefer PASTORAL drama *Aminta* for a part of its inspiration.

The pastoral drama was Renaissance Italy's most original contribution to theatrical history. Pastoral theater is rooted in the notion that the Edenic Golden Age—the earliest age of human existence—partly survived for a time, despite humanity's fallen estate, in the Greek region of Arcadia, where nymphs, shepherds, huntsmen, noblemen, and priests lived their lives and conducted their amours in an idyllic landscape.

Adam and Eve's fall had, of course, occurred, so even in Arcadia there were difficulties to be overcome, and Guarini exploits all of them in his play. These included the failure of some shepherdesses, nymphs, and shepherds to return the love that others felt for them or even to love at all. Also, the lustful appetites of another set of Arcadian inhabitants, the half-human, half-goat satyrs, threatened the virtue of unwary maidens. Most ominous of all, perhaps, was the annual necessity for sacrificing a maiden's life to the moon goddess Cynthia/Diana to atone for the sins of Arcadia.

As Europe's earliest theorist of TRAGICOMEDY, Guarini thought of his play as representing a third genre of theatrical production beyond COMEDY and TRAGEDY. In *The Faithful Shepherd* Guarini interweaves multiple situations—each with the potential for a tragic outcome—into the fabric of his play, but he is careful never to let the situation grow overly tragic and to ensure that all outcomes remain essentially comedic.

The main plot concerns a young man, Mirtillo, who feels a secret passion for Amarillis. She, however, is promised to Silvio—a hunter who prefers sport to love. Her father thinks that she and Silvio are destined to marry and that, should she oppose that destiny, she is fated to become the next sacrifice at Cynthia's altar. Another young woman, Corsica, loves Mirtillo. Corsica, moreover, knows that if Mirtillo spurns her love, it will change to hate and that she will exact vengeance on both Mirtillo and Amarillis. Corsica, in turn, is beloved by a satyr. On being spurned by her, the satyr seizes her by the hair. Things appear grim for Corsica, but she easily escapes from the satyr, leaving him with a wig in his hand. An attempted ravishment by a satyr becomes a stock requirement of the pastoral drama

Early in the play, Mirtillo's friend, Ergasto, recounts the origin of the annual sacrifice: Amintas, a priest of Cynthia/Diana, has been led on and then spurned by a nymph, Lucrina. Amintas prays to Cynthia for redress. The goddess demands a life for the insult to her priest. Lucrina is the chosen sacrifice. Rather than kill his beloved, Amintas plunges the sacrificial knife into his own heart. Realizing too late the consequences of her behavior and her love for Amintas, Lucrina commits suicide at the goddess's altar.

This history sets the scene for the partial reenactment of the original sacrifice when Amarillis indeed becomes its intended victim. Like Amintas before him, however, Mirtillo volunteers to die in her place. Montano, the priest, accepts the substitution, and his axe is raised to strike down Mirtillo when Mirtillo's foster father, Carino (a character who may bear a distant resemblance to the author) interrupts the ritual. Carino recounts the tale of the infant Mirtillo's rescue from the river Alpheus during a flood 19 years before. The circumstances surrounding Carino's adoption of Mirtillo convince Montano that Mirtillo is his own son, lost as a baby during that self-same flood.

After many changes in fortune and unlikely invention, including Silvio's at last falling in love with Dorinda, people in wolf's clothing, and a brilliant tour de force in which Echo predicts Silvio's future by repeating with new meaning the last phrase of his every statement, Mirtillo and Amarillis marry, and, with the possible exception of Corsica, all the young people of the play end up happily matched in love relationships.

Though Guarini has often been accused of pedantry and *The Faithful Shepherd* unfavorably compared with Tasso's *Aminta,* the truth of the matter is that, though Tasso is much the superior poet, Guarini's sense of stagecraft seems surer. Whereas in Tasso the characters comment on and describe past action, in Guarini action usually happens as the characters speak. Certainly George Frederick Handel recognized the dramatic possibilities in *The Faithful Shepherd* when he chose it as the basis for his opera of the same name.

Bibliography

Guarini, Giovanni Battista. *The Faithful Shepherd.* Translated by Thomas Sheridan. Edited by Robert Hogan and Edward A. Nickerson. Newark: University of Delaware Press, 1989.

Familiar and Invective Letters, The
Hélisenne de Crenne (1539)

This was the first work in the French language to attempt to tell a story through a series of letters with no connecting commentary. The *Letters,* which appeared in eight editions by 1560, is composed of 13 personal missives and five invective ones. All 13 of the personal letters ostensibly come from the pen of the fictive HÉLISENNE. So do four of the five invectives, but her husband ostensibly writes the second letter of that series. In it he accuses Hélisenne of intolerable infidelities and of many of the faults that men have alleged against women in person and in print from time immemorial.

The letters reveal a pattern of growing self-knowledge in the development of the central character. In the first letter the writer addresses an abbess and explores the idea of becoming a nun. In the next letter Hélisenne refuses an invitation so that she can care for her ailing mother. The epistles that follow offer conventional advice to a series of friends. To one whose character has been besmirched she suggests chaste forbearance. To another, banished unfairly from court, she counsels patience. To a friend involved in an illicit love affair she recommends the triumph of reason and breaking off the liaison.

The next two letters console friends. One has lost money and the other his wife. Finally in this first part of her series of personal letters, the writer counsels a friend to give up both her lover, her objections to the spouse her parents have chosen for her and to marry advantageously.

Now, however, the mood shifts, and the reader discovers that the letters so far have only revealed the public face of Hélisenne. In the ninth letter she withdraws the advice she has just given, telling her friend Clarissa to conceal from her parents her love for someone they have not approved. In the 10th she apologizes for her prudishness to the friend with an illicit lover, confessing that she herself is in the same situation, and the 11th—again to the same friend—reveals Hélisenne's distress at the conflict she feels.

In the 12th personal letter the reader discovers that Hélisenne's husband knows of her infidelities and has virtually imprisoned her, so the unhappy woman pleads with her correspondent for help in escaping. The last letter in the personal series, which is to her lover, describes in code all her suffering on his behalf and her willingness to go on even if it means more pain.

The five invective letters involve an exchange between Hélisenne and her husband. In her first letter she attempts to cloak her activities by suggesting that fiction is not the same as autobiography. The husband does not believe her. His letter accuses her of infidelity and adds virtually every misogynistic charge ever made against women.

In the last three of the invective letters, Hélisenne rises for a while above personal agendas to become the champion of women everywhere. She refutes her husband's general accusations against women with Scripture, with the arguments of the ancients, and with the writings of early churchmen. She then returns to more personal matters, defending a woman's right to compose and publish and denouncing small-minded bumpkins who criticize her for doing so.

The invective letters reintroduced into France a long quiescent, medieval literary subgenre, the "quarrel of women." Works in this tradition asserted the rights of women to learn and write and defended women's characters and their right to control their own persons.

Bibliography

Crenne, Hélisenne de. *A Renaissance Woman: Hélisenne's Personal and Invective Letters.* Translated and edited by Marianna M. Mustacchi and Paul J. Archambault. Syracuse, N.Y.: Syracuse University Press, 1986.

Faydī (later Fayyādī), Abu 'L-Fayd
(b. Shaykh Mubarak Al-Madawi)
(1547–1595)

A commentator on the Koran, a scholar, a physician and a poet in the Persian language, Faydī came to be regarded as one of the nine *jewels* of the court of the Mughal Emperor of India, AKBAR (1542–1605). In 1566, Faydī persuaded his outlaw father to surrender and seek the forgiveness of the emperor in his court at Agra. Accompanying his father to the interview, Faydī so impressed Akbar that he took the young poet into his service. There he rapidly rose to important positions and began the composition of a collection of five poems, only two of which he ever completed. He did however complete a collection of lyric poems in Persian. He also wrote two books in Arabic, one on ethics and another that conducted a commentary on the Koran. Although later scholars have praised his work as very influential among Turkish writers, his reputation in his own day does not seem to have been quite as secure. He chose to write both his Arabic works without using any dotted letters. This meant that his Arabic vocabulary was unusually extensive and that he could find synonyms for common words that contained dotted letters. Some, therefore, have dismissed these works as vulgar showmanship, and some have gone so far as to accuse him of having written them while drunk and ritually impure, but the best scholarship deems this unlikely. Among his contemporaries, however, he does seem to have been regarded with some suspicion because he became an adherent of Akbar's revisionist Islamic religion, which traditional believers denounced. Akbar hoped to reconcile Islam and Hinduism.

A translator as well as a poet, Faydī translated a Sanskrit treatise on arithmetic and, on Akbar's orders, parts of the Indian EPIC poem *The Mahabharata* into Persian. A posthumous collection of Faydī's letters was made by his nephew. The letters are notable for a simple, readable style at odds with the flowery language favored by many of his contemporaries. Very few of his apparently voluminous writings survive, and only a few of his poems have been translated into English and anthologized.

Fehím   (Unji-záda Mustafá Çelebî)
(d. ca. 1647)

One of a very few Turkish poets of the 16th and 17th centuries who were not members of the legal profession, Fehím apparently lived by his wits and by the support his patrons provided. When one of his patrons, Eyyúb Pasha, became the Ottoman governor of Egypt, Fehím accompanied him to Cairo. Unhappy there, Fehím wrote uncomplimentary verses about Egypt. Displeased with these poems, his patron dismissed him.

A generous Egyptian took pity on Fehím and in exchange for one of his poems gave the poet enough money to support him on his return journey overland by camel caravan to Constantinople. On that journey, however, Fehím fell ill and died.

He is chiefly remembered for his contributions to lyrical poetry like GHAZELs and QASÍDAs. Unlike most of his predecessors, Fehím drew both his subjects and his images from familiar surroundings instead of from earlier poems. This practice made him a forerunner of the following period of Turkish poets. He writes, for instance, *ghazels* about dancers and about dervishes whom he observed in the market.

Feng Menlong   (Feng Meng-lung)
(1574–1646)

An accomplished late-Ming period dramatist, editor, and short-story writer from the Chinese city of Suzhou (Soochow), Feng, like most Chinese writers of his epoch, became a member of the imperial civil service. Unlike most of them, he did not achieve this honor until he was 60 years old—10 years after his first collection of stories appeared. He also served as a soldier and eventually died while fighting against the Manchu.

His best remembered works include his contributions to three collections, each containing 40 stories. Chinese literary tradition alludes to these works as the *Three Words* because *words* appears in the title of each collection: *Clear Words to Instruct the World* (1620), *Common Words to Warn the World* (1624), and *Constant Words to Awaken the World* (1627). The literary historian Jenna Wu suggests that Feng likely contributed 19 stories to the 1620 collection—also known as *Stories Old and New*—16 to the 1624 collection, and only one or two to the third collection. He drew his material from anecdotes, from history, and from the stories of his predecessors, editing or reworking them to suit the tastes of his readers. In his process of revision he rescued from oblivion several stories and even novels not his own that would surely have otherwise been lost. Some of the works rescued clearly were intended for public performance, for they command audiences to be attentive and repeated action for the benefit of late arrivals. Such stories live in the oral rather than the written tradition and disappear more easily.

Several topics commanded Feng's interest. He liked to write and rework love stories. He was fond of depicting historical military, political, and patriotic leaders and courageous and generous men who are willing to sacrifice themselves for their beliefs or their loved ones. A historical person in the last category was Wang Hsin-chih. Wrongfully accused of sedition, Wang sacrificed his life to save his family and his estate.

Feng also wrote about scholars and courtesans, about able men whose talents went unrecognized because they lacked the connections necessary to bring them to official attention—a situation that reflected Feng's own late-blooming official career. He wrote about love and fidelity, and he penned works designed to disseminate the values of the Confucian religion—sexual morality, loyalty, trust in benevolence, and fear of demons. In Feng's stories, the good are rewarded in this world or the next and the evil are punished. POETIC JUSTICE seeks out and finds the evildoers through complex and ingenious plots that sometimes need ghosts or visits to the underworld to unravel them.

Good English translations of many of Feng's original stories and of those he edited are widely available. The titles of some serve to suggest Feng's whimsical sense of humor: "Love in a Junk," or "The Mandarin-duck Girdle." Even a detective story appears in Feng's work with the tale, "Censor Ch'en Ingeniously Solves the Case of the Golden Hairpins."

Bibliography

Feng Menglong. *Stories Old and New: A Ming Dynasty Collection Compiled by Feng Menglong.* Translated by Shuhui Yang and Yunqin Yang. Seattle: University of Washington Press, ca. 2000.
———. *Four Cautionary Tales.* Translated by Harold Acton and Lee Yi-hsieh. London: J. Lehmann, 1947.
———. *The Perfect Lady by Mistake and Other Stories.* Translated by William Dolby. London: P. Elek, 1976.
———. *Stories from a Ming Collection: The Art of the Chinese Story-Teller.* Translated by Cyril Birch. New York: Grove Press, 1958.

Fernández de Oviedo y Valdés, Gonzalo (1478–1557)

An early arrival in the Spanish New World, Fernández de Oviedo y Valdés received his education at the court of King Ferdinand and Queen Isabella of Spain. In 1513 he traveled to Tierra Firme in newly Spanish America with a dual responsibility. He supervised the smelting of gold ore and objects acquired by the Spaniards, and his rulers had charged him as well with chronicling the natural history of their transatlantic possessions. He spent the rest of his life fulfilling the second responsibility. His *General and Natural History of the Indies* eventually expanded to fill 50 books, and he was still engaged in adding material to each of its major sections at the time of his death. Both the staggering magnitude of the effort and its author's method of working produced a document very uneven in its literary quality. Sometimes Fernández de Oviedo y Valdés simply copied whole documents from reports the governors of various

Spanish dominions sent him. At other times, he abstracted source documents so severely that readers feel shortchanged of relevant detail. Sometimes his work rises to eloquence, but more usually he rambles. On balance, however, the work provides us with a valuable and unique source of factual material about geography, geology, aboriginal peoples, and the political goings-on of 16th-century Spanish America.

The entire Spanish version of the *General and Natural History* has only once appeared in print in an edition of 1851–55. Extractions from the various sections of the work organized around topics of special interest have appeared in English translation. Among others these include portions relating to Christopher Columbus, Ponce de León's exploration of Florida, the discovery of the Amazon River, de Soto's explorations and discovery of the Mississippi, and Cabeza de Vaca's expedition across the North American continent.

Fernández de Oviedo y Valdés penned other works as well. In his later years he wrote a series of personal recollections in the form of dialogues, *Batallas y Quinquagenas* (Exchanges of fire [battles] and my 50s, ca. 1550.). He talks in these about his happy memories of his country, about notable families and persons with whom he was acquainted, including members of Spanish royalty, and about such high church officials as Cardinal Ximenes, the founder of the University of Alcalá and the motivating force behind the production of the COMPLUTENSIAN POLYGLOT BIBLE. Beyond this, Oviedo wrote a similarly titled, 7,500-line poem *Las Quinquagenas* (The fifties, 1556). This poem drew more character sketches of his distinguished contemporaries. As a younger man, Oviedo had also written a CHIVALRIC ROMANCE entitled for its principal character, *Claribalte* (1519) and a work of religious asceticism that he said he translated from Italian: *Reglas de la Vida* (Rules for life, 1548.)

Bibliography

Carrillo, Jesús, ed. *Oviedo on Columbus.* Translated by Diane Avalle–Arce. Turnhout, Belgium: Brepols, ca. 2000.

Fernández de Oviedo y Valdés, Gonzalo. *Batallas y quinquagenas: batalla primera.* Edited by Juan Pérez de Tudela y Bueso. Madrid: La Real Academia de la Historia, ca. 2000–02.

———. *Claribalte.* Edited by Maria José Rodilla León. Mexico City: Universidad Nacional Autónoma de México, 2002.

———. *Historia General y Natural de las Indias.* Edited by José Amador de los Rios. Madrid: La Real Academia de la Historia, 1851–55.

———. *The conquest and settlement of the island of Boriquen or Puerto Rico.* Translated and edited by Daymond Turner. Avon, Conn.: Limited Editions Club, 1975.

———. *The Hernando de Soto expedition.* Edited by Jerald T. Milanich. New York: Garland, 1991.

Krieger, Alex D., ed. *We Came Naked and Barefoot: the Journey of Cabeza de Vaca across North America.* Austin: University of Texas Press, 2002.

Ferreira, António (1528–1569)

A Portuguese native of Lisbon, Ferreira received a thorough HUMANIST education and specialized in canon law. As a poet and dramatist, he pioneered the introduction of both Italian and ancient classical forms of poetry into Portugal. His literary reputation rests principally upon a verse play, *THE TRAGEDY OF INÊS DE CASTRO* (1598). Both Ferreira and his contemporary LUÍZ VAZ DE CAMÕES (ca. 1524–80) treat the same incident from Portuguese history as the subject of a portion of their verse.

In 1355 Inês de Castro was condemned to die by legal assassination. Camões's version of this sad episode appears in the third canto of his *LUSIAD*. Ferreira instead devotes his entire play to unraveling her love story, to exploring the moral dilemma of a king who must, for the greater good, justify to his own conscience the unpalatable act of ordering the death of an innocent subject who is also secretly his son's second wife and the mother of the king's grandchildren. Ferreira also sets forth the relevant concerns of Christian humanism—a movement whose precepts formed the core of Ferreira's thinking. Those precepts, together with patriotism and popularizing in Portugal the poetic models of PETRARCH and the ancients, constituted the rationale of Ferreira's poetic output.

In addition to *Castro*, Ferreira also wrote a pair of prose comedies constructed on classical models but Portuguese in theme, *Bristo* (1552), and *Cioso* (ca. 1553). He also penned a significant body of lyric verse. His collected works, *Poemas Lusitanos* (Portuguese or Lusitanian poems) were published in 1598 but, aside from *Castro*, have not as yet appeared in English.

After a career as a jurist, a first brief marriage to a beloved wife who died young, and a second marriage later in life, Ferreira died of the plague in 1569.

Bibliography

Earle, T. F. *The Muse Reborn: The Poetry of António Ferreira*. Oxford, U.K.: The Clarendon Press, 1988.

Ferreira, Antonio. *The Tragedy of Inês de Castro*. Translated by John R. C. Martin. Coimbra, Portugal: Universidade de Coimbra, 1987.

Ficino, Marsilio (1433–1499)

A Florentine polymath, gifted as a philosopher, linguist, physician, theologian, and translator, Ficino was intimately connected throughout his life with the ruling Medici family of Florence. His father was Cosimo de' Medici's physician, and Cosimo knew of the young man's intellectual capacities very early on, arranging to have him trained so that he would qualify to teach Greek philosophy. Ficino also took orders as a Roman Catholic priest.

After mastering Latin and studying the writings of the ancients and of medieval churchmen, Ficino accordingly moved on to Greek. Like the rest of the Florentine intelligentsia, Cosimo was deeply interested in the HUMANIST recovery of Greek works. He also collected manuscripts. In 1463, therefore, the Florentine grandee gave Ficino an income-producing farm, a residence, and a Greek manuscript containing PLATO's then-known works and set Ficino to translating it into Latin. Almost as an afterthought Cosimo also requested a similar translation of The body of hermetic [secret] knowledge (*Corpus Hermeticum*)—a treatise concerning alchemy, astrology, and other arcane pseudosciences and magical lore. Within five years

Ficino had finished drafting his Latin translation of the works of Plato—a daunting task. He revised them and saw them through the press in 1484. Thereafter many revised editions of this influential work appeared. Although he was not Plato's first Renaissance translator—BRUNI and others had preceded him—he was reputed to be the best.

He also translated into Italian both Dante's Latin treatise on Monarchy (*De monarchia*) and Plato's Banquet (*Symposium*). Arguably these translations from the Latin and the Greek, together with the many others that he did—notably of the neoplatonist Greek philosophers—constitute Ficino's most important lasting contribution to the world of letters. His translations, however, were not the project nearest his heart.

Ficino most ardently wished to synthesize Christianity with ancient philosophy—particularly with that of the first neoplatonist, Plotinus (205–270 C.E.). In this enterprise he was partly successful. He dismissed ordinary reasoning in favor of fervent, enraptured thinking informed by intellectual love and the goal of fusing the human mind with Christ conceived of as the "Wisdom and Understanding of God." He played an important role in undergirding the church's 16th century assertion of the immortality of the human soul on rational grounds. His mystical theology has been considered a precursor of Jungian psychology.

His study of Neoplatonism, however, also led Ficino into arenas that the church found suspect. Via humoral medicine and the idea that one's astrology determined one's physical makeup, Ficino became interested in ancient magical theory (see MAGIC), demonology, numerology, and other arcane ideas. These he explored in his work, About life (*De vita*, 1489), which raised ecclesiastical eyebrows.

A complex and perplexing figure, Ficino wrote so prolifically, profoundly, and eclectically that much work remains to be done on the body of his writings to unravel his ideas. Among the leading figures currently involved in that effort is the scholar Michael J. B. Allen.

Bibliography

Allen, Michael J. B. *Nuptial Arithmetic: Marsilio Ficino's commentary on the Fatal Number in Book*

VIII of Plato's Republic. Berkeley: University of California Press, ca. 1994.

———. *Synoptic Art: Marsilio Ficino on the History of Platonic Interpretation.* Florence, Italy: L. S. Olschki, 1998.

Ficino, Marsilio. *Marsilio Ficino: His Theology, His Philosophy, His Legacy.* Edited by Michael J. B. Allen, Valery Rees, and Martin Davies. Leiden, Netherlands: E.J. Brill, 2002.

———. *Platonic Theology.* Edited by James Hankins and William Bowen. Translated by Michael J. B. Allen and John Warden. Cambridge, Mass.: Harvard University Press, 2001–2002.

Hankins, James. *Plato in the Italian Renaissance.* Leiden, Netherlands: E. J. Brill, 1990.

———. *Icastes: Marsilio Ficino's Interpretation of Plato's Sophist: Five Studies and a Critical Edition.* Edited and translated by Michael J. B. Allen: Berkeley: University of California Press, ca. 1989.

Finnish language and literature

Although Finnish people share the Scandinavian peninsula with the Norwegians, the Swedes, and some far northern tribal peoples, the Finnish language is unrelated to others in the region. The non-Finnish peoples mentioned all speak North Germanic languages and, along with Danish and Icelandic, these tongues are closely related descendents of Old Norse. Finnish, on the other hand, is a Finno–Ugric language related to Hungarian. Reportedly, in the Middle Ages Finland produced a largely oral tradition of folk poetry, and though some examples of it survived into the Renaissance, no texts have come down to us. Rather it was during the Renaissance that the PROTESTANT REFORMATION gave impetus to a new spurt of literary activity in the Finnish language.

The need to promote the new faith and to create a literate populace motivated the early literary productions of Finnish writers of the period. Michael Agricola (ca. 1509–57) translated the New Testament (1548) into his native tongue. A Lutheran bishop, Agricola also encouraged literacy by publishing an *A–B–C Book* (1542). He continued to encourage the Lutheran faith by publishing a Finnish version of *The catechism* (1543). The year 1544 saw the publication of his *Book of prayers,* and in 1551 his *Book of hymns* completed his literary contributions.

The work Agricola had begun, one of his successor bishops, Ericus Erici (ca. 1545–1625), continued with two editions of a large collection of sermons in 1621 and 1625. These collections continued to influence the Finnish pulpit and populace for the next 200 years. Finally, in 1642, the entire Bible became available in Finnish. Additionally, religious poems and occasional verse appeared, but the Bible and the work of the two bishops were the most important literary productions of the Finnish Renaissance.

Bibliography

Bach, Giovanni, Richard Beck et al. *The History of Scandinavian Literatures.* New York: Dial Press Inc., 1988.

Blankner, Frederika, editor and translator. *The History of the Scandinavian Literatures: A Survey. . . .* 1938. Westport, Conn.: Greenwood Press, 1975.

Schoolfield, George C., ed. *A History of Finland's Literature.* Lincoln, Neb.: University of Nebraska Press, ca. 1998.

Firenzuola, Agnolo (1493–1543)

Acceding to his father Bastiano's wish that he study law and follow an ecclesiastical career, Firenzuola was educated in Siena and Perugia while at the same time pursuing his own HUMANIST interests. In 1518 he became the Roman attorney for the Vallombrosian monastic order. His residence in Rome gave him the opportunity to renew his acquaintance with an old friend, the celebrated and sometimes notorious PIETRO ARETINO. The two had been wild students together. In Rome, Firenzuola enlarged his literary and scholarly acquaintance as well. Also in Rome, Firenzuola fell in love in 1523. His relationship with an anonymous woman he called Costanza Amaretta in his writings lasted until her death in 1525.

Under her influence he turned his attention away from the law to the pursuit of his scholarly and literary interests. In 1524 he attacked Gian Giorgio Trissino's abortive attempt to introduce letters from the Greek alphabet into the Italian spelling system. Firenzuola's discussion attracted the favorable attention of many literary contemporaries, including the most influential of Renaissance Italian literary pundits, PIETRO BEMBO.

Encouraged, Firenzuola merged the short Italian narrative in the manner of GIOVANNI BOCCACCIO with the dialogue narratives of classical antiquity in a collection of stories called Discussions about love (*Raggionamenti d'amore*). Many of the stories deal humorously with the moral lapses of the clergy—both male and female. The work's major characters, Don Giovanni, Sister (*Suor*) Appellagia, and Brother (*Fra*) Cherubino became the standards for subsequent Italian comedy about dissolute clerics.

There followed a period during which Firenzuola, apparently depressed by the death of his beloved and ill from the effects of venereal disease, kept largely to himself, attending to his duties with the Vallombrosians. They may have assisted him financially by granting him incomes from San Prassede (St. Praxeds) in Rome and Santa Maria di Spoleti. They advanced him to the post of abbot of their monastery of San Salvatore a Vaiano in the city of Prato where Firenzuola once more took up his pen.

In Prato he wrote his *Dialogo delle bellezze delle donne* (Dialogue on the beauties of women, 1541). In this important work Firenzuola discusses the way that women are represented in 16th-century painting and sculpture and points out the connections between that representation and the philosophy of PLATO. He applies the Platonic doctrine that contemplation of physical beauty leads in turn to the consideration of intellectual and moral excellence and finally to philosophical contemplation of the ideal. The women whom he pretends to have interrupted in a discussion about the beauty of Mona Amelia della Torre Nuova and whom he disguises with names not their own were actual persons in Prato.

Firenzuola also translated the Roman poet Horace's *Ars Poetica* (The art of poetry). He wrote two comedies and set forth in Italian some folk stories from India in The first version of the discourses of the animals (*La prima veste dei discorsi degli animali*). This work is composed of a series of jewellike little novels. Late in his career Firenzuola composed an adaptation of the Roman author Apuleius's novel, *The Golden Ass* (second century C.E.). This free adaptation (published 1550) contains interesting autobiographical detail and illustrates Firenzuola's style at its best.

At first lionized by the citizens of Prato, Firenzuola somehow made enemies, finding himself at length both shunned and poor.

Bibliography

Firenzuola, Agnolo. *The Bawdy Tales of Firenzuola.* Translated by Jules Griffon. Covina, Calif.: Collectors' Publications, 1967.

———. *Tales of Firenzuola.* Translated anonymously. New York: Italica Press, 1987.

———. *On the Beauty of Women.* Translated by Konrad Eisenbichler and Jacqueline Murray. Philadelphia: University of Pennsylvania Press, 1992.

Five Friends (*Panch-Sakhas:* Oriya language Poets of India) (16th–17th centuries)

Devotional poets of Orissa province in northern India, the five friends shared a common theological view. They considered that the supreme god is Nirakar, or the void, and that one could come to know that deity through difficult yogic practices. The group included the poets Achyutananda, Ananta, Balarama, Jagannatha, and Yasovanta.

The poems of the group are addressed to initiates of the yogic practices they employed. Therefore, their poems were never intended for the general public. Rather they employ esoteric images serving as codes that the initiates understood. A broken boat, for instance, stood for the human body—the vehicle of the soul. The human mind was figured forth in their poems by various images: a talking bird, an unbaked earthen pot, or a cow ready for milking.

These poets also participated in the BHAKTI devotional movement by writing *bhajans* addressed to the Hindu deity, Lord Krishna. *Bhajans* were poems that named the gods by their several names and informed them of the writer's sufferings. They are expressions of pure devotion, love, and surrender to the divine will.

Five Women Who Loved Love Ihara Saikaku (1686)

SAIKAKU's collection of five novellas concerns impetuous women whose lives are sometimes lost and always deeply changed when they act on their emotional impulses. In the first of the five tales, "The Story of Seijuro in Himeji," an extraordinarily handsome young man named Seijuro has acquired a name for himself by enjoying the favors of all the 89 courtesans in the Japanese town of Murotsu. All the courtesans were besotted with Seijuro and besieged him with so many love letters that he was hard pressed to answer them.

He genuinely fell in love, however, with one of the courtesans, Minakawa. Convinced that they can never marry, he tests her love by proposing joint suicide. At first she rejected the idea but then agreed to it. When she brought knives to do the deed, however, others in her brothel prevented them. As a result of the consequent scandal, Seijuro had to enter a Buddhist monastery, and Minakawa commited suicide at the first opportunity.

Fearing Seijuro would do likewise, people tried to keep the news from him. About 10 day later, though, he heard about it. His mother's entreaties prevented his suicide, but he ran away to begin a new life in the town of Himeji. He flourished there, finding employment as an assistant innkeeper. His employer had a lovely 16-year-old sister named Onatsu.

One day the women of Onatsu's household discovered and read some of the love letters the courtesans of Murotsu had written Seijuro. Thinking that Seijuro would be an experienced lover, Onatsu fell desperately in love with him. She managed to communicate that fact to Seijuro, who returned the feeling. For some time, the two sought opportunities to escape the watchful eyes of those about them. Eventually, a fleeting opportunity presented itself. The lovers seized it and agreed to run away together.

Pursued by Onatsu's brother and others, they boarded a ship but were captured when the vessel returned to port. The lovers were separated, and Onatsu learned in a dream that, though she would live a long life, Seijuro was destined to die soon. The dream proved accurate, for Seijuro was accused of having stolen 700 gold pieces from the inn. Convicted of the theft, he was executed. Too late his employer discovered that the gold had only spilled from its bag and was still in the inn. To do penance for the way her impetuous love led to her lover's demise, Onatsu became a nun and lived out the rest of her days as a holy woman.

The theme of the consequences of impetuosity continues in Saikaku's next tale, "The Barrel Maker Brimful of Love." In this story the barrelmaker, or cooper, falls in love with Osen, the maid of a household in his town. An old matchmaker volunteers her services, and after a humorous digression in which the girl, the matchmaker, the cooper, and a would-be seducer all go on pilgrimage together, Osen and the cooper marry, have children, and enjoy a happy and prosperous life together until a chance incident intervenes.

Osen volunteers to assist in the preparations for a feast celebrating the 50th anniversary of the death of a neighbor's father. As Osen is helping out, the master of the house, Chozaemon, accidentally drops a bowl on her head and disarranges her hairdo. Chozaemon's wife thinks that Osen and her husband have been misbehaving. She accuses Osen, refuses to believe her denial, and gossips about Osen at every opportunity. Osen decides that since her reputation is ruined, she will avenge herself by in fact doing what she has been accused of. Chozaemon reaches a similar conclusion, and the two arrange a halfhearted liaison. The cooper catches them naked and chases Chozaemon. Osen commits suicide, and Chozaemon is eventually executed. Their bodies are both exposed in "the field of shame." If the punishment seems too severe for the crime, Saikaku's point is that the consequences of impetuous impropriety are neither predictable nor always just.

The third story of Saikaku's collection, "What the Seasons Brought the Almanac Maker," begins with a description of the almanac maker's beautiful wife and the notoriety of her behavior. Then the scene immediately flashes back to a group of jaded girl chasers who are amusing themselves by watching women pass and embarrassing them with unwelcome remarks. The loveliest woman that passes, the loafers learn, is nicknamed "modern Komachi." Saikaku prepares his reader for what follows with the remark: "Only later did they learn how much devilry was hid beneath that beauty."

The lovely girl proves to be named Osan. A lonely almanac maker falls desperately in love with her at first sight and arranges to marry her with the help of a matchmaker. After three happy years with her, the almanac maker must travel on business. He arranges to have a trusted employee, Moemon, assist Osan with business affairs. Moemon moves in, and a maid, Rin, falls for him while administering a precautionary remedy against winter illness.

Observing her illiterate maid's feelings, Osan writes Moemon a love letter on Rin's behalf. That missive begins an exchange of correspondence that concludes with an assignation between Rin and Moemon. Osan plans to make a joke of everything and to take Rin's place to embarrass Moemon. Instead, in a hardly credible episode, Osan falls so deeply asleep that when Moemon comes to visit the woman he thinks is Rin, he makes love to the woman he finds in bed without awakening her. On realizing what has happened, Osan abandons herself to her unintentional situation, and she and Moemon throw caution and reputation to the winds in a wild love affair.

Eventually, they go on pilgrimage together and feign a joint suicide, intending to begin life together in a new city. Starving in the wilderness, they appeal to an aunt of Moemon for help. The aunt is suspicious, and under her cross-examination, Moemon claims that Osan is his sister. The aunt then proposes that Osan marry her son, who proves to be a dangerous and churlish oaf. To avoid the proposed match, the lovers slip away together in the night.

Again, however, the operations of the universe intervene. Moemon returns to his native city because he feels compelled to know what people are saying about him. A peddlar has recognized the pair in the village where they are hiding and tells the almanac maker. He investigates, finds the pair alive, and files charges. Both are executed for their crimes. Again, the storyteller invokes an unforgiving universe.

"The Greengrocer's Daughter with a Bundle of Love," stands fourth in the collection. The refugees from a city fire take shelter in a Buddhist temple, and while helping extract a splinter from the finger of a young samurai named Onogawa Kichisaburo, the greengrocer's daughter, Oshichi, falls in love with him and he with her. The two exchange love letters, and Oshichi seeks him out one stormy night. Both are only 15, but after some awkwardness the two become lovers. In the morning, Oshchi's mother finds the two together. She separates them and takes her daughter home. Some time later, Kichisaburo visits her home in disguise, and the two are once again together for a single night, but this time her father separates the pair.

Desperate, Oshichi thinks that perhaps if she starts another fire she will have to return to the temple as a refugee. She no sooner sets the fire, however, than townspeople discover her at it and arrest her. As punishment, she is exposed to public ridicule in several locations, and she simply decides to die. On learning of her death, Kichisaburo wishes to commit suicide, but the monks prevent him.

An interesting complication in "The Greengrocer's Daughter . . ." arises from the fact that Kichisaburo is involved in a lifelong, sworn relationship with an older samurai warrior whose place in the young man's affection Oshichi takes. Eventually, learning that Oshichi wanted him to become a monk and care for her spirit with his prayers, Kichisaburo does so, though everyone thinks it a shame and that his fate is harder than hers.

The last tale in Saikaku's stories of love in the city, "Gengobei, the Mountain of Love," recounts the story of the 25-year-old Gengobei who loves another young man named Hachijuro. One night as they are together, Hachijuro dies suddenly. Gengobei promises his dead companion that he will "mourn . . . for three years" before joining him "among the ghosts."

In the next chapter, though, Gengobei meets a beautiful boy who drives all thoughts of dying from his mind. The two spend a single night together and promise undying friendship. Gengobei completes a pilgrimage that he has undertaken but then hurries back to his new companion. In his absence, however, his new friend has also died. In his grief, Gengobei resolves to live a hermit's life and retires to a shack near the sea. There a young woman named Oman observes him and falls in love with the hermit. She becomes aware of his preference for men, sees a vision in which the spirits of his two dead loves appear, each making advances toward him. She then assumes the character of a man and confesses her feelings. Not knowing she is a girl, he accepts her. When he discovers her sex, he decides that love is love, and he loves her.

As the story continues, going with Oman in search of his father, Gengobei discovers that his own former spendthrift life of pleasure has ruined the family fortune. Gengobei and Oman join a group of itinerant actors, and Gengobei ironically gets to play himself, for the story of his profligacy has become legendary. Eventually, Oman's wealthy parents find the pair, have them properly married, and turn over the keys to their vast fortune to Gengobei. It occurs to him that he is rich enough to buy up all the female prostitutes of three Japanese cities and have enough left over to finance all the theaters.

Only in this final story is Oman's impetuosity rewarded with a happy ending.

Bibliography

Saikaku, Ihara. *Five Women Who Loved Love*. Translated by William Theodore De Bary. Rutland, Vt.: Charles E. Tuttle Company, 1959.

Fleming, Paul (1609–1640)

A German poet, itinerant businessman (1634–36), physician, and poet, Paul Fleming attended the University of Leipzig for both his undergraduate and medical studies. There he apparently became a close friend of a better-known poet, MARTIN OPITZ.

The business ventures with which Fleming was associated for two years proved unsuccessful commercially, and his absence while trying to make contacts in Russia and in Persia cost him his fiancée, Elsabe Niehus, who tired of waiting and married someone else. Her sister Anna, however, took Elsabe's place in Fleming's affections.

His prospects for making a living improved after he decided to study medicine. He completed his M.D. in 1639 and had secured an appointment as the medical officer for the city of Reval. On his way to assume that position, however, Fleming took sick and died in the city of Hamburg.

Only his literary endeavors achieved—and continue to achieve—notable success. Sadly even that success came posthumously. He had composed both Latin and German poetry, and two volumes appeared in the decade after his death: *Prodromus* (1641) and *Teutsche Poemata* (1646). His collected works appeared in a three-volume edition between 1863 and 1865. Both his Latin and German poems are available in 20th-century editions.

A world-weary Christian stoicism, low expectations for a world whose few joys pass quickly, and a philosophical resignation to this fact of life characterize many of his poems. The forms he chooses to employ are those typical of his epoch: He translates the Psalms into German verse, he writes SONNETS, love poems, ODES, religious poems, and poems built from rhymed couplets and from sestettes. (See POETIC METER.) Much of Fleming's verse is in the PETRARCHIST tradition. Sometimes he seems overfond of repetitive phrasing and elaborate contrasts. Yet despite such quirks and despite the conventionality of the forms he chooses, his verse rises above that of many of his German contemporaries. This stems partly from its musicality and partly from the freshness with which he incorporates his personal experiences into his poems. The effect is to make a reader feel like an intimate friend.

Perhaps it was this quality that led the German composer Johannes Brahms (1833–97) to set one of Fleming's religious poems to music. Only this poem seems as yet to have been translated into English in a bilingual score for chorus and organ. In the year following Fleming's death, 12 of his love poems—all odes—were also set to music.

Fleming personally subscribed to the stoic practice of facing the inevitable with calm resignation. This appears most poignantly in the fact that, when he realized he would die in Hamburg, he wrote a sonnet to serve as his own epitaph.

Bibliography

Brahms, Johannes, and Paul Fleming. *Sacred Song: Lass dich nur nichts nicht dauern* (Let nothing ever trouble you at all. Musical score in English and German.) Bryn Mawr, Pa.: Thorpe Music Publishing Company, ca. 1999.

Fleming, Paul. *Gedichte.* Leipsig: Insel–Verlag, 1970.

Sperberg-McQueen, Marian R. *The German Poetry of Paul Fleming: Studies in Genre and History.* Chapel Hill, N.C.: University of North Carolina Press, 1990.

Fletcher, John (1579–1625)

An English playwright and the son of Bishop Richard Fletcher, John Fletcher may have been educated at Cambridge. By 1596 surviving records indicate that he was working in some capacity in London theaters. It may be that his friend BEN JONSON introduced him in about 1605 to another member of his circle, FRANCIS BEAUMONT. However they met, Beaumont and Fletcher quickly became close friends and discovered that they had a talent for working together as playwrights. This discovery eventually led to an enduring collaboration that produced more than 50 plays either by the both of them, by one or the other, or by one of them in collaboration with another playwright.

The plays of the two friends mark a transition from the earlier days of the theater during the reigns of ELIZABETH I and JAMES I. In place of the psychological penetration and the questions of high morality that characterized the golden age of British theater, Beaumont and Fletcher substitute lavish romanticism, pathos, and emotionalism. Their verse, though competent, makes metrical compromises and falls off from the high standard of SHAKESPEARE, MARLOWE, and MIDDLETON. Together they introduced to London audiences a kind of slick and ingenious, predictably formulaic TRAGICOMEDY that anticipated the theater of the 18th century. Those reservations aside, they produced theatrical entertainment of a very high order.

Among the plays that Fletcher wrote on his own, *The Wild-goose Chase* (1621) is his best-remembered

comedy. In it the action centers on the quest of Oriana to marry a bachelor confirmed in his solitude, Mirabel—the wild goose. In her pursuit of Mirabel, Oriana has help from her brother, De-gard, and from Lugier, who tutors Oriana in strategy for catching Mirabel. Though Mirabel despises Oriana at first, when she disguises herself as someone else he falls madly in love with her and proposes without considering her fortunes or her rank. She accepts and casts off her disguise. Mirabel declares himself pleased that she has trapped him. After he promises in jest that he will beat her no more than once a week (if she deserves no more) and promises in earnest that he will father her child (if only in revenge for her tricks), the goose chase ends with all the characters heading off to church for the wedding.

Bibliography

Beaumont, Francis, and John Fletcher. *The Dramatic Works in the Beaumont and Fletcher Canon.* Cambridge, U.K.: Cambridge University Press, 1966; reissued 1996.

———. *The Works of Beaumont and Fletcher.* Edited by Alexander Dyce. New York: D. Appleton and Company, 1877.

Fletcher, John. *A Critical Edition of John Fletcher's Comedy, The Wild-goose Chase.* Edited by Rosa Herzberg Lister. New York: Garland, 1980.

Oliphant, E. H. C. *The Plays of Beaumont and Fletcher: an Attempt to Determine their Respective Shares and the Shares of Others.* New Haven, Conn.: Yale University Press, 1927.

Fletcher, Phineas (1582–1650)

A British poet in the manner of EDMUND SPENSER, Fletcher also composed verse in Latin. While a student at Cambridge he wrote a play, *Sicelides,* a sort of PASTORAL drama having to do with fishing. Except among specialists, it has passed into obscurity. Writing as a Protestant opponent of the Jesuit order, he penned a Latin poem, *Locastae* (Locusts, 1627), vilifying the order's members as "locusts," "priests–cannibal," and "incarnate fiends." This poem appeared with an English paraphrase and expansion, *The Locusts, or The Apollyonists.* To Fletcher's poem, the later English poet JOHN MILTON is deeply indebted for his depictions of Sin and Death as the guardians of the gates of Hell in *Paradise Lost*.

In the same year appeared Fletcher's poem *Britain's Ida*—a poem based on Virgil's *Aeneid*. It recounted the love between Anchises, King of Troy, and the goddess Venus. This poem so resembled Spenser's work that it was misattributed to him.

The subject of fishing continued to interest Fletcher, and he returned to it in his *Piscatory Eclogues and other Poetical Miscellanies* (1633). Again a reader observes echoes of Spenserian style that hark back to *The Shepherd's Calendar* (1579). Even Fletcher's stanzas are adaptations of the elder poet's.

In his own time, readers knew Fletcher best as the author of one of the other works that appeared in the same volume with *Piscatory Eclogues*—a verse ALLEGORY (again a la Spenser), *The Purple Island* (1633). The shape of the island and its topography represent human physiology. Those who dwell there and their activities stand for human emotions, actions, and psychological traits.

American composer Steven Stucky (b. 1949) has set at least one of Fletcher's poems of 1633 ("Drop, drop, slow tears") to music for double a cappella chorus. A reproduction taken from Stucky's holograph (a manuscript written in his own hand) score has recently become available.

Bibliography

Fletcher, Phineas. *Locustae, vel, Pietas Jesuitica*. Edited and translated into English by Estelle Haan. Leuven, Netherlands: Leuven University Press, 1996.

———. *The Purple Island; or, The Isle of Man*. Amsterdam: Theatrum Orbis Terrarum, and New York: Da Capo Press, 1971.

Stucky, Steven. *Drop, Drop, Slow Tears*. Score arranged for double a cappella chorus. King of Prussia, Pa.: Merion Music, ca. 2001.

Florentine Codex, The: *General History of the Things of New Spain*
Bernardino de Sahagún (ca. 1577–1580)

A bilingual document whose text appears in Spanish in the left-hand column and the Nahuatl language on the right, the Florentine Codex (manuscript) is bound in three volumes and preserved as MSS. Palat. 218–220 at the Laurentian Library (Biblioteca Medicea–Lorenziana) in Florence, Italy. The manuscript represents a major part of the life work of the Spanish Franciscan missionary, teacher, and scholar, Fray BERNARDINO DE SAHAGÚN (1499–1590). It also reflects the efforts of teams of Sahagún's native Mexican collaborators. Some of those collaborators were trilingual Aztec who had been trained in Franciscan schools from childhood to read and write Spanish and Latin and to transliterate their native Nahuatl language into Latin script. Others were Aztec tribal elders who were acquainted with the vast literature written in the pictographic and ideographic characters that represented the Aztec tongue. This second set of collaborators advised Sahagún as he set about revising the drafts of his work and translating the Nahuatl version into Spanish. They also provided him with copies of the great painted codices that the Aztecs and Mayans had prepared. Other examples of Sahagún's manuscripts containing additional pertinent material are preserved at various libraries in Europe and America. Studied carefully as parts of a set, they reveal much about Sahagún's planning, his working methods, and his tireless industry. His work has deservedly earned him a reputation as one the most important ethnographers who ever lived. His methods anticipate by more than 400 years those of today's best scientific ethnography.

The Codex itself is divided into 12 parts or books, and each of these is subdivided into a numbers of chapters. The first book devotes each of 21 chapters to a description of an Aztec deity and the manner of that deity's worship. Chapter 13 considers several lesser gods together. To book one, Sahagún appends a number of addenda, Aztec adages, a prologue, and information that supplements several sections. The second book devotes each of its 38 chapters to a discussion of the feasts and sacrifices—including human sacrifices—with which the Aztec honored their gods, and Sahagún again supplements that material with appendices. In its 14 chapters and nine appendices, the third book recounts myths associated with several of the gods, and the appendices tell of funeral customs, rewards and punishments in the afterlife, education, the rearing of nobles and rulers, penances, and the selection of Aztec priests and advancement within their order.

The fourth book discusses in 40 chapters and the usual appendices the signs associated with each day of the 260-day Aztec ceremonial year and the predictions for the good or ill fortune for persons born on each day. A 13-day-long cycle, for instance, beginning with the first day of the ceremonial year contained such signs as One-Crocodile (the first day)—a favorable sign, One-Ocelot (the second day)—an unfavorable sign, One-Reed (the fifth day)—a terrible sign, and One-Death (the sixth day)—a very fortunate sign. The fifth book's 37 chapters contain discussions of and stories about the omens in which the Mexica believed. The 43 chapters of the sixth book report prayers and consider rhetoric and moral philosophy. Book seven is devoted to astronomy and meteorology and to a discussion of the 52-year cycle the Aztec called "the binding of the years." At the end of each 52-year cycle, all fires were extinguished and new ones lit. Household gods would be thrown into the water and new ones venerated. Out with the old and in with the new was the watchword at the beginning of each new cycle.

Book eight is devoted to the rulers of the Aztec, their education, their dynasties, their ordinary and ceremonial dress, their standards of success, and their apparel when they went into battle. It also tells of the rulers' dwellings, their entertainments, dancing, furniture, diet, and the adornment and training of the women. In its sixth chapter, the eighth book recounts as well the omens that appeared before any European had set foot in Mexico that foretold the Spaniards' coming. Book nine principally concerns itself with commerce and with describing the work of artisans, particularly those who work with precious materials. Book 10 continues that discussion, focusing on such artisans as carpenters, tailors, and weavers, but also dealing with sorcerers, magicians, pimps, and prostitutes. It begins with a consideration of kinship affiliation.

The 11th book discusses geography, the metallurgy, and the fauna and flora of the land. It devotes several chapters to a consideration of Mexico's beautiful birds, others to serpents, especially the rattlesnake, and many to insects. Others still focus on crops and the bounty of the harvest. One needs to recall that what we presently consider high French and Italian cooking has its roots in such New World crops as tomatoes and potatoes, which were unknown in Europe before the discovery of America.

The last book of the Codex is perhaps the one of greatest interest to historians, for its 41 chapters detail the Spanish conquest of Mexico from the first omens, through the first landing of the Spaniards, their reception by Montezuma, their treachery, the battles, and their eventual victory.

We find much to praise in the monumental work Sahagún accomplished in producing the Florentine Codex and its associated documents. Regrettably, he also deserves the blame for the destruction of the irreplaceable painted manuscripts of the Aztecs and Mayans from which he worked. It was he who, thinking them diabolical, had them burned after he had described them and copied many of their characters. We can perhaps derive some comfort from remembering that he was not the first to burn the painted books. Some 100 years earlier—in about 1430—it seems that the Aztecs themselves, who were then extending their power throughout the surrounding lands, had burned the great painted histories of their predecessors and had written revisionist histories lest the old books mislead the peoples the Aztecs conquered.

Bibliography

Sahagún, Bernardino de. *Florentine Codex: General History of the Things of New Spain.* Translated from Aztec by Charles E. Dibble and Arthur J. O. Anderson. Monographs of the School of American Research, no. 14. 12 volumes. Santa Fe, N. M.: The School of American Research and the Museum of New Mexico, 1961–1975.

Florio, John (1553–1625)

The first English translator of the *Essais* of MICHEL EYQUEM DE MONTAIGNE, John Florio in his *Montaigne's Essays* (1603) produced a free but at the same time lively translation of Montaigne's influential work. Florio's translation was widely read in England

and influenced the development of the essay genre there. It also provided grist for the dramatic mills of English playwrights. WILLIAM SHAKESPEARE; for example, read his Montaigne in Florio's version.

Born of Italian parents in London, Florio was fluent in Italian as well as French and tutored in foreign languages at Oxford University. In 1578 he published a work addressed to the British and the Italians who were students of each other's language. It consisted of two parts: *First Fruits,* which contained examples of Italian, and *A Perfect Induction to the Italian and English Tongues.* Florio's translation of JACQUES CARTIER's *Navigations to New France*—the second in English—appeared in 1580. The year 1591 saw the publication of a volume containing some 6,000 Italian proverbs and entitled *Second Fruits.* In 1598 he published an English and Italian dictionary, *A World of Words,* and expanded on this in several later editions.

Florio's translations also attracted royal attention. In 1603 he became the Italian reader for Queen Anne and the following year was promoted to the post of groom of the privy chamber in the royal household.

Florio's translation of the Italian Traiano Boccalini's political treatise, *New Found Politicke . . .* appeared posthumously in 1626. Modern editions of several of Florio's translations—particularly of Montaigne—remain available.

Bibliography

Cartier, Jacques. *Navigations to Newe Fraunce.* Translated by John Florio. 1580. Ann Arbor, Mich.: University Microfilms, 1966.

Florio, John. *Firste Fruites.* 1578. New York: Da Capo Press, 1969.

———. *Queen Anna's New World of Words.* 1611. Reprint, Menston, U.K.: Scolar Press, 1968.

———. *Florio's Second Fruites.* 1591. New York: Da Capo Press, 1969.

Montaigne, Michel de Equyem. *The Essays [of] Michel de Montaigne.* Translated by John Florio. 1603. Reprint, Menston, U.K.: The Scolar Press, 1969.

Fonte, Moderata (Modesta Pozzo Zorzi) (1555–1592)

Born into a well-to-do Venetian family and orphaned as an infant, Fonte had an elementary convent education, was tutored by the grandfather who reared her, and learned Latin from her brother who recited his lessons for her as she brought him home from school. Before her marriage, she had begun to publish under the pen name of Moderata Fonte. In 1583 she married a lawyer, Fillippo Zorzi, bore him four children, and tragically died while bearing the fourth.

Her principal work, *Il merito delle donne* (The worth of women), was written late in life—likely in the year she died—and appeared in print eight years later. Framed as a conversation among friends who agree to discuss a set subject, Fonte's work breaks new ground for this established Renaissance genre. In the first place, no men are present during the conversations; all the speakers are women. Generally, in the preceding Italian examples of such fictive conversations, the men do most of the talking, and the women confine themselves to asking tactful questions. In the second place, the subjects of the discussion depart from the preconceived domestic concerns of women. The conversations address medicine, politics, science, and philosophy. They examine the place of women in the family and in society as a whole, and they explore women's treatment at the hands of men. In the conclusion, the men fare badly. The women conclude that men have conspired to enslave women both socially and emotionally. This conspiracy, moreover, violates the natural equality of the sexes.

Seven Venetian women participate in the conversation. Their discussion leader, the unmarried Corinna, prefers study and writing, celibacy, and independence to the unremitting round of housewifery and child bearing. The other discussants represent a typical spectrum of Venetian womanhood. The eldest, a widow named Adriana, participates with her daughter Virginia, who is about to enter the marriage market. Next in age to Adriana is a middle-aged wife named Lucretia. Also present are a younger married woman, Cornelia; a recent bride, Helena; and a young widow, Leonora. The tenor of the conversations, the arguments the women offer, and the quality of the thinking all go far toward the demonstration of Fonte's belief in women's superiority. Ironically, though a few likeminded women in the Italian literary community knew Fonte's work, it was the late 20th century's concern with women's issues that brought her work once again into the light it richly deserves.

Fonte's earlier writings included part of a verse CHIVALRIC ROMANCE, Thirteen cantos about Floridoro (*Tredici canti del Floridoro,* 1581), and two religious poems, The passion of Christ (*La Passione di Christo,* 1582) and The resurrection of Jesus Christ (*La Resurrettione di Giesu Christo,* 1592). She also authored anonymously an allegorical, musical entertainment that was performed for the doge (duke) of Venice in 1581. It was published in 1582. According to a contemporary chronicler, she also authored numerous poems in several of the traditional Italian forms—canzoni (songs), madrigals, and SONNETS. These, which probably existed only in manuscript, appear to have been lost.

Bibliography

Fonte, Moderata. *The Worth of Women: Wherein Is Clearly Revealed Their Nobility and Their Superiority to Men.* Edited and Translated by Virginia Cox. Chicago: University of Chicago Press, 1997.

Malpezzi Price, Paola. "Moderata Fonte." *Italian Women Writers: A Bio-Bibliographical Sourcebook.* Pages 128–137. Westport, Conn.: Greenwood Press, 1994.

Ford, John (ca. 1586–ca. 1639)

A British poet and dramatist, John Ford certainly ranks in the top 10 playwrights of the British Renaissance and is generally regarded as the best one during the reign of Charles I (1625–49). John Ford, like WILLIAM SHAKESPEARE, largely led his life out of the public view. A record of his baptism exists in Devon. He may have briefly attended Oxford in about 1601. He undertook legal studies at London's Middle Temple in 1602, was expelled in 1605 for nonpayment of his bill for meals, but was reinstated in 1608. Presumably he eventually became a lawyer.

While on involuntary leave from the Middle Temple, Ford began his literary career. In 1606 he authored a poem, *Fame's Memorial,* and a pamphlet, *Honor Triumphant.* That year he also wrote verses in praise of two works by other writers. In Renaissance Europe such verses played the role that reviewers' praise of new works often does today. The year 1613 saw publication of another poem, *Christ's Bloody Sweat,* and another pamphlet *The Golden Mean.* In 1620 still another pamphlet followed: *A Line of Life.* Ford's pamphlets, though not particularly distinguished, advocated a philosophical stoicism in the face of the world's adversities.

Just how Ford became a collaborator with playwrights THOMAS DEKKER and WILLIAM ROWLEY is unclear, but 1621 saw the production at Whitehall of *The Witch of Edmonton.* This collaboration was one of a number of plays produced on the subject of witchcraft. Some of them like this one were based on trials and popular accounts of real cases. Another play of 1623, *The Spanish Gypsy,* may have been Ford's, or he may have collaborated with THOMAS MIDDLETON and Rowley. That same year saw more of his commendatory verses in the front matter of other's works. Still other such verses appeared in 1632 and 1636. Ford wrote another for BEN JONSON's memorial volume *Jonsonus Virbius,* in 1638.

In 1624 Ford had collaborated with Dekker again on a play, *The Sun's Darling.* Another of Ford's plays, *The Lover's Melancholy,* was licensed for performance in 1628 and published in 1629. This TRAGICOMEDY concerns the unhappy consequences that follow from a father's passion for his son's intended bride and the resolution to that and other problems when all disguises are thrown off, the father recovers his senses, and the young people can finally marry.

All the works, however, for which literary history particularly praises Ford appeared in 1632–33. These include THE BROKEN HEART (probably written around 1628), 'TIS PITY SHE'S A WHORE (between 1629 and 1633)—Ford's most notable play—and *Perkin Warbeck.*

Bibliography

Anderson, Donald K. *John Ford.* New York: Twayne Publishers, 1972.

Ford, John. *'Tis Pity She's a Whore and Other Plays.* Edited by Marion Lomax. Oxford and New York: Oxford University Press, 1995.

Fortune (*Fortuna*)

Although the ancient Romans had worshiped *Fortuna* as a goddess, by the Renaissance the widespread concept that people were subject to accidental circumstances over which they exercised no control had experienced a literary and quasi-religious development. God, some thought, operated in human affairs through two agencies: nature and fortune. For literary purposes these agencies often became personified as two demigoddesses who ran matters for God on Earth. Fortune was regularly represented in literature and ICONOGRAPHY as a female figure who arbitrarily affected the affairs of people by rotating a metaphorical wheel to which each person was theoretically bound. A person born to a wealthy family, for example, could lose everything and wind up begging as the result of the revolution of Fortune's wheel. Similarly, a beggar might undeservedly become a king.

SHAKESPEARE's King Lear, who was used to having everything just his own way, finds himself "bound / upon a wheel of fire" (*KING LEAR*, Act IV, scene vii) as his world comes apart. That wheel belongs to Fortune. LORENZO DE' MEDICI repeats the ancient tale that Jove, the king of the gods, keeps two jars near his throne. One, which he pours out on the heads of those he particularly dislikes, contains nothing but ill fortune. The other, reserved for people he particularly favors, contains half ill fortune and half good.

Renaissance writers made frequent and effective use of METAPHOR involving fortune—sometimes personified and sometimes not.

Foxe, John (1516–1587)

An English student of Christian history, particularly the lives and deaths of modern and ancient Christian martyrs, Foxe was a fiery Protestant controversialist. A member of a Lincolnshire family, Foxe took three degrees, B.A., M.A., and B.D., from Oxford University. In 1538 he was appointed a fellow of Magdalen College, but he resigned that appointment in 1545 when the college's rules and his Protestant convictions came into conflict. He then became a tutor serving the family of the duke of Norfolk. In about 1547, after he had mastered Greek, Hebrew, and Latin and had studied the writings of the early church fathers and modern church history, Foxe began to publish theological treatises supporting the PROTESTANT REFORMATION.

On the accession of the Roman Catholic Queen Mary I to the throne of England in 1553, Foxe fled to the Continent. The following year he published at Strasbourg a Latin work whose title meant, *Commentaries on matters in church affairs.* This became the first modest installment of what, once it had been translated, became after the Bible itself the English-speaking world's most influential book of Renaissance Protestantism: *ACTES AND MONUMENTS . . .* or more popularly, "*Foxe's Book of Martyrs* (1563)." A much-expanded, second Latin edition of his work appeared at Basel in 1559. It included entries on Englishmen martyred under Bloody Mary's rule.

New and ever-larger editions appeared in 1570, 1576, and 1583. Posthumous ones have continued coming out ever since. A recent one even modernizes Foxe's Renaissance English.

In addition to his book of martyrs, Foxe continued writing anti-Roman Catholic treatises throughout his life. He also penned a pair of Latin plays on the subject of martyrdom: *Titus et Gesippus* (Titus and Gesippus, 1544–45) and *Christus triumphans* (Christ triumphant, 1556). Two of his English sermons also appear in a modern edition.

Bibliography

Foxe, John. *Foxe's Christian Martyrs of the World.* Westwood, N.J.: Barbour Books, ca. 1989.

———. *The English Sermons of John Foxe.* Edited by Warren W. Wooden. Delmar, N.Y.: Scholars' Facsimiles and Reprints, 1978.

———. *The New Foxe's Book of Martyrs.* Rewritten and updated by Harold J. Chadwick. North Brunswick, N.J.: Bridge-Logos, ca. 1997.

———. *Two Latin Comedies by John Foxe the Martyrologist: Titus et Gesippus* [and] *Christus triumphans.* Edited and translated by John Hazel Smith. Renaissance text series, 4. Ithaca, N.Y.: Cornell University Press, 1972.

Francis I (1494–1547, reigned 1515–1547)

In the world of letters, King Francis I of France is best remembered as the father of Renaissance French literature. In addition to extending his protection and encouragement to such French HUMANISTS as the classical editor and BIBLE translator Lefèvre d'Étaples (1455–1536) and to authors and intellectuals whose ranks included such writers as RABELAIS (1483–1553) and the printer Robert Estienne (1503–59), Francis appointed the erudite and energetic GUILLAUME BUDÉ (1467–1540), to the post of royal librarian. The consequences of this appointment were far reaching, for in that capacity Budé assembled the collection that became the core of the French national library, the great Bibliothèque Nationale. Also at Budé's suggestion, the king established a trilingual national academy for the study of Greek, Latin, and Hebrew. That academy eventually developed into the Collège de France.

The king shared his literary interests with his sister MARGARET OF ANGOULÊME (1492–1549), and he read with enthusiasm the works of the humanist thinker ERASMUS (1466–1536), those of the Italian polymath and artist, Leonardo da Vinci (1452–1519), and those of the founder of the European Renaissance, FRANCESCO PETRARCA (PETRARCH, 1304–74).

Francis I is also remembered for his variously successful wars in Italy, for his participation with Henry VIII of England in the Field of the Cloth of Gold, and for his religious persecutions of nonconforming peasants late in his career.

Franco, Veronica (1546–1591)

A Venetian courtesan, Franco is listed among those of that calling whom the citizens of Venice considered honored. That tribute resulted from the artistic and intellectual accomplishments that qualified certain courtesans as suitable female companions for men of the highest social standing. In Franco's case, her clientele included King Henry I of France.

Franco took pride in her Venetian citizenship. Evidence exists of her civic mindedness, her generosity, and her philanthropic concern for those, especially women, less fortunate than she. As a literary figure, she was an accomplished poet and a thoughtful and voluminous writer of letters.

Although she had been married to a physician, the couple did not long live together, and he fathered none of her six children, of whom three survived and were acknowledged by their respective fathers.

A tactful but direct and sometimes stern proponent of the essential superiority of women's dispositions, Franco constructed a myth to counter the creation story of Genesis that held men to be women's masters. In Franco's view, men enjoy the benefits of women's usually more penetrating intelligence, thoughtfulness, and patience. In women's understanding of their place in repopulating the world, they submit to men rather than resist them—as she thought men often deserved. To their discredit, those men who fail to understand women's freely given gift of themselves often assert mastery over women. Those men who do understand the sacrifices women make for them feel appropriately grateful, and they respect women and honor them.

Her poems appeared in 1575. Written in TERZA RIMA, the work contains a number of poetic exchanges with men of her acquaintance. Exchanging poems was a popular form of complimentary correspondence as well as a way to carry on polite arguments and exchanges of ideas. It was not unusual for such exchanges of correspondence to appear in the collected works of poets; what is unusual is the direct eroticism of some of Franco's poems as she celebrates her skill in lovemaking and the delights she can confer. Beyond this, she rejects the PETRARCHIST pose of her correspondent who sings his lover's anguish. She insists that he engage her as an intellectual equal and drop the sort of conventional wooing that made Lord Byron call Petrarch "the pimp of all Christendom."

After a group of seven such exchanges, Franco devotes the rest of her work to a spirited defense of women in general and of herself personally against the nasty written attacks of Maffio Vernier (1550–86). Sometimes playful, sometimes serious, and always eloquent, Franco's work stands among the most compelling written by courtesan poets of the Italian Renaissance.

Although Franco enjoyed a decade of opulent wealth when she was at the height of her popularity, a selection of her letters, published in 1580, reveals that during the plague years in Venice (1575–77) her fortunes had ebbed, and they never totally recovered. In the year her letters appeared, when she was down on her financial luck, she also had to defend herself from charges before the Venetian INQUISITION that she practiced magic.

She was always concerned about women who practiced her profession, especially those who were the poorest, and when she was able she was generous in trying to provide shelters and dowries for them. She unsuccessfully proposed to the city of Venice that they appoint her the administrator of such a shelter. She was convinced that the intellectual differences between women and men arose from women's lack of educational opportunities, not from any innate predisposition, and she points to the natural differences among men in support of her argument.

Bibliography

Franco, Veronica. *Poems and Selected Letters*. Edited and translated by Ann Rosalind Jones and Margaret F. Rosenthal. Chicago and London: The University of Chicago Press, 1998.

Fries, Peder Clausson (1545–1614)

A Norwegian HUMANIST, topographer, natural historian, translator, and clergyman, Peder Clausson Fries's principal claim to literary fame rests on a translation. He rendered into Norwegian from Icelandic the medieval *Sagas of the Kings of Norway* (*Heimskringla*) by the Atlantic island nation's greatest poet, Snorri Sturluson (1179–1241). Beyond that signal achievement, Fries also wrote a natural history of Norway and provided an early topographical account of his country.

Fuzûlî (Fuḍūlī) of Baghdad, Mehme (Mehmet) ibn Süleyman (ca. 1495–1556)

A poet of Baghdad, Fuḍūlī (his pen name) composed with equal facility in Arabic, Persian, and Turkish. He is remembered as a major poet of the first two languages and as the finest poet of all classical Turkish literature. A court poet during the reign of the Safavid dynasty's Shah Ismāʿīl I, who conquered Baghdad in 1508, Fuḍūlī authored two collections of lyric poems, one in Persian and one in Turkish. In these collections, Fuḍūlī's lyrics treat the mystical love between soul and soul and examine the love of the soul for the divine. They also bewail the fleeting experience of life in this world, and several contain complimentary poems addressed to important figures of his time. He also wrote a Persian work entitled *Health and Illness*. Another of Fuḍūlī's major compositions retells in Turkish the Islamic allegorical romance LEYLÁ and MEJNÚN (*Leylâ ve Mecnun*). This poem concerns the desire of the human spirit (*Mecnun*) for union with divine beauty (*Leylâ*). He also composed an account of Shiite martyrs and retold the 40 traditions of the Prophet. In these works, Fuḍūlī departs from the formal rules that had governed earlier Islamic poetic composition. He introduces a more personal style distinguished by its sincerity, its ardor, and a characteristic plaintiveness. He sometimes symbolically equates wine with mystic love. Some 14 of his compositions and a collection of a few of his letters survive. He himself explains that he chose his pen name because it could simultaneously be read as *inappropriate, improper,* and *of great value.* His collections of riddles both in Turkish and Persian also attest to a lively sense of humor.

After the Ottoman Turks conquered Baghdad in 1534, Fuḍūlī tried to maintain his officially favored status and to improve on it by addressing complimentary verses to Turkish officials and applying to become the court poet to the sultan of the Ottoman Empire at Istanbul, Süleyman I. Fuḍūlī's failure to achieve that appointment occasioned one of his best-remembered poems. Written in Turkish and entitled Complaint (*Şikâyetname*), the poem scornfully derides the judgment of those who failed to recognize his preeminence as the finest Muslim poet of his era. He is still the most popular poet of Turkey. Some of his poems have been set to music, and his work remains influential in the Islamic world where critical editions continue to appear. Only *Leyla and Mejnun* is available in English.

Bibliography

Fuzûlî, Mehmet. *Leyla and Mejnun*. Istanbul: The Turkish National UNESCO Committee, 1959.

Galilei, Galileo (Galileo) (1564–1642)

Born at Pisa, Galileo (as he is universally known) grew up in Florence, where he received his early education. He also studied for a period before 1578 with the monks at the monastery of Santa Maria of Vallombrosa. From there he moved on to the University of Pisa, where he began to study medicine in 1581. A precocious intellect, Galileo was also interested in astronomy, natural philosophy, and mathematics. He discovered in 1583 that all pendulum vibrations were uniform, and he perceived the value of that observation for measuring the passage of time. His mathematical studies and his application of them to the solution of various practical problems led to his appointment in 1589 as professor of mathematics at the University of Pisa. His experimental approach to problems, however—particularly those concerning the acceleration of falling bodies—led to fierce opposition from the Aristotelian faculty of the institution, which preferred logical argument by syllogism. They angrily insisted that heavier objects would fall faster, whereas Galileo was certain, despite his inability to create a vacuum, that in a vacuum, objects would accelerate at a uniform rate regardless of their weight. The unpleasantness led to his resignation in 1591.

The next year he accepted the chair of mathematics at the more congenial University of Padua, where students flocked from all over Europe to work with the increasingly celebrated professor on both his theoretical and his applied work.

In his private life, about 1598 he formed a long-lasting liaison with a beautiful Venetian woman, Marina Gamba. In due course, Gamba bore Galileo three children: Virginia (1600), Livia (1601), and Vincinzo (1606). Both girls would eventually enter convents and become, respectively, Sister Maria Celeste and Sister Arcangela at the Convent of San Matteo at Arcetri (1614).

In 1606 Galileo invented a compass and published a book about it. Then he became intrigued with a new Dutch invention—the telescope. He acquired one, made modifications to it, and in 1609 perfected the first instrument suited to doing serious astronomy. The following year he published his first astronomical treatise, *Sidereus Nuncius* (*The Starry Messenger*). That publication, together with his other distinctions, led to his appointment as the chief mathematician and philosopher to the grand duke of Florence, Cosimo II de' Medici (1590–1620).

For a time, Galileo was lionized as an intellectual hero. The year 1609 saw his election to the

Lincean Academy of Rome, which in 1613 published his *Letters on Sunspots*. In 1615 he wrote a letter to the grand duchess Cristina di Lorena in which he discussed the use of the BIBLE in scientific argumentation. Behind the scenes, however, opposition was building to the way in which his scientific approach undermined Aristotelian, Ptolemaic, and clerical opinion. The Dominican preacher Tommaso Caccini attacked him in a public sermon in 1614. In a series of episodes that eerily presage the contemporary disagreements between science and Scripture about evolution, churchmen and laymen who opposed NICHOLAS COPERNICUS's heliocentric observations of 1513 (published 1543) mounted an attack both on Copernicus and on Galileo. The church banned Copernican theory and forbade Galileo to support it. In 1625, by which time the church had somewhat softened its views about Copernicus, Galileo began working on his *Dialogo dei massimé sistemi* (Dialogue concerning the chief world systems: Ptolemaic and Copernican). He finished the work in 1630 and sought and obtained permission to publish it. Pope Urban VIII (1623–1644), in fact, supported Galileo. The head of the Lincean Academy, however, who was supposed to have supervised printing the book died suddenly, and not until 1631 did the book appear with permission in Florence. When its contents were discovered to support Copernicus's views with Galileo's astronomical observations, in 1632 Rome put a stop to sales of the book. In the face of a political firestorm Pope Urban withdrew his support for Galileo's views, even though the pope agreed with them. In 1633, over the protests of his physicians and of Cosimo II, a gravely ill Galileo was hauled before the Roman INQUISITION. Following a pair of examinations by inquisitors, the threat of torture ("severe inquisition") led to Galileo's acquiescence in the views of the church. He spent the rest of his life under various types of house arrest. Even his total blindness did not dissuade his persecutors. He was nonetheless at liberty to write, and write he did. In 1638 he managed to have his work, *Dialogues Concerning Two New Sciences*, published at Leiden in Holland. It humorously maintained the truth of his positions. That same year, the celebrated English poet and statesman JOHN MILTON visited Galileo at his dwelling in Arcetri. During his long involuntary retirement from the public scene, Galileo also penned some rhyming verse that has recently been collected in Italian but has yet to be translated into English.

Ill and dispirited, Galileo took to his bed in November 1641, and, after lingering there for two months, the man who had proved by observation that the Earth was not the center of the universe died on January 8, 1642.

Bibliography

Brophy, James, and Henry Paolucci, eds. *Achievement of Galileo*. Smyrna, Del.: Griffon House Publications, ca. 2001.

Galilei, Galileo. *Dialogue Concerning the Two Chief World Systems, Ptolemaic and Copernican*. Translated by Stillman Drake. New York: Modern Library, 2001.

———. *Discoveries and Opinions of Galileo: Including The Starry Messenger (1610). Letter to the Grand Duchess Christina (1615), Excerpts from Letters on Sunspots (1613), The Assayer (1623)*. Translated by Stillman Drake. New York: Anchor Books, 1990.

———. *Le Rime* [Rhymes]. Edited by Antonio Marzo. Rome: Salerno Publishers, 2001.

Gàmbara, Veronica (1485–1550)

An Italian regional ruler and poet and the wife of the hereditary ruler of Correggio in northern Italy, Gàmbara was widowed in 1518. She took over her husband's responsibilities. As the governor of the region, she proved to be an able administrator and diplomat, establishing and maintaining advantageous relationships with such powerful Italian ruling families as the Farnese of Parma and Piacenza and the Medici of Florence. She also secured for her small state the protection of Charles V, the Holy Roman emperor.

As a girl, Gàmbara had received a careful education in Italian and classical letters. This led in turn to her becoming a precocious poet while still in her teens. Some of her verse is imitative of the PETRARCHIST manner. Other poems celebrate gracefully the love she shared with her husband, Giberto. Others still invoke the newly popular PASTORAL style to recount the pleasure she took in nature and in rural landscapes and her aversion to cities. She was a literary adherent of the views of the influential PIETRO BEMBO.

Gàmbara's correspondence also commands literary interest. Among her correspondents she numbered Bembo himself as well as the colorful and unruly PIETRO ARETINO. She notably exemplifies the influential, well-educated, and cultured Renaissance Italian noblewoman.

Bibliography

Russell, Rinaldina, ed. *Italian Women Writers: a Biobibliographical Sourcebook*. Westport, Conn.: Greenwood Press, 1994.

Garcilaso de la Vega (1503–1536)

A Spanish soldier, diplomat, and poet, Garcilaso is not to be confused with another person of the same name, GARCILASO DE LA VEGA, THE (EL) INCA (1534–1616). The earlier Garcilaso who concerns us here led a busy life filled with military exploits, diplomacy, a brief period of exile on an island in the Danube River, and service at the Spanish court in Naples, Italy. He also formed a close friendship with the poet JUAN BOSCÁN. To that friendship we ultimately owe the preservation of Garcilaso de la Vega's poetry, for like many gifted gentlemen of his day, he circulated his poems in manuscript among his friends. It may be that he himself made a selection of what he considered to be his best work and left it in the hands of Boscán during a visit in to his friend in Barcelona in 1533.

The year 1534 found Garcilaso back in Naples preparing for a military incursion into North Africa the following year. There he was severely wounded, but by 1536 he was well enough to fight in the Holy Roman Emperor Charles V (King Charles I of Spain)'s invasion of France. Garcilaso received a mortal wound on September 19, 1536, while fighting in the southern French region of La Muy. He died a few days later.

Late in his own life, Boscán, who had come into possession of copies of some of Garcilaso's lyric poems and ECLOGUES, prepared to publish his deceased friend's work along with his own. Though Boscán died in the course of that preparation, his widow saw the project through and in 1543 brought into print The works of Boscán and some of Garcilaso de la Vega, divided into four books (*Las obras de Boscán y algunas de Garcilaso de la Vega, repartidas en cuatro libros*).

The works of Garcilaso can be generally categorized into his lyric poems and his eclogues. Although it seems likely that some of Garcilaso's early poems followed the conventions of medieval Spanish verse, little of his surviving work displays those characteristics, and the few poems that do are not datable. The majority of his lyrics together with those of Boscán are the first in the Spanish language to take their inspiration from the Italian forms of PETRARCH, and the surviving verse is among the finest of the Spanish Renaissance. The lovelorn sorrow of the Petrarchan mode was congenial for Garcilaso since, like the earlier Italian poet, the Spaniard had loved a woman he lost—first to marriage with another and then to death. Garcilaso's love was named Isabel Freire. Like Petrarch as well, Garcilaso had fathered an illegitimate child. Unlike Petrarch, however, Garcilaso had a wife, Elena de Zuñiga, whom he had married the year before he met Freire. It is Isabel Freire, however, whom Garcilaso memorializes as Elisa, his heavenly lady, in his poems. The themes of Garcilaso's lyrics involve sorrow in a world largely devoid of happiness. That sorrow, nonetheless, the poet reports in beautiful verse. A substantial body of these poems survives. The lyrics also include ODES written in the manner of the Roman poet VIRGIL.

The collection of 1543 also contained three short dramatic eclogues that Garcilaso had composed in Naples in the mid-1530s. Conceivably he had written them for stage production, though no external evidence exists that they were ever performed. These eclogues embodied the PASTORAL conventions of the era. The speakers largely describe action among shepherds and nymphs that has taken place offstage. Only in the second of the three do the players actually enact a portion of the story.

The poems of Garcilaso de la Vega and Juan Boscán forever altered the direction of Spanish poetry by bringing the Petrarchan conventions of the Italian Renaissance to Spain.

Bibliography

Gicovate, Bernard. *Garcilaso de la Vega*. Boston: Twayne Publishers, 1975.

Garcilaso de la Vega. *Works: A Critical Text with a Bibliography*. Edited by Hayward Keniston. New York: Hispanic Society of America, 1925.

Garcilaso de la Vega, The (El) Inca
(1534–1616)

The son of an Incan princess and a noble Spanish conquistador related to the powerful Infantado family, Garcilaso was born in the Incan capital of Cusco, Peru, and educated there as the Spanish conquest of his native land continued. At the age of 20 he moved to Spain and enrolled as a soldier in the army of Don John of Austria, then engaged in fighting the Moriscos of Granada.

His literary career began relatively late in life. In 1590 he translated JEHUDAH BEN ISAAC ABRAVANEL's influential Platonic and kabbalistic document, *The Dialogues of Love*. From the perspective of the Spanish INQUISITION, however, Vega's choice did not prove fortunate. The inquisitors found his translation suspect in part because of its Jewish material and in part because of the impetus they perceived it might give to free thinking. Not long after publication, therefore, the inquisitors placed his work on the INDEXES OF FORBIDDEN BOOKS. Garcilaso next turned his attention to a safer subject, Fernando de Soto's early explorations of Florida. This work appeared in 1605 as *The History of Florida*.

As Garcilaso grew older, the subject of Peru increasingly attracted him. It may seem strange that writing about his personal recollections and about the land of his birth did not strike him much earlier as a subject worthy of his attention. He had the reputation of being a model Spanish courtier, so perhaps he did not wish his personal history—one that his contemporaries surely must have considered exotic—to become the principal ground for public interest in him. More likely he feared the renewed scrutiny of an Inquisition that might have suspected him of paganism. However that may be, relying on his own memory, on Spanish records of the conquest, and on such materials as his relatives in Peru could furnish, Garcilaso undertook his *ROYAL COMMENTARIES OF THE YNCAS*. The work appeared in two parts, the first in 1609, and the second posthumously in 1617. As part II of the work had been licensed for publication in 1613, its deferred appearance once again raises the specter of the Inquisition.

Throughout both volumes of his work, Garcilaso de la Vega, the Inca, takes pains to assure his readers that he is a thoroughly convinced Catholic Christian who utterly rejects the polytheistic idolatry of his royal ancestors while at the same time feeling pride in their accomplishments and in his descent from them. Among his contemporaries Garcilaso had the reputation of being a trusting and gentle person who was proud of his military service to the Spanish Crown.

Bibliography

Castanien, Donald Garner. *El Inca Garcilaso de la Vega*. New York: Twayne, 1969.

Varen, John Greier. *El Inca: The Life and Times of Garcilaso de la Vega*. Austin, Tex.: The University of Texas Press, 1968.

Garcilaso de la Vega. *First Part of the Royal Commentaries of the Yncas, by the Ynca Garcilasso de la Vega*. Hakluyt Society, 1869—71. Translated and edited by Clements R. Markham. New York: B. Franklin, 1963.

Gascoigne, George (ca. 1525–1577)

Remembered chiefly as an early innovator in English literature, Gascoigne also lived a colorful and contentious life. After periods at Cambridge University, from which he apparently did not take a degree, and as a student of law at Gray's Inn (1555), he was elected to Parliament. There he served from 1557 to 1559. In 1562 Gascoigne married a well-to-do widow, Elizabeth Breton. Breton was apparently engaged to another man at the time. A lawsuit and, as it seems, a street riot resulted from her divided allegiances.

In 1566 one of the most remarkably original literary careers of the English Renaissance began with a collaborative translation of Lodovico Dolce's Italian tragedy, *Jocasta.* Based in turn on Euripedes' play *Phoenissae,* when *Jocasta* was performed at Gray's Inn it became the first Greek tragedy acted in England. The collaborating translator was Gascoigne's friend, Francis Kinwelmersh. The same year Gascoigne translated alone ARIOSTO's Italian play: *The pretenders* (*I suppositi*). Another first, the performance of Gascoigne's play, *Supposes,* marked a milestone in the development of the popular English theater. It introduced a subplot for SHAKESPEARE's *The Taming of the Shrew* and also became the first Italian prose comedy to appear in English on an English stage. Ariosto's play is the ultimate source for the 20th-century Broadway musical *The Fantastics.*

Apparently a spendthrift, Gascoigne found himself disinherited by an angry father in the early 1570s. With his financial prospects spoiled, he ran again for Parliament and was elected. He was prevented from serving, however, by the success of a petition his creditors circulated. They accused him not only of owing them money but also of "slander, manslaughter, and atheism." Barred from politics, Gascoigne undertook a military career but not before delivering to his publishers a volume that appeared while he was serving in the Low Countries. This work, *A Hundreth Sundry Flowers,* issued anonymously in 1573, contained the text of the plays mentioned above as well as SONNETS by his own and possibly some by other hands. Those certainly by Gascoigne anticipated the popular Renaissance genre of the sonnet cycle by linking series of sonnets together. Appearing in this collection as well was a prose piece, THE ADVENTURES OF MASTER F. J., which has the distinction of being the first original short story in English during the Renaissance.

For a while Gascoigne fought in the Netherlands. There he was captured and remained a prisoner for four months before being ransomed and returned to England. Back at home he arranged for republication of the 1573 volume and supplementary material under the title, *The Posies of George Gascoigne* (1575). He included a prose essay called "Certayne Notes of Instruction." This essay contained the first discussion of PROSODY and versification in English. The year 1575 also saw publication of a moralistic tragi-comedy, *The Glass of Government.* The year following Gascoigne's BLANK-VERSE SATIRE, *The Steel Glass* appeared. If it is not the first genuine, nondramatic satire in English, it is very early.

Also in 1576 Gascoigne originated the English version of OVIDian verse narration in *The Complainte of Philomene.* This was the form that William Shakespeare later chose for his narrative poems, *The Rape of Lucrece* and *Venus and Adonis*—an iambic pentameter, six-line stanza, rhyming ababcc.

To complete the recital of Gascoigne's firsts in the field of English letters requires only a word identifying him as the first English war correspondent. In his 1576 prose effort, *The Spoyles of Antwerp,* he describes the war in the Netherlands in a clear and remarkably unbiased series of graphic reports. In addition to the influential works discussed here, Gascoigne authored numerous others.

Paying tribute to Gascoigne's influential originality 12 years after his death, THOMAS NASH credited him with being the first to "beat the path to that perfection . . . our best poets have [since] aspired to."

Bibliography

Gascoigne, George. *A Hundreth Sundrie Flowers.* Edited by G. W. Pigman III. Oxford: Clarendon Press; New York: Oxford University Press, 2000.

———. *The Green Knight: Selected Poetry and Prose.* Edited by Roger Pooley. Manchester, U.K.: Carcanet New Press, 1982.

———. *The Complete Works.* Edited by John W. Cunliffe. Grosse Pointe, Mich.: Scholarly Press, 1969.

Wallace, William L., ed. *George Gascoigne's The Steele Glas* and *The Complainte of Phylomene.* Salzburg: Institut für Englische Sprache und Literatur, Universität Salzburg, 1975.

Gelosi, The

An Italian acting troop specializing in the COMMEDIA DELL' ARTE—a largely improvisational form of popular theater, the Gelosi were owned and managed by ISABELLA ANDREINI (1562–1604) and her husband Francesco.

The troop performed with atypically great success throughout Western Europe, and Isabella became one of the most celebrated actresses of her time. Her *mask*—as the stereotypical roles played by actors in the commedia were called—became a stock character, that of *Isabella,* in the subsequent history of the commedia.

Gerhardt, Paul (1607–1676)

The best-remembered writer of German Protestant hymns of the 17th century, Gerhardt was born to the family of the mayor of the small community of Gräfenhainichen in the vicinity of Wittenberg. At Wittenberg University he studied theology. Thereafter he supported himself for a period by tutoring in Berlin. In 1651 he succeeded in procuring a pastorate at Mittenwalde and in 1657 moved to a major appointment at St. Nicholas's Church in Berlin.

A not atypical dispute between Calvinists and Lutherans led Gerhardt to resign his post at St. Nicholas in 1667. Until 1669 he relied on the support of members of his former parish and that of friends. Then, however, he was appointed to the church at Lübben—a post he held until his death.

His personal life was troubled by sadness. Of the five children born to him and his wife, four died. Nonetheless, the poems that he wrote to be set to music and sung sound notes of optimism, appreciation for the beauties of nature and the way those beauties resonate with human sensibilities, Christian fortitude, gratitude for Christ's sacrifice on the cross, and the benefits that Gerhardt believed people derived from Christ's death and resurrection.

Several of Gerhardt's works continue to be included in the Lutheran hymnody, and some of their verses are familiar to all lovers of Johann Sebastian Bach's *St. Matthew's Passion,* where they appear as the chorales *"Befiehl du deine Wege,"* (Command your ways. . . .) and *"O Haupt voll Blut und Wunden"* (O bloody, wounded Lord). Felix Mendelssohn also set the latter work to music. Bach created still another musical setting for one of Gerhardt's hymns, "A Lamb goes Uncomplaining Forth" (*"So gehst du nun, mein Jesu, hin"*—literally: Thus now, my Jesus, you go forth).

ghazel (ghazal)

A form of lyric poem widely popular in the Muslim world, the *ghazel,* a form of lyric poem traces its origins at least as far back as the eighth century. Particularly identified with Persian, Turkish, and North Indian Mughal poets in the 16th and 17th centuries, the *ghazel* displays a variety of forms. The word *ghazel* has been variously translated. Some say it means "spinning" in Arabic. Others claim its literal translation is "talking to your women" or "small talk among women." Others still give its meaning as "love poem." Another identifies it with "a small, graceful, soft-eyed antelope." All are probably true.

In Persian and Turkish poetry the *ghazel* may have as few as four or as many as 14 lines. Whatever its length within those bounds, its first two lines rhyme, and lines four, six, eight, and so on through all the even-numbered lines repeat the initial rhyme. The odd numbered lines, three, five, seven, and so on do not rhyme with lines one or two or with each other. Each couplet of a *ghazel* stands as an independent poetic unit. Customarily, the last line of the poem contains the name or the pseudonym of the poet.

Translated examples of *ghazels* have lines whose length varies from poem to poem, but whose length is uniform within a single poem. Generally poets treat erotic or mystical subjects in *ghazels* characterized by tranquility of mood. Here is an example of my own composition:

A Brief Autumn ghazel
The autumn leaves change color with the chill
Fall days and bring the work-cloyed heart a thrill.
With brilliant hues—red, yellow, orange, pied—
Old Mother Nature paints her canvas still.
She makes one hope the world might yet improve
If, Jimmy thinks, folks stopped to look their fill.

(J. W. C.)

European poets of the 19th century, like Goethe, adapted the form to their languages. The German romantic poets who employed it lengthened it to as many as 30 lines.

In India the *ghazel* spread by degrees from the Persian poems of the north Indian Mughal court poets to the various tongues of the subcontinent. Among the Indian practitioners of the form in Persian in the 16th and 17th centuries were Fughani (d. 1519) and 'URFI OF SHIRAZ (1555–90). From Persian, the *ghazel* form early spread south where it appeared in both Marathi and Telegu versions that combined Persian technique with native word stock in a poetic dialect resembling Urdu that its writers called *Dakhini* or *Dakkani* after the name of the earliest of the southern poets, Vali Dakhini or Dakkani (1635–1707) and his successor Siraj Dakhini or Dakkani (1714–64). A bit later the form appears in Urdu proper. From all these sources the *ghazel* spread throughout the languages of India in the 18th, 19th, and 20th centuries. Each tongue has made its additions and amendments to the *ghazel* tradition, which is a living, growing one.

Bibliography

Akbar, Fatollah. *The Eye of an Ant: Persian Proverbs and Poems Rendered into English Verse*. Bethesda, Md.: Iranbooks, 1995.

Globe Theatre

Built of materials salvaged from an earlier playhouse called simply *The Theatre*, the Globe was half-owned by actor Richard Burbage and his brother Cuthbert. Several members of the acting company called the Chamberlain's Men, one of whose principal members after 1594 was WILLIAM SHAKESPEARE, jointly owned the other half.

Erected on the south bank of the Thames River in Southwerk in 1599, the Globe joined the Swan and the Rose theaters as members of a popular theater district. Though the details of the Globe's design have not been preserved, a consensus has emerged about what it probably looked like. The original structure was probably more or less cylindrical with a thatched roof covering the audience seating and the attic of the theater.

The apron of the main stage certainly projected into the area where standing room was available to the groundlings—the audience members who paid the least to see performances. The apron proved useful for group scenes. The three witches who open Act I, scene i, of *Macbeth* probably appeared there as did crowd and battle scenes. At the rear center of the projecting stage, an inner chamber could be curtained or revealed to the audience. Private scenes with no more than two or three characters might be performed there or scenes, say, in which the setting represented a prison cell as in *Richard II* and *Richard III*. Trap doors on the stage led to an area below stage known as hell. These might have served for the grave-digging scene in *Hamlet* or as a source for the voice of the ghost of Hamlet's father as he moved about under the stage at the end of Act I, scene v. An upper stage directly above the inner chamber made a useful place from which a speaker might survey the scene below. One imagines Prince Malcolm speaking from there as he describes the battle between Scottish and Norwegian forces in *Macbeth* I, ii. On one side and possibly on both sides of the upper stage were windows from which actors might speak. Perhaps from a window stage Juliet spoke her lines "Romeo, O, Romeo, wherefore art thou Romeo?" (Her question means, "Why are you named Romeo, and why did I have to fall for the son of my blood enemies?" not "Where are you, Romeo?").

Higher still, above the central upper stage stood a small acting area called heaven. This could well have served as the point from which the ship's lookout called out in Act I, scene i of *The TEMPEST*.

Above heaven an attic invisible to the audience housed the stage machinery.

This rich variety of available acting areas meant that no time needed to be lost changing scenes. In his own lifetime, Shakespeare heard his lines spoken very rapidly as the action flowed from one part of the several available acting areas to another with no breaks or intermission. The effect was cinematic. One scene dissolved into another as the action and poetry swept the audience along.

The Globe Theater burned to the ground in 1613 when, during a performance of Shakespeare's *Henry VIII,* a blazing wad of tow that had been shot from a cannon ignited the thatched roof. By June of the following year, the reconstructed theater reopened. In this incarnation it seems to have been more circular, and the dangerous thatch was replaced with tile. Performances continued in the building until the CLOSING OF THE ENGLISH THEATERS. In 1644 the Puritans demolished the Southwerk theaters to make room for low-cost housing.

In the year 2000, a new Globe Theater, constructed as a near replica of the one destroyed in 1644, opened near the original Southwerk site. Essentially a museum theater, it provides a venue where audiences can see Shakespeare and other Renaissance playwrights' works performed much as their authors envisioned them.

Bibliography

Kiernan, Pauline. *Staging Shakespeare at the New Globe.* New York: St. Martin's Press, 1999.

Wells, Stanley, ed. *Shakespeare and the Globe.* Cambridge, U.K., and New York: Cambridge University Press, 1999.

Glückel von Hameln (1645–1724)

An extraordinary Jewish memoirist, Glückel was born in the city of Hamburg into the family of Leib Pinkerle, the wealthy chief functionary of that community's synagogue. Her father was called both Judah Leib and Judah Joseph and her mother Beila Melrich. Both worked in trading and business. At age 14 Glückel married a well-to-do jeweler, Chaim of Hameln. She lived happily with him, presenting him with 12 children. But her husband died, leaving Glückel a widow at age 44. At first disconsolate, she conceived the idea of writing a memoir to lift herself from her depression. She also wanted her children to have a memorial of their father and, beyond that, to be acquainted with the importance, piety, and charitable works of their ancestors. She remarried 10 years later, but her second husband, a banker named Cerf Levy, died a bankrupt.

Following Chaim's death, Glückel planned a work in seven volumes that would make the storehouse of her prodigious memory accessible to the world. She began to work on it in 1691 and brought her design to completion in 1719. Her work gives readers a remarkable insight into the life of a caring, family-centered, devout, and artistically talented woman. Had Glückel been a highly educated woman, her memoir would have been remarkable enough. All the more extraordinary, therefore, is the fact that she had only some elementary schooling. To guide her she followed her own reading of a growing body of folk and ethical literature addressed principally to an audience of German-speaking, Jewish women. She also emulated some popular treatises on medicine, child care, and arithmetic.

Among these, Glückel particularly recommended to her children's close attention the "godly books," for they made accessible the sorts of descriptions and examples of Jewish social and ethical culture that are important to a community that wishes to preserve its identity among the influences of a Christian society. From her counsel to her children one gains a sense of Glückel's own deep and abiding faith. She repeats Talmudic parables and borrows material from books of private devotional materials (called *techinnot* in Hebrew) written in Yiddish.

Glückel's *Memoirs,* however, move far beyond being just a family history or merely a personal memoir with moral advice. She also provides a chronicle concerning social and economic conditions and the business dealings and relationships among members of the Jewish community in Hamburg and the surrounding communities. Her work is a principal primary source for historians of those locations. Without Glückel's seven volumes, little detail would be available to the students of her age. Finally, however, the personal quality of Glückel's narrative gives the work its lasting appeal.

Bibliography

Glückel of Hameln. *The Memoirs of Glückel of Hameln.* Translated by Marvin Lowenthal, and introduced by Robert S. Rosen, New York: Schocken Books, 1977, ca. 1932.

Davis, Natalie Zemon. *Women on the Margins: Three Seventeenth Century Lives.* Cambridge, Mass.: Harvard University Press, 1995.

Golden Lotus, The *(Jinpingmei ci hua, Chin Ping Mei tz'u hua)* (ca. 1619)

The original Chinese title of this anonymous work means literally: "A story interspersed with *ci* songs of three women named Chin, Ping, and Mei." Critics usually call it simply *Jinpingmei.* An anonymous novel, it is the earliest in China to deal realistically with social problems in the context of private vice. Prior to its appearance, the Chinese novel dealt with history and legend set in a world of fantasy. Instead *Jinpingmei* details the daily activities of a wealthy but dishonest Chinese businessman, Qing Ximen (Ch'ing Hsi Men), through his life to his death and then explores the subsequent history of members of his household.

Alcoholic and sexually promiscuous, Qing marries six wives and uses the female servants of his household as concubines. After his fourth marriage, Qing's passion for a married woman named Golden Lotus (Pan Jinlian, P'an Chin-lien) leads him to become her accomplice in poisoning her husband. As corrupt and as insatiable in her appetites as Qing, Golden Lotus eventually inadvertently poisons him with an overdose of aphrodisiac.

Before that occurs, however, Qing has acquired a new mistress who becomes his sixth wife, Vase (Li Ping-erh). Also unscrupulous at first, Vase undergoes a reformation, becoming a model of virtue. She bears a sickly child. The jealous Golden Lotus sees to its death before its first birthday.

Throughout all this, the first wife, Moon Lady (Yueniang, Yüeh-niang) has borne everything in resigned desperation while both seeking solace and advice among Buddhist nuns and swallowing magical potions in an effort to become pregnant. That effort belatedly succeeds, and she gives birth to Qing's son almost at the moment of his father's death.

In the 21 chapters that follow, the novel details the lives and fortunes of the major characters, culminating in the decision of Moon Lady to allow her 15 year-old son Xiaogo (Hsiao-ko) to become a Buddhist monk in atonement for his father's sins. Some have reasonably argued that this novel, despite its many unabashedly pornographic passages, illustrates the Buddhist doctrine of redemption through retribution. The last chapter predicts the necessity for the characters to atone for their evil ways through a series of rebirths. Yet the author sometimes undermines this Buddhist emphasis by conducting a Confucian critique of Buddhist doctrines.

Critics have naturally sought to identify the work's author, but their efforts have not thus far borne fruit. They have, however, made clear that the novelist enjoyed an encyclopedic mastery of preceding Chinese literary tradition and that he or she intended to appeal to the tastes of a popular audience. *Jinpingmei* includes material drawn from earlier Chinese novels, contains descriptive passages in verse, frequently employs songs as its original title implies, incorporates folk tales, draws on histories of the Sung period, on the drama, and on several sorts of short story. The latter include those about crime and eroticism. Two factors further complicate the task of identifying the author. First, Chinese novelists of the period often preferred that their work be anonymous. Second, the pornographic content of *Jinpingmei* would have provided added incentive for anonymity.

The work has been widely revised in Chinese, translated into European languages, and edited to suit the tastes of the audiences for whom the revisions, translations, and editions have been prepared.

Bibliography

The Golden Lotus. Translated by Clement Egerton. London and New York: Kegan Paul International, 1995.

———. Chin P'ing Mei: *The Adventurous History of Hsi Men and His Six Wives.* Translated into English from the German of Franz Kuhn by Bernard

Miall. New York: Putnam, 1940. Reprint, New York: Capricorn Books, 1962.

Hsia, C. T. *The Classic Chinese Novel: A Critical Introduction.* Reprint, Ithaca, N.Y.: Cornell University Press, East Asia Series 1996.

Gómara, Francesco López de
(1511–1564)

The sometime chaplain and secretary to the returned Spanish conquistador Hernan Cortés, Gómara later became professor of Rhetoric at the Spanish University of Alcalá. Though he himself had benefited from travel chiefly in Italy and though he never went to the New World, his interest in exploration and explorers consumed him, and he was the first professional historian to undertake writing up their discoveries. His first work, *History of the Indies,* deals mainly with the discoveries of Christopher Columbus and with the discovery and conquest of Peru. Like many Spanish historians, Gómara sees the hand of Providence at work in selecting Spain for contemporary greatness, so he begins his work with the creation of the world.

His second work, *The Chronicle of New Spain,* relying chiefly on written and verbal reports from Hernan Cortés, gives a grossly untrue and unbalanced account of Cortés's explorations in the New World and a biography of his former employer. The inaccuracies in Gómara's history led BERNAL DÍAZ DEL CASTILLO, a member of the Cortés expedition, to occupy the leisure of his retirement by writing a true, eyewitness account of the matters Gómara had misrepresented. Gómara is the better writer, but Díaz gives a much more reliable account of the conquest of Mexico by Spain.

Gómara's other principal work was translated into English in the 1590s under the title, *The Debate and Stryfe betwene the Spanyardes and Portugales.*

Bibliography

Díaz del Castillo, Bernal. *The Discovery and Conquest of Mexico: 1517–1521.* New York: Farrar, Straus, and Cudahy, 1956.

Gómara, Francisco López De. *Cortés: The Life of the Conqueror by His Secretary. . . .* Translated and edited by Lesley Byrd Simpson. Berkeley: University of California Press, 1964.

———. *The Debate and Stryfe betwene the Spanyardes and Portugales.* London: Westminster, 1895.

———. *The Pleasant Historie of the Conquest of the West India, now called New Spayne, atchieved by the Worthy Prince Hernando Cortes, Marques of the Valley of Huaxacac, Most Delectable to Read.* London: Henry Bynneman, 1578.

Góngora y Argote, Luis de (1561–1627)

The Spanish poet who introduced to Spain a cultivated literary style that ever after bore his name, Góngora founded the *Góngorist* school or *Góngorism.* Born at Córdova, to a noble but poor family, Góngora was supposed to study law at the University of Salamanca, but he had already developed the taste for writing poetry that was to last throughout his lifetime. In 1580 he took minor religious orders and left the university without a degree.

Despite the fact that his prolific output of graceful verse attracted much favorable attention, including that of CERVANTES when Góngora was only 23, he did not succeed in attracting a patron until his seventh decade. This seems especially strange since Góngora enjoyed great popularity, and he and the famous and successful playwright LOPE DE VEGA long contended in their short ballads for top literary honors. Several of Góngora's poems appeared in anthologies or with the work of others in 1580, 1584, 1585, 1589, and 1600. Nonetheless, to keep body and soul together, Góngora's poverty forced him in 1585 to take a deacon's orders and enter a priesthood he found uncongenial. Even in the church, significant advancement for a person of his talent did not prove to be forthcoming. On the contrary, his bishop accused him of negligence—an accusation against which Góngora successfully defended himself.

A collection of poetry by illustrious poets, published by Pedro Espinosa in 1605, included most the poems he had thus far written. Too late a famous and powerful patron of the arts, the Count Duke Olivares, underwrote the publication of Góngora's collected works. At the age of 66, while he was in process of preparing his manuscripts for the press,

Góngora died. Yet the poetry that survived him was remarkable in many ways and extraordinarily influential—especially in the New World where such poets as SOR JUANA INÉS DE LA CRUZ emulated his style. He managed to combine the polish of Renaissance Italian verse with subjects sometimes taken from the ancient classics and the native vigor of Castilian Spanish forms, themes, and cadences.

A brief flirtation with the theater early in his career produced a pair of unsuccessful plays. After their failure he turned his attention to works better suited to the intellectuality and complexity of his creative processes. He early produced SONNETS written in the Italian manner that nevertheless bore marks of an unprecedented originality in Spanish treatments of the Italian style. He reworked and made popular several genres of brief Castilian verses. Many of these quickly were set to music and were sung and danced to by the people.

His lasting reputation and his enormous influence, however, rest principally on works he wrote and circulated in manuscript during the last 15 years of his life. His *Solitudes* (ca. 1613), for example, are two long, complex narrative poems, dense with INTERTEXTUALITY and full of unusual figures of thought and speech. *Solitudes* really have no exact parallels elsewhere in earlier literature. His overall plan for the *Solitudes* involved two more similar poems, but he never finished them. Equally intertextual but also highly erotic is his earlier written *POLYPHEMUS AND GALATEA* (ca. 1613)—a work taking its inspiration from the Roman poet OVID's *Metamorphoses*, book 13. *Polyphemus* conducts a parody of Ovid, of the Italian Poet, PETRARCH, and a self-parody of Góngora's own poetic practices.

In the year of Góngora's death, his friend Juan López de Vicuña finally published his collected works as *The Poetic Works of the Spanish Homer*, but the Spanish INQUISITION prohibited its sale. Not until 1633 did his complete works become widely available. Thereafter Góngora's verse continued stimulating great literary controversy and much critical discussion during his own time and throughout the 17th century both in Europe and in Spanish America. His intellectuality, his departure from what many considered social norms, his continual use of allusive METAPHORs that required readers to be as scholarly as he to understand them, and his multiple points of view made his work less popular in the two centuries that followed. The readers of the 20th century, however, once more found Góngora's poems appealing and intriguing to modern sensibilities. Some of his poems were set to music, and translations of 20 of his sonnets on women, for example, were chosen to accompany Pablo Picasso's portraits of women in a 1985 art book devoted to that subject. The same book appeared in Spanish in 1986 and has recently (2003) reappeared. Góngora's previously unpublished correspondence has also now seen print (2001). The publication and republication of Góngora's work and discussion of it is a thriving industry in Spain and elsewhere.

Bibliography

Aramo, Juan F. *Veinte sonetos: con ochenta y una páginas ilustradas fácsimiles del pintor / Luis de Góngora, Pablo Picasso.* 1986. Madrid: Casariego, ca. 2003.

Foster, David William, and Virginia Ramos Foster. *Luis de Góngora.* New York: Twayne Publishers, Inc., 1973.

Góngora y Argote, Luis de. *Fourteen Sonnets and Polyphemus.* Translated by Mack Singleton. Madison, Wisc.: Hispanic Seminary of Medieval Studies, 1975.

———. *Luis de Góngora: Selected Shorter Poems.* Translated by Michael Smith. London: Anvil Press Poetry, 1995.

———. *The Fable of Polyphemus and Galatea.* Translated by Miroslav John Hanak. New York: P. Lang, ca. 1988.

———. *The Solitudes of Luis de Góngora.* Translated by Gilbert F. Cunningham. Baltimore, Md.: Johns Hopkins University Press, 1968.

Russell, John, ed. *Góngora/Pablo Picasso.* Translated by Alan S. Trublood. New York: G. Braziller, 1985.

Gorboduc; or Ferrex and Porrex Thomas Sackville and Thomas Norton (1561)

First acted in the Inner Temple and then a year later at Whitehall before Queen ELIZABETH I, SACKVILLE and NORTON'S SENECAN TRAGEDY *Gorbo-*

duc has the distinction of being the first play written in BLANK VERSE in English.

The source of the plot for WILLIAM SHAKESPEARE's *KING LEAR*, *Gorboduc* explores the same themes. In a mythical old England the play presents authority divided, a kingdom split apart, civil war, and the tragic effects that follow from foolishly establishing multiple chains of command. It is also the first English play to observe the conventions of the UNITIES of time, place, and action. In his translation of ARISTOTLE, the Italian LUDOVICO CASTELVETRO had elevated these unities to the status of rules for composing tragedy.

Despite the unfortunate truth that *Gorboduc* is dull, overblown in its oratory, and plodding in its verse, it does have historical importance. It gave SIR PHILIP SIDNEY hope that the undisciplined British theater of his day might—as it soon did—overcome some of the silliness that resulted from the early 16th-century practice of randomly mixing slapstick comedy with serious material.

Playwrights other than Shakespeare imitated *Gorboduc*. GEORGE GASCOIGNE and Francis Kinwelmersh appropriated aspects of it for *Jocasta* (1566)—the first Greek tragedy performed on the Renaissance English stage. Robert Wilmot rewrote his rhymed tragedy *Gismond of Salern* in blank verse as *Tancred and Gismond* to make his play conform to the fashion that *Gorboduc* introduced. While the use of blank verse took hold and became the Renaissance standard for serious drama, the British playgoing public, except for the few whose tastes had been formed by specialized knowledge about *proper* tragedy, did not long reward such slavish imitation of ancient Greek and Roman practices as interpreted by Castelvetro.

Bibliography

Cauthen, Irby B., Jr., ed. *Gorboduc; or, Ferrex and Porrex [by] Thomas Sackville and Thomas Norton.* Lincoln, Neb.: University of Nebraska Press, 1970.

Tydeman, William, ed. "*Gorboduc*" in *Two Tudor Tragedies.* London and New York: Penguin Books, 1992.

Gournay, Marie Le Jars de (1565–1645)

First a devoted reader and admirer and then a surrogate daughter of the great French essayist, MICHEL DE MONTAIGNE, Marie Le Jars de Gournay became the great essayist's confidante and editor in the last years of his life. It seems likely that this father–daughter relationship with one of the principal literary figures of Europe to a degree inhibited de Gournay's own development as an independent literary figure.

After her mentor's death, however, de Gournay began to work through both her sorrow at his loss and her own need for literary independence. Her first work, a novel entitled The promenade of Monsieur Montaigne (*Le proumenoir de Monsieur de Montaigne*, 1594), belonged to a type that Montaigne had hated—the melodramatic tragic novel. In it she tells the tale of a princess ruined by her own wild passion and by the betrayal of an unworthy lover. In that novel, whose plot was evidently imagined in a conversation she had once had during a stroll with Montaigne, she develops for the first time some of the feminist views she would eventually refine and publish. She treats the sorrows of women and asserts women's equality with men.

As Montaigne's editor she brought to press in 1595 a magnificent new edition of his essays, including some that he had written late in life. She introduced it with a preface praising her mentor for his genius and characterizing herself as a combatant in the war of women against male dominance. Also in this vein was her "Apology for the Woman Writing" and "The Ladies' Grievance."

An essayist herself, de Gournay also wrote autobiography and poetry. She was a tireless reviser. Her collected works appeared in 1626 under the title The Shadow of Miss Gournay (*L'Ombre de la Damoiselle de Gournay*). Long neglected, de Gournay has begun to reemerge as the important writer she was.

Bibliography

Gournay, Marie Le Jars de. *Apology for the Woman Writing and Other Works.* Edited and translated by Richard Hillman and Colette Quesnel. Chicago: University of Chicago Press, 2002.

———. *Preface to the Essays of Michel de Montaigne by his Adoptive Daughter. . . .* Translated by

Richard Hillman and Colette Quesnel. Tempe: Medieval and Renaissance Texts and Studies, University of Arizona Press, 1998.

Great Mirror of Male Love, The
(*Nanshoku ōkagami*) Saikaku (Ihara Saikaku) (1687)

Homoerotic relationships between adult males and boys in their adolescence had for centuries been institutionalized in Japan. Such relationships were common, for example, between samurai warriors and the younger men they trained in martial skills. They also occurred frequently between cloistered Buddhist monks and their disciples. In Buddhist circles, love between teacher and disciple was thought to contribute to spiritual enlightenment. The translator and literary historian Paul Gordon Schalow tells us that when the adolescent partner, who was termed a *wakashu,* reached age 19, a coming-of-age ceremony marked his passage to adult status.

Less formal, more ephemeral relationships took place between Kabuki actors or members of the merchant classes and boy prostitutes. The cultural expectation that marriage involved romantic love was not a feature of 17th-century Japanese society, and no stigma attached to men who sought the company of either male or female prostitutes. On the contrary, books devoted to the manner of loving women and to the manner of loving boys had for centuries flourished among an eager readership.

SAIKAKU organizes the 40 stories in *The Great Mirror of Male Love* into two sections. The first 20 stories sometimes exalt and sometimes ironically depict the ideal of committed, homoerotic love as it had long been practiced among the samurai. The second half of the book concerns itself with the interactions of actors in the Kabuki theater and their adolescent male partners. Each of the 40 stories is organized as a biographical account of one of the boys. The men depicted fall into two categories: married men who cultivated a taste for both women and boys, and bachelors who hated women. The culture, however, that seems to elicit Saikaku's approval is that of the bachelors. He registers distaste for those who pursued women as well as boys.

A list of some of the titles from each section of the work conveys something of the character of Saikaku's work. In the first section we find such stories as: "Love: The Contest Between Two Forces," "The ABC's of Boy Love," "The Boy Who Scarificed His Life in the Robes of His Lover," and "Handsome Youths Having Fun Cause Trouble for a Temple." In the second section appear stories with such titles as: "A Secret Visit Leads to the Wrong Bed," and "A Terrible Shame He Never Performed in the Capital." In "Bamboo Clappers Strike the Hateful Number," Saikaku pokes fun at the samurai whose values he had elevated in the first part of the book.

Based on the positive depictions of homosexual love in this work, some have wondered about Saikaku's own sexual orientation. Gordon Schalow convincingly argues, however, that the work was a part of Saikaku's program of fictively exploring love in all its manifestations for the explicit purposes of entertaining his audience and contributing to his own support. Given the laissez-faire attitude of 17th-century Japanese culture toward recreational sex, attributing any preference to this author on the basis of his work seems a mistake.

Bibliography
Saikaku, Ihara. *The Great Mirror of Male Love.* Translated and edited by Gordon Schalow. Stanford, Calif.: Stanford University Press, 1990.

Greene, Robert (1558–1592)

After taking the B.A. and M.A. degrees at Cambridge, Greene may have traveled for a period on the Continent, living a confessedly wild and dissolute life. Except for a brief period between his wedding in 1584 and his financial insolvency in 1585, after he had wasted all his wife's money and deserted her and their child, Greene struggled to live on the money his writing produced—his only source of income. This necessity made him the first genuinely professional man of letters (some would say "first literary hack") in Renaissance England.

On leaving his wife, Greene settled in London and established himself among the more dissolute of London's literary inhabitants. He had a popular writer's unerring instinct for shifts in public taste and a quick capacity to provide material that satisfied those shifts. When JOHN LYLY's novel *Euphues* (1579) was fashionable, Greene wrote in the Euphuistic style, as in the two parts of his Italianate prose romance *Mamilla*. In it he also emulated Lyly's subject matter with discourses on love and adopted the characteristics of the hero of Lyly's novel for his own. Seeing in the success of SIR PHILIP SIDNEY's *Arcadia* (1588) a market for pastoral romances, Greene addressed it with his *Menaphon* or *Arcadia* (1588). If plays were selling well, Greene with notable success tried his hand at plays—either alone or as a collaborator.

The exact order of his first efforts as a dramatist is uncertain. Likely, his first play was *The Comical History of Alphonsus, King of Aragon*—an imitation of CHRISTOPHER MARLOWE's *Tamerlaine the Great*. Apparently Greene's play—a SENECAN TRAGEDY with a paradoxically happy romantic ending—did not find an enthusiastic audience. More successful, one of his next two plays is loosely based on the 23rd song from ARIOSTO's *ORLANDO FURIOSO* and bears that title. The central interest for Greene in this portion of his great Italian original seems to have been Orlando's going mad from jealousy. Greene took great liberties with Ariosto's material and introduced thoroughly English clowns into the action. About the same time (ca. 1589), he collaborated with THOMAS LODGE on *A Looking Glass for England and London*—a sort of moralistic play with INTERLUDES whose composition may have coincided with one of his periodic efforts at reforming his life. This play enjoyed considerable success on stage and in printed editions.

A Looking Glass ended the period in Greene's development during which he drew his direct inspiration from Italian and other foreign sources. In his next play, his *Scottish History of James IV*, Greene sets three historical figures in situations drawn exclusively from the realm of his occasionally grotesque imagination. A remarkable attribute of Greene's drama appears in his sympathetic and often realistic treatment of working-class people. He seems to have been the first among his fellows to perceive the interest, nobility, and worth of ordinary lives. As a result, the servants in *James IV* prove to be the most fascinating characters. One of them, a rogue named

Slipper, became one of the most enduringly popular characters on the Elizabethan stage.

The two plays for which Greene is best remembered as a dramatist round out the account of those of his plays that have come down to us. The first, *Friar Bacon and Friar Bungay*, is loosely based on the tales and legends that surrounded Roger Bacon, a scholar and churchman who rejected medieval scholastic philosophy in favor of mathematical and experimental proof, but who was popularly remembered as a magician. The play features MAGIC mirrors, a brass head created by magic and alchemy that will have the power to prophecy, philosophize, and build a protective wall of brass around England. Regrettably Bacon's apprentice fails to waken his master at the critical moment, and the head does not come to life. The play also contains a meeting with the devil, disguises, wounds, lovers' quarrels, and reconciliations. Though it was one of Greene's most popular plays, modern readers may find it improbable and tedious.

More to 21st-century taste, *The Pinner* [one who makes pins] *of Wakefield* seems to have been performed with Greene himself in the title role of George-a-Greene. Democratic in ideology, George considers himself as good a man as any. He strikes a peer of the realm for pursuing a fox into George's cornfield, and George eventually murders him, overcoming the peer and his retainers by tactics when he cannot oppose the numbers the nobleman brings against him.

Greene continued to keep his finger on the pulse of public preference. He addressed readers' interest with political pamphlets such as *The Spanish Masquerado* and such love pamphlets as *Gwendonius* and *Morando*—both written during his Italianate period. Perceiving that Euphuism had fallen from favor and that tracts of moral edification were in, Greene simplified his style and used his own biography to illustrate the dangers of a dissolute life with its resultant regrets, confessions, and repentance. He used the occasion of the threat posed by the Spanish Armada to remember he was a Protestant and to mount virulent attacks on Roman Catholicsm.

Observing that reports of the London underworld were in vogue, Greene gathered all the earlier accounts of it he could find and rewrote them as firsthand news of the schemes and plots of the London criminal classes. He added credibility to such reports by insisting that the criminals had threatened his life for revealing too much about theirs. Many of Greene's accounts lay bare the strategies by which the criminal classes separated the gullible of London from their money. Such gullible persons were called *conys* (rabbits), and duping them was termed *cony-catching*. Thus, this series of Greene's works (reflecting one of his varying spellings of the phrase) became known as the *Conny-catching* pamphlets. The first of them appeared in 1591: *A Notable Discovery of Cosenage*. The series it initiated was probably Greene's most financially successful venture.

His dissolute life had, however, taken its toll. By 1592 it was evident that he was dying. He may have penned *The Repentance of Robert Greene, Maister of Arts*. Some have thought it insincere, but its tone suggests otherwise; others question Greene's authorship. He also repented the "folly of his pen" in *Greene's Vision, Written at the Instant of his Death*—another work whose origin some people doubt. Greene's final work, *A Groatsworth of Wit, Bought with a Million of Repentance* (1592) was delivered to the publishers by Henry Chettle and published posthumously. In it Greene has bequeathed to literary historians a continuing puzzle. In the pamphlet, Greene essentially accuses WILLIAM SHAKESPEARE of having plagiarized his work, calling the Bard an "upstart crow, beautified with our feathers."

Given the way Greene produced much of his own writing, it may seem strange that Shakespeare's borrowings or plagiaries should have so concerned him—especially since British Renaissance playwrights continually collaborated and often reworked each other's material. There seems, however, to have been a history of bad blood between the two authors, and Shakespeare undeniably had borrowed much from Greene. These borrowings included subjects, plots, characters, treatments, forms of versification, and perhaps sometimes phraseology. What probably infuriated Greene even more, however, was that Shakespeare seemed to use his borrowings to greater effect than Greene's originals achieved. This may have been particularly galling in view of Greene's pride in his own academic credentials (he had received a second M.A. from Oxford in 1588). That an *upstart* from Stratford, apparently without benefit of a university education, should outshine the older and three-degreed Greene as a dramatist must have rankled. On Shakespeare's side, one critic has suggested that Shakespeare based the life and death of Sir John Falstaff in *HENRY IV, Parts 1 and 2* on Greene's riotous life and pitiable passing. After Greene's death, Shakespeare used Greene's *Pandosto* (1588) as a source for the plot of *A Winter's Tale* (1610–11).

Greene's surviving literary output is vast, running in the standard edition of his works to 13 volumes. A masterful study by Charles W. Crupi, Greene's most recent biographer, demonstrates that uncertainties surround the authorship of some of the works assigned to Greene and some of the reports of events in Greene's life.

Bibliography

Crupi, Charles W. *Robert Greene*. Boston: Twayne Publishers, 1986.

Grosart, Alexander B., ed. *The Life and Complete Works in Prose and Verse of Robert Greene, M.A.* Cambridge and Oxford. 15 vols., 1881–1886. New York: Russell and Russell, 1964.

Gregorian Calendar

From the year 8 C.E. until the year 1582, the Julian calendar remained in common use throughout Europe. Named for Julius Caesar, who had introduced the calendar to Rome in 45 B.C.E., the Julian calendar eventually proved to overestimate the length of a solar year by 11 minutes, 45 seconds. Thus a considerable mistake accrued over time—about a day every 314 years.

Throughout the Christian world the most important festival, Easter, is supposed to be celebrated on the Sunday after the first full moon after the vernal equinox. By the 16th century, the nominal equinox, March 21, was fully 10 days behind the actual equinox. The error meant a confusion of the dates on which Christendom celebrated Easter—some figured it from the real equinox, and some from the artificial one.

Compounding that confusion, the New Year was celebrated on different dates in different places. March 15 was the date of the new year in most places, but Florence, Italy, and all of England celebrated it on March 25.

In 1573 Pope Gregory XIII formed a commission to study the problem and make recommendations. They came up with a solar calendar that, though still not perfect, only required the addition of an extra day every four years to keep the calendrical year very close to the actual solar one. A day's error still accrues in a period of 25 centuries.

Rome adopted the Gregorian calendar in 1582, and most Roman Catholic countries quickly followed suit. Protestant countries in Europe were slower to perceive the benefits of the Gregorian calendar, but in time they did. Protestant England waited until September 3, 1752, to make the change and to move New Year's Day to January 1. The Orthodox churches of Eastern Europe continued to employ the Julian calendar to determine the date of Easter and its attendant festivals, Ash Wednesday and Pentecost.

From the perspective of literature, many literary works celebrate the return of the spring and the greening of the earth, which, of course, in temperate climates would closely coincide with the March dates of the Julian New Year. Students of older literatures might wish to bear this in mind. The 16th-century shift in calendars also bears on the year of birth or death of certain authors who came into or left the world under one or the other calendrical system.

Greif, Andreas (Andreas Gryphius)
(1616–1664)

More celebrated among his contemporaries than any other writer of his era in Germany, the learned Greif, or Gryphius, had mastered all the major European languages of the Renaissance and Latin, Greek, and Hebrew as well. He wrote many lyrical poems in Latin and German—EPIGRAMS, ODES, and SONNETS. These are pervaded by a woeful seriousness and by a melancholy sense of the world's vanity and the ultimate futility of all human enterprise.

Greif also wrote several examples of TRAGEDY and of COMEDY. Among those in the former category we find a play based on the murder of Leo Armenius, the king of Byzantium, a second based on

the execution of the widowed Christian Queen Catherine of Georgia, a prisoner of the shah of Persia, who chooses to die rather than marry her captor. A third tragedy is based on the beheading of the English monarch, Charles I, and a fourth concerns the execution of an ancient Roman lawyer, Amilius Paulus Papinianus, who refused to invent legal grounds to justify murders and fratricide committed by the Roman emperor, Caracalla.

Among his comedies we find a farce drawn from the play-within-a-play in SHAKESPEARE's A MIDSUMMER NIGHT'S DREAM. This work features Peter Quince—or Squenz as he appears in Greif's version. Another, Horribilcribrifax (1663), concerns the aftermath of the Thirty Years War and the attempt of the survivors to return their society to a semblance of normalcy. Greif wrote other comedies as well.

Despite his fame during his lifetime, his highly decorative baroque style of composition fell out of favor in the 18th century. As a result his works still languish largely unknown and neglected. None of his plays and only four of his poems in a musical setting, for instance, have been translated into English. This is a pity, for Greif's stoic view of the world's vanity would resonate well with the global situation in the early 21st century.

Greiffenberg, Catharina Regina von
(1633–1694)

Born at her family's estate at Castle Seisenegg in Austria, von Greiffenberg received a splendid education under her mother's tutelage and that of the uncle who, after 1641, became her guardian, Rudolph Freiherr von Greiffenberg. Although he was her father's half brother and 30 years her senior, in 1664 Rudolph also became Catharina's husband. Because of their close blood relationship, their marriage required a special dispensation from a Protestant cleric.

As a poet and literary artist, von Greiffenberg considered herself to be in the vatic tradition. (See VATES.) She felt that God had called her to be a poet and that the exercise of her literary gifts amounted to a divinely appointed responsibility. This included the obligation to learn everything she could so she might better exercise her high calling. She early learned Latin, French, Italian, and Spanish. Late in life she would also master Hebrew and Greek. Beyond this she read incessantly throughout her lifetime.

When the Turks assaulted Austria, von Greiffenberg moved in 1663 to the city of Nuremberg, the home of a talented circle of poets and artists with whom she became associated. There she composed a long (more than 7,000 alexandrine stanzas) heroic poem on the subject of the long-standing feud between Islam and Christianity. A Protestant herself in largely Roman Catholic Austria, von Greiffenberg viewed Islam as a thorn in the flesh of Christendom. God had put it there, she thought, to plague the Roman Catholics and to encourage the Protestants, led, as she hoped, by the royal house of Habsburg, to mount a final, triumphant crusade against the followers of the Prophet Muhammad. Women, she thought, had a responsibility to become involved in the crucial issues of the day as their intellects and educations equipped them to do so. Her heroic poem, Triumphal column of penance and faith . . . (*Sieges-Seule der Busse und Glaubens . . .*, 1675) represented her contribution to the war effort. An ardent nationalist, she became the first female member of the German Patriotic Society of Nuremberg.

Though she wrote that work in part to fulfill her sense of responsibility to her high calling as a poet and to the religious precepts she believed, the poetic mode that she found most congenial was the short lyric. She composed SONNETS and individual alexandrines of great beauty and freshness. She also wrote a number of devotional poems and prose pieces that she drew together into a sizable collection of meditations. This eventually grew to eight volumes. All of her work is characterized, first, by a sense of personal immediacy and, second, by a sense of intense, mystical devotion to a God of spirit for whom human experience plays the role of sense organs in the natural world.

Although von Greiffenberg was and is considered the best German poet of her time, her work has not yet been translated into English. A sense of it, nonetheless, may be gained from the commentary of the authors cited below.

Bibliography

Browning, Robert Marcellus. *German Baroque Poetry, 1617–1723*. University Park: Pennsylvania State University Press, 1971.

Foley-Beining, Kathleen. *The Body and Eucharistic Devotion in Catharina von Greiffenberg's "Meditations."* Columbia, S.C.: Camden House, 1997.

Kimmich, Flora. *Sonnets of Catharina von Greiffenberg: Methods of Composition*. Chapel Hill: University of North Carolina Press, 1975.

Greville, Fulke, first baron Brooke
(1554–1628)

The author of a pair of tragedies, more than 100 sonnets, some didactic poems, and a posthumously published work, *Life of the Renowned SIR PHILIP SIDNEY* (1652), Greville was educated at Cambridge University. Besides his literary activities, Greville enjoyed the confidence and patronage of Queen ELIZABETH I, who named him secretary for Wales. He served in that office from 1583 to 1628, undertaking several diplomatic embassies in the Netherlands, France, and Ireland. For seven of those years, under James I, Greville also served as chancellor of the Exchequer (1614–21). Near the end of that term of service (1620) JAMES I created him the first Baron Brooke.

As a sonneteer, Greville departed from the PETRARCHIST norm followed by many Elizabethan lyricists. His sonnet cycle *Cælica* (published posthumously in *Certain learned and Elegant Works*, 1633) avoids the affectations of overwrought CONCEITS. His work strikes a reader as at once more philosophical, realistic, and satirical than many of his contemporary sonneteers. While it seems that the sonnets in *Cælica* are addressed to more than one lady, some critics have speculated that Greville may have admired Queen Elizabeth herself. Perhaps that admiration reflects itself in Greville's lines, "For I have vowed in strangest fashion/To love, and never seek compassion." In keeping with that sentiment, Greville never married.

Greville's didactic poems reveal a Calvinist religious allegiance as in his somber *Sion Lies Waste*—a work that appeared in the same collection of

1633. His longer poems also reveal a profound talent for philosophic speculation in verse.

His prose is clear, straightforward, and readable and includes maxims, essays, and CHARACTERS. His biography of Sir Philip Sidney remains valuable for its style as well as for the portraits it contains of contemporary persons and events. Greville and Sidney had begun their friendship as children and had attended Shrewsbury school together until Greville went to Cambridge and Sidney to Oxford in 1567.

Reunited at the royal court around 1577, their close friendship continued until Sidney's untimely death in 1586, and Greville cherished Sidney's memory until his own tragic murder. Before that event, Greville had written his own epitaph: "Servant to Queen Elizabeth, councilor to King James, and friend to Sir Philip Sidney."

Greville was stabbed to death by a distracted family retainer who was angered by the apparently groundless notion that Greville was about to dismiss him after years of loyal service without having made provision for his old age. After killing Greville, the servant committed suicide.

Though Greville wrote voluminously, he did not belong to "the scribbling classes." As a result the only one of his works to appear during his lifetime was a probably pirated edition of his Oriental tragedy, *Mustapha* (1609). A work of uncertain attribution, *Narrative History of King James, for the First Fourteen Years* was published in 1651. First editions of Greville's works continued appearing until as late as 1670, when another compilation of unpublished works was mined from his manuscripts and appeared as *The Remaines of Sir Fulk* [sic] *Greville, Lord Brooke: Being Poems of Monarchy and Religion.*

Bibliography

Caldwell, Mark, ed. *The Prose of Fulke Greville, Baron Brooke* and *Life of the Renowned Sir Philip Sidney.* New York: Garland, 1987.

Greville, Fulke, Baron Brooke. *Selected Poems.* Edited by Neil Powell. Manchester, U.K.: Carcanet Press, 1990.

Grimald, Nicholas (1519–1562)

The author of both English and NEO-LATIN plays and poems, Grimald studied at Christ's College, Cambridge, and at Brasenose and Merton Colleges, Oxford. He took religious orders and, until Mary I revoked the Anglican establishment, served as a Protestant chaplain. Under Mary, he recanted his Protestantism and returned to the Roman Catholic fold.

During his first year at Oxford, Grimald penned a play in Latin, The resurrection of Christ (*Christus Redivivus*, 1541). It was produced there in the spring of that year. Eventually he took master's degrees from both Oxford and Cambridge and became a lecturer at Oxford. Apparently in preparation for his lectures there, he translated and commented upon a wide range of Latin, Greek, and Hebrew texts. He also composed his second neo-Latin play—a tragedy based on the life of John the Baptist and entitled the Archprophet (*Archipropheta,* ca. 1547). This may have been the first tragedy written by an Englishman. In 1556, the printer Richard Tottel published the first edition of Grimald's translation of CICERO's Concerning duties (*De Officiis*), and brought out a second edition in 1558.

The connection between Grimald and Tottel probably explains why some 40 of Grimald's lyric poems appear in the most influential collection of English lyric poems of the early British Renaissance, *Songes and Sonettes,* otherwise known as TOTTEL'S MISCELLANY (1557). This collection began the vogue for English lyric that continued through the 17th and into the 18th and even the 19th centuries. Until late in the 19th century, the British reading public preferred reading verse to reading prose. Tottel's work seems to have helped to form—and its many subsequent editions to sustain—that taste.

Although Grimald's production of translations and other works seems to have been extensive, much of it was not printed and the manuscript remnants have largely been lost. His work is principally represented, therefore, by the two plays named above, by the translation of Cicero, by the 40 English lyric poems printed in *Tottel's Miscellany,* and by six Latin lyrics preserved elsewhere. L. R. Merrill has usefully brought all Grimald's surviving texts together in the volume cited in the bibliography below.

Bibliography

Cicero, Marcus Tullius. *Marcus Tullius Ciceroes thre bokes of duties, to Marcus his sonne, turned out of Latine into English, by Nicolas Grimalde.* Washington, D.C.: Folger Shakespeare Library, ca. 1990.

Merill, L. R. *The Life and Poems of Nicholas Grimald.* 1925. Hamden, Conn.: Archon Books, 1969.

Tottel's Miscellany. *Songes and Sonettes by Henry Howard, Earl of Surrey, Sir Thomas Wyatt, the Elder, Nicholas Grimald, and Uncertain Authors.* New York: AMS Press, 1966.

Grimmelshausen, Hans Jacob Christoph von (ca. 1621–1676)

A gifted and original German novelist and satirist, Grimmelshausen is remembered for 10 novels and for the development of a highly distinctive style that he named for the hero of his best known work and labeled the "Simplician manner." Orphaned young, reared by his grandparents, and afflicted with the uncertainties of the Thirty Years' War. Grimmelshausen nonetheless managed to begin a basic education by studying at a Lutheran Latin school in his native Gelnhausen.

His informal education at Gelnhausen proved more disturbing. The town was afflicted with a mania for identifying and persecuting witches. In 1633–34 this public furor reached its peak with those accused of witchcraft being tried, tortured until they confessed, and then publicly beheaded. As Grimmelshausen lived very near the jail, he likely witnessed some of this horror. One of his biographers, Kenneth Negus, attributes the deep vein of the occult and the Satanic in Grimmelshausen's later writings to this teenage trauma.

By 1636 the 15-year-old Grimmelshausen was serving in some capacity in the army—a role in which he continued, eventually serving as a musketeer and in the cavalry. This experience also appears in his fiction both in terms of the characterization of his protagonist, Simplicissimus, and in various episodes of the plot.

In 1639 and for about three to five years following, Grimmelshausen was assigned a garrison post in the town of Offenburg. There he attracted the attention of the regimental secretary, Johannes Witsch, who undertook to supplement the young man's education. Grimmelshausen succeeded Witsch as regimental secretary. He then left that post, served elsewhere, though just where is unknown, and finally mustered out of the army in 1649 after 15 years of service.

In the fall of the same year he managed to secure both a bride and a job. He married Catharina Henniger, the daughter and sister of fellow soldiers. His former commander, Col. Hans Reinhard von Schauenburg, employed him as his family's steward. There followed a period of financial ups and downs and the arrival of several children. Though Grimmelshausen eventually left the Schauenburgs' regular employ, he continued to perform occasional tasks for them and supplemented his small income by becoming an innkeeper.

He then found uncongenial employment with a physician, Dr. Küeffer, who seems to have become a model for one of the author's unsavory characters, Dr. Canard. It was during this three-year stint that Grimmelshausen began his literary career in earnest, perhaps making good use of his employer's connections with polite literary society—though Grimmelshausen did not share their refined aesthetic preferences. Before he published anything, though, he gave up his employment and, from 1665 to 1667, returned once again to innkeeping. While fulfilling this function, he completed his first two books, The satirical pilgrim (*Satyrischer Pilgram*, 1666) and The chaste Joseph (*Keuscher Joseph*, 1666). He also wrote about half of his masterpiece, ADVENTUROUS SIMPLICISSIMUS (*Der abendteuerlich Simplicissimus Teutsch*, 1668). In 1667 he at last found congenial employment as mayor of Renchen. This post left him free to pursue his literary career as well.

Grimmelshausen's first two works were standard SATIRE, exposing human folly and vice and by implication promoting reason and virtue. With the publication of *Simplicissimus,* however, Grimmelshausen arrives at a new vision of satiric possibility—one that presents alternative viewpoints side by side without making an effort to judge between them. The realistic, the comic, the satiric, the moral, the religious, the roguish, and the bestial all intertwine without a pervading authorial guide to privilege one position over another. Above all, perhaps, *Simplicissimus* presents an unblinking picture of the horrors of the Thirty Years War—a picture that would compel anyone who reads to think at least twice before embarking on its like. The 20th-century playwright Bertholt Brecht drew inspiration for his play *Mother Courage and Her Children: A Chronicle of the Thirty Years War* (1949) from Grimmelshausen's narrative—especially from the part whose title appears in two separate English translations: *Mother Courage* and *The Runagate Courage* (both 1965)—which its author published in German in 1670.

Once Grimmelshausen had worked out his complex manner of presentation (and once it had proved stunningly successful), he continued to employ it on his future works. He even rewrote *The Chaste Joseph* (1669), as Grimmelshausen said, to "Simplicianize" it. There followed in 1670, first, a sequel to *Simplicissimus*, *The Singular Life of Heedless Hopalong* (*Der seltzame Springinsfeld*, 1670), and then *Trutz Simplex: Lebensbeschreibung der Ertzbetrügerin und Landstörtzerin Courasche* (*The Runagate Courage*, 1670). Several commentators see as the capstone work of Grimmelshausen's Simplician series the as yet untranslated, two-part The enchanted bird's nest (*Das wunderbarliche Vogelnest*, 1672 and 75).

Some critics argue convincingly that Grimmelshausen's 10 novels and some of his treatises as well constitute part of a grand design that in essence makes up one very long book—a bit like what the Scottish writer J. K. Rowland claims for her *Harry Potter* sequence. Only pieces of Grimmelshausen's overarching design have as yet become available in English, but the ones that have command the greatest interest. "The enchanted bird's nest" needs a good English translator. Otherwise, Grimmelshausen's work was sometimes of uneven quality, and some of the installments in the series seem to have been written principally to give his publishers something to sell and capitalize on his renown.

Bibliography

Grimmelshausen, Hans Jakob Christoph von. *An Unabridged Translation of Simplicius Simplicissimus. . . .* Edited and translated by Monte Adair. Lanham, Md.: University Press of America, ca. 1986.

———. *The Adventures of Simplicius Simplicissimus . . . A Modern Translation.* Translated by George Schulz-Behrend. Columbia, S.C.: Camden House, ca. 1993.

———. *The Runagate Courage.* Translated by Robert L. Hiller and John C. Osborne. Lincoln, Neb.: University of Nebraska Press, ca. 1965.

Menhennet, Alan. *Grimmelshausen the Storyteller.* Columbia, S.C.: Camden House, 1997.

Negus, Kenneth. *Grimmelshausen.* New York: Twayne Publishers, 1974.

Guarini, Giovanni Battista (1538–1612)

Remembered principally for his PASTORAL TRAGICOMEDY *Il pastor fido* (*THE FAITHFUL SHEPHERD*, 1590), Guarini found himself in the uncomfortable position of being a courtier in an aristocratic Italian society whose system of patronage he despised. For a decade and a half after 1567 he labored as a diplomat in the service of the duke of Ferrara, Alfonso II, in Italy at Rome and Turin and abroad in Poland. He nonetheless found time to write, completing a comedy *La Idropica* (The woman with dropsy) in 1583. He also composed lyrical verse—chiefly madrigals—that such important composers of his era as Vittoria Aleotti and Claudio Monteverdi set to music.

Aside from his creative writing, Guarini penned considerable criticism and tracts on political subjects as well. He deplored what he considered the fallen state of Italian popular theater as represented by the COMMEDIA DELL'ARTE. He joined the ever-growing ranks of Renaissance persons who published their correspondence. He objected to church censorship of the work of creative artists. On several occasions he defended *The Faithful Shepherd* against the attacks of other critics, asserting his drama's importance as something new in the world of letters. The new sort of drama that he espoused was tragicomedy. Guarini objected to the neo-Aristotelian point of view that insisted on a sharp distinction between the staging of comedy and tragedy. In what is likely his own *Compendio della Poesia tragicomica* (Compendium of tragicomic poetry, 1601) and a series of pamphlets that preceded it, Gurarini lucidly developed the fundamental and definitive theoretical basis for mixing the two genres and for the interweaving of multiple plot lines to achieve the third sort of drama that tragicomedy represented.

The literary historian Jane Tylus catalogues some of the influence that *The Faithful Shepherd* exercised, not only in Italy but in England, France, and Spain as well. George Frederick Handel turned Guarini's play into an opera of the same name. SHAKESPEARE's dark comedy from his later period is indebted to Guarini's technique of setting up situations whose outcome is potentially tragic but which avoid tragedy through forgiveness and reconciliation. A similar influence appears in Pierre Corneille's French play about the Spanish hero, *The Cid* (*Le Cid,* 1633). Sir Richard Fanshawe first translated *The Faithful Shepherd* into English in 1647. Tylus considers Fanshawe's rendering among the best English translations of any Italian work. It is available in a bilingual, modern edition. Fanshawe, however, seriously truncates Guarini's play. A fuller version, also in an attractive translation that catches more of the poetic flavor of the original, is the 18th-century translation by Dr. Thomas Sheridan—also available in a recent edition.

Bibliography

Donno, Elizabeth. *Three Renaissance Pastorals: Tasso, Guarini, Daniel.* Binghamton, N.Y.: Medieval and Renaissance Texts & Studies, 1993.

Guarini, Battista. *Il Pastor Fido: The Faithfull Shepherd.* Translated (1647) by Richard Fanshawe. Edited by J. H. Whitfield. Edinburgh, U.K.: Edinburgh University Press, ca. 1976.

———. *The Faithful Shepherd.* Translated by Thomas Sheridan. Edited by Robert Hogan and Edward A. Nickerson. Newark, N.J.: University of Delaware Press, ca. 1989.

Tylus, Jane. "Guarini, Giovanni Battista." In *Encyclopedia of the Renaissance.* Volume 3, edited by Paul F. Grendler. New York: Charles Scribner's Sons, 1999.

Gul-Badan Begum (1523–1603)

A princess and daughter of Zahir al-Din Muhammad Babur Padishah (Babur, 1483–1530), the first Mughal emperor of India, Gul-Badan Begum (Princess Rose-Body) was the daughter of the Emperor Babur and Dildar Begum, one of his wives. Adopted and educated by Babur's principal wife Maham Begum, Gul-Badan Begum learned both Persian and dialectical Turkish, mastered calligraphy, and wrote poetry.

Her brother, Nasir Al-Din Muhammad Humayun Padishah (Humayun, 1508–56), inherited the empire and consolidated his power until his untimely death in a fall. His son and successor, Akbar the Great, asked his aunt to write a personal memoir of her recollections of his father's reign. After pleading her lack of qualification for the task, Gul-Badan Begum acceded to her nephew's insistent request and penned The history of *Humāyūnnāma* (Humayun). Only one incomplete copy of this work still exists. It is in the archives of the British Library. In it, rather than the usual chronicle of military and political events recorded in such works, Gul-Badan Begum follows the life of the ruling family from the perspective of the women of the household. The men come and go to their wars while the women wait and weave close friendships. Although she focuses on the daily activities of the royal household, she does recount one battle at Khanua, where her brother fought and won against the Rajput princes. She also details a four-year-long pilgrimage to Mecca made by the women of the royal household, recalling both its pleasures and its near disaster when the pilgrims were shipwrecked.

Written in lively, colloquial Persian prose sprinkled with Turkish words and phrases, at the turn of the 20th century, Gul-Badan Begum's work was rendered into a superlative English version by British scholar Annette S. Beveridge. Beveridge found that Gul-Badan Begum's work "lights up a woman's world."

Bibliography

Gul-Badan Begum. *Humāyūn-Nāma*. Translated by Annette S. Beveridge. London: The Royal Asiatic Society, 1902.

Tharu, Susie, and K. Lalita. "Gul-Badan Begum." In *Women Writing in India 600 B.C. to the Present*, edited by Susie Tharu and Ki Lalita, 99–102. New York: The Feminist Press at The City University of New York, 1991.

Hakluyt, Richard (ca. 1552–1616)

A tireless collector of the logbooks of voyages and writings about the accomplishments of navigators, a cosmographer, a visionary of the field of exploration, and a clergyman, Hakluyt had since boyhood been consumed with sailing, voyages of discovery, and the idea of making England great through discovery and commerce.

The geographical and economic knowledge he amassed about distant places made him invaluable to newly formed British trading companies seeking to establish commercial ties overseas. He served, for instance, as a consultant for a newly formed company seeking trading partners in the Middle East.

He studied for the Anglican priesthood and from 1583 to 1588 served as chaplain to the English embassy in France. Before assuming that post, however, Hakluyt published *Divers Voyages Touching the Discovery of America* (1582). Dedicated to SIR PHILIP SIDNEY, this volume contained not so much Hakluyt's own writings, but rather reports of voyages that he had collected and edited. He keenly wished to encourage English colonization of the New World.

On a brief return from France in 1584, Hakluyt instantly began to edit materials he had collected and sent home from across the channel. This material he published under the title *The Discourse of Western Planting* (1584). It presented a plan for colonizing North America and was designed to capture the interest of Queen Elizabeth I in promoting the scheme.

Now utterly consumed by his passion for accounts of exploration present and past and driven by his vision of a far-flung British empire based on exploration and trade, his next major publication appeared in 1589: *The Principal Navigations, Voyages, and Discoveries of the English Nation.* Once he had the idea of using the triumphs of past and present British seamanship to promote an interest in the creation of a seagoing, imperial power, Hakluyt assembled and edited or rewrote every report of travel to far-off places he could find. This included accounts by sailors, those translated from other languages, and even those from the medieval and ancient worlds. He included in subsequent editions, for instance, a translation of the Old English account of the Voyages of Ohthere and Wulfstan—intrepid English seafarers who had coasted the Scandinavian peninsula to very high latitudes during the seventh century and had described the non-European peoples and the fauna they encountered. He also included a condensed version of GEORGE BEST's account of the three voyages of Martin Frobisher to the New World in 1576, 1577, and 1578.

Though Hakluyt neither explored nor sailed except as an occasional passenger nor ever discovered any new places, his energy and zeal and the knowledge he assembled inspired and enabled others, finally making possible the achievements he was among the first in England to imagine.

Hakluyt's industry and obsession produced an enormous amount of text. The works discussed above represent some of the high points. Modern editions of the works are generally abridged, though the bibliography below contains one reference to an almost complete 20th-century reprint of perhaps his most important work, *The Principal Navigations.* . . . The Canadian author, Delbert A. Young, has used the works of Hakluyt as source material for a charming collection of sea yarns for teenagers.

Bibliography

Hakluyt, Richard. *A particuler discourse concerninge the greate necessitie and manifolde commodityes that are like to growe to the Realme of Englande by the Westerne Discoveries lately attempted. . . .* [*Discourse of Western Planting.*] Edited by David Quinn and Alison M. Quinn. London: Hakluyt Society, 1993.

———. *The Principal Navigations, Voiages, and Discoveries of the English Nation made by Sea or Overland to the Remote and Farthest Distant Quarters of the Earth at Any Time within the Compasse of these 1600 Yeeres.* 12 vols. 1903–1905. New York: A. M. Kelley, 1969.

Young, Delbert A. *According to Hakluyt: Tales of Adventure and Exploration.* Toronto: Clarke, Irwin, 1973.

Halacha, Halachism

The *halacha* is that portion of Jewish literature that deals with the law. Halachism is the practice of appealing to the *halacha,* either in the Scripture or in later Jewish literature, for the resolution of disputes or the key to understanding issues.

Háletí ('Azmi-záde Mustafá) (1570–1631)

A distinguished Turkish jurist who served the Ottoman Empire in numerous responsible posts,

Háletí enjoys a reputation both as one of the best poets and one of most cultured and widely read persons of his epoch. He left a library of between three- and four-thousand books and manuscripts. Each of them bore his handwritten annotations.

Particularly remembered for his 460 RUBÁ'ɪs (four-line poems), Háletí imitated Persian models in these short verses that have come to be regarded as the best of their sort in the Turkish language. Some are considered equal to the Persian ones collected and translated by Edward Fitzgerald in *The Rubbaiyat of Omar Khayyám* (1859). In addition, Háletí composed a separate collection representing the other varieties of Turkish verse—MESNEVÍs, QASÍDAS, and GHAZELs.

Háletí contributed notably to a subcategory of Arabic–Persian–Turkish poetry, the CUPBEARER book, with his poem of the same name: *Sáqí-Náme.* This sort of poem praised the joys of wine drinking and revelry. Although Islamic law forbade the actual consumption of alcoholic beverages, individuals sometimes complied with that prohibition more in the breach than in the observance. Literary descriptions of revelry, moreover, were meant to be taken as ALLEGORY. The ecstatic states resulting from drinking, as poems described them, were to be understood as the joys of life—especially the religious life. Lest the abstemious devout misunderstand that intention, cupbearer poets regularly included, as Háletí did, a section explaining how to interpret the allegory.

The opening and closing sections of Háletí's 15-section *Cupbearer Book* address the poet's praises to God. Some of the other 13 sections of the work's 515 couplets (*mesneví*) contain the author's complaints about the sad conditions of his life. Some address compliments to the bearer of the cup, to the minstrels whose songs and recitations enliven the evening, to the poet's fellow revelers, and to the lovely women who contribute to the party's gaiety. The poem details the characteristics of the wine, of the bowl in which it is served, of the tavern where the party is held, and of the seasons of the year. Háletí's verses also contain instructions for enjoying each season to the fullest.

At the same time, the poet both criticizes conventional persons who do not make the most of life's party and invites them to join the revelry. FORTUNE is fickle; life is short; situations change by the minute. Take advantage of life's pleasures, the poet advises, when they present themselves.

The message of cupbearer books had much in common with Renaissance Europe's mistaken notions about the practices of the Greek philosopher EPICURUS, who was popularly thought to have advised that we ought to "eat, drink, and be merry, for tomorrow we die."

Bibliography

Gibb, E. J. W. *A History of Ottoman Poetry.* Edited by Edward G. Browne. London: Luzac and Company, 1965.

Hall, Joseph (1574–1656)

An English clergyman, scholar, poet, Utopian visionary, religious controversialist, and eventually the Anglican bishop of Norwich and of Exeter, Hall is considered to be the first English poetic satirist in the manner of the ancients.

Joseph Hall was educated at Emmanuel College, Cambridge, where he received four degrees—the highest a doctorate in divinity—between 1592 and 1610. His career as an English satirist began in 1597 with the publication of a volume of iambic-pentameter couplets entitled *Virgidemiarum: First Three Books of TOOTHLESS SATIRES.* These were followed the next year by a similarly titled three books of *BITING SATIRES.*

Hall married Elizabeth Winiff in 1603 and published a poem, "The King's Prophecy," dedicated to King JAMES I on his accession to the throne that same year. The following year, 1604, saw the publication of religious writings and, a year later, of his one sally into the field of Utopian (or in this case *distopian*) literature. Written in Latin his *Mundus alter et idem* (*Another world and yet the same,* 1605) was ostensibly published abroad, though it may not have been. Hall never claimed this work as his own. Neither did he disclaim it, but his authorship nevertheless seems to have been an open secret. In the work, which John Healy translated into English

in 1609 as *The Discovery of a New World,* Hall anticipates Jonathan Swift's *Gulliver's Travels* (1726) by having his hero, Mercurius Brittanicus, travel to Antarctica where he visits four kingdoms: *Crapulia,* the kingdom of gluttons; *Viraginia,* the kingdom of shrews; *Moronia,* the kingdom of fools; and *Lavernia:* the kingdom of thieves.

Located at the southern pole, these kingdoms and their laws and customs turn the norms of European society upside down. Hall's splendid biographer, Leonard D. Tournay, observes that in Crapulia "the atmosphere . . . is that of an Elizabethan tavern: a riot of gluttony and dyspepsia." Punning on the British–American colony of Virginia, named for ELIZABETH I, the virgin queen, Hall's Viraginia is a country ruled by women where all the household chores and so-called women's work gets done by men. Hall shared the misogynist preconceptions of his era and his religion, so he considered this role reversal an appropriate subject for SATIRE. In Moronia, of course, Hall subjects all sorts of folly to his satiric scrutiny, and in Lavernia the populace is trained in thievery from childhood, and alchemists and lawyers abound.

Like a number of his contemporaries, Hall authored a collection of brief essays, *Characters of Virtues and Vices* (1608). In his prose CHARACTER WRITING he pictured persons with stylized virtues and vices. His depiction of vices generally follows the model provided by the ancient Grecian originator of the character genre, Theophrastus (ca. 372–ca. 278 B.C.E.). Like Theophrastus, Hall's exploration of the faults of the vicious has moral reform as its central objective. This seriousness of purpose, although it lacks some of Theophrastus's good humor, lends conviction to the portraits Hall draws in "The Hypocrite," for example, or "The Busybody."

Hall's exploration of virtues, on the other hand, seem less heartfelt and more conventional, didactic, and less convincing as portraits either of individual people or of character types. "The Humble Man," provides a case in point. Both as a satirist and a clergyman, perhaps, Hall found more and better examples of vice to ridicule than instances of virtue to praise.

Throughout his literary career, Hall also penned both religious and secular verse, including what the Indian poet P. Lal calls verse "transcreations" of several Psalms and in 1613 introductory poems for JOHN DONNE's *Anniversaries*. Throughout his life, he regularly published a number of moving religious meditations, and as a preacher he was counted among the greatest of his era—a claim his collected sermons fully support.

Hall's lifetime stretched from the glory days of the high English Renaissance under Elizabeth I through the English civil strife between Cavaliers (the longhaired, aristocratic supporters of the Stuart dynasty and the established Anglican church) and Roundheads (the puritan commoners whose hair was close cropped and who wished to install a Puritan government and a Presbyterian style of church governance.) As the Puritans became more vocal and critical of the Anglican hierarchy, Hall stepped into the fray, criticizing the Presbyterians as he sometimes did the Roman Catholics. First in 1610 he rebutted puritanical arguments against the established church. He defended the episcopacy as divinely established. Dissenting preachers and finally JOHN MILTON engaged him in a war of words. This latter debate between Hall and Milton grew ever more rancorous, peaking in the early 1640s during the British civil war, as two of the most learned men of their time took opposite sides on religious issues.

Hall had become bishop of Exeter in 1627. In 1641 he added to that distinction the bishopric of Norwich. The Anglican king, Charles I, and the Presbyterian Parliament by that time, however, stood tottering on the brink of civil war. Before Hall could take up the duties of his new office, in December of 1641, Archbishop of York John Williams, Hall himself, and 11 other Anglican bishops were all charged with high treason and imprisoned in the Tower of London. The charges were excessive, and in 1642 Hall was released and permitted to assume his bishopric. He was not destined to serve long in that office. On August 22 of that year Charles I took up arms. The next year Parliament passed a law that stripped Hall of his bishopric and income. For five years he was allowed to remain in the official residence, but eventually that privilege too was taken away. He moved to a little house outside Norwich. There between 1648 and 1651 he wrote three more devotional pieces before falling into literary silence for the last five years of his life.

Bibliography

Hall, Joseph. *Another World and Yet the Same: Bishop Joseph Hall's Mundus alter et idem*. Translated by John Millar Wands. New Haven, Conn.: Yale University Press, ca. 1981.

———. *The Collected Poems of Joseph Hall*. Edited by A. Davenport. St. Claire Shores, Mich.: Scholarly Press, 1971.

———. *The Works of the Right Reverend Joseph Hall*. Edited by Philip Wynter. New York: AMS Press, 1969.

Tourney, Leonard D. *Joseph Hall*. Boston: Twayne Publishers, 1979.

hamartia   (tragic flaw)

Originally a Greek archery term, *hamartia* meant missing the target or the mark. Used in the Greek New Testament to mean "sin," it is also the term ARISTOTLE uses in his *POETICS* to describe the flaw in the character of a tragic protagonist that contributes to that person's eventual downfall. Often the flaw results from hubris (overweening pride). Always the flaw paradoxically results from an excess of some virtue. Pride, for example, is an excess of the virtue of self-respect. One of Hamlet's virtues, his willingness to suspend judgment and defer action while awaiting further evidence, when it continues too long, becomes a flaw—a kind of moral sloth—with tragic consequences.

Hardy, Alexandre   (ca. 1572–ca. 1632)

A prolific French playwright who wrote or had a hand in producing literally hundreds of plays, Alexandre Hardy's surviving works include five PASTORALS, 11 tragedies, and 25 tragicomedies. Most of what he wrote lived only for the duration of its production. What survives is what he took the trouble—or found the time—to publish.

Before Hardy, French Renaissance drama had been written principally by poets and literary theorists such as ÉTIENNE JODELLE, Jacques Grévin, Jean de la Taille, and Louis Demasures who subscribed to the rigid rules of Aristotelian drama as fixed in stone by the Italian critic LUDOVICO CASTELVETRO. The audience for such work mainly included upper-class people with HUMANIST educations. Such folk knew the Greek and Roman classics and expected their theater to observe the conventions of the ancients. It also included those who subscribed to the ideas of the marquise de RAMBOUILLET. She was the social arbiter who established rigid standards of refined taste and permissible vocabulary and action. Plot was drawn largely from the ancient Greeks and Romans or from the Bible, and incident tended to be spoken about rather than acted.

Left out of all this was the French person in the street whose taste tended in an entirely different direction. Hardy addressed his plays to an audience composed of common people and in so doing, despite what many consider to be his inferior talent, breathed life into a moribund French theater.

In general Hardy heightened the action as he does in *La mort d'Alexandre* (The death of Alexander). He did away with the ancient Greek convention of having a chorus comment on the public significance of the main events. He ignored his predecessors' insistence on the rigid preservation of the unities of time, place, and action. Hardy's version of the history of the Roman Emperor Coriolanus—a subject also treated by Shakespeare—illustrates this shift. His treatment of the story of Herod and the Macabeean princess Miriam achieves psychological interest by having a repentant Herod regret the rash action of having his wife beheaded. This story was also the subject of the first verse tragedy to be written by an English woman. (See *THE TRAGEDY OF MIRIAM* ELIZABETH CARY NÉE TANFIELD.)

Hardy introduced tragicomedy to the French stage, and he shifted the focus of such plays to bring out the audience's interest in the psychology of the characters. In the English-speaking world, Hardy's plays did not arouse enough interest to attract a collector and translator. Despite their often improbable plots, their pedestrian style, and their failed attempts to imitate his betters, however, they found favor with French audiences and helped to change the direction of the development of French theater away from the self-consciously exclusive and toward the popular taste.

Hátifí, 'Abudu'lláh (d. 1521)

A Shiite Persian poet, Hátifí composed a verse history of the career of the Turkic conqueror, Tamerlane (*Timur–nama*). He also undertook to create a cycle of five poetic romances—a kind of exercise that established a poet's claim to major status in Hátifí's time. In the event, however, he left the collection unfinished, and only two of his romances survive: *LEYLÁ AND MEJNÚN* and another tale of lovers, *Shirin and Farhad*. Both of these borrow traditional subjects from the treasure trove of Persian topics for romance.

Hátifí also seems to have composed a considerable number of lyric poems, but again only a few samples have survived.

Bibliography

Hátifí, 'Abudu'lláh. *Laili Majnun, A Persian Poem of Hátifí.* Calcutta: M. Cantopher, 1788.

Henry IV, The History of, Part I William Shakespeare (1589–90)

Perhaps the most artistically successful of SHAKESPEARE'S plays concerning the Wars of the Roses between the English princely houses of York and Lancaster, *Henry IV, Part I* opens with King Henry IV consulting with Lord John of Lancaster, Sir Walter Blunt, and the earl of Westmoreland. The year is 1400. The Lancastrian Henry IV has come to power by an act of rebellion against his cousin, the Yorkist Richard III. Worse, he bears responsibility for what his contemporaries considered the most blameworthy act in Christendom—regicide. Either through secret edict or merely by turning a blind eye, Henry approved the assassination of his cousin, Richard III, whose abdication from the English throne Henry and his allies had forced. Because kings were believed to be God's appointed agents for governing the nonspiritual affairs of people, regicide opposed human will to God's will.

Consequently England has fallen under God's curse, and for the next century the only bright spot in the chronicles of her kings will be the reign of Henry V (Prince Hal in this play) whom history considered "a mirror for all Christian princes."

That time has not yet come, however, and as the play opens we meet a Henry IV crushed by guilt and by the weight of his heavy responsibilities. Both the Scots and the Welsh are in arms against him. The successor to his throne that Richard III named, Edmund Mortimer, the earl of March, led an army against the Welch for Henry but lost. Mortimer has defected to the Welch and married a Welsh woman. The powerful members of the Percy family, the earls of Northumberland and Worcester—allies who supported Henry's coup—are having second thoughts. They are beginning to perceive Henry IV as uncontrollable and dangerous to them.

Henry had hoped to expiate some of his guilt for his cousin Richard's death by leading a crusade to free the Holy Land from Muslim rule. His troubles at home, however, have made such a campaign impossible.

As if all that were not enough, Henry is concerned about the unseemly behavior of his son, the heir apparent to the throne, Prince Hal. Hal seems to spend his time in taverns with rough company and displays little apparent interest in affairs of state. In fact Henry compares him unfavorably with the scion of the Percy family, Henry Percy (Hotspur in this play), wishing that, instead of Hal, Hotspur were his son.

The first scene's only bright spot for Henry arises from a victory Hotspur has won over the Scots where he captured many Scottish nobles. Hotspur sends word, however, that he is withholding a number of the prisoners, meaning that Henry will not be able to ransom them.

Henry IV, Part I is principally a verse DRAMA whose scenes concerning the nobility are penned in iambic-pentameter blank verse, while those concerning the commoners are mostly in prose. In Act I, scene i Shakespeare introduces one of several astronomical poetic IMAGES that will reappear in various guises throughout the play. The first of these is the image of meteors. Renaissance astronomy and astrology viewed meteors and comets as disorderly phenomena that predicted disaster. Increasingly throughout the play, they become associated with the parties intent on disordering the realm. Hotspur proves himself the most meteoric of all the characters. Subsequent action and language identifies Sir John Falstaff and his accomplices with images of moon and night—predictable but shifty. King Henry and particularly Prince Hal, however, become increasingly identified with images of sun and day—images associated with predictability and order. Shakespeare's interweaving of this set of astronomical images helps to unify the main plot—Prince Hal's political policy and filial responsibility and the restoration of order in the realm—with its two principal subplots: Falstaff's unruly character and unreliability and Hotspur's unbridled ambition and rebellion. Both image and action reinforce the major thematic oppositions of the play: honor against dishonor, familial loyalty versus disloyalty, and responsibility versus irresponsibility.

While much of the play is deadly serious, it is also side-splittingly funny. Sir John Falstaff was such a popular comic character that, after his death in *Henry IV, Part II,* Shakespeare's audience demanded his resurrection in a COMEDY about Falstaff's antics, *The Merry Wives of Windsor* (1597).

For Prince Hal, Falstaff represents the attractions of the world—attractions the prince firmly rejects. In the closing speech of Act I, scene ii Hal makes clear that his own loose behavior is political policy and that his reformation will gain him a greater reputation than simply seeming dutiful all the while. In Act II, scene iv Hal and Falstaff perform a play within a play. At first Falstaff plays the role of King Henry and Hal plays himself. Falstaff does not rise adequately to the king's dignity, so the two exchange roles, and Hal becomes a father figure to the aged libertine and thief, taking the occasion to reveal jokingly his true opinion of Falstaff as "a villainous abominable misleader of youth."

Falstaff defends himself, growing serious as he does so, and pleads that he not be banished from the prince's company. He ends this plea with, "Banish plump Jack, and banish all the world."

To this Prince Hal replies, "I do, I will." This utterance becomes prophecy, for in *Henry IV, Part II* Falstaff stations himself along the route of the coronation procession where the new King Henry V will have to pass within earshot. Falstaff calls out, "Hal, Hal!" The newly crowned ruler cuts him dead with, "I know thee not, old man." Although Hal provides for Falstaff's old age, he forbids him to come within several miles of the royal presence.

Falstaff deserves his banishment. Hal appointed him a captain of infantry and gave him a chance to prove himself. Falstaff stole the money entrusted to him for recruiting and equipping his troops, using his authority to empty the prisons and madhouses without paying the recruiting bonus the law required. He equipped his troops by having them steal laundry from the hedgerows on which it was drying. At their first engagement, he led his troops to a spot where the first artillery barrage would free him of his responsibility.

In the thick of battle (Act V, scene iii) Hal and Falstaff meet, and Hal asks Falstaff to loan him a weapon. In his pistol cases, however, Falstaff keeps only bottles of wine. To avoid having to fight, he pretends to be dead. Here and elsewhere, he lives up to his name. Hal cannot depend on his support. He is a false staff. We also find his name appropriate in Act II, scene iv when Hal picks Falstaff's pockets while he sleeps off his liquor. Hal discovers receipts for gallons of sack (a dry sherry) and only a halfpenny's worth of bread—the staff of life. Falstaff lives on wine—also a false staff. Hal saves his father's life in battle when a moment's hesitation would have made Hal king. Hotspur's relatives, by contrast, desert him at the crucial moment, leaving him alone to fight the royal army.

Just as in Act II, scene iv Hal's intervention restores to the royal treasury money that Falstaff and his confederates stole, so his victory over Hotspur in single combat in Act V, scene iv makes him the agent who gathers up the multiple strands of the action and resolves its conflicts.

Henry IV, Part I provides a model of the characteristic way in which Shakespeare weaves together poetic image and METAPHOR, the behavior of his characters, and elements of theme and plot. Whether or not viewers or readers are consciously aware of these interactions, they unify the plays and help drive their power.

Bibliography

Shakespeare, William. *The First Part of Henry the Fourth.* In *The Riverside Shakespeare*, edited by G. Blakemore Evans et al., 884–927. Boston: Houghton Mifflin Company, 1997.

Heptameron Margaret of Navarre (1558)

MARGARET OF NAVARRE had intended to emulate BOCCACCIO's *Decameron* by composing 100 tales— 10 each told by a group of 10 travelers, five male and five female, while storms held them marooned in an abbey in the Pyrenees Mountains. She did not, however, complete her design. Only 72 tales were finished, hence a title meaning seven instead of 10 days was chosen for her posthumous collection by her editor.

All 72 stories, their author insists, are true and happened recently. Their tellers are real persons, all well known to Margaret, though they travel together under assumed names. Unlike many of Boccaccio's tales, Margaret of Navarre's are generally refined, high-minded tales of love, of the forms it takes, and of its sometimes sorrowful consequences. After each tale, the travelers discuss it. Pleased with the elevated tone of many of the stories, Margaret herself in the guise of her character Parlamente often denounces with high-minded moral conviction and theological vigor the more lubricious sorts of stories with which her predecessor raconteurs, like Boccaccio, had amused their contemporaries.

Margaret's tales interest social historians as well as students of literature and general readers because of their descriptions of the daily life of the top ranks of French society in the early to mid-16th century.

Bibliography

Navarre, Marguerite de. *The Heptameron.* Translated by P. A. Chilton. Harmondsworth, U.K.: Penguin Books, 1984.

Herbert, George (1593–1633)

An Anglican priest, musician, translator, and religious poet, Herbert received his education at Trinity College in Cambridge University, receiving his B.A. in 1612 and his M.A. in 1616. Having made an early decision to enter the priesthood and also feeling deeply attracted to the study and practice of poetry, Herbert decided that writing poems was too high a calling to waste on trivial matters like celebrating earthly love. His poetic production, therefore, became exclusively religious.

He was temporarily distracted from his religious vocation by an opportunity to become the public orator for the University of Cambridge in 1619. He competed for the post and won it, and his performance there won the approval both of King JAMES I and the powerful duke of Buckingham. This notice temporarily turned his head, and he began to think of a career in the civil service that might prove more distinguished than one he might aspire to in the church. The king died, however, and the duke's favor proved fickle, so Herbert, after some soul-searching, turned again to the church, ultimately confirming his commitment to the life of a cleric after his marriage to Jane Danvers in 1629. His period of indecision behind him, Herbert distinguished himself with his piety, eventually becoming the subject of one of IZAAK WALTON's biographies.

As a translator, Herbert rendered into English a discourse on healthful living by the Italian Luigi Cornaro (1475–1566). Herbert's English title perhaps provides a key to one of his goals: *How to Live for a Hundred Years and Avoid Disease.* If this was a goal, Herbert did not achieve it.

As a poet, though Herbert set some of his own verses to music and participated as a lutenist in their performance, he made no attempt to publish them until illness convinced him that his time was short. Then he put his collected poems in the hands of a retired merchant and Protestant monk, Nicholas Ferrar. With the blessing of the vice-chancellor of Cambridge University whose license was required for publication, the collection appeared not long after Herbert's death in 1633, entitled *The Temple.* Its 169 poems reveal Herbert's mastery of poetic form. He employed techniques unusual in his era, such as the employment of CONCRETE POEMS where the type is set so that it pictures the thing being written about. Both "The Altar" and "Easter Wings" provide examples of this technique.

The letter Herbert sent to Ferrar along with his manuscript assured his friend that a reader of his verse would discover there "a picture of the many spiritual conflicts . . . betwixt God and my soul." *The Temple* achieved rapid renown, and other poets including RICHARD CRASHAW and Henry Vaughn soon emulated Herbert's work, penning and publishing their own religious verse.

Bibliography

Cornaro, Luigi. *How to Live for a Hundred Years and Avoid Disease.* Translated by George Herbert. Oxford, U.K.: The Alden Press, 1935.

Herbert, George. *The Complete English Poems.* Edited by John Tobin. New York: Penguin Books, 1991.

———. *The Temple: The Poetry of George Herbert.* Edited by Henry L. Carrigan, Jr. Brewster, Mass.: Paraclete Press, 2001.

Walton, Izaak. *The Lives of Dr. John Donne, Sir Henry Wotton, Mr. Richard Hooker, Mr. George Herbert.* Menston, U.K.: Scolar Press, 1969.

Herbert, Mary

See PEMBROKE, MARY HERBERT, COUNTESS OF.

Heywood, Thomas (1574–1641)

A prodigious writer of plays (about 220 according to his own testimony—though only 24 survive), a literary critic, a translator, a crafter of a considerable body of nondramatic work, and an actor in the immediately post-Shakespearian English generation that included THOMAS DEKKER, BEN JONSON, and THOMAS MIDDLETON, Heywood was born in Lincolnshire, probably to a country parson, Robert Heywood and his wife Elizabeth. His father's death in 1593 obliged him after two years at Cambridge to forego further study and to earn his living. This he contrived to do by moving to London and writing. His first published work was a poem, *Oenone and Paris,* in imitation of the work of the Roman poet OVID (1594). With at least this work to his credit, he managed to find employment with the theatrical producer Philip Henslowe. Heywood served first, apparently, as an apprentice playwright and on-call actor, and Henslowe's diary records payment to him in 1596 for an unspecified book and in 1598 for a play that has not survived.

That same year Heywood signed on for a two-year period with the Lord Admiral's company of players. His earliest extant plays date from this period and include a city play, *The Four Prentices of London* (probably written and performed ca. 1599, published 1615) and two history plays based on the reign of King Edward IV. FRANCIS BEAUMONT satirized *The Four Prentices . . .* in his THE KNIGHT OF THE BURNING PESTLE.

In 1601 Heywood moved into management, becoming an actor for and part owner of the Earl of Worcester's Company (later Queen Anne's Company). The following two years saw two surviving comedies produced, *How a Man May Choose a Good Wife from a Bad* and *The Royal King and the Loyal Subject.*

In an age whose theater often pandered to the lowest common denominator of the popular culture, Heywood kept before him the classical motto that the objective of literature is both to please and to instruct. To those aims Heywood added another objective in his *An Apology for Actors* (1612)—"to polish the English tongue." As a result of his firmly keeping these principles in view, though his plays enjoyed great popularity, the depth of their feeling and their high mindedness also distinguished them from the flood of drama that the Elizabethan and Jacobean theatrical machine cranked out for popular amusement. In 1603 these qualities appeared in a domestic tragedy usually considered Heywood's masterpiece and one of his most characteristic plays, *A WOMAN KILLED WITH KINDNESS.* "Here," says the literary historian Hazleton Spencer, "is an Elizabethan tragedy . . ." that "reaches its pathetic end without shedding the blood of any important character."

A representative sample of Heywood's surviving plays among the 220 in which he reports he "had a whole hand or a main finger" includes the two parts of *If You Know Not Me You Know Nobodie* (1605 and 1606), *The Rape of Lucrece, a True Roman Tragedie* (1608), *The Golden Age* (1611), *The Silver Age* and *The Brazen Age* (both 1613). *The Fair Maid of the West, Or A Girle Worth Gold* appeared in 1631 and *The Iron Age* in 1632. Following these came *The English Traveller* (1633). Then, written in collaboration with the playwright Richard Brome, a piece appeared that appealed to the popular interest in witch hunting and actual trials for allegedly practicing the black art: *The Late Lancaster Witches* (1634). That same year saw published *A Pleasant Comedy, Called a Maiden Head well Lost,* and in 1636 came *Love's Maistresse: Or The Queens Masque* and *A Challenge for Beauty.* *The Royal King and Loyal Subject* and *Pleasant Dialogues and Drammas* appeared in 1637 and *The Wise Woman of Hogsdon* in 1638. The last of Heywood's dramatic works to see print resulted from a collaboration with WILLIAM ROWLEY: *Fortune by Land and Sea* appeared posthumously in 1655.

Few writers as good as Heywood have managed to write with such industry and across such a broad field of endeavor. He wrote poems for royal and state occasions like weddings and funerals and pageants for royal entertainments. He wrote two works portraying famous women in history: *Gunaikeion . . .* (1624), and *The Exemplary Lives and Memorable Acts of Nine . . . Worthy Women of the World* (1640). He penned a sort of epic on the mythic subject that traces the founding of Britain to ancient Trojans who sailed there after Troy's fall, *Troia Britanica* (1608). He prepared a biography of Queen ELIZABETH I (*England's Elizabeth Her Life and Troubles . . . from the Cradle to the Crowne,* 1631). Beyond this he wrote about angels and the fall of Lucifer (1635) and in that same year published *Philocothonista, or, The Drunkard, Opened, Dissected and Anatomized.* He wrote about wonders, like a 152 year-old man, about ships, about Merlin and prophecy, and he published a history of the mythic and actual kings of England from prehistory to Charles I. Again, this list is suggestive, not exhaustive. To all of that work Heywood added the first complete English translation of the Roman poet Ovid's *Art of Love* and other translations as well from the Latin of the ancient Roman Sallust (86–34 B.C.E.), but even then Heywood's industry was not exhausted.

For 10 years, between 1630 and 1640, he occupied the post of poet of the city of London. As such he was responsible for writing the annual pageants that were performed at the inauguration of the lord mayor. Heywood's was a long, fruitful, and distinguished literary career.

Bibliography

Baines, Barbara J. *Thomas Heywood*. Boston: Twayne Publishers, 1984.

Brome, Richard, and Thomas Heywood. *The Witches of Lancashire*. Edited by Gabriel Egan. London: Nick Hern Books, 2002.

Cromwell, Otelia. *Thomas Heywood: A Study in the Elizabethan Drama of Everyday Life*. New Haven, Conn.: Yale University Press, 1928.

Heywood, Thomas. *The Dramatic Works of Thomas Heywood. . . .* 1874. New York: Russell & Russell, 1964.

———. *Thomas Heywood's Art of Love: The First Complete English Translation of Ovid's Ars Amatoria*. Edited by M. L. Stapleton. Ann Arbor, Mich.: University of Michigan Press, ca. 2000.

———. *Thomas Heywood's Pageants: A Critical Edition*. Edited by David M. Bergeron. New York: Garland Publications, 1986.

Hindi language, the golden age of
(1500–1700)

Though literary works had appeared in the Hindi language as early as the eighth century, in the 16th and 17th centuries Hindi came into its own as a major literary language of northern India. A part of this development resulted from Hindi's employment by major figures in India's ongoing religious reawakening—the bhakti movement. Among these figures we find first the poet and saint KABIR (1440–1518) who hoped to see Hinduism and Islam combine into a single religion. Following in his foot-

steps and to some degree achieving Kabir's goal, we find the founder of the Sikh religion, NĀNAK, who compiled—mostly in Hindi—the first version of what eventually became the enormously influential ADI GRANTH (in Hindi and Punjabi).

One of the most influential authors to employ Hindi and to continue its emergence as a significant literary language was the poet and saint TULSĪDĀS (1532–1623). In addition to lyric poems and songs based on the life of the Hindu deity Rama, Tulsīdās reworked that deity's ancient Indian EPIC the *Ramayana* into a Hindi retelling that focused on Rama as the supreme deity and on his brother, Bharata, as the prototype of the devout man of faith—the man of bhakti. With this verse epic THE HOLY LAKE OF THE LIFE OF RAMA (*Ramcharitmânas,* late 16th century), Tulsīdās demonstrates Hindi's capacity to incorporate many elements of the scholarly Sanskrit tongue and to convey high poetic art. In his lyric works, by contrast, he achieved similar artistic outcomes for popular Hindi dialectical vernaculars. He sometimes composed his lyrics in the Braj dialect and sometimes in the Avadhi dialect of Hindi. In both cases his composition expanded the capacity of Hindi for poetic expression.

Other important poets who contributed to the 16th- and 17th-century canon of Hindi religious letters include VALLABHA (1479–1541) and his son BITTALNÂTH (VITTHALNÂTH, ca. 1515–88) both of whom promulgated the worship of Krishna in their poems. Vallabha founded a school of eight poets that included his son. Among the eight the most prominent and possibly the most accomplished Hindi lyricist was SŪRDĀS (1483–1563), the author of many devotional poems celebrating in the Braj dialect the love of Krishna and his consort Radha.

The famous female poet Princess MĪRĀ BĀĪ wrote sometimes in Gujerati and sometimes in Hindi. MALIK MOHAMMAD JAYISI (1477–1542), although himself a Moslem, composed an important mystical epic that revealed his enormous interest in Hindu letters—the *PADUMĀVATI* (1540). Finally, among the important religious poets who participated in the literary development of Hindi, we find NABHĀDĀS (1570–ca. 1662) and KESHAVDĀS (1556–1605). Nabhādās wrote a verse biographical history of the holy men who had spread the renewed worship of the deity Vishnu throughout India during the preceding century. Keshavdās, on the other hand, is principally remembered for having formalized the poetic practice of Hindi and for having illustrated poetic form and rhetoric with numerous religious and secular examples.

Following him, the poet BIHARI LAL (1559–1663) produced a collection of 700 stanzas in the year before his death. Although his models come from poems venerating Krishna, his own content is largely secular.

It was this collection of seminal figures and others like them that turned an originally countrified dialect of Sanskrit into one of the most important literary languages of modern India and created for Hindi its golden age.

Bibliography
Lal, Mohan, ed. *Encyclopedia of Indian Literature.* New Delhi: Sahitya Akademi, 1992.

Renou, Louis. *Indian Literature.* Translated by Patrick Evans. New York: Walker and Company, 1964.

Hŏ Kyŏngbŏn (Xu Jingfan) (1563–1589)
A Korean lyric poet, Hŏ Kyŏngbŏn was the daughter of a widely reputed literary family. Throughout a life made unhappy by marital problems, children who died young, a comfortless mother-in-law, and political turmoil, Hŏ Kyŏngbŏn wrote prolifically in both the Chinese and the Korean languages. Shortly before her death, however, she burned many of her works. One of her brothers nevertheless collected the Chinese works she had spared and presented them to Zhu Zhifan, the Chinese ambassador to Korea. He in turn arranged for their publication in China where readers received Hŏ Kyŏngbŏn's verses with great enthusiasm.

Late in the 17th century a Korean edition of all her surviving poems appeared, and in 1711 her poems were published in Japan as well. Hŏ Kyŏngbŏn's works include poems about love, about nature, and about the folly of youthful men. They also include epistolary poems to friends, rhymes in imitation of and answers to some of her brother Hŏ KYUN verses, and rhymes in which she grieves for her dead children.

Hŏ Kyŏngbŏn is widely regarded as the leading female poet of Korean letters. Her brother, Hŏ KYUN is remembered as the writer of the first work of fiction in the Korean language, THE TALE OF HONG KILTONG.

Bibliography
Widmer, Ellen, Editor and Translator. "Hŏ Kyŏngbŏn (Xu Jingfan)." *Women Writers of Traditional China: An Anthology of Poetry and Criticism.* Edited by Kang-i Sun Chang and Haun Saussy. Stanford, Calif.: Stanford University Press, 1999.

Hŏ Kyun (1569–1618)
A Korean writer and social thinker, Hŏ Kyun thought his contemporary Korea too rigidly stratified by class, and he looked to Chinese literary models for a way to offer a fictional social critique. Finding a model in Chinese stories about bandits who challenge central authority—as they do in THE STORY OF THE WATER MARGIN and PEONY PAVILION— Hŏ Kyun wrote in Chinese a story about a Korean bandit king of his own era, HONG KILTONG. Chinese was the principal Korean literary idiom of Hŏ Kyun's time. Regrettably Hŏ Kyun's own version of the story has not survived. We know it, however, through a later rendition of his tale by an anonymous imitator. Elements of the story emulate the Chinese interest, not only in banditry itself, but also in military strategy and campaigning. Parts of the tale also imitate Chinese fantasy fiction like that found in THE JOURNEY TO THE WEST.

Hobbes, Thomas (1588–1679)
Though he wrote and published as early as 1620, Hobbes's most important contributions to literature came relatively late in life. From about the age of 40 Hobbes became a tireless translator, political philosopher, historian, and autobiographer and was one of the most important theorists of the modern world. A thoroughgoing materialist, Hobbes studied the Greek mathematician Euclid's geometry in 1628. Its clarity and conviction

spurred him to literary action. He wished to apply the same careful reasoning to the study of humankind and politics that Euclid had applied to mathematics.

Preparing for this effort, Hobbes first published a translation of the Greek historian Thucydides's (ca. 460–ca. 400 B.C.E.) work, *History of the Peloponnesian War*. The stresses between the English king and Parliament and between Puritans and high-church Anglicans were about to tear the political fabric of England with civil war, and Hobbes strove to understand the underlying causes by studying history.

He finished a first effort at codifying the laws of political science in 1640, and this work finally appeared 10 years later as *Elements of Law Natural and Politic*. A thoroughgoing monarchist, Hobbes hurried to France in 1640 ahead of the coming confrontation between the English factions. In France he continued to clarify his theories, publishing a critique of RENÉ DESCARTES's *Meditations about the First Philosophy* (1641) and a fuller exposition in Latin of his own theories in 1642. This work, *On the Citizen* (*De Cive*) appeared in English in 1651 as *Phillosophical [sic] Rudiments Concerning Government and Society*.

In Paris in 1648, Hobbes became the tutor in mathematics for Prince Charles—destined to become King Charles II of England. This connection would stand him in good stead later (1666) when Hobbes's religious view that the church had a social origin and function that often veered toward idolatry would subject him to the threat of being tried as a heretic. This threat the king was able to avert, and he provided his old tutor with a pension as well.

The year 1651 also saw the publication of Hobbes's masterwork, LEVIATHAN. In it he set forth the principles that he thought explained the mechanical operation of the universe, the utter selfishness of human interests, the social contract that people formed to limit the effects of that selfishness, and the necessity for a rigidly hierarchical system of government to enforce the contract.

Until the end of his life, Hobbes continued to translate, write, and publish. He completed verse translations from Homer's Greek EPICS *The Iliad* (1675) and *The Odyssey* (1676). Another historical and political treatise, *Behemoth: a History of the Causes of the Civil Wars of England*, had been completed in 1668, but King Charles thought it too incendiary and had it suppressed. It finally appeared posthumously in 1682. The writings that did escape censorship provoked controversy: *About the Body* (*De Corpore*, 1655) and *About Mankind* (*De Homine*, 1658) belong to this category.

He wrote on a wide variety of topics. A suggestive list of topics includes works about heresy; about the politics of the Scottish church; about mathematics, necessity and chance as they relate to politics; and about the history of elegiac poems in churches. He penned his own autobiography late in life in Latin verse.

Interest in Hobbes and his work has never been higher than it is at the beginning of the 21st century.

Bibliography

Condren, Conal. *Thomas Hobbes*. New York: Twayne Publishers, 2000.

Hobbes, Thomas. *Leviathan*. Edited by A. P. Martinich. Peterborough, Ont.: Broadview Press, ca. 2002.

———. *On the Citizen*. Edited and translated by Richard Tuck and Michael Silverthorne. New York: Cambridge University Press, 1998.

———. *The Collected Works. . . .* Edited by Sir William Molesworth. Introduced by G. A. J. Rogers. London: Routledge Thoemmes Press, 1992.

Martinich, Aloysius. *Hobbes: A Biography*. Cambridge, U.K., and New York: Cambridge University Press, ca. 1999.

Hoby, Sir Thomas (1530–1566)

Educated at Cambridge, Hoby became friends with both Sir John Cheke and ROGER ASCHAM. Identified early on as a potentially gifted diplomat, Hoby traveled throughout Italy and France, and for a time in 1547 he lived with the German reform minister, Martin Bucer, whose *Gratulatoria* Hoby translated into English. He served the government of King Edward VI as a diplomat on several missions.

The diary that he kept from his student days onward provides valuable glimpses into the life of a 16th-century English student, traveler, and diplomat. When Queen Mary I ascended the English throne in 1553, he went to Padua where he visited her exiled supporters Sir Anthony Cooke and Sir John Cheke. In was perhaps at that time that he became acquainted with Sir Anthony's daughter, Elizabeth. His diary records that in 1558 he "communed . . . [with her] in the way of marriage." His communing connected and she accepted, thereby making Hoby the uncle by marriage to SIR FRANCIS BACON.

Hoby made his principal contribution to English letters with his translation of BALDEASSARE CASTIGLIONE's THE BOOK OF THE COURTIER (Hoby's title: *The Courtyer of Count Baldessar Castilio*, 1561), which he withheld from publication until the restoration of a Protestant monarchy. Introduced by Sir WALTER RALEIGH, Hoby's *Courtier* became a widely influential book about the manner in which courtiers should conduct themselves. Hoby's rendering is valuable not only for its content and for the straightforward and unaffected style of his English, but also because it marked the beginning of the long-standing affinity between the English and the Italians. It also accelerated in England the spread of Neoplatonic ideas about PLATONIC LOVE that had their origin for many Englishmen in PIETRO BEMBO's discourse on love in *The Courtier*'s fourth book. These ideas reflected themselves everywhere in the amorous poetry of the English Renaissance. In fact, they eventually became so hackneyed that they provoked unflattering verse responses.

Bibliography

Hoby, Sir Thomas. *The Book of the Courtier . . .* New York: AMS Press, 1967.

Hofmannswaldau, Christian Hofmann von (1617–1679)

A German nobleman, translator, educational theorist, lyric poet, and disciple of MARTIN OPITZ and ANDREAS GREIF, Hofmann (as he is known) traveled in Europe and England before settling down in about 1642 in his native Breslau. There he served as a member of the city council and later as its president.

He translated the Italian poet GIOVANNI BATTISTA GUARINI's THE FAITHFUL SHEPHERD into German (printed, 1678). In his *Emma und Eginhard* (1663) he composed a series of verse love letters ostensibly exchanged between Emma, the daughter of Emperor Charlemagne, and Eginhard, who may have been in real life a certain Einhard, the emperor's biographer. Hofmann achieved a high degree of technical mastery in his poems. He wrote erotic lyrics, moral reflections, sonnets, and alexandrines. (See POETIC METER.)

Interested in education as well as in literature, Hofmann also published a series of letters in Latin commenting on the curriculum that he thought should be studied by young people in Breslau and elsewhere. Although a modern edition of Hofmann's work is available in German, his writings have not as yet found an English translator.

Holinshed, Raphael (d. ca. 1580)

Born in Cheshire, Raphael Holinshed later moved to London where he found employment as a translator with the printer Reginald Wolfe. Wolfe commissioned from Holinshed and his collaborators a work that, as its title makes clear, would eventually include the *Chronicles of England, Scotland, and Ireland* (1577). In composing and editing this famous work, Raphael Holinshed made use of Edward Hall's earlier book, *Union of the Two Noble and Illustre Families of Lancaster and York* (1542), and of SIR THOMAS MORE's (1487–1535) earlier written (1513–14) but later published (1577) *History of Richard III*, which More had originally penned in Latin.

The original plan for Holinshed's *Chronicles* envisioned a "universal cosmography," but the scope of the actual publication narrowed appreciably to focus exclusively on the British Isles. Treating geographical as well as historical subjects, Holinshed's work included sections written by other hands. William Harrison provided the *Description of England*. He also translated from the Scottish dialect of John Bellenden's *Description of Scotland*. This geographical treatise Bellenden had in turn translated from Hector Boece's (ca. 1465–1536) Latin *History of Scotland* (1527). The second edition of Holinshed's *Chronicles* included Irish as well as English and Scottish history. Also contributing to Holinshed's *Chronicles* were the historians Richard Stanyhurst and William Harrison. These men provided, respectively, the history of Ireland and the geographic description of that island.

Though an interesting document in its own right, the *Chronicles*, particularly the second edition, and their author as well are chiefly remembered as an important source for much of the historical material that WILLIAM SHAKESPEARE incorporated into his plays about earlier monarchs, real and legendary, in England and Scotland. These include the three parts of *Henry VI*, *Richard II*, *Richard III*, *King John*, the two parts of *HENRY IV*, *KING LEAR*, *Henry V*, *Macbeth*, and *Henry VIII*.

Bibliography

Evans, G. Blakemore, et al., eds. *The Riverside Shakespeare*. Boston: Houghton Mifflin Company, 1997.

Holinshed, Raphael. *Holinshed's Chronicles—England, Scotland, and Ireland.* Edited by Vernon F. Snow. New York: AMS Press, ca. 1976.

Taufer, Alison. *Holinshed's Chronicles.* New York: Twayne Publishers, ca. 1999.

Holy Lake of the Acts of Rama, The

(*Rāmcaritmānas*) Tulsīdās (1579)

The masterpiece among the Hindi language works of the 16th-century Indian saint and poet TULSĪDĀS, *The Holy Lake*, retells in Hindi the Sanskrit EPIC the *RAMAYANA* (ca. 400 B.C.E.) The Hindu sage Vālmīki penned that epic with the purpose of following the career of a royal hero and divinity, Rama, and tracing his heroic interactions with human beings, deities, and demons.

Tulsīdās, however, had other objectives in retelling the story. He belonged to a spiritual movement that repeatedly swept across the length and breadth of India during a period of several hundred years—the BHAKTI, or devotional movement, and one of the poet's objectives was the elevation of Rama to new heights as a manifestation of God.

Therefore, while Tulsīdās follows the general outline of his predecessor's work, he suppresses incidents that strike him as too racy sexually, and he adds philosophical reflections. He also modifies Rama's status, elevating him from a heroic leader who achieves divinity to the status of a member of a divine triumvirate that includes Rama among the principal deities Brahman and Vishnu. In Tulsīdās's version, Rama assumes human form so that he can inspire people to worship in the right way.

Both Tulsīdās and Vālmīki organize their basic material in the same way. The first section of the work recounts Rama's childhood and youth up to his wedding with his lovely bride Sita. Whereas Vālmīki plunges directly into the story after a brief introduction, however, Tulsīdās inserts many pages of introductory material. These include an invocation seeking inspiration, stories about earlier events that provide background Vālmīki neglected, a sarcastic rebuttal to his critics, and a wordy apology for the quality of his poetry. Elsewhere Tulsīdās omits tangential legends that interrupt the flow of Vālmīki's narrative.

The second section, entitled "Ayodhyā"—the name both of Rama's capital city and its district—picks up the story after Rama and Sita's honeymoon. Rama, not yet king, becomes regent of Ayodhyā, but jealous gods conspire to thwart his purposes. The queen, deceived by a chambermaid who is the gods' emissary, prevails on the king to suspend Rama's regency, appoint her son Bharat in Rama's place, and exile Rama as a religious hermit to the forest for 14 years. The king resists this advice, but on hearing the plan Rama thinks it a good idea. After much discussion and the king's fainting several times when he considers life at court without Rama nearby, Rama takes Sita with him and the two depart for the forest. Bharat follows them and becomes Rama's disciple for a while until he thinks the time has come to take up his regency. The group's adventures on the journey to the forest, Rama's sympathy with the plight of the common people, and their recognition of Rama as the incarnation of the Lord occupy the rest of the second section. So does the theme of Rama's ascendancy over the entire pantheon of lesser Hindu deities who fear his power and try to resist with magic and guile what is fated to occur.

In the third section, "The Forest," Rama must overcome a formidable army of 14,000 demons, but they cannot match his strength, and his arrows cut the demons' entire host to pieces. Eventually Rama makes each demon see the other as Rama's image. The demons fight among themselves and finally kill each other.

What the demons cannot accomplish by combat, they attempt to achieve by guile. The 10-headed demon–king, Ravan, kidnaps Sita and, overcoming a rescue attempt by the Vulture King, carries her off to the south there with Rama in hot pursuit. The narrative suspends as Tulsīdās seizes the opportunity to make explicit the ALLEGORY of the section. "Lust, wrath, greed, pride, and all the passions form the strong army of infatuation," he explains. He also digresses to attack sensual women as the enemies of religion. A sensual woman, he declares, will wither religion as winter frost withers lotuses. He exhorts the faithful to "Abandon lust and pride, worship Rama and . . . seek the fellowship of the saints."

The book's next three sections, *"Kiskindhā," "The Beautiful,"* and *"Lankā,"* recount the famous story of the recovery of Sita by the joint efforts of Rama, his brother Laksman, and their wonderful ally, Hannuman, the monkey king. Hannuman's magical talents and millions of monkey subjects locate Sita on the island of Sri Lanka and rescue Rama's wife from the demons, overcoming them both in battle and by trickery.

Throughout his version of the story, Tulsīdās has taken great care to expunge sections of the original epic that might undermine his view of Rama's ideality. The poet is careful to accord Sita the same courtesy. In Vālmīki's version, Rama sends the rescued Sita into exile when gossips suggest that she had been unfaithful during her long captivity with the demon king. In that version, the demon king had ravished his captive. In *The Holy Lake*, instead, Tulsīdās borrows a device from yet another retelling of the story. In this account, Sita saves herself from rape by burning herself when Rāvan makes advances. A false Sita is substituted for her. When the

substitute is rescued, the real Sita emerges from the flames. Her chastity is never in doubt.

It would be difficult to overestimate the influence of *The Holy Lake* on Hindu devotional life. Just reading the poem or hearing it read is considered a devotional act that confers extraordinary blessing. A performance of the poem called the *Rām Līlā* takes place annually in every community, regardless of size, in North India. Many think that Tulsīdās himself initiated the custom. Writing in the 1950s, the English translator of the poem, W. Douglas P. Hill, reports witnessing a particularly elaborate performance at Rāmnagar. That presentation began in the vast compound of the maharaja of Benares. In a performance that lasted three weeks, the actors silently depicted the story, moving from place to place as they simulated the story's itinerary. The spectators, some afoot and some mounted on elephants, trailed along behind the actors. Accompanying the performance, a choir chanted the Hindi words of the epic in antiphonal fashion. The final scene of the performance took place in the center of the city of Benares—perhaps the holiest spot in all Hindu India.

Bibliography

Aruna, Rājendra. *Rama, the Lord of Decorum.* New Delhi: Ocean Books, 2000. Tulsīdās. *Sri Rāmacharitamānasa, or, The Manasa Lake Brimming over with the Exploits of Sri Rama.* Gkorakhpur, India: Gita Press, 1991.

———. *Sri Rāmacharitamānasa: . . . Transliteration and Translation in English.* Translated by G. B. Kanungo and Leela Kanungo. New Delhi: Muni Bhagwan Kanungo Charitable Society, 2000.

———. *The Holy Lake of the Acts of Rama: An English Translation of Tulsīdās Rāmacharitamānasa.* Translated by W. Douglas P. Hill. Calcutta and New York: Oxford University Press, India Branch, 1952.

Honest Whore, The Thomas Dekker and Thomas Middleton (Part I, 1604; Part II, 1605)

THOMAS DEKKER'S most celebrated achievement, *The Honest Whore*, is a play in two parts. Part I (1604) resulted from Dekker's collaboration with

THOMAS MIDDLETON, but part II (ca. 1605) is considered the better play, and Dekker wrote it alone.

Set in and around the Italian city of Milan, both parts focus on the life of a woman named Bellafront who has been ruined by a seducer, Matteo, and forced into prostitution. Part I details her preservation of her dignity despite the loss of her virtue and her eventually successful efforts to recover that virtue by marrying the man who initially seduced her. This she achieves by feigning madness and by winning the duke of Milan to her cause. The duke orders Matteo to marry her. Matteo says that he cannot because she is crazy, but that if she recovers her wits, he will comply with the duke's order. She reveals her deception, and Matteo marries her. In part II, however, Matteo, who has not undergone a rehabilitation that parallels Bellafront's, attempts to persuade her to return once again to the streets and ply the prostitute's trade. She firmly resists his efforts. As she does so, her father, Orlando Friscobaldo, keeps a secret and protective watch over her.

Orlando is one of the most fully realized and memorable characters of the Jacobean stage. His characterization has often been compared to the 19th century novelist Charles Dickens's greatest. While the setting of *The Honest Whore* is Italian, the language of the common characters is strictly lower-class London—a dialect of which Dekker was a master.

Bibliography

Dekker, Thomas. *The Honest Whore.* London: Globe Education: New York: Theatre Arts Books and Routledge, 1998.

Hong Kiltong, The Tale of Hŏ Kyun
(ca. 1600)

The Tale of Hong Kiltong recounts the life history of its title character. A story of social criticism that borrows from Chinese models, Hŏ Kyun's narrative exposes the ill effects of the rigidity of the class system and the corruption of 16th- and 17th-century Korean society.

The love child of an important civil servant named Hong and his maidservant Ch'unsom,

Hong Kiltong's birth is predicted by his father's dream. The child proves to be gifted, but because of his mother's low status in the household, he is not permitted to claim Hong as his father or his half brother, In-hyŏng, as his sibling. Feeling discriminated against, Hong Kiltong complains to his father. Minister Hong is secretly sympathetic but is too bound by convention to side openly with his son and reproves him for harboring ambitions above his station. Hong Kiltong resolves to make a name for himself and undertakes the study of MAGIC and of the martial arts. The better to make his way in the world, Hong Kiltong also decides to leave his father's house. He tells his mother of this decision and the reasons for it. Before he can act on it, however, the enmity of another member of the household, his father's favorite but childless concubine, Ch'onan, threatens his very existence.

Ch'onan first hires a physiognomist to predict that the boy will cause trouble. On seeing the lad, however, the physiognomist perceives a hero who will become the marvel of his age. She conceals this, however, and lies to the father, predicting that Kiltong will be the ruin of his father's household. Worried, Minister Hong isolates his son, intending to keep careful watch over him. His enemy, Ch'onan, however, now hires an assassin, T'ŭkchae, to murder the lad. Forewarned by a raven's croaking, Hong Kiltong makes himself invisible. Eventually he confronts the assassin who explains that Ch'onan has hired him and that the physiognomist is also implicated. Then the assassin attempts to carry out his commission. Hong Kiltong wrests away his weapon and kills T'ŭkchae instead. Furious, Kiltong next seeks out the physiognomist and slits her throat.

Knowing that he can no longer stay, Kiltong takes formal leave of his father. The elder Hong gives his son permission to call him *father* and his half-sibling *brother,* and the two exchange affectionate farewells. After also saying goodbye to his mother, Kiltong heads for the mountains.

When the bodies are discovered, Ch'onan's part in the affair also comes to light. Minister Hong drives her away and instructs his servants never to mention anything further about the night's events.

Kiltong chances upon a bandits' hideaway. Perceiving in him a potential leader, the bandits challenge him to lift a great stone. He does so, carrying it 10 paces. Impressed, the bandits appoint the young man their leader. He proves a clever strategist as good at plotting a robbery as he is at deceiving the police. Kiltong becomes a Korean Robin Hood. He leads his band—which he names the Save-the-Poor Party—all over Korea, stealing from the rich and giving to the poor. He also splits his forces into seven groups and appoints seven surrogates to lead them. To his victims, he seems everywhere at once.

Eventually the Korean king becomes sufficiently alarmed that he is about to send out all his forces to corral the bandit. A brave captain, however, Yi Hŭp, volunteers to find him with just three helpers. As he searches, he encounters a young man who first challenges the captain to a test of strength and then leads him to the outlaws' lair. The young man, of course, proves to be Hong Kiltong in disguise. He has Yi Hŭp captured and then entertains him in his hideout, impressing the captain with his seemingly invincible power.

Increasingly bold, Hong Kiltong impersonates a royal official. In that guise he travels about accusing, trying, and punishing corrupt officials of the regime. Eventually the king discovers that Kiltong's father and half brother are still living. He arrests them but finding them innocent forgives them and appoints In-hyŏng the governor of a province with a year to capture Hong Kiltong. In-hyŏng posts notices appealing to Kiltong's family loyalty. A magic surrogate turns himself in and, when brought before the king, changes first into all eight Kiltongs and then into eight men of straw.

Other complications of this sort follow. Finally however, Hong Kiltong promises to end his career as an outlaw if the king will appoint him minister of war. After some delay in which the king becomes convinced of Hong Kiltong's invincibility, the king accedes to this demand. Satisfied, Kiltong comes to court, pays his respects to everyone, accepts the post, and rises up into the clouds to begin a new life elsewhere.

In subsequent episodes Kiltong kills monsters, gains two wives, divines by the stars the end of his father's life, and selects and prepares a gravesite for his burial.

In the final episodes of the story, Hong Kiltong gathers his crew of bandits into a proper army and leads them to the island of Lü-tao. There he conquers and is acknowledged as king. He rules wisely for 30 years, dies, and is succeeded as king by his son.

Although several Korean editions have appeared in the past 25 years, only one English version is available at this writing.

Bibliography

Ho Kyun. "The Tale of Hong Kiltong." *Anthology of Korean Literature from Early Times to the Nineteenth Century,* edited by Peter H. Lee. Honolulu: University of Hawaii Press, 1981.

Honnamma, Sañchiya (late 17th century)

A female poet in the Kannada language of INDIA, Sañchiya Honnamma appears to have been a maidservant in the household of Queen Yelandur Devajammani in Mysore state. Despite that lowly status, Honnamma seems to have also been a disciple of the court poet, Alasingararya. Her mentor suggested to the king, Chikkadevaraja Wadeyar, that he ask the queen to require a poem from Honnamma. The queen did so, and the result has become a widely known, standard text. Lines from Honnamma's poem, *Hadibadeya Dharma* (Duties of a devoted wife), are still recited in Indian households today. Her work was a remarkable, possibly unique, achievement at a moment in history when as a rule only holy men and noble women penned poetry.

Although for the most part the duties that her poem presents are the standard ones that one would expect from a woman of her time, place, and station in life and although they generally reflect the attitudes of a society with a masculine bias, one does find exceptions. She criticizes, for example, the bias against female children that still characterizes much of Indian society. She reminds her readers that women bear the children of both sexes and can bring as much value to a family as boys can when girls are afforded opportunities to develop their skills and intellects. She therefore advises parents not to be stingy with their daughters but to be sure they have "clothes and ornaments."

Honnamma's didactic poem contains 479 stanzas organized into nine cantos. It does not develop a coherent story line, but it often invokes or summarizes such ancient Hindu texts as the RAMAYANA, the *Bhagavata*, the MAHABHARATA, and the *Manusmriti* as those works apply to the proper points of view and the duties of housewives.

Bibliography

Lal, Mohan, ed. *Encyclopedia of Indian Literature.* Vol. 4. New Delhi: Sahitya Akademi, 1991.

Tharu, Susie, and K. Lalita. *Women Writing in India, 600 B.C. to the Present.* Vol. 1. New York: The Feminist Press at The City University of New York, 1990.

Hooker, Richard (1554–1600)

An English churchman of broad, traditional, and sophisticated views and a writer of distinguished prose, Hooker was educated at Corpus College in Oxford University where he became a fellow in 1577. He took orders in the Anglican priesthood in 1581 and went to London to preach at Paul's Cross. While there he married his landlady's daughter, Joan Churchman.

After a further preaching assignment, Hooker competed against a Calvinist Puritan named Travers for appointment to the post of master of the temple. Through the influence of a patron John Whitgift, Hooker prevailed. Relying exclusively on the authority of the Bible, Travers attacked Hooker publicly for his latitudinarianism—that is, for his broadly inclusive views concerning the authority of Scripture, of church tradition, of human reason, and of the ecclesiastical establishment.

Forced to defend himself against the railing fundamentalist, Hooker destroyed Travers's arguments with sweet reason. He then felt obliged, however, to provide a more detailed account of the grounds for the positions that he took. He asked Whitgift to assign him to a less demanding parish, moved to Boscomb near Salisbury, and there planned to write eight books that would definitively treat his positions on ecclesiastical matters

and the grounds on which he based them. Four of the books he finished at Boscomb, and the other four after he moved in 1595 to Bishopsbourne in the neighborhood of Canterbury.

Hooker's monumental *Of the Laws of Ecclesiastical Polity* began to appear with the publication of the first four books in 1594. The fifth volume appeared in 1597, and the last three were printed posthumously in the next century.

Hooker enjoys the reputation of having been 16th century's finest crafter of English prose. His measured clarity set the style and tone for all subsequent Anglican theological writing.

Bibliography

Hooker, Richard. *Of the Laws of Ecclesiastical Polity,* edited by W. Speed Hill et al. Binghamton, N.Y.: Medieval and Renaissance Texts and Studies, 1993.

———. *The Sermons of Richard Hooker: The Power of Faith, the Mystery of Grace.* Edited by Philip B. Secor. London: SPCK, 2001.

Kirby, W. J. Torrance. *Richard Hooker and the English Reformation.* Boston: Kluwer Academic Publishers, ca. 2003.

———. *Richard Hooker, Reformer and Platonist: A Reassessment of his Thought.* Burlington, Vt.: Ashgate Publishers, Ltd. 2004.

Voak, Nigel. *Richard Hooker and Reformed Theology: A Study of Reason, Will, and Grace.* Oxford, U.K.: Oxford University Press, 2003.

Howard, Henry, earl of Surrey

See SURREY, HOWARD HENRY, EARL OF.

Huang Xiumei (Hsiu-mei) (1498–1569)

The daughter of a high official in the Ming dynasty's administration, Huang Xiumei had been carefully educated by a loving father. In 1519 she married the recently widowed heir of an equally well-to-do family. After five idyllic years, however, her husband Yang Shen was beaten and exiled for opposing the will of the new Chinese emperor Shizong (Shih-tsung; also known as Jiajing). Separated from her husband thereafter, except for one three-year reunion and some occasional brief meetings, Huang Xiumei conducted with him a 35-year-long exchange of verses and letters until his death in 1559. Although the letters have perished, the verses have survived.

Although Huang herself made no attempt to publish her poems, she and her husband both seem to have shared manuscript copies of them with others. In time they became well known and began to be included in Ming and Qing (Ch'ing) dynasty poetic anthologies.

The 16th century in China saw a revival of poems that emphasized sincere feeling as a primary poetic value. A number of women proved central to that revival with their contributions to it. Talented courtesans, for example, were often prized for their literary accomplishments. Women of the administrative class—like Huang herself—also played a crucial part in writing works that appealed the public taste for romantic lyric poems.

Huang Xiumei stands out among the members of the latter class, however, because of the intensely intimate, unabashedly erotic subject matter of her verse as well as for the depth of its feeling and the lyricism of her poems. She weaves her sense of loss, her loneliness, her erotic fantasies, and her devotion to Yang Shen—despite her sardonic knowledge that he did not forego the company of other women as she did men—reflect themselves in a lovely *sanqu* (*san-ch'ü*) lyric she penned for him. Like most Chinese lyrics of its sort, Huang Xiumei intended it to be sung to a traditional tune, "a song for breaking of Cassia twigs."

Huang first recalls the times when the two of them shared a home, a bed, and a happy life that seemed immune to sadness. But then her thought turns to the way in which her husband's exile and their separation has blighted her marriage and wasted away her spirit so that she is lost in sighing and in gloom. She ends her poem by rejecting as hollow his promises of eternal love, his recollection of their love making, and his assertion that just 15 minutes together would be worth a thousand gold pieces.

Huang Xiumei survived Yang Shen by a decade.

Bibliography

Huang Xiumei. "*Sanqu* lyric to the tune *Zhe gui ling.*" Translated by Ch'en Hsiao-Lan and F. W. Mote. *Women Writers of Traditional China: An Anthology of Poetry and Criticism.* Page 176. Stanford, Calif.: Stanford University Press, 1999.

Mair, Victor H., ed. *The Columbia History of Chinese Literature.* New York: Columbia University Press, 2001.

Huarochiri Manuscript (Peru, 1608)

Written in the Quechua language of the Peruvian Andes at Huarochiri, a locale situated between the Spanish capital of Lima and the Inca capital city of Cuzco, and penned after 70 years of contact between the Quechuans and Europeans, this manuscript chronicles many important aspects of Andean religion, culture, and history. First, its 31 chapters contain accounts of the local mythology. Second, it recounts from the perspective of the Quechuans the integration of various subethnic groups into a more or less unified culture. Finally, it recounts the domination of the Quechuans, first by the Incan Empire and then by the Spanish during and after their 40-year-long conquest of the Inca in the 16th century.

We owe the document's existence to the efforts of a Jesuit missionary, Francisco de Avila. Following the usual Jesuit strategy of seeking parallels between Christianity and the local mythology with the aim of substituting the former for the latter, Avila commissioned the collection both of written and oral accounts of local myth and history. These purposes and methods, the confrontations and interpenetrations of cultures, the probability that portions of the document were composed by Quechuans literate in Spanish, and the fact that the document marks a shift from oral tradition to preservation in writing all conspire to produce a fascinating composite.

A reader discovers a broad structural similarity between the Christian BIBLE and the chapters of the Huarochiri Manuscript. Chapter 1, for example, alludes to a time before time when the idols of old warred among themselves and insisted on eating one of the two children that human beings were allowed to bear. As in Genesis, deities and people are in direct contact. Chapter 2 contains the story of the deity Cuni Raya Vira Choca. Through trickery, this deity causes a beautiful virgin to swallow his seed in a fruit. She subsequently bears his child but runs away. As he pursues her he asks directions of birds and animals, rewarding those who encourage him and punishing those who discourage him. He rewards the condor with the carcasses of dead animals and a promise of revenge should anyone kill it. He punishes the skunk with his odor. Chapter 3 contains a flood story.

Despite many rough parallels with the Bible, a reader of the manuscript will soon discover a radically unfamiliar culture. Various Quechuan communities venerated local deities who were connected to groups of kindred, villages, mountains, and other topographic features. This localism characterizes the religious dimensions of the manuscript to a much greater degree than does the simultaneous veneration of more powerful but less locally familiar deities. These include Cuni Raya Vira Coca—favored as the principal deity of the empire by the Quechua's Incan masters. His story asserts that though he began as a relatively minor god, he both founded Incan towns and asserted his mastery over the other deities, eventually supplanting them altogether as a creator and solar deity. Other regional deities include Paria Caca and Chaupi Ñamca who may be identified with mountains.

Solar eclipse led to a number of mythic accounts of the periodic death and rebirth of the sun. Into one such account, Avila inserts or caused to be inserted a Christian interpretation, identifying the darkness with that which the Bible says followed Christ's crucifixion.

The history of the Andean people as unfolded in the pages of the Huarochiri Manuscript chronicles a repetitive cycle of conquest and assimilation. Victorious new arrivals become identified with the offspring of figures in the pantheon of local deities. This pattern applies as well to the domination of the Quechua by the Inca whose victory is detailed in chapters 18, 19, 20, 22, and 23.

Chapter 18 also contains a foreboding prediction: After examining the entrails of a sacrificed llama, a mountain man named Quita Pariasca foretells that a time is coming when "Paria Caca will be abandoned." His prophecy is scorned until a few days later when someone reports that the Spanish have been seen in nearby Caxa Marca. A bit later the Spanish arrive, seeking silver and valuables stored for the god by the priests of Paria Caca's order. Infuriated by one priest's refusal to cooperate, the Spanish order that he be burned. A strong wind, however, blows away the straw they use for fuel before the priest is burned to death. He survives, and the other priests hand over the valuables.

The manuscript's compilers also fit into its mythic structure many natural phenomena, such as the eclipses and floods already mentioned and like volcanic eruptions and hurricanes as well. A wonderfully readable bilingual (English and Quechuan) edition has recently appeared.

Bibliography
Avila, Francisco de. *The Huarochiri Manuscript: A Testament of Ancient and Colonial Religion.* Translated by Frank Salomon and George L. Urioste. Austin: University of Texas Press, 1998.
Spalding, Karen. *Huarochirí, an Andean Society Under Inca and Spanish Rule.* Stanford, Calif.: Stanford University Press, 1984.

Hubbi Qadin (Ayishe, fl. ca. 1600)
A writer of both Turkish and Arabic verse, Hubbi Qadin (Madame Hubbi) enjoyed a reputation among the BIOGRAPHERS OF TURKISH POETS as the best female poet of the Ottoman Empire. She was the author of a long, narrative, romantic poem of more than 3,000 couplets chained together (a MESNEVÍ). Its subject was the love between Khurshíd and Jemshíd—the only such love poem composed by a Turkish woman. She also penned numerous QASÍDAS and GHAZELS.

hubris

The variety of overweening human pride that the gods in ancient European literature found most objectionable, hubris invariably led those who displayed it into difficulty. Homer's Odysseus, for instance, after having been given a favorable wind to send him home to Ithaca, attempted to exceed the capacities of human beings by refusing to allow any but himself to handle the ship's tiller while he stayed awake for nine days and nights. He also kept to himself the knowledge that a bag he brought on board contained all the unfavorable winds. Finally and inevitably, within sight of his goal, Odysseus dropped, exhausted. His crew, thinking that Odysseus meant to keep without sharing a treasure concealed in the bag, opened it. All the imprisoned winds rushed out at once, producing a hurricane that blew the ship back to its starting point on the Island of Aeolia.

Because Homer's *Odyssey* is essentially comic, that episode is only one of a series of setbacks Odysseus experiences before reaching his home in Ithaca and recovering his former kingdom and his family. Such, however, is not the case for those who display hubris with tragic outcomes.

SHAKESPEARE displays the consequences of hubris in some of his dramas. KING LEAR attempts to remain in control of matters both beyond his retirement and beyond his lifespan by dividing his kingdom among his daughters. In doing so against wise advice, he displays both hubris and folly, and he and those about him suffer the tragic consequences of his pride and foolishness. Coriolanus, in the play by the same name, sacrifices himself, his family, and his city, Rome, to his uncompromising certainty of his own nobility and innate superiority.

JOHN MILTON in *PARADISE LOST* makes his Satan (Lucifer) the archetype of hubris. Created the brightest archangel in heaven, Lucifer (whose name means "the bearer of light") finds himself dissatisfied with being second and, thinking that one more step would set him highest, declares war in Heaven, winning a third of the angels to his side with tragic consequences and eternal punishment for all who revolt.

humanism, humanist

When discussing Renaissance humanism one must bear firmly in mind that the term has little or nothing to do with what 21st-century Americans call secular humanism—a phrase that implies a particular orientation toward religious belief. Instead, as it applies to the Renaissance, the word *humanism* alludes to the study and mastery of the languages and literatures of the great authors of ancient Greece and Rome, and the word *humanist* applies to those persons who were engaged in those studies and in the activities that enabled those studies to occur. These activities included, but were not limited to, the translation of texts, the creation of grammars and lexicons as aids to the study and mastery of ancient languages, and the development of methods of comparing ancient texts—including biblical texts—with a view to correcting the errors that had crept in during centuries of hand copying, mistranslation, and editorial misunderstanding. They also included the development of humanistic curricula for all levels of education and improvements in methods of teaching.

The studies central to the Renaissance humanist enterprise included grammar, history, moral philosophy, poetry, and rhetoric. Mastery of these subjects, the humanists who taught them were convinced, had the power both to improve the lives of those who studied them and to make civic life more refined and livable. The humanists placed great confidence in the power of education to cultivate the skills required for good government and for personal morality.

From a literary perspective, the study of the writings of classical antiquity provided models Renaissance people could emulate. Although the roots of the activities associated with literary humanism are traceable into the late Middle Ages, the marker that is often thought to divide the mindset of the Medieval period from that of the Renaissance appears in the life and career of the Italian poet and scholar PETRARCH (FRANCESCO PETRARCA, 1304–74), who for the first time since imperial Roman days used his own life and love as the subject for his Italian lyric verse. He also emulated the Romans by composing works in Latin and in the genres the ancients had produced. These included a history, *Of illustrious men* (*De Viris Illustribus*), and the EPIC that he considered his masterpiece, his *Africa,* based on the career of the Roman general, Scipio Africanus. He also emulated the ancients by collecting his own letters and organizing them into letters written in his youth and in his old age.

Though the roll of important humanists is far too long to enumerate here, a few who deserve particular mention include LORENZO VALLA (ca. 1405–57), who developed the standards for textual criticism that resulted in recovering better versions of ancient writing; DESIDERIUS ERASMUS (1466–1536), who applied those standards to improving the available text of the BIBLE and who wrote influentially on education, morality, and Christian conduct. Coluccio Salutati (1331–1406), who carried on the initiatives of Petrarch in the city of Florence and who was responsible for bringing the first professor of Greek, MANUEL CHRYSOLARAS, to Italy; and the Spaniard Juan Luis Vives (1492–1540) whose concern for the welfare of the poor brought an important new social dimension to the humanist enterprise. In England, SIR THOMAS MORE (1478–1535) became the outstanding humanist of his era, reflecting the movement's political thinking in his *UTOPIA* (1516) and organizing his household and the education of his children into a working model of applied humanist ideals. In France, GUILLAUME BUDÉ (1467–1540) was probably the leading exponent of the humanist cause, writing encyclopedic works about Roman law and founding the Collège Royal (1530) to teach classical languages.

Humanism also attracted numbers of brilliant women to its standard. The French MARGARET, DUCHESS OF ANGOLÊME and queen of Navarre (1492–1549) surrounded herself with and supported with her patronage many of the most brilliant French humanists of her era. Like her, Queen ELIZABETH I of England had benefited from a humanist education and was influenced by humanist thought. In a highly individualistic way MARGARET CAVENDISH, DUCHESS OF NEWCASTLE (1623–73) treated matters of humanist interest, such as Utopian society, from an early feminist perspective. Isotta Nogarola (1418–66) of Verona, Italy,

mastered Latin and Greek and became extremely learned in humanist studies. Latinists and humanists as well were the Venetian Cassandra Fedele (1465–88) and the Brescian LAURA CERETA (1469–99).

Bibliography

Burckhardt, Jakob. *The Civilization of the Renaissance in Italy.* Translated by S. G. C. Middlemore. New York: Modern Library, 2002.

Goodman, Anthony, and Angus MacKay, eds. *The Impact of Humanism on Western Europe.* New York: Longmans, 1993.

Nauert, Charles Garfield. *Humanism and the Culture of Renaissance Europe.* Cambridge, U.K., and New York: Cambridge University Press, 1995.

Rabil, Albert. *Erasmus and the New Testament: The Mind of a Christian Humanist.* Lanham, Md.: University Press of America, ca. 1993.

———. *Renaissance Humanism: Foundations, Forms, and Legacy.* Philadelphia: University of Pennsylvania Press, 1988.

Trinkaus, Charles Edward. *In Our Image and Likeness: Humanity and Divinity in Italian Humanist Thought.* Notre Dame, Ind.: University of Notre Dame Press, 1995.

humanist cursive handwriting

In the late 14th century, PETRARCH complained about the crabbed handwriting of medieval calligraphers. So did others who became associated with the HUMANIST movement, notably the Florentine humanist Coluccio Salutati and two members of his school Niccolò Niccoli and Poggio Bracciolini. As humanism developed as a self-conscious movement, its adherents wished to distance themselves in as many ways as possible from the Medieval scholastic thinkers and scholars. As a part of that effort both Niccoli and Bracciolini busied themselves at developing a distinctive handwriting and associating it with the humanist school.

Bracciolini developed a new script ironically called ancient letters (*lettera antica*) that soon became known as humanist round hand or humanist book script. He borrowed it from a script that flourished in the 11th and 12th centuries, but that because of its clarity, he assumed to be older. It differed from its predecessors, says Christopher S. Celenza, by running all the way across a page, by using fewer vertical strokes or minims and fewer abbreviations, by adopting a system of uniform spacing, and by differentiating the letters more clearly. Niccoli studied Bracciolini's script and combined it with his own cursive writing. Niccoli's handwriting became the standard toward which humanist cursive script aspired and, with the advent of the printing press, became the basis for *italic type, which these phrases exemplify.*

Bibliography

Celenza, Christopher S. "Calligraphy." In *Encyclopedia of the Renaissance,* edited by Paul F. Grendler. New York: Charles Scribner's Sons, 1999.

Davies, Martin. "Humanism in Script and Print in the Fifteenth Century." In *The Cambridge Companion to Renaissance Humanism,* edited by Jill Kraye, 47–62. Cambridge, U.K.: Cambridge University Press, 1996.

De la Mare, Albinia. *The Handwriting of the Italian Humanists.* Oxford, U.K.: Oxford University Press, 1973.

humoral medicine

From the time of ancient Greeks until late in the 18th century, the art of medicine depended on ideas derived from Greek physics and from the pseudoscience of astrology. Throughout this entire period, European and Arab physicians believed that each person's basic physical and psychological nature were determined by the configuration of the stars at the moment of his or her birth. They also learned that four bodily fluids corresponded to the four elements of Greek physics. Black bile corresponded to earth, yellow bile to air, blood to fire, and phlegm to water.

The configuration of a person's natal stars caused one of these fluids, or *humors* as they were labeled, to predominate in the makeup of each individual. If black bile dominated, a person was said to be melancholy. A predominance of yellow bile made one bilious. If blood were the predominate humor, a person had a sanguine disposition. A tendency to be phlegmatic resulted from the watery humor's predominating.

In healthy persons, whatever their predominate humor might be, the humors remained in the same balance the stars dictated at the moment of birth. Sickness, medical theory asserted, resulted from an imbalance of the humors. When someone fell ill and called the doctor, therefore, the first step in the physician's diagnostic procedure often involved casting the sufferer's horoscope. Fever was thought to result from a surplus of blood, so opening a vein or putting a live leech on an ill person removed the excess blood. Depression and the temperament of artists associated itself with the melancholy humor. Laxatives were often the treatment of choice.

All of this is important for the literature of the Western world, first, because many authors made use of these theories when drawing their characters and sometimes when describing themselves. Both LORENZO DE' MEDICI and ROBERT BURTON, for example, described themselves as "melancholy." Burton spent his life in the exhaustive study of the various forms taken by the condition from which he suffered, publishing his findings in his ANATOMY OF MELANCHOLY. Cheerful and assertive characters belong in the sanguine group. Cowardly, sneaky ones show the symptoms of the phlegmatic. Characters who were forever criticizing and finding fault had bile as their predominate humor.

Not until microscopes revealed the existence of disease-causing bacteria and microbes did the humoral theory of medicine pass entirely into history. The terms associated with the humors themselves, however, remain a part of the everyday vocabulary of many speakers.

I

Ibn Iyās (1448–1524)

An Egyptian historian, Ibn Iyās set out to write a comprehensive history of Egypt from the time of the pharaohs until his own. His discussion of the earliest periods is very brief, but as he nears his own time he begins to give year-by-year accounts of events. These become increasingly detailed until he gives his readers a famous eyewitness account of the psychological and physical consequences for the inhabitants of Cairo when in 1516 the Ottoman Turks, under the leadership of Sultan Selim (Selim the Grim), defeated the troops of the Mamluk Sultan al-Ghawri, who had ruled in Egypt. That defeat left the citizens of Cairo in panic. The installation of a new regime meant that life in Cairo as people had known it was about to change in all its details, and the populace found itself gripped by fear of the unknown and of the behavior of the Ottoman troops. Some of their worst fears were realized, and Ibn Iyās records what happened in his Arabic work, The choicest blooms concerning the incidence of dooms (*Badā'i' al-zuhūr fī wāqa'i' al-duhūr*). He discusses daily life, gives obituaries, records market trends and prices, and includes his own poems that are addressed to important people. He blames Sultan al-Ghawri for the financial difficulties of Cairo and attributes the defeat of the Mamluk regime to internal quarreling within the government and to the sultan's failure to procure and defend adequately against artillery.

Ibn Iyās also wrote a cosmography (1517) and may have written other works, though their attribution is doubtful.

Bibliography

Ibn Iyās. *An Account of the Ottoman Conquest of Egypt in the year A. H. 922 (A.D. 1516)*. Translated by W. H. Salmon. Westport, Conn.: Hyperion Press, 1981.

Icelandic linguistic law

The golden age of Icelandic literature came during the three and a half centuries after the settlement of the island between 874 and 930 C.E. by immigrant Norwegian seafarers who spoke Old Norse. That tongue was then only beginning to differentiate into the modern Scandinavian languages of Swedish, Danish, Norwegian, and, most conservative of all, Icelandic.

The great medieval documents of Iceland included the very early poetic *Edda*—a collection of manuscripts that contains myths, heroic legends, and moral teachings. The works also included Snörri Sturluson's (1179–1241) later prose chronicle of Norway's kings down to the year 1177 and his prose *Edda* that was a handbook about the composition of verse illustrated with his own poems. Beyond that so-called Skaldic poems were preserved from the work of the professional entertainers who sang and recited them first in Norway and later in Iceland. A number of sagas also preserved the real and mythic histories of Scandinavian heroes.

The legislature of Iceland, the Althing, recognized that linguistic change is an unstoppable phenomenon. Nonetheless, they sought a way to preserve the legibility of Iceland's classic literature for future generations of readers. They therefore crafted a strategy to slow or avoid a succession of linguistic events like the ones that have rendered *Beowulf* and the works of Chaucer and, increasingly, of Shakespeare virtually incomprehensible to contemporary English readers who lack special training.

In their wisdom, the Icelandic legislators required that all new inventions or ideas introduced into the country must be named with native elements—no foreign expressions allowed. So, instead of using the word *telephone* for the invention of that name, for example, in Icelandic one refers to the instrument with a phrase that means "the distance speaker." Similar combinations from native word stock apply to computers and television sets.

Iceland's relative isolation from the rest of the world has until recently, at least, helped this rearguard policy work. Time will tell whether or not Icelandic literary culture and language will be able to withstand the onslaught of foreign words contained in the lyrics of songs enjoyed by young people around the world.

Icelandic poets, hymnodists, and preachers

In the 16th and 17th centuries, Icelandic poets and preachers often proved to be the same persons, and their poetic inspiration regularly expressed itself in the composition of hymns. This certainly was the case with one of the most talented hymnodists of Lutheranism ever, Hallgrímur Pétursson (1614–74). Having gone through over 50 editions and still in print, Pétursson's *Hymns of the Passion: Meditations on the Passion of Christ* (*Passíusálmar*) are regularly

performed. He was also the author of some of the most skillful secular poetry written in Iceland during the Renaissance, and although a modern edition of it exists in Icelandic, no translation is available.

Another clergyman who composed poems on matters both sacred and secular was Stefán Ólafson (ca. 1620–88). Unlike Pétursson, however, Ólafsson's secular poems proved to be his most successful work. He is best remembered as a satirist and humorist and for his contributions to a 1665 collaborative Latin translation of samples of and a commentary on Icelandic works including the *Edda* of the 13th-century Icelandic author, Snörri Sturluson.

Finally, numerous clergymen collected their sermons and published them, and most of these have passed into history unremembered and unmourned. The sermons, however, of Bishop Jón Thorkelssom Vídalín (1666–1720), which he collected and published in installments during the four years preceding his death, continue to be read in Iceland and throughout the world. Their readers find them impassioned, eloquent, and informed by a gift for careful observation of human behavior and its wellsprings. They remain influential in the development of the national Icelandic character.

Bibliography

Pétursson, Hallgrímur. *Hymns of the Passion: Meditations on the Passion of Christ*. Translated by Arthur Charles Gook. Reykhjavík: Hallgríms Church, 1978.

———. *Passíusalmar*. Sound Recording. Reykjavík: Ever, 1989.

Vídalín, Jón. *Whom Wind and Waves Obey: Selected Sermons of Bishop Jón Vídalín*. Translated by Michael Fell. New York: Peter Lang, 1998.

Icelandic translators, balladeers, annalists and biographers

After the composition of the great Icelandic poetic and prose sagas following the Scandinavian settlement of the island, and aside from the work of Bishop JÓN ARASON (1484–1550), little of literary interest happened in Iceland until the forced introduction of Lutheranism in 1536 at the behest of the king of Denmark.

This change produced predictable results. Two Lutheran translations of Scripture and a new Lutheran hymnal appeared on the scene. The first of these is Oddur Gottskálksson's Icelandic New Testament (1540). Then came the whole Bible, translated by Bishop Gudbrandur Thorláksson (1584), and then his hymnal (1589). The church took possession of the only printing press in Iceland—that originally imported by Arason—and this meant that secular literature circulated only in manuscript. Circulate it did, however, and in addition to the doggerel mentioned above, a new sort of ballad appeared in the 16th century that remained in vogue until the 19th. One of the best composers of such songs was a Lutheran pastor named Einar Sigurdsson (1538–1626).

Biographies and annals were composed in abundance. These are chiefly interesting as historical rather than as literary documents, but some of their authors rose above the common herd. Among the more notable annalists were Jón Egilsson (1548–1634) and Björn Jónsson (1574–1655). Three historians deserve mention: Arngrímur Jónsson (1568–1648), Thormódur Torfason (1636–1719), and Arní Magnússon (1663–1730). The last named was especially important for the work he did collecting and preserving Icelandic manuscripts that are now housed in Copenhagen, Denmark as part of the Arna–Magnean collection.

iconography

Iconography is the representation in the graphic arts of an IMAGE that is regularly associated with an abstract idea or concept or with powerful persons or families. In contemporary Western society, a blindfolded woman with a scale in one hand and a sword in the other is the icon of justice. The Statue of Liberty is an icon of freedom. In the Renaissance and earlier, a female figure with a wheel represented fortune or the goddess FORTUNA. Often, Renaissance writers borrowed icons from the graphic arts and conveyed the ideas they represented through description. The coats of arms of powerful families had iconographic status. The heraldic device of the

Medici family of Florence, for example, was a series of six balls (Italian, *palle*) mounted on a shield. The balls represented pills because the family's founder had been an apothecary. Medici supporters often cheered *"palle, palle, palle,"* thereby invoking the icon that represented the family and its power. Many iconographic images, whether written or depicted, were widely recognized by Renaissance people and could thus be used to convey ideas and associations—often without particular comment—and add significantly to the meaning of a work. ALLEGORY that depended on the presentation either of verbal or visual iconography regularly appeared in both literary and graphic art works.

Ihara Saikaku

See SAIKAKU.

image

In literature an image may be defined as a verbal appeal to the senses. This can be visual, as with a word picture, or tactile as when one describes, for instance, the scrape of chalk on a blackboard. It can be olfactory, as when poets evoke the fragrances of flowers in a garden at night simply by naming the blooms. It can be aural as is Edgar Allen Poe's invocation of the sound of bells in his choice of the word *tintinnabulation.* If a verbal image appeals to more than one of a reader's senses at the same time, the phrase that does so is called a synaesthetic image:—Longfellow describes a blacksmith's face as "wet with honest sweat," where a reader both envisions a face bathed in perspiration and remembers how the heat and dampness feel. Cultivating one's responses to poetic imagery opens a door to greater enjoyment of reading verse.

incunable

Derived from the Latin word for "cradle," in literature *incunable* means a book printed during the first 100 years after the invention of printing in Europe (ca. 1450). WILLIAM CAXTON, for example, opened the first printing business in England in 1476. Thus his editions of Chaucer's *Canterbury Tales* and Mallory's *Morte d'Arthur* (death of King Arthur), both of which appeared between 1476 and 1500, would be considered incunables or incunabula. So would the books printed by the ALDINE PRESS before 1550.

indexes of forbidden books

From as early as the second century the Roman Catholic Church has expressed its concern with the power of the written word both to promulgate and to undermine its teachings. Throughout the first 14 centuries of the church's history various councils and popes had discriminated between what was and was not authentically scriptural and had condemned or forbidden works judged to be spiritually dangerous to their readers.

With the 15th-century invention of movable type and the printing press and the resultant explosion both of books and literacy, the problems posed by potentially dangerous writings increased exponentially. In 1469, therefore, Pope Innocent VIII issued a decree requiring the submission of all books to the authorities of local churches before circulating them among the general public. Pope Leo X issued a similar directive in 1515.

Church, national, and civil authorities all felt endangered by the rapid circulation of the writings of MARTIN LUTHER and other religious reformers, and many authorities undertook to prohibit their books' being printed, transported, sold, bought, or read. In England, France, Italy, Spain, and Portugal, ecclesiastical and civil authorities at the national, regional, and local levels attempted to stem the tide of dangerous print by issuing edicts, drawing up lists, and passing legislation. These efforts proved variously successful. In Spain and Portugal the efforts achieved many of their goals. Venetian publishers and booksellers, on the other hand, joined forces to suppress an Index of 1549 that the government and the Venetian INQUISITION had prepared.

In 1557 Pope Paul IV assigned to the Congregation of the Inquisition the responsibility for compiling a definitive list of forbidden books. Pope Paul found the contents of its first draft too narrow and rejected it. A more comprehensive revision was approved and published in 1559 as the first Roman Index. This list stirred up much controversy within the church leadership because its contents presented obstacles to the reconciliation between Protestants and Roman Catholics that was an objective of the COUNCIL OF TRENT (1545–63). The Council of Trent itself, therefore appointed a commission to revise the index, and in 1564 Pope Pius IV approved the revision. This so-called Tridentine Index both listed the banned books and established 10 standards to be applied in considering future publications. The standards confirmed the condemnations of earlier popes and councils. The standards prohibited all works by the leaders of movements judged heretical; obscene works; and works about magic, astrology, and the occult. Some works by heretical authors were to be permitted if they did not deal with religion. Also permitted were works not in Latin that dealt with matters of controversy between heretics and Catholics. Some works could be published after the parts judged objectionable were deleted. Only licensed translations of the Bible were allowed.

Under Pope Sixtus V the index was once again revised, and 22 new standards substituted for the Tridentine's 10. Two further major revisions occurred during the Renaissance: The first (1596) was commissioned by Pope Clement VIII, and the other by Pope Alexander VII in 1664. The later one was the first to list forbidden books alphabetically.

Works appearing on the index during the Renaissance included unauthorized translations of the Bible, such as those of John Wycliffe and WILLIAM TYNDALE. Works promoting heliocentric views of the universe, such as those of Galileo and Copernicus, also were listed. So were works by the HUMANIST priest ERASMUS of Rotterdam. Since 1966 the index itself has been abandoned except as a document relating to church history. Some of its principles governing approved and forbidden reading, however, remain in effect because they derive from canon law as it relates to spiritual health.

A monumental French language compendium of the principal Renaissance regional and papal indexes appeared in 10 volumes between 1984 and 1996.

Bibliography

Bujanda, J. M., ed. *Index des livres interdits.* [Index of forbidden books.] Sherbrooke, Québec, Canada.

Centre d'études de la Renaissance, Editions de l'Université de Sherbrooke, 1993.

Grendler, Paul F. *The Roman Inquisition and the Venetian Press, 1540–1605.* Princeton, N.J.: Princeton University Press, 1977.

McCabe, Joseph. *The History and Meaning of the Catholic Index of Forbidden Books.* Girard, Kans.: Haldeman-Julius Company, ca. 1931.

Tedeschi, John. *The Prosecution of Heresy: Collected Studies on the Inquisition in Early Modern Italy.* Binghamton, N.Y.: Medieval & Renaissance Texts & Studies, 1991.

India, languages of

To say that the linguistic situation in India is complex may seriously understate the matter. Literally hundreds of languages, many with regional variants, are actually spoken in India today. The Sahitya Akademi (National Academy of Letters) of India recognizes 22 official ones, including English, and all 22 of them have significant literatures.

The major language groups of India are usually categorized by their historic origins. In the north of India one finds languages belonging to what is called the Indo-Iranian subfamily of the Indo-Aryan group. The ancient roots of these languages are traceable to a long-dead common ancestor—Indo-European—that also gave rise to most of the languages of modern Europe.

The theory holds that five or six thousand years ago a group of people speaking a common language and living either in the Anatolian region of Turkey or in what is now Russia near the Black Sea began to migrate east and west from their original homeland. As their descendants traveled over a period of several millennia, the language they originally spoke continually changed in quite regular ways and eventually produced several families of related but mutually unintelligible languages.

Speakers of one of the descendant subgroups, Indo–Aryan, began to infiltrate northern India in about 1500 B.C.E. Their now dead common language, called Indic, produced a literary language called Vedic Sanskrit. That tongue, too, changed over time to produce numerous linguistic off-spring. Modern descendent tongues spoken in India include: Assamese, Bengali, Bhili, Bhojpuri, Braj, Gujerati, Hindi in two main dialects, Kacchi, Kashmiri, Konkani, Lahnda, Maithili, Nepali, Oriya, Nuristani, Punjabi, Rajasthani (several dialects), Sinhala, and Urdu. Most of those named have literary cultures. One other family member, Romany, is the language spoken by the Gypsies in Europe, the Middle East, and elsewhere. Other member languages still survive in India—meaning that they have native speakers—but some of them had as few as two or three thousand speakers in the early 1970s. A few others survive as important second languages or liturgical languages (tongues used only for religious purposes, such as church Latin). Pali, Sanskrit, and Sauraseni exemplify this sort of survival.

When the Indo-European immigrants entered India, they did not find an unpopulated land. Rather, they encountered, probably subjugated, and eventually coalesced with an indigenous population who principally spoke languages in the Dravidian family. Almost 70 members of this family survive on and near the Indian subcontinent in Pakistan, India, and Sri Lanka. Those languages have a manuscript and/or print literary tradition include Kannada, Malayalam, Tamil, and Telegu. The Dravidian languages spoken in India have as few as 100 native speakers to as many as 57 million. Most of the Dravidian languages without written literary traditions have oral ones.

Other language families are represented in India and in nearby regions whose speakers have often felt Indian intellectual, religious and literary influences. They include, first, the 32 Kiranti languages, which are spoken in Nepal, Tibet, and Sikkim. Next, tribal peoples in the northeastern regions of Assam, Manipur, and Nagaland speak some 19 Konyak tongues. Finally, other tribal peoples in northeastern India and Bangladesh speak some 38 Kuki-chin languages. The languages and language families named above by no means exhaust the list of tongues spoken in India and its immediately adjacent sphere of cultural influence. I hope, however, that the foregoing discussion conveys a sense of the subcontinent's convoluted linguistic situation.

India's enormous linguistic diversity helped define the literary outcomes that followed from the bhakti spiritual movement that began in about 1450 and continued through the 16th and 17th centuries and beyond. For one thing, important literary figures retold the great EPICS of India in the various languages of the authors. In the retelling of epics such as the RAMAYANA, of the MAHABHARATA, or of stories connected with the worship of Krishna, authors such as the Bengali-speaking Kasiram Das and KRISHNADĀSA KAVIRĀJA GOSVĀMI, the Braj-speaking KABIR, the Punjabi-speaking NĀNAK, the Malayalam-speaking ERUTACAN, and the Oriya-speaking Dānakrishna Dāsa modernized the works for their contemporary audiences. A higher degree of eroticism, for example, characterized the retellings. So did a greater emphasis on the individual's relationship with the deities of India. Social criticism and dissatisfaction with the ancient inflexibilities of the caste system appeared in their writings.

An important story that was often retold in various languages with different emphases was the CHAITANYA BHĀGAVATA —a verse life of the Hindu poet–saint Chaitanya (1485–1533). Chaitanya was thought to be an incarnation of the deity Krishna himself. In a related development Dānakrishna Dāsa's poetic composition RASAKALLOLA brought to hearers and readers in the Oriya language the wonderfully entertaining, erotic stories that center on the deity Krishna's adventures among an amorous group of milkmaids called *gopi*. Also of great literary significance was the compilation in the Punjabi language of the holy book of Sikhism, the ADI GRANTH.

Beyond the language families described, the introduction into northern India in the 16th century of Chaghtai Turkish and of Persian as the literary language of court culture among the emperors of the Mughal Empire also had literary consequences. In the former language a Mughal princess, GUL-BADAN BEGUM (1523–1603) possibly drafted a work that she subsequently translated into Persian, *The History of Humayun* (*Humāyūn-nāma*). A long series of Muhgal court poets and scholars wrote Persian poems such as GHAZELS and MESNEVÎ, prose histories of other imperial reigns, and translations of works from Indic languages into Persian.

This ongoing reworking in the 16th and 17th centuries of earlier literary works and traditions played an important role in unifying Indian culture despite the complex differences in languages spoken. Language differences often play a divisive role in human affairs. The efforts of Indian writers in the epoch we are considering helped overcome some of the suspicions that arise when people speak different languages.

Bibliography

Bright, William, ed. *International Encyclopedia of Linguistics.* New York and Oxford, U.K.: Oxford University Press, 1992.

Pollock, Sheldon, ed. *Literary Cultures in History: Reconstructions from South Asia.* Berkeley: University of California Press, 2003.

Pyles, Thomas, and John Algeo. *The Origins and Development of the English Language.* 4th edition. New York: Harcourt, Brace, Jovanovich College Publishers, 1993.

India, literature in (1500–1700)

The literature of 16th- and 17th-century India constitutes a vast mosaic. It includes both new texts and survivals into written culture of oral literary works and traditions whose roots finally disappear into the mists of very ancient times. It also involves literary output in at least 21 of the 22 languages of INDIA that are officially recognized by The Sahitya Akademi (National Academy of Letters) of India. This academy was founded in 1954, six years after the emergence of India from British rule. Its objectives are partly historical and partly political. Among its purposes is demonstrating that, despite the linguistic diversity of the subcontinent, its literature and intellectual culture make it a unified whole. At this writing, literary histories for 18 of the 22 regional and transregional tongues of India have appeared with the academy's support. One of the recognized languages of modern India is English, but the events that led to this fact occurred in and after the 18th century.

In treating the literature of any arbitrarily defined time period, to set the stage properly requires looking briefly at some important precursors.

Among these are the introduction on the Indian subcontinent of writing and the production and copying of manuscripts—activities that in India date as far back, at least, as the beginning of the first millennium. These ancient innovations made possible the preservation and, to some degree, the reconstruction of stories, literary types, and literary traditions that had been even earlier preserved in the memories of the singers of songs, the tellers of stories, the preachers of sermons, and the performers of drama. The ability to preserve such materials in writing, of course, encouraged the authors of literary works. It also gave rise to the usual associated set of professionals that accompany literature transmitted principally in manuscript. These persons include professional calligraphers, literary critics, exegetes who explain the meanings of metaphors and works, literary historians, biographers, patrons of literature, and appreciators—both readers and hearers of literature. The rise of a manuscript literature like India's often also involves an increase in the level of literacy among the populations.

At the same time, one does well to remember that literacy, though increasing, had not become widespread. So throughout the long period of manuscript culture, an oral literary culture continued (and continues) to flourish in India as well, and the two cultures interacted and interact.

All of these developments were in place on the Indian subcontinent before the beginning of the 16th century. They needed only a trigger to spark an important widespread literary flowering in Hindu India.

Though more than one trigger appeared, no single figure is more important for our considerations in this work than the poet-saint KABIR(1440–1518). His contributions to Indian letters were remarkable. His influence was instrumental in making the various Indian vernaculars widely acceptable as media for literary composition of the philosophic and religious sort and for poetic social criticism as well. He is revered as the founder of a movement of spiritual reawakening called BHAKTI that eventually spread to the furthest reaches of the subcontinent and that continued to inspire the production

of literature in many languages throughout the 16th and 17th centuries and beyond. Kabir's rejection of class distinctions, his unquestioned authority, his acceptance and preaching of individualism, and a kind of populism became hallmarks of a wide range of Indian texts and oral compositions in many languages in the succeeding centuries.

The 16th and 17th centuries also saw the emergence of several of India's regional languages themselves. The science of linguistics makes clear that language variation in the ages before mass electronic media was a local phenomenon. The language of your village and my neighboring village might be very much alike with just a few noticeable differences. Further afield, however, distinctions would become increasingly clear, and far enough away we would discover that, while what people were saying sounded familiar, we really could not understand much of what they said. Beyond that point, we might move into an area where we understood nothing. We might be in a separate language zone or, if the language we were hearing arose from the same source as our own, in the zone of a mutually unintelligible dialect. The process suggested here works in time as well as in space. Brajbasha, Hindi, and Bengali—important literary languages of North India—developed from Sanskrit and became languages of literary discourse during the 16th and 17th centuries.

Extra–Indian cultural contact and military activity also radically influenced the literary scene, particularly in northern India in the same time period. For 2,000 years the subcultures of India had exchanged mutual influences of many sorts with the culture of Persia. An era, however, of specifically literary, Persian, Islamic influences began to make themselves felt with increasing vigor from the 10th century on. Trade, warfare, and conquest brought Iranian–Persian literary culture (and military rule) into northwestern India along the Indus River. This expanded as far to the east as Delhi with the 12th- and 13th-century invasions of northern India by the Turks, who participated in Iranian–Persian literary culture. A further expansion of that culture occurred when a vast influx of refugees arrived, fleeing the invasion of Persia and north India by hoards of Mongolian and Turkish nomads under Timur (Tamerlane, 1336–1404; see *TAMBURLAINE*).

At the same time, native Indian elements were influencing the development of Persian letters with translation from indigenous Indian tongues appearing in Persian. Indeed, for a time in the early 16th century, it appeared that native languages would displace the Persian of the Islamic ruling classes in several regions.

These bidirectional influences had prepared the North Indian soil for a flowering of Indo–Persian literary activity that may well represent the high point of Persian poetry's achievement. This flowering accelerated with the arrival of the Mughals under BABUR (1483–1530).

Although the Mughals themselves were Chaghtai Turks who spoke a Turkish dialect called Turki, Babur and each of his successors, Humayan (1530–56) and AKBAR (1542–1605), also spoke Persian with varying degrees of mastery. All had occasion to call upon the Persian-speaking Iranians to assist them in military campaigns or, in Akbar's case, to counterbalance the revolutionary tendencies of some of his own people. All these Mughal emperors, but especially Akbar, developed a taste for Persian poetry and culture. Akbar made a special effort to import Persian-speaking scholars, intellectuals, and poets into his court at Agra.

Although Akbar himself had little if any formal education, he was interested in and patronized literary endeavors, and he especially enjoyed being read to in Persian. He established the post of poet laureate at his court, and of the several occupants between his reign and that of his Taj Mahal-building successor, Shāh Jahān (1592–1666), all but one laureate had Persian as a first language. It was the literary culture inspired by the Mughal court that produced many of the gems of Persian composition that compare favorably with others regardless of their place of origin.

Two native Indian developments and one foreign one effectively stemmed and eventually played an important role in reversing the spread of Persian literary culture in India. The first of these arose from a continuation of the bhakti movement mentioned above. Poets in the bhakti tradition wrote almost exclusively in the Indian vernacular languages. This meant that they shifted away from composition in Sanskrit—the ancient classical language of Indian letters and high culture—to the languages spoken and understood by common people. As many of the bhakti compositions were sung, they comprised the popular music of their epoch and, then as now, quickly won the hearts of the younger generation. Those who enjoyed the compositions of the poets in the bhakti tradition surely viewed the encouragement and cultivation of Persian court poetry as a hyperrefined taste of little interest to the masses. The bhakti poets were also more likely to feature individualism and social issues in their works—subjects of greater popular appeal than the traditional ones of the Persian tradition.

The second force countervailing the spread of Persian arose from the founding and growth of the Sikh religion and the eventual compilation of its holy book, the ADI GRANTH. Sikhism incorporated the humanistic emphasis of the bhakti poets. Like them, the Sikhs rejected caste distinctions and allowed for divine interest in individual human beings. Unlike the Hindu bhakti poets, the Sikhs rejected miracles, ritual purification, and idolatry. Because, like Christianity, Judaism, and Islam, Sikhism is a religion of the book, the massive literary enterprise that accompanied the compilation of the Adi Granth and its subsequent dissemination to every Sikh household encouraged literacy and preserved both a native tongue, Punjabi, and its native Gurmukhi script. Because the Sikhs were warlike and capable, they also posed a formidable barrier to further Islamic military expansion in northwestern India.

The foreign force that helped stem the tide of Persian language and Persian–Arabic script for the representation of native Indian languages was the 18th-century success of the British East India Company in dominating the subcontinent for about 200 years, but that is another story.

Bibliography

Datta, Amaresh, et. al. *Encyclopedia of Indian Literature.* 6 volumes. New Delhi: Sahitya Akademi, 1987–1994.

Gonda, Jan J. *History of Indian Literature.* 10 vols. Wiesbaden: Harrassowitz, 1974–?

Pollock, Sheldon, ed. *Literary Cultures in History: Reconstructions from South Asia.* Berkeley: University of California Press, 2003.

Varma, Siddheshwar. *G. A. Grierson's Linguistic Survey of India; a Summary.* Hoshiapur, India: Vishveshvaranand Institute, Panjab University, 1972–76.

inkhorn terms

Writers of the English Renaissance often felt that the word stock of the ENGLISH LANGUAGE did not provide as flexible an instrument for the full expression of their thoughts and feelings as had ancient Latin and Greek. A number of authors attempted to remedy that perceived defect by introducing into English terms that had been borrowed from other languages. Such terms often struck their readers or auditors as strange and un-English, and as those who introduced them were often pedants and preachers with ink-stained fingers who used hollow cows' horns as portable inkwells, the words came to be known as inkhorn terms. Some of them appeared once or a few times and found their way to history's trash heap. Others became standard fixtures in a language forever growing, changing, and open to novel vocabulary and usage.

Here is a list of words that many considered inkhorn terms when they first appeared but that have become standard in the language: *affability, capacity, celebrate, expending, frivolous,* and *ingenious.* Here is a list of inkhorn terms that did not survive in the standard tongue: *fatigate, ingent, magnifical,* and *revoluting.*

inquisition

Early in the 13th century, regional authorities of the Roman Catholic Church began to appoint individual clergymen to look into alleged cases of heresy—that is, of serious nonconformity to the official views of the church on matters of belief and doctrine. In the Renaissance, however, four separate offices of Inquisition were established, in Spain in 1478, in the New World in 1522, in Portugal in the late 1530s, and finally in Rome in 1542.

The Renaissance Spanish and Portuguese Inquisitions differed from the others by being under at least the nominal control of secular rather than of religious authority. Clergymen, however, administered the day-to-day operations of the inquisitions in both countries. In Spain, numerous Jews had converted to Christianity. Many anti-Jewish Christians erroneously suspected that such converts (*conversos*) privately continued to observe the faith of their fathers. The Inquisition in Spain concerned itself particularly with looking into the Christian orthodoxy of such nominal converts. More persons found guilty were pardoned than were executed, and persons who had never converted to Christianity either from Islam or Judaism were not subject to the inquisitors' authority. Nonetheless, during its bloodiest years, ca. 1480–1530, the Spanish Inquisition put to death as many as 2,000 converts found, rightly or wrongly, to have reverted to their original religions.

The Portuguese Inquisition proceeded from similar concerns about backsliding former non-Christians. It also looked into allegations of bigamy, Protestantism, sacrilege, and witchcraft. Not only did the Portuguese Inquisition conduct its work on the European mainland, but it also operated in Goa, Portugal's colony in India. From there it also kept watch over Portugal's other Asian possessions. No office of the Inquisition was established, however, in Portuguese Brazil. Officers in the homeland conducted whatever business was necessary there. Between 1536 and 1674, 1,515 people died at the stake in Portugal proper and at least another 103 in Goa between 1562 and 1605. These figures take no account of other punishments meted out by the inquisitors, such as condemnation to serve as galley slaves, confiscation of belongings, exile, and beatings.

In comparison, the activities of the Roman inquisitors were hedged about with greater safeguards for the accused. Torture was the recourse of last resort in the examination of the accused and never occurred until the defense had made its case. Life sentences were usually commuted after three years, and only the most recalcitrant among the accused found their way to the stake. Even there, John Tedeschi tells us, the Romans usually eased the passing of those sentenced to burn. Noblemen were first beheaded, commoners strangled, and even those who could under no circumstances be persuaded to return to the fold had bags of gunpowder hung around their necks to hasten their passing. Fewer than 200 persons seem to have died at the hands of the Roman Inquisition.

With respect to literature, of course, the work of the Roman Inquisition among writers is widely known. The astronomer Galileo Galilei famously recanted rather than face the possible sentences open to the inquisitors. The pantheistic philosopher, GIORDANO BRUNO, who supported the views of the astronomer NICHOLAS COPERNICUS, suffered death by burning in 1599 after a seven-year-long trial. The Italian theologian and writer, TOMMASO CAMPANELLA, whose theological opinion favored Galileo in the run-up to the astronomer's trial, also found himself the victim of the Spanish Inquisition. He fell under their authority because the Spaniards ruled the Kingdom of Naples. Condemned to death both as a heretic and as a traitor to the Spanish state, Campanella escaped burning by feigning madness. Insane people, because they were irresponsible, could not be condemned.

To be published in the territories where the inquisitors held sway, of course, books required licensing. Many a book was long suppressed, and others totally lost because their contents did not satisfy the inquisitors. In the countries where the Inquisitions held sway, many disapproved books never found their way to the press. Disapproved books imported from other countries were subject to seizure so that the work of the Inquisition had a chilling economic effect on some aspects of the book trade. The ALDINE PRESS in Venice, Italy, played a long cat-and-mouse game with the Venetian office of the Roman Inquisition to publish important books that seemed likely to raise questions. Unauthorized translations of the Bible were particularly disapproved. The English translator WILLIAM TYNDALE suffered a heretic's death (1536) in Antwerp, then under the authority of the Spanish Inquisition, for making available a fine but forbidden translation of the BIBLE IN ENGLISH.

Ironically, the activities of the Inquisition continued longest in the New World—in Mexico until 1834. There, in addition to overseeing the adherence of the faithful to the faith, the Inquisition extended its jurisdiction to include priests who abused the confessional by soliciting sexual favors and to impersonators of clerics. In its zeal to uncover backsliding Jewish converts, in 1596, the Mexican Inquisition brought to trial the notable Jewish family of Luis de Carvajal.

Bibliography

Giles, Mary E. *Women in the Inquisition: Spain and the New World*. Baltimore: Johns Hopkins University Press, ca. 1999.

Haliczer, Stephen. *Sexuality in the Confessional: A Sacrament Profaned*. New York: Oxford University Press, 1996.

Herculano, Alexandre. *History of the Origin and Establishment of the Inquisition in Portugal*. Translated by John C. Banner. New York: Ktav Publishing House, 1972.

Netanyahu, Benzion. *The Origins of the Inquisition in Fifteenth Century Spain*. New York: New York Review Books, 2001.

Tedeschi, John A. *The Prosecution of Heresy: Collected Studies on the Inquisition in Early Modern Italy*. Binghamton, N.Y.: Medieval & Renaissance Texts & Studies, 1991.

Toro, Alfonso. *The Carvajal Family: Jews and the Inquisition in New Spain in the Sixteenth Century*. El Paso: Texas Western Press, ca. 2002.

interlude

A short dramatic entertainment sometimes presented between the courses at banquets, the interlude has roots that penetrate back into the medieval morality play. By Renaissance times in England the interlude had developed two apparently conflicting characteristics. It often treated as an ALLEGORY some moral subject. By contrast, it also often developed some bawdy theme, like a priest and a housewife deceiving her husband. As the interlude continued its development in England, it also revealed an interest in HUMANIST topics.

Among the first exclusively secular plays in England, Henry Medwall's (fl. 1490) interlude *Fulgens and Lucres* (ca. 1499) has as its source a short story written in Latin by the Italian humanist, Bonaccorso da Montemagno. Medwall makes significant changes in the story, however. Lucretia is the daughter of Fulgentius, a Roman senator. She has two suitors, a worldly, rich aristocrat and a virtuous poor young man. Whereas Bonaccorso's Fulgentius gives the choice to the Roman Senate for decision, Medwall sensibly leaves the choice to the girl. He also adds a subplot in which two servants of the principals compete for the hand of Lucretia's maid. The main plot is serious, but the subplot is comic—a practice that sets the stage for many later plays in the annals of English theater.

Topics of interest to humanists also provided grist for the mills of the authors of interludes. John Redford's (d. 1547) interlude *Wit and Science* (ca. 1535) follows the allegorical career of a student, Wit, as he pursues the hand of Science, the daughter of Reason and Experience. In his efforts to win her, Wit must overcome a series of obstacles familiar to students everywhere. Attractive characters tempt him (sometimes successfully) to drink and party. A giant, Tedium, whom Wit must defeat, presents a particular challenge, and the would-be groom of Science must also complete a pilgrimage to Mount Parnassus. In a similar vein, John Rastell's (d. 1536) interlude, *The Nature of the Four Elements* (early 16th century), mines the popular interest in exploration and discovery. Allegorical characters instruct Humanity in geography and the latest scientific findings. Humanity, in the meantime, must resist the temptations of various characters who represent the several vices. These two plays mark the beginning of a serious educational thrust in the English theater.

A popular author of interludes that emphasized pleasing over instructing, John Heywood (ca. 1497–ca. 1580), wrote to order for entertainments given by aristocrats and the wealthy. Several of his works survive: *Witty and Witless* and the *Play of Love* amuse by offering spirited debates between characters that represent types. *The Play Called the Four PP* is a favorite among Heywood's works. In it a palmer (a religious mendicant), a peddler, a pardoner (one who sold church indulgences that were supposed to reduce the time a sinner spent in Purgatory), and a 'pothecary (apothecary), fall in together as they travel along a road. Discussing the tools of their trades, they discover that what they share in common is the ability to tell lies. Thus they decide that, with the peddler as judge, they will pass their time on the road with a lying contest. The apothecary goes first, recounting in bawdy detail a miraculous cure he affected. The pardoner follows, telling how the husband of a champion shrew, Margery Corson, found himself desolate after his wife died. He missed her abuse. The husband hired the pardoner to go to Hell and bring his wife back. In Hell, the pardoner asks Satan to restore Margery to life. Complaining that Hell has not been a fit place for anyone since Margery came, Satan agrees, and the pardoner takes her home.

At the end of this story, the palmer observes that he finds the lie difficult to believe since he has never known a shrewish woman. At that the peddler awards the palmer the prize—a sack of flour—without further ado.

Other examples of Heywood's interludes survive including a bawdy deception of a husband by his wife and a priest, *A Merry Play between Johan Johan the Husband, Tyb his Wife, and Sir Johan the Priest.* Still another is *The Play of the Weather* that amusingly demonstrates that since everyone prefers a different sort of weather, things are best left as they are.

The interlude sometimes served as propaganda in the Protestant cause in England. John Bale (1495–1563) wrote such dramas as *King John.* In this play the king is presented as a character who flaunts papal edicts to make the Bible accessible to English readers. The allegorical characters of the earlier morality plays appear here, not as the traditional vices, but rather as abstract representations of what Bale considered Roman Catholic faults: Clergy, Dissimulation, Sedition, and Usurped Power. What Bale views as Protestant virtues also appear as such characters as Nobility and Civil Order. Sometimes the allegorical figures morph into historical ones, as when Usurped Power becomes the pope. Bale wrote other interludes on religious subjects—all in the interests of militant Protestantism.

Bibliography

Axton, Richard, ed. *Three Rastell Plays: Four Elements; Calisto and Melebea; Gentleness and Nobility.* Cambridge, U.K., and Totowa, N.J.: D. S. Brewer and Rowman & Littlefield, 1979.

Bale, John. *The Complete Plays of John Bale.* Edited by Peter Happé. Dover, N.H.: Boyell and Brewer, 1985.

Heywood, John. *The Plays of John Heywood.* Edited by Richard Axton and Peter Happé. Cambridge, U.K.: D. S. Brewer, 1991.

Moeslin, M. E., ed. *The Plays of Henry Medwall: A Critical Edition.* New York: Garland Publishing, 1981.

Recently Recovered "Lost" Tudor Plays with some Others. [Includes Redford's *Wit and Science.*] 1907. New York: Barnes and Noble, 1966.

intertextuality

Intertextuality may be described as the conversation that literary texts conduct with one another through direct or veiled allusion to their predecessors. Julia Kristeva, who labeled the idea, suggests that all discourses operate under the control of rules established by earlier works. Some writers in the Renaissance, like EDMUND SPENSER, JOHN MILTON, and ERASMUS seem to perceive many of those rules quite consciously so that the fabric of their writing bristles with both overt and subtle allusion to earlier texts. The degree to which texts and readers participate in that intertextual conversation varies as both the writer and the reader are aware or unaware of the system of prior texts within which a new one operates.

Bibliography

Kristeva, Julia. *Desire in Language: A Semiotic Approach to Literature and Art.* Edited by Leon S. Roudiez. Translated by Thomas Gora, Alice Jardine, and Leon S. Roudiez. New York: Columbia University Press, 1980.

Iphigénie (*Iphigenia*) Jean Racine (1674)

Many ancient poets and dramatists wrote versions of the story of King Agamemnon's sacrifice of his daughter, Iphigenia, to procure a favorable wind for the Greek fleet's invasion of Troy. RACINE carefully studied several of them and combined their stories to give French theater a new version.

Racine's play opens with Agamemnon's describing for his officer, Arcas, the conflict the king feels at the gods' price for a following wind. At the urging of his followers, Agamemnon has lured his daughter and his wife to the Greek camp by pretending to have arranged Iphigenia's marriage to Achilles. As they are enroute, however, he repents, changes his mind, and sends them a message to remain where they are. He alleges that Achilles has postponed the wedding until after the war. He tells Arcas to find the women and escort them home.

At that moment (Act I, scene ii) Achilles and Ulysses enter. Achilles has learned of his engagement to Iphigenia and is very pleased. When the young hero leaves, however, Ulysses reminds Agamemnon of his duty and of the precedence that public welfare takes over private happiness. Agamemnon argues ineffectually against Ulysses but nevertheless resolves to save his daughter by sending her home.

Ulysses once more urges public duty, and Agamemnon assures him that he would feel differently if his son Telemachus were the designated victim. At that moment another officer, Eurybates, arrives to announce the landing of Iphigenia, Clytemnestra, and a Trojan subject, a slave girl and captive of Achilles, Eriphyle. Act I ends with the torn Agamemnon opting once again for doing his duty.

Act II opens with Eriphyle expressing to her companion, Doris, the grief she feels because she is ignorant of her parentage. An oracle has told her, moreover, that if she learns her true parentage she will die. Doris tries to gloss over that prophecy by suggesting that she will die to her old identity to assume a new one.

The conversation then turns to the topic of Eriphyle's capture and ravishment (which can mean kidnapping or rape or both) at Achilles' hands. In the next instant it emerges that she is in love with her captor and that her true reason for having asked Iphigenia and Clytemnestra to bring her with them is to try to prevent the wedding.

In the next scene, Agamemnon and Iphigenia meet. Iphigenia is surprised at her father's reserve and sadness at seeing her. She mentions that she has heard of an upcoming sacrifice, and her father promises that she will be there. They part with the daughter confused at her reception but happy and confident about her future.

Scene iv finds Clytemnestra attributing her cool reception to Achilles' having postponed the wedding. Although Eriphyle has given as her reason for coming a desire to find out her parentage from the seer Chalchas, Clytemnestra shrewdly guesses that another man (Achilles) is her real motivation. In the following scene, Iphigenia picks up on her mother's hint and accuses Eriphyle of wanting Achilles for herself. After an exchange of ladylike remonstrances, an emotional Iphigenia accuses Eriphyle of reveling in Iphigenia's grief at her postponed wedding.

In scene vi, Achilles, delighted at Iphigenia's arrival, enters, only to be greeted with scornful chilliness; then Iphigenia withdraws. In view of the confusion, Eriphyle senses a turmoil in the offing—a storm in which fate may advance her interests.

As the third act begins, Agamemnon, who has resolved once more to proceed with the sacrifice, tries to convince Clytemnestra not to accompany her daughter to the altar to give her away in marriage, as was customary. When Clytemnestra objects, Agamemnon commands her to obey.

In the fourth scene of Act III, Iphigenia asks Achilles for a wedding present. She pleads that he free his slave, Eriphyle; Achilles willingly does so. That happy scene, however, is followed by one in which Arcas reveals to Clytemnestra Iphigenia's upcoming sacrifice. Clytemnestra consigns her daughter to Achilles' protection and vows that, before anyone will strike her daughter, they will have to burn her mother.

In scene v Achilles rants against Agamemnon to Iphigenia. She, however, seeks to calm Achilles and suggests that her sacrifice may be necessary for the success of the Greek cause and for the public good. Clytemnestra then enters and reports she has been barred from the ceremony. Achilles is about to go forth and attempt a violent resolution to the entire problem when Iphigenia stops him and says that if she is late, her father will soon come for her.

The fourth act opens with Eriphyle claiming to envy Iphigenia's fate. Then a plan occurs to Eri-

phyle. She can thwart the Greeks' designs on Troy, she thinks, by telling everyone everything she knows. In the next scene, confronted with evidence of his own duplicity, Agamemnon confesses to his wife and his daughter but claims that he is forced to this sacrifice by the will of the Greeks. In the face of their determination, he says, a king is only a pawn to the will of the people. He encourages Iphigenia to die with the honor and dignity befitting her royal blood.

Not buying her husband's self-serving rationalization, Clytemnestra retorts that he is a true son of Atreus. The house of Atreus, Agamemnon's forbear, is cursed through all its generations because of the horrible revenge Atreus visited on his enemy Thyestes. He fed Thyestes the flesh of Thyestes' own murdered children at a banquet. The very sun turned its back in horror.

In Act V, scene vi, Achilles confronts Agamemnon. Hot words are exchanged. Agamemnon, however, surprises Achilles by saying that it is his own overweening desire to conquer Asia that is the real culprit in the situation. Had Achilles not whipped up the Greeks' greed and bloodlust, a favorable wind would not be necessary. Angered by Achilles, Agamemnon resolves once more to go through with the sacrifice. At the next moment, however, he recoils from that decision, calls Clytemnestra, and instructs her to flee with Iphigenia but not to let Chalcas or Ulysses see them go.

Eriphyle, however, has overheard these instructions. She resolves to reveal all to Chalcas. As a result, the escape attempt fails as the alerted Greeks herd the women back to the camp. Achilles then tries to convince Iphigenia to allow him to take her to his tents where he and his troops can protect her against all comers. She refuses, praying that a thunderbolt will strike her dead and resolve the entire issue.

Now Achilles and the others learn that Eriphyle has betrayed them and that the Greeks have taken sides and are fighting each other.

The prophet Chalcas, however, in the final scene steps between the warring factions and clarifies the gods' intentions. Helen, he explains, by a secret first marriage to Theseus of Athens, bore a daughter who was also named Iphigenia. Fearing to reveal that marriage to Menelaus, Helen exiled her first daughter under the name Eriphyle. It is Helen's Iphigenia, not her sister Clytemnestra's, whom the gods want for a sacrifice.

Recognizing the truth of the seer's words and the fulfillment of the fateful prophecy about her, the melancholy Eriphyle forestalls the necessity for a sacrifice by taking her own life on the altar. No sooner has she plunged the knife into her body than the audience hears thunder, and an offshore wind begins to ruffle the heretofore glazen sea.

Bibliography

Racine, Jean. *The Complete Plays*. 2 vols. Translated and edited by Samuel Solomon. New York: Random House, 1967.

Italian language, the issue of (*La questione della lingua*)

Writing just before the end of the Italian Middle Ages, in his Latin treatise *On the eloquence of the language of everyday life* (*De vulgare eloquentia*), DANTE ALIGHIERI (1265–1321) defended the use of the Italian language as a medium of literary expression. Even now, many regional and even local dialects are heard in Italy. Some of those dialects are mutually unintelligible although most Italians share in common at least a basic mastery of school Italian.

In Dante's time, the Italian linguistic situation was even more confused, and, in a polyglot Europe, many shared the opinion that serious writing should be done in Latin—a language that literate people throughout the British Isles and Continental Europe shared as a second tongue. Dante, however, thought that the vernacular languages—particularly his Tuscan tongue—possessed all the same resources for the expression of thought and feelings as did the great literary languages of the past. In Italy, Tuscan seemed particularly privileged for literary discourse as the tongue shared by the "three crowns" (*tre corone*) of Italian letters: Dante himself, GIOVANNI BOCCACCIO (1313–75), and the writer whose life and work marked the transition in Italy from the Middle Ages to the Renaissance, FRANCIS PETRARCH (FRANCESCO PETRARCA, 1304–74).

Following Dante the cause of the vernacular language found a champion in LORENZO DE' MEDICI (1449–92), the uncrowned prince of Florence. A gifted poet in his own right, Lorenzo also wrote defending the use of the vernacular, restating many of Dante's arguments, and adding some of his own. In his influential *Treatise on Italian Prose* (1525), Cardinal PIETRO BEMBO (1470–1547) also took up the cause of the Tuscan vernacular as the appropriate tongue for writers in Italian. Bembo weakened his case among writers more gifted than he by insisting that only a purified version of the now archaic language as Petrarch and Boccaccio had used it was appropriate for serious literary work. For the most part, though, Bembo's contemporaries were grateful for his support of vernacular letters and ignored the specifics of his advice. Only a few, such as the unsavory but brilliant PIETRO ARETINO (1492–1556), were rude enough to challenge Bembo's pedantry openly. Bembo's friend and admirer BALDESSARE CASTIGLIONE (1478–1529), however, did suggest in his enormously influential book, THE BOOK OF COURTIER (1528), that the use of antiquated Tuscan phrases amounted to an affectation and should be avoided in favor of harmonious and graceful, contemporary expressions.

Around 1540 Cosimo de' Medici founded the Florentine Academy, which took up the cause of the Tuscan tongue. It was succeeded in 1582 by the ACADEMY OF THE CROSS, which proposed to purify the Italian language and provide for it a literary standard. During centuries of activity and with much help from gifted Italian writers, the academy has succeeded in this mission. Today the best Italian is considered to be the language of Tuscany, spoken with a Roman flavor.

Italian sonnet

The Italian sonnet appeared sometime during the second decade of the 13th century. The earliest surviving example is a sonnet by the Sicilian Giacomo da Lentino. Practiced by the poets of "the sweet new style," the form served DANTE for a sequence of sonnets entitled *La Vita Nuova*. The greatest Italian practitioner of the form was

FRANCESCO PETRARCA. Petrarch's Fragments of things in the language of ordinary life (*Rerum vulgarium fragmenta*) or Songbook (*Canzoniere*) as it is everywhere known, became the model for sonnet cycles throughout Europe. Although Antonio da Tempo identified 16 possible varieties and more subvarieties of Italian sonnet, Petrarch's examples usually consisted of eight lines rhyming abba abba—an octave or two quatrains—and six lines rhyming *cde cde*, *cde dce*, or *cdc dcd*. The Italian sonnet's line was typically 11 syllables long—a hendecasyllabic line—and the meter was usually iambic. Sonnets were also exchanged as letters between friends (see EPISTOLARY SONNETS) and were written about an enormous variety of subjects. LORENZO DE' MEDICI, the uncrowned ruler of Florence, was himself a talented poet who wrote sonnets. He considered the form the noblest in the Italian language because a sonnet's formal requirements challenged poets to express deep thought and intense feeling in a concentrated package.

From Italy, the sonnet fanned out across the Continent. The marqués de Santillana brought it to Spain in the 15th century. In France, RONSARD wrote some with Alexandrine lines (with 12 syllables and four emphatic beats in French). Others favored the 10 syllable line, and DU BELLAY composed a Petrarchan sonnet sequence, *L'Olive,* in 1549. FRANÇOIS DE MALHERBE established the conventional from of the French sonnet.

After Petrarch himself, CAMÕENS in Portugal was perhaps the most notable Renaissance sonneteer on the continent. MARTIN OPITZ and G. R. Weckerlin introduced it to Germany. (See ENGLISH SONNET.)

Cycles of sonnets were written on every imaginable topic. One, still in manuscript in the Marciana Library in Venice, gives directions for sailing to various places in the Mediterranean Sea.

Bibliography

Medici, Lorenzo de'. *The Autobiography of Lorenzo de' Medici: A Commentary on my Sonnets.* Translated and edited by James Wyatt Cook, 1996. Reprint, Phoenix: University of Arizona Press, 2000.

Petrarca, Francesco. *Petrarch's Songbook: Rerum vulgarium fragmenta.* Translated by James Wyatt Cook. Introduced by Germaine Warkentin. Binghamton, N.Y.: Medieval and Renaissance Texts and Studies, 1997.

Shipley, Joseph T. *Dictionary of World Literary Terms.* Boston: The Writer, Inc. 1970.

J

Jack of Newberry
See *Pleasant Historie of John Winchcomb . . .*

James I of England (James VI of Scotland) (1556–1625)

James, who was the son of Mary Queen of Scots, founded the Stuart line in England when he succeeded his cousin, Queen Elizabeth I, on England's throne in 1603. Best remembered from a literary perspective for his nominal sponsorship of the so-called King James version of the English Bible, James was in fact a scholarly person. He patronized the arts and learning, encouraging dramatic performance by underwriting a portion of the expenses of the King's Men—William Shakespeare's dramatic company. Playwrights such as Ben Jonson and the landscape architect Inigo Jones enjoyed royal favor and were commissioned to produce elaborate and spectacular court entertainments and masques for James and his aristocratic entourage.

Before Sir Francis Bacon's political disgrace, he enjoyed James's favor and during his reign was appointed to a succession of high offices. Bacon dedicated some of his best work to the king.

Sometimes called "the wisest fool in Christendom," James insisted on the doctrine of the divine right of kings that held rulers to be God's appointed viceroys for secular matters on Earth. This conviction did not sit well with Englishmen whose hereditary freedoms suggested that, like them, the king was subject to the operation of the law. Some have thought that Shakespeare's play *King Lear* presents a tactful reminder to the king of royalty's essential humanity and mortality.

Jayisi, Malik Mohammad (1477–1542)

An Islamic poet and saint of the Sufi sect, Jayisi lived in India and wrote in early Hindi (also called Avadhi). Jayisi drew his inspiration largely from ordinary Hindu life, from Hindu narrative, and from Hindu poetic form—though not so much from Hindu scriptural or philosophic writings. Considerations of love, both worldly and otherworldly, provided him with his central topic. One of the tenets of Sufism calls to mind the Western concept of Platonic love. The lover, by progressively and devotedly loving a beloved's physical, intellectual, and moral attributes, rises at last to an understanding of love as the central principle of the cosmos. Jayisi subscribed to this belief. As a disciple of the Hindu poet saint Kabir, Jayisi subscribed to Indo–Muslim thinking that reflected his belief in the peaceful coexistence of Islam, Hinduism, and all other religions. He thought they represented varying paths to the same central truth.

According to literary historian Abdul Qavi Desnavi, Jayisi penned as many as 24 books. In the author's own lifetime, of course, these circulated in manuscript. Up until now, only six have been printed. Four of Jayisi's books are poetic narratives. The first, his EPIC masterpiece, *The PADUMĀVATI* (1540), tells the tragic love story of the Princess Padumavati and King Rata Sen. The poem is considered the outstanding epic achievement of its era. Readers value it for its lush descriptions of the physical charms of the princess and for its emphasis on social justice. Jayisi values the virtue of charity as the highest of human qualities. He despises wrath and killing and encourages self-control, chastity, nonviolence, the preservation of human life, and justice.

A shorter piece of narrative verse, *Chitrarekha* (ca. 1530–40), tells the comedic story of a princess of that name and her love for Prince Pritam Singh. It features ironic humor and a series of dramatic coincidences. Still another short narrative poem, *Akhiri kalam*, recounts in Hindi verse the Koran's version of the day of doom.

The earliest written of Jayisi's narratives, *Kaharanama* (The history of Kahara, ca. 1477–1504) provides the first exploration of subjective experience in the Hindi language. Another love story, it begins a small subgenre of Hindi verse that deals with the exploration of internal emotional states.

The other two works that have seen publication are both collections of couplets. One, *Maslanama*, is a collection of Hindi proverbs that takes its title from an Arabic word with the meaning "proverb." The other, entitled *Akhravat*, is an alphabetically organized series of couplets that illustrate the concepts of the Sufi way of life.

The importance of Jayisi's work derives first from the wonderful musicality of his verse and also from the way he interweaves the themes of Islamic Sufi culture with material from the daily lives of his Hindu neighbors and the forms and meters of Hindi poetry.

Bibliography

Jayisi, Malik Mohammad. *The Padumawati* [sic] *of Malik Muhammad Jaisi*. Edited and translated by G. A. Grierson and Sudhākara Dvivedi. Calcutta: Asiatic Society, 1911.

Pollock, Sheldon, ed. Literary Cultures in History: Reconstructions from South Asia. Berkeley: University of California Press, 2003.

Jerusalem Delivered (*Gerusalemme liberata*) Torquato Tasso (1580 and 1581)

At the time of the unlicensed publication of his great verse EPIC, the Italian poet and playwright TORQUATO TASSO was languishing in an asylum for the insane. With a feigned regard for the poet's health his patron, Duke Alfonso II d' Este of Ferrara, had confined Tasso there. In fact, however, the duke wished to keep Tasso from defecting to the Medici family of Florence who had offered the poet their patronage. Duke Alfonso did not want the major epic of the CATHOLIC COUNTER-REFORMATION in Italy dedicated to his Florentine rivals.

Composed in 20 cantos of *ottava rima*—the eight-line rhymed stanza favored by many Italian poets of the epoch—*Jerusalem Delivered* takes as its subject the factual and imagined events that occurred during a 40-day period in the first Christian crusade against the Muslims in the year 1099. Much of the action occurs in the Christian encampment outside the city walls of Jerusalem. The poem brings together the events of the crusade, the courage and zeal of Jerusalem's Christian community, the cruelty of Aladine, king of Jerusalem, and the usual material of the CHIVALRIC EPIC—the loves of knights and ladies, feats of arms, and charms and wizardry.

When the epic opens, the Christian forces—called the Franks by the Muslim defenders—have already campaigned for six years in the Middle East and have captured Antioch from the Syrians. Wearied with campaigning, many of the principal heroes of the Christian cause are focused on enhancing their own chivalric reputations or on the love affairs they find themselves conducting. The new Christian governor of Antioch, however—Behemondo—is busy consolidating his position there, and the French nobleman Godfrey of Bouillon (ca. 1060–1100) is pressing his allies for an all-out assault on Jerusalem. In his determination to attack, Godfrey has the support of supernatural allies. Both the angel Gabriel and the Eternal Father himself urge Godfrey to the attack.

Convinced at last that the time for assault has come, with Godfrey as their general, thousands of Crusaders representing the nations of Europe pass in review under the banners of their leaders and march toward Jerusalem.

In response to news of their coming, King Aladine imposes oppressive taxes on the Christian inhabitants of Jerusalem to pay for the city's defense against the Christians' co-religionists. A former Christian convert to Islam, the magician Ismero advises Aladine that Jerusalem could become impregnable if the statue of the Virgin Mary were stolen from the Christian temple and installed in the mosque. Aladine accepts the advice, but the statue immediately disappears. Enraged, the king condemns all his Christian subjects. A heroic Christian girl, Sophronia, however, falsely confessed to the theft to spare her people. Olindo, a young man in love with Sophronia, tries in turn to save her by claiming responsibility. The king thinks that the two should die together at the stake. At the last moment, however, a Muslim amazon, Clorinda, convinces the king that Allah had been offended by the statue and has removed it.

Coming at last to Jerusalem, the Christians, fervent with zeal at the sight of the city, weep, remove their shoes and helmets, and walk barefoot as pilgrims toward the holy place. Inside the city's walls, the defenders prepare for siege. Under the leadership of Clorinda, a raiding party rides out from the city and attacks the Christian column. One of the Christian heroes, Tancredi, has for some time been in love with Clorinda. Recognizing her, he refuses to fight. This action continues for some time with losses on both sides until the Muslim raiders are finally driven back into the protection of the city walls. The Christians bury their dead and begin to build battering rams and siege engines that will enable them to breach Jerusalem's fortifications.

Now the Muslims receive help from supernatural allies. Satan musters Hell's forces, rallying them to the cause of the Islamic defenders. (One must remember that Tasso was a Christian partisan.) The hellish forces resolve to work by means of guile, employing the abilities of a magician of Damascus, Idraotes. This sorcerer sends his niece, a matchless beauty named Armida, to make the Christians love her and divert them from their objective. She works her wiles on Godfrey but finds him proof against them. When she leaves camp, however, several enchanted young Christians follow her—including Godfrey's younger brother Eustace and the hero Rinaldo.

As is usual in chivalric epics, one situation evolves rapidly into another. Jealous of Rinaldo, founder of the Este line, the besotted Eustace spreads false rumors to undermine the warrior's reputation. The Egyptians mount an effort to relieve besieged Jerusalem. One of its defenders, Argantes, issues a general challenge to meet any Christian in single combat. Many volunteer, but Tancredi is chosen. On his way to fight, Tancredi sees his beloved Clorinda among the spectators and falls into such a love-struck reverie that another Christian, Otho, has to ride out to remind him of his duty. Though they fight furiously, neither Tancredi nor Argantes can get the better of the other. They fight until the light fails, and, both suffering from many wounds, they agree to continue on the next day. Just as Tancredi loves Clorinda, so the king of Antioch's daughter, Erminia, loves Tancredi. Skilled in medicine, she wishes to help heal his wounds. She therefore disguises herself as Clorinda and rides out of Jerusalem in search of Tancredi. The crusaders, however, intercept her and pursue her to a forest where she finds shelter with a shepherd and his wife. Hearing that Clorinda is about, Tancredi rides out in search of her but instead finds Armida, who enchants him with her beauty and, to his endless shame, imprisons him.

A substitute, Count Raimondo, fights Argantes in place of Tancredi. A treacherous arrow from the pagan ranks, however, starts a general melee that the Christians seem about to win when Satan sends a storm that ends the battle. More bad news follows. Sweno, king of Denmark, had been bringing up reinforcements from Greece but had been intercepted, defeated, and slain. Of all his forces, only one man survived to bring news to Godfrey and Sweno's sword to Rinaldo.

Further near disasters afflict the Christians. Godfrey must endure a mutiny, the Sultan Suleyman arrives with reinforcements for the king of Jerusalem, and only the intervention of the archangel Michael saves the crusaders from Suleyman's night attack. Clorinda succeeds in destroying the crusaders' siege engines—though she in turn is slain by Tancredi when she refuses to tell him her name. Before she dies in his arms, she converts to Christianity. Still, the Christian cause often seems on the verge of being lost. Despite their many difficulties—including suffering from great heat and lack of water—Godfrey's unfailing piety assures the crusaders the continual intervention of heavenly supporters.

Before the Christians can overcome the Muslim defenders of the city, however, they must regain Rinaldo's services. A lengthy digression takes the reader and several of the Christian crusaders on a search for the hero. This includes a stop at the abode of Peter the Hermit who explains how the searchers can avoid Armida's enchantments. Then the search party gets a flying boat tour of much of the known world, complete with a prequel to the voyages of CHRISTOPHER COLUMBUS and the discovery of the New World. The worldly landscape, however, soon fades from the reader's view, and an imaginary one takes its place as Tasso leads his reader past the Fortunate Isles and the Elysian Fields of ancient story to a dragon-guarded island where the sensuous Armida keeps the enchanted Rinaldo, with his head in her lap, under her amorous spell.

The searchers have been equipped with the diamond shield of a friendly wizard. On locating Rinaldo, the searchers show him his reflection in its MAGIC surface where he sees himself as he appears to others. Disgusted with himself, he deserts Armida, who by this time has fallen in love with him, and rejoins the crusaders. Furious, Armida offers her hand in marriage to anyone who kills Rinaldo.

Safely away from Armida's garden, Rinaldo confesses his sins to Peter the Hermit and sees reflected in the diamond shield both the past and future glories of his ancestors and descendents of the house of Este. The Egyptians meanwhile advance to try to raise the siege of Jerusalem. Tancredi's clever squire, Vafrino, disguises himself, planning to infiltrate the Egyptian camp and spy on the enemy. A captured carrier pigeon's message informs the Christians that the Egyptians will arrive in four days to support Jerusalem's defenders.

Hoping to overthrow the city before that time, Godfrey has his troops receive the last rites of the church, and the crusaders attack. Tasso's descriptions of the ensuing battle are exciting, graphic, and bloody. They include wizards and witches, medieval battering rams and assault towers, and individual acts of heroism as well. Tancredi and Argantes renew their duel. Tancredi triumphs but faints from loss of blood. Erminia, the Syrian princess who loves him, finds him senseless on the field and joyfully has him carried to safety and her tender care.

The Egyptians arrive before the crusaders can overcome a determined resistance. With them comes a troop of suitors for the hand of Armida. Rinaldo vanquishes each of them in turn, and the tide of battle turns in the crusaders' favor. Catching sight of Armida, Rinaldo pursues her, overtaking her just in time to prevent her suicide. At the sight of Rinaldo, Armida's hatred evaporates. She confesses her love and promises to become a Christian and wed him.

Finally the crusaders prove triumphant. Godfrey behaves as generously to his former enemies in victory as he was their determined foe in battle. The victorious Christians celebrate their success by devoutly praying at the Holy Sepulcher.

Bibliography

Tasso, Torquato. *Jerusalem Delivered.* Translated by Anthony M. Esolen. Baltimore: Johns Hopkins University Press, 2000.

Jew of Malta, The Christopher Marlowe (ca. 1588)

The title character of MARLOWE'S play, Barabas, is a Jewish merchant on the island of Malta who regularly suffers from the anti-Jewish behavior of his Christian neighbors. Essentially all Barabas would have liked was the opportunity to practice his trade unmolested. Regrettably, this never happens. He is taxed at a higher rate than his Christian neighbors, and he endures harassment at their hands. Finally Barabas suffers a blow that exhausts his patience. His daughter, Abigail, runs off with a Christian. That in itself is bad enough, but when they elope, the couple also steals a considerable part of Barabas's working capital.

The young couple flees to a nunnery where they take refuge among the sisters. Barabas's spies sniff them out. When Barabas discovers their whereabouts, he exacts a terrible revenge. He poisons the convent's well, killing not only Abigail and her new husband but also all the nuns.

The island of Malta is a Christian maritime stronghold against the expansionary ambitions of the Ottoman Turks. As a longtime smuggler of goods, Barabas knows the city's weaknesses. These he is willing to reveal to the Turks—for a price. The Turks willingly pay it, and Barabas shows them the way to bypass the citadel's defenses by sneaking in through the sewer system.

With the Turks in power, Barabas overnight becomes a highly respected Maltese citizen. Unable in his greed, however, to let well enough alone, Barabas turns double agent. He conspires with the Christians to overthrow the Turks. On a solemn feast day, the nobility of the Turks hold a banquet in the palace courtyard. Their common soldiers and sailors also banquet in the citadel's armory, where the gunpowder is stored. Barabas arranges to have the gunpowder set off with all the common soldiers and their weapons inside. This will leave the Turkish nobility at the mercy of the Christians who, according to the customs of the time, will imprison them and hold them for ransom. The Christians promise Barabas a handsome reward.

Barabas keeps his part of the bargain. The powder magazine goes up on schedule, and the Christians rush in. They have decided, however, that Barabas is far too unreliable an ally to let live. Reinstalled in power, with the enthusiastic encouragement of their Turkish prisoners, the Christians boil Barabas in oil—*on stage.*

In the surviving text of the play (1633) a number of scenes depict the activities of a prostitute, Bellamira. It seems likely, however, that these scenes come from the pens of BEAUMONT and FLETCHER rather than Marlowe's. They were prob-ably later interpolated to please a London audience that had come to like its TRAGEDY mixed with a little COMEDY or bawdy. Possibly Marlowe's most popular play, *The Jew of Malta* was frequently acted in the century after his death and still enjoys an occasional resurrection.

Bibliography

Marlowe, Christopher. *The Jew of Malta.* Edited by Havelock Ellis. 1887. New York: Dover Publications, 2003.

Jodelle, Étienne (1532–1573)

A French poet, HUMANIST, playwright, and neo-classical theorist, Étienne Jodelle was a member of an influential group of literary figures called the PLÉIADE. In response to the call of another member, JOACHIM DU BELLAY, for a more dignified French theater, Jodelle and others answered. They rejected the farces and morality plays that had dominated the immediately preceding French stage, opting instead for a comic theater that revived the practices of ancient Roman and Greek theater.

Whereas many who responded to Bellay's call contented themselves with translations and adaptations from the ancients, Jodelle undertook to provide an entirely original work on the model of classical COMEDY, initiating that effort in 1552 with the completion of his play *Eugène.* Most commentators take issue with the premise that *Eugène* represents a *complete* break with the farcical tradition. While it is true that the formal characteristics of Jodelle's comedy reflect classical practice—the use of eight- syllable verse lines to reflect Roman hexameters and a five-act structure—it is also the case that the play's plot borrows heavily from farcical themes—a cheating husband and a priest with a roving eye.

Jodelle did not limit himself to comedy. In 1553 his verse TRAGEDY, *Cléopâtre captive* (The captive Cleopatra), was performed before King Henry II and the cardinal of Lorraine. *Cléopâtre* was the first original French verse tragedy of the Renaissance to be performed in France. In an elaborate compliment to his king, Jodelle seated Henri on stage in the center of the action. Another tragedy, however, preceded *Cléopâtre* as the first one written in the language. Performed in Lausanne, Switzerland, in 1550, *Abraham sacrifant* (The sacrifice of Abraham) by the influential Calvinist Théodore de Bèze claims that distinction. Another verse tragedy by Jodelle, *Didon* (ca. 1560), subsequently appeared.

Beyond his contributions to French drama, Jodelle also composed verse, some of it on Christian themes. Selections from his Christian poems—including those about the religious wars in France—were included in collections with anti-Huguenot, pro-Roman Catholic propagandistic objectives. He also wrote love poems and satirical verse.

Possibly because many of his European contemporaries read French, because the themes and subjects of Jodelle's work were so widely known, or because, despite his membership in the Pléiade, his talent as a poet was not much valued, Jodelle's production has not been translated into English.

Bibliography

Hollier, Denis, ed. *A New History of French Literature.* Cambridge, Mass.: Harvard University Press, 1989.

Nitze, William A., and E. Preston Dargan. *A History of French Literature.* New York: Henry Holt and Company, 1922.

Jones, Inigo (1573–1652)

Famous both as a designer of buildings and as a landscape architect, Jones brought the Palladian style of architecture from Venice to England. Although his greatest triumphs undoubtedly occurred in the field of planning and constructing Italianate buildings, he also made significant contributions to the development of British theater. He collaborated with BEN JONSON in staging elaborate court masques until the two began to bicker in public. As a result of their open quarreling, Jonson fell out of favor, though Jones continued to enjoy royal patronage, eventually rising to the post of surveyor-general of the royal buildings. Beyond his work designing the settings for royal entertainments, Jones also brought the proscenium stage and movable scenery to England from the Continent.

Jonson, Ben (1572–1637)

One of the more colorful characters of the English Renaissance and also one of its best playwrights, Ben Jonson was probably born in London where he studied for a while under the tutelage of William Camden in the Westminster School. He may have enrolled briefly at Cambridge. If so, he seems to have been obliged to leave university and work with his father for a time as a bricklayer, "with a trowel in one hand" and a book in the other, as one early biographer reports.

He then fought as a British soldier in Flanders in the 1590s. There, when he once represented the British army as its champion in single combat, he killed his opponent. On his return to England, he became an actor and, after killing a colleague in a duel, nearly was hanged for murder. Jonson escaped this fate on a technicality. During the 14th century, scholars at the English universities were essentially permitted one free murder because they could read and write, and those skills were in high demand. If convicted of murder, they could escape hanging by "pleading their clergy"—that is, their literacy. Instead of hanging, their punishment was to be branded on the thumb so that all would know they had used up their license. Though this law was not much used by the 1590s, it was still in force and provided the loophole through which Jonson ducked, much preferring branding to hanging.

In 1598 he enjoyed his first major theatrical success with the performance by the Lord Chamberlain's Men of his *Every Man in His Humor.* SHAKESPEARE acted in the play. The following year saw a sequel, *Everyman out of his Humor.* During the next three decades, Jonson's plays, sometimes coauthored with such playwrights as MARSTON, DEKKER, and CHAPMAN, premiered at a great rate with general but varying success. One coauthored play, *EASTWARD HO!,* landed Jonson and his collaborators in jail because it smelled of sedition to the Scottish supporters of England's new king, JAMES I.

Deeply versed in Roman and Greek literature, Jonson mastered many genres. He wrote satirical COMEDY, classical TRAGEDY, and revised the work of others for production. For inspiration, he looked to the ancient Roman models, employing in his comedies STOCK CHARACTERS in the manner of PLAUTUS and TERRENCE. In his tragedies he frequently followed both the Romans and the unities of time, place, and action that were recommended by LUDOVICO CASTELVETRO.

Jonson was also one of the greatest lyric poets of his age, remembered not only for EPIGRAMS, ELEGY, and SATIRES, but also for such verses as the lovely "Song: to Celia" (1616) that begins: "Drink to me only with thine eyes / and I will pledge with mine...."

In 1603 Jonson secured an appointment that made him responsible for writing various sorts of entertainments for the royal court's revels and for state occasions. In all he authored 28 of these. In this connection the year 1605 saw the beginning of Jonson's collaboration with the notable landscape architect INIGO JONES in the production of court masques—a popular mode of entertainment among the fashionable aristocrats of the time. The first production they staged together at Whitehall Palace was called *The Masque of Blackness*. Though together they produced many of these spectacular entertainments, Jones and Jonson eventually disagreed publicly, and the upshot of their wrangling was Jonson's loss of favor with the royal court—a psychological blow that devastated him and from which he never fully recovered. He apparently considered his court masques his most notable achievement, for it was in them, he felt, that a writer could exercise his civic and social responsibilities by influencing the chief officers of the state with dramatic performance. A prolific and multitalented author, Jonson also wrote a grammar of the English language. He could very well lay claim to having been the first literary critic in England, as revealed in his interesting COMMONPLACE BOOK, published posthumously in 1641, *Timber or Discoveries Made upon Men and Matter*. In it he passes judgment on popular praise for bad poets. He also suggests that the proper use of classical authors as authorities is to consider them "as Guides, not Commanders."

On the work of his friend and colleague, William Shakespeare, he observes that he recalls the actors thought it "an Honour to Shakespeare" that "he never blotted out a Line." Intending no malice because he cared deeply for Shakespeare, Jonson nevertheless thought it would have been best if his friend had blotted a thousand lines. Shakespeare's creativity was so fertile that Jonson thought it sometimes needed reining in.

Though Jonson was an extremely active playwright throughout his career, the decade beginning in 1606 saw the production of the most memorable of his dramas—plays still regularly performed on the professional stage today to the continuing delight of audiences. These include: *VOLPONE, OR THE FOX* (1607); *EPICOENE, OR THE SILENT WOMAN* (1609); *THE ALCHEMIST* (1610), and *BARTHOLEMEW FAIR* (1614).

Jonson may have been the first English dramatist to enjoy a fan club. Younger writers and wits had formed an admiring association around him: "The Tribe of Ben." After his death, calling themselves The Friends of the Muses, they published a commemorative volume: *Jonsonus Virbius: or, the Memory of Ben Jonson Revived*. The often-quoted epitaph on his simple monument in the poet's corner of Westminster Abbey reads merely: "O rare Ben Jonson." His work is his real monument. He needs no greater.

Bibliography

Bloom, Harold, ed. *Ben Jonson*. Broomall, Pa.: Chelsea House Publishers, 2001.

Fraser, Russell A., and Norman Rabkin. *Drama of the English Renaissance*. Vol. 2, *The Stuart Period*. New York: Macmillan, 1976.

Herford, C. H., and Percy and Evelyn Simpson, eds. *Ben Jonson*. 11 vols. Oxford: Oxford University Press, 1925–1952.

Kay, W. David. *Ben Jonson: A Literary Life*. New York: St. Martin's Press, 1995.

Joseph and Zelíkhá Hamdí (ca. 1500)

Throughout Islamic letters the biblical and Koranic story of Joseph and his Egyptian master Potiphar's unnamed wife has appeared in many languages, usually in the form of a long narrative verse in rhyming couplets—a MESNEVÍ. Early in the development of this romantic, narrative verse tradition, the woman acquired the name Zelíkhá. One version, written in Turkish just before the turn of

16th century by the poet Hamdí (d. 1509), became the most popular of its type for the next 50 years and continued attracting an enthusiastic readership for centuries.

Apart from the straightforward Scriptural accounts of the story, Hamdí's version draws on two Persian variants. One by Firdawsi (d. 1020–21) is also straightforward. When Hamdí follows it, he generally paraphrases. Another richly allegorical and rhetorical version by Jámi (1414–92) is considered the best of the type. When Hamdí follows his second source, he tends to translate the Persian original into Turkish. To narrative and stylistic material drawn from both sources, Hamdí also adds elements from his personal experience, and he enriches the formal characteristics of his sources by interspersing among the couplets of the MESNEVÍ genre other verse forms.

Ordinarily, retellings of the story open with dedicatory verses to patrons. Hamdí's version does not, legend suggests, because his patron had mistreated him and the author cut out the dedication. Hamdí's poem begins instead with the poet's praising God, the Prophet and his ascension into heaven, and his first four successors. He next encourages the soul to be vigilant and remember that the day is coming when it will go forth naked from the body. He recalls his aged father's weeping at the thought that when he died, Hamdí's brothers, like Joseph's, would expose the child to the chances of fortune. This did in fact occur, the poet tells us, with the result that he always felt a special affiliation with Joseph. He acknowledges his sources, pleads his own lack of poetic skill, and, with a brief summary of the lives of the patriarchs Abraham, Isaac, and Jacob, launches into his tale.

The Islamic tradition considers Joseph the most beautiful of human creatures. When his mother dies, an aunt takes care of Joseph in his father's extended absence. The aunt becomes so fond of Joseph that she plots to keep him when his father, Jacob, sends for him. Eventually, however, Joseph returns to his father, whose favorite child the beautiful lad rapidly becomes. Jealous, his brothers conspire to imprison him in a pit and sell him into Egyptian slavery. The brothers tell their father various stories about what happened to Joseph, including that a wolf ate him, but since the brothers have returned Joseph's coat of many colors undamaged, Jacob remains unconvinced. The brothers capture a wolf and bring it home, saying that this was the one. God miraculously allows the wolf to speak, deny the accusation, and explain his purposes.

The story then follows Joseph's miraculous adventures on the trail to Egypt. Some people are converted to the true faith at the sight of his beauty. Others make an image of him and worship it as an idol. A dragon appears to protect him while he bathes in the Nile. On his arrival in Egypt, an angel proclaims his coming. His keeper, Málik, is delighted to be able to charge admission for a sight of the marvelous lad. Among the crowds who come to see him is the occupant of the office Joseph will eventually hold, the chief administrator or grandee of Egypt, Potiphar and his wife Zelíkhá.

With the arrival of Zelíkhá on the scene, the story flashes back to her girlhood. The reader learns that, years before, she had dreamed three times about a wondrously beautiful young man and had fallen in love with him. When she asked who he was, he replied that he was the grandee of Egypt.

When the time comes for her to marry, the seven monarchs of Yemen, Abyssinia, Iraq, Syria, the Frankish (Mediterranean) Sea, Rúm (Turkey), and Tibet seek her hand. But she refuses for her heart is set on the grandee of Egypt. Her indulgent father writes the grandee imploring a proposal. Startled but delighted, Potiphar returns one by carrier pigeon. The happy Zelíkhá at once accepts and starts out to Egypt where her retinue is met by Potiphar and a magnificent parade of his retainers. Peeking out through a slit in her tent, Zelíkhá is unimaginably distressed to discover that her husband is a withered old man instead of the radiant youth of her dreams. Beyond hope she spends her days in lovesick yearning for a lad she believes must somewhere be real.

The story then returns to the slave market of Egypt where Joseph is about to be sold. The bidding is fierce; the offers grow astronomical. Finally Zelíkhá, who is fabulously wealthy in her own right, silences the other bidders by doubling the sum total offered by all of them.

Hamdí then briefly digresses, telling of a potential rival for Zelíkhá. Arriving at the auction in all her finery, the rival—Bázigha—is so dazzled by Joseph's beauty that she asks him who made him. He replies that his creator is the one God of whose heavenly beauty his own faintly reflects. He offers other moral advice, and Bázigha feels moved to give all her belongings to the poor and dedicate her life to prayer and worship.

With Joseph under her roof, Zelíkhá can enjoy his company and conversation. She discovers that her first dream of him occurred exactly at the moment his brothers cast him in the pit.

The story goes on to recount Zelíkhá's increasing ardor and her attempts to seduce Joseph, his steadfast resistance, his being jailed when Zelíkhá tries to cover her own guilt by accusing him to Potiphar. In jail, Joseph gains a reputation as an interpreter of dreams. Word of this capacity reaches the king who asks Joseph to interpret his. As matters fall out, Joseph interprets the dreams, discusses the reasons for his imprisonment with the king, who investigates and wins from Zelíkhá a confession that Joseph is blameless. The king instantly promotes Joseph to the office of grandee of Egypt in place of the recently retired Potiphar.

Still obsessed with Joseph, Zelíkhá spends her fortune seeking news of him. White haired with grief and blind from weeping, she lives in a reed hut beside a road he uses so she can hear the sound of his chariot's wheels. An idolater, she prays to the image of her god to restore her sight, but her prayer is fruitless. When she next hears his chariot she stands in the road and calls out, "Glory to Him who raises up the fallen and makes the slave a king!" Joseph hears her and, not recognizing her, has her brought before him.

Asked who she is, she identifies herself and confesses that she has loved him all her life. Asked what she wishes, she requests the restoration of her beauty and her sight. Joseph prays, and his prayer is answered. Asked what else he can do, she admits that she wants to be his love and spend her life with him. Joseph hesitates, a voice tells him that she has found favor with God, and so they are married.

Hamdí then recounts the story of Joseph's reunion with his brothers and father. After that, he closes his story with an account of Joseph's death away from his wife, her grief, and her death at the tomb of her husband.

The story, greatly abbreviated here, appears largely as Hamdí recounted it and as it appears in Islam's holy book, the Koran, where the narrative consumes most of the 12th chapter.

Bibliography

Browne, E. G. *A Literary History of Persia.* Vols. 2 and 3. Cambridge, U.K.: Cambridge University Press, 1963.

Gibb, E. J. W. *History of Ottoman Poetry.* Edited by Edward G. Browne. London: Luzac, 1965.

Journey to the West, The (Xiyuji, Hsi yu Chi) Wu Cheng'en (ca. 1592)

One of the major surviving monuments of Chinese literary endeavor, the 100 chapter-long prose and verse novel, *The Journey to the West,* usually attributed to the 16th-century writer WU CHENG'EN, has at its core an actual journey from China to India. The novel turns this pilgrimage, undertaken in the seventh century C.E. by a Buddhist monk, Xuanzong (Hsüan–tsang), into a vast tapestry of fantasy, philosophy, religious teaching and reflection, humor, adventure, and wonder. Wu Cheng'en, moreover, proves to write poetry as well as he does prose.

Xuanzong's historical objective involved the acquisition in India of Buddhist texts for use in Chinese monasteries. To the account of his journey, however, during the course of almost 1,000 years, mythic and fantastic elements attached themselves. So did elements of Taoist and other religious teachings. The principal American expert on and the only English translator of the entire text, Anthony C. Yu, traces those teachings and elements. In the introduction to his monumental, four-volume edition Yu also explores what can be gathered about the history of the attachment of various elements to the core story. Suffice it to say here that, for centuries, as the landscape covered by the increasingly legendary monk became less and less literal and was more and more drawn from the realms of the imagination, folklore, and ALLEGORY, Xuanzong acquired companions with similarly imaginary origins.

Chief among these companions is the remarkable monkey, Sun Wukong (Sun Wu-k'ung), whose story occupies the first seven chapters of the book. Sun Wukong becomes, first, the king of the monkeys and then an extraordinary magician who can increase or decrease his size by a hundredfold. He studies, and he acquires a MAGIC rod that grows and shrinks with him and that renders him invincible. He learns to fly. He invades heaven and fights heavenly beings to a draw. He eats immortal peaches. All the while that he accomplishes such extraordinary things, he retains a monkey's mischievous behavior and curiosity. Even the king of heaven, the Jade Emperor, gives him the title of Great Sage to pacify him. Finally, however, Buddha himself brings the monkey's obstreperous behavior under control. First the enlightened one pinions Sun Wukong under a mountain and then, once the monkey is eventually released (in chapter 14), equips him with a nonremovable golden coronet that inflicts pain if he thinks unbecoming thoughts or behaves badly. Eventually the monkey also achieves enlightenment and gains immortality. The manner in which Wu Cheng'en develops and recounts this early section of the narrative is funny, satirical, and richly imaginative. The enlightened monkey will later become the monk's disciple and chief protector.

The eighth chapter provides a transition. In it, Buddha announces to his celestial council his intention to share the great texts of Buddhism with the Chinese people. He selects the female bodhisattva Guanyin (Kuanyin) to scout the trail from China to India for a "scripture–pilgrim" whom she will select. (A bodhisattva is a person who has already achieved enlightenment but who defers becoming one with godhead—achieving nirvana—out of the compassionate desire to help others attain the same goal.) Traveling on a cloud, Guan-yin carefully notes the way. On her journey she finds the monkey still languishing under the mountain. Convinced by their conversation that Sun Wukong has genuinely reformed, Guan-yin

promises him that the scripture–pilgrim will rescue him as he passes that way.

The next three chapters shift to an examination of Xuanzong's personal history. A reader discovers that bandits murdered his father and kidnapped his pregnant mother. When her baby is born, the bandit leader intends to destroy him, but his mother floats him down the river on a plank. A monk named Faming rescues the child, names him River Float, and rears him until his 18th year. He decides to pursue the monastic life and acquires the name Xuanzong. Obsessed with a desire to know something of his parentage, the young man begs Faming for information. Faming presents him with the garment in which his mother had wrapped him. On it she had written him a letter in her own blood recounting his father's history and naming his murderers. Faming tells his foster son where to find his mother. Eventually, he avenges his father's murder, and after a series of incidents that include the death, descent into the underworld, and resurrection of the Tang dynasty emperor Taizong (T'ai-tsung), Xuanzong accepts his commission from the bodhisattva, who reveals her identity. She explains that there are three collections of scriptures that the monk must seek, and from them he takes his nickname: Tripitaka.

A huge section of the text, chapters 13–97, follows in detail the adventures that Tripitaka/Xuanzong encounters on the long journey from China to India. Like JOHN BUNYAN's *The PILGRIM'S PROGRESS* (1678), the long journey toward India is an ALLEGORY of the Buddhist's (and the Taoist's) journey toward understanding and enlightenment. The tigers, dragons, demons, and monsters that repeatedly face Xuanzong and the disciples he acquires along the way represent the temptations and distractions that confront the human soul in its quest for enlightenment.

At the transition between chapters 13 and 14, Wukong realizes that the scripture–pilgrim has at last arrived and cries out from his stone box beneath the mountain—formerly named the Mountain of the Five Phases but now called the Mountain of the Two Frontiers. The pilgrim liberates Wukong, who acquires the title Pilgrim Sun and therewith his full name, Sun Wukong. In chapter 14 the pilgrims confront and overcome six robbers who represent the distractions of the senses that can impede a pilgrim's journey to enlightenment. Here too the monkey acquires the golden behavioral control device earlier mentioned.

The scripture–pilgrim is destined to confront 81 temptations, distractions, ordeals, and dangers as he and his small band—himself and four disciples—travel westward. Chapters 13–97 are principally occupied with recounting each of these in turn. In the words of Anthony C. Yu, these episodes develop "through a long series of captures and releases of the pilgrims by monsters, demons, animal spirits, and gods in disguise."

The final three chapters conclude the account of the fantastic journey. First the pilgrims receive rewards from Buddha's own hands. Then they complete the return trip to China, deliver the sacred texts, and they all achieve sainthood.

Despite the daunting length of the novel, it is a gripping read. Yu's translation is a delight. His workmanlike prose, spiced as Wu Cheng'en's is with frequent poems, makes the novel difficult to put down.

Bibliography

Wu Cheng'en. *Monkey.* Translated by Arthur Waley. New York: Grove Press, 1958.

———. *The Journey to the West.* 4 vols. Translated and edited by Anthony C. Yu. Chicago: The University of Chicago Press, 1977–1983.

K

Kabir (Kabirdas) (1440–1518)

An enormously influential Hindu saint, a mystic, and the most important poet of the Indian devotional tradition of BHAKTI, Kabir was born to a Muslim family in the holy city of Benares (Varanasi), India. He grew up in the family of a weaver who cared for him after he was orphaned early in life. He became a disciple of a Hindu holy man, Rāmānanda, who initiated him into the worship of the Hindu deity, Rama.

As an initiate he began to preach a new kind of popular religion that equally venerated Allah and Rama. He disdained idolatry, ritual bathing, and the authority of the Brahmans who practiced an elitist brand of Hinduism with themselves as the elite. His disrespectful attitude earned him the enmity of the Brahmans, and they tried to tempt him by sending a prostitute to him. He converted her, and his reputation as a holy man spread throughout the community.

Whereas the Brahmans often drew their livings from temple offerings, Kabir made his by practicing the weaver's trade of his adoptive father. The passionate devotion that Kabir felt for a mystical religion requiring no temples, icons, idols, priests, or rituals and whose purpose was the union of the individual human being with the Divine Essence drew the masses to his point of view. All a believer needed to do to be saved, Kabir preached, was devotion to God and good will and behavior toward others.

The beauty and clarity with which Kabir expressed his creed attracted both poets and thinkers to emulate his verse and to incorporate his religious views into their own programs. JAYISI MALIK MUHAMMAD (1477–1542), himself a poetic innovator, followed Kabir's religious example. Kabir's verse and theology made a particular impression on NĀNAK (1469–ca. 1539), the founder and first guru of the Sikh religion. When the fifth and last human guru of Sikhism, Arjun (1562–1606), decided to transfer the gurus' authority permanently to a book—the ADI GRANTH (1604)—rather than to continue vesting that authority in persons, Arjun included many of Kabir's verses as scripture. Indeed, this work preserves in a Punjabi language translation of the Hindi originals most of the verses and sermons of Kabir during the last 14 years of his life. (See INDIA, LANGUAGES OF.) The Adi Granth serves as a principal source for modern collections of Kabir's work. Another authoritative source for the huge surviving body of Kabir's verse has been variously titled KABIR GRANTHAVALI, Bijak, or Kabir bijak.

It would be difficult to exaggerate the influence that Kabir's life and work has exercised—and still exercises—on Indian devotional life and on Indian letters. At least representative samples of his verse have been translated into all the major Indian languages—including English. Perhaps the most famous of the English translations is the brief sampling of Kabir's verse offered by India's winner of the Nobel Prize in Literature, Rabindranath Tagore (1861–1941). Other modern editions and translations, however, continue to appear with regularity. About a million people in India are today the direct disciples of Kabir. Countless millions feel his indirect influence.

Literary historian Herbert H. Gowen recounts a moving legend about Kabir. On the poet–saint's death, runs the story, both Hindus and Muslims attempted to claim his body for a funeral in keeping with their traditions and customs. The Hindus wished to burn the body on a funeral pyre, and the Muslims wanted to bury it. On lifting Kabir's shroud, however, the arguing parties found under it only a mass of flowers. Shamed, they respectfully shared the blooms equally, and each group dealt with its half according to the customs of its faith.

Bibliography

Gowen, Herbert H. *A History of Indian Literature.* New York: D. Appleton and Company, 1931.

Kabir. *Bijak of Kabir.* Translated by Linda Hess and Shukdev Singh; edited by Linda Hess. Oxford and New York: Oxford University Press, 2002.

———. *Songs of Kabir.* Translated by Rabindranath Tagore. Mineola, N.Y.: Dover Publications, 2004.

———. *Songs of Kabir from the Adi Granth.* Translated by Nirmal Dass. Albany, N.Y.: State University of New York Press, ca. 1991.

———. *The Ocean of Love: The Anurāg Sāgar of Kabir.* Translated by Raj Kumar Bagga, Partap Singh, and Kent Bicknell. Sabornton, N.H.: Sant Bani Ashram, 1982.

Kabir Granthavali (*Bijak* or *Kabir Bijak*)
(late 15th–early 16th century)

Universally regarded as the most authoritative collection of the Hindu poet and saint KABIR's surviving popular work, the poems in the *Granthavali* address three overriding themes. First, it contains devotional poetry associated with the spiritual reawakening of the Indian masses that reached its high point with Kabir and his work—the BHAKTI movement. Second, it contains poems—some of them satirical—that address the ills of society and some potential remedies for them. Philosophical poems round out the rest of the collection.

In the devotional poems, Kabir attempts to form a relationship with God. The poet addresses the Almighty by many names—Allah, Gobind, Hari, Rama (Kabir's favorite), and others. This variety of addresses makes the point that, whatever one calls the Supreme Deity, Deity remains the same. Addressing the Deity also focuses a person's attention on God, causing one to remember the nature of the rapport between created and Creator and leading to the purity of purpose and action essential to a life of sanctity and devotion. He develops metaphors of the union between God and the human soul, comparing that bond to the one between husband and wife.

In his poems of social protest, Kabir attacks the people and institutions that he perceived as misleading and abusing the common workers of his time. Impatient with formal religion, dogma, sects, priests, and rituals, he especially condemns the caste system whose effect is to preserve the status quo for the upper classes. He encourages an enlightened, egalitarian humanism leavened by a large pinch of mystic devotion and charitable behavior.

His philosophical poems seek metaphors that will help people understand the operation of the universe, the role of the supernatural in it, and the nature of the human soul. He concerns himself with the difference between the illusory world that human senses perceive (*Maya*) and ultimate reality. Finally, his philosophical poems attempt to clarify the relationships among these elements.

Kabir himself did not arrange the order of his collection. His editors performed that task long after his death. Many of his verses are metrical couplets, strung artfully together to great effect. The editors have arranged 409 of Kabir's couplets under 59 headings.

Some of the telling effect of Kabir's poems among the people of his time and ours is doubtless traceable to the heightened effect his verses achieved when set to popular music. He often intended them to be sung to popular tunes (*ragas*). The editors have arranged together 403 stanzas (*padas*). These are of varying length but often several lines, and they are linked to compose descriptions or narrations. Their subject is often the love of the soul for God.

In the third section of the *Granthavali*, Kabir's editors have grouped seven longer poems—some of four, some of seven, and some of eight stanzas. These too are designed to be sung. In a useful appendix, the editors have included from the Sikh Holy Book, the ADI GRANTH, several of Kabir's verses that occur there but that were not included in the *Granthavali*. Each of the three sections of the work has a name: the first, *sakhi* (the couplets); the second, *padavali* (the stanzaic section); and the third, *ramainis* (verses of other sorts).

This collection of Kabir's verses and selections from it continue to be translated and regularly appear not only in the languages of India, but throughout the world as well.

Bibliography

Kabir. *Bijak of Kabir.* Translated by Linda Hess and Shukdev Singh; edited by Linda Hess. Oxford and New York: Oxford University Press, 2002.

———. *Selected Couplets from the Sakhi in transversion: 400-odd Verses in Iambic Tetrameter Stanza Form.* Translated by Mohan Singh Karki. Delhi, India: Motilal Banarsidass Publishers, 2001.

Sethi, V. K. *Kabir, the Weaver of God's Name.* Amritsar, Punjab, India: Radha Soami Satsang Beas, 1984.

Singh, Pushappal. "Kabir Granthavali." *Encyclopedia of Indian Literature.* Volume 3. Edited by Amaresh Datta. New Delhi: Sahitya Akademi, 1989.

Karagöz

Both the name of a Turkish shadow play theater and the name of the shadow comedy's principal character, the word *karagöz* literally means "black eye" in Turkish.

Made of leather, the *Karagöz* shadow puppets are manipulated by a puppeteer who moves them with a stick across a screen illuminated by a lamp behind the figures. The puppeteer recites the parts, sings songs, and handles the sound effects—including shaking a tambourine whenever a new character appears on the shadow screen. The leather figures themselves fall into four categories. First, there are the characters. Some of these are associated only with a single play, but others appear in all the plays. In this latter group appear Karagöz himself and Hadjivad. Karagöz is a comic, adventuresome, thoughtless, greedy, ne'er-do-well, rough sort of character reminiscent of Punch in British Punch and Judy shows. Hadjivad, on the other hand, represents an educated, highly respected person of the middle classes. He is nonetheless Karagöz's best friend. Also appearing in many plays are the *zenni* (ladies), a European foreigner, an Arab, a young man named Çelebî, a strong man named Matiz, and characters typed by physical defects or moral failings. Second, we find a sort of puppet drawn from fantasy: dragons, MAGIC trees, and sorcerers. Animals that are sometimes associated with the characters constitute the third sort of puppet. In this category we find Karagöz's donkey, or another character's horse, for example. Finally, there are pieces of scenery and props, such as sections of landscape, trees, and working implements.

The shadow plays themselves follow fairly set patterns with variations possible. The plays always begin with Hadjivad chanting a kind of verse called a *semai*, which asks a series of questions that the play will address. This is followed by a GHAZEL—in this context a curtain poem that points up the important meaning of the play and its benefit to the viewers. Following this opening, Hadjivad shouts for his friend Karagöz, who enters from the right and beats him. They then conduct a dialogue on whatever subject the play addresses. This dialogue constitutes the second part of the play and is often improvised.

The play itself constitutes the third part of the performance. The subject matter of the play may be drawn from popular romances, from stories, from popular novels, or from farces composed on themes drawn from everyday life. In this latter category are plays in which Hadjivad gets the unemployed Karagöz a job, and the fun arises from the latter's utter unsuitability for the work. Sometimes the plays have been used to conduct political commentary and have therefore not always enjoyed official sanction.

Shadow theater came to Turkey in the 17th century when it achieved its current form, and its origin there has traditionally been attributed to Ewliyâ Çelebî. Earlier, the Egyptian historian IBN IYĀS mentions a shadow puppet show performed at Cairo before the Ottoman Sultan Selim I in 1517.

As it developed in Turkey, *Karagöz* was publicly performed in cafes during the holy month of Ramadan. As a private entertainment, it whiled away the hours of winter evenings in private homes or was performed in connection with circumcision festivities.

Bibliography

And, Metin. *Karagöz: Turkish Shadow Theatre and Popular Entertainment in Turkey.* Ankara: Dost Yayinlari, 1975.

Spatharis, Sotiris. *Behind the White Screen.* New York: Red Dust, 1976.

Tietze, Andreas. *The Turkish Shadow Theater and the Puppet Collection of the L. A. Mayer Memorial Foundation.* Berlin: Mann, 1977.

Karo, Joseph Ben Ephraim (1488–1575)

Both an initiate of the mysteries of the Kabbalah and a systematic codifier of the rabbinical law of his medieval predecessors, the Sephardic Jewish scholar Karo spent the two decades from 1522 to 1542 writing the definitive compendium of rabbinical law for both Sephardic Jews (those dwelling on the Iberian penisula and, after their expulsion from Spain and Portugal, their descendents throughout the world) and for Ashkenazic Jews (those living in Germany and Eastern Europe and their descendants). Karo's four Hebrew volumes, the House of Joseph (*Bet* or *Beit Yosef*), with its very full citations, commentary, and argument, was intended to provide an encyclopedic reference of precedent and rationale upon which future rabbis could base their judgments when deciding issues brought before them.

Once the *House of Joseph* was fully drafted, Karo spent another dozen years editing it. As he did so he also prepared an abridgment that was intended for the use of less learned folk in the conduct of their lives and decision making. This work was called The well-set table (*Shulhan àruch,* published after 1558). Contrary to Karo's wishes and expectations, it was the abridgment rather than the much more scholarly work that became the foundation stone of subsequent rabbinic Judaism. The *Table* went through six editions in Karo's lifetime. Certain Ashkenazic rabbis, moreover, felt that Karo had given too much weight to Sephardism at the expense of the Ashkenazi. They therefore provided in Hebrew a supplementary work called *The Table Cloth* that substituted Ashkenazic precedents for some of Karo's.

As a mystic, Karo was a friend and disciple of the martyred Solomon Molcho (d. 1532). From him Karo had learned the mysteries of the kabbalah, and throughout Karo's adult life he received frequent nightly visits from a spirit or heavenly messenger (a *maggid*) who regularly gave him instruction, reproved him for failure, and made him promises of future fame.

Other works by Karo include a diary in which he records the visits of the *maggid,* his *Maggid mesharim* (written ca. 1533), and a commentary on the *Mishneh Torah* (the postbiblical body of codified Jewish law) of the medieval philosopher and physician Maimonides (1135–1204).

Bibliography

Zinberg, Israel. *A History of Jewish Literature.* Vol. 5. Translated and edited by Bernard Martin. Cincinnati, Ohio, and New York: Hebrew Union College Press and KTAV Publishing House, 1974.

Kathākali

A dramatic performance retelling the old legends of ancient India, *Kathākali* employs recitation by a single actor alternating with poetic dialogues. The actors in a *Kathākali* performance wear highly stylized makeup that masks the features. While they speak, the actors assume a series of traditional, dancelike poses that particularly emphasize the use of the hands and fingers to complement the stories being performed. Both the *Kathākali* performers and the members of the audience must learn these poses and their hundreds of subtle variations, for they communicate a wide range of nuanced emotions and abstract ideas. Though it may have roots in ancient performance traditions, in its current manifestation the form was invented in Kerala on the southwestern coast of India in the 17th century, and its earliest examples appear in the Malayalam language. Subsequently, *Kathâkali* has become popular throughout India and is regularly performed in numerous tongues.

Bibliography

Govindan Kutty, Kalamandalam. *Kathakali, the Dance Theatre.* Calcutta: Asiatic Society, 1999.

Zarrilli, Phillip B., ed. *Kathakali Dance-Drama: Where Gods and Demons Come to Play.* London and New York: Routledge, 2000.

Kâtib Çelebî (Hajii Khalifah) (1609–1656)

A Turkish cavalry officer until a substantial inheritance made possible his full-time pursuit of a literary career, Kâtib Çelebî thereafter became an encyclopedist, a bibliographer, and a charming essayist and autobiographer.

His most ambitious project was a huge encyclopedia and bibliography called *Kashf al-Zunun* (The removal of doubts, after 1635). His last work, THE BALANCE OF TRUTH (*Mīzzān al-Hāqq*), addressed disputed issues of Islamic behavior, observance, and doctrine. It concluded with a short autobiography. Its only English translator, C. G. Pfander, considers it a model of "liberalism and good sense"—one "enlivened" by Çelebî's sense of humor.

After making an obligatory pilgrimage to Mecca, Hajii Khaifah, as he thereafter called himself, penned an account of his journey that includes him among travel writers. He died in the midst of drinking a cup of coffee. This fact gains significance from his having written entertainingly on the subject of coffee and its consumption in *The Balance of Truth.*

Bibliography

Kritzeck, James, ed. *Anthology of Islamic Literature from the Rise of Islam to Modern Times.* New York: Holt, Rinehart and Winston, 1964.

Kemalpasazâde (Ibn Kemal) (1468–1534)

Having begun a career as a soldier, the Turkish Kemalpasazâde found himself attracted by the scholarly life, so he shifted careers as a young man. His natural capacities and insatiable appetite for hard work soon distinguished him above all his fellows and attracted the attention of influential superiors. They in turn recommended him to the sultan with the result that he became principal of a college immediately on completion of his studies. This proved to be merely the first step in a meteoric rise that carried him to the chief academic and legal post of the Ottoman Empire, the Shayk of Islam or Grand Muftí.

Although Kemalpasazâde was a distinguished poet and literary figure, composing with equal facility in Turkish, Persian, and Arabic, his unparalleled contributions to the scholarship of his time overshadow his purely literary output. He wrote his scholarly work mainly in Arabic. In that language he penned treatises concerning each of the sciences of his time. He also wrote on the methods and levels of interpretation of the Koran, on Islamic theology, and on jurisprudence. At his death, he had begun some 300 separate works and finished most of them. So renowned did Kemalpasazâde become that his tombstone bears a title that has never been conferred on any other person who occupied his high office. He is called The Muftí of the Two Ponderables, which means that he was the supreme scholar and jurist of the two classes of beings that, because both are composed of matter, have weight: people and genies. Genies are a class of mythic beings with superhuman powers, and legend has it that they chose Kemalpasazâde as their chief advisor, paying him well to perform the office.

Only one of Kemalpasazâde's Persian works seems to have been known to the BIOGRAPHERS OF TURKISH POETS—apparently a series of verse biographical sketches. His Turkish works include a discussion of Persian lexicography, a history of the Ottoman Empire through the year 1526, a collection of GHAZELS, a MESNEVÍ retelling the Biblical story of JOSEPH AND ZULÍKHÁ, and two translations commissioned by the sultan. One of these translations is a work of history about Egypt. The other, a medical treatise, bears the intriguing title The return of the elder to his youth (*Rujú'-ush-Sheykhi ila Sibá*).

Bibliography

Gibb, E. J. W. *A History of Ottoman Poetry.* Edited by Edward G. Browne. London: Luzac, 1965.

Keshavdās (Keśvamiśra) (1556–1605)

A court poet in the princely state of Orccha in central India, Keshavdās participated in an elitist culture that expressed itself in both the Sanskrit and Brajbhasha (early Hindi) tongues. A master of the poetic theory and practices of ancient Sanskrit, Keshavdās chose to write in the vernacular language of the region and to merge the nascent poetics of Brajbhasha with the fully developed poetic practice of Sanskrit. He regularly employed Sanskrit meters in his Hindi verse, and the range of his composition is greater than that of any subsequent Hindi poet. In making that choice, he modeled in his own work the standard toward which all subsequent poets in Hindi aspired. His work taught poets "the way of delight" (*rasa-rīti*). His poems also supplied the readers of Hindi poetry both with the knowledge required to read and understand Hindi verse and with a theoretical yardstick that they could apply to judge it.

Some modern critics think that his frequent preference for Sanskritic vocabulary as well as for its forms and meters makes his poetry too mannered to feel completely natural. At the same time, the commentators credit him with introducing a heightened dramatic element into his narrative verse, with helping to refine the emerging Hindi language with his polished diction, and for his great originality.

Keshavdās enjoyed the patronage of members of the princely household, one of whom, Prince Indrajit, commissioned his Companion to love (*Rasikpriya,* 1591). Among other matters, this work instructs poets in a method for achieving emotional unity in their verse and was considered indispensable for budding writers. It also details the sorts of heroes and heroines whom love poems should develop and the emotions the characters should display.

When Indrajit inherited an estate some 20 miles southeast of Orccha, Keshavdās moved there with his patron. In a work written in that location, Companion to rhetoric (*Kavipriyā,* 1601) describes Indrajit's generous support of artists, dancers, and musicians. Among them Keshavdās describes several talented courtesans. One named Rāyprabīn, Indrajit's special favorite, herself composed poetry. She recited or sang it while accompanying herself on the vīnā—an Indian stringed instrument. In the same work, Keshavdās also makes clear his own awareness of his role in transmitting Sanskritic literary culture to Brajbhasha/Hindi as a means of preserving the older tradition. Aside from its pictures of life at court, *Kavipriyā* explores figures of speech, metrics, and poetic forms. Though Keshavdās's vernacular works have apparently not been translated into English, his Sanskrit work *Alankāra'sekhara* (Figures of speech . . .) treats issues similar to those in his Brajbhasha *Kavipriyā.* This work is available under the Sanskrit title in a bilingual English/Sanskrit edition and gives one a sense of Keshavdās' literary interests.

The numbers of surviving manuscripts of the two works outlined above attest to the widespread influence of Keshavdās's work in his own time. A younger contemporary and more famous poet, BIHARI LAL (1559–1663), followed Keshavdās advice. The same sort of manuscript evidence also suggests the importance of the poet's reworking of a literary tradition associated with the veneration of the name of the Hindu deity Rama. Keshavdās's book, *Ramchandrika* (1600), says the literary historian Stuart McGregor, constructed "a new image of Rama." The poet assimilated Rama's age-old characteristics to the central Indian situation at the turn of the 17th century, and in retelling the ancient legends surrounding Rama, made more or less direct allusions to contemporary events.

Contemporary events themselves become the subject of—or at least the occasion for—other works. The most notable, The deeds of the noble Virsingh or Birsingh (*Virsingdev charitra,* 1607), recounts the rise to power of Prince Virsingh and his contentious relationships both with his brothers and with the Mughal Emperor AKBAR the Great. More, however, than just a straight historical account of these matters, the work romanticizes the state of Orccha, life at its court, and its countryside. It also makes an ALLEGORY of Virsingh's eventual success. Historically speaking, Virsingh supported Akbar's son, Jahangir, as successor to his father's throne at Agra and became his feudal subordinate. Allegorically, Keshavdās presents this material as the beneficent operation of fate (of dharma in the Indian context). Krishna has preselected Virsingh's dynasty for greatness and for forwarding a divine agenda of religious devotion, piety, and charity toward one's neighbor.

In The song of Vijanan (*Vijanan gita*, 1610) Keshavdās reworked a 14th century Jain allegorical drama that damns the vice of hypocrisy. As was often his practice, the poet selected it as a means of transmitting the literary culture of an earlier time into the present with a contemporary flavor.

Surviving and available works include *Rathanbhavani* (1583). Though I have not been able to locate a description of this work, I believe it to be a reworking of an ancient COMEDY depicting court life. *Barahmasa* (1600) presents a substantial narration by a young woman who describes her emotions as they fluctuate throughout the year. It is a traditional form. *Chhandmala* (1602) likely concerns the veneration of the goddess Chandi, and *Jahagiryash chandrika*, Keshavdās's final work, concerns the reign of the Mughal Emperor Jahāngir (1612), praising his virtues as a leader.

Bibliography

Datta, Amaresh. *Encyclopedia of Indian Literature.* New Delhi: Sahitya Akademi, 1987.

Gowen, Herbert H. *A History of Indian Literature.* New York and London: Appleton and Company, 1931.

Keśavamiśra. *Alamkāra-śekhara.* Translated by Bijoya Goswami. Calcutta: Sanskrit Pustak Bhandar, 1998.

McGregor, Stuart. "The Progress of Hindi, Part I: The Development of a Transregional Idiom." *Literary Cultures in History: Reconstructions from South Asia.* Edited by Sheldon Pollock. Berkeley: University of California Press, 2003.

Winternitz, M. *History of Indian Literature.* Vol. 3, Part 1. Translated by Subhadra Jhā. Delhi: Motilal Banarsidass, 1963.

Khágání (Muhammad Bey)
(d. ca. 1606–1607)

The author of a small collection of otherwise unremarkable poetry, Khágání is warmly remembered in the literary history of Turkey for a single poem that he wrote, *The sacred physiognomy* (*Hilya-i Sherífa*, ca. 1598). Based on an ancient, simple, and traditional Arabic account of the appearance of the prophet Mohammed, The prophetic physiognomy (*El-Hilyat-un-Nebeviyya*), which catalogues details like the black color of the Prophet's eyes and his aquiline nose, Khágání's poem takes each of the items in the list and adds from 12 to 20 supporting couplets.

Khágání achieves his expansion by writing multiple SIMILEs that enlarge on the simple statements of fact in his source. Whereas, for instance, the earlier catalogue of the Prophet's features describes his complexion and face as "bright," Khágání assures his reader that the Prophet's features were ruddy as a rose, that the stubble of his beard was the "verse of grace," and that when he perspired it was like the dew on a rose. The available partial English translation employs antiquated poetic conventions that probably do not reflect very accurately the craftsmanship of the Turkish original. Its translator, E. J. W. Gibb, however, remarks that Khágání's poem is more valued for its subject matter than for its poetic merit.

Khayriyya (For Khayr) Nábí (ca. 1662)

A poem of fatherly advice addressed by the Turkish poet NÁBÍ to his son Ebu 'l-Khayr, this work introduced a new poetic subject into the Turkish language. In the form of a MESNEVÍ—a long series of rhyming couplets—the work is divided into chapters. Each of them either tries to encourage a particular virtue in the young man or to discourage a particular vice. Nábí exhorts his son to observe his religious responsibilities as a good

Muslim. He is to be generous in almsgiving and dutiful in fasting, praying, and going on pilgrimage, and he must work hard at his studies. He must be patient and avoid avarice. He must also avoid making jokes at the expense of others, must be dependable, stay sober, be conservative in dress, not oppress the poor, and tell the truth.

Avoid the legal profession, Nábí tells his son. In fact, the poet advises, try to avoid any official position at all. If he must work in the civil service, says Nábí, the son should seek to become head clerk in the sultan's judicial assembly. This was, the poet thought, the least onerous among official positions.

His father further counsels Ebu 'l-Khayr to learn something of medicine and literature but to avoid studying astrology, alchemy, and other occult subjects. He should also avoid using opium and should play checkers and chess only in moderation.

Avoid marrying, the father suggests. Rather, he recommends, take concubines (who enjoyed a legal status under Turkish law)—but only female concubines, preferably from what is now the Russian-speaking Republic of Georgia.

Despite parallels that might be drawn with 21st century concerns, the *Khayriyya*'s fatherly advice may seem quaint and distant. The picture it draws, however, of 17th-century Turkish society with its corruption and cruelty, the hopelessness of its poor, and the oppression of the masses by the authorities is of great interest to historians. In its own time the book was highly valued for the quality of its good counsel.

Bibliography

Gibb, E. J. W. *A History of Ottoman Poetry.* Edited by Edward G. Browne. London: Luzac and Company, 1965.

Nábí. "The Counsels of Nabi Effendi." *Turkish Literature.* Translated by Epiphanius Wilson. New York and London: The Co-operative Publication Society, 1901.

Kim Man-jung (1637–1692)

Principally remembered for a romance novel that he wrote in both Chinese and Korean, Kim Man-jung was forced into exile as a relatively young man, and his mother was exceedingly distraught. Hoping to console her, Kim wrote *Kuun mong* (*A dream of nine clouds,* mid-17th century). Associated with a tradition of stories and novels whose titles contained the word *dream*, Kim's central message to his mother advises her not to worry overmuch: Life is a dream, and its apparent reality ought not to be taken too seriously.

Kim sets the story during the Tang dynasty of 10th-century China. In the prologue a Buddhist monk, Xingzhen (Hsing-chen), studies with his master, Liuguan (Liu-kuan). The master intends that his student succeed him as head of the monastery. Volunteering to visit the Dragon King's water palace as an emissary of his master, Xingzhen drinks the Dragon King's wine, converses with eight fairy maidens that serve the Lady Wei, and gives them presents of blossoms that turn into pearls. On his return to his cell, he cannot get the fairies' loveliness out of his mind. His thoughts of them interfere with his meditation and lead him to consider Confucian studies and an important career in the Chinese civil service rather than the anonymous life of the Buddhist monk. Aware of these sinful thoughts, Liuguan summons his erring student and reproves him. Then he sends him to the underworld to serve Lord Yama who rules there. On Xingzhen's arrival, Lord Yama is considering what to do with Xingzhen when all eight fairies are escorted in. Lady Wei has punished them for tempting Xingzhen. Lord Yama decides that none of the nine have merited their exile in the realm of the dead, and he sends them back to earthly lives. Xingzhen finds himself reborn as Shaoyu, who becomes a gifted young scholar trained in the Confucian tradition.

The story itself is divided into two parts and describes the *dream* of his life. The first part follows Shaoyu's itinerary through eight different locales. At each one he meets the reincarnation of one of the eight fairies. In the meantime, he rises rapidly through the ranks of the civil service. Incidents command the reader's primary attention through the first part.

In the second part, Shaoyu marries two of the young women he met in the first part and enjoys the other six as concubines. All live happily together. He rises to the very top of the civil service and experiences much success and happiness. Yet he feels impelled to undertake a religious pilgrimage. Dialogue provides the principal interest of the second part.

Kim rounds out his novel with an epilogue. In it Liuguan arrives at Shaoyu's household just before he sets out on his journey. Liuguan restores Shao–yu's memory of his former existence as a monk and promises to teach him the *Diamond Sutra* of Buddhism to awaken his soul, though he must await the arrival of other initiates. On cue, the eight maidens of Lady Wei appear and announce their determination to become Buddhist nuns.

Liuguan accepts them and teaches all nine the *Diamond Sutra,* which explains that all existence is dharma—illusion—nothing but shadow, a bubble, a dream. This the good Buddhist must understand. Having taught them all that doctrine, Liuguan hands over authority in the monastery to Shaoyu —once more now Xingzhen. Then the old monk returned to his native India while Xingzhen and the eight nuns practiced their religion, and eventually all entered paradise together.

A dream of nine clouds illustrates the Chinese–Korean romance genre in a number of ways: It displays repetitive patterning; includes adventure, coincidence, and fantasy; moves from one self-contained episode to the next; sees life as a quest or journey in pursuit of understanding; and contains many mythic elements whose themes resonate with those of Western cultures of the ancient world.

Bibliography

Kim Man-Jung. *A Nine Cloud Dream* in *Virtuous Women: Three Masterpieces of Traditional Korean Fiction.* Translated by Richard Rutt and Kim Chong-un. Seoul: Korean National Commission for UNESCO, 1974.

King and no King, A   John Fletcher and Francis Beaumont (acted 1611, published 1619) A prose and blank-verse romantic COMEDY, BEAUMONT and FLETCHER's *A King and no King* opens with two Iberian captains, Mardonius and Bessus, discussing Bessus's lack of valor as it contrasts with his bragging about his military exploits—like

being forced to fight while trying to run away and to his own surprise achieving victory.

In the second scene, the undeniably valiant king of Iberia, Arbaces, is reproved by his prisoner, Tigranes, the king of Armenia, for boasting. Mardonius concurs in this reproof and further counsels King Arbaces to be less volatile in his passions and more self-effacing.

After years of campaigning in Armenia, Arbaces has bested Tigranes in single combat to win the war. Rather than demand ransom, however, Arbaces offers his prisoner the hand of Arbaces's sister, the princess Panthea, in marriage. Tigranes, however, is secretly in love with Spaconia, the daughter of his courtier, Lygones. He therefore refuses Panthea as a bride . Arbaces nonetheless demands that Tigranes see Panthea before he will accept his prisoner's refusal. Tigranes arranges to have Bessus conduct Spaconia to Iberia and install her in Panthea's household. Tigranes instructs his beloved to dissuade Panthea from accepting him.

As the first act ends, the audience learns that in his long absence, Arbaces's mother, Arane, has led a failed rebellion against him and that she is under house arrest back in Iberia.

Act II opens with a conference between Gobrias, the lord protector of Iberia in the king's absence, and the queen mother, Arane. Bessus enters, interrupting their conference and bearing letters from Arbaces. One of the letters forgives his mother and releases her on her own recognizance. Asked for news of the king, the vain and foolish Bessus can speak only of himself and his dangers and exploits. He eventually introduces Spaconia to Panthea with silly remarks concerning Spaconia's virtue. Spaconia introduces herself as Thalestris. When she and Panthea are alone, Spaconia begs Panthea not to accept Tigranes as her husband and reveals her true identity. Panthea pledges that she will reject Tigranes.

The next scene pictures common people awaiting the king's return. On his arrival they cheer him, and Arbaces boasts of capturing Tigranes. Tigranes once more reproves his captor, this time for exposing him to popular scorn. When the royal party arrives at court, Arbaces, who has not seen Panthea since she was a child, fails to recognize her as his sister and falls desperately in love with her at first sight. Told that she is indeed his sister, he refuses to believe it and flies into one of his characteristic passions.

Despite his promise of fidelity in his love for Spaconia, Tigranes also falls in love with Panthea. When he begins to woo her as Arbaces had encouraged him to do, however, Arbaces experiences another of his mood swings and forbids Tigranes's suit. The two quarrel, and Arbaces has Tigranes hauled off to prison.

Arbaces finally acknowledges Panthea as his sister in Act III, scene 1. Fearing his incestuous thoughts, however, he places her under house arrest as a traitor rather than be tortured by his own feelings in her presence. In the next scene, the king confesses his secret to Mardonius and tries to enlist him as a go-between to arrange a liaison with Panthea. The upright and courageous Mardonius refuses and shames Arbaces. When the king tries to recruit the unprincipled Bessus for the same office, however, Bessus immediately accepts. Enraged at Bessus's lack of principle, Arbaces threatens to banish him to the desert and vows to overcome temptation.

As Act IV begins Spaconia begs Panthea to arrange a visit to Tigranes in prison. Panthea gives Spaconia a ring as a token to get her past the jailers. While she is enroute to the jail, the scene shifts to Tigranes. He bemoans his hasty refusal of the offered marriage to Panthea and his having arranged to have Spaconia on hand. On arriving, Spaconia tells Tigranes that he is false and that she plans to die. Just then, Arbaces arrives to visit Tigranes and comfort him, promising him early liberty. When Arbaces discovers Spaconia, however, he jumps to the conclusion that she is a go-between sent by Panthea. His friendly feelings toward Tigranes immediately evaporate, and in a fit of pique he imprisons Spaconia with the man she loves. This development suits her just fine.

The fourth scene of Act IV presents Bessus being advised by two experts in the etiquette of dueling. He wants their advice on whether or not he is valiant. The logic-chopping considerations that contribute to resolving that issue ridicule the whole convoluted code of dueling, which was a popular passion in the early 17th century. By a series of irrelevant and wrongheaded arguments, the experts conclude that the cowardly Bessus is indeed valiant.

In the next scene, Arbaces at last confesses his feelings to Panthea and explains why she cannot be near him. Panthea admits that she harbors similar sentiments but firmly rejects any suggestion of the sin of incest. Narrowly avoiding yielding to their mutual passion, they agree to remain away from one another.

Act V opens with the arrival of Spaconia's father, Lygones. Assuming that his daughter had run off with Bessus, he comes to avenge himself on Bessus and to disown the disgraced Spaconia. After Lygones beats Bessus, Bessus explains his role as her escort. Lygones then assumes that Spaconia is the king's mistress, and in scene ii, he accuses her of unchaste behavior and reproves King Tigranes for seducing his daughter. Both deny his allegations, and Tigranes tells Lygones that he intends to make Spaconia his queen. Spaconia reminds the king of his fickle interest in Panthea, but Tigranes assures her that was a momentary aberration and that it will not happen again.

The next scene returns, rather tiresomely, to Bessus and his experts. They arrive at the home of a courtier Bacurius to advise him of the experts' conclusion about Bessus's valor. Bacurius beats all of them and exposes the experts as Bessus's equals in cowardice.

In the last scene, Lord Protector Gobrias, despite many interruptions and wrong conclusions by the volatile Arbaces, explains that, to provide an heir for the realm, Queen Arane, who thought her elderly husband the king impotent, feigned a pregnancy. At its end, Gobrias substituted his and his wife's son Arbaces as the heir and held a mock funeral to cover the absence of their child. Then, contrary to all expectations, Arane did become pregnant with Panthea. During Arbaces's absence the revolution was designed to restore the legitimate heir to the throne. Delighted to find himself a subject rather than a king, Arbaces asks Panthea, who now enters, to promise to marry him if he can prove it legal for them. She does so willingly, and the king, who has now become no king, gains a new status as the prospective prince regent of Iberia.

Though this is not one of Beaumont and Fletcher's best theatrical efforts, it nonetheless typifies the fare that appealed to the tastes of London audiences at the beginning of the second decade of the 17th century. It included overtones of popular Orientalism with characters in supposedly Armenian costume, a satiric treatment of dueling, a good deal of slapstick beating of cowardly braggarts, and a series of hardly credible improbabilities that lead to the triumph of true love over not only the baser passions, but also the darkest of them, incest.

Bibliography

Beaumont, Francis, and John Fletcher. *The Dramatic Works in the Beaumont and Fletcher Canon.* Cambridge, U.K.: Cambridge University Press, 1966; reissued 1996.

———. *A King and no King.* Edited by Robert K. Turner, Jr. Lincoln: University of Nebraska Press, 1963.

King Lear, The Tragedy of William Shakespeare (ca. 1605)

Indebted for its plot to SACKVILLE and NORTON's earlier SENECAN TRAGEDY, *GORBODUC* (1561), and perhaps to the *Chronicle History of King Leir* (ca. 1590), as well, *King Lear* occupies a special place in the Shakespearean canon. If it has not always been SHAKESPEARE's most popular tragedy, it is almost universally regarded as his greatest. This is true both from the point of view of the play's construction as drama and from the point of view of the nobility of its poetic achievement. Some have also considered the possibility that Shakespeare intended the drama as an object lesson for the recently crowned King James I that in England the king was not above the law.

The story concerns an octogenarian monarch, Lear, who has wearied of the responsibilities of governing. Wishing to lay aside the burdens of leadership, he nevertheless means to retain its perquisites. In the natural order as defined by the English system of primogeniture the eldest child, Lear's daughter Goneril, should inherit the title

and estates. Lear, however, has a favorite child, his youngest, Cordelia, whose name means "heart's ease." To demonstrate his care for her, Lear decides that he will bestow a third of his kingdom on each of his daughters, the two already named and his middle daughter, Regan.

The exercise of absolute power throughout a long rule has led Lear to perceive himself as different in *kind*—that is, different in his basic nature—from other people. Implicit in his decision to divide his kingdom into thirds is a desire to manage affairs from beyond the grave—a situation that would upset the natural order.

The play opens with a conversation among the Earls of Gloucester and Kent, and Gloucester's illegitimate son Edmund. In it the elderly Gloucester introduces Edmund as a "whoreson" and makes other belittling remarks about him that at least subliminally establish the grounds for one of the subplots.

Entering the chamber where the three have been talking, Lear publicly announces his living legacy to each child, asking each in turn to describe the quality of her love for her father. Both Goneril and Regan recognize the old man's expectation that they flatter him outrageously, and they do so. Each swears that she loves Lear far beyond the bounds of filial duty. Lear then rewards each of his elder daughters by pointing on a map to the domains over which she and her consort will preside. When, however, Lear asks Cordelia what she can say to "draw a third more opulent than her sisters," she surprises and enrages him by answering, "Nothing."

"Nothing?" Lear retorts.

"Nothing!" Cordelia repeats.

"Nothing will come of nothing," Lear threatens, "Speak again."

From that moment forward, the dreary repetition of the word *nothing* tolls through the play like the ringing of the funeral knell. By the end of the play, the total sum of Lear's hopes and expectations amounts precisely to nothing.

In enunciating that threatening line, moreover, Lear unwittingly makes the first of his many mistakes. He forgets that *nothing* is God's raw material for creating *everything*, and the entire action of the play springs from Cordelia's reply.

Cordelia explains that she loves Lear exactly as much as she should and that a future husband will command half of her devotion.

In his fury at this answer, Lear cuts Cordelia off and disinherits her.

Lear's faithful retainer, the Earl of Kent, intervenes and attempts to persuade Lear that Cordelia has it right. Lear, however, will have his own way. He cuts Kent off and threatens him, revealing again that the king has lost his sense of his own humanity and frailty. He tells Kent to keep out of the matter, warning, "the bow is drawn," and cautioning, "come not between the dragon and his wrath." This speech reveals Lear's second mistake. Dragons live forever, not so aged kings.

Kent continues trying to advise Lear, and Lear continues to prevent him and threaten until Kent tries to shock his ruler into reason by dropping polite forms of respectful address like "Royal Lear." Instead he suggests that Lear is mad and reminds the king of his basic nature: "What wouldest thou do, *old man*?" (Emphasis mine.)

In the exchange that follows, Lear swears by Apollo, revealing himself to be a pagan, and Kent tells the king that he swears by his gods in vain.

Appalled, Lear banishes Kent on pain of death.

As Kent withdraws, two suitors for the hand of Cordelia, the Duke of Burgundy and the King of France enter. On discovering that Cordelia will bring him no dowry, the Duke of Burgundy declines to wed her. The King of France steps forward, however, and claims Cordelia as his queen. Lear objects that he would not so far dishonor his colleague as to foist his disgraced daughter off on him, but France holds Cordelia precious beyond price.

Just before leaving for France, the newly betrothed Cordelia, who has not been at all impressed by her sisters' expressions of devotion for their father, exhorts them to take good care of Lear, expressing her conviction that she would have "preferred him to a better place" than they will.

Goneril and Regan snub her and confer privately, revealing their conviction that their father has lost his mind and that he will soon regret his decision and endanger their new authorities. They

resolve to take quick action to avoid that possibility, and Act I, Scene i, ends. It has established most but not quite all of the themes and images that help give the play its marvelous unity.

Act I, Scene ii, finds Gloucester's bastard son Edmund alone and plotting the downfall of his elder and legitimate brother, Edgar. Edmund convinces his gullible father, who wishes to manage his own authorities in his dotage and who is a foil for Lear, that Edgar is plotting against him. Misled and enraged, Gloucester orders Edgar's arrest. Edmund then advises Edgar to go armed and hide out until Gloucester's rage blows over. In Act II, Scene i, Edgar is forced into hiding as Gloucester has ordered his arrest.

At the level of IMAGE and METAPHOR, Shakespeare's language in Act I, Scene ii, introduces eclipses, comets, and meteors, thought by the Renaissance to be disturbances in the natural order and to portend disaster. Shakespeare also explores the ambiguity of the term *natural* in the context of a *natural*—that is, illegitimate—child versus the *natural* affection between children and parents. The Gloucester subplot begins here to reflect and reinforce the main plot. In terms of age and their misperceptions of their children's characters, Gloucester and Lear find themselves in similar circumstances. Misunderstood and victimized, Edgar and Cordelia mirror aspects of one another. Also alike are the filial disloyalty and corruption of Edmund, Goneril, and Regan. When Edgar next appears (Act III, Scene iv), he will be disguised as a mad beggar, Poor Tom o' Bedlam. By that time the king is really mad, and the play explores moral issues in the context of real and feigned madness.

Scene iii of Act I reveals that the predicted difficulties between Lear and his daughters have begun. Lear has struck Goneril's retainer Oswald, and Goneril instructs her servant to treat the old king with "weary negligence." In scene iv, the faithful Kent returns disguised as Caius, craves employment with Lear, and, by tripping Goneril's man, helps the king when Oswald behaves disrespectfully. Scene iv introduces the last important character of the play, Lear's jester, the Fool. Because a jester is able to say whatever he pleases in the presence of a king, Lear's Fool continually acts as Lear's conscience, focusing Lear's attention on his folly in giving his daughters authority over him. When Lear asks if the jester calls the king a fool, the Fool replies: "All thy other titles thou hast given away, that thou wast born with."

The utter corruption of the natures of Goneril, of Regan and her husband the Duke of Cornwall, and of Edmund continues to appear throughout the play. Cornwall offends against diplomatic privilege by locking Lear's messenger, Kent disguised as Caius, in the stocks. The sisters thrust Lear out of doors in a howling tempest where Lear's last reserves of reason desert him and, after commanding the tempest to rage and blow, he orders it to "strike flat the thick rotundities of the world" and spill at once all the seeds "that make ingrateful man." Almost through the entire play, Lear gives orders. When Lear meets the nearly naked Edgar disguised as the madman Tom o' Bedlam, the old king in his own madness at last realizes that a human being in essence is no more than a "naked, forked animal," and that the trappings of office are of no consequence. The old king tears off his clothes, still giving orders to the clothing as he strips: "Off, off you lendings!" he cries, "Come, unbutton here!"

When old Gloucester helps Lear by sending him to Dover, where Cordelia and a force of French troops have landed, Gloucester's bastard son Edmund betrays his father to Cornwall. After torturing and insulting the old man, Cornwall blinds him by plucking one eye out with his sword and grinding the other out with his heel—on stage (Act III, Scene vii). The enormity and inhumanity of this action so offends the moral sensibilities of one of Cornwall's retainers that he stabs the duke, giving him his death wound.

Edmund soon after has made mistresses of both sisters—the widowed Regan and Goneril, wife to the well-intentioned but ineffectual Duke of Albany. The illegitimate son of the blinded duke is trying to promote himself to a kingdom. Jealous of one another, the sisters plot. Goneril poisons Regan and, after the elder sister's own infidelities become public and her lover is mortally wounded, she commits suicide.

In the other camp, both plot and subplot present reconciliations. Disguised first as Poor Tom and then as a Kentish peasant, Edgar accompanies his blind and distracted father (Act IV, Scene vi). First, Edgar saves his father from suicide by pretending to lead him to the edge of a cliff. Gloucester falls forward to the ground. Then, in the latter disguise, Edgar first convinces his father that he has fallen from a great height and miraculously survived. Then Edgar saves Gloucester from Goneril's servant Oswald. Edgar fights Oswald and kills him. Letters that Oswald carries reveal Goneril's infidelity.

Reunited with Cordelia and restored to sanity by a physician's care, Lear recognizes his daughter and prays that she will "forget, and forgive," since he is "old and foolish" (Act IV, Scene vii). The King of France has been called home, and when the opposing armies finally meet, the English win the day and Lear and Cordelia are captured.

King Lear has been called a play about the belated education of a prince with much justification. In Act V, Scene iii, the captive Lear has finally figured out what really matters. He looks forward to spending his remaining time in prison with Cordelia where the two of them "will sing like birds i' th' cage." Cordelia will ask Lear's blessing, and Lear Cordelia's forgiveness. The old king envisions happiness with his favorite child at last. That expectation, however, will be thwarted. Edmund arranges for a captain to murder the two in prison.

In this same scene, Goneril poisons Regan, and the Duke of Albany, who has finally become aware of Goneril's infidelity, announces Edmund's arrest on capital treason, challenging him to fight against an anonymous champion who will prove the truth of the accusation in trial by combat. On the third sounding of a trumpet, Edgar appears armed and unrecognized. He and his half brother fight, and Edmund falls mortally wounded. Distracted, Goneril runs off and stabs herself to death.

The dying Edmund, in a gesture of death-bed repentance, remembers the order he has given for Lear and Cordelia's death and sends his sword to the captain as a sign that its bearer has authority to countermand that death sentence. It comes, however, too late.

Lear enters bearing the dead Cordelia in his arms. We learn that he killed the captain who hanged her. In a riveting final scene, the old king thinks for a moment that perhaps Cordelia lives. Convinced at last that she is gone, he addresses her and grieves, "Thou'lt come no more / Never, never, never, never, never."

Then, for the first time in the play, instead of giving an order, Lear makes a request: "Pray you," he says to Kent, "Undo this button. Thank you, sir." Three brief sentences later, Lear dies thinking he sees motion on Cordelia's lips.

The kingdom passes to a reluctant Edgar, now next in line, and the play closes with a "dead march"—a funeral procession. The bodies of Lear, Cordelia, Edmund, Goneril, and Regan all are borne offstage to the beating of a muffled drum. The best of Shakespeare's tragedies, *King Lear* is also the darkest of them. It offers little optimism about the human condition.

Anyone seeing a good performance of *King Lear* will understand experientially what ARISTOTLE meant by CATHARSIS. Typically, audiences seem so deeply moved that they sit emotionally drained, stunned by what they have just witnessed. Shakespeare typically makes no effort to conform to the artificialities of the UNITIES of time, place, and action imposed by Italian critic LUDOVICO CASTELVETRO in his interpretation of Aristotle. The action of Lear covers a span of many months—not a single day. It takes place in a variety of locations—further than one could travel afoot or on horseback in a 24-hour period. But the play sweeps from beginning to end with such an unremitting series of disasters and tragic and pathetic incidents portrayed in such deeply moving language that it achieves total unity of action in a genuinely Aristotelian sense.

Bibliography

Shakespeare, William. *The Tragedy of King Lear*. In *The Riverside Shakespeare*, edited by G. Blakemore Evans et al. Boston: Houghton Mifflin Company, 1997.

Kingo, Thomas Hansen (1634–1703)

A Danish poet and hymnodist, Kingo focused his work on translating into the Danish language the great hymns of earlier Protestant Europe. The intensity with which he expresses his feelings for nature, particularly, sets Kingo's work above that of other Danes of his epoch who were engaged in similar efforts.

Two of his collections are remembered as particularly noteworthy: his *Spiritual Chorus* (1673–81) and his *Morning and Evening Songs* (1677–84). Some of these, set to music by various composers, are available on a sound recording in Danish.

Knight of the Burning Pestle, The
Francis Beaumont (ca. 1611)

Partly inspired by CERVANTES's *DON QUIXOTE*—or by reports of it—the play begins when George, a grocer, rises from the audience to interrupt the prologue in a London theater. George proclaims that he wants to see a play celebrate an ordinary Londoner as its hero. Nell, George's wife, chimes in, proposing that the play feature a grocer who kills a lion with a pestle—an implement ordinarily used to grind things in a bowl, but also a policeman's nightstick or club. In this play the term is also frequently a phallic pun on *pizzle*—the penis of a bull or other animal that was often used to flog prisoners. George proposes that his apprentice, Ralph, who has a neighborhood reputation as an actor, play the hero's part. The speaker of the prologue agrees to all this, Ralph demonstrates his acting ability by misquoting Hotspur's speech on honor from SHAKESPEARE's *HENRY IV, PART I*, and the play begins anew.

As it progresses, George and Nell conduct a frequent and spirited commentary on its action. They make suggestions for the actors' behavior. They occasionally participate in the action. They eventually become so engrossed in the play that they forget for a time that everything is only make-believe. The subject matter regularly adjusts itself to comply with the couple's demands. When they want more of Ralph, they get more. When they want him in a more exotic setting than London, he appears in the royal court of Moldavia, whose princess's heart he breaks by reproving her Roman Catholicism, remaining true to his quest, swearing his undying affection for Susan, a cobbler's maid in Milk-street, and leaving.

When George and Nell want Ralph to die in a sad ending, despite a boy's advice to George that Ralph's death will be unfit for comedy, Ralph obliges, appearing with an arrow through his head. Instead of bleeding, the dying Ralph treats the audience to a foolish parody of Hieronymo's dying speech from THOMAS KYD'S TRAGEDY, *Hieronymo is Mad Againe*. Vastly pleased with the outcome, Nell invites the entire audience home for "a pottle of wine" and a "pipe of tobacco," ending the play with a peremptory, "Come, George."

BEAUMONT'S stunning innovation of ostensible audience participation in the play proved wildly successful with London audiences. Beyond this, *The Knight*'s plot mixes the traditional stuff of romantic COMEDY, with STOCK CHARACTERS, and the occasional situation drawn from *DON QUIXOTE*. Young lovers, Luce Venturewell and Jasper Merrythought, are thwarted because Luce's father has chosen a dolt, Master Humphrey, as Luce's future husband. At the same time he has dismissed Jasper to separate him from Luce. Luce convinces Humphrey that he must kidnap her to win her affection and must take her to Waltham Forest. There she intends to meet Jasper and elope with him. Ralph in the meantime parodies *Don Quixote* by reading a CHIVALRIC EPIC about "Palmerin of England." Consumed with an appetite for knight-errantry, he dubs himself the Knight of the Burning Pestle, acquires a pair of apprentices as followers, and outlines for their bemused benefit the regulations of chivalric questing. Eventually the lovers are united through a variation on the ancient device of feigning death and being carried into each other's presence in coffins.

In another allusion to Cervantes, Ralph mistakes the Bell Inn for a castle, a barber for a giant, and his customers for his victims. Everyone humors Ralph in his misperceptions. In the character of the giant Barbarossa, the Barber of Waltham swears on the pestle to forego his evil ways.

The Knight of the Burning Pestle helped develop a public taste for *City Comedies*—light fare that featured situations and characters drawn from the London audiences' familiar daily lives.

Bibliography
Beaumont, Francis. *The Knight of the Burning Pestle*. Edited by Sheldon P. Zitner. Manchester, U.K., and Dover, N.H.: Manchester University Press, ca. 1984.

Kong Shangren (K'ung Shang–jen) (1648–1718)

A premier Chinese dramatist and critic of the later Qing (Ch'ing) dynasty, Kong Shangren authored, among others, a long (40 acts), famous, historical play, THE PEACH BLOSSOM FAN (1699), over whose text and songs he labored for 10 years before deeming it ready for public presentation. He figured as well among a new generation of Chinese authors whose works were in part designed to illustrate their literary principles. As a result, when his work was published, Kong appended to it an introduction and interlinear analysis that conducted a careful and ongoing criticism and explanation of what he hoped to achieve.

Kong's reputation as a teacher and scholar earned him imperial favor. At the request of the Emperor Kangxi (K'ang-hsi), Kong presented a lecture before him in Shandong (Shantung) in 1684. As a result, the emperor employed Kong as a civil servant. He occupied several imperial offices from around 1684 until, for reasons unknown, the emperor dismissed him in 1699.

Kong also enjoyed the distinction of being a direct descendant of Confucius at a remove of 64 generations. This fact inspired him to pen a voluminous genealogy of his family (1684) and to re-edit historical materials dealing with the region of Confucius' birth.

Bibliography
Dolbey, William. *A History of Chinese Drama*. London: Elek Books Limited, 1976.

Mair, Victor H., ed. *The Columbia History of Chinese Literature.* New York: Columbia University Press, 2001.

Korean alphabet, invention of
(1443–1444)

After KING SEJONG of Korea came to the throne in 1418, he soon established an Academy of Worthies to improve the state of arts and sciences in Korea. The academy's learned members identified as a major problem the lack of an indigenous system of writing in Korea. Literate Koreans were constrained to learn Chinese and to use the ideographic and phonographic system of characters employed to represent that language.

The members of the academy saw that the alphabetic system of writing used to represent the languages of the Middle East and Europe had a major advantage over the Chinese system. A small number of symbols could be used to represent the sounds of the language and put together as the vocabulary required. The Chinese system—and any system that represents ideas with symbols—needs thousands of characters to do the same job. In the days before computers, Chinese typewriters would have needed about 5,000 keys.

With the king's approval, the academy's members devised a system of 28 letters to represent all the sounds of Korean. Their system is still in use, although now the number of letters has been reduced to 24. The first work to be produced in Korea using the new alphabet appeared between 1445 and 1447. Appropriately, the volume, entitled *Songs of flying dragons,* contained a series of eulogies in honor of King Sejong's father and his grandfather who founded the Yi dynasty in 1392.

After the Korean alphabet's introduction Korean writers used both Korean and Chinese as languages of formal literary expression.

Bibliography

Lee, Peter H., ed. *Anthology of Korean Literature From Early Times to the Nineteenth Century.* Honolulu: University of Hawaii Press, 1981.

Korean language works

The literary culture of Korea until the mid-15th century was a mixture of Korean folk elements and Buddhist devotional elements. Although the high literary culture of Korea remained Chinese owing to the education of the literary elite who were also the imperial civil servants, the invention of the KOREAN ALPHABET in 1443–44 did give rise to a number of works in the native tongue of the country. The earliest of these, *Songs of Flying Dragons,* was a cycle of poems eulogizing the founding of the Yi dynasty in 1392 and praising the ancestors of King Sejong (1397–1450), the literary father of his country.

During the Yi dynasty, which lasted for 518 years, Korea's official religion became Confucianism, and poets continued using Chinese alongside Korean to pen the native *sijo*—a form of short verse lyric designed for singing or oral recitation. Literally thousands of *sijo* were and continue to be produced on topics ranging from patriotism to love to SATIRE to court manners to time and its vicissitudes. The point of view of the *sijo* poets generally manages to combine Taoist and Confucian points of view with respect to nature and society.

A more rambling and discursive sort of prose poem, the *kasa,* also developed alongside the *sijo.* There are no set limits on the *kasa*'s length, and it ranges widely in the subjects it treats. Often realistic, some *kasa*s reflect on love unfulfilled, others on the grief that exile brings. One celebrates the retired and bucolic life of the farmer. The form became a favorite with women writers chaffing against the restraints that their country's culture imposed upon them. Like *sijo, kasa* were intended for singing.

Prose narratives of the Yi dynasty, which of course encompasses the period this encyclopedia addresses, followed the pattern of Chinese models. KIM MAN-JUNG (1637–92) uses the familiar situations of the Chinese romance novel to explore across a series of reincarnations the lessons one can learn in earth and heaven in his *A DREAM OF NINE CLOUDS.* HŎ KYUN introduces the theme of discrimination against illegitimate children into his story of social criticism about a heroic title character *The Tale of Hong Kiltong.* SATIRES and personal portraits also appear among the prose narratives of the Yi dynasty and diaries occasionally achieve literary status as well.

Bibliography

Lee, Peter H. *Anthology of Korean Literature from Early Times to the Nineteenth Century.* Honolulu, University of Hawaii Press, 1981.

Krishnadāsa Kavirāja Gosvāmi
(1527–1607)

A Bengali poet, biographer, and hagiographer, Krishnadāsa wrote a more complete biography of the saint and religious reformer, CHAITANYA DEVA (1486–1533) than did the earlier biographer, VRINDĀVĀN DĀS. Written as an EPIC poem, Krishnadāsa's biography is considered the only one of that genre in 16th century Bengali literature. Critics praise (*Chaitanya Charitamrita*) The nectar of Chaitanya's life history for being at the same time a model of a saint's life that mingles "imagination with erudition" in great poetry and a "serene religious treatise" filled with spiritual fervor, philosophy, and devotion. They also admire it for the beauty of its lyric verse.

Krishnadāsa follows the example of his predecessor in dividing the life of Chaitanya into three parts. The later biography, however, picks up the story at about the point the earlier book stops. A reader follows the religious ascetic Chaitanya up, down, and across the Indian subcontinent as he expounds and clarifies for his listeners his religion of love. Whereas Dās's earlier work concentrates on Chaitanya as a Bengali figure, Krishnadāsa follows him throughout the land, clarifying his national importance. We discover Chaitanya's appeal to persons of all ranks, castes, and religions. We come to understand the power of the reformer's personality and to appreciate his followers' conviction that somehow that personality incarnated the Hindu deity Lord Krishna—one of the manifestations of the god Vishnu whose cult Chaitanya spread. Of the several verse biographies of Chaitanya in Indian languages, that of Krishnadāsa is the definitive one.

Bibliography

De, Sushilkumar. *Early History of the Vaishnava Faith and Movements in Bengal.* 2nd ed. Calcutta: Firma K. L. Mukhopadhya, 1961.

Krishnadevaraya (ruled 1509–1530)

The most remarkable of the south Indian dynasty of Vījayanagara emperors, Krishnadevaraya was also a patron of writers and himself a notable poet both in the ancient and most scholarly of the LANGUAGES OF INDIA, Sanskrit, and in the vernacular language of his region, Telugu. His one Telugu work ranks among the outstanding verse creations of his language.

The poem *Amuktamalyda* tells the story of a girl of the same name and how she came to marry the Hindu deity Andravishnu. As special as the poem itself is the way in which Krishnadevaraya reports that he came to write it. The god Andravishnu, himself, the emperor explained to his courtiers, visited him in a dream and instructed him to write a poem on the topic of the god's wedding to the girl. The god told the emperor to write the work in Telugu because he was the god who lived in the Telugu-speaking region and because "Telugu is as sweet as sugar-candy."

Though modern editions are available in Telugu, no English translation has as yet appeared.

Kyd, Thomas (1558–1594)

The son of a London scrivener or notary, Kyd was born in London and educated there at the Merchant's Taylors' School, one of the schools established for the education of the children of the rising middle classes. There he was able to acquire at least the rudiments of Latin, French, Spanish, and Italian. Though his father had intended that Thomas follow in his footsteps, Kyd opted instead for the theater, for which he principally wrote and translated tragedies. His most notable play is the SENECAN TRAGEDY, *THE SPANISH TRAGEDY, OR HIERONYMO IS MADDE AGAINE* (1592). Kyd is also known to have translated the Frenchman Robert Garnier's play, *Pompey the Great his Fair Cornelias Tragedie* into English. Beyond this, two anonymous tragedies are thought to be his: *The Rare Triumphs of Love and Fortune* (1598) and *The Tragedye of Solyman and Perseda* (ca. 1592). Kyd may also have had a hand in composing *A True Chronicle History of King Leir* (1605), a version of the story that WILLIAM SHAKESPEARE's *KING LEAR* also recounts.

Bibliography

Kyd, Thomas. *The Spanish Tragedy.* Edited by David Bevington. Manchester, U.K.: Manchester University Press, 1996.

———. *Tragedy of Solyman and Perseda.* Edited by John J. Murray. New York: Garland Press, 1991.

Tydeman, William, ed. *Two Tudor Tragedies.* New York and London: Penguin, 1992.

Kynaston, Sir Francis (1587–1642)

A minor English poet and a Renaissance editor of Chaucer's *Troilus and Crisseide,* Sir Francis Kynaston's work is of interest principally because he carried the PETRARCHIST CONCEIT to its furthest point among English versifiers of the Renaissance. Not merely satisfied, for instance, to compare his lady's lips with roses, her teeth with pearls, her breast with snow, and so forth as run-of-the-mill imitators of PETRARCH regularly did, Kynaston added to those features of his beloved's praise the notion that her beauties provided the Platonic ideals from which the universe drew its models.

"Do not conceal," he advises his lady, "those eyes of thine," lest the stars forget how to shine. Similarly, coral and pearl draw their inspiration from her lips and teeth, and so on through the lady's several stylized attributes. Most important, Kynaston insists, the lady's virtue gives the universe a model for its goodness.

Kynaston's work provides a useful reference point for persons interested in understanding the way in which a skillful poet could still gracefully handle material that had become hackneyed from centuries of overuse.

Lady of Pleasure, The   James Shirley (1635)

SHIRLEY's best known COMEDY, *The Lady of Pleasure* opens to find Aretina Bornwell, a recent arrival in London and an enthusiastic participant in the city's social scene, arguing first with her steward and then with her husband. Aretina prefers the whirl and gallantry of London, whereas her steward praises peaceful country pleasures. Her husband, Sir Thomas Bornwell, objects to the expense of city life with its balls, dinners, and costly entertainments and is concerned as well about his wife's reputation. A high-class bawd, Madame Decoy, appears briefly, and she means to arrange a love affair for Aretina. Two town fops, Alexander Kickshaw and John Littleworth, pay a call on the Bornwells, repeating all the tattle of the town and swearing their devotion to Aretina. Unable to persuade Aretina, who has noble family connections, that her spendthrift ways could ruin him, Bornwell resolves to appear to join her in the unbridled pursuit of town pleasures in hopes of reforming her.

Shirley introduces a parallel situation in the second scene. Lady Celestina Bellamour—a rich and beautiful young widow—receives a visit from a man named Haircut who claims to be a courtier and wants to marry her. Although Celestina intends like Aretina to participate in the pleasures of the town, she has no intention of submitting her person or her fortune to another husband, and she toys with Haircut (who is a

barber in the service of a lord), wittily encouraging his hopes while keeping him at a distance.

Back at the Bornwell's in Act II we find Aretina upset at the appearance of her nephew Frederic, who has arrived on a visit from his university dressed in black academic garments. She wants him to give up study, dress fashionably, and become a town gallant. He agrees to do so.

At Celestina's once more, more company arrives including the perfumed and powdered Sir William Scentlove and later Bornwell. Already knowing the Bornwell's reputation, Celestina shrewdly guesses that Bornwell is feigning gallantry just as she is enjoying bilking her foppish suitors. She and Bornwell lead the company in a dance symbolic of the potential for the coexistence of moral uprightness and honorable pleasure. They begin a mock flirtation.

Act III introduces a widower, Lord A., who still grieves over the loss of his wife, Bella Maria. It is he whom Haircut serves as a barber. Madame Decoy calls on Lord A. and suggests that she arrange a liaison between him and Aretina Bornwell. Lord A. threatens to call the law on Decoy for procuring and begins writing a letter warning Aretina of Decoy's character. In the meantime, Kickshaw and Littleworth visit Lord A. They sing the praises of Celestina's beauty, and Lord A. agrees to meet her.

Aretina receives Lord A.'s letter. Alerted to Decoy's character and intentions, Aretina decides to use Decoy to defame Celestina, of whose beauty Aretina has become jealous. Aretina also engages Kickshaw and Littleworth in the same enterprise, but Celestina is far too intelligent for them, and they fail. Aretina finds herself appalled at her own intrigues but also unable to forego them.

In the first scene of Act IV Decoy disguises herself in an effort to seduce Kickshaw for whom she has developed a passion. Kickshaw is an easy target. The second wittily satirical scene presents the formerly scholarly Frederick showing off his new and fashionable finery to Littleworth and the Bornwell family's steward. In the second scene the major characters begin to question their own motives. Aretina acknowledges Celestina's superior gifts and attractiveness. Bornwell begins to think that perhaps he finds Celestina too attractive and that his motives may not be altogether honorable. In the third scene Celestina and Lord A. meet and in a witty, careful, and polite conversation take each other's measure and discover that they are mutually attracted.

In the fifth act Bornwell's imitation of a rakish, London fop and profligate finally has an impact on Aretina. She begins to see herself in his behavior but pretends commitment to her spendthrift ways despite the specter of imminent bankruptcy. Her nephew Frederick, moreover, has become a drunk and a lecher as well as a fop and makes amorous advances to her. So does Kickshaw, and Madame Decoy tries ever more insistently to achieve Aretina's dishonor. At last convinced of the error of her ways, Aretina reforms herself, talks Frederick into returning to college, and undertakes the reformation of Kickshaw and Decoy.

Act V is presented as a single scene, and its second part brings together Lord A. and Celestina, who acknowledge their feelings for one another and agree to wed. The final part portrays the reconciliation of Aretina and her husband, both of whom reject the false pleasures of a fashionable but dishonorable London society in favor of the honorable pleasures of conjugal affection in a simpler, country setting.

Bibliography

Shirley, James. *The Dramatic Works of James Shirley.* 1883. Edited by William Gifford and Alexander Dyce. New York: Russell and Russell, 1966.

La Fayette, Marie-Madelaine Pioche de la Vergne, comtesse de La Fayette
(Madame de Lafayette) (1634–1693)

The daughter of a family whose social status was rising from the upper bourgeoisie to the lesser nobility, La Fayette (or Lafayette) received a private education from tutors and from her teenage years participated in the literary salons of the doyenne Catherine de Vivonne, marquise de RAMBOUILLET and the novelist MADELAINE DE SCUDÉRY. A friend and admirer of the nun Mother Angélique de La Fayette, who headed the Convent of Chaillot, the young Marie-Madelaine came to know the mother superior's brother, Comte François de La Fayette. The couple married in 1655 and produced two sons during the next four years. After that time, the comtesse moved to Paris, where she and the count occasionally got together as friends. When Princess Henrietta of England married Philippe d'Orléans, brother of King Louis XIV of France, in 1661, Madame de La Fayette joined her at court and remained a courtier for the rest of her life, acting as a diplomat to the Duchy of Savoy on the king's behalf and participating fully in the intellectual and literary life of Paris. She formed an intimate and enduring association with the duc de La Rochefoucauld, who penned the celebrated *Maximes* and who may have had a hand in writing some of the works now attributed to her.

Madame de La Fayette apparently shared to a degree the aversion that upper-class women felt in having their names attached to their literary productions. Moreover, as her translator John D. Lyons explains, her works may have arisen to a degree from the joint efforts of members of the literary salons she frequented. Lyons notes that notions of authorship and literary ownership differed in 17th-century France from our contemporary ideas. Moreover, the work for which Madame de La Fayette is most famous did not appear in print under her name until 1781. That work, *THE PRINCESS CLEVES*, however, is celebrated as a watershed novel. It marks the transition away from the older sort of multivolume, complex French romances like HONORÉ D'URFÉ's *ASTREA* or Madelaine de Scudéry's *Clélie, histoire romaine* (Clélie, a Roman story). In the place of settings and characters distant in time and space and of magical incidents and improbable plots, Madame de La Fayette and her putative collaborators offered a new realism. Settings were recognizable. Historical situations and personages were wedded to imaginary incident to achieve a kind of historical fiction within a shorter and more readable text. In addition to her groundbreaking novel, *The Princess of Cleves,* Madame de La Fayette is sometimes credited with two earlier works in the manner of her predecessors, *La Princesse de Montpensier* (The princess of Montpensier, 1662) and, coauthored with Jean-Regnauld Segrais and the duc de La Rochefoucauld, *Zaïde* (Volume I, 1670; published under the name of Segrais; Volume II, 1670–71). Other attributions to her pen have been disproved.

Bibliography

Haig, Stirling. *Madame de Lafayette.* New York: Twayne Publishers, 1970.

Lafayette, Marie-Madelaine de. *The Princess of Cleves.* Edited and translated by John D. Lyons and Thomas S. Perry. New York: W. W. Norton & Company, 1994.

La Fontaine, Jean de (1621–1695)

Trained in the law, La Fontaine preferred the life of a poet who depended on the generosity of patrons to support his literary endeavors. He was passionately attached both to the writings of ancient authors and to those of many of his immediate predecessors and contemporaries in the French, Italian, and Spanish tongues. He described himself as "a butterfly on Mount Parnassus"—one who sampled the sweetness of the various literary offerings of those inspired by the MUSES. In the ongoing quarrel that he started about whether ancient times or modern times were better, La Fontaine firmly backed the ancients. He flirted with a religious vocation in 1641–42 but left the order of the Oratorians after less than a year with them. In 1645–46, he studied law.

Although he married Marie Héricart in 1647 and subsequently fathered a child, Charles, La Fontaine apparently found family life as uncongenial as he had the church and the law, and he often lived apart from his wife and son. This situation

suited her as well as him, for casual affairs were the norm for persons of their social status, and neither took the other's peccadilloes very seriously.

Thereafter the poet moved from one patron to another as he penned his numerous works. The year 1654 saw the publication of his unsuccessful imitation of the Roman Terence's comedy, *The Eunuch.* About this time, La Fontaine attracted the attention of an important official who was also a patron of the arts, Nicholas Fouquet; in 1658 the poet presented his patron with a splendid manuscript of a major poem, his mythological work, *Adonis.* He worked on a verse comedy, *Clemène* (1671) in this period as well.

Fouquet was arrested in 1661 for abuses connected with his official position. In 1662 appeared La Fontaine's anonymously published poem, his *Élégie aux Nymphes de Vaux* (Elegy to the nymphs of Vaux). This poem implores the animistic spirits of the region to plead that King Louis XIV be merciful toward Fouquet. In 1663 La Fontaine made a more direct appeal to the king on his patron's behalf in an ode addressed to the monarch. It seems not to have helped Fouquet, but it brought the poet to the favorable attention of the royal family. In that same year, La Fontaine wrote a series of charming letters to his wife. These would be published after his death as *Le Voyage en Limousin* (The journey in Limousin).

The widowed dowager duchesse d'Orléans, the sister-in-law of Louis XIII, now came to the poet's assistance. He became a member of her household in 1664, and she became his new patron. Her support freed him to work on what would become one of the centerpieces of his life work, his *Novels and Tales in Verse* (Part I, 1665; Part II, 1666). In 1668 followed the first installment of the masterpiece for which he is principally remembered, his verse *FABLES OF LA FONTAINE.* This work he continued to expand throughout his lifetime, with installments coming in 1678–79 and in 1693.

La Fontaine set his hand to a number of other literary projects. Among them, he collected poems on Christian subjects and dedicated the anthology to the prince de Conti (1671). Also in a religious vein La Fontaine dedicated to the cardinal de Bouillon a religious poem on the subject of St. Malc's captivity (1673). He composed libretti for operas *Daphné* (1674) and *Astrée, tragédie lyrique* (Astree, a lyrical tragedy, 1691). He also wrote a number of miscellaneous poems for his patrons and translated tales from BOCCACCIO. This list is suggestive; by no means is it exhaustive.

The highpoint of La Fontaine's literary recognition came with his election to the Académie française in 1683, but King Louis XIV had another candidate, Boileau, and so he delayed La Fontaine's induction into the august body. Another opening for Boileau soon came along, however, and Louis withdrew his objections. La Fontaine achieved France's highest literary honor in 1684.

His recent biographer, Marie–Odile Sweetser observes that, like any truly great artist, La Fontaine was obliged to create his own genre. Though he pretended to be following the ancient Greek fabulist Aesop, La Fontaine was busy reworking Aesop's material, making it self-referential, satirical, funny, sometimes scandalous, and always entertaining.

Bibliography

La Fontaine, Jean de. *La Fontaine's Bawdy: of Libertines, Louts, and Lechers: Translations from the Contes et nouvelles en vers.* Translated by Norman R. Shapiro. Princeton, N.J.: Princeton University Press, ca. 1992.

———. *Love and Folly: Selected Fables and Tales of La Fontaine.* Translated by Marie Ponsot. New York: Welcome Rain Publishers, 2002.

———. *Once again, La Fontaine: Sixty more Fables.* French and English with accompanying CD. Translated by Norman R. Shapiro. Hanover, N.H.: University Press of New England, ca. 2001.

———. *The complete fables of Jean de la Fontaine.* Translated and edited by Norman B. Spector. Evanston, Ill.: Northwestern University Press, 1988.

———. *The Tales and Novels of Jean La Fontaine. Completely Translated into English.* New York: Privately printed, 1929.

Sweetser, Marie–Odile. *La Fontaine.* Boston: Twayne Publishers, 1987.

Lámi'í of Brusa ('Osman-zade Mahmùd) (ca. 1472–ca. 1531)

A disciple of a noted mystical teacher, the author Lámi'í composed both prose translations and poems in Turkish. His most renowned prose work, an ethical romance *Sheref-ul-Insán* (The nobility of humanity), freely translates an Arabic work, The contest of man with the animals. Other prose translations included some farfetched ALLEGORIES and the Arabic biographer Jami's lives of mystic saints.

In mixed verse and prose, Lámi'í penned an allegorical representation entitled—depending on the source one follows—either *Munázara i Behár u Shitá* (The contention of spring and winter) or *Munázara i Behár u Khazán* (The contention of Spring and Fall). In either case Lámi'í presents the progression of the seasons as warfare between rival kings. In the original the work is said to be very beautiful, and the writer has developed his material into a full-length romance.

Lámi'í's verse principally includes romantic MESNEVÍs. These lengthy narrative works composed of couplets bypass the usual subjects for such tales—such as the highly embroidered biblical story of JOSEPH AND ZELÍKHÁ. Instead, Lámi'í sought his subjects among the less familiar narratives of ancient Persia, thereby treating subjects new to Turkish letters. Five of his seven romantic verse narratives—the greatest number composed by an Eastern poet—look to Persian originals for their inspiration. Edward Fitzgerald translated one of these, *Selámán and Absál,* from Persian into English in the 19th century. All five recount the legendary love stories of ancient persons.

Perhaps the most interesting of Lámi'í's other romances is his *Heft Peyker* (The seven effigies). This tale details the way in which King Behrám V sees the portraits of seven beautiful princesses, falls in love with them all, and resolves to make them his brides. He successfully achieves this quest, and on each of his seven wedding nights each bride recounts for her new husband a subsidiary romance. As a result, a reader benefits from having eight tales within the framework of the main one. This feature characterized many Middle Eastern stories going all the way back to Scheherezade's *A Thousand and One Nights.*

The other two of Lámi'í's *mesnevís* present allegorical romances of a sort once very popular among Eastern readers. Entitled *Shem' u Perváne* (The taper and the moth) and *Gúy u Chevgán* (The ball and the bat), this class of narrative personifies, in the first case, irrational creatures and, in the second, inanimate objects as lover and beloved. English parallels might be found in a nursery rhyme like "The Owl and the Pussycat," and in the line about the dish that ran away with the spoon. In any case, the Ball (a polo ball in this case) represents the persistent lover who returns as often as the Bat drives him off, only to be knocked away again. The Moth, of course, is attracted to its own destruction by the irresistible appeal of the Taper's flame.

Lámi'í numbers one other *mesneví* among his works, *Maqtel-i Hazret-i* (The martyrdom of St. Huseyn). In it Lámi'í recounts the story, familiar to all the faithful of Islam, of the martyr's death suffered by the Prophet's grandson. Hearing about the poem's existence, a cleric maintained from his pulpit that publicly reciting such poems on religious subjects constituted blasphemy. Told of this opinion, Lámi'í issued a general invitation to the citizens of Brusa and a special one to the cleric to hear him read his poem in the city's great mosque. The poet's reading moved the entire audience to tears, and, presumably, the cleric withdrew his objections.

In addition to the works described above, Lámi'í wrote a collection of GHAZELS and QASÍDAS. He also wrote a poetic description of his native city, Brusa.

Bibliography

Gibb, E. J. W. *A History of Ottoman Poetry.* Edited by Edward G. Browne. London: Luzac and Company, 1965.

Later Seven Masters *(Hou qizi)*

A group of Chinese poets, founded by Hsieh Chen and eventually led by LI PANLONG (1514–70), the later seven masters included WANG SHIZHEN (1526–90), Hsü Chung-hsing (1517–78), Liang Yu–Yü (ca. 1520–56), Tsung Ch'en (1525–60), and Wu Kuo-lun (1529–93). Although these men spent only a few years together in Peking in about 1550, they shared an interest in and an advocacy of the application of ancient poetic practice and technique to the creation of mid-16th century Chinese poetry.

Their predecessors, the EARLIER SEVEN MASTERS, had been something of a retrospective grouping together of poets who, though they knew each other and shared common literary interests and ideals, did not often if ever operate as a literary coterie. The same could well be said of the seven later masters.

Of their number, Wang Shizhen was the best and most influential writer. He is often considered the principal writer of SHI POETRY in the second half of the 16th century. Hsieh Chen is remembered for his important criticism, and Li Panlong collected materials for widely read anthologies of poetry. On balance, however, the work of the earlier seven masters proved of higher quality and more lasting interest.

Legend of the Suns in *The Codex Chimalpopoca* Anonymous (1558)

Catalogued as *Códice Chimalpopoca,* Colección Antigua 159, of the Historical Archive of the National Museum of Archaeology in Mexico City, this important colonial manuscript contains two works written in Nahuatl language and a shorter Spanish work. One of the Nahuatl documents is *THE ANNALS OF CUAUHTITLAN* (1570), and the other is the *Legend of the Suns.* Although the manuscript itself seems to have been missing since about 1949, a photographic facsimile is available for study.

A creation EPIC, *Legend of the Suns* was composed by a different author from *The Annals.* Internal evidence suggests that the author may have composed the work while following a pictographic version of the story. The same evidence implies that readers are sometimes expected to use the *Legend* to help interpret a pictorial manuscript. At other times the author recounts associated myths in detail.

The *Legend of the Suns* does not begin the Aztec creation story quite at the beginning. From other sources, however, we learn that gods created the Earth from the body of an enormous reptile. That done, the god Tezcatlipoca became the first sun exactly 2513 years before May 22, 1558—the date composition of the *Legend* began and the place at which *The Legend* picks up the story.

The first sun's name was 4 Jaguar. The people who lived in that period ate 7 Straw (probably wild seeds and fruits). Names like those in the preceding two sentences are taken from the names of years in the

52-year cycle of the Aztec calendar. The people of the first sun were eaten by Jaguars, and after 676 years, as the last of them succumbed, the sun also died.

The second sun was called 4 Wind. People of that period ate 12 Snake (corn). The period of the second sun was 364 years, and at its end both sun and people were blown away, and the people turned into monkeys.

The third sun, 4 Rain, lasted 312 years. The people ate 7 Flint (?). Sun and people all died in a rain of fire, and the people turned into turkeys.

The fourth sun, 4 Water, brought 52 years of water. That sun lasted 676 years. An analog to the biblical story of the flood occurs in the time of the fourth sun. As the cycle ended the rains came and the skies fell down. Before that occurred, the god Titlacahuan commanded that Tata and his wife hollow out a cypress log and seal themselves inside. They did this and survived the ensuing flood. All the other people died and turned into fish. Tata and his wife, however, did not entirely escape the general destruction. Safely ashore after the waters receded, they found and cooked a fish. The smoke from their cooking fire offended the gods. They expressed their disapproval by cutting the people's heads off and turning them into dogs.

The fifth sun, 4 Movement, is the sun that shone on the author and that shines on us his readers. He tells us that this sun is represented by two different names: first, a combination of the pictographs for eagle, jaguar, falcon, and wolf; second, a combination of the pictographs for 6 Wind and 6 Flower.

Interspersed among these accounts of the five suns and following them, the author recounts several myths and legends. He also gives a quasi-historical account of the decline and fall of the city of Tollan and an apparently accurate catalogue of the rise of the Mexica (Aztec) and their dynasties and rulers.

Bibliography

History and Mythology of the Aztecs: The Codex Chimalpopoca. Translated from the Nahuatl by John Bierhorst. Tucson, Ariz., and London: The University of Arizona Press, 1992.

Leland, John (ca. 1506–1552)

One of the earliest of Elizabethan chroniclers, Anglican priest John Leland understood that when the Anglican establishment closed Roman Catholic monasteries, the contents of their libraries would inevitably be scattered and that much material existing only in manuscript would disappear. The correctness of Leland's prediction appears in the single datum that some people used discarded documents from monastery libraries as toilet tissue. Leland, who was chaplain to King Henry VIII, persuaded the king of the importance of the documents. Henry appointed Leland a royal antiquary and authorized him to sift through the holdings of abbey, church, and monastery libraries throughout England and to preserve what he considered important.

Leland accordingly began a patient and laborious, six-year-long search for manuscripts composed by early British authors. This effort culminated most importantly in a Latin work whose title translates *Commentaries on British Writers.* Among his other works one finds *The Itinerary* and another Latin work in which he describes the "world of things very memorable" that he discovered in British collections. To Leland, to his contemporary John Bale (1495–1563), and to his successor John Pits (1560–1616)—scholars who sought out and chronicled the unprinted work of early English writers—belongs the credit for the foundation of English literary scholarship.

Bibliography

Leland, John. *John Leland's Itinerary: Travels in Tudor England.* Edited by John Chandler Stroud. Gloucestershire, U.K.: Sutton Publishers, 1998.

Leviathan Thomas Hobbes (1651)

Hobbes argued in his masterpiece, *Leviathan,* that the human creature in a state of nature is as "the wolf is to the wolf." Unfamiliar with the amicable social structure of actual wolf packs, Hobbes thought his phrase meant that without the intercession of government, people, motivated only by self-interest, would be in a continual state of the war of all against all and people's lives would necessarily be "solitary, poor, nasty, brutish and short." Government, Hobbes reasoned, with an absolute monarch at its top, provides for individual and general self-preservation by making and enforcing the rules whose observation makes possible going to sleep without fear of being murdered in bed by one's neighbors.

Such a jaundiced view of basic human nature offended Hobbes's religious contemporaries when he set forth ideas directly contrary to the biblical story of the Garden of Eden and the primordial innocence of human beings, created in God's image and living in a state of nature. Some of his countrymen even attributed disasters like the outbreak of the plague in 1665 and the great London fire of 1666 to God's anger that England would tolerate an atheist like Hobbes.

Hobbes, however, was not deterred by what he considered irrational disapproval. The physical universe, he felt certain, works like the gears in a machine—a material system driven by forces that attract and forces that repel. Human psychology, likewise, arises from the same material causes, and human behavior too results from attraction and repulsion. Government arises from a necessary *social contract* in which each individual gives up aggression and the right to kill another person to a central, absolute authority with responsibility for enforcing observation of the contract.

Bibliography

Hobbes, Thomas. *Leviathan.* Edited by A. P. Martinich. Peterborough, Ont.: Broadview Press, 2002.

Leylá and Mejnún Hamdí (1500) and Fuḍūlī (ca. 1550)

The allegorical love story of *Leylá and Mejnún* has often been retold in the Islamic world since late in the 15th century. In the 16th, both Hamdí and, more successfully from the perspective of style, Fuḍūlī told the story.

The story goes that a handsome and love-obsessed youth named Qays attends a coeducational school where he meets a maiden, Leylá. The two fall madly in love, neglect their studies, and become the talk of the school despite their efforts to conceal their feelings. Qays is so smitten that his school-

mates dub him *Mejnún*—one possessed by a spirit. The name sticks, and he is thereafter known by it.

Word of the young people's feelings for each other reaches Leylá's mother. She instantly withdraws her daughter from the school and locks her away. Twice, however, Mejnún contrives to disguise himself and see her, but the servants grow so watchful that he finds further contact impossible; in his distress he goes wandering about the countryside and is so often taken for a madman by townspeople that he dwells instead in the wilderness.

There his father eventually finds him and entices him home by promising to try to arrange a marriage. After a couple of false starts, the father fulfills his promise and is well received by Leylá's people until her father discovers who the proposed groom is to be. Convinced that Mejnún is mad, the father considers him unsuitable. Mejnún retreats even further into his obsession.

His father takes him on pilgrimage to Mecca, instructing the lad to pray for release from his passion. Mejnún thanks God for it instead and prays that it will grow. His defeated father leaves Mejnún to his fate and returns home. The young man's relatives also consider him a disgrace, and the fact that he is also a poet who writes very popular *GHAZELS* on the subject of his love fuels their disapproval. His tribal chief threatens to kill him. The father tries once more to rescue the youth from his passion. Unable to do so, he advises him to flee; Mejnún does so, traveling to the city of Nejd where he continues writing his love poems.

Meanwhile Leylá, equally in love with Mejnún but much more circumspect and crafty, spends time on her roof where the wind blows phrases from Mejnún's verse to her. She answers his poems on scraps of paper that she throws into the road. Strangers pick them up, memorize them, and recite them to others until they make their way at last to Mejnún. For over a year the lovers correspond in this way.

In the spring Leylá's mother, touched at last by her daughter's sorrow, counsels patience and puts off the suit of another lover who wants the girl for his bride. Mejnún in the meantime has made a friend of a warrior chief, Nevfel, who promises to aid him in gaining the girl. Much to Mejnún's distress, he mounts an attack on Leylá's clan, overcomes them, and claims the girl. Her father agrees to give her up if Nevfel promises not to marry her to the madman Mejnún. If that is to be her fate, her father promises, he will kill her himself. Thwarted once more, the unhappy lover runs away and is nowhere to be found.

Wandering again, he trades his arms and his horse to a hunter in exchange for the freedom of two gazelles and an antelope the hunter has snared, and he tells a passing crow his troubles. He then hopes to find a way to approach Leylá, so he exchanges places with a beggar in the service of an old woman who keeps him chained and roped as a madman to arouse charity in the generous. In that guise he comes at last to her parents' tent, and, madder now than ever, Mejnún falls howling to the ground before their tent flap.

The public discussion this strange business has provoked has spread the fame of Leylá's beauty far and wide. Many proposals now arrive, and against her will her parents marry her to Ibn-us-Selám. She, however, will not permit him to touch her. A doting husband, he agrees to be satisfied just to look upon her, and so matters stand for a long time while Leylá continually asks passersby for news of Mejnún.

Learning of her marriage, Mejnún writes Leylá, reproving her for marrying. Leylá replies with the truth of her situation and asks him not to judge her unfairly.

There follows a series of unlikely incidents in which Mejnún lives as a hermit in the desert, tames animals, shuns the company of people, and again refuses to accompany his father back home. The father dies. The disconsolate Mejnún visits his grave but returns immediately to his isolation.

Eventually worn down by Leylá's coldness to him, her husband sickens and dies. She summons Mejnún to her, and both faint at the sight of each other. When they come to, a tender scene ensues between them. Surrounded by the wild beasts that have accompanied Mejnún, they exchange recitations of love poems.

Mejnún's madness, however, by this time has become incurable, and, seized by another fit, he rushes back to the wilderness. Leylá soon dies broken-hearted. Mejnún now travels back and forth between the wilderness and her tomb until, worn out with grief and illness, he dies among the wild beasts. They guard his body for over a year, allowing no one to approach it. Eventually the animals abandon their vigil, and the people gather his bones and bury them next to Leylá's tomb.

Thereafter, a stalwart friend of both, Zaid, has a vision. He envisions himself in Paradise where he sees a shining young couple seated in loving conversation and surrounded by glory. Leylá and Mejnún have been united at last.

Bibliography

Gibb, E. J. W. *A History of Ottoman Poetry.* Edited by Edward G. Browne. London: Luzac and Company, 1965.

Li Dongyang (Li Tung-yang) (1447–1516)

The Chinese poet Li Dongyang became a central figure in a 16th-century Chinese literary movement that looked back to the poets of the Tang dynasty (700–ca. 1000 C.E.) for inspiration. His verse revived the SHI (*shih*) form of poetry that the Tang writers had favored. Beyond that he wrote critical commentary in which he advised close attention to poetic form, meter, and word choice in the manner of the ancients.

Perhaps his most important literary contribution was his generosity as a nurturer of younger poets' talents, he recognized and encouraged the fine work of several poets of the early 16th century including Shao Bao (Shao Pao; 1460–1527), He Mengchun (Ho Meng-ch'un; 1474–1536), and Li MENGYANG (Li Meng-yang; 1473–1530).

Based on the poetic theories Li Dongyang developed, a school of poetry that favored archaism—the Ch'a-ling school—grew up. Eventually, however, some of his early protégés found that Li Dongyang's poetry overemphasized formal elements at the expense of true feeling and moving subject matter. They therefore moved beyond his ideas, created poetic theories of their own and some became associated with a group collectively called the SEVEN EARLIER MASTERS or Gentlemen.

Li Mengyang (Li Meng-yang)
(1473–1530)

A Chinese civil servant, literary theorist, and poet, Li was a leader among the so-called EARLIER SEVEN MASTERS of Chinese letters. This label was retrospective and applied to the group by a pair of its members who wanted to be sure that literary history did not forget them.

Li made his most significant contribution to Chinese literature as a literary theorist. He deplored the literary taste and standards of his own period. He and his associates therefore sought models from which they might establish standards for the production of better poetry. In the case of the traditional style of Chinese poetry, they found these models among the poets of the Han dynasty (206 B.C.E.–220 C.E.) and the Wei dynasty (221–264 C.E.). In the case of the innovative style of poems in which Li's contemporaries principally worked, Li's models came from among the poets of the Tang dynasty (618–906 C.E.).

In Li's view great poetry was not about individual self-expression. Instead, though some individual variation was a given of poetic expression, great poetry rested on a well-established series of precepts that individual poets ignored at their peril. Because he looked to ancient poets as exemplars of great poetry, Li is considered a founder of the 16th century "archaist movement" in Chinese letters. This movement gained and retained a great many followers. Female and male poets both found the models that Li recommended congenial to their lyric talents. His views remained influential among Chinese writers for the next 400 years.

Li Panlong (Li P'an-lung) (1514–1570)

A prominent Chinese civil servant, a minor poet, and the eventual leader of the group called the LATER SEVEN MASTERS of Chinese poetry, Li is remembered chiefly as the compiler of an influential collection of representative poetry from the Tang dynasty (618–906 C.E.). This collection illustrated the aesthetic principles promoted by the seven masters. They held that the dignity and principles of poetry from the Tang period provided a better model for poets than did innovation and individual expression. This point of view gained wide acceptance among poets in China, Korea, and Japan, and the collection provided models that many poets in those countries have emulated ever since.

Li Yu (Li Yü, Li Li-weng) (1611–1679)

At first the owner and manager of a touring female Chinese theater troop that gave private performances in the homes of important people, Li Yu eventually established himself in Nanjing (Nanking) as a writer and as the owner of a publishing company called The Mustard Seed Garden. Among his publications he brought together a collection of his as yet untranslated prose writings, *Random Notes on Leisurely Enjoyments*, or as one sometimes translates the title, *Casual Expressions on Idle Feelings*. In this anthology Li Yu included a series of essays in which he propounded a very practical theory of theatrical writing and performance that bore in mind the kind of audience likely to attend—one that included many illiterates in its number. On such an audience the dense web of arcane literary allusion that sometimes characterized earlier Chinese theater would have been utterly lost.

Li Yu also authored 16 plays. Of these, six have been lost, but the other 10 survive because he published them together in a collection. In the surviving examples we see the pragmatic working out of his theories. He wrote what would sell. His plays are racy and witty. They concern themselves with matters like hetero- and homosexual love, funny situations arising from mistaken identity, the situation of three wives married to the same ugly husband, life in the theatrical world, or a fantasy situation in which the hero meets a dragon princess. He composed these plays in classical Chinese rhymed verse and intended the lyrics to be sung as they are in all Chinese drama.

Beyond the plays Li Yu authored two collections of brief, dramatic novels in the vernacular language of Nanjing. The stories in the first collection, because they were intended for private reading, he called SILENT OPERAS. The second collection contained 12 novellas. Because each of those stories contained the word *tower* in its title, the book is called TWELVE TOWERS. A pornographic novel, THE CARNAL PRAYER MAT, is also thought to be his work.

Li Yu's publishing house brought works to light beyond Li's own. A famous one by three brothers named Wang was published very near or just after Li's death: *The Mustard Seed Garden Manual of Painting* (1679–71).

Bibliography

Li Yu. *Silent Operas [Wusheng Xi]*. Translated and edited by Patrick Hanan. Hong Kong: Research Centre for Translation, Chinese University of Hong Kong, 1990.

———. *The Carnal Prayer Mat.* Translated by Patrick Hanan. Honolulu: University of Hawaii Press, 1996.

———. *Twelve Towers: Short Stories by Li Yu; Retold by Nathan Mao.* Hong Kong: Chinese University Press, 1979.

Wang Gai, Wang Shih, and Wang Nieh. *The Mustard Seed Garden Manual of Painting.* 1956. Princeton, N.J.: Princeton University Press, 1977.

Lianja and Nsongo   (date unknown)

An episodic EPIC performed among the Mongo people of the northeastern Congo, *Lianja and* [his sister] *Nsongo* shares enough attributes with other CENTRAL AFRICAN EPICS to serve as an example of the type. It contains creation myths about the origins of creatures but not of the world itself. It reveals a central concern with food production and eating and the competition for available food, sometimes between members of the same family and sometimes between members of different generations.

Lianja and Nsongo contains quasi-historical reports of migration and conquest and reflects in general the matrilineal social organization of the Mongo people, their marriage customs, and their hunting and farming practices. It also details Lianja's genealogy—certainly partly mythic and perhaps partly real.

This is an oral epic, only recently committed to text. It is composed of many more episodes than are ever enacted at a single performance, and the performers apparently tailor the episodes they choose to include to suit the occasion for the production. A typical selection might include the story of Lianja's earliest ancestor, who journeys across a body of water to steal the Sun and to find a wife. He succeeds in these ventures, and his new wife bears him a son named Lonkundo.

Lonkundo comes with a curse. If anyone ever gives him a direct order, he will die. Despite this threat, Lonkundo's maternal grandmother twice directs the lad to give her his food. As expected, Lonkundo dies on both occasions. The first time, a magical remedy brings him back to life. The second time, the grandmother destroys the remedy before it can work, and Lonkundo stays dead. His father, perceiving that his wife's family means no good to his progeny, kills them all, his wife and her mother included, and once again restores his son to life. The thankless youth then kills his father and goes to the center of the world. There his father's spirit, seemingly bearing no ill will toward the son who executed him, gives Lonkundo hunting lessons in the lad's dreams.

Now Lonkundo marries, and he and his wife dwell in the jungle. When she becomes pregnant, the little food Lonkundo has been able to stockpile begins to disappear. Suspecting a thief, they set a trap. In it they are surprised to catch their own still unborn child who has been sneaking out of the womb at night and eating them out of house and home. Quite naturally alarmed by these developments, and suspecting that the monster is no child of theirs, the parents name the child Itonde and abandon him, setting traps to keep him from following. He eludes all their snares, however, and when his parents invent ordeals to test his parentage, Itonde survives them all, convincing them at last that he is indeed their son. Lonkundo and his wife then give the lad a new name: Ilelangoda.

Ilelangoda seeks a wife and wins one, Mbombe, by besting her in a wrestling match. But he refuses to share with her the fruits of his hunting expeditions. She at last convinces him to do so, but she eats so fast and so much that a spirit described as the forest's owner warns that, unless Mbombe becomes a vegetarian, her appetite will empty the forest of game. Unrepentant, Mbombe borrows Ilelangoda's hunting equipment but encounters an animal that is too strong for her. When she calls for help, Ilelangoda comes on the run and throws his spear at the struggling pair, not much caring which combatant he hits. When he misses both, Ilelangoda runs away, assigning names to all the animals he encounters as he flees. He eventually comes to a village of cannibal women who promise they will eat him unless he can learn their names. He conspires with an old woman to do so. Now safe, he makes the village his home, and eventually Mbombe turns up pregnant.

She develops an obsessive appetite for safou nuts that only grow on one tree in the neighboring land of the Sausau, and supernatural creatures carefully guard the tree. Ilelangoda successfully steals nuts from the tree for a long time. Eventually, however, a turtle captures him, and Ilelangoda is killed, butchered, and eaten.

In the meantime, learning of her husband's death, Mbombe goes into labor and produces a prodigious progeny: First she bears red ants, then other sorts of ants and all kinds of insects. Next she bears a variety of birds. There follow several clans of human beings, including the Balumbe who emerge singing. Next come a number of individuals who are destined to assist Lianja in his various enterprises. Finally, first Nsongo and then Lianja is born. Lianja comes into the world, not from the womb, but from a cut in Mbombe's leg. He arrives already a full-grown adult complete with war gear and, in some versions of the story, with his wife. Parallels to Greco–Roman stories concerning the birth of Dionysius and that of Athena appear in this episode.

Next, with some difficulty, Lianja wrests the truth about his father's death from Mbombe. Her entire progeny then march against the Sausau, who are governed by a chief of the same name. In most versions of the story, this produces general carnage, with only Lianja and Nsongo left alive. Nsongo, however, prevails on Lianja to bring everyone back to life, and in some versions of the story she marries Sausau. The safou tree, which had caused all the trouble in the first place, is cut down with specially water-sharpened axes. The parallels to the creation accounts in Genesis and in the Koran may or may not be accidental. If they are not, of course, they suggest a post-European or post-Islamic-contact date for this part of the epic.

Lianja, Nsongo, and their entourage, which now includes the Sausau, march forth through the forest, conquering and assimilating as they travel. They overcome all opposition and win their erstwhile opponents to their cause. As they migrate, they also learn new technologies from the peoples they conquer. They learn to fish, to make beer, and to weave cloth.

Some episodes in some versions include the widespread folkloristic element of Lianja's encounters with a trickster. Sometimes Lianja himself becomes the trickster. Though many more episodes exist, including several MAGIC ones, some that involve Lianja's going to heaven and his death and rebirth, and several that recount Nsongo's colorful love life, an episode that often brings performances to a close reports the people's crossing a river to a spot where they at last settle down while Lianja and Nsongo rise up to heaven.

Bibliography

Belcher, Stephen. *Epic Traditions of Africa.* Bloomington, Ind.: The Indiana University Press, 1999.

Johnson, John William, Thomas Hale, and Stephen Belcher, eds. *Oral Epics from Africa: Vibrant Voices from a Vast Continent.* Bloomington: The Indiana University Press, ca. 1997.

liberal arts

European universities in the Renaissance inherited from preceding generations the medieval organization of the curriculum into two parts: the trivium and the quadrivium. Taken together the subjects in this curriculum made up the liberal arts. The study of grammar, rhetoric, and logic constituted the trivium, and that of arithmetic, astronomy, geometry, and music the quadrivium. Along with that curriculum the universities inherited a highly structured method of disputation called scholasticism that, at its worst, enabled interminable arguments on totally banal subjects such as the number of angels that could dance on the head of a pin—an infinite number since angels have no corporeal essence and can intermingle their spiritual essences.

Renaissance HUMANISTS developed highly successful methods of instruction that emphasized the early study of classical languages, especially Latin, but also Greek and Hebrew so that a pan-European, largely male elite of readers and speakers of classical Latin began to emphasize the study of the subjects included in the trivium, though not necessarily to the total neglect of the quadrivium. A tendency did develop, however, to view the quadrivium as more practical and mechanical than the trivium and thus of less use to gentlemen than to the working classes.

See also EDUCATION IN EUROPE.

Life Is a Dream (*La vida es sueño*) Pedro Calderón de la Barca (ca. 1630, revised 1635)

Generally regarded as CALDERÓN's supreme dramatic achievement, *Life Is a Dream* combines a conventional disguise and recognition plot with a philosophical, psychosocial one that sets the play apart from all but one of Calderón's other dramas.

As the play opens we find the lady Rosaura and her maid, Clarín, arriving in Poland in search of the fickle lover, Astolfo, who has jilted Rosaura and taken up with Estrella. Disguised as men, Rosaura and Clarín happen upon a castle in which the crown prince of Poland, Segismundo, is imprisoned. Finding their way inside, Rosaura and Clarín encounter Segismundo, who regales the disguised women with a self-pitying soliloquy on his loss of freedom.

His speech is interrupted by the arrival of Segismundo's tutor, Clotaldo, who doubles as the prince's jailer. Displeased at finding two unauthorized young persons inside his jurisdiction, Clotaldo arrests them as trespassers. In the ensuing discussion, Clotaldo recognizes as his own the sword Rosaura is wearing. He penetrates her disguise and realizes that she is his daughter. Once he knows who she is, he is able to interpret the story that she tells and realizes that she is trying to recover her lost honor. Clotaldo also recognizes his own paternal responsibilities in the matter, but he does not reveal to Rosaura his identity as her father.

The opportunistic Astolfo and his newfound love and cousin Estrella, in the meantime, have come to visit their uncle, Basilio, the king of Poland. With Segismundo jailed and disgraced, they may be next in line for the throne. They and the audience learn of a prophecy stemming from Segismundo's horoscope. Born under an unlucky star, Segismundo, according to the prophecy, will be a tyrant if he succeeds to the kingdom. It is for that reason that the king has sentenced his son to languish as a prisoner.

As the king begins to consider the matter of the succession, he realizes that he has no grounds for believing the prophecy. He therefore decides to test Segismundo. He will bring the prince to the palace. If the prince behaves nobly and justly there, he will succeed to his father's throne. If, on the other hand, he behaves as predicted, he will be reimprisoned and informed that the palace experiences he remembers were merely dreams.

Accordingly, the king has a narcotic administered to Segismundo, and while he sleeps deeply he is transported to the palace. Awakening there and being convinced that his memories of prison are merely dreams, Segismundo begins to behave like a self-centered eight year old in a room full of toys. He lords it over others and pursues his pleasure. Eventually he loses his temper and kills someone. He also falls in love with Roseaura and behaves caddishly.

Convinced by all this of the birth-prophecy's accuracy, the king has Segismundo once again put to sleep and returned to the prison. This time, however, his father, Basilio, accompanies the prince and secretly observes his reawakening. He watches his son as he awakens to possession of his reason and learns to distinguish between appearance and reality. Having shown himself capable of reasoning and learning from experience, Segismundo promises to use his lessons to control his emotions—especially anger.

In the meantime, a group of revolutionaries, unhappy about the prospect of a nonnative ruler, attacks the prison and sets Segismundo free. The audience watches the liberated Segismundo as, with some false steps, he rises by degrees to master himself. Nonetheless, while the education of the prince goes forward, civil war is rampant in the land. This culminates when Basilio surrenders, throwing himself on Segismundo's mercy. Segismundo lectures Basilio on the king's mistakes and then prostrates himself before King Basilio for forgiveness. The king grants it, restoring the natural order. Father and son end up the better for the lesson.

With a Spanish sense of sexual rectitude that a modern reader can only regard as quaint, Segismundo upon the throne orders the cheating Astolfo to restore Rosaura's honor by marrying her.

The philosophical questions that the play raises about the relationship between and the identity of appearance and reality are central to the speculations of representatives of many philosophies around the world.

Bibliography

Calderón de la Barca, Pedro. *Life Is a Dream/La vida es sueño.* Edited and translated by Stanley Appelbaum. Mineola, N.Y.: Dover Publications, ca. 2002.

Life of Benvenuto Cellini, The Benvenuto Cellini (begun 1558, published 1730)

The goldsmith BENVENUTO CELLINI began to dictate his biography in his 58th year. On its completion it circulated widely in numerous manuscript copies until its eventual 18th-century publication. The circumstances of its composition together with Cellini's extraordinary combination of talent, temperament, memory, ego, and curious forthrightness open a unique window for modern readers not only on a Renaissance man of remarkable accomplishment but on 16th-century Italian life as well.

The work displays the charm of Cellini's lively if not always grammatical spoken language—an idiom largely uncluttered with literary adornment. The author's faults as well as his achievements stand out in bold relief. In sharing his life with the world, Cellini principally intended to share his personal history as it relates to his work as an artist. We discover in its pages his lifelong devotion to the goldsmith's trade. We also follow his father's disappointment at Cellini's preferring that craft to music—the discipline his father had the young Benvenuto trained for and the one that the father repeatedly attempted to persuade his son to practice.

Basically honest in his reporting and self-examination, Cellini's occasional tendency toward exaggeration arises largely from the high value he set on his own intrinsic worth. He credits, for example, a demonstrably false tale of the origins and naming of Florence. It appealed to him because, in the version he reports, the city derives its name from that of Fiorino of Cellino, a Roman captain serving under Julius Caesar. Cellini claims Fiorino as an ancestor.

Cellini also credits himself with having shot and killed the constable of Bourbon and thereby saving the Vatican from invading French troops under the Constable's command. Though no evidence supports Cellini's claim, none belies it either. Cellini's best 19th-century English translator, John Addington Symonds, suggests that in Cellini's version of events his thinking went something like this: *I was firing on the invading French from the ramparts of Rome. The Constable of Bourbon was leading the French attack. Someone on the Ramparts shot and killed the Constable. I am the best shot among the defenders. It follows that my shot probably—nay, almost certainly—killed the Constable, and the Constable's death led to raising the French seige. I am largely responsible for raising the siege.* In Cellini's mind, if the truth bends, it does not do so from conscious mendacity; the possibility just morphs into fact.

Cellini's extraordinarily robust ego shines through his text at every turn. With some justice he ranks himself as the greatest goldsmith of his day. At the same time, he does not fail in praising the talent of other skilled craftsmen. His artistic judgments, moreover, in praise of the work of MICHELANGELO BUONAROTI and Leonardo da Vinci accord impeccably with the value that history sets on their work. History has also borne out Cellini's unfavorable evaluation of the graphic and plastic art works of the imminent biographer of Italian artists, GIORGIO VASARI.

Cellini values his own physical courage and his skill with sword, pistol, and dagger as much as he does his artistic accomplishment. He frequently turns aside from the history of his art to recount tales of insult, challenges, duels, and his single-handed stands against multiple adversaries. He also confesses to more than one murder in his pages. Renaissance Italian justice did not view murder, however, as the heinous crime it has since become. People were granted license to settle their own scores in matters of honor, dueling was a sanctioned method of settling insults, and Cellini wore his easily offended honor on his sleeve. He reports his brawls and killings with the same insouciance with which he treats a tumble in the hay with a teenage prostitute.

The irascible Cellini's capacities as a goldsmith, moreover, led such powerful figures as the pope to view him as a national treasure. Cellini literally got away with murder because, as the pope remarked, laws were not meant to apply to extraordinary persons like Cellini. Cellini liked blood sport, and he excelled at the use of weapons. His prowess on that front was as much a part of his character as his artistic sensibility. By contrast we also discover that he was a dutiful son (except for hating music) and a strong financial support for his birth family. He also believed in Divine Providence and thought himself to be under its special protection. Cellini approves of himself as he is. He holds back from his readers little or nothing of his view of himself. The accessibility of his text arises in part from Cellini's frank self-approval. He likes himself the way he is, and his faults, viewed from his perspective, usually look like virtues.

Through Cellini's eyes we see celebrated figures of the epoch—LUIGI PULCI, whom Cellini at first liked but then grew to despise; cardinals and kings, particularly the king of France, who liked Cellini and encouraged him to remain in Paris. We also meet art patrons, false friends, society women, prostitutes, and artisans—people whose names have long been forgotten and those whose names echo down the corridors of history. Thus, despite Cellini's work not having become a part of print culture for almost 200 years after its completion, today's readers and scholars consider his autobiography a quintessential document of the high Italian Renaissance. Once a reader begins turning its pages, *The Life of Benvenuto Cellini* is a hard book to put down.

Bibliography

Cellini, Benvenuto. *The Autobiography of Benvenuto Cellini.* Translated by George Anthony Bull. Hammondworth, U.K.: Penguin, 1956.

———. *The Treatises of Benvenuto Cellini on Goldsmithing and Sculpture.* Translated by C. R. Ashbee. London, 1888. Reprint, New York, 1967.

Life of Lazarillo de Tormes, His Fortunes and Adversities, The
Anonymous (1554)

A little book of only six chapters and a prologue appeared in three separate editions in Spain in 1554. Perhaps there was an earlier, lost original. Despite Herculean efforts, the work's author has never been certainly identified. Internal evidence, however, suggests that the author was well educated, probably a HUMANIST, perhaps a follower of ERASMUS of Rotterdam, and the work's most recent Spanish editors have been convinced by the case for Alfonso de Valdés. A reader clearly recognizes the identifying marks of a skeptic and a satirist. Whoever its author may have been, the slender volume proved to be one of the most influential works of Renaissance prose fiction, for it was something genuinely new in the world, the prototype of the PICARESQUE NOVEL and a foundation stone of modern prose fiction in general.

Ostensibly a first-person narrative spoken by an adult town crier of Toledo by the name of Lázaro, the fiction masquerades as an autobiography and displays some of the trappings of that already established Renaissance genre. The novel begins with a prologue whose classical allusions effectively satirize the displays of erudition common to Renaissance autobiographies. The work has ostensibly been written to satisfy the curiosity of a nobleman about Lázaro's history. As the adult narrator, who is both corrupt and unrepentant, tells the first-person tale of his childhood and adventures, the reader sees Lázarillo's history colored by the adult Lázaro's retrospective interpretations of events as recounted in the child's words. The resultant ironic and sarcastic distancing between the teller and the hero was to become a standard narrative technique of the picaresque or rogue novel.

The son of a miller and his wife, Lázarillo was born literally on the bank of the River Tormes—whence his surname. Convicted of stealing flour from the customers, his father was punished and then joined a military force going off to fight the Moors in Africa, where he fell in battle. To eke out a living, Lázarillo and his mother move to the city where she is employed as a cook and washerwoman. She takes an African lover, and Lázarillo soon acquires a dark skinned half brother and a de facto stepfather, Zaide. Zaide too, however, is caught stealing, suffers severe physical punishment, and is forbidden from continuing his relationship with Lázarillo's mother. She moves away, is hired as a servant, and accepts a request from a blind man that she allow Lázarillo to become his guide. She agrees, and the boy goes forth in the world with his sightless master.

From that point on in the story the new characters cease to have names. The Blind Man proves to be clever, meanspirited, and abusive. To teach Lázarillo caution, the blind man tells him to put his ear close to a stone statue of a bull and listen for a loud noise. When the lad does as he is told, the Blind Man violently pushes his head against the stone. The loud noise he hears is the ringing in his ears for several days afterward.

Suffering from hunger, Lázarillo devises methods of stealing food and drink from the Blind Man but is always caught and severely punished—the last time so severely that only the intervention of nearby people saves the boy. Having had enough and having learned both cruelty and duplicity from his master, Lázarillo turns the tables on the Blind Man and contrives to have the fellow smash his own head on a stone column. As the man lies senseless, Lázarillo runs away.

The boy next takes up with a miserly priest from whom he must steal food to keep body and soul together. This time the lad has a key to a chest where his new master keeps food. He bores holes in the chest to make the Priest think that rats or snakes are getting into it. Lázarillo hides the key in his mouth when he sleeps. One night his breathing through the key sounds to the Priest like snakes' hissing, and in the dark the Priest flails away at the serpents with a club. This has disastrous consequences for Lázarillo's teeth, and when the Priest discovers the lad's deception, he sends him away saying that the boy is as tricky as a blind man's servant.

These adventures occupy the first two chapters of the book. In the third, Lázarillo takes up with a squire whom the boy thinks is rich but who proves to be as poor as the youngster himself. When the Squire runs off and leaves Lázarillo to face his creditors, the boy narrowly escapes being punished in the Squire's place.

A friar of the Order of Mercy is Lázarillo's employer in the very brief fourth chapter. The Friar provides the boy with a pair of shoes—his first—but requires Lázarillo to accompany him on so many presumably amorous visits that the boy wears them out in a week. Finding himself overworked and the Friar disgustingly busy with a series of women who claim the brother of the Order of Mercy as a relative, Lázarillo seeks other employment.

One of the principal religious abuses of the late Middle Ages and the early Renaissance was the sale of indulgences that were supposed to relieve the purchaser of a certain period of suffering in purgatory. Geoffrey Chaucer in *The Canterbury Tales* had castigated pardoners, and Lázarillo also exposes their greed and trickery in the fifth chapter of his tale in which the Pardoner and a confederate fake a miraculous cure to separate credulous parishioners from their money.

In chapter six the nearly grown Lázarillo finds his first decent employment as a water seller and is able to earn a living wage. But after four years, when he has saved enough to buy good secondhand clothing and a sword, he decides to move on. He works for a while as a bailiff but decides, in chapter seven, that the work is too dangerous. He lands a government job as a town crier and finally reaches the part of his story that in the first place interested the nobleman to whom he is ostensibly telling it. He recounts the way in which he has married a servant girl (and the mistress) of a priest. He considers himself very fortunate in this connection, for the priest rewards Lázarillo's family generously. He ends the book by recounting how, when anyone tries to broach the subject of his wife's behavior with the priest, he refuses to listen. He explains that he will not consider anyone a friend who "sows discord" between his wife and himself, that he loves her, and thinks that she has brought him to "the zenith of good fortune."

Bibliography
Alpert Michael, trans. *Lazarillo de Tormes and The Swindler (El Buscón).* London and New York: Penguin Books, 2003.

Valdés, Alfonso de [presumptive author]. *La Vida de Lazarillo de Tormes, y de sus fortunas y de sus adversidades.* Edited by Milagros Rodríguez Cáceres. Barcelona: Octaedro, 2003.

Life of the Admiral Christopher Columbus by His Son Ferdinand, The
Ferdinand Columbus (1571)

A lifelong bibliophile with a scholarly disposition, FERDINAND COLUMBUS was moved to write his father's biography by a number of factors. First, having accompanied his father to the New World on the admiral's fourth voyage in 1502, Ferdinand was acquainted firsthand with his father's seamanship, with the dangers and difficulties that faced him in the Americas, and with his father's strengths as a visionary leader and his weaknesses as an administrator.

Second, Ferdinand was in possession of his father's papers so that he had at hand all he needed to compile an accurate history of the elder Columbus's life. Third, lives of Columbus by other authors had already appeared. Ferdinand correctly felt that these sometimes misrepresented the facts of the case, as did biographies by GONZALO FERNÁNDEZ DE OVIEDO Y VALDES or LÓPEZ DE GÓMARA, by putting words into the mouths of speakers, by lengthy digressions that left readers with spurious impressions, and by silence where important matters needed full discussion.

Most important, perhaps, Ferdinand wished to set the record straight concerning the unfulfilled promises King Ferdinand and Queen Isabella made to Columbus and his heirs—promises that had been the subject of lengthy litigation between the Columbus family and the Spanish Crown. The younger Columbus's work dwells at length on some of the issues disputed by the litigants.

While substantial portions of the material in this invaluable biography is available elsewhere, that which treats Christopher Columbus's early life in Italy is not, and for that alone history has occasion to be grateful to Ferdinand.

Ferdinand may have died before having the opportunity to put the finishing touches on his manuscript, or he may have been reluctant to publish it because of passages that took issue with the king's views about contentious matters. In any case, Ferdinand did not attempt to bring it to the press. The manuscript languished from the time of Ferdinand's death (July 12, 1539) until Christopher Columbus's grandson sold it to a physician, Baliano de Fornari, in Genoa, Italy, in about 1570. Fornari took the precious Spanish manuscript to Venice, where three editions were planned—one in Spanish, one in Italian, and one in Latin. Translation into Italian fell to Alfonso Ullúa, and that version appeared in 1571. Fornari, who subsidized the publications, died before the other two editions were readied for the press. Astonishingly, the precious Spanish original simply disappeared. While, therefore, this foundational work of New World history is available in many languages, including Spanish, all current editions trace their origins to Ullúa's Italian translation. Happily, competent scholar–editors have been able to correct evident textual errors. There is, of course, no way to be sure whether such errors are attributable to the author, to the translator, or to the printer.

The biography begins with an account of Christopher Columbus's family, place of birth, and name. It goes on to describe his person, correct the mistakes of another biographer, and follow Columbus's career before arriving in Spain. Ferdinand then traces through several chapters the process by which his father conceived his project, his search for support, and his eventual success in convincing the Spanish sovereigns to support his enterprise. There follow accounts of the outfitting of the ships, the voyage itself, the first sighting of land in the Bahamian archipelago, encounters with the indigenous population, the discovery of Cuba, shipwreck, and hostilities between the Spaniards and the Amerindians of the island of Española.

Ferdinand goes on to recount Columbus's voyage home, his reception in Europe, the pope's approval for the conquest of the newly discovered territories, the arrangements made for governing them, and Columbus's return to the New World. The account thus far summarized consumes 46 of Ferdinand Columbus's 108 chapters. Chapters 47 through 107 present the reader with a detailed account of Columbus's activities, ending with his successfully defeating a mutiny and capturing its leader.

The last chapter traces Christopher Columbus's final voyage home and his death in the city of

Valladolid. For anyone interested in the discovery of the Western Hemisphere, Ferdinand Columbus's biography of his father is the absolutely essential first requirement.

Bibliography

Colón, Fernando. *The Life of the Admiral Christopher Columbus by His Son Ferdinand.* Translated by Benjamin Keen. New Brunswick, N.J.: Rutgers University Press, ca. 1992.

———. *Historia del Almirante Cristobál Colón.* Edited by Luis Arranz Márquez. Madrid: Dastin, 2000.

Lives of the Artists, The (*Delle Vite de' più eccelenti pittori, scultori, ed architectori*) Giorgio Vasari (1550 and 1568)

The Italian artist GIORGIO VASARI began the most famous and important biographical work of the Renaissance almost by accident. In 1546 he promised the Roman Cardinal Farnese to make a classified list of notable artists for Bishop Paolo Giovio to use in preparing a treatise on notable artists. When Vasari showed the bishop his list, Giovio realized he could not write the work he had proposed and suggested that Vasari do it instead. Four years later, the first edition of *The Lives of the Artists* appeared with 133 biographical sketches of earlier Italian artists.

Vasari began his compendium with a life of Giovanni Cimabue (ca. 1240–ca. 1302), the earliest Italian artist to achieve a distinctive style uninfluenced by Byzantine conventions. Vasari duly notes Cimabue's initiative, documenting his discussion with reference to the artist's works in Florence. The mode of presentation of an artist's life and work in the Cimabue entry establishes the frame within which Vasari presents the subsequent artists. Chatty and novelistic, Vasari elucidates both the characters of his subjects and the aspects of their work that both casual viewers and art historians would find helpful.

Older scholarship has sometimes criticized Vasari's inclusion of unlikely details about some of his subjects. More recent scholars with better access to documents contemporary with the artists Vasari includes have often found confirmation of Vasari's particulars. This is little short of amazing. Specialized research libraries did not exist in Vasari's day. He had to rely on the stories that continued to circulate among the people in the regions where the artists had worked, on such documents as might casually surface or that he could trace with significant effort, and particularly upon his own professional and informed eye as he considered the work of the artists he chose to include.

At first Vasari seems to have been an insecure annalist. He disclaims any particular skill as a writer in his first edition, pointing out that he is primarily a painter and an architect. In fact, he sought feedback on style from literary friends before his work went to press. The principle advice he got back was to be more direct and less flowery. He followed it.

The public reception of Vasari's *Lives of the Artists* proved so overwhelmingly enthusiastic that Vasari overcame his initial diffidence as a writer. He had a strong sense of his own abilities and worth as a graphic artist and architect, and that same sense expanded to include his *Lives* as well. So in the second, expanded edition of the *Lives* 1568), Vasari has come to think that his work will prolong the reputations and renown of artists and that they are lucky he undertook the project. The second edition includes 168 lives and expands its scope to include both earlier artists and some of his contemporaries. In the 1568 edition Vasari begins with the ancient Chaldeans. Among the contemporary artists whose lives he discusses he includes himself in a charming autobiographical sketch. Some of Vasari's lives, like that of his teacher and close friend, MICHELANGELO BUONARROTI, are very nearly of book length on their own. Other lives, like that of the Bolognese painter and goldsmith, Francesco Francia, occupy only a few pages.

Some of Vasari's art history has been superseded by later, more professional work, and he did not get everything right. The quality of his discussion also varies. Nonetheless, Vasari's work is still a valuable source of pleasure and profit for both professional students and casual readers. The availability, moreover, of the fine recent translation by the Bondanellas makes the work a joy to read in English.

Bibliography

Vasari, Giorgio. *The Lives of the Artists.* Translated by Julia Conaway Bondanella and Peter Bondanella. Oxford and New York: Oxford University Press, 1998.

Lo Guanzhong (Lo Pen, Lo Kuan-chung) (1330–1400)

A major author of 14th-century China, Lo is credited with writing two of the most celebrated, partly historical novels of the Chinese classical tradition: THE ROMANCE OF THE THREE KINGDOMS and THE STORY OF THE WATER MARGIN. In the 16th and 17th centuries, several authors revisited these texts, expanding or shortening them for the benefit of more- and less-literate audiences and capitalizing on the interest in older literatures sparked by critical schools such as the EARLIER SEVEN MASTERS and such theorists as their leader, LI MENGYANG (1473–1530). Lo apparently also authored a number of dramas.

Lodge, Thomas (1558–1625)

Educated at the Merchant Taylors' School in London and later at Trinity College at Oxford University, Lodge, whose father had briefly been Lord Mayor of London, became a student of law at Lincoln's Inn in 1578 and soon was attracted to the London theatrical scene.

When Stephen Gosson wrote a tract attacking the theater, his *School of Abuse* (1579), Lodge replied with *A Defense of Plays* (1580). For about a decade and a half, Lodge pursued a career in literature—one that he interrupted briefly to join an expedition to South America led by the English explorer and circumnavigator of the world, Thomas Cavendish (1560–1592).

Although Lodge seemingly tried his hand at writing for the theater, drama did not prove to be his forte. He turned his attention, therefore, to writing lyric poems, verse SATIRE, prose fiction in the style of *EUPHUES,* and PASTORAL romance in prose and verse. While on Cavendish's expedition, Lodge wrote a pastoral romance, *Rosalynde* (1590). This work achieved notable success and had appeared in four editions when SHAKESPEARE borrowed its plot for *As You Like It. Rosalynde* went through seven more editions between 1600 and 1640. In 1590 he published a narrative, mythological poem, *Scilla's Metamorphosis,* together with some lesser pieces including a satire and some lyrics. He also authored a cycle of SONNETs, *Phillis* (1593), and a successful verse satire, *A Fig for Momus* (1595), which became a model for later authors.

Finally tiring of the uncertainties surrounding the literary life and having found the law uncongenial, Lodge turned to the study of medicine, taking M.D. degrees at Avignon (1600) and Oxford (1602). He practiced in London for a quarter century. During that time he limited his literary activities to translation. Lodge had already done a translation (1602) from the work of the first century Jewish historian, Flavius Josephus. A little more than a decade later, he published translations from the Roman philosopher and tragedian, SENECA (1614).

Bibliography

Lodge, Thomas. *Complete Works of Thomas Lodge.* New York: Russell and Russell, 1963.

———. *Life and Death of William Longbeard.* Edited by Allan H. Findlay. Copenhagen, Denmark: Department of English, University of Copenhagen, 1983.

———. *Rosalynd.* Edited by Brian Nellist and Simône Batin. Oxfordshire, U.K.: Ryleran Publishers, 1995.

———. *The True Chronicle History of King Leir.* New York: AMS Press, 1970.

London Company of Stationers

Incorporated in 1557, the Company of Stationers included distinguished city publishers of the day. The company also became the office through which new works about to be printed were licensed for publication. The records of the company, therefore, provide researchers with information about the first licensed publications of 16th-century works in England. Among the original members of the company was the publisher Richard Tottel, whose edition of *Songs and Sonnets* (also called *TOTTEL'S MISCELLANY,* 1557) proved extremely influential in furthering the cause of English Renaissance poetry.

Lope de Vega Carpio, Félix (1562–1635)

The most famous and prodigiously productive Spanish literary figure of his own or any era, Lope de Vega in his colorful life and career served as a soldier in Portugal, sailed with the Spanish Armada against England, and worked as secretary to a series of noble Spaniards. Although as a young man he was twice married and involved himself in some love affairs, later (1614) he became a priest and joined the Office of the Spanish INQUISITION.

A precocious talent, Lope could compose verses in his head before he had learned to write. He bribed other children with bits of his breakfast to copy his verses from his dictation. Following his first period of military service as a teenager, and a stint as a student at the University of Alcalá, Lope found employment as secretary to Antonio, the duke of Alva (Alba). On the advice of the duke, Lope wrote his first substantial work, a PASTORAL drama entitled *Arcadia* (written ca. 1590, first printed 1598) that drew upon CERVANTES's *Galatea* and Montemayor's *Diana*. Though this prose work is pedantic and tedious, some passages show promise of the eloquence and descriptive power that would characterize Lope's later efforts.

At about the time he wrote *Arcadia* Lope married. His bride, Isabela de Urbina, belonged to the circle of aristocrats surrounding the Spanish throne. Soon after, Lope foolishly allowed himself to be drawn into a quarrel, dueled with and wounded his opponent, and, as a result, was first jailed and then exiled for two years to Valencia, where his theatrical career began. Within a year of his return to Madrid, Isabela died. Before her death, however, Lope had already conceived an affection for another woman whom he addressed as Filis in his verse. She, however, seems to have rejected him as a suitor after Isabela died.

Overcoming his disappointment, Lope enthusiastically enlisted in the ill-fated Spanish Armada. During the course of his four months at sea with that famous military disaster, Lope penned most of a long poem, *The Beauty of Angelica*, a work designed to continue LUDOVICO ARIOSTO's *ORLANDO FURIOSO*.

His personal history included another marriage in 1597 to Juana de Guardio. She bore Lope a son, Carlos, who died at age seven. Then Juana herself died while giving birth to the couple's daughter Feliciana. Lope was devastated by Juana's loss notwithstanding that during his second marriage and after it he continued an attachment to Maria de Luxan. In the course of time, she bore Lope two children, a daughter Marcela, who eventually became a nun, and a son Lope, who entered military service and whose ship was lost at sea when the junior Lope was only 15.

As Lope de Vega grew older, his thoughts turned away from his youthful peccadilloes toward religion and charitable works. He became a daily communicant at mass, visited the sick, and gave generous alms to the poor. At last, in 1609, he became a priest and rose to become the chief chaplain of the congregation of the native priesthood of Madrid as well as a member of the Holy Office of the Inquisition. In that role he actually presided in January 1623 at the public execution of a man burned at the stake for being "a Lutheran, a Calvinist," and "of Jewish descent."

None of those developments, however, interfered with his tireless literary activity. The year 1599 saw the publication of a 10,000-line poem on the subject of St. Isidro, the ploughman. This popular piece went through four editions in the next nine years. In 1602 appeared the poem he had begun aboard ship, his now 11,000-line *Angelica*. Along with one edition of that work (1604) Lope published an EPIC poem that is possibly unique in the history of that genre. Taking as its subject the last voyage and death of the English privateer, Sir Francis Drake, the poem *La Dragontea* devotes all of its 10 lengthy cantos to vilifying the British scourge of Spanish shipping around the world. The word *dragon* appears in the title because *Drake* is a synonym for that word. Even among Lope's patriotic countrymen, the poem did not meet with great success.

A prose work punctuated with a number of poems was published in the same year. *"The Pilgrim in his Own Country,"* enjoyed a more enthusiastic reception among Spanish readers. This work is among the earliest examples of the prose romance in Spanish literature and enjoys a reputation as being among the finest of its sort. Lope then returned to poetry, publishing in 1609 a 22,000-line tragic epic called *Jerusalem Conquered*. As the title suggests the poem consciously challenges TORQUATO TASSO's epic *GERUSALEMME LIBERATA*. Lope's subject, however, the ill success of Richard the Lion-Hearted's failed 12th-century crusade to liberate the Holy Land, as compared with Tasso's epic, failed.

Once he became a priest, Lope from time to time turned his attention to religious subjects. This was the case with a long, pastoral, prose-and-verse poem, *The Shepherds of Bethlehem* (1612), which has the shepherds of Bethlehem reenacting the history of the Virgin Mary from her birth, through the nativity and the holy family's flight from Israel, to their safe arrival in Egypt. This charming play, whose end Lope never wrote, is dedicated to the memory of his lost seven-year-old son, Carlos.

He wrote such mock-heroic poems as his "Battle of the Cats," in which two tomcats battle through 2,500 lines for the love of a female. He wrote caricatures and verses based on classical mythology. He penned literary criticism. In 1609 he drafted in verse a manifesto, "The New Art of Making Plays." It rejected rules and praised the popular taste. He also attacked the densely allusive and arcane school of poets who followed LUIS DE GÓNGORA Y ARGOTE. In 1625 he published a poem in five cantos that emulated PETRARCH's famous *Triumphs* in form but which set that classical subject in a Christian context.

It was his contributions to the theater, however, that make Lope de Vega an unparalleled literary phenomenon. Some claim for him as many as 1,500 secular dramas plus another 400 religious ones, not to mention a steady stream throughout his career of miscellaneous works. Lope himself names hundreds of them. About 400 secular and 40 religious plays survive. We know the names of another 250 or so, but have no trace of their texts. Thus in a brief essay of this sort one can only indicate Lope's range

and give a passing glimpse of a few works that represent classes within his enormous output.

When Lope began writing for the theater in Madrid, only two companies of itinerant players existed there. By the time of his death, 40 theaters employed 1,000 people, and Lope's pen provided much of their employment. He had also taken the nascent Spanish theater as he found it and, without appealing to the rules of classical drama that LUDOVICO CASTELVETRO had popularized throughout the rest of European theater, shaped its subsequent development based on public taste.

Perhaps his most characteristic innovation on the Spanish stage was the drama of CAPE AND SWORD. Plays of this sort featured gallant action by a hero who captured and defeated assassins, fought duels, and carried on noble love affairs. Such plays also contained comic subplots in which clownish characters parodied the puff and bluster of the gallants. Lope wrote cape-and-sword dramas both for public performance and for private shows as COURT ENTERTAINMENTS. A particularly notable example of the latter sort is his *SAINT JOHN'S EVE*. Devotees of modern cinema will recognize the survival of the genre in movies about Zorro.

A somewhat more dignified and serious category of Lope's drama appears in his heroic or historical plays. Examples of this sort include his *Rome in Ashes* (*Roma Abrasada, Tragedia Famosa*, 1629) based on the career of the Roman emperor Nero, his *The Perfect Prince* (*Principe perfeto*), whose hero is Don Juan of Portugal, his *THE DISCOVERY OF THE NEW WORLD BY CHRISTOPHER COLUMBUS*, and his *PUNISHMENT WITHOUT REVENGE*, based on a dark incident in the annals of medieval Ferrara. Even these plays, however, generally feature a comic subplot, though an occasional exception like *The Star of Seville* does occur. In writing these plays, Lope virtually emptied Spanish history of playworthy material, and, when that source ran dry, he looked further afield, basing historical drama, for instance, on the career of the Russian Boris Godunov.

Another category of Lope's drama was drawn from the lives of common people. *The Wise Man at*

Home illustrates this category as does a play whose plot Lope stole from his contemporary and rival Miguel de Cervantes's autobiographical play about his captivity in Algeria. In Lope's version he introduces a character named Saavedra in the captive's role.

In 1598 the church, viewing secular plays as a danger to public morality, prevailed upon the crown to ban such drama from Madrid. Lope responded to that prohibition by switching to religious drama, and performance of his works went on just as if no prohibition were in effect. The playwright, moreover, never deserted his principle of pleasing the crowd. As his sources he substituted for history and contemporary biography the Bible, saints' lives, and stories about converting the heathen. To these he added his usual comic subplots, and he spiced the devotional stories with romance. His plays based on the stories of Queen Esther, St. Francis, St. Thomas Aquinas, and even on THE BIRTH OF CHRIST (1641), follow his usual formulas. In 1600 the ban was lifted.

Lope also continued to pen AUTOS SACRAMENTALES—a more traditional version of Spanish religious drama—as well as interludes and introductory scenes. Regardless, however, of the category of drama in which he worked, he always gave precedence to plot. Character, credibility, traditional morality, and historical fact were matters of little concern as long as the action held the audience's interest.

Lope made and spent a fortune. But as fast as the money came in, it went out, much of it given away to friends and spent on church charities. He died poor and so fanatically religious that he may have hastened his death through fasting and self-flagellation. All Europe mourned his passing. His last patron gave him a magnificent, nine-day funeral and honored Lope's cloistered daughter Marcela's request that the cortege bearing her father's body pass by her convent window so she could see his face one final time.

Bibliography

Rennert, Hugo Albert. *The Life of Lope de Vega.* 1904. Reprint, New York: B. Blom, 1968.

Vega, Lope de. *Desire's Experience Transformed: A Representative Anthology of Lope de Vega's Lyric Poetry.* Translated by Carl W. Cobb. York, S.C.: Spanish Literature Publications, 1991.

———. *Fuente Ovejuna [The sheep's well]. The Knight from Olmeda. Punishment without Revenge.* Translated by Gwynne Edwards. Oxford and New York: Oxford University Press, 1999.

———. *Obras completas de Lope de Vega.* 1993. Madrid: Turner, 2003.

———. *Porfiar hasta morir: Persistence until Death.* Edited by Antonio Cortijo Ocaña and Adelaida Cortijo Ocaña. Translated by Antonio Cortijo Ocaña, Jessica Ernst Powell and Erin M. Rebhan. Pamplona, Spain: Ediciones Universidad de Navarra, 2004.

———. *The Best Boy in Spain/ El mejor mozo de España.* Translated by David Gitlity. Tempe, Ariz.: Bilingual Press, ca. 1999.

———. *The Discovery of the New World by Cristopher Columbus: A Critical and Bilingual Edition. A Comedy in Three Acts by Lope De Vega.* Translated by Robert M. Shannon. New York: Peter Lang, ca. 2001.

———. *Translations of the American Plays of Lope de Vega: The Discovery of the New World, The Conquest of Araucania, Brazil Restored.* Edited and translated by Kenneth Stackhouse. Lewiston, N.Y.: E. Mellen Press, 2003.

Love Poems, The (*Les Amours*) Pierre de Ronsard (published 1552–1578)

Always a self-conscious artist, RONSARD kept one eye fixed on techniques for conveying in verse his own experience; he kept the other on a refined musicality. He also tried to expand the capacity of the French language to convey the subtleties of intellectual and emotional complexity.

His early love poems often cloaked the steaminess of his private amatory experience with the sometimes-pedantic trappings of classical mythology. This was assuredly the case in such a poem as the fourth sonnet of his 1552 collection of love poems, addressed to Cassandre Salviati. There a reader needs either a recent and sophisticated classical education or a classical dictionary of names to trace Ronsard's allusions to minor figures and dimly remembered places relevant to the Greek siege of Troy—all brought on by the identity of Salviati's first name with that of a Trojan priestess, Cassandra, the sister of Hector. Also, the poem's point was already conventional and trite by the time Ronsard made it. The lover is shot with Cupid's bow. For a reader willing or already able to wend her way through the thicket of recondite allusion and through the disappointment of the poem's conventional ending, nonetheless, the music of the verse rewards the effort of reading and understanding it.

Ronsard's love experiences during the decades resulted in poems addressed to many ladies. So did experiences not his as he wrote poems on behalf of patrons. Yet the history of these many affairs, from a literary point of view, falls largely beside the point. As Ronsard wrote to and about these real and sometimes perhaps fictive women—Cassandre, Genèvre, Jeanne, Marguerite, Marie, and Hélène, he polished and refined his art. He did the same thing when he turned his attention to politics and religion (he was a cleric) and to history. History and belief were, of course, important. So was the public taste, which he helped to shape as a member of the French PLÉIADE, but for Ronsard poetic craftsmanship and its capacity for displaying the interior person in the intrinsically beautiful prism of an art object took center stage.

A critical consensus holds that Ronsard's poetic mastery reached its high point in the poems he addressed to Hélène de Surgères—a young member of the nobility who was a lady-in-waiting at the French royal court. He may have felt attracted by the identity of her name with that of Helen of Troy. She was surely flattered by the attention of the older man, the most celebrated poet of France. She was also, however, a devotee of the cult of PLATONIC LOVE. For her, love was supposed to be a spiritually purifying experience that need not descend to crass physicality, and she was confirmed in that view by the taste and the staid morality of the *précieux* school of French literature and manners, much influenced by the other-worldly spirituality

of LEONE EBREO. Experienced in the ways of the world, on the other hand, Ronsard thought love to be entirely otherwise, and he pressed her for a less spiritual expression of her feelings. Offended, she quarreled with Ronsard, and the pair parted.

The poems he offered her in *Sonets pour Hélène* (1578), however, are on balance the loveliest he ever penned. In them he returns to the Italianate style, employing with new skill the METAPHOR and themes of PETRARCH. To his Italian models, however, he conjoins the worldview of a rather jaded lover. His devotion to love as a center for living has been shaken. He sees love, rather, as a social game whose genuine ends have, for propagandistic reasons, been spiritualized by the sentimental followers of NEOPLATONISM and its love theory. The poet, however, sees love's joys and pangs in terms of his own bodily appetites. A surprising sense of irony and of multiple viewpoints that were largely absent from earlier collections join forces with the high point of Ronsard's command of poetic diction and metrics to produce what is surely his finest lyric work.

A particularly lovely English translation of a selection of the poems of Ronsard—a version including examples in French and English from the poet's earlier as well as his later work—is that of Nicholas Kilmer, listed below.

Bibliography

Kilmer, Nicholas, trans. and ed. *Poems of Pierre de Ronsard*. Berkeley: University of California Press, 1979.

Love Suicides at Sonezaki, The
Chikamatsu Monzaemon (1703)

The first of the Japanese playwright Chikamatsu Monzaemon's domestic tragedies, *The Love Suicides* was based on events that had in fact occurred only a month before the play's initial performance. Thus, like other similar plays the author composed, the story has a journalistic quality. It was originally composed for performance in a puppet theater.

The hero, Tokubei, is an honest though too trusting young man who is involved in a passionate love affair with a prostitute, Ohatsu. His employer is pleased with the young man's work and wishes to advance him to partnership in the business by marrying him off to the boss's niece. Because Tokubei is reluctant to accept this offer, his employer pays the promised dowry of two silver *kamme* (roughly $2,000) to the young man's mother, hoping to trap Tokubei into marriage.

Offended and devoted to Ohatsu, Tokubei definitively refuses the match and with considerable difficulty recovers the dowry money from his mother. Hearing that he has done so, Tokubei's best friend, an oil merchant named Kuheiji, pleads to borrow it, promising to repay it before it must be returned. Kuheiji, however, has no intention of repaying the money and arranges matters so that his promissory note to Tokubei appears to have been forged. The two fight, but the first scene ends with Tokubei both beaten and disgraced.

The second scene takes place in the brothel where Ohatsu works. By coincidence, Tokubei, concealed under the train of Ohatsu's kimono, and Kuheji happen to be in the brothel at the same time. Tokubei overhears Kuheji gloating over his former friend's ruin. All agree to Ohatsu's suggestion that, dishonored as he is, Tokubei has no alternative but suicide. The lovers communicate their determination to die together by a series of gestures as Ohatsu presses her foot against Tokubei questioningly and he assents by pressing her foot to his lips.

The play's third, final, and most touching scene traces the lovers' journey from the town of Dōjima to the Sonezaki Shrine—a Buddhist temple. They promise each other to be wed eternally. On arriving they tie themselves to a tree trunk, and Tokubei clumsily and agonizingly kills Ohatsu with his dagger. Satisfied that she is rapidly dying, he twists the blade in his own throat and both die. A narrator, who has commented on the action throughout the play, assures the audience that both in the future will "attain Buddha hood," as they are "models of true love."

The popularity of this play encouraged Chikamatsu and others to write on similar themes and also led to a rash of love suicides in real life. To discourage the fad the government eventually prohib-

ited using the word that meant "love suicides" in the titles of any works published or performed.

Bibliography

Chikamatsu Monzaemon. *The Love Suicides at Sonezaki* in *Major Plays of Chikamatsu*. Translated and edited by Donald Keene. 1961. Reprint, New York: Columbia University Press, 1990.

Lucretius (Titus Lucretius Carus)
(ca. 99–55 B.C.E.)

A Roman materialist philosopher and a poet, Lucretius is chiefly remembered for his dactylic hexameter poem in six books, *De rerum natura* (*On the nature of things*). (See POETIC METER.) Lucretius felt convinced of the falsity of all religious belief with its accompanying notions that whatever one believes and does is God's will and that whatever contradicts one's cherished faith is evil. That kind of credulity, he thought, is the source of most human misery. The poet hoped that his monumental poem would popularize a thoroughgoing philosophical materialism in the place of such superstition.

Though most Renaissance Europeans did not agree with Lucretius about religion, they nevertheless considered his poem a reliable source of scientific knowledge. They mined it for wonders that Lucretius described as natural facts, like a magnetic rock that sank ships by drawing the nails from their timbers so that their hulls disintegrated, or like his assertion that people living near the source cataract of the Nile River were deafened by the roar of its falling water. Both PETRARCH and LORENZO DE' MEDICI, for instance, used Lucretius in this way.

Lusiad: or The Discovery of India, The
Luís de Camões (1572)

An EPIC poem in 10 cantos, CAMÕES's masterpiece, *The Lusiad*, draws its title from the ancient name for Portugal and focuses on the historical voyages of the Portuguese explorer Vasco da Gama around the Horn of Africa. The voyages of da Gama succeeded in opening a new trade route to the east and establishing the colonies where Camões had served. With this historical strand Camões combines, as VIRGIL's *Aeniad* had done for Rome, the mythic origins of Portugal, its past history, and a hopeful future development in which the nation would achieve its divinely appointed destiny. With these narrative threads, always pointing toward Christian Portugal as the inheritor of Roman greatness, Camões interweaves Roman and Trojan history, gods and goddesses from the Roman pantheon, and mutually reflecting events on Earth and in the heavens.

Practically from the moment of its publication, *The Lusiad* has been considered the great national epic of Portugal, though its celebrity did little to relieve its author's poverty during his life.

Bibliography

Camões, Luís de. *The Lusiad: or The Discovery of India: An Epic Poem . . . with a Life of the Poet.* Translated and edited by William Julius Mickle. Fifth edition revised and edited by E. Raymond Hodges. New York: Gordon Press, 1975.

Luther, Martin (1483–1546)

Born to a German miner's family, Martin Luther was destined to become the prime mover of the Protestant Reformation. A person of enormous gifts and great energy, Luther studied the Scriptures and entered an Augustinian monastery in the city of Erfurt, Saxony, where he spent three years. He next attended the University of Erfurt, where he graduated in 1505. Ordained as a priest in 1507, he became a lecturer at the University of Wittenberg, discussing both philosophy (1508) and Scriptural interpretation (1509). During this time he also preached in churches, and his powerful sermons attracted a large following among the faithful.

In 1510–11 Luther undertook a pilgrimage to Rome. The realities of conditions there and the greed and superstition surrounding the sale of indulgences in the Holy papal See disappointed Luther's high expectations. Indulgences, which were papal dispensations that released the soul of the recipient from a certain period of suffering in Purgatory, had origi-

nated as rewards for particularly meritorious service to the Catholic Church. In time, however, the sale of indulgences instead became a source of income for Rome as they were hawked all over Christendom as a way of relieving the postmortem sufferings both of those still living and of their departed loved ones.

On his return to Wittenburg, Luther took aim both in his sermons and in his lectures at the abusive sale of indulgences carried on in Saxony by a Dominican, Johann Tetzel. Luther also attacked the idea that forgiveness of sin rested in human hands, and he scorned the veneration of the relics of saints and of other mostly false Christian memorabilia such as supposed fragments of the true cross.

On October 31, 1517, Luther posted NINETY-FIVE THESES detailing his views about indulgences on the door of the church at Wittenburg. These stirred up much local controversy, and Tetzel left Saxony. Another noted theologian, Philip Melancthon, joined Luther's initiative. Eventually Pope Leo X summoned Luther to Rome to recant his position. Fearing that Rome might execute the intransigent Luther as a heretic, the authorities of the University of Wittenburg and the elector (prince) of Saxony stepped into the dispute, insisting that Rome negotiate.

Though ineffectual negotiations did occur, Rome and Luther had by now become irreconcilable, and Luther began to publish his central objections to the papal system. Taking the position that salvation was available by faith, Luther published two of the documents now viewed as central to his position, the address he made to the CHRISTIAN NOBILITY OF THE GERMAN NATION . . . and ON THE BABYLONIAN CAPTIVITY OF THE CHURCH OF GOD (both 1520). Many think that Luther's Ninety-five Theses, the two works named in the previous sentence, and his work *Concerning Christian liberty* (1520) contain the theoretical core of the reformer's position. The last named document posits the simultaneous freedom and bondage of every Christian and lays the groundwork for a Reformation ethic.

As a writer, Luther produced a vast array of works both in Latin and in German. The standard American edition of the surviving works (which leaves out several) runs to 54 volumes plus two more of apparatus. Often Luther wrote quickly without an outline. Sometimes, when he himself viewed a work as particularly important, he planned it carefully. In both languages his writing flows easily. His word choice is apt and colorful and his comparisons telling. He avoids many of the stylistic contrivances that HUMANISTS of his era employed. When attacking his opponents, he is a master of ridicule. He views himself with an attractively ironic detachment. His prose reveals a hearty sense of humor and an active imagination. Above all he seems utterly without the pride of authorship that many if not most writers feel.

One of Luther's major literary accomplishments was the translation into German of the entire BIBLE. His New Testament—also called "the September Testament"—appeared in 1522. Thereafter, installment-by-installment, his Old Testament appeared until by 1539 he had completed the daunting task. The extant corpus of his other work includes lectures, biblical commentary and interpretation, sermons, meditations, and disputations with other professors of theology. Luther also drafted arguments against his critics, discussions of church liturgy and sacraments, pamphlets and tracts on questions of church and civil government, writings about educating young children and preachers, anti-Semitic tracts about the relationship between Jews and Christians, and works designed to comfort those who were grieving. Particularly he wrote a series of tracts that he hoped would hasten the end to hostilities in the Peasants War. To these one can add a host of marginalia and commentary on his reading. His writings about the Ottoman Turks reveal his view that they presented an increasing danger to Europe.

In addition to all this, Luther was one of the greatest poet–hymnodists ever to compose for congregational singing. On any given Sunday, his hymns such as "A Mighty Fortress is Our God" can still be heard across Protestant Christendom.

In 1525 Luther married a former nun, Katherina von Bora, who had withdrawn from the religious life. Some of his supporters found this shocking, but Luther defended his devotion to his wife as a means of thwarting Satan's temptations.

After more than 30 years in the tireless pursuit of the goals of his theological reforms, Luther died, having forever changed the character of Western European Christian belief and practice, both Protestant and Roman Catholic.

Bibliography

Luther, Martin. *Basic Luther*. Springfied, Ill.: Templegate Publishers, ca. 1994.

———. *Faith and Freedom: an Invitation to the Writings of Martin Luther*. New York: Vintage Books, 2002.

———. *Luther's Works*. 56 vols. Edited by Jaroslav Pelikan et al. Philadelphia: Fortress Press, 1956–ca. 1959.

———. *On Christian Liberty*. Translated by W. A. Lambert. Minneapolis: Fortress Press, 2003.

Lycidas John Milton (1637)

A PASTORAL ELEGY written in rhymed iambic-pentameter verse to commemorate the death of MILTON's friend Edward King, *Lycidas* opens with an address to laurel, myrtle, and ivy—symbolic funeral plants that the poet is gathering to scatter on the imagined bier of the dead poet–clergyman. King had drowned crossing from England to Ireland in an unseaworthy vessel. His body was not recovered, so Milton's poem becomes the funeral that King, here figured forth as the shepherd Lycidas, could not have.

Milton invokes the classical muses to inspire him and then recalls the time he and King spent together at Cambridge, transforming their times together there into the idylls of shepherds in a classical landscape. The poem follows the psychology of grief, moving from memories to grief to an imagined scenario in which King/Lycidas might have escaped his fate. Then the poet recognizes the inevitability of death and wonders why he should spend his own brief lifetime in laborious writing when he might instead enjoy life's pleasures. He answers his own question by saying that "fame is the spur" that leads him to work so hard, despite death's approach. Praise, he says, will outlast life and he suggests that God will reward the poet's labors eternally.

After a transposed account of how Lycidas died, the poem presents a funeral procession. The river Cam, personified as an elderly father, passes by. Next comes St. Peter, who grows angry when he considers the loss of a worthy clergyman while so many who are unworthy occupy church offices.

Milton then imagines that the mourning shepherds cast symbolic flowers on Lycidas's hearse, and that wherever his remains actually are, dolphins will find them and push them toward the shore. The poet then comforts the grieving shepherds with the assurance that Lycidas is not dead but instead enjoys eternal life in the company of the saints in heaven and that Lycidas himself will become the patron saint of voyagers on the Irish Sea.

The elegy ends with the rededication of the poet himself to the business of life and to work in "fresh woods and pastures new."

Lyly, John (ca. 1554–1606)

Educated at Magdalen College, Oxford, Lyly was the son of a notable family that had included educators and civil servants. After receiving both a bachelor's (1573) and a master's (1575) degree from Magdalen, Lyly hoped to become a fellow there. When that hope was disappointed, he entered the service of the chancellor of the exchequer, Lord Burghley, and of Burghley's son-in-law, the earl of Oxford.

In 1578 Lyly published a work that instantly became a bestseller and remained one for a decade, EUPHUES: THE ANATOMY OF WIT. Though Lyly had not been the first to use the alliterative, flowery, parallelism of its style, his book popularized the technique that has ever after been labeled the *euphuistic style*. In addition to his most successful work and its sequel, *Euphues and his England* (1580), Lyly also wrote comedies for COURT ENTERTAINMENTS. He received appointments as the assistant master to the children's companies that performed plays at the Chapel Royal and at St. Paul's Cathedral. For the children he wrote a series of allegorical dramas, based both on the classics and on events of the day. These plays were often presented before Queen ELIZABETH I, and Lyly hoped their success would result in his appointment as Elizabeth's master of the revels, in charge of all court entertainments. Again, however, his hope was to be disappointed.

Nonetheless, Lyly's work with the highly professional acting companies of children made him, together with THOMAS KYD and CHRISTOPHER MARLOWE, one of the three most celebrated playwrights of the early Elizabethan era. His most notable play is *Endymion, The Man in the Moon*. This prose drama was performed for Queen Elizabeth in celebration of Candlemas on February 2, 1588. All eight of Lyly's court plays survive. The first of them, *Campaspe*, was acted in 1584. The last, *The Woman in the Moon*, was performed around 1595. All Lyly's plays but one were in the euphuistic prose that his novel had popularized. *The Woman in the Moon* was the one verse exception.

Like other literary men of his era, Lyly was pressed into service as a propagandist when the PURITANS attacked the established Anglican bishops in a series of anonymous tracts called the Martin Marprelate pamphlets. Lyly responded against them with a pamphlet, *Pappe with an Hatchet* (1589). That same year Lyly was elected to Parliament and served as a member of four parliaments before his death in 1606.

Bibliography

Lyly, John. *Campaspe, Sappho and* Phao. New York: Manchester University Press, 1991.

———. *Complete Works*. Edited by R. Warwick Bond. Oxford, U.K.: The Clarendon Press, 1967.

———. *Endymion*. Edited by David Bevington. Manchester, U.K., and New York: Manchesters University Press, 1996.

———. *Euphues: The Anatomy of Wit: and Euphues and his England*. Edited by Leah Scragg. Manchester, U.K., and New York: Manchester University Press, 2003.

————. *Galatea and Midas.* Edited by George Hunter and David Bevington. Manchester, U.K.: Manchesters University Press, ca. 2000.

————. *Selected Prose and Dramatic Work.* Edited by Leah Scragg. Manchester, U.K.: Carcanet Press, 1997.

Machiavelli, Niccolò (1469–1527)

Born to the family of a Florentine notary, Machiavelli spent his formative years in the Florence of LORENZO DE' MEDICI, where he received a Latin, HUMANISTIC education. Perhaps assisted by his boyhood friendship with Lorenzo's son Giuliano, in 1498 he became involved in the politics of his native city, in the supervision of its outlying dependencies, and in its foreign diplomacy both in and out of Italy. In 1501 he married Marietta Corsini, and during the course of the next two decades the couple had seven children together.

Troubled by the heavy reliance of his city on mercenary troops, Machiavelli effectively championed the formation of a local militia. After the Florentines exiled the Medici family in 1502 and elected Piero Soderini as their leader, or standard bearer (*gonfalniere*), for life, Machiavelli received his chance to form and train the militia that he advocated. Though effective in regional hostilities—his militia overcame the revolted city of Pisa in 1509—his local force proved to be no match for the papal and French alliance that soon arrayed itself against the Republic of Florence. That coalition returned the Medici to power in 1512, and Machiavelli found himself imprisoned and tortured on the mere suspicion that he had conspired against them. He spent much of the rest of his life in a mostly frustrating but finally modestly successful effort to repair his fences with the Medici so that he could return to significant public service. Ironically his small success worked against him in 1527 when the Medici once more retreated into exile.

As a writer Machiavelli authored a wide variety of works, all of which have literary merit but some of which are less specifically literary than others. He wrote history and political analysis and theory. In this category of his production he is most famously remembered for one of the most influential works of the European Renaissance, *THE PRINCE* (written 1513, published 1532). Almost as well remembered are his *Art of War* and his *Florentine Histories* (1520–24). He also conducted a detailed analysis of the political lessons to be learned from the ancient Roman republic in his *Discourses on the First Ten Books of* [the Roman historian] *Titus Livy* (1531). In his *Life of Castruccio Castracani of Lucca* (written ca. 1520, published 1532), he used Castracani's life as the basis for a romance that showed some of the principles recommended in *The Prince* at work in a fictionalized version of the real world.

Works that critics specifically assign to the literary realm include Machiavelli's contribution to the ongoing discussion of the ISSUE OF THE ITALIAN LAN-GUAGE. In this discussion of the comparative merits of the tongues of classical antiquity and of modern vernacular Tuscan, Machiavelli sided with the vernacular, and he always wrote in his contemporary Florentine dialect. He also followed the example of PETRARCH by preserving his correspondence for publication. His most self-consciously literary writings included two comic plays, his famous and racy *MANDRAGOLA* (THE MANDRAKE ROOT, ca. 1517) and *Clizia* (ca. 1525). A third comedy, *The Clouds,* has been lost. He also penned a novella, *Belfagor, The Devil Who Married* (written ca. 1515, published 1549). Beyond this he authored some social satire.

Machiavelli's poetic writings are preserved, first, in two collections of verse, his *First* and *Second Decenale.* Each of them sets out to review 10 years of Florentine history. Writing in TERZA RIMA, Machiavelli completed the first project, which covered the decade from 1494 to 1504. The second project got as far as 1509 and was left unfinished. Another incomplete offering from Machiavelli the poet appears in a satirical dream vision, an ALLEGORY in the medieval manner, his *Asino* or *Asino d'oro* (*Golden ass*). Beyond this, other miscellaneous verse survives, including CARNIVAL SONGS, terza rima poems on subjects like ambition and envy, and a trio of SONNETs addressed to Giuliano de' Medici and imploring his intervention when Machiavelli was jailed. That effort seems to have failed: Machiavelli owed his release to a general amnesty.

A Machiavelli myth grew up after his death. His utilitarian views on a ruler's exercise of power without reference to the concerns of Christianity for meekness and humility, led many—particularly those who had not read him—to imagine him as a godless and even demonic figure. This view of Machiavelli led to stage portrayals, particularly in England, of "Machiavellian" villains who believed that the end justified the means and that the ethics of naturalism should prevail. Edmund in SHAKE-SPEARE's *KING LEAR* is such a villain. Barabas in CHRISTOPHER MARLOWE's *THE JEW OF MALTA* is another. In fact "Machiavel" himself speaks the prologue to Marlowe's play. This view of Machiavelli derived principally from tracts written against him rather than from his own writings.

A more accurate view of the man, perhaps, derives from Machiavelli's own description of his activities during his years of retirement at his familial country place at Sant' Andrea in Percussina south of Florence. There, he reports, he spent his days in the village in conversation with the country folk and joining the men in their rural pastimes. In the evening, however, he returned home, put on his best clothes, and spent the waning hours reading the great classics of the ancient and modern worlds, lost in the interior conversation with geniuses long dead that books make possible—the highest and most ennobling definition of leisure.

Bibliography

Falco, Maria J. *Feminist Interpretations of Niccolò Machiavelli.* University Park: Pennsylvania University Press, 2004.

Machiavelli, Niccolò. *Art of War.* Translated by Christopher Lynch. Chicago: University of Chicago Press, 2003.

———. *The Comedies of Machiavelli.* Translated by David Sices and James B. Atkinson. Hanover, N.H.: Published for Dartmouth College by the University Press of New England, 1985.

———. *The Letters of Machiavelli: a Selection.* Translated by Allan Gilbert. Ca. 1961. Chicago: University of Chicago Press, 1988.

———. *The Prince and Other Writings.* Translated by Wayne Rebhorn. New York: Barnes and Noble Classics, ca. 2003.

Viroli, Maurizio. *Niccolò's Smile: A Biography of Machiavelli.* Translated by Antony Shugaar. New York: Farrar, Straus, and Giroux, 2000.

magic

Renaissance magic assumed that the chain of events in the universe was governed by FORTUNE and by NATURE. The mechanism for the operation of these forces was a vast network of interacting rays given off by every object in the universe from stars, whose rays principally governed the destinies of things, to the tiniest creatures. Human beings and animals also were supposed to give off rays through the eyes. Magicians thought that by interrupting the network of rays and creating a tiny flaw in it, they achieved a momentary opportunity to create an unnatural effect. So, for example, by sacrificing a chicken or destroying a plant and stopping the rays they emitted, magicians might create a brief hole in the network into which they could insert a spell or some other magic practice to work their will. Witchcraft and magic are frequent subjects in the literature of the Renaissance.

Bibliography

Couliano, Ioan P. *Eros and Magic in the Renaissance.* Translated by Margaret Cook. Chicago: University of Chicago Press, 1987.

Magnússon, Jón (ca. 1610–1696)

An Icelandic clergyman who imagined that he spent most of his career at war with witches, Magnússon penned a colorful account of his campaigns against them. The work is important for the cultural and anthropological look it gives us at the folly and fixations of an earlier age and the inhumane practices to which they led. The title of the work, *Píslarsaga* (The story of torments), indicates the treatment that presumptive witches could expect at the hands of religious authorities. Though a new Icelandic edition appeared in 2001, the work has not as yet become available in English.

Mahabharata Vyasa (Vyas, ca. 350 B.C.E.)

The great EPIC of ancient India, the *Mahabharata* contains the myths, songs, poems, legends, philosophical viewpoints, and, some argue, historical accounts whose retelling and reworking from at least the fourth century B.C.E. have played major roles in shaping the cultural identity of India—especially Hindu India. Containing more than 100,000 verses, the *Mahabharata* may be the world's longest epic. Both its immensity and the variety of literary forms that make up its contents suggest that it grew by accretion over time to its present length and complexity. Tradition attributes its composition in its current form in the Sanskrit

language to the poet Vyasa, who brought a remarkable degree of unity to the epic's diversity.

Identifying this legendary seer and poet with a single historical personage may not be possible. Indian tradition assigns the name Vyasa to almost 30 poets who may have been engaged in compiling the *Mahabharata*. Whatever the apparently irrecoverable facts of this matter, Hindu belief has deified Vyasa, considering him to have been a fractional share of the deity Lord Vishnu in his 17th human incarnation and also the son of the Hindu goddess of poetry and the arts, Saraswati.

Despite its great antiquity, the *Mahabharata* appears in this discussion of 16th- and 17th-century literature because those centuries saw the epic or portions of it repeatedly translated from Sanskrit into the emergent, vernacular, regional, and transregional LANGUAGES OF INDIA. Moreover that impulse for translating the *Mahabharata* was fueled at the same time by the spiritual reawakening and widespread religious fervor associated with the bhakti movement and the veneration of Vishnu—the principal wellsprings of Indian letters in the period. These repeated retellings of the *Mahabharata* often reshaped its material in response to local issues and concerns and to contemporary popular interests rather than to the elitist interests of the Brahman priestly classes.

At the core of the *Mahabharata*'s story the reader finds an ongoing competition for control of a kingdom between the Kauravas and the Pandavas—two branches of the royal family, the Purus. Their internecine struggle intensifies over several generations until war eventually results. The war proves disastrous for both parties, and though the Pandavas gain nominal victory, everybody loses more than they win, and the central unlearned lesson of history presents itself once again: Warfare rarely brings advantage to anyone.

Within this general framework, a vast cast of characters takes the stage. Their interest springs in part from their actions and the roles they play in the story. In part their attraction for a reader arises from their participation in the epic's ALLEGORY. The character Karna, for instance, allegorically represents the ongoing struggle between people and their fates. Karna's principal opponent on the field of battle is the heroic Arjuna, who inadvertently sins while trying to do good. The Pandava queen, Draupati, represents in her own person the grievances that finally drive the contending parties to take up arms. The deity Krishna, who directs most of the action, represents both divine involvement in and unconcerned detachment from the affairs of human beings. Though generally, for instance, he seems to favor the Pandavas and to shape things to go their way, he can also be totally unconcerned with their virtual annihilation in battle—an annihilation he could have forestalled.

As the principal repository of Hindu myth, legend, belief, and philosophy, the impact of the *Mahabharata* on all subsequent Indian thought and literature can hardly be exaggerated. The epic is available in English in good verse and in good prose versions.

Bibliography

Lal, P. *The Mahabharata of Vyas condensed from Sanskrit and Transcreated into English.* New Delhi: Vikas, ca. 1980.

Narayan, R. K. *The Mahabharata: a Shortened Modern Prose Version of the Indian Epic.* Chicago: University of Chicago Press, 2000.

The Maid's Tragedy Francis Beaumont and John Fletcher (1611)

Among the tragedies produced by the joint effort of FRANCIS BEAUMONT and JOHN FLETCHER, *The Maid's Tragedy*, typical of the tragedy of revenge, is generally considered the best and to be mostly Beaumont's work. In this play the main plot concerns the maiden Aspatia who has agreed to marry her beloved Amintor. Before that wedding can take place, however, the king commands that Amintor marry Evadne, the sister of Melantius, instead. Ostensibly, the king arranges this wedding to honor Melantius, but in fact Evadne is the king's mistress. The wedding is a ruse to preserve Evadne's reputation should she become pregnant with the king's offspring. Adding insult to injury, Aspatia serves as a bridesmaid for Evadne. While accompanying the bride to the bridal chamber, the forsaken Aspatia sings mournfully of her impending funeral when she dies of a broken heart.

Amintor, in the meantime feels a pang of perfunctory guilt for deserting Aspatia, but instantly transfers his affections to Evadne. When he proposes that they consummate the marriage, however, Evadne refuses, telling him that she has sworn an oath "never to be acquainted with [Amintor's] bed." She confesses that she is the king's mistress and that she only agreed to marry to "cover shame." Perceiving that the king has shamed them both, they agree to pretend to be happily married while Evadne secretly pursues her course with the king. In the third act this ruse confuses the king himself. The king accuses Evadne of forswearing herself, for she had promised never to have another man. She disagrees, telling him that she promised "never to love a man of lower place." "I love," she says, "with my ambition."

Convinced that Evadne has slept with Amintor, the king recalls him. Confronted, Amintor accuses the king of tyranny and threatens to kill him. This threat of regicide was a major shock for the audience. When Beaumont and Fletcher were overheard discussing this scene while writing the play, one of their listeners accused them of high treason until he understood they were talking about a play rather than an assassination plot. No doubt anticipating the shock, the playwrights have Amintor withdraw the threat. When he asks for an explanation, the king impatiently tells him to "wink" at the situation and exits.

In the meantime, Aspatia's father, Calianax grows distressed at his daughter's depression and feels convinced that Melantius has arranged his sister Evadne's marriage to Amintor. Calianax challenges Melantius to a fight. Melantius talks the old man out of it but resolves to get to the bottom of the matter with Amintor.

Amintor tells him the truth. Unbelieving, Melantius draws his sword and challenges Amintor. Amintor accepts the challenge, welcoming death if he loses and swearing not to outlive Melantius long if he loses. Convinced, Melantius sheaths his sword and asks his friend for pardon. Seeing that the king has dishonored his family, Melantius plans regicide and sets his plot in motion, sending his brother Dilphius to call their friends to arm themselves for a coup. When Calianax, who is in charge of the fortress, reenters still angry, Melantius attempts to calm him and enlist his aid, asking him to surrender the fortress. Unconvinced, Calianax goes to warn the king. In the fourth act, Melantius confronts Evadne with her guilt. Stricken with conscience, she allows her brother to make her the instrument of revenge. She swears to kill the king. Reformed, she begs Amintor for forgiveness, which he grants, and goes forth to fulfil her vow. Calianax tells the king that Melantius means to occupy the fortress. Melantius, who is the most accomplished soldier of the realm, convinces the king that the old man is mad. Seeing that unless he surrenders the fort, Melantius will hound him to his grave, Calianax does so.

In the final act, Evadne enters the king's bedchamber. Finding him asleep, she binds him. The king awakens; she announces her intention and stabs him twice—once for herself and once for Amintor. As the king dies, she forgives him for dishonoring her. She exits, and two servants enter and discover the murder. Melantius occupies the castle and negotiates pardons for the rebels, agreeing to recognize Lysippus, the king's brother, as the successor. Aspatia in the meantime disguises herself as a man. She finds Amintor, and, claiming to be her own brother, provokes him to fight with her. He wounds her. Evadne enters with a bloody knife in her hand and kills herself. Amintor announces that he will right the wrong he did Aspatia. Hearing that, Aspatia rallies briefly but then, happy at last, dies. Amintor, overcome with grief, commits suicide. Melantius tries to join him but is prevented by the new king, Lysippus, who declares: "on lustful kings . . . deaths from Heaven are sent; / but curs'd' is he that is their instrument."

Bibliography

Beaumont, Francis, and John Fletcher. *The Maid's Tragedy*. Edited by T. W. Graik. 1988. Reprint, Manchester, U.K.: Manchester University Press, 1999.

Mairet, Jean (1604–1686)

A French playwright, Mairet became the first to subscribe fully to the neo-Aristotelian view of the Italian LUDOVICO CASTELVETRO that the unities of time, place, and action were essential to the creation and production of genuine TRAGEDY. Though Castelvetro's views on the matter had earlier been echoed both by PIERRE DE RONSARD and Jean de la Taille, Mairet became the first to apply them stringently to his own writing. This is particularly apparent in his tragedy *Sophonisbe* (1634), which is generally thought to have been the first French tragedy written so that the action took place in a single day, occurred no further from the initial location than one could travel in a 24-hour period, and swept with an uninterrupted movement to its inevitably tragic outcome.

In addition to *Sophonisbe*, Mairet is remembered for his contributions to PASTORAL TRAGICOMEDY. Three plays of this sort are his *Chryséide et Arimant* (1625), his *Sylvie* (1626), and his *Silvanire* (1630). Mairet felt a natural bent for unified plots, and he was encouraged in that direction both by theater critics and by adherents of the powerful patron, the marquise de Rambouillet, who encouraged Mairet in his neo-Aristotelian efforts. The year following *Silvanire*'s production, Mairet published the play with a preface in which he discussed the unities. He also suggested that the plot of a tragedy should be drawn from history so that the audience would recognize it and that a tragedy should be true to life.

Mairet participated in a heated competition with the other dramatists of his era, particularly CORNEILLE and SCUDÉRY. Of the three, Mairet was perhaps the least gifted, but he followed the suggestions of the critics and the tastes of his supporters to good effect. None of his work has as yet appeared in English.

Bibliography

Nietze, William A., and E. Preston Dargan. *A History of French Literature From the Earliest Times to the Great War*. New York: Henry Holt and Company, 1922.

Malherbe, François de (1555–1628)

A French poet and poetic theorist, François de Malherbe was born in Normandy and studied law both in France and Germany. Although his own poetic production was small, and though he is better remembered as a theorist than a practicing poet, at age 50 Malherbe became the most important judge of good and bad poetry in France. He accomplished this coup by first using his connections to be nominated as the de facto poet laureate of the Bourbon dynasty. Then he wrote a genuinely charming poem that flattered the king, the *"Prière pour la Roi allant en Limousin"* (A prayer for the king on going into Limousin, 1605).

Though Henry IV had at first felt dubious about granting Malherbe his patronage, that poem overcame his objections. The queen, Marie de' Medici, was equally charmed by an ode Malherbe had written in praise of her beauty and accomplishments, and she supported him through her husband's reign and that of her son Louis XIII. Until his death, Malherbe maintained a tight grip on his role as the foremost critic of French letters, fending off repeated attacks from poets who took issue with his principles.

He was an intellectual poet. He objected to poems that merely expressed emotion. He wished poetry to contain feeling, but feeling rationalized. Although, for example, he lost both his own children, he never attempted a poem of consolation for his own grief. When, however, his friend Monsieur du Périer lost a child, Malherbe penned the poem for which he is best remembered: *"Consolation à Monsieur Du Périer, geuilhomme d'Aix en Provence, sur la mort de sa fille,"* (A consolation for Mr. du Périer, gentleman of Aix . . . on the death of his daughter, 1598).

He preferred the language of the common man and resisted learned and Latinate poetry. He also preferred poems with political subjects that called for a highly oratorical style of verse that the French were to perfect. An ode that he wrote in his 72nd year to celebrate the victory of Louis XIII at La Rochelle is a prime example of the style and one of his greatest successes. He celebrated purity, precision, and clarity in verse. While admirable in principle, his practice was often eccentric and grounded in private taste with the result that to a degree his principles confined poets' practice too severely. Poets and writers who took issue with Malherbe's principles included MARIE LE JARS DE GOURNAY, THÉOPHILE DE VIAU, and Mathurin Régnier. These

poets preferred a poetics of emotion to Malherbe's decorous and intellectualized classicism.

Malherbe also published an edition of his letters and some translations from Latin during his lifetime. No English translation of Malherbe has yet appeared, but a good modern edition is available in French.

Bibliography

Hollier, Denis, Editor. *A New History of French Literature.* Cambridge, Mass.: Harvard University Press, 1989.

Malherbe, François de. *Les Poésies.* Edited by Jacques Lavaud. Paris: Société des textes français moderne, 1999.

Mandrake Root, The (Mandragola)
Niccolò Machiavelli (1517)

By consensus the most successful neoclassical COMEDY of the Italian Renaissance, *The Mandrake Root* skillfully combines elements of Aristotelian classicism as it was understood in early 16th-century Florence with elements of folk tale, with elements of the Roman comedy, and with the author's own invention to produce something new and lively in the Italian theater.

The play's folk-tale elements have to do, first, with the mythic properties of the mandrake root itself. The root is bifurcated and resembles the legs of a human being. A woman who drinks a potion made from the root is almost certain to conceive a child. The catch is that a person who uproots the mandrake will die, and so one must tie a dog to the plant and have the dog pull it up. The dog dies, but its master has the magic plant that will make barren women fertile. MACHIAVELLI modifies this legend. Instead of the dog or the uprooter, the first man to sleep with a woman after she has drunk the potion will die. This becomes the central device that makes the play work.

The elements of neo-Aristotelianism in the play derive from its form. It is presented in five acts as Renaissance HUMANISTS thought ancient plays had been staged. Also, in translating and interpreting Aristotle, LUDOVICO CASTELVETRO had insisted on the unities of time, place, and action as requirements for classical theater—especially TRAGEDY. Machiavelli, however, applies those requirements to comedy, and *Mandragola* scrupulously observes them all.

The Roman comedy makes its contribution to Machiavelli's creative mix by providing him with STOCK CHARACTERS: a young lover, a flattering schemer, a foolish old man, his frustrated young wife, and a priest who acts as procurer. Although he makes use of these stereotypes, Machiavelli's fertile talent endows them with new and vibrant life.

As the play opens, we find Callimaco, a young Florentine recently returned from Paris, confessing to his servant, Siro, that he has fallen madly in love with Lucrezia, the young and beautiful wife of the elderly and foolish lawyer, Messer Nicia. Moreover, he has procured the promise of Nicia's rascally companion, Ligurio, to act as his ally in seducing Lucrezia.

Ligurio and Callimaco hatch a plot: Callimaco will pose as a doctor and advise Nicia concerning the causes of Lucrezia's barrenness. After examining Lucrezia's urine and muttering medical gibberish in Latin, Callimaco assures Nicia that a mandrake-root potion will certainly cure her, but he also explains the catch: Whoever next sleeps with her will die within eight days. Thus, to achieve all the objectives, someone other than Nicia must first sleep with his wife. Nicia of course objects at first but eventually comes around. They settle on a priest, Brother Timoteo, Lucrezia's confessor, as the sacrificial victim. It remains to talk Lucrezia into the idea; her mother Sostrata is brought into the plot to convince Lucrezia. With everyone at her to cooperate so she can give her husband an heir, against her better judgment, Lucrezia capitulates.

After a series of other complications and ingenious solutions, Callimaco rather than Brother Timoteo is finally brought to bed with Lucrezia. The audience learns of the encounter, which takes place off stage, by report. Once with the girl, Callimaco identified himself, swore his eternal love, promised to marry her on Nicia's death, told her how easily they both could both enjoy an extended affair, and threw himself on her mercy. She considered the matter, sighed, and responded that since Callimaco's cunning, Nicia's stupidity, her own mother's unscrupulousness, and her confessor's

evil nature have led her to do what she otherwise would never have done, some divine power must be at work and she will go along.

The play continues to be regularly performed before enthusiastic audiences.

Bibliography

Bondanella, Peter, and Mark Musa, eds. and trans. "The Mandrake Root." *The Portable Machiavelli.* Harmondsworth, U.K.: Penguin, ca. 1986.

Cairns, Christopher, Editor. *Ariosto's "The Supposes;" Machiavelli's "The Mandrake;" Intronati's "The Deceived:" Three Renaissance Italian Comedies.* Translated by Jennifer Lorch. Lewiston, N.Y.: Edwin Mellen Press, ca. 1996.

al-Maqqari of Tlemcen, Ahmed, b. Muhammad (d. ca. 1632)

The principal source for our knowledge of the literary history of Muslim Spain, al-Maqqari was both a biographer and a historian. His best known work, a biography of Ibnu 'l Khatib, a celebrated vizier of Granada, also contains a lengthy and wide-ranging introduction. The introduction's eight chapters treat, first, a general description of Spain. The second chapter details the Arab conquest of Spain. The third examines the history of the Arabic ruling dynasties in Spain. In the fourth chapter, al-Maqqari discusses the city of Cordova, and in the fifth he follows the itineraries of Spanish–Arabian scholars who journeyed to the Arab homelands. The sixth chapter treats Oriental travelers who came to Spain. The seventh chapter brings together a miscellany of extracts from other writers, short prose anecdotes and poems that discuss or illustrate the literary history of Spain. The last chapter in the introduction chronicles the reconquest of Spain by the Christians and the subsequent expulsion of the Spanish Arabs. After this discursive beginning, the biography proper begins. A portion of the memorable title of Al-Maqqari's Arabic work is: *Nafh al-tib min ghusn al-Andalus al-ratib . . .* (Waft of fragrance from Andalus' luscious branch . . .).

Other works written by al-Maqqari include a biography of Iyad ben Musa and another of Muhammad, the Prophet. Al-Maqqari's works, especially the *Waft of Fragrance,* are available in modern Arabic editions, but only that portion of the *Waft of Fragrance* dealing with the Arabic ruling dynasties in Spain has ever been translated into English.

Bibliography

al-Maqqari, Abmed ibn Muhammad. *The History of the Mohammedan Dynasties in Spain.* Edited and translated by Pascual de Gayangos. London: W. H. Allen, 1840–43.

Marguerite de Navarre (Marguerite d'Angoulême) (1492–1549)

A brilliant star among literary women of her age, Marguerite was the sister of King Henry I of France. Her first husband, the duc d'Alençon, died in 1525, and two years later she married Henri d' Albret who, though a vassal of the king of France, was also in his own right the king of Navarre.

As a girl, Marguerite of Angloulême gave evidence of extraordinary intellectual gifts. Accordingly she received a thoroughgoing HUMANIST EDUCATION. Although Marguerite remained a Roman Catholic throughout her life, her second husband was a Protestant and Marguerite herself a Protestant sympathizer. She shared certain points of view with MARTIN LUTHER, and she found the writings of ERASMUS of Rotterdam particularly convincing—though like her he remained at least nominally within the Catholic fold. Scholarly Protestants could generally count on Marguerite's protection if they could find their way to her court, which was one of the most intellectual on the Continent. Her protégés included CLÉMENT MAROT and JOHN CALVIN as well.

She commanded several languages both ancient and modern, including Latin, Spanish, and Italian. She also worked at learning Hebrew. As a writer, Marguerite worked in a number of genres. Early in life she wrote a *Recipe for a Happy Life* (1500). Her HEPTAMERON (published and entitled posthumously, 1558) is a framework series of tales modeled on BOCCACCIO's *Decameron.* She penned a collection of mystical poems, *Prisons*—a monumental work containing 5,000, 10-syllable lines in which she details errors peculiar to the human species. Her confessional poems *Mirroir de l'âme pécheresse, Chansons spirituelles* (1548) were translated into English by ELIZABETH I of England as *The Glass of the Sinful Soul.* Marguerite of Navarre also wrote a pair of comic plays: *Comédie à dix personnages* (A comedy for 10 characters, 1542) and *Comédie jouée à Mont-de-Marsan en 1547* (A playful comedy at Mont-de-Marsan in 1547.) Also available in English translation are a pair of poems, "The Coach," and "The Triumph of the Lamb."

Generally her prose is thought to be superior to her verse.

Bibliography

Marguerite de Navarre. *Les Prisons.* Translated by Claire Lynch Wade. New York: Peter Lang, 1989.
———. *Recipe for a Happy Life . . . Amplified . . .* from the Works of Various Writers. Edited by Marie West King. San Francisco, Calif.: P. Elder and Company, ca. 1911.
———. *The Coach; and The Triumph of the Lamb.* Exeter, U.K.: Elm Bank Publications, 1999.
———. *The Heptameron.* Translated by P. A. Chilton. Harmondsworth, U.K.: Penguin Books, 1984.
Shell, Marc, Editor. *Elizabeth's Glass: with "The Glass of the Sinful Soul. . . ."* Lincoln: University of Nebraska Press, 1993.

Marinella, Lucrezia (1571–1653)

A Venetian poet who was the daughter of one physician and the wife of another, Marinella received a superior, probably private, education in the splendid library of her father, Giovanni Marinelli. She and her husband Girolamo Vacca had two children.

As a poet, Marinella celebrated the historic involvement of Doge Enrico Dandolo of Venice as the leader of the fourth Crusade in an EPIC poem modeled on TORQUATO TASSO's *GERUSALEMME LIBERATA.* Marinella's epic, entitled *L'Enrico, overo Bisantio acquistato* (Enrico, or Byzantium acquired, 1635), tells how Enrico saved Constantinople from its Greek Orthodox rulers and places its government in the hands of the Venetian Republic.

Historically, the people of the Byzantine Empire murdered its Emperor Alexius in an uprising. The crusaders, or the Franks as they were called, happened to be encamped nearby and laid siege to the city. They subdued the rebels and established a Latin monarchy (1204). Although the by-then-blind Dandolo was offered the empire, he refused it. With Dandolo's support, a Flemish count, Baldwin I was crowned emperor. The requirements of the CHIVALRIC EPIC did not include too close a correspondence with history.

An expert on the works of Marinella, the critic Letizia Panizza, points to significant differences in the treatment of women in Tasso's and Marinella's epics. In Tasso, female warriors are subdued in love or in battle by their male counterparts. Not so in Marinella's versions. They remain undefeated. Though the women value male friendship, Panizza continues, they reject male lovers and husbands, and they are the full moral and intellectual equals of the men.

Marinella was attuned to the literary currents of her time. She participated in the vogue for PASTORAL plays with a pair of her own contributions: *Amore innamorato e impazzato* (Love [the god of love, Cupid] in love and insane, 1598) and *Felice arcadia* (Happy Arcadia, 1605).

The work for which she is most celebrated in the early 21st century is her prose treatise *THE NOBILITY AND EXCELLENCE OF WOMEN AND THE DEFECTS AND VICES OF MEN* (1600). Marinella undertook this distinguished contribution to the Renaissance genre of works defending women against an ingrained patriarchal, misogynistic tradition because she felt thoroughly irked. In his *I doneschi difetti* (The defects of women, 1599), Giuseppe Passi had attacked women as completely dissolute without hope of redemption. Marinella's angry, cogent, informed, and lively response left Passi looking as utterly foolish as his arguments. She expanded her work and her range of targets in a later, revised edition (1601) with similar results.

Marinella also authored several saints' lives in verse, a prose and verse biography of the Virgin Mary, and some scholarly commentary on poetry.

Bibliography

Marinella, Lucrezia. *The Nobility and Excellence of Women and the Defects and Vices of Men.* Edited by Anne Dunhill with an introductory essay by Dunhill and Letizia Panizza. Chicago: University of Chicago Press, 2000.

Panizza, Letizia. "Marinella, Lucrezia," in *Encyclopedia of the Renaissance.* Volume 4. Edited by Paul F. Grendler. New York: Scribner, 1999.

Marlowe, Christopher (1564–1593)

The most brilliant of the early Elizabethan playwrights, Christopher Marlowe, was born at Canterbury to a family of humble origins. There in 1579 he received a scholarship as a Queen's scholar to the King's School—a school with a reputation for producing and performing plays. The following year he entered Cambridge and matriculated at Corpus Christi College as a candidate for the Anglican priesthood. He received his B.A. in 1584. That same year, Marlowe apparently became a spy in the service of the Star Chamber of Lord Burghley, and although he was enrolled in college as a master's candidate, he was often absent on secret government business. The following year (1585) began his recorded period of literary activity with his translations of OVID's *Amores* and Lucan's EPIC *Pharsalia* on the subject of the war between Pompey and Caesar. In 1586, perhaps in collaboration with THOMAS NASHE, Marlowe wrote his first drama, *Dido, Queen of Carthage,* and he began his pair of historical dramas tracing the career of the 14th-century Turkic conqueror, Tamerlane, who led an army of nomadic Mongols in wars of conquest against Transoxania, Persia, northern India, the Ottomans, the Mamluks, and, unsuccessfully, the Chinese. The Lord Admiral's Company acted the first of these dramas, *Tamburlaine the Great, Part I,* in 1587.

That same year Cambridge University was about to deny Marlowe his master's degree, ostensibly on charges of atheism, when the Queen's Privy Council intervened on Marlowe's behalf and the degree was granted. In 1588 a production of *Tamburlaine the Great, Part II* was staged. At about the same time Marlowe learned of the publication in Germany of a history of a reputed necromancer Dr. Johann Faustus. Using that document as his source, Marlowe wrote *THE TRAGICAL HISTORY OF DOCTOR FAUSTUS.* It was performed in 1588 and is one of

Marlowe's two most notable tragedies. The other, THE JEW OF MALTA, appeared on stage in 1589.

Marlowe was apparently a friend of another of the three most notable playwrights of his era, THOMAS KYD. The two shared a study in 1590. They were both also thought to share dangerous, possibly atheistic points of view. In was perhaps during this period of working in close proximity to Kyd that Marlowe turned his attention to British history as the source for his next drama, *Edward II*, which was performed in 1592. French history and the St. Bartholomew's Day Massacre that would inspire such a notable French work as THÉODORE AGRIPPA D' AUBIGNÉ'S *The Tragic Ones* (1616) became the subject of one of Marlowe's darkest tragedies, *The Massacre at Paris* (1593).

Later that year Marlowe came under suspicion again for atheism. Though earlier the Queen's Privy Council had protected Marlowe as an agent of the crown, on this occasion it was the council who brought the charges, and, as an upshot, from May 20, 1593, Marlowe was under orders to put in a daily appearance at the council's sessions. What more might have come of these charges no one can say. On May 30, Marlowe, who had a hot temper and who had been in trouble before for armed brawling in the streets, fought in a tavern and was stabbed to death through the eye. His killer, Ingraham Frizer, was acquitted and pardoned on grounds of self-defense.

Marlowe's work continued to issue and reissue from the press. The year 1594 saw the publication of *Edward II* and of a theretofore unpublished work, *Dido, Queen of Carthage*. In about 1596 an unlicensed edition of Marlowe's translation of a book of Lucan and of Ovid's *Elegies* appeared. Marlowe's *Hero and Leander* followed this in 1598.

Even posthumously Marlowe managed to arouse animosity among the religious. In 1599 the bishops of England denounced Marlowe's translation of Ovid's *Elegies* and publicly burned copies of his book. Nonetheless, Marlowe's works have remained in print ever since. Of the great verse dramatists of the English Renaissance, Marlowe had no peer as a poet or playwright before the appearance of the plays of SHAKESPEARE. From time to time a recurrent species of academic silliness puts in an appearance. Because Shakespeare lacked a university education, the argument usually begins with the assertion that someone else must have written his plays. At this writing, MARY SIDNEY HERBERT, the countess of Pembroke, is an unlikely candidate. Earlier candidates have included BACON and Edward de Vere, the earl of Oxford. Marlowe too has been put forward as the real Shakespeare. That theory must overcome the inconvenient datum of Marlowe's well-documented death well before most of the bard's plays were penned. Resurrecting Marlowe and having his pseudonymous Shakespearian plays sent from an ostensible exile in France boggles the boldest ingenuity.

Bibliography

Knoll, Robert E. *Christopher Marlowe.* New York: Twayne Publishers, 1969.

Kuriyama, Constance Brown. *Christopher Marlowe: A Renaissance Life.* Ithaca, N.Y.: Cornell University Press, 2002.

Marlowe, Christopher. *Complete Poems.* Mineola, N.Y.: Dover Press, 2003.

———. *Doctor Faustus. A Two-Text Edition.* Editor: David Scott Kastan. New York: W. W. Norton, 2004.

———. *Edward the Second.* Edited by William-Alson Lundes. Studio City, Calif.: Players Press, 1997.

———. *Tamburlaine the Great.* Edited by J. S. Cunningham and Eithne Henson. Manchester, U.K.: Manchester University Press, ca. 1998.

———. *The Jew of Malta.* Mineola, N.Y.: Dover Press, 2003.

Marot, Clément (ca. 1496–1544)

One of the earliest among French poets to be influenced by the literary winds of change sweeping north from Italy, Marot was a transitional figure between the French Middle Ages and the Renaissance. Until 1527 he used the meters and manner of Medieval French poetry. In that year, however, he abandoned the old and began to introduce into or adopt new meters and forms for French poetry. For the first time in French, he imitated in his sonnets the increasingly fashionable Italian example of PETRARCH. Marot was also familiar with and modeled French works on the classical Latin ECLOGUE, ELEGY, and EPIGRAM.

He wrote a significant body of court poetry. This was sometimes lighthearted and droll, and at other times, when addressed to his enemies, including the theological faculty of the Sorbonne, keenly witty and satirical.

Marot's father had also been a poet and a courtier, and in 1518 the young Marot became an attendant in the court of the Protestant Marguerite of Alençon, who later was crowned Queen MARGUERITE DE NAVARRE. Marot apparently shared his employer's Lutheran religious sentiments. He was imprisoned in 1526 for breaking the Lenten fast. This experience occasioned a verse satire, *L'Enfer* (Hell, 1532). Routinely suspected of religious unorthodoxy, Marot returned to prison in 1527. This time the king, whom Marot now served, intervened on his behalf. The second imprisonment moved him to write a defense of his faith. He included that defense in a work commemorating a recently deceased French treasurer: *Defloration de Florimond Robertet* (The withering, or decline, of Florimond Robertet). It appeared together with other early works in a 1532 collection, *Adolescence Clémentine* (Clement's juvenilia).

Continuing harassment over his religious beliefs and practices forced him to seek refuge outside Paris in 1535. He traveled to Navarre, Ferrara, and Venice. At length he was permitted to return to France on condition that he disavow his errors. He did so.

A collection of his poetic works appeared in 1538. For some time Marot had been translating the Psalms into French and in 1539 dedicated to the king a collection of 30 Psalms in French verse that appeared in 1541. These translations outraged the Roman Catholic clergy, and Marot once again sought refuge in exile, this time in Geneva where JOHN CALVIN welcomed him. There he continued expanding his collection of Psalms and published an enlarged edition. Marot, however, proved too lighthearted and free spirited for the sober Calvinists of Geneva. He seems to have been reproved for indulging in a game of backgammon on a Sunday. Obliged to seek asylum elsewhere, he once again headed south to Savoy and Italy. He resided in Turin at the time of his death.

Among his works one also finds a long allegorical poem, *Le Temple de Cupidon* (The temple of Cupid), and shorter forms—rondeaus, songs, elegy, ballads, epigram, and other translations, notably of a portion of OVID's *Metamorphoses*. He also prepared editions of medieval works. The year 1527 saw his edition of *The romance of the rose* and 1533 an edition of the work of his great medieval predecessor, François Villon (1431–ca. 1463).

Most of Marot's contemporaries considered him the preeminent French poet of his generation. Since then his reputation has waned from time to time, but just as often it has recovered. His fame was eclipsed by the poets of the next generation.

Bibliography

Clive, H. P. *Clément Marot: An Annotated Bibliography.* London: Grant & Cutler, 1983.

Glidden, Hope, and Norman R. Shapiro, eds and trans. *Lyrics of the French Renaissance: Maro, Du Bellay, Ronsard.* New Haven, Conn.: Yale University Press, 2002.

Smith, Pauline M. *Clément Marot: Poet of the French Renaissance.* London: Athlone Press, 1970.

Williams, Anwyl. *Clément Marot: Figure, Text, and Intertext.* Lewiston, Mass.: E. Mellen Press, 1990.

Marston, John (1576–1634)

An English poet, satirist, and dramatist, Marston was the son of a Coventry lawyer and his wife, Marie Guarsi. The young Marston attended Brasenose College in Oxford University, taking his B.A. in 1594. His earliest surviving entry into the literary arena came in 1598 with the publication of a poem based on the Roman poet OVID's *Metamorphoses*. The work's title, *The Metamorphosis of Pigmalion's Image*, describes its content. A sculptor, Pigmalion [*sic*], falls in love with a statue he has carved and prays to Venus, the goddess of love, to bring his creation to life. Venus grants his prayer. An apprentice work that provoked much unfavorable comment, Marston's tasteless, erotic poem is written in iambic-pentameter, six-line stanzas rhyming ababcc. The 1598 version of the poem is accompanied by *Certaine Satyres*. The outraged critical response to *Pigmalion's Image* convinced

Marston, a better verse satirist than love poet, that satiric rather than amorous verse was his province. The work was followed later the same year by another set of verse satires, *The Scourge of Villanie,* which went into second and third editions with expansions in 1599.

One of Marston's biographers, R. W. Ingram, points out that Marston belonged to a species of Elizabethan intellectual known to their contemporaries as "malcontents." The perennial dissatisfaction of such persons with virtually everything took root in their predisposition toward melancholy—a condition exhaustively explored by ROBERT BURTON in his ANATOMY OF MELANCHOLY (1621). According to the precepts of HUMORAL MEDICINE, melancholia arose principally from an excess of black bile in a sufferer's constitution. The same condition also became associated in the popular imagination with an artistic temperament. Perhaps for this reason, being perceived as a malcontent (and therefore as a creative person) became fashionable among some Elizabethans.

As a verse satirist, Marston was too certain of the corruption of the world, too inexperienced to make well-informed judgments about what were and were not proper objects and methods of satire, and too sure of his own capacities and rectitude to achieve success in accomplishing the prime objective of SATIRE—moral reform. At the same time, when he describes the minor foibles of fops and sportsmen addicted, say, to fencing, his early verse satires can be effective and amusing.

Marston's failure to recognize his own limitations brought him into conflict with persons whose satirical pens were sharper and whose intellects were perhaps keener than his own, such as JOSEPH HALL and BEN JONSON. Marston's quarrel with Hall seems to have been grounded in professional jealousy, with Marston taking vocal exception to Hall's claim to be the first English satirist.

The quarrel with Jonson arose after Marston transformed himself into a satirical dramatist. This happened in 1599 when the records of the theatrical producer Philip Henslowe show a loan to Marston for an unnamed play. This may have been his *Robert II, King of Scots.* In any case, Marston apparently intended the character of Chisoganus in

his first play *Historiomatrix* (written 1599) to be based on Jonson and to compliment him. Unfortunately, the characterization proved both recognizable and sufficiently ambiguous that Jonson felt insulted. He replied in kind with an uncomplimentary barb directed at Marston in *Every Man Out of his Humor* (1599). The quarrel grew to epic proportions, fanned by the encouragement of rival theater owners who understood that the battle of the satirical playwrights improved the box-office receipts. If Jonson is to be believed, the quarrel at least once reached the level of fisticuffs and armed confrontation. On stage, after THOMAS DEKKER had become involved as Marston's ally, the quarrel finally blew itself out with a full-scale exchange of vitriol in Jonson's *The Poetaster,* in which Jonson directly attacks Marston, and Dekker and Marston's *Sociomatrix* (1602), in which the two collaborate in gleefully lampooning Jonson.

Marston's theatrical career, however, was by no means limited to his quarrel with Jonson. The year 1599 had also seen the production of two Marston plays: *Historiomatrix, or The Player Whipt,* and a drama in two parts, *The Historie of Antonio and Melinda.* Both these SATIRE plays mix dramatic forms almost indiscriminately. While *Historiomatrix* (the play that began the quarrel with Jonson with the characterization of the principal interlocutor, Chrisoganus) is a satire, it is a satire that is also a sort of medieval morality play in six acts. Each of the acts is an ALLEGORY featuring as its principal character Peace, Plenty, Pride, Envy, War, and Poverty. The play reads more like a series of declamations than like an acted drama despite the fact that it includes snatches of scenes presented by a company of itinerant players led by Sir Oliver Owlet.

Also a comic satire, *Antonio and Melinda* combines with its satirical and moral purposes the romantic elements of melodrama and the violence of SENECAN TRAGEDY. Following the two parts of *Antonio and Melinda* came *Jack Drum's Entertainment or the Comedy of Pasquill and Katherine* (performed 1600). Marston partly deserts for the moment his satiric MUSE in *Jack Drum's Entertainment,* and although he has not yet fully mastered the playwright's craft, he creates a mostly good-natured romp through the overplotted, complicated love lives of Katherine and Camelia, two daughters of Sir Edward Fortune. Sir Edward has decreed that the daughters can marry whomever they choose as long as their husbands are gentlemen. Some darker moments are included to hold audience interest, as when a disappointed suitor, Mamon, throws poison in Katherine's face, temporarily disfiguring her, or when Camelia's suitor, Brabant, Jr., plots his friend's death because he mistakenly considers him a rival. The modicum of satire that this play retains is directed at the conventional plots, stock characters, and repetitive stage business that are included in popular comedies based on the lives of typical citizens of the London plays known as city comedies.

The year 1601 saw the production of *Antonio's Revenge*, one of the bloodiest and least restrained of the so-called tragedies of the blood ever performed on the Elizabethan stage. Depicting both murder and torture, *Antonio's Revenge* nonetheless avoids the accusation of bloody spectacle for its own sake by embedding that action in a genuinely dramatic series of ritualistic stage pictures. The effect of the violence is also muted by Marston's inclusion of music and interchanges among the actors as several of them complete each other's speeches in contrapuntal, musical fashion.

By 1603 Marston and Jonson had stopped attacking each other on stage and had apparently buried the hatchet. In that year, in fact, Marston wrote complimentary prefatory verses to Jonson's historical drama *Sejanus*. In 1605 the two reconciled playwrights collaborated with GEORGE CHAPMAN to write *Eastward, Hoe!*—a play that got all three in trouble with the authorities. Before that, however, in 1604 Marston purchased a one-sixth interest in a company of child actors, Children of the Queen's Revels. Having mastered his art, he wrote all his remaining plays for performance by this highly professional company of young people.

These plays included *The Malcontent* (1604), *The Fawne* (ca. 1605), *The Dutch Curtezan* (1605), and *Sophonisba* (ca. 1606). Marston's work for this company also included some plays designed as COURT ENTERTAINMENT: *The City Spectacle* (1606), performed before King JAMES I and the king of Denmark, and an *Entertainment of the Dowager-*

Countess of Darby (1607). He also had a hand in a play *The Insatiate Countess* that the playwright William Barksted completed.

In 1608 Marston ran afoul of the law again and spent some time in jail, but the circumstances surrounding that experience are unclear. Whatever they were, Marston apparently decided that his continued participation in the world of theater was ill advised. He divested himself of shares that he owned in Blackfriar's Theater and in 1609 moved to Oxfordshire in the village of Stanton Harcourt. There he became first the deacon and then the ordained priest of its church where he served until 1616. That year he was attacked and robbed. He moved with his wife Mary to Christchurch, Hampshire. He remained the priest of its church until 1631.

Bibliography
Ingram, R. W. *John Marston*. Boston: Twayne Publishers, 1978.

Jackson, Macdonald P., and Michael Neil, eds. *The Selected Plays of John Marston*. Cambridge, U.K.: Cambridge University Press, 1968.

Marston, John. *Antonio and Melida, Antonio's Revenge, The Malcontent, The Dutch Curtezan, Sophonisba*. Edited by Keith Sturgis. Oxford: Oxford University Press, 1997.

———. *The Plays of John Marston*. Edited by H. Harvey Wood. Edinburgh: Oliver and Boyd, 1934–1939.

———. *The Poems of John Marston*. Edited by Arnold Davenport. Liverpool: Liverpool University Press, 1961.

Marvell, Andrew (1621–1678)

Educated at Hull Grammar School and at Trinity College, Cambridge, Marvell is principally remembered and most highly regarded for his lyric poems. These include his "garden poems," which were inspired by the time he spent in the 1650s as a tutor to Mary Fairfax at Nun Appleton House in Yorkshire—a country estate with magnificent gardens. A long poem of 776 lines, *Upon Appleton House*, is one of many elaborate lyrics inspired by Marvell's stay with the Fairfax household.

Marvell's reputation as a lyric poet rests in part upon his having reinvigorated the METAPHYSICAL CONCEIT in his poems. He is also identified with the *CARPE DIEM* tradition. In his poem *To His Coy Mistress*, Marvell laments his lady's reluctance on the grounds that "at my back I always hear \ time's winged chariot hurrying near" and on the swift approach and finality of death. His later satires grew from his extraordinarily faithful service in the English parliament (1659–78)—he actually reported regularly to his constituents—and from his critical view of government chicanery, self-deception, and corruption. Among his literary acquaintance he numbered JOHN MILTON, with whom he was very friendly, and JOHN DRYDEN, who disliked Marvell intensely.

Bibliography

Marvell, Andrew. *The Complete Poems*. Edited by George de F. Lord. New York: Alfred A. Knopf, ca. 1993.

———. *The Poems and Letters of Andrew Marvell*. 2 vols. Edited by H. M. Margoliouth; revised 3rd edited by Pierre Legouis and E. E. Duncan–Jones. Oxford: Oxford University press, 1971.

———. *The Prose Works of Andrew Marvell*. Edited by Martin Dzelzainis and Annabel Patterson. New Haven, Conn.: Yale University Press, 2003.

———. *"To His Coy Mistress" and Other Poems*. Mineola, N.Y.: Dover Publications, 1997.

Massinger, Philip (1583–1640)

Born in Salisbury and reared in London, British dramatist Philip Massinger attended St. Alban's Hall at Oxford University for a period of years but left without a degree. Back in London after 1610 Massinger was among the many London playwrights collaborating with others to meet the playgoing public's insatiable appetite for new material. During the decade from 1610 to 1620 his name appears as a collaborator in almost 20 plays, some of which have not survived. Among those collaborations that have survived we find *The Second Maiden's Tragedy* (ca. 1611), *The Faithful Friends* (ca. 1614), *The Queen of Corinth* (ca. 1617), and *The Bloody Brother* (ca. 1618). With THOMAS MID-DLETON and WILLIAM ROWLEY at about the same time Massinger collaborated in staging *The Old Law*. Massinger is also thought to have had an anonymous hand in several of the plays of FRANCIS BEAUMONT and JOHN FLETCHER.

Around 1620, plays exclusively or mostly penned by Massinger began to appear. Again, a number of these plays have been lost, and the earliest survivor of a play in which he was the lead writer seems to be *The Virgin Martyr* (published 1620). *The Duke of Milan* (1623) is probably the earliest play securely attributable to his hand alone, though a SENECAN TRAGEDY, *The Unnatural Combat*, is also a candidate. *The Bondman* (1623) came next. It is a romantic TRAGICOMEDY set in Sicily. *The Renegado* (1624) concerns the rescue of a Venetian lady, Paulina, from an eventually reformed pirate, Grimaldi, and the conflict between the Muslim and the Christian worlds. As in many of his plays, what seem to be topical references to events of the time appear. Massinger was at his best in comedy. His play, *The Parliament of Love* (1624), provides a merry romp through the era's stock comic and spectacular devices that many a playwright used to evoke positive responses from audiences. They approved and enjoyed the repetition of familiar stage situations—confused love affairs, profligate husbands reformed by virtuous wives' comic remedies, and onstage swordplay.

That Massinger was much in demand as a playwright, whether working singly or with others, appears in his providing material for COURT ENTERTAINMENT. *The Virgin Martyr* had been first publicly performed, but with a fresh scene added it was performed before King JAMES I for the king's revels. Later Massinger composed works for companies that included the King's Men where he succeeded John Fletcher as the leading playwright. He also wrote for the Queen of Bohemia's Men, Lady Elizabeth's Men, and, after the accession to the throne of Charles I, Queen Henrietta's Men. For the last named of these companies in 1630 Massinger wrote *The Maid of Honour*. This play explores within the life of its heroine, Camiola, the eternal conflict between virtue and vice and the dangers that viciousness pose for the national character. Camiola's character is loosely but recognizably based on Queen ELIZABETH I.

A NEW WAY TO PAY OLD DEBTS (1625?), a comedy slightly atypical of Massinger's more characteristic work, has proved to be his best-remembered play. It is at once a comedy of manners in the new style of Massinger's time and a morality play that opposes traditional virtues to the typical vices of the time.

Massinger continued writing plays into the reign of King Charles I. His industry produced many plays, several of which have not survived. He seems to have completed the plays that Fletcher left unfinished and then to have penned his own. One of the latter, *The Roman Actor* (1626), explores in a notable play the relationship between the state and the theater. In a moving scene, the title actor, Paris, explains to Emperor Diocletian's corrupt counselors the benefits of theater to national virtue and the pitfalls awaiting the nation that, like Massinger's England, ignores its lessons. The year 1627 saw the performance of *The Great Duke of Florence* by Queen Henrietta's Men. His other surviving plays include: *The Picture* (1629), *The Maid of Honour* (1630), *Believe as You List* and *The Emperor of the East* (both 1631). These were followed by *The City Madam* (1632), *The Guardian* (1633), *The Tragedy of Cleander* and *A Very Woman* (1634), and *The Bashful Lover* (1636). Though the records of performance show that Massinger's new plays continued to be produced until six weeks before his death, those written after 1636 no longer survive.

In addition to his long and fruitful career as a playwright Massinger also penned occasional verse throughout his working life. Examples of such poems include "A Newyeares Guift," dedicated to the countess of Chesterfield in 1621, a plague poem "London's Lamentable Estate" (1625), and a funeral poem for Charles Herbert, son of the earl of Pembroke, in 1636.

Bibliography

Adler, Doris Ray. *Philip Massinger.* Boston: Twayne Publishers, 1987.

Fletcher, John, et al. *The Bloody Brother: A Tragedy.* [Refurbished ca. 1630 by Massinger as *Rollo, Duke of Normandy.*] Edited by Bertha Hensman. New York: Vantage Press, ca. 1991.

Massinger, Philip. *Selected Plays of Philip Massinger.* Edited by Colin Gibson. Cambridge, U.K.: Cambridge University Press.

———. *The Plays and Poems of Philip Massinger.* Five volumes. Edited by Philip Edwards and Colin Gibson. Oxford, U.K.: The Clarendon Press, 1976.

———. *The Roman Actor.* London: Nick Hern Books, 2002.

——— et al. *Three Turk Plays from Early Modern England: Selimus, A Christian Turned Turk, and* [Massinger's] *The Renegado.* Edited by Daniel J. Vitkus. New York: Columbia University Press, ca. 2000.

master of the revels

The official in charge of organizing English royal COURT ENTERTAINMENT, the master of the revels early became the unofficial arbiter of what was and was not permissible on the London stage. In 1589 Queen ELIZABETH I made her master of the revels officially responsible for licensing and censoring all plays to be performed in London. The touchy political situation in which Elizabeth found herself made this move expedient. Plays were popular and could be used to foster sentiments uncongenial to Elizabeth's rule. JOHN LYLY, the author of the famous *EUPHUES,* unsuccessfully aspired to become Elizabeth's master of the revels; instead in 1579 the queen appointed Edmund Tilney. Tilney continued to fill the office until 1610, serving JAMES I in the same capacity.

Matsuo, Bashō

See BASHŌ.

Medici, Lorenzo de' (1449–1492)

The son of the uncrowned ruler of Florence, Piero di Cosimo de' Medici and Lucrezia Tornabuoni and the grandson of Cosimo, the father of his country as he was known, Lorenzo reluctantly succeeded to his father's role as the leader of the Florentine Republic in 1469. He also succeeded Piero as head of the Medici's far-flung banking empire.

Although he was famously in love with his mistress, Lucrezia Donati, for reasons of state he married a Roman noblewoman, Clarice Orsini, in June of 1469. Three years after assuming command of Florence, Lorenzo was faced with rioting in one of her dependencies, the city of Volterra. Inexperienced in such matters, Lorenzo made a decision that he regretted as long as he lived. He authorized the military suppression of the riot, with the result that he lost the hearts and minds of the Volterrans.

On April 26, 1478, the Pazzi family, hoping to rid Florence of the Medici and perhaps take over its reins themselves, conspired to assassinate both Lorenzo and his younger brother Giuliano in the cathedral of Florence. The assassins struck down Giuliano before the high altar of the church, but Lorenzo narrowly escaped through a side door and made his way to his dwelling a few blocks distant. Lorenzo's revenge on the Pazzi family was swift and terrible. Their kinsman and confederate Cardinal Salviati of Florence was among those whom Lorenzo hanged in reprisal. Also an accessory to the plot, Pope Sixtus IV saw to it that Lorenzo was excommunicated from the Roman Catholic Church and that all of Florence came under papal interdict, which meant that Florentine citizens were denied the sacraments of their religion. In a formidable alliance with Naples, Calabria, and others, the Vatican made war against Florence.

In Lorenzo's most successful diplomatic coup, however, he went to Naples where he convinced King Ferrante to withdraw from the papal alliance. Thereafter a series of carefully considered moves and a great deal of carefully spent money reconciled Lorenzo with his foes.

A patron of the arts and learning, Lorenzo financed the revival of the University of Pisa and made it a great intellectual center. In Florence, painters and sculptors benefited from his largesse. In Florence, too, Lorenzo participated in a literary coterie that included some of the finest and most talented persons of his era, GIOVANNI PICO DELLA MIRANDOLA, for example, and AGNOLO POLIZIANO. Lorenzo numbered all the members of the literary PULCI family among his acquaintance, and he himself was among the best poets of Italy in his period.

As early as 1474–75 Lorenzo decided to collect his poetic work, as PETRARCH had done, and to comment on it himself as Dante had done. In other words, he put himself directly in the succession of the best poets in the Italian language. Like Dante, too, Lorenzo wrote a defense of the use of the vernacular language for serious literary production. All his adult life, he worked on a collection that, at his death, contained 41 of his sonnets together with his own extensive discussion of his reasons for writing them and his own interpretations of them: *The AUTOBIOGRAPHY OF LORENZO DE' MEDICI: A COMMENTARY ON MY SONNETS* (*Il Commento*). He worked on his collection periodically throughout a very busy life. It broke off unfinished when he died and was published posthumously.

Beyond his *Commentary* and his defense of the use of vernacular Italian, Lorenzo also wrote bawdy CARNIVAL SONGS and a religious play about Saints Peter and Paul that Lorenzo designed for production at his son's school. As the historian of drama Nerida Newbiggin has observed, the play contained a part for every child.

Lorenzo's wife, Clarice Orsini, died in 1488. The following year Lorenzo was able to negotiate an agreement that made his 14-year-old son Giovanni a prince of the church, a cardinal. He would later become Pope Leo X.

On December 29, 1491, an attack of a hereditary case of gout afflicted Lorenzo. He never fully recovered from it, and on April 8, 1492, he died.

Bibliography

Cook, James Wyatt, trans. *The Autobiography of Lorenzo de' Medici, a Commentary on My Sonnets.* 1995. Tempe, Ariz.: Arizona Center for Medieval and Renaissance Studies, 2000.

Kent, F. W. *Lorenzo de' Medici and the Art of Magnificence.* Baltimore: Johns Hopkins University Press, 2004.

Martines, Lauro. *April Blood: Florence and the Plot against the Medici.* New York and London: Oxford University Press, 2003.

Medici, Lorenzo de'. *Carnival Songs.* New York: Raphael Fodde Editions, 2001.

Meistersinger

The *Meistersinger,* or mastersingers, of the German Renaissance were generally drawn from among craftsmen and middle-class residents of German towns who competed annually in composition and singing contests in several locations in Germany. The competitions included songs on both spiritual and secular subjects. The first were performed in churches during a ceremony called *Singschule* (singing school); the latter were performed in taverns after the spiritual performance.

The competitions were conducted according to very strict rules. In the beginning the prize of the title *Meister* (master) was awarded to the person who came up with the best words for an old tune. As the contests evolved, however, they came to require both new words and new tunes as well.

The fame of Richard Wagner's opera *Die Meistersinger von Nürnberg* (*The Meistersinger of Nuremburg*), has led to a popular perception that exaggerates the importance of these competitions during the Renaissance. Only initiates of the societies could attend their performances. The winning songs could not be published or publicly performed elsewhere. Thus they exercised little influence on the development of German music or German poetry. Nonetheless, the societies of Meistersingers persisted from the 15th and well into the 19th century, and the still-active male choirs composed of members of German trades and crafts may trace their origins to them.

Despite the virtual impossibility of the general public's hearing the master songs of the winning composers at the competition, a number of them gained considerable fame. Wagner, of course, has immortalized Hans Sachs of Nuremburg. But in their own time others were at least as celebrated. Hans Folz, also of Nuremburg and earlier of Worms, was perhaps the most highly regarded among the masters. Adam Puschman and Georg Hager of Breslau, and Onophrius Schwarzenback and Johannes Spreng of Augsburg are among the 16th-century *Meistersinger* whose renown has survived.

mesneví

A traditional type of poetic composition in the Islamic world, a *mesneví* is a verse narrative, often quite long but of varying length, that is composed of a series of rhyming couplets. Most Turkish, Per-

sian, and Arabic poets of the 16th and 17th centuries left at least one *mesneví* among their works. One celebrated Turkish poet, LÁMI'Í OF BRUSA (ca. 1472–ca. 1531) left eight examples of the type among his poetic works.

The subjects a *mesneví* might treat included the romantic stories of lovers—stories that often presented an ALLEGORY of a matter like the relationship between physical and spiritual love. A *mesneví* could also treat a moral or religious subject, or it might take inanimate objects like polo balls and mallets or like candles, or an irrational creature like a moth, personify those objects and creatures, and then construct didactic allegories about their relationships.

Messenius, Johannes (1579–1636)

A Swedish historian and dramatist, Messenius conceived the notion of combining the styles of biblical drama and student comedy to present Swedish history. He planned a grand cycle of 50 plays that he hoped would stir up patriotic fervor among the Swedes in the same way that biblical drama had fanned the flames of religion. Though he put his plan into action, the result came far short of his original hopes: Only six of the plays ever saw production.

Messenius also wrote a religious drama based on the life of the Swedish Saint Bridgid and a Latin history of all the Scandinavian countries including Greenland and Iceland from the time of the biblical great flood to the 16th century.

metaphor

The Greek roots of the word *metaphor* suggest a transfer of meaning. A metaphor is a comparison that takes the qualities associated with one word or phrase or object and attributes them to another. If you say, "skiing is a trip," in theory, you take whatever qualities you associate with taking a journey and apply them to sliding down a hill. The same principle works in a more complex way in the metaphors that poets employ. If a poet says that a woman's eyes are starry, the author applies the qualities of stars to the eyes of the subject—brilliance, the emission of light, beauty. Because astrology suggests a person's destiny is determined by the stars, the metaphor also suggests that the poet was fated to love the woman.

Metaphor is divided into various subcategories: The simplest is simile, a comparison that states the words *like* or *as*. Some Renaissance poets were fond of a simile that announced a woman's blond hair was "like golden wire."

The word *metaphor* itself has both the broader meaning described above and a more specific meaning: a comparison that does not state *like* or *as*.

All metaphors, according to I. A. Richards, bear in common two elements: a *tenor* and a *vehicle*. *Tenor* is used in the sense of its Latin root word, which means "to hold." So the tenor of a metaphor is the part of the comparison that holds the meaning—the idea—it receives from the vehicle. The *vehicle* is the part of the comparison that conveys the meaning by means of a poetic image. *Image* one may define as a verbal appeal to the senses. "To burst joy's grape against my palette fine" is a vehicle that conveys a tactile image and appeals to the sense of taste as well, so the idea or tenor of the metaphor involves comparing joy to the pleasant sensation of popping a ripe grape between the tongue and the roof of the mouth and of the sweet taste of the fruit or, perhaps, of wine.

Some metaphors have multiple vehicles. When this is true, they become symbolic. When someone says, "My love is like a red, red rose," the many qualities of a rose—tenderness, fragrance, delicacy, the complexity of the multifoliate form of the flower, and perhaps thorniness—are verbally transferred to the speaker's beloved. Sometimes poets create new symbols within the context of a poem; on other occasions they make use of symbols that their readers may have seen frequently before, that they will recognize and respond to. When a symbol has more or less the same set of ideas attached to it over time in the work of several artists, it is said to be a conventional symbol. These can be verbal, or they can also be visual or auditory.

In those bygone days when films were more suggestive and less direct in their handling of steamy material, one might have seen two would-be lovers in bathing suits walking on the beach as night approached. They regard each other longingly, they clinch; the camera pans to pounding surf, and everyone in the audience knows what goes on off camera. Such camera work became a conventional visual symbol.

Similarly, Renaissance poets had a repertoire of verbal and visual symbols that they and their predecessors regularly endowed with sometimes complex significance, both conventional and novel. When Francesco Petrarca (Petrarch) in the 366th and final poem of his *Songbook* addresses the Virgin Mary as *"vera beatrice"* (true bearer of bliss or blessing), his Italian phrase evokes his reader's recollection, first, of Dante's *La Vita Nuova* (The new life), whose sonnets are addressed to Dante's beloved Beatrice). Next, it reminds the reader that the sainted spirit of Beatrice takes over as Dante's guide in purgatory after the Dante pilgrim in his *Comedy* passes through the refiner's fire. She leads him to Paradise. Petrarch's phrase seems to imply that, among women, only the Holy Virgin has that power. Attributing to mortal women like Petrarch's Laura or Dante's Beatrice the power to guide one to Heaven is a mistake, Petrarch's phrase seems to suggest. All Italian and most Continental and English Renaissance poets had read their Dante and their Petrarch. Moreover, as readers, they expected more from text than information of a surface sort, and they understood the codes of their predecessors. The best of the poets borrowed the conventional symbolism of their forebears and endowed it with new significance of their own.

In thinking about reading Renaissance works, it may be helpful to remember that our contemporary audiences have exactly the opposite problem from Renaissance readers. Whereas we can barely find time to look at all we need to read for our jobs and our studies, the Renaissance readership came mainly from the leisure classes who had time on their hands. Thus they looked for ornament, surprise, and implicit meaning in the texts they read as well as for story and information. Also, as mostly Roman Catholic Christians, European readers of the Renaissance were used to finding evidence of divine providence both in natural phenomena and in the writing of gifted authors, whom they considered inspired (see Vates and typology). Metaphor, both simple and complex, enriched the texts they read.

All language is essentially metaphoric. There is no necessary connection between the object we call a potato and the sounds that stand for it. The word *potato*, however, is the verbal *sign* of the object rather than a metaphor in the sense described above.

Bibliography

Cook, James W. *Poetry: Method, and Meaning.* Chicago: Educational Methods, 1968.

Ohly, Friedrich, ed. *Sensus Spiritualis: Studies in Medieval Significs and the Philology of Culture.* Translated by Kenneth J. Northcott. Chicago: University of Chicago Press, 2004.

Petrarca, Francesco. *Petrarch's Songbook: Rerum vulgarium fragmenta.* Vol. 151. Translated by James Wyatt Cook. Introduced by Germaine Warkentin. Binghamton, N.Y.: Medieval and Renaissance Texts and Studies, 1995.

metaphysical conceit

Just as a CONCEIT compares the qualities of unlike objects in the hope of producing a fresh effect, a metaphysical conceit seeks likenesses in sometimes startlingly far-fetched comparisons. Principally identified with the British school of metaphysical poets that included JOHN DONNE, RICHARD CRASHAW, and GEORGE HERBERT among others, the metaphysical conceit, well handled, can produce telling effects. Donne, for example, was forced to separate for a time from his wife, Anne, age 17, who had not obtained her parents permission to marry before she came of age. For her he wrote *A Valediction* (a farewell) *Forbidding Mourning*. In this poem he uses several metaphysical conceits with telling effect. He suggests that, though the pair must separate, their two souls, which have become one, will expand "like gold to airy thinness beat," without being torn apart. This conceit takes its effect from the capacity of gold to be beaten to a thinness of a single molecule without tearing. Though this scientific truth was unknown to Donne, the process by which thinly beaten gold leaf was applied to objects as large as cathedral domes was common knowledge. In the same poem, he also compares the lovers' fidelity to the two legs of a drawing compass. (He calls the legs

"stiff twin compasses," but, like *scissors, compasses* is a singular with a plural form.) The further one leg leans, the more the other leans toward it, keeping the circle just. The implicit psychosexual imagery evoked by the successful employment of metaphysical conceits in this poem is breathtakingly effective. In another case, Donne compares the morning sun that awakens lovers to a "busy old fool"—a disorderly and senile peeping Tom—with humorous effect.

Not all metaphysical conceits achieve similar success, unfortunately. Crashaw compares the eyes of the weeping Mary Magdalene to "two walking baths, two weeping motions, / two portable and compendious oceans"—all of which seems a bit much.

metaphysical poetry

The British poet John Dryden first associated the word *metaphysics* with the poetry of JOHN DONNE. Whereas preceding love poets had often concerned themselves with exploring the feelings that arose in connection with passion and the effects those feelings produced in lovers, Donne interested himself in the philosophy of love and in analyzing love's components. He also explored ethical and religious issues in his poems.

Beyond that, Donne and the poets who emulated him—poets such as GEORGE HERBERT, VAUGHAN, and CRASHAW in the religious vein and Cleveland, Cowley, and MARVELL in the secular—introduced into the poetry of the 17th century a language more closely approximating the usage of ordinary speech than that employed by their predecessors. "For God's sake hold your tongue and let me love!" Donne exclaims in the opening of his poem, "A Canonization."

Metaphysical poems were also characterized by a search for fresh comparisons and metaphors. At their best such comparisons were marvelously clarifying, as when Donne in "A Valediction forbidding Mourning," compares the effect of absence on lovers to the way that gold can be beaten to "airy thinness" without tearing, or the way in which the legs of a compass stretch out and come together as one leg "roams" away from or approaches the other. At their worst, such comparisons can seem laughable, as when Richard Crashaw compares the eyes of the weeping Mary Magdalene to "walking baths" and "portable and compendious oceans." Such comparisons were labeled "METAPHYSICAL CONCEITS."

The final quality that distinguishes metaphysical poems is their high degree of intellectuality. This characteristic appealed to English poets of the 20th century and brought the Renaissance metaphysical poets, who had fallen out of favor for more than 100 years, back into the limelight.

Michelangelo Buonarrotti
(Michelagniolo di Lodovico Buonarroti)
(1475–1564)

Michelangelo is best remembered as the finest sculptor of the Renaissance and as a peerlessly superb painter who, because he preferred sculpting to painting, only reluctantly agreed to adorn the Vatican's Sistine Chapel. Michelangelo, however, also enjoys an enviable reputation as a literary figure. This reputation rests principally on his poems, circulated in manuscript during his life and published posthumously. His literary reputation rests also to a degree upon his letters. He composed the poems during a long period that ran from 1503 to 1561, and they were of such outstanding quality that his contemporaries PIETRO BEMBO and the humanist writer, Benedetto Varchi, considered Michelangelo to be 16th-century Italian poetry's "Apollo-Appelles" (the one who calls or invokes the god Apollo, patron deity of the arts).

A modern critic of Michelangelo's poems, like James M. Saslow, displays more reserve in evaluating his work. On the positive side Saslow notes with earlier critics Michelangelo's straightforwardness, his intellectual capacities, his willingness to grapple with ideas, and the confessional quality of many of the poems. On the negative side, Michelangelo sometimes tried too hard, and his meaning and purposes become obscure, or he leaves a poem unfinished because he loses control of it. Like other Italian poets of his time, Michelangelo followed the models provided by DANTE and PETRARCH. Unlike them, however, Michelangelo found himself harboring homoerotic thoughts and

homosexual desires. Two significant poetic innovations followed from his sexual orientation: In the first place, he produced the first extended body of homoerotic poetry in a modern European language; in the second, as Saslow points out, Michelangelo developed a consciously androgynous continuum on which to express his feelings. Sometimes he addressed his friend and benefactress, VITTORIA COLONNA, in both male and female terms, and sometimes he conceives of himself in female roles. The actress and poet ISABELLA ANDREINI would later apply a similar strategy both to her role-playing on stage and to the voices of the speakers in her poems.

Michelangelo's NEOPLATONIST views on art also emerge from his poems. In several of them he develops the view that God has implanted in the living rock the forms that the skillful hands of God's elected artists can draw forth. In a poem about his hammer's ability to find the forms in the stone, Michelangelo also maintains that God sustains the strength that makes his art possible. He also expresses the view that when an artist portrays the friends he loves, he bestows immortality upon them.

Michelangelo's love poems are addressed to two persons. Vittoria Colonna, in addition to being his friend, became a patroness and the MUSE who inspired him. Several poems are addressed to her. Those poems that concern his homoerotic yearnings are written to an aristocratic and handsome youth, Tommaso de' Cavalieri. Some 50 of these exist. Springing as always from Michelangelo's personal experience, they communicate his feelings of yearning, ecstasy, joy, rejection, and the guilt about his feelings that his Christian faith sometimes imposes. Principally, however, his love poems assert the views of PLATONIC LOVE that through the contemplation of physical beauty one can be drawn to consider, first, moral and intellectual beauty and, eventually, divine beauty itself. Divine beauty is the same as divine truth and divine good. They are three aspects of the same unity.

Occasionally, Michelangelo used his poems to vent his frustrations about the disdain and neglect he suffered at the hands of Pope Julius II, one of his early patrons. Having vented his frustrations, however, Michelangelo apparently had the good sense not to send his verse to the pope. He also chaffed in verse at the constraints that authorities attempted to impose on artists. Although Michelangelo complained about being dragooned into decorating the Sistine Chapel in fresco—a medium that he did not know well—he managed to convert some of his annoyance into humorous verse, as when he describes a goiter that he attributes to working all day in awkward positions. He also describes in a sardonic vein other physical changes that he attributes to his burdensome task. Nonetheless, he felt so pleased with his depiction of the creation of the Sun and the Moon on the Sistine ceiling that he celebrated its completion with a SONNET. He similarly composed verses about the sculptures that adorn the Medici Chapel in the Church of San Lorenzo in Florence—particularly the figure of the personified Night.

As Michelangelo grew older, his religious nature more frequently appeared in his verses. He often comments on the changes that time has wrought in his physical appearance and capacities, and he follows Petrarch in excoriating Rome for its immorality and venality. World weariness, regret at his failing faculties and growing infirmities, and the anticipation of death provide the subjects of many of his late poems.

Many of Michelangelo's letters have been preserved. Although he himself was far too modest to publish them as many of his contemporaries did, he was also far too famous to imagine that others would not collect and publish them posthumously. From them one can glean his views about many of his contemporaries, including BENVENUTO CELLINI whose capacities as a goldsmith Michelangelo admired. They reveal much about his sometimes stormy but always affectionate relationship with his teacher Leonardo da Vinci, his views about the Florentine religious reformer Girolomo Savonarola, the modesty that made him uncomfortable when he received public praise, but his pleasure, nonetheless, when Benedetto Varchi publicly read and commented upon and then printed two of Michelangelo's poems along with his commentary.

Dissatisfied with the biographies of Michelangelo that had appeared by the early 1960s, Renaissance scholar Robert J. Clements assembled in a single volume the translations of the texts of many poems, letters, and conversations of Michelangelo that persons present had preserved. Clements has grouped these materials under a number of useful topic headings. Although his work has been superseded by subsequent scholarship and improved biographies, Clements' work remains a helpful introduction to the study of this fascinating Renaissance genius.

Bibliography

Bull, George, and Peter Porter, trans. and eds. *Michelangelo, Life, Letters, and Poetry.* [Contains Ascanio Condivi's 16th-century biography of Michelangelo.] Oxford, U.K., and New York: Oxford University Press, 1999.

Clements, Robert J., ed. *Michelangelo, A Self-Portrait.* Englewood Cliffs, N.J.: Prentice Hall, Inc., 1963.

Michelangelo Buonarroti. *Love Sonnets and Madrigals to Tommaso de' Cavalieri.* Translated by Michael Sullivan. London: P. Owen, 1997.

———. *The Complete Poems of Michelangelo.* Translated by John Frederick Nims. Chicago: University of Chicago Press, ca. 1998.

———. *The Complete Poetry of Michelangelo.* Translated by Sidney Alexander. Athens: Ohio University Press, ca. 1991.

———. *The Poetry of Michelangelo: An Annotated Translation.* Translated by James M. Saslow. New Haven, Conn., and London: Yale University Press, 1991.

Vasari, Giorgio. *Life of Michelangelo.* Translated by Gaston du C. de Vere. Edited by Frank Sadowski. New York: Alba House, ca. 2003.

Microcosme Maurice Scève (1562)

The French poet MAURICE SCÈVE'S last major work, *Microcosme* (Microcosm), was finished in 1559 and published in 1562. For its form, Scève chose alexandrine couplets (see POETIC METER) for use in the body of his poem. That body he divided into three books, each 1,000 lines long. This organization reflects both the Trinitarian and the millenarian traditions of Christian numerology. The entire work is enclosed at either end by an introductory and a final sonnet—a parenthesis that suggests the beginning and the ending of time.

The first book of *Microcosme* begins with a definition of God and then uses as the book's superstructure the Old Testament story of the world's creation as far as Cain's archetypal murder of his brother Abel. On this biblical framework, Scève constructs a typically Renaissance philosophical edifice by bringing to bear the insights of the early church fathers, Platonic doctrine, and ancient materialist authors. Scève also embroiders the biblical story with invented incidents that serve to dramatize aspects of the Old Testament's story. When humankind falls, for example, the predatory animals become ferocious, and briars and nettles flourish among the plants. The reality of Adam and Eve's fall from grace is brought home to them by the death of Abel. To the story of this first murder Scève adds a note of touching pathos as he describes the primordial couple's burial of their son's cold body.

The second book turns its attention to tracing the history and development of humankind after the fall. Like the first book, the second begins with a definition, this time of man as a virile, divinely created and shaped, insatiably curious, but often self-deceptive creature. Then Adam has a lengthy dream in which Scève examines the outcomes of the way fallen human nature operates. On the one hand, human beings discover how to make bread and wine, clothing and shelter, and how to hunt. On the other, they learn to make weapons and war, use the things they fabricate as status symbols, and use dressed stone to construct the tower of Babel that, in its presumption, offends God. Human beings domesticate animals and explore the world on horseback, foot, and by tree-trunk canoe. They also develop the alphabet, learn to write, and preserve knowledge from generation to generation. They invent mathematics and develop musical scales and theory. Adam awakens from his dream, and from its grandeur he and Eve go once more to visit Abel's tomb, reminding themselves and the reader of the common fate of humankind and, in the long run, of all its achievements.

The pair then climbs to a mountaintop where Adam explains astronomy to Eve. Impressed with Adam's innate mastery of such complex subjects,

Eve's quick intelligence leads her to ask astute questions, and the pair's interactions confirm the divine spark of intelligence that they share. Adam goes on to discuss astrology. He does not reject it, as many of Scève's contemporary theologians would have done. Rather he treats it as a mechanism for the expression of God's will in the universe. Not everything in Book III is positive, however: Human beings are flawed creatures, and Scève discusses with horror man's invention of gunpowder.

Yet the final note is optimistic. God's gift of intelligence and reason will lead to philosophy, to self-knowledge, to accepting Christ, and to eventual reunion with God in the afterlife. That conviction encourages Eve about the future, and the poem ends praising God's goodness.

Ironically, the wars of religion were already under way in France, and the grounds for Scève's optimism were soon carried away by the flood waters of religious strife and inhuman behavior.

Bibliography

Mulhauser, Ruth. *Maurice Scève.* Boston, Mass.: Twayne Publishers, 1977.

Staub, Hans, ed. *Maurice Scève, Oeuvres poétiques complètes.* 2 vols. Paris: Union Générale d'Editions, 1971.

Middleton, Thomas (1570–1627)

The son of a London bricklayer, Middleton began a university career at Queen's College, Oxford, but did not take a degree. His literary career began early with poems published when he was only 17. By the age of 22, he had begun writing plays, of which more than 20 survive. In addition to his busy theatrical career, Middleton served as the official chronologer of the city of London, a post he held until his death, when BEN JONSON succeeded him. Despite his enviable output, he does not seem to have been able to save much. His wife, Magdalene Middleton, had to apply for public assistance the year after his death. She received 6£ 13s. 4d.

The master of many styles and genres, Middleton's range as a playwright included, first, TRAGEDY that included *The Second Maiden's Tragedy* (ca.

1606) and the bloody *Revenger's Tragedy* (1607). His most effective and original forays into the tragic medium, however, came first with a play coauthored with WILLIAM ROWLEY, *The Changeling* (1622). This Middleton followed with *Women beware Women* (1625). Both these plays explore the traps that evil sets for people, and the disintegration of character and the chain of destruction that follows from yielding—even reluctantly—to one's baser nature. Both plays also rely heavily on stock situations and STOCK CHARACTERS—girls who try to avoid marrying their fathers' favorites, seductions, murders that succeed and those that accidentally claim the wrong victim. Yet both plays are powerful in evoking pity for persons caught in the toils of situations they tried to avoid.

In *The Changeling's* principal plot, Beatrice and Alsemero fall in love. Her father, however, has pledged her to Alonzo. Casting about for a way to avoid marrying him, Beatrice approaches her father's servant De Flores—a man she despises and ordinarily shuns—and enlists his aid in ridding her of Alonzo. De Flores obligingly murders Alonzo, bringing her the corpse's ring finger as proof. The killer then demands as his price Beatrice's virginity. Try as she might, she cannot refuse.

Assuming that Alonzo's disappearance means that he has decided not to marry Beatrice, her father, Veramando, consents to her marriage to Alsemero. Fearful lest her loss of maidenhood be discovered, Beatrice gets her maid, Diaphanta, to substitute for her on the wedding night. The maid, who also admires Alsemero, is pleased both with the situation and the money Beatrice pays her. Diaphanta remains so long in the bridal chamber, however, that she arouses Beatrice's jealousy. Now thoroughly a creature of the dark side, Beatrice plots again with De Flores, who starts a fire to flush Diaphanta from Beatrice's wedding bed. When the maid runs out, De Flores pursues her and kills her. After further complications Alsemero becomes suspicious of Beatrice and De Flores. Under Alsemero's close questioning, Beatrice, to her husband's horror, confesses all—though she insists she did it all for him. Unmoved, Alsemero has the pair arrested pending trial. Rather than undergo that

indignity, De Flores first stabs Beatrice and then commits suicide.

Middleton took the main plot of *Women beware Women* from an Italian novel, *Hippolito and Isabella.* He then interwove multiple plots with great deftness, resolving them all in a grand finale of death and destruction. Here his themes involve forced marriage (Isabella's father, Fabricio, wants her to marry the Ward); incest (Hippolito is in love with his niece Isabella); seduction of innocence—(a) Isabella's aunt, Livia, lies to her niece, telling her that she is not her father's daughter so she can return Hippolito's love; (b) Livia and Guardiano collaborate with the Duke of Florence in the seduction of Bianca, the young, beautiful, and initially innocent and morally attractive wife of Leantio. Beyond these Middleton gives us lust, blood vengeance, true love poisoned by vice, the destruction of the characters of both Isabella and Bianca, and a final act play within a play. Staged to celebrate the nuptials of the Duke and Bianca, this wedding masque with principal characters from the earlier plots playing gods and cupids dissolves into onstage mayhem. Poisoned arrows do in Hippolito; poisoned smoke accounts for both Isabella, who introduces it, and her intended victim, Aunt Livia. Bianca has prepared a poisoned cup that the Ward—in the guise of Ganymede, cupbearer of the gods—is supposed to present to her brother-in-law the Cardinal of Florence. Instead, the duke, her new husband, gets the cup, drinks, and dies. Realizing her guilt, Bianca also drinks, joining him in death.

After a decade's dry spell in the production of effective tragedy, these two plays must have moved and gratified their London audiences.

Middleton also wrote an allegorical play, *A Game at Chess* (1624). This play, in which the characters assume the roles of chess pieces, assails the Spanish and the Catholics from an English and Protestant point of view. Although this play got an enthusiastic public reception, it did not amuse the Spanish ambassador. His official complaint resulted in a summons to appear before a magistrate for everyone connected with the play. Along with the actors, Middleton failed to appear. This made matters worse, and finally his son appeared in his place and posted a bond for his father's appearance.

Middleton may have been jailed because of this incident, but the record is unclear.

His most characteristic dramatic mode was bitter SATIRE. In *A CHAST MAYD IN CHEAPSIDE* (1611), for instance, multiple plots interlace to expose the darker undercurrents of city life in the notorious London district.

Many of Middleton's other plays deserve mention: *A Trick to Catch the Old One* (1604–06); *A Mad World My Masters* (1608); *The Roaring Girl* (1610); *No Wit, No Help Like a Woman's* (1613); and *Michaelmas Term* (1607). One other play, *The Witch* (1610–16), although not one of his best, has nonetheless provoked a good deal of critical attention because of the scenes in which witches appear. Much of that attention focuses on the relationship, if any, between SHAKESPEARE's *Macbeth* and Middleton's drama. No real connection has been convincingly demonstrated. A sort of subgenre of witch plays by several playwrights appeared on the stages of Elizabethan and Jacobean theaters. The subject has always commanded the attention of an interested audience, and perhaps that is why Middleton addressed it.

In the plays that deal with events and characters in the city of London, Middleton's sense of dialect and class mannerisms seems unerring, and he mimics them with great skill and conviction. His mastery of the tricks of stagecraft seems equally impressive as far as these can be imagined from the editions of his plays.

Middleton's texts presented both his 17th-century and modern editors with significant problems of reconstruction. Sometimes he wrote poetry and sometimes prose, but he did not capitalize poetic lines in his manuscripts, and he ran blank verse lines together. These practices together with similar space-saving tactics in early printed editions make unraveling his intention exceedingly difficult. Modern editors have performed heroically in reconstructing his plays in anthologies and in single play editions. No one, however, has undertaken to edit the whole body of his work since the late 19th century.

Bibliography

Dutton, Richard, ed. *Thomas Middleton: A Chaste Maid in Cheapside; Women beware Women; The Changeling; A Game at Chess.* New York: Oxford University Press, 1999.

Esche, Edward J. *A Critical Edition of Thomas Middleton's The Witch.* New York: Garland Publishers, 1993.

Ellis, Havelock, ed. *Thomas Middleton.* 1887. Reprint, New York: Scribner, 1904.

Midsummer Night's Dream, A William Shakespeare (ca. 1595–1596)

A COMEDY that caps SHAKESPEARE's early period of experimentation with the comic form, *A Midsummer Night's Dream* introduces royal characters drawn via English intermediaries including Chaucer from ancient Greek myth and legend into its framing plot. Theseus, the Duke of Athens is about to marry Hippolyta, the Queen of the Amazons. In the Athenian court we also find two young men, Lysander and Demetrius, both in love with Hermia, a daughter of the aged courtier Egeus. Hermia returns Lysander's love, but Hermia's close friend Helena loves Demetrius, who scorns her. Egeus, despite his daughter's preference in the matter, has arranged a marriage between Hermia and Lysander and has asked Duke Theseus to enforce his choice. Theseus gives her three options: marry Demetrius, remain single for life, or be put to death. Hermia and Lysander agree to run away together, but Helena overhears them and to show her own self-sacrificing love for Demetrius, decides to tell him.

In the meantime, preparations for the royal wedding are going forward, and Philostrate, MASTER OF THE REVELS to Duke Theseus, has organized a contest for an original nuptial entertainment to be presented before the court. Competing for the honor, a group of workmen have an original play in rehearsal. Undistinguished by education or remarkable intelligence, these good English workmen are nonetheless well intentioned and confident of their theatrical skills. The group includes the play's author and director, Bottom the Weaver; Peter Quince, a carpenter; Flute, a bellows mender; Snout, a tinker; and Starveling, a tailor. In Act I, scene ii, Bottom assigns parts in their tragedy about the ill-fated classical lovers Pyramus and Thisbe. The group agrees to meet outside the city that night to rehearse their play by moonlight.

Act II, scene 1 introduces characters drawn from English folklore. Robin Goodfellow, also called Puck, is a mischievous spirit in the service of the King of the Fairies, Oberon. We discover that Oberon and his queen, Titania, are at odds over Titania's doting on a young Indian boy kidnapped to Fairyland by exchanging a fairy child for him. Puck hopes to keep Oberon and Titania apart, but they meet by moonlight and mutually accuse each other of loving Hippolyta and Theseus. After Titania's departure, Oberon sends Puck for a flower whose juice dropped in a sleeper's eyes will make that person fall madly in love with the first living thing he or she sees on waking. Just then Demetrius passes by pursued by Helena, and Oberon instructs Puck to also administer the potion to Demetrius so he will return her love. In the next scene Oberon administers the drug to Titania. Then Lysander and Hermia enter and, wearied by wandering in the wood, fall asleep. Thinking them to be Demetrius and Helena, Puck drops the magic fluid in Lysander's eyes. Helena and Demetrius enter, and when Demetrius runs away, Helena sees Lysander on the ground and wakes him. He instantly forgets his love for Hermia and declares his passion for Helena, who thinks he is tormenting her. She flees. He follows. Hermia awakes and finds herself deserted.

The opening of Act III finds Bottom and company in the wood near Titania's bower. They rehearse their play and work out a technical problem. They realize that they need an actor to represent the wall through whose chink Pyramus and Thisbe declare their love. Puck happens by, comments on the play, and sets a donkey's head on Bottom's shoulders. Terrified at Bottom's changed appearance, the other actors flee. Attempting to follow, Bottom stumbles upon the sleeping Titania, who awakens and falls passionately in love with the donkey-headed tailor. His hee-hawing voice seems like sweetest music to her ears, and she orders her fairy attendants to wait on him.

In the next scene Puck reports Titania's passion for Bottom to a delighted Oberon. Demetrius and Helena enter. The fairies discover their mistake, and Oberon gives orders to remedy it. Before that occurs, however, the audience is treated to the exchanges that occur among the enchanted lovers. These include some amusing repartee between Hermia and Helena whose friendship temporarily turns to insulting rivalry. Lysander and Demetrius are about to fight a duel, but the fairies intervene, put all four to sleep, and sort out the young lovers' difficulties.

Act IV, Scene I begins with the lovemaking of an increasingly asinine Bottom and a doting Titania. They fall asleep. Oberon and Puck enter. Oberon explains to the audience that the Titania has given him the changeling Indian child and that the fairies' rulers are reconciled. He releases her from the spell, and she remarks: "Methought I was enamor'd of an ass." Theseus and Hippolyta and their attendants enter; they find the four young people asleep. Though Egeus is furious at his daughter's disobedience, Demetrius explains that his affections have changed, and Theseus decrees a triple wedding for himself and Hippolyta, Demetrius and Helena, and Hermia and Lysander. Bottom in the meantime recovers from his apparent dream and seeks out his companions.

In Act V, the courtiers choose *Pyramus and Thisbe* as the wedding entertainment, and a thoroughly hilarious performance follows, but not before Bottom has assured the ladies of the court that the lion is not real and that no one really dies. After the play within a play has ended, the mortals exit, leaving the stage to the fairies. They bless the royal household and the marriages, and Puck speaks the epilogue.

The psychological depth and richness of the play have encouraged much ingenuity in modern productions. The play is sometimes performed as a risqué farce whose highpoint is the lovemaking between donkey-headed Bottom and Titania. It has at least once been performed on trapezes. Perhaps the most thought-provoking recent production, however, presented the play as a psychosexual dream sequence whose action took place in a pool on stage. An acrobat mimicking the movements of a crab played Puck, and the forest-chase scenes featuring the young lovers occurred above the waters of the pool on a series of brass beds.

Bibliography

Shakespeare, William. *A Midsummer Night's Dream*. *The Riverside Shakespeare*. Edited by G. Blakemore Evans et al. Boston: Houghton Mifflin Company, 1997.

miles gloriosus (the overbearing soldier, the braggart warrior)

A stock character borrowed from Roman COMEDY for the Renaissance stage, the *miles gloriosus* had his origin in the self-glorifying military figures of the comedies of PLAUTUS and TERENCE—especially Plautus's play *Miles Gloriosus*. English examples of the type include WILLIAM SHAKESPEARE's Sir John Falstaff, who appears in HENRY IV, PART 1 and 2, and in *The Merry Wives of Windsor* in which Falstaff is the principal character. Other examples of the type appear both as the title character in NICHOLAS UDALL's *Ralph Roister Doister* (ca. 1552), and as Roister Doister's foil in the same play, the character Merrygreek.

Milton, John (1608–1674)

The last major literary figure of the high English Renaissance, Milton was born in London and educated both by private tutelage and in St. Paul's Cathedral School. He attended Christ's College in Cambridge University beginning in 1625 and earned a bachelor's degree in 1629. His extraordinary, almost girlish good looks earned him the nickname *Our Lady of Christ's*. Milton remained at Cambridge until 1632, the year he took his M.A. While there he composed a series of elegies in Latin and other early verse works including his celebrated "Nativity Ode."

By 1631 he had composed some of his minor poems and some that are better known, including a famous pair of poems comparing two poetic styles, "L'Allegro" (The joyous style) and "Il Penseroso" (The thoughtful style). Though a church vocation might have seemed natural for the devout Milton, his religious sympathies lay more with the PURITANS than with the Anglican establishment. He strongly objected to its Episcopal system of governance.

While he continued to consider his career options, he wrote a pair of COURT ENTERTAINMENTS: his masques *Arcades* and *Comus*, the latter of which was acted at Ludlow Castle. In 1637 Milton suffered a double loss: His mother died, and his best college friend, the clergyman and poet Edward King, was drowned crossing from England to Ireland in an unseaworthy vessel. To commemorate King's passing Milton wrote a PASTORAL ELEGY, LYCIDAS. The poem is probably the best example of its type in the English language. It mourns King's passing, rejoices in his transfiguration into the eternal realm of spirit, and serves as Milton's own dedication to the high and, in Milton's view, priestly calling of poet. (See VATES.)

Milton spent 1538 and 1539 traveling in Italy and Switzerland. While on this journey he began work on preliminary drafts for his major religious EPIC, PARADISE LOST (1667).

Throughout Milton's youth the debate between the Anglican Church establishment and the Puritan dissenters had grown increasingly rancorous, finally erupting into civil war. Strongly attached to the Puritan cause, Milton joined the discussion in 1641. During the next two years he penned a succession of antiepiscopal tracts: *Of Reformation, Of Prelatical Episcopacy, Animadversions, Reason of Church Government*, and *Apology for Smectymnus*. *Smectymnus* was the name of a group of Puritan apologists to which Milton belonged.

In 1642 Milton married Mary Powell. From the outset the marriage was a disaster. The only grounds in effect, however, for a British divorce were those of adultery. Many unhappy couples offered that reason to dissolve their marriages whether or not it was true. Not Milton and Powell, however. Eventually, after a three-year separation, they achieved reconciliation, and before her death in 1652 the couple had three daughters. Based on his experience, however, Milton campaigned to have Parliament change the divorce laws. He wrote *The Doctrine and Discipline of Divorce* in 1643, and the following year translated and commented upon the writings on the subject of divorce of the German Protestant and HUMANIST Martin Bucer. Milton's final treatises on the subject of divorce, *Tetrachordon* and *Colasterion* appeared in 1645. Before that, however, he also discussed the subject of education (1644) and wrote the definitive argument in the English language on the reasons that the state and its representatives should not become involved in censoring books: *Areopagitica, a Speech for the Liberty of Unlicensed Printing* (1644). The Greek title of this work flattered the British Parliament by comparing its legislators with those who had met in Athens during the Golden Age of Greece on Ares Hill.

In the meantime, the debate between Puritan and Anglican had boiled over into civil war between the royalist faction and the supporters of OLIVER CROMWELL, who wished to disestablish both the Anglican Church and the monarchy. The victory of Cromwell's forces led eventually to the beheading of King Charles II in 1649, and to Milton's appointment as the Latin secretary of England. This post is comparable to the position of secretary of state. It was the chief diplomatic post in England and took its name from the fact that diplomatic correspondence was conducted in the Latin language. In that role, Milton undertook to justify Charles's execution in two short works: *The Tenure of Kings and Magistrates* and *Eikonoklastes* (both 1649). The Greek title of the second work is the Greek form of English *iconoclasts* (those who tear down idols).

The burdens that both his own commitment to writing and the expectations of his government post put on Milton's eyesight eventually destroyed it, and the poet went absolutely blind in 1652. Milton took his blindness as God's will. He discusses his feelings on the subject in the famous "Sonnet on His Blindness," and he developed coping strategies. As he could compose in his mind and remember vast passages of prose and verse both in Latin and in English, he often composed at night and dictated to secretaries during the day. His political tracts continued to issue throughout the 1650s until 1660. In 1656 he married for the second time. His second wife Katherine Woodcock died in 1658.

Oliver Cromwell also died in 1658. His son Richard Cromwell succeeded him briefly but soon demonstrated that he was no statesman and abdicated in 1659. Under the leadership of General George Monck (1608–70), Parliament reconvened and invited the pretender to the throne, Charles Stuart, to return from France and assume his father's crown. On the day of Charles II's restoration to England's throne Milton was arrested. He was stripped of public office and then immediately released.

During the 20 years Milton labored as a public servant, he had published only one collection of early poetry (1645). Otherwise his very considerable output of English and Latin prose had addressed public issues. To a degree Milton's participation in a nominally democratic form of government had disenchanted him with the notion that good Puritans and their party would necessarily govern better than proud bishops and theirs. "New presbyter," he wrote "is but old priest writ large." Freed of public responsibilities, he returned to work on *Paradise Lost,* this time composing iambic-pentameter blank verse in his head at night and dictating lines to his daughters during the day. While that work went forward, he married Elizabeth Minshull in 1663. He finished *Paradise Lost* in 1665 and published it in 10 books in 1667. The year 1671 saw the publication of another religious epic, *Paradise Regained* and a drama, *Samson Agonistes.* Milton identified strongly with the blinded biblical hero. His text became the basis of an oratorio of the same name by George Frederic Handel.

In 1673 he entered the public area once more in a foredoomed effort to unite Protestants with a pamphlet, *Of True Religion.* He died the year of publication of the second edition of *Paradise Lost.*

Bibliography

Lewalski, Barbara Kiefer. *The Life of John Milton: A Critical Biography.* Oxford, U.K.; Malden, Mass.: Blackwell Publishers, 2000.

Milton, John. *Complete Poems and Major Prose: John Milton.* Ca. 1957. Reprint, edited by Merritt Y. Hughes. Indianapolis, Ind.: Hackett Publications, 2003.

———. *John Milton: The Major Works.* Edited by Stephen Orgel and Jonathan Goldberg. 1991. Oxford: Oxford University Press, 2003.

———. *Paradise Lost and Other Poems.* Edited by Edward M. Cifelli and Edward Le Comte. New York: Signet Classic, ca. 2003.

Mīrā Bāī (Princess Mira) (1450–1547)

Little can be said with certainty about the princess Mīrā Bāī, a famous 16th-century saint and devotional poet who composed in the old Rajastani language of northern India. Much, however, has been handed down over the centuries. The problem arises when one tries to distinguish fact from folklore.

Among the certainties we know that she was a princess in a family whose members were devotees of the Indian deity Vishnu. We know that Mīrā Bāī became a mystic and worshiped that deity in his manifestation as Krishna. We are quite sure that her mystical devotion to Krishna expressed itself in some of her verse in the METAPHOR of human love and that she perceived herself as a manifestation of Krishna's consort—his beloved Radha. Her ideas about Krishna arise exclusively from her devotion and do not parallel those found in traditional Hindu scriptures. Although she perceived herself in this mystic relationship as the bride of God, she nevertheless was said to have taken a human husband in an arranged marriage of convenience with Prince Bhoj of Medwa.

The scholar Hermann Goetz has made a careful attempt to separate fact from legend in reconstructing Mīrā Bāī's biography. On the basis of Goetz's work it is likely that, after the death of her husband and her father-in-law, she suffered political persecution at the hands of her brothers-in-law and moved around India, sometimes as a religious pilgrim, for a number of years to avoid her husband's brothers.

Uncertainty, however, surrounds the precise canon of Mīrā Bāī's work. Many poems have been ascribed to her that she likely did not write. The total number of verses bearing her name approaches 1,400. It is also unclear whether she wrote only in Rajastani or she composed in other Indian languages as well. We can nonetheless feel certain that an agreed-upon core of those poems are indeed Mīrā Bāī's and that the works in that group share common characteristics that identify her as a very gifted poet indeed. Her language is the simple, dialectical language of the people. Her poems tend to be short and convincing in their emotional appeal. She is a master of matching linguistic rhythm to the varying mood of her verse. Her language conveys her feelings with clarity and immediacy.

The poems she addresses to her beloved Krishna in his manifestation as Giridhar Naagar throb with erotic ecstasy.

Her life and work made her a legend in her own lifetime, and her songs and verse have remained from then until now far and away the most popular work of any poet–saint associated with the Indian spiritual reawakening known as the BHAKTI or devotional movement. Many poems and songs by or attributed to Mīrā Bāī are available in translations in many LANGUAGES OF INDIA including English, and a number are available set to music on sound recordings.

Bibliography

Mirabai. *Mira: the Call of the Heart: Mira Bhajans.* Translated by Sushil Rao. Forest Hills, N.Y.: Hrdaipress, 2000.

———. *For Love of the Dark One: Songs of Mirabai. Translated by Andrew Schelling.* Prescott, Ariz.: Hohm Press, 1998.

———. *Mīrā Bāī and her Padas.* Translated by Krishna P. Bahadur. New Delhi: Mujnshiram Manoharlal, 1998.

———. *Mystic Love: Music for the Soul.* Sound recording. Jaipur: Ninaad Music and Marketing, 1998.

———. *Sweet on my Lips: The Love Poems of Mirabai.* Translated by Louise Landes Levi. Brooklyn, N.Y.: Cool Grove Press, ca. 1997.

miracle-play cycles

In 1264 the pope decreed a new European holiday, Corpus Christi Day, or the festival of the body of Christ—a festival that was celebrated by carrying the Host in procession and displaying it at several predetermined locations. In several English towns including Chester, York, Coventry, Newcastle, and Wakefield Corpus Christi Day came to be celebrated with the performance of cycles of short, religious dramas. These were presented from pageant wagons—horse-drawn truck beds fitted out with scenery above and sometimes with a space below the wagon's floor where actors could conceal themselves and change costumes. Emulating the processional display of the Host, the wagons rolled around a fixed route, stopping at established locations. At each location the plays were performed. It became customary for particular plays to become performed by members of particular trades or guilds with whose profession the theme of the play had a connection. Chandlers, for example, often performed "Jonah and the Whale" because candles were made from whales' blubber. The carpenters typically presented the story of "Noah and the Ark" since Noah had practiced their trade in building the ark.

The plays represented moments in biblical history from the Creation to the Resurrection to the Last Judgment. They could be very serious, as when they presented Christ's Crucifixion or the angel Gabriel's appearance to Mary to announce her important role in God's plan for human salvation. They could also be hilariously funny, as when an aging and somewhat befuddled Joseph attempts to figure out how an enormously pregnant Mary came to be in that condition.

Although they were a medieval phenomenon, the plays continued to be performed into the Renaissance until Henry VIII established the Anglican Church and disallowed the continued practice of Roman Catholicism. During his reign the morality-play cycles were repressed because the government feared that they would encourage popery. Elements of the cycles, however, were passed along to the nascent British secular theater. The early tendency of British theater, for example, to combine comedy and tragedy on stage traces its origins in part to the traditions surrounding the miracle play cycles.

Misanthrope, The (Le Misanthrope)
Molière (1666)

Among the bitterest of Molière's satiric comedies is *The Misanthrope*. Its principal character, Alceste, establishes himself as the moral, intellectual, and literary arbiter of everything. Secure in the sufficiency of almost all his own judgments, he scorns the conventions of polite exchanges of compliments. They arise, he thinks, from insincere sentiments, and he values plain and honest speaking regardless of the consequences.

Alceste voluntarily blinds himself to the roles played by influence and false witness in court pro-

ceedings. He insists that truth will win the day without his intervention, even though he is himself the defendant in a legal action that, though it has no merit, has the potential of ruining him. In the event, of course, he loses.

Despite his jaundiced view of society and his distaste for people in general, Alceste nonetheless is in love with a flirtatious woman named Célimène. He acknowledges that she is too flighty for him, and he knows that a worthier woman, Eliante, would be pleased to have his affections. A considerable portion of the play, however, occupies itself with Alceste's attempts to elicit an unequivocal declaration of devotion from Célimène. Even after it becomes clear that she has made similar declarations of love to several admirers, Alceste gives Célimène one last chance to move with him to some isolated spot away from the duplicity of human creatures. Horrified at the thought of isolated boredom with a man whom a recent translator and adapter of the play, Liz Lochhead, has labeled *miseryguts*, Célimène turns him down.

Even his admirer, Eliante, who has long hoped that Alceste might turn to her for a more settled affection, decides when he finally does that she will be better off with Alceste's friend, Philinte. Though Eliante and Philinte provide the sensible and principled touchstones by means of which an audience can find something admirable in the human condition, the other characters both male and female demonstrate that Alceste is right in his evaluation of the species in general, though self-deluding about his own capacity to judge.

Bibliography

Molière. *The Misanthrope and Tartuffe.* Translated by Richard Wilbur. New York: Harcourt Brace Jovanovich, Publishers, 1965.
———. *Miseryguts* [*The Misanthrope*]; and *Tartuffe: Two Plays by Molière.* Translated and adapted by Liz Lochhead. London: Nick Hern, 2002.

Miser, The (L'Avare) Molière (1668)

First performed at the Thèâtre du Palais-Royal in Paris in 1668 with MOLIÈRE himself in the lead role of the miser, Harpagon, *The Miser* is by consensus one of the playwright's greatest triumphs. The comedy imitates the ancient Roman play, *Aulularia* by PLAUTUS.

Harpagon's young steward, Valère, has rescued his employer's daughter Élise from drowning, and the two young people have fallen in love and secretly pledged themselves to each other. As the play opens we find Valère calming his beloved's fears that he will prove unfaithful. Satisfied on that score, she worries that Valère will prove an unacceptable suitor from her father's perspective. Valère explains that he has been seeking to ingratiate himself with Harpagon by seeming to share his points of view in all matters. He also advises Élise to enlist her brother Cléante's aid in the lovers' cause.

Act I, scene ii finds Cléante confessing to Élise that he is in love with Mariane, a young woman recently moved to the neighborhood with an ill and widowed mother. Cléante complains bitterly of Harpagon's miserliness. Élise intimates to her brother that she too has found love, and the two agree to flee if Harpagon opposes their desires.

The third scene focuses on some comic business between Harpagon and Cléante's valet, La Flèche. Harpagon reveals his pathological concern for money by causelessly searching La Flèche's pockets and eventually driving the young man from the house.

In the next scene, Harpagon's soliloquy reveals to the audience that he has just buried 10,000 gold crowns in his garden. On his children's approach, he fears that they may have overheard him talking to himself. They tell him, however, that they have come to discuss marriage. Harpagon immediately picks up on this topic and asks what Cléante thinks of the new neighbor, Mariane. For a moment it appears that Cléante will be matched as he would wish. Harpagon reveals, however, that he has chosen Mariane for himself. For Cléante he has selected a widow, and for Élise an elderly widower, Anselme. When Élise objects, Harpagon suggests submitting his decision to his steward, Valère. Delighted, Élise agrees to be bound by Valère's opinion. Although always beginning with "some might say," Valère marshals the principal rational arguments against a January–May marriage, he nonetheless pretends to be persuaded by the argu-

ment that Harpagon finds most convincing: Anselme will require no dowry with Élise.

When Élise reproves Valère for agreeing with her father's choice, Valère explains that the only way to deceive the miser is to appear to agree with him. Charmed by Valère's apparent concurrence in his viewpoints, Harpagon gives him absolute control over Élise.

Act II, scene ii finds Cléante arranging to borrow money from an anonymous lender at outrageous rates of interest and under bone-crushing conditions. The lender, of course, proves to be Harpagon. When a go-between brings father and son face-to-face, they exchange heated remonstrance, each blaming the other for folly and criminality.

In the next scene, the valet La Flèche tells a matchmaker, Frosine, that Harpagon is so tight that he never says, "I give you good day," but only, "I lend you good day." Frosine, however, is the go-between who is arranging Harpagon's match with Mariane. Skilled at her trade, she manages the miser by flattering his vanity and by telling him that Mariane prefers older, bespectacled men. When, however, she seeks payment for her services, Harpagon remains unmoved.

Act III opens with Harpagon giving instructions for an engagement dinner to be held at his house and trying to scrimp at every turn. He shows the servants how to conceal their stained and torn clothing and instructs his cook to make do with little money, to prepare enough food for eight, and to stretch it so that it serves 10. Maître Jacques acts both as cook and coachman and changes to the appropriate costume to receive Harpagon's instructions for each of his responsibilities. We learn that Harpagon starves his horses in the same fashion that he intends to famish his guests. The scene ends with Harpagon beating Maître Jacques for truthfully reporting what people say about his master's miserliness.

The match with Mariane is arranged, and in scene vi when she comes to the party she is surprised to discover that Harpagon's son is the young man whom she loves. In Act III, scene vii Mariane and Cléante express their mutual distaste at becoming mother-in-law and son-in-law. At the same time they convey to one another their true affection. Harpagon misses the subtext and thinks they do not get on.

Cléante next offends his father by providing expensive snacks for the company and by removing a diamond ring from Harpagon's finger and slipping it on Mariane's. For Mariane, Cléante interprets the miser's muttered objections as his insistence that she keep the ring. The young man next arranges to confer privately with Mariane, Élise, and Frosine about how to break off his father's match and further his own prospects. Frosine hits on the plan of having someone impersonate a wealthy noblewoman who wants to marry Harpagon. All agree that the miser's obsession will make him break off the match with Mariane.

In Act IV, scene iii, however, Harpagon asks Cléante what he thinks of Mariane. Cléante disparages her. Harpagon says that, having seen Mariane, he has decided that he is too old for her and was going to substitute Cléante. Since his son does not like the girl, however, Harpagon will go forward with his plan to marry her himself. Cléante retorts that despite his distaste, he will be a dutiful son and take his father's place. Harpagon insists that he would not force an uncongenial bride on his son. Cléante finally reveals his true feelings, and Harpagon instantly instructs his son to forget Mariane. The miser has all along intended to marry her. An argument follows. Cléante defies his father, and Harpagon calls for a stick to beat his son.

In an effort to settle everything down, father and son appeal to Maître Jacques to negotiate their feud. Jacques runs back and forth between them, telling each what he wishes to hear, proclaims the feud settled, and leaves. The two seem reconciled until Cléante reveals that he now thinks Mariane his. Then the quarrel erupts again.

In the next scene, La Flèche finds Harpagon's garden treasure and gives it to Cléante. Discovering the money missing, Harpagon cries out "thieves" and "murder!" He is distracted with grief.

Act V opens with the arrival of a magistrate. Harpagon wants him to arrest the whole town. The magistrate questions Maître Jacques, who takes the opportunity to settle a score with Valère. In a series of patently obvious lies, he accuses the steward. When Harpagon confronts Valère, the young man

thinks that his passion for Élise has been discovered. He confesses that, and in a comedy of errors that depends largely on the French feminine pronoun *elle* and its capacity to point either to Élise or to the chest containing the treasure, the two men argue at cross-purposes for several minutes. When the matter is finally clarified, Valère reveals that he has saved Élise from drowning and, moreover, that he is a Neapolitan nobleman of high birth. He gives an incredible but nonetheless true account of shipwreck, survival, rescue, and separation. Knowing it to be true, Mariane confirms Valère's account and announces that he is her brother. Anselmo, who is also present, reveals himself as their father, the also providentially rescued husband of Mariane's mother and the very wealthy nobleman in question.

In return for the promise of the recovery of his stolen money and the payment of certain other expenses, Harpagon consents to the marriages of Mariane and Cléante and of Élise and Valère. The young people's happiness and the reunion of the Neapolitan family constitute the comic portion of the play's outcome. Harpagon's continuing psychopathic absorption with money and its accumulation is the tragedy. The 19th-century German poet Johann Wolfgang von Goethe thought the play to be "pre-eminently great," and "sublimely tragic."

Bibliography
Molière. *The Miser and Other Plays.* Translated by John Wood and David Coward. London and New York: Penguin Books, 2000.

Mithradates, Flavius (Shmuel Ben Nissim Ben Shabbatai Abu al-Faraj) (ca. 1450–1483)

Seemingly a native of Agrigento, Sicily, Flavius Mithradates (a pen name) converted from Judaism to Christianity. He assumed the name Guglielmo Raimondo de Moncada and traveled through Italy, Germany, and France as an itinerant scholar and teacher of Aramaic, Arabic, Greek, and Hebrew. His students endowed him with a further nickname, Guglielmus Siculus (William the Sicilian).

Mithradates's encyclopedic learning earned him an appointment as a lecturer in Rome at the university named the Sapienza, where he taught theology. He was among the teachers of the important Florentine HUMANIST GIOVANNI PICO DELLA MIRANDOLA.

His principal contribution to literature was as a translator and an enabler of the humanist writers and scholars who came after him. He translated several works into Latin from Arabic, Greek, and Hebrew. Often these translations were commissioned. Duke Federigo da Montefeltro of Urbino, for example, commissioned a translation of sections of the Koran, and Giovanni Pico commissioned a translation of a Hebrew commentary on the Torah, Maimonides's treatise on resurrection, and various works about the kabbalah—the Jewish mystical system of interpretation of Scripture and invocation of spirits. He translated other works as well.

In the pope's presence Mithradates once preached a sermon on the sufferings of Jesus that used material from the Muslim and the Jewish as well as the Christian traditions. He often participated in learned discussions with practicing Jews in Florence.

Molière (Jean-Baptiste Poquelin)
(1622–1673)

The son of a well-to-do interior decorator who enjoyed royal favor, Molière received a fine education at the Collège de Clermont. With some like-minded friends and neighbors, Molière formed an itinerant acting company, the Illustre Théâtre. Although the troupe performed in Paris and in Rouen, the venture proved too risky and failed. As Molière was the financial backer and could not cover the bills, he was imprisoned for a time for debt. Undeterred by this first failure, Molière and some of his former partners, the Béjarts family, formed a second touring company and for 13 years operated throughout France. Molière became adept at all aspects of the business including acting, managing, and playwriting. The troupe performed his first dramatic works.

The success of the company and Molière's connections led in 1658 to an invitation to perform at the Louvre—then still a royal residence. Louis XIV,

charmed by the troop's work, assigned them a theater, the Petit-Bourbon, and favored them with his ongoing patronage, naming them *la troupe de Monsieur* (that is, the troupe of the king's brother). Just two years later, the troupe was transferred to a more splendid hall, the Palais Royale, and in 1665 they became the troupe of the king himself—*la troupe du Roi*. In addition to the plays that Molière crafted for general performance, he was in demand as a collaborator with the musician and composer Lulli in creating COURT ENTERTAINMENTS. In 1662, during this period of rising fortunes, Molière married an actress, a member of the family with whom he had founded the business, Armande Béjart. Their union, however, did not prove to be a happy one.

Molière's system of values ran counter to the rather stuffy, conventional, and some might say hypocritical piety and behavior of some middle-class Frenchmen of the period. As a result powerful persons and organizations representing conventional points of view often attacked him. The king's favor and that of influential writers like LA FONTAINE and Boileau, however, shielded him from the worst of conservative rancor.

Between 1653 and 1673 Molière wrote more than 30 comedies in a variety of comic genres: farces, comedies with dancing, comedies of manners, and comedies that skewered his critics—comedies for special occasions. He is best remembered, however, for four splendid comedies of character that he wrote in the mid-1660s: *TARTUFFE* (1664), *DOM JUAN* (1665), *LE MISANTHROPE* (The misanthrope, 1666), and *L'AVARE* (The miser, 1668).

Molière remained actively involved in theater until the last day of his life. He collapsed during a performance and died an hour later.

Bibliography

Molière. *The Misanthrope and other Plays*. Translated by John Wood and David Coward. London and New York: Penguin Books, 2000.

Scott, Virginia. *Molière: a Theatrical Life*. Cambridge, U.K.: Cambridge University Press, 2000.

Molina, Tirso de (Gabriel Téllez)
(ca. 1580–1648)

The son of a poor family in Madrid, Gabriel Téllez rose to become in 1601 a monk in the order of Our Lady of Mercy (the Mercedarian order). His early years in the order were devoted to study. He pursued the arts in Salamanca from 1601 to 1603, and studied theology in Toledo and Guadalajara from 1603 to 1607. He may have continued his theological studies for two more years at in Alcalá de Hernares. He somehow also acquired a fluent command of Portuguese and Galician.

With the Mercedarians he traveled as a missionary in 1616 to Santo Domingo in the West Indies, remaining there until 1618. Well before that journey, however, in 1610 Téllez had begun a parallel career as a playwright. Then active in the city of Toledo, Téllez wrote both religious and secular plays. Among the former we find *La Peña de Francia* (The rock of France, ca. 1610). In this play an artless French rustic finds a statue of the Virgin Mary in the cleft of a rock. Fray Gabriel Téllez also composed three plays about SOR JUANA INÉS DE LA CRUZ (before 1614), and one about the rise to the papacy of Pope Sixtus V: *La elección por la virtud* (Elected for his virtue, 1612). Representatives of secular COMEDY can also be attributed to this period. *El vergonzoso in palacio* (The shy man at court, before 1611) may have been the first. His hilarious *Don Gil de las calzas verdes* (Don Gil of the Green Breeches), *Marta la piadosa* (The pious Martha), and others also date from sometime in this period.

Just before his departure for the New World, Brother Gabriel Telléz adopted the penname under which he became, along with LOPE DE VEGA and PEDRO CALDERÓN DELLA BARCA, one of the three most celebrated Spanish playwrights of the Golden Age of Spanish theater: Tirso de Molina. Some time in 1620–21, likely under the patronage of the powerful Cardinal Archbishop Don Bernardo de Sandoval y Rojas, Tirso moved to Madrid where he began devoting the lion's share of his attention to writing plays and short stories. Some of the works of this period landed him in trouble by including lightly veiled attacks on dependents of the Spanish king's chief minister, the count–duke of Olivares. This was the case with *Los cigarrales de Toledo* (The country houses of Toledo, published 1624)—a prose miscellany organized around conversations and entertainments among the country-house dwellers. The entertainments include three of Tirso's plays. As a result of Olivares's displeasure, Tirso was deemed to have set a bad example and was banished to the provinces, where he spent three years away from the center of theatrical activity. This pattern of theatrical production and banishment would later (1640–48) repeat itself a second time.

In theatrical exile Tirso continued to write plays, but he also became the official chronicler of his order. He wrote a magnificent history of the Mercedarians, but politics caused it to be suppressed, and it languished unpublished for 300 years.

Collections of his theatrical works and short stories, however, continued to appear during his lifetime. His nephew Francisco Lucas de Avila either in fact or ostensibly edited some of the five collections that eventually appeared. Tirso's biographer Margaret Wilson, after detailing the extraordinary difficulties associated with determining the authorship of many of the almost 80 surviving plays ascribed to Tirso, nevertheless suggests that his total output—if not the 800 he claimed—probably numbered in the hundreds.

Outside Spain Tirso is best remembered for having originated the character of Don Juan or Don Giovanni in a play whose title has been variously rendered in English translation as *Don Juan* or *The Joker*, or *The Seducer*, or THE TRICKSTER OF SEVILLE (*El Burlador de Sevilla*). In other representatives of his secular drama, romantic comedy predominated. In such plays Tirso's insights into the wellsprings of human amorous feeling and psychology have led some to wonder where he acquired his expertise.

Tirso's religious drama included a selection of AUTOS SACRAMENTALES—the Spanish drama written for performance on church feast days. Four—perhaps five—representatives of Tirso's contribution to this genre survive. Three of them, *El colmenero divino* (The divine beekeeper), *Los hermanos parecidos*

(The identical brothers), and *No le arriendo la ganancia* (Much good may it do him!), appear in his collection of miscellaneous works, *Deleitar aprovechando* (Pleasure with profit, published 1635). The fourth appears in a manuscript not in his hand but bearing his name, and the fifth is simply ascribed to him in a miscellaneous collection of 1664.

A sampling of Tirso's plays is available in English—a small representation in view of his historical importance—and good Spanish modern editions of his works remain in print.

Bibliography

Molina, Tirso de. *Damned for Despair: El Condenado por desconfiado.* Warminster, Wiltshire, U.K.: Aris & Philips, 1986.

———. *Don Juan of Seville.* Translated by Lynne Alvarez. New York: Theatre Communications Group, ca. 1989.

———. *La vida y muerte de Herodes—The Life and Death of Herod: A Christmas Tragedy and Epiphany.* Edited and translated by Frederick H. Fornoff. New York: Peter Lang, 1991.

———. *Obras completas de Tirso de Molina.* Edited by Pilar Palomo and Isabel Prieto. Madrid: Turner, 1994–97.

———. *Tamar's Revenge: La venganza de Tamar.* Translated by John Lyon. Warminster, Wiltshire, U.K.: Aris & Philips, ca. 1988.

———. *The Joker of Seville & O Babylon.* New York: Farrar, Straus, and Giroux, ca. 1978.

Sprague, Frank A. *The Biblical Material of Tirso de Molina.* Lewisburg, Pa., 1950.

Wilson, Margaret. *Tirso de Molina.* Boston: Twayne Publishers, 1977.

Molla, Atukuri (early 16th century)

Although critics disagree about the residence of the first female poet in the Telegu language of India, all agree that Atukuri Molla brought to that language for only the second time in the tongue's history the great ancient Hindu EPIC THE RAMAYANA. Her objective in doing so, moreover, was to make the text available to simple people in their own language so that they might understand the greatness of Rama—a principal deity of the Hindu pantheon.

To achieve her objective Molla summarizes the story in her version, the *Molla Ramayana.* While she at least touches upon most of the really important incidents in the story, she leaves out great swatches of the original. Again, her object was to make the text accessible to the common folk with little time for reading and perhaps with not much practice at the task. Even so, her poem runs to 900 lines disposed in 138 verses divided into six sections. She also keeps her language simple to make the poem more accessible to her audience, mostly composed of simple villagers. At the same time, evidence appears in many places that, in bringing *The Ramayana* into Telegu, Molla had before her many poets' versions of the ancient text and that hers benefits from the exercise in comparison.

Molla's text confirms her genuine talent as a poet. Her descriptions of natural phenomena create mental images of their beauty, and METAPHORS and meters evoke the moods she wants them to. Her characterizations, moreover, seem particularly notable and convincing. Only the brief, introductory, autobiographical sections of her version of the epic and a suggestive selection of verses in the translation of B. V. L. Narayanarow have until now appeared in English.

Bibliography

Datta, Amaresh, ed. *Encyclopedia of Indian Literature.* Volume III. New Delhi: Sahitya Akademi, 1989.

Tharu, Susie, and K. Lalita, Eds. *Women Writing in India: 600 B.C. to the Present.* Vol. I. New York: The Feminist Press at the City University of New York, 1991.

Montaigne, Michel Eyquem de
(1533–1592)

Born a member of the French nobility, Montaigne is widely credited with inventing the personal essay. Certainly, he is the first to apply to a prose discourse the term *essay,* by which he meant trying out something in the crucible of his own experience.

Between the ages of six and 13, he received a careful education—one he discusses critically in his essay *Of the Education of Children.* (He married and fathered five children of his own.) Montaigne later studied law and worked in the Court of Justice as a counselor for the Parliament of Bordeaux. In that capacity, he attracted the favorable attention of the French king, Henry II, who employed him as a diplomat, entrusting the young man with very important missions. In 1570, however, when only 37 years old, Montaigne put aside his diplomatic and legal career. He chose to return to his own chateau to a life spent in reflection, in reading, and in writing. His preferred tranquility was interrupted, however. First he traveled for 15 months to Germany, Switzerland, and Italy. Then King Henry recalled him from Italy to France, where, at the king's insistence, Montaigne served reluctantly as mayor of Bordeaux. First appointed by the king and later elected to a second term, Montaigne performed his duties faithfully in an extraordinarily difficult period of armed conflict between French Catholics and Protestants. In 1585, at the end of his term, he returned to his own estates and a life of scholarly and literary pursuits.

His *"Essais"* had begun to appear in 1580. A revised and enlarged version was published in 1588, and another, a posthumous one, in 1595. Though several other editions appeared, these three were the ones Montaigne scholars consider authoritative. MARIE DE GOURNAY, a brilliant young literary protégée whom Montaigne regarded with paternal affection, edited the last two of those editions.

As a thinker, Montaigne resists pigeonholing. He avoids preconceptions and authorities, testing his own conclusions and those of others against his own experience. He is skeptical but kindly and positive in his outlook. His style is witty, tasteful, sometimes rambling. His development of subjects often takes unexpected turns. He willingly includes autobiographical material in his examples. In fact he makes himself the object of his closest study. He sometimes fuses this introspection with the thinking of Greek and Roman writers, and sometimes, based on his study of himself, he demurs from their conclusions. Yet he is no egoist, as his essay, "That It Is Folly to Measure Truth and Error by Our Own Capacity," attests. His object is to live a life that is good, graceful, fulfilling, and useful to himself and others. His *Essays* are a means for him to examine his own life, to track its development,

and to give others a method for tracking and examining theirs. He does not demand that others reach conclusions similar to his own. Though at times he seems both stoic and Christian, from the points of view of his using himself as a standard and his trying to live according to what he discovers there, one might also consider him the first and the most attractive of the French existentialists.

The subjects Montaigne addresses are many and highly individualized. Among his most often anthologized essays is *Of Friendship*, a discussion detailing what it means to be a friend and what he had learned on that subject as a result of his own close association with Étienne de La Boétie, who died young in 1563. *OF CANNIBALS* asserts the essential humanity of all people everywhere and lays the groundwork for the influential notion of "The Noble Savage." In one of his most famously skeptical essays *The Apology for Raymond Seybond*, Montaigne seems momentarily to doubt the sufficiency of human reason for knowing anything. His thinking in this essay led him to adopt the motto "What do I know?" He certainly understood that much bloodshed followed from people's certainty about the correctness of their dubious convictions and points of view. He had before him the example of the religious wars of France and their attendant horrors. In his essay "About Solitude," Montaigne disparages the ambitions associated with public careers and the compromises of principle they necessitate. Here Montaigne follows Socrates in counseling that "the greatest thing in the world is to know oneself." Following that advice, Montaigne concludes in the third book of his essays, written in 1586–88, that each person "bears the entire form of the human condition." Thus, by studying oneself, one studies humankind. Sometimes vain, sometimes epicurean, a lover of peace, worldly and tolerant, Montaigne is among the most intellectually honest of all writers.

It would be hard to overestimate the influence of Montaigne on his immediate successors and on the thinkers of later periods. If the work of any one person captures the quintessence of the Renaissance, Montaigne's does, and his work continues to be retranslated and widely published. Among his French successors, René Descartes arrived at his syllogism proving his own existence ("I am thinking; therefore I exist.") with Montaigne's sort of introspection. Jean-Jacques Rousseau adopts Montaigne's methods and reexamines some of his subjects. Even in the mid-20th century, Montaigne's wise and often existential individualism resonated within the work of thinkers and writers such as Jean-Paul Sartre and, Montaigne's sense of civic responsibility considered, Albert Camus.

In Britain, JOHN FLORIO translated Montaigne's *Essais* and published them in 1603. The book became one of the mostly widely sought after and influential texts in Elizabethan England. FRANCIS BACON borrowed both the title of Montaigne's work and his method, and SHAKESPEARE echoes Montaigne in THE TEMPEST.

Bibliography

Cottingham, John, Robert Stoothoff, and Dugald Murdoch, Translators and Editors. *The Philosophical Writings of Descartes*, 2 vols. Cambridge, U.K.: Cambridge University Press, 1985.

Montaigne, Michel de. *Essays*. Translated by J. M. Cohen. New York: Penguin, 1993.

———. *The Complete Works: Essays, Travel Journals, Letters*. Translated by Donald M. Frame. Introduced by Stuart Hampshire. New York: Alfred A. Knopf, 2003.

Montalvo, Garci Rodríguez de (fl. 1500)

The governor of the city of Medina del Campo in Spain, Montalvo played an early role in the development of the Renaissance and therefore of the modern novel. Sometime between 1492 and 1504, working from a lost source with much apparent originality, perhaps in Portuguese, Montalvo reworked the fabulous adventures of a knight-errant, Amadis of Gaul. Though editions were said to have been printed as early as 1504, the earliest editions extant date from 1508 and 1519. The work was a smash hit, not only in Spain where it went through 12 editions in the next five decades, but also in Italy (six editions in 30 years) and France where it has remained popular ever since. AMADIS OF GAUL subsequently appeared in Germany (translated in

1583), England (1619), and most recently in the United States (2003).

To the four-book-long story that he adapted, Montalvo appended a wholly original fifth book that recounts the adventures of Esplandian, the son of Amadis and his consort Oriana. Not as highly regarded as the first four books, Esplandian's adventures drew the following remark from the curate in *Don Quixote de la Mancha* as he examined the books in Don Quixote's library: "the merits of the father must not be imputed to the son."

Amadis became the most popular work of those that continued the tradition of CHIVALRIC ROMANCE into the Renaissance. If Montalvo only made one contribution to the letters of his age, it proved to be an important one.

Bibliography

Montalvo, Garci Rodríguez de Montalvo. *Amadis of Gaul: A Novel of Chivalry . . . Books I and II*. Translated by Edwin B. Place and Herbert C. Behm. 1974. Reprint, Lexington: University Press of Kentucky, 2003.

———. *The Labors of the very Brave Knight Esplandián*. Translated by William Thomas Little. Binghamton, N.Y.: Center for Medieval and Early Renaissance Studies, State University of New York at Binghamton, 1992.

Montpensier, Anne-Marie-Louise d'Orléans, duchesse de (La Grande Mademoiselle) (1627–1693)

A French novelist, memoirist, and historical biographer, La Grande Mademoiselle, as almost everyone referred to Montpensier, was the niece of King Louis XIII of France. Early on, she had imagined she would become the consort of some ruling European king or prince. Partly owing, no doubt, to her direct participation as a military leader in a pair of uprisings against the French Crown that pitted the nobility of France and the Parisian bourgeoisie against royal autocracy, her ideas on that subject changed. Also, the royal court arranged no match for her. As a result, she deferred marriage until late in life. She fell in love in her 40s with the comte de Lauzun, and the French court was thunderstruck when *she* proposed marriage to *him*. He accepted, and King Louis XIV at first granted his approval. Dissuaded by his advisers, however, the king rescinded his initial consent to the couple's marriage and threw Lauzun into prison until the comte agreed to give back the titles to the lands that the enamored duchess had showered on him. After his release in 1581, he and the duchess were probably wed in secret (1582). She was then 53. After all their trials, the couple unfortunately did not get on, and they separated in 1584.

Mademoiselle Montpensier wrote two novels that her secretary, Jean Regnault de Segrais (1624–1701), allowed her to publish under his name: *La Relation de l'île imaginaire* (The tale of the imaginary island) and *La Princesse de Paphlagonie* (The princess of Paphlagonia). These romances are regarded as her apprentice efforts under the tutelage of Segrais. Her correspondence and memoirs, on the other hand, have attracted both literary admiration and serious scholarly attention. A recently discovered exchange of correspondence between Montpensier and her friend Madame de Montville has appeared in English as *AGAINST MARRIAGE: THE CORRESPONDENCE OF LA GRANDE MADEMOISELLE*.

In addition to the works named above, Mademoiselle Montpensier also wrote biographical sketches of her friends including one of the marquise of Fouquesolles, Jeanne Lambert d'Herbigny, and her activities at the French court.

Bibliography

Pitts, Vincent. *La Grande Mademoiselle at the Court of France, 1627–1693.* Baltimore: Johns Hopkins University Press, 2000.

moralized geography

Map making is both a science and an art. Before Mercator-grid projections, maps made according to the system of the Greek mathematician Ptolemy represented the known world, if not accurately, at least scientifically. Before the age of exploration required better and better maps that more closely represented locations, directions, and distances, European maps often tended to have more to do with ALLEGORY than with geographical content. There were "T in O" maps that represented three continents, Europe, Asia, and Africa, surrounded by ocean and separated by two great rivers, the Nile and the Don, and by the Mediterranean Sea. Jerusalem, as the city most closely identified with Christian salvation, sat squarely in the middle of the map. The top of the map pointed east, for there, closest to Heaven, the Garden of Eden was located. On one such surviving map, a figure of Christ is superimposed on the continents, and Jerusalem sits at his heart. Thus these allegorical maps presented a moralized geography whose purpose was teaching relationships between God and the world.

Maps of another sort, zonal maps, also depicted frigid, temperate, and equatorial zones. The directions on the maps also became laden with moral significance. In a famous English play *THE CASTLE OF PERSEVERANCE* (15th century), north was the direction of the devil and of Hell. South was the direction of sensuality and sins of the flesh. Heaven was, of course, to the east, and west was the direction of the world and worldliness. Sometimes other values were assigned to the directions on maps. In SHAKESPEARE'S *THE TEMPEST*, we find the Neapolitan fleet sailing home from Claribel's wedding in Africa from the south, the direction of emotionality, toward Europe in the north, the direction of the rational. The action of the play takes place on an island somewhere between, and therefore, in terms of moralized geography, a region where balance between reason and passion may be expected to prevail.

Celestial maps also bore allegorical significance. By the time that JOHN MILTON finished *PARADISE LOST* (1665), a heliocentric solar system was a well-established fact. The Ptolemaic system, however, which put the Earth at the center of a system of concentric, crystalline spheres beyond which, as the church and poets had it, God, the Prime Mover, dwelt in eternal, unchanging light. The older system provided a moral framework that suited Milton's literary purposes so that science gave way to art.

More, Sir (Saint) Thomas (1478–1535)

An English HUMANIST, scholar, historian, NEO-LATIN (that is, classical Latin as written in the Renaissance) writer, statesman, and historian, More was educated in classics at Oxford and in the law at New Inn and Furnivall Inn in London. Thereafter he taught law for a period of three years and then withdrew from the world to the Charterhouse, a religious foundation, for a period of prayer and religious reflection.

Toward the end of the reign of King Henry VII, More became a member of Parliament and served as an undersheriff of London. Cardinal Wolsey, King Henry VIII's influential power broker and chancellor of the exchequer, introduced More to the king, and More occupied a series of increasingly important governmental and diplomatic posts. When Wolsey fell from power (1529), Henry, over More's strenuous objections, appointed More to the chancellorship. He served in that post with dignity and honor, though some found him too harsh a judge in religious matters.

When Henry VIII established himself as the head of the Church of England in 1534, More, who had resigned his chancellorship two years earlier, would have none of it. He remained steadfast in his allegiance to the pope despite repeated efforts to force him into the Anglican fold. Finally, after a year in prison proved unavailing, he was convicted of high treason, given a last chance to change his mind, and beheaded when he refused. A Roman Catholic martyr, More was canonized in 1935.

A great friend of the Dutch humanist, ERASMUS of Rotterdam, More played host to the eminent scholar in England, and Erasmus punned on More's name in the Latin title of his THE PRAISE OF FOLLY, *Encomium moriae*. As a literary figure More is best remembered for two works. His *History of King Richard III* (1513) is the first piece of English historiography that approaches modern standards of scholarship. His Latin work, *Utopia* (Noplace, 1516), provides the model for all subsequent Utopian literature. It was translated into English in 1556. Beyond these two works, More wrote religious polemics that influenced subsequent English prose writing. He attacked MARTIN LUTHER and WILLIAM TYNDALE as members of a "pestilent sect" in a 1528 *Dialogue*. While he was awaiting execution in the Tower of London, he also penned a *Dialogue of Comfort against Triubulation*. It candidly

explores his fear of his execution while detailing his hopes as a Christian. In this most personal of his works—though it is cast in the form of a conversation between two Hungarians—More reveals his charming good humor, his serious thoughtfulness, and his religious resolution.

Bibliography

More, Sir (Saint) Thomas. *Selected Writings: Saint Thomas More. Together with, The Life of Sir Thomas More by William Roper* [1496–1535]. Edited by John F. Thornton and Susan B. Varenne. New York: Vintage Books, 2003.

———. *The Complete Works of St. Thomas More.* 1963. New Haven, Conn.: Yale University Press, ca. 1986.

———. *Utopia: Thomas More.* Translated by Paul Turner. London and New York: Penguin Books, 2003.

Morgante: The Epic Adventures of Orlando and His Giant Friend Morgante (*Morgante maggiore*)
Luigi Pulci (1483)

In 1461 Lucrezia Tornabuoni de' Medici, wife of Piero and mother of LORENZO DE' MEDICI, commissioned LUIGI PULCI to write a pious CHIVALRIC EPIC in tribute to the Christianizing influence of the Holy Roman Emperor Charlemagne (747–814 C.E.). The literary historian Mark Davie suggests that the initial idea for the poem's production may have been part of a Medici effort to cement an alliance with the new French king, Louis XI. Fulfilling that commission consumed most of the rest of Pulci's literary working life as his poem developed through numerous additions and revisions that circulated from 1462 until the final version appeared in 1483, the year before the poet's death.

Given Pulci's playful sense of humor, his bent for sarcasm, his distaste for medieval versions of chivalric epics in general, and his distinctly impious (though often denied) ambivalence about the received doctrines of Roman Catholicism, he may have been a dubious choice for achieving Lucrezia's objectives. Yet the book that he left the world is one of the most stunningly original, funniest, and most influential works of the late 15th-century Italian Renaissance.

Pulci began his work with a roughly contemporary version of the story of Charlemagne's heroic general Roland (Orlando) as an apparent source document, but from the outset Pulci's uniquely ambivalent authorial voice imparts a fresh, mock-heroic tone and perspective to the narrative. The voice of the narrator also sometimes turns autobiographical so that the life, times, quarrels, and troubles of Luigi Pulci figure as a part of the fabric of the poem. That fabric helped to form Pulci's readers' responses to his epic, and because of his serial revisions of the work, audience response helped to shape the poem's final form.

Many of Pulci's characters and situations remain the familiar ones of the medieval *Song of Roland*. Gano, the duplicitous troublemaker, and Orlando, the king's nephew, appear early on. Enchanters, journeys, battles against pagans and Amazons, maidens in need of escort and rescue, and giants also figure prominently in the narrative.

As the poem opens, Orlando, annoyed by Gano's complaints about his influence with Charlemagne, departs angrily from the emperor's court and travels to a distant monastery. There the abbot, Orlando's cousin, reports that three giants are plaguing the neighborhood and asks for the hero's assistance. Just then a rock that one of the giants has thrown breaks the back of Orlando's warhorse. Remounted, Orlando rides off to battle the giants, kills two of them handily, but the third giant, the title character Morgante, begs for mercy since his dream of Christ's rescuing him from a serpent has made him desire to become a Christian convert.

Orlando grants Morgante's request, and the fun begins in earnest. When the abbot and his monks overcome their initial fear of Morgante, they send him off after water so that they can baptize him. He comes back with a huge container of water on one shoulder and two wild boars that he has strangled on the other. The boars provide the main course of the first of many giant-sized banquets that occur regularly through the poem. A good deal of the poem's humor results from these culinary excesses. One of the poem's major threads then follows the exuberant, fast-paced, and largely unconnected adventures of Orlando and Morgante. They are soon joined by another of Charlemagne's knights, Rinaldo, with whom they journey eventually back to Charlemagne's court.

Surely contrary to Medician expectations, Pulci sometimes depicts Charlemagne himself as a weak and indecisive ruler whose confidence in the treacherous Gano leads, among other disastrous consequences, to an invasion of the Christian empire by the forces of the pagan emperor, Erminione. Charlemagne reveals himself to be a duplicitous ruler as well. He encourages a duel between Rinaldo and Orlando when the two fall out. Charlemagne hopes that Rinaldo will be killed. Instead, Rinaldo leads a rebellion against the emperor, and Orlando has to put it down and rescue Charlemagne.

Canto 18 sees the introduction of a totally original character, Margutte. Neither quite a human being nor quite a giant, the dark-complexioned Margutte answers a conventional question about whether he is Christian or pagan with an affirmation of his credo. This proves to be a litany of his vices and of his sins against every conventional social and religious expectation of his era. He believes, he says, "in food and drink." He is able to dominate everyone he meets both by trickery and by means of verbal pyrotechnics. As Margutte robs and cheats his way through the canto, Pulci builds an underlying tension between the trickster and Morgante. This tension is eventually resolved when Morgante hides Marguette's boots, and challenges Margutte to guess where they are. When Margutte sees that a Barbary ape is putting his boots on and taking them off, he is so amused that he dies of laughter. The Morgante–Margutte episode is interrupted along the way by the story of the pair's rescue of the damsel Florinetta from other giants who have captured her. Morgante and Margutte restore her to her father, King Filomeno.

After 23 increasingly long cantos, Pulci turns his attention in the next five to the traditional matter of the *Song of Roland*—the destruction of the rear guard of Charlemagne's army by the pagan forces at Roncevalles. As author and commentator Pulci in part returns to the commission of his patroness by claiming two sources for his material on

Charlemagne—a false one that presents the emperor as weak and gullible and a reliable source by the English scholar Alcuin who paints Charlemagne as the Christian hero Lucrezia Tornabuoni thought him to have been.

Morgante, though a giant, is also mortal. Eventually he dies, and Pulci turns his attention to other aspects of his kaleidoscopic poem. He creates such wonderfully imaginative characters as Malagigi the magician or Astarotte, a pedantic devil who does Malagigi's bidding and makes speeches so tedious that they become funny. Pulci's multiple perspective on his material—at once a telling and a commentary, comic and tragic, distanced and involved, satiric and serious, linguistically brilliant and sometimes nonsensical—establishes a new possibility for simultaneous multiple perspectives in European writing.

Many learned Pulci's lessons. FRANÇOIS RABELAIS's *Gargantua et Pantagruel* (Gargantua and Pantagruel) profited from Pulci's example. So did MIGUEL DE CERVANTES Y SAAVEDRA's *DON QUIXOTE DE LA MANCHA*. At another level both BOIARDO and ARIOSTO in Italy are Pulci's literary heirs. They learned his lessons of narrative stance, verbal music, and irony. As late as the 19th century, Lord Byron undertook a translation of *Morgante*. Byron completed only a single canto—the text is full of thorny problems for a translator. Nonetheless Byron perceived the basic duality of Pulci's enterprise and coined a descriptive phrase for his verses: "half-serious rhymes."

Bibliography

Davie, Mark. *Half-Serious Rhymes: The Narrative Poetry of Luigi Pulci*. Dublin: Irish Academic Press, 1998.

Pulci, Luigi. *Morgante: The Epic Adventures of Orlando and His Giant Friend Morgante*. Translated by Joseph Tusiani. Introduction and notes Edoardo A. Lébano. Bloomington, Ind.: Indiana University Press, 1998.

muses

By the time of the Renaissance, the number and function of the muses—the Greek divinities who presided over the arts and inspired their practitioners—had long been firmly fixed in mythology and in iconography on the model of the Greek poet Hesiod (eighth century B.C.E.). His list included Calliope, the patron goddess of EPIC poetry and the principal muse; Clio, the muse of history; Erato, the muse of love poetry and lyrics in general; Euterpe, the muse of music; Melpomene, the muse of TRAGEDY; Polymnia, the muse of sacred poetry and mimicry; Terpsichore, the muse of dancing and choral singing (which on the Greek stage was accompanied by dance movement); Thalia, the muse of COMEDY, and Urania, the muse of Astronomy.

From the perspective of literature, in keeping with the view of the poet as VATES or as priest, the artist was thought to act as a medium through which the deities spoke. Just as poets might accompany themselves on musical instruments, so the muses used the artists as *their* instruments. Homer and following Homer most epic poets ever after start by invoking the muse. Homer begins his *Odyssey* by praying, "Sing in me, Muse [presumably Calliope], and in me tell the story . . ." and the adventures of the wandering king of Ithaca unfold.

Seeking to overtop his predecessor poets by singing an epic about a universal history that began before the creation of the world, JOHN MILTON in his *PARADISE LOST* invokes as his Christian muse the Holy Spirit: "Of man's first disobedience . . . With loss of Eden, till . . . [we] regain the blissful seat, Sing heavenly Muse. . . ."

In *iconography,* or mythography the muses, including Milton's, are regularly associated with identifying visual symbols. A representation of a dove often stands for the Holy Spirit. Calliope is pictured with a writing tablet, Clio strumming on a lyre, Euterpe with a flute, Melpomene with the mask of tragedy, and Thalia with that of comedy. The thoughtful expression on Polymnia's face identifies her while Terpsichore is represented dancing and accompanying herself on a lyre. Urania is usually pictured holding either a terrestrial or a celestial globe.

Nabhādās (1570–ca. 1662)

Writing in the Brajbasha language—a tongue closely allied with Hindi but that developed a literature earlier—the Indian poet Nabhādās was born to a destitute family. When he was five years old, poverty and desperation forced his mother to abandon him in a forest. There, a Hindu holy man and poet named Agradas found and adopted him, rearing him as his own child and, according to legend, curing him of his congenital blindness.

A devotee of the sect of the Hindu deity Rama, Agradas encouraged Nabhādās to compose a verse history that recounted the biographies of the lives of poet–saints in the BHAKTI tradition of spiritual revival generally, but especially of those who particularly venerated Rama. This Nabhādās did, producing his celebrated *BHAKTAMALA*—a catalog of those biographies. The first such work in India, the *Bhaktamala* initiated a genre much imitated throughout the subcontinent.

In addition to that work, Nabhādās also wrote a less famous devotional one, *Ramashtayam* (Verses in honor of Rama). Though I have been unable to locate modern editions of that work, several exist of the *Bhaktamala*. The most recent appeared in 1998.

Bibliography

Nābhādāsa. *Srī Bhaktamāia . . .* Rājakota, India: Prarīna Prakāśna, 1998.

Nábí (ca. 1630–1712)

The last considerable poet of the Turkish classical age, Nábí belonged to that class of Turkish poet and prose writer who emulated both the art and the language of the Persians. A self-conscious artist, he took the entire field of literary endeavor as his province. In prose he became a biographer, a travel writer, and a historian, and he published collections of his own letters. In poetry, he tried his hand at all the traditional forms—*GHAZELS, MESNEVI*, and *QASÍDA*. He also dealt with all the traditional subjects: CUPBEARER poems, love poems, poems of moral instruction, mystic experience, worldly experience, religious poems, and poems that taught philosophy.

Throughout much of the 16th and 17th centuries, Turkish poets looked to their Persian contemporaries for inspiration. This is the central defining characteristic of the classical age of Turkish poetry. Though in the following period this would change, Nábí is the last poet of importance in the classical period to continue the practice. He found his model in the work of the Persian poet ṢĀ'ĪB OF TABRIZ (ca. 1601–1670). Both poets encouraged a commonsense philosophy. Particularly fond of proverbs and parable, Nábí often dispensed small doses of wisdom in couplets that both stated a proverb and made an application of it.

Paradoxically, Nábí's most famous poem neither imitates a Persian model nor introduces Persian words. Rather it is composed in plain, straightforward Turkish. Constructed of a lengthy series of couplets, the work is in the *mesneví* form. Entitled KHAYRIYYA (For Khayr, ca. 1662), the poem is addressed to Nábí's son, Ebu 'l-Khayr. It is filled with fatherly advice about how the young man should conduct his life.

This sort of book represented a new genre in Turkish literature, and its novelty made it an immediate success.

Ná'ilí (Yeni-záda Mustafá Efendi)
(d. 1666 or 1667)

Earning his living as a government clerk in the department of mines in his native Constantinople, Ná'ilí gained a reputation as one of the three or four best Turkish poets of the 17th century. This evaluation rests partly on his introduction into traditional subjects and forms much fresh and daring language and METAPHOR deriving from the Persian tradition. It also rests on the highly (some would say *over*) refined polishing of his vocabulary. Literary historian Elias Gibbs judges that Ná'ilí finally represents a dead end in the development of Turkish verse. Much of his brilliantly fresh metaphor derives from Persian vocabulary that Ná'ilí tried to introduce into the Turkish language. Unfortunately, some of his word selections were impossible to intuit from the context in which they appeared. A Turk who spoke no Persian would have found some of Ná'ilí's poems as lexically incomprehensible as Lewis Carroll's "Jabberwocky."

Ná'ilí's production consists mainly of GHAZELS and QASÍDAS.

Nānak, Dev Guru (1469–ca. 1539)

A poet in the Punjabi and Hindi languages of India, Nānak founded the Sikh religion of northern India and was its first guru or teacher (see ADI GRANTH). He objected to the Hindu caste system, to idol worship, and to Hinduism's ritualism and, as he thought, superstition. He also spurned Muslim formalism and the Islamic veneration of prophets, saints, and martyrs. An unusual religious thinker in his time and place, Nānak believed in the power of reason as the only vehicle for exploring the ground of being. Where rationality failed, he thought, mystery took over, and Nānak was satisfied to leave matters there rather than appeal to special revelation, divine inspiration, and mysticism. At the same time, Nānak believed in religious freedom and peoples' right to follow the faith that suited them—as long as they refrained from trying to impose their beliefs on others.

Also remarkable in his country and his era, Nānak strongly advocated the dignity and rights of women. A social critic, too, he wrote bitingly about the invasion and takeover of northern India by Babar and his armies, and he was indignant about social arrangements that perpetuated poverty for those in certain castes and occupations.

His collected writings appear, along with those of his successors as gurus and of other Indian poet–saints of the BHAKTI devotional movement in a collection of Sikh scriptures, the Adi Granth.

Nānak wrote mainly in verse and principally in Punjabi and Hindi. His vocabulary, however, was very cosmopolitan, and one finds in his works words from Persian, Arabic, Sanskrit, Sindhi, and Khariboli in addition to the lexicon of his principal tongues. All of his work is available in good English translation.

Bibliography

Nānak, Guru. *Five Hundred Thoughts of Guru Nanak. . . .* Chandigarh, India: Panjab Government Department of Public Relations, 1977.

———. *Guru Nanak's Asa di vara: Text, Translation, and Study.* Translated by G. S. Randhawa. Amritsar, India: Guru Nanak Dev University, 1997.

———. *Guru Nanak's Siddha Goshti.* Translated by Piar Singh. Amritsar, India: Guru Nanak Dev University, 1996.

———. *The Japuji: Sikh Morning Prayer.* Translated by Kartar Singh Duggal. New Delhi: UBS Publishers' Distributors, 2000.

Songs of the Saints from the Adi Granth. Edited and translated by Nirmal Dass. Albany: State University of New York Press, ca. 2000.

Sri Guru Granth Sahib in English Verse. Translated [freely] by Swami Rama. Dehra Dun, India: Himalayan Hospital Trust, ca. 1998.

Nandadāsa (fl. ca. 1585)

An influential poet from several points of view, this Indian scholar, poet, and saint helped set the literary standard toward which poets in the Brajbhasha language (a literary predecessor of Hindi) would aspire for at least two centuries. It was he who introduced into the Braj tongue many of the traditional modes of poetic artwork from other LANGUAGES OF INDIA—principally from Sanskrit. His *Quintet on Krishna's Dance,* generally considered his masterpiece, introduces into the literary culture of Braj—the area just north of Agra—the literary device of attributing to Krishna's amorous dancing with Braji women the ancient theme of the soul's yearning for God and God's responsive grace and love. This theme appears in the ancient Sanskritic text the *Bhāgavatapurāna,* which is the most popular and perhaps the most influential work of Sanskritic philosophical literature. Nandadāsa borrows sections and themes from the ancient work and assimilates them to the situation of his time and place. (See ROUND DANCE OF KRISHNA, THE.)

In addition to his efforts as a seminal poet, Nandadāsa also felt a teacher–scholar's responsibility to help his audience understand poems and how they work. He provides, for example, versified vocabulary lists in two of his compositions, *Anekārthamañjarī* (Bouquet of senses) and *Mānmañjarī* (Bouquet of synonyms), to assist readers and hearers of verse with hard words or words with Sanskritic roots. His *Rasmañjarī* (Bouquet of the sudden bliss of recognition) was designed to acquaint his public with the methods for achieving those flashes of insight about poetic meaning that make the informed reading of good poetry so addictive.

As a man of religious devotion, Nandadāsa reworked an 11th-century Sanskritic allegory into a CLOSET DRAMA. He meant his *Prabodhancandrodaya* (The rising of the moon of understanding) as a text for private devotional study rather than as a play for performance. He also adapted for his Braj audience a Sanskritic text that had already been re-

worked by others for audiences of Marathi speakers (centuries before) and Gujerati speakers (in the 15th century). That work, his *Bhavargīt* (Bee's song) emphasizes Krishna's status as a divine incarnation among human beings of the deity Vishnu. Also, in an ongoing ALLEGORY that pits the relative importance of knowledge against that of devotion—the latter position, argued by the milkmaids of Braj—easily wins the day. This emphasis departs significantly from the Sanskritic model.

Adaptations of Nandadāsa's work continued to appear as late as the 20th century, and Stuart McGregor tells us that some of his verses still were recited accurately to accompany dancers into at least the middle of that century. More important, perhaps, Nandadāsa himself achieved sainthood, and his scholarly works, particularly, achieved the status of scripture early in the century following his death.

Bibliography

McGregor, Stuart. "The Progress of Hindi, Part I: The Development of a Transregional Idiom." In *Literary Cultures in History: Reconstructions from South Asia,* edited by Sheldon Pollock. Berkeley: University of California Press, 2003.

Nandadāsa. *The Round Dance of Krishna, and Uddhav's Message.* Translated by R. S. McGregor. London: Luzac, 1973.

Nashe (Nash), Thomas (ca. 1567–1601)

The son of an Anglican vicar, Nashe was educated at St. John's College, Cambridge, taking his B.A. in 1586, and working toward an M.A. that he never completed. Apparently St. John's had become a center of PURITAN activity by that time, and Nashe may no longer have found it congenial, or his father's death may have made it financially impossible for him to remain.

After traveling in Italy and France for a time, Nashe returned to London to try his luck as a writer. He became a satirist and a dramatist and a member of the group of early writers called the UNIVERSITY WITS. In London Nashe's first venture as a professional writer was a pamphlet, *The Anatomie of Absurditie* (registered, 1589, published 1590). Posing as a critique of women (except for

Queen ELIZABETH I), Nashe's SATIRE was mainly directed against contemporary popular romances. Written in the style of JOHN LYLY's *EUPHUES*, *The Anatomie* decried the imitators of medieval Arthurian legend. In this section of the work Nashe seems more modern than most early Elizabethan prose writers. Toward the end, however, he returns to his announced theme, pedantically citing examples of the inconstancy of women taken from the work of ancient writers. Nashe's biographer, Donald J. McGinn, characterizes *The Anatomie* as the first piece of Elizabethan journalism.

Before that work actually saw print, however, Nashe's preface to ROBERT GREENE's *Menaphon* appeared. In it Nashe attacks many literary trends of his time and defends the theater against the mounting attacks of its PURITAN opponents. As a result Nashe was immediately himself attacked by those same Puritans and became involved in a celebrated exchange of insults, the *Martin Marprelate* controversy. Puritan writers attacked the Anglican establishment in a series of propagandist pamphlets written under the penname Martin Marprelate. Vehemently anti-Puritan, Nashe was immediately recruited to answer for the Anglicans. An anti-Martinist pamphlet, *An Almond for a Parrot* (1590), is very likely Nashe's. In it Nashe deserts the euphuistic manner and develops a highly individualized style compounded of elements from RABELAIS, ARETINO, and the racy colloquialism and invective of the Marprelate pamphlets themselves. His anti-Puritan views also involved him in an ongoing controversy with the English academic and minor poet, Gabriel Harvey.

Nashe's best-remembered work is his novel, *THE UNFORTUNATE TRAVELLER* (1594). The first historical novel in English, it also displays characteristics of the PICARESQUE novel. It initiates in English the joining together of fictive characters with historical persons and events. It also satirizes and parodies many of the literary trends and tendencies that appeared in Elizabethan letters.

On at least two occasions, Greene collaborated with others in writing drama for the English stage. With CHRISTOPHER MARLOWE he collaborated on *The Tragedy of Dido, Queene of Carthage* (1594). He also worked with BEN JONSON on a play now lost, a COMEDY, *The Isle of Dogs* (1597), whose satire was so objectionable to the authorities that Jonson was jailed, the license of its producer, Thomas Henslowe, withdrawn, and Greene himself constrained to flee London for Yarmouth. While there he wrote his last notable work, *Nashe's Lenten Stuffe* (1599). This amusing pamphlet satirically celebrates both the city of Yarmouth and its principal export, red herring.

Bibliography

Brooke, C. F. Tucker. *The Life of Marlowe, and The Tragedy of Dido, Queen of Carthage.* 1930. New York: Gordian Press, 1966.

McGinn, Donald J. *Thomas Nashe.* Boston: Twayne Publishers, 1981.

Nashe, Thomas. *The Unfortunate Traveller and Other Works.* Edited by J. B. Steane. Harmondsworth, U.K.: Penguin, 1972.

———. The Works of Thomas Nashe. 1904–10. London: A. H. Bullen, 1958.

Nature (*Natura*)

Since ancient times Mother Nature has been personified in a variety of ways, and aspects of nature have been deified as animistic spirits associated with natural phenomena like trees, springs, waterfalls and so forth. In the Renaissance, a system of ICONOGRAPHY developed that represented Nature as a goddess. She was one of two (FORTUNE was the other) who mediated between God and the affairs of the world. They were the means by which God's will was accomplished on Earth. The visual, the plastic, and the literary arts all frequently represented Nature in this guise.

neo-Latin writing

Commentators mean different things by *neo-Latin writing*. Some use it to mean an artificial international language. Others apply it to Latin writings during the European Middle Ages after the fall of Ancient Rome. Here I mean by *neo-Latin writing* any work of literature written in the Latin language by authors beginning with FRANCIS PETRARCH (1304–74) and his fellow HUMANISTS in Europe and elsewhere until the end of 17th century in Continental Europe, England, and newly discovered realms, and, in the Scandinavian countries, a bit later.

The people of Europe speak many languages. Hikers through the countryside today would not only hear spoken the official tongues of the geopolitical units through which they passed; they would also sometimes hear mutually unintelligible regional dialects and languages such as Basque, whose speakers have no independent geopolitical unit. In the Renaissance, the European linguistic situation was even more complex than it is today, for the leveling influences of mass media, print excepted, had not yet begun to operate.

Despite that polyglot environment, Europe in the early Renaissance was united as Christendom, and the Latin language had for a millennium provided the lingua franca by means of which literate persons could communicate across the boundaries of their native vernaculars. With the rise of humanism, students of the literature of ancient Rome beginning with Francis Petrarch in the 14th century sought to purify Vulgate Latin by making their Latin writing correspond more closely with the language as the great writers of ancient Rome had used it. The humanist interest in education, moreover, established a new standard of Latin EDUCATION that eventually included most upper-class men and some women all across Europe. By the 16th and 17th centuries a common, Latin-based, well to do, largely masculine, educated class had produced a pan-European readership for literature written in Latin. This fact produced a dilemma for many writers interested in the development of their native tongues and the capacities of their birth languages to convey the complex fabric of idea and feeling. They wished to write in their own idioms, but they also wanted a broad readership beyond the boundaries of their native countries.

Some writers, including PETRARCH, resolved the dilemma by writing in both languages. Others such as the Dutch DESIDERIUS ERASMUS and the English SIR THOMAS MORE composed principally in Latin—the original language of Erasmus's THE PRAISE OF FOLLY and of More's *Utopia*. Latin became the language of choice for most humanists who wished to communicate with each other across national boundaries, and many works of literature appeared in that language as well as in the various European vernaculars. In the 17th century when the English poet JOHN MILTON served at the cabinet level of the English government under OLIVER CROMWELL, Milton's function was similar to that of a U.S. secretary of state. Milton was the chief diplomat of the realm. His title, however, was Latin secretary, for Latin was the language of international diplomacy. Milton composed voluminously in Latin as well as in English.

Neo-Latin moved north with Renaissance humanism into the Scandinavian countries where such writers as the Dane, Peder Palladius and Christiern Pedersen, practiced it. In Scandinavia neo-Latin composition remained in vogue well into the 18th century.

The age of exploration spread Europeans practicing neo-Latin composition to the far reaches of the globe. Many churchmen working in the New World used neo-Latin as did such missionaries as ROBERTO DI NOBILI as far away as India.

Bibliography

IJswijin, Joseph. *Companion to Neo-Latin Studies.* Leuven, Belgium: Leuven University Press; Peeters Press, 1990–1998.

Neoplatonism

A term that alludes to the thought of the Greek philosopher PLATO (ca. 428–ca. 348 B.C.E.), *Neoplatonism* describes that thought as it was reinterpreted and modified both in ancient times and in Renaissance Europe. Many of Plato's writings, though they had been continuously transmitted in the Byzantine world, for centuries had been lost to Western scholars. In part this loss resulted from the disintegration of the Roman Empire, and in part it resulted from the triumph of the thought of ARISTOTLE among medieval Christian theological scholars. The capacity to read and understand Greek, moreover, survived only in isolated pockets in Western Europe.

In the Greco–Byzantine world, however, an active interest in Platonic thought continued to flourish, and expansions and reinterpretation of Plato regularly appeared. An early and important Platonic thinker was the Roman–Egyptian Plotinus (ca. 205–270 C.E.), who moved to Italy and tried to set up a Platonic republic. His student and biographer, the Syrian Porphyry, commented influentially on the works of Plato and on those of Plotinus and Aristotle as well. Proclus (ca. 410–485 C.E.), who was one in a long line of leaders of Plato's academy in Athens, is still regarded as the founder of Neoplatonism in the classical world. Following him, the sixth-century writer known as Dionysius the Areopagite, living in Alexandria in Egypt, wrote a series of important theological treatises reconciling Christian theology with Platonic mysticism. Christian enthusiasts misidentified this writer as the apostle Paul's Athenian convert to Christianity named in Acts 17.34. This error conferred special authority on the later writer and became the basis for several Renaissance attempts to reconcile Plato's philosophy with Christian doctrine.

In the 15th century a Greek scholar named Georgios Gemistos, who took as his surname Plethon or Pletho, inspired a number of Florentines with an enthusiasm for Platonic thought and writings. Although an interest in Greek had already been spreading among European HUMANISTS, who had made unsystematic efforts to translate recovered works of Plato and his followers into Latin, Gemistos's passion for Plato focused the efforts of gifted Florentine humanists and other Italians into a program of recovery and translation. Among those making major contributions to this effort, MARSILIO FICINO translated the then known works of Plato into Latin at the request of Cosimo de' Medici. Before Ficino, LEONARDO BRUNI translated four Platonic dialogues and parts of others. GIOVANNI PICO DELLA MIRANDOLA followed Ficino's lead in attempting to reconcile Plato's thought with that of Aristotle and with elements of the mystical Jewish kabbalah.

Though these attempts and later ones to bring Platonic thought first into Latin and then the vernacular tongues of Europe proved influential among philosophers, the most widespread popular application of Platonic theory appeared in poetry, and particularly in a kind of poetry celebrating the benefits of PLATONIC LOVE. JEHUDAH BEN ISAAC

ABRAVANEL's influential Platonic and kabbalistic document, *The Dialogues of Love* gave currency to the concepts involved in Platonic, Renaissance love theory. The poems of LORENZO DE 'MEDICI provide examples of the theory's application. So do those of EDMUND SPENSER and many others. In CASTIGLIONE'S *THE COURTIER*, a character named for Cardinal PIETRO BEMBO rises to the ethereal contemplation of divinity, borne there by first admiring the physical beauties of a lady, then her moral virtues, and finally the perfections of divinity itself. Poets throughout Europe made much of this progression and of the unity of goodness, beauty, and truth as the essential and interchangeable attributes of godhead according to Renaissance love theory, or Platonic love. In all the courts of Europe, the devotees of the cult—for such it became—attempted to achieve new levels of human perfection grounded in a love for the physical beauties of a beloved person. It was in this Neoplatonic religion of love that the modified thought of the most influential of all philosophers appeared most prominently in the literature of the Renaissance.

Bibliography

Ficino, Marsilio. *Platonic Theology.* Edited by James Hankins and William Bowen. Translated by Michael J. B. Allen and John Warden. Cambridge, Mass.: Harvard University Press, 2001–2002.

Hankins, James. *Plato in the Italian Renaissance.* Leiden, Netherlands: E. J. Brill, 1990.

Leone Ebreo [Abravanel, Jehudah]. *The Philosophy of Love.* Translated by F. Friedeberg-Seely and Jean H. Barnes. London: 1937.

Pico della Mirandola, Giovanni. *Commentary on a Poem of Platonic Love.* Translated by Douglas Carmichael. Lanham, Md.: University Press of America, ca. 1986.

Nev'í (Nasúh-záde Pír-záde Yahya)
(ca. 1533–1599)

A Turkish poet and encyclopedist of science, in his childhood Nev'í had been a classmate of the poet BÂKÎ. Like him Nev'í belonged to the class of civil administrators of the Ottoman Empire. He rose through the ranks of that bureaucracy until Sultan

Murád III picked Nev'í to become the tutor to his son, the Crown Prince Mustapha. Pleased with the poet's performance, the sultan entrusted the education of three of his other sons to Nev'í's care. When Mustapha succeeded his father, however, he followed the practice of his ancestor Muhammed the Conqueror and had all 19 of his brothers summarily executed. He was the last Ottoman emperor to practice that particular barbarity.

Among Nev'í's poems, one especially touching ELEGY mourns the deaths of his royal students. His poetic style is modeled on that of his friend Báqí but lacks his skill and clarity. Nev'í's erudition burdens his verse and costs it the quality of graceful spontaneity that critics attribute to Báqí. Nonetheless the royal tutor's poems have merit. His love poems resemble those of the PLATONIC LOVE cult of Renaissance Europe in that they perceive human love (called typal-love by the Turkish commentators) as a bridge to the love of God. This should seem none too surprising, for Arabic love lyrics are the likely foundation stone of the European development as well as of the Turkish one.

Nev'í wrote prose prolifically. His most important work was his encyclopedia, *Netá'ij-ul-Funún ve Mehásin-ul-Mutún* (The results of the sciences and the virtues of the texts). At the request of the sultan, Nev'í also translated Arabic works into Turkish.

New Way to Pay Old Debts, A   Philip Massinger   (1625)

A New Way to Pay Old Debts is the best remembered play of the prolific British playwright, PHILIP MASSINGER, whose career spanned the reigns of King JAMES I and King Charles I.

The plot concerns a social climber and financial schemer, Sir Giles Overreach, who has by every crooked scheme imaginable amassed an extravagant fortune and owns vast tracts of land. He is able to employ down-on-their-luck English aristocrats as his servants, but he has not himself been able to rise to hereditary, noble rank. He hopes, however, to marry off his virtuous daughter Margaret to a member of the old nobility so that her children, at any rate, can achieve the status that is his goal.

Margaret, however, loves Alworth, a page in the household of Lord Lovell. Overreach schemes to arrange a marriage between Margaret and Lovell. Helping to thwart Overreach's ambitious trickery, we find his nephew, Welborne. Welborne's spendthrift youth has left him with no avenue of appeal except to his despicable uncle. Despite the power that Overreach exercises over him, Welborne resolves to thwart his uncle's plans and help Margaret and Alworth.

Welborne plots with Alworth's wealthy, widowed stepmother. She pretends to have fallen in love with Welborne. Seeing an opportunity to enrich himself further by duping Welborne of the wealth he will acquire by this advantageous marriage, Overreach gives Welborne money and returns clothing he had held in pledge against debts his nephew owed him.

The trickster, Sir Giles Overreach, is tricked and defeated at every turn. Margaret and Alworth run away and marry. Welborne reacquires title to lands his uncle had cheated him of. He also pledges to redeem a wasted youth by becoming a member of the British military forces and serving his country. Sir Giles Overreach, however, disappointed in his hopes and for the first time denied the objective of his greed, goes stark raving mad and has to be institutionalized.

For Lord Lovell and Lady Alworth, who assisted the young people in Overreaches' overthrow and the achievement of their hopes, there is also a happy ending. The two mature representatives of solid British virtue also fall in love and marry.

Massinger's play focused his audience's attention on the destructive potential of the greedy pursuit of wealth and on the value of traditional virtue to the British national character.

Bibliography

Massinger, Philip. *The Plays and Poems of Philip Massinger*. Five volumes. Edited by Philip Edwards and Colin Gibson. Oxford, U.K.: The Clarendon Press, 1976.

Ninety-five Theses   Martin Luther   (1517)

The 95 theses that MARTIN LUTHER reputedly posted on the door of the church in Wittenberg are widely regarded as being among the foundational documents of the Protestant Reformation. It seems entirely likely, however, that when Luther wrote them, he did not view them as revolutionary. For the most part, the theses were directed against the sale of indulgences. Indulgences were papal dispensations that reputedly relieved their recipients from a degree of punishment in Purgatory for venial sins they had committed during their lifetimes. Originally created as a freely given reward for faithful and extraordinary service to the church, over time the sale of indulgences and relics had instead become a major source of income for the papal See. Luther saw the practice as nondoctrinal, and the theses that he posted principally take that position. Luther felt perfectly within his priestly rights in doing this because the church had not elevated its views with respect to indulgences to the status of official dogma.

Essentially, Luther objected to the idea that forgiving sin was a part of the church's prerogative. He thought that indulgences could only legitimately be used to lessen the severity of penances that the church had imposed. It is unlikely that Luther envisioned the firestorm that would result from his rather scholarly commentaries. As it happened, however, a Dominican, Johann Tetzel, was the chief and abusive purveyor of indulgences in Saxony at that moment, and Luther's theses had the effect of coalescing public opinion against Tetzel and his huckstering.

The Vatican eventually took Tetzel's side. As one issue led to another, the pope's authority came into question, and a major division once again tore the fabric of Christendom.

Bibliography

Lohse, Bernhard. *Martin Luther: An Introduction to His Life and Work.* Translated by Robert C. Schultz. Philadelphia: Fortress Press, 1986.

Nobili, Roberto de (1577–1656)

In 1604 an Italian Jesuit priest, Roberto de Nobili, accompanied a number of missionaries on the dangerous voyage to the Portuguese colony of Goa on India's southwestern shore. Although forced to endure a shipwreck in route, he eventually arrived safely. Once ashore, he mastered some of the LANGUAGES OF INDIA including both Sanskrit and Tamil and assumed his duties in Madura—the first missionary to be sent to the interior.

He wrote numerous religious books in several languages, both European and Indian. De Nobili saw many correspondences between Hinduism and Christianity and employed them in his missionary efforts. Moreover, he rightly perceived that the methods of his predecessors, which required the assimilation of converts to the European manner of dress, diet, and behavior, amounted to a form of cultural domination that led both converts and priests to be despised widely.

De Nobili therefore assumed the saffron-colored robe, the diet, and the identifying brow markings of a Hindu holy man and teacher. The fact that his father was an Italian count, when the Indians discovered it, overcame his formerly untouchable status and gained him access to the upper classes of Hindu society.

This blending together of Christian and Hindu—even though de Nobili did it in the cause of the former religion—landed him in trouble with the Portuguese office of the INQUISITION. Church authorities censured his practices in 1610. As a result, de Nobili was forced to suspend using the methods he had developed until 1623. Then, in response to de Nobili's petition, Pope Gregory XV and the grand inquisitor of Portugal found in his favor, overturning the opinions of the church hierarchy in Goa. De Nobili's pioneering method, earlier used successfully in China, came to be called missionary adaptation and was widely adopted thereafter by missionaries throughout the world.

He resumed his writing and publication program, becoming one of the important, albeit nonindigenous, voices among the writers of India in the 17th century.

Bibliography

Cronin, Vincent. *A Pearl to India: The Life of Roberto de Nobili.* New York: E. P. Dutton, 1959.
Nobili, Roberto de. *Preaching Wisdom to the Wise: Three Treatises.* Translated by Anand Amaladass

and Francis X. Clooney. Saint Louis, Mo.: Institute of Jesuit Sources, 2000.

————. *Adaptation [by] Roberto de Nobili.* Palayamkottai, India: De Nobili Research Institute, 1971.

Nobility and Excellence of Women and the Defects and Vices of Men, The
Lucrezia Marinella (1600)

In 1599 Giuseppe Passi published a vitriolic diatribe against women, *The Defects of Women,* that infuriated Lucrezia Marinella. She responded to it in a white heat of intensity, publishing the first edition of *The Nobility and Excellence of Women* the following year. In it she brings to bear a level of erudition much superior to Passi's, a keen debater's edge, a more logical mind, and an appropriate sense of outrage. Her strategy for defeating Passi at his misogynist game involved a pincers movement. In the first part of her argument she adopts Passi's own tactics.

Passi begins by exploring the etymologies of various terms for *woman.* This form of debate was grounded in the notion that the names of things reveal their natures. Passi manages to find mostly false etymological roots for Italian terms for *woman* that suggest the word stands for such descriptors as "an error of nature." Marinella responds in kind, expounding much more clearly than Passi the theory of why names contain fundamental truths about the things they label, and then finding mostly accurate etymologies that reveal women to be superior, not inferior creatures.

Passi next fulminated against the inbred evil inclinations of women, citing authorities in support of his arguments. Marinella effectively destroys these arguments with a virtuoso intertwining of arguments from Aristotle, from Neoplatonist authorities, and from St. Augustine and other early church fathers. She demonstrates that God is the ultimate cause of everything, including women, and that excellent causes produce excellent effects. From that perspective, men and women proceed equally from a perfect idea in God's mind. Women, however, are more beautiful. Since, in the view of Platonic doctrine, the beautiful, the true, and the good are one, women's greater beauty means they must come from truer and better ideas than men. On this subject Marinella cites both ancient and modern authorities. Closely reasoned variations on this argument together with citations demonstrating the high esteem in which all civilizations have held women and a refutation of Passi's arguments for their depravity occupy Marinella's text through chapter 4. In chapter 5, with a host of examples that result in Marinella's literary anticipation of such 20th-century feminist artwork as Judy Chicago's *The Banquet,* Marinella gives examples of women from many centuries and all walks of life—women who equaled or surpassed men in terms of reason and will power (qualities Passi denied to women), and in the cardinal VIRTUES of prudence, temperance, and fortitude as well.

In these first five chapters Marinella destroys Passi's arguments and shows herself to be a far more skilled debater than he, appealing not only to argument but to her readers' emotions and imaginations as well.

Having done this, she turns in chapter 6 to a point-by-point refutation of Passi's arguments against women and those of other misogynists. She shows how they generalize from a single bad example to indict all women.

As Marinella's work went into subsequent editions, she expanded its first section. In 1601 she added four chapters that addressed works written by men in which they slandered women. She refuted GIOVANNI BOCCACCIO's *Corbaccio* (1355), Sperone Speroni's *Dialogue on the Dignity of Women* (1542), TORQUATO TASSO's treatise *On Female and Womanly Virtue* (1585), and Ercole Tasso's *On Taking a Wife* (1595).

The second part of Marinella's treatise (the other jaw of her pincers) considers failings she thinks more characteristic of men than of women. These include wrathfulness, eccentricity, brutality, obstinacy, stubbornness, ingratitude, discourtesy, inconstancy and fickleness, hatred, and effeminacy. Marinella also accuses men of a greater tendency toward patricide, matricide, fratricide, and infanticide.

Neglected for centuries, Marinella's treatise reemerged in the 1970s as the subject of intense and rigorous study. It remains a central document in the history of women's struggle for equality in the Western world.

Bibliography

Marinella, Lucrezia. *The Nobility and Excellence of Women, and The Defects and Vices of Men.* Edited and translated by Anne Dunhill. Introduced by Letizia Panizza. Chicago: The University of Chicago Press, 1999.

Norton, Thomas (1532–1584)

An English Protestant translator, poet, playwright, and attorney, Norton translated JOHN CALVIN's *Institutes of the Christian Religion* from Latin into Engish in 1561. With Thomas Sackville, the first earl of Dorset, Norton collaborated in writing a blank verse, SENECAN TRAGEDY, *Ferrex and Porrex* or *GORBODUC*, which has the distinction of being the first such tragedy in the English language. The play was performed at the Inner Temple in 1559 or 1560, and the following year it was performed at Whitehall before Queen ELIZABETH I, who was Sackville's second cousin. *Gorboduc* is one of the sources for WILLIAM SHAKESPEARE's *KING LEAR*.

ed652d

ode (*canzone*)

Meaning simply a "song," in ancient times the ode developed into a form of high poetic art, often highly ornamental and complex. In ancient drama the form took on regularity as it was composed of a strophe (a unified group of lines on a given subject), an antistrophe (a group of lines identical in form to the strophe but with a different message), and an epode (a verse with a different structure whose content mediates between strophe and antistrophe.) In the Renaissance PETRARCH to a degree followed the models of the ancients. His *canzoni* (odes), though they are not a fixed form like the SONNET, display a three-part structure composed of an introductory section, called a *frons* or *fronte* followed by an often lengthy development of several stanzas—the *sirima*. He closes his odes with a stanza containing a direct address to the song itself as he sends it on its way to do its work.

Petrarch's odes provided the model that many European poets emulated in the early Renaissance. BEN JONSON and ROBERT HERRICK typify the poets who emulated Petrarch by composing their odes in stanzas that were usually of the same length. In 1655 Abraham Cowley changed the English model by introducing the Pindaric ode—that is one modeled on the odes of the ancient Greek poet Pindar.

Elsewhere in Europe, Petrarch's example was widely followed, and odes modeled on his appeared throughout the Renaissance in Italy, France, Spain, Portugal, Germany, and elsewhere.

"Of Cannibals" Michel Eyquem de Montaigne (1578–1580)

A pioneering essay on the subject of cultural relativism, "Of Cannibals" begins with MONTAIGNE'S recollection of sayings from ancient Greek generals. The Greeks were accustomed to dividing human beings into two sorts: Greeks or barbarians. When the Greek kings Pyrrhus and Philip beheld the battle order of Roman legionaries, though, they concluded that however barbarous their enemies might otherwise be, the Roman's military tactics were certainly sophisticated.

The author next describes his untutored servant who had lived for over a decade in the newly discovered region we now call Brazil, then called Antarctic France. The man's very simplicity of mind made him trustworthy, and Montaigne learned much from him about the quality of life of the indigenous people in the regions where his servant had dwelled.

After a digression considering the topic of whether or not the New World might be identical with the lost Atlantis or with other regions dis-

395

cussed in ancient sources with which he was familiar, Montaigne returns to his major topic. On the basis of what his servant has told him, on the author's knowledge of scraps of indigenous song and poetry from the New World, and on his conviction that each man thinks barbarous all customs but his own, Montaigne concludes that dwellers in the newly discovered regions of the earth are not at all barbarous. Rather he considers that they are living in a state of nature closely resembling the fictive golden age of Euro-Asian culture. He imagines (incorrectly from an anthropological point of view) that the cannibals of the New World have no commerce, "no knowledge of letters ... science of numbers," or social hierarchy, and he imagines that their time is devoted to leisure pursuits. He rightly discerns that they have little use for clothing and that their social organization is based on kinship ties.

Montaigne describes their fishing and hunting, their absence of envy and avarice, and, again mistakenly, their freedom from treachery. He describes a faintly alcoholic beer made from roots, and he celebrates the two principal values of the male community: valor in warfare and love of one's wife. He thinks that a desire for riches beyond one's natural needs is unknown among them.

Montaigne discusses at length the customary treatment of prisoners taken in war. They are held for a long time and treated very well except that the captor attempts to break the captive's spirit by taunting him with impending death. On their parts, the captives, whose universal fate is to be killed, roasted, and eaten, hurl unflagging insults at their captors. They remind their jailers that, when they eat the captive's cooked flesh, they will also be eating the flesh of their own ancestors on which the captive and his comrades have earlier dined. When the day of execution finally comes, the captives go to their deaths defiantly.

The author mentions some Indians who have been brought to France and with whom he had an opportunity to speak through an interpreter. Montaigne feels sorry that in France the Indians may develop new desires that will lead to their moral ruin. Through his interpreter, Montaigne asked his informants what about Europe had most amazed them. He recalled two things they said. First, they had seen the boy king, Charles IX, surrounded by his Swiss guard. They were amazed that the guardsmen obeyed the orders of a child and a guardsman was not in command. Second, it seems that Montaigne's informants shared the idea that men were part of each other, or, as Montaigne expresses it, that each one had another half in some other person. The Indians were surprised that, in France, some men ate to excess while their other halves starved at their doors in direst need of food, clothing, and shelter.

Montaigne clearly admired the Indians, and from this essay sprang the notion of the *noble savage* that influenced such thinkers as DESCARTES and Rousseau and that continues to inform the thinking of some who consider the matter. Montaigne himself might have been surprised at his essay's long-lasting influence, for in its final sentence he despairs of convincing Europeans of the Amer-Indians' nobility since the latter do not wear britches.

Bibliography

Montaigne, Rene. "Of Cannibals." In *The Complete Works of Montaigne*. 1943. Reprint, Stanford, Calif.: Stanford University Press, 1957.

Omer (Nefʻi of Erzurum) (1572–ca. 1635)

A Turkish poet and satirist, Nefʻi (as Omer was known) is principally remembered as the author of incomparably brilliant QASÎDAS—poems that praise, compliment, or eulogize others. Whereas most of his predecessors and contemporaries closely followed the expectations established by earlier poets and their works, Nefʻi's style is wholly original. His brilliance and originality reveal themselves particularly in the introductory material that leads up to the portion of the poem that mourns a person's passing. If a deceased person had been a soldier, for example, Nefʻi might describe the battles in which that person had fought. In doing so his extraordinary imagination for detail, his subtle handling of language to make the tone of the poem reflect the emotions implicit in the scenes he describes, the flawless musicality of his word choice, and the perfection of his diction have all commanded the admiration of commentators and critics. Elias Gibb suggests that when Nef'i writes a battle scene one "can almost hear . . . the rush of . . . soldiers . . . and the clash of arms." In writing of a garden, Nef'i equally well evokes the perfume of the flowers and the sounds of water playing in a fountain. Though occasionally his verbal brilliance leads him to overshoot his mark, generally his verse is delicate, fresh, charming, and tasteful. The effect of Nef'i's mastery of the *qasida's* idiom was its institutionalization as a sort of Turkish national poetic standard. Many subsequent writers sought to follow his example.

The same cannot be said, however, for Nef'i's SATIRE—verses that he called *Shafts of Doom.* Their personal attacks on people obscure the purpose of satire, which has always been the exposure of vice and folly with the object of moral reform. Nef'i's obscene and abusive text merely heaps his displeasure on anyone who has offended him. His practice, here, of course, may reflect to some degree the taste and manner of his epoch. His satires may have offended people less than they now would, though subsequent events suggest the contrary.

Similarly, while our contemporary readers might find another sort of Nef'i's verse offensive, he was not the only poet to write self-glorifying poems. Many others did too, but Nef'i's are the most famous in the Turkish language. Despite the fact that modern taste may disapprove self-praise, the language in which the poet congratulates himself is glorious and on its own account pleasing to a reader.

The popularity throughout the Islamic world in the 16th and 17th centuries of CUPBEARER POEMS (*Sáqí Náma*) virtually demanded that every good poet write one. In keeping with this expectation Nef'i did so. His work, however, differed radically from all the others. Most followed the expectations of the MESNEVÍ form, constructing a long narrative from rhymed couplets. Nef'i instead addresses five little jewellike stanzas to the wine cup itself.

As an author of GHAZELS Nef'i adopted a quieter and more contemplative style than in his *qasídas.* At the same time he maintains the same purity of language and exemplary diction as well as the traditional form of these short, rhyming poems.

To a degree, Nef'i's career did for the Turkish language what the Renaissance vernacular poets of England, France, and Italy did for theirs. He purified the language and polished its capabilities for expression. The difference between the Turkish and the European poets, however, arose from Nef'i's emulation of Persian language and literature instead of the Europeans' fascination with Greek and Latin. In this respect, Nef'i followed in the footsteps of BÂKÎ. Taken together these poets inaugurated a school of Turkish poetry that, in addition to emulating Persian models, worked on technical mastery, purity of vocabulary, and diction. The school concerned itself less, however, with introducing nontraditional subject matter or with exploring a new palette of emotional possibilities.

In the end, Nef'i's *Shafts of Doom* boomeranged, dooming the poet himself. Sultan Murad was reading Nef'i's book one day when a bolt of lightning struck right at the sultan's feet. Feeling that this represented Heaven's judgment on Nef'i's satire, the sultan temporarily exiled the poet but then readmitted him to favor—provided that he write no more satire. Nef'i agreed and returned. For a while Nef'i' tried to keep his promise. Unfortunately he was addicted to this darker side of his art.

On the return from temporary exile of the sultan's brother-in-law, the Vezir Beyrám Pasha, Nef'i yielded to an impulse and satirized him, giving full vent to his penchant for gross insult. Infuriated, the vezir petitioned the sultan for redress. The sultan complied by turning Nef'i over to his enemy. Beyrám Pasha then sought and obtained the official permission of the Ottoman civil service hierarchy to execute Nef'i. As many civil servants in its ranks had been former subjects of Nef'i's lampoons, that permission proved easy to obtain. The vezir had Nef'i strangled with a bowstring and his body thrown into the sea without benefit of funeral or even one of the eulogizing *qasídas* of which the luckless poet remains the undisputed master.

Bibliography

Andrews, Walter G., Jr. *An Introduction to Ottoman Poetry.* Minneapolis: Bibliotheca Islamica, 1976.

Gibb, E. J. W. *A History of Ottoman Poetry.* Edited by Edward G. Browne. London: Luzac and Company, 1965.

Opitz, Martin (1597–1639)

Often considered the initiator of Renaissance and therefore of modern German literature, Opitz was a poet, an operatic librettist, a translator, and a prose writer as well. Despite a remarkably large and varied body of work, his principle contribution to the literature of his and of following epochs in German letters rests mainly on his contributions to the science of poetics and POETIC METER.

Like HUMANIST poets across Europe, German writers interested themselves in applying the principles of composition of the ancient classics to their German works. Before Opitz, however, their efforts had been random trial and error. Opitz systematically developed a PROSODY for German poetry that replaced the singsong meters of HANS SACHS's earlier, indigenous, eight- or nine-syllable line, rhymed couplets called *Knittelvers*. Opitz created a series of metrical possibilities that much more fully exploited the musical potentialities of the German language. His work made available to German poets the sort of sophisticated prosody already available to poets in southern Europe and in England. Once German poets had Opitz's models available to them, moreover, people developed a greater appreciation for poets' work.

Opitz's own poetic career began early with the inclusion of some of his Latin verses in a little volume dedicated to a teacher, *Strenarum libellus* (A little book of New Year's wishes, 1616). That same year Opitz became the tutor in the household of an important imperial counselor, Tobias Scultatus. In his employer's fine library, Opitz gained a sense of Germany's literary backwardness as compared to the rest of Europe, and he penned a Latin treatise, *Aristarchus sive de Contemptu Linguae Teutonicae* (Aristarchus or concerning the contempt for the German Language.) He began to think about ways to overcome the low regard into which German letters had fallen.

In 1620 he translated a song of praise for Jesus Christ from the Dutch of the scholar–humanist Daniel Heinsius. By this time Opitz was living in Heidelburg. But the Thirty Years' War had begun in 1618, and in 1620, threatened by the hostilities, Opitz and others fled Heidelburg for Denmark. Enroute, Opitz detoured to Holland, spending a winter in Jutland. There he composed his most notable poetic work, *Trostgedichte in Wiederwetigkeit dess Krieges* (Poems of consolation in the adversity of war, published 1633.) In 1622 Opitz moved to Transylvania. There he visited the gold-mining town of Zlatna, whose name means "gold." He borrowed the name for a second highly regarded work, a utopian poem tinged with ironic humor: *Zlatna oder von Ruhe des Gemüts* (Zlatna or concerning the repose of the soul, 1623). *Zlatna* continues to attract considerable interest among Romanian as well as German critics.

The following year (1624) saw twin triumphs for Opitz. First his collected German poems appeared in Strasbourg. Then the 50-page, eight-chapter work that became the cornerstone of German Renaissance poetry was published in Brieg: *Buch von der Deutchen Poeterey* (Book of German poetry or poetics). Opitz said he wrote it in five days. He expanded it with a second part in 1629. His reputation as a major poetic theorist and poet was now secure, but further laurels soon crowned him. The Holy Roman Emperor Ferdinand II (reigned 1619–37) named Opitz poet laureate in 1625.

Despite occasional dislocations arising from religious disputes, the warfare between Protestants and Catholics, and the ongoing Thirty Years' War, Opitz continued his enviably successful career as a man of letters. His further accomplishments included such verse translations from the classics, as the Roman Seneca's *The Trojan Women* (1625). He translated too from biblical sources; one finds the *Lamentations of Jeremiah* (1626), *The Song of Songs* (1627), and 10 Psalms of David and Judith (both 1635). He also translated the Scottish satirist John Barclay's treatise on ALLEGORY, *Argenis* (written 1621, Part I translated 1626, Part II, 1631). Other translations continued to follow throughout his life including a Roman Catholic tract and the Dutch scholar Hugo Grotius's *On the Truth of the Christian Religion*.

Opitz managed as well to write the libretto for the first opera in the German language (*Dafne*, 1627). He also penned the first German PASTORAL, *Schaefferey von der Nimpfen Hercinie* (1630). This charming poem fictively catalogues the poet's adventures on a country ramble with friends. In 1637

King Wladislaus IV of Poland appointed Opitz his court archivist in Danzig. In that capacity the prolific Opitz penned essays and notes about Polish history. During this period he also prepared volumes containing his spiritual and secular poems. Both of these appeared in 1638. The works discussed in this entry represent but do not exhaust the results of Opitz's industry.

Opitz's varied and highly successful literary career terminated abruptly in Danzig during an outbreak of the bubonic plague. He caught it and died in a few days. His works continued to appear posthumously within the five years after his death and intermittently since. Modern editions are available in German.

Bibliography

Becker-Cantarino, Barbara. "Martin Opitz." *German Baroque Writers, 1580–1660, Dictionary of Literary Biography.* Volume 164. Edited by James Hardin. Detroit, Mich.: Gale Research, 1996.

Ulmer, Bernhard. *Martin Opitz.* New York: Twayne Publishers, 1971.

oral tradition

Self-evidently, human language is far older than writing, and storytelling and singing must be almost as old as language itself. Language, in turn, is the principal identifying mark of the human species, so telling stories must be a very old practice indeed. Preliterate societies survived (and here and there still survive) in odd corners of the world as late as the 20th and 21st centuries. Their survival gave anthropologists, folkloreists, and others with professional interests in such matters the opportunity to study at firsthand what oral literary traditions were like before they became written.

One example of such an oral poetic culture survived among Yugoslavian shepherds into the mid-20th century, and the students of the poems those shepherds passed down through the generations discovered that the traditional works had much in common with the Homeric EPIC of ancient Greece. They displayed a high degree of metrical regularity, and they used set phrases to fill out lines where the singer's or the reciter's invention might mo-

mentarily fail—a phrase like "rosy-fingered dawn." The same and other common characteristics typify such early Germanic heroic epics as *Beowulf*, the *Niebelungenlied*, or the *Njalsaga*. There such phrases as "the swan-necked one" or "the foamy-necked one" were used elegantly both to signify a ship and to meet the metrical expectations of a line of verse. The students of such matters concluded that the Homeric poems and the Germanic heroic poems named above reflected transitional moments in the development of literature as it moved from the mouths of storytellers and singers (including poets) onto the pages of manuscripts. Those early epics carry many of the characteristics of preliterate poetic practice into the written literature of the cultures they represent.

Similar traditions emerged elsewhere in the world (or are descended at a great distance from very early common cultures). The peoples of POLYNESIAN OCEANIA, for instance, developed a rich and complex oral literature that was preserved from generation to generation by remarkable feats of rapid memorization. Examples of AFRICAN ORAL EPIC, though clearly infiltrated with elements of foreign print culture, still survive, as do examples of folk tales in India and among the indigenous peoples of North America.

Bibliography

Chadwick, H. Munro, and N. Kershaw Chadwick. *The Growth of Literature.* Vol. 3. 1940. Cambridge, U.K.: Cambridge University Press, 1986.

Orlando furioso Ludovico Ariosto (1532)

ARIOSTO spent more than half of his lifetime penning and polishing the verse CHIVALRIC EPIC that many consider the highest achievement of 16th-century Italian letters. The poet dedicated his poem to his overlord, Ippolito d' Este, the duke of Ferrara, drawing a genealogical connection between the Este family and Ruggiero, one of the heroes of the court of Emperor Charlemagne. Ruggiero, says Ariosto, founded the Este line.

"I sing," the vast poem begins, "of knights and ladies, of lovers and arms, of courtly chivalry . . . of courageous deeds." In the introduction to the story, Ariosto explains that Orlando (the Italian version of the name *Roland*) goes mad with his love for Angelica, a princess of Cathay. In a parenthetical compliment to his own mistress, Alexandra Benucci Strozzi, the widow of Tito Strozzi, Ariosto tells us that his love for her has driven the poet almost as mad as the titular hero of his epic.

The poem's beginning finds Emperor Charlemagne's forces camped near the Pyrenees Mountains. At war with the Moors of North Africa and Spain, Charlemagne plans to capture their leaders, the African, Agramant, and the Spanish Moor, Marsileus.

Meanwhile, having searched all over the world for his beloved Angelica, Orlando finds her and brings her to Charlemagne's camp. Also in love with the princess and also in camp is Orlando's cousin, Rinaldo, who fell in love with Angelica at first sight after drinking from the Fountain of Love. Angelica, for her part, finds Orlando distasteful and detests Rinaldo. He was the first man she encountered after drinking from the Fountain of Hate. To avoid conflict between the love-struck cousins, Charlemagne takes charge of Angelica, entrusting her care to Duke Namus of Bavaria.

The Moors attack, routing Charlemagne's Christian forces, and Angelica seizes the chance to flee, intending to make her way back to Cathay. Riding through the forest, she encounters the despised Rinaldo and tries to outdistance him. As she does so she meets a Moorish knight, Ferrau—another ardent admirer. The pursuing Rinaldo and Ferrau duel, and, as they fight over her, Angelica escapes again. Now, however, she encounters the knight Sacripant. He is an Oriental admirer of Angelica and has followed her from Cathay to France. A female knight, Bradamante, who is also Rinaldo's sister, challenges and defeats Sacripant, to whom Angelica has temporarily entrusted her safety.

The method of *Orlando furioso* is kaleidoscopic—one scene and set of its enormous cast of characters dissolves into the next in a series of incidents drawn from medieval and classical literature and from Ariosto's fertile imagination. At the same time the poem continues the epic, ORLANDO INNAMORATO, by Ariosto's predecessor at the Court of Ferrara, MATTEO MARIA BOIARDO.

In *Orlando furioso* a reader encounters, wonders that include a winged steed, the hippogriff, which carries off Bradamante's beloved Ruggiero only moments after she had freed him from the enchanted steel castle of the magician Atlantes. The reader then follows for a time the fortunes of Ruggiero, whom the hippogriff has carried off to an island ruled by two sisters. Alcina, an enchantress like Circe in Homer's *Odyssey,* who controls men through their passions, rules most of the island. Her sister, Logistilla, who represents rationality, rules a smaller but more pleasant and profitable part of the island. The island represents the human mind and its division into its larger passional and smaller rational parts.

Having learned to control the formerly unruly hippogriff, Ruggiero, though anxious to return to his beloved Bradamante, goes touring around the world on his MAGIC steed. This journey presents him with various opportunities, such as rescuing the chained Angelica from a monstrous Orc to which she was destined for sacrifice.

The scene sometimes shifts to follow the fortunes of Charlemagne in his efforts to vanquish the Moors. Sometimes it follows Ruggiero, who manages to fall into the clutches of Atlantes again. Actually trying to save Ruggiero from his predestined fate, Atlantes magically leads the knight to imagine himself in search of Bradamante. In fact, Ruggiero is trapped in a fantasy of inaction in another of Atlantes' enchanted castles.

At other times the story follows Angelica and the constant quarreling and fighting among her unwanted admirers. She chances, however, upon a wounded young Moorish soldier, Medoro. She nurses him back to health, and, in the course of his cure, she falls in love with him and plans to take him home with her to Cathay.

Leaving these lovers, Ariosto turns his attention to the adventures of the knight Astolpho, whom the reader first met back in Logistella's realm. She has provided Astolpho with a book that lets him overcome all magic. She also gives him a horn whose sound will turn to jelly the knees of his boldest potential adversaries.

Astolpho's book enables him to break the enchantments of Atlantes, who by this time has both

Ruggiero and Bradamante in his power. Set free, the pair agrees to marry as soon as Ruggiero accepts Christianity; but, a series of unexpected events separates the lovers again.

Chivalric romances of this sort and parodies of them enjoyed an enormous vogue in Renaissance Europe until CERVANTES's *DON QUIXOTE*'s brilliant SATIRE of them ended their popularity.

A summary account of this sort fails to convey the richness of Ariosto's invention, the wonderful musicality of his verse, or the delightful quality of his humor. A summary description also neglects the emotion that Ariosto is able to evoke in his readers by bringing them to care about his unlikely cast of characters.

A case in point appears in the sad death of Isabel, who remains faithful to her love, Zerbino. Rather than yield to the passion of another suitor, Rodomonte, Isabel tricks that ardent admirer into killing her. She pretends to be magically invulnerable to attack, and Rodomonte kills her when he tests her claim.

Readers might also marvel at the almost inexhaustible chain of difficulties with which Ariosto besets the love relationship of Ruggiero and Bradamante. They, however, finally overcome all obstacles.

As for the title character, owing to Astolpho's intervention, Orlando, raving mad for his unachievable love of Angelica, is ultimately restored to his right mind when Astolpho ties Orlando down and makes him inhale again his own lost good senses.

Bibliography

Ariosto, Ludovico. *Orlando Furioso.* Translated by Guido Waldman. Oxford: Oxford University Press, 1974.

———. *The Orlando Furioso.* Translated by William Stewart Rose. London and New York: G. Bell, 1892.

Orlando innamorato Matteo Maria Boiardo (1494)

Orlando innamorato, on which BOIARDO's literary reputation principally rests, first became wholly available in English only in 1989. Boiardo's work continues threads of the medieval *Chanson de Roland* that recounts the adventures and death of Charlemagne's nephew Roland. Roland (*Orlando* in Italian) commands the rear guard that, while protecting Charlemagne's retreating army, is utterly demolished by Saracen forces. Boiardo's continuation follows the practice of LUIGI PULCI's earlier work about the giant Morgante by telling Orlando's tale in rhymed octaves. Thereafter, that verse form became the norm for Italian verse romance and CHIVALRIC EPIC. So did an element of plot that had not characterized the medieval French versions. In the Italian versions, a Christian knight questing or crusading abroad in pagan lands regularly falls in love with a pagan heroine. He pursues her, they suffer many difficulties and undergo many adventures, and the knightly hero evangelizes his beloved's people.

The novelty of Boiardo's work rests on his assembling and intertwining elements from a variety of literatures, including Italian, French, Latin, and Greek, together with a broad spectrum of literary genres, including TRAGEDY, COMEDY, lyric poetry, short fiction, and history. Thus he is able to keep several stories moving forward as he advances from one plot or theme to another, holding his reader in suspense about the other strands.

The first of the poem's three books concerns the siege of Paris by the infidel Gradasso; the second a war waged over the hand of a beautiful pagan woman—Angelica; and the third an attack on the city of Paris by the combined pagan forces of Africa and Asia. Ruggiero, the ideal knight and a descendant of Hector of Troy, would, in the end, have defeated the pagans and, together with Angelica, founded the Este family line. Before, Boiardo could achieve that courtly compliment to his patrons and overlords, however, he died, leaving his masterwork incomplete. Its unfinished state served as an invitation to successors to rewrite the work, and many did so. Most notable among those who took up the challenge was Boiardo's successor to the patronage of the Este family, LUDOVICO ARIOSTO. The Venetian celebrity PIETRO ARETINO also penned a satirical continuation, the *Orlandino* (little Roland) that mocked Boiardo's poem. Many others in Italy either rewrote the work or continued it. It was well known throughout the European Renaissance, though in later years the burlesque version by Francesco Berni was better known than the original and sometimes confused with it. In Spain, MIGUEL DE CERVANTES DE SAAVEDRA knew it as did John Milton in England. Although the poem was clearly influential outside Italy in helping to spawn a spate of chivalric romances, its influence on specific authors is still much debated.

Bibliography

Boiardo, Matteo Maria. *Orlando Innamorato.* Translated by Charles S. Ross. Berkeley and Los Angeles: University of California Press, 1989.

Ovid (Publius Ovidius Naso) (43 B.C.E.–17 C.E.)

The most prolific of Roman poets, Ovid became enormously influential in the Renaissance. Most important for Renaissance authors, was the narrative stance that Ovid took in his love poems, his *Amores.* This was particularly true for the first of the authors, the Italian FRANCIS PETRARCH (Francesco Petrarca, 1304–74). Ovid's subject was his own experience of love, and when Petrarch sang the history of his inner life in the 366 poems of his *Songbook,* or *Canzoniere,* he emulated in his verses the autobiographical stance of Ovid for the first time in 1,200 years. The subsequent interiority of Euro-American lyric poetry from Petrarch's time until our own can be traced directly to that influence.

The Renaissance also felt Ovid's influence as a result of a series of love letters he imagined to have been written by the women of the heroic age to their beloveds, his Letters (*Epistolae*), also called his *Heroides.* Highly influential among Renaissance authors were Ovid's Arts of Loving (*Ars Amandi* or *Amatoria,* ca. 1 B.C.E.), his Remedy of Love (*Remedia amoris*), his *Metamorphoses,* his *Fasti,* and his Elegies (*Tristia*). English poet GEORGE GASCOIGNE, for example, adapted Ovid's narrative verse stanza to English in his *The Complainte of Philomene,* and SHAKESPEARE used it in his narrative poems *Venus and Adonis* and *The Rape of Lucrece.* The English playwright FRANCIS BEAUMONT may have written a long, erotic elaboration of Ovid's *Metamorphoses,* entitled *Salmacis and Hermaphroditus.* These examples only suggest the frequent and varied uses to which Renaissance authors throughout Europe put the work of this widely read, much emulated, and greatly respected classical model for Renaissance letters. Ovid was translated, imitated, and rewritten in new settings. His major attraction for Renaissance writers and thinkers arose from the importance that Ovid assigned to personal as opposed to typical experience.

P

Padumāvati, The   Malik Mohammad Jayisi (1540)

That a Muslim saint of the Sufi sect should have elected to master Sanskrit and early Hindi to tell in the latter language a 10th-century Hindu story familiar to virtually every practitioner of that faith suggests a spirit of greater religious toleration in 16th-century India than one perhaps finds there today. In any case, JAYISI'S story of Queen Padumāvati recounts the history of the queen of Chitor. It follows her biography from her birth on the Island of Ceylon (now Sri Lanka) through her love match with Rata Sena, the Rajput ruler of Chitor.

Then the story shifts its focus to the plotting of a Brahman named Rāghava, who wishes to make trouble between the followers of the Hindu pantheon and the faithful adherents of Allah. To achieve his purpose, Rāghava carries tales of the Rajput queen's beauty to the Sultan of Delhi, Emperor Alā-ud-Dīn Khilji. The Brahman's steamy descriptions of Padumāvati's charms so inflame the ardor of the emperor that he resolves to assault the previously invincible Rajput citadel of Chitor.

Jayisi's story details the military preparations of both Hindu and Muslim forces, describes the organization and discipline of the Muslim army, and celebrates the valor and gallantry of the Rajput soldiers as they try to resist Muslim conquest and protect the honor of their wives and daughters.

The poet builds suspense by describing first the capture of Ratna Sena, next his imprisonment in Delhi, and then his escape to Kambhalner. There, Ratna Sena is killed as a result of his host's treachery.

With Padumāvati now a widow and the Muslim forces victorious on the battlefield, the sultan marches to Chitor expecting to claim its queen as his bride. She, however, defeats his purposes by performing *suti*. Miraculously without suffering pain, she burns herself to death on the funeral pyre of her beloved husband. Arriving at the palace as conqueror, the sultan finds only the ashes of the woman who had been his obsession.

Displaying both the classical Muslim literary taste for ALLEGORY and the Sufi doctrine of the representation of Divine Love through human passion, Jayisi assimilates this ancient Hindu story to his contemporary Islamic milieu by turning Padumāvati's tragic story into an instance of the transfiguring power of human love as both a reflection of and a road toward divinity. He clearly approves her sacrifice, having his narrator remark that a person like Padumāvati dies happy since, although the flower perishes, the fragrance lingers forever.

Although modern Hindi editions of Jayisi's *The Padumāvati* exist, the only English version seems to have been a provisional translation by the celebrated G. A. Grierson.

Bibliography

Jayisi, Malik Mohammad. *The Padumawati* [sic] *of Malik Muhammad Jaisi*. Edited and translated by G. A. Grierson and Sudhākara Dvivedi. Calcutta: Asiatic Society, 1911.

———. *The Padumāvati of Malik Mohammad Jaisi* [Hindi]. Edited by Surya Kanta Shastri. Lahore: University of the Punjab, 1934.

Palladius, Peder (Peter Plade)
(1503–1560)

A Danish Protestant clergyman, moralist, and diarist, Peder Palladius rose to become the bishop of Zeeland and a professor of theology at the University of Copenhagen. During his lifetime he wrote several moral tracts. One of them, written in Danish, treated the subject of drunkenness. He also wrote in Latin, and a religious treatise in that language on the subject of penitence and justification by faith appeared in 1559. In 1598 Edward Vaughn translated from Latin into English Palladius's work, *An Introduction into the Books of the Prophets and Apostles*.

Perhaps the most interesting literary remnant of Palladius is a daybook he kept describing the calls he made while performing his duties as a pastor in visiting his parishioners. This work lay neglected in manuscript until the mid-19th century when it was discovered and published (*Visitatsbog*, 1867). It has since been translated into French and provides lively pictures of 16th-century life and government in Denmark. The work is not available in English as yet.

Pantagruel and Gargantua François
Rabelais (1532 and 1535)

Although modern editions of RABELAIS's comic masterpiece print the story of the giant Gargantua first and of his giant son Pantagruel second, that order was reversed when Rabelais first wrote and published the works.

Ostensibly written by a deceased author, Master Alcofribas Nasier—an anagram of François Rabelais—the work was inspired in part by tales of giants in LUIGI PULCI's MORGANTE. Rabelais seems also to have been inspired by the financial success of an anonymous work about giants, including one named Gargantua. In any case, Alcofribas becomes Rabelais's narrative persona in the work—a comic mask that the author, who was both a clergyman and a physician, could wear as he romped through his sprawling, lusty, hilariously irreverent and delightfully tasteless tale. Two years later he wrote—perhaps invented—a prequel that traces the history of Pantagruel's colossal father, Gargantua. It is well to note, however, that these giants are not always giants, and, when they are, they don't always stay the same size. Like characters in the Chinese novel THE JOURNEY TO THE WEST, Pantagruel and Gargantua are also shape shifters whose size varies with the tasks they undertake.

Perhaps in beginning with the son and following with the father, Rabelais also looked back to the classical EPIC, which, like Homer's *Odyssey*, began in the middle of things with a portion of the history of the son, Telemachus, before treating the history and adventures of Odysseus, the father. If so, subsequent editors have undermined Rabelais's original vision. In any case, *Pantagruel* begins with the birth of the title character and the simultaneous death of his mother, Badebec. It traces Gargantua's alternate grief at his wife's death and his joy and pleasure in his newborn, monstrous son, who nursed on the milk of 4,600 cows at each meal. Then a reader follows Gargantua from his destruction of his too confining cradle, through his playtime activities, to his education at Poitiers and other schools and universities in France, his early educational travels, and his responses to other students.

In the sixth chapter Rabelais satirizes those Frenchmen who Latinized their language by introducing the French equivalents of INKHORN TERMS—words whose meanings can, with effort, be rooted out but that have no standing in either of the languages from which the terms are cobbled together. In the following chapter Pantagruel comes to Paris where he visits the Library of Saint-

Victor. In it Rabelais lists for his readers several pages of titles of the trivial books he finds there. Nonetheless his desire to profit from his studies is reinforced by a sensible and heartfelt letter from Gargantua encouraging him to learn. As a result, his mind among his books became "like fire amid the heather."

Pantagruel next meets the character who will become his constant companion and tutor, Panurge. Only after exhausting a store of modern and classical, European and Middle Eastern tongues—not a word of which Pantagruel can follow—does Panurge confess that French is his native tongue. In the next several chapters, Pantagruel reveals his wisdom by settling a dispute between Lords Kissass and Shitniff. He reconciles the disputants by rendering a verdict no word of which either can understand. They accept it and depart good friends.

Panurge then recounts his escape from the Turks and presents a novel plan for rebuilding the walls of Paris from women's undergarments. Rabelais often attributes to Panurge tales of an extremely bawdy and scatological nature, like that of the lion, the fox, and the old woman in chapter 15. The author then devotes chapters 16 and 17 to a detailed description of Panurge, his behavior, and his disposition. Essentially, the reader discovers that Panurge behaves like a brilliant but antisocial practical joker. He enjoys an ingenious jest at the expense of others, and he appears never to pity his victims.

The next three chapters are devoted to exchanges between Pantagruel and Panurge, on the one hand, and, on the other, to those between both of them and an English scholar who has heard of Pantagruel's encyclopedic learning and has come to debate him. After introductory pedantic sallies, the scholar and Panurge perform a debate without language, using only ingenious but incomprehensible sign language. At the end of this unusual debate, the scholar declares Panurge the indubitable winner. He is less successful, however, in his straightforward efforts to seduce a Parisian lady in the next two chapters. Eventually her screams drive him away and he leaves cursing her. Seeking revenge, he smears on the lady's clothing in church on the following Sunday a mixture that attracts every male dog in Paris to try to mount her.

This collection of bawdy adventures complete, Pantagruel learns in chapter 23 that his father, Gargantua, has been magically transported to Fairyland. As a result the Dipsodes (the thirsty ones or the drunkards), who had been held in check by their fear of Gargantua, seize the opportunity to invade the land of the Amaurots. With his companions, Pantagruel sets out to confront his father's enemies. A sea voyage leads to a confrontation with 660 knights whom Panurge defeats almost single-handedly with a trick involving nooses and gunpowder.

Among the marvels that follow, Pantagruel's farts turn into 53,000 little male dwarfs and his "fizzles" into the same number of little women. He marries them to each other and gives them an island to live on where they prospered and multiplied. Then Panurge demonstrates a tactic for vanquishing the Dipsodes.

That tactic was to send a drug by a captive. One tried it, and it made him so thirsty he was able to drink an enormous amount. Impressed, the others tried it with the same effect. All the Dipsodes got so drunk that they were unable to defend themselves the next day against Pantagruel's attack as they were still sleeping off their inebriation. Finding them asleep with their mouths open, Pantagruel sprinkled salt down all their throats, incapacitating his enemies further. Then, feeling the necessity for making water, Pantagruel urinated so copiously that he drowned all his enemies and created a flood for 10 leagues around.

The Dipsodes' reserves, however, included a company of giants under the command of Captain Werewolf—a giant approximately the size of Pantagruel. They engage in single combat, which of course Pantagruel wins. The other 300 giants rally to the attack, but Pantagruel, using the body of the now defunct Werewolf as a weapon, neatly dispatches all 300.

Surveying the carnage, Pantagruel and his party find all their enemies dead, and all their companions safe except for Epistémon. He is lying decapitated with his head cradled in his arms. Panurge, however, assures the party that he can restore Epistémon, and he keeps the head warm in his codpiece until he can fit the head precisely to the body, sew it in place, and apply a medicine that brings Epistémon back to life.

Thus far, Pantagruel and his company have been engaged in driving the Dipsodes out of lands they had conquered. In the last three chapters, he and his companions invade their land, and everyone surrenders right away and swells the number of Pantagruel's soldiers. As the army marches along a sudden rainstorm engulfs them. Pantagruel, at the moment taller than the rain clouds, assures everyone it will soon pass, orders them to close up ranks, and sticks out his tongue to cover the army like an umbrella.

The ostensible author of the story, Alcofribas Nasier, assures the readers that while the tongue was out, he took the opportunity to have a look around inside Pantagruel's mouth and discovered a whole country within, complete with the populous cities of Larynx and Pharynx, whose citizens were dying of the plague. On issuing from Pantagruel's mouth, Alcofribas attracts Pantagruel's attention and learns that he has been gone six months during which time Pantagruel has become king of the Dipsodes. He rewards Alcofribas with a castle.

The Very Horrific Life of the Great Gargantua Father of Pantagruel followed three years later. Still in the guise of Alcofribas, Rabelais refers the reader to Pantagruel's genealogy for an understanding of how giants came into the world. He then digresses with a translation of the remnants of an ostensibly Etruscan treatise inscribed on elm bark, *The Antidoted Frigglefraggles*. Chapter 3 reports how Gargantua gestated for a period of 11 months in his mother Gargamelle's womb, and the next three chapters detail the events leading up to his remarkable birth from his mother's left ear. On arriving in the world, Gargantua first cried and then called for a drink. The following chapters discuss Gargantua's naming, his clothing, his livery and colors, and his childhood, including his hobbyhorses. The totally scatological chapter 13 devotes itself to the way Gargantua's father, Grandgousier, discovered Gargantua's intellectual capacities.

Several chapters next recount the details of Gargantua's education, the way he took the great bells from the Cathedral of Notre-Dame du Paris as bridle jinglers for his horse, and the bells' subsequent recovery. The reader learns how Gargantua came under the tutelage of Ponocrates, who taught him discipline.

In all of this, despite his earthy humor, Rabelais essentially follows the classical format for the development of an EPIC hero. Just as Pantagruel faced the Dipsodes, therefore, Gargantua too must confront and overcome his enemies. These appear when Picrohole, the king of Lerné, and his minions first mount a surprise attack on Gargantua's shepherds, and then follow that with assaults on Grandgousier's people and eventually, on the ill advice of his military advisers and intelligence operatives, with a grand design for the conquest of the world.

Grandgousier calls on Gargantua for assistance, and with his companions, Ponocrates, Gymnaste, and Eudémon, Gargantua rides to the rescue. After individual combats, battles, and digressions Gargantua and his supporters defeat the minions of Picrohole, and Gargantua distributes rewards all around to those who have supported him. His supporters include a monk, and, when Gargantua offers to make him abbot of an existing monastery, the monk proposes that instead Gargantua construct for him a new abbey on principles opposite to those on which abbeys have traditionally been founded. Gargantua agrees to this plan, and chapters 52 through 57 contain some of the most serious and famous passages in Rabelais's work. They describe the Abbey of Thélème. In many respects the principles on which the abbey is founded anticipate precisely the de facto situation at coeducational, secular colleges and universities found in the West in the 21st century. For Rabelais, however, Thélème represented the principles and ideals of the new HUMANIST EDUCATION as against those of the old, medieval notions of SCHOLASTICISM.

The buildings of the abbey are magnificent, the libraries well stocked, and activities proceed on self-selected schedules. The men and women who study and live in the abbey are all good-looking and good-natured. Unlike other religious orders, the members can come and go as they see fit. They can marry or not as they choose. They can possess worldly goods. Chapter 54 contains the list, posted above the abbey's gates, of the sorts of people who are not welcome in the abbey and a list as well of the sort who are. The latter include the beautiful people and the well to do, but especially the merry regardless of social class. Only one rule governs the lives of Thélème's inhabitants: Do What You Will. That rule, however, optimistically presupposes that well-born and well-bred free people who are accustomed to honorable companions and behavior will always be moved to virtue rather than to vice.

Gargantua ends with a prophetic riddle that Gargantua interprets as a call to religious fervor, but that the monk interprets as a description of a tennis game. Rabelais constructs and deconstructs the riddle's moral in juxtaposed speeches.

Bibliography
Rabelais, François. *The Complete Works of François Rabelais.* Translated by Donald M. Frame. Berkeley: University of California Press, 1991.

———. *Gargantua and Pantagruel.* New York: Alfred A. Knopf, 1994.

Paradise Lost John Milton (1667)

An EPIC poem on the theme of the history of the universe as figured in the BIBLE and in associated myth and legend, *Paradise Lost,* like all classical epics, begins with an invocation of the MUSE and the poet's prayer for inspiration. The muse whom MILTON addresses, however, is not one of the nine who inhabited Mount Parnassus in classical myth. Rather, Milton's muse is the Holy Spirit, who was present before the beginning of time as one of the three personalities of Godhead. Milton prays for support as he attempts his high purpose to "assert Eternal Providence/ And justify the ways of God to men."

Milton asks the muse who caused Adam and Eve to sin. "Th' infernal Serpent," comes the answer, and after a very brief account of Lucifer's rebellion against God in Heaven, Milton leads his reader to fall with Satan and his crew to Hell, whose horror Milton describes in terms both concrete and abstract, like "darkness visible" and "floods and whirlwinds of . . . fire."

Once in Hell the principal fallen angels hold a council to consider how they may best continue their attempt to battle against God. Although their circumstances are pitiable and their cause foredoomed, their rhetoric is puffed up with HUBRIS. They imagine that the outcome of their battle against God's omnipotent power was "dubious," and that they "shook" God's throne. In their discussion of God's purposes, they accidentally hit upon what God has in mind for them—to do God's work unwillingly and, as they strive to defeat God's purposes, to heap upon their own heads further punishment and frustration. At that point, ironically, they fail or pretend to fail to recognize the truth of that possibility.

Unlike Heaven, which is a benign monarchy, Hell is a nominal democracy. In its councils, however, only Satan's voice really counts. He has heard of a new creation and its principal inhabitants who are just a little below angels in their capacities. These new creatures are destined after a period of testing to occupy the heavenly places vacated by the fallen angels. At Satan's suggestion the devilish council agrees to make subverting these beings their first priority. Satan volunteers to go look for them, and all the others cheer him on.

Milton conceives of angelic glory in terms of intellectual capacity. An observant reader will notice that Satan's thinking is increasingly flawed as the epic proceeds. "The mind is its own place," he says, "and in itself / Can make a Heaven of Hell, a Hell of Heaven (I, 255)." Later on, however, the archfiend realizes that wherever he goes he carries Hell inside himself.

Satan flies through the vast reaches of Hell and eventually arrives at its closed gates. Guarding them he finds two horrible creatures. The first is Sin, who is a lovely woman above her waist but serpentine below and who hourly gives birth to hellhounds that kennel in her womb and gnaw her innards. The other is Death, a shadowy phantasm who is Sin's firstborn child and the forcible father of the hellhounds. Satan is appalled by the appearance of the two, and Death strides forward to do battle with him. Sin, however, intervenes, addressing Satan as "father." The reader then learns that Sin sprang fully armed from the left (the sinister) side of Satan's head at the instant he decided to rebel against God. Moreover, seeing his own image in his daughter, Satan fell in love with her and, coupling with her, produced Death, their firstborn son.

Satan negotiates with the monstrous pair, promising them prey and food if he is successful in his mission. They agree to open Hell's gate for him, and Satan flies off through chaos in search of Earth. Sin and Death follow, building a long, broad bridge from Hell to Earth. Satan's way is not easy. He makes an ally of a personified Chaos who points the way to Earth and the solar system, which God has recently carved from Chaos's dominions.

At the beginning of Book III, Milton interrupts his epic to speak in his own voice in a celebrated address (also called an *apostrophe*) to light. "Hail holy Light," he says, and compares himself with predecessor blind poets, regretting the loss of his sight, but calling on light to shine within him so that he may recount "things invisible to mortal sight."

The scene then shifts to Heaven where God and Christ in heavenly council work out mankind's salvation and the role of the paradoxically fortunate fall in that plan. When Satan arrives at the edge of the solar system, he has just enough residual glory left to disguise himself as a cherub—the lowest order of angel. Pretending to be a heavenly sightseer, the fiend inquires his way to Earth from Uriel, the guardian angel of the solar system. Unable to penetrate Satan's hypocritical disguise, Uriel directs him.

Landing on Mount Niphates, Satan in Book IV looks over the world, the Garden of Eden, and the sun. Thinking himself alone, he gives vent to his true feelings. As he does so his glory fades. The DEADLY SINS of ire, envy, and despair appear in his countenance, and the watchful Uriel penetrates his disguise and warns the angel Gabriel, the guardian angel of Paradise. On first glimpsing Adam and Eve in their natural bliss, Satan is overwhelmed by sexual jealousy. He overhears Eve report her recollections of her dawning of self-consciousness. Milton borrows the story of Narcissus for this episode. As soon as she becomes aware of herself, Eve looks into a pool. There she is surprised by her reflection and she starts away. The reflection also does. She and the reflection both come again and as she looks at it lovingly in the pool, the reflection answers with looks of the same sort. A voice tells her that she is seeing herself and that another being is her destined mate—though Eve thinks Adam is less fair and mild than the image that she saw.

Satan decides that Adam might prove to be too strong an adversary for him and resolves to tempt Eve by guile. That night while Adam and Eve sleep, Satan squats like a toad at her ear, sending her tempting dreams. Guardian angels, warned of his presence, discover him there and drive him away.

In Books V and VI God sends the archangel Raphael to give Adam a lesson in universal history and to warn him of the danger Satan poses. Milton follows classical epic tradition in returning to the beginning and detailing the events that led to the current situation. The battle in Heaven is now described in full. Satan, we learn, invented artillery for his assault on Heaven, which continued for three days until God sent his son Messiah to defeat Satan and his host. Book VII continues Adam's education with Raphael's account of God's creation of the world. Adam's curiosity is still not satisfied, and in Book VIII he gets an astronomy lesson. Raphael finally admonishes Adam that natural history is not his principal concern. People should concern themselves with understanding God's will for them and fulfilling it.

Adam then discourses about the dawn of his self-awareness, his first divinely conducted tour of Paradise, and the admonition to eat freely of every tree except the one whose fruit, if eaten, would confer knowledge of the difference between good and evil. Eating that fruit, Adam learns, will result in loss of Paradise and eventual death. Adam next describes the creation of Eve from his rib and the joy he felt at wooing and winning her.

Book IX elaborates the biblical account of the fall. Satan occupies the serpent while it sleeps. Eve proposes to Adam that the two of them work separately around the garden so they can accomplish more. Adam objects, citing the danger against which they have been forewarned. Eve, however, prevails and goes off on her own. Finding her alone, a phallic and resplendent serpent rises before her and addresses her with flattery, surprising her by having gained the power of speech. Milton has the serpent string together several series of sibilant *s* sounds so that a subtextual hiss runs through Satan's discourse.

Satan appeals to Eve's narcissism by arguing that if eating the fruit can empower a dumb animal with speech and reason, it should confer God-like capacities on human beings. Eve is suspicious of the serpent's reason since she recognizes his flattery. She clearly chaffs, however, at the hierarchical organization of the world that makes Adam her intellectual superior and director. Though she cites God's prohibition against eating the fruit, eventually she yields to the serpent's blandishments. She eats the fruit. "Earth felt the wound," Milton says, and nature began to show signs that decay and death had entered the world.

The effects of the fruit are like those of wine. Though Eve thinks the outcomes have been beneficent, she nonetheless cannot bear the idea that she might die and an immortal Adam take another mate. She resolves to tempt Adam to join her. Adam understands the consequences of what she has done and what will happen if he joins her, but he loves her so much that he cannot bear the thought of life without her. He voluntarily eats as well. Whereas Eve falls through self-love—a form of the deadliest of the SEVEN DEADLY SINS, pride—Adam falls through uxory—too much love for one's wife.

Not surprisingly, Milton's male chauvinism throughout *Paradise Lost* draws the regular disapproval of critics sympathetic to the causes of women. The unbending and patronizing patriarchy that *Paradise Lost* espouses underscores the objections of feminist critics to the operation of a male dominated world. Why, to cite one instance, did the angel educate only Adam? Why not Eve as well?

In any case, in Book X the predicted punishments follow from the disobedience of the primordial pair. Both will die. He is doomed to earn his bread by the sweat of his labor. She will experience pain in childbirth. Both are driven from the Garden of Eden. The serpent will forever crawl in the dust. Satan in the meantime flies triumphantly back to Hell—his journey this time made easy by the highway Sin and Death have built. When he arrives at the city of Pandemonium, which the other fallen angels have constructed in his absence, his legions prepare to cheer his triumph. At the moment of their shout all are turned instead to serpents and their cheer comes out as a universal hiss.

Christ in Heaven in Book XI intervenes on repentant humankind's behalf and offers to suffer

death himself to redeem them. God accepts, but implements the punishments. He mitigates them somewhat, however, by having the archangel Michael take Adam to a high hill and reveal the biblical future to him until the time of Noah's flood. The vision of the future continues in Book XII. It includes Christ's birth, death, and resurrection, the foundation and growth of the church, and the second coming and last judgment. Adam is comforted by what he learns, and the epic ends with Adam and Eve, hand in hand, slowly making their way out of the Garden of Eden.

Bibliography
Milton, John. *Complete Poems and Major Prose: John Milton.* Edited by Merritt Y. Hughes. 1957. Reprint, Indianapolis, Ind.: Hackett Publications, 2003.
———. *John Milton: The Major Works.* Edited by Stephen Orgel and Jonathan Goldberg. Oxford: Oxford University Press, 2003.
———. *Paradise Lost and Other Poems.* Edited by Edward M. Cifelli and Edward Le Comte. New York: Signet Classic, ca. 2003.

pastoral poetry and drama

The pastoral poetry of the Renaissance looked back through classical Rome to ancient Sicily for its roots. Around 280 B.C.E. a Greek poet, Theocritus, took the simple songs of shepherds and developed from them three sorts of poems that have proved very influential throughout the following ages. The most imitated sort of poem that Theocritus initiated was the ELEGY or lament. JOHN MILTON's poem "Lycidas" (1637) displays all the conventions that Theocritus established for the pastoral elegy. In a rural landscape, a grieving poet invokes the MUSES, and all nature joins in the general sorrow. Grief leads to a despairing questioning of the processes of nature. Mourners file past the poet's view, and these include aspects of personified nature like rivers. The mourners lay flowers on the bier of the deceased—imagined in Milton's case since the friend he commemorates, Edward King, was lost at sea. The flowers all have symbolic significance and stand for aspects of sorrow, hope, immortality, and the abilities of the deceased. At length the elegy closes with a consoling thought and a recommitment of the living to the tasks that confront them.

A second sort of Theocritan pastoral less widely emulated was a singing match among shepherds. The contest was supposed to settle their not-very-serious disagreements about who was most in love or whose girlfriend was prettiest. The judge was seldom able to reach a decision about whose songs were best. Elements of this sort of pastoral appear in EDMUND SPENSER's *The Shepherd's Calendar* (1579).

The third pastoral mode that Theocritus popularized was the pastoral lyric, ostensibly written by a shepherd, which celebrates his mistress's charms and bemoans her neglect. This form of pastoral poem became very popular in the Renaissance. As it developed, a third party often narrated the poem and commented on the shepherd's sorrowful condition. Several of the lyric poems of the Italian ISABELLA ANDREINI adopt this device.

The Renaissance found some new uses for the material of pastorals, first with the introduction of the pastoral romance—a fairly extended story told in verse and in prose, most of whose action takes place in pastoral settings and whose pages are peopled by shepherds and lords and ladies playing at being shepherds. The Neapolitan poet JACOPO SANNAZARO began the vogue for the pastoral romance with his *Arcadia* (1504). His example was followed in Portugal with Jorge de Montemayor's unfinished work *Diana* (written in Spanish, published 1558), in France with HONORÉ D' URFÉ's *Astrée* (1610), and in England with SIR PHILIP SIDNEY's *ARCADIA* (1590). IZAAK WALTON's *THE COMPLEAT ANGLER* (1653) belongs to an offshoot of the genre—the piscatory pastoral.

What some have characterized as Italy's most original contribution to Renaissance theater, the short-lived genre of pastoral drama, also developed in the 16th century. Representatives of this sort of play include TORQUATO TASSO's *AMINTA* (1573), GIOVANNI BATTISTA GUARINI's *THE FAITHFUL SHEPHERD* (*Il Pastor Fido,* 1590) that George Frederick Handel turned into an opera, and ISABELLA ANDREINI's *La Mirtilla,* 1588. An English example appears in JOHN FLETCHER's *Faithful*

Shepherdess (1602), and certain elements of the type turn up in WILLIAM SHAKESPEARE's *As You Like It* and his late DARK COMEDY.

Bibliography

Andreini, Isabella. *La Mirtilla: A Pastoral.* Translated by Julie D. Campbell. Tempe, Ariz.: Arizona Center for Medieval and Renaissance Studies, 2002.

Doelman, James, ed. *Early Stuart Pastoral.* Toronto: Centre for Reformation and Renaissance Studies, 1999.

Hubbard, Thomas K. *The Pipes of Pan: Intertextuality and Literary Filiation in the Pastoral Tradition from Theocritus to Milton.* Ann Arbor: University of Michigan Press, 1999.

Paternal Tyranny Arcangela Tarabotti (written ca. 1621, published 1654)

Forced by her father to enter the Benedictine convent of Santa Anna against her will and without a religious vocation, TARABOTTI struck out against the patriarchy of the Republic of Venice whose laws made possible the unwilling, lifetime incarceration of unwanted or potentially expensive daughters behind convent walls. Venice, she wrote, was a republic that took pride in the political liberties that it accorded its citizens and even its foreign residents, but a republic that nonetheless deprived many of its daughters of their freedom.

She decries important, antifeminist texts of her time that lent support to such practices and on the basis of Scripture and other authoritative religious works, she brought evidence to bear that attested to the God-given equality of women.

Bibliography

Tarabotti, Arcangela. *Paternal Tyranny.* Edited and translated by Letizia Panizza. Chicago: University of Chicago Press, 2003.

patronage

Before a royalty system made it possible for some writers to support themselves with their pens, many authors found it necessary to depend on the support of wealthy persons, who were often members of the aristocracy, in order to pursue their literary craft. ARIOSTO and BOIARDO in Italy, for instance, enjoyed the patronage of the Este family, the dukes of Ferrarra. The relationship between patron and poet or writer often implied that writers would take some pains to sing the praises of their employers. Both the Italian poets named in the last sentence certainly fulfilled that part of the bargain.

Many members of the MEDICI family of Florence helped support not only writers but also artists and scholars. In England, BEN JONSON for a time enjoyed the patronage of the royal Stuart family and an appointment to write COURT ENTERTAINMENTS. Although royalties have made freedom from patronage possible for writers who appeal to popular tastes, those whose works are important but unlikely to achieve commercial success still have access to a form of patronage that has been institutionalized and is managed by organizations like foundations or the various National Endowments or academies and universities.

Peach Blossom Fan, The   Kong Shangren
(1689)

In this long (40 acts) and famous play Kong SHANGREN interweaves a love story (the main plot) with a series of historical incidents that examine the reasons for the fall of the Ming dynasty (1644) and the subsequent ascendancy of the Qing (Ch'ing) or Manchu dynasty (1644–1912) in China.

Like most CHINESE DRAMA, this play is largely written in rhyming verse, and the actors sing much of the verse to traditional tunes. Ever a perfectionist, Kong submitted his play to the scrutiny of experts who evaluated both the play's factual material and its conformity to musical tradition. The author revised his play significantly over a decade before he judged it ready for public performance.

The love story follows the affair between a courtesan, Li Shiang-chün, and a student, Hou Fang-yü. Both are politically active and deplore the corruption among the officials who administer the affairs of the Ming dynasty. Hou Fang-yü's political loyalties, however, are tied less to principle than they are to his pocketbook. He agrees to join the faction of a certain official, Juan Ta-Ch'eng, when Juan offers to provide him with the money to marry Li. She, however, proves unwilling to compromise her principles in this way, and Hou Fang-yü despairs.

Later, another suitor, T'ien Yang, a Ming official, ardently pursues Li Shiang-chün. Again she refuses to marry, even resisting T'ien's attempt to kidnap her from the bordello in which she works. In this attempt, Li receives serious wounds, spattering a fan with her blood. Later on an artist who carries messages between the two lovers turns the blood spots on the fan into the peach blossom decoration that gives the play its name.

Li becomes a supporter of the triumphant Qing dynasty while Hou continues to cooperate with an increasingly hopeless Ming insurgency. Despite their differing political allegiances the lovers manage a last fleeting tryst at a Buddhist monastery, but the ongoing political turmoil destroys any hope of marriage the pair might still entertain. Here the playwright makes a major departure from preceding dramatic tradition. Any of his predecessors would have had the lovers live happily together ever after. Instead, in *The Peach Blossom Fan*, both young people enter religious vocations and altogether reject the world.

While all this is going forward, the historical scenes—every one of which is dated—scrupulously follow the events that rendered the fall of the Ming dynasty unavoidable. Kong Shangren uses the actual names of the participants in the debacle, sparing no one and exposing the corruption in Nanking that undermined all efforts to resist the foreign Mongolian invasion that established the Qing dynasty.

The Peach Blossom Fan is one of the world's great historical dramas, and, although modern audiences seldom have the patience to see all of it, parts of it are frequently still performed.

Bibliography

Kong Shangren. *The Peach Blossom Fan* (*T'ao-hua-shan*). Translated by Chen Shih-hsiang and Harold Acton. Berkeley: University of California Press, ca. 1976.

Pedersen, Christiern (1480–1554)

A chronicler, theologian, translator, lexicographer, and poet-psalmodist, Christiern Pedersen is considered by many to be the father of Danish literature. Pedersen studied for the Roman Catholic priesthood in Paris, where he published a Danish-Latin dictionary containing some 13,000 entries (1510). Also in Paris he published a Psalter, the *Missale Lundense* (The Lund missal), which has often been reprinted.

After Pedersen's return to Denmark, Lutheranism officially became the state religion, and Pedersen converted. He turned his attention to translating the Bible into Danish, completing the New Testament in 1529 and the Old Testament in 1543. Among his religious writings he also published a number of commentaries on the writings of Martin Luther, a collection of sermons for the winter and another for the summer, a collection of the Psalms of David, a missal in Danish, and books concerning the Mass. In the 16th century, the Scotsman John Gau included translations from Pedersen's sermons among the texts in a Scots-English work entitled *The Richt vay to the Kingdom of Heuine.*

Secular letters also occupied Pedersen's attention. He translated Saxo Grammaticus's (ca. 1150–ca. 1220) huge Latin chronicle of the history of the Danish kings—both mythic and historical—into the Danish language and brought it up to date. He also translated the 12th century French CHIVALRIC ROMANCE *Ogier danois* (Olger the Dane), rendering it into Danish as *Kong Olger Danskes Kronike* (The history of King Olger the Dane, ca. 1530). King Olger had been the Danish retainer among the heroic knights of Emperor Charlemagne. Pedersen was interested in not only his parishioner's spiritual and intellectual well-being but also their physical health. He published a little manual of medicine in Malmö in 1533.

The Lund missal is available in Denmark in a facsimile edition, as is Pedersen's Latin-Danish dictionary. His complete Danish works last appeared in the mid-19th century (1850–56.)

Bibliography

Pedersen, Christiern. *Missale lundense av år 1514.* Malmö, Sweden: J. Kroon, 1946.

———. *Vocabularium ad usum dacorum. . . .* [Latin-Danish dictionary.] Edited by Inger Bom and Niels Haastrup. Copenhagen: Akademisk Forlag, Eksp.: 1973.

Pembroke, Mary Herbert, countess of (Mary Sidney) (1561–1621)

A member of a respected English noble family and a distinguished English literary coterie, Mary Sidney Herbert became a generous patron of poets whose work she admired. These included BEN JONSON, EDMUND SPENSER, SAMUEL DANIEL, and others. A sister to SIR PHILIP SIDNEY, Mary Herbert became her brother's editor and literary executor on his death in 1586. Sir Philip had left unfinished a translation of the Psalms into English verse, so his sister took up where he left off and completed the work. Some 44 of the versions were Sir Philip's and the remaining 128 his sister's. A critical consensus agrees with Grossart, an early editor of Sir Philip Sidney's work, that Mary Herbert's translations stand "infinitely in advance of her brother's in thought, epithet and melody." Because they were slated for private devotion rather than congregational singing, Mary Herbert's versions of the Psalms catch more of their potential for ALLEGORY and interpretation, and they employ more sophisticated metrical and rhyming patterns in support of their intellectual and emotional content. They are, in short, brilliantly done.

Herbert translated from the French Phillipe de Mornay's *A Discourse of Life and Death.* Her choice of this work may have rested in part on her brother's association with Mornay. The translation may have helped her work through her multiple griefs as well. She had lost her daughter Katherine in 1584, and her mother died the same year as her brother. The work combines Calvinist Protestantism with HUMANIST stoicism in the face of the world's accidents and impermanence. With that discourse she also published in 1592 her blank verse version of Robert Garnier's tragedy, *Antonius.* Later (1595) the tragedy appeared alone as *The Tragedy of Antony.* One of the poets who benefited from her patronage, Samuel Daniel, wrote a companion tragedy, *Cleopatra,* in 1593. In bringing these tragedies before the English public, Herbert and Daniel and another member of their circle, FULKE GREVILLE, sought to model for playgoers a *proper* sort of classical tragedy. Herbert's verse translation displays her mastery of English versification and the benefits of blank verse for theatrical presentation.

When Edmund Spenser published his *Astrophel* in 1595—a work honoring Sir Philip Sidney—Herbert prefaced the edition with her own pastoral ELEGY on the death of her brother: "The Doleful Lay of Clorinda."

Mary Herbert's was an early and important female voice on the English publishing scene, not only because of her talent but also because, as one of the most respected and admired women in the kingdom, her example opened doors for the women of talent who followed her.

Bibliography

Herbert, Mary, trans. *The Tragedy of Antonie.* In *Three Tragedies by Renaissance Women.* Edited by Diane Purkiss. Harmondsworth, U.K.: Penguin Books, 1998.

Rathmell, J. C. A., ed. *The Psalms of Sir Philip Sidney and the Countess of Pembroke.* New York: New York University Press, 1963.

Waller, Gary, Betty Travitsky, and Patrick Cullen, eds. *Mary Sidney Herbert.* Volume 6 in *The Early Modern Englishwoman: A Facsimile Library of Essential Works.* Aldershot, U.K.: Scolar Press, 1996.

Peony Pavilion, The Tang Xianzu (1598)

Considered by many the greatest Chinese play ever written, *The Peony Pavilion* reworks the central incident of an earlier fantasy tale about a deceased young woman's resurrection for love into a drama of epic proportions. Its central theme celebrates the power of passion to ennoble human existence and overcome seemingly insurmountable obstacles. The devotion of Ming dynasty poets to this idea was a defining feature not only of this play but also of the epoch it represented.

TANG skillfully interweaves into his 55 scene play several central plot lines. The main one concerns a maiden, Bridal Du, who dreams of a young scholar and falls in love with the man in her dream. Love-struck, she pines away and dies. The scholar, Liu Mengmei, whose name is composed of elements meaning *willow* and *apricot*, has had a similar dream about Bridal Du. His life, however, is focused on competing in national examinations, being first in them, being named Prize Scholar, and achieving high office. That quest contributes another plot line.

A third line traces the rise of Bridal Du's father, Du Bao, from his post as a district governor to a military commissioner whose responsibilities run from saving a city besieged by an outlaw prince in the service of the Mongols to his becoming the chief minister of the Chinese empire. Still another line concerns the outlaw prince, Li Quan, and his Amazon-like wife Lady Li. The play traces their joint development of military strategy, the dangers of playing a double game, Du Bao's successful tactic of offering the outlaws high office and rewards to switch sides, and the Lis' prudent decision to go to sea as pirates rather than risk the emperor's wrath because of their initial treachery.

Bridal Du's death and resurrection provides this elaborate structure's central support. Realizing that she is dying for love of a man who carried her off by force in her dream but who in reality may not even exist, she paints her own portrait and asks that it be placed near her grave. When she dies, her father establishes an Apricot Shrine and grants her wish to be buried beneath an apricot tree in its garden. Du Bao then appoints her tutor, Chen Zuiliang, and a bawdy but kindly Taoist nun, Sister Stone, as guardians of the shrine. Almost three years pass as Bridal Du's body lies buried beneath the tree.

During that time, down in the underworld, Bridal Du's spirit awaits judgment because the central administration of Hell has failed to appoint a judge. (Details such as this one satirize government inefficiencies and frequently appear throughout the play.) In scene 23, the judge in charge of Bridal's case finally arrives and is at first disposed to condemn her soul to rebirth as a bird. On learning all the circumstances of her Karma, however, the judge discovers that Bridal is destined to return to earth as the wife of Liu Mengmei. Bridal will be allowed to return to life if Liu Mengmei takes quick action and digs up her body.

Having taken shelter at the Apricot Shrine, Liu Mengmei discovers Bridal Du's self-portrait and recognizes the girl of his dream. Aided by a mass said by Sister Stone for the rebirth of Bridal's soul in Heaven, her ghost manifests itself to Liu Mengmei. Not realizing that she is a spirit, Liu Mengmei pleads that Bridal stay with him. She agrees to come to him each night as long as he consents to let her leave before the cock crows at dawn. In scene 32 the lovers exchange wedding vows, and Bridal Du hesitantly reveals her ghostly nature. Terrified at first, Liu settles down and listens to Bridal Du's instruction for her disinterment. She tells him that haste is necessary if she is not to be doomed to wander by the nine springs of Hell.

Liu employs Scabby Turtle, the nephew of Sister Stone, to open the grave. When the coffin is opened, Bridal Du revives, coughs up some mercury that had been used to delay her body's decomposition, and rises weak but alive. Sister Stone strengthens her with food and drink. Having regained her strength, Bridal Du, whose dream life had been impetuously passionate, becomes very concerned with the conventions. She wants to defer her marriage until a go-between has been appointed and until her father's approval for the match is forthcoming. Liu is impatient and presses her to marry. In the event, he wins the debate. Grave robbing is a capital offense, and Tutor Chen, having discovered the empty grave and casket but no corpse, thinks Sister Stone and Liu have opened the tomb to steal the jewels buried with Bridal Du and thrown her body in a neighboring pond. He notifies the authorities.

In the meantime, Sister Stone takes ship with the lovers for Hangzhou, where they marry. Liu then goes off to take the examinations. He arrives late but is admitted and writes the prize essay. Announcement of his victory, however, gets deferred because of the military situation in the empire. He returns home, and his wife asks him to find her father and introduce himself.

Liu arrives at the court of Du Bao and presents himself as the governor's son-in-law. He has been so introducing himself along the road. Hearing of it, Du Bao has issued a proclamation ordering his arrest as an imposter. As the plot continues to develop complications, Du Bao and Liu develop a deep enmity that culminates in Du Bao's having Liu beaten unmercifully with peach wood. Moreover, on learning of his daughter's resurrection, only imperial inquiry and the emperor's edict convince Du Bao that his daughter is again alive. Even then he conditions accepting her on her willingness to leave Liu Mengmei. Eventually, however, imperial edicts and rewards all around restore order in both family and empire. A false report is corrected that had convinced Du Bao of the deaths both of his wife and of Bridal Du's girlhood companion, Spring Fragrance. Plots and subplots are all satisfactorily resolved and all loose ends are tied up.

In its original form, the play took two or three days to enact. A number of conventions unfamiliar to Western playgoers were necessarily employed for the benefit of audience members who might wander in and out or come late or fail to have seen an earlier segment. Characters regularly announce who they are. Summaries of past action occasionally appear—perhaps at points that the play resumed after an overnight break. The serious matter of the play is regularly punctuated with comedy, often overtly sexual in nature. The incompetence of several public officials and examiners becomes the butt of SATIRE.

The play, like Western opera, was largely sung, though some passages were also spoken. Both major sorts of Chinese poetry, CI and SHI, appeared. In Chinese the play is largely in rhymed verse, though some prose also appears. Moreover, the power of the play gets continual reinforcement from its deep and almost constant INTERTEXTUALITY. The lines of earlier poets often appear in the mouths of the characters as they vie in displays of their erudite mastery of older classics. Moreover, many characters speak in CENTOS composed from lines borrowed from older poets. For readers or members of the audience to whom these lines were familiar, a pleasant sensation of recognition undoubtedly further enriched their enjoyment of the performance.

Remarkably, the magnificent English translation by Cyril Birch catches most of this play's delightful complexity. In China, portions of the play still appear on stage with considerable regularity, though performances of the whole play seem few and far between.

Bibliography

Tang Xianzu. *The Peony Pavilion (Mudan Ting)*. Translated by Cyril Birch. Boston: Ching & Tsui Company, 1999.

periodic prose

Periodic prose is composed of very long, complicated sentences. The underlying concept of such a sentence assumes that all ideas directly subordinate to the main idea of a sentence should be grouped together within a single grammatical unit called a *period*. Many Renaissance thinkers composed in periodic prose, but one of the clearest examples comes from the writing of LORENZO DE' MEDICI. Though in translating some of Lorenzo's prose, I broke his sentences up for the benefit of modern readers, as an illustration of a single periodic sentence from his AUTOBIOGRAPHY (*Il Comento*), I have put the following one back together:

> My lady was not only above all the others most lovely and endowed with most worthy manners and elegant habits, but she was also full of love and grace; and it could truly be affirmed of her that she was so excellent in all the attributes that a woman ought to have, that any other woman would have been most excellent among the others if she had been perfectly endowed with only one portion of what my lady so thoroughly had.

In English, word order comes to the reader's rescue. In languages that indicate their grammatical relationships by the endings on words rather than primarily by word order, a periodic sentence can present readers with a very difficult tangle.

peripeteia

Deriving from ARISTOTLE's discussion of TRAGEDY in his *Poetics*, the *peripeteia* is that moment in the action of a tragedy at which the fortunes of a tragic hero or heroine reverse. Though things may at first seem favorable for the main character, from the moment of the reversal, matters rapidly go from bad to worse. For Macbeth in WILLIAM SHAKESPEARE's tragedy of the same name, the protagonist recognizes his fortunes have turned at the moment in Act V, scene v, when Birnam Wood appears to begin advancing on Macbeth's stronghold of Dunsinane. In *KING LEAR* the moment comes much earlier. His descent into despair begins as soon as he gives away his kingdom to be managed by his daughters (Act I, scene i).

Persian poets of the classical tradition
(1500–1700)

Throughout the 16th and 17th centuries, writing poetry was at least as popular an avocation as it had earlier been in Persia and as it continues to be in contemporary Iran. Both the works of many poets and critical commentaries on their writing have come down to us. In separating the poets of greater from those of lesser talent, however, critical commentaries offer little help. Their authors' criteria for inclusion often had less to do with quality than with tangential issues like the degree of political influence the poets exercised, poets' personal appeal, or whether or not the critic perceived a poet's religious views as adequately orthodox. A consensus respecting poets' capacities, nonetheless, does emerge among the critics. The Persian poets whose names appear in this volume represent that critical agreement.

Some Persian poets of this period worked in their native land. Others, attracted by the encouragement and rewards that the Mughal emperors of India offered talented poets, journeyed eastward and often found employment and fame at the imperial court in Agra, or at the courts in Delhi and Kabul. Some enjoyed enviable reputations both at home and abroad.

FAYDĪ (1547–95) exemplifies this last category of poet. At the court of AKBAR in Agra, he was considered one of the "nine jewels" among the more than 100 poets who enjoyed the emperor's patronage. Another Persian poet at Akbar's court was 'URFĪ OF SHIRAZ (d. 1590–91). His reputation has grown over time, for he seems to have been one whose personality offended some contemporaries.

A poet of Persia who built his reputation at home was FŪZŪLĪ of Baghdad (ca. 1495–1556). Equally skillful in Persian, Arabic, and Turkish, Fûzûlî worked in the court of Shah Ismmā'īl I in Baghdad and later tried unsuccessfully to obtain a similar appointment in Istanbul, Turkey.

HÁTIFÍ (d. 1521) represents a class of Persian poet whose work has largely been lost. We do have two allegorical verse romances on subjects traditional in the Arabic world to give evidence of his talent.

Widely considered to be the last of the great poets of Persia, ṢÃ'IB OF TABRIZ (d. ca. 1670) migrated from Persia to India and back again. He was a court poet in Kabul, Afghanistan, at Agra, India, and at the imperial court in Baghdad. He somehow offended the emperor in Baghdad, however, and was dismissed. This fall from favor influenced his contemporary critics, and his reputation dropped in their esteem. Later criticism, however, has restored him to the top rank of Persian poets.

Petrarch, Francis (Francesco Petrarca) (1304–1374)

If a single person can be credited for the impetus that resulted in the flowering of the European Renaissance, that person is Francis Petrarch, who among many other achievements was the earliest of the great Italian HUMANISTS. The son of an exiled Florentine notary, Ser Petracco, Petrarch was born in Arezzo just south of Florence, and in 1312 moved with his father, his mother, and his brother Gherardo to the papal court in Avignon. The family resided in the village of Carpentras near Mount Ventoux, and there the young Francesco acquired an ardent love of literature—a subject to which he swore he would devote his life. His father, however, had other ideas for his eldest son and sent the lad when he was just 12 years old to study civil law at Montpellier in France. After four years there, he moved on to the law school at Bologna, Italy—Europe's finest legal institution of the epoch—where he spent much of his next five years.

Petrarch's upbringing in a Tuscan family in a district of Provence gave him mastery of the two most important literary vernaculars of 14th-century continental Europe: the Italian of Tuscany, of DANTE, and of BOCCACCIO, on the one hand, and the Provençal used by the Troubadors of southern France. The poems of the Troubadors modeled for Italian poets of the generation immediately preceding Petrarch's the manner of writing love lyrics—mainly SONNETS—that the Italians would develop into the "Sweet New Style."

Petrarch also mastered Latin—not just the Vulgate Latin of the Middle Ages but also the classical Latin of the great age of Roman letters, and throughout his life he worked at purifying his own command of that idiom in his Latin writings. He was probably the first 14th-century European to perceive the potential for the construction of modern poetry that lay largely unexplored in the secular writings of the ancients. He haunted libraries in search of lost and neglected manuscripts. As a law student he rediscovered several lost portions of Livy's history of Rome and edited them. He found in Liège, now in Belgium, two orations of Cicero previously unknown to medieval Europe. In Florence he discovered a lost portion of Quintilian (ca. 35–ca. 100). In the Capitoline Library of the Cathedral of Verona, Italy, he found the letters of Cicero. He was one among few persons in Europe who could have recognized them for what they were. On their model, he early decided that he would preserve his own correspondence, and he did so in two famous collections of letters, those of his youth and those of his old age.

If the secular literature of the ancients inspired Petrarch, so did a religious work. When the poet was 19, the Augustinian monk Dionigi da Borgo San Sepulchro had presented Francesco with a manuscript copy of St. Augustine's *Confessions*—a work that modeled for Petrarch the interiority and the dividedness that reappears throughout Petrarch's best-remembered 366-poem vernacular collection, PETRARCH'S SONGBOOK (*Rerum vulgarium fragmenta* or *Canzoniere*), and throughout his Latin work, *Petrarch's Secret*—an imagined dialogue with St. Augustine on the subject of Petrarch's own lifelong consuming passion for a woman he called Laura.

His parents' early death meant that Petrarch could desert the law and devote himself to study and writing. Doing so, however, also meant that he would ever afterward be dependent on the generosity of a series of patrons who supported him throughout his career, both directly by giving him access to their libraries and with gifts of money and less directly by bestowing upon him the income from ecclesiastical livings. Petrarch seems to have taken minor orders that allowed him to accept livings from churches he did not in fact serve, but he seems never to have become a priest.

That his Italian poems made him the most influential European lyric poet of all time would have come as a surprise to Petrarch. He staked his claim to glory on his Latin writings. While they are far from forgotten, they did not bring him posterity's acclaim as his Italian poems did. He expected that his EPIC poem *Africa* would be regarded as his masterpiece. This poem celebrates the career of the Roman general Scipio Africanus (237–183 B.C.E.), who conquered Spain for the Romans and forced the withdrawal from Italy of the Carthaginian general, Hannibal. When a grateful populace offered Scipio the offices of Roman consul and dictator for life, he refused them and instead retired to a secluded, private life. Petrarch's other Latin writings include his *Lives of Illustrious Men,* his work in praise of *The Solitary Life,* his treatise about the ease of the religious life, the letters mentioned above, *Remedies against Adverse Fortune,* his description of his *Ascent of Mount Ventoux,* and INVECTIVES.

Petrarch aspired to glory and he achieved it. During his lifetime he became the most famous private person in Europe. The subsequent history of lyric poetry in Europe and the Americas can accurately be regarded as a series of footnotes (sometimes very great ones) to the achievement of Francesco Petrarca. His admirers imitated him—often badly—and his detractors reacted against his imitators—especially the bad ones. Those who imitated him well are called PETRARCHANs and those who did it badly are labeled *PETRARCHISTS*.

One of Petrarch's primary goals was to reestablish in his own person the ancient Roman honor of the office of poet laureate. His unparalleled achievement and some careful finagling conspired to accomplish this objective. Almost simultaneously Petrarch received invitations from the University of Paris and from the Senate at Rome to accept the honor. Petrarch opted for Rome, and, on Easter Sunday 1341, he delivered an oration on the steps of the capitol and was crowned with the traditional wreath of laurel leaves.

After moving from court to court under the auspices of first one patron and then another, in his old age Petrarch agreed to leave his books to the Republic of Venice as a founding collection for the Marciana Library in exchange for what amounted to an old-age pension. He moved into a pleasant house just outside Arqua in the Eugenian Hills between Venice and Padua. There he died. His books were taken over by the local Paduan ruler and his library dispersed to the highest bidders across Europe. Venice nonetheless considers the Marciana to be Petrarch's monument, and the poet's brooding statue presides over it. Behind glass, his stuffed cat presides over his residence at Arqua Petrarca. The home has been preserved as a literary tourist site. Petrarch's bones have recently been disinterred from his monument in the town square in the interests of scientific study and of television and journalistic voyeurism.

Bibliography

Petrarca, Francesco. *Letters of Old Age.* Translated by Aldo S. Bernardo, Saul Levin, and Reta A. Bernardo. Baltimore: Johns Hopkins University Press, ca. 1992.

———. *Invectives.* Translated and Edited by David Marsh. Cambridge, Mass.: Harvard University Press, 2003.

———. *On Religious Leisure: De otio religioso.* Edited and translated by Susan S. Shearer. New York: Italica Press, 2002.

———. *Petrarch's Songbook: Rerum vulgarium fragmenta.* Translated by James Wyatt Cook; introduced by Germaine Warkentin. Binghamton, N.Y.: Medieval and Renaissance Texts and Studies, 1995.

———. *The Portable Petrarch.* Edited by Mark Musa. Harmondsworth, U.K., and New York: Penguin, 2004.

———. *The Secret Book: The Private Conflict of Your Thoughts.* Edited by Silvia Girardi. Translated by Geoffrey Rowland. Oregon House, Calif.: Ulysses Books, 2003.

Petrarchist, Petrarchan, Petrarchism

Petrarchists were European and Euro-American poets of the Renaissance who imitated the surface features of the verse of the Italian poet FRANCIS PETRARCH (FRANCESCO PETRARCA) but who failed to perceive or understand the creative complexity and the evocative quality of the poet's work. The English poet, SIR FRANCIS KYNASTON, exemplifies a not altogether bad poet whose grasp of Petrarch's idiom was unidimensional in this way and who could well be included among the Petrarchists. SIR THOMAS WYATT, HENRY HOWARD, THE EARL OF SURREY, and EDMUND SPENSER, on the other hand, exemplify Petrarchans who brought to English verse much of the novelty and depth that their Italian exemplar achieved. WILLIAM SHAKESPEARE in his early SONNETS was indebted to the Petrarchan model.

Poets who elsewhere either successfully or unsuccessfully modeled their work on Petrarch's include RONSARD and DU BELLAY in France, BOSCÁN and Herrera in Spain, CAMÕES in Portugal, and OPITZ in Germany. It was *Petrarchism*—a term that encompasses the work of both successful and unsuccessful followers of the master—that liberated many poets from the traditional, medieval forms that had been current in their languages and brought a new refinement to the poetry of Europe.

Petrarch's Songbook (Canzoniere)
Francesco Petrarca (ca. 1373)

In its final form, *Petrarch's Songbook*, to which he assigned the Latin title *Rerum vulgarium fragmenta* (Fragments of things in the language of ordinary life), contains 366 Italian poems. These include, SONNETS, madrigals, sestinas and double sestinas, and *canzoni* or ODES. From the perspective of numerology, 365 of the poems suggest the days of a year, and the 366th, which is addressed to the Virgin Mary, points toward eternity.

PETRARCH began work on his collection of vernacular verse in the 1330s and, though he circulated manuscript versions as an open text throughout his lifetime, he did not close the text in final form until around 1373. From a literary perspective the collection, known for centuries in Italian simply as *Il Petrarca*, marks the passage in the West from the medieval to the modern world. The medieval Dante in his *The Divine Comedy* had perceived the Dante pilgrim's dream journey through Hell and Purgatory to a final, inexpressible, mystic vision of Heaven itself as the progress of a representative human being. The Dante pilgrim was at once a persona of the author and Everyperson. Petrarch, by contrast, for the first time in Europe in 1,000 years sang his own experience at a level of emotional, INTERTEXTUAL, and intellectual complexity and evocativeness hardly matched elsewhere in the canon of Western letters. The Dante pilgrim trod a well-traveled path to a certain Salvation, Petrarch's literary persona and perhaps its creator remained lost in a labyrinth of alternative pathways and uncertainty.

At 7:00 A.M. on April 6, 1327 (a Good Friday), at the church of Saint Claire in Avignon, France, Petrarch fell in love at first sight with a woman he thereafter called Laura. This date was convenient for a poet because April 6 was traditionally considered to be the day on which the world had been created, the day on which Christ was crucified, and the day on which the world will end. Early on the morning of April 6, 1348, Laura died of the plague. Her death made it possible for Petrarch to see her as a heavenly intercessor who could plead for his sinful soul in Heaven. Many editors of *Petrarch's Songbook* have divided the poem into those written during the life of Madonna Laura and those written after her death.

It is likely that the historical Laura was Lauretta de Sade—an ancestress of the famous marquis from whose name *sadism* derives. She was, of course, already married, and eventually she became the mother of six children. Thus Petrarch's expression of his ardor was almost certainly confined to the sublimated form he achieved in his poems. And her husband seems to have tolerated—perhaps even been flattered by—the literary attention of Europe's most famous poet. Her name made it possible for Petrarch to assimilate the historical woman to his hopes and aspirations. For him she came to symbolize his pursuit of fame as poet *laureate*. She also represented the *laurel* tree. In mythology, Zeus had turned the nymph Daphne into a laurel to protect her from the ardent attentions of Apollo—the patron god of poets. Her hair was the color of gold, *l'oro* in Italian. Throughout his work Petrarch rings changes on these themes and on the patterns of sound the similarities allowed him exploit in his verse.

Petrarch believed in the priestly mission of the poet—the poet as VATES. Sometimes, particularly in his odes, he speaks out in the voice of a prophet as he does in the 28th poem of the collection, the *canzone* "O fair and blessed soul whom Heaven awaits." In it the poet encourages Cardinal Giacomo Colonna to provide leadership in mounting the crusade of 1333. In this poem and elsewhere, however, the voice of the prophet is often flawed by the obsessions of the lover. This is not the case, however, in the noblest patriotic poem of the Italian language, the 128th poem in *Petrarch's Songbook*, "My Italy." There the voice of the prophet remains in full force throughout the poem, encouraging the lords of Italy to unite in driving German mercenaries from Italian soil.

Interspersed throughout the collection are poems that Petrarch addressed to friends and epistolary sonnets that answer poems Petrarch received. There are poems that mark anniversaries of the beginnings of the poet's love and others that commemorate the deaths of friends. In a series of three sonnets called "the Babylonian sonnets" (poems 136–138) Petrarch vents his wrath at the worldliness and sexual license of the papal court at Avignon. Some of the loveliest nature poems in any language also appear. Again and again, however, the poet's eye turns to the effects that his obsession with Laura have produced upon his inner being, upon his hopes for this world, and upon his expectations for salvation in the next.

Renaissance poets throughout Europe and the European New World emulated Petrarch. The better ones perceived at least some of the depths of his accomplishment and tried to approach them. The lesser ones imitated his more obvious CONCEITS—his comparisons—and strewed the world with similes of pearly teeth, hair like golden wire, lips like rubies, skin like snow, and so forth. Fed up with that sort of imitation, other poets sought different approaches and new metaphors. Lord Byron in the 19th century had the ill grace to call Petrarch

"the pimp of all Christendom." But the most influential poet of the European tradition deserves much better than that. If an aspiring poet in any language could choose only one Italian poet to study as a model, that aspirant could choose no better than to study *Petrarch's Songbook*.

Bibliography

Petrarca, Francesco. *Petrarch's Songbook: Rerum vulgarium fragmenta, A Verse Translation*. Translated by James Wyatt Cook; introduced by Germaine Warkentin. Binghamton, N.Y.: Medieval and Renaissance Texts and Studies, 1995.

Phaedra (*Phèdre*) Jean Racine (1677)

Like most of RACINE'S TRAGEDY, his last play for the Paris theater and his masterpiece, *Phaedra*, is traceable to classical sources. Racine combines elements of the Greek Euripedes' drama *Hippolytus* with elements of the Roman Seneca's play of the same name. Racine also introduces new material of his own.

Hippolytus is the son of the Greek ruler Theseus and the Amazon queen Antiope. Theseus's new wife, Phaedra, is secretly in love with her stepson. Unaware of his stepmother's feelings, Hippolytus is secretly in love with Aricie, an Athenian princess under house arrest as a hostage at his father's court. As the play begins, Theseus has long been absent, and a report of his death—mistaken as it turns out—reaches the court at Troezen. Phaedra, thinking herself no longer married, confesses her feelings to Hippolytus. The youth is repulsed by the revelation, and Phaedra feels utterly humiliated by his reaction.

Just at this moment, a messenger arrives with the news that Theseus is alive and at the very gates. On his arrival, his son greets him with a request that he be permitted to live elsewhere. Distressed, Theseus inquires of members of his court why his son wishes to leave. Phaedra's lifelong companion and nursemaid, Oenone, to whom Phaedra confided her feelings, answers and accuses Hippolytus of having tried to seduce Phaedra.

In his fury, Theseus curses his son by calling on the God Neptune to destroy him. Hippolytus maintains his innocence, confessing his love for Aricie. Aricie tells Theseus that she also loves Hippolytus and that his son is innocent of Oenone's charges. Theseus begins to doubt his son's guilt, but the damage has been done. The god of the sea has heard the curse. Neptune sends a sea monster to frighten Hippolytus's chariot horses. Even though the young man defeats the monster, the horses nevertheless drag him to his death, leaving his mutilated corpse near the tombs of his ancestors. All this sequence of events occurs offstage, but it is reported in gory and graphic detail by Hipploytus's tutor, Théramène, in a long soliloquy.

Oenone, in the meantime, has committed suicide, and the audience must now endure the shocking spectacle of Phaedra's poisoning herself and dying onstage. This innovation shocked the theatergoing public of Racine's Paris who expected French playwrights to observe the ancient Greek convention of having death occur offstage and be reported as Hippolytus's was.

Chastened and appalled by the sequence of events that his rash curse initiated, Theseus assumes the role of Aricie's foster father and forswears any further invocations of Neptune.

Phaedra is one of a series of female characters in whose depiction Racine explores the darker recesses of the human psyche. His view of people was not an optimistic one. He did not believe that education or attempts at self-improvement could reform essentially flawed humanity. Only God's predestined grace, the playwright believed, could lead an individual to salvation.

A wonderful, modernized film version of the play is available.

Bibliography

Racine, Jean. *Phèdre: A Tragedy in Five Acts.* Translated by Wallace Fowlie. Mineola, N.Y.: Dover Publications, 2001.

Philips, Katherine (1631–1664)

A British poet and translator of the mid-17th century, Katherine Philips, nee Fowler, was celebrated as a writer under a poetic name: The Matchless Orinda. Royalist in her politics and a devotee of the country life rather than of the social whirl of the city, she published her earliest poems in 1651. They ap-

peared as a preface to the work of HENRY VAUGHAN. Much to her irritation, in the year of her death a pirated edition of her collected poems appeared. They reappeared posthumously in an authorized version in 1667. Her poems reflected her royalist sentiments in that they continued the themes of love and of seizing the moment that had appeared in the work of court poets like THOMAS CAREW, Richard Lovelace, and SIR JOHN SUCKLING—poets who wrote what came to be called the CAVALIER LYRIC.

As a translator, Philips drew favorable notice for her rendition of PIERRE CORNEILLE's work, the TRAGEDY, *La mort de Pompée* (*The Death of Pompey,* 1643). Her version was performed in Dublin before enthusiastic audiences in 1663. She had begun work on a verse translation of the works of the Roman poet Horace when she succumbed to smallpox in 1664. Her good friend, the Irish poet and architect SIR JOHN DENHAM (1615–69), completed her translation after she died.

Bibliography

Souers, P. W. *The Matchless Orinda.* Cambridge, Mass.: Harvard University Press, 1931.

picaresque novel

A picaresque novel tells the life story of a rascal, a confidence man, or a male or female criminal of some sort. Often the book is told in the first person, so that as the main character tells his/her own story, the audience comes by that means to understand the rogue's point of view. A Spanish tale sometimes attributed to the Spaniard Diego Hurtado de Mendoza, *LA VIDA DE LAZARILLO DE TORMES* (The life of Lazarillo de Tormes, ca. 1554) established the model for the type. Other stories following its example rapidly appeared on the European continent and in England. In France the four-volume work *Gil Blas* (1715, 1724, and 1735) by Alain-René Le Sage (1668–1737) represents the genre. So in England does THOMAS NASHE's *THE UNFORTUNATE TRAVELER* (1594). Though the picaresque novel originated in the Renaissance, the form remains popular today, and contemporary examples can be found on bookshelves throughout the world.

Pico, Giovanni della Mirandola
(1463–1494)

An Italian nobleman, the count of Mirandola in the province of Ferrara, the philosopher Giovanni Pico studied in both France and Italy. Eventually he moved to Florence where he met MARSILIO FICINO and came under his intellectual influence. Pico was among the most brilliant and sometimes controversial polymaths of his age.

In an early Italian work, *A Platonic Discourse on Love* (1486) Pico explained and commented on a CANZONE by the poet Girolomo Benivieni. In his only other composition in Italian, Pico dedicated to his host at the time, LORENZO DE' MEDICI, a posthumously published collection of ITALIAN SONNETS. Its title in a good English translation is *Heptaplus: or, Discourse on the Seven Days of Creation.* The work's original Greek and Latin title, however, *Heptaplus de septiformi sex dierum geneseos enarratione* is more literally and descriptively translated as Heptaplus: a seven-level explanation of the six days of Genesis (written ca. 1489). In his *Heptaplus* Pico imputed mystical meaning to the story of the Creation in Genesis. Always interested in mystical matters and under the influence of ELIJAH DEL MEDIGO of Padua, Pico studied the Jewish Kabbalah and incorporated its complex and arcane numerology into his thinking on the subject of religion. In Latin prose he undertook a similar interpretative discussion of the Psalms, which, though it was translated into Italian in 1997, does not as yet seem to have found its way into English.

He was a syncretic philosopher—always trying to find an overarching intellectual framework within which he could reconcile disparate points of view. He tried in his *Of Being and Unity (De ente et uno)* to bring Aristotle's materialist view of the nature of the universe under the same theoretical umbrella with PLATO's view, which saw ultimate reality not as material but as a realm of prototypical ideas. The perceptible forms of these ideas, Plato argues in his *Republic,* are presented to the senses of human beings as no more than the shadows of images of the ultimate ideas themselves.

Pico's theological views, which drew on the Muslim as well as on the Jewish and Christian traditions, seemed heterodox to the Vatican and landed him in serious trouble. His difficulties began in 1483 when he enunciated in Rome his theories about many intellectual matters in 900 theses called his *Conclusiones* and offered to debate all comers in defense of his positions. Pope Innocent VIII, however, forbade the proposed debate on the grounds that many of Pico's views were heretical. Pico remained suspect in the judgment of the Vatican until 1493 when Innocent's successor, Pope Alexander VI, absolved him of his former sinful errors. Before the authorities intervened in the matter, however, Pico had given an oration as a preamble and invitation to his proposed debate. This Latin oration, published and titled posthumously, has become the work for which Pico is best remembered: his *Oration on the Dignity of Man (De hominis dignitate oratio,* composed ca. 1483).

At the time of his death (perhaps by poison), Pico was working on another ambitious project. Pico's final work was in the NEO-LATIN of the HUMANIST tradition he so capably represented. This last unfinished treatise attacked the widespread use of the pseudoscience of astrology as a means of predicting the future. Pico had also earlier set his hand to the composition of poems in Latin. These apparently remained in manuscript until 1964 when a selection of 10 of them appeared in a slender volume in the Netherlands. Gavin Bryars set some of the Latin poems to music in 1988.

Both Pico's nephew Giovanni Francesco Pico della Mirandola and SIR (ST.) THOMAS MORE wrote biographies of this learned and original thinker.

Bibliography

Bryars, Gavin. *Glorious Hill:* [a musical score for] *Countertenor, 2 Tenors and Baritone.* London and New York: Schott, ca. 1994.

Farmer, S. A., trans. and ed. *Syncretism in the West: Pico's 900 Theses (1486): The Evolution of Traditional, Religious, and Philosophical Systems.* Tempe, Ariz.: Medieval & Renaissance Texts and Studies, 1998.

Pico della Mirandola, Giovanni. *Commentary on a Poem of Platonic Love.* Translated by Douglas Carmichael. Lanham, Md.: University Press of America, ca. 1986.

———. *Heptaplus: or, Discourse on the Seven Days of Creation.* Translated by Jessie Brewer McGaw. New York: Philosophical Library, ca. 1977.

———. *Of Being and Unity.* Translated by Victor Michael Hamm. Milwaukee, Wisc.: Marquette University Press, 1943.

———. *On the Dignity of Man; On Being and the One; Heptaplus.* Translated by Charles Glenn Wallis, Paul J. W. Miller, and Douglas Carmichael. Indianapolis, Ind.: Hackett Publications, 1998.

Pilgrim's Progress, The John Bunyan
(Part I 1678; Part II 1684)

Firmly rooted in the medieval tradition of allegorical dream vision exemplified by DANTE's *Divine Comedy* and by Geoffrey Chaucer's *Parliament of Fowls, Pilgrim's Progress* belongs as well to a tradition of rudimentary, one-to-one ALLEGORY. In one sense, BUNYAN's allegorical method draws on the tradition of TYPOLOGY also practiced by EDMUND SPENSER. As compared with Spenser's complex web of multiple sorts of allegory, however, Bunyan's much simpler method would only parallel Spenser's entry-level comparisons. In other ways, however, the book constitutes a sophisticated examination of the human condition within a specifically evangelical Protestant context. Mark Twain's character Huckleberry Finn read the book. In his opinion, *Pilgrim's Progress* was "interesting, but tough."

Like the pilgrim Dante and the dreamer Chaucer, in Part I of *Pilgrim's Progress,* a narrator who is traveling through the world's wilderness grows weary, finds a place that reminds him of a jail or of a den, and there lies down to rest. He sleeps and dreams of a man wearing tattered clothing—a man we later discover to be named Christian. His family considers him mad because he roams about wondering how he can be saved. Another character named *Evangelist* gives the man a scroll, tells him to avoid the coming wrath, and sends him off toward a destination that Christian can't quite make out.

Along his pathway, Christian encounters events and characters that hinder and endanger him on his journey and others that lend him a helping hand. All bear names and labels that make their natures clear. Obstinate tries to impede his journey; Pliable decides to go along. Pliable distracts Christian, however, with the result that both fall into the Slough of Despond. Pliable quits the quest, but Christian moves forward through the mire until Help rescues him. Encountering Mr. Worldly Wise-man of Carnal Policy, Christian again detours and is threatened by a volcano. Evangelist, however, comes to his aid and points him once again on the right path. This leads to a gate with the inscription: "Knock and it shall be opened to you." Christian knocks. Goodwill answers and pulls him inside—away from the danger of the arrows of the devil Beelzebub.

As the journey continues Christian follows a road walled off from the dangers of the open country by the Wall of Salvation. Along his way he has been carrying a kind of heavy rucksack that stands for the burden of original sin. When he arrives, however, at the foot of the cross, this burden tumbles from his shoulders into a tomb below. Three radiant persons called "shining ones," now clothe him in fresh garments, mark his forehead with a sign that identifies him as one of the saved, and give him a scroll that will so identify him when he arrives at the gates of Heaven—his ultimate goal.

Despite Christian's successes thus far, the way ahead is not easy. He has yet to climb the Hill of Difficulty although the most evident impediments to success in that effort are chained at the bottom. These are Sloth, Presumption, and a character named Simple—meaning foolish. Moving up the incline, Christian next encounters Hypocrisy and Formalist. These men have jumped the wall rather than follow the more difficult way, and they insist on their right to salvation. They are unwilling, however, to follow the steep incline and detour via the easier appearing paths of Danger and Destruction.

Further misadventures delay Christian on his way up the hill, but with some difficulty he survives them and makes his way eventually past Timorous and Mistrust and his own inattention and mistakes to the Palace Beautiful. There he meets and talks with Prudence, Charity, and Piety, who invite him to rest in the Chamber Peace.

After a refreshing night's sleep, Christian tours the palace and sees its biblical mementos and wonders. From the roof he can see far off a goal of his journey, the Delectable Mountains. Then, preparing him for trials yet to come, the Porter of Palace Beautiful gives him weapons and reports that a former neighbor, Faithful, has passed that way and has preceded him along the road. Young women from the castle next provision him for the journey, caution him about the Valley of Humiliation, and go along with him for a little way to see him off.

As he goes along, the way narrows and darkens. He meets others running away from dangers he has yet to face. In the Valley of Humiliation, after fighting and narrowly overcoming the monster Apollyon, an emissary of the Devil who would force him into his master's service, Christian continues on his way. Worse is to come. He arrives at the Valley of the Shadow of Death, where the mouth of Hell itself threatens him with showers of fire and a deafening din. Christian sheathes the sword he has been carrying, exchanging it for a more specialized weapon—All-prayer. He sees visions; he hears misleading and threatening voices; and he must pass through the booby-trapped valley of death with its rotting carcasses and skeletons. Finally he passes the cave of two formerly dangerous giants. One of them, named Pagan, has died. The other, Pope, is past threatening Christian.

As he follows the trail up from the valley, Christian can see Faithful ahead. He calls out to him, but Faithful won't wait. Annoyed, Christian begins running and passes faithful, only to trip himself on his prideful behavior. Chastened, Christian now waits for Faithful who reports on the snares that have impeded him on his journey—a different set than Christian encountered. The devil's temptations are custom-made for the weaknesses of the sinner.

Arriving at the town of Vanity Fair, the newcomers are assailed by vendors who want them to buy the town's attractive goods. The two, however, stop their ears against such temptations, and, though some of the townsmen are converted by their good behavior, most revile and persecute the strangers. They are charged under the town's worldly laws and tried by Judge Hate-good. Bearing witness against them are Envy, Superstition, and Pick-thank. Although Christian manages to escape, a jury headed by Blind-man finds Faithful

guilty. He is tortured mercilessly and finally burned at the stake. On his death, however, a heavenly chariot bears him off to Heaven to the accompaniment of victorious trumpets.

On his way once more, Christian meets Hopeful and By-ends. The silver mines of Hill Lucre successfully tempt By-ends and others who join him. Christian, however, manages to keep the wavering Hopeful firmly on the narrow path.

After they pass a pillar of salt, representing Lot's wife who was transmuted into that object when she looked back longingly on Sodom and Gomorrah when God's wrath destroyed those cities, the pair arrive at a delightful oasis on a riverbank. Road weary and footsore, they detour into a pleasant field named By-path Meadow. Their adventures there culminate in their falling into the hands of the Giant Despair, who imprisons them in doubting castle. There the giant's wife Diffidence encourages the giant to try to drive the pair to suicide. Despair is on the point of success when Christian remembers that he is carrying a key named Promise. He tries it, the door to the travelers' cell opens, and they escape, once more regaining the straight and narrow way.

At length they come safely to the Delectable Mountains and meet the shepherds who abide there: Experience, Knowledge, Sincere, and Watchful. These worthies point out dangers to the travelers—hills named Error and Caution where men whose eyes the Giant Despair has put out wander aimlessly.

Not yet in sight of their goal, the Celestial City, the pair presses on, warned by the shepherds of other dangers to avoid. Christian and Hopeful have yet to pass through the town of Conceit, must remain vigilant against pausing to rest on the Enchanted Ground, and avoid a flatterer, resist Atheist, and eschew Ignorance, who prefers not to discuss the doctrine of Christian justification.

As they near their journey's end, the weary travelers come to the land of Beulah. They still must cross the River of Death, and final apparitions beset Christian. His faith and his hope overcome them, however, and they are at last welcomed into the Celestial City and its ineffable joys by the saints who rejoice in their victory.

Looking back, they see Ignorance rowed across the River of Death by Vain-hope. He is refused admission, however, and conducted by heavenly beings to a nearby entrance to Hell. The narrator awakes and realizes that all has been a dream.

Critical opinion seems almost unanimous in preferring Part I of *Pilgrim's Progress* to Part II. In the second part Bunyan seems to tire of his tried-and-true method and rushes through his transitions. Nonetheless, Part II is not without interest, for it recounts the story of Christian's wife, Christiana, her four sons, and their companion, Mercy, as they follow the road Christian has taken before them. Though their adventures often differ markedly, the characters of Part II often find accounts of Christian's adventures and mementos of them as they pass along the way. Some of the young men marry on the journey. Christian and Christiana's son Matthew, for example, weds Mercy. When the party reaches the land of Beulah, only Christiana is called to cross the River of Death, though the narrator suggests that he will give accounts of her children and grandchildren later on. Bunyan takes some pains to feminize the situations Christiana encounters as she, for example, is called on to play nurse to one of her sons when he falls ill. Part II also contains a greater emphasis on music and hymnody than does Part I, and songs and verse play a greater role. Finally, Bunyan seems more playful in Part II, having greater recourse to humor and to riddles that he seems to enjoy including and that the company uses to entertain themselves along the road.

Bibliography

Bunyan, John. *The Complete Works of John Bunyan.* Edited by Henry Stebbing. New York: Johnson Reprint, 1970.

Plato (ca. 428–ca. 348 B.C.E.)

A disciple of Socrates and the teacher of ARISTOTLE, the ancient Greek Plato is arguably the most influential thinker of the Western philosophical tradition. Though all of his works have probably not survived, many of his most influential ones have. Though their exact order will probably always remain a puzzle, those that feature Socrates as a probing questioner concerning moral virtue probably represent Plato's earlier work. Included among these we find his *Laches,* where the virtue in question is courage and his *Euthyphro,* which looks at the virtue of piety. Three of his so-called *Socratic* dialogues, *Apology, Crito,* and *Phaedo* catalogue for posterity the last days of Socrates from his trial through his execution.

A middle period in Plato's work is likely represented by his *Symposium* (Banquet), in which a group of friends that includes Socrates gathers for food, wine, entertainment by flute girls, and conversation so stimulating that the flute girls are excused. Direct and indirect imitations of the *Symposium* abounded in the late Middle Ages and the Renaissance. DANTE modeled his work of the same name on it. BALDESSARE CASTIGLIONE borrowed many of its conventions in composing his *BOOK OF THE COURTIER.* The list of Renaissance works indebted to the *Symposium* in one way or another could grow tedious.

To this middle period Plato's *Gorgias, Phaedo,* and *Republic* also belong. They seem to present his views on matters like knowledge, whose acquisition he theorized represented the soul's recollecting things known from a previous state. He also considers the immortality of the soul, for which he argues, and its division into three parts. The *Republic* is perhaps Plato's most influential work. In it he develops his famous allegory of the cave, in which he illustrates the tripartite nature of reality. The mind of the true philosopher, he implies, can rise by degrees to understand the timeless and unchanging world that underlies the temporal and mutable natural world. In that other reality ideas or the underlying forms of literally everything exist and have always existed. In the natural world, those essential forms are represented by individual phenomena that are their reflections. What human beings experience of the ultimate forms or ideas is further mediated by their senses, so that people see mere shadows of images. Only the philosophical mind can by degrees rise to apprehend the truth, which is at once also the good and the beautiful. Plato's discussion of these matters was enormously influential during the Renaissance, and a cult arose that drew an analogy between the intellectual progress of the philosopher and the spiritual progress of true lovers. The result of this analogy was the tradition of PLATONIC LOVE that generations of poets made their stock in trade and that continues to undergird the more starry-eyed notions of romantic love.

The *Republic* also describes Plato's views on the nature of the ideal state and its structure—views that drew both admiration and horror from readers in the Renaissance and beyond. It is clearly the foundational document of the entire genre of the literature of UTOPIA. SIR (ST.) THOMAS MORE's book of the same name is the prime Renaissance example, but the ideal society was a theme dear to the hearts of Renaissance writers, and we see developments of the theme in writers as disparate as RABELAIS, MACHIAVELLI, and MARGARET CAVENDISH, THE DUCHESS OF NEWCASTLE. In the 18th century, as well, Jonathan Swift would take the inflexible society Plato described to its logical conclusion in the fourth book of *Gulliver's Travels*.

Plato's apparently late dialogues grew increasingly self-critical and less literary. They have proved more attractive to professional philosophers than to poets and utopian novelists. They include works like his *Theaetetus,* his *Sophist,* and his *Parmenides.* The Italian polymath GIOVANNI PICO DELLA MIRANDOLA was at pains to find an overarching intellectual framework that would make possible reconciling Plato's idealistic view of the nature of being with the materialistic view of his student, ARISTOTLE.

From the perspective of western Europe, the 15th century marked an important age during which platonic writings that the West had either not known or had lost sight of were rediscovered. As trade increased between Byzantium and the West, and as more scholars and HUMANISTS like LEONARDO BRUNI learned ancient Greek from teachers like MANUEL CHRYSOLARAS, editions in Greek and translations into the languages of Europe made Plato's works increasingly accessible to Renaissance readers.

Finally, Plato had founded an academy at Athens (ca. 387 B.C.E.)—a school that survived him for centuries. On its spiritual if not its organizational model, academies both formal and informal arose across Europe. Famous informal ones included those of the Florentine Coluccio Salutati and the circle surrounding LORENZO DE' MEDICI. Cities across Europe organized academies, which their intellectual and accomplished citizens were invited to join, as did ISABELLA ANDREINI, at the invitation of the Academy of the *Intenti* at Pavia. Some of the more formally organized academies, such as the ACADEMY OF THE CROSS in Florence or the national Académie Française, continue to exist to this day with missions and ideals similar to those on which they were founded in emulation of their Platonic original.

Bibliography

Duerlinger, James, trans. *Plato's Sophist: A Translation with a Detailed Account of Its Theses and Arguments.* New York: Peter Lang, 2005.

Hankins, James. *Plato in the Italian Renaissance.* Leiden and New York: E. J. Brill, 1994.

Jayne, Sears Reynolds. *Plato in Renaissance England.* Dordrecht and Boston: Kluwer Academic Publishers, ca. 1995.

Plato. *Complete Works.* Edited by John M. Cooper and D. S. Hutchinson. Indianapolis, Ind.: Hackett Publications, ca. 1997.

———. *Republic.* Translated by Elizabeth Watson Scharffenberger. New York: Fine Creative Media, 2004.

———. *The Last Days of Socrates.* Translated by Hugh Tredennick and Harold Tarrant. London and New York: Penguin Books, ca. 2003.

Platonic love

The Greek thinker PLATO had suggested that the mind of the philosopher could by degrees rise from the contemplation of the appearances of the illusory physical world as the senses perceive them, through the consideration of the world's physical realities unmediated by the senses (as a chemist or physicist, say, might think of apparently solid iron as a collection of atoms in motion), to the direct intellectual apprehension of the ultimate reality—a realm of ideas that underpins the physical world. Plato thought the attributes of that ideal realm to be at once and interchangeably the true, the good, and the beautiful.

Renaissance love theorists and poets borrowed Plato's ideas and built a cult of love on an analogy to them. A lover, they thought, might be initially attracted to a beloved by the beloved's physical beauties. But just as a philosopher could move beyond appearances, so a true lover could move beyond the physical, first to an appreciation of the beloved's moral excellence, and finally to an absorption with the beloved's spiritual attributes. As the lover progressed through these stages, the lover became ennobled and, in theory, might be led not only to intellectual purification but also to a state of religious grace through a love that transcended both physicality and time.

At its best, this theory of Platonic love produced numerous delightful literary applications. In BALDESSARE CASTIGLIONE'S BOOK OF THE COURTIER, for example, Castiglione has his character PIETRO BEMBO (ostensibly the real cardinal of the same name) rise to empyrean heights of platonic ecstasy from initially thinking about a lady's charms. Castiglione's Bembo becomes so distracted that a lady has to tweak his garment to call him back to the ordinary world. At a more serious level JOHN DONNE attempts to explore the geography of true and ennobling love in a Platonic context in poems like "The Good Morrow," "The Relic," "A Valediction Forbidding Mourning," and "The Ecstasy." In them he illustrates the triumph of love over separation, time, and death. He also illustrates the necessary connection between the physical, the moral, and the spiritual aspects of true love.

At their most cynical, cults of Platonic love as practiced in the courts of Europe became a game of gallantry and coquetry whose objective was a more or less interminable series of affairs among members of the upper classes. At its worst the language of Platonic love was applied to varnish over with a coat of respectability straightforward seduction, lust and recreational sex, and even prostitution. Writers did not overlook these seamier sides of the uses of the tradition. PIETRO ARETINO, for example, parodied the *Book of the Courtier* in his salacious *La Cortigiana* (The courtesan). The English courtier THOMAS CAREW was personally a member of the English chapter of the cult of Platonic love, and he led a very colorful life in pursuit of its pleasures. He also wrote one of the most tastefully erotic poems in the English language, "The Rapture." He and others were convinced that the trappings of the Platonic love tradition merely served to sugarcoat a game of musical beds.

Arguably the Western practice of basing marriages on romantic love and the cinema's formulas for boy-meets-girl movies can trace their genealogies to the traditions involved in the cults of Platonic love.

Bibliography

Fletcher, Jefferson Butler. *The Religion of Beauty in Woman, and Other Essays on Platonic Love in Poetry and Society.* New York: Haskell House, 1966.

Gould, Thomas. *Platonic Love.* Westport, Conn.: Greenwood Press, 1981.

Plautus, Titus Maccius (ca. 250–184 B.C.E.)

One of two Roman playwrights (the other being TERENCE) whose works provided classical models of comedy for Renaissance dramatists, Plautus stirred especially intense interest after 1427. In that year a dozen of his lost plays were rediscovered, so that now 21 of his comedies—those definitively attributed to him by the Roman writer Varro—are known to survive.

Plautus based much of his comedy on the second wave of Grecian comic theater. Both he and the later Greek comedians treated social life rather than political life as the older Greek comedy had done. His plays tended to revolve around stock situations, often involving a pair of lovers whose path to happiness was bestrewn with obstacles. These often took the form of disapproving parents and rich but elderly rivals. Another stock situation involved a confidence artist attempting to separate the foolish and unwary or the greedy from their money.

STOCK CHARACTERS populated the Plautine stage. These included the young lovers themselves, bawds and go-betweens, soldiers of fortune, lickspittles, hypocrites, and fools.

Playwrights in Renaissance Europe learned much about the construction of comedy from Plautus. In England, BEN JONSON put Plautus's example to effective use in such plays as *VOLPONE* and

THE ALCHEMIST. WILLIAM SHAKESPEARE is much indebted to him for the character of Falstaff, particularly as that Plautine soldier of fortune appears in the *Merry Wives of Windsor.* In many of Shakespeare's comedies, other Plautine elements also appear as they do in the plays of most Elizabethan and early Stuart comedians. The English seem to have found the Plautine comedy particularly congenial.

In Italy, LUDOVICO ARIOSTO blended Plautus's example with other sources of inspiration in plays like his *Cassaria* (1508) and *The Pretenders* (*I Suppositi,* 1509), and many other Italian playwrights followed a similar course. In Spain, the king's physician, Francisco de Villalobos prepared a prose translation of Plautus's *Amphitryon* (published, 1515), but we have no evidence it was ever performed. Other Spanish translations of the same play followed.

In France, though some early Renaissance playwrights like ROTROU dipped their quills in the Plautine example, it was MOLIÈRE whose exquisite ridicule of vice in plays like *TARTUFFE* (1669) and *THE MISANTHROPE* (1670) combines the satiric social mockery of Plautus with the moral authority of an Erasmus to lay bare an essentially pessimistic, though still ridiculous, view of the human condition.

Eventually the influence of Plautus seems to have followed the HUMANIST impulse north to the Scandinavian Peninsula. Plautine elements appear in the social SATIRE of the DANISH DRAMA, especially in the plays of Mogens Skeel (1650–94).

Play of Ollantay, The (*Afu Ollantay*)

Anonymous (ca. 1700)

An Incan DRAMA in the Quechua language and belonging to a cycle of kingship plays that were regularly performed in precolonial and colonial times, *Afu Ollantay* chronicles the rebellion of a regional prince, Ollantay, against Pachacuti, the Incan emperor at Cuzco. Ollantay's uprising, as the play reports it, resulted from his love for Cusi Coyllur Ñusta, a princess of the royal family whose name means Joyful Star.

With the approval of her mother, Ollantay has secretly married Joyful Star. The High Priest of the Sun, Uillac Uma, Ollantay's foster father, has discovered the prince's secret passion and predicts

dire consequences if he doesn't give it up. Ollantay tells the priest that it is too late, and he goes to the emperor to plead his case.

After enumerating his many services to the crown but without revealing that he has already married the princess, Ollantay asks for her hand in marriage. The emperor grows furious. Custom forbids members of the royal household from marrying outside their immediate kinship circle. He condemns Ollantay and imprisons his heretofore-beloved daughter in a secret dungeon in the gardens of the Virgins of the Sun.

Ollantay flees. An army led by Rumi Ñaui, his old friend and the emperor's faithful soldier, pursues him. Ollantay's troops destroy the pursuers by raining boulders on them in a mountain pass. Rumi Ñaui is the only survivor. Reporting his failure to the emperor, Rumi Ñaui proposes to become a secret agent. He succeeds in infiltrating Ollantay's camp, learning his plans, and causing the prince's rebellion to fail.

In the meantime, Joyful Star has a daughter, Yma Sumac, whose name means How Beautiful. Yma Sumac learns the secret of her birth and that the woman imprisoned in the dungeon is her mother. Yma's grandfather, Emperor Pachacuti, dies and is succeeded by her uncle Tupac Yupanqui.

Owing to Rumi Ñaui's good work, the new emperor's troops capture Ollantay and his principal supporters. They are hauled before the emperor and condemned to death. Just before the execution, however, the emperor commutes their sentences and demonstrates his merciful nature by promoting Ollantay to viceroy, first at Cuzco and then of the whole empire. He offers Ollantay a bride, but Ollantay responds that he is already married, though he has no idea where his wife might be.

Just then, Yma Sumac gains admission to the royal presence and pleads that the emperor rescue her dying mother. All troop to the dungeon and rescue Joyful Star, who is chained between a puma and a snake. Ollantay introduces his long lost wife. Her brother the emperor blesses the union, and all presumably live happily ever after.

The play features music and spectacle, and parts of it have inspired later writers like Peter Shaffer, who incorporates some of its songs in his drama about the Spanish execution of the Incan emperor Atawallpa, *The Royal Hunt of the Sun.*

Although the Spanish attempted to stamp out the native cycle of kingship dramas after the Inca Tupac Amaru rebelled in 1780, the plays survived—some in print and others in the memories of the actors. They continue to be widely performed in the Andean region. Moreover, the play, at least in its main outline, recounts history. A Spanish viceroy interviewed the historical Ollantay in the winter of 1570–71.

Bibliography

Garay, J. Paz, et al., editors and translators. *Ollantay: Drama Quechua* [Spanish and English]. Lima, Peru: Ediciones Markham, 1964.

Markham, Clements R., trans. *Ollanta: An Ancient Ynca Drama.* London: Trübner & Company, 1871.

Shaffer, Peter. *The Royal Hunt of the Sun.* Edited by Nicole Ridgeway. Pretoria: Unisa Press, ca. 1999.

Pléiade

A group of seven of the most influential writers of the French Renaissance, the Pléiade was named, first, for the cluster of seven stars into which, in Greek mythology, the seven daughters of Atlas had been turned. In the second place, the group of French luminaries was named after an assemblage of similarly illustrious poets that had operated in Alexandria, Egypt, during the period when Greek pharaohs and queens of the Ptolemy dynasty (including Cleopatra, who was of decidedly Mediterranean European rather than African heritage) governed Egypt. Among the members of that ancient Pleiad of Graeco-Egyptian poets, Theocritus, Lycophron, and Aratus figured prominently.

The founding members of the French Pléiade included the poets JEAN-ANTOINE DE BAÏF (1532–89), JOACHIM DU BELLAY (ca. 1522–60), Remi Belleau (ca. 1528–77), Jean Dorat, a HUMANIST teacher who transferred his love of classical literature to Baif, du Bellay, and PIERRE DE RONSARD (1524–85). Also members of the group were the playwright and poet ÉTIENNE JODELLE (1532–73), and the bishop and sonneteer Pontus de Tyard or Thyard (1521–1605). As a group these men were

responsible for moving French letters along the road that Italian letters had already traveled. They introduced such new poetic forms as the SONNET, stimulated interest in and emulation of classical letters, and worked at standardizing and "purifying" the French language.

At the outset, the oldest member of the group was not yet 24 years old. As time passed and each of the founders died off, the organization became a permanent fixture of the French literary scene and perpetuated itself by electing a candidate to fill the vacant seat. To become a member of the Pléiade is the highest mark of national literary distinction a writer can achieve.

Pleasant Historie of John Winchcomb, in his Younger Years Called Jack of Newberry, the Famous and Worthy Clothier, The   Thomas Deloney (1597)

A fictive account of the career of a real person, DELONEY'S first published novel, usually called simply *Jack of Newberry,* traces the history of Jack from his early days as a foreman in a clothing shop to his enviable success as the premier clothier of the nation.

When Jack's master in a small clothing business dies, in preference to her other suitors the master's widow woos Jack, and he marries her. As the head of the firm, Jack implements changes that rapidly propel his business into a thriving enterprise with branches in many parts of England. At its central factory in Newberry 400 men and boys operate 200 looms, 200 women card wool, 200 more spin yarn, 140 children pick wool, and numerous others are employed at other tasks. The entire picture is of a beneficent employer who sees himself as one of his workers and obliged to be concerned with their welfare. He pays generous wages, and he sees to their sustenance with full-scale cooking, baking, and brewing operations. Jack is also aware of the value of his operation to the well-being of the kingdom.

Offered a knighthood by the king, Jack refuses it, preferring not to erect artificial social barriers between himself and his employees, understanding himself to be both a clothier by trade and, because of his great success, "a gentleman by condition." At the same time, Jack is sensitive to the national interest. When the king requires troops for his war in France, Jack outfits and maintains at his own expense a troop of 150.

Upon the death of his first wife, Jack woos and wins a good-looking young woman, the daughter of a Buckinghamshire peasant. The simple old father speaks regional dialect with a sprinkling of humorous malapropisms, and he is overwhelmed by his prospective son-in-law's success. The father provides his daughter with the most generous dowry he can afford, and Jack, valuing the daughter's person and virtues above all, arranges a 10-day wedding party.

Jack is not by any means overawed by royalty and provides Henry the VIII with an allegorical entertainment in which Jack himself plays the role of the Emperor of the Ants. The entertainment proposes to instruct the king in the importance of such businesses as Jack's to the national interest. The king's minister, Cardinal Wolsey, becomes Jack's adversary because some of the cardinal's policies have the effect of restraining trade.

Such serious themes alternate with humorous ones, as when Deloney borrows a scene from BOCCACCIO's *Decameron* and locks his wife out in the cold when she returns home late. When Jack at last is moved by his wife's piteous entreaties, and lets her in, she pretends to drop her wedding ring outside. Jack gets down on hands and knees to search for it, his wife whisks into the house, and she turns the tables on him by locking him out.

Another delight of Deloney's novel arises from his sensitivity to language and the variety of styles that he uses to entertain his reader. He generally mocks the alliterative, repetitious style of EUPHUES, and he mocks members of the upper classes by having them use that style in their speech. Jack himself speaks clear, straightforward, unaffected English. The novel was exceedingly popular. It appealed to a rising audience of middle-class reader who enjoyed seeing the lives of ordinary persons represented fictively.

Bibliography

Deloney, Thomas. *The Novels of Thomas Deloney.* Edited by Merrit E. Lawlis. Westport, Conn.: Greenwood Press, 1978.

Wright, Eugene Patrick. *Thomas Deloney.* Boston: Twayne Publishers, 1981.

poetic justice

One idea of poetic justice stems from drama. There, especially on the European Renaissance stage until the middle of the 17th century, poetic justice meant that heroes would be rewarded in ways particularly suited to the merits of their case and that villains would be punished in ways specifically appropriate to their crimes. A case in point might be that of Barabas in CHRISTOPHER MARLOWE's play THE JEW OF MALTA. Barabas has been repeatedly treacherous to Christian and Muslim overlords and has poisoned a convent's well. He is punished by being boiled in oil on stage.

Another view of poetic justice is more general and stems from an ethical perspective. Whenever in literature good and evil are represented, poetic justice requires rewarding goodness and punishing evil. Audiences no longer require close adherence to the expectations that poetic justice establishes.

poetic meter (scansion)

Conventions of line length and *either* degrees of vocal emphasis (stress) *or* the relative duration of vowel sounds (quantity) characterize the production of poetry all over the world. In the Western world in classical times, the relative duration of vowel sounds in long or short syllables determined the way in which a metrical foot was measured. This system still typifies verse in Arabic.

Virgil's opening lines in The Aeneid give an idea of the metrical line the Romans and Greeks preferred for EPIC poetry: *"Arma virumque cano, Troiae qui primus ab oris / Italiam, fato profugus, Laviniaque venit. . . ."* (I sing of arms and the man who first came from distant Troy to Italy and the Lavinian [shore].) Without belaboring the details (since quantitative verse is rare in the European Renaissance) each of Virgil's Latin lines illustrates dactylic hexameter—a six-foot line composed mainly of dactyls, that is, of one long syllable followed by two short.

In the modern languages of Europe, by contrast, the lines of verse are usually measured according to patterns of stress. English, a four-stress language with two relatively heavy stresses and two relatively lighter ones in ordinary speech, groups heavier stresses together as one for purposes of scansion and does the same with lighter ones. A "metrical foot" is a pattern of stress. A combination of one light stress, followed by one heavy stress, - ', (y' KNOW?) is called an "iamb" or "iambus." Its opposite, '-, (MAny) is a "trochee." A foot of two light stresses - - (uh-uh), is a pyrrhus; one of two heavy ' ' (OH, NUTS!), a spondee. Two light stresses followed by one heavy - - ', (holy SMOKE!) is an anapest: its opposite, ' - - (FABulous!) an English and European dactyl.

A line of measured verse is written by combining metrical feet in conventional ways. Lines are classified by the number of feet they contain and by the stress pattern of the most frequent foot. Meter, like the sides of geometric shapes, get counted in words derived from Greek. Monometer means one metrical foot; dimeter, two; trimeter, three; tetrameter, four; pentameter, five; and hexameter, six. One rarely encounters lines longer than hexameter in English, but if one did the system would carry on. Sometimes poets write lines of iambic hexameter. These are called *alexandrines.*

Here is a very short poem each of whose lines, without the title, illustrates trochaic monometer:

> *A Poem to Answer the Question: What*
> *should I do with the billiard balls and cue*
> *sticks?*
> *Rack'em*
> *Stack'em*
>
>   (J. W. C.)

Iambic pentameter is the chief meter of ENGLISH SONNETS and of WILLIAM SHAKESPEARE's plays. If a line has four iambic feet and one dactyl, it still gets classified as iambic pentameter. The English language seems to fall naturally into iambic patterns. French poets of the Renaissance favored the alexandrine line.

Bibliography

Drake, Barbara. *Writing Poetry.* 1983. New York: Harcourt Brace Jovanovich, 1994.

Harrison, Michael, and Sue Heap. *Splinters: A Book of Very Short Poems.* Oxford: Oxford University Press, 1988.

Kirby, David. *Writing Poetry: Where Poems Come from and How to Write Them.* Boston: The Writer, 1997.

Poliziano, Angelo (1454–1494)

A gifted protégé of LORENZO DE' MEDICI, Poliziano was the son of Benedetto Ambrogini and Antonia Salimbeni— both representatives of notable families in the Tuscan town of Montepulciano near Siena. As a translator and poet, Poliziano worked with facility in Italian, Latin, and Greek. Before his 20th birthday he had translated Homer's *Iliad* into Latin hexameter verse—a feat that led to his lifelong connection with Lorenzo.

His reputation as an Italian poet rests in considerable measure upon an unfinished work, *The Stanze* (Stanzas) *of Angelo Poliziano* (ca. 1428). Though Giuliano de Medici's assassination seems to have interrupted the poem's composition, its finished portions establish Poliziano's claim to be regarded among the great innovators of Italian poetry. Whereas CARDINAL PIETRO BEMBO advocated the univocal imitation of the language and practice of PETRARCH as the proper direction for Italian verse to follow, Poliziano clearly understood Petrarch at a much more profound level than the cardinal did. The young poet perceived the way that Petrarch had used his immense mastery of the work of his predecessors to inform his poems with a learned variety that grew from subtle INTERTEXTUAL allusion. It was this aspect of Petrarch's work that Poliziano developed in seeking a new poetics for vernacular Italian. Another celebrated work in the Italian language was his play *Fabula di Orfeo* (The fable of Orpheus, ca. 1480). This work, as the literary historian Paul Colilli tells us, is reputed to be the earliest nonreligious drama in the history of Italian literature.

Poliziano also chronicled in Latin the conspiracy of the Pazzi family that took the life of Giuliano de' Medici and that had threatened Lorenzo's. Following the example of the Roman historian Sallust (86–34 B.C.E.), Poliziano wrote his *Pactianae coniurationis commentarium* (Commentary on the

Pazzi conspiracy, 1478). Beyond that, a scholarly, encyclopedic work in Latin appeared in 1489, a miscellany in which Poliziano discussed and re-established variant readings of ancient manuscripts, anticipating as he did so many of the methods of modern codicology—the science of manuscript study and documentation.

As a priest, Poliziano also authored sermons. He composed poems and EPIGRAMS in Latin and in Greek, and he collected his letters for posthumous publication. He also penned miscellaneous Latin collections of verses, notes, and commentary called *Silvae*.

Bibliography

Lord, Louis E., trans. *A Translation of the Orpheus of Angelo Politian and the Aminta of Torquato Tasso.* Ca. 1931. Westport, Conn.: Greenwood Press, 1986.

Poliziano, Angelo. *Silvae.* Translated and Edited by Charles Fantazzi. Cambridge, Mass.: Harvard University Press, 2004.

———. *The Stanze of Angelo Poliziano.* Translated by David Quint. University Park: Pennsylvania State University Press, ca. 1993.

Polynesian Oceania, oral literature of

Widely dispersed across the Pacific Ocean from New Zealand to Hawaii and from Fiji to Easter Island, the seafaring Polynesian peoples share a common oral literary culture and mutually intelligible dialects of a common ancestral language. The Polynesians apparently migrated in great double canoes and outriggers and settled on their islands between the 10th and 14th centuries. So hardy were these mariners that there is reason to think they may have reached and returned from Antarctica. In the process of their early migrations and also later on they developed a varied and complex oral literature. They did not, however, invent a written method of recording and preserving their poems and stories. A possible exception to that generalization may have existed on Easter Island where as yet undeciphered glyphs may be some sort of script.

To preserve their creative efforts in the absence of writing, Polynesians trained a class of storytellers to memorize flawlessly at one hearing lengthy recitations in verse (which is sung) or prose (which is spoken). M. H. Chadwick tells us that they called this mnemonic method *apo*—literature catching. A 19th-century European witness and recorder of some of the stories, W. K. Rice, listened to Hawaiian bards reciting unfamiliar works to a literature catcher for as long as three hours. Rice took notes. At the recitation's end, the literature catcher repeated the bard's entire performance exactly.

While this may seem incredible to those of us who supplement our powers of recollection with computers and filing systems, many preliterate peoples display astounding feats of memory—though none perhaps equal to the art of *apo*. Certain Renaissance Europeans, as well, carefully cultivated their memories. PETRARCH is said to have been able to quote 20,000 verses from Virgil by heart. The Italian writer GIORDANO BRUNO and the Spaniard Ramon Lull also had prodigious memories and both wrote books and gave instruction in the art of memorizing.

One class of Polynesian literature involved the recitation of genealogies that seem to be accurate back to as many as 25 generations and to very distant degrees of kinship. Because these memorized genealogies had legal status and could prove or disprove whether or not people were who they claimed to be, they were kept secret within families. A person whose ancestors had moved from one Pacific island to another generations before could, on returning to the original island, claim specific legal rights and inheritance if he could prove his identity by reciting his genealogy correctly beyond the point where his ancestor had emigrated. Someone claiming such rights and failing to meet the standards of proof was summarily executed. The accuracy of these genealogies has been cross-checked by comparing the histories of royal lines of the Hawaiians, the Tahitians, the Maori of New Zealand, and the Rarotongan islanders back through time until they intersect. Beyond the point where the groups first separated, the shared genealogies, though centuries old, have proved to be identical and more reliable near their beginning than later. Some of the later variance arises from the tendency of politicians to revise history in their own interests.

The public histories of Polynesian peoples were likewise recorded in songs that bards memorized and passed down from generation to generation until finally the meanings of some archaic words were lost though the words themselves survived. HISTORIC POEMS OF TONGA survive, for example, that record long, 16th-century sea voyages to several islands by mariners from the island of Tonga. After the age of European exploration began, Tongans recorded in their songs the visits of explorers such as Schouten in 1616 and Tasman in 1643. Only in cases like these are exact dates usually ascertainable. Scholars rely on counting generations for their estimates of the age of particular accounts. Some estimate 30 years to a generation, others 25, and others still argue for a shorter period given the prominent role of warfare in Polynesian society.

Chronicling the novel visits of European explorers did not, of course, constitute a principal focus of the historical sagas of the Polynesian peoples. They focused rather on the heroic deeds of early kings and priests and their monumental voyages of exploration. They report such matters as the discovery of the previously uninhabited island of New Zealand by two chiefs from Ra'iatea in the Society Islands and the description of the now extinct, enormous wingless bird, the Moa. The sagas concerning kings, also called heroic sagas, detail warfare, bloodshed, valor, and treachery.

A nonheroic saga concerning a priest tells the tale of Umi (ca. 16th century). The younger son of a hereditary Hawaiian chieftain, Umi inherited the temples and gods of Hawaii while his brother inherited the kingdom and the secular power. Umi overthrew his brother by intellect and treachery and extended his rule to other islands.

Other sorts of poems are often embedded in the sagas. Speech poems purport to record the words of particular individuals. Other poems praise people. Others still eulogize the dead. Dances such as the Hawaiian hula were performed to the singing of poems in praise of the rulers.

Another line of Polynesian poetry is that relating to religion. It includes poems in praise of divinities, prayers, incantations, oracles, myths, and prophecies. One also finds in abundance exemplary poems that feature nameless individuals but give edifying examples of behavior appropriate to a variety of circumstances. Sometimes the poems and stories of Polynesia record the unhappy circumstances of a nontechnological people (seafaring excepted) who relied for food mainly on fishing and gathering fruit and tree sap on limited landmasses in a virtually boundless ocean. The stringent necessity for population control was a fact of daily life. To keep population from overwhelming the supply of available food, all sorts of unpleasant expedients were brought into play, and these too appear in the literature of Polynesia: infanticide, cannibalism, almost constant warfare with an attendant veneration of warriors—both those who survived and those who died heroic deaths.

Finally, among many others, there is a class of poem that enabled Polynesian sailors to maneuver their canoes across apparently trackless wastes of thousands of miles of ocean—navigation poems. These record distances by the time it takes to chant a certain number of verses. They give directions and note landmarks. They tell where to look for sky marks like constellations at night or, by day, clouds that regularly gather over an island below the horizon. They also call attention to currents and to phenomena like a log that might be caught for centuries in the same eddy. Gerald Knight has recently translated into English examples of such navigation poems and other stories from the Marshall Islands. Among them is the story of "TARA-MALU AND LA ENJEN." It details some of the methods used to navigate the open ocean.

Bibliography

Chadwick, H. Munro, and N. Kershaw Chadwick. *The Growth of Literature,* Vol. 3. 1940. Reprint, Cambridge, U.K.: Cambridge University Press, 1986.

Knight, Gerald, trans. and ed. *Man that Reef.* Majuro, Republic of the Marshall Islands: Micronitor News & Print Company, 1982.

Polyphemus and Galatea   Luis de Góngara y Argote (ca. 1613)

A long and highly original retelling of a myth recounted by the Roman poet OVID (43 B.C.E.–17 C.E.) in the 13th chapter of his *Metamorphoses,*

GÓNGARA'S *Polyphemus* marks the transition to the poet's most characteristic and mature period. That period, some think, is best represented by two slightly later poems, the *Solitudes,* that Góngara intended to expand to four but never completed. In view of Góngara's plan for his *Solitudes* remaining unfulfilled, *Polyphemus,* many think, provides our best indicator of the direction of the development of the most remarkable poet of the 17th-century, Spanish baroque period.

Polyphemus was the Cyclops—the one-eyed giant and shepherd—that we first meet in Homer's *Odyssey.* The son of Poseidon, the god of sea and earthquake, Polyphemus displays volcanic behavior in Homer's work, throwing boulders and causing rockslides and tidal waves. In Ovid's story and in Góngara's we meet Polyphemus in love with the beautiful sea nymph, Galatea. She does not return the monster's affection. Instead she has fallen for the handsome youth Acis and he with her. Galatea snubs Polyphemus, and she and Acis consummate their passion in a lovely bower. Enraged, Polyphemus invades the bower and smashes Acis with a rock. The slain lover is metamorphosed in both versions into a river.

While that synopsis gives the minimal essentials of both versions, Ovid requires only 160 lines to tell his story and focuses close attention on the slain Acis's conversion to a river. Góngara, by contrast, writes 63 eight-line stanzas and dramatically heightens the erotic attention paid to the love affair of Acis and Galatea and to Galatea's fatal attraction for all manner of would-be lovers. Though other Renaissance poets had treated this material, none did so with the originality of Góngara, who humanizes the emotional responses of the monstrous Polyphemus.

From an interpretative point of view, an emergent and convincing critical consensus suggests that Góngara's message is an amoral and deterministic one at odds with the optimism of Renaissance HUMANISM, with the romantic sentimentality of the PASTORAL school of poetry, and perhaps even with the Christian message—though the dead Acis's conversion into a more-or-less immortal river may partly avert that suggestion. Polyphemus may be thought to represent the inescapable forces of the operation of the natural world in love with the creative principle as embodied in the female but finally destroying the creatures love brings into being. If there is optimism here, it rests in the thought that the life that comes and goes recycles into something else even though the edifice of love on which it pins its hopes crumbles just like mortal dust itself.

Bibliography

Foster, David William, and Virginia Ramos Foster. *Luis de Góngara.* New York: Twayne Publishers, 1973.
———. *The Fable of Polyphemus and Galatea.* Translated by Miroslav John Hanak. New York: P. Lang, ca. 1988.

Popul Vuh (1558)

The earliest known complete literary document in a native American tongue, the *Popul Vuh* is a mytho-historical poem composed in the Mayan-Quiché language represented in the Latin alphabet by an anonymous, Spanish-educated, Guatemalan Indian between 1554 and 1558. As one of its leading students, Margaret McClear, describes the poem's preservation, a Dominican priest named Francisco Ximenez came upon the manuscript between 1701 and 1703. He borrowed it, transcribed the 5,237 lines of the original text down the left side of each of 112 pages, and then added his own Spanish translation on the right. When his work was finished, he returned the original manuscript—now called the Chichicastenango Manuscript—to its owner. That original has never again been seen. Ximenez's manuscript, however, survives in the Edward E. Ayer Collection at the Newberry Library in Chicago, and it was there that McClear did her work on it.

Although the Ximenez manuscript contains no divisions, subsequent editors and translators have given the work section and chapter divisions that prove useful in gaining a sense of a document whose conventions of composition and presentation of material are unfamiliar to European and American readers.

The *Popul Vuh* recounts the rise and fall of the Quiché nation from two narrative perspectives—a mythic perspective that begins in a time before time and a historical perspective that never loses sight of the interactions between the people and their deities. A prologue states the author's purposes and methodology in a manner so perplexing that it raises a question as to whether the original lost source or sources of the *Popol Vuh* was a written document or a body of myth and history preserved in the corporate recollection of a group of Indians with the responsibility for remembering such matters.

The narrative proper begins by describing an empty, silent, static time when only sky and sea existed. There follows a creative word—a sort of divine verbal big bang—that animates the creative processes of the world. The book then continues with two juxtaposed stories. The first tells how the gods, after creating animals, vegetables, and minerals, at first failed to create creatures on earth to worship and obey them and keep their altars. The gods' efforts to turn animals, mud, or wood into people all fail. The second story recounts how two not-yet-human twins named Hunahpú and Xbalanqué annihilate a family of proud and overbearing heavenly creatures who refuse to acknowledge the gods as their creators or their own creaturely limitations.

The second part of the Popul Vuh recounts how the evil lords of Xibalba—the equivalent of Hell—challenge the still-not-quite-human sons of the mythic forebears of the Maya-Quiché people to a ball game whose stakes are life or death. The evil ones covet, as it turns out, the paraphernalia of the game. The boys, Hun-Hunapú and Vucub-Hunapú accept the challenge, but when they show up without equipment the evil ones torture, sacrifice, and bury them without even playing the game. A fruit-laden tree springs up on their grave, and the lords of Xibalba forbid sitting under it or picking the fruit. An Eve-like character named Xquic, however, ignores the prohibition. The fruit of the tree turns out to be talking skulls, and one of them asks the maiden if she wants one. She does, and when she stretches forth her hand to pick, the skull spits in her hand. By this means she becomes pregnant. Her father, one of the hellish lords, condemns her to be burned for harlotry and sends messengers off with her to accomplish the deed. She talks her executioners out of killing her, however, and goes to Earth while they deceive her father into thinking

they have burned her. In due course she finds her mother-in-law and bears twins who turn out to be the same two not-yet-quite-human twins of the first part of the story.

After numerous complications that, among other matters, explain the origin of monkeys from almost men, the twins accept another challenge to play ball with the evil lords of the underworld. This time they take their father's equipment with them and beat the hellish team twice. They then avoid various unpleasant fates their hosts have planned for them. Eventually they voluntarily allow themselves to be burned and, as they have achieved mastery over death, resurrect themselves for the entertainment and edification of the lords of Xibalba. They ask to be killed and resurrected too, and the twins grant the first half of their request. Thus the twins overcome the lords of the underworld and avenge their father.

The first two parts of the *Popol Vuh* concern themselves with mythic elements in the prehistory of the Mayan-Quiché people. So do the first three chapters of the third part in which the first four fully realized human beings at last appear shaped from cornmeal dough by the creator-mother Xmucané and her helpers. As soon as they are sentient, the four thank the gods who created them. This immediate evidence of human intelligence worries the gods; they think that people know too much. They therefore dim the vision of the first human beings by blowing dust in their eyes, clouding both their vision and their intellectual powers.

The balance of the book concerns itself both with the history of the Maya-Quiché people and with their myths. On the historical side of the ledger, for example, we learn of their rise to power, their dominance over other peoples in their region, the genealogies of some of their rulers, and descriptions of religious rites. We also read of the gods they worshipped and of the eventual destruction of the people. On the mythic side we learn of the people's acquisition of fire, of further descents into and ascents from the underworld, and of periodic visits to the sky and the underworld of the great King Gucumatz, under whom the Maya-Quiché reached the pinnacle of their power.

Bibliography

Goetz, Delia and Sylvanus Griswold Morley, trans. *Popul Vuh: The Book of the Ancient Maya.* Mineola, N.Y.: Dover Publications, 2003.

McClear, Margaret. *Popul Vuh: Structure and Meaning.* Madrid: Coleccion Plaza Mayor Scholar, 1973.

Recinos, Adrián, trans. and ed. *Popol vuh: Las antiguas historias del Quiché.* 1960. Reprint, Mexico City: Fondo de cultura económica, 1976.

Praise of Folly, The (*Encomium Moriae*)
Desiderius Erasmus (1514)

In the summer of 1509 as he traveled across the Alps on horseback, the most influential HUMANIST thinker of the northern European Renaissance, DESIDERIUS ERASMUS, conceived of writing an ironic, mock oration that would mimic a device of the ancient Greek playwright Aristophanes by having the person delivering an oration be at once its speaker and its subject. The work is at once a joke and a serious treatise. Even the title contains a Latin pun since it is simultaneously translatable as *The Praise of Folly* and *Praise by Folly.* An English edition entitled *Folly's Praise of Folly* would catch Erasmus's recondite double meaning. The title's joke is even more complex, however, because Erasmus was a close friend of the English humanist SIR (ST.) THOMAS MORE. Thus the accidental correspondence between More's name and the Greek word for *fool* became another level of Erasmus's jest. (It is well not to lose sight of the etymological heritage of the word *sophomore* whose elements taken together mean "a wise fool.") One of Erasmus's principal objectives in writing the work was to entertain More.

Folly as Erasmus presents her would make a wonderful 21st-century politician or entertainer. She tells us that she is the daughter of Plutus—the god of wealth—and of Youth. Her nurses were Drunkenness and Ignorance. She herself is fun loving, and she wholeheartedly approves of fun. She proves by false logic that folly is of greater value than wisdom. She explains that people worship her because, in her various manifestations, she makes them happy. To be happy, people need illusions to make the world seem more habitable than it is. Leaders need to deceive both themselves and their followers into thinking that their irresponsibility, ineptitude, and mistakes are the equivalents of valuable service.

For about 30 chapters Folly continues in this vein. She sometimes forgets things, and she contradicts herself. In the 31st chapter, however, Folly begins to talk about fools of another order and the light-hearted tone begins to dissipate. She begins to point to elderly men who dye their hair and old women who chase young men. Christians need Folly to convince them that the promise of life eternal is worth foregoing the pleasures of this world. But this, Erasmus clearly thinks, is folly of another order. Whereas ordinary folly leads to disaster, Christian folly leads elsewhere. But Folly herself does not concur in this judgment. She takes credit, for example, for the production of courage, the arts, and hard work. In order to gain a reputation in the world, she points out, people are prepared to spend sleepless nights, untold effort, and even shed their life's blood. She asks if working that hard and taking such risks do not represent the height of foolishness. She concludes that they do, but the outcomes justify the effort, and Folly again congratulates herself.

Erasmus intentionally makes it difficult for readers to perceive a dependable relationship between his own authorial viewpoint and the opinions of Folly. That relationship shifts, and just when readers think they have Erasmus's intention figured out, it slips through their fingers like quicksilver. Only when Folly levels her scornful gaze at the corruption of the clergy does there seem to be a clear and certain correspondence between the operation of her scalpel and that of Erasmus. Folly credits foolish self-love with the importance that underpaid, student-plagued professors and teachers assign themselves.

Of all of Erasmus's enormously influential works, *The Praise of Folly* is at once the most fondly and the best remembered. If a person could choose only one representative text of humanistic Renaissance letters to read, that reader could hardly make a better choice than *The Praise of Folly.*

Bibliography

Erasmus, Desiderius. *The Praise of Folly.* New Haven, Conn.: Yale University Press, 2003.

Prince, The Niccolò Machiavelli (written 1513, published 1532)

In some ways MACHIAVELLI'S *The Prince* continues a long tradition of treatises that give advice to rulers. It discusses the relative merits of love and fear, the way a ruler should handle his executive staff, the prince's liberality, and how to treat flattery. In a more important way *The Prince* breaks completely with its predecessors because it ignores their theological overlay. It breaks with their pious advice that rulers should subordinate themselves to the conventional morality espoused by church authority.

Machiavelli wants his ruler to be a good person and an example to the citizens, but that goodness is grounded not in a desire to serve God but rather in a desire to serve the best interests of the citizens and to preserve the state. Enhancing and protecting the common good was above all the ruler's responsibility. For that reason Machiavelli advises a prince to adopt a sliding scale of morality; the good of the state may require a ruler to act in a manner inconsistent with conventional ethical and moral principles.

In arriving at this conclusion, Machiavelli had before him the model of Rome—not of imperial Rome, but of the Roman Republic. In his personal political convictions, Machiavelli ardently favored republics. Nonetheless he perceived the potential benefits of a constitutional monarchy and looked to France as a model of such a state. He thought that there were times when only a monarch could hold in check the corruption of the populace at large. He also believed that at times of imminent danger to the state no consideration of justice or injustice, pity or cruelty, or praise- or blameworthiness should inhibit a ruler from acting in the best interests of the state. In particular, the interests of the church are subordinate to those of the state—an important departure from the thinking of his predecessors. A prince whose private morality is unassailable can ruin his people in the name of conventional virtue, for it often masks wickedness. Anything a prince does that benefits his people is virtuous regardless of the point of view of conventional morality.

Machiavelli devotes the first 11 chapters of *The Prince* to defining the idea of a principality, to examining its various forms, and to explaining how princes typically acquire, maintain, and lose principalities. These chapters include advice about gaining people's support and about defense against besieging enemies. In them Machiavelli often uses examples of contemporary or recent rulers in Italy and France. Among them we find Cesare Borgia (1476–1507). The illegitimate son of Pope Alexander VI, Borgia became captain-general of the armies of the church and parlayed that command into the control of much of central Italy. Though Borgia was popularly remembered as a heartless tyrant, Machiavelli viewed him as a prince who had saved Italy by overcoming the forces of roving bands of foreign mercenaries. The French king, Louis XII, is also the object of Machiavelli's admiration.

Chapters 12 through 14 concern themselves mainly with military matters and the harm that can come to governments controlled by princes. Chapter 15 turns its attention to issues of foreign and domestic policy and the way rulers should treat their allies and their subjects. The question of whether a prince should be generous or stingy occupies Chapter 16. On balance, Machiavelli advises stinginess. Maintaining a reputation for liberality can ruin a prince, whereas the outcome of stinginess produces "a bad reputation without hatred."

Machiavelli next turns his attention to a prince's cruelty or pity and whether a prince might better be loved or feared. Machiavelli advises that a few well-chosen, seemingly cruel acts will deter general lawlessness and avert the necessity of broader acts of cruelty. In the best of situations, Machiavelli thinks, a prince will be both loved and feared, but such an outcome is difficult to achieve. Faced with a choice, Machiavelli advises that a prince will find being feared more useful. A subject will break faith with a beloved prince if he sees the potential for profit but will think twice in the face of a certain punishment. The prince should, however, be careful not to become so feared that he is hated. Machiavelli concludes that men "love as they please," but "fear as the prince pleases."

The famous METAPHOR of the lion and the fox appears in chapter 18. Lions cannot avoid traps, and foxes cannot protect themselves from wolves. A prudent ruler will therefore adopt the qualities of both animals, but particularly of foxes. Machiavelli wants his ruler both to seem and to be "compassionate, trustworthy, humane, honest, and religious." Yet the same ruler, especially if new to the job, must act in ways "contrary to faith . . . charity . . . humanity . . . and religion," to continue in power. The chapter also discusses foreign policy.

To avoid the hatred and contempt of the citizens, Machiavelli advises in chapter 19 that a ruler should avoid being perceived as "variable, volatile, effeminate, cowardly, or irresolute." To preserve the subjects' respect, a leader must give the impression of "greatness, spirit, gravity, and fortitude." Princes should have their agents do whatever will attract the people's hatred, and they should personally do whatever will please them.

In the discussion of fortresses in Chapter 20, Machiavelli concludes that, for a ruler, a better fortress than one of stone and mortar is the people's love. Chapter 21 treats the reputation of the ruler at home and abroad, and the two chapters following address the subject of those who advise the ruler. A summary of many earlier points appears in chapter 24, and chapter 25 moves on to a consideration of the power of FORTUNE. Renaissance ICONOGRAPHY represented Fortune as a goddess who, together with NATURE, implements God's will in the world. Princes, therefore, are also subject to the vicissitudes of Fortune and cannot avoid them. They can, however, lessen them sometimes through hard work and prudent policy.

The final chapter, chapter 21, encourages a prince to lead Italy out of the control of the mercenary bands who continued throughout this period to plunder her. Machiavelli expresses the hope that the Medici, restored to Florentine power in 1512, might be the ones to produce a prince who can bring relief to Italy—the ones who will unite the Italians against the mercenaries. In this hope Machiavelli ends *The Prince* by quoting from the noblest patriotic poem in the Italian language, PETRARCH's "My Italy" (*Italia mia*). If the princes of Italy will resolve their differences and do their duty, Petrarch says:

Then Virtue will seize arms
'Gainst madness, and the battle will be brief
For ancient valor is
Not dead, as yet, within Italian hearts.

Bibliography

Machiavelli, Niccolò. *The Prince.* Translated by George Bull. New York: Penguin Books, 2003.

Petrarca, Francesco. *Petrarch's Songbook: Rerum Vulgarium Fragmenta.* Translated by James Wyatt Cook. Binghamton, N.Y.: Medieval and Renaissance Texts and Studies, 1995.

Princess of Cleves, The (*La Princesse de Clèves*) Madame de La Fayette (1678)

MADAME DE LA FAYETTE's celebrated book marks the 17th century's most significant shift in the manner and content of the French novel. Before its appearance, French novels were typically long, multivolume affairs whose principal interest arose from action—often military. They tended to be set in far-away, exotic places and in the distant past. Their casts of characters were enormous. They appeared in installments whose publication stretched over decades. They were filled with incredible incidents, identities concealed and revealed, magicians, and sorcerers.

The appearance of *The Princess of Cleves* changed all that. The book is short and readable in a single sitting. Its principal interest arises from a highly repressed love triangle and from the curiosity, conversations, and speculations about that triangle by the lovers themselves and those in their social circle. The work is set in the recent past in Paris and nearby locations. Madame de La Fayette's late-17th century Paris, transposed into the France of the mid-16th century at the court of King Henry II, provides the social milieu. The author peoples her pages with historical personages, and she draws the framing incidents from well-known French history. Thus the reader meets Henry's mistress, Diane de' Poitiers, the duchesse de Valentinois, and his queen, Catherine de' Medici, together with other members of his court. Only those intimate details of interpersonal relationships that give the novel its unique character and charm arise from the brilliant invention of its author and, perhaps, of members of her social circle.

The central plot of the novel opens with the introduction to court of the 16-year-old beauty, Mademoiselle de Chartres. Unlike many of her peers, the young woman had been carefully instructed by her mother about men and their insincerity, about love and its joys and snares, and about the benefits of preserving one's virtue. Madame de Chartres had particularly emphasized the dangers of illicit love affairs and the domestic unhappiness that they were certain to engender. The mother had also convinced the daughter that in their social circle virtue was difficult to preserve and that only in the mutual commitment of a husband and a wife was happiness to be found.

Mademoiselle de Chartres's introduction at court produced a great stir, and more than one young man fell immediately in love with her. Among the aspirants to her hand was the Prince of Cleves. After carefully reporting the jockeying and negotiations of the prince and his rivals, the author reports the success of the prince's suit and his joy at fulfilling his heart's desire. The marriage is arranged, and Mademoiselle de Chartres willingly becomes the Princess of Cleves. Although she feels respect and affection for her husband, she does not love him, and the prince's perception of that fact undermines to a degree his happiness in his union with her. He nevertheless remains hopeful that time will remedy the defect.

On the day before the couple's wedding the Duke of Nemours arrived in Paris, and, on seeing Mademoiselle de Chartres, fell immediately in love with her. On her side, the young woman also found that the Duke of Nemours stirred her feelings in ways that no other man had ever done. That impression strengthened on the numerous subsequent occasions when court life brought the two into each other's presence.

The young woman discussed her feelings with her mother, and the mother repeated all her former warnings. The mother, however, fell ill and died, and the daughter was deprived of her advice and support. As time passed, convinced of the danger of her feelings for the duke, the princess takes pains to avoid being alone with him. She observes him stealing a miniature portrait of her, but she says nothing to him lest she give him an opportunity to discuss his feelings for her.

Though he had earlier been something of a rake, the duke now silently serves his devotion to the princess. Increasingly distressed by her own

feelings and by her perceptions of the duke's, the princess takes the unusual step of telling her husband of her feelings. She assures him that she will never act on them, and she refuses to identify the object of her affections, but she explains that she will often be at pains to avoid company in order to dissuade her admirer from seeking opportunities to express his feelings. This unparalleled frankness on the one hand increases her husband's admiration of his wife's forthrightness and, on the other, distresses him since she evidently feels for another man what he wished her to feel for him.

Madame de La Fayette introduces further complications into the main plot. A dropped letter from a mistress endangers a confidant of the queen who asks his friend, the Duke of Nemours, to pretend the letter is his. Hiding in the garden of the private retreat of the princess for an opportunity to see her without her knowing, the Duke of Nemours overhears a conversation between the princess and her husband that confirms Nemour's suspicion: she loves him. Claiming that he is dicussing the situation of a friend, Nemours confides in the Princess of Cleves's uncle. The uncle shrewdly guesses that Nemours is really discussing himself, but he does not suspect that the lady who secretly returns the duke's love is the princess. The uncle then reports that juicy bit of gossip to his mistress. She passes it on to others, and soon the entire court is trying to find out the name of the lady whom the duke loves and who secretly loves him. No one, however, suspects the virtuous Princess of Clèves.

When the gossip reaches her ears, however, not knowing that the duke has secretly overheard her conversation with her husband, the princess concludes that he has violated her confidence. When she confronts him, he denies it and says that the princess herself must have told some other person. The ensuing recriminations further separate the increasingly estranged pair. The princess isolates herself at her country home to avoid all contact with Nemours. The duke requests the king's permission to leave the court. He means to observe the princess secretly and gain access to her if he can. Suspicious, the prince has the duke followed. Misinterpreting his spy's report, the prince assumes the worst.

When he confronts his wife, she denies her guilt and convinces him of her innocence.

Dealing with the whole situation, however, has become more than the husband can bear. He complains that he wishes his wife could either have loved him or had at least let him think so and, like other women, indulged her passion. He sickens, and reproving his wife as the cause of his death, soon dies. Disconsolate, the princess isolates herself. As time passes, however, she comes to terms with her grief. Eventually she discovers that the Duke of Nemours is secretly observing her comings and goings. Able at last to speak directly with him, she does so.

It may be that readers expected a resolution in which the lovers, free at last, would wed and live happily ever after. If so the readers were doomed to disappointment. Although the princess feels free at last to express her feelings and to confirm that she does indeed love Nemours, she tells him that she has no intention of ever marrying him. "You have loved before," she tells him. She is convinced that after marriage to her he would love again and find another mistress. She thinks it was her unkind fate to be married to the only man in the world who could preserve love into marriage, and she could not love him back. In the event, she enters a convent and spends half the year as a religious recluse and half equally isolated on her own estates. She did not, La Fayette tells us, live long. As she predicted, the duke eventually finds other loves.

This woeful tale is interspersed with historical reporting. We learn of the unfortunate death of Henry II in a jousting accident and the prediction of that death by an astrologer. We hear the story of ANNE BOLEYN. We learn that the Duke of Nemours rejected the opportunity to become Prince Consort of England by marrying ELIZABETH I. We learn of Catherine de' Medicis' revenge against her dead husband's longtime mistress, the Duchess of Valentinois.

Perhaps, as some have suggested, the radical change from its predecessors in the structure and focus of this novel arises from a corresponding change in the view of the nature of history. What drives history, Madame de La Fayette may have thought, is less its great military events and heroic actions and more the intimate feelings, activities, and decisions of persons in their day-to-day existences.

Bibliography

Lafayette, Marie-Madelaine de. *The Princess of Cleves*. Edited and translated by John D. Lyons. New York: W. W. Norton & Company, 1994.

printing

Using wooden word-blocks set in presses, printing developed in China as early as the ninth century C.E. Because Chinese ideographic and phonographic symbols generally represent entire words, printing in Chinese required many different blocks. By the 13th century, the Chinese technology of printing had migrated to Korea. The impetus for the development of printing in both countries seems to have arisen as a result of the demand for Buddhist texts. Chinese remained the literary language of Korea until the time of the European Renaissance. Printing of texts in the Korean language developed only after scholars developed a Korean alphabet based on Arabic sources. The first work printed in Korean appeared around 1446. A celebrated 13th century Korean edition of a long Buddhist text in the Chinese language required some 80,000 word-blocks to print.

Chinese books of the 16th and 17th centuries continued to have the appearance of Chinese calligraphy, and the same technologies that allowed for word-block printing made possible illustrating editions with pictures as well. In Asia the era of the European Renaissance saw the rise of Chinese social and erotic novels as well as the increasing popularity of collections of secular short stories, poems, and drama that contained interlinear commentary on and criticism of the text. LI YU and DONG YUE figure among the many authors whose printed works survive from the period and illustrate some of its trends.

In Europe experiments in combining moveable type with screw presses were going forward early in the 15th century. Johann Gutenberg is generally credited with having invented the first practicable printing press, which he began operating in Strasbourg, Germany, between 1436 and 39. He moved to Mainz and went into partnership with Johann Fust in 1450. Shortly thereafter work began on the Gutenberg or 42-line BIBLE. But pioneering the printing business proved financially risky, and Fust acquired

Gutenberg's interest in 1455. Like Gutenberg, several pioneers succeeded at learning the trade but failed at running the business. Others, however, successfully established themselves in Germany in the 1450s and 1460s, and all of them at first served mainly the markets that education and religion made profitable.

From Germany practitioners of the printers' craft fanned out across the continent. The year 1465 saw the establishment of a press about 50 miles from Rome, where the printers Arnold Pannatz and Conrad Sweynheim soon moved their operation. By 1480 Italy had 50 presses in operation—more than Germany. Venice was an especially active center of Italian printing and before 1500 had more than 4,000 titles to its credit. The rise of HUMANISM created new markets for books in Latin, Greek, and Hebrew. This also meant that typefaces had to be invented to represent those languages as well as the vernacular languages of Europe. A famous example of the printer's art, the COMPLUTENSIAN POLYGLOT BIBLE, was prepared at the new University of Alcalá de Henares in Spain with the three ancient languages all represented.

WILLIAM CAXTON brought the printing press to England from Belgium in the 1480s and made a success of the business. Caxton translated and edited many of the works he printed, and his associate, Wynkyn de Worde, succeeded him in the business in the early 16th century.

A rise in literacy accompanied the spread of printing, and the enormous drop in the price of books that printing occasioned meant that the age of literary mass marketing had arrived. It was accompanied by all the abuses that new technologies usually bring to a market. Editions were pirated, authors were done out of their payments, and printers were ruined. On the other hand, the thirst for books, secular and entertaining as well as religious and scholarly, meant that writers no longer depended exclusively on the generosity of patrons and PATRONAGE for a living. It became possible to scrabble together a living with one's pen, and even, in rare instances, to become wealthy.

The historian of printing Martin J. C. Lowrey argues that printing made possible the success of reform movements like the Protestant Reformation. Writings like MARTIN LUTHER's could be broadly disseminated to a critical mass of like-minded readers. The sheer weight of numbers that this made possible undermined the established power of the Roman Catholic hierarchy and allowed Luther to succeed where earlier religious reformers like John Wycliffe in England had failed.

If one considers carefully, one can see that the book and its predecessor the manuscript codex are technological achievements of a very high order. The codex, that is, pages bound in book format, is much easier to use than was its predecessor, the scroll. Equipped with a good index, a book is still at least as quick and efficient a way to find information as is electronic surfing and scrolling, and, at least in the view of this reader, a much more user friendly way of working. The combination of the book's format with the mass production that printing made available can certainly be credited with the preservation and transmittal of information that made the rise of the industrial age a possibility.

From Renaissance Europe the printing press spread during the age of exploration to those parts of the world, such as India and America, where the Chinese system of printing had not arrived ahead of the European printing press.

Bibliography

Barker, Nicolas. *Form and Meaning in the History of the Book: Selected Essays.* London: British Library, 2003.

Chappell, Warren. *A Short History of the Printed Word.* Point Roberts, Wash.: Hartley and Marks Publishers, ca. 1999.

Febvre, Lucien P., and Henri Jean Martin. *The Coming of the Book: The Impact of Printing, 1450–1800.* New York: Verso, 1990.

Jensen, Kristian, ed. *Incunabula and Their Readers: Printing, Selling, and Using Books in the Fifteenth Century.* London: British Library, 2003.

Steinberg, S. H. *Five Hundred Years of Printing.* New Castle, Del.: Oak Knoll Press, 1996.

prosody

Any system of analysis that attempts to account for the sequences of sounds and silence, the rise, continuity, and falling of pitch, the duration of vowel, consonant, and syllable sounds, and the clustered components of phrase and clause structures in any language is called *prosody*. Prosody includes but is a broader category than POETIC METER.

Protestant Reformation

In 1517 MARTIN LUTHER attacked the sale of indulgences and the theological right of the Vatican to authorize release from after-death punishments that the church neither had imposed nor, he argued, could impose. That attack began a process that irreparably tore the fabric of what had for over a thousand years been European Christendom. Luther, JOHN CALVIN, JOHN KNOX, HULDRICH ZWINGLI, and DESIDERIUS ERASMUS—though Erasmus never broke officially with the church—foreswore the veneration of relics and religious icons, espoused the priesthood of every Christian, called the efficacy of certain sacraments into question, and denied the authority of the pope.

The roughly simultaneous development of the PRINTING PRESS resulted in the widespread dissemination of Protestant ideas and won many converts to the cause of religious reform. People took their religion very seriously, and disagreements between the Protestants and the Roman Catholics soon warmed from debate to civil war in France, Germany, Iceland, the Netherlands, and Scotland. One of the primary lessons of history is that religious disagreement often becomes a prime cause of armed belligerence.

Whereas the reforming impetus in Continental Europe involved theological and doctrinal matters, in England the Protestant break with Rome came instead as a result of Henry VIII's roving eye and his wish to divorce Catherine of Aragon to wed ANNE BOLEYN. When Rome refused a divorce or an annulment, Henry made himself the head of an English state church and denied the pope's authority. When, however, his daughter, Mary I, became queen, she returned England to the Roman Catholic fold for the brief five years of her reign. Her sister and successor ELIZABETH I, however, pursued an adroit religious policy by reestablishing an Anglican state church that did not look very different theologically from the Roman Catholic one. Elizabeth, however, tolerated a wide spectrum of religious conviction.

The literary influence of this series of religious upheavals can hardly be exaggerated. Not only were the works of the principal reformers widely disseminated, so were the works of their opponents. BIBLE translation into the vernacular languages of Europe—a practice the Roman Catholic Church had opposed—became a thriving industry. In countries like Spain and Italy where the Roman Church had the power to impose its will on the book trade, printers were theoretically prohibited from publishing and selling publications on the INDEXES OF FORBIDDEN BOOKS. Though being on the index made certain books difficult to come by, it also made them more desirable to persons who chaffed at the notion of church censorship.

Impressively imaginative works of literature flowed from the pens of writers and poets on both sides of the religious controversy. On the one hand we see works like THÉODORE AGRIPPA D'AUBIGNE's LES TRAGIQUES (1616) chronicling the tragic outcomes of the French civil war from a Protestant perspective, or JOHN MILTON's Protestant EPIC of universal history, *PARADISE LOST*. On the other hand we see the great epic poem of the Roman CATHOLIC COUNTER REFORMATION, the Italian TORQUATO TASSO's *GERUSALEMME LIBERATA*. In England a new butt for SATIRE arose in the persons of undereducated, grasping, Scripture-spouting hypocrites who began to populate the English stage to the vast amusement of everyone but the Puritans they parodied.

Bibliography

Lindberg, Carter. *The European Reformations*. Oxford and Cambridge, Mass.: Harvard University Press, 1996.

McGrath, Alister. *The Intellectual Origins of the European Reformation*. Oxford: Oxford University Press, 1987.

psychomachia

This term, formed from the Greek words for "soul" and for "warfare," alludes to a conflict that often provides a subject for literature in many times and places. Frequent in the literature of the Renaissance, a "psychomachia" describes the ongoing warfare between the forces of good and evil for the soul of an individual. In a sense, all of PETRARCH's lyrical verse in his cycle of 366 poems is part of an unresolved psychomachia—unresolved because at the work's end the author is uncertain about the state of his soul. The German play *Everyman* and the English play THE CASTLE OF PERSEVERANCE both belong to this type. So does CHRISTOPHER MARLOWE's THE TRAGICAL HISTORY OF DR. FAUSTUS.

Pu Songling (1640–1715)

The most accomplished of several Chinese prose writers who specialized in the literature of the supernatural, Pu Songling described himself as the "historian of the strange." Both terms of this self-description are accurate. Pu always claimed that he was merely passing along what he had learned from others who considered them factual accounts of historical happenings. What he passed along was regularly from the realm of the fanciful. His reports feature ghosts, love stories with supernatural twists, and characters who move with relative ease across the boundaries between the natural and the supernatural worlds.

Pu's masterpiece is STRANGE TALES OF LIAOZHAI (not published until 1766). It contains over 500 stories, some very brief but others long and involved, that Pu apparently assembled over a period of 40 years, pretending they were all by an earlier writer. The collection is famous for its imaginative and credible characterizations both of men and of women, for the inventiveness of its incidents, for its humor, and for the physical and psychological credibility of the physical and the spectral worlds.

Critics have also celebrated Pu's originality in including domestic interactions and disagreements into the general framework of the classical Chinese tale. Commentators also point to another feature of Pu's writing: his sometimes outspoken social criticism of administrative corruption, the examination system (Pu himself never passed), and the social ills that afflicted his era. His language is readable, colloquial, and straightforward. Pu is also thought by some to have written verse plays for production in his local theater in Shandong (Shantung) Province, but his authorship remains a matter of controversy.

Bibliography

Pu Songling. *Chinese Tales: Zhuangzi, Sayings and Parables, and Chinese Ghost and Love Stories.* Translated from Martin Buber's German translation of the Chinese by Alex Page. Amhurst, N.Y.: Humanity Books, 1998.

———. *Strange Tales of Lioazhai . . .* [Selections]. Translated by Lu Yunzhong. Hong Kong: Commercial Press, 1982.

———. *The Bonds of Matrimony.* Translated by Eve Alison Nyren. Lewiston, N.Y.: Mellen Press, ca. 1995.

Pulci, Antonia Tannini (1452–1501)

An Italian poet and playwright who authored a number of charming sacred plays in verse, Tannini Pulci was early married to BERNARDO PULCI, a member of a Florentine literary family who benefited from the patronage of LORENZO DE' MEDICI. It is likely that Lorenzo's wife Clarice Orsini de' Medici furnished the dowry that made this Pulci-Tannini union possible. Conceivably Bernardo and Antonia Pulci were the first husband-wife playwriting team ever to operate in Italy.

Following Bernardo's death in 1487, Antonia became an Augustinian tertiary—that is to say, an affiliate of the Augustinian order but not a full-fledged nun. Because no children had been born of her union with Bernardo, Antonia's dowry reverted to her on his death. Resisting her brother's suggestion that she remarry, she used the dowry to found a religious order, Santa Maria della Misericordia (Saint Mary of Mercy), in Florence. She wrote further plays and was herself the subject of a contemporary biography written by an Augustinian friar, Antonio Dulciati, whom she mentored and who, upon taking orders, chose the religious name Antonio in her honor.

Among the several plays securely attributable to Pulci we find a play about the life of St. Francis of Assisi, *The Play of St. Anthony the Abbot,* and *The Sacred Representation of the Prodigal Son*—written while Bernardo was still living. We also find what is perhaps her most characteristic play, THE SACRED REPRESENTATION OF SAINT GUGLIELMA. Antonia Tannini Pulci's plays are all of interest because they illustrate the high point of a development of the genre of sacred representations from a crude folk form to a polished poetic art. Pulci displays in her verse dramas an impressive mastery of the Italian *ottava rima* stanza. Some of her plays, including *Guglielma* and *The Play of Saint Domitilla*, command special interest not only for their sensitive portrayal of aspects of the lives of women but also because of the intriguing possibility that autobiographical elements may appear in them.

Pulci finally took orders as an Augustinian nun shortly before her death.

Bibliography

Pulci, Antonia. *Florentine Drama for Convent and Festival: Seven Sacred Plays*. Translated by James Wyatt Cook; edited by James Wyatt Cook and Barbara Collier Cook. Chicago: University of Chicago Press, 1996.

———. *Florentine Drama for Convent and Festival: Seven Sacred Plays*. 2nd edition. Edited by Elissa Weaver. Translated by James Wyatt Cook and Elissa Weaver. Chicago: University of Chicago Press, ca. 2005.

Pulci, Bernardo (d. 1487)

One of three brothers of the literary Pulci family of Florence, the very devout Bernardo married ANTONIA TANNINI PULCI in 1470 when she was 18 years old. Both spouses were playwrights and poets. Bernardo is known to have authored two sacred plays: *Barlaam and Josaphat* and *The Angel Raphael*. In 1464 he wrote a poem in Dantean TERZA RIMA that eulogized Cosimo de' Medici as the father of his country. His other poems are of a religious cast. He wrote a long series of triplets in praise of the Virgin Mary, SONNETS lamenting scandals at the papal court in Rome, and a series of visions in which he praises the virtues of poverty and condemns wealth. He and his wife shared an extremely ascetic vision of the virtuous life and lived in very straitened financial circumstances.

In the year of the couple's marriage Bernardo's brother LUCA PULCI died. Bernardo and Antonia assumed a portion of the responsibility for taking care of Luca's children. It may well be that necessity

led the couple to become the first Italian husband and wife playwriting team, supplying the Florentine market with plays for religious performances and with printed versions of the plays.

In 1471 Bernardo Pulci appealed to LORENZO DE' MEDICI for help. Though Lorenzo's assistance was slow in coming, it did finally arrive in 1476 when Lorenzo facilitated Bernardo's appointment as a chamberlain of the district of Mugello. After only a year, however, Pulci's health deteriorated and he had to resign. Before 1484 Lorenzo again helped him find employment, this time as a kind of steward serving officials at both the universities of Florence and Pisa. He held that post until his death in 1487.

Bibliography

Pulci, Antonia. *Florentine Drama for Convent and Festival*. Edited by James Wyatt Cook and Barbara Collier Cook. Chicago: University of Chicago Press, 1996.

———. *Florentine Drama for Convent and Festival: The Plays of Antonia Pulci*. Revised and expanded bilingual edition. Edited by Elissa Weaver, translated by James Wyatt Cook and Elissa Weaver. Chicago: University of Chicago Press, ca. 2005.

Pulci, Luca (d. 1470)

One of three literary Pulci brothers, Luca's poetic output was the least consequential among the three. Like his brothers, Luca was at least a marginal member of the circle surrounding LORENZO DE' MEDICI. Among his poetic remnants are several stanzas he contributed to his brother LUIGI PULCI's poem in celebration of a ceremonial tournament that Lorenzo is said to have staged to honor his mistress, Lucrezia Donati. Entitled *La giostra di Lorenzo de' Medici* (The joust of Lorenzo . . .), the poem is of interest principally to specialists. Luca also apparently had a hand in a work for which his brother Luigi Pulci claimed principal credit though another poet seems also to have been involved: *"Il Ciriffo Calvaneo."*

Perhaps the most interesting story about Luca Pulci is the persistent though unsubstantiated rumor that he died in the notorious debtor's prison of Florence, the Stinche. The records of the prison do not bear this out, but he did die young and his brothers were obliged to rear his children.

Pulci, Luigi (1432–1484)

The eldest of three literary Pulci brothers, Luigi was descended from a noble family that had fallen on financial hard times. By the time their father Iacopo Pulci died, his debts were so great nothing was left for his sons. Luigi was fortunate to attract the attention of Cosimo de' Medici, the uncrowned ruler of Florence. Cosimo invited Luigi into his household where Pulci's poetic talent made him a great favorite of Cosimo's daughter-in-law Lucrezia Tornabuoni de' Medici, wife to Piero and mother of LORENZO DE' MEDICI.

Lucrezia prevailed on Pulci to undertake a CHIVALRIC EPIC that she hoped would add a major, pious poem to the Charlemagne cycle. The result, Pulci's enormous, elaborate, bizarre, influential, and sometimes impious MORGANTE: THE EPIC ADVENTURES OF ORLANDO AND HIS GIANT FRIEND MORGANTE (Morgante maggiore, 1483) bore little resemblance to Lucrezia Tornabuoni's expectations.

Pulci's nature was saturnine and sarcastic, and he was a free thinker. He was also more of a populist than an aristocrat. Perhaps these very qualities attracted Lucrezia's son Lorenzo de' Medici to the poet who was more than 16 years his senior. In any case, the two became great friends and are said to have roistered together through the streets of Florence during the pre-Lenten carnival singing bawdy CARNIVAL SONGS.

In addition to Morgante, Pulci's work includes his contributions to a poem, La giostra di Lorenzo (Lorenzo's joust, 1482), celebrating a tournament sponsored by Lorenzo in honor of his mistress Lucrezia Donati. Pulci had earlier prepared a peculiar wordlist, his Vocabolista (Lexicon, 1465.) About this work the literary historian Edoardo A. Lébano speculates that Pulci wrote it so he would be considered a member of Florence's HUMANISTIC intelligensia. He also parodied one of Lorenzo's works, wrote a short novel in the manner of BOCCACCIO, and composed some songs. His well deserved and lasting claim to poetic fame, however, rests solidly if not exclusively on his mock chivalric epic, Morgante.

Eventually, however, Pulci's individualistic view of matters led him to exceed the bounds of what Florentines, including Lorenzo, considered pious and proper. Pulci wrote a series of irreverent sonnets leveled at the Neoplatonist MARSILIO FICINO. In them the poet called into question both the immortality of the soul and the notion of post-mortem heavenly rewards. Furious, Ficino accused Pulci of making war on God, and Florence was horrified. Pulci tried to beat a strategic retreat. He wrote a long confessional poem as a public apology, but the damage had been done. Lorenzo withdrew his patronage, and the church and the people adjudged him a heretic. At his death his corpse was denied a place in consecrated ground.

Bibliography

Davie, Mark. Half-Serious Rhymes: The Narrative Poetry of Luigi Pulci. Dublin: Irish Academic Press, 1998.

Pulci, Luigi. Morgante: The Epic Adventures of Orlando and His Giant Friend Morgante. Translated by Joseph Tusiani. Introduction and notes by Edoardo A. Lébano. Bloomington: Indiana University Press, 1998.

Punishment without Revenge (El Castigo sin Veganza) Lope de Vega Carpio (1631)

Based on a historical incident that occurred in Ferrara in 1405, LOPE'S TRAGEDY recounts the story of a duke of Ferrara who, in his middle years, contracted a marriage with a young and passionate daughter of the ducal house of Mantua.

Engaged in warfare in command of papal armies, the Duke of Ferrara sends his illegitimate son Federigo as a stand-in to conduct his youthful bride to Ferrara. On the way, she is almost swept away in a flash flood, but Federigo saves her from drowning, and passionate feelings develop between the two young people. When, after her marriage, her husband the duke proves inattentive, the young duchess and Federigo become lovers.

In due course the duke discovers the liaison. He imprisons his wife in a cell and covers her person with a veil so that she is unrecognizable. He then charges his son with the task of assassinating a person who represents a threat to the duke's life. Unaware of the identity of the person he is to kill, the obedient Federigo stabs his beloved to death. As Federigo emerges from her cell with his bloody knife in his hand, the duke raises a hue and cry, proclaiming Federigo as the assassin of his stepmother. The duke's retainers cut Federigo down on the spot. The duke has seen his version of justice served without ever appearing to others to have been vindictive.

Bibliography
Lope de Vega. *Fuente Ovejuna [The sheep's well]. The Knight from Olmeda. Punishment without Revenge.* Translated by Gwynne Edwards. Oxford and New York: Oxford University Press, 1999.

Purandaradasa   (1484–1564)

An Indian poet, musician, and saint whose medium of expression was the Kannada language, Purandaradasa has been said by some to have written 475,000 songs. This output seems mythically exaggerated, but about 1,000 of his works survive to attest to his industry and skill.

As the lyrics of his work are often autobiographical, it is possible to trace something of Purandaradasa's religious development through his work. A reader finds the poet often depressed and complaining not only about his difficulties but also about a God who would allow a good person to suffer. Eventually, however, he underwent a religious epiphany, and from that moment forward he sang of an intimate personal relationship with the Deity, proclaiming that he could see God in all his splendor and beauty. His poems praising that personal Deity are widely considered the best exemplars of the type.

His reputation as a theoretical musician, if anything, exceeds his fame as a poet and hymnodist. Historians of music credit him with having imposed a system on a variety of music (Carnatic music) that had its origins in the region of southeastern India now occupied by Madras state.

Bibliography
Jackson, William J. *Songs of Three Great South Indian Saints.* Delhi and New York: Oxford University Press, 1998.

Purandaradāsa. *Anthology of Saint-Singer Purandara Dasa.* Translated by D. Seshagiri Rao. Bangalore, India: Parijatha Publications, 1978.
———. *Purandara Dasa Krithis.* Sound recording. Koel Music: KDV 098 DDD. Sung by M. Balamuralikrishna. New Delhi: World Media, 2000.

Puritan, Puritanism

These controversial terms are now widely used by scholars to describe the members and creed of a 16th- and 17th-century English religious movement in the tradition of JOHN CALVIN. The Puritans venerated Holy Scripture as the source of all necessary knowledge, and they valued learning languages like Greek and Hebrew and the study of the explanation of the Scriptures according to various interpretative systems. They did not regard other studies as nearly so important. Their opposition both to Rome and to the established Church of England proved an important contributing factor to the civil war that began in England in 1642.

One reason that the term *Puritan* remains controversial arises from its having originally been coined as an insult. Many Englishmen perceived Puritans as BIBLE spouting know-nothings and disturbers of the peace. A sense of the general public's scornful attitude toward them during the English Renaissance can be gained from their depiction on the English stage during the reigns of ELIZABETH I and JAMES I, her successor.

Ben Jonson's BARTHOLOMEW FAIR provides a useful illustration of Puritans' low regard in popular esteem. There Jonson depicts the rich widow, Dame Purecraft, and one of her fortune-hunting suitors, Zeal-of-the-Land Busy. The playwright pokes fun at the naming practices of Puritans and represents the general perception of Puritan hypocrisy. These characters satirize ignorant, proselytizing, grasping Puritans who loudly proclaim virtue and denounce vice, but who are themselves running confidence schemes to bilk their more simple-minded co-religionists of their money.

qasída

A traditional poetic form in Arabic, Persian, and Turkish poetry, a *qasída* regularly praises someone or is often an ELEGY or a eulogy. The *qasida* is the most characteristic form of Arabic poem.

As contrasted with most verse in modern European languages, the metrical patterns of verse in the Semitic languages and Turkish are quantitative. In quantitative verse, a metrical foot is measured by a combination of traditionally defined long and short syllables rather than by a system of accentual emphasis. (See POETIC METER.) Thus, English translations of *qasida* have regularly been normalized on English accentual models. As a result, they fail to reflect very accurately that aspect of their originals. On the other hand, the *qasída* employs a regular rhyme scheme, and English translators have often captured that characteristic of the form successfully. They have also succeeded in reflecting the ingenuity and appeal of the often striking IMAGES of the original poems.

In Arabic and Persian, the *qasida* varies in length from 30 to 120 lines. In Turkish, the form is sometimes longer. The two halves of the first line of the poem rhyme, and most and sometimes all of the other lines end in the same rhyme. Sometimes poets intersperse couplets with a different rhyme for the sake of variety or to mark a change of subject.

A famous writer of Turkish *qasídas* was the poet BÂKÎ (1520–1600). Among the most celebrated examples of the form is his 213th *qasída*, a poem that usually stands first in collections of the poet's work. It honors his patron, Sultan Suleymán, to whom in the fiction of the poem all the then-known seven planets pay tribute one starry night. Mercury, for example, is pictured as the scribe of Heaven, recording Suleymán's accomplishments with a "meteor-pen." E. J. W. Gibbs's English translation of this work runs to 84 lines.

Rabelais, François (ca. 1494–1554)

The son of a French lawyer, Rabelais was educated with members of the prestigious Du Bellay family. He entered the Franciscan order at about 17. Fascinated with the new HUMANISM, he embarked on the study of languages, learning Latin, Arabic, Greek, and Hebrew. The Franciscans, however, took a dim view of the newfangled humanist learning and confiscated Rabelais's Greek books. In response, with the help of another boyhood school friend, Geoffrey d' Estissac, now bishop of Mailezais, Rabelais sought and obtained permission to shift to the Benedictine order in 1525. Among the Benedictines his impulse for study was not restrained, and he spent six years among them with his books. His interests were by no means limited to the humanities; he also avidly pursued the sciences, including mathematics, astronomy, and medicine. Although the medicine of the early 16th century was in some ways a more literary than scientific study, it was nonetheless unusual for anyone to master that science in such short order as did Rabelais.

He was admitted to the School of Medicine at the University of Montpellier on September 17, 1530. A month and a half later, on November 1, 1530, he received a bachelor's degree in medicine. By April of the following year he was lecturing on the Greek physicians Hippocrates and Galen at the university. He became a resident physician at the hospital, the Hotel-Dieu, in Lyon in 1532, and, the following year, he set out for Rome with his boyhood friend, Cardinal Jean Du Bellay, whom Rabelais served both as a secretary and as a personal physician. In 1537 he returned to Montpellier to take his M.D., and he undertook further studies in anatomy by conducting the dissection of the body of a criminal who had been executed by hanging.

In 1532 Rabelais's literary career had begun, not with the books for which he is widely remembered as a humorist, but with editions of the medical *Epistles* of the Italian Giovanni Manaradi and of works by those same ancient physicians, Galen and Hippocrates, about whom he had lectured. That same year also saw the publication of his pseudonymous PANTAGRUEL. For its ostensible author, Rabelais chose Alcofribas Nasier—an anagram of François Rabelais. *Pantagruel* came as a response to a short pamphlet that Rabelais may have had a hand in editing: *Les Grand et inestimables chroniques du grand et énorme géant Gargantua* (The great and inestimable chronicle of the great and enormous giant, Gargantua). That work is not to be confused with Rabelais's own later GARGANTUA (1535), which, since Gargantua is the father of

Pantagruel, is now printed as the first section of Rabelais's four-part masterpiece. Also in 1532 Rabelais wrote the first of a series of mock almanacs, his *Pantagrueline Prognostication* for the year 1533. This series continued for each year until 1550.

In Rome in 1534 Rabelais edited the Latin *Topographia Antiquae Romae* (Topography of Ancient Rome) by Marliani. In 1535 Rabelais successfully petitioned Rome to absolve him from violations of his priestly vows. He had fathered a child (who died at age two) and there may have been some irregularities connected with his 1530 conversion from Benedictine monk to secular priest. A papal dispensation absolved him of these errors and permitted him to continue the practice of medicine as long as he performed neither surgery nor cautery. The papal document also allowed him to return to the Benedictines whenever he wished.

From 1538 to 1543 he served in the French diplomatic service with another Du Bellay, Guillaume, who was the French equivalent of a secretary of state. During the same period he was also charged with collecting manuscripts for the library of King FRANCIS I.

Both *Pantagruel* and *Gargantua* had been condemned by the theological faculty at the Sorbonne for their scatological content as well as for heresy. In 1545, therefore, when the third installment of his series of related texts was complete, Rabelais obtained royal permission to publish it. The Sorbonne banned it nonetheless, and the uproar in Paris led Rabelais to work in Metz as a physician from 1546 to 1549. Then he once more joined Cardinal Du Bellay in Rome, and while there wrote an account, *Sciomachie,* of the celebrations in honor of the birth of the second son of the newly crowned King Henry II.

By Henry's favor, a royal decree lifted the Sorbonne's ban against Rabelais's books, and he published the fourth and final section of *Gargantua and Pantagruel* in 1552. Undeterred by the king's influence, the Sorbonne censured the book during the ruler's absence from Paris. On his return, he lifted the ban. After a life filled with enviable accomplishment, Rabelais died the following year.

Bibliography

Bowen, Barbara C. *Enter Rabelais, Laughing.* Nashville, Tenn.: Vanderbilt University Press, ca. 1998.

Frame, Donald Murdoch. *François Rabelais: A Study.* New York: Harcourt Brace Jovanovich, ca. 1977.

Rabelais, François. *Gargantua and Pantagruel.* New York: Knopf, 1994.

———. *Oeuvres complètes: Rabelais.* Edited and translated from Middle into Modern French by Guy Demerson. Paris: Editions du Seuil, ca. 1995.

———. *The Complete Works of François Rabelais.* Translated by Donald M. Frame. Berkeley, Calif.: University of California Press, ca. 1991.

Racine, Jean (1639–1699)

Orphaned at two, Jean Racine was reared by his grandmother. She saw to it that he received a first-rate education at Port-Royal from members of the Jansenist sect to which the grandmother herself belonged. Unlike Protestants, the Jansenists wished to reform Roman Catholicism from within. Although like the HUMANISTS the Jansenists interested themselves in classical literature, unlike humanists, who believed in the reforming power of education, the Jansenists viewed human capacities for improvement with much greater pessimism. They thought human beings to be deeply flawed creatures whose only hope for individual salvation lay in God's predestined plan. When he became the foremost poet-playwright of his era, the young Racine would bring with him to his tragedies that Jansenist pessimism with its conviction concerning the destructive power of unrestrained human passion and appetite.

MOLIÈRE produced Racine's first two plays, *The Thebiad* (1664) and *Alexander the Great* (1665). Writer and producer disagreed, however, concerning the second production, and Racine took his play to another theater. The two master playwrights of their times never overcame the resultant animosity.

The Thebiad deals with the enmity between Polynices and Eteocles, the incestuous sons of Oedipus and Jocasta, and the war the sons fight over their father's throne. Knowing them to be irreconcilable, their uncle Creon advises them to share the throne. As Creon hopes, the brothers kill each other. Creon proposes to his niece Antigone. She responds by committing suicide. A guilty Creon does likewise, and the tragic history of Oedipus's family continues into another generation.

Alexander (*Alexandre le Grand*) focuses on a series of incidents that occur during Alexander's march toward India. Two Indian kings and their armies stand in Alexander's way. One, Porus, wants to fight at once. The other Indian ruler, Taxile, however, has a sister whom Alexander loves, and he makes a secret treaty with the invader. Both Porus and Taxile are in love with an Indian queen named Axiane. When Porus attacks Alexander's army, he finds that he faces both Alexander and Taxile, and Porus's army is soundly beaten. Alexander offers Axiane to Taxile, but she rejects the traitor. Furious, Taxile rides to the battlefield where Porus and a few of his personal bodyguards are still fighting. Porus slays Taxile in personal combat, and he submits to Alexander. Impressed with his enemy's courage, Alexander returns Porus to his throne and gives him a now willing Axiane.

The great drama of the ancient world often provided Racine with inspiration. His ANDROMACHE (1667) appeared in 1667. It was a stunning success, and in the following years Racine demonstrated his versatility with a comedy *The Suitors* (*Les Plaideurs,* 1668), and a political history play, *Brittanicus* (1669). In the decade of the 1670s Racine reached the height of his poetic and dramatic powers. *Bazjazet* (1672) departed from his usual practice by being set in contemporary Turkey. *Mithradates* appeared in 1673, the year Racine was inducted into the French Academy. *IPHIGÉNIE* followed next in 1674, and then came his masterpiece PHAEDRA (*PHÈDRE*, 1677).

His *Phaedra*, however, ended Racine's dramatic career—at least for the Paris stage. Probably he had always felt some tension between his theatrical calling and his religious convictions. At least once, in fact, he had felt compelled to defend his work against the disapproval of his Jansenist friends. In any case 1677 marked a watershed in the poet's life. During that year he married and was appointed as one of two historiographers in the service of King Louis XIV. In that capacity, he traveled with the king and accompanied him to war. At the request of Madame de Maintenon, first the mistress and eventually the wife of the king, Racine wrote his last plays. They were two religious pieces, *Esther* and *Athalie*. These dramas were staged by the young women enrolled in the St. Cyr school for girls—one of Madame de Maintenon's charities.

Beyond this in his later years Racine wrote four spiritual canticles (*Cantiques spirituels*) and completed a short history of Port-Royal (*Abrégé de l'histoire de Port-Royal, 1767*), a part of which he had earlier published (1742).

Bibliography
Racine, Jean. *Bajazet.* Translated by Alan Hollinghurst. London: Chatto & Windus, 1991.

———. *Brittanicus; Phaedra: Athalia.* Translated by C. H. Sisson. Oxford and New York: Oxford University Press, 1987.

———. *Complete Plays.* Translated by Samuel Solomon. New York: Random House, 1967.

———. *Oeuvres complètes.* Edited by Georges Forestier. Paris: Gallimard, ca. 1999.

———. *Phèdre: A Tragedy in Five Acts.* Translated by Wallace Fowlie. Mineola, N.Y.: Dover Publications, 2001.

———. *The Suitor.* Translated by Richard Wilbur. New York: Dramatic Play Service, ca. 2002.

Raleigh, Sir Walter (1552–1618)

Born in Hayes Barton, a community in Devon near Sidmouth, Raleigh eventually matriculated at Oriel College, Oxford. Passionately devoted, however, to the cause of the Protestant Huguenots, he withdrew from university and enlisted as a Huguenot soldier in France. There he fought in two pitched battles at Moncontour and Jarnac. Still in the service of Protestant ideals, in 1578 he became a de facto pirate—a privateer who fought alongside his half brother, Sir Humphrey Gilbert, in a sea raid against the Spanish. Still ruthlessly opposing the Roman Church and its supporters, in 1580 he participated in a punitive expedition against the rebellion in Ireland of the Ulsterite Desmonds.

Back in England, Raleigh became a courtier who for a time enjoyed the special favor of Queen ELIZABETH I. During the period between 1581 and

1587, his status in the queen's affections brought him profitable offices, land holdings, and privileges that among others included the vice-admiralty of Devon and Cornwall, a seat in Parliament as the representative for Devon, and appointment as Lord Warden of the Stanneries.

Between 1584 and 1589, Raleigh financed efforts to settle Roanoke Island in North Carolina and to establish colonies in Virginia. Though both these efforts failed, Raleigh is responsible for the introduction into England of two New World crops, potatoes and tobacco. The latter product, of course, has borrowed his name as a brand.

In 1587 the earl of Essex supplanted Raleigh in the queen's affections. Raleigh moved to Ireland, where, with the help of English Protestant immigrants who came at his invitation, he became a planter of potatoes. While in Ireland Raleigh also became a close friend of the poet EDMUND SPENSER. This association occasioned Spenser's letter to Raleigh explaining "allegory's dark conceits," as Spenser claimed to have employed them in composing his unfinished EPIC, *The FAERIE QUEENE*.

During his lifetime, Raleigh himself enjoyed a reputation as a witty and satirical poet in the manner of GEORGE CHAPMAN and Sir JOHN DAVIES. Much of Raleigh's poetry, however, has been lost, and some is insecurely attributed to him. Most secure, perhaps, is the attribution of "The Nymph's Reply to the Shepherd" (1600)—a poem that humorously responds to one by Christopher Marlowe, "The Passionate Shepherd to His Love" (ca. 1599). Whereas in Marlowe's poem the shepherd invites the nymph to live with him and be his love, in Raleigh's the nymph has a number of pragmatic conditions that puncture the shepherd's overly romantic notions about what such a relationship might entail.

As a prose writer and historian, Raleigh enjoys a more certain reputation. He set out on an ambitious project to chronicle the history of the world. In 1614, however, he decided to publish what he had so far accomplished. He had reached the year 186 B.C.E. He did not resume the project.

In 1595 he led a voyage of exploration to the Caribbean Sea, where he explored the coasts of the island of Trinidad. He continued by attempting the navigation of the Orinoco River. The results of this voyage he recounts in his *The Discovery of Guiana*.

The year 1596 saw his participation in the British sack of Cádiz, and in 1600 he was appointed the governor of the island of Jersey.

Although he generally distanced himself from political plotting, Raleigh did not avoid serious scrapes with the law. The first of these resulted from his impetuous and passionate nature. He offended the queen in 1592 by engaging in a secret affair with one of her maids of honor, Betsy Throckmorton. This resulted in a stint in the Tower of London and a four-year exclusion from the queen's presence. Raleigh and Throckmorton subsequently married. His next skirmish with the law was much more serious, despite the probability that he was entirely innocent. In the year of Elizabeth's death, 1603, he was arrested and jailed. After a failed attempt at suicide, he was condemned to death as a conspirator in Essex's attempt to overthrow the crown. Innocent, Raleigh attempted suicide before his trial. Despite a convincing defense, he was found guilty and condemned to death. He had actually mounted the scaffold to be executed when his death sentence was suspended and provisionally commuted to life imprisonment. He spent the years from 1603 to 1616 as a prisoner, occupying his time, in part, by composing further political and historical prose. Other than his abortive *History of the World*, his other prose writings (published posthumously) include: *A Discourse of War* (1650), *The Prerogative of Parliaments* (1628), and *The Cabinet Council* (1658). He also penned an introduction to Sir THOMAS HOBY's translation of BALDASSARE CASTIGLIONE's *Book of the Courtier*.

In 1616 Raleigh was released to lead another expedition to the Orinoco—this time in quest of rumored gold. The expedition proved to be a disaster. His fleet foundered; the son who accompanied him was killed; and Raleigh, who was under orders not to raid Spanish possessions, nonetheless destroyed a Spanish colonial town. Raleigh's return, the predictable complaint of the Spanish ambassador in London led to the reinstitution of Raleigh's death sentence. He was beheaded at Whitehall.

Bibliography

Raleigh, Walter. *Discoverie of the Large, Rich, and Beautiful Empyre of Guiana.* Edited by Neil L. Whitehead. Norman: University of Oklahoma Press, 1997.

———. *Sir Walter Raleigh: Selections from his History of the World . . .* Edited by G. E. Hadow. St. Claire Shores, Mich.: Scholarly Press, 1978.

———. *The Letters of Sir Walter Raleigh.* Edited by Agnes Latham and Joyce Youings. Exeter, U.K.: Exeter University Press, 1999.

———. *The Poems of Sir Walter Raleigh: A Historical Edition.* Edited by Michael Rudick. Tempe: Arizona Center for Medieval and Renaissance Studies and the Renaissance English Text Society, 1999.

Ramayana (date unknown)

The earliest surviving poem in a LANGUAGE OF INDIA and commonly attributed to the poet Valmiki, the EPIC story of Rama has deeply and continually influenced Indian thought and letters throughout the ages. In the 16th and 17th centuries the poem, secular in its original version, became spiritualized in its many retellings in various Indian languages as part of the BHAKTI movement of devotional fervor that rolled in repetitive waves across the Indian subcontinent. An instructive example of the poem's spiritualization and updating in the period on which this volume focuses appears in THE HOLY LAKE OF THE ACTS OF RAMA (*Ramcharitmânasa*, 1579) by the Hindi poet TULASÎDÂSA. In that version Rama, a human emperor and epic hero in Valmiki's version, becomes one of the principal deities of the Hindu pantheon.

Bibliography

Sagar, Ramananda, producer. *Ramayana* [television serial]. Transcribed and edited by Girish Bakshi and Tomio Mizokami. Osaka, Japan: Osaka University of Foreign Studies, 1992.

Rambouillet, Catherine de Vivonne, marquise de (1588–1665)

The most prominent of a number of women who established literary salons in France, the Italian-born marquise de Rambouillet found both the wit and the manners of the royal court of France beneath her standards. In response she established what became essentially a counter-court at her townhouse in Paris. There at what became known as the Hôtel de Rambouillet, aristocrats, witty conversationalists, and literary figures gathered to discuss all sorts of topics. Prominent among these were questions of proper behavior, the origins and meanings of varying shades of emotion, current news and scandals, and the quality of literary works.

Though other salons of the sort had preceded that of Madame Rambouillet, hers established the model upon which subsequent salons, such as that of Madeleine de Scudéry, were established. Such salons—and there were eventually many—turned their hostesses into the arbiters of an important segment of French literary taste. Rambouillet had brought with her from Italy a taste for the literary principles of Cardinal PIETRO BEMBO. These stressed refinement both of subject and of language. Rambouillet and others like her extended these principles with mixed results. Among those who shared their views, writers such as RABELAIS, who had written about earthy subjects in less than refined language, fell out of official favor.

The movement to which Rambouillet gave impetus was called *preciosity.* Influential for a time, it eventually fell out of favor and became an object of ridicule among writers, including MOLIÈRE and RACINE. Throughout the 17th century, however, salons such as Rambouillet's empowered women as the arbiters of literary taste and refinement.

Bibliography

Krajewska, Barbara. *Mythes et découvertes: Le salon littéraire de Madame de Rambouillet dans les lettres des contemporains.* Paris and Seattle: Papers on French Literature, 1990.

Rasakallola Dānakrishna Dāsa (17th c.)

The *Rasakallolla* (Waves of delight) is the best-remembered poem of an important poet in the Oriya LANGUAGE OF INDIA. Among its other distinctions, it displays a unique form. Each line throughout its entire 34 cantos begins with the syllable *ka*. Each line is thus one of the delightful waves. This highly wrought artistry places the poem in a category labeled *ornate poetry*.

Like many of the prominent productions of the period, the Waves of delight grows out of the BHAKTI devotional movement in India. In the Hindu pantheon, different aspects of a single holy being often manifest themselves as other beings. *Rasakallolla* joins the poems that first celebrate Vishnu in his manifestation as Jagannath, and then in his incarnations as Krishna and Radha, divine beings themselves and also aspects both of Vishnu and Jagannath.

Rasakallolla's first canto traces the significance of Jagannath and praises the accomplishments of ancient scholarship. The second canto traces the birth of Lord Krishna. The third deals with the fascination of a group of milkmaids called *gopi*s with the infant. Other episodes describe Krishna's childhood, his liking for butter, and an attempt to assassinate him. The seventh and eighth cantos introduce the theme of Krishna's passionate enchantment with the *gopi*s and theirs with him. In the ninth, Krishna overcomes a dangerous snake, and in the 10th the reader meets the overwhelmingly beautiful Radha. Krishna and Radha represent two sides of the same coin: Krishna the eternal adorer, and Radha, the eternally adored. The 10th canto concludes the introductory section of the work.

The poem pays by far the closest attention to the highly erotic love play between Krishna and Radha and Krishna and the other *gopi*s. Other adventures include his journey to the region of Mathura, the *gopi*s' devastation at his absence, and the delight of the women of Mathura at his arrival.

The 32nd and 33rd cantos pursue a more didactic course as they encourage the development of the philosophy associated with the worship of Vishnu and stress the importance of the worshippers' love and devotion for and submission to the will of the God.

In the last canto of the poem, an emissary from the *gopi*s, Udeb, seeks out Krishna in Mathura and reports how terribly the milkmaids miss him. The poem's ALLEGORY suggests that complete union of the worshiper and the God is the goal of worshiping the deities on whom the story focuses.

DĀSA displayed his technical mastery of his language's verse forms and contributed to his poem's delight by composing each of the 34 cantos of the poem in a different meter.

Bibliography

Mishra, Gopal Chandra. "Rasa Kallola." *Encyclopedia of Indian Literature.* Volume IV. Edited by Mohan Lal. New Delhi: Sahitya Akademi, 1991.

Ratnākaravarni (b. 1557)

An Indian poet who wrote in the Kannada language, Ratnākaravarni belonged to the Jain religion. The most important of his several surviving works is a lengthy EPIC, the *Bharatatesha Vaibhava*, which recounts the life story of Lord Bharata, the son of the founder of the Jain religion, Adinatha. The work runs to 10,000 stanzas organized in 80 books. Though the story of Bharata had earlier been told, Ratnākaravarni embellished it in two ways. He elevated the title character to the status of an epic hero, and he shaped the story in a way that conformed to the tenets of the Jain religion. Ratnākaravarni explains how Bharata became emperor and conquered the entire world—except for his own brother.

Ratnākaravarni authored several poetic works concerning religious and philosophical topics. Among these are examples of a new poetic form in the language, poems each 100 verses (lines) long. Each poem offered advice on some moral or behavioral topic. The poet intended the poems to celebrate the greatness of God while at the same time illustrating the insignificance of human achievement.

Widely translated into the other LANGUAGES OF INDIA, Ratnākaravarni's verse established the standard toward which other Kannada poets aspire.

Bibliography

History of the Kannada Literature, Jaina, Veereshaiva, and Brahmanical Times. Jyotnsa Kamat. "Jaina, Veerashaiva and Brahmanical Epics." Available online. URL: http://www.Kamat.com/Karlanga/Kar/literature/epics.htm. Downloaded on March 20, 2004.

Regnier, Mathurin (1573–1613)

Although he made his living as a priest, Regnier operated as a philosophical disciple of MONTAIGNE. Like the famous essayist, Regnier subscribed to a worldview of rationalist relativism. Unlike Montaigne, Regnier's mode of life was reputedly dissolute. Clearly a gifted poet whose work attracted the favorable attention of King Henry IV, of the poet and poetic theorist, François de MALHERBE, and of a successor, Nicholas Boileau (1636–1711), Regnier wrote comparatively little—some 7,000 lines all told. These include a few songs, ODES, and EPIGRAMS, five examples of ELEGY, and three verse epistles. He was chiefly admired by his contemporaries and is principally remembered for his satirical CHARACTER WRITING in verse. Following the example of the ancient Roman satirists Horace and Juvenal, Regnier penned some 16 verse satires that expose the failings of persons such as hypocrites, poets, and physicians.

Although Regnier's works are available in a relatively modern French critical edition, they have not as yet appeared in English translation.

Bibliography

Regnier, Mathurin. *Oeuvres complètes.* Edited by Gabriel Raibaud. Paris: M. Didier, 1958.

Religio Medici Thomas Browne (1635)

THOMAS BROWNE apparently first intended his spiritual autobiography *Religio Medici* (The religion of a physician) as a private devotion, but he shared it with others who passed it along and in copying and emending changed it until unauthorized editions of 1642 made him feel obliged to publish an authentic version (1643). After stating his reasons for making his work public, Browne goes on to declare himself a Christian and an adherent of the Church of England. Except for the minimal requirements of his sworn allegiance to that church, however, and except for the authority of Scripture, he considers his reason to be a better guide to his worship than sermons, synods, councils, priests, popes, or kings.

He next confesses former beliefs that he has come to consider errors, such as the simultaneous death of the body and soul, and that God would eventually forgive all sinners and would release them from the torments of Hell (which Browne locates in the hearts of men). Later he suggests that Holy Scripture and the Book of Nature are the objects of his study. He sets great store by good works and charity and finds that the object of human existence is to achieve happiness. Yet he cautions, "there is no felicity in that [which] the world adores." He critiques the ancient philosophers and rejects their notions of happiness as idle fancies. He rather prays: "Bless me in this life with but peace of my conscience, command of my affections, the love of thy self and my dearest friends, and I shall be happy enough to pity *Caesar*." Browne's sense of humor, his encyclopedic learning, his keen intellect, and his occasionally naive credulity all appear in this work that, from a literary perspective, may well belong in a category unique to itself.

Reply to Sor Philotea Sor Juana Inés de La Cruz (1691)

At the insistence of her friend, Manuel Fernández de Santa Cruz, bishop of Puebla, Mexico, the extremely learned and talented Jeronymite nun, SOR JUANA INÉS DE LA CRUZ, wrote a critical treatise that took issue with a number of theological arguments raised in a sermon preached 40 years earlier by a Portuguese Jesuit, Antonio de Vieyra. Perceiving that her commentary's contents were potentially inflammatory in an atmosphere pervaded by concerns about holding opinions contrary to those approved by the Spanish INQUISITION, Sor Juana acceded to the bishop's request and wrote the piece on the condition that her treatise not be published.

This condition the bishop apparently ignored. Nobel Prize Laureate Octavio Paz argues that the bishop instead had the document published at his own expense, covering his tracks by attributing the edition to a Sor Philotea (Sister Love-God). Further complicating this bizarre scenario, Bishop Fernández de Santa Cruz, posing as Sor Philotea, then penned a fork-tongued letter to Sor Juana. Couched in terms of loving concern and admiration, Sor Philotea's letter cuttingly suggests that Sor Juana spend less time studying humane letters and more studying the Bible. Moreover, it reminds her of St. Paul's admonition that women should keep silent in church and neither teach nor preach.

Paz speculates that the bishop's objective for undertaking this improbable project involved, first, his desire to attack indirectly the archbishop of Mexico City, Francisco de Aguiar y Seijas, whose position Fernández coveted, and the archbishop's Jesuit friends. The impersonation served, second, to assign the blame for the attack to Sor Juana. Third, the bishop could claim to have had Sor Juana reproved for presuming to argue theology with a priest.

Sor Juana's response came three months later. Perhaps she knew both who had published her treatise and who was posing as Sor Philotea. In any case, she acknowledges her embarrassment at its publication, thanks the ostensible sister nevertheless for having gone to the expense and trouble, and then conducts a classic justification of her life and pursuits.

She traces her history as a child, explaining that study and speculation came naturally to her and that for her both were utterly unavoidable. She defends her study of secular subjects as preparation for the study of religious ones, including the Scriptures, the writings of the saints and doctors of the church, and the queen of the sciences—theology. The list of subjects she has mastered would prove daunting for any but the most gifted students. Yet she disclaims any credit. Her passion for study, she maintains, is totally involuntary, and she thanks God that study rather than some vice has obsessed her.

Sor Juana's letter to Sor Philotea bristles with quotations from Scripture and from classical and modern writers and with learned commentary on both. Clearly she has already followed the advice the letter presumes to give her. Then Sor Juana considers the issues that concern her particular status as a woman involved in the world of letters. She masterfully demonstrates that the construction a male church hierarchy has chosen to give the admonitions of St. Paul against the participation of women in theological discourse was conditioned on special circumstances peculiar to the time and place in which Paul's letters were written. She argues convincingly that such prohibitions were never intended to apply to women in general. She also demonstrates with myriad examples from Scripture and church history that scriptural prohibitions against preaching applied equally to the unlearned of both sexes. She needed to make no mention of the woeful ignorance of many pre–Counter-Reformation male clergy.

She turns her attention to the benefits that would accrue to girls and young women if mature women had not been prohibited by a determined patriarchy from acquiring the knowledge requisite to teaching. Particularly she tactfully cites the dangers that arise from the frequent instances of female students and male tutors falling in love.

In conducting a spirited defense of her life and activities, Sor Juana moves beyond the specific accusations and innuendos of Sor Philotea's letter. She discusses the jealousy that the less accomplished often feel for the more accomplished and the desire to belittle that such jealousy provokes. She discusses the objections that some have raised to her writing in verse and defends that capacity, first, as a God-given natural talent and inclination, and, second, as an emulation of Scripture, many of whose books and verses, like the Magnificat of Mary, the Psalms, and the Book of Job are written in poetry, not prose, in their original language. She also cites the approval of church authority and the example of authors ancient and modern.

The tone of Sor Juana's letter is never accusatory, it is always grateful for Sor Philotea's concern. It even offers to make Sor Philotea the arbiter of Sor Juana's future activities. At the same time, although the letter affirms her obedience to the order of nuns in whose ranks she is enrolled and to the authorities to whom she owes obedience, it offers no apology for the woman or the person that Sor Juana is, nor any for the way she has spent her life.

Sor Juana's life and career have become icons for persons interested in women's issues both of her era and of ours.

Bibliography

Mirrim, Stephanie. *Early Modern Women's Writing and Sor Juana Inés de la Cruz.* Nashville, Tenn.: Vanderbilt University Press, 1999.

Paz, Octavio. *Sor Juana or, The Traps of the Faith.* Translated by Margaret Sayers Peden. Cambridge, Mass.: Belknap Press of Harvard University Press, 1988.

Trueblood, Alan S., editor and translator. *A Sor Juana Anthology.* Cambridge, Mass.: Harvard University Press, 1988.

Reuter, Christian (1665–ca. 1712)

A German humorist of the baroque era, Reuter's reputation rests on a single example of a grotesque novel in the PICARESQUE mode. Translated into English as *Schelmuffsky*—the name of the main character—Reuter's novel bore rather a more descriptive title in German: *Schelmuffskys kuriose und sehr gefährliche Reisebeschreibung zu Wasser und Lande* (Schelmuffsky's account of his curious and very dangerous travels on water and land, 1696).

Schelmuffsky himself is a curious mixture of literary types. He belongs on the one hand to the picaresque tradition begun by the anonymously authored LIFE OF LAZARILLO DE TORMES, HIS FORTUNES AND ADVERSITIES (1554), and on the other to a tradition of the grotesque that includes such characters as RABELAIS's Pantagruel and Luigi PULCI's MORGANTE. These two elements come together in the context of a native German forebear, Hans Jacob Christoph von Grimmelshausen's partly autobiographical character and soldier of fortune, SIMPLICISSIMUS.

Schelmuffsky's sphere of operation is much greater than those of his literary forebears. Before describing Schelmuffsky's fabled journeys, however, Reuter describes the unusual circumstances of his birth. When Schelmussky's mother was in the fifth month of her pregnancy with him, she found a rat gnawing holes in her favorite silk dress. She chased the rat with a broom. It darted between her daughter's legs and into a hole in the wall. The exertion caused the mother to faint and for 24 days she lay unconscious. At the end of that time, curious to see where the rat had gone, Schelmuffsky terminated his mother's pregnancy by crawling forth into the world.

Later on, having failed as a university student and as an apprentice to a merchant, he sets out to see the world and to become a "famous fellow." After seeing Hamburg, Stockholm, and Amsterdam, he travels by ship through real and fabled seascapes. He crosses the equator. He finds himself becalmed in the "sea of the dead" where ships can remain motionless so long their crews die for lack of water. In Mughal India he seeks out the emperor at Agra. The emperor receives him with great pomp and splendor and presents him with rare and costly gifts including 1,000 valuable coins.

As a naive narrator who survives fabulous adventures, Schelmuffky reminds one of an 18th-century literary descendant from England, Jonathan Swift's Gulliver.

Bibliography

Reuter, Christian. *Schelmuffsky.* Translated by Wayne Wonderley. Chapel Hill: University of North Carolina Press, 1962.

Revenger's Tragedy, The Cyril Tourneur (1607)

As its title suggests, *The Revenger's Tragedy* belongs to the genre of TRAGEDY OF THE BLOOD. It also belongs with JOHN WEBSTER's *The White Devil* to a theatrical tradition that sees Italy as a setting in which vice rules and manslaughter occurs with horrifying frequency.

The action takes place at an unspecified Italian ducal court where both the duke and the duchess are steeped in intrigue and adultery. Both duke and duchess have children from earlier marriages. The duke has fathered two sons, one legitimate, Lussurioso, and one, Spurio, out of wedlock. The duchess has three sons: Ambitioso, Supervacuo, and an unnamed younger son. Keeping an eye on all of them is the play's central character, Vindice, who, as the curtain rises, comments for the benefit of the audience on each member of the royal family as they pass in procession. Vindice also reveals to the audience the skull of his poisoned love, Gloriana, whom the duke murdered when she spurned his advances. As his name indicates, Vindice seeks vengeance, and an opportunity presents itself when Vindice learns that Lussurioso is looking for a procurer to find women for him. Vindice steps into the role.

After the opening scene, the play becomes a succession of murders, executions, and attempted and successful seductions, with Vindice playing the central role. His most successful moment of revenge comes when, playing pander for the duke, in the dark Vindice has the duke kiss the poisoned lips of the skull of Gloriana. Then, while the poison takes its slow course, Vindice makes the duke watch while his duchess cuckolds him with his bastard son Spurio.

In Samuel Schuman's view, the play rises well above the generality of Italianate revenge tragedies because it achieves a double irony. Not only does Vindice succeed in avenging his own loss, quite against his will he becomes the instrument of a vengeful Providence as well. His stratagems largely depopulate the drama of its characters by the time the final curtain falls.

Bibliography

Tourneur, Cyril. *The Revenger's Tragedy: Thomas Middleton; Cyril Tourneur.* Manchester, U.K., and New York: Manchester University Press, 1996.

Ritual of the Bacabs (ca. 1650; Quiche–Maya Language)

Although all the verse rituals in this book of healing spells originated before the Maya made contact with Europeans, the version in which the rituals have survived is a transliterated one. Either from memory or from a now lost Mayan manuscript the rituals were copied out in Roman letters during the 17th century.

The prayers for healing are addressed both to natural and to supernatural creatures. Some of the poems address birds. Others appeal to colors or to winds that blow from various points of the compass. The English title of the work comes from the verses that address the company of mythic Bacabs who hold up the sky.

romance

As a literary term, *romance* can apply either to a kind of narrative fiction or to the plots of narrative poems or of plays. Novels that recount somewhat unrealistic tales of heroism, strange events, and high-minded love are characterized by the word *romance.* Poems and plays that focus upon sentimental subjects, swashbuckling adventure, and PASTORAL pleasures also are usually covered by the broad literary label *romance.* Verse epics like ORLANDO FU-RIOSO fall into the category of CHIVALRIC ROMANCE. A play like SHAKESPEARE's *A MIDSUMMER NIGHT'S DREAM* also exemplifies the romance mode.

Romance of the Three Kingdoms
(Sanguo zhi yanyi, the San-kuo yen-i)
Lo Guanzhong; Luo Kuan-chung (1522)

One of the three foundational novels of Chinese historical fiction, *The Romance of the Three Kingdoms* first appeared in the 14th century. In the 16th, however, it was several times rewritten—sometimes shortened and sometimes expanded—to accommodate the literary tastes of audiences in the later century for longer or shorter narrative. Falling somewhere on the middle of a scale that runs from history to fiction, it presents largely historical characters in mostly but not always historical situations. Its most authoritative form is that of Lo.

Although the story compiles for its readers material that was first presented in the streets by storytellers and that had become encrusted with supernatural and folkloristic material, Lo judiciously sorts through the work's material reliably for its readers the political and military exploits of second- and third-century warlords contending for control of the empire of China at the end of the Han dynasty. Despite that effort, remnants of mythic material remain, and, in the absence of reliable biographical detail for some of the personages, authorial invention has often been necessary.

From the perspective of plotting, the action of *Three Kingdoms* may well strike a Western reader as a virtually interminable series of narrative summaries of military encounters. Lo does interrupt these summaries from time to time with more gripping, descriptive scenes detailing personal combat. In one instance the Wei faction's general, Xiahou Dun (Hsia-hou Tun), despite being treacherously shot in the eye during an ostensibly single combat, runs his lance through his adversary, the general Cao Xing (Ts'ao Hsing).

From the perspective of character development, however, the skill with which Lo brings members of his immense cast to life for a reader is one of the most memorable characteristics of the work. We meet, for instance, a local magistrate Chen Gong

(Ch'en Kung), who leaves his home to follow first the unscrupulous general Cao Cao (Ts'ao Ts'ao). Disillusioned with the general, however, he deserts him to join Cao Cao's enemy, the warrior Lu Bu (Lü Pu). Though the latter displays great courage and personal fighting skill, he lacks leadership ability. That failure leads directly to Chen Gong's capture by Cao Cao, who seems inclined to spare his former subordinate. Chen Gong, however, does not give his earlier leader the chance to spare him. Rather, Ch'en places in Cao Cao's hands the well-being of the former magistrate's family, and he walks unhesitatingly to the headsman's block.

Other characters that populate the pages of the book include writers and thinkers who, sometimes at the risk of their lives, openly poke fun at powerful members of the court and even of the royal family. The scholar Ni Heng is one of these. In his confidence in his own intellectual superiority, he scorns and reproves his social betters, including Cao. Yet from the author's perspective it is Ni Heng who deserves the readers' contempt as a conceited boor.

The literary historian C. T. Hsia suggests that Lo is more successful as a popular historian than as a writer of fiction. Nonetheless Lo's 16th-century reworking of a 14th-century source produced one of the most influential examples of Chinese historical fiction.

Bibliography

Hsia, C. T. *The Classic Chinese Novel: A Critical Introduction.* 1968. Ithaca, N.Y.: Cornell University Press, 1996.

Luo Guanzhong. *Three Kingdoms (Condensed Version).* English and Chinese. Translated by Moss Roberts. China: Foreign Language Press, 1999.

Roman comique (A comic novel) Paul Scarron (Part 1, 1651; Part 2, 1654)

The incomplete masterpiece of the French humorist PAUL SCARRON, his *Roman comique* expresses by its example Scarron's disdain for the precious novels of his predecessors. They had focused the plots of their work on classical themes set in ancient times, had dealt with noble and rather effete characters, had used a high-flown, artificial verbal style, and had written principally for an aristocratic audience with hyperrefined tastes.

Scarron, by contrast, set his novel in the contemporary city of Le Mans, focused the work on the problems and challenges that beset an itinerant acting troupe, used a straightforward, colloquial French, and frequently interjected personal commentary on the action as it proceeds.

The novel opens with the arrival of La Caverne, Destin, and La Rancune—three members of an acting troupe—in an oxcart at the market square of Le Mans. Though they are shorthanded since the other actors have not arrived, the players agree to perform in an inn and tavern where they mean to stay. No sooner do they get under way than a fight breaks out in the tavern. The town's chief law officer, La Rappiniére, invites the actors to his home for their first night in Le Mans, and the reader comes to know the actors' host as grasping, self-important, and wary.

The rest of the acting company arrives. It includes Angélique, Estoile, Léandre, Olive, and Roquebrune. Soon after they come, Scarron introduces a stage-struck lawyer, who wants to join the actors. The lawyer, Ragotin, auditions by telling a story, "The Invisible Mistress," which he falsely claims to have composed. The harder Ragotin tries to become an actor the more ludicrous he becomes. At one point he confesses that he has fallen in love with one of the actresses, but he isn't sure which one. He allows La Rancune to steer his affection to Estoile.

The story now develops along two lines. Someone kidnaps a priest from the town of Domfort, and Destin tells his own life's story. His early experiences include the possibility of his having been exchanged for another infant, an education with the sons of a nobleman, and a trip to Rome. There he falls in love with Léonore. He defends her honor against two masked assailants who seriously wound Destin. His courage wins the approval of Léonore's mother, who interjects the story of her own secret marriage to Léonore's father. An acquaintance lies about Destin at this point, accusing him of being a servant. The mother withdraws her approval.

Brokenhearted, Destin goes off to fight the Turks, hoping to be killed in battle, but he fails in this goal and returns to Paris. There he again encounters

Léonore and her mother, who dies after a further series of adventures. Eventually the only recourse for Destin and Léonore is to turn to acting. Léonore changes her name to Estoile, and she and Destin, posing as brother and sister, join La Rancune's troupe.

Further complications follow. The law officer, La Rapiniére, falls in love with Estoile, and Roquebrun and La Rancune both fall for a married Spanish lady. A horse throws Rogantin and Roquebrun. Then Angelique is kidnapped, and as everyone prepares to search for her, Part I of the story ends.

Six years later Part II resumed the story with the actors' search for Angelique. Again, entertaining complications and jokes at Ragoutin's expense interrupt the flow of the action. So do attempted seductions of both the male and the female members of the troupe.

At this point Angelique reappears with the news that the kidnappers had mistaken her for Estoile. They have therefore now captured her and released Angelique. Destin is inconsolable until his boyhood friend Verville appears and finds out that a certain Saldagne, who regularly pursues Estoile, is her kidnapper. Further kidnapping and attempted kidnapping continue to drive the main plot. One of these attempts is made by La Rappiniére, who proves to have a portrait of Estoile/Léonore's father on a jewel.

Back in Le Mans, the troupe performs Scarron's play DOM JAPHET OF ARMENIA and CORNEILLE's *Nicomède*. Further complications and tale telling ensue, and Part II ends with the foolish Ragoutin being butted by a billy goat.

Though Scarron was certainly at work on Part III at the time of his death, no portion of the final installment has ever surfaced. Some speculate that his wife suppressed it.

Bibliography

Scarron, Paul. *The Whole Comical Works of Monsieur Scarron.* 2 vols. New York: Garland Publishers, 1973.

Ronsard, Pierre de (1525–1585)

The most famous poet of 16th-century France, Pierre de Ronsard was also a soldier and courtier who in his boyhood served as a page both to the crown prince of France (the dauphin) and to his brother the duc d'Orleans. He went for three years to Scotland in the retinues of Madelaine de France and Mary of Guise when first Madelaine and, after her death, Mary married the Scottish king, James V.

On his return to France Ronsard turned his attention to literature and HUMANISTIC studies. He and his friend JEAN ANTOINE DE BAÏF received private tutelage in classical languages and letters from the renowned HUMANIST teacher, Jean Dorat, at the home of Baïf's father. This prepared the two friends to study together at the College de Coqueret where they encountered two other young men, JOACHIM DU BELLAY and Remi Belleau, who, with Ronsard, Baïf, and their teacher Dorat, were destined to be among the founders of the French PLÉIADE.

Ronsard devoted seven years of study to preparing for the career in letters to which he would devote the rest of his life. That career's first fruits appeared in 1547 with the publication of a single poem, and, next, in his collection of his ODES in 1550. More odes and a collection of SONNETS, *Amours,* saw print in 1552. These love poems he addressed to a Florentine woman in Paris, Cassandre Salviati. Further editions followed in the mid-1550s, and, in 1560, all his works to that point were collected and published.

In the mid-century religious and civic warfare that afflicted France, Ronsard supported the Catholic and royalist causes. Some of his most moving poems are political in nature and address such subjects as the misery of the times (*Discours des misères de ce temps*), the responsibility of the populace to support the king against the Protestant Huguenots (*Remonstrance au peuple de France* [A remonstrance to the people of France]), and the mutual obligations of a ruler and the ruled (*Institution pour l'adolescence du Roi très chrètien* [Institution for the youth of the most Christian king]; "Most Christian," was an official title that the pope had conferred upon the kings of France.) At the request of King Charles IX, Ronsard also attempted a national EPIC, the *Franciade,* but the poet permanently suspended work on it when Charles IX died.

Ronsard and the members of the Pléiade shaped French poetic taste for almost three generations. In keeping with the main literary currents of the Renaissance, his work was based on classical and Italian models. His early odes rather slavishly and pedantically followed the example of the Greek poet Pindar (ca. 522–ca. 440 B.C.E.) and were intended to be sung to instrumental accompaniment. Later, as his own voice grew more confident, Ronsard divided odes into light and serious categories, and his palette of models broadened to include the Roman poets Horace, Catullus, and OVID, the Greek Anacreon, and the Italian precursor of Renaissance lyric poetry, PETRARCH.

In addition to the works listed above Ronsard also wrote poems praising important people, allegories, and moral, narrative, and philosophical poems. Still, he is principally remembered for the moving love poems that he addressed to a series of women over the decades: to Cassandre Salviati, to Marie—a peasant girl whose last name is unknown—and to one of Queen Catherine de' Médici's maids of honor, Hélène de Surgères. To the woman last named he wrote many of his last and loveliest lyric poems in his collection, *Sonnets pour Hélène* (Sonnets for Helene).

Bibliography

Ronsard, Pierre de. *Poems of Pierre de Ronsard.* Translated by Nicholas Kilmer. Berkeley: University of California Press, ca. 1979.

———. *Les amours de Pierre de Ronsard.* [Sound Recording]. Set to music by Guillaume Boni. Paris: Arion, ca. 1999.

Shapiro, Norman, R., trans. *Lyrics of the French Renaissance: Marot, Du Bellay, Ronsard.* New Haven, Conn.: Yale University Press, ca. 2002.

Rosenhane, Gustaf (Skogekär Bergbo) (1619–1684)

A Swedish poet who wrote under the pen name Skogekär Bergbo, Rosenhane was among those influenced by the late arrival of the Renaissance in Scandinavia. Particularly moved by the poems in *PETRARCH'S SONGBOOK,* Rosenhane penned a SON-NET cycle entitled *Wenerid* (1680). He later published another work, *Fyratijo små Wisor* (1682), but details as to its content seem unavailable.

Though *Wenerid* has not been translated into English, it has been summarized in that language.

Bibliography

Rosenhane, Gustaf. *Wenerid/ Skogekär Bergbo.* Edited with English summary by Lars Burman. Stockholm: Svenska vitterhetssamfundet, 1993.

Rotrou, Jean de (1609–1650)

A friend and associate of the dramatist PIERRE CORNEILLE, the French playwright Jean de Rotrou was a protégé of the power behind the French throne, Cardinal Richelieu. Richelieu maintained a group of five writers to furnish plays for the entertainment of his many guests, and Rotrou and Corneille were among them. He wrote plays in all three major genres, COMEDY, TRAGICOMEDY, and TRAGEDY.

French audiences, like audiences everywhere, demanded frequent changes of program to feed their insatiable appetites for fresh entertainment. Invention alone seldom sufficed to meet that demand, so like other members of the playwrights' fraternity Rotrou drew the plots for his plays from numerous sources. Prominent among them were plays that had been written by Spanish playwrights like LOPE DE VEGA and Francisco de Rojas. Rotrou's plays, in turn, became sources for MOLIÈRE.

Rotrou's first play, *L'Hypocondriaque ou le mort amoureaux* (The hypochondriac or amorous death) was performed before its author had turned 20, and a tragedy, *Hercule mourant* (The dying Hercules) followed in 1634. Rotrou reached the height of his powers in the 1630s and 1640s. Those years saw the production of comedies like *Les Sosies* (1636), and *La Soeur* (The sister, 1645). Among his tragicomedies of the same and slightly earlier periods he penned a play drawn from Lope, *Laure persécutée* (The persecuted Laura, 1627) and *Don Bernard de Cabrére* (1648). Tragedies of his mature period included another based on Lope, *La véritable Saint Geneste* (*The True Saint Genest*, 1646), one drawn from Rojas, *Venceslas* (1647), and *Cosros* (1649).

In addition to his theatrical career, Rotrou occupied a civil office in the city of Dreux. He died a heroic death when he insisted on remaining at his post in the city during the plague of 1649–50, caught the disease, and died from it.

Round Dance of Krishna, The
Nandadāsa (17th c.)

A poem in the early version of the Hindi language called Brajbhasha, this work by the poet and saint NANDADĀSA celebrates in an extended allegory the human soul's love of and desire for union with God. It also represents God's reciprocal love for the human soul and the grace God extends to it. The context in which Nandadāsa develops that allegory is the traditional Indian legend of the blue Hindu deity Krishna—at once human and divine— among the village girls who herd cows—the *gopis*.

Drawn by the soft autumn evenings on the banks of the Jumna River near Vrindavan, Krishna plays his flute to summon the *gopis* from the homes of their husbands and fathers to dance with him through the groves along the river. The *gopis* find the divine music irresistible, and they come to dance.

Krishna lovingly welcomes them but at the same time reminds them of their worldly responsibilities, suggesting they should return home. The lovely girls refuse, reminding him that he is what makes life worth living. Krishna's love for the girls is stirred, and as he runs along the riverbank playing his flute, they follow. Perceiving impurities of pride and selfishness in the girls' devotion to him, however, at the end of the first section of the poem Krishna vanishes from among them.

Through the next two much shorter sections of the poem the *gopis* search fruitlessly for Krishna, begging the local deer and vegetation to reveal his whereabouts. Eventually they come upon two sets of footprints that they recognize as belonging to Krishna and one of their own number. Drawing a self-evident but mistaken conclusion, they begin to envy their comrade. But they discover Krishna has also deserted her.

The *gopis* now both lament Krishna's desertion and grieve at the sufferings they imagine he must be enduring in the forest. Just at that moment, he returns. The *gopis* question him about the nature of love. Touched by their devoted affection, Krishna begins to play and an ecstatic, erotic dance follows whose mood Nandadāsa exactly catches. Finally all bathe together in the waters of the Jumna.

The poem ends in a less ecstatic and more didactic vein as Nandadāsa draws lessons concerning the nature of the dance, how difficult it is to find the sort of ecstatic union with the Absolute that the dance represents, and how the poem can point the way for one who seeks that union and the ineffable ecstasy it evokes.

I am unable to read the poem in its original language, but the translation of R. S. McGregor, for me at least, evokes something of the emotional charm that must appear in the Hindi version.

Bibliography

Nandadās. *The Round Dance of Krishna and Uddhav's Message.* Translated by R. S. McGregor. London: Luzac & Company, 1973.

Rowley, William (ca. 1585–ca. 1642)

An English playwright and actor, Rowley collaborated with several 17th-century playwrights for the London stage. These included DEKKER, FORD, HEYWOOD, MASSINGER, MIDDLETON, and WEBSTER. Rowley seems not to have written anything outside such collaborations. Several plays survive that Rowley had a hand in writing, one TRAGEDY, *All's Lost by Lust* (1633); a city COMEDY that catered to Londoners taste for seeing members of the rising middle classes presented on the stage, *A Shoemaker a Gentleman* (1638); a satiric comedy, *A New Wonder, a Woman Never Vexed* (1632); and a romantic comedy, *A Match at Midnight* (1633).

Perhaps Rowley's most effective collaborations were those with Thomas Middleton. Together the two wrote their most notable work, *The Changeling* (acted ca. 1622, published 1668), and Rowley also participated in the production of Middleton's *A Fair Quarrel*, *The Spanish Gipsy*, and *Women Beware Women* (1625).

Rowley apparently collaborated with Thomas Heywood on a PASTORAL play, *The Thracian Wonder.*

Bibliography

Middleton, Thomas, and William Rowley: *The Changeling.* 1958. Edited by N. W. Bawcutt. Manchester, U.K.: Manchester University Press, 1998.

Rowley, William. *A Shoemaker, a Gentleman.* Edited by Trudi L. Darby. London: Nick Hern Books, 2002.

Rowley, William, and Thomas Heywood. *The Thracian Wonder.* Edited by Michael Nolan. Salzburg, Austria: Institut für Anglistik und Amerikanistik, Universität Salzburg, 1997.

Royal Commentaries of the Yncas
Garcilaso de la Vega, The (El) Inca (Part I, 1609; Part II, 1617)

The literary historian George Ticknor characterizes the first section of the Inca GARCILASO DE LA VEGA's *Commentaries* as a "garrulous" and "gossiping" book, filled with not altogether relevant personal anecdotes. In addition to the work's subject, however, precisely those qualities make the book attractive and interesting.

Part I of the book deals with the 18 Incan rulers whose history had been preserved in Peru both in a system of writing, *quipu,* that involved tying knots in strings of various colors, and in a cycle of royal dramas that were then held and that continue to be performed annually in the Andes mountains. Garcilaso dedicates this first volume as a tribute to his royal ancestors. He is aware of the duality of his obligations as the product of two societies. As the son of an Incan princess descended from a line called the Children of the Son, Vega feels bound to discuss the attributes of the Peruvian people, their manners and customs, and their institutions and traditions. It is that obligation he undertakes to fulfill in Part I of his work.

In Part II, on the other hand, he undertakes to fulfill the equal obligations he feels as the descendant of a conquistador with noble connections and as a writer who is himself a soldier and courtier in the service of the Spanish crown. The second volume of the work recounts the history of the conquest of Peru. It details the disagreements that arose among the Spanish conquerors and lingers over the details of the history of his father's Castilian ancestors—members of the Infantado family—and the glories of their accomplishments.

Garcilaso takes few pains to discriminate fact from fiction. Whatever casts the best light on his Peruvian ancestors, whether it be fact or fable, he includes as fact. He takes a similar approach in dealing with his Infantado ancestors. In both volumes he takes pains to present himself as a right-thinking Catholic Christian who has absolutely no personal interest in his Peruvian ancestors' idolatrous polytheism. His first literary effort, a translation of JEHUDAH BEN ISAAC ABRAVANEL's influential Platonic and kabbalistic document, *The Dialogues of Love,* had incurred the disapproval of the Spanish Inquisition and been listed on THE INDEX OF FORBIDDEN BOOKS. Garcilaso wished at all costs to avoid a similar fate for his life's crowning literary achievement.

Bibliography

Glubok, Shirley. *The Fall of the Incas.* New York: Macmillan, 1967. [Contains abridgments and adaptations of writings by Garcilaso de la Vega and Pedro Pizzaro.]

Ticknor, George. *History of Spanish Literature.* Vol. 3. New York: Gordian Press, 1965.

Vega, Garcilaso de la. *First Part of the Royal Commentaries of the Yncas, by the Ynca Garcilasso[sic] de la Vega.* Hakluyt Society, 1869–71. Translated and edited by Clements R. Markham. Reprint, New York: B. Franklin, 1963.

Rubá'i

A quatrain principally popular among poets in Persian and Arabic, but also sometimes employed by poets in other languages of the Islamic world, the *rubá'i* (a word whose plural is *rubáiyát*) became widely known in the English-speaking world as the result of Edward FitzGerald's translations and publication of quatrains by the mathematician 'Umar al-Khayyām in the 19th century.

Almost all the Islamic poets mentioned in this volume, including ŞĀ'IB OF TABRIZ (OR ISFAHAN), NEV'Ī-ZÁDE 'ATÁ'Í, and HÁLETÍ, penned at least some examples of the form. Readers of translations of such quatrains should bear in mind that Arabic verse, like that of ancient Latin and Greek, depends on arbitrarily defined vowel lengths rather than on a pattern of stresses as English does.

See also POETIC METER.

Bibliography

Saberi, Reza, trans. and ed. *A Thousand Years of Persian Rubáiyát: An Anthology of Quatrains from the Tenth to the Twentieth Century.* . . . Bethesda, Md.: Ibex Publishers, 2000.

S

Sachs, Hans (1494–1576)

See MEISTERSINGER.

Sackville, Thomas (1536–1608)

The first earl of Dorset and a second cousin of Queen ELIZABETH I of England, after studying both at Oxford and at Cambridge, Sackville pursued a career as a lawyer and as a diplomat. For a time his spendthrift ways brought him into official disgrace, but Elizabeth relented and entrusted important offices and missions to him. One of his least palatable responsibilities was announcing to Mary, Queen of Scots, that she had been sentenced to death (1586).

Together with a fellow lawyer and poet, THOMAS NORTON, Sackville authored the first blank verse, English SENECAN TRAGEDY, GORBODUC. The play was performed as part of an ongoing theatrical program sponsored by the lawyers of the Inner Temple around 1559–60. The following year, Queen Elizabeth witnessed a performance at Whitehall. Also known as *Ferrex and Porrex, Gorboduc* is one of the primary sources for WILLIAM SHAKESPEARE's *KING LEAR*.

Sahagún, Bernardino de (1499–1590)

Educated at the University of Salamanca in Spain, Sahagún, a Franciscan friar, came from Spain to Mexico in 1529 and devoted his life to the study and preservation of the high culture of the Aztecs. He mastered the Nahuatl tongue and taught the children of upper-class indigenous families both in Spanish and in their own languages. His GENERAL HISTORY OF THE THINGS OF NEW SPAIN, rediscovered in manuscript in the FLORENTINE CODEX in the 19th century, is a model of ethnographic writing that anticipates the best scientific anthropological and ethnological practices of today.

Sahagún championed the causes of the indigenous peoples of Mexico and took the trouble to understand and to try to preserve at least portions of a culture that he recognized as, in some ways, more advanced than his own. Politics contributed to the eventual confiscation and suppression of his writings. His influence, however, lived on among the students that he trained. His views and methods, moreover, were carried on at the College of Tlaltelolco in what is now Mexico City and among the members of the Franciscan order who succeeded him.

The rediscovery of his books in the 19th century has made the foundation stones of early

Meso-American scientific study and exposition once again available to the world.

Bibliography

León Portilla, Miguel. *Bernardino de Sahagún, First Anthropologist*. Translated by Mauricio J. Mixco. Norman: University of Oklahoma Press, ca. 2002.

Schwaller, John Frederick, ed. *Sagagún at 500: Essays on the Quincentenary of the Birth of Fr. Bernardino de Sahagún*. Berkeley, Calif.: Academy of American Franciscan History, 2003.

Ṣā'ib of Tabriz (or Isfahan) (Alí, Mirzá Muhammad) (d. ca. 1670)

Born in Persia (now Iran) near the city of Isfahan to the family of a wealthy merchant, the young poet Ṣā'ib was privately educated and studied the arts of composing poetry and of calligraphy. Perhaps drawn by news of the generous reception accorded poets among the Mughal rulers in Afghanistan and India, the poet set out for India about 1625–26. In Kabul his skill as a Persian poet earned him the friendship and patronage of the city's administrator, Zafar Khan—a member of the Mughal nobility. When Zafar Khan was posted to central India, Ṣā'ib accompanied him. On his patron's recommendation, the Mughal emperor appointed Ṣā'ib commander of 1,000 cavalrymen—a post that paid a handsome salary.

The poet's aged father, however, so missed his son that the elderly man trekked from Isfahan to Agra in India to persuade the young man to return to Persia. With the permission of his friend and patron, Ṣā'ib acceded to his father's wishes and returned to Persia after a brief stay in Kashmir, becoming poet laureate to the court of Shah 'Abbás II. The shah's successor, however, dismissed Ṣā'ib from that high post when the poet offended the ruler. Until his death Ṣā'ib remained quietly in Isfahan, writing his own verse and teaching budding poets their art.

Throughout his career, Ṣā'ib displayed a deep appreciation for other poets—particularly Indian poets in the Persian language like FAYDÍ. This appreciation sets him apart from some of his fellow Persian poets who looked upon their Indian counterparts with the same sort of disdain some big city dwellers sometimes display toward rural residents. His careful study of other poets' works led to his compilation of an extensive anthology of his predecessors' and colleagues' best verses. A manuscript of this anthology found its way to the city of Hyderabad in central India where the work became a source document for later anthologists and biographers.

Ṣā'ib became renowned for his quick wit and ingenuity. A late 19th- early 20th-century literary historian, Edward G. Browne, translated a selection of his favorite lines from the poet's verses. I offer two of Browne's translations here as examples of Ṣā'ib's trenchancy:

1. When poison becomes a habit it ceases to injure: make thy soul gradually acquainted with death.
2. All this talk of infidelity and religion finally leads to one place: The dream is the same dream, only the interpretations differ.

Considered the last of the great poets of Persia, Ṣā'ib is especially remembered for the novelty, grace, and fluidity of his ghazels. His total production of lyric poems, not all of which survive, is thought to have encompassed some 80,000 to 125,000 verses. In addition he penned a history of Kandahar, Afghanistan, and CUPBEARER poems. Several of these and some of his amorous poems he organized into volumes according to their subject matter with Persian titles that translate "Tavern," "The mirror of beauty," and "The mirror of thought."

Ṣā'ib 's literary reputation, like that of most poets, has had its ups and downs. At the moment, judging from the recent appearance in print of many of his surviving poems and a spate of critical articles in Iran and India, his popularity seems to be on the rise.

Bibliography

Browne, Edward Granville. *A Literary History of Persia*. Volume 4. 1902. Reprint, Bethesda, Md.: Iran Books, 1997.

Saikaku (Ihara Saikaku) (1642–1693)

A Japanese poet and fiction writer, Saikaku (as Ihara Saikaku is familiarly known) enjoys a reputation as the first major novelist in the Japanese language since the 11th century. As a young man he began a family, but his wife died young and his blind daughter soon followed her mother in death. Alone, Saikaku withdrew from conventional life. Instead of joining a religious order as might have been expected, however, he devoted himself to a literary career.

He began that career as a *haikai* poet and the disciple of Nishiyama Soin, the founder of the Danrin school of poetry. This school sought to liberate poetry from constraining rules of composition and to open it to new subjects. An extreme advocate of that position, Saikaku drew his subjects from the daily lives of ordinary citizens and from such commonplace events that the greatest contemporary *haikai* poet of the Danrin school, MATSUO BASHŌ, judged Saikaku's work both vulgar and lacking inspiration.

Whatever qualitative faults Saikaku's verse may have displayed, quantitatively his output was so enormous that his contemporaries dubbed him *old master twenty thousand*. His facility in composition was such that he put on demonstrations and competitions to see who could write the most *haikai*. In 1678 he set a record, producing 1,600 *haikai* in a single performance. In 1681 he broke that record, composing 3,000 of the 17-syllable verses in one day. He far overshot that mark, however, when in 1685, in a 24-hour exhibition, he produced 23,500 *haikai*. That effort, at least temporarily, appears to have drained the wellspring of Saikaku's poetic inspiration. For the last decade of his life he shifted his attention to writing prose. In doing so he fundamentally altered the shape of Japanese fiction.

In prose, he penned some plays. He did several character sketches of people involved in theatrical production, especially depicting attractive young actors and details about their personal lives. He also wrote some short fiction. His novels—or perhaps better, linked novellas—assured him his distinguished place in the annals of Japanese letters.

Their subjects remained the ones he had favored in his verse, namely, the lives and activities of ordinary citizens—a subject matter for which there was a large and receptive audience.

His first and most realistic novel, *Koshoku ichidai otoko* (*The life of an amorous man*, 1682) follows the career of a Japanese Don Juan who moved about the country taking any work he could find and seducing "3,742 women and 732 young boys." This does not count his preadulthood affairs. In the end the hero, Yonosuke, sails at the age of 60 from a completely picked-over Japan in search of a legendary Isle of Women, which will afford him new opportunities to practice his avocation. A sequel depicts the career of Yonosuke's illegitimate son as he emulates his father's career, but only among women in the houses of pleasure. This book raised a subliterary genre, books comparing the charms of courtesans, to the level of literary fiction.

In the opening lines of his first work Saikaku tells his readers that the way of love can follow two paths—the path of the love between male and female or the path of love between male and male. In his subsequent writings, Saikaku traces the permutations of these itineraries and of another one as well—the love of people for wealth.

One of his most notable works, FIVE WOMEN WHO LOVED LOVE (*Kōshoku gonin onna*, 1686) links five short novels that follow the amorous careers of five headstrong, love-struck women, four of whom suffer death as the outcome of their passion. A sequel the same year explores the sexual indignities suffered by a maid at the hands of her mistress. Another famous book, THE GREAT MIRROR OF MALE LOVE (*NANSHOKU ŌKAGAMI*, 1687), brings together 40 nonjudgmental short stories about love relations between boys and adult men—usually Samurai or Buddhist monks.

In reading Saikaku's works, Western readers should bear in mind that marriage in 17th-century Japan involved many considerations, but that romantic love was seldom one of them. The Japanese cultural bias of the period held rather that romantic love—though highly prized—was much more likely to develop among prostitutes of both sexes with members of their clientele than between a husband and a wife. Romantic feelings were also likely to develop between a Buddhist monk and a novice or a Samurai warrior and his page. Homosexual relationships of this sort were institutionalized to the degree that, at age 19, a youth who had been beloved by an older man underwent an initiation ceremony. After that ritual the adult role in similar relationships became the initiate's.

Saikaku explores the love of money in a pair of books entitled *Eitai Gura* (Treasury for the ages) and *Seken mune-zanyo* (The calculating world).

Other works include, first, a little volume depicting examples of filial disrespect (1686). The next year saw a series of books containing stories of Samurai vengeance. *Budō denrai ki* (Record of the transmission of the martial arts, 1687) and two others that followed within a year examined various aspects of the martial code and behavior of the Samurai class. Beyond this Saikaku raised another subliterary genre to the level of literature in a series of critiques of Kabuki actors.

Bibliography

Saikaku, Ihara. *Five Women Who Loved Love.* Translated by William Theodore De Bary. Rutland, Vt.: Charles E. Tuttle Company, 1956.
———. *The Great Mirror of Male Love.* Translated by Paul Gordon Schalow. Stanford Calif.: Stanford University Press, 1990.

Saint Guglielma, The Play of Antonia Tannini Pulci (before 1487)

The plays of ANTONIA TANNINI PULCI were probably performed by nuns taking both men's and women's roles. Their audiences were probably composed of women from the surrounding neighborhoods, possibly accompanied by some of their children. Tannini Pulci's plays regularly opened with an actress attired as an angel who spoke a prologue to give the audience an idea of what was coming and to inspire a properly reverential mood.

The Play of St. Guglielma opens in England where Guglielma is a daughter of the king. An embassy from the king of Hungary begs that Guglielma will agree to marry their king. Though Guglielma would rather choose a religious life, she obeys her father and travels to Hungary where she marries and lives happily with the king. Her pious devotion proves infectious, and she instills in her husband her own desire to make a pilgrimage to the Holy Land. Rather than take her with him, however, the king decides to go alone and to leave Guglielma in charge of the kingdom with his brother as her adviser.

In the king's absence the brother attempts to seduce Guglielma, but she remains faithful. The incident, however, leaves her utterly confused about what action to take when her husband returns. As soon as word comes that the royal entourage is nearing home, rather than risk the king's potential wrath, the brother rides out to meet him, intercepts the king at an inn, and accuses Guglielma of all sorts of lewd behavior and bad stewardship of the kingdom. The king uncritically accepts his brother's account of affairs and condemns Guglilma to death without even waiting to hear her side of the story.

Convinced of her innocence, the officials, who have been ordered to burn her, let her go. Protected by angels, Guglielma travels far by ship, eventually taking up residence in a convent where, though as a married woman faithful to her husband she never takes orders, she nonetheless acquires a reputation as a very holy person with the power of healing the sick through prayer.

In due course, the false brother develops leprosy. The royal physicians fail to cure him, and their professional ineptitude becomes the butt of playful satire. Seeking a cure the king and his brother travel abroad, learn of the reputation of a wise and holy healer, and seek her out. The woman of course proves to be Guglielma. She recognizes her husband and his brother, but they don't know her.

Guglielma promises to pray that God will cure the brother provided that he will confess any wrong he has ever done his brother and provided that the king will promise to love and forgive his brother when he learns of his crime. Both men agree, the brother confesses all, the king fulfills his promise, Guglielma prays, the leper is healed, and Guglielma reveals her identity to her husband. Reunited, they return to Hungary where the barons are overjoyed to see their queen, who had been in fact an exemplary ruler.

Guglielma, the king, and the brother who has been healed both physically and morally distribute their power and wealth among the barons and retire from the world to a religious hermitage. The angel who spoke the prologue now reappears, pronounces an epilogue, and dismisses the audience.

The general outline of Guglielma's behavior in the play resonates with Antonia Tannini Pulci's biography. Like her play's heroine, Pulci retired from the world to a religious retreat but stopped short of becoming a nun.

Bibliography

Pulci, Antonia. *Florentine Drama for Convent and Festival: Seven Sacred Plays.* Translated by James Wyatt Cook; edited by James Wyatt Cook and Barbara Collier Cook. Chicago: University of Chicago Press, 1996.

———. *Florentine Drama for Convent and Festival: The Plays of Antonia Pulci.* Revised and expanded bilingual edition. Edited by Elissa Weaver, translated by James Wyatt Cook and Elissa Weaver. Chicago: University of Chicago Press, ca. 2005.

Saint John's Eve   Lope de Vega Carpio (1631)

An example of a Spanish CAPE AND SWORD DRAMA, *Saint John's Eve* was offered as a COURT ENTERTAINMENT for the Count Duke Olivares's party for the Spanish king on Saint John's Eve in June 1631. In Spain that holiday was akin to carnival in Venice. In the city of Madrid on that evening crowds were in the street seeking amorous entertainment and diversion. LOPE's play brings to the stage in the Count Duke's garden the activity that is actually going on in the town outside its walls.

A lady, Leonora, shares with the audience her tender feelings toward a wealthy Spanish adventurer just back from the West Indies, Don Juan de Hurtado, who has been wooing her. Leonora's brother, Don Luis, unaware of the growing understanding between the two, gets to know Don Juan and enlists his aid in arranging a match for Luis with Doña Blanca, the sister of Juan's dear friend Bernardo.

Glad for a chance to help the brother of the woman he loves, Don Juan goes to Bernardo and describes the preparations for the play that the au-

dience is in progress of watching. In the course of that description Lope has Juan pay a number of courtly compliments to dignitaries present at the performance.

When Juan gets around to proposing the match between Blanca and Luis, Bernardo is pleased, but suggests that he himself marry Leonora. Juan's hyperrefined but typically Spanish sense of honor requires him to give up his suit of Leonora. Moreover we discover in an exchange between Blanca and Leonora that Blanca loves Don Pedro, and wants nothing to do with Luis. Leonora becomes upset that Juan (because of his sense of honor as the audience knows) has suddenly grown cold toward her. She thinks he may have found someone else.

Act two begins with Blanca's describing Don Pedro and the way she found out he loves her. She is preparing to run off with him and marry him, but is interrupted by her brother, Bernardo, who wants Blanca to help him win Leonora. Leonora in the meantime goes out with a companion into the crowds in Saint John's Eve. There she encounters Don Juan's servant who tells her that his distraught master is about to flee Madrid and his unhappy fate. Don Juan enters, Leonora faints, and, when she comes to, she and Juan agree to marry in secret. Just then, however, Juan's servant quarrels with some impudent revelers (clad, of course, in capes). Swordplay follows, and the watch arrests Don Juan. Leonora seeks refuge in an empty house. It proves to belong to Don Pedro who is out searching for Blanca. He returns to find Leonora, whom he has never met, up on his balcony trying to spot Don Juan. Trusting her plight to his honor, Leonora tells him all, and he vows to protect her and her secret. Then he returns to the streets.

Juan in the meantime has bribed the officers and gained his freedom. He and Pedro meet, and Juan inquires about Leonora. Pedro thinks that Juan is Leonora's brother instead of the lover she seeks. Just then, Blanca arrives at Pedro's house where she intends to hide until their marriage can be performed. On finding Leonora there, Blanca assumes the worst and rushes out again. Leonora pursues her to set her straight, and the women both encounter their brothers. After a good deal more amusing confusion, matters get sorted out, and the lovers pair off in keeping with the ladies' preferences.

Lope de Vega himself took the stage at the end to observe in a pedantic joke that he had bettered one of the classical UNITIES by more than 14 hours since the action of his play had required only 10 hours instead of the 24 permitted.

Salluste, Guillaume, seigneur du Bartas
See BARTAS, GUILLAUME DE SALLUSTE, SEIGNEUR DU.

Sankaradeva (1449–1568 or 1569)
An extraordinarily long-lived saint, the founder of an influential cult, a poet and dramatist in the Assamese LANGUAGE OF INDIA, and the inventor of an artificial dialect, Sankaradeva became a one-man literary movement. He wrote actively throughout his life, completing and directing a play, *Rama-vijaya* (The conquests of Rama) in his last and 119th year.

Like many of the other literary figures of the period in India, Sankaradeva found inspiration in the BHAKTI movement of spiritual renewal that for a period of some centuries swept repeatedly through the country. Among other writers, he looked to the ancient EPIC literature of India for material that he could reshape into vehicles for his fresh ideas and his religious convictions.

His earliest surviving work, probably written around 1469, reworks in 615 verses an episode concerning King Harishchandra from the ancient *Markandeya-purana* (Traditional stories relating to Brahma). The poet alters little of the plot, but he shapes the material in keeping with the emergent ideas of the cult he was to found. He develops those ideas further in his *Bhakti-pradipa* (The lamp of devotion), where he instructs his followers to repeat God's name as the main road to salvation.

Still borrowing from ancient materials, Sankaradeva penned 795 verses retelling the story of the abduction of Rukmini. Here the poet's reshaping of the original Sanskritic texts reveals itself in the heightened characterizations of his people and the colloquial quality of his language. Song lyrics from this work, the scholar Maheswar Neog tells us, are still memorized by Assamese village women for performance at their weddings.

The popular theology that characterized the resurgent worship of the Deity Vishnu associated with the bhakti movement achieves its fullest expression in Assamese in the 2,264 verses of Sankaradeva's *Kirtana-ghosha* (The book of songs and refrains).

Others of his works retell the accomplishments of various members of the Hindu pantheon. They give the saint's views on theology (the contention between the forces of creation and destruction), cosmology (where the earth is located on the water that surrounds the universe), and philosophy. He also paints a frightening picture of the torments of the damned in another work, assuring his followers that the simple repetition of God's name can save them from directly experiencing those sufferings.

A series of Sankaradeva's works contains stories about the Hindu Deity Lord Krishna and his earthly adventures. Among these the one considered most characteristic of his maturity is *Krishna-prayana Pandava-niryana*. It recounts Krishna's departure from the world, the Pandava family's demise as a result of their own folly, the sorrow of Krishna's consorts—the milkmaids of Braja—and the grief of other major characters at Krishna's departure. It also details the horrid treatment of Krishna's beloved milkmaids at the hands of the bestial cowherds among whom they work. A work in the Krishna series, *The Kirttana,* is the only one of Sankaradeva's works in full English translation.

This brief account merely represents Sankaradeva's narrative verse production. A full listing would require a much longer discussion. One must, however, also glance at the master poet's drama, crafted mostly in verse but also containing the first instances of Assamese dramatic prose.

For these plays, Sankaradeva invented the artificial dialect mentioned above—Assamese Brajabuli. This dialect contains an idiosyncratic blending of Assamese, Hindi, and Maithili elements spiced with phases from a few other tongues. Its popularity suggests that his audiences possessed the linguistic facility to follow appreciatively, helped along by an interlocutor who takes the stage, speaks a prologue, and then sings, dances, explains, and directs the action throughout. At least five of these plays survive.

Bibliography

Neog, Maheswar, ed. *The Bhakti-ratnākara of Sanka-radeva . . . with a Résumé in English and History of . . . Bhakti. . . .* Patiala, India: Publication Bureau, Punjab University, 1982.

Sankaradeva. *The Kirttana.* Translated by Chandrakanta Mahanta. Johat, Asom, India: Asom Satra Sangha, 1990.

satire

Though the term *satire* can be applied to a wide spectrum of literary works, the word almost always implies a literary attack on someone or something. The tone of the attack can range from virulent to gentle. When satire is employed for moral purposes, it is often used to attack vice. The Renaissance abounds with examples of satire of this sort. Agrippa d'Aubigné in France, for example, uses bitter satire in his attack on the French system of justice in the third book of his Protestant EPIC *LES TRAGIQUES* (The tragic ones) when he exposes the justice system as systematically unjust. A more humorous variety of satire often appears on the English Renaissance stage to expose the false piety of some Puritans, the false virtue of some women, or the hypocrisy of con artists. Examples of these occur in BEN JONSON's *THE ALCHEMIST* and his *BARTHOLOMEW FAIR*. We also find examples of a similar sort in MOLIÈRE's *TARTUFFE*.

Satire can also be used to attack affectation. We see examples of this sort in PIETRO ARETINO's *The Courtesan* (*La cortegiana*), which conducts a mocking parody of BALDESSARE CASTIGLIONE's *BOOK OF THE COURTIER* (*Il cortegiano,* 1528). Whereas Castiglione sought to outline the characteristics of an ideal member of the Italian nobility, Aretino considered the entire institution of nobility an imposition on the lower classes whose ill-rewarded efforts supported them. Castiglione's work, however, also supplies an example of satire at its gentlest. As a character representing Cardinal PIETRO BEMBO considers PLATONIC LOVE, he becomes so distracted from ordinary reality that a lady present in the company must pluck at his sleeve to call him back to earth. Aretino, however, considered Bembo's hyperrefined but very influential literary tastes to be a roadblock to the development of Italian literature.

Satire can be used for political, literary, religious, moral, or personal purposes. Writers such as DESIDERIUS ERASMUS use it to expose folly and vice. Many playwrights use it to make laughing stocks of dull-witted persons. Writers such as CERVANTES, however, or RABELAIS use satire very broadly to expose a wide variety of pretense, silliness, self-delusion, dogma, notions about life, and the vacuity of many of the tastes of the popular culture of their times.

In its broadest application, however, satire sometimes pokes bitter fun at the human condition itself and at the pretensions of human beings who identify their own purposes with those of Divine Providence. Sometimes satirists who operate in the existential spirit have even been known to lampoon those who seek to discern preestablished meaning in a universe whose only meaning derives from individual choices and commitment. Though such a point of view more often characterizes 20th- and 21st-century writers than those of the Renaissance, foreshadowing of such ideas appears in the work of such Italian writers as LUIGI PULCI, TOMMASO CAMPANELLA, or such as the English writer, ROBERT GREENE. For satirists with such convictions about life and the nature of things, the proper response to the human condition is laughter.

Scarron, Paul (Monsieur Scarron) (1610–1660)

Paul Scarron deserved his reputation as the most notable writer in the burlesque manner of 17th-century France. Yet, as his biographer Frederick A. de Armas argues, Scarron was much more than that. His burlesque works are hardly read at all today. His later work, heavily influenced by the Spanish theater of the Golden Age, on the other hand, moved in the direction of TRAGICOMEDY and therefore in the direction of greater realism. Scarron's reputation principally rests on his later work, whose greater complexity of plot anticipated the developments of French theater and provided useful models for MOLIÈRE.

After a childhood made difficult by the loss of his mother, Gabrielle Gouguet, and by a domineering stepmother, Françoise de Plaix, who was not fond of her husband's children by his first marriage, Scarron was educated at a Paris academy. While there he discovered the Spanish theater of the Golden Age and began writing verse. Hoping to pursue a literary career, Scarron took minor orders in the church. This step provided him access to the literary world and, together with an allowance from his father, would underpin his financial security by giving him access to church stipends that required little if any actual work.

As a young man in Paris, Scarron's activities could hardly be called priestly. He became involved in numerous love affairs and in duels with rivals. Until 1639, in fact, his adventures remained colorful to the point of debauchery. He fictionalized and recorded in a series of early poems his passionate involvements with several women. His stepmother, however, objected to her husband's continued support of a wastrel son, and his father soon found a position for Scarron as secretary to the bishop of Maine, Charles de Beaumanoir, in the city of Le Mans. The young poet and the bishop immediately became good friends, and in 1635 Scarron accompanied his new mentor to Rome.

On their return from Rome, the bishop not only secured a church salary for Scarron, he also introduced the poet to persons who could help further his literary career. One of these, François d'Averton, the count of Belin, encouraged Scarron to write pamphlets that mounted violent attacks against PIERRE CORNEILLE—a playwright whose works Scarron much admired. Scarron felt obliged to do so as he was heavily dependent upon the count's continued good favor, and in 1637 two venomous pamphlets appeared.

They were hardly published before fortune turned her wheel to Scarron's disadvantage. Both the count and the bishop died within a year leaving Scarron without their protection and with no place to live. His church stipend was contested in the courts. In 1638, moreover, the young man was afflicted with a crippling disease—multiple rheumatoid arthritis, according to his biographer Naomi Phelps—that eventually left him shaped, as he himself said, "like the letter Z." His physical disability, however, also required him to undertake making a living with his pen, and in 1639 he met Marie de Hautfort, a woman beloved by King Louis XIV. Cardinal Richelieu wielded his power to exile Madame de Hautfort from Paris to Le Mans. There she and Scarron met. She undertook to reform his life and to encourage his writing. He responded with utter nonsensual devotion and complete dedication to her goals for him.

In 1640, with his modest church income at last secure, Scarron returned to live in Paris. In 1642, after seeking relief from his illness at the baths of Bourbon-l'Archambault, he wrote two verse pieces recalling his experiences there. Their success confirmed his decision to write for a living. He also wrote a verse description of the annual fair at St. Germain and a poem requesting that Cardinal Richelieu rescind his edict exiling Scarron's father from Paris.

Responding to the popularity of burlesque poems among the readers of the French capital, in 1643 Scarron published his *Collection of Some Burlesque Verses* (*Recueil des quelques vers burlesques*). Its instant popularity encouraged successors, his *Suite of Burlesque Works* and *Typhon* (1644). Named for a mythical Greco-Roman monster with a hundred snakes' heads, eyes of fire, and an eardrum-shattering voice—a monster both the enemy of Zeus and the son of Tartarus, ruler of the underworld—*Typhon* satirizes the Olympian gods. By extension it also satirizes the hyperclassical tastes of Renaissance French poets such as RONSARD. Scarron dedicated both of these works to Cardinal Jules Mazarin, who had succeeded to Richelieu's power as minister of France. In 1656 Scarron once more returned to satiric verse in his *Leander and Hero*. The literary critic Robert Berens argues that this poem shows a markedly improved and much more mature poet at work.

Scarron's first comic play, *Jodelet, or the Master Valet*, took Paris by storm in 1643. The entire city admired the visibly deteriorating, crippled young writer who laughed in the face of his personal adversity and charmed the populace with his wit. A less successful sequel, *The Three Dorothys or Jodelet Affronted,* followed in 1645 (published, 1647).

Scarron's view of Cardinal Mazarin changed radically after the cardinal and the queen mother, Anne of Austria, conspired in exiling Scarron's good angel, Mme. de Hautfort, to a convent. Instead of having Scarron's work dedicated to him, the cardinal became the object of the poet's SATIRE in his unfinished *Virgil parodied* (*Virgile travesti, 1648–49*) and in Scarron's *Mazarinade* (1651). Particularly the cardinal's role in events leading to the two popular uprisings called the *Frondes* (1648 and 1651) receives the brunt of Scarron's unsparing invective.

In 1650 Scarron received a courtesy call from Françoise d'Aubigné, the granddaughter of THÉODORE AGRIPPA D'AUBIGNÉ. On seeing the state of the poet's affliction, the girl wept openly. Over the next two years, she became a frequent, then a constant visitor. Knowing that she lacked a prerequisite for an advantageous marriage—a dowry—in 1652 Scarron offered to supply one. She refused. He then proposed that she marry him. She accepted. He was 42, she 16. He was deformed by his illness; she was one of the great beauties of her era. Until Scarron's death eight years later, the couple seems to have shared an idyllic marriage. (Clerics who only take minor orders are not subject to the vows of poverty, chastity, and obedience sworn by ordained priests.) Later on, Mme. Scarron became first the mistress and then the wife of Louis XIV of France. With the king's help she purchased a marquisate and is remembered as Madame de Maintenon, a persecutor of Protestants and a benefactor of impoverished noblewomen.

Throughout the period from 1647 until his death, literary works continued flowing from Scarron's pen. These included COMEDY like the one-act drama, *The Jests of Captain Matamore* (1647), *DON JAPHET OF ARMENIA* (performed 1647, published 1653), and *The Ridiculous Heir* (1648). His next play *The Scholar of Salamanca* (1654), a serious tragicomedy whose plot was drawn from the work of the Spanish playwright Rojas Zorilla, represses all elements of the burlesque. It was a box-office failure. Perceiving that the public was not yet ready to accept his serious mode, Scarron returned to plays that moved between the poles of farce and seriousness. Two plays of that kind, *His Own Guardian* (1655) and *The Ridiculous Marquis* (1656) proved more successful with the public.

Scarron's posthumously published writings reveal that he had not lost interest in the Spanish theater nor in writing serious plays, even if the public was not ready to watch them. Two complete plays and fragments of others appeared after his death. The first finished work, *The False Appearance,* adapts a work by PEDRO CALDERÓN DE LA BARCA. In this play Scarron, for the first time, troubled himself to observe the unities of time, place, and action that the Italian theorist LUDOVICO CASTELVETRO had added to ARISTOTLE's *Poetics.* The second complete drama, *La Prince Corsaire* (The Pirate Prince), is a swashbuckling play with murders, saber rattling, two sets of lovers happily married, and a pirate who is really a prince. No source for this play is known, and it is different from anything else Scarron wrote.

Scarron's reputation among posterity depends mainly on his unfinished novel *ROMAN COMIQUE* (A comic novel, part 1, 1651; part 2, 1654; part 3, apparently lost). Set in the city of Le Mans, it seems in part to objectify the author's own internal reality, integrating his interior biography with the fiction of admired predecessors like MIGUEL DE CERVANTES.

Bibliography

De Armas, Frederick Alfred. *Paul Scarron.* New York: Twayne Publishes, 1972.

Phelps, Naomi Forsythe. *The Queen's Invalid: A Biography of Paul Scarron.* Baltimore: The Johns Hopkins University Press, 1951.

Scarron, Paul. *The Whole Comical Works of Monsieur Scarron.* 2 vols. New York: Garland Publishers, 1973.

Scève, Maurice (1501–1560)

A translator and the foremost poet of the Lyon school, Scève came to public notice during his student years by reputedly finding the tomb of PETRARCH's celebrated Laura in Avignon. If true, that happenstance together with his admiration for the poetry of the Italian school, both Petrarch's own and the work of his 15th- and 16th-century disciple

Cardinal PIETRO BEMBO, led Scève to emulate the Italians in his own poems.

Scève's literary career seems to have begun with a 1535 translation of a Spanish novel by Juan de Flores, whose title translates as "The deplorable end of Fiametta." About this time, as well, he composed several short descriptive poems called *blasons* on subjects like an eyebrow, a tear, a neck, a forehead, and a sigh.

Around 1536 Scève met Pernette Du Guillet when she was 16 years old, and they became affectionate friends. On Du Guillet's side, the relationship appears to have been entirely platonic, and she married Antoine Du Molin. Scève, by contrast, entertained sexual fantasies about Du Guillet and felt jealous of her husband. His sublimated feelings about her became the subject matter of his 4,490 line poem, *Délie, Obiect de plus haulte vertu* (Delie, a subject of the highest virtue, 1544). Organized into 10-line stanzas, the poem presents the poet's views about life as well as his often obscure and sometimes occult references to his feelings for his lady.

The year 1547 saw the publication of a different sort of work, a PASTORAL ECLOGUE entitled *La Saulsaye* (The willow grove). In this 732-line dialogue, written in 10-syllable couplets, two shepherds discuss their loves and their views about life. Two shepherds, Philerme, whose name means one who loves solitude, and Antire (one who contradicts), propound their outlooks. Rejected in love, Philerme has fled to the peace of the rural shepherd's life where he can avoid the pain life in society exposes him to. Antire argues that life outside society is dangerous. The ensuing debate restates in a pastoral setting the medieval argument about the attractions of the active life versus those of the contemplative life.

In 1548 Scève wrote a description of the magnificent entry of the royal procession of Henry II into the city of Lyon in September of the same year.

The poet's last major work, *MICROCOSME* (Microcosm) was finished in 1559 and published in 1562. This time Scève chose alexandrine couplets (see POETIC METER) for the body of his poem, which is divided into three books, each a thousand lines long. This organization reflects both the Trinitar-

ian and the millenarian traditions of Christian numerology. The entire work is enclosed at either end by an introductory and a final sonnet.

Bibliography

Coleman, Dorothy Gabe. *Maurice Scève, Poet of Love.* Cambridge, U.K.: Cambridge University Press, 1975.

Hallett, Ronald A., trans. "A Translation, with Introduction and Notes of the "Dèlie of Maurice Scève." Ph.D. diss. Ann Arbor, Mich.: University Microfilms, 1973.

Mulhauser, Ruth. *Maurice Scève.* Boston: Twayne Publishers, 1977.

Scève, Maurice. *Emblems of Desire: Selections from the "Délie" of Maurice Scève.* Edited and Translated by Richard Sieburth. Philadelphia: University of Pennsylvania Press, ca. 2003.

———. *The Entry of Henry II into Lyon: September 1548.* Edited by Richard Cooper. Tempe, Ariz.: Medieval & Renaissance Texts & Studies, 1997. [Critical discussion in English; text in Middle French.]

Staub, Hans, ed. *Maurice Scève, Oeuvres poétiques complètes.* 2 vols. Paris: Union Générale d'Editions, 1971.

scholasticism

During the Middle Ages, scholasticism was the principal system of philosophical discourse and proof taught in universities. Assuming that the universe was a rational place that operated according to the laws of logic, scholasticism applied the logical syllogisms of ancient philosophers to all sorts of moral and theological questions—even sometimes to those that made no practical or empirical sense. The proofs that scholasticism offered were, nonetheless, subordinate to the official positions of the church and to the authority of Scripture.

One of the principal philosophical and educational movements of the Renaissance, HUMANISM, reacted against the methods of scholasticism, which had come to seem hopelessly outmoded and trivial.

Scudéry, Georges de (1601–1667)

The brother of the better remembered MADELEINE DE SCUDÉRY, in his own time Georges was a soldier, an EPIC poet, and a prolific dramatist. As a soldier, he acquired a reputation as a swaggerer and something of a bully.

As an epic poet he penned an 11,000-line work based on the life and conquests of the king of the Visigoths, *Alaric* (ca. 370–410 C.E.). This poem he addressed to Queen Christina of Sweden. Whether or not the queen read it, the French poet and critic Nicholas Boileau did, and he found the work ludicrous.

Scudéry's numerous plays, though sometimes flawed by verbosity and florid language, were nonetheless imaginatively plotted. He penned COMEDY, tragicomedy in both verse and prose, and TRAGEDY. The best remembered among his comedies was his *Comédie des Comédiens* (The comedy of the comedians), which follows the adventures of a company of actors. He enjoyed for a time the patronage of Cardinal Richelieu, and the cardinal commissioned Scudéry to write a verse tragicomedy, *L'Amour tyrannique*. French writers and their patrons frequently involved themselves in disputes with their contemporaries, and Richelieu encouraged Scudéry not only to pen that work to compete with PIERRE CORNEILLE's *Le Cid* (ca. 1635–36) but also to criticize it officially before the French Academy. The Academy found Corneille's tragedy deficient with respect to issues of style and grammar. Although the public loved Corneille's play, Scudéry's action disheartened the younger playwright, and Corneille fell silent for three years.

Another of Scudéry's tragicomedies, this time in prose, was *Axiene* (1643). Georges Scudéry's French work found an audience in England as well as in France. Companies of French players acted in that language in England, and in 1635 they performed *Le Trompeur Puni*, a play based on material from HONORÉ D'URFÉ's ASTREA (L'ASTRÉE).

Bibliography

Schweitzer, Jerome W. *Georges de Scudéry's Almahide; Authorship, Analysis, Sources, and Structure*. Baltimore, Md.: The Johns Hopkins University Press, 1939.

Scudéry, Madeleine de (1608–1701)

Scudéry was one of the French literary women who, like the MARQUISE DE RAMBOUILLET, established a literary salon. Scudéry's salon was called "Saturdays." In such salons the witty and the literary figures of the day gathered for refined and amusing conversation. During the regency of Anne of Austria and her chief minister, Cardinal Mazarin, the salons of France also became a focal point of political dissent. The popular uprising called the Frondes (the Slings) had gained impetus in the salons, and Mazarin suppressed them for a time.

Madeleine de Scudéry, an important author in her own right, became the retrospective, novelistic voice of the rebellion. Publishing under the name of her brother, GEORGES DE SCUDÉRY, she penned several lengthy and popular romances. The earliest of these, *Ibrahim* (1641), recounts the tale of a Christian slave in Turkey who becomes the sultan's favorite general and at length wins the hand of an Italian aristocrat, Isabel, whom he rescues from captivity. She published her most popular, longer, and more political later works in installments. In them she depicted herself and other contemporary people lightly disguised as ancient Greeks, Persians, and Romans.

These works included, first, *Artemenes, or the Grand Cyrus* (*Artemène, ou Le Grand Cyrus*, 1649–53), in which she herself plays a role under her salon name, Sappho. This novel, as the literary historian Joan DeJean tells us, fictionalized the love affairs and military heroism of the leaders of the Fronde, and was enthusiastically received by the salon readership. Scudéry's most popular work, perhaps, was her 10-volume romance novel, *Clelie, a Roman story* (*Clélie, histoire romaine*, 1654–60). The first volume of that work contains a celebrated allegorical map, *Le carte de Tendre* (The map of the land of Tenderness), which DeJean cites as a predecessor of board games like Monopoly.

Following a map of the roads to a lady's favor or disfavor, a suitor begins at *Nouvelle Amitié* (New Friendship). From there the suitor follows paths appropriate to his objectives. Each objective appears as a city situated on the three rivers of the land of Tenderness: *Tendre sur Estime* (Tenderness on the river of Regard), *Tendre sur Inclination*

(Tenderness on the river of Passion), and *Tendre sur Reconnaissance* (Tenderness on the river of Gratitude or Recognition). A suitor can reach his goal by passing through a series of correct stages toward each. Exchanging love notes, for example, is a step in the direction of either of the first two objectives. Suitors can, however, go astray, and by taking wrong steps—like seeming lukewarm—can end up in the lake of Indifference or in the rugged mountains of Enmity.

Later on, Scudéry wrote other, now largely unread romances including *Almahide ou l'Esclave reine* (Almahide or the slave queen, 1660–63)—a novel set in Moorish Spain. In 1671, an essay she wrote won a prize for eloquence.

Bibliography

DeJean, Joan. "The Salons, 'Preciosity,' and the Sphere of Women's Influence." *A New History of French Literature*. Edited by Denis Hollier, et al. Cambridge, Mass., and London: Harvard University Press, 1989.

McDougall, Dorothy. *Madeleine de Scudéry: Her Romantic Life and Death*. New York: B. Blom, 1972.

Scudéry, Madeleine. *Selected Letters, Orations, and Rhetorical Dialogues*. Edited and Translated by Jane Donawerth and Julie Strongson. Chicago: University of Chicago Press, 2004.

———. *The Story of Sappho/Madeleine de Scudéry*. Translated by Karen Newman. Chicago: University of Chicago Press, 2003.

Sejong, king of Korea (1397–1450)

A learned Korean ruler who came to the throne at age 21, King Sejong's interests in philology, music, literature, and medicine led him to establish a royal academy for research in the arts and sciences—the Academy of Worthies. Under Sejong's patronage and encouragement a movement akin to the European Renaissance took hold in Korea.

The members of the academy devised a system to represent the sounds of their language phonetically. They invented, in other words, a KOREAN ALPHABET. Before that invention, literate Koreans had been constrained to learn Chinese and the thousands of ideograms and phonograms used to represent that language.

Under Sejong's careful supervision, an aristocracy of culture rather than of lineage arose in Korea that nurtured literary activity. In a very real sense King Sejong can be considered the father of his country's literature.

Seneca, Lucius Annacus (the younger)
(ca. 4 B.C.E.–ca. 65 C.E.)

A Roman philosopher, statesman, essayist, and verse tragedian, Seneca wrote plays that very much influenced Renaissance playwrights, particularly in England. There his name became attached to TRAGEDY OF THE BLOOD or *revenge tragedy*, which was also called SENECAN TRAGEDY. THOMAS KYD's *The Spanish Tragedy, or Hieronymo is Madde Againe*, provides a signal example of the type as Hieronymo's terrible vengeance leaves the stage strewn with corpses.

Seneca suffered a personal tragedy of the blood when the Roman emperor Nero commanded him to commit suicide. With characteristic stoicism, he obeyed by opening his own veins in a hot bath and bleeding to death.

Senecan tragedy
See TRAGEDY OF THE BLOOD.

seven deadly sins

In the Christian scheme of things, there are seven sins that put the immortal soul in jeopardy of eternal damnation. The most dangerous is pride, for that is the sin from which all others follow. Pride was the sin that, in JOHN MILTON's *PARADISE LOST*, caused Satan and the rebellious angels to fall. The others include: avarice, envy, gluttony, lust, sloth, and wrath. Many Renaissance literary works examine the effects of sin on the human condition, often in the context of a PSYCHOMACHIA—a war between the forces of good and evil for the soul of a human being.

Bibliography

Herbermann, Charles G., et al. *The Catholic Encyclopedia*. Vol. 14. New York: The Gilmary Society, 1913.

Shakespeare, William (1564–1616)

By virtually unanimous consensus the finest poet-dramatist of the European Renaissance, Shakespeare also stands with a very few other verse playwrights at the very pinnacle of world poetic and dramatic achievement. One of eight children, he was born in Stratford to the family of a glove-maker and burgess of that city, John Shakespeare and his wife Mary Alden. Though no record exists of Shakespeare's having attended the excellent grammar school of that city, his plays bristle with allusions to material included in its standard curriculum, and his father had a right to send young William there free of charge.

In 1582 Shakespeare, then 18, married a 26-year-old farm girl, Anne Hathaway, who was carrying his child. That child, Susanna, was christened on May 26, 1583. The year 1585 saw the birth of twins, Judith and Hamnet. At about this time, Shakespeare appears to have left Stratford, perhaps in search of employment, and an actor who knew him reported that he worked for a while as a country schoolmaster. Little else is known of him until around 1589 when he appears to have been a member of the acting troop that resulted from the combination of two companies, Lord Strange's Men and The Lord Admiral's Men. In 1589–90, as well, Shakespeare wrote his first known play, Part I of the history play *Henry VI*, and he continued with Parts II and III the following year.

These plays initiated a spectacularly successful, 25-year-long career as an actor, playwright, theater owner, producer, and lyric poet. By June 1592, when the plague necessitated a 23-month closure of London theaters, Shakespeare had added to his list another history play, *Richard III* (1592–93), *The Comedy of Errors* (1592–94), and a SENECAN TRAGEDY, *Titus Andronicus* (1593–94).

The hiatus in theatrical performance also permitted Shakespeare's sustained attention to other sorts of poetic endeavor. He completed his mythological-erotic poem in the style of OVID, *Venus and Adonis* (1592–93). A poem of 1,194 iambic pentameter lines organized in sestettes and rhyming ababcc, *Venus and Adonis* bore a dedicatory preface addressed to Henry Wriothesley, the Earl of Southampton. While the theaters were closed Shakespeare also began writing his lovely SONNET cycle that he completed around 1599 and that appeared in print in 1609. ROBERT GREENE's famous attack on Shakespeare as a dramatic upstart—a "shake-scene"—also occurred in 1592.

"The Bard," as Shakespeare has come to be called, did not neglect preparations for the reopening of the theater, completing his romantic comedy, *The Taming of the Shrew,* in 1593–94. The latter year also saw the completion of another poem dedicated to Southampton, one earlier promised as "a graver labor"—*The Rape of Lucrece.* For this more serious, 1,855-line poem based on the attempted violation of the Roman matron Lucretia by King Tarquin and her preservation of her honor by suicide, Shakespeare chose the rhyme royal stanza (a seven-line, iambic pentameter stanza, rhyming ababbcc) that Geoffrey Chaucer had used in his *Troilus and Criseyde.* The poem proved popular and went through six editions in the poet's lifetime.

In 1594, *Two Gentlemen of Verona* appeared, and Shakespeare began writing *King John,* finished in 1596. To this period his tragedy of *Romeo and Juliet* (1595–96) also belongs. So does his delightful romantic comedy, *A MIDSUMMER NIGHT'S DREAM,* which has proved a perennial favorite of audiences ever since. So too do the history plays, *Richard II* (1597), HENRY IV, PART I (1596–97), and the Italianate tragicomedy, *The Merchant of Venice* (1596–97).

Responding to the demands of his audiences that the rotund and merry Sir John Falstaff of *Henry IV, Part I,* star in his own play, Shakespeare penned *The Merry Wives of Windsor* (1597), where a pair of women conspire to punish Sir John for his inappropriately amorous advances. In *Henry IV, Part 2* (1598), Shakespeare has Falstaff die in miserable circumstances that suggest he was more to be pitied than censured. The playhouse most closely associated with Shakespeare's later career, THE GLOBE THEATER, opened in 1599. At about the same time came the romantic comedy, *Much Ado about Nothing* (1598–99).

The year 1600 saw the production of *Henry V, Julius Caesar,* and *As You Like It.* Drawing its essential situations from earlier works by THOMAS KYD,

Hamlet, one of Shakespeare's darkest and most perplexing tragedies, followed in 1600–01. During this period Shakespeare contributed a 67-line, allegorical ELEGY, "The Phoenix and the Turtle," to Robert Chester's *Love's Martyr* (1601). Other notable poets of the time also contributed verses. No one is sure whose death "The Phoenix and the Turtle" commemorates, and its manner and content make it unique among Shakespeare's works, though another late elegiac poem has been recently discovered. To the period 1601–02 also belong *Twelfth Night* and *Troilus and Cressida.*

All's Well that Ends Well followed in 1602–03, and in 1604 came *Measure for Measure* and one of Shakespeare's most moving tragedies, *Othello.* In 1605 came KING LEAR, perhaps the most profoundly tragic of all Shakespeare's plays. *Macbeth* (1606) was succeeded by a quartette of plays on classical subjects: *Antony and Cleopatra* (1606–07), *Coriolanus, Timon of Athens,* and the romance *Pericles* (all 1607–08).

In 1609 Shakespeare's sonnets appeared in an unauthorized edition, and his romance, *Cymbeline* (1609–10) appeared. The following year saw the production of the romantic TRAGICOMEDY, *The Winter's Tale* (1610–11). Shakespeare's tragicomedies are deeply moving for they contain all the seeds for a disaster that is finally averted through the operation of virtue and forgiveness. In *The Winter's Tale,* which draws inspiration from Italian PASTORAL drama, the operation of virtue and forgiveness eventually restores to the mistakenly jealous and originally vengeful King Leontes the queen he accused of adultery and thought long dead, Hermione. He also regains his daughter, Perdita, whom he thought lost. *The Winter's Tale* portrays, as well, one of Shakespeare's triumphs of comic characterization, the rogue seller of BROADSIDE BALLADS, Autolycus.

THE TEMPEST, perhaps Shakespeare's crowning achievement in the realm of romantic tragicomedy, was performed in 1611. Another history play, *Henry VIII,* which may have been a collaboration with JOHN FLETCHER, appeared in 1613. About the same time, Shakespeare and Fletcher collaborated as well on a play now lost, *Cardenio.* Their association continued with the appearance of *The Two Noble Kinsmen* the same year.

Until at least as late as 1603 Shakespeare not only wrote plays but also acted in them. That year his name appears on the role of "principal tragedians" who performed in BEN JONSON's *Sejanus,* and Shakespeare had earlier (1598) been listed among the "principal comedians" playing in Jonson's *Every Man in His Humor.* Shakespeare also owned interests in more than one London theater, so that he was a producer as well as a playwright and actor.

Around 1610 Shakespeare seems to have returned to Stratford to live. Although he remained involved in theatrical production, his participation from that time forward seems sharply reduced, and his career in theater had made him a wealthy man. It is clear that through the years he had been using his money to improve the situation of his family back in Stratford.

Shakespeare remains big business in the modern world. His plays have been translated into every major language and many lesser ones, and Shakespeare festivals occur around the globe. Not every organization associated with his name, however, treats Shakespeare with the same reverential awe. The Oxford University Shakespeare Society begins each meeting with a motion that "the Bard *not* be read tonight."

Bibliography

Evans, G. Blakemore et al., eds. *The Riverside Shakespeare.* Boston: Houghton Mifflin Company, 1997.

Shaking of Skull Caps, The Yūsuf Al-Shirbīnī (16th c.)

A satirical work in two parts, the Egyptian Al-Shirbīnī's Arabic text opens by making gross fun of the behavior and preferences of peasants in the Nile River valley. It also holds up to ridicule their ignorant teachers who mis-instruct them in the tenets of their faith. The author next satirizes folk poetry and then takes on the critics of serious poetry by mimicking them in a spurious discussion of awful poems he wrote for the occasion. Al-Shirbīnī carries this jest even further by next composing a self-important, 196-line Arabic verse commentary on the activities of the peasants he has just vilified.

The second part of the poem continues the game of literary parody. Al-Shirbīnī invents a peasant-poet named Abū Shādūf and his 47-line poem, written in colloquial Arabic, whose every line ends in the same rhyme. Al-Shirbīnī analyzes the poem in the fashion of classical critical commentary and has enormous fun at the expense of the hyper-refined interests and posturing of literary critics.

The text also gives a few otherwise unknown facts about the life of the author, including the name of the person who suggested he write the work, the identity of one of his teachers, and the fact that Al-Shirbīnī became a religious pilgrim to Mecca in 1664–65.

No English edition has as yet appeared.

Shi Naian (Shin Nai-an) (14th c.)

Shi Naian has often been credited with having authored or coauthored the original version of an important Chinese quasi-historical novel, THE STORY OF THE WATER MARGIN. Though most current English translations of the work list Shi Naian as its author, the Chinese literary scholar C. T. Hsia argues forcefully for the primary or exclusive authorship of LO GUANGZHONG (1330–1400).

shi poetry (shih)

The classical mode of the Chinese lyric poem, shi or shih is usually translated into English as ODE. Shi poems feature lines of regular length, clear organization of subject matter, and language that is apparently quite assertive and often ornate. Written since very ancient times in China, shi poetry gained new vigor in the 16th and 17th centuries, partly as a result of an antiquarian movement among Chinese writers, such as Li Mengyang, who looked to the past for models to follow and partly because women poets of the period found shi a congenial mode of expression.

Shi poems generally took the form of a rhymed, four-line stanza. Each line contained either 7 or 10 syllables. The Chinese language is tonal. The configuration of vowel and consonant sounds that constitutes a word, when pronounced with one tonal pattern, can mean something entirely different when pronounced with another. Nonnative speakers attempting the language have sometimes experienced both funny and humiliating situations as the result of selecting the wrong tone pattern. Shi poetry capitalizes on this feature of Chinese linguistics. Its rhythmic patterns rely on the opposition of tones, but the poet often gives the reader a choice of multiple tonal possibilities with the result that the poem's meaning shifts around.

Beyond this, shi attempts to achieve a compression of language by leaving out words that only convey grammatical as opposed to lexical or dictionary meanings. An English word of that sort is "be." (Try defining it.) Together with a minimalist, evocative language, shi as it developed also incorporated a dense web of literary allusion into its fabric. This feature might be compared to the European and colonial, Spanish American school of Gongorism, founded on the practice of the Spanish poet, LUIS DE GÓNGORA Y ARGOTE.

To all of those characteristics, we must add one more. Shi was often written for vocal performance to particular tunes. Converting shi poems into non-Chinese equivalents is a translator's worst nightmare.

Bibliography

Lévy, André. Chinese Literature, Ancient and Classical. Translated by William H. Nienhauser, Jr. Bloomington and Indianapolis: Indiana University Press, 2000.

al-Shirbīnī, Yūsuf (d. 1659)

An Egyptian satirist, al-Shirbīnī wrote a very well remembered satirical work in Arabic. Its Arabic title is a pun that can be translated either as "THE SHAKING OF SKULL-CAPS," or as "The stirring of yokels." Other works that the author himself mentions having written include a similar diatribe on the subject of weddings among the Egyptian peasantry and a work on morality that has either been lost or remains somewhere in manuscript.

Shirley, James (1596–1666)

An English educator, scholar, poet, and a prolific dramatist, James Shirley was educated in London at the excellent Merchant Taylor's School and attended university both at St. John's College, Oxford, and at Catherine Hall, Cambridge. He entered the Anglican priesthood and served for a time as a cleric at St. Albans. Moved by his conscience to convert to Roman Catholicism, as many think, Shirley tried his hand at school teaching (1623–24). After a year as a schoolmaster, he moved to London where, in 1625, he became a playwright, producing all his works during the reign of King Charles I.

Shirley's first play was a satirical comedy, *Love Tricks* (1625). Later entitled *The Schoole of Compliment* (1631), and later still *Love Tricks with Compliments*. Its SATIRE targeted the pretensions of London's newly rich, and Shirley combined that satire with the romantic entanglements of three sets of frustrated lovers and with scenes of low comedy. The play's witty and morally upright hero, Gasparo, displays the same ingenuity and know-how that Shirley displayed in making a living for his family. In addition to at least 30 plays that flowed from Shirley's pen before the CLOSING OF THE ENGLISH THEATERS in 1642, as early as 1618 Shirley published nondramatic verse. Though no copy of his 1618 work, "Echo, or the Unfortunate Lovers," survives, that poem is thought to be the same as "Narcissus, or The-Self Lover," which appeared in a collection of his works in 1646. His production of such works, however, was modest when compared with his drama. All in all, some 54 poems were included in the 1646 collection. Another nine are extant in manuscript, and one of Shirley's modern editors, R. L. Armstrong, attributes 10 more poems to Shirley. The published works include quite conventional love poems whose heroines have much in common with the

heroines of his plays. His lyrics reveal the influence of JOHN DONNE.

Though tragicomedy was his principal dramatic mode, Shirley most successfully wrote romantic comedies of manners. He penned tragedies and COURT ENTERTAINMENTS as well. In the latter mode, Shirley wrote masques like *The Triumph of Peace* (1633) that was presented before the king and queen. This was followed by *The Triumph of Beauty*, a masque that presents the Trojan Paris's giving the goddess Aphrodite first prize in a mythic beauty contest among three Greek goddesses. Shirley's third and final masque, *Cupid and Death*, introduces a period during which Shirley apparently tried unsuccessfully to make a living by writing moral allegories instead of prohibited plays. When the theaters closed in 1642, of course, Shirley suddenly became unemployed. He turned again to schoolteaching to survive, and, in that capacity in the 1650s, he wrote several examples of moral ALLEGORY, such as *The Contention of Ajax and Ulysses for the Armour of Achilles*, or *Honoria and Mammon*, or *A Contention for Honour and Riches*. He wrote these allegories for performance by his students. Theater survived under the Puritans in private performance.

Although the number of Shirley's plays almost equals that of SHAKESPEARE, Shirley is generally regarded as belonging to the second or third rank of late Renaissance English playwrights. Nevertheless, some of his comedic efforts rise at least to the top of the second rank. These include *Hyde Park* (1632) and *THE LADY OF PLEASURE* (1635), which to a degree anticipate the urbane, upper class wit of a 20th-century playwright such as Noel Coward and presage the 18th century's comedy of manners. Other notable plays include the SENECAN-TRAGEDY *The Cardinal* (1641) and a romantic comedy *The Opportunity* (1634). *The Opportunity* distinguishes itself by containing more examples of disguise, mistaken identity, and impersonation than does any other play in the canon of a playwright who liberally employed all three devices in his work.

Shirley was of a scholarly disposition, and when he was forced once more to become a schoolmaster, he tried his hand at writing grammatical textbooks that ironically became more influential after his death than were his plays. One of these appeared in each decade from the 1640s to the 1660s. His *Rudiments of Grammar* (1656) made an attempt to assist students in learning grammatical rules by writing some of them in rhymed verse that Shirley hoped would make the rules easier to memorize.

Although as long as the theaters remained open Shirley apparently made a better living than most writers, after they closed he was financially pressed for the rest of his life. He and his wife struggled to make a living. They are said to have died of exhaustion on the same day in October 1666.

Bibliography

Lucow, Ben. *James Shirley.* Boston: Twayne Publishers, 1981.

Mekemson, Mary J., ed. *A Critical, Modern-spelling Edition of James Shirley's* The Opportunity. New York: Garland, 1991.

Shirley, James. *The Cardinal.* Edited by E. M. Yearling. Manchester, U.K.: Manchester University Press, 1986.

———. *The Dramatic Works of James Shirley.* Edited by William Gifford and Alexander Dyce. 1883. Reprint, New York: Russell and Russell, 1966.

Sidney, Sir Philip (1554–1586)

Regarded as the model of English Tudor chivalry and intellect, the soldier, poet, and literary patron, Sir Philip Sidney, was born at his family's estate of Penshurst in Kent. He attended Christ Church College in Oxford University and may have enrolled for a time at Cambridge. Between 1572 and 1575 he traveled on the continent at Europe, spending a year in Italy. There he studied ethics and history, and the Italian Paolo Veronese (ca. 1528–88) painted his surviving portrait.

He was knighted in 1582, married Frances Walsingham in 1583, and became the governor of Flushing in Holland in 1585. Among the poets who benefited from Sidney's largesse as a literary patron the most prominent was EDMUND SPENSER when he wrote his *Shepherd's Calendar* (1579). RICHARD HAKLUYT dedicated to Sidney his prose collection of narratives about the exploration of the New World, *Divers Voyages Touching the Discovery of America* (1582).

Sidney was part of a literary circle whose membership included FULKE GREVILLE, SIR EDWARD DYER, Gabriel Harvey, and Sidney's sister Mary. His own posthumously published literary work had circulated in manuscript during his lifetime and included the foundation stone of English critical writing, *The DEFENCE OF POESIE* (1595). *A Defense* probably indirectly answered Stephen Gosson's attack on plays and poetry, *The School of Abuse,* which Gosson had dedicated to Sidney.

Sidney also penned a PETRARCHAN SONNET sequence, *ASTROPHEL AND STELLA* (1591). *Astrophel* was probably written in honor of the woman he lost to another, Penelope Deveraux. His PASTORAL ROMANCE *THE COUNTESS OF PEMBROKE'S ARCADIA* (1593), was partly written in verse and partly in prose. It honored Sidney's sister Mary Sidney who was the Countess of Pembroke. An early COURT ENTERTAINMENT, a masque presented before Queen ELIZABETH I in 1578, *The Lady of May,* also survives.

As a soldier and governor, Sidney served in the Low Countries, leading assaults against towns controlled by Spain and against Spanish transport. On one of the latter sorties Sidney was shot in the thigh. Although the wound did not at first appear mortal, it became infected, and Sidney died after 26 excruciating days while the infection spread. His gallantry is illustrated by the fact that he wrote a song about his death wound, *"La cuisse rompue"* (The broken thigh), and had it sung to entertain him.

Bibliography

Sidney, Sir Philip. *The Major Works.* Edited by Katherine Duncan-Jones. Oxford and New York: Oxford University Press, 2002.

———. *Sir Philip Sidney's an Apology for Poetry, and Astrophil and Stella: Texts and Contexts.* Edited by Peter C. Herman. Glen Allen, Va.: College Publications, 2001.

Silent Operas (Wusheng xi) Li Yu (ca. 1655–1656)

A collection of short stories by the best and most distinctive of Chinese writers of short fiction in the golden age of that form, Li Yu's *Silent Operas* is a collection of 12 brief tales. A copy of its first edition survives in the Sonkeikaku Library in Japan.

The title of the collection suggests that Li Yu had a use for his material beyond publishing it. Also a playwright, Li extensively revised at least some of the stories from the collection for performance. Because Chinese drama was sung, it qualified as opera. The title thus probably means, *operas intended for silent reading*. The success of the volume quickly led to a sequel, a second collection of silent operas. Although, as Li Yu's English editor, Patrick Hanan, tells us, no copy of the second collection survives independently, the stories appearing in it were also published in a volume combining the first and second collection, *Priceless Jade*.

Li Yu organized the stories in *Silent Operas* in six pairs. "An Ugly Husband Fears a Pretty Wife but Marries a Beautiful One," is followed by, "A Handsome Youth Tries to Avoid Suspicion but Arouses It Instead." These stories make up the first pair. Sometimes recognizing the relationship between the titles of the paired stories depends on a reader's prior acquaintance with Chinese literature. The titles, for instance, of the fifth and sixth stories contain the names of contrasting characters, Chen Ping and Mencius, who would have been familiar to Chinese readers of the era.

All 12 of the stories from the first collection do not yet seem available in English. Patrick Hanan's translation brings English readers three pairs of tales. Thus one can get a sense of the interactions between Li's stories and a feeling for Li Yu's style and methods as well.

In the first story of the collection, Li tells a story to illustrate an old Chinese proverb: "pretty face; sorry fate." It recounts the tale of a rich but slow-witted fellow, Que Lihou, who was very ugly and afflicted with body odor, bad breath, and stinky feet as well. Que wishes to marry, but when women get a look at him, they shudder. His father had, however, arranged a marriage for him with a Miss Zou when she was only a child of four. The nuptials were delayed until she was beyond the usual marriageable age, and Que managed to wed her without her seeing him. He also kept the room dark during their wedding night. He could not, however, disguise his unfortunate aromas.

When Miss Zou finally managed a look at her husband, she realized that she could not suffer through life with him. She contrived to become a Buddhist nun within her husband's house. By that means she avoided contact with him altogether.

As the Chinese of the era practiced polygamy, the frustrated, angry Que sought another wife, this time employing the services of a matchmaker. When the family of his prospective bride, Miss He, insisted on seeing him before the betrothal, Que persuaded a handsome friend to stand in for him. When the bride entered her bridal chamber and saw the ugly ogre she had married, she let fall two tears. Que, however, intimidated her into getting drunk with him, and in that condition their union was consummated.

At her earliest opportunity, however, Miss He arranged to meet Miss Zou. Greeting her predecessor spouse as "reverend mother," she announced herself as Miss Zou's disciple, and she too escaped her wifely role.

Desperate now for a wife who will tolerate his defects, Que sends the matchmaker to arrange for him to marry one of two concubines of a scholar named Yuan. Yuan's jealous wife was taking advantage of his absence to get rid of the two women. The matchmaker arranged for a match with Miss Zhou. On seeing Que, however, she said she'd rather die than marry him. When Mrs. Yuan insisted, Miss Zhou hanged herself. Mrs. Yuan then substitutes the brilliant and beautiful Miss Wu, who had been engaged to someone else. After a series of other complications, including Que's failed attempt to return Miss Wu to the Yuan household and Que's sealing off the door to the room where the two nuns are holed up, Miss Wu observes her bridal obligations.

Eventually, Que allowed her to meet her predecessor wives. She was more beautiful and cleverer than either. She explained to them that beautiful, talented women did not get good husbands, and that it was their karmic fate to be married to Que for sins committed in an earlier existence. Tricking them out of their sanctuary and locking the door behind them, Miss Wu proposed a solution that would both help expiate their former sins and make life married to Que bearable for all three. She proposed equipping each of three separate bedchambers with two beds and an incense burner. Que would sleep with each woman in turn in a different chamber each night, and except for the period Li Yu delicately described as "that critical time," he would sleep in one of the beds alone. The incense would spare the wives' delicate nostrils. Of necessity the women agreed to this plan, and over time each bore Que a child that took after its mother in both good looks and intelligence—karmic rewards for the wisdom of the arrangements.

In terms of form, style, and ingenuity of incident this first story in the collection anticipates the manner of the others. Each tale begins with a poem that points up the tale's moral. This is followed by explanatory passages that illustrate the moral to be drawn. Next comes the action of the tale proper. In some of the stories, that action is annotated, or there are authorial asides that comment on the action—for instance, one that asks why puritans don't have puritanical children.

When the tale ends, Li Yu provides a moral and religious interpretation of the action from a Buddhist or Confucian perspective. That leads in turn to a final critique of the story itself, sometimes ostensibly written by a literary critic named Du Jun. It seems likely, however, that Li Yu is the author of the critical commentary as well.

Bibliography

Li Yu. *Silent Operas (Wusheng xi)*. Edited and translated by Patrick Hanan et al. Hong Kong: The Research Centre for Translation, Chinese University of Hong Kong, 1990.

Sommi, Judah Leone Ben Isaac (Leone de' Sommi Portaleone, Leone Ebreo di Sommi, Leone di Somo, Leone de' Sommo Portaleone, Yehuda Sommo) (1527–1592)

An Italian Jewish dramatist and prolific writer in both Italian and Hebrew, Sommi received both a Renaissance HUMANIST and a traditional Jewish education from his teacher the rabbi David ben Abraham Provençal.

After a few years spent as a copier for a publishing firm and as a tutor, Sommi broke with the Jewish antitheatrical tradition of his era and penned what is now the earliest extant Hebrew play, a five-act, prose comedy: *A COMEDY OF BETROTHAL* (*Tsaohoth B'dihuta D'Kiddushin*, 1560). Sommi's theatrical interests led him to become associated with the powerful Gonzaga family, the rulers of Mantua. The Gonzaga required that their Jewish subjects present an annual play at the court theater, and Sommi soon became the manager and director of such performances. Stagecraft in all its aspects fascinated him, and he studied the arts of theatrical production and wrote about them. As in many Italian cities an academy flourished in Mantua. It enjoyed the patronage of Cesare Gonzaga and rejoiced in being named the Academy of the Lovesick (Accademia degl' Invaghiti). For Cesare's benefit Sommi wrote out the fruits of his labors and submitted them to his patron in a manuscript entitled *Dialoghi in materia di rappresentazione sceniche* (Dialogues on the art of the stage, 1565). Though the work discusses many aspects of stagecraft, it is particularly notable for its descriptions of the ways in which Sommi manipulated torchlight to brighten and darken the stage according to the time of day or night being represented or according to the mood of action. Gonzaga named Sommi an official writer for the academy the following year as a mark of the nobleman's approval of the dialogues. Sommi was the only one of his coreligionists so honored.

Sommi's fame as a dramatist and director, as a designer of scenery and stage effects, as a make-up artist, and as a theatrical innovator spread across all of Europe. His work survived in manuscript in 16 volumes until the beginning of the 20th century. It was an impressive collection. There were 13 plays that included both prose and verse. Of these, 45 were based on the Psalms of David and were in the mode of the Italian theater's sacred plays (*sacre rappresentazioni*). There were also INTERLUDES, examples of PASTORAL DRAMA, and both prose and rhymed comedies in the Italian language, SATIRES, and various lyric poems and ODES. In 1904, regrettably, 11 of the volumes that contained Sommi's works in Italian were consumed in a fire in the National Library of Turin. Only two of the Italian plays, a prose comedy entitled *Le tre sorelle* (The three sisters), and a pastoral play *L'Hirifile* (Eriphyle—the name of a Greek woman), together with a few examples of the writer's Italian poems survived. Happily however, most of the Hebrew works also did. These include the *Comedy of Betrothal* and the earliest surviving example of Hebrew children's literature, *Shetei Sihot Tinok Omenet ve-Horim.* That work, as far as I know, has not been edited. At least some of the other work that survived has seen both print and translation.

Bibliography

Nicoll, Allardyce. *The Theatre and Dramatic Theory.* Westport, Conn.: Greenwood Press, 1978. [Contains discussion of Sommi's stagecraft.]

Sommi, Leone de'. *A Comedy of Betrothal* (*Tsahoth B'dihutha D'Kiddushin*). Translated by Alfred S. Golding. Ottawa: Dovehouse Editions Canada, 1988.

Sommi, Leone de'. *Quattro dialoghi in materia di rappresentazioni sceniche.* Edited by Ferruccio Marotti. Milan: Il Polifilo, 1968.

songs in the Nahuatl language of Mexico (16th c.)

Following contact with Europeans in the late 15th and early 16th centuries, speakers of the Nahuatl language learned, often at mission schools, to transcribe their language into the Latin alphabet. Among other benefits, this capability resulted in the preservation of both traditional songs that had existed before European contact and some that were later composed.

Tony and Willis Barnstone have assembled a brief representative sample of the texts of such postcontact songs in English translation. One of these, the anonymously authored "Orphan Song," catches the sense of despair among a people separated from both their families and their old gods and uncertain of their reception by the new, monotheistic God they have learned to address as *Dios,* and who find themselves among a strange people trying to educate them in new ways.

Another gemlike, eight-line poem by the poet Nezahualcoyotl reflects on the brevity of a never-to-be-repeated life. Still another, "Death and Rebirth at Tula" begins with an ELEGY in which the speaker, an orphan named 10-Flower, laments the destruction of the city of Tula, the death of its ruler, Nacxitl, and the speaker's own sense of irreparable loss. In the second half of the poem, however, 10-Flower takes heart, declaring the poet's faith that as a child of God and a creator of song, 10-Flower can leave a "song-image" on the earth that, like a flower, will take root, sprout, and flourish under the gentle inspiration of the cocoa flower and the peyote bud.

Rounding out the Barnstones' selection are three brief Nahuatl poems translated by William Carlos Williams. Their predominant tone conveys a sense of loss and nostalgia for a precontact world that is no more.

Bibliography

Barnstone, Willis, and Tony Barnstone, eds. *Literatures of Asia, Africa, and Latin America from Antiquity to the Present.* Upper Saddle River, N.J.: Prentice Hall, 1999.

Sorel, Charles (1597–1674)

One of the founders of the so-called *libertine* movement among French writers and intellectuals of the 17th century, Sorel was a novelist and a writer of counter-PASTORAL romance. He belonged to a group of men and women whom the literary critic Jean Alter characterizes as "protointellectuals." These were persons of wit and learning for whom society had as yet no well-defined institutional roles, but who were loosely united in their rejection of religious dogmatism. They also abhorred the hyperrefined taste for pastoral moralizing and for the precious, elevated language that had characterized the work of their immediate literary forbears. The libertines also rejected the notion that one's social status and capacities were fixed by one's genealogy.

Although Sorel wrote serious bibliographical studies, he is today chiefly remembered for two novels. The first, his *The Bawdy Adventures of*

Francion (*Vrai histoire comique de Francion* [The true comical history of Francion], 1622), looks for inspiration to the Spanish PICARESQUE novel. It follows the amorous career of a young student of good birth as he moves through the lowest ranks of French society in search of sexual adventure. Along the way the reader acquires a sense of the daily life of a Parisian college student in the 17th century and views similarly interesting representations of life in a French village. A reader also meets representatives of the lower end of the French social spectrum. These include prostitutes, impoverished poets and would-be poets, self-important pedants, ruffians, and crooked lawyers. Sorel's freewheeling narrative includes its author's assurance that his book would "teach men to live like gods." In his more mature years, however, Sorel concluded that such utter freedom of action as Francion displayed did not necessarily lead to that outcome.

Sorel's other work that can still be read with pleasure, his antipastoral romance, *Le Berger extravagant* (The extravagant shepherd, 1627), punctures the self-congratulatory didacticism and pastoral artificiality of HONORÉ D' URFÉ's encyclopedic novel, *L'ASTRÉE*. For his second novel, Sorel once again finds inspiration in a Spanish work, this time in DON QUIXOTE DE LA MANCHA. Whereas Don Quixote was driven mad by reading CHIVALRIC ROMANCE, however, Sorel's hero, Lysis, has had his wits turned by reading too many pastorals. Wishing like their heroes to enjoy the bucolic life, Lysis dresses like a shepherd and, encouraged in his delusions by associates who find them amusing, becomes entangled in a web of strange adventures. Finally, his friends relent and help him regain his sanity.

Just as *Don Quixote*'s appearance tolled the death knell of chivalric romance's popularity, Sorel's addlepated shepherd marked a shift in French public taste away from the pastoral mode. Unlike CERVANTES, Sorel's prose tended toward the pedantic, and he lacked his Spanish model's human touch.

Bibliography

Alter, Jean. "Figures of Social and Semiotic Dissent." *A New History of French Literature.* Edited by Denis Hollier. Cambridge, Mass.: Harvard University Press, 1989.

Howells, R. J. *Carnival to Classicism: The Comic Novels of Charles Sorel.* Paris and Seattle: Papers on French Seventeenth-Century Literature, 1989.

Sorel, Charles. *The Bawdy Adventures of Francion.* Translator unknown. Fort Lauderdale, Fla.: Intermedia, 1999.

Suozzo, Andrew G. *The Comic Novels of Charles Sorel: A Study of Structure, Characterization, and Disguise.* Lexington, Ky.: French Forum, ca. 1982.

Verdier, Gabrielle. *Charles Sorel.* Boston: Twayne Publishers, ca. 1984.

Spanish Tragedy, The, or Hieronymo Is Madde Againe Thomas Kyd (1592)

An early English example of SENECAN TRAGEDY, Kyd's verse, four-act play, *The Spanish Tragedy,* opens with a prologue spoken in Hades. The allegorical figure, Revenge, converses with the ghost of the murdered cavalier, Andrea. Revenge promises Andrea that the person responsible for his death, the Portuguese prince Balthazar, will die by the hand of Andrea's beloved Bel-imperia.

In the first act, Horatio, the son of Hieronymo, and Lorenzo, the brother of Bel-imperia, have captured Balthazar in battle, and are contending for the resultant honors. The king of Spain rewards them both, and Bel-imperia transfers her love of the fallen Andrea to his friend, Horatio. Balthazar also desires her, however, and he and Lorenzo surprise the lovers at a tryst in Hieronymo's bower, stab and hang Horatio, and kidnap Bel-imperia. Hieronymo finds his son's body and swears vengeance, but reminds himself to be cautious until he can identify the murderers and develop a plan. At the end of each act, Andrea's ghost and Revenge comment in the role of a Greek chorus on the progress of the action.

In the second scene of Act 2 Hieronymo receives from Bel-imperia a letter written in her own blood, naming Lorenzo and Balthazar as Horatio's murderers, and calling on Hieronymo to avenge him. Lorenzo, the most villainous of the characters, regularly bribes others to do his dirty work and then betrays them. Bel-imperia's treacherous servant Pedringano is one of Lorenzo's pawns. He commits a murder on Lorenzo's promise of a royal pardon, but ends up swinging from a hangman's rope instead. Before he dies, Pedringano confirms for Hieronymo Bel-imperia's accusations against Lorenzo and Balthazar.

The next scene interrupts the main action of the play to show Isabella, Hieronymo's wife, gone mad with grief over the death of her son. Against her real madness Hieronymo pretends madness. His feigned madness is overcome by careful policy, however, and, as Act 3 ends, he pretends to be reconciled to his son's murderers and to believe that they are innocent.

As Act 4 begins, Bel-imperia, convinced by Hieronymo's apparent reconciliation with his enemies, reproves him and announces her intention of being avenged by her own hand. Hieronymo takes her into his confidence, and the two agree to cooperate. She then goes along with his deceits.

Balthazar and Lorenzo ask Hieronymo to prepare a COURT ENTERTAINMENT for the duke and his guests as Hieronymo had done for the king in Act I. He agrees, and describes a tragedy he has written in which he himself, Bel-imperia, Balthazar, and Lorenzo will all have parts. Hieronymo describes the story of Perseda and Soliman—another play Kyd is thought to have written.

The scene then shifts to the place in which Horatio was murdered, where the distracted Isabella seeks vengeance by cutting down the grove in which her son was hanged and then turns her knife on herself.

Back at court the play is to be presented with each character speaking a different language, but the king has a transcript in English that will enable him, the duke, and the Portuguese viceroy to follow the action. In quick succession, Bel-imperia stabs Balthazar and herself. Then Hieronymo stabs Lorenzo, and explains to the onlookers that this has not been a play. He draws aside a curtain revealing the body of Horatio with its wounds, and then runs off to hang himself. He is prevented, and the king threatens to have him tortured until he tells the names of his confederates. Rather than submit to this, Hieronymo bites out his own tongue. His captors then order him to write. He makes signs that he needs a knife to sharpen his pen. They foolishly give him a knife, and he stabs the Duke of Castille and himself. The stage is littered with corpses.

In the play's final scene, Andrea's ghost and Revenge call the role of the dead, and the ghost suggests that each of Hell's new arrivals take over suffering a famous punishment from several of the damned of classical times, such as those of Tityus whose liver was daily eaten by a vulture or Sisyphus who continually rolled a stone uphill.

Elements of the play anticipate parts of SHAKE-SPEARE's *Hamlet*. Kyd's verse, moreover, is of a very high order indeed. *The Spanish Tragedy* was one of the great early successes of Senecan tragedy on the Renaissance English stage.

Spee von Langenfeld, Friedrich
(1591–1635)

A Jesuit priest, a professor of moral theology, a social critic, and a religious poet, Spee made novel contributions to German poetics. Working without reference to the poetic innovations of MARTIN OPITZ, Friedrich Spee von Langenfeld developed a similar new metrics and versification for the German language. He wrote both in Latin and in German and composed works in both prose and verse.

His earliest social criticism, the Latin *Cautio Criminalis, or, A Book on Witch Trials* (1631), condemned as un-Christian the practices employed in the accusation and trial of women who were thought to be witches. The only one of Spee's works available in English, the *Witch Trials* especially mounted an attack on the practice of torturing accused women to elicit confessions. This work occasioned considerable furor among his Jesuit superiors, many of whom approved of torture in these circumstances. The reaction of his superiors briefly threatened Spee's membership in his order.

Spee authored a Latin textbook compiled from his lectures: *Theologia moralis explicata* (Moral philosophy explained, ca. 1630). His other, more poetic

German works, however, he deferred publishing, and they appeared posthumously. Spee presented one of these as a prose dialogue whose conversation is punctuated at intervals by poems and songs. Essentially devotional in tone, this work, *Güldenes Tugend-Buch* (The golden book of virtue, 1649) seeks to help the faithful develop the principal Christian virtues of faith, hope, and charity. To that end the work includes many poems and songs. Jakob Gippenbusch in Cologne set a number of the songs to music in 1642, when 26 of Spee's works appeared in a Psalter for church performance throughout the liturgical year. The musical score for this Psalter reappeared in 1662 and again in 1991. Much of the same poetic material also reappeared in a broader collection of Spee's mystical and spiritual verse: *Trutz-Nachtigal, Oder Geistlichs-Poetisch Lust Waldlein* (The nightingale's shelter or a spiritual-poetic grove of pleasure, 1649).

This last collection of Spee's verse employs TY-POLOGY to model itself on traditions that interpret the Song of Solomon from the Old Testament, on the one hand, as Christ's addressing the church as his spiritual bride, and, on the other, as Christ the bridegroom wooing the souls of individual Christians. In this collection Spee, like Opitz before him, demonstrated the viability of PETRARCHAN verse forms in the German language.

Spee died of the bubonic plague in the city of Trier while performing his priestly functions and caring for the sick.

Bibliography

Gippenbusch, Jakob, and Friedrich Spee von Langenfeld. *Mein ganze* Seel *dem Herren Sing: 72 Gesänge durch das Kirchenjahr. . . .* (My whole soul sings to the Lord: 72 songs throughout the church's year). [Musical score with texts of songs in German and Latin.] Trier: Friedrich Spee Gesellschaft, 1991.

Spee, Friedrich von. *Cautio Criminalis, or, A Book on Witch Trials.* Translated by Marcus Hellyer. Charlottesville: University of Virginia Press, 2003.

———. *Güldenes Tugend-Buch.* Edited by Theodorus Gerardus Maria van Oorschot. Nijmegen, Netherlands: Dekker & Van de Vegt, 1969.

———. *Theologia moralis explicata. . . .* Edited by Helmut Weber. Trier: Spee Buchverlag, 1996.

Spenser, Edmund (ca. 1552–1599)

Widely regarded as one of the most skillful and musical craftsmen of English verse, Spenser was born in London and educated at the Merchant Taylor's School in that city. In the last year of his attendance there, 1569, Spenser published several verse translations in Jan van der Noodt's *Theater of . . . Voluptuous Worldlings.* These expert early translations held promise of greater things to come.

Spencer spent the next eight years at Pembroke Hall, Cambridge University, taking his B.A. in 1573 and an M.A. in 1576. While at Cambridge he formed a friendship with one of the faculty, Gabriel Harvey, and, through that connection, he came to the attention of SIR PHILIP SIDNEY, who became Spenser's early literary patron.

In 1579, the year of his marriage to Machabyas Chylde, Spenser's first major literary work appeared, *The Shepheardes Calender.* The work is composed of 12 PASTORAL ECLOGUES, one for each month of the year. The 12 are framed at the beginning with the poet's address "To His Booke," and by a 12-line epilogue in couplets at the end. The work appeared complete with full scholarly apparatus that attested to the young Spenser's early status as a major poet. It has a preface and a gloss remarking on Spenser's consciously archaic English. The poet was concerned with expanding the poetic resources of the language by reintroducing vocabulary from native sources rather than relying exclusively on new words, INKHORN TERMS as they were called, borrowed from classical and continental European languages. The gloss, provided by someone identified only as E. K., emphasizes Spenser's learning, his mastery of poetic tradition, and his expansion of the pastoral tradition by bringing to it specifically English elements. Spenser also employs a variety of verse forms and metrical patterns throughout the work. Together with this array of qualities, Spenser, who firmly believed in the priestly function of the poet as *VATES,* wove moral matter and ALLEGORY together with the love story of the work's principal English shepherd, Colin Clout, and his beloved shepherdess, Rosalinde. In emphasizing the specifically English elements of *The Shepheardes Calender,* Spenser to a degree followed the example of the poets of the French PLÉIADE, who also had been concerned with forging a poetic language that emphasized native elements and did not follow slavishly the examples of the ancients or of the early Renaissance Italians.

The year 1580 saw the publication of a collection of correspondence between Spenser and Gabriel Harvey, the initiation or continuation of work on Spenser's masterpiece, his national English, Protestant EPIC, THE FAERIE QUEENE. That year also saw his appointment as secretary to Lord Grey of Wilton, the lord deputy of Ireland. For 18 years Spenser occupied this post, living mainly in Ireland at Kilcolman Castle, but also traveling to England as necessary. In 1590 the first three books of *The Faerie Queene* appeared with a letter addressed to Sir WALTER RALEIGH that purported to explain the poem's complex allegory. Allegorically represented in the work as Gloriana, the Faerie Queene herself, and as Belphoebe, the virgin huntress, in 1591 a pleased Queen ELIZABETH I granted Spenser an annual stipend of £50. Allegedly it would have been more, but her chancellor, Lord Burleigh, is said to have remarked, "All that for a song!" and to have reduced the amount.

Other works appeared in 1591: *Daphnaida* and *Complaints.* Having lost his first wife, Spenser remarried in 1594, this time wedding Elizabeth Boyle. The following year, his EPITHALAMION (On the bed chamber) appeared. This remarkable poem seems to have been one of Spenser's wedding presents to his bride. Also appearing in 1595 was a SONNET cycle, the *Amoretti.* While to a degree this cycle appears to trace the development of Spenser and Boyle's relationship, the literary critic Hugh Maclean reasonably suggests that sonnets written as early as 1580 and perhaps originally addressed to other women were pressed into service to fill out the sequence. Another pastoral poem,

"Colin Clouts Come Home Againe," also appeared in 1595.

In 1596 appeared the next installment of *The Faerie Queene,* this time including books I–VI. Also that year *Fowre Hymnes* and *Prothalamion* were published. Political troubles were brewing for the English rulers of Ireland, however. In 1598 the Irish rose in rebellion. Under the leadership of an Irishman named Tyrone, Spenser's estate was attacked and Kilcolman Castle burned. Spenser and his wife fled to Cork. There he was given letters for delivery to the Queen's Privy Council in London, where he arrived on December 24, 1598. The winter sea voyage and the stress of recent events, however, overcame Spenser's reserves. A cold apparently developed into pneumonia, and he died on January 13, 1599. Before the sacking of Kilcolman, however, Spencer had written a pamphlet in prose: *A View of the Present State of Irelande* (not published until 1633). In it he proposed a final solution to the Irish question—essentially genocide. Not surprisingly, Spenser's anti-Irish, anti-Catholic sentiments have fundamentally and negatively influenced Irish points of view and discussions concerning Spenser's abilities and poetic accomplishments, notably that of the 20th century's most gifted Irish poet and outstanding literary figure, William Butler Yeats. Yeats considered that Spenser pandered to the literary tastes of the English moneyed, merchant classes.

Bibliography

Anderson, Judith A., Donald Cheney, and David A. Richardson, eds. *Spenser's Life and the Subject of Biography.* Amherst: University of Massachusetts Press, ca. 1996.

Spenser, Edmund. *Edmund Spencer's Poetry.* Edited by Hugh Maclean. New York: W.W. Norton, 1982.

———. *The Faerie Queene.* Edited by A. C. Hamilton and Toshiyuki Suzuki. New York: Longman, 2001.

———. *The Shorter Poems: Edmund Spenser.* Edited by Richard A. McCabe. London and New York: Penguin Books, 1999.

Stampa, Gaspara (1523–1554)

Among the most highly esteemed female poets of the Italian Renaissance, Stampa was born in Padua, but on her father's death around 1530, she moved to Venice with her mother and two siblings. There the children received classical educations that included Greek, Latin, music, literature, and rhetoric. She early on acquired a reputation as a talented vocalist.

A three-year long, sometimes stormy, love affair with Collaltino di Collalto, Count of Treviso, seems to have triggered her poetic sensibilities, and she began to write sonnets in the PETRARCHAN manner. Like Petrarch's, Stampa's poems document her interior life in response to her consuming passion and her lover's cruelty and neglect. Though her poems lack the deep INTERTEXTUALITY of the older poet's work, her temperament, more volatile than that of her model, lends freshness to her verse.

Almost certainly, her poems circulated in manuscript among an admiring Venetian readership, and, together with her status as a respected singer, her work resulted in an invitation in 1550 to become a member of the Accademia dei dubbiosi (the academy of the doubtful). She accepted the invitation and was initiated under the academic pseudonym, Anaxilla—a name by which she sometimes alludes to herself in her poems.

The differences in the social status of Collalto and Stampa probably doomed their relationship from the outset. When their troubled liaison ended in 1550, she formed a new one with the Venetian Bartolemeo Zen. The years 1551–52 brought relative quiet and peace of mind, but then Stampa's health began to fail, and she died on April 24, 1554.

Stampa's sister Cassandra set about editing Gaspara's work for publication, and in October of 1554 from the press of Pietrasanta appeared the first edition of the work that would bring Gaspara Stampa fame throughout Italy.

Bibliography

Bassanese, Fiora. *Gaspara Stampa*. Boston: Twayne Publishers, 1982.

Stampa, Gaspara. *Gaspara Stampa: Selected Poems.* Translated and edited by Laura Anna Stortoni and Mary Prentice Lillie. New York: Italica Press, 1994.

Stiernhielm, Georg (1598–1672)

A Swedish *Renaisssance man,* Stiernhielm mastered much of his epoch's body of knowledge as it related to archaeology, jurisprudence, the ancient and modern Germanic languages, Greek, Latin, mathematics, natural science, and philosophy. He came to be regarded, moreover, as the founder of modern Swedish poetry. Beyond that he worked as an editor of historic legal texts and of what seems to have been the first POLYGLOT BIBLE that included several Germanic languages. He wrote the libretto for a ballet, and he also conceived a plan for a definitive dictionary of the Swedish language, but he did not take it past the letter A.

From the point of view of high literary art, his most ambitious and enduring work was his verse poem *Hercules* (1648). Subtitled "An Anacreontic Idyll," this ambitious poem recounts for the first time in Swedish the story of the labors of Hercules. Stiernhielm's ballet libretto, on the other hand, concerns itself with Cupid, the god of love.

Perhaps inspired by the work of DESIDERIUS ERASMUS and of Cardinal Francisco Jiménez de Cisneros in bringing out Bibles with facing passages in several languages that would help scholars make comparative textual analyses and arrive at more authoritative texts, Stiernhielm edited a polyglot Scripture that contained the Gothic text of the Bible that had been prepared by the 4th-century bishop of the Goths, Ulfilas. With the Gothic also appeared comparative texts in Swedish, Icelandic, and vulgate Latin.

Stiernhielm's scientific writing included a revision of the work of the ancient Greek mathematician Archimedes—particularly as it related to hydrostatics and engineering problems of various kinds. His legal work included a compilation of Swedish and Scandinavian jurisprudence that looked back to its origins among the Old West Germans and the Ostrogoths. He also preserved his correspondence, and it has appeared in a 20th-century edition. None of his work has as yet been translated into English.

Bibliography

Blanker, Frederika, et al. *The History of the Scandinavian Literatures.* New York: Dial Press, 1938.

Stiernhielm, Georg. *Hercules.* Stockholm: Almquist & Wiksell, 1967.

———. *Brev till* [Letters of] *Georg Stiernhielm.* Edited by Per Wieselgren, Gerhard Bendz, and Maria Widnäs. Lund, Sweden: Gleerup, 1968.

stock character

Those characters in a drama who conform to a recognizable type are designated *stock characters.* In the Renaissance the most extreme European examples, perhaps, were to be found in the Italian COMMEDIA DELL' ARTE (comedy of the guild), where each character wore a recognizable costume and mask that defined an actor's role in the play. The clown, Pucinello; the plague doctor from Bologna; and the romantic heroine, Isabella—a role created by the famous actress ISABELLA ANDREINI—exemplify the type.

Stock characters also typify the performances of the Turkish shadow puppet theater called *KARAGÖZ* after its principal character. Karagöz is a comic, adventuresome, thoughtless, greedy, ne'er-do-well, rough sort of character reminiscent of Punch in British Punch and Judy shows. His friend, Hadjivad, always appears as an educated, highly respected person of the middle classes.

Elsewhere, European playwrights borrowed stock character types from the Roman comedies of PLAUTUS and TERENCE. BEN JONSON's title character in *VOLPONE* is a stock confidence artist. Young lovers and their greedy parents who attempt to marry them off to others appear all across the European stage in situations borrowed from the ancient comedians. Other stock characters include the lickspittle flatterer, the bombastic soldier or *MILES GLORIOSUS,* and the male or female go-between or procurer.

In the Orient, stock characters like the student and the courtesan in love and heroic criminals also appeared in the Chinese COMEDY called *ZAZU.*

Story of the Water Margin, The Lo Guanzhong (Luo Kuan-chung) (ca. 1550)

Like many other classical Chinese novels, *The Story of the Water Margin* (*Shuihuzhuan; Shui Hu Chuan*) developed over time from a series of historical incidents to which a host of legendary events and characters attached themselves in many retellings. Several dramas also borrowed incidents from the tale and over the course of time added material to it. Ming dynasty commentators generally agree that the *Water Margin*'s author was LUO GUANZHONG (1330–1400), but many others thought that the 14th-century writer SHI NAIAN either authored or coauthored the work. No authoritative texts, however, exist before the 16th century. About 1550 a patron of the arts, Marquis Guo Xun (Kuo Hsün) of Wu, commissioned a 20-volume, 100-chapter version of the story. In the 16th and 17th centuries other versions of the work appeared. Though some of these were divided into fewer chapters and some into more, all of them were abridgments of the 1550 version. A 70-chapter version has become the standard.

The literary historian C. T. Hsia considers the novel divided in its purposes. On the one hand it purports to recount history. On the other it attempts to develop experimental fiction. In Hsia's view the failure to reconcile these opposing purposes flaws the novel. He finds the fictional part much more interesting.

The Water Margin recounts the adventures of a band of 12th-century outlaws who inhabited the Liangshan marshes. Although 108 hardy heroes appear in the novel, its story focuses on a central group of the principal outlaws. Song Jiang (Sung Chiang) is the greatest of the outlaw leaders, and the others obey him willingly. The group's principal military strategist is named Wu Yung. Li Guei (Li Kuei) is a typical man of action who never wants to wait for plans to be developed. As with these characters, the author proves very successful in differentiating the members of his large cast and in making them credible as people. This holds true not only for the principal outlaws but also for robbers and prostitutes, Buddhists and Taoists, monks and priests, bureaucrats and publicans, and all the other figures that populate the book's pages.

As Lo tells the story, the band of heroic outlaws, some of whom really are historical, repeatedly engage the most accomplished generals that the Chinese emperor can send against them. Their success is stunning. In the end, however, they surrender and the emperor makes use of their military prowess to help put down a more dangerous uprising. Most of the book deals with military exploits and with the adventures the band encounters traveling to and from their many battles.

The outlaws can be likened to the knights-errant of the European CHIVALRIC ROMANCE. Like those knights, the outlaws practice a code of honor. They are also devoted to their fathers. They hold the brotherhood of man as an ideal, but, like street gangs of today, they value group loyalty, esteeming above all the responsibilities imposed by friendship within the band.

Though the outlaws are usually puritanical with respect to sex, they are great eaters of meat and drinkers of wine. Much humor arises from the drunken behavior of such characters as the military officer disguised as a monk, Lu Chih-shen, who gets drunk, destroys the tutelary idols of his monastery, and forces his brother monks who are vegetarians to eat dog meat. A reader can welcome the fact that a good deal of humor enlivens the novel, especially since much graphically described violence is also present in its pages.

Although the central episodes of the novel and its basic text originated in an earlier period of literary history, *The Story of the Water Margin* in its 16th- and 17th-century retellings participates in the broader literary movement of the times. This movement looked to earlier epochs in Chinese literary history for inspiration and for material that could be reworked to suit popular tastes.

Bibliography

Dent-Young, John, and Alex Dent-Young, trans. *The Marshes of Mount Liang . . . or Water Margin of Shi Nai'an and Luo Guanzhong*. Hong Kong: Chinese University Press, ca. 1994.

Chang Cheh, director. *The Water Margin*. Videocassette. 1972. Chinese with English subtitles. Hong Kong: Shaw Brothers Ltd., 1999.

Hsia, C. T. *The Classic Chinese Novel: A Critical Introduction*. 1968. Ithaca, N.Y.: Cornell University East Asia Program, 1996.

Strange Tales of Liaozhai Pu Songling
(finished 1679, published 1766)

A collection of more than 500 stories about supernatural and unusual happenings, *Strange Tales of Liaozhai* features stories about ghosts, about supernatural love stories, and about persons who can cross the borders between the visible and invisible worlds. A catalogue of some of the stories' titles suggests the variety of material that Pu includes in the volume's pages: "A Chinese Jonah," "A Chinese Solomon," "Death by Laughing," "The Donkey's Revenge," "The Disembodied Friend," "Chou K'o-chang and His Ghost." The list could be vastly extended, but perhaps a few more titles will suffice to hint at the variety of strange stories that Pu includes: "The Flying Cow," "The Fighting Cricket," "The Elephants and the Lion," "Miss Lien-hsiang, The Fox-Girl," "The Resuscitated Corpse," "The Thunder God," "The Three Genii," "A Supernatural Wife."

For more than 200 years Pu's masterpiece has been among the most widely read of Chinese texts. Not surprisingly it has also been a book that has drawn a great deal of attention from literary critics and scholars. One of Pu's later editors, T'ang Mêng-Lai, observes that Pu devoted his youth to learning about the marvelous and his later years to sharing what he had learned. Tang continues his commentary, observing that Pu was both an extraordinarily skilled craftsman and a commendable moralist whose work was meant "to glorify virtue and to censure vice." Tang concludes that in fulfilling his moral objectives, Pu's work must be counted among the most important philosophical treatises in the Chinese language.

One of Pu's English translators, Herbert A. Giles, considers Pu one of the most gifted stylists in the Chinese language. Giles praises the terse economy of Pu's style, the rich allusiveness of his references to the entire body of earlier Chinese literature, and his skillful manipulation of vocabulary that results in the expansion of a word's capacity for conveying meaning. Pu's originality founded a school of writers who imitated him with varying degrees of success but who never succeeded in surpassing him. Giles selected 164 of Pu's stories for translation. His edition, though admirable and including stories elsewhere unavailable in English, excludes some of the racier stories that offended Giles's Victorian sensibilities. Readers wishing to experience an English approximation of Pu's full range, therefore, need to consult more than one volume of selections.

Bibliography

Pu Songling. *Chinese Tales: Zhuangzi, Sayings and Parables, and Chinese Ghost and Love Stories.* Translated from Martin Buber's German translation of the Chinese by Alex Page. Amhurst, N.Y.: Humanity Books, 1998.

———. *Strange Stories from a Chinese Studio.* 1916. Translated by Herbert A. Giles. New York: Dover Publications, 1969.

———. *Strange Tales of Lioazhai . . .* [Selections]. Translated by Lu Yunzhong. Hong Kong: Commercial Press, 1982.

Suckling, Sir John (1609–1642)

A British writer of CAVALIER LYRICS, a political polemicist, a soldier, a member (very briefly) of Parliament, and a playwright, Suckling entered Trinity College, Cambridge, in 1623. He spent the period following his father's death in 1627 as a participant in a variety of military campaigns and at the University of Leiden in the Netherlands, where he apparently studied astrology. As was often the practice in his era, he purchased a post at court and a knighthood that King Charles I bestowed on him in London in 1630. The following year found him in Germany as a member of a diplomatic mission.

The year 1637 saw his debut as a public literary figure with a brief prose essay, *An Account of Religion by Reason.* As its title suggests, Suckling, whose private life was apparently very colorful and included brawling and wenching, must be counted among the moderates in his views about religion. One of his three finished plays also appeared the same year. A verse TRAGICOMEDY that Suckling supplies with two endings, one tragic and one comic,

Aglaura, was first performed as a COURT ENTERTAINMENT for King Charles I, and, in 1638, it was produced at Blackfriar's Theater for public consumption. The play features complex relationships of love and lust, conventional disguises, plots, and confusions among multiple sets of lovers and a lustful and villainous king. Despite Suckling's strange insistence that the audience take its choice between endings and notwithstanding the overwrought though conventional plot, the public found the play pleasing as a kind of collection of familiar set pieces, and it secured Suckling's reputation as a dramatist.

Less care and attention, however, characterizes Suckling's next play, a verse romantic COMEDY called *The Goblins* (ca. 1640). Though Suckling again uses the technique of portraying a series of not-necessarily related scenes, *The Goblins* often confuses the viewer or reader with its disjointed tales of attempted assassination, thieves who disguise themselves in devils' costumes, imprisonments and escapes, duels, singing, dancing, and the love of Reginella and Orsabin that is modeled on that of Miranda and Ferdinand in SHAKESPEARE's *THE TEMPEST.* It is this love affair, finally, that, in a feeble reflection of the grandeur of Shakespeare, finally sorts everything out and gives the play its happy ending.

Suckling's last play, his TRAGEDY *Brennoralt,* also known as *The Discontented Colonel* (ca. 1640), succeeds somewhat better as stagecraft. For this play, Suckling made use of the plot of a French play by Jean Pierre Camus, *L'Iphigene* (1625). The parallels between the movement of Camus's play and the contemporary political situation in England drew Suckling to borrow its plot. Just as the Scots really rose in rebellion against their English masters, so the play's Lithuanians rebel against their Polish ruler. The play manages to intermingle a substantial dose of love interest together with its military main plot. Suckling's biographer, Charles L. Squier, sees *Brennoralt* as Suckling's attempt to state his political views in a more public arena than Parliament, where he served as a member for a period of six days in 1640. About that time, Suckling wrote an epistolary political tract: *To Mr. Henry German, in the Beginning of Parliament, 1640.* Parliament, however, was dissolved six days after it convened.

Suckling's private political activity, participating in planning a proposed military coup called "the Army plot," resulted in his fleeing England for France in 1641. There, desperate and depressed, he ended his own life, probably by taking poison.

Whatever Suckling's shortcomings as a playwright, he did have a knack for SATIRE and laughter. He was, moreover, a gifted and musical poet. Had the plays never been written, Suckling would be remembered for his accomplished satirical and sometimes irreverent lyric verse. His love poems tend to strip away romantic window dressing and to focus on sensual gratification. His poetic works appeared posthumously in a pair of collections that included letters and other miscellaneous writings: *Fragmenta Aurea. A Collection of all the Incomparable Peeces, Written by Sir John Suckling. And Published by a Friend to Perpetuate his Memory* came first (1646). It was followed in 1659 by *The Last Remains of Sir John Suckling. Being a Full Collection of All His Poems and Letters Which Have Been So Long Expected and Never Till Now Been Published.*

As literary reputations go, Suckling's has fared very well for such a short-lived writer. Almost every quarter century since his death collections of his works have appeared, and his reputation seems secure for a while longer, at least among an antiquarian readership that values irony.

Bibliography
Squier, Charles L. *Sir John Suckling.* Boston: Twayne Publishers, 1978.

Suckling, John, Sir. *The Works of Sir John Suckling.* Oxford: The Clarendon Press, 1971.

Süleyman I (1494–1566)
Sultan of the Ottoman Empire from 1520, Süleyman I himself wrote very creditable poetry. His patronage and encouragement of literature, however, proved more significant for the subsequent history of Turkish letters than his own literary creation. At his court he appointed a rhyming chronicler—the *Sheh Námaji* or writer of the book about kings. This writer's job included chronicling current events in verse and adding those events to verse histories he created of earlier Ottoman events.

Though models for this sort of poem existed in earlier Persian works, it was an innovation in the Turkish language.

Süleyman I encouraged the composition of poetry in his family as well as in the court and elsewhere throughout the empire. Five of his sons composed poems well enough to be included in the BIOGRAPHIES OF TURKISH POETS that long continued as a standard genre in the country. One of those sons, Süleyman's heir, Selim II (1524–74), reputedly wrote the best and most graceful verse of any produced by a long succession of royal poets.

The reign of Süleyman I (1520–66) initiates the classic age of Ottoman poetry, which continued until the early 18th century.

Sullam, Sara Coppio (ca. 1592–1641)
The daughter of a well-to-do Venetian Jewish family, the poet Sara Coppio received a thorough HUMANIST EDUCATION. She married a distinguished member of the Jewish community, Jacob Sullam, in 1614. Throughout her life, she and her birth family sustained a passionate interest in literature, and they helped support the writer, Leone Modena, by underwriting the expense of publishing several of his books.

In 1615–16, a Genoese monk and nobleman, Ansaldo Cebà, published a verse EPIC recounting the life and times of the biblical queen Esther. It came to Coppio Sullam's attention, and she liked it so well that she initiated a correspondence with Cebà. She was especially pleased that Cebà had unconventionally selected for the subject of his poem a tragic heroine from the Jewish tradition in place of a male figure from Greco-Roman antiquity. The two poets began exchanging letters, sonnets, and tokens of mutual admiration. The NEOPLATONIC tradition of COURTLY LOVE was still very much in vogue in the second decade of the 17th century, and the two writers opted to employ it in their exchanges. At one point Coppio Sullam even expressed her spiritual affection for Cebà. He in turn complimented her upon her mastery of the humanist tradition and her purity of soul. He also, however, repeatedly attempted to convert her to Christianity. Eventually Cebà published the letters he had written Coppio Sullam, but he did not include her side of the correspondence. Her letters and her verse waited until the 19th century for their publication, though copies of both circulated fairly widely in manuscript.

Asserting that in her verse Coppio Sullam denied the immortality of the soul, the eventual cardinal of Capo d'Istria, Baldassar Bonifaccio, published an attack on her and her poems. In a droll and ironic prose response, she refuted Bonifaccio point by point. She also replied with a pair of sarcastic sonnets that asserted her pride in her Jewish heritage.

Bibliography

"Coppio Sullam, Sara." *The Feminist Encyclopedia of Italian Literature.* Edited by Rinaldina Russell. Westport, Conn.: Greenwood Press, 1997.

"Sullam, Sara Coppio," *Encyclopeaedia Judaica.* Vol. 15. Jerusalem: Macmillan Company, 1971.

Sullam, Sara Coppio. *The Works of Sara Coppio Sullam.* [Includes letters to her from Ansaldo Cebà.] Translated and edited by Don Harran. Chicago: University of Chicago Press, ca. 2006.

Sūrdās (Sūradāsa) (1483–1563)

A musician and devotional poet who was either born blind or later became so, Sūrdās is regarded as the outstanding devotional poet in Brajbhasha, the early Hindi language OF INDIA. Early in his career Sūrdās became a disciple of VALLABHA, another Hindu poet-saint only a few days his senior. The story goes that Vallabha asked Sūrdās to sing some of his own compositions and, on hearing them, invited the younger man to devote his talent to singing the praises of the Hindu Deity Krishna.

Sūrdās became an initiate of Vallabha's sect and spent the rest of his life fulfilling his guru's request. The outcome was the *SUR-SAGAR*—a collection of 4,937 interconnected short songs arranged to tell a story in music and verse. Scholars debate the issue of whether or not all the songs were composed by Sūrdās. It may well be that his own production was preserved in writing by others and that songs he did not write crept in. The masterful and sometimes complex flow of the narrative and the uniform delicacy of style, however, suggests that the author at least had a hand in arranging his works.

Sūrdās's remarkable talents for composing verse and singing soon brought him regional fame, and his reputation reached the ears of the Mughal emperor AKBAR the Great in his court at Agra. The emperor, who had a passionate interest in the poetry of several languages and in song, is said to have received the poet at his palace. There Sūrdās likely gave a command performance—always, however, praising Krishna and his consort Radha rather than earthly potentates.

The scholar Najendra points to a number of extraordinary qualities that characterize Sūrdās's work. The poet's major achievement arose from his fusion of classical and pastoral culture. His poems capture especially well the psychology of villagers, particularly women and children. Sūrdās is a sure master of IMAGE, both aural and visual. The scholar also praises the poet's musicianship.

Although Sūrdās was not an original philosopher and relied upon Vallabha for that aspect of his devotional poems, his work nonetheless greatly influenced the cultural development of the region around the city of Agra and the literary traditions of the Hindi language. Sūrdās brought the benefits of ancient culture to the masses while at the same time blending into the older tradition the folk culture of his area. In doing so, he preserved for the study of socioethnographers much that would otherwise not be known about life in his time and place.

Bibliography

Hawley, John Stratton. *Sūr Dās [sic]: Poet, Singer, Saint.* Seattle: University of Washington Press, ca. 1984.

Sūrdās . *The Poems of Sūradāsa.* Translated and edited by Krishna P. Bahadur. New Delhi: Abhinav Publications, 1999.

———. *Rosary of Hymns (Selected Poems) of Surdas.* Translated by Jaikishandas Sadani. New Delhi: Wiley Eastern, ca. 1991.

———. *Songs of Surdas, Bhramargit* [digital sound disc]. Performed by Purshotamdas Jalota. Thornton Heath, U.K.: Audiorec Limited, 1991.

Surrey, Henry Howard, earl of
(1517–1547)

A literary innovator in English and one of the most prominent and colorful of King Henry VIII's courtiers, Surrey himself descended from royalty on both sides of his family. His father, Thomas Howard, third duke of Buckingham, traced his ancestry to the last hereditary Anglo-Saxon king of England, Edward the Confessor (ca. 1003–66). His mother—Elizabeth Stafford, daughter of the duke of Buckingham—traced hers to King Edward III (1312–77). This heritage together with a fierce pride, a hot temper, and frequent experience as the commander of large bodies of land and sea forces in putting down rebellion, keeping Scotland under control, and warring against the French made Surrey a sometimes controversial figure. Though he rose to become lieutenant general of the king on sea and land for all Continental possessions of England, he was more than once jailed for quarreling and rioting, and he came near to having his right hand cut off when he struck another courtier within the royal precinct at Windsor Castle.

His royal connections and his willingness to assert them finally led to his execution. As an overweight and syphilitic Henry VIII neared the end of his life, Surrey quartered his family's coat of arms with the heraldic device of King Edward III. His enemies maliciously, but perhaps rightly, construed this action as laying claim to the royal succession. He was accused of high treason, arrested, and confined in the Tower of London in December 1546. On January 21, 1547, only a week before the death of Henry VIII, Surrey was found guilty and beheaded. As the penalty for treason was usually much crueler, involving torture, hanging but not till death, and drawing and quartering, the quicker death suggests that not everyone was convinced of Surrey's guilt.

John Clere, a deeply learned scholar, had carefully tutored Surrey, teaching the boy Latin, Spanish, Italian, and French. He early developed a taste for poetry and while traveling on the continent he learned something of the style of PETRARCH that was sweeping across Europe. In England, he became friends with SIR THOMAS WYATT. Wyatt had brought the Italianate and French manners of composition to England, and Surrey both emulated them and made poetic experiments of his own.

When the London printer Richard Tottel published his famous *Songs and Sonnets* (1557)—better known as TOTTEL'S MISCELLANY—he included some of the most important works by both Wyatt and Surrey. Surrey's included love SONNETS and songs or ODES. Some autobiographical poems also appear, for one "Prisoned in Windsor, he recounteth his pleasure there passed." Written after he was jailed in Windsor Castle for striking the courtier, Surrey recalls his childhood pleasures there when he was a playmate for and companion to the duke of Richmond, Henry Fitzroy. Another is addressed to friend Thomas Ratcliffe, third earl of Sussex, advising him to "learn by others' troubles." Perhaps as early as 1542 Surrey had also published a moving tribute for his friend Wyatt under the title "An Excellent Epitaph."

Though Surrey lacked the inspiration and raw poetic talent of Wyatt, he was nonetheless the better technician. Surrey's biographer William A. Sessions praises the poet for his ability to filter the Petrarchist material of continental love poetry through a web of classical matter and allusion in the HUMANIST tradition. The enormous popularity of Tottel's collection inspired a legion of imitators both of the collection itself and of the poems it contained. As a result, Surrey's work became almost overnight the influential model on which poets aspiring to the latest fashion based their work. He set the tone of lyric poetry in English for at least the next generation.

Another and surely even more influential contribution appeared in Surrey's innovative experiments with and invention of blank verse in his translations of the first two (1557) and the fourth (1542?) books of VIRGIL's *Aeneid*. He emulated the example of Italian humanist translators who had also sought an unrhymed equivalent for the dactylic hexameter of the ancients. Surrey, though, found a successful approximation by using Chaucer's pentameter line and excising the rhyme. (See POETIC METER.) He did not, however, stop at that deceptively simple solution. Rather, he perfected the blank verse line in ways that made it an incomparably apt vehicle, not only for rendering Virgil in English, but also for reflecting the dactylic music of other classical poets and, as SHAKESPEARE and others also demonstrated, for exploiting the inherent musical possibilities of unrhymed English as well.

Bibliography

Howard, Henry, Earl of Surrey. *Selected Poems*. Edited by Dennis Keene. Manchester, U.K.: Carcanet Press, 1985.

Sessions, William A. *Henry Howard, the Poet Earl of Surrey: a Life*. Oxford, U.K.: Oxford University Press, 1999.

Tottel, Richard, ed. *Songs and Sonnets (Tottel's Miscellany)*. Menston, U.K.: Scolar Press, 1970.

Sur-sagar   Sūrdās (16th c.)

A collection of 4,937 Hindi devotional songs organized into an intricate narrative pattern, the *Sur-sagar* is valued among the major poetic achievements in the language. In about 225 of the songs, Sūrdās views himself as a representative, sinful human being and prays that the Lord will bestow his grace on the poet himself and on the people who share his shortcomings.

Around 150 of the songs humbly invoke the Hindu Deity, Lord Rama. Another 200 or so allude to portions of various Hindu myths that appear in ancient classical texts—particularly those having to do with Krishna. In these poems Sūrdās adopts the persona of a saint-poet who suffers from the awareness of his own human frailty. He finds himself proud, wrathful, overemotional, and covetous of worldly things. He seeks to shelter himself from these weaknesses in his devotion to the Lord Krishna, who in Hindu thought represents eternal bliss.

Nearly 3,500 of the songs draw inspiration from stories about Krishna's amorous encounters with the milkmaids (*gopis*) of Braj—an area of India that includes the city of Agra. Some of these also celebrate Krishna's rapturous relationship with Radha. In the ALLEGORY of these songs, all the characters and their lovemaking represent the eternal bliss that a human soul can expect to experience once released from the cycle of death and rebirth into union with the eternal. Still other songs recount Krishna's adventures in Braj and the grief-stricken reactions of the residents to his departure.

Bibliography

Hawley, John Stratton. *Sūr Dās [sic]: Poet, Singer, Saint*. Seattle: University of Washington Press, 1984.

Sūrdās . *Sūrāsāgara* [poems]. Translated and edited by Usha Nilsson. New Delhi: Sahitya Akademi, 1982.

———. *The Poems of Sūrāadāsa*. Translated and edited by Krishna P. Bahadur. New Delhi: Abhinav Publications, 1999.

al-Suyūtī, Jalāl al-dīn (1445–1505)

Celebrated as the most prolific writer in all of Islamic letters, the Egyptian al-Suyūtī was descended from a Persian family. His being born in the family library earned him the nickname "the son of books." In the course of a busy life, he became deeply learned in the arts and sciences of his day—particularly in the law and in religion. From the age of 18 he taught and lectured in religious law at a major mosque in Cairo.

By the time he reached the age of 30, his religious opinions (*fatwas*) and his works on Islamic law—all written in Arabic—had circulated throughout the Middle East. He apparently enjoyed a prodigious memory and attempted to master all Islamic knowledge and all the secular subjects of his day as well. He wrote about the history of the Arabic language and about cosmology. He commented on the Koran, and he discussed Islamic mysticism, lexicography, pharmacy, dietetics, erotic subjects, philology, ethics, philosophy, and prophecy. He also wrote works of history—including a history of Egypt—and books of biographical sketches of notable persons organized according to their employment. In addition he assembled books of aphorisms. Though the total count of all al-Suyūtī 's writings varies from authority to authority, most estimate his output at between 900 and 1,000 separate works.

Although an enormous representation of this production is available in very recent modern editions in Middle Eastern languages, only a minimal and spotty selection can be found in Western languages—some in Latin, and a very few in French and English. A good English biography of al-Suyūtī, however, is available.

Bibliography

al-Suyūtī, Jalal al Din. *History of the Caliphs.* Translated by H. S. Jarrett. Amsterdam: Oriental Press, 1970.

———. *History of the Temple of Jerusalem.* Translated by James Reynolds. London: A. J. Valpy, 1836.

———. *Revival of Forgotten Virtues.* Translated by Chowdhery Muhammad Ibrahim. Karachi, Pakistan, Peermahomed Ebrahim Trust, 1970.

Sartain, E. M. *Jalāl al-Dīn al-Suyūtī: Biography and Background.* Cambridge, U.K. and New York: Cambridge University Press, 1975.

Tamburlaine the Great, Parts I and II

Christopher Marlowe (ca. 1587)

MARLOWE based two plays on the career and conquests of a Turkic shepherd, Tamburlaine (anglicized from Timur-i-Lang, which means *lame Timur*, 1336–1404), who became the leader of a military horde of Turks and Mongols. In the late 15th and early 16th centuries the historical Timur, who was called "the scourge of God," led his hosts in the conquest of Transoxania (the region east of the Oxus River). He then conquered Persia and northern India and defeated both the Ottoman Turks and the Mamluks of Egypt. He died while campaigning against the Chinese.

The first of Marlowe's BLANK VERSE, history plays begins in Persia. There, Mycetes, Persia's king, orders his troops to destroy Tamburlaine's smaller force. Mycetes's brother Cosroe, however, accuses the king of weakness and demands his abdication. When it is not forthcoming, Cosroe accepts the title and crown of emperor from the generals of Persia and, with 10,000 cavalrymen, rides to assist Tamburlaine against Mycetes.

The next scene finds Tamburlaine in his camp. He and his 500 foot soldiers have captured a caravan of travelers that includes Zenocrate, a princess of Egypt. She disdains her captor, calling him "shepherd." He nonetheless woos her, promising that he will become the emperor of all the East and make her his queen. While this conversation continues, the Persian captain, Theridamas, won over by Tamburlaine's personality, leadership qualities, and self-confidence, enlists his 1,000 armored Persian cavalry under Tamburlaine's banners. The African members of Zenocrate's escort also join Tamburlaine, so she is compelled to remain in his camp.

In Act II Cosroe's 10,000 horsemen join forces with Tamburlaine's infantry against Mycetes. One of Mycetes' spies reports in scene ii that Tamburlaine's forces now outnumber the Persians, but Mycetes' dismisses them as an undisciplined rabble. The battle is joined in scene iii, and, in scene iv, a defeated Mycetes enters carrying his crown in his hand. He encounters Tamburlaine, who first takes the crown but then restores it, promising to win it in battle—which he does. Then, as a little joke, Tamburlaine makes Cosroe the emperor of Persia and India. Cosroe sets out for Persepolis to assume his throne, but Tamburlaine calls him back to fight against his Turkic-Mongol army. Cosroe loses, and Tamburlaine himself becomes king of Persia.

Act III opens with the rulers of several African kingdoms and the sultan of Egypt conferring about Tamburlaine's threatened invasion of Africa. They haughtily warn the upstart against presuming any such attempt. Back in Tamburlaine's camp, we find that Zenocrate has fallen in love with her captor, who continues to treat her with courtesy, consideration, and chivalry. A Medean lord, Agydas, however, tries to woo Zenocrate. Tamburlaine observes the attempt and sends his Scythian lieutenant, Techelles, bearing a dagger to suggest to Agydas the fate Tamburlaine desires for him. Knowing his fate is sealed, Agydas takes the hint and commits suicide. His courage earns him a hero's funeral.

In Act III, scene iii, the African emperor, Bajazeth, and Tamburlaine parley and exchange threats and insults. Both the African empress, Zabina, and Zenocrate are present, and the men call on them to witness their predictions about the havoc each will wreak upon his enemy. Following the men's lead, Zabina and Zenocrate each promise to make the other a servant to slave girls. Tamburlaine proves victorious once again. Rejecting the customs of the epoch, he refuses to ransom his royal prisoner Bajazeth. Instead, Tamburlaine imprisons Bajazeth in a cage and takes him wherever he goes, using him as a human footstool and subjecting him to all sorts of gross indignities. True to her word, Zenocrate appoints Zabina her slave girl's servant. By the fifth act, Bajazeth decides death is preferable and on stage beats his own brains out against the bars of his cage. On finding her husband dead, Zabina follows suit.

Tamburlaine has by now adopted a custom that contributes to his rapid military success. On the first day his forces appear before a besieged city, his tents, all his forces' clothing and armor, and all his insignias are white. If the city capitulates without a fight, Tamburlaine welcomes it to his empire. On the second day, all the colors are blood red and there is no way for a city to avoid an attack. If the city's resistance continues until the third day, all Tamburlaine's colors are black. The city's inhabitants are doomed to execution, its buildings and battlements to destruction, and even its fertile ground will be sown with salt so nothing will grow. Having resisted through the second day, the city of Damascus sends its virgins to plead with Tamburlaine for mercy. Although he pities them, he is implacable. They have come a day late. Wearing black, he sends them to their deaths.

Tamburlaine's mercy and consideration, however, are reserved for Zenocrate. When his forces overcome her father, the sultan of Egypt and his allies, she is certain that the sultan's resistance will result in the same fate that befell Damascus. With respect to her former fiancé, she is correct. He, the king of Arabia, appears wounded on stage and dies in her presence. When her captive father is led in, however, for her sake Tamburlaine spares his life, restores to him his throne and kingdom, and requests his fatherly blessing on Tamburlaine's forthcoming marriage to Zenocrate. The conqueror crowns her queen of Persia and all his other conquests. He also rewards his faithful lieutenants with kingdoms of their own. Theridamas becomes the king of Argier (Algeria), Techelles of Fez, and Usumcasane of Morocco.

Many of the exchanges among the characters of this play involve boasting and threatening. In fact, except for the spectacular onstage deaths of several characters, little else happens. Yet this play and its sequel enjoyed long and successful runs on the London stage for two centuries. The secret of its popularity lies in Marlowe's poetry. His stirring iambic pentameter lines move with such stately majesty that they command an audience's rapt attention.

Marlowe's second play on the subject of Tamburlaine traces his history, that of his three sons, and that of Zenocrate to her death in Act II, scene iv. The drama details a fruitless military alliance between Christians and Muslims against the seemingly innumerable forces that Tamburlaine is able to field. The second play focuses as well on Tamburlaine's imprisonment of Callapine, the orphaned pretender to the empire of Egypt, in his father Bajazeth's cage. Eventually Callapine escapes, and at the play's end is still at large and still working to field troops against Tamburlaine.

The drama follows Tamburlaine's continued successes against the escaped Callapine and his Muslim and Christian allies. Late in the play, the audience is treated to the spectacle of Tamburlaine as he is drawn in his chariot by kings Trebizon and Soria. They have bits in their mouths, and Tamburlaine lashes them liberally with his whip. In place of a spare horse, Tamburlaine keeps a spare king, Orcanes, the king of Natolia and Jerusalem.

Though no mortal foe succeeds in overthrowing Tamburlaine, his final illness does. He lives to see his son Amyras crowned as his successor. Then just before the final curtain Tamburlaine dies, regretting only his loss of Zenocrate, in whose hearse his corpse will be transported, and the fact that he had not yet conquered the entire world.

In preparing to write the two dramas and to achieve geographical accuracy, Marlowe apparently studied closely the cartographer Ortelius's 1584 map of Asia included in his *Theatrum Orbis Terrarum* (Theater of the earthly globe).

Bibliography

Marlowe, Christopher. *Tamburlaine the Great, Parts 1 and 2*. Edited by David Fuller. *The Massacre at Paris: with the Death of the Duke of Guise*. Edited by Edward J. Esche. Oxford: Clarendon Press; New York: Oxford University Press, 1998.

———. *Tamburlaine the Great*. Edited by J. S. Cunningham and Eithne Henson. New York: Manchester University Press, ca. 1998.

Tang Xianzu (T'ang Hsien-Tsu)
(1550–1617)

A Chinese civil servant and playwright, Tang was dismissed from the civil service and banished in 1590 to the backwater province of Guangdong (Kwangtung) for openly criticizing the government. Though he reentered government service in a minor capacity, he apparently found it uncongenial. In 1598 he arranged to be fired and afterward devoted himself exclusively to a literary career.

Though he was skillful in composing both verse and prose and also as a literary critic, in his own time his reputation principally rested on four plays whose plots were drawn in part from his own career experiences. These plays, whose texts were sung like opera, contributed to the rising popularity of a kind of drama called *kunqu* or *ch'an-ch'i* or *chuanqi* plays.

The *kunqu* drama combined a plaintive style of singing to the accompaniment of strings, of instruments like pan pipes, and of bamboo flutes. This melodic mix was called "water polished music." Its tunes undergirded text featuring ele-gant diction, highly romantic if sometimes improbable plots, and a dreamy manner of delivering lines that had its origins in southern China. The music that accompanied the drama, a new musical idiom in Tang's China, continued to grow in popularity for centuries after his death.

Tang's first play, *The Purple Flute*, reworked an earlier tale of Chiang Fang. Tang later rewrote his drama under the title *The Purple Hairpin*. His greatest play—and some think the greatest play ever written in China—came next: PEONY PAVILION, or *The Return of the Soul*. Following that work, he penned *The Tale of Han-tan*—another adaptation of an older story, "Record of the World within a Pillow," by Shen Jiji (Shen Chi-chi). Tang's final play adapted "The Story of the Prefect of South Branch," by Li Gongzuo (Li Kung-tso). That revision appeared on stage as "The Tale of South Branch." Because dreams prove to be crucial in resolving the complications of the plot in each play, as a group they are called "Four Dreams of Lin-chu'an."

Though all Tang's plays are exceedingly well written, only *Peony Pavilion* is informed by a view that sees *qing* (*ch'ing*) or passion as the defining characteristic of human existence—a characteristic that overcomes all distinctions of epoch, place, and culture. The other plays seem more philosophical and less passionate.

Bibliography

Dolbey, William. *A History of Chinese Drama*. London: Elek Books, 1976.

Mair, Victor H., ed. *The Columbia History of Chinese Literature*. New York: Columbia University Press, 2001.

Tang, Xianzu. *The Peony Pavilion (Mudan ting)*. Translated by Cyril Birch. Bloomington: Indiana University Press, 2002.

Tarabotti, Arcangela (Elana Cassandra Tarabotti, Galerana Baratotti)
(1604–1652)

In 1620 Elana Cassandra Tarabotti, clearly forced by her father and despite the fact that she felt no particular religious vocation, entered the Benedictine Convent of Santa Anna as Sister Arcangela.

Despite her lack of formal education, she spent the rest of her life as a polemicist arguing in support of women and against the familial and societal institutions that deprived them of their full rights of participation in life and society.

Her first foray in support of women against the ensconced patriarchal institutions of her day, PA-TERNAL TYRANNY only appeared posthumously in 1654 as *La simplicità ingannata* (Simplicity deceived) and under the anagrammatic authorship of Galerana Baratotti. In this work she accused both fathers and the Venetian government of unjustly condemning daughters like herself to a lifetime of almost penal servitude behind convent walls in order to avoid paying for daughters' education and providing daughters with dowries to make them marriageable.

A second work, a discussion of the difficulties encountered by nuns who felt no religious vocation, *L'Inferno monocale* (Convent hell) did not see print until the 20th century. A sequel, "Il Purgatorio della malamaritate" (The Purgatory of the ill-married), has been lost. Tarabotti wrote a third book in this quasi-Dantean set, *Il paradiso monocale* (Convent paradise, written 1643, published 1663), and it has survived in print. This work is most convincingly read, the literary historian Elissa Weaver suggests, as Tarabotti's "failed attempt to reconcile herself to . . . [a nun's] vocation."

Tarabotti's dissatisfaction with her cloistered existence found expression not only in her writings but also in her preference for secular literature, and the Italian literary historian Elena Urgnani tells us that Tarabotti's brother-in-law smuggled books for her into the convent. Many of these, in turn, were discovered during inspections of her cell and consigned to the flames.

Throughout her literary life Tarabotti, in both her public utterances and her eventually published correspondence, continued to support the cause of women against the misogynist attacks of male writers. The Italian Francesco Buoninsegni's antifeminist tract *Contro il lusso donesco, satira menippea* (Against the luxuries of women, a Menippean satire) drew a spirited response from Tarabotti, her *Antisatira* (Antisatire, 1644). This time she signed her work DAT for Donna Arcan-gela Tarabotti. She responded in a similar fashion to Orazio Plata's translation of the German Acidalius Valens Latin tract, *Women are not Human*. This tract infuriated Tarabotti, and she heaped scorn on it in her response *That Women Are of the Human Species* (*Che le donne siano della spetie degli uomini; Difesa delle donne de Galerana Baratotti*).

Her edited letters appeared in 1650, and in them she followed the same themes. Women are the natural equals of men; only denying women education makes them seem inferior, and even then their natural reason often enables them to rise above the handicap of being untrained. She turns men's accusations of vanity and luxury back on the males, making it clear that men are just as subject to minor vices as women are.

Bibliography

Anonymous [Acidalius Valens]. *"Women are not Human": An Anonymous Treatise and Responses.* [Includes Tarabotti, *That Women Are of the Human Species.*] Edited and translated by Theresa M. Kenney. New York: Crossroad Publications, 1998.

Tarabotti, Arcangela. *Paternal Tyranny.* Edited and translated by Letizia Panizza. Chicago: University of Chicago Press, 2004.

Urgnani, Elena. "La ragion di stato monacale nel pensiero di Arcangel Tarabotti incontro con Nicolletta Lissone." Available online. URL: http://www.url.it/donnestoria/incontri/tarabotti.htm. Downloaded on June 14, 2004.

Weaver, Elissa. "Ancangela [sic] Tarabotti." *An Encyclopedia of Continental Women Writers.* Edited by Katharina M. Wilson. New York and London: Garland Publishing Company, 1991. Available online. URL: http://www.pinn.net/sunshine/~book-sum/contentl.html. Downloaded on June 14, 2004.

"Taramalu and La Enjen" (date unknown)

A legend of the Marshall Islands first recorded by Gerald Knight in the 1970s from its recitation by the Majol islander, La Bedbedin (Man This Reef), the tale of the mother and son navigators named Taramalu and La Enjen contains an oral folk description of the way in which the inhabitants of the islands of Pacific Oceania acquired some of the skills they needed to navigate from island to island in the broad reaches of the Pacific Ocean.

The story recounts the manner in which Taramalu, a girl of Kwajalein, learned to navigate the open sea. Floated over a reef in a wooden bowl, Taramalu was blindfolded and required to swim around and around a great rock until she could point to the rock from any direction. She could do this because she learned to discriminate between the kind of waves that the winds create and the kind of waves born from what the islanders call the four waves or swells of the world—those that always originate from the north, south, east, and west. Among them the swell from the east is always strongest.

She learned that these basic rolling motions of the ocean do not "bend" around islands. If a sailing canoe approaches an island from the west, say, even if that island is still far below the horizon, the forward motion of the canoe will increase as the eastern swell diminishes (as the island *eats* the swell), and the skillful navigator will know land lies ahead. Away from land, knowledge of the relative strength and interaction of the four basic "world waves," informs the skillful navigator of her position and speed—and therefore of sailing distances to known islands.

Once Taramalu had mastered her lessons around the rock, her teachers put her in a boat and took her into the open ocean as a final exam. She passed with flying colors since the roll of the waves and the rock of the boat told her the location of the island below the horizon regardless of her position with respect to it.

In time, Taramalu passed her special knowledge on to her son, La Enjen. Later, as a young crewmember on a flotilla of canoes, La Enjen kept his silence when he realized the captain was lost. Captains of such expeditions did not tolerate corrections from juniors. When, however, the entire flotilla ran out of drinking water, La Enjen, who always knew exactly where he was on the ocean's surface, finally said so.

Everyone expected the captain to throw La Enjen overboard, but instead the captain gave the boy command of the expedition. Though he knew the way to the two nearest islands, La Enjen did not sail directly to either. He knew everyone on the flotilla would die of thirst before they made landfall. Instead he navigated to a spot where freshwater springs bubbled up from the ocean floor and sent down divers with water pots. Once in the plume of fresh water, the divers were able to fill their earthenware vessels and plug their narrow spouts. The entire expedition was saved.

La Enjen became a famous navigator. Then one day he met a man who had sailed with Taramalu on her last expedition. The man had jumped overboard in a moment of panic at unfamiliar conditions, but when he reached for the canoe's stern it was not there. Neither was the ocean. The man told La Enjen that he had found himself falling a long way until he landed in the sea. Taramalu's last known expedition had ended up sailing, he said, not on water but in the sky.

La Enjen sailed west in search of his mother and, according to La Bedbedin, on the return trip composed a navigation poem that others could use to follow his course. La Bedbedin did not know all the poem, but he recited what he remembered. It includes landmarks, information about currents and fish populations, and sailing directions that typify the navigation poems of the seafaring peoples of Polynesia.

Bibliography

Knight, Gerald, trans. and ed. *Man This Reef.* 1982. Majauro, Republic of the Marshall Islands: Micronitor Press, 1986.

Tartuffe Molière (1664)

A COMEDY of character, *Tartuffe* satirizes the folly that results from the mid-life crisis of a principal character, Orgon, and the late-life crisis of his mother, Madame Pernelle.

Orgon, the husband of a sensible and capable younger wife, Elmire, has retired from a distinguished career in public service. Turning his attention to piety, Orgon becomes obsessed with respect and admiration for Tartuffe. Tartuffe and his servant are a pair of confidence men who pretend to virtue and godliness. Besotted by his admiration of Tartuffe's apparent saintliness, Orgon moves him into his household in the role of moral adviser.

Orgon's mother, an aging and no longer attractive coquette, has replaced her former flirtatiousness with a blind and hypocritical piety that leads her to exceed even her son's unhealthy respect for Tartuffe.

Tartuffe's real objective, however, is simply to steal property and whatever else he can from the foolish Orgon. Credulously Orgon breaks off his daughter Marianne's engagement to her beloved Valère and proposes to force her to marry Tartuffe. Though he is pleased with this arrangement, the hypocrite Tartuffe hotly lusts after Orgon's wife Elmire. This illicit passion and Tartuffe's ego eventually lead to the con man's exposure. Not before Orgon has already signed over his estate to Tartuffe, however, does Tartuffe's host see through the pious fraud. Moreover, Orgon has jeopardized himself by giving Tartuffe a strongbox filled with the incriminating papers of a friend who rebelled against the king in the French civil wars.

Throughout the play the voice of reason issues from the mouth of a servant in Orgon's household, Marianne's maid Dorinne. It is she who mounts a spirited though ineffectual opposition to Orgon's plan to force Marianne to wed Tartuffe. Dorinne also reconciles the young lovers when they bullheadedly work at cross purposes in the affair.

So thoroughly and effectively does Tartuffe scheme to ruin Orgon and his family that only the king's seemingly omniscient and enlightened intercession saves Orgon's estate. The king pardons Orgon for hiding the papers, rewards him for past services, and sends Tartuffe off to a well-deserved prison sentence.

The five-act play is written in French rhymed verse, and the rhymed English translation of Richard Wilbur catches much of the charm of the original. In *Tartuffe* Molière combines the Renaissance fascination with stock characters and situations from the Roman comedy of PLAUTUS and TERENCE with the moralistic conventionality of segments of French society to achieve a moral comedy that lauds common sense and satirizes false piety.

Bibliography

Molière. *The Misanthrope and Tartuffe.* Translated by Richard Wilbur. New York: Harcourt Brace Jovanovich, 1965.

———. *Miseryguts* [*The Misanthrope*]; and *Tartuffe: Two Plays by Molière.* Translated and adapted by Liz Lochhead. London: Nick Hern, 2002.

Tashköprü-záde family (1423–1591)

Three generations of the Tashköprü-záde family of Turkish scholars from the northern region of Anatolia produced notable literary figures. The first of them, Muslih al-Din Mustafa (1453–1529), served as a teacher for Sultan Selim I of the Ottoman Empire and composed poetry under the pen name Hilmī.

His son, Isām al-Dīn Ahmed (1495–1561), became the most celebrated member of the literary dynasty. Writing in Arabic, he left 19 works of theology and an important work detailing the biographies of famous people during the reigns of 10 Ottoman sultans. Others continued this work through the reigns of later sultans. Isām al-Dīn Ahmed also dictated an encyclopedia and a second collection of biographies. Some of his work has been translated into German, but none thus far appears in English.

Isām's son, Kemāl al-Dīn Mehmed (1552–1621), continued the literary activity of his family into the third generation. Like many Turkish writers he became a member of the legal profession, holding judgeships at various locations in the Ottoman Empire. He penned a short history of that empire through the year 1617 and enlarged it with brief looks at other Muslim dynasties. He composed poetry in both Arabic and Turkish under the pen name Kemālī. He also translated several Persian and Arabic works into Turkish, including his father's encyclopedia.

Tasso, Torquato (1544–1595)

Perhaps the most gifted Italian poet of his era, Torquato Tasso led a life that reads like a Spanish CAPE AND SWORD romance. The son of Bernardo Tasso and his wife Porzia, Torquato was born at Sorrento and given the name of an elder brother who had died in infancy. His father was an aristocrat of ancient lineage, a lesser poet than his son, and a wandering dependent on a series of patrons who employed him in various stations, often as a civil administrator.

If his biographers can be credited, Torquato Tasso's linguistic gifts became apparent during the first year of his life. At age six months he is said to have begun speaking fully formed, properly pronounced words. As a schoolboy he was hard working and scholarly from the very beginning. His father was involuntarily separated from his family as an undeservedly proclaimed rebel in the Kingdom of Naples and had fled to Rome. Remaining with his mother in Sorrento, Torquato studied with the Jesuits. He worked with them for three years from 1551 to 1554, learning Latin, some Greek, public speaking, and composition. By the age of 10 he was reading his own poems in public.

Prevented by many difficulties from being reunited with his family, Bernardo eventually brought Torquato to stay with him in Rome. The boy also accompanied his father as a companion in his subsequent wanderings from patron to patron. The father managed to assure, nonetheless, that Torquato received careful tutoring from the best teachers he could find.

Concerned for his son's future and worried lest Torquato's literary aspirations lead him to the kind of gypsy dependency on the generosity of noble patrons that Bernardo himself endured, the father insisted that Torquato study law. Though the aspiring poet found this pursuit totally uncongenial, Torquato dutifully enrolled at the University of Padua in 1561. There he attended not only the lectures on law but also those on philosophy, poetry, eloquence, and mathematics. He found time, moreover, to pen his first epic poem, *Rinaldo*, a CHIVALRIC EPIC based on the adventures of a cousin of ORLANDO, the hero of epics by BOIARDO and ARIOSTO. Bernardo reluctantly consented to the publication of his son's poem. Dedicated to Cardinal Luigi d'Este of Ferrara, *Rinaldo* appeared in Venice in April 1562, and became an instant success. Overnight the son, only 19, achieved the fame that the father had sought throughout his life, but that his own chivalric epic, *Amadigi*, had failed to bring.

Torquato's newly minted poetic eminence brought with it an invitation to change university in 1563. This call came from Pier Donato Cesi and

Gio-Angelo Papio, respectively, the rector and a celebrity professor of the newly refurbished and restaffed University of Bologna. Pleased and flattered, Tasso accepted and, with his father's consent, also gave up legal study. During the year at Bologna, Tasso not only continued his studies but also lectured on heroic poetry, and he began work on the epic that would be his masterpiece, JERUSALEM DELIVERED (GERUSALEMME LIBERATA). Unfounded accusations against him, however, provoked an official inspection of his quarters and seizure of his papers. Though nothing incriminating was discovered, Tasso was so offended that he did not return to Bologna the next year but reenrolled at Padua.

At Padua once more, Tasso met GIOVANNI BATTISTA GUARINI, author of the PASTORAL DRAMA, *THE FAITHFUL SHEPHERD*. Guarini would be a rival sometimes, but also a faithful friend. Also in Padua Tasso joined the Academy of the Ethereals, taking the academic name, *Il Pentito* (the penitent). He pressed ahead as well with *Jerusalem Delivered*, and found time to write three discourses on the art of poetry. These treatises another friend would arrange to have published in 1587. He also contributed 38 SONNETs, two madrigals, and two ODEs to a joint publication by the members of the Ethereals.

At about this time, however, Cardinal Luigi d'Este invited Tasso to join his retinue at the court of Ferrara. Against the advice of Professor Speroni Sperone, who had just come from a similar and disappointing appointment in Rome, Tasso joined the cardinal's court and moved to Ferrara.

With the cardinal in 1570–71 Tasso traveled to Paris, where he was warmly received at the French court. Not only did the king treat him with kindness, but Tasso also formed a special bond with the poet PIERRE RONSARD, and the two exchanged their work for each other's criticism. In December of the same year Tasso and the cardinal moved on to Rome, where a warm reception at the papal court once again awaited the young poet.

On the cardinal's recommendation, his brother Duke Alfonso d'Este took Tasso into his service at Ferrara, granting him a comfortable income and, at last, the leisure to write. Tasso thanked his patron for that latter gift when, in his pastoral play

AMINTA, he speaks in the guise of its shepherd hero, Tirsis: "A god [the duke] has given me this ease, [commanding me to] Sing and take . . . [my] leisure." [Translation mine.]

In addition to *Aminta* (1573) Tasso wrote a discussion of the comparative attributes of Italy and France, and an unfinished discussion of the French religious wars. In 1574 Duke Alfonso recognized Tasso's remarkable intellectual range by appointing him to the chair of Mathematics at the University of Ferrara, and *Aminta* was performed at the court. The duke's sister Lucrezia, duchess of Urbino, invited Tasso to come there and read *Aminta* to her. He accepted. That year as well, Tasso began writing the first Italian tragedy in the classical style, *King Torrismondo*.

In 1575 Tasso at last finished JERUSALEM DELIVERED. In keeping with his usual practice, he circulated it among his respected acquaintances for comment, and apparently received much advice and some unfavorable criticism. The advice of his critics and his responses to them are preserved in his letters and in his defense of his work.

At this point, the story grows confused. Some say Tasso and the duke's sister Leonora were in love and that Tasso aspired too high. Others say that several courtiers, jealous of the generosity and regard with which the duke favored Tasso, conspired together and poisoned the duke's mind against him. It is certainly true that the grand-ducal family of Florence, the Medici, repeatedly tried to attract Tasso to Florence with offers of money and vastly more generous patronage than he received in Padua, and it appears that Tasso may have seriously entertained their offer and other invitations from Rome. Others maintain that the conflicting advice from the readers of his epic addled the poet's wits so that he fell into a paranoiac melancholy. His suspicions and accusations, perhaps, turned the duke against him. In any case, the duke had Tasso arrested as a madman in 1579 and confined, at first to his quarters and then to the hospital of Santa Anna. Once Tasso escaped, he made his way to his sister's house in Sorrento where he remained for a year. Then he was invited back to Ferrara, accepted either from folly or from need, and was again incarcerated. Altogether Tasso spent over

seven years confined in a madhouse on Duke Alfonso's orders.

To make matters worse, unauthorized, severely flawed editions of Tasso's *Jerusalem Delivered* began appearing. The first of these in 1580 published the first 10 cantos in recognizable but lamentable condition. Cantos 11 and 12 appeared in prose, and 13 through 16 in fragments with the text of early versions used instead of current ones.

Friends tried to come to the rescue of Tasso's work. The theatrical producer Angelo Ingeniere possessed a quite recent manuscript version of the poem, and he brought out two simultaneous, improved editions. Tasso's college friend and sometime rival Guarini, perhaps with Tasso's help and approval, brought out a faithful version—by now the poem's fifth edition—that contained Tasso's retrospective interpretation of the poem's religious ALLEGORY.

In the meantime, Tasso's pitiable condition had become a matter of concern to Pope Sixtus V. Together with many other important Italians, including Prince Vincenzo Gonzaga of Mantua, the pope mounted a concerted effort to win the poet's freedom. Reluctantly yielding at last to public pressure, but only then with many reservations and conditions, Duke Alfonso allowed Tasso to depart Ferrara to Gonzaga's care in Mantua.

Tasso, like his father before him, became a disappointed wanderer. Yet his output was much greater than Bernardo's, and, despite all his difficulties, he produced many works, not all of which there is space here to name. He wrote a lively defense of his great poem; then he tried to revise it, taking into account all the comments of its critics. The result, *Jerusalem Conquered* (*Gerusalemme Conquistata*, 1593), was greatly inferior to its original. He traveled as a pilgrim to Loreto, and throughout Italy he found many willing to open their doors to him and offer their hospitality.

Pope Clement VIII determined at last to honor Italy's premier poet by having him crowned poet laureate at the Roman Capitol. Tasso no sooner arrived in Rome to accept the honor, however, than he fell ill and died in the care of the monks at the monastery of Sant' Onofrio. The comedienne and poet, ISABELLA ANDREINI, was among those who wrote moving funeral lamentations on the occasion of Tasso's death.

Bibliography

Boulting, William. *Tasso and His Times.* New York: Haskell House Publishers, 1968.

Rheu, Lawrence F. *The Genesis of Tasso's Narrative Theory: English Translations of the Early Poetics and a Comparative Study of Their Significance.* Detroit, Mich.: Wayne State University Press, ca. 1993.

Tasso, Torquato. *Aminta: A Pastoral Play.* Edited and translated by Charles Jernigan and Irene Marchegiani Jones. New York: Italica Press, 2000.

———. *Discourses on the Heroic Poem.* Translated by Cariella Cavalchini and Irene Samuel. Oxford: Clarendon Press, 1973.

———. *Jerusalem Delivered.* Edited and translated by Anthony M. Esolen. Baltimore, Md.: The Johns Hopkins University Press, 2000.

———. *King Torrismondo.* Translated by Maria Pastore Passaro. New York: Fordham University Press, 1997.

———. *Mondo Creato* (*The Creation of the World*). Translated by Joseph Tusiani. Binghamton, N.Y.: Center for Medieval and Early Renaissance Studies, State University of New York, 1982.

Tausen, Hans (1494–1561)

Originally a Roman Catholic monk, Tausen converted to Protestantism and preached the new religion with such conviction and zeal that his hearers in the city of Viborg are said to have dismantled 12 Roman Catholic churches. His slender contribution to Danish letters included a translation into Danish of the first five books of the Old Testament and a brief treatise on truth and falsehood.

Tempest, The William Shakespeare (ca. 1611)

A late romance or TRAGICOMEDY, *The Tempest* illustrates the way that SHAKESPEARE, then at the height of his powers as a poet and dramatist, can establish all the conditions for a disaster of hatred and vengeance and avert the tragic outcome through the operation of reason and forgiveness.

Prospero, the lawful duke of Milan, has been deposed, exiled, and cast adrift by his brother, Antonio. With Prospero in a leaky boat is his infant daughter, Miranda. Though Antonio intended that his brother and niece be lost at sea, Gonzalo, a counselor, provisioned their craft, and the castaways drift ashore on a desert isle whose only inhabitant is Caliban, reportedly the offspring of the devil and a witch, Sycorax.

As a duke, Prospero had neglected governing in favor of study, especially the mastery of white MAGIC, and the loyal Gonzalo saw to it that his most important books went with him. On the island, Prospero perfected his art and used it to set free a spirit, Ariel, whom the witch Sycorax had imprisoned in the knot of a tree. In return, Ariel has become Prospero's magic servant until such time as Prospero sets him free.

By means of his craft Prospero knows what goes on back in Italy. He knows that to consolidate his control of Milan Antonio secured an alliance with Alonso, the king of Naples, turning Milan into a feudal vassalage of Naples. He also knows that Alonso's daughter Claribel is to be married in North Africa and that Antonio, the counselor Gonzalo, King Alonso, and Alonso's son, Prince Ferdinand, are traveling together in the same ship, homeward bound from the wedding.

Using his magical powers, Prospero has Ariel stir up a tempest that will drive the wedding party's ship to the shores of the island where he and Miranda are marooned. The play opens in the midst of the tempest with the ship's captain trying to save his vessel. The nobles attempt to take charge, but the sailors tell them to keep out of the way. Under Prospero's spell the ship seems to founder on rocks and split. All its occupants survive unscathed, however, and Prospero disperses them singly and in small groups around the island, so that each person thinks himself and his companions to be the only survivors. Equidistant from Africa and Europe, which from the perspectives of ALLEGORY and MORALIZED GEOGRAPHY, respectively, represented passion and reason, the island suggests a balance between the two.

In the second scene Prospero for the first time reveals to Miranda her princely heritage and the circumstances that brought them to the island. He then causes his daughter to sleep and the spirit Ariel enters, claiming his freedom. Prospero reminds Ariel of his duty, but promises to free him soon. Then the two discuss Caliban. We discover that Prospero had taught Caliban language and treated him as another child until Caliban had attempted to violate Miranda. After that Prospero turned him into a menial servant.

Prince Ferdinand enters believing himself the shipwreck's only survivor. Invisible to him Ariel sings a funeral song for the ostensibly drowned king. Then Ferdinand and Miranda see each other and fall in love at first sight. This, of course, has been Prospero's objective all along. Not only has he arranged matters so that he will return to his dukedom, his daughter and her progeny will rule in Naples. But Prospero doesn't want the young people's love to develop too quickly or easily lest Ferdinand think his bride too easily won. So Prospero accuses him of spying and threatens harsh treatment. When Ferdinand tries to resist, he finds himself too weak to draw his sword.

Meanwhile around the island we find the others. The largest group includes King Alonso, the usurping Duke Antonio, Gonzalo, and others, including Sebastian. Alonso grieves for Ferdinand, whom he thinks drowned. Eventually he and Gonzalo fall asleep, and Antonio and Sebastian conspire to kill them so that Antonio will become king of Naples. Ariel awakens Gonzalo at the crucial moment, and the opportunity passes. Elsewhere on the island two common sailors, Trinculo and Stephano, have come ashore on a barrel of liquor. They have filled their bottles from the source and are already drunk when we meet them. They encounter Caliban, who is frightened of them. They give him liquor to drink, and he thinks they must be gods. Accordingly, he worships them and recruits them to help him rid the island of Prospero. Shakespeare has woven the themes of the subplots together in such a way that they reflect those of the main plot—usurpation and the potential for disaster are implicit in each strand of the plot.

At the end of Act 3 Ariel, in the form of a harpy, accuses Antonio and Alonzo of their crimes against Prospero. The three grow desperate, and Prospero sends Ariel to keep them from doing themselves harm. In the meantime, Prospero thinks that Ferdinand has endured enough harsh treatment and ac-

cepts him as a prospective son-in-law. The magician has Ariel provide a magical entertainment for the newly affianced young people—a play within a play, "The Masque of Ceres."

Reminded of the plot of Stefano, Trinculo, and Caliban, Prospero has Ariel deal with them by having spirits chase them through bog, brake, and bramble, and brings all the aristocrats together. He reveals his identity and his plans for the young people. Forgiveness is exchanged on all sides, and the former enemies are reconciled. Caliban, Trinculo, and Stefano are chastened. The play ends with Prospero freeing Ariel and foreswearing his magic art.

Numerous readers have thought that this play may be interpreted as Shakespeare's farewell to his theatrical art. Like Prospero on the island, Shakespeare could make tempests and spirits appear onstage. Just as Prospero gave up his magic, it was about the time of this play's performance that Shakespeare retired to live in Stratford and limited his participation in London theatrical production, leaving the magic of the Shakespearean stage to others.

Bibliography

Shakespeare, William. *The Tempest. The Riverside Shakespeare.* Edited by G. Blakemore Evans, et al. Boston: Houghton Mifflin Company, 1997.

Terence (Publius Terentius Afer)
(ca. 190–159 B.C.E.)

Born in Carthage on the North African coast of the Mediterranean Sea, as a child Terence was purchased as a slave by the Roman senator P. Terentius Lucanus. Finding his servant equipped with an extraordinary intellect, the senator saw to it that Terence became well educated and set him free. Terence opted to become a comic playwright. He lived both in Rome and in Athens and modernized the plays of the earlier Greek playwright Menander into an especially lucid Latin.

During the Renaissance, Terence's plays, together with those of PLAUTUS, became models for writers of COMEDY throughout Europe. Not only did such European writers as BEN JONSON in England and MOLIÈRE in France imitate his plots, they imitated his character types as well, and Terentian

STOCK CHARACTERS populated the European stage for centuries. To a degree, they continue to do so, for self-promoting braggarts, young lovers whose parents try to keep them apart, and con artists remain a standard part of the repertoire of comic writers' devices.

terza rima

A verse form invented by the Italian poet DANTE ALIGHIERI for his *Divine Comedy* (*Commedia*, begun ca. 1307), terza rima has a stanza composed of three 11 syllable lines called tercets or triplets. Lines 1 and 3 rhyme: a, a. Line 2 rhymes with lines 4 and 6: b, b, b. Line 5 rhymes with the first and third lines of the following tercet. The subsequent sets of 3 lines continue to interlock in this way until Dante reaches the final tercet of each of the three books comprising his *Divine Comedy*. The last tercet closes off the interlocking rhyme scheme in each book and is followed by a single line whose last world is *stelle* (stars). *Stelle* completes the rhyme scheme by appearing in the final position of each book, thus tying all three together in a final tercet whose rhyming elements are widely separated.

Many Italian poets of the Renaissance including ISABELLA ANDREINI, PETRARCH, and others followed Dante in using terza rima. The English poetic innovator, HENRY HOWARD, EARL OF SURREY (1517–47) experimented with the form. So did JOHN MILTON and other later poets, but the consensus seems to be that the form does not work very well in English. Here is an English doggerel example that I wrote to illustrate the form:

> *If ever I should try to write a verse, dear,*
> *Please call the men in white coats to our*
> *dwelling.*
> *Explain to them that madness has crept in*
> *here,*
> *And tell them that the tears from my eyes*
> *welling*
> *Can be staunched by a sharp rap on the*
> *nuckles,*
> *And never mind the opiates they're selling.*
> *Tell them to strap me down with belts and*
> *buckles. . . .*

textual criticism

The science of textual criticism, developed during the Renaissance, tries to arrive at a version of a text—usually an ancient one—that more closely approximates that text's original state. LORENZO VALLA (1407–57) became the most influential contributor to the effort to reverse in ancient texts the effects of centuries of misreading, copying errors, interpolation, and revision to suit those with vested interests in reinterpretation of texts. The essential method of scientific textual criticism involved accumulating the earliest and most authoritative texts available, comparing them with more modern ones, and sifting out the cumulative errors of the ages.

Those who followed Valla strove to improve the versions available to Europeans of the ancient Greek and Roman authors. They also labored to arrive at a more pristine version of Scripture. DESIDERIUS ERASMUS, for example, applied Valla's principles to the BIBLE and retranslated both the Old and the New Testaments. He then applied the same principles to his own texts, using Valla's methods as a way to improve his own work.

Because the power and authority of religious leaders rested on biblical texts, especially on the Vulgate Latin Bible, Erasmus's work was suspect. This fact led Cardinal Francisco Jiménez de Cisneros to form a team to produce an alternative text, the COMPLUTENSIAN POLYGLOT BIBLE. Cisneros insisted on giving precedence to the Vulgate when revision on textual grounds produced text that conflicted with official doctrine.

The application of the principles of textual criticism to ancient texts has produced versions of many texts that are much closer to the originals than were the versions available at the beginning of the European Renaissance.

'Tis Pity She's a Whore John Ford (between 1629 and 1633)

'Tis Pity She's a Whore strikes a viewer as one of the most unremittingly bleak REVENGE TRAGEDIES of the British Renaissance. Only three secondary characters seem in any way admirable: Friar Bonaventura, Philotis, and Florio. Most are moral monsters, both vengeful and pitilessly cruel. The

play opens with Giovanni's confession to Friar Bonaventura that he is in love with his own sister, Annabella. Giovanni uses logic-chopping arguments in an effort to justify his unnatural passion.

Annabella's father, Florio, has sworn not to give his daughter in marriage to a man she does not love. She has two suitors. One is Bergetto, a dunce who really doesn't care much for her and whose unfailing stupidity provides what little laughter the play provokes. The other is Soranzo, who has fallen desperately in love with Annabella. Soranzo, as we discover, had earlier seduced a married woman, Hippolyta, promising that he would marry her when her husband, a physician named Richardetto, died. To heighten that probability, Hippolyta encourages Richardetto to undertake a journey to Leghorn to collect his orphaned niece, Philotis. Richardetto knows about his wife's affair and her motives. He therefore sends home a report of his own death so that he can return disguised and catch her.

On learning of Richardetto's presumed death, in Act II, scene ii, Hippolyta confronts Soranzo, reminding him of her seduction and his promise to wed her. Soranzo scorns her and advises her to repent of her sins. She then attempts to win over Soranzo's old, Spanish servant, Vasques, as an accomplice in her plan for vengeance. She promises to marry him and make him lord of her estate. Vasquez, despite all his other faults, at least displays the virtue of unwavering loyalty and appears to agree so he can protect Soranzo.

Unable to bear the burden of his secret love any longer, in Act I, Scene ii, Giovanni confesses his feelings to his sister. Annabella responds by assuring him she feels the same way about him. With the help of Annabella's guardian, an old bawd named Putana, the siblings consummate their passion (Act II, Scene i) and Annabella eventually becomes pregnant by her brother.

In the meantime, Bergetto presents his halfhearted proposal of marriage to Annabella, and she rejects him. Soranzo also proposes. Annabella refuses him in the hearing of Giovanni, who has grown jealous of his sister's suitors. She adds, however, that, though she intends never to marry, were she to do so, Soranzo would be the man.

Meanwhile, in Leghorn, Richardetto and a Roman nobleman, Grimaldi, have discovered that they share a mutual hatred for Soranzo. They plot his murder with a poisoned sword. Disguised as a new doctor in town, Richardetto returns to Parma, bringing his niece Philotis with him. Philotis and the dunce Bergetto encounter one another on the street and fall in love. Their respective uncles agree to their match, and they become engaged.

Still defending his behavior, Giovanni tells Friar Bonaventura all about his liaison with his own sister. The friar assures the unrepentant Giovanni that he is damned. Bonaventura also hopes that he can gain access to Annabella so that he can offer her a chance at repentance and salvation.

In Act III, Scene iii, Putana discovers Annabella's pregnancy. Hoping to disguise it for a while as illness, Giovanni arranges for Friar Bonaventura to visit his sister, ostensibly to hear her confession in the event of her death. The friar seizes the opportunity to describe the torments that await the brother and sister in Hell and to encourage her to repent and sin no more. Unlike Giovanni, Annabella is moved by the friar's warning and seeks forgiveness.

Informed of Soranzo's hope to marry Annabella, and not knowing of her refusal, Richardetto and Grimaldi resolve to waylay and murder Soranzo on his way to Friar Bonaventura's cell, where they think the ceremony will take place. Armed with the poisoned sword, Grimaldi waits. Hearing a man call someone "sweetheart," he thinks he has his victim and stabs—not Soranzo—but poor Bergetto who was on his way with Philotis to the friar who was to marry them. Bergetto dies, and his uncle, Donado, Florio, Richardetto, officers of the watch, and others pursue Grimaldi to the gate of the cardinal's palace. They pound on the door until the cardinal appears with Grimaldi. Grimaldi confesses the murder, explains he has killed the wrong man, and submits to the cardinal's judgment. The cardinal protects him, saying Grimaldi is too high born to taste local justice.

Anabella's pregnancy and her repentance encourage her to seek an honorable way out of her predicament. She therefore agrees to marry Soranzo. Vasques tells Hippolyta of this and informs her of the time and place of the wedding. Act IV, Scene i, opens with the postnuptial banquet. Giovanni refuses to drink to his sister's and Soranzo's happiness, but before anything can come of that insult, Hippolyta and a group of women appear at the door to offer a wedding entertainment as a present. She says she forgives Soranzo for the way he treated her. She asks Vasquez for a cup of wine to drink Soranzo's health, knowing that he will pledge hers in return. Vasquez hands her the poisoned cup she had intended for Soranzo, and she poisons herself on stage. As Hippolyta dies she curses Soranzo and Annabella and any children she may bear. Florio rightly considers all this a bad omen for Annabella's marriage.

In Act IV, Scene ii, Ford wraps up one strand of subplot by having poor Philotis resign herself to life in a convent in Cremona. In the next scene, however, a furious Soranzo has discovered Annabella's condition. She refuses to tell him who the father is, and Soranzo is about to kill her when Vasquez suggests he has a way to discover the culprit. He advises Soranzo to treat his wife as if he is reconciled to her and to their situation until Vasquez can put his plan in motion. Soranzo agrees.

Vasquez guesses that Putana will know who Annabella's lover was. Without much effort, he worms it out of her. Once she has identified Giovanni, Vasquez has a group of ruffians seize Putana, blind her, and lock her up until he needs her later.

The final act opens with Friar Bonaventura overhearing Annabella's heartfelt confession. He absolves her and has her write her brother a letter informing him of her repentance. Soranzo and Vasques lay a plot to have the ruffians murder Giovanni at a banquet for the cardinal. The friar delivers Annabella's letter to Giovanni and makes a final effort to encourage him to repent. Giovanni refuses. Scene iv ends with the arrival of the guests for the banquet.

Act V, Scene v finds Giovanni and Annabella alone, and Annabella tries to warn him that the banquet is a ruse to lead them to their destruction. Giovanni is beyond caring, however, and, after asking his sister to kiss him and forgive him, which she does, he stabs her to death. In the next and final scene, he enters the banquet with her heart transfixed on his dagger. There before the entire company, he confesses both his incest and his crime. His father, Florio, dies of shock on the spot.

Giovanni then stabs Soranzo, at which point the ruffians and Vasquez attack him. He fights until he is overwhelmed and dies without a word of remorse. Soranzo also dies. Vasquez produces Putana to confirm all. The cardinal then passes judgment, ordering the burning of "this woman," who may be either Putana or the dead Annabella, and sending Vasquez into exile. Richardetto comes out of disguise, and the cardinal ends the play by regretting the unhappy life and untimely death of Annabella and wondering who would not agree with the play's title.

Some critics of this play have played the dangerous game of psychoanalyzing its author based on its text, concluding that Ford was himself amoral and a defender of free love where no marriage was a marriage without a union of hearts and minds. Ford's tracts, however, suggest otherwise. They promote stoicism as the philosophy with which to confront a world like the barren one this play depicts. A balanced and historically tenable view is one offered by critic Mark Stavig. Stavig suggests that Ford here as elsewhere follows the sort of thinking ROBERT BURTON collected in his *Anatomy of Melancholy* (1621). In his discussions of lover's melancholy Burton distinguishes honest or natural love—the kind that leads to and is maintained within good marriages—from violent, "heroical" love. This latter sort, says Burton is "immoderate, inordinate," and boundless. It begets "rapes, incests, and murders." Heroical love undermines the social order and the sanity of persons suffering from its associated melancholy. Surely this is Giovanni's kind of love, and Hippolyta's, and perhaps Soranzo's as well. From the melancholy of heroical love springs their wild behavior—particularly Giovanni's.

Thus Ford's play is not an apology for unrestrained passion but rather a critical example of how unbridled love upsets the ordinary working relationships of the world and destroys lives. A still living play, *'Tis Pity . . .* has been frequently performed during the 20th century.

Bibliography

Ford, John. *'Tis Pity She's a Whore and Other Plays.* Edited by Marion Lomax et al. Oxford and New York: Oxford University Press, 1995.

Stavig, Mark. *John Ford and the Traditional Moral Order.* Madison: University of Wisconsin Press, 1968.

Tlatelolco, Annals of (1528)

Appearing as the last 41 chapters of THE FLOREN-TINE CODEX, *A GENERAL HISTORY OF THE THINGS OF NEW SPAIN* by Fray BERNARDINO DE SAHAGÚN (ca. 1577–80), the Annals of Tlateloco report the genealogies of important figures and the histories of the principal centers of civilization in central Mexico prior to European contact.

They go on to summarize the fall of Mexico-Tenochtitlán and the events preceding and following HERNÁN CORTÉS's conquest of the city. The account begins with a report of eight signs and omens that warned the people of impending disaster. Strange lights appeared in the sky; the temple of a devil spontaneously combusted, lightning struck another temple, a tripartite comet or meteor was observed falling. The water in the lake around Mexico City bubbled and boiled up, flooding portions of the city and washing out the foundations of buildings. The emperor, upon being presented with an unusual bird, had a vision of people outfitted for war riding, as he thought, on the backs of deer. Also, strange, thistlelike people appeared and disappeared.

The annals next report the arrival of news that strangers had been sighted navigating the Gulf of Mexico and details the embassy and gifts that Montezuma sent to them. It recounts the ambassadors' reception by the Spanish who, after accepting their gifts, clapped the Mexican ambassadors in irons and fired off a cannon, causing them all to faint with fright. Cortés next proposed a test of strength between the Mexicans and the Spaniards using weapons and shields.

The annals continue, detailing the failure of Montezuma's witches and wizards to enchant the Spaniards, the emperor's instructions to receive the Europeans hospitably, the Spaniards' treachery, and the Mexican's driving them from the city. The arrival of smallpox in the Mexican capital is described, as is the Spaniard's siege of Mexico-Tenochtitlán and their eventual success in conquering the Aztecs.

Bibliography

Sahagún, Bernardino de. *Florentine Codex: General History of the Things of New Spain.* 12 vols. Translated from Aztec by Charles E. Dibble and Arthur J. O. Anderson. Monographs of the School of American Research, no. 14. Santa Fe: The School of American Research and the Museum of New Mexico.

Tonga, historic poems of

Because it seems fairly certain that the events these poems record and the composition of the poems themselves both occurred in the 16th century, I have chosen them as minimal representatives of the vast, rich, complex, but usually difficult to date ORAL LITERATURE OF POLYNESIAN OCEANIA.

Sir Basil Thompson records a poem chronicling the deeds of a Polynesian seafarer named Kau-ulu-fonua. The poem reports this sailor's adventures as the leader of an expedition whose members arrived at Tonga by oceangoing canoe and who settled the islands. Tongans apparently date their history from Kau-ulu-fonua's reign. Not very long afterward, European explorers arrived at Tonga in their sailing vessels without paddles. Poetic descriptions of even the smallest observations of metal objects, equipment, and human and nonhuman passengers survive in Tongan poems of the period. Thompson reports, for instance, a description of a ship's cat. *Pusi,* as the cat is called in the poem, is pictured sitting atop the forecastle. The cat would have been an exotic animal from the Tongan's perspective.

The arrival in 1616 of the Dutch explorers Willem Schouten (ca. 1580–1625) and Jakob Lemaire (1585–1616) is also recorded in poetic song—particularly the strength and warlike prowess of Schouten. Thompson speculates that perhaps that detail, preserved in song, restrained the piratical propensities of the Tongans when, in 1643, the Dutch discoverer of Tasmania, Abel Janszoon Tasman (1603–59) arrived on Tonga. His visit is also recorded in minute detail in a Tongan poem.

Bibliography

Andersen, Johannes Carl. *Myths and Legends of the Polynesians.* 1928. New York: Dover Publications, 1995.

Thompson, Basil. *The Diversions of a Prime Minister.* Edinburgh and London: W. Blackwood and Sons, 1894.

———. *Savage Island: An Account of a Sojourn in Niué and Tonga.* London: J. Murray, 1902.

Toothless Satires and *Biting Satires*
(*Virgidemiae* or Harvests of Switches)
Joseph Hall (1597 and 1598)

In these works Hall strove to apply in iambic pentameter couplets in the manner of the Roman poet Juvenal (ca. 55–ca. 140 C.E.) to the matter he found around him on the contemporary Elizabethan scene. The works are often thought to be the first true poetic satire in the English language. (See POETIC METER.)

Book I of the *Toothless Satires* surveys the literary situation in England and, in a carefully conducted literary critique, concludes that the excesses and follies of English artists have prostituted the MUSES. Though Hall exempts EDMUND SPENSER from his general harangue, he scorns the theater (Christopher Marlowe's *TAMBURLAINE* is his chief example). He skewers the patronage system, the borrowings of English poets from CHIVALRIC ROMANCE, English poems that warn people against suffering disasters that have afflicted the famous, English love poems, and the attempts of poets such as THOMAS CAMPION who tried to write English poetry according to the rules for Latin prosody— tried, that is, to use a quantitative instead of an accentual system of poetic meter. Hall also disdains the state of religious poetry and bitterly castigates obscenity and sexual titillation. The entire performance reveals a discriminating intellect with a preference for classical high art and little patience with the pandering of the popular entertainment culture to the ill-formed tastes of the crowd.

The second and third books of *Toothless Satires,* respectively, examine the foibles and pretenses of professional people of Elizabethan England and the decay of manners in English society. In connection with his examination of manners, Hall begins to draw in verse the sort of portraits of personality types that he would later sketch in his prose CHARACTER WRITING. In the ongoing debate about whether people in ancient or modern times were better off and more virtuous, Hall was firmly in the camp of the ancients. The further humankind moved away from the biblical Garden of Eden, Hall was convinced, the more fallen people became. When, therefore, he turned to *Biting Satires,* after first defending his methods, he launched into an exposé of sexual transgression, to which he devotes over two books. Dissatisfaction with hereditary roles in society becomes the object of his next invective. Hall also excoriates what he considered to be the lavish ritual of Roman Catholicism. He turns next to social satire, examining economic issues, such as enclosing land formerly held in common, and abuses such as rent gouging that exacerbated the social tensions between the aristocracy and the commons and between landlords and their tenants.

Hall's satires instantly spawned a spate of imitators, among them JOHN MARSTON, William Rankin, and THOMAS MIDDLETON, who rushed their satires into print in 1598. To the authorities, however, satire seemed potentially incendiary material. In June 1599, shortly after the appearance of Hall's *Biting Satires,* the government issued orders forbidding the publication of satire.

Bibliography

Hall, Joseph. *The Collected Poems.* . . . Edited by A. Davenport. St. Clair Shores, Mich.: Scholarly Press, 1971.

Tourney, Leonard D. *Joseph Hall.* Boston, Mass.: Twayne Publishers, 1979.

topos, topoi (locus, loci)

Topos and its plural, *topoi,* are terms, meaning "place" and "places," that literary criticism has borrowed directly from Greek. Some critics prefer the Latin equivalents, *locus-loci.* The Renaissance concept of the structure of the human mind pictured a vast series of ranked pigeonholes, like open mailboxes in a post office. Into each pigeonhole, learning stuffs a topic. These topics then become available to a person for consideration or for recombining as required. Those subjects that literature regularly treats are called *topoi* or *loci*. Many topoi have names, often in Latin, like *"locus amoenus"* (an amiable place, like the Garden of Eden) or *"vestigia"* (vestiges, like footprints in the sand). As poets and writers repeatedly treat such topoi in a wide variety of contexts, they acquire layers of both conventional and novel significance and contribute to the construction of ALLEGORY. For example, PETRARCH uses the topos of vestiges to suggest his adoration of Laura as he searches everywhere for some hint of her having passed by. At the same time, the same topos evokes an association with the footprints of Christ that might have remained after his passing. It is not necessary for a reader to recognize all topoi to understand or enjoy the work of a Renaissance author. Recognizing some topoi does, however, enrich one's experience of reading and contribute to one's appreciation of an author's talent. It also helps a reader understand how a text pays tribute to its predecessors by evoking their meanings in a kind of intertextual conversation. (See INTERTEXTUALITY.)

Some Renaissance authors, such as BEN JONSON in England, kept COMMONPLACE BOOKS, filled with entries that approximated on paper the topoi in the pigeonholes of the mind.

Bibliography

Petrarca, Francesco. *Petrarch's Songbook: Rerum vulgarium fragmenta.* Translated by James Wyatt Cook. Introduced by Germaine Warkentin. Binghamton, N.Y.: Center for Medieval and Renaissance Texts and Studies, 1999.

Salstad, M. Louise. *Text as Topos in Religious Literature of the Spanish Golden Age.* Chapel Hill: University of North Carolina Press, 1995.

Smith, Susan L. *The Power of Women: A Topos in Medieval Art and Literature.* Philadelphia: University of Pennsylvania Press, ca. 1995.

Tottel's *Miscellany* (*Songs and Sonnets*) (1557)

In 1557 there issued from the press of the English printer, Richard Tottel, the first and most widely influential of a series of collections containing the new poetry that a group of poets—principally noblemen grouped under the label "the COURTLY MAKERS"—were writing. Taking their models from Italy and the Continent, from PETRARCHAN lyric and HUMANIST discourse, poets like SIR THOMAS WYATT; HENRY HOWARD, THE EARL OF SURREY; THOMAS, LORD VAUX; and others less securely identifiable were represented in Tottle's pages.

The popularity with which Tottle's *Miscellany,* or more accurately his *Songs and Sonnets,* was received by an eager reading public spawned numerous imitators. Taken together these collections of verse helped establish the reputations of numerous early modern English poets.

Tourneur, Cyril (ca. 1575 or 1580–1626)

A skillful British poet, dramatist, civil servant, and elegist, Tourneur authored two surviving blank-verse tragedies: *THE REVENGER'S TRAGEDY* (1607) and *THE ATHEIST'S TRAGEDY* (1611). His play *The Nobleman,* now lost, was performed as a COURT ENTERTAINMENT twice in 1612.

Tourneur's first published poem, *The Transformed Metamorphosis* (1600), presents a rather confused satirical, sometimes PASTORAL, ALLEGORY that contains echoes of both EDMUND SPENSER's *FAERIE QUEENE* and his *Shepheard's Calendar.* On the one hand, Tourneur's poem decries and bitterly mocks the sorry state in which the human race finds itself. On the other hand, it complains that the poet himself is trapped in the same ignorance and vexation as the fallen world he pictures. Yet transformations continue throughout the work, and if evil can come from good, then good can also come from evil, so that in darkness one finds the prospect of light, and in a poetic wasteland the promise of renewal for both society and the poet.

That prospect of hopeful renewal disappears from the second poem attributed to Tourneur, *Laugh and Lie Down, or The World's Folly* (1605). Less original than *The Transformed Metamorphosis,* this allegorical presentation of the sad state of England draws inspiration from a variety of sources that suggest Tourneur's erudition: Spenser, Chaucer, Dante. Although it is a familiar sort of diatribe against human and particularly English foolishness, its employment of dialogue suggests a developing dramatist at work.

Ironically, the authorship of the play on which Tourneur's reputation as a dramatist principally rests, *The Revenger's Tragedy,* remains a matter of dispute, with THOMAS MIDDLETON also a candidate for authorship. Tourneur's biographer, Samuel Schuman, traces the technicalities of the argument and essentially calls it a draw.

The Atheist's Tragedy does not enjoy the same high critical regard as does its predecessor, but its authorship at least does not seem in doubt. It represents the last minute triumph of good after five acts of onstage evil.

As a writer of ELEGY, Tourneur is remembered, first, for his 604-line *A Funeral Poem on the Death of the Most Worthie and True Soldier, Sir Francis Vere* (1609). Vere had employed Tourneur as his secretary. Tourneur's next elegy took the form of CHARACTER WRITING. His "Character of Robert, Earl of Salisbury" (1612) mourned the earl's passing. Later that same year Tourneur penned "A Grief on the Death of Prince Henry," who had died on November 6th.

Thereafter Tourneur appears to have deserted both stagecraft and the poetic MUSE and returned to duties as a civil servant and diplomat. For reasons unknown he was arrested in September 1617 and jailed for over a month. He was released into the custody of Sir Edward Cecil, whose secretary he continued to be until at least October 8, 1625, when Tourneur participated in an unsuccessful attack on the Spanish city of Cadiz. Considered one of the mortally ill on the return voyage, Tourneur was abandoned on December 11, 1625, at Kinsale in Ireland. He died there on February 18, 1626.

Bibliography

Foakes, R. A. *Marston and Tourneur.* Harlow, U.K.: Longman Group, 1978.

Schuman, Samuel. *Cyril Tourneur.* Boston: Twayne Publishers, 1977.

Tourneur, Cyril. *The Revenger's Tragedy: Thomas Middleton; Cyril Tourneur.* Manchester, U.K., and New York: Manchester University Press, 1996.

———. *The Plays of Cyril Tourneur.* Edited by George Parfitt. Cambridge and New York: Cambridge University Press, 1978.

Tower of Myriad Mirrors, The (*Xiyoubu, Hsi Yu Pu*) Dong Yue; Tung Yüeh (ca. 1641)

A sequel to the Chinese masterpiece JOURNEY TO THE WEST, *The Tower of Myriad Mirrors* continues the fantastic adventures of one of its heroes, Monkey, whose activities one can take as an ALLEGORY representing inquisitive and irrepressible human intelligence. Dong Yue displays great originality in his short novel by weaving it from a dream that Monkey is supposed to have had about halfway through *Journey to the West.* Sometimes called, *More about the Pilgrimage, The Tower of Myriad Mirrors* enjoys a unique place among the novels of its era because it reflects the way that dreams operate in their sudden shifts to unconnected situations. The book is structured on the logic of dream life.

As the work opens, Monkey is trying to obtain a magic fan so he can blow out the fire on Flaming Mountain (an allegorical representation of the temptations of the flesh). In a parallel but illusory world lives Monkey's counterpart and evil doppelgänger, the Jing (Ching) Fish Spirit, a mackerel. Born at the same moment as Monkey, the spirit is one of several characters that allegorically represent aspects of human desire. The Jing Fish Spirit hypnotizes Monkey, and, while he under the spirit's spell, Monkey has a dream. He must ask the First Emperor of Qin (Ch'in) to loan him a bell that will enable him to remove Flaming Mountain.

Still under the spell and on his dream quest, Monkey finds himself meandering about in the Tower of Myriad Mirrors. As he regards himself in the mirrors' reflections, he sometimes looks into the future and sometimes into the past. The hero dreams that he flies through space and through time, occasionally landing unpredictably in the wrong century. At times he sees himself as the ruler of Hell. At other times he sees himself as a beautiful young woman. In that situation Monkey becomes Lady Yu, who reproves her overardent husband for kneeling before her to beg a smile.

The Master of Nothingness finally releases Monkey from his spell and instructs him concerning the nature of truth and illusion. Monkey must learn this principal lesson: all desire is only illusion. Desiring things is a vain and foolish enterprise. If Monkey can come to learn this, he can begin to perceive the truth that exists beyond desire.

To deliver its serious moral message *The Tower of Myriad Mirrors* draws on the great religious traditions of China: Buddhism, Confucianism, and Taoism. Its manner of presentation, however, displays both wit and SATIRE. Dong's biographer, Frederick P. Brandauer, suggests five main targets for the book's satirical attacks. Four of these involve social satire. First the imperial court is pictured as sleepy, stagnant, and essentially useless. Second, the positive and negative effects of the imperial examination system come under Dong's satirical scrutiny. The other two objects of social satire include the military establishment and traitors to China. Dong directs his moral satire against historical figures that allowed themselves to be dominated by their attachment to worldly things, as was Lady Yu's husband, General Xiangyu (Hsiang-Yü). Not only does Dong portray him as overly smitten with his wife, the author also draws the general as mightily impressed by his own exploits. He is always willing to recount them at great length.

The Tower of Myriad Mirrors is probably the best and most imaginative of a number of sequels that continued the story of *The Journey to the West*. A recently discovered copy of the 1641 edition contains 16 woodblock prints illustrating aspects of the story. A facsimile edition is available, and the prints are interesting even if one cannot read the Chinese text.

Bibliography

Brandauer, Frederick P. *Tung Yüeh*. Boston: Twayne Publishers, 1978.

Dong, Yue. *The Tower of Myriad Mirrors: A Supplement to Journey to the West*. Translated by Shuenfu Lin and Larry J. Schulz. Ann Arbor: Center for Chinese Studies, University of Michigan, 2000.

Mair, Victor H., ed. *The Columbia History of Chinese Literature*. New York: Columbia University Press, 2001.

Toxophilus Roger Ascham (1545)

Addressed by ASCHAM to King Henry VIII of England, *Toxophilus* is a treatise on archery modeled on the dialogues of CICERO. This work presents a discussion between Toxophilus, whose name means "one who loves the bow," and Philologus, "one who loves the word."

After apologizing to King Henry for not having written the book in Latin or Greek, and after defending his use of English on the grounds of its potential benefit to English readers, Ascham advises the king to require all Englishmen to become proficient in the use of the English long bow. Not only would universal training in wielding this armor-piercing weapon be useful in time of war, practicing with the bow, Ascham maintains, is also an "honest . . . pastime for the mind . . . wholesome for the body, not vile for great men . . . [nor] costly for poor men."

Beyond its implications for national policy, *Toxophilus* provides an early example of an effort to improve English prose style by being at the same time both scholarly and popular. Though it follows a classical model, it avoids INKHORN TERMS (unfamiliar borrowings from ancient tongues) while at the same time employing words of Greek and Latin derivation as appropriate to enrich a discourse that reflects good, plain, conversational English. (See ENGLISH LANGUAGE.) The work so pleased Henry VIII that he rewarded Ascham for the book with a pension.

Bibliography

Ascham, Roger. *Toxophilus*. Edited by Peter E. Medine. Tempe: Arizona Center for Medieval and Renaissance Studies, 2002.

tragedy

In its earliest manifestations in Europe, Egypt, and the Middle East, tragedy seems to have been associated with religious ritual, with the cycle of death and rebirth in the vegetative world, and with such deities as the Egyptian Osiris or such mythic figures as the Greek Adonis or the god Dionysus who were connected with that cycle and with the sacrifice of goats at Dionysian rites. *Tragedy* means "goat song."

Some argue that ancient Greek theatrical tragedy sprang partly from eulogies given at the funerals of influential people. One scenario suggests that the most interesting episodes of the lives of notable persons began to be acted out at graveside and attracted such large audiences that someone got the bright idea of staging the action in a roomier venue.

Early on, "tragedy" applied to any serious play, even those with happy endings such as Sophocles' play, *Philoctetes*. Together with Sophocles, Aeschylus and Euripides were the principal Greek tragedians. About 70 years after the death of Euripedes in 406 B.C.E., ARISTOTLE developed a theory of tragedy in his *POETICS*. He thought of tragic figures as persons who, owing to a tragic flaw, somehow contributed to their own downfall or destruction. The phrase, *tragic flaw* translates Aristotle's Greek word, "*HAMARTIA*." That word is a term used in archery. It means missing the target or what one aims at. It is the same word usually translated "sin" when it occurs in English versions of the Greek New Testament. So, to Aristotle, a tragic hero was a person whose judgment or character was flawed, but who was otherwise a person of some importance, with high morals and with intellect sufficient to her or his station and responsibilities.

Aristotle arrived at his definition of tragedy and his analysis of its elements empirically. That is, he attended the theater, watched many tragedies, and conducted an analysis of the way they seemed to operate. He noted that the action of tragic plays regularly took place in a 24 hour span, usually (but not always) occurred in a space limited by the distance one could travel in that time, and swept inescapably from beginning to end without interruption or remission. (This observation later became the basis for the Italian LUDOVICO CASTELVETRO's concept of the UNITIES of time, place, and action—a concept Aristotle himself never mentioned.) Aristotle's analysis proposed that the action be complete in itself and of a sufficient magnitude, that its language (always verse) be lofty. Because the flaw led to the protagonist's downfall, the tragic hero's situation had fi-

nally to reach a turning point (a *peripeteia*). This resulted in the hero's suffering in a way audience members identified with. That identification evoked in them the emotions of pity and fear, and the end of the play served to purge the audience of those emotions. The resultant CATHARSIS, or cleansing, left the audience members morally improved.

Over time, other theories developed. During the European medieval period, one notion of tragedy involved the fall of a person from a high station in life to a low one as the result of the operation of FORTUNE. For example, a person born a king who lost his kingdom would be considered a tragic figure. Another idea presupposed that tragedy was connected with the suffering caused by the bad behavior of autocratic rulers. With the European rediscovery of classical texts, however—particularly of Aristotle's *Poetics*—the definition of tragedy on the European continent shifted.

Swept up in the fascination of the rediscovery of ancient Roman and Greek texts that characterized Renaissance HUMANISM, some continental theorists like Castelvetro, took Aristotle's observations as virtual rules for the construction of tragedy, and some playwrights, such as the Frenchmen PIERRE CORNEILLE and JEAN RACINE, followed closely every neo-Aristotelian precept so as to please a learned, aristocratic audience whose tastes were partly formed on the basis of Castelvetro's view of Aristotle.

In England, native and Roman theatrical traditions took hold before knowledge of Aristotle became widespread. Particularly, native British theater of the Renaissance looked to the English religious drama of the Middle Ages, to BIBLICAL TROPES, and to INTERLUDES (entertainments during banquets). Also, the bloody tragedies of the Roman playwright SENECA, some of whose plays had survived through the Middle Ages, provided models for English playwrights such as THOMAS KYD and GEORGE CHAPMAN. Others, however, contributed to emerging British traditions of tragedy that concerned themselves very little if at all with Aristotelian precepts. Thus the most celebrated Elizabethan tragedians of England largely ignored the unities that some of their continental counterparts regarded as rules. CHRISTOPHER MARLOWE and WILLIAM SHAKESPEARE both wrote tragedies whose action required years and whose characters traveled far. Shakespeare and others frequently inserted scenes that interrupted the inexorable sweep of the action, perhaps to appeal to the taste of those members of his mainly working-class audience who didn't know or care about neo-Aristotelian requirements. Among these scenes, famously, is "The Drunken Porter Scene," Act II, scene iii of MACBETH, which has long been tarred with the dubious brush of COMIC RELIEF. Whereas ancient Greek and the early Renaissance French playwrights avoided depicting violence on stage, the British were much less reticent. Marlowe's character Barabas, in THE JEW OF MALTA, gets boiled in oil in full view of the audience.

In Spain, too, native traditions and a concern with innovation and stagecraft took precedence over Aristotle *à la* Castelvetro. Whereas Greek characters often had to contend with their fates, or were overcome by the tragic flaw of hubris, or pride, Spanish tragedy often developed a conflict between honor and love, as in PEDRO CALDERÓN DE LA BARCA's *Love, Honor, and Power*. In Asia and the Islamic world, with the exception of the Japanese No Drama, a dramatic tradition that developed in the 14th and 15th centuries, tragedy in the theatrical sense discussed here did not usually appear in our period. An exception to that generalization occurs in the Bengali verse opera Beautiful Malua (*Sundari Malua*), sometimes attributed to the 16th-century Indian female poet CHANDRABATI. Malua, the heroine, is driven to suicide in tragic circumstances.

Bibliography

Shipley, Joseph T. *Dictionary of World Literary Terms.* Boston: The Writer, 1970.

Tragedy of Iñes de Castro, The Antonio Ferreira (1598)

Based on historical events in the life of a 14th-century Portuguese woman who was first the mistress and then the secret second wife and mother of the children of Prince Pedro, heir to the Portuguese throne, the verse tragedy *Castro* represents the high point of FERREIRA's dramatic and poetic achievement.

The play centers on the innocence of the title character and on the quandary of King Alfonso IV when he allows his advisers to convince him that, for reasons of state, de Castro must be put to death. The widowed Prince Pedro had a child by his first marriage—a lad who will presumably succeed him as king someday. King Alfonso's advisers fear—not without good reason—that, should Prince Pedro openly acknowledge de Castro as his wife, the stage will be set for civil strife between the supporters of her offspring and those of the heir apparent. The advisers therefore consider her judicial execution a prudent course.

In the play, Iñes de Castro appears as a wholly admirable woman devoted to the prince and his children and loyal to the king. King Alfonso is torn between the advice of his counselors and his admiration for de Castro. At one moment he is convinced of the necessity for her death and at the next assures her that she "will live as long as God wills."

But the fateful portents of disaster with which Ferreira has filled Iñes's dreams are unavoidable. The king again changes his mind and leaves Iñes's fate in the hands of his advisers, disclaiming his own responsibility. This of course seals her fate.

Ferreira emulates Greek models of tragedy in his play and observes many of their conventions. A chorus that represents public opinion discourses with the prince and the king. After the execution the chorus judges that, while the king's counselors were loyal, and the king zealous in his duty, his action was cruel. Observing the unities of time, place, and action that the Italian HUMANIST LUDOVICO CASTELVETRO had characterized as Aristotelian requirements for good tragedy, the play's action occupies a single day, focuses exclusively on events surrounding the heroine's situation and death, and takes place within the precincts of the palace. The execution of the heroine by beheading takes place off stage, and the fifth act is consumed entirely by Prince Pedro's return from afar, his learning the news of his beloved's execution and its circumstances, and his expressions of his grief and devotion.

In history, but not on the stage, the real Prince Pedro joined Iñes's brothers in a rebellion against King Alfonso. Eventually, however, king and prince were reconciled, and an orderly succession occurred after Alfonso's death in 1357.

Bibliography

Ferreira, Antonio. *The Tragedy of Iñez de Castro.* Edited and translated by John R. C. Martin. Coimbra, Portugal: University of Coimbra Press, 1987.

Tragedy of Miriam, The Elizabeth Tanfield Cary, viscountess Falkland (1613)

The first verse tragedy by an English woman, *The Tragedy of Miriam* also enjoys the distinction of being the first original play printed in England to have been penned by a woman. Drawing its interlinked plots from THOMAS LODGE's translation of the First-century historian Josephus's *Antiquities of the Jews* (1602), the play focuses on the intrigues at the court of King Herod and on relationships between Herod's second wife, Miriam, his first wife, Doris, and between Miriam and Herod's hateful, murderous, and self-centered sister, Salome.

The main plot deals with the relationship between Miriam and her husband. Herod's consuming passion for Miriam has spawned the psychotic fantasy that, should he die, someone else would enjoy her favors. Preferring her death to that eventuality, Herod leaves secret instructions that, in the event of his death, she is to be executed.

Herod, descended from Esau who sold his birthright for a mess of pottage, owes his throne both to the patronage of Mark Anthony of Rome and to his own bloody determination to destroy any potential rivals. Miriam herself is a princess of the royal house of Israel—the Maccabees. Her brother, Aristobolus, was the rightful heir to the throne, but Herod has had him and his grandfather, Hircanus, who was next in the line of royal succession, murdered.

Thus Miriam is caught in an emotional trap. She has deeply loved her husband—indeed still loves him. She is the mother of his second family, and her eldest son stands to inherit the throne of Israel. At the same time she grieves for her brother and grandfather and rightly blames Herod for their deaths. Her distress at his cruelty and her desire for vengeance leads her, on another emotional level, to hate Herod and wish him dead.

A false report of Herod's death in Rome has reached Judea, and, as the play opens, Miriam, alone on stage, recites a soliloquy that touchingly reveals the emotional quandary in which she finds herself. Given the way she blamed Herod for her brother's death, she is surprised at the depth of her grief on hearing the report of her husband's death.

Miriam's wonderful soliloquy reveals much about Elizabeth Cary's poetic and dramatic artistry. Cary makes Miriam's emotional ambivalence totally credible and draws the audience at once to empathize with the play's protagonist. The quality of the verse, moreover, is stellar. Composing in perfectly crafted, iambic pentameter quatrains that rhyme abab, Cary almost instantly convinces her readers or viewers that they are in the presence of a major poetic talent. Though the quatrain remains her principal vehicle throughout the play, she varies her stanzaic forms, sometimes using rhymed couplets when a speech is short and sometimes employing sestettes rhyming ababcc. Cary reveals a preference for fairly lengthy set speeches. In the hands of a lesser poet, this practice could ruin the play, but the grace of Cary's versifying draws the reader on. It may well be the case that Cary thought of this work as a CLOSET DRAMA rather than one intended for public performance.

The other subplots begin unfolding in the first two acts. Miriam and her friend Alexandra have been discussing Herod's reported demise when his sister Salome appears and exchanges accusations and insults with Miriam. We subsequently learn that Salome has colluded in the death of her first husband, Josephus, to free her to marry her second, Constabarus. We also discover that she has now tired of him and wishes to be free to marry an Arabian, Silleus. To accomplish that end, Salome takes into her own hands the Hebrew law that permitted husbands to divorce wives, but not vice versa. When in Act I, scene 6, Constabarus reproves her for spending time alone with Silleus, she announces that she is divorcing her husband whether he is willing or not. Constabarus concludes that he is well rid of her and that he is better off than the murdered Josephus. Nonetheless, his final soliloquy is full of foreboding. He reflects on Miriam's innocence and on Salome's hatred for her sister-in-law. He speculates that, had Herod returned, Salome would have found a way to work Miriam's ruin.

At the end of each act, Cary introduces the device of the ancient Greek tragedians, the chorus. Typically, the chorus represents the views of the public at large. Tragedians employed choruses as well to focus the audience's attention on important issues in the act just past and to draw moral lessons from the drama—a sort of review session. Cary's chorus is no different. At the end of Act I, it focuses on the moral depravity of persons, like Salome, who live only for delight, and it reminds the audience of Miriam's ambivalence in grieving that Herod is dead. Were he to live again, the chorus says, she would grieve at that as well.

Act II begins with the prenuptial pledges of Herod's brother, Pharoas, and his beloved, the commoner Graphina. It is clear that their planned wedding would not receive the king's approval. Scene ii presents a discussion between Constabarus and the two sons of Babus. They predict that the news of Herod's death is false and that he will rule in Jerusalem once more. Scene iii introduces Herod's first wife Doris in conference with Antipater, the incestuous son of Herod and Salome. They are already plotting to supplant Miriam's children as royal heirs apparent. Scene iv details a quarrel between the supplanted Constabarus and his replacement in Salome's affection, Silleus. Silleus works hard to provoke a fight over Salome, but Constabarus doesn't consider her worth fighting about. Finally Silleus gets his rival to fight by calling Constabarus a coward. Constabarus quickly gets the better of Silleus, wounding him severely. They stop the fight and Constabarus helps Silleus home to have his wounds dressed, and the two adversaries pledge friendship.

This summary puts in place most of the play's major threads. One other involves Miriam's learning of Herod's unpleasant instructions concerning her future should he die. It is a tribute to Cary's literary talent and her sense of what holds audience interest that she can make so many elements of plot credibly converge.

Herod's return alive, of course, pulls all the disparate threads together. He is overjoyed to find Miriam alive despite his instructions to the contrary, and her ambivalence toward him reasserts itself as she reproaches her husband for her brother's death. A standard feature of revenge tragedies—a poisoned cup—now appears on Salome's orders. Its bearer, Salome's servant, first says it is a love potion Miriam has ordered for her husband. Then, however, the servant reveals the cup is poisoned. He alleges that Miriam has learned of Herod's instructions concerning her in the event of his death. Herod is convinced that Miriam is trying to poison him and, on Salome's advice (Act IV, scene vii) rashly gives orders for Miriam's beheading. Before that sentence can be carried out, Doris and Miriam confer in a scene where Doris vents her anger at being supplanted and curses both Miriam and her children.

In keeping with the conventions of Greek tragedy, Miriam's death does not take place upon the stage. Rather a messenger reports it to Herod. Repenting of his rashness, Herod at first hopes that Miriam still lives. Then he snatches at straws, asking if there is no medical or magical art to restore her life. "Is there no tricke to make her breathe againe?" he asks.

"Her body is divided from her head," the messenger replies—perhaps the artistic low point of the play.

The messenger ends the act with a long soliloquy that predicts Herod's death and with the chorus's reflection on what has passed.

Cary's play throughout generally observed the conventions of Greek tragedy as LUDOVICO CASTELVETRO had interpreted them. The action takes place in a single place in a single day and sweeps from beginning to end with an admirable unity of action—especially considering all the lines of subplot.

Bibliography

Ferguson, Margaret W., et al., eds. *The Tragedy of Miriam the Fair Queene of Jewry: Works by and Attributed to Elizabeth Cary.* Aldershot, U.K.: Scolar Press, 1997.

tragedy of the blood or Senecan tragedy

A kind of tragedy popular on the English stage in the 16th and 17th centuries, the tragedy of the blood originated in imitations of plays by the first-century Roman statesman and playwright, Lucius Annacus Seneca. Also called revenge tragedy, such plays left the stage strewn with corpses as the result of a principal character's obsession with getting even for a grievous wrong suffered at the hands of his or her enemies.

Thomas Sackville and Thomas Norton wrote the first such blank verse tragedy in English, Gorboduc (1561). Other notable plays of the sort include Cyril Tourneur's admirable The Revenger's Tragedy (1607 and his The Atheist's Tragedy (1611). In the latter play, Tourneur modifies the type by counseling patience and leaving revenge to Divine Providence. William Shakespeare's Hamlet brings the subgenre to what is likely its highest point of artistic achievement in Renaissance England.

Les Tragiques (The tragic ones) Agrippa d'Aubigné (1616)

Begun some five decades before its publication, Les Tragiques draws its inspiration from the bloody religious disputes that ripped the political fabric of France in the 16th century. A long epic poem (9,302 lines plus a 414-line preface), it shares with du Bartas's The divine weeks and works (La Semaine ou la Création du monde, 1578) the distinction of being one of the two major Protestant poems of the French Renaissance.

Begun after d'Aubigné had been very seriously wounded in the fifth of the French religious wars in June 1577, the poem provides a personal and emotional expression of his responses to the unjust and bloody persecution of French Protestants at the hands of the French Crown and the Roman Catholic establishment. That persecution had continued throughout the 16th century but especially from the 1550s onward and most particularly after the St. Bartholomew's Day massacre of August 24–25, 1572. That massacre targeted the French Protestant nobil-

ity for death while they were guests at the wedding of Margaret de Valois and Henri of Navarre.

The French queen mother, Catherine de' Medici had conspired with Catholic nobles to assassinate Admiral Gaspard de Coligny, the powerful Protestant adviser to Catherine's son, King Charles IX. The attempt failed; angry Huguenots demanded an investigation. Fearing her complicity would be exposed, Catherine plotted to exterminate the Huguenot nobility who were celebrating the wedding in Paris. Her son joined in this plot. Because Henri of Navarre was second in line for the French throne, he himself was spared, but even his personal retainers were murdered. Though some, like Salluste du Bartas escaped, the violence spread and Huguenot tradesmen and shopkeepers also became victims. Estimates of the murdered ranged between 2,000 and 70,000, depending on the religious views of the estimators. Historians put the figure at something more than 3,000.

To console his fellow religionists, to give his own feelings tongue, and to record the sufferings and heroism of the Protestant martyrs, d'Aubigné undertook the composition of his epic. Perhaps reflecting the seven days of creation as recounted in Scripture, Les Tragiques contains an introduction and seven parts. The introduction sets out the author's purpose; he wants to move the reader to share his feelings. The first book of the seven, entitled Misères (the troubles or miseries), invokes both divine inspiration and Melpomene, the Muse of tragedy, to guide his pen. The muse speaks to a France personified as a monstrous and putrefying mother whose children are at war with one another. The kings have become the wolves and have turned the world and the civil order upside down. D'Aubigné excoriates Catherine de' Medici and the cardinal of Lorraine, identifying them with such Old Testament villains as Jezebel and Achitophel and accusing them of impure lives and practicing the black arts. The Jesuits come in for a generous share of d'Aubigné's vitriol. The book ends with a prayer that God will exact retribution for the slaughter and mistreatment of his people.

The second book, entitled Princes, is a verse satire on the satanic corruption of rulers who are supposed to be the temporal viceroys of God on earth. Like all good satire, it seeks to reform the morals of the satirized by exposing their vices to ridicule. The rulers confuse appearances with reality, and they pretend to piety while they undermine the common good. Pretending to operate in the interests of the people, the rulers instead oppress the ruled. D'Aubigné then turns the lens of his scrutiny on the private vices of the rulers: illicit sex, sodomy, and sumptuous living while the people starve. A day of retribution, however, will be coming.

The third section, *La chambre dorée* (The gilded chamber), opens in Heaven where God receives a report on the sorry state of French affairs from a somewhat battered and tattered Justice, Piety, and Peace, who have been sorely mistreated in France. God decides to conduct an inspection tour of the heavily gilded French Palace of Justice. He finds it constructed on the skeletal remains of the dead and held together by mortar made from mixing the ashes and blood of Protestant martyrs. D'Aubigné then proceeds to draw a sometimes tedious picture of the tutelary deity of the palace—ironically Injustice—and of the 27 vices who attend her. Since He is on Earth anyway, God decides to call in on Spain where He becomes distinctly annoyed with the INQUISITION. To predict the coming destruction of the forces of Roman Catholic evil, d'Aubigné describes a triumph, which is a kind of procession. At its head marches the wise Themis, the goddess of Justice. Following her come the ancient Greeks, the Persians, the Romans, the French of antiquity, and a small group of contemporary French. Before them the unjust flee, and d'Aubigné once more predicts a coming day of judgment.

Les Feux (The fires), the fourth book of d'Aubigné's epic, often follows a popular history of the martyrs by Crespin and sometimes supplies d'Aubigné's own examples of those who died for their Protestant faith. In any case, God now reviews a procession of martyrs whose deaths d'Aubigné describes in fearsomely graphic detail. Having seen enough, an angry and disgusted God departs for Heaven in a flurry of imagery that invokes several sections of the Old and New Testaments.

At the beginning of the fifth book, *Les Fers* (Those bound in irons), Satan pays a call on God and asks permission to test the firmness of God's

Protestants. God agrees, and Satan swoops down to Earth, where he takes over the body of Catherine de' Medici, and recruits allies in the royal court, the church, the law, the Vatican, and elsewhere. An ALLEGORY featuring Bellona, the goddess of war, follows. This sets the stage for a sickeningly graphic description of the horrors of the St. Bartholomew's Day massacre, the ensuing warfare, and a picture of the rivers of France clogged with the bodies and choked with the blood of the dead of both sides. A personified Ocean complains that he doesn't wish to be burdened with receiving the blood and corpses of those responsible for starting these horrors—that is, the Roman Catholic royalty and nobility and their retainers and supporters.

The sixth book, *Vengeances,* opens with the poet's praying that God will free him from worldly dross so he will be worthy to accomplish God's high purposes in making d'Aubigné his instrument. That done, d'Aubigné draws an analogy between the fratricidal atrocities of St. Bartholomew's Day and the Bible's account of Cain and Abel with its archetypal example of the murder of brother by brother. Then the poet leads the reader through biblical and church history and example after example of treachery, murder, and martyrdom. God uses such means, the poet assures the reader, to test the faithful, but God's justice also demands a fitting punishment for the perpetrators of such heinous acts.

In *Jugement,* the seventh book of his epic, d'Aubigné begins by again calling on God to exercise his wrath on those who oppose his will so that the faithful will have reason to fear the Lord. The poet fulminates against his former ally, Henri de Navarre, who had recanted his Protestantism and turned Catholic in part to save his own life and in part to assure his succession to the French throne. He then turns his apocalyptic vision to the last judgment, to the survival of reason in the faithful, to the terrible punishments of the wicked, and to the joys of Heaven for the saved. His vision of Heaven and the rigors of having described what he has seen having exhausted the poet, he faints into God's lap, and the poem ends.

Good modern editions of the entire work and of selections from it are available in French, but only summaries of it have as yet appeared in English.

Bibliography

Aubigné, Agrippa d'. *Les tragiques.* Edited by Jean-Raymond Fanlo. Paris: H. Champion, 1995. [Critical edition.]

Aubigné, Agrippa d'. *Les tragiques.* Edited by I. D. McFarlane. London, Athlone Press, 1970. [Selections.]

Cameron, Keith. *Agrippa d'Aubigné.* Boston: Twayne Publishers, 1977.

Traherne, Thomas (1637–1674)

Writing both poems and prose, Traherne continued and perhaps wrote the last chapter in the traditions of METAPHYSICAL POETS such as JOHN DONNE and HENRY VAUGHAN. Traherne also initiated a prose form that he called *centuries.* Each one contained about a hundred religious meditations in prose.

A cleric himself, Traherne had been educated at Brasenose College, Oxford, and had served for a time as a parish priest before he became the chaplain to the powerful Sir Orlando Bridgeman, Lord Keeper of the Great Seal. Traherne continued in that post until his death.

He is best remembered for the spiritual nostalgia with which he celebrates childhood—a very uncommon viewpoint in his times when children were rarely regarded sentimentally. That celebration has inevitably led to comparisons between Traherne's literary spirituality and that of the later English poets, William Blake and William Wordsworth. Traherne, however, develops an evocative style uniquely his own in his moving reflections.

Comparisons with the later poets partly arise from the fact that Traherne's religious works in prose and verse lay unpublished until the late 19th and early 20th centuries.

translation in the Renaissance epoch

In many ways, translation was at the heart of much that defined the European Renaissance. Translation also characterized the BHAKTI devotional movement in India as it developed in bringing Sanskrit and Dravidian texts into the Indian vernacular languages of the 16th and 17th centuries. Translation contributed as well to the spread of Indian and Chinese cultures into their respective and often overlapping spheres of Asian influence. During the age of exploration translation acquainted Europeans with the pre– and-post–European contact literatures, written and oral, of the Americas. Translation performed the same service for the oral compositions of POLYNESIAN OCEANIA during the age of exploration. In the Muslim world, 16th- and 17th-century retellings and translations of traditional stories, often originally in Persian or Arabic, into Turkish, say, or into Syrian became one of the principal unifying forces of Muslim literary culture.

Although the person who is often credited for beginning the European Renaissance, FRANCIS PETRARCH, could not read Greek, the fact that he carried a Greek manuscript of Plato in his saddlebags evinced both his desire and his never fulfilled intention to learn to do so. His younger contemporary Giovanni Boccaccio, however, did learn Greek. So did a number of other northern European and Italian HUMANISTS, including RUDOLPHUS AGRICOLA, LEONARDO BRUNI, and MARSILIO FICINO. Among these, the last two named translated the known works of Plato available into the Latin that all educated persons could read. The Belgian physician and professor at the University of Padua, Andreas Vesalius, also prepared a Latin translation of many of the works of the Greek physician Galen. That work contributed to modern medicine by exposing Galen's errors and the superiority of the experimental method.

From the perspective of many Renaissance Christians, especially those who felt displeased by papal and episcopal edicts against translating the Scriptures into vernacular languages, the most important of Renaissance European translation projects concerned making the text of the BIBLE available in the vernacular languages. In this respect as well the principles of criticizing and emending ancient texts that LORENZO VALLA developed led to improved methods of establishing texts that proved influential among biblical translators such as DESIDERIUS ERASMUS, WILLIAM TYNDALE, MARTIN LUTHER, and the team of translators under the auspices of Cardinal Francisco Jiménez de Cisneros at the University of Alcalá in Spain as they prepared the COMPULTENSIAN POLYGLOT BIBLE.

Translation was also responsible for spreading Renaissance culture across national borders as translators made new works written either in Latin or in the then modern languages of Europe accessible in other tongues. This process began in Italy and moved north, arriving latest on the Scandinavian Peninsula. A new style of poetry, written in the manner of Petrarch, became a pan-European phenomenon as translations and imitations of the poet's work appeared. Plays composed in Spain or Italy soon appeared in French or English translations. The development of printing created a readership as well as an audience for vernacular works, and the possibility of a mass market for books made it possible for authors and for translators to make a living. Many capable writers who had received a humanistic education continued to write in NEO-LATIN, particularly in the 16th century. Some, such as SIR (ST.) THOMAS MORE, felt they were addressing an international audience that would find Latin more accessible than their native tongues.

But translation made its influence felt vertically as well as horizontally, and works like More's soon found their way into the vernaculars among a new readership that spoke no Latin but wanted to read in the tongues they knew. Translation in Europe, then, became a principal means for spreading new cultural norms both across political and linguistic borders and among persons literate only in the languages they spoke. It also brought Jewish thought into the matrix of Renaissance thinking—and vice versa.

The age of exploration brought learned European missionaries into contact with persons more and less literate in the tongues they spoke. Such contacts resulted in Europeans' becoming familiar with Native American texts in the translations of people like Brother BERNARDINO DE SAHAGÚN, and a reader of postcontact Incan kingship drama like *THE PLAY OF OLLANTAY* (*AFU OLLANTAY*) will be hard pressed not to think that some of the conventions of Spanish drama did not find their way into the native art form.

Translations of ancient, venerated texts in India like the MAHABHARATA or the RAMAYANA or of stories about Krishna and his beloved cowgirls, the GOPIS, also occurred on the Indian subcontinent as new literary vernaculars emerged such as Hindi, Bengali, Rajastani or the two-score other languages now officially spoken in India. Many more that are not official, of course, are in fact spoken. Many if not most of these translations took place in the context of the spread of the fervent worship of Vishnu and the other deities associated with him. The translations of ancient religious texts in India were often transcreations that emphasized new values: emotionalism in place of intellectualism, social equity in place of caste hierarchy, an emerging, if hard to come by, place for women in the social scheme of things, and an emphasis on purity of heart that was in some unconnected ways analogous to the emphases developed by the writings of convinced Protestants in Europe.

Indian devotional works found their way in translation into China via the translation efforts of Buddhist scholars. The Chinese, however, had an ancient literature of their own and a means for printing it long before movable type became a reality for Europeans. Chinese literature had, of course, heavily influenced the literary efforts both of Japan and of Korea. In Korea, in fact, writers until the mid-15th century composed principally in Chinese. That situation changed abruptly with the invention of the Korean alphabet in the mid 1400s. Based on Arabic script, a method for representing Korean sparked not only a brushfire of Korean composition, but also a good deal of translation and borrowing from pre-exiting Chinese literature. A prime example is HŎ KYUN's story *HONG KIL-DONG*. It mimics many narrative elements of Chinese fiction.

In Turkey especially the translation of Persian and Arabic stories, some of them both biblical and Koranic—such as the story of Potiphar's wife—helped cement the intellectual bonds that united the Muslim world.

Trickster of Seville, The (*Burlador de Sevilla*) Tirso de Molina (early 1620s)

In this prototype of the Don Juan or Don Giovanni story, the motivation of the lead character differs markedly from that of his counterpart in the more familiar Mozart opera. Whereas Mozart's

Don Giovanni is motivated by seemingly insatiable sexual appetites and an unrestrained sense of entitlement, Don Juan in TIRSO DE MOLINA'S original version is instead motivated by the satisfaction of having tricked and dishonored his victims. If Don Giovanni is an unrepentant sinner, Don Juan seems Satanic in his seductions. Tirso's biographer, Margaret Wilson puts it this way: "[Don Juan] is the enemy of light . . . he extinguishes the light of honor in his victims." Tirso always represents Don Juan as a creature of the night. Wilson interprets the Don's longing for nightfall as a foreshadowing of his own approaching physical and spiritual death.

Some of the women tricked in the play are themselves hardly models of comportment: Ana and Isabella are ready targets for Don Juan's blandishments and to a degree participate in their own falls. Aminta, a country girl whom Don Juan seduces on her wedding day, though she is short on brains, also fails in respecting her betrothed husband, Batricio, enough to resist Don Juan.

Two characters most attract the audience's sympathy in Tirso's play: the first is Don Juan's servant, Catalinón. He sees where his master is headed and tries unsuccessfully to warn him against his wicked ways. The other is the ambassador to Lisbon, Don Gonzalo. Killed by Don Juan, it is his living statue that appears in the final scene to speed the reprobate trickster on his way to Hell.

The play sounds a solemn warning, reminding the audience that God is just and that retribution awaits persons who prey upon the weak and on the easily misled. As an ordained theologian, Tirso took seriously in this play as in many others the dramatic imperative both to please and to instruct.

Bibliography

Molina, Tirso de. *Don Juan of Seville.* Translated by Lynne Alvarez. New York: Theatre Communications Group, ca. 1989.

———. *The Last Days of Don Juan.* Adapted by Nick Dear. Bath, U.K.: Absolute Classics, 1990.

Wilson, Margaret. *Tirso de Molina.* Boston: Twayne Publishers, 1977.

Tristan L' Hermite (François L'Hermite) (1601–1655)

A poet, novelist, and playwright who both wrote comedy and tragedy, Tristan L'Hermite (a pseudonym) belonged to the generation of tragedians who succeeded the French HUMANIST playwrights. Born François L'Hermite to Pierre L'Hermite and his wife Ysabeau Miron, François came from an illustrious but not very wealthy family. His father was the lord of Soliers. This connection stood him in good stead, for before 1609 King Henry IV of France took little François into his inner circle as a page, playmate, and classmate of his son, the duc de Verneuil. As a result François received a royal education. He continued in this role until, as he alleges in his partly autobiographical, partly fictional novel, *Le Page disgracié* (The disgraced page, 1643), he wounded someone in a fit of pique and fled the court and France for England, where he stayed until he worked his way back to France via Scotland and Norway around 1617.

On his return, he first found employment with the poet and dramatist Nicholas de Sainte-Marthe, and then as a librarian with his employer's uncle, Scévole de Sainte-Marthe. After about two years in this post, he moved on to work for the marquis de Villars and then the duc de Mayenne. During a royal visit to the duke in 1620, King Louis XIII recognized his brother's former playmate. The king brought François into his own service and, the following year, passed him along to his obstreperous brother, Gaston d'Orléans. Under Gaston's patronage, which was interrupted at intervals, François's literary career began to flourish, though, owing to Gaston's parsimony, François hardly became wealthy. Finally, at Gaston's behest, he left Gaston's service entirely around 1645. He then briefly became the lover of the Duchess of Chalnes, but by this time he had developed tuberculosis and no longer had the strength to accompany the duchess on her travels. In addition to that physical affliction, he also suffered from severe mood swings, sometimes finding himself elated, but more often, as it seems, depressed.

Fairly early on François adopted the penname *Tristan,* which identified him among the knowledgeable as the descendent of celebrated ancestors.

Under that soubriquet he published a wide range of writings. These included, first, a libretto: *Vers du ballet pour Monsieur Frère du Roi* (Verses of a ballet for *Monsieur* the king's brother, 1626). [*Monsieur* was the traditional title for French kings' eldest brothers. They were next in line of succession until a male heir appeared.] A lengthy triumph of descriptive verse, *La mer* (The sea), followed in 1628. The collection that brought him lasting poetic fame came next: *Les Plaintes d'Acante* (The lamentations of Acante, 1633). He wrote this series of poems bemoaning a lover's sufferings not on his own account, but rather as a stand-in for the Duke of Bouillon, who had fallen head over heels for Mademoiselle de Bergh. Whether or not the poems contributed to the duke's success, they appealed to the general public. They went through an edition a year for the next three years.

The year 1636 saw the triumph that established Tristan L'Hermite's reputation as a playwright, his very first verse play, a historical tragedy, *Mariane*. Perhaps he had learned of ELIZABETH TANFIELD CARY, FIRST VISCOUNTESS FALKLAND's tragedy on the same subject, THE TRAGEDY OF MIRIAM (1613), during his self-imposed exile in England. If not the story was widely known in any case: The usurping Jewish king Herod marries a princess, Mariane or Miriam, from the Maccabean royal line that he has displaced. When he has to travel to Rome, Herod's jealousy prompts him to leave orders for Mariane's execution in the event of his death. He cannot stand the idea of her taking another husband. In his absence Mariane learns of his order and blames him aloud. Her sentiments are grossly exaggerated and reported to Herod by her enemies. He orders her beheaded and, too late, repents of his rashness. Playgoers flocked to see *Mariane;* almost 90 performances were staged by 1703, and the play went through 10 printed editions in the 17th century. Its profits, regrettably, did not line Tristan's pockets.

A much less successful verse tragedy, *Panthée,* followed, appearing on the stage in 1637 or 1638. Cirus captures Panthée, wife of Abradate, in battle and leaves her in the care of a trusted friend, Araspe. Panthée must reject Araspe's advances and suffer his threats of forcing her. She appeals to Cirus and convinces him to become allied with Abradate. In the next battle, however, Abradate falls. Panthée takes her own life on her husband's body, and Araspe, who really loved her, commits suicide.

MOLIÈRE's acting company, the Illustre Théâtre, often performed Tristan's plays. This was the case for Tristan's next two historical, verse tragedies: *La mort de Sénèque* (The death of Seneca, 1644) and *La mort de Chrispe* (The death of Chrispe, 1645). No record exists that Tristan's last verse tragedy, *Osman* (1646–47)—a piece of Orientalia based on Ottoman Turkish history—was ever staged.

Only once did Tristan L'Hermite try his hand at TRAGICOMEDY. His *La Folie du sage* (The wise man's folly, 1645) seems loosely related to the real-life, swashbuckling adventures of Tristan's sometime patron, Gaston d'Orleans, who rebelled against his brother, King Louis XIII; married against his sovereign's wishes, fought and lost, and, as a result, was separated from his wife from 1633 to 1643. They were reunited when the king died. The parallels between this actual scenario and Tristan's appear more directly in the determination of the characters than in the action of the play. The play draws its moral from real life: before true love even royalty must bow down. The play enjoyed a brief success. Tristan also tried his hand at a PASTORAL DRAMA, *Amaryllis* (1652). This work adapted a play by another to the pastoral mode. In his last play *La Parasite* (1653), Tristan turned for inspiration to the Italian COMMEDIA DELL'ARTE. Using its STOCK CHARACTERS and broadly incorporating the spirit of the Italian comedy into its fabric, even as his tortured lungs gave out, Tristan gave the world a jewel of a comedy that is RABELAISian in spirit and the equal of the comedies of Molière.

Another collection of Tristan's poems appeared in 1638, *Les Amours* (The loves), which expanded on the 1633 edition of *Les Plaintes*. Sprinkled throughout his collections among his many serious poems a reader finds a number of riotously funny, burlesque poems that seem to reflect his more somber poems from a comic point of view, distorting them, as his biographer Claude Abraham suggests, like a mirror in a funhouse.

The following year (1639) saw the publication of *La Lyre* (The lyre). Tristan also published a miscellaneous collection of his letters in 1642, and, in 1648, his collection, *Vers héroïques* (Heroic poems). Beyond this, if the work next mentioned is really his (the attribution seems doubtful), Tristan penned a vast and scholarly tome on cosmography: *Principes de Cosmographie* (Principles of cosmography, 1637). Finally Tristan occasionally included pious poems in his various collections, and, in 1646, he addressed his attention specifically to a religious topic, namely, the Office of the Virgin Mary, in his work: *Office de la Sainte Vierge* (Office of the Holy Virgin).

In 1655, the poet's lungs failed him at last. Several works, however, including a new edition of *La Mariane* and the first published text of *Osman,* appeared posthumously.

Bibliography

Abraham, Claude K. *The Strangers: The Tragic World of Tristan L'Hermite.* Gainesville: University of Florida Press, 1966.

———. *Tristan L'Hermite.* Boston: Twayne Publishers, 1980.

Tudor

The family name of the monarchs of England beginning with Henry VII (born: 1457; ruled 1485–1509). Succeeding him in the Tudor line were his son, Henry VIII (born 1491; ruled 1509–47), grandson, Edward VI (born 1537; ruled 1547–53), and granddaughters, Mary I (born 1516; ruled 1553–58), and ELIZABETH I (born 1533; ruled 1558–1603). Used as a literary term, *Tudor* describes works written and authors who flourished under any of the monarchs in the line. Works written and writers who flourished under the last of the Tudor monarchs, Elizabeth I, are often alternately labeled *Elizabethan*. NICHOLAS UDALL, for instance, is a Tudor writer. EDMUND SPENSER and his EPIC, *THE FAERIE QUEENE,* are both Elizabethan.

Tukārāma (1608–ca. 1650)

A saint and a poet in the Marathi and Hindi LANGUAGES OF INDIA, Tukārāma is the generally acknowledged master of the ABHANGA form. In these short and pithy verses Tukārāma conveyed impor-

tant religious and ethical ideas in a form at once easy to understand and laden with emotional power. As a result, when taken all together, the 5,000 or so *abhanga*s that the poet composed form a kind of popular Scripture. They convey in a way that common people can grasp the essence of the BHAKTI devotional movement that Tukārāma helped foster throughout Maharashtra.

Born to a family of moneylenders, Tukārāma married and became a father. In 1630, however, both his wife and child starved to death in a great famine. Tormented by the loss, he devoted himself to a period of mystical contemplation whose outcome was an experience of unity with the infinite so intense that he could hardly bear it. Many of his poems attempt to convey that intensity of experience.

A social and religious progressive, Tukārāma had little patience with religious hierarchies, the domination of the priestly classes, or the Indian system of caste.

Throughout the villages of Maharastra to this day one can hear the *abhanga*s of Tukārāma on the lips of the people as they go about their daily tasks. His *abhanga*s have been gathered together in a collection containing 4,500 examples. Though some of these are doubtless interpolations of work by other hands, many of the verses in his ABHANGA GATHA (Collection of *abhanga*s) are both undoubtedly his and clearly autobiographical. He is the first poet in an Indian tongue to discuss his private life and feelings so openly in his verse.

Undoubtedly the most popular author among the vast array of Indian poet-saints and affectionately known as *Tuka,* the poet has been widely translated into the other Indian tongues including English, which is among India's officially recognized languages.

Bibliography

Tukārāma . *An Indian Peasant Mystic: Translations from Tukaram.* Translated by John S. Hoyland. London: H. R. Allenson, 1932.

———. *Eating Hunger: Selections from the poems of Tukarama.* Translated by J. Nelson Fraser and K. B. Marathe. Cambridge, Mass.: RhwymBooks, 1998.

———. *Meditations of St. Tukarama.* Jodhpur, India: Marudhar Publishers, 1976.

———. *Says Tuka: Selected Poetry of Tukaram.* Translated by Dilip Chitre. New York: Penguin Books, 1991.

———. *The Poems of Tukârâma.* 1909–1915. Translated by J. Nelson Fraser and K. B. Marathe. Reprint. Delhi: Motilal Banadarsidass, 1981.

Tulasīdās (Tulsīdāsa) (1532–1623)

A towering figure among the poet-saints of the BHAKTI devotional movement of India, Tulasīdās commanded several closely related tongues among the LANGUAGES OF INDIA. He wrote in Braj, Avadhi, and Hindi, choosing his language of composition according to the character of the work in hand.

At his birth, his horoscope looked inauspicious. His credulous parents therefore abandoned him, and a kind benefactor, Baba Narhari Das, reared the child. After being married to a wife whom he adored but who reproved him for too much devotion to her, Tulasīdās left home for 19 years and consecrated himself to a religious life, to writing, and to the service of the Hindu Deity, Lord Rama.

Although he wrote examples of virtually every literary genre then current in India, his masterpiece was his Hindi verse EPIC, *THE HOLY LAKE OF THE ACTS OF RAMA*, (*RAMCHARITMÂNASA*, 1579). Apart from that major accomplishment, posterity remembers Tulasīdās for his narrative verse accounts of the marriages of members of the Hindu pantheon: Rama's with Sita and Shiva's with Parvati. He also wrote a poem on the subject of a bridegroom's prewedding rituals ("*Ramala nahachhu*," ca. 1586.) In it the groom gets his hair cut, his beard shaved, and his nails manicured. The poem takes the groom through all his prenuptial preparations.

Tulasīdās also compiled a long series of lyric poems on the model of the *SUR-SAGAR* of SŪRDĀS. One of these, his Braj work *Gitavali*, celebrates Rama in 329 verses. Another important collection, the *Kavitavali* celebrates Krishna. A third is a devotional work, *Vinay-Patrika*, in which the poet implores salvation in poetic prayers addressed to a broad collection of Hindu deities who, the poet hopes, will intercede for him with Rama, the master of the universe.

Unlike many other poets in the *bhakti* tradition, many of whom sprang from humble origins, Tulasīdās came from a high-caste background. Perhaps for that reason he tended to be more socially conservative than many of his contemporary poets. He believed in the obligation of the governed to obey their governors and in the caste system. He also advocated the status quo with respect to women's deferential behavior toward men. At the same time, he thought everyone capable of achieving salvation.

His works have been translated into many of the languages of the world. They are all available in English, though their titles are sometimes left untranslated.

Bibliography

Sundd, Mishr D. K., and Sheo Nandan Pandey, eds. *Goswami Tulsidasji's . . . Sri Sankat Mochan Hanuman Charit Manas: The Holy Lake Containing the Acts of Sri Hanuman.* New Delhi: Aravali Books International, 1998.

Tulasîdâsa. *Complete Works of Gosvami Tulsidas.* Translated by S. P. Bahadur. Banares, India: Prachya Prakashan. 1978–79.

———. *Couplets from Thulasee Das.* Translated by G. N. Das. New Delhi: Abhinav Publications, 1997.

———. *Kavitavali.* Translated by F. R. Allchin. New York: Barnes, 1965.

———. *Sri Ramacharitamanasa.* Translated by G. B. Kanungo and Leela Kanungo. New Delhi: Muni Bhagwan Kanungo Charitable Society, 2000.

Twelve Towers, The Li Yu (ca. 1658)

A collection of 12 short stories, LI's *Twelve Towers* is the only anthology of Li's original stories to have come down to us intact. The title of each story contains the Chinese word, *lou. Lou* can translate as "*tower*," "*pavilion*," or "*hall*." This device links together all 12 stories. The tales' subjects provide further internal links within the collection. Li's literary reputation suffered during his lifetime owing to his nonconformist way of life and his habit of living beyond his means. His literary abilities however, increasingly command the attention of literary scholars and readers around the world today.

The first story of the collection, "The Reflections in the Water," tells the history of two first cousins, a boy and girl, whose mothers are sisters who married husbands of opposite temperaments. Though the sisters inherited a large house, the increasing incompatibility of the families led to their dividing the house until the only common area was a pavilion extending over the water. The girl's parents built a wall separating the halves of the pavilion, but it remained possible for a person on one side of the wall to see in the water the reflection of the person on the other side.

This of course happens to the two cousins. They discover that they look as much alike as identical twins. Of course they fall in love and manage to exchange poems. The girl's father, Mr. Guan (Kuan), wants absolutely nothing to do with the boy's family. The boy approaches his father, Mr. Tu (T'u), explaining that he wishes to marry his cousin. Tu has no objection and asks a mutual friend of the Guans and the Tus to act as a go-between. Guan refuses to discuss the matter, writing out his objections so that the go-between, Mr. Lu, will drop the subject.

Faced with Guan's adamant refusal, Lu proposes that the Tu son, Zhensheng (Chen-sheng), marry his adopted daughter instead. The parents eagerly agree, but Chen-sheng will not hear of the arrangement. Then a brilliant idea occurs to Mr. Lu. He already has one adoptive son. He will also adopt Zhensheng and propose a match between his adoptive son and the Guan daughter, Yujuan (Yü-chüan). Both weddings will occur at his house on the same day. His solution is to have Chen-sheng marry both girls simultaneously. The idea works. Everyone is happy. The estranged families reconcile, the barriers between their houses come down, and Zhensheng moves freely back and forth between his spouses.

The second story, "The Jackpot," recounts the tale of two exceedingly beautiful daughters of ugly, quarreling parents. Each parent arranges marriages for the girls so that each girl has two fiancées. As neither parent will budge, the matter first provokes a street riot when the father's candidate tries to kidnap the girls. Then the issue ends up in court, where a wise judge releases the girls from their engagements to totally unsuitable young men. In sympathy for their plight, the judge then arranges a contest of scholarship whose winners will receive the girls in marriage as the prizes. The same young man writes both winning essays. Perceiving the extraordinary talent of the writer, the judge awards him both girls as wives. The young man hits the jackpot.

The third tale, "Buried Treasure," recounts the ill fortune of a man who spends a fortune building and rebuilding an estate that he eventually has to sell for a fraction of its worth. A wealthy friend, as the reader learns at the end of the story, buries 20 silver bars on the one piece of property—a tower—that the builder manages to keep. The friend buries the treasure hoping that the builder will find it and his poverty be relieved. The silver, however, is not found until the next generation. Then to resolve the puzzle of the true owner of the silver a wise judge figures out the sequence of events. He awards the treasure to the builder's heirs, who use the money to reacquire their father's estate. Li Yu explicitly draws from his story this moral: "It pays to be generous and kind, wealthy people should accumulate virtues . . . [and] monetary gain can bring only sorrow."

The fourth tale, "The Magic Mirror," explains the way a young scholar uses information he collects with a telescope to convince, first, the girl he loves and then her reluctant father that the youth and his beloved are predestined to marry.

The fifth story, "The Swindler," begins with Li Yu's advice to the wicked that they should attempt to give up their evil ways and change their lives. He then tells the story of a clever swindler and a prostitute who do just that. Though the swindler is a master at his profession, he also is kind-hearted. He twice buys the prostitute out of the bondage into which her husband has sold her. The second time she becomes a Buddhist nun. The swindler himself employs the tricks of his trade one last time to persuade two wealthy men to build neighboring temples for the nun and for him. Successful in this last swindle, he reforms his life by becoming the Taoist priest in charge of the temple.

"The Elegant Eunuch," the sixth story, tells a bitter story of cruelty and revenge. Yen Shifan (Yen Shih-fan), a powerful official and son of the prime minister, is overcome by desire to possess as a male concubine a handsome young dealer in rare goods, Chuan Ruxiu (Ch'üan Ju-hsiu). To accomplish this end he arranges to have a subordinate drug and castrate the youth. Forced into servitude, Chuan (Ch'üan) bides his time while collecting evidence of the treasonable activities of Yen and his father. Eventually Chuan has the opportunity to share that evidence with the emperor and to tell the ruler his wretched history. The emperor has both Yens executed. Chuan acquires the skull of the man who had him mutilated and thereafter uses it as a urinal.

Li Yu begins the seventh story of his collection, "The Crafty Maid," with an anecdote about a maid who betrays her mistress and a warning against the trickery of maids. But the story succeeds by disappointing the expectations that warning arouses. Instead, in a plot complex enough to provide material for a novel, the story reveals the way in which a crafty maid serves her own best interests, and those of and her mistress by arranging marriages for them both. Both women become the wives of a man from whom the maid has procured a signed contract that regulates his behavior toward them. Li's story surprises by describing a maidservant who is both crafty and faithful.

The remaining five stories include, "Marital Frustrations," "The Stoic Lover," "The Male Heir," "Father and Son," and "The Hermit."

"Marital Frustrations" tells the story of a young man who marries a girl he loves only to discover that she is physically deformed and unable to consummate the marriage. The parents exchange her for first one sister and then another, but the son can't bear either. Eventually, after nine unsuccessful marriages, he weds the tenth time only to discover that he has remarried his original bride. His loving attention causes a miraculous change in her, and, late in life, they discover happiness together.

Li insists that "The Stoic Lover" tells a true story. In it two young men marry lovely women whom the emperor wanted for concubines. To punish the men, the emperor sends them away on missions that will keep them from home for years. One of the men, a stoic, cautions his wife not to expect much happiness and predicts that he will never return. Convinced that he is cold and unfeeling, the wife relies on herself and becomes a

successful weaver. The other man declares his love and assures his wife he will return as soon as he can. His wife expects him every moment, and when he finally does return he finds her unburied in the coffin where she has lain since her death three years before.

"The Male Heir" illustrates that female fortitude and sacrifice can involve as much resolution and long-suffering as that of men. When bandits besieged a city, the men all fled. They had to leave their wives behind since the Chinese custom of binding women's feet made their flight afoot impossible. Babies not yet weaned had to stay with the mother. Everyone knew that the bandits would rape all the women left behind unless the women chose to die to preserve their virtue. Mr. Shu's infant son was the only male child in his extended family. His preservation, everyone thought, took precedence over Mrs. Shu's virtue. Shu and all the relatives on both sides of the family advise Mrs. Shu to endure the bandits' violence and preserve her life and the life of her child. She reluctantly agrees. Her fortitude impresses the bandits, who take her and the child away with them. Years later, exhausted by a fruitless search for his wife and child, Shu is captured by bandits who make him a forced laborer. His wife, who is now the wife of the bandit general, recognizes her former husband and has him cruelly chained for four days until the chieftain returns. The chaining preserves Shu's life. Otherwise the bandit would have thought his wife unfaithful. He returns Shu's son to him, and when his wife attempts suicide, returns her as well with the advice that Shu pay tribute to the lost wife as if she were dead and treat the restored Mrs. Shu as a new mate.

Yi Lu continues the theme of the return of kidnapped women in the collection's penultimate tale. "Father and Son," is a hardly credible tale of multiple kidnappings, separations, and coincidental reunions in which father and son, husband and wife, mother and son, lover and beloved are lost to one another and then all happily restored.

The writer concludes his collection with "The Hermit," a story of a man who wishes to leave the city and retire to the country. His friends miss him and his good counsel so much that they stage an elaborate plot to get him to move just outside the city so that he can be near them once more. The plot works, and the closest one of his friends builds a house next door so he can constantly benefit from the hermit's advice and criticism. People who can benefit from criticism, Yi Lu remarks at the story's end, are the rarest of all individuals.

Bibliography

Li Yu. *Li Yü's Twelve Towers Retold by Nathan Mao.* Hong Kong: Chinese University of Hong Kong, 1975.

Twenty Sacred Hymns (1554)

Brother BERNARDINO DE SAHAGÚN, the indefatigable recorder of native Central American literary and subliterary culture, set down 20 hymns that he heard chanted in the Nahuatl language by Meso-American, post–European contact, Nahuan tribal elders.

These hymns have been translated into English verse, and examples of them are available from several sources. (See bibliography below.) The hymns are addressed to various members of the Meso-American pantheon and their priestly servants. A "Hymn to Xipe Totec," for example, was addressed to a priest who presided over the sacrifice of gladiators, and it included reference to Xipe Totec, a deity identified as "our flayed lord." Rainfall, warfare, the growth of the life-giving food staple maize, the need for blood from human sacrifice to fertilize the soil and assure the harvest, and reverential devotion to the god constitute the subject matter of the hymn.

Similar themes that underscore the connection between the shedding of human blood and the bounty of the harvest appear in a hymn entitled "Song of Cihuacoatl." "A Hymn to Tlaloc," on the other hand, contains a lengthy incantation asking the rain god to end the evils of pestilence, famine, drought, and human sufferings that plague the land. An "Invocation of Tezcatlipoca," on the other hand, seeks deliverance from the destruction of Nahuan cities and the destruction of Nahuan civilization. It is difficult to read this hymn without thinking of the catastrophic destruction of the old Meso-American world by the military activity of the Spanish conquistadors. The tone of this song

is full of irony. It entertains the notion that the people may have somehow offended their god, and that he is visiting destruction upon them in retribution. It also suggests the ironic possibility that the god is simply entertaining himself at human expense. Given the round of more or less constant warfare, however, that Meso-American societies carried on among themselves, seeing allusions to Europeans in the stanzas may be self-deceptive.

Other hymns in the group pray for cleansing from taboo-breaking sexual activity, like the "Prayer to Tlazolteotl." That goddess was the patron deity of filth. She had the power to cleanse those who had strayed from clean and upright behavior.

Bibliography

Anderson, Arthur J. O., and Charles E. Dibble. *Florentine Codex of Fray Bernardino de Sahagún.* Vol. 6, chap. 7. Santa Fe, N.M.: School of North American Research and the University of Utah Press, 1950–1982.

León-Portilla, Miguel, Earl Shorris, et al. *In the Languages of Kings: An Anthology of Mesoamerican Literature—Pre-Columbian to the Present.* New York: W. W. Norton, 2000.

Sullivan, Thelma D. *Primeros Memoriales.* Norman: University of Oklahoma Press, 1997.

———, and T. J. Knab. *A Scattering of Jades.* New York: Simon and Schuster, 1994.

Tyndale, (Hutchins) William
(ca. 1494–1536)

A Greek and Latin linguist who had been educated at Magdalen Hall in Oxford University, William Tyndale was also a HUMANIST versed in TEXTUAL CRITICISM. He saw the need for a new English translation of the BIBLE, and he asked permission from Bishop Cuthbert Tunstall of London to do the work and publish it (see BIBLE IN ENGLISH). When Tunstall refused, Tyndale visited MARTIN LUTHER in Cologne. The plots of Tyndale's enemies forced him to flee, but, in 1526 in the city of Worms, Germany, he succeeded in publishing between 3,000 and 6,000 copies of the English New Testament that he had translated directly from the Greek. To get the book into England, Tyndale and his confederates hid copies in bales of cloth and smuggled them past customs both on the Rhine and in the ports of England. Once ashore, Tyndale's Testament was quickly distributed.

The ecclesiastical authorities, however, sought out most of the copies and publicly burned them in a ritual at St. Paul's Cathedral in London. As a result, only two copies are known to survive today. Enough copies remained in the Renaissance, however, that Tyndale's version provided the underpinning for all subsequent English New Testaments. David Daniell reports that the Christmas stories, the parables of Jesus, the reports of the Crucifixion, and certain passages of Paul's writing, such as his Epistle to the Romans, have all come down to us mainly in Tyndale's words.

Doubtless disappointed at the fate of his translation but nonetheless undaunted, Tyndale, still in Germany, mastered Hebrew and began work on translating the Old Testament. He completed the first five books of the Old Testament, the Pentateuch, and those books of the Old Testament that detail the history of the Jewish people. Then he was tricked into going to Antwerp. In Tyndale's time, Antwerp was a part of the Spanish Netherlands and under the ecclesiastical scrutiny of the Spanish INQUISITION. In Antwerp, Tyndale was arrested, tried for heresy, convicted, and, as an object lesson to other would-be translators, both strangled and burned to death on October 6, 1536.

Beyond his work as a translator, Tyndale also authored a pair of devotional tracts, *The Parable of the Wicked Mammon* (1528), and in the same year his most ambitious such work, *The Obedience of a Christian Man*. He vented his frustrations with the ecclesiastical establishment in his disputatious *Practyse of Prelates* (1530).

Bibliography

Daniell, David. *William Tyndale: A Biography.* New Haven, Conn., and London: Yale University Press, 1994.

Tyndale's New Testament. Edited by David Daniell. New Haven, Conn., and London: Yale University Press, 1995.

Tyndale's Old Testament: Being the Pentateuch of 1530, Joshua to 2 Chronicles of 1537, and Jonah. Edited by David Daniell. New Haven, Conn., and London: Yale University Press, 1992.

typology

A variety of ALLEGORY in which one term of a stated or implied comparison is a historical event or figure. Thus, in PETRARCH's lyric poems the figure of Laura may be said to be typological. She was a real woman, probably a member of Avignon's minor aristocracy named Lauretta de Sade. In his poetry, however, she variously stands for Petrarch's hope and inspiration for literary fame as poet laureate (which he achieved), for his hope of heavenly salvation (about which he isn't so sure), for his way to that salvation, his spiritual undoing, and for numerous other comparisons as well. Another sort of typological interpretation finds suggestions of divine intention in naturally occurring objects. Some, for example, point to the five perforations on sand dollars as typological precursors of the wounds of the crucified Christ. Still another kind involves matching incidents in the Old and New Testaments to see how the Old Testament prefigures Christ's coming.

Bibliography

Ohly, Friedrich, ed. *Sensus Spiritualis: Studies in Medieval Significs and the Philology of Culture.* Translated by Kenneth J. Northcott. Chicago: University of Chicago Press, 2004.

Petrarca, Francesco. *Petrarch's Songbook: Rerum vulgarium fragmenta.* Translated by James Wyatt Cook. Introduced by Germaine Warkentin. Binghamton, N.Y.: Center for Medieval and Renaissance Texts and Studies, 1999.

U

Udall, Nicholas (1504–1556)

An English HUMANIST, clergyman, educator, translator, publisher, poet, and playwright, Nicholas Udall was born in Southampton and attended Winchester College there, entering when he was 12 years old. From Winchester he graduated to Corpus Christi College in Oxford University—then a major center of humanist activity and the new learning—where he mastered Greek as well as the Latin he had learned at Winchester. While at Oxford he may have authored an INTERLUDE, *Thersites.*

In 1533 with JOHN LELAND, Udall wrote verses for the coronation of Queen ANNE BOLEYN. The following year he published a textbook designed to assist schoolboys in perfecting their spoken Latin, *Floures for Latyn Speakynge,* an influential work whose success, thinks his biographer William L. Egerton, led to an important appointment. In June 1534 Udall became headmaster of Eton School—a post he held for seven years but lost owing to a scandal whose outcome led to a prison term in the Marshalsea jail.

Eventually, however, Udall was able to reestablish himself in the good opinion of his patrons. The year 1542 saw the first fruits of a new career, this time as a translator. He translated, annotated, and added fresh material of his own to DESIDERIUS ERASMUS's *Apophthegemata* under the title *Apoph-*

tegmes. Both versions present a collection of memorable and witty sayings of the ancients for the benefit of Renaissance readers. The following year Queen Catherine Parr selected Udall to head a group of scholars charged with translating Erasmus's *Paraphrases of the New Testament.* Udall himself seems to have translated the paraphases of Luke, Matthew, and the Acts of the Apostles. This widely circulated book remained in print for generations and secured Udall's scholarly reputation.

Udall's career as a translator continued with the appearance in 1550 of a translation of a treatise by the Italian humanist and Oxford professor Peter Martyr (Pietro Martiri Vermigli). He also acquired the privilege of publishing, not only that treatise, but the Bible as well—a privilege with enormous financial potential for the militantly Protestant Udall.

The work that secured Udall's reputation in the annals of the British theater, *Ralph Roister Doister,* was probably performed at Windsor Castle for the young but sickly King Edward VI late in 1552 or early 1553. Drawn from the Roman playwright PLAUTUS's play *MILES GLORIOSUS,* Udall's play brings to the English stage for the first time the STOCK CHARACTERS of the Roman theater. Ralph Roister Doister is the antecedent of WILLIAM SHAKESPEARE's Sir John Falstaff. His servant, Matthew Merrygreek, anticipates the stock character of such a parasite, as Mosca in BEN JONSON's *VOLPONE.* The plot of Udall's play, moreover, is a model for Shakespeare's *The Merry Wives of Windsor*. Udall's Ralph Roister Doister inappropriately woos Dame Custance, but she and her maids give him a well-deserved comeuppance.

We know that Udall wrote one other play, now lost, *Ezechias* (ca. 1545?). He may also have written another *Respublica* (1553). If so the timing was bad, for that piece was Protestant propaganda, and the Roman Catholic queen Mary I ascended the throne in July of that year. As a result, Udall lost an ecclesiastical post at Windsor. His services as a producer of COURT ENTERTAINMENT, however, remained in demand, for Queen Mary's disbursement records show that her MASTER OF THE REVELS paid Udall for staging such performances in December 1554 and January 1555.

Udall ended his life as an educator, becoming headmaster of Westminster School in December 1555. He occupied the post until his death a year later.

Bibliography

Axton, Marie, and D. S. Brewer, eds. *Three Classic Tudor Interludes: Thersites, Jack Jugeler, Horestes*. Totowa, N.J.: Rowman and Littlefield, ca. 1988.

Erasmus, Desiderius. *Apophthegms*. Translated by Nicholas Udall. New York: Da Capo Press, 1969.

Edgerton, William L. *Nicholas Udall*. New York: Twayne Publishers, 1965.

Terence (Publius Terentius Afer), and Nicholas Udall. *Flowers for Latin Speaking*. Menston, U.K.: Scolar Press, 1972.

Udall, Nicholas. *Ralph Roister Doister*. Edited by Clarence Griffin Child. Reprint, 1912. New York: Octagon, 1979.

———. *Respublica: The Macro Plays, no. 4.* 1910. New York: AMS Press, 1970.

Unfortunate Traveller, The Thomas Nashe (1594)

NASHE'S *The Unfortunate Traveller* appears to many of our contemporary critics to anticipate important attributes of 20th-century fiction. Its main character, Jack Wilton, for instance, acts as the novel's not-altogether-reliable narrator. Sometimes Jack speaks for himself. Sometimes Thomas Nashe speaks through him. The novel revels in violence, but the violence itself sometimes transforms into something scandalously funny. Morally ambiguous at best, the novel provokes an accusation of nihilism—another 20th-century attribute, among others. Like the exhibitionist Jack Wilton and like Thomas Nashe himself, the text is always verbally brilliant.

After introducing Jack and establishing him as a young military page, Nashe turns the narration over to him. The novel begins with Jack's gleefully reporting a complex prank he plays on a Falstaffian supplier of food and drink to the army. After worming his way into the victualer's confidence by appealing to his pride in a baronial heritage, Jack convinces the supplier that he is about to be charged with spying for the enemy and with smuggling secret messages in and out of camp in ale barrels and other containers. After much slapstick comedy, Jack's commander uncovers the joke and punishes Jack with a beating. For Jack the fun has been worth the price.

Jack travels around the continent, and, in Rome, he becomes witness to scenes of unspeakable violence. He, and through his eyes the reader, watches an Italian matron, Heraclide, being raped on the murdered body of her husband. Jack describes the vengeance that a character called Cutwolf takes on his brother's murderer, Esdras. As Esdras pleads for his life, Cutwolf offers to spare him if he will consign his soul to the devil. Esdras does so, writing the contract in his own blood. As soon as Esdras signs it, Cutwolf shoots him in the mouth and send him off to hell. Jack himself narrowly misses execution after Heraclide's rape, and only the intervention of a British nobleman saves him from the gallows.

In many of the violent scenes, however, Nashe finds material for a grisly humor. Like MARGARET CAVENDISH and others in his era, the brilliant and classically educated Nashe seems to have sought freshness and originality by combining or juxtaposing literary modes. Nashe can be drawing a moral at one moment and, at the next, indulging in scatological humor arising from the same circumstances. The critic Neil Rhodes has seen this tendency to combine or alternate between opposite modes as characteristic of novels of the grotesque—a genre to which FRANÇOIS RABELAIS's novels about GARGANTUA AND PANTAGRUEL also belong. Others have argued for assignment to other genres, particularly the PICARESQUE.

As compelling as 21st-century readers find Nashe's novel to be, the readers of ELIZABETHAN FICTION seem not to have found it so attractive. It went through two small editions in 1594 and then did not again see print for a very long time. Yet no other work of the much-emulated Tom Nashe offers greater proof of the author's unparalleled mastery of an easy, colloquial, and at the same time verbally brilliant Elizabethan English prose style.

Bibliography

Nashe, Thomas. *The Unfortunate Traveller and Other Works.* Edited by J. B. Steane. Harmondsworth, U.K.: Penguin, 1972.

Rhodes, Neil. *Elizabethan Grotesque.* London and Boston: Routledge and Kegan Paul, 1980.

Salzman, Paul. *English Prose Fiction, 1558–1700: A Critical History.* Oxford: Clarendon Press, 1985.

unities

The unities of time, place, and action, though widely attributed to ARISTOTLE's description of TRAGEDY in his *Poetics,* were actually the Italian HUMANIST LUDOVICO CASTELVETRO's elaboration of Aristotle's discussion. Schooled by Castelvetro's discussion, erudite audiences came to expect that new plays, aspiring to equal the stature of the ancients, would observe the unities. The action of a play would ostensibly occupy no more than 24 hours. The location of that action would not move further than an audience could imagine someone could travel in the same period of time. The plot of the play would focus on a single event or series of closely related events and sweep uninterruptedly from beginning to end following the steps of development that Aristotle had outlined in his discussion of tragedy.

Some Renaissance playwrights, particularly in France, treated the unities as rules of dramaturgy and carefully observed them. Better playwrights,

like LOPE DE VEGA CARPIO in Spain and WILLIAM SHAKESPEARE in England simply ignored them.

university wits

A label applied to a group of English writers, resident in London from about 1585–95, the university wits were young men who had graduated from the British universities and who had there received classical educations. They gathered at such places as the Mermaid Tavern to discuss literary issues of their day. The membership of the group is a bit variable, but usually it includes ROBERT GREENE, THOMAS KYD, THOMAS LODGE, JOHN LYLY, CHRISTOPHER MARLOWE, and George Peele. As a group and individually they were responsible for many of the literary innovations of their day: blank-verse TRAGEDY, bringing SENECAN tragedy to the English stage, the popularization of euphuistic prose (see *EUPHUES*), the rise of British journalism and naturalistic prose, and the development of TRAGICOMEDY.

Urfé, Honoré d' (1567/8–1625)

A French aristocrat, soldier, novelist, epic poet, and playwright, d'Urfé grew up in a family that owned one of the finest libraries in France. His encyclopedic mastery of Renaissance thought and literature would later demonstrate that he made good use of it.

Perhaps the most significant circumstance of d'Urfé's personal life was his passion for his sister-in-law, Diane du Châteaumorand. The two fell in love not long after Diane's marriage to d'Urfé's brother Anne in 1574. Although Anne was impotent, his marriage survived, at least in name, for 25 years. Finally, in 1599, the union was dissolved on the grounds of nonconsummation. In February 1600 Honoré and Diane were at last married. They did not, however, live happily ever after. Around 1614 they decided to go their separate ways. They lived together only occasionally after that time. Nonetheless, d'Urfé's situation led him to be deeply interested in all aspects of human passion, both the theoretical ones and the practical ones. The exploration of that subject would eventually form the intellectual and narrative spine of his masterpiece, ASTREA (L'ASTRÉE).

While still a student, d'Urfé had begun his writing career with a poetic description of a grand wedding procession and the accompanying festivities in the city of Tournon, *Le Triomphante Entrée de trés illustre Dame Magdeleine de la Rochefoucald* (The triumphant entrance of the very illustrious lady Magdeleine of Rochefoucald, 1583). Later, he penned a trio of epistolary works containing a number of letters addressed to an imaginary mentor. His *Épîtres morales* (Moral letters, Book I, 1598; Book II, 1603; Book III, 1608) recorded portions of his personal history and political difficulties, and they expressed the rational, Christian, HUMANIST philosophy that he espoused.

He undertook his early military career as a member of the Catholic League whose objective was to stop the spread of Calvinism in France. When the league's enemy, the Protestant king Henry of Navarre, became Henry IV of France and converted to Roman Catholicism, d'Urfé became at least nominally reconciled with his sovereign. Nonetheless, he spent significant periods of time in Savoy. Its dukes were his maternal relatives, and he owned an estate there. The history of the dukes of Savoy and its ruling family's glorious founder, Bérold, would provide the topic for d'Urfé's epic poem, *La Savoysiade,* of which he published two installments in 1509 and 1606, but which, despite further work, he never finished. Apparently he became bogged down in the details.

D'Urfé's first venture into the briefly popular PASTORAL mode came with the publication of his poem, *La Sirene*. Inspired by the work of the Spanish pastoralist Jorge de Montemayor, the poem recounts the story of the shepherd Sirene's separation from his beloved Diana and their eventual reunion. D'Urfé's biographer, Louise K. Horowitz, suggests that the pastoral manner was particularly congenial to d'Urfé, both from the point of view of his own biographical circumstances and from that of the opportunities he found in pastoral for exploring the wellsprings of the human motivation and the human condition. The poet would write another pastoral play toward the end of his life, *La Sylvanire,* which appeared posthumously in 1627. Notable for its author's choice of unrhymed verse as his medium of expression, *La Sylvanire* looks to TORQUATO TASSO's *AMINTA* and to GIOVANNI BATTISTA GUARINI's pastoral TRAGICOMEDY *THE FAITHFUL SHEPHERD* as the models for its form and plot. A lovesick shepherd desires a huntress who disdains love, but, after a series of difficulties that usually include a mistaken report of death, long delays, uncooperative parents, and, in the Italian versions, attempted violation of a nymph by a satyr, the shepherd persuades the nymph to love him, and all ends happily.

The work, however, for which d'Urfé is principally remembered is his mind-numbingly lengthy, encyclopedic, pastoral novel *Astrea* (*L'Astrée*, Part I, 1607; Part II, 1610; Part III, 1619; Part IV, 1627.) This work, in part and in very complicated ways autobiographical, occupied him until his death. His secretary, Balthazar Baro, loyally completed Part IV from notes that d'Urfé left, and he published the final installment after his employer's death.

Bibliography

Hinds, Leonard. *Narrative Transformations from L'Astrée to Le berger extravagant.* West Lafayette, Ind.: Purdue University Press, 2002.

Horowitz, Louise K. *Honoré d'Urfé.* Boston: Twayne Publishers, 1984.

Urfé, Honoré d'. *Astrea, Part I.* Translated by Steven Randall. Binghamton, N.Y.: Medieval and Renaissance Text Society, 1995.

'Urfí of Shiraz   (d. 1590–1591)

A gifted Persian poet born in the city of Shiraz, like many of his contemporaries 'Urfí traveled to India to seek his fortune among the Islamic conquerors of northern India, the Mughals. Fortunate in his connections, 'Urfí passed from patron to patron until those connections and his skill brought him a presentation to the greatest patron of his age, Emperor AKBAR THE GREAT. 'Urfí accompanied Akbar's train on its march from Agra to Kashmir in 1588–89.

Although Akbar's taste for Persian poetry assured the talented 'Urfí's future, the poet's arrogance and conceit soon made him an unpopular figure among his fellow writers at court. They found particularly objectionable 'Urfí's propensity for comparing himself favorably with former poets who were regarded as the wonders of their ages. 'Urfí was not unaware of his contemporaries' opinion, and he complains of it in a poem in which he likens himself—sick at the time—to the biblical Job and compares the friends who drop in to visit him to Job's cold comforters who blamed the sufferer for his troubles.

A nearly contemporary chronicler of Persian poets, Shiblí, praises 'Urfí for his forceful diction and for his ability to find fresh and striking combinations of words, his apt similes and metaphors, and the ease with which he moves from one topic to another.

'Urfí composed, in addition to his poems, a little-read prose work on the Islamic sect of Sufism. Otherwise, everything he wrote followed a pattern typical among Persian poets. He imitated earlier poets, retelling romances on traditional topics. He made a collection of his own lyrics—a *Diwan*—in 1588. This collection contains 270 GHAZELs, 26 QASIDAs, and several hundred fragmentary poems and quatrains.

Vaishnava religious reform in India

The Vaishnavite movement in India produced a devotional reformation called *BHAKTI* that repeatedly swept through the length and breadth of the country for centuries. Some might argue that the movement has yet to run its course.

At the center of the movement was the special veneration of the Hindu Deity Vishnu and his various manifestations, like Krishna, and submanifestations, such as Krishna's consort Radha. From a literary perspective, although the movement itself began as early as the 15th century, its flowering in the 16th and 17th centuries resulted in the translation and often in the re-creation of the ancient Indian Sanskrit EPICs and Scriptures in the emergent LANGUAGES OF INDIA. The social results were akin to the effects of the Bible being translated into the vernacular languages of Europe. The high-caste guardians of the old Sanskritic texts and their wisdom found themselves displaced or marginalized by a new class of poet-saints, many of humble origins, who composed their ardent devotional verses in languages that people understood.

In addition to translating the old texts and upgrading some of their heroes, such as Rama or Arjuna, to the status of deities, the poet-saints also simplified, broke up, or truncated the sometimes enormously long ancient texts. The MAHABHARATA, for instance, is the world's longest poem. Vaishnavite poet-saints often spoon-fed bits of the poem to their flocks in short and easily memorized songs. Moreover, the availability of manuscript documents in the vernacular languages cultivated literacy in those tongues. Literally hundreds of vernacular poets emerged, and I have tried to include a generous sampling of them in this volume: SANKARADEVA, SŪRDĀS, TULASĪDĀS, KRISH-NADĀSA KAVIRĀJA GOSVĀMI, Princess MIRABAI, and TUKÂRÂMA represent a sampling of the Vaishnavite poets to be found in these pages.

Many of these poet-saints introduced into their teachings elements of social reform that called into question the caste system and the doctrine of untouchability. All insisted that everyone could find the way to salvation regardless of sex, wealth, station, or intellectual accomplishments. Taken together these poets, most writing in the vernaculars but a few still using Sanskrit, represent the mainstream of Indian Hindu letters in the 16th and 17th centuries.

Bibliography

Pollock, Sheldon, ed. *Literary Cultures in History: Reconstructions from South Asia.* Berkeley: University of California Press, 2003.

Valla, Lorenzo (1407–1457)

Valla was probably the most influential theorist of the early Renaissance. A self-educated scholar and thinker, an independently minded Christian, and a classical linguist, he contributed significantly to the resurgence of interest in classical letters that characterized Renaissance HUMANISM. First, he argued that the Roman author Quintilian was a better Latin model for the scholar-writer than was Cicero—the Roman author favored by Valla's predecessors and many of his contemporaries. He believed the Latin language capable of expressing subtleties of thought and nuances of feeling much better than the vernacular European languages of his day. He felt that restoring the purity of Latin would lead to the improvement of European and particularly Christian culture, which had fallen off from the high standards of classical Rome and from the purity of the early church. He therefore wrote his major works in Quintilian Latin. His most notable work in this vein was *De elegantiis linguae latinae* (The elegances of the Latin language, 1471), a book he worked on sporadically for almost 40 years.

He also developed new standards of textual criticism. By comparing later, more corrupted classical texts with earlier versions, he was able to restore, to a greater or less degree, works of Roman and Greek writers to a more pristine condition. In applying those techniques, he would influence DESIDERIUS ERASMUS, who later employed the methods that Valla proposed in his *Annotations on the New Testament* (after 1448). Following Valla's method, Erasmus produced a more reliable translation of the Bible than the Latin vulgate.

Based on the techniques for textual criticism he developed, Valla was able to prove, for example, that a famous document, *The Donation of Constantine*, attributed to the fourth century C.E., was in fact an eighth-century forgery. As the church based its claim to temporal authority on this spurious document, it was fortunate for Valla during the INQUISITION that others, including Cardinal Nicholas of Cusa, had also discovered the manuscript's forgery. Even so, Valla's work *De falso credita et ementita Constantini donatione declamation* (On the falsely believed and fictive donation of Constantine) provoked the wrath of powerful Roman clerics.

Valla also called into question the very foundations of medieval thinking about theology, philosophy, and formal argument. He critiqued ARISTOTLE, BOETHIUS, and the SCHOLASTICISM of the medieval church, first, in his *Dialectical Disputations* (1439, 1448, and 1452) and then in his *Dialogue on Free Will* (1439). In the latter document he argues that people cannot achieve salvation merely through the exercise of free will. Both Erasmus and MARTIN LUTHER (German) allude to Valla's work on the freedom of the will. Some of his critique of scholasticism reappears comically in the work of FRANÇOIS RABELAIS.

A prolific NEO-LATIN writer, Valla translated from the Greek as well. He translated Aesop's *Fables*, Herodotus, a portion of Homer's *Iliad*, Thucydides, and Xenophon's *Cyropedia*. Valla's work provided important foundation stones for both the Renaissance and the Reformation.

Bibliography

Trinkaus, Charles. "Valla, Lorenzo." In *Encyclopedia of the Renaissance*. Vol. 6, edited by Paul F. Grendler. New York: Scribner, 1999.

Valla, Lorenzo. *Dialogue on Free Will*. Translated by Charles Trinkaus. In *The Renaissance Philosophy of Man*, edited by Ernst Cassierer, et al. Chicago: University of Chicago Press, 1948.

———. *The Treatise of Lorenzo Valla on the Donation of Constantine*. Translated by Christopher B. Coleman. Toronto: University of Toronto Press, 1993.

Vallabha (Vallabhāchārya) (1481–1533)

An Indian thinker and philosopher, Vallabha continued to compose in the ancient Sanskrit LANGUAGES OF INDIA considerably after most writers had shifted to writing in their respective vernaculars. His principal verse contributions were to the fields of scholarly philosophy and religion and learned commentary thereon. Among these we find a celebrated commentary on one of the basic texts of Indian thought, the *Bhāgavata Purana*—a compendium of the ancient stories associated with the Deity Vishnu. Vallabha also composed devotional verse works, as in his 16 verse treatises included in *The Grace of Lord Krishna*. He was one of the great theorists of the

Vaishnavite movement that flourished in India for centuries and that promoted the veneration of all that deity's manifestations, including Krishna.

In addition to his by no means modest literary output, Vallabha was indirectly responsible for the production of a vast amount of poetry, for it was he who convinced the poet SŪRDĀS to devote his life and poetic talent to the adoration and celebration of the Hindu Deity Krishna.

A major publication effort is currently underway to provide parallel Sanskrit and English texts of all Vallabha's work.

Bibliography

Vallabhāchārya. *Collected Works of Shri Vallabhāchārya.* Translated by [our contemporary] Vallabhāchārya. Delhi: Sri Satguru Publications, 2003.

———. *Srī Subodhiniī: Text with English Translation, Commentary on Srimad Bhāgavata Purāna.* Delhi: Sri Satguru Publications, 2003.

Vasari, Giorgio (1511–1574)

An enviably successful artist in the mannerist style, a skillful architect, a genial man who was in demand among princes and popes as an interior designer, a muralist, a designer and builder of palaces, and a painter of portraits, Giorgio Vasari surprised himself by making his most notable contribution to posterity as the foremost and best remembered biographer of the Renaissance.

Vasari was born in the Tuscan hill town of Arezzo. There his parents noticed his budding talent for sketching and took the advice of friends to have little Giorgio trained as an artist. His teachers were among the best artists working. Luca Signorelli, Andrea del Sarto, and MICHELANGELO BUONAROTTI all had a hand in perfecting Vasari's artistic skills. He soon came to the attention of the Medici family in Florence, and they kept him busy with commissions. A notable example was the commission of Grand Duke Cosimo de' Medici to have Vasari design the Uffizi Palace in Florence. Now among that city's premier art museums, the Uffizi originally served as Cosimo's governmental offices.

Vasari and his biographers tell the story of how he came to write his masterpiece, The LIVES OF THE ARTISTS (*Delle Vite de' più eccelenti pittori, scultori, ed architectori,* 1550 and 1568). At dinner one evening in 1546 at the palace of Cardinal Farnese in Rome, Bishop Paolo Giovio mentioned that he was considering writing a sort of biographical dictionary that would bring together discussions of all notable artists. Cardinal Farnese asked Vasari his opinion of the project, and Vasari thought the plan a good one provided that "a painter" or other knowledgeable person helped the bishop "put the facts into their proper order" and explained "the technicalities to him."

The cardinal inquired if Vasari could provide the bishop with a summary and a classified list of artists. Although Vasari was already overwhelmed with commissions and though others were lined up clamoring for his services, he agreed to do so. When after some time Vasari gave Giovio the promised list, the bishop realized that he himself was not qualified to undertake the project. Instead he encouraged Vasari to do it.

After four years, working in such moments as he could spare, Vasari's two-volume work with 133 biographical sketches of earlier artists appeared. In its first edition Vasari apologized for his ineptitude as a writer, but the work's instant success and the public's continuing demand made him proud of the project. In 1568, therefore, he brought out a second edition—this time with 168 lives, one of which was his own.

In an era characterized by frequent jealousies and disagreements among persons in the arts and letters, Giorgio Vasari seems to have been liked and admired by everyone. Hardworking and upright, Vasari continued to practice his arts until the day of his death. That day, June 27, 1574, interrupted him just before he could complete the project he had in hand. He was putting the final touches on the figures of the biblical prophets and elders around the eye of the lantern in the cupola of the Cathedral of Santa Maria del Fiore, in Florence.

Bibliography

Vasari, Giorgio. *The Lives of the Artists.* Translated by Julia Conaway Bondanella and Peter Bondanella. Oxford and New York: Oxford University Press, 1998.

Vates

"*Vates*" (rhymes with "Ma says") is the Latin word for *priest*. Serious poets around the world have historically viewed themselves and been viewed by others as performing a priestly function when they speak in verse or write poetry. When they were performing ordinary tasks, poets were thought to be just like everybody else. When they wrote or performed, however, they became the mouthpiece of the gods, for they were thought to be inspired by the MUSES. Thus Homer begins his epics by invoking the muse as he does in *The Odyssey:* "Sing in me, Muse, and in me tell the story." JOHN MILTON calls upon the Holy Spirit for inspiration so that Milton may, "assert eternal Providence/ and justify God's ways to men." This vatic view of the role of the poet imposes serious responsibilities on those who feel called to the profession. They must carefully and diligently prepare for it through practice and study.

See also COMPOSITION; TOPOS.

Vaughan, Henry (1621–1695)

A Welch poet in a modified PASTORAL tradition, Henry Vaughan attended Jesus College in Oxford University with his twin brother Thomas. After two years there, Henry moved to London to pursue a career in civil law. Once in the city, he became a member of a group of poets called the "tribe of Ben," associating himself with other poets of the era, including THOMAS CAREW.

Following completion of his legal studies Vaughan returned to Wales and entered the civil service. He may have served as a soldier on the royalist side during the First English Civil War (1642–45).

In 1646 his first collection of verse and translations appeared: *Poems, with the tenth Satyre of Juvenal Englished.* The original poems in this book deal with love in a sort of idealized pastoral mode that looks back to the lyrics of such predecessor English poets as BEN JONSON. From Vaughan's translation of the Roman poet Juvenal emerge the twin themes of his preference for the rural over the urban life and for the pursuit of virtue rather than becoming a disciple of FORTUNE.

The next year he completed another collection, *Olor Iscanus* (The swan of the river Usk, published 1651). This work contains 47 verse translations and original poems in both English and Latin. These lyrics deal with such subjects as war, politics, behavior, and literature. Only two of the poems concern love. Of special interest are Vaughan's translations of several lyrics from the fifth-century Roman BOETHIUS's *Consolation of Philosophy.* They address the defenses that faith and virtue provide against the operations of adverse fortune. Other translations in the book come from the works of the ancient Romans OVID and Ausonius. Vaughn also translates the Latin lyrics of a contemporary Polish Jesuit, Maciej Kasimierez Sarbiewski (Casimirus). In addition to the poems, Vaughan includes four brief prose translations that focus on the characteristic themes of the volume: 1) retreat from the miseries of the world, especially the decadence of the city, to the country life; 2) Christian stoicism in the face of unpredictable and adverse fortune.

Perhaps his most memorable verse collection, *Silex Scintillans* (The sparkling flint), appeared first in 1650 and in an expanded second edition in 1655. Inspired by GEORGE HERBERT's *The Temple,* Vaughan considers the two books of God: the BIBLE and the book of nature. In this collection, Vaughan reveals a mystical side and a yearning for the arrival of the Day of Judgment. The poems seek to kindle anew faith in the hearts of faithless and hope for the hopeless. The poems are among the most attractive of their sort in the late English Renaissance.

Vaughan later turned his hand to devotional prose. *The Mount of Olives or Solitary Devotions* (1651) contains three pieces: "Admonitions for Morning Prayer," "Man in Darkness," and "Man in Glory,"—the last being a translation of St. Anselm's "On the Happiness of the Saints." The next year saw the composition of Vaughan's *Floris Solitudinis* (Flowers of solitude). In this most successful of his devotional prose compositions, Vaughan merges the pastoral tradition of a happy golden age with nostalgia for the simplicity of the primitive Christian Church.

Bibliography

Friedenreich, Kenneth. *Henry Vaughan*. Boston: Twayne Publishers, 1978.

Vaughan, Henry. *The Complete Poetry of Henry Vaughan*. Garden City, N.Y.: Doubleday, 1964.

Vaux, Thomas, Lord (1510–1556)

A skillful early Tudor lyricist included in a group of poets called the COURTLY MAKERS, Thomas, Lord Vaux's verses first appeared with those of SIR THOMAS WYATT, of HENRY HOWARD, THE EARL OF SURREY, of NICHOLAS GRIMALD and others in Richard Tottel's MISCELLANY (*Songs and Sonnets*, 1557.) Most of the other surviving verses securely attributable to him appeared in a later collection *The Paradise of Dainty Devices* (1576).

Witty and sometimes self-deprecating, Vaux wrote a poem that is widely remembered because Shakespeare has the gravedigger in *Hamlet* sing bits of it: "The Agèd Lover Renounceth Love." Written in iambic quatrains rhyming abab, with lines 1, 2, and 4 composed of three and line 3 of four metrical feet, the poem lists the incapacities of the aging lover as he stumbles toward the grave losing his hair, good looks, capabilities, and his interest in the game of love, one by one.

Vaux was among those who introduced a new sort of poetic practice into Renaissance England and who helped establish an eager audience for the sort of poetry that he and the other courtly makers wrote. His total known output fills approximately 30 pages.

Bibliography

Vaux, Thomas, Baron. *The Poems of Lord Vaux*. Edited by Larry P. Vonalt. Denver, Colo.: A. Swallow, 1960.

Viau, Théophile de (1590–1626)

A poet, translator, and dramatist whom the French regime exiled as a freethinking Huguenot in 1619, Théophile (as he is universally called) published his collected works in 1621. These contained translations from PLATO that included the *Phaedo*, *Traicté de l'immortalité de l'âme ou la Mort de Socrate* (A treatise on the immortality of the soul or the death of Socrates), and all the poems Théophile had written until that time. In the same year he was pardoned for his former offenses.

In 1623, however, a collection of satirical and dissolute verse by many hands appeared in a second edition, *Le Parnasse des poétes satiriques* (The Parnassus of satirical poets). Whereas in its first edition the year before, no authors' names appeared, this time Théophile's did. The authorities were quick to blame him for all in the work they found objectionable. Théophile was quickly imprisoned and soon thereafter exiled once again in 1625.

His mocking verse found a more sympathetic audience in England, where SIR JOHN SUCKLING in some of his verse emulated Théophile's satiric style. His SATIRE found a congenial reception as well with those who disapproved of the literary worship of ancient writers, and fragments of his verse dealing with that subject found their way into print in English translation.

Bibliography

Warman, S. A., ed. *Selected Poems of Théophile de Viau, André Chénier, Victor Hugo*. Bristol, U.K.: University of Bristol, 1976.

Vijayavilasam Venkata Kavi Chemakura (ca. 1630–1640)

The most notable work of VENKATA KAVI CHEMAKURA, *Vijayavilasam* retells in the Telegu language of southern India the adventures of the heroic figure Arjuna as they appear in the great EPIC poem of ancient India, the MAHABHARATA.

Arjuna, seeking to come to the aid of a needy Brahman, has inadvertently interrupted the privacy of Queen Draupadi and King Dharmaraja. This sin requires expiation. Arjuna therefore undertakes a pilgrimage to wipe the slate clean. In the course of his journey he meets and marries two princesses, Uluki of Nagaloka and Chitrangada of Pandya. Finally he meets and marries Subhadra, the sister of the Deity Lord Krishna himself. He fights and wins a victory over an army of the Yadavas, eventually freeing himself from the consequences of his unintentional sin.

Though the Telegu version contributes nothing new to the plot of the story, it exploits the linguistic resources of the Telegu language in fresh and delightful ways. For example, as literary historian Goparaju Sambasiva Rao tells us, the poet uses words whose meaning varies depending on how the reader perceives they might be split up. Rao gives the word *mammakagamanavarta* as an example. Perceived as *mamaka agamana varta,* it means "news of my coming." Read as *mamaku agamana varta*—only one sound different, the phrase conveys: "the news of my arrival to my prospective father-in-law." Understood as *mama kaga mana varta,* the meaning becomes "my word to marry his daughter."

Despite this sort of verbal acrobatics, the poem's meanings are clear, and its language and diction gracefully convey those meanings to an attentive reader. Both the poet's patron, King Raghunatha Nayaka, and generations of Telegu readers have considered *Vijayavilasam* a poem unique in the annals of Indian literature.

Bibliography

Rao, Goparaju Sambasiva. *"Vijayavilasam."* In *Encyclopedia of Indian Literature,* vol. 5, p. 4572, edited by Mohan Lal. New Delhi: Sahitya Akademi, 1992.

Virgil (Publius Virgilius Maro) (70–19 B.C.E.)

The work of the most celebrated poet of imperial Rome, Virgil, and the purity and grace of his Latin composition, provided models to which the EPIC and PASTORAL poets of the Renaisance looked for inspiration. His *ECLOGUES* (37 B.C.E.), poems that Virgil had modeled on the Greek poems of the Sicilian Theocritus (310–250 B.C.E.), inspired such poets as EDMUND SPENSER in England, and GUARINI and TASSO in Italy to work in the pastoral mode. Virgil's *Georgics* (30 B.C.E.) stimulated interest in the literary treatment of rural and bucolic subjects. His masterpiece, however, undertaken at the urging of the first emperor of Rome, Augustus Caesar, was the Roman national epic, *The Aeneid* (ca. 19 B.C.E.). *The Aeneid* was designed to trace the founding of the Roman imperial family to the Trojan prince Aeneus and to demonstrate that the fall of Troy was itself a part of a divine plan to establish Rome as a world power under Aeneus's descendants, Rome's emperors.

Though Virgil borrowed his epic structure from Homer before him, his modifications established the form that poet after poet in the European Renaissance would emulate as they strove to claim the same sort of divine foreordination for their own countries and rulers in regional and national epics, and in at least one case a universal epic. A merely suggestive list of such Renaissance epics includes the Portuguese LUÍZ VAZ DE CAMÕES's *THE LUSIADS;* the Italian MATTEO MARIA BOIARDO's *ORLANDO INNAMORATO,* LUDOVICO ARIOSTO's *ORLANDO FURIOSO,* and TORQUATO TASSO's *JERUSALEM DELIVERED.* The list also includes the French THÉODORE AGRIPPA D'AUBIGNE's, *LES TRAGIQUES,* Honoré d'URFÉ's unfinished *La Savoysiade,* and the English EDMUND SPENSER's *THE FAERIE QUEENE,* and JOHN MILTON's *PARADISE LOST.* Whatever else they have in common, and whatever other INTERTEXTUAL resonances appear, all to a greater or less degree look back to Virgil's *Aeneid* as their great exemplar.

virtues

Lists of virtues vary in their details, but Renaissance theological thinking concurred in believing that the so-called *infused virtues* of faith, hope, and charity were given to human beings by divine grace. Beyond those three, chastity, courage or fortitude, gentleness, harmony, humility, justice, obedience, perseverance, patience, prudence, and temperance generally made the list, with courage, justice, prudence, and temperance being considered the cardinal virtues. EDMUND SPENSER in his Protestant EPIC, *THE FAERIE QUEENE,* planned to make the hero of each of the work's 12 books a knight who allegorically personified one of the virtues. Spenser claimed, however, in a famous letter to Sir Walter Raleigh, to have taken his list of virtues from Aristotle's *Nichomachean Ethics.* No scholar, however, has been able to demonstrate a precise match. To the list of virtues above, Spenser added holiness, and the Redcross Knight of the epic's first book depicts that virtue. He also added the British prince Arthur who rolled all the virtues into one.

Sometimes both literary and pictorial ICONOGRAPHY paired or contrasted the virtues with the vices and sins whose opposites they were. Thus the 12 books of the unfinished *Faerie Queene* pitted the knights who represented each of the virtues on SPENSER's list against figures representing various aspects of the SEVEN DEADLY SINS, which attacked the soul and the vices, which sought to undermine human virtue by continually assaulting the five senses.

Vitthal (Vitthal Anant Kshirsagar or Vitthal Bidkar) (1628–1690)

Vitthal is remembered principally as a member of a group of poets who made examples of ancient Sankrit EPIC available in the Marathi language of INDIA and thus to an audience who could not read the ancient tongue. He also combined with that older tradition some of the retellings and devotional emphasis of his near contemporaries, such as the poet EKNATH.

Although modern critics consider Vitthal's work unoriginal in terms of plot and emphasis, they nevertheless remark upon his high degree of poetic craftsmanship, particularly his introduction of meters new in Marathi and his experiments with poetic form.

Vitthal also penned accounts of his annual pilgrimages to Pandharpur that provide interesting glimpses of 17th-century devotional life.

Volpone Ben Jonson (1605)

First acted in 1605 and published in 1607, the blank-verse *Volpone* exemplifies the original use to which JONSON put the character types of the ancient Romans, PLAUTUS and TERENCE. It features a main plot suggested by a hint in the *Satiricon* of the Roman Petronius Arbiter, songs borrowed from the Greek poet Philostratus and the Roman Catullus, and a British development of the Roman COMEDY, the comedy of humors, in which English stereotypes are added to the list of STOCK CHARACTERS drawn from Roman comedy.

A wealthy Venetian bachelor, Volpone (the fox) makes his living by disappointing the hopes and expectations of persons no more admirable than he. Though in his prime, he pretends to be old and ill, just one cough away from his deathbed. A parade of dupes whose names, like Volpone's, provide the keys to their characters, enrich Volpone with expensive presents, each one hoping to be named his exclusive heir. The entourage of the gullible includes a lawyer, Voltore (the vulture), Corbaccio (the large, ugly crow or raven), a merchant, Corvino (a small crow), and an English woman, Lady Would-Be, the wife of Sir Politick Would-be—an ineffectual know-it-all who expects at any moment to become rich as the result of his impractical schemes.

Also present in the cast are the members of Volpone's household, Mosca (the fly, a parasite); Nano (a dwarf); Castrone (a eunuch), and Androgyno (a hermaphrodite). Mosca is the play's principal character. To him falls the responsibility of convincing each of Volpone's false friends that he or she will soon become the Fox's sole heir.

In the course of swindling his dupes, Volpone discovers that Corvino has a beautiful and virtuous wife, Celia. The jealous Corvino keeps Celia closely at home in virtual imprisonment, but disguised as a seller of false medicines—a mountebank, Volpone manages to get a look at her and wants her for his mistress. His scheme to achieve that end becomes the play's main subplot. Volpone has Mosca tell Corvino that only by having a young woman share the presumably impotent Volpone's bed can Mosca assure that the woman's kinsman will become Volpone's heir.

Mosca's plots begin to backfire when he tells Corbaccio's son, Bonario, that his father means to disinherit him in favor of Volpone. Bonario comes to Volpone's house in time to save Celia from being forced into sexual relations with Volpone.

Consequently, a lawsuit comes before the judges of Venice. All the presumptive heirs to Volpone's fortune lie to discredit Bonario and Celia. Having suborned the witnesses and duped the judges and wishing to enjoy the discomfort of his victims, Volpone makes Mosca his heir, thinking that Mosca will continue to do his bidding. Mosca, however, seizes his opportunity to become wealthy, confirms the false report that Volpone has indeed died, and spurns the claims to his inheritance of the hopeful foolish.

The judiciary of Venice, deceived at first into thinking that Celia and Bonario are illicit lovers, eventually realize that they too have been duped, and, in the play's final scenes, they punish the guilty and exonerate the innocent. Volpone is exposed for the fraud he is and his wealth is confiscated for the poor. Celia is taken from Corvino and returned to her father with a triple dowry payment. Mosca and the others are also convicted of crimes against morality and the state.

This brilliant play shares with WILLIAM SHAKE-SPEARE's *Hamlet* the distinction of having been performed both at Oxford and at Cambridge Universities as well as in London.

Bibliography

Jonson, Ben. *Volpone and The Alchemist.* Mineola, N.Y.: Dover Publications, 2004.
———. *Volpone or the Fox; Epicene or the Silent Woman; The Alchemist; Bartholomew Fair.* Edited by Gordon Campbell et al. Oxford and New York: Oxford University Press, 1998.

vulgate Latin

Even before the fall of the Roman Republic and the rise of the imperium after the assassination of Julius Caesar in 44 B.C.E. the Latin language as spoken in the city of Rome was divided into class dialects. The upper social strata spoke a Latin illustrated by the writings of VIRGIL, CICERO, and Caesar himself—the language that the few who still study Latin learn in school. The vast majority of the Roman populace—the workers, the slaves, the tradespeople, and, most significantly, the military—however, spoke a Latin that differed significantly from the language of the Roman aristocracy. The lower classes spoke the vulgate—the language of the common people. The differences were not merely matters of accent; they extended to vocabulary and grammar as well. For example, the upper-class word for horse was *equus*—from which comes English *equestrian.* The vulgate term

was *caballus*—from which come French *cheval,* Spanish *caballo,* Italian *cavallo,* and, by way of French, English *chivalry.* It was the vulgate language, as the example suggests, that the Roman legionaries spoke when they went forth carrying Rome's banners across Europe and around the Mediterranean Sea as far as Asia Minor.

It was this language, too, that indigenous people in conquered territory learned to speak if they wanted to prosper by doing business with the Romans. Thus, over time, vulgate Latin became the lingua franca of the Roman world. After the official Christianization of that world under Emperor Constantine in 324 C.E., vulgate Latin also became the language into which St. Jerome translated the Scriptures during the period 383–405. Jerome's Vulgate translation eventually superseded an earlier Latin version of the BIBLE, and from the ninth century on became the translation stamped with the approval of the Roman Catholic Church. Revised under the auspices of Popes Sixtus XIV and Clement VIII, the Vulgate Latin Bible of 1592–93 is the standard to which Roman Catholic vernacular translations in all other languages appeal.

Renaissance HUMANISTS however, considered vulgate Latin a corruption of the flexible and subtle capacities of classical Latin and did their best to reintroduce classical Latin in preference to the vulgate, which, in their view, was a debased tongue. The Protestant upheavals of the 16th century shifted the terms of the debate from linguistic and literary critical grounds to issues of authority and faith. Humanist and Protestant points of view often became identified in the eyes of their opponents. Sometimes, in fact, those points of view did coincide. The pragmatic outcome from the viewpoint of Scripture was that new translations based on careful comparisons of ancient texts benefited both the Protestant and the Catholic faithful—with one essential difference. When new Catholic translations undermined the received doctrinal authority of Jerome's Vulgate Bible, they tended to be suppressed, as they were in the COMPLUTENSIAN POLYGLOT BIBLE. In humanist and Protestant translations, on the other hand, the antiquity and authenticity of the text from which the translator was working provided the authoritative yardstick for including, modifying, or rejecting a passage. For such doctrinal rather than scientific and linguistic reasons, the work of such a Roman Catholic humanist as DESIDERIUS ERASMUS was considered as reprehensible as the proscribed versions of Scripture produced by such reform-minded translators as the martyred WILLIAM TYNDALE.

Vyas, Harriram (ca. 1510–1598)

A learned poet who served as tutor to King Madhukar Shah of Orccha in the Indian region of Madhya Pradesh, Vyas authored a number of poems, mainly lyrical. A writer who composed in both the Hindi and the Sanskrit LANGUAGES OF INDIA, Vyas is principally remembered for a collection of 787 Hindi verses, *Vyasa vani*. Organized in two parts, the work first presents a reader with a series of devotional songs whose ALLEGORY reminds one of interpretations imposed on the erotic images occurring in the Song of Solomon in the Old Testament. Vyas compares the devotion of a worshipper of Krishna with the ardor of a woman for her lover. The collection goes on to offer a number of poems devoted to the exploration of moral and ethical issues.

Like many of his contemporaries, Vyas was associated with the widespread BHAKTI devotional movement and with the veneration of Krishna. Still in manuscript is a work in Hindi that includes a series of 604 couplets on the art of music and Vyas's two surviving Sanskrit works.

Vyāsa (Krishna Dvaipāyana, Vedavyā)
(fl. ca. 1500 B.C.E.)

In the folklore of India, Vyāsa receives credit for having written or at least assembled the great Indian EPIC, the *MAHABHARATA*. He is said to have been a holy man, and to have dictated this longest of the epics of the ancient world to the elephant-headed deity of the Indian Pantheon, Ganesha, the remover of obstacles.

Wali (Valī, Walī Muhammad, Walī Dakhanī) (ca. 1668–ca. 1707)

Considered by many to be the father of poetry in the Urdu LANGUAGE OF INDIA, the Islamic poet Walī composed his poems first in a dialectical form of Urdu called Dakhinī. He is reputed to have shifted to Urdu as spoken in Delhi, and, with that change, as the tale is told, to have brought about a poetic revolution that established the Urdu of Delhi as the language of choice for poetic composition among north Indian Islamic writers. Persian, which had formerly been the language of Mughal court composition, was displaced as the result of Walī's revolution.

The British scholar C. Shackle suspects this tale as in part revisionist history designed to support the notion of the political ascendancy of the Delhi court. Nonetheless, Walī's work does represent a transitional phase in the development of the poetry of northern India even though the extant body of his work does not bear out the notion of a sudden linguistic shift.

Love was the principal subject of Walī's poems, some of which were hetero- and some homoerotic. All are delightful. His poetic form of choice was the GHAZEL—a poetic form traditionally in favor for lyric poems throughout the Islamic world. His collected works contain some 400 *ghazels*. They proved enor-mously popular among his contemporaries. Some critics have attempted to find a spiritual ALLEGORY in Walī's sexually explicit poems, but it seems that he was a poet of the body rather than of the soul.

All of Walī's extant poems have been translated into French, and a selection appears in English versions.

Bibliography

Hāshimī, Nūrulhasan, editor and translator. *Wali.* English and Urdu selections. New Delhi: Sahitya Akademi, 1986.

Sadiq, M. *A History of Urdu Literature.* Delhi: Oxford University Press, 1984.

Shackle, C. "Walī." *The Encyclopaedia of Islam.* Vol. II. Leiden: Brill, 2002.

Waller, Edmund (1606–1687)

An English poet, translator, and verse eulogist of important persons, a member of Parliament, and a conspirator against Parliament on behalf of King Charles I, Waller studied at Cambridge without taking a degree. He served various constituencies in several parliaments during the period 1624–43.

His best remembered poems were written around 1636–39, a period that coincided with his courtship of Lady Dorothy Sidney, whose attributes he celebrated in the person of his poetic heroine, Sacharissa (the sweetest one).

When the politics of the period became increasingly heated, and King Charles I and parliamentary leaders were at each other's throats, Waller and others conspired in a plot against Parliament that history remembers as "the Waller Plot." The conspiracy was discovered, and, though other plotters were executed, Waller was able to save himself by an abject apology, a splendid defense, giving evidence against his co-conspirators, and payment of a fine of £10,000—an enormous sum that he was able to afford because his first wife had left him a fortune. Although his life was spared, he was disenabled from ever serving again in Parliament, incarcerated in the Tower of London for a time, and banished from the kingdom in 1645.

That same year, several different printings of his poems appeared. All were probably pirated. Some of the volumes contained examples of his political speeches as well. Six years later, however, probably as the result of the intervention on his behalf by the Lord Protector of England, OLIVER CROMWELL, Parliament pardoned Waller, and he was able to come home (1652) and reenabled as a member of Parliament. Three years later, he expressed his thanks in what many regard as his best political poem, "A Panegyric to My Lord Protector." Despite his having healed his breech with Parliament and the Puritan cause, with the restoration of the British monarchy in 1660, Waller penned a similar panegyric for King Charles II, "To the King upon His Majesty's Happy Return."

Among the forms of verse in which Waller particularly distinguished himself is a sort that describes places and settings. The consensus candidate for his best effort at that sort of poem is his description of one of the lovely places of London: "On St. James's Park."

The year 1661 saw his return to Parliament, where he served as the representative for Hastings, Cinque Ports, until 1679. In 1664 a new edition of his poems appeared, this time both with his authorization and the inclusion of his translation of PIERRE CORNEILLE's tragedy, *Pompey the Great*. The popularity of Waller's verse demanded new editions with additional poems in 1664, 1682, and 1686. To that list he added a collection of religious verse, *Divine Poems,* in 1685. A posthumous edition of all his poems appeared in 1689.

While Waller lived and worked, his contemporaries considered him the finest poet of the period, and his biographer, Jack G. Gilbert, attributes that popularity, which has since waned, partly to Waller's capacity for looking on the bright side of everything in a dangerous and difficult time.

Bibliography

Gilbert, Jack G. *Edmund Waller.* Boston: Twayne Publishers, 1979.

Stockdale, Edmund. *The Life of Edmund Waller.* New York: Garland Publishers, 1971.

Waller, Edmund. *Poems, 1645, Together with Poems from Bodleian MS Don d 55.* Menston, U.K.: Scolar Press, 1971.

Walton, Izaak (1593–1683)

A biographer and a craftsman of careful English prose, Izaak Walton achieved fame with THE COMPLEAT ANGLER, *or the Contemplative Man's Recreation* (1653). This work has the distinction of being, with the exception of the Bible, the best selling book ever written in English. By 1952, Walton's partly autobiographical treatise on fishing had gone through no fewer than 265 editions, and it continues to reappear to the delight of almost all who read it. While not all anglers have approved Walton's often valuable advice about fly fishing, his delight in the charms of the countryside, his contentment with his friends, his religious conviction, and his love of nature appear engagingly on every page.

Before his early retirement from business, he had been an ironmonger in London. In that capacity, he seems to have made friends with many clergymen, a profession whose members' company he seems especially to have cherished. To his wide acquaintance among the clergy he may owe introductions to both his first wife, Rachel Floyd (or Floud), whom he married in 1626, and to his second, Anne Ken, whom he wed in 1647. Both were related to notable preachers. Literary people were also his friends. Among them he numbered poets

Charles Cotton and Michael Drayton as well as poet and playwright BEN JONSON.

Walton's clerical connections seem also to have resulted in his being appointed steward to his close friend, George Morley, who was successively bishop of Worcester and then of Winchester.

Though now remembered chiefly for *The Complete Angler,* Walton's contemporaries also valued his skills as a biographer. His first effort in that field was his finishing *The Life of John Donne* that his friend, Sir Henry Wotton had been writing at his death. Walton had been Donne's parishioner and had known him well. This biography by two hands appeared in a posthumous collection of Wotton's writings, Wotton's relics (*Reliquiae Wottonianae,* 1651). The same volume also included Walton's biographical commemoration of his deceased friend.

Having thus established his credentials as a biographer, Walton responded to a request from another clerical friend, Archbishop Sheldon, by writing a life of the celebrated philosopher, scholar, theologian, and advocate of the Church of England, RICHARD HOOKER—the first of Walton's subjects not personally known to him. That work appeared in 1665. In 1670 Walton's life of GEORGE HERBERT appeared. At age 85, Walton agreed to write a life of clergyman Robert Sanderson, which appeared in 1678 and, in a revised edition, in 1685. At his death in 1683 he was engaged in collecting notes toward a life of John Hales, who was provost of Eton College Oxford from 1624 to 1639 and whom Walton probably knew.

In constructing these biographies, Walton seems to have relied on whatever sketchy biographical notices may have appeared concerning his subjects, on interviews with persons among his own circle of acquaintance who had known them, and, for the first time among English biographers, on his subjects' correspondence. Where his facts are thin, he lets the reader know it. Sometimes, though, to increase reader interest, he heightens the facts he does have as well as the conversations he reports. Sometimes, too, he is overly literal in reading from JOHN DONNE's poems, for example, into John Donne's life. Nonetheless, he was the dean of 17th-century British biographers. No modern editions of Walton's biographies are in print, but electronic versions of early editions are widely available in university libraries.

Bibliography
Stanwood, P. G. *Izaac Walton.* New York: Twayne Publishers, 1998.

Walton, Izaak. *The Complete Angler.* Edited by Jonquil Bevan. New York: Oxford University Press, 1983.

Wang Duanshu (Wang Tuanshu) (1621–ca. 1706)

Before she became a writer, an editor, and a political loyalist to the fallen Ming dynasty, Wang Duanshu was a better student, as her father thought, than any of her eight brothers. One of her English-language translators, Ellen Widmer, observes that Wang was one of only a few women of her era who managed to create for herself a real literary career. Like some European Renaissance women, Widmer continues, Wang's learning and literary mastery led her contemporaries to regard her as an "honorary man."

Born in Shaoxing (Shaohsing), Wang lived with her husband in or near Beijing (Peking) until the fall of the Ming dynasty in 1644. After that she moved first to her home province and eventually to Hangzhou (Hangchow) where she participated fully in the life of a sparkling literary society there.

In the first half of the 1650s, financed by her husband and some friends, Wang published her most celebrated collection of poems, a work whose Chinese title translates "Red chantings." This collection featured many sorts of poems in many forms and showcased Wang's remarkable talent and her wide-ranging mastery. The poems in this collection concerned themselves mainly with political topics rather than personal ones, and some considered this unusual in a female poet.

In 1651 appeared her introduction to Li Yu's play, "Soul mates." Much more important, however, was a collection of poems by women. These she edited and published in 1667. Wang describes her selection process for inclusion in this collection. She ruled out long dead women, and decided to include the works of fairly recent "women of note," about whom she could write with confidence. When she had written notes about the women and comments on the selections she had made from their poems, Wang observes, her "anthology was . . . more than 40 chapters long."

Wang organized her material in several ways. She considered social status, era (all recent), and respectability (wives of officials, gentry, and "upright commoners"). She included a section for the work of reformed "disorderly" women and another for erotic poems by women who remained "disorderly." She lumped together poems by Buddhist nuns, Taoist priestesses, and foreigners. When these categories failed to serve, she used subject matter as an organizing principle, so works about ghosts and the strange, jokes, predictions, and recluses fall together under fiction and mysteries. Song lyrics share a section with "random" but elegant writing and scattered notes. She even has a section to remember women whose poems had vanished but about whom something was known or samples of whose calligraphy were extant.

Clearly, Wang had learned from her own experience how difficult it could be for a woman to find outlets for her literary pursuits—even in a society that generally valued women's artistic creations. Her anthology creates a memorial both to women whose works survived them and to women whose works were lost, but whose names survive owing to Wang's efforts.

Bibliography

Kang-i Sun Chang, and Haun Saussy, eds. *Women Writers of Traditional China: An Anthology of Poetry and Criticism.* Stanford, Calif.: Stanford University Press, 1999.

Wang Jiaoluan (Wang Chiao-luan)
(16th c.)

Wang Jiaoluan's poetic efforts are partly preserved in an anthology of poems by notable women. As a girl in the city of Nanyang, Wang Jiaoluan had taken a lover named Zhou Tingzhang (Chao T'ing-Chang). The two exchanged poems and swore eternal fidelity. Zhou, however, moved away and married another woman.

Inconsolable, Wang Jiaoluan secreted all the poems the lovers had exchanged in a packet with a military report her officer father was sending to the provincial court in Suzhou (Soochow). After the report was safely on its way, Wang took her own life by hanging. When the poems arrived and were read, officials at the court summoned the faithless Zhou and punished him—presumably for breach of promise—as the law allowed.

Later, some of Wang's verse and her touching story found their way into a popular anthology, *Mingyuan shi gui* (Compendium of poetry by renowned ladies). Wang's story and a representative poem are available in English translation.

Bibliography

Kang-i Sun Chang, and Haun Saussy, eds. *Women Writers of Traditional China: An Anthology of Poetry and Criticism.* Stanford, Calif.: Stanford University Press, 1999.

Wang Shizhen (Wang Shih-chen)
(1526–1590)

A member of a group of influential writers called the LATER SEVEN MASTERS of Chinese letters, Wang Shizhen was the major poet among them. He wrote prose as well as verse, and around 1576 he collected a large body of his work together in a single volume. This work he divided into the four traditional categories of a Chinese library: creative writing, including poems and fiction; classics; history; and the products of his literary critical thinking and philosophical speculations.

As a group, the seven later masters were principally associated with the antiquarian movement that sought to persuade contemporary Chinese writers to follow the models of earlier periods and encouraged poets, especially, to look to the Tang dynasty for models to follow. Wang, however, never felt confined by this limited view. Throughout his career, he remained flexible in his notions of what constituted good poetry. Sometimes he followed the models of older writers, penning lovely examples of SHI POETRY—odes in the ancient manner. Through most of his life, however, Wang also wrote popular, modern, 16th-century

CI POETRY (*ci* is also transliterated as *tz'u.*) These poems avoided the refined overlay of literary allusiveness and the difficult multiple meanings of his odes. His tastes for the poems of other writers were similarly broad.

Despite critical controversy, Wang continues to be a candidate for the authorship of a splendid novel, THE GOLDEN LOTUS. Western translations of this work often list him as author, and so does a Chinese edition that appeared in 1993. If he is, a wonderful though quite possibly apocryphal story concerns his authorship. Wang is alleged to have avenged himself by giving an enemy who loved pornography a copy of *The Golden Lotus* with poisoned pages. When the reader licked the pages to turn them, he envenomed himself and died. Literary historians credit Wang's book with shifting the focus of the Chinese novel from national history to domestic interactions and intrigue.

Wang continued writing throughout his life. He left much still unpublished when he died, and his grandson gathered much of that material into a very substantial posthumous collection.

Bibliography

Hsia, C. T. *The Classic Chinese Novel: A Critical Introduction.* 1968. Ithaca, N.Y.: Cornell University East Asia Program, 1996.

Yu, Pauline, ed. *Voices of the Song Lyric in China.* Berkeley: University of California Press, 1994.

Wang Shih-chen. *The Golden Lotus.* Translated by Clement Egerton. London: Routledge, 1939; New York: Paragon Book Gallery, 1962.

Wang Shizhen II (Wang Shi-chen II) (1634–1711)

A sometime police magistrate and a high official during the early years of the Qing (Ch'ing) dynasty of China (1644–1911), Wang was the grandson of an earlier poet by the same name. The grandfather had committed suicide when the Ming dynasty fell. The second Wang Shizhen enjoys a continuing reputation as the most influential Chinese poet of the 17th century.

Wang brought to his poems a vast store of knowledge, a refined emotional sensibility, and a gift for musical language. He also based his poetry on a carefully thought out system of composition. Its elements, as the literary historian Richard John Lynn tells us, included "classical diction," "esthetic distance . . . and standards," and "prosodic harmony."

In his most serious work, Wang was a disciple of the literary theories earlier proposed and practiced by both the EARLIER and the LATER SEVEN MASTERS. In Wang's poems, some think, poetic practice founded on those theories reaches its fullest expression. Wang's SHI (*Shih*) poems—his more traditional odes—are characterized by technical mastery and by a sort of Buddhist version of the 19th-century idea of "emotion recollected in tranquility" so that it becomes separated from its sensory roots and achieves the purity and distance that true spirituality requires.

Poems focusing on spirituality, however, characterized Wang's later production rather more than it had the poems he wrote in his youth. Although he always composed in both the high and the popular style, his youthful work more eagerly explored the byways of popular CI, or TZ'U, poems. Written for musical performance to traditional tunes, some of his earlier work was descriptive, catching his emotional responses to scenic vistas. He addressed poems to lovely women. He explored his own feelings of depression or his loneliness for absent friends.

In addition to his verse, Wang also penned important literary criticism, literary history, and discussions of technical poetics. No English translations of this influential poet's work appear to be available.

Bibliography

Lynn, Richard John. "Poetry of the Seventeenth Century." In *The Columbia History of Chinese Literature,* edited by Victor H. Mair. New York: Columbia University Press, 2001.

Webster, John (ca. 1580–ca. 1634)

Widely regarded as the most skillful British Renaissance verse tragedian apart from WILLIAM SHAKESPEARE, John Webster worked as a playwright who both collaborated extensively with others and wrote highly successful dramas independently as well. What little we know of his personal life, however, we principally owe to the determined scholarship of recent researchers, including Mary Edmond and Mark Eccles.

Webster was the son of a successful London carriage maker, John Webster Sr. and his wife Elizabeth Coates Webster. As a nine-year-old, young John may have entered the famous Merchant Taylor's School. His father was a successful member of the Merchant Taylor's Company. Webster's later apparent unfamiliarity with classical languages, however, casts doubt on his long-term attendance. There is a higher degree of certainty, however, that he acquired a legal education at the New Inn of the Inns of Court—the training ground for members of the London legal profession.

Unquestionably in 1602 the theatrical impresario, Philip Henslowe, paid Webster among the authors collaborating on plays named *Two Shapes, Caesar's Fall, Lady Jane,* and *Christmas Comes but Once a Year.* That same year saw Webster's verse in a preface to the third part of *Palmerin of England* by Anthony Munday. In 1604 Webster collaborated with Thomas Dekker on *Westward Ho!* and in 1605 on *Northward Ho!*—plays written for the children's theatrical company of St. Paul's Cathedral. Webster also wrote introductory verses for other plays, including John Marston's *The Malcontent* that was performed in 1604 by Shakespeare's company, The King's Men.

The year 1607 saw the publication of Webster's independently authored *The Famous History of Sir Thomas Wyatt*—a play that likely included the text from the earlier *Lady Jane.* Sometime after 1610 but before the end of 1619, Webster wrote *The Devil's Law-Case*—a play whose legal technicalities help make the case that Webster was educated in the law. The theatrical company Queen Anne's Men performed it between 1617 and 1620.

In 1612 and 1613 The Red Bull Company and The King's Men, respectively, performed Webster's best-remembered tragedies, The White Devil and The Duchess of Malfi. These were followed in 1614–15 by a play now lost, *The Guise.* Webster may have then collaborated with Thomas Middle-

ton on *Anything for a Quiet Life*—a play of uncertain date and authorship.

Further collaborations followed, some of them less certain than others. *A Late Murther of the Son upon the Mother, or Keep the Widow Waking,* written by Webster in collaboration with Dekker, John Ford, and William Rowley was performed in 1624 but has not survived. Returning to his merchant roots, Webster provided the text for a pageant for the inauguration of the Merchant Taylor, John Gore, as lord mayor of London. About the same time he *may* have collaborated with William Rowley on *A Cure for a Cuckold,* and a year or so later with Webster, Fletcher, Ford, and Philip Massinger on *The Fair Maid of the Inn.* No one is certain.

No one is certain either when he died. It could have been as early as 1628 or, more likely, between 1632 and 1634. In addition to the plays he authored either alone or in collaboration, he also wrote occasional verses and tributes—sometimes introducing plays or even, on one occasion, a dictionary.

We do know something of his manner of working. He was apparently a slow and meticulous artist who wrote with difficulty and revised a lot. He was particularly gifted at taking the work of earlier writers and playwrights and transforming it into a drama that, though its origins might be recognizable, had become in his hands an exquisitely wrought piece of poetic stagecraft. He preferred to work from translations of originals written in foreign tongues—a fact that raises questions about his early schooling.

Bibliography

Ranald, Margaret Loftus. *John Webster.* Boston: Twayne Publishers, 1989.

Webster, John. *The Duchess of Malfi: John Webster.* Edited by Dympna Callaghan. New York: St. Martin's Press, 2000.

———. *The White Devil; The Duchess of Malfi; The Devil's Law-case; A Cure for A Cuckold.* Edited by René Weis et al. New York: Oxford University Press, 1996.

———. *The White Devil by John Webster.* Stratford, U.K.: Nick Hern Books [with] the Royal Shakespeare Company, 1996.

White Devil, The John Webster (1612)

The White Devil and THE DUCHESS OF MALFI present a pair of complex and gripping tragedies that have gained JOHN WEBSTER a reputation as the finest British Renaissance tragedian after WILLIAM SHAKE-SPEARE. Based recognizably but loosely on historical figures and incidents, the play asserts the moral ambiguity its title suggests. The historical Vittoria Accoramboroni came from Gubbio. Her family used her spectacular beauty to arrange a Roman marriage advantageous to themselves. Webster turns the stunning young woman into Vittoria Corombona, making her a Venetian prostitute who, though equally beautiful to the eye, is a repository of vicious appetite and wickedness within.

In the first act we discover that Vittoria's brother, Flamineo, is serving as a pander to the Duke of Brachiano, Paulo Giordano Orsini. Flamineo is trying to persuade Vittoria to accept the duke as her lover. Over the objections of his and Vittoria's mother Cornelia, one of the few moral characters of the play, Flamineo proposes encouraging Brachiano to arrange the assassinations of his wife, Isabella de Medicis, and of Vittoria's elderly husband, Camillo.

The second act portrays the attempt by the Duchess Isabella to regain her husband Brachiano's affection. When he coldly rejects her, however, and privately swears in legal terminology never to sleep with her again, Isabella protects Brachiano's reputation by publicly repeating the legal forms he has just used to separate herself from him.

Two silent scenes follow that depict the murders of Isabella and Camillo. Knowing that, following her prayers, Isabella nightly kisses her husband's portrait, her assassins fumigate his picture with poisoned smoke. She kisses it and dies. Camillo, who is celebrating his appointment as commander of a fleet charged with clearing the Italian coasts of pirates, has his neck broken in a tavern while competing in a vaulting contest—a murder ineffectually arranged to look like an accident.

Suspected of complicity in her husband's death, Vittoria stands trial in Act 3. A lawyer accuses her in Latin, and when she objects to the foreign tongue, he continues in INKHORN TERMS—flowery, almost incomprehensible English. She also objects to that jargon. In plainer language, Cardinal Monticelso, ostensibly her judge, also acts as her accuser. Vittoria staunchly denies her guilt, not only as a murderess but also as an adulteress. Her brothers, however, bemoan her loose ways, and while the murder charge does not stick, she is nonetheless sentenced to life in a religious house for reformed prostitutes.

Cardinal Monticelso and Duke Francisco de Medicis, in the meantime, pursue separate strategies in Act IV to avenge the death of their sister, Isabella. Confronted by the murdered Isabella's ghost, the duke lays a plan for vengeance. At this juncture, however, the pope dies and in the following election, Cardinal Monticelso is elected Pope Paul IV. Duke Brachiano and Vittoria seize the confusion surrounding the papal elevation as a moment to flee Rome together and to marry.

Enraged at this development, Pope Paul excommunicates both. In a further twist to a complex plot, the pope also learns in the confessional from Francisco's retainer, Ludovico, that Duke Francisco has hired him to murder Duke Brachiano and that Ludovico has a private reason for vengeance since he was in love with the murdered Isabella. The pope tries to dissuade Ludovico from committing the murder by withholding absolution. Francisco, however, sends Ludovico a thousand ducats in the pope's name, and Ludovico thinks the pope really wants him to avenge Isabella.

The last act opens in Padua where a tournament will be held in honor of Vittoria's wedding to Brachiano. New plot complications follow rapidly on one another. Flamineo confesses an affair with Vittoria's African maidservant, the Moor Zanche, whom he falsely promised to marry. He next commits fratricide, killing his brother, Marcello, at the feet of their mother, Cornelia. Cornelia's grief drives her instantly mad.

During the final preparations for the wedding tournament, Duke Francisco, disguised as the Moor, Mulinassar, and Flamineo put poison in Duke Brachiano's helmet. As soon as he begins to perspire in the tournament, the poison acts. Writhing in agony Brachiano is carried to his deathbed. There the assassins Ludovico and Gasparo await him disguised as monks. Ostensibly present to administer extreme unction, in Vittoria's presence they strangle Brachiano instead, assuring him that his eternal damnation is unavoidable.

The villainous Flamineo now undergoes a hardly credible change of heart, and guiltily rushes off to tell Vittoria of his vow that neither he nor she will long outlive Brachiano. As he prepares to shoot Vittoria, his paramour Zanche intervenes, suggesting that he should show the women how to die. He agrees, giving them pistols. They shoot him, and, thinking him dead, they taunt him. He, however, has anticipated their ploy and gave them weapons charged only with powder—no bullets. Just then Ludovico and Gasparo, still disguised as monks, enter to kill Flamineo and the two women. Vittoria faces death without a qualm. So does Flamineo, and, Zanche, who had had a hand in the murders of Camillo and Isabella, dies in silence.

Lodovico and his companions are arrested, tried, and executed, and the play ends with Giovanni, the son of the Duke of Brachiano, preparing to succeed his father.

Bibliography

Webster, John. *The White Devil by John Webster.* Edited by Simon Trussler. London: Nick Hern Books [and] . . . the Royal Shakespeare Company, 1996.

Wickram, Jörg (Georg) (ca. 1505– ca. 1560)

A novelist, editor, and playwright, Wickram was the first to write novels concerning the middle classes in 16th-century Germany. He initiated a trend away from the romances of the Middle Ages that had earlier dominated the German prose literary scene. One such work is his *The Golden Thread* (*Der Goldfaden,* 1557), the only one of Wickram's works available in English. While the work displays elements of the medieval romance tradition— knightly valor and the pursuit of a fair maiden's hand, its hero, Lionel, springs from humble origins. Lionel is a shepherd's son who, in addition to bravery, displays extraordinary kindness, virtue, and perseverance. As a result he marries a nobleman's daughter. The tale's subtitle advertised the

work to its readers as "a most useful narrative for all who love virtue." Other novels by Wickram include *Der jungen Knaben Spiegel* (The mirror for young boys, 1554), and *Von guten und bösen Nachbarn* (About good neighbors and bad, 1556). Like *The Golden Thread,* these novels are didactic in their purposes. They show how virtue, community service, and hard work get rewarded and conversely how crime and vice are punished.

Wickram also continued the practice that HANS SACHS had earlier begun of writing religious plays for performance at Shrovetide. Wickram authored, for instance, a version of the biblical story of the prodigal son in 1540. He also founded a MEISTERSINGER school in the city of Colmar in 1549. Beyond his work in the genres above, Wickram modeled at least one effort on the literature of fools founded by SEBASTIAN BRANT. Wickram rewrote and enlarged Thomas Murner's work, *Narrenbeschwörung* (Exorcism of fools, 1512). In 1549 Wickram also edited and modernized Albrecht von Halberstadt's earlier translation of OVID's *Metamorphoses.*

Wickram also began a popular subgenre in Germany. His *Das Rollwagenbüchlein* (The little book for stagecoach travel, 1555) became a model for other authors who addressed the market for diverting reading material to while away the uncomfortable hours on the road. Within the next five decades, as the literary historian Richard Ernest Walker tells us, eight other writers followed Wickram's example of providing travelers with collections of stories.

Wickram's own life followed the course he proposed for his heroes. The illegitimate son of a city councilor of Colmar, Wickram received no formal education. Nonetheless, by dint of hard work and perseverance he learned to be a goldsmith, occupied offices in the civil service of two cities, and became one of the most notable German authors of his period. His complete works run to some 12 volumes in the standard, late-20th-century German edition.

Bibliography

Walker, Richard Ernest. "Georg . . . Wickram." In *Encyclopedia of German Literature,* edited by Mathias Konzeit. Vol. 2. Chicago and London: Fitzroy Dearborn Publishers, 2000.

Wickram, Jörg. *The Golden Thread.* Translated by Pierre Kaufke. Pensacola: University of West Florida Press, ca. 1991.

Wilson, Thomas (ca. 1525–1581)

An English statesman and diplomat, Thomas Wilson also used his deep mastery of the Latin prose of CICERO and Quintilian to construct an early system of rhetoric and composition for the English language. Born in Lincolnshire, he studied at Eton and later at King's College, Cambridge.

In his most influential book, his *Arte of Rhetorique* (1553), Wilson advocated speaking plain, straightforward English that an ordinary person could understand. He condemned INKHORN TERMS, the resurrection of archaic terms, and the introduction of unfamiliar coinages. At the same time, he recognized that a certain amount of classical ornament and musical language could make prose more readable. He was fond of SATIRE, and approved of ridicule and illustrative anecdotes to make writing more interesting.

Earlier Wilson had written *The Rule of Reason, Conteyning the Arte of Logike* (1551). Like the *Arte of Rhetorique*, *The Rule of Reason* found a ready audience. By 1593 both works had gone through eight editions. Wilson's third book did not enjoy as much success. His *A Discourse upon Usurye, by way of Dialogue and Oracions* (1572) saw only one further edition (1584) in the Renaissance.

A pair of colorful episodes enlivened his personal story. In 1555 he found it prudent to flee England for a time while Queen Mary I occupied the throne. While visiting Rome in 1557, however, he was accused of plotting against Mary's adviser, Cardinal Pole. The queen summoned Wilson back to England. When he ignored the summons, the Roman INQUISITION charged him with heresy and arrested him. Just then, however, a discontented Roman citizenry rose in arms. Wilson used the resultant confusion to cover his escape.

With the restoration of an Anglican monarchy under ELIZABETH I, Wilson returned to public service as a diplomat in Portugal and the Netherlands. In 1579 he became Elizabeth's secretary of state.

Bibliography

Wilson, Thomas. *The Art of Rhetoric.* Edited by Peter E. Medine. University Park, Md.: Pennsylvania State University Press, ca. 1994.

———. *The Rule of Reason, Conteinyng the Arte of Logique.* Edited by Richard S. Sprague. Northridge, Calif.: San Fernando Valley State College, 1972.

Wivallius, Lars (1605–1569)

A Swedish lyric poet whose works are infused with a spirit of enlightened nationalism, Lars Wivallius anticipated the patriotic work of a better known 18th-century successor, Carl Michael Bellman. Wivallius welcomed into Swedish culture positive influences from the other countries of Europe. For that reason, he is considered to be the father of modern Swedish poetry. Although Wivallius's work is available in a 20th-century Swedish edition, it has not been translated into other languages.

Bibliography

Wivallius, Lars. *Svenska dikter* (Swedish poems). Edited by Erik Gamby. Stockholm: Minerva, ca. 1990.

Woman Killed with Kindness, A Thomas Heywood (1603)

A domestic TRAGICOMEDY written principally in rhyme and blank verse, *A Woman Killed with Kindness* opens at the wedding feast of Mr. Frankford and his wife Nan. Amidst the celebrations and much sexual punning, two of the wedding guests, Sir Charles Mountford and the bride's brother Sir Francis Acton, agree to hunt the following day with hounds and falcons. They wager about whose falcon will make the first kill.

In Act I, Scene iii, Sir Charles wins the wager, but Sir Francis disputes the outcome. As tempers flare the men first exchange insults and then draw their weapons. In the ensuing fight, Sir Charles kills two of Sir Francis's men. This event leaves the killer conscience-stricken. The sheriff, whom Acton has summoned, arrives and arrests the repentant Sir Charles for murder. Also on the scene,

Sir Charles's sister, Susan Mountford, is much distressed on her brother's behalf.

The second act opens with Mr. Frankford reflecting upon his own happy situation in the world. He congratulates himself on his wife's beauty and chastity, and on his own wealth. The arrival of his friend, Wendoll, with news of Sir Charles's arrest interrupts Frankford's soliloquy. Wendoll reports on the quarrel and its outcomes, and Frankford generously takes Wendoll into his service as a companion and second in command of the household.

Some years pass, and in Act II, Scene ii, the audience discovers that, despite the efforts of his enemies to see him hanged for murder, Sir Charles Mountford has managed to be pardoned for his crimes. Doing so, however, has cost him everything he owns except for a small cottage and 500 pounds. A scheming, secret enemy, Shafton, presses a loan on Sir Charles.

In the next scene we find that, despite Wendoll's gratitude for Mr. Frankford's generosity, Wendoll has fallen violently in love with Mrs. Frankford. He reveals his feelings to her, and though she reproves him, she nonetheless allows herself to be seduced. A servant, Nicholas, discovers the affair and resolves to report it to Frankford.

The third act opens with Shafton's intrusion upon Sir Charles and his sister Susan. By hard work the two have managed to make a meager living on the one bit of family property they still own. Shafton covets both the property and Susan. He offers to buy the place, and, when Mountford refuses to sell, Shafton demands immediate repayment of the 300-pound loan and its interest. Sir Charles cannot pay, so Shafton has him clapped in irons and flung into the worst dungeon of the local prison. Just then, Sir Francis Acton passes by, and his enmity toward the Mountfords evaporates as he finds himself suddenly smitten with love for Susan.

The servant Nicholas follows through in Act III, Scene ii and tells Frankford about his wife's illicit liaison with Wendoll. Incredulous, Frankford makes arrangements to see for himself, but first the audience is prepared for his discovery with a conversation over a card game. The repartee is filled with double meanings that allude to Wendoll and Nan Frankford's adultery.

The fourth act opens with Susan Acton's canvassing her friends and relatives in an effort to raise enough cash to pay her brother's debts. Everyone refuses—some even disclaiming kinship now that the Mountfords have lost everything. To relieve her distress, Sir Francis Acton offers to pay Mountford's debts. Susan, however, thinks that her honor is for sale and refuses. Sir Francis nonetheless pays the debts, thereby purchasing his former enemy's freedom. Mountford at first gives credit to his relatives until his jailer tells him of Acton's generosity. Susan surmises that Acton is trying to buy her chastity. This plot line resolves itself in the second scene of Act IV with the reconciliation of Acton and Mountford and Susan's agreeing to marry Sir Francis, declaring that she "will yield to fate / And learn to love where . . . [she] till now did hate."

After two more scenes of suspenseful preparation, Frankford discovers his wife and Wendoll asleep together. Frankford restrains his fury against his wife, though with sword drawn he chases Wendoll, dressed in his night gown, offstage. Frankford then promises his wife that he'll kill her with kindness. He provides her with a house, income, and servants, but he never wishes to see her again or let her near the children.

Stricken with remorse, Mrs. Frankford starves herself. From her deathbed she pleads with her husband to come to see her and forgive her. Frankford relents and visits her. On his arrival he finds her dying and repentant. He forgives her, weds her again with a kiss, and she dies. The play ends with Frankford's composing his wife's epitaph: "Here lies she whom her husband's kindness killed."

A Woman Killed with Kindness, with its parallel plots, with its contrasts between the wages of sin and the rewards of virtue, and with its tasteful avoidance of onstage bedroom scenes is generally considered Heywood's masterpiece. In it Heywood attempts, as he regularly does, to please and to instruct.

Bibliography

Heywood, Thomas. *A Woman Killed with Kindness.* Edited by R. W. Van Fossen. London: Methuen, 1970.

women, the quarrel or debate about

A heated debate about the comparative capacities of men and women began in Europe in the late Middle Ages and continued throughout the Renaissance and beyond. Though the French phrase *Querelle des Femmes* is frequently limited to the 15th and 16th centuries' continuation of this discussion, the issue appears here in a somewhat broader context.

GIOVANNI BOCCACCIO wrote on both sides of the debate about women and their moral and intellectual capacities. In his Italian *Elegy for Madonna Fiametta* and his Latin work *About Famous Women* (*De mulieribus claris*, 1361) he praises women and lauds their capabilities and accomplishments. In his *Corbaccio* (Ugly crow, after 1354), on the other hand, his criticism of women becomes fiercely misogynistic.

Writing in France at the end of the 14th century, the Venetian-born Christine de Pisan, translated Boccaccio's account of famous women and incorporated that translation into her *The Book of the City of Ladies* (1405). This work together with her *Letter to the God of Love* (1399) and her *Poem of the Rose* asserted the moral and intellectual excellence of women and defended them against the antifeminist assertions of Jean de Meung in his earlier *Romance of the Rose*. Christine de Pisan's work remained an important source document for women writing throughout the Renaissance.

The literary historian Albert Rabil points to a widely translated Latin lecture delivered in 1509 by Heinrich Agrippa von Nettesheim, his *Declamation on the Nobility and Preeminence of the Female Sex* (published 1529), and to Mario Equicola's *De mulieribus* (On women, 1500) as major, early-16th-century contributions to the debate. Agrippa argued that women had been more privileged in the ancient world than they were in 16th-century Europe and contended on the basis of authoritative ancient texts, including the Bible, that women were men's superiors. On the basis of the first chapter of Genesis, Agrippa asserted that men and women had been created equal in soul, and, on the basis of the New Testament, he shows that women in the primitive Christian Church had been leaders and had both preached and prophesied. Both Agrippa and Equicola agreed, Rabil tells us, that their contemporary male domination of women was a result of socially constructed gender roles and not of biologically rooted capacities.

Many joined the debate on both sides of the issue. In Italy such writers as VERONICA FRANCO, TULLIA D'ARAGONA, BALDESSARE CASTIGLIONE in his *THE BOOK OF THE COURTIER*, LUDOVICO ARIOSTO in his *ORLANDO FURIOSO*, and perhaps most heatedly of all, LUCREZIA MARINELLA in her *The NOBILITY AND EXCELLENCE OF WOMEN AND THE DEFECTS AND VICES OF MEN* (1600) entered the fray on the side of women. So did AGNOLO FIRENZUOLA who, in his *Dialogue on the Beauties of Women* (1541), approached the issue from the perspectives of the plastic arts and the philosophy of PLATO. Taking up cudgels against women, we find among others the writer whose work had so annoyed Marinella. In his *I doneschi difetti* (The defects of women, 1599) Giuseppe Passi summarized and presented most of the antifeminist arguments that his predecessor woman haters had mustered.

Turning to France we find the women's side of the argument represented by writers such as MARIE DE GOURNAY; PERNETTE DU GUILLET; HÉLISENNE DE CRENNE; ANNE-MARIE-LOUISE D'ORLEANS, DUCHESSE OF MONTPENSIER; and MARGUERITE DE NAVARRE.

The example of numerous women rather than or in addition to their pens argued their case. Queen Catherine de' Medici of France was its de facto ruler. In England first Mary then Elizabeth Tudor (Mary I and ELIZABETH I) occupied the throne, and another Mary ruled in Scotland. Margaret of Navarre both wrote literary works and maintained one of the most enlightened and intellectual courts of Europe. Vittoria Colonna both governed a small principality and maintained a court where the intellectual lights of Italy gathered to exchange ideas with their hostess and with each other.

In England the Duchess of Newcastle wrote outspokenly profeminist works while she strove to fashion for herself a gender-neutral public persona, and EDMUND SPENSER voiced his unequivocal support for Elizabeth I as Gloriana in his *THE FAERIE QUEENE*. In Scotland, however, John Knox fulminated against women and their capacities in his *First Blast of the Trumpet against the Monstrous Regiment of Women* (1558).

The New World saw an attack on SOR JUANA INÉS DE LA CRUZ by her supposed friend the bishop of Puebla. The bishop wrote pseudonymously, pretending to be a nun named Sor Philotea (Sister Love-God). In her response, Sor Juana wrote a brilliant, courteous, tactful, and impassioned defense of her activities and intellectual pursuits. Her *REPLY TO SOR PHILOTEA* (1691) has become a fundamental document of modern feminism.

Elsewhere in the world, though the terms of the argument differed and were traceable to causes unlike those in Europe, analogues of the debate sometimes surfaced in the literary sector. The Bengali novel *Sundari Malua* (Beautiful Malua), which has been controversially attributed to a female Bengali poet CHANDRABATI, becomes a novel of social protest against Mughal India's "black laws." These gave village and regional authorities the power to hold women hostage as pledges against the unpaid taxes of their families. In China, particularly in poems authored by women, one finds a good deal of unhappiness occasioned by the subordinate roles most women played to their fathers and husbands. Occasionally, however, Chinese women in the novels break out of the mold and appear as military figures and leaders as in *THE PEONY PAVILION*.

Bibliography

Agrippa, Heinrich. Declamation on the Nobility and Preeminence of the Female Sex. Translated by Albert Rabil. Chicago: University of Chicago Press, 1996. [For further bibliography, please see the cross-referenced entries.]

women writers in India, 1500–1700

The comparatively few women writers in India during this period spanned a broad spectrum of social classes from princesses to members of the artisan class, to village entertainers and housewives and menial servants. The princesses included GUL-BADAN BEGUM, daughter of the Mughal emperor BABUR and sister to the emperor Humayun. Writing in Persian liberally sprinkled with words and phrases in her native Turki, at the request of her nephew, the emperor AKBAR, she penned a history of his father, Humayun. The work is famous for its intimate histories of the royal family and for its description of a 16th-century pilgrimage to Mecca.

Also a princess was MIRABAI or the Princess Mira. Mira became a devotee of the Indian devotional movement called BHAKTI. Although identifying the poems she actually wrote among the more than 1,400 attributed to her has proved difficult, those that seem genuine are characterized by an intense religious ecstasy in which she pictures herself as the beloved of the Hindu deity Krishna. Many of the poems attributed to her are in the Gujerati language

CHANDRABATI was the daughter of a poet-singer named Banidas who eked out a subsistence living with his oral art in a village in what is now Bangladesh. Jilted by the man she loved, she entered the religious life and composed a Bengali version of a Hindu sacred epic, the *Ramayana* and a bandit story *Dasyu Kenarum* (The bandit Kenarum). The literary historians Susie Tharu and K. Lalita have controversially also attributed to her a novelistic poem of feminist social protest, *Sundari Malua* (The beautiful Malua).

A village wife of the Brahman caste and a religious mystic, poet, and saint, BAHINABAI wrote in the Marathi language a series of 473 ABHANGAS that begin with an ATMANIVEDANA—a spiritual biography that traces the progress of her reincarnated soul through several lives. She too was a devotee of the BHAKTI movement.

Writing in the Kannada language in the late 17th century, SANCIYA HONNAMMA was a servant in the royal household of Mysore. She wrote a verse book of instruction, *Hadibadeya Dharma* (Duties of a devoted wife).

Bibliography

Tharu, Susie, and K. Lalita, eds. *Women Writing in India, 600 B.C. to the Present*. Volume I. New York: The Feminist Press at the City University of New York, 1991.

Wonderful Year, The Thomas Dekker (1603)

DEKKER'S plague-pamphlet *The Wonderful Year* illustrates the sprightliness of the prose of an Elizabethan writer who was a poet, a playwright, and an early English journalist as well. During the year the pamphlet discusses, 1603, several major events had occurred in London. First, England's long-reigning queen ELIZABETH I had fallen ill and died in March. Her death was accompanied by all the pomp and circumstance of a state funeral and Elizabeth's interment at Westminster. Her burial was followed by the unexpectedly peaceful succession of her cousin James VI of Scotland as King JAMES I of England, and the colorful ceremonies surrounding his coronation.

In addition to these events of national consequence, during the summer of 1603 the bubonic plague broke out in London with the consequent death of tens of thousands and all the fear, medical quackery, largely ineffectual public health measures, and religious fervor that a premodern epidemic entailed.

Not only does Dekker vividly paint the scenes associated with these events, he also depicts, particularly in his descriptions of the plague, his own horrified reactions to the appalling scenes he witnesses and recounts, such as the story of the bride who went ill to her own wedding and came home a corpse. In addition to playing on his readers' heartstrings with such pathetic tales, Dekker also expresses with effective SATIRE his total disgust for the ineffectual fraternity of physicians whose best efforts against the plague were total failures.

Bibliography

Dekker, Thomas. *The Plague Pamphlets of Thomas Dekker.* Edited by F. P. Wilson. Norwood, Pa.: Norwood Editions, 1977.

———. *The Wonderful Year and Selected Writings.* Edited by E. D. Pendry. London: Edward Arnold, 1967.

Wroth, Lady Mary (Mary Sidney Wroth) (ca. 1587–ca. 1653)

The first daughter of the Earl of Leicester, Sir Robert Sidney and Barbara Gamage Sidney, and the niece of SIR PHILIP SIDNEY, Mary Sidney was named for her aunt, MARY SIDNEY HERBERT, THE COUNTESS OF PEMBROKE. In 1604 the earl arranged for his daughter to marry Sir Robert Wroth. As the wife of a wealthy knight, Mary Wroth joined the court of King JAMES I, where, along with other members of her circle, she participated in COURT ENTERTAINMENTS. She is known to have performed, for instance, in BEN JONSON's *The Masque of Blackness.*

Following the example of other members of her famous literary family, Wroth began writing sonnets and circulating them in manuscript. Other poets, including Ben Jonson and GEORGE CHAPMAN admired them, and the literary historian Josephine Roberts tells us that Jonson said reading Wroth's poems had made him both a better poet and a better lover.

Familial tragedy dogged Wroth's footsteps for a time. She lost her husband in 1614, and her son James followed his father in death in 1616. Her husband's untimely passing left her deeply in debt, and she faced financial hardship throughout the rest of her life as she tried to clear his obligations. She chose not to remarry, but she later became the mistress of a cousin, William Herbert, the third Earl of Pembroke, and bore him two children.

Around 1618–20 she began writing the first work of original fiction certainly authored by an Englishwoman. Dedicated to her cousin, Susan Herbert, Countess of Montgomery, THE COUNTESSE OF MOUNTGOMERIES URANIA (1621, second part 1999) is an enormous prose ROMANCE. It combines Wroth's thinly veiled eyewitness experiences of life in King James' court with the distillation of her reading of European poetry and prose. To a considerable extent Wroth modeled her work on her uncle Sir Philip Sidney's PASTORAL work, ARCADIA, but one also finds echoes of CHIVALRIC ROMANCES such as GARCI RODRIGUEZ DE MONTALVO's AMADIS OF GAUL, LUDOVICO ARIOSTO's ORLANDO FURIOSO, and EDMUND SPENSER's THE FAERIE QUEENE. The influence of MIGUEL DE CERVANTES SAAVEDRA's DON QUIXOTE DE LA MANCHA also appears. To the 1621 edition of *Urania,* Wroth appended her SONNET sequence *Pamphilia to Amphilanthus.* Although in that edition the text of *Urania* simply breaks off as Sidney's *Arcadia* also does, a 20th-century scholar, Josephine Roberts, discovered in the Newberry Library in Chicago a second part of the work that continues from the end of Part I. Owing to Robert's efforts and, following her untimely death, those of successor editors, Suzanne Gossett and Janel Mueller, the second part of Wroth's groundbreaking work finally saw print in 1999. Beyond her *Urania* and her sonnet sequence, Wroth also penned a pastoral TRAGICOMEDY, *Love's Victory,* which remained in unpublished manuscript until 1988.

Lady Mary Wroth pioneered the participation of women in the literary marketplace of Renaissance England. The British aristocracy had considered print publication déclassé—especially for a woman—as compared with circulating their writings in manuscript. The appearance in 1621 of Wroth's romance, *Urania,* and her sonnet sequence, *Pamphilia to Amphilanthus,* provoked a sexist response that had as its objective the exclusion of women from writing and publishing.

Bibliography

Wroth, Lady Mary. *Lady Mary Wroth's Love's Victory: The Penshurst manuscript.* Edited by Michael G. Brennan. London: Roxburghe Club, 1988.

———. *Pamphilia to Amphilanthus by Lady Mary Wroth.* Edited by G. F. Waller. Salzburg, Austria: Institut für Englische Sprache und Literatur, University of Salzburg, 1977.

———. *Poems: a Modernized Edition: Lady Mary Wroth.* Edited by R. E. Pritchard. Keele, Staffordshire, U.K.: Keele University Press, 1996.

———. *The First Part of the Countess of Montgomery's Urania.* Edited by Josephine A. Roberts. Binghamton, N.Y.: Renaissance English Text Society ... [and] Medieval and Renaissance Texts and Studies, 1995.

———. *The Poems of Lady Mary Wroth.* Edited by Josephine A. Roberts. Baton Rouge: Louisiana State University Press, ca. 1983.

———. *The Second Part of the Countess of Montgomery's Urania.* Edited by Josephine A. Roberts and completed by Suzanne Gossett and Janel Mueller. Tempe, Ariz.: Renaissance English Text Society ... [and] Arizona Center for Medieval and Renaissance Studies, 1999.

Wu Cheng'en (Wu Ch'Eng-en) (1500–1582)

Very possibly but not certainly the author of one of the greatest of Chinese classical novels, THE JOUR-

NEY TO THE WEST, Wu Cheng'en belonged to a very large group of Chinese authors who made their livings in the vast network of the Chinese civil service. He apparently never rose to very high office. The theory that he authored *The Journey to the West* only emerged in 1923 when an entry listing him as the writer of the work was discovered in *The Gazeteer of Huaian-fu,* dating from the period 1621–27. The question of Wu's ostensible authorship continues at the center of an unusually polite scholarly controversy.

Seventeenth-century sources allude vaguely to Wu as a writer of SATIRE and as a skillful poet. If he was *The Journey*'s author, in addition to a marvelous talent for imaginative, fantasy fiction, he also displayed considerable mastery of both Buddhist and Taoist religious and philosophical lore.

A useful summary of the debate concerning Wu's authorship and the evidence on both sides of the issue appears in the introduction to the first volume of Anthony C. Yu's magnficent translation of *The Journey to the West.*

Bibliography

Yu, Anthony C., trans. and ed. *The Journey to the West.* 1977. Chicago: University of Chicago Press, 1980.

Wyatt, Sir Thomas (1503–1542)

An English diplomat, soldier, and statesman, Wyatt was also the foremost poet during the reign of Henry VIII. Together with HENRY HOWARD, THE EARL OF SURREY, Wyatt brought to England the Italian manner of writing lyric verse in the tradition of PETRARCH. He also introduced into English the practice of writing letters in verse, and he established a widely imitated form for the verse translation of the Psalms.

During his lifetime his lyrics circulated in manuscript, as was the fashion among the English nobility and upper gentry. In the decade before his death, however, some of his lyrics appeared in print in an early verse anthology *The Court of Venus* (ca. 1537–39). His other lyrics appeared in print posthumously. The year 1549 saw NICHOLAS GRIMALD's publication of Wyatt's verse translations—one might say *transcreations*—of the penitential psalms that bring to the biblical text both King David's and Wyatt's interest in eroticism. That eroticism reappears in the lyrics published in TOTTEL'S MISCELLANY (*Songs and Sonnets, 1557*). Wyatt was among those accused of adultery with Queen ANNE BOLEYN. He was in fact a prisoner in the Tower of London when she was beheaded there. Unlike some of the others accused, however, Wyatt was released. Yet before Anne became queen, Wyatt's famous sonnet beginning, "Whoso list to hunt, I know where is an hind," gives evidence that he was among her admirers.

One of Wyatt's recent biographers, Stephen Mirriam Foley, argues that Wyatt, who was always at or near the center of important national events, became a spokesman in his verse for the English nation. He reflected in his writing the ambiguities and challenges that characterized a kingdom in the throes of religious and political change. He also reflected the personal ambiguities of an able politician and courtier who experienced personal disappointments as well as successes and sometimes expressed a stoic resignation to his sense of injured merit.

Bibliography

Foley, Stephen Merriam. *Sir Thomas Wyatt.* Boston: Twayne Publishers, 1990.

Rollins, Hyder E., ed. *Tottel's Miscellany (1557–87).* 1928. Cambridge, Mass.: Harvard University Press, 1965.

Wyatt, Sir Thomas. *Sir Thomas Wyatt: The Complete Poems.* 1978. New Haven, Conn.: Yale University Press, 1981.

Xu Wei (Hsü Wei) (1521–1593)

A Chinese essayist, wit, eccentric, painter, and playwright, Xu became an advocate of importing into the Chinese literature of his era features from that of much earlier times. He belonged to a literary movement that favored looking within to discover truth and wisdom.

Xu is best remembered for his reinvention with new rules of a Chinese genre of farce called ZAZU, or *tsa-chü*. By the late 16th century, except at court where the emperor's taste for farce kept the older form alive, public taste had shifted to more melodramatic fare. Moreover, because all CHINESE THEATER is musical, because all Chinese plays fit new text to old tunes, because the tunes for *zazu* all came from northern China, and because audiences had come to prefer plays set to tunes from southern China, the older comedy had ceased to be publicly performed.

Xu changed all this with his quartette of short plays called *Four Shrieks of the Gibbon* (ca. 1580). He made the length variable—one, two, or five scenes. Three of the plays used northern melodies and one of them southern melodies as the musical bases for the texts. His new idea for what was essentially a mixed form reinvigorated the popularity and changed the definition of the farcical drama.

The four plays link together with common threads of dramatic performance and impersonation. In the first and shortest of the quartette, *The Mad Drummer,* the spirit of a second-century poet reenacts in the underworld a scene he had written while alive. In it he both curses and criticizes bitterly the tyrant who ruled him while both were living.

In the second, *Zen Master Yu Tung,* a prostitute poses as a respectable widow to seduce a monk. As punishment for his fall, the monk is reborn as a courtesan. One of the other women in the house reenacts the monk's original seduction to help him (now her) understand the punishment.

The third play, *A Female Mulan,* dramatizes the career of a girl who impersonates a man to serve as a soldier. In the fourth, *A Female Top Graduate,* when a government official offers his daughter in marriage to a promising, multitalented young clerk who had graduated with top honors, the clerk is forced to admit that he is a girl. Happily, the official also has a son—also a top graduate—so the official ends up keeping his very able subordinate in the family. She, of course, must give up her disguise.

Hsü Wei's work both made his new kind of *zazu* a popular success and initiated a vogue for writing short plays in sets of four. He is also remembered as an insightful critic of drama. His successes came late in life. Earlier the poet had endured periods of suicidal depression, manic behavior, and imprisonment.

Bibliography

Dolby, William. *A History of Chinese Drama.* New York: Harper and Row Publishers, 1976.

Leung, K. C. *Hsu Wei as Drama Critic: An Annotated Translation of the Nan-tz'u hsü-lu.* Eugene: University of Oregon, 1988.

Mair, Victor H., Editor. *The Columbia History of Chinese Literature.* New York: Columbia University Press, 2001.

Yahyá Effendi (ca. 1553–1644)

One of the most eminent Ottoman Turkish officials during the reign of Sultan Murad IV (1609–40), the learned, wise, virtuous, and incorruptible Yahyá Effendi rose through the legal ranks to become the Muftí or Shaykh of Islam—at once a judge, the supreme head of the learned professions, and a close personal adviser to the sultan. To his many other distinctions, Yahyá Effendi added becoming one of the most accomplished poets of his age.

He founded a school of poetry whose principles ran partly counter to those of the contemporary group of poets for whom the work of BAQÍ and, particularly, of NEF'Í provided models and inspiration. Whereas Nef'í imitated the forms and subjects of Persian poetry, and whereas the members of his school had as their objective the purification of the Turkish language on the Persian model, Yahyá Effendi led and perhaps founded what one critic has labeled the *natural* school of poetry. Although he modeled his style on that of BÂKÎ, Yahyá Effendi sought to draw subjects from his own experience in everyday life instead of always from traditional topics. As the last great poet of the classical age of Ottoman poetry, his treatment of innovative subject matter in a conservative manner provides the link between his predecessors and those, such as his successor poet NEDÍM (1681–1730), whose work is regarded as part of a transitional period between the classical age of Turkish poetry and the early modern period.

Particularly in his composition of GHAZELs literary history regards Yahyá Effendi as an innovator. In them he moves from an almost exclusively imitative and decorative manner to a simpler style and more realistic subjects, drawing, for example, his similes from commerce by comparing the sweet bouquet of his beloved to those scents wafting abroad when Chinese merchants open their bales of perfumed spices.

Yahyá Effendi also wrote an example of the obligatory CUPBEARER POEM. His writing differs from many other examples of this sort of work by being unambiguously and unmistakably mystical and allegorical in its intentions. Many such poems claim to celebrate the joys of drinking only as an ALLEGORY of the rewards of the religious life. Yet many seem to employ that allegory in a suspiciously ambiguous fashion and celebrate the life of the senses as well.

Bibliography

Andrews, Walter G. *An Introduction to Ottoman Poetry.* Minneapolis: Bibliotheca Islamica, 1976.

Gibb, E. J. W. *A History of Ottoman Poetry.* Edited by Edward G. Browne. London: Luzac & Company, 1965.

Yang Jishen (Yang Chi-sheng)
(1516–1555)

In real life Yang Jishen was a city official who risked and lost everything to denounce the corruption and cruelty of a powerful dictator, Yen Song (Yen-Sung) (1480–1565), and his equally cruel and corrupt son, Yen Shifan (1513–65). In literature he became the hero of a play, *The Crying Phoenix* (ca. 1570), which detailed Yang's eventually successful campaign against the pair. In subsequent drama of the period the two villains became quasi-allegorical figures representing the abusive exercise of power and accompanying greed.

Yang Shen (1488–1559)

A brilliant scholar and the son of a very high official in the imperial court, Yang Shen performed brilliantly on the Chinese examinations for entry into the civil service, receiving the top score in 1511. He wrote both poetry and prose. His prose generally took the form of brief essays and notes on historical subjects and about issues in literary criticism.

Widowed, Yang married a second wife, the notable poet HUANG XIUMEI (1498–1569). Despite his brilliant promise, Yang fell from imperial favor when he openly resisted imperial policies. He was exiled and never permitted to return to his home estates. Huang Xiumei was obliged to remain there and manage the estates so she could contribute to Yang's support in exile. The pair spent only a little time together thereafter.

Many of Yang's poems—both those in the classical SHI (*shih*) form and those in the more popular idiom of CI (*tz'u*) verse—were exchanged with Huang over the years of their separation. His literary production was considerable and a large body of his work survives. Much if not all of it is available in modern Chinese editions, but none has as yet found its way into English translation.

Yuan Hongdao (Yuan Hung-tao)
(1568–1610)

One of a pair of poet brothers from Kung-an in the Chinese province of Hubei (Hupei), Yuan Hongdao expressed determined opposition to slavishly following the practices of ancient poets of the Tang dynasty. Both the theoretical schools of the EARLIER and the LATER SEVEN MASTERS had articulated a preference for the finely wrought poetry of a former age. They claimed that with its overlay of literary allusion and its multiple levels of meaning, the ancient Tang poets represented the best China had to offer. The masters of both schools advised those who would write good poems to emulate the archaic style.

In contrast, many recent critics have argued, Yuan preferred personal expression, a freer narrative development, topics drawn from the real lives of real people, a poetic diction that more closely approximated conversational speech, and a more casual approach to crafting verse. Yuan's literary declaration of independence from the old masters attracted a coterie of those who shared his views, and 20th-century critics have celebrated him as a man of "truly modern consciousness."

Close examination, however, of Yuan's poems and of those associated with him in what has come to be called the "Kung-an school," says the literary historian Daniel Bryant, reveals little difference in the actual poetic practice of Yuan and his adherents and the practice of the masters. Perhaps one real difference was the Kung-ans' choice of a broader subject matter. In some of his poems as well, Yuan's speaker assumes a feminine as well as a masculine persona, and such androgyny has been thought a sign of new times.

In the generation following Yuan's death, however, his theory and practice both became very influential in Japan. There a Buddhist monk named Genzei (1623–68), after studying Chinese poetry with a tutor, repeatedly read Yuan's works. Then, having internalized their style and Yuan's practice, Genzei burned Yuan's poems and wrote his own in Yuan's style. Yuan's work produced a similar formative effect on the Korean poets of the 18th century.

Modern editions of Yuan's work and of biographic and critical commentary about him are available in Chinese. Only illustrative fragments of a few of his lines, however, have as yet made their way into English.

Bibliography

Idema, Wilt, and Lloyd Haft, eds. *A Guide to Chinese Literature.* Ann Arbor: Center for Chinese Studies, University of Michigan, 1997.

Mair, Victor H., ed. *The Columbia History of Chinese Literature.* New York: Columbia University Press, 2001.

Zhou, Zuyan. *Androgyny in Late Ming and Early Qing Literature.* Honolulu: University of Hawaii Press, 2003.

Yu Tong (Yu T'ung) (1618–1704)

Born in Zushou (Soochow), Yu early tried to embark on an official career with the Chinese civil service, but despite his remarkable learning he was not able to pass the exam. He did secure a position as magistrate of the police, in which he served from 1652 to 1656.

Following a scandal that suggested the examination results were subject to fraud, Yu wrote a satirical play exposing the corruption in the system. This play was performed in Suzhou, and it so offended the authorities that, immediately after its opening, all the members of the cast were arrested and beaten until they revealed the names of the play's author and its producer. With help from influential friends, Yu avoided the consequences that might otherwise have followed.

He left police work in 1657 to become an independent scholar and writer. So successful was he in these endeavors that his work came to the attention of Emperor Shunzhi (Shun-chi); ruled, 1644–61). Yu's work so pleased the emperor that he made Yu his personal poet. Yu's poems in praise of the emperor were rewarded with both official recognition and the emperor's further favor. In the reign of Shunzhi's successor, Emperor Kangxi (K'ang-hsi) (ruled 1662–1722), Yu continued to enjoy imperial patronage and a special personal relationship with the ruler. Perhaps as a result of the emperor's esteem, in 1679 Yu finally passed the examination. The emperor immediately rewarded the poet with a post in the Hanlin Academy that carried the title, "Elder Celebrated Scholar."

By no means a sinecure, this post involved serious research and writing. Yu compiled a huge bibliography of works that authors had written during the Ming dynasty (1368–1644). It also seems that Yu had a hand in writing that dynasty's official history. By 1683 Yu had amassed the means that enabled him to resign his academic post and return to the role he loved best—independent scholar and writer. He continued in it for the rest of his life.

His surviving works include drama, prose, and verse. He was also an avid anthologist. In this capacity, like several other compilers of anthologies in the 17th century, he became interested in bringing together CI poems by Chinese women. He admired the lyrics of female writers and argued that their gender particularly qualified them to write better song lyrics than men.

Bibliography

Dolby, William. *A History of Chinese Drama.* London: Elek Books Ltd., 1976.

Yu, Pauline, ed. *Voices of the Song Lyric in China.* Berkeley: University of California Press, 1994.

Z

Zacuto, Moses ben Mordicai
(ca. 1620–1697)

A poet and a student and devotee of the Hebrew kabbalah, Zacuto grew up as a member of a small community of Jews called the Marrano. In the late 16th and early 17th centuries the Marrano settled in the Netherlands after having been expelled from Spain and Portugal as a result of the anti-Semitic fervor that arose as a part of the CATHOLIC COUNTER-REFORMATION.

Later Zacuto traveled in Poland and eventually migrated to Italy, living first in Verona and then, after 1645, in Venice where he became a rabbi. He authored a number of commentaries on religious matters, annotations on the works of earlier Jewish writers, prayers, and discussions of kabbalistic matters. He penned a great dramatic poem, *Tofteh Gnarukh*. Modeled on *The Divine Comedy* of DANTE ALIGHIERI, the poem opens with a recently dead person recalling his last illness and funeral arrangements. Thereafter, the deceased is taken by an angel named Duna through seven parts of Hell, where he witnesses the punishments meted out to sinners. The poem ends with a celebration of the rewards of the righteous and of God's wisdom as the one true judge. Though the poem has been twice translated into Italian, once in verse and once in prose, it has not as yet appeared in English. Among Zacuto's very substantial body of work some occasional poetry also appears.

Literature especially remembers Zacuto for his early effort at writing in the Hebrew language the sort of poetic drama that was springing up in the countries from which the Marrano had been forced to migrate. His verse play *Yesod Olam*, however, languished in manuscript for centuries before being rediscovered and published in 1874. That the play did not appear in Zacuto's lifetime resulted from its fulfilling only a portion of the author's plan for a much longer work. The play concerns the Jewish patriarch Abraham, a righteous man who is the Old Testament's common ancestor of Muslims, Jews, and Christians. The part of the work that Zacuto completed tells about Abraham's legendary destruction of household idols in the home of Terah, a trial with King Nimrod as judge, Abraham's miraculous experience in and delivery from the fiery furnace, and Haran's death.

The play reveals Zacuto's familiarity with the dramatic precepts of ARISTOTLE as interpreted by the Italian LUDOVICO CASTELVETRO, for the drama observes the UNITIES of time, place, and action. Little stage business occurs in the play. The characters speak lengthy monologues, and Abraham himself is represented as a rationalist HUMANIST attempting to hold both hedonists and idolaters in check. The play is the first biblical drama in all of Hebrew literature. It has not been translated into English or other western European languages.

Bibliography

Foa, Cesare. *Tofte Gnaruch ossia il castigo dei reprobi: poema ebraico del secolo XVII di Mose Zacut* (Tofte gnaruch or the punishment of the damned: A Jewish poem of the 17th century). Padua: Prosperini, 1901.

Zinberg, Israel. *A History of Jewish Literature.* Translated and edited by Bernard Martin. Cincinnati and New York: Hebrew Union College Press and KTAV Publishing House, 1974.

zazu (*tsa-chü,* Chinese comedy)

The *zazu,* or *tsa-chü,* variety of Chinese comedy originated at least as early as the 13th century. With the arrival of the Ming dynasty in 1368, the form was adopted as the official drama of the Chinese court. Although around 30 manuscripts of plays from the Ming dynasty or earlier survive, the examples of *zazu* best known to modern scholarship date from the mid-16th through the early 17th centuries. The plays as most of them exist, then, contain modifications that reflect the tastes of audiences— particularly court audiences—living in those centuries.

Though they are regularly called plays, from the perspective of European and American theatergoers, *zazu* productions might better be called operas, for, in addition to spoken passages, many of the interchanges on *zazu* stages were sung. The *zazu* theater had originated in northern China and it became identified with its roots. A later sort of theater, *chuanqi* or *ch'uan-ch'i,* originated in southern China.

As compared with other examples of Chinese theater, *zazu* productions tended to be comparatively short. Though the plays could present a wide variety of subjects, Chinese history became a perennial favorite—though just what period of history shifted according to the tastes of the rulers. The plots of these history plays often coalesced to become the source of plots for much longer novels, such as THE ROMANCE OF THE THREE KINGDOMS or THE WATER MARGIN. Stories about criminals and their apprehension and punishment achieved a high degree of popularity. So did romance, warfare, and the corruption of public officials. The stories about love often involved a gifted student and a courtesan and the difficulties that impeded the progress of their affair. THE PEACH BLOSSOM FAN, though not a *zazu* play, exemplifies such a plot.

By the 16th century, *zazu,* which had once been widely popular outside the royal court, fell largely out of public favor except at court. There the novel THE JOURNEY TO THE WEST seems to have originated as six separate *zazu* performances. So did *The Journey to the Western Ocean.* This history play celebrated 14th-century Chinese voyages to the Indian Ocean under the command of Zheng He (Cheng Ho).

Bibliography

Idema, Wilt, and Lloyd Haft. *A Guide to Chinese Literature.* Ann Arbor: Center for Chinese Studies, University of Michigan, 1997.

Levy, André. *Chinese Literature, Ancient and Classical.* Translated by William H. Nienhauser, Jr. Bloomington: Indiana University Press, 2000.

Mair, Victor, ed. *The Columbia History of Chinese Literature.* New York: Columbia University Press, 2001.

"Zithuwa Hymns" (1575?)

Performed at the Incan capital of Cuzco as part of an annual purification ceremony, these hymns celebrate the power of the principal Incan deity, Viracocha. This patriarchal figure is represented as a herdsman, not of sheep, but of the Andean llamas—animals to which Viracocha's people are compared. Among other matters, the hymns celebrate the harvest with its abundance and the life-giving rainfall that is personified as a goddess princess.

These hymns were translated from the Quecha language of the Inca into Spanish by the Spanish-Incan courtier GARCILASO DE LA VEGA, THE (EL) INCA. Several examples are available in English translation.

Bibliography

Barnstone, Willis, and Tony Barnstone. "Zithua Hymns." *Literatures of Asia, Africa, and Latin America from Antiquity to the Present*, pp. 1520–21. Upper Saddle River, N.J.: Prentice Hall, 1999.

Zwingli, Huldrych (Ulrich) (1484–1531)

A militant Swiss opponent of the superstition with which he believed the Roman Catholic Church to be infected, Zwingli anticipated MARTIN LUTHER's theses against indulgences by at least a year. By 1516 he was already preaching what would become central doctrines of the Reformed Church. Zwingli did not think that original sin damned unbaptized infants to Hell or Limbo. Rather he considered that divine mercy would save them. The same salvific grace, he believed, applied to virtuous non-Christians. Zwingli also abhorred the veneration of saints and images. He considered the doctrine of transubstantiation of bread and wine into the body and blood of Christ during the Eucharist to be another example of superstitious folly. He subscribed to the doctrine of predestination, which held that those whom God intended to be saved would be saved. Like other Protestant reformers, Zwingli appealed to Holy Scripture as the source of authority and dismissed the papal hierarchy as a worldly intrusion into the realm of true religion.

Zwingli's 67 theses were adopted as the basis of the officially reformed religious position of the Swiss canton of Zürich in 1623. As a result all images were removed from the churches of Zürich or destroyed. Also the Mass ceased to be celebrated and a communion substituted for it. Some of the other Swiss cantons followed Zürich's lead. The Forest Cantons (Uri, Schwyz, and Unterwalden), however, remained staunchly Roman Catholic, and five of them allied themselves with Archduke Ferdinand of Austria in opposition to the reformers. Zürich officially declared war on the alliance in 1529, but fighting was temporarily avoided through negotiation. In the fall of 1531, however, a force of 8,000 men from the Forest Cantons and Austria invaded. Zwingli, who had been a military chaplain in Italy from 1513 to 1515, joined a force of 2,000 defenders and fell in the ensuing battle.

From a literary perspective, Zwingli must be numbered among the reforming HUMANISTS of his era. He composed his works in Latin and in vernacular German, and he had taught himself the Greek language. His most influential work was his *Commentary on True and False Religion* (1525). He also wrote on subjects that included educating young persons. In that arena he emphasized religious instruction and classical languages. He laid special emphasis on training that would produce churchmen. He also discussed such matters as baptism, controversies about the Lord's Supper, faith, and the clear and certain nature of Holy Scripture.

Bibliography

Luther, Martin, and Ulrich Zwingli. *Luther's and Zwingli's Propositions for Debate: The Ninety-five Theses of 31 October 1517 and the Sixty-seven Articles of 19 January 1523*. Translated by Carl S. Meyer. Leiden: E.J. Brill, 1963.

Zwingli, Huldrych. *Early Writings*. 1912. Edited by Samuel Macauley Jackson. Durham, N.C.: Labyrinth Press, 1987. [Includes 1532 biography of Zwingli by Oswald Myconius.]

———. *Huldrych Zwingli: Writings*. 2 vols. Translated by E. J. Furcha and H. Wayne Pipkin. Allison Park, Pa.: Pickwick Publications, 1984.

SELECTED BIBLIOGRAPHY

⤞⤝

Note to readers: Individual entries usually contain ample bibliographies that, taken together, reflect the scope of this volume. For that reason, I have included here only general and specialized reference volumes and works that, in addition to those in the entry bibliographies, I found especially helpful in thinking about and preparing this encyclopedia.

Reference Works

Bright, William, ed. *International Encyclopedia of Linguistics.* New York and Oxford: Oxford University Press, 1992.

Brockhaus Enzyklopädie. Wiesbaden: F. A. Brockhaus, 1969.

Crystal, David. *The Cambridge Encyclopedia of Language.* Cambridge and New York: Cambridge University Press, 1997.

Datta, Amaresh, ed. *Encyclopedia of Indian Literature.* New Delhi: Sahitya Akademi, 1989.

Encyclopaedia of Islam. Leiden: E.J. Brill and London: Luzac and Company, 1963–1980.

Encyclopaedia Judaica. Jerusalem: Macmillan Company, 1971.

Garland, Mary, and Henry Garland. *The Oxford Companion to German Literature.* Oxford: Oxford University Press, 1997.

Grendler, Paul F., ed. *Encyclopedia of the Renaissance.* New York: Scribner, 1999.

Konzett, Matthias, ed. *Encyclopedia of German Literature.* Chicago and London: Fitzroy Dearborn Publishers, 2000.

Mair, Victor H., ed. *The Columbia History of Chinese Literature.* New York: Columbia University Press, 2001.

New Catholic Encyclopedia. New York: McGraw Hill, 1967.

Singer, Isidore, et al., eds. *The Jewish Encyclopedia.* New York and London: Funk and Wagnalls, 1924.

The Feminist Encyclopedia of Italian Literature. Edited by Rinaldina Russell. Westport, Conn.: Greenwood Press, 1997.

Primary Sources

Bowen, Barbara C., ed. *One Hundred Renaissance Jokes: An Anthology.* Birmingham, Ala.: Summa Publications, 1988.

Columbus, Christopher. *A Synoptic Edition of the Log of Columbus' First Voyage.* Edited by Francesca Lardicci et al. Translated by Cynthia L. Chamberlin and Blair Sullivan. Turnhout, Belgium: Brepols, 1999.

Elizabeth I. *The Letters of Queen Elizabeth I.* Edited by G. B. Harrison. Westport, Conn.: Greenwood Press, 1981.

Ficino, Marsilio. *The Philebus Commentary.* Translated by Michael J. B. Allen. Tempe: Arizona Center for Medieval and Renaissance Studies, 2000.

La Fontaine, Jean de. *Once Again, La Fontaine: Sixty More Fables.* Translated by Norman R. Shapiro. Hanover, N.H.: Wesleyan University Press, 2000.

Lodge, Thomas. *Treatise on the Plague.* 1603. Norwood, N.J.: Theatrum Orbis Terrarum, 1979.

———. *Wounds of Civil War.* Edited by Joseph W. Houppert. Lincoln: University of Nebraska Press, 1969.

Luther, Martin, and Desiderius Erasmus. *Luther and Erasmus: Free Will and Salvation.* Philadelphia: Westminster Press, 1969.

Milton, John. *Paradise Lost and Selected Poetry and Prose.* Edited by Northrup Freye. New York: Rinehart Editions, 1951.

———. *Paradise Lost: John Milton, David Hawkes.* New York: Fine Creative Media, 2004.

Rabelais, François. *Œuvres complètes.* Edited by Michel Renaud et al. Translated from Middle French and Latin into Modern French by Guy Demerson and Geneviève Demerson. Paris: Editions du Seuil, ca. 1995.

Scudéry, Madeleine de. *Artemenes: or The Grand Cyrus.* 5 vols. London: H. Moseley et al., 1653–1655.

———. *Clelia: an Excellent New Romance . . .* London: Herringman et al., 1678. [Because Scudéry published under her brother's name, both the translators and the publishers assumed these works of Madeleine were written by Georges.]

Vasari, Giorgio. *Lives of the Artists.* Selections translated by E. L. Seeley. New York: The Noonday Press, 1958.

Wroth, Lady Mary. *The Countesse of Montgomeries Urania* [microform] *written by the right honourable the Lady Mary Wroth, daughter to the right noble Robert earle Leicester, and niece to the ever famous, and renowed Sr. Phillips* [sic] *Sidney knight, and to . . . Lady Mary countesse of Pembroke late deceased.* London: I. Marriott and I. Grismand, 1621.

———. *[Selected works of] Mary Wroth.* Edited by Josephin A. Roberts. Brookfield, Vt.: Ashgate Publishing Company, ca. 1996.

Secondary Sources

Aronson, Nicole. *Madame de Rambouillet, ou, La magicienne de la Chambre bleue.* Paris: Fayard, ca. 1988.

Atchity, Kenneth John, ed. *The Renaissance Reader.* New York: HarperCollins, ca. 1996.

Baker, Earnest A. *The History of the English Novel: The Elizabethan Age and After.* London: H. F. & G. Witherby, 1929.

Bradbrook, Muriel Clara. *John Webster, Citizen and Dramatist.* New York: Columbia University Press, 1980.

Brittin, Norman A. *Thomas Middleton.* New York: Twayne Publishers, 1972.

Fenster, Thelma S., and Clare A. Lees, eds. *Gender in Debate from the Early Middle Ages to the Renaissance.* New York: Palgrave, 2002.

Hampton, Timothy. *Literature and Inventing Nation in the Renaissance: Sixteenth Century France.* Ithaca, N.Y.: Cornell University Press, 2001.

Hopkins, Lisa. *Christopher Marlowe: A Literary Life.* New York: Palgrave, 2000.

Jusserand, J. J. *The English Novel in the Time of Shakespeare.* Translated by Elizabeth Lee. London: T. Fisher Unwin, 1903.

Kendall, Roy. *Christopher Marlowe and Richard Bains: Journeys through the Elizabethan Underground.* Madison, N.J.: Fairleigh Dickinson University Press, ca. 2003.

Kristeller, Paul Oscar. *Medieval Aspects of Renaissance Learning: Three Essays.* Edited and translated by Edward P. Mahoney. New York: Columbia University Press, ca. 1992.

———, and Philip P. Wiener. *Renaissance Essays.* Rochester, N.Y.: University of Rochester Press, ca. 1992.

Levin, Carole, et al., eds. *"High and Mighty Queens" of Early Modern England: Realities and Representations.* New York: Palgrave Macmillan, 2003.

Levin, Richard A. *Shakespeare's Secret Schemers: The Study of an Early Modern Dramatic Device.* Newark: University of Delaware Press, ca. 2001.

Miller, Naomi J. *Changing the Subject: Mary Wroth and Figurations of Gender in Early Modern England.* Lexington: University of Kentucky Press, 1996.

Milman, R. *The Life of Torquato Tasso.* London: Henry Colburn, Publishers, 1850.

Mozley, James Frederic. *William Tyndale.* New York: Macmillan Company, 1937.

Pinciss, Gerald M., and Roger Lockyer. *Shakespeare's World: Background Readings in the English Renaissance.* New York: Continuum, 1989.

Schelling, Felix E., and Matthew W. Black. *Typical and Elizabethan Plays by Contemporaries and Immediate Successors of Shakespeare.* New York and London: Harper and Brothers Publishers, 1931.

Spitz, Lewis William, ed. *The Northern Renaissance.* Englewood Cliffs, N.J.: Prentice Hall, ca. 1972.

Stoll, Elmer Edgar. *John Webster: The Periods of his Work as Determined by His Relations to the Drama of His Day.* Philadelphia: R. West, 1978.

Symonds, John Addington. *The Life of Michelangelo Buonarroti: Based on Studies in the Archives of the Buonarroti Family at Florence.* Philadelphia: University of Pennsylvania Press, 2002.

Upham, Alfred Horatio. *The French Influence in English Literature from the Accession of Elizabeth to the Restoration.* New York: Columbia University Press, 1911.

Warkentin, Germaine, and Carolyn Podruchny, eds. *Decentring the Renaissance: Canada and Europe in Multidisciplinary Perspective, 1500–1700.* Toronto and Buffalo: University of Toronto Press, ca. 2001.

Washington, Charles J. *Michelangelo: In the Footsteps of the Master: An Account of Michelangelo's Life and Art for the Modern Traveler.* Fort Collins, Colo.: Advantage Publications, ca. 2001.

Wilson, Katharina M. *Women Writers of the Renaissance and Reformation.* Athens: University of Georgia Press, ca. 1987.

INDEX